CAMPING
FRANCE 2016

Selection 2016
2,300 selected camping sites including:
2,000 with chalets, gîtes and mobile homes
1,200 with campervan facilities

Dear Reader,

The Michelin Camping Guide is perfect for all those who love the great outdoors and enjoy spending their leisure time in a tent, caravan, campervan, chalet or mobile home. We have selected the best campsites in France with our usual care, listing those with the best facilities in the most pleasant surroundings.

Using the traditional Michelin classification method, this guide provides you with an easy, speedy reference for assessing the category of each site: 1 to 5 tents (see pages 8–9).

The guide is updated each year, so consult the latest edition for the most up-to-date information and pricing.

Here are a few tips on how to use the guide

→ To select a campsite

The guide covers all 22 regions of France – see the map and list of regions on pages 4–5. Each region has been colour-coded so that you can find your way around the guide easily: the band at the top of the page matches the colour used in the map. Once you have selected a region, turn to the detailed map at the start of that region's section. It shows all the localities that have at least one campsite. The localities with campsites and their descriptions are listed alphabetically within each region section.

→ To find a specific locality

Refer to the index on page 500, where all the places are listed in alphabetical order.

→ To make a selection based on specific criteria

See the list of campsites on pages 26–33 for an at-a-glance summary of selected facilities available at sites, listed region by region.

→ For a detailed description of each individual site

The essential information and brief description given for each site are supplemented by symbols, which provide a wealth of additional information and detail. See pages 10–12 for the key to the symbols used in both the campsite entries and the maps.

→ Glossary of French terms

For a list of useful words, turn to the Glossary on page 14 for a translation of common terms.

→ Descriptions of the sites start on page 34

For more information on visiting particular towns or regions, consult the relevant regional Michelin Green Guide. We also recommend you use the appropriate Michelin regional map to locate your selected campsite, to calculate distances and to work out the best route.

→ To get the most out of this guide, read pages 6–12 carefully.

© Jharela / Fotolia.com

We welcome your feedback on our listed campsites.

Please email us at:
campingfrance@tp.michelin.com

Many thanks in advance!

Nanterre 92 | Bobigny 93 | PARIS 75 | Créteil 94

62 | Lille
NORD-PAS DE CALAIS
Arras | 59
Amiens | 80
76
Rouen
02
Laon
Charleville-Mézières
08
PICARDY
Beauvais
60
50
Caen | 27
St-Lô | 14 | NORMANDY
Evreux
Pontoise | 95
Versailles 78 | 77
ILE DE FRANCE
91 Évry | Melun
51 | Châlons-en-Champagne
55 | Metz
LORRAINE | 57
Nancy | 67
Strasbourg
CHAMPAGNE-ARDENNE
Bar-le-Duc | 54
ALSACE
22 | St-Brieuc
29 | Quimper
BRITTANY
35 | Rennes
56 | Vannes
61 | Alençon
Chartres
28
53 | Laval
Le Mans
72
PAYS DE LA LOIRE
Troyes | 10
Chaumont
52
88 | Epinal
Colmar | 68
70 | Vesoul | 90 | Belfort
FRANCHE-COMTÉ
44 | Nantes
Angers | 49
41 | Blois
Tours | 37
CENTRE
Orléans | 45
89 | Auxerre
21
BURGUNDY | Dijon
Besançon | 25
85 | la Roche-s-Yon
79 | Poitiers | 86
36 | Châteauroux
18 | Bourges
Nevers | 58
71
Lons-le-Saunier
39
La Rochelle
17 | 16
Niort
POITOU-CHARENTES
87 | Guéret | 23
Limoges
LIMOUSIN | 19
Moulins | 03
Clermont-Ferrand | 63
42 | 69 | Lyon
Mâcon
Bourg-en-Bresse | 01
74 | Annecy
Angoulême
Périgueux | 24
Tulle
AUVERGNE | St-Étienne
Chambéry | 73
38
RHÔNE-ALPES
Bordeaux | 33
AQUITAINE
47 | Agen
46 | Cahors
15 | Aurillac
le Puy-en-Velay | 43
Grenoble
Privas | Valence | 26
Gap | 05
Mont-de-Marsan | 40
32 | Montauban | 82
MIDI-PYRÉNÉES | Auch
Albi
Rodez
12
Mende | 48
30
Nîmes
84 | Avignon
Digne-les-Bains | 04
PROVENCE-ALPES-CÔTE D'AZUR | Nice | 06
Pau | 64
31 | Tarbes | 65
Toulouse | 81
Foix | 09
Carcassonne | 11
Montpellier | 34
LANGUEDOC-ROUSSILLON
13 | Marseille
83 | Toulon
Bastia
CORSICA
2B
Ajaccio | 2A
Perpignan | 66

Practical information for each location with cross reference to Michelin maps

Michelin classification of selected sites

Services and leisure facilities available

Brief description of the site and its capacity

Peak season rates

For key to the symbols, see pages 10 to 12

CENTRE

BRACIEUX

41250 – Michelin map **318** G6 – pop. 1 256 – alt. 70
▶ Paris 185 – Blois 19 – Montrichard 39 – Orléans 64

⚠ Indigo Les Châteaux

☎ 02 54 46 41 84, www.camping-indigo.com
Address : 11 rue Roger-Brun (take the northern exit, follow the signs for Blois; beside the Beuvron)
Opening times : from end March to beginning Nov.
8 ha (350 pitches) flat, grassy
Tariff : (2015 price) 30,20€ ✚✚ ⚎ 🔲 🔲 (10A) –
Extra per person 6.35€ – Reservation fee 13€
Rental rates : (2015 price) (from end March to beginning Nov.)
🔥 (1 chalet) – 6 'gypsy' caravans – 30 🔲 – 6 🔲 – 26 tent lodges. Per night from 40 to 108€ – Per week from 224 to 719€ – Reservation fee 13€
🔲 local sani-station 7€
In a wooded setting comprised of different types of trees.

Surroundings : ⚓ ♨♨
Leisure activities : ▾ ✕ 🔲 🔲 ♾ ✕ 🔲 🔲
Facilities : ⅄ ⚬➡ ♈ launderette

G P S Longitude : 1.53821
Latitude : 47.55117

BRIARE

45250 – Michelin map **318** N6 – pop. 5 688 – alt. 135
▶ Paris 160 – Orléans 85 – Gien 11 – Montargis 50

⚠ Onlycamp Le Martinet

☎ 02 38 31 24 50, http://lemartinet.onlycamp.fr
Address : at Val Martinet (located 1km north via the town centre, between the Loire river and the canal)
Opening times : from beginning April to end Sept.
4.5 ha (160 pitches) flat, grassy
Tariff : (2015 price) 20.50€ ✚✚ ⚎ 🔲 🔲 (10A) –
Extra per person 4.40€
🔲 local sani-station 5€

Surroundings : ⚓ ♨♨
Leisure activities : 🔥
Facilities : ⅄ ⚬➡🔲🔲 🔲 🔲 🔲
Nearby : 🔲 🔲

G P S Longitude : 2.72441
Latitude : 47.64226

BUZANÇAIS

36500 – Michelin map **323** E5 – pop. 4 501 – alt. 111
▶ Paris 286 – Le Blanc 47 – Châteauroux 25 – Châtellerault 78

⚠ La Tête Noire

☎ 02 54 84 17 27, www.camping-latetenoire.com
Address : to the northwest along the r. des Ponts; beside the Indre river, near the stadium
Opening times : from beginning April to mid Oct.
2.5 ha (100 pitches) flat, grassy
Tariff : (2015 price) 15€ ✚✚ ⚎ 🔲 🔲 (16A) – Extra per person 4€
Rental rates : (2015 price) (from beginning April to mid Oct.)
4 🔲 – 2 yurts. Per night from 45 to 60€ – Per week from 315 to 420€ – Reservation fee 10€
🔲 9 🔲 15€ – 🔲 🔲 11€

Surroundings : ⚓ ♨♨
Leisure activities : ▾ 🔲 🔲 hammam 🔲
Facilities : ⅄ ⚬➡🔲🔲 🔲 🔲
Nearby : 🔲 ✕ 🔲

G P S Longitude : 1.41805
Latitude : 46.89285

ANDÉ-SUR-BEUVRON

20 – Michelin map **318** E7 – pop. 1 462 – alt. 70
Paris 199 – Blois 15 – Chaumont-sur-Loire 7 – Montrichard 21

La Grande Tortue

0254441520, www.la-grande-tortue.com

dress : 3 route de Pontlevoy (500m south along the D 751, follow
e signs for Chaumont-sus-Loire and take the turning to the left,
ow the signs for La Pieuse, not far from the Beuvron river)

ening times : from mid April to mid Sept.

a (169 pitches) flat and relatively flat, grassy, sandy

iff : 42€ ★★ ⇔ 📧 (10A) – Extra per person 10.50€ –
servation fee 12€

ntal rates : (from mid April to mid Sept.) ⅃ – 39 🖼 – 3 🏠
night from 62 to 150€ – Per week from 290 to 930€ –
servation fee 12€

local sani-station 10€

urroundings : 🐾 🚗 🎣
eisure activities : 🍴🗙 🛶 🛥 🛝🐎🏊 🔲
pen air in season) 🏊 water park
acilities : ⅃ ⚲ 🔲🚿♿🚾🍴🔲🔥🍴

Longitude : 1.2583
Latitude : 47.48992

*This guide is updated regularly, so buy your new copy
every year!*

HAILLAC

310 – Michelin map **323** D8 – pop. 1 136 – alt. 180
Paris 333 – Argenton-sur-Creuse 35 – Le Blanc 34 – Magnac-Laval 34

Municipal les Vieux Chênes

0254256139, www.chaillac36.fr

dress : allée des Vieux Chênes (southwest of the town, 500m from
ke)

a (40 pitches)

ntals : 3 🏠.

reen, well-kept site with flowers, close to the stadium and
side a lake.

urroundings : 🐾 🚗 🎣
eisure activities : 🛝🐎 🎣 fitness trail
acilities : ⚲ 🔲🚿🔲
earby : 🍴 🛶🏊 pedalos

Longitude : 1.29539
Latitude : 46.43224

HARTRES

00 – Michelin map **311** E5 – pop. 39 122 – alt. 142
Paris 92 – Orléans 84 – Dreux 38 – Rambouillet 45

Les Bords de l'Eure

0237287943, www.auxbordsdeleure.com

dress : 9 rue de Launay

a (110 pitches) flat, grassy

ntals : 2 'gypsy' caravans – 1 🖼.

a pleasant wooded setting near the river.

urroundings : 🎣
eisure activities : 🛶 🛝🐎 🎿 pedalos
acilities : ⅃ ⚲ 🔲🚿🍴🔲
earby : 🍴 🎣 sports trail

Longitude : 1.4951
Latitude : 48.43265

Directions to campsite

Rental options and rates

Sani-station (borne) and fee (see page 12)

Address of campsite

GPS

The Michelin Camping Guide selection lists the best sites in each 'comfort' category:

⩕⩕ ⩕⩕ Extremely comfortable, equipped to a very high standard

⩕⩕ ⩕⩕ Very comfortable, equipped to a high standard

⩕⩕ ⩕⩕ Comfortable and well equipped

⩕⩕ ⩕⩕ Reasonably comfortable

⩕ ⩕ Satisfactory

Exceptional campsites in each category are awarded an additional rating:

⩕⩕ … ⩕ Particularly pleasant setting, good quality and range of services available.

How the selection works:

• Campsites are ranked according to their location, facilities, etc., and awarded tent symbols.

• In order for the guide to remain wholly objective, the selection is made on an entirely independent basis. There is no charge for being selected for the guide.

• The Michelin classification (⩕⩕ … ⩕) is totally independent of the official star classification system awarded by the local prefecture or other official organisation.

• All practical information and classifications are revised and updated annually so that the information is as reliable and up to date as possible.

• Our inspectors make regular visits to campsites; our readers' comments are also a valuable source of information, and regular follow-up visits are undertaken.

26 campsites have been classified ⩕⩕ / ⩕⩕ and 90 ⩕⩕ / ⩕⩕ in 2016. See below and opposite for this selection.

⩕⩕ 2016

BERNY-RIVIÈRE	La Croix du Vieux Pont
BISCARROSSE	Club Airotel Domaine de la Rive
CANET-PLAGE	Yelloh! Village Le Brasilia
CARNAC	Les Castels La Grande Métairie
DOL-DE-BRETAGNE	Les Castels Domaine des Ormes
GHISONACCIA	Arinella-Bianca
LABENNE-OCÉAN	Yelloh! Village Le Sylvamar
LECTOURE	Yelloh! Village Le Lac des 3 Vallées
PERROS-GUIREC	Yelloh! Village Le Ranolien

⩕⩕ 2016

ARZANO	Les Castels Ty Nadan
AZUR	FranceLoc La Paillotte
BELVÈS	RCN Le Moulin de la Pique
BIRON	FranceLoc Le Moulinal
BISCARROSSE	Mayotte Vacances
CANET-DE-SALARS	Les Castels Le Caussanel
CARANTEC	Yelloh! Village Les Mouettes
CHASSIERS	Sunêlia Domaine Les Ranchisses
CONTIS-PLAGE	Yelloh! Village Lou Seurrots
DIENNÉ	DéfiPlanet au Domaine de Dienné
FRÉJUS	Yelloh! Village Domaine du Colombier
GHISONACCIA	Homair Vacances Marina d'Erba Rossa
GRANVILLE	Les Castels Le Château de Lez-Eaux
GRIMAUD	Les Prairies de la Mer
HOURTIN-PLAGE	Club Airotel La Côte d'Argent
LACANAU-OCÉAN	Yelloh! Village Les Grands Pins
LONGEVILLE-SUR-MER	MS Vacances Les Brunelles
MÉZOS	Club Airotel Le Village de Sen Yan
MONTCLAR	Yelloh! Village Domaine d'Arnauteille
MUROL	Sunêlia La Ribeyre
PYLA-SUR-MER	Yelloh! Village Panorama du Pyla
QUIMPER	Les Castels L'Orangerie de Lanniron
RAMATUELLE	Village Vacances Toison d'Or
RUOMS	Sunêlia Aluna Vacances
ST-CAST-LE-GUILDO	Les Castels Le Château de la Galinée
ST-CRÉPIN-ET-CARLUCET	Les Peneyrals
ST-JULIEN-DES-LANDES	Les Castels La Garangeoire
ST-JUST-LUZAC	Les Castels Sequoia Parc
ST-LÉON-SUR-VÉZÈRE	Le Paradis
SAMPZON	Yelloh! Village Soleil Vivarais
SARLAT-LA-CANÉDA	La Palombière
SOMMIÈRES	Les Castels Le Domaine de Massereau
SOUSTONS	Sunêlia Village Vacances Framissima Nature
VALLON-PONT-D'ARC	Les Castels Nature Parc L'Ardéchois
VIAS-PLAGE	Yelloh! Village Club Farret
VITRAC	Domaine Soleil Plage

ᴧᴧᴧᴧ 2016

AGAY	Esterel Caravaning	ROQUEBRUNE-SUR-ARGENS	Domaine de la Bergerie
ARGELÈS-GAZOST	Sunêlia Les Trois vallées	ST-ALBAN	Sunêlia Le Ranc Davaine
ARGELÈS-SUR-MER	La Sirène et l'Hippocampe	ST-AVIT-DE-VIALARD	Les Castels St-Avit Loisirs
BADEN	Yelloh! Village Mané Guernehué	ST-BREVIN-LES-PINS	Sunêlia Le Fief
BÉNODET	Sunêlia L'Escale St-Gilles	ST-RAPHAËL	Les Castels Douce Quiétude
FRÉJUS	La Baume – La Palmeraie	SÉRIGNAN	Yelloh! Village Le Sérignan Plage
MESSANGES	Club Airotel Le Vieux Port	VALRAS-PLAGE	Domaine de La Yole
PIERREFITTE-SUR-SAULDRE	Les Alicourts	VIELLE-ST-GIRONS	Sunêlia Le Col Vert
RAMATUELLE	Yelloh! Village Les Tournels		

ᴧᴧᴧ 2016

AIGUES-MORTES	Yelloh! Village La Petite Camargue	MARSEILLAN-PLAGE	Les Méditerranées - Beach Club Nouvelle Floride
ARGELÈS-SUR-MER	Le Front de Mer	MEUCON	Le Haras
ARGELÈS-SUR-MER	Club Airotel Le Soleil	MIMIZAN-PLAGE	Club Airotel Marina-Landes
AVRILLÉ	FranceLoc Le Domaine des Forges	MOLIETS-ET-MAA	Le Saint-Martin
BELVÈS	FranceLoc Les Hauts de Ratebout	LA PALMYRE	Village Siblu Bonne Anse Plage
BÉNODET	Le Letty	PARENTIS-EN-BORN	Yelloh! Village Au Lac de Biscarrosse
BIDART	Les Castels Le Ruisseau des Pyrénées	PORNIC	Club Airotel La Boutinardière
BIDART	Yelloh! Village Ilbarritz	PORTIRAGNES-PLAGE	Les Sablons
BONIFACIO	Pertamina Village - U-Farniente	RUOMS	Domaine de Chaussy
BORMES-LES-MIMOSAS	Le Camp du Domaine	RUOMS	Yelloh! Village La Plaine
CARNAC-PLAGE	Les Menhirs	ST-AYGULF	L'Étoile d'Argens
CASTELLANE	Les Castels Le Domaine du Verdon	ST-CYPRIEN-PLAGE	Cala Gogo
CHAMBON-SUR-LAC	Yelloh! Village Le Pré Bas	ST-HILAIRE-DE-RIEZ	Les Biches
COL-ST-JEAN	Yelloh! Village L'Étoile des Neiges	ST-JEAN-DE-LUZ	Club Airotel Itsas Mendi
CORCIEUX	Yelloh! Village Le Domaine des Bans	ST-JEAN-DE-MONTS	Les Amiaux
DOUCIER	Le Domaine de Chalain	ST-JEAN-DE-MONTS	Le Bois Joly
FOUESNANT	Sunêlia L'Atlantique	SARLAT-LA-CANÉDA	Les Castels Le Moulin du Roch
FRÉJUS	Sunêlia Holiday Green	SÉRIGNAN-PLAGE	Yelloh! Village Aloha
GHISONACCIA	Sunêlia Perla Di Mare	TALMONT-ST-HILAIRE	Yelloh! Village Le Littoral
GIEN	Kawan Village Les Bois du Bardelet	TORREILLES	Sunêlia Les Tropiques
ÎLE DE RÉ	Sunêlia Interlude	TORREILLES	Mar I Sol
ÎLE DE RÉ	L'Océan	VARENNES-SUR-LOIRE	Les Castels Domaine de la Brèche
ÎLE D'OLÉRON	Club Airotel Les Gros Joncs	VIAS	Sunêlia Le Domaine de la Dragonnière
LACANAU-OCÉAN	Club Airotel L'Océan	VINSOBRES	Franceloc Le Sagittaire
LARNAS	FranceLoc Le Domaine d'Imbours	VOGÜÉ	Domaine du Cros d'Auzon
LIT-ET-MIXE	Tohapi Les Vignes	VOLONNE	Sunêlia L'Hippocampe
LES MATHES	La Pinède		
MARIGNY	Les Castels La Pergola		

You can find a particular village or town in the index at the end of the guide.

CAMPSITES

Michelin classification

⋀⋀⋀⋀ ⋀⋀⋀⋀	Extremely comfortable, equipped to a very high standard
⋀⋀⋀ ⋀⋀⋀	Very comfortable, equipped to a high standard
⋀⋀ ⋀⋀	Comfortable and well equipped
⋀ ⋀	Reasonably comfortable
⋀ ⋀	Satisfactory

• **Campsites are ranked according to their location, facilities, etc., within each category and are awarded a number of tent symbols – see page 8.**

• **Michelin classification (⋀⋀⋀⋀ ... ⋀) is totally independent of the official star classification system awarded by the local prefecture or other official organisation.**

Opening times

Permanent	Site open all year round

Special features

❄	Winter caravan sites: these sites are specially equipped for a winter holiday in the mountains. Facilities generally include central heating, electricity and drying rooms for clothes and equipment.
👥	Child-friendly sites, including washing facilities for young children, playgrounds and activities monitored by professionals

Exceptional in its category

⋀⋀⋀⋀ ... ⋀	Particularly pleasant setting, quality and range of services available.
🐦 🐦	Tranquil, isolated site – Quiet site, particularly at night
⋴⋴	Exceptional view – Interesting or panoramic view

General information

Access	Direction from the city centre
☎	Telephone
⚷	24 hour security: a warden usually lives on site and can be contacted during reception hours, although this does not mean round-the-clock surveillance outside normal hours
⚷	Day security only
🐕	No dogs (if dogs are permitted, a current vaccination certificate is required)
Ⓟ	Cars must be parked away from pitches
℞	Reservations not accepted
⊘	Credit cards not accepted
⊘	Chèque-vacances (French holiday vouchers) not accepted
cc	Chèque-vacances accepted

Site information

3 ha	Area available in hectares (1ha = 2.47 acres)
60 ha/3 ha for camping	Total area of the property/total area available for camping
90 pitches	Number of pitches
⊡	Marked-off pitches
♀ ♀♀ ♀♀♀	Shade: fair amount of shade to well shaded
⚐	Waterside location with swimming area

Facilities

▥	Heating facilities
♿	Facilities for the disabled
🚼	Baby changing facilities
⚱ 🚰	Each bay is equipped with water/drainage
▣	Washing machines, laundry
🛒 ▣	Supermarket – Grocery
☕	Takeaway meals
((•))	Internet or Wifi point

Facilities for campervans

	Services for campervans
sani-station 4 €	Type of service point and rate (see page 12)
3 ▣ 15.50 €	Number of pitches equipped for campervans/daily rate per pitch
	Special FFCC price for campervans at site (Fédération Française de Camping et Caravaning)
8 to 13 € [₺]	Daily charge for special FFCC price (with or without electricity)

Sports and leisure facilities

♀	Bar (serving alcohol)
✕	Eating places (restaurant, snack-bar, etc)
	Common room or games room
	Miscellaneous activities (sports, culture, leisure)
	Children's club
	Exercise room or gym
⸌s	Sauna
	Playground
	Cycle hire
✂	Tennis courts: open air/indoor
m	Minigolf
	Swimming pool: indoor/open air
	Bathing allowed (or supervised bathing)
	Waterslide
	Fishing
	Canoeing
	Sailing (school or centre)
⚓	Mooring pontoon (river mooring)
	Pony trekking or riding

• **The majority of outdoor leisure facilities are only open in season and during peak periods; opening times are not necessarily the same as those of the site and some facilities are only available during the summer season.**

Nearby   The guide only features facilities that are in the vicinity of the campsite (500 m)

Charges in euros

Daily charge:

♀ 5 €	per person
2 €	per vehicle
▣ 7.50 €	per pitch (tent/caravan)
[₺] 2.50 € (4A)	for electricity (calculated by number of ampere units)

Inclusive rates:

25 € ♀♀ pitch for 2 people

▣ [₺] (10A)   including vehicle and electricity

• **The prices listed were supplied by the campsite owners in autumn 2015 (if prices were not available, those from the previous year are given). The fees should be regarded as basic charges and may fluctuate with inflation.**

• **Listings shown in** light type **(i.e. not bold) indicate that not all revised charges have been provided by the owners.**

• **Additional charges may apply for some facilities (e.g., swimming pool, tennis courts), as well as for long stays.**

• **Special rates may apply for children – ask owner for details.**

• **Some information or pricing may have changed since the guide went to press. We recommend you check the price list online in advance or at the entrance to the campsite and enquire about possible restrictions.**

Rentals

12 🚐	Number of mobile homes
20 🏠	Number of chalets
6 🛏	Number of rooms to rent
Per night 30 to 50€	Minimum/maximum rates per night
Per week 300 to 800€	Minimum/maximum rates per week

LOCALITY INFORMATION

23700	Postcode
343 B8	Michelin map reference
Rennes 47	Distance in kilometres to place/town named
1,050 pop.	Population
alt. 675	Altitude (in metres)
⚕	Spa
1200/1900m	Altitude (in metres) of resort/highest point reached by lifts

• **Should you have grounds for complaint during your stay at a campsite about your reservation, the prices, standards of hygiene or facilities available, we recommend that you first try to resolve the problem with the proprietor or with the person responsible.**

• **If you are unable to resolve the disagreement, and if you are sure that you are within your rights, you could take the matter up with the relevant prefecture of the department.**

• **We welcome all suggestions and comments, whether in criticism or praise, relating to the campsites recommended in our guide. However, we must stress that we have neither the facilities nor the authority to deal with complaints between campers and proprietors.**

A sani-station, known in French as a 'borne', can be one of several proprietary commercial makes or a local, home-made 'artisanale' device. In return for a payment of a few euros or using a 'jeton', a pre-paid token, you receive fresh water, mains electricity and access to rubbish bins, plus grey and black wastewater disposal.

Types of sani-station (borne)

sani-station	specific type not known
local sani-station (borne artisanale)	locally made, a non-proprietary brand of sani-station
Aire Service/Eurorelais/Flot Bleu/ Raclet/Urbaco sani-station	different types of commercial sani-station
borne autre	other type of sani-station

Many addresses are given in French simply as 'lieu-dit', meaning 'place known as', e.g. lieu-dit Les Gravières. In this guide, we translate such addresses as 'at Les Gravières', or just 'Les Gravières'. These are names given locally to very small places, the names often deriving from a historical or topographical detail. The places they indicate may consist of just a few houses, or even no houses at all and simply represent a certain location.

YOU ALREADY KNOW THE GREEN GUIDE, NOW FIND OUT ABOUT THE MICHELIN GROUP

A better way forward

accès difficile	difficult access	emplacement (empl.)	pitch
accès direct à	direct access to…	entrée	way in, entrance
accidenté	uneven, hilly	entrée fleurie	attractive floral entrance/ reception area
adhésion	membership		
aire (de repos)	rest area	essence	petrol, gas
après-midi	afternoon	étang	lake, pool
arrêt	stop (traffic instruction)	été	summer
Ascension	Feast of the Ascension		
assurance obligatoire	insurance cover compulsory	falaise	cliff
août	August	famille	family
automne	autumn	fermé	closed
avenue (av.)	avenue	feu rouge	traffic lights
avril	April	février (fév.)	February
		forêt	forest
baie	bay		
bain	bath	garage	parking
base de loisirs	leisure and activity park/ centre	garage pour caravans	covered parking for caravans
bois, boisé	wood, wooded	garderie (d'enfants)	(children's) crèche
bord	shore, riverbank	gare routière	bus/coach station
au bord de la mer	by the sea	gare (S.N.C.F.)	railway station
borne	sani-station (see page 12)	à gauche	on/to the left
boucher	butcher	gazole	diesel
boulanger	baker	goudronné	surfaced road
boulevard (bd.)	boulevard.	GPL	LPG
au bourg	in town/in the village	gratuit	free, no charge
		gravier	gravel
cadre agréable	attractive setting	gravillons	fine gravel
cadre sauvage	natural setting		
carrefour	crossroads	hammam	Turkish-style steam bath with plunge pools
cases réfrigérées	refrigerated food storage facilities	herbeux	grassy
cedez le passage	give way (on roads)	hiver	winter
centre équestre	equestrian centre	hors saison	out of season
chambre d'hôte	guesthouse, B&B		
château	castle	île, îlot	island
chemin	path	incliné	sloping
conseillé	advised	indispensable	essential
cotisation obligatoire	membership charge obligatory	interdit	forbidden, prohibited
		intersection	junction
en cours d'aménagement	rebuilding work in progress		
croisement difficile	difficult access	janvier (janv.)	January
crêperie	pancake restaurant/stall	jeudi	Thursday
		jour	day
décembre (déc.)	December	juillet (juil.)	July
déjeuner	lunch	juin	June
derrière	behind		
dimanche	Sunday	lac	lake
dîner	dinner	lande	heath/moorland
douche	shower	licence obligatoire	camping licence/ international camping carnet compulsory
à droite	on/to the right		
		au lieu-dit	in the small locality of/at the place known as
église	church		
embouteillage	traffic jam	lundi	Monday

mai	May
mairie	town hall
marché	market
mardi	Tuesday
mars	March
matin	morning
mer	sea
mercredi	Wednesday
mineurs non accompagnés non admis	under 18s must be accompanied by an adult
montagne	mountain
Noël	Christmas
non clos	open site (landscape)
novembre (nov.)	November
nuit	night
à la nuitée	per night, on a nightly basis
octobre (oct.)	October
ouvert	open
ouverture prévue	opening scheduled
en panne	broken down
Pâques	Easter
parcours de santé	fitness trail
passage non admis	no touring pitches
péage	toll
pelouse	lawn
pente	sloping/slope
Pentecôte	Whitsun
personne (pers.)	person
petit-déjeuner	breakfast
pierreux	stony
piéton	pedestrian
pinède	pine trees, pine wood
place (pl.)	square
places limitées pour le passage	limited number of touring pitches
plage	beach
plan d'eau	stretch of water, artificial lake
plat	flat
pneu	tyre
pont	bridge
port	port, harbour
prairie	grassland, lawn
pré	meadow
près de	near
presqu'île	peninsula
prévu	projected
printemps	spring
en priorité	as a priority

priorité à droite	priority to right (give way to traffic from right, traffic joining roundabouts has priority, traffic on minor roads has right-of-way onto major roads, sign: black cross inside red triangle)
à proximité	nearby
quartier	quarter, district, area
Rameaux	Palm Sunday
réservé	reserved, booked
rive droite, gauche	right, left bank
rivière	river
rocailleux	stony, rocky, rugged
rocheux	rocky
rond-point	roundabout
route (rte)	road
rue (r.)	street
ruisseau	stream
sablonneux	sandy
saison (tourist)	tourist season
samedi	Saturday
avec sanitaires	with sanitary facilities
schéma	local map
semaine	week
à la semaine	per week, on a weekly basis
septembre (sept.)	September
soir	evening
sortie	way out, exit
sous-bois	undergrowth
(face) à la station	(opposite) at the filling station
supplémentaire (suppl.)	extra
en terrasses	terraced
toboggan aquatique	water slide
torrent	torrent (river/stream)
Toussaint	All Saints' Day (1 Nov)
tout compris	all inclusive
tout droit	straight ahead
unleaded	sans plomb
vacances scolaires	school holidays
vallonné	undulating
vendredi	Friday
verger	fruit trees, orchard
vers	in the direction of/towards
Voie Verte	green route (usually for pedestrians/cyclists)
voir	see

SPA FACILITIES ON THE CAMPSITES

Spas are back in fashion! And outdoor campsites are only too keen to ride the crest of this wave of enthusiasm for relaxation and health by expanding their range of services to include spa treatments. More and more tourists are attracted to the idea of spending a few hours on holiday in a spa, especially in the resort where they are actually staying.

But what do we really mean when we talk about spa facilities? The term 'spa' covers any kind of treatment with hot water (20–34°C) involving hydro massage, such as jacuzzi and whirlpool bathing. Often these are combined with other treatments using dry or wet steam (saunas and hammams), as well as massage and body sculpting massage.

Hot water and water vapour have many benefits: relaxing the muscles, stimulating blood circulation, eliminating toxins and dead skin, and dilating the pores. It is an excellent way to treat rheumatic and skin conditions and helps reduce stress.

© T. Pepeira / Iconotec / Photononstop

On campsites, spa centres – areas specifically dedicated to providing these treatments – are not medical facilities as such, but they are run by healthcare professionals. Nor are they open access, as the amenities provided generally have to be paid for.

© Image Source G / Photononstop

Particular attention is given to the decor of such centres, often utilising a Greco-Roman or contemporary type design, special lighting effects, background music and an array of aromas: everything is designed to make you feel completely relaxed. We have carefully chosen campsites with the finest spa facilities (see the names and detailed descriptions of the selected campsites), where you will find jacuzzis, saunas, hammams and massages. What a great way to relax!

Club Airotel Domaine de la Rive

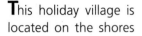

AQUITAINE
Biscarrosse (40)
See page 55

This holiday village is located on the shores of a lake (Cazaux-Sanguinet) and has direct access to the beach. It offers accommodation in chalets tucked away in the pine forest with wooden terraces that provide a sense of warmth and (something important to hard-core campers) space. But the real plus point of this place is Aquarive Park, with its slides, banana boats and other colourful attractions, which children will love, whilst for adults there is a wave pool and the more adventurous can safely learn water sports (such as sailing, water skiing, racing between buoys) at La Rive Watersports.

Village Vacances Port Lalande

AQUITAINE
Castelmoron-sur-Lot (47)
See page 58

Port Lalande is a small harbour built on the banks of the Lot. Located in a huge area of greenery, this resort offers accommodation in extremely comfortable air-conditioned chalets with terraces and outdoor garden lounges. You can safely leave children aged 6 to 10 in the care of childminders to supervise their activities (including paddling) while you explore the area, swim in the outdoor pool or head for the spa facility, one of the best features of the place, offering sauna, hammam and massages. It has all you need to eliminate toxins or stress.

Mayotte Vacances

AQUITAINE
Biscarrosse (40)
See page 55

This feels like a tropical island! The Indian Ocean my be a long way from the Atlantic, but you could quite easily believe that's where you are once you arrive here, right down to the lovely mobile homes and tented lodges in bright colours. As well as all the usual amenities of a luxury campsite (including 450 square metres of shops), Mayotte Vacances offers a large area for aquatic activities, complete with lagoon pool, water slides and paddling pools, gym, spa, restaurant, sports facilities for beach volleyball, basketball and minigolf, four children's clubs (grouped according to age), cabaret evenings and even a beauty salon. You almost never need to set foot outside the place!

Yelloh! Village Le Sylvamar

AQUITAINE
Labenne-Océan (40)
See page 65

If you head to the heart of the pine forest, you'll discover Le Sylvamar hidden away. Located in the Labenne-Océan district, this resort on the Landes coast offers a wide variety of camping accommodation from simple pitches to Palombière, beautiful cabins built in the trees. Comfortable cottages and chalets are also available. Then you are spoiled for choice in terms of sports; you can enjoy a huge area for aquatic activities and two heated pools. And for those who want to explore the country, Spain and the Pyrenees are virtually next door.

Yelloh! Village Les Grands Pins

AQUITAINE
Lacanau-Océan (33)
See page 66

Just a few yards from the beach, this campsite is a great holiday village, with the typical hilly terrain and shady pine trees that are common to the Landes. It has first-class amenities too, of course. These include partially covered swimming pools and a small shopping centre for everything you might need during your stay, not to mention the comfortable mobile homes located on the main site itself. Some have a tall wooden design that blends in with the surroundings and wooden decor reminiscent of the pine trees. Finally, part of the place is closed off to motor vehicles, in order to protect the environment and for the comfort of holidaymakers, especially those with children.

Le Paradis

AQUITAINE
St-Léon-sur-Vézère (24)
See page 81

Located in the heart of the Périgord Noir (in the Dordogne), this verdant site stretches down to the banks of the Vézère river, where guests can swim or enjoy wonderful canoe or kayak excursions. Each pitch is well defined by dense vegetation comprising a variety of flowers, bushes and trees. The site boasts a hundred different plant species. There are some mobile homes along with Canadian-style tents boasting 25 square metres of living space on a wooden base (complete with covered terrace) and an opportunity to return to nature. Some tents are situated on the riverbank, just a stone's throw from the water.

Club Airotel Le Vieux Port

AQUITAINE
Messanges (40)
See page 68

A short walk from the ocean and the large sandy Landes beaches, Le Vieux Port has a landscape lined with trees. You can even ignore the Atlantic if you like, since the aquatic area of the campsite has several pools, a paddling pool and slides for children, both younger (from aged 3) and older (from aged 10). Other attractions include an equestrian centre, activities and sports facilities. Relax and recharge your batteries at this lovely spot while all the family has fun.

Sunêlia Village Vacances Fram Nature

AQUITAINE
Soustons (40)
See page 88

This resort is unusual in that it was built only recently. Just a few years ago it was simply a stretch of Landes pine forest. Then the Fram Group, travel specialists, decided to open their first site here, building wooden mobile homes and tented lodges with large covered terraces and all the latest facilities on the beach, in the shade of the pine trees. To blend in with the natural environment, the buildings are made of Landes pinewood and the pool is drained naturally into the surrounding greenery. In addition to its spa facilities, this new holiday resort benefits from being close to Lake Soustons and the sea.

Yelloh! Village Le Pré Bas

▲▲▲

AUVERGNE
Chambon-sur-Lac (63)
See page 97

These camping facilities lie on the shore of Lake Chambon, which is overlooked by an enormous mountain range. High hedges, mostly flat or slightly inclined, surround the buildings, offering some privacy. The floral spaces are well laid out and you can swim in the lake or in one of two heated pools, complete with four slides. There is entertainment galore, plus a play area for children and fitness facilities for adults. Walkers or sports enthusiasts into hiking, biking or climbing will love the clean air in the vast surrounding open space.

Yelloh! Village Mané Guernehué

▲▲▲▲

BRITTANY
Baden (56)
See page 114

In the Gulf of Morbihan, the small town of Baden is home to one of the most beautiful campsites in the area, set on gently sloping grassy terrain. The accommodation consists of tents or caravans, as well as mobile homes, chalets and even traditional 'gypsy' caravans. And, appropriately enough, there is also a riding farm. The site offers a wide selection of activities and entertainment, including a partially covered aquatic area with slides. For those who prefer to relax while on holiday, new facilities include a jacuzzi, sauna, hammam and gym, with massages and facials also available. It's a great place in which to unwind.

Sunêlia L'Escale St-Gilles

▲▲▲▲

BRITTANY
Bénodet (29)
See page 116

L'Escale St Gilles is ideally located right on the coast. There is a magnificent first class spa centre on site, a large heated and partially covered aquatic area and beautiful beaches with straw huts providing shade. It remains open on some evenings in season to the great delight of those who enjoy slides and other water games. On other nights you can enjoy cabaret entertainment, quizzes and karaoke. Whether you bring your own equipment (tents/caravans) or choose to stay in one of the very comfortable mobile homes, you will be on a clearly marked pitch covering at least 100 square metres.

Sunêlia L'Atlantique

▲▲▲

BRITTANY
Fouesnant (29)
See page 124

The Atlantic is exactly the right name for this campsite. A stone's throw from the sea, this holiday village has some 150 mobile homes with facilities for families but also has 100 pitches on which to put up your tents or park your caravan in the shade of large trees. The water park complex is particularly impressive with several different pools with marine themes, complete with lighthouses, coconut palms, waterfalls and cliffs. The indoor pool takes up the baton on rainy days. The spa is ultra modern and there to be enjoyed by all those wanting to try its facilities.

Yelloh! Village Le Ranolien

⋀⋀⋀⋀

BRITTANY
Perros-Guirec (22)
See page 133

There is plenty of variety at Le Ranolien. The campsite has pitches for tents or caravans and boasts atmospheric 'gypsy' caravans and top-quality chalets. The latter are equipped with a 1.8-metre bed, two flat screen TVs, hi-fi system and dishwasher. Le Ranolien is also a holiday club with many activities, sports during the day, entertainment or cultural events in the evening, plus superb facilities for health and relaxation treatments: spa, hammam, sauna, massage. It has a unique location in the heart of a protected natural site. What more could one want?

Arinella-Bianca

⋀⋀⋀⋀

CORSICA
Ghisonaccia (20)
See page 197

Located on the east coast of Corsica, known as the 'Isle of Beauty', Ghisonaccia is a small resort offering several campsites but Arinella Bianca stands out because of the quality of its services and its great location. It is right next to the sandy beach, and the vegetation, including palm trees, eucalyptus and oleander, make this a particularly pleasant resort. Many of the available activities revolve around water: sea fishing or in the small inland lake, outdoor fitness facilities and an indoor spa, a sailing club and, for fun, buoy-to-buoy racing! There are plenty of things to do in the evening as well and sometimes it may even be your turn to take to the stage!

Les Alicourts

⋀⋀⋀⋀

CENTRE
Pierrefitte-sur-Sauldre (41)
See page 179

You'll never be bored at Les Alicourts. The resort offers plenty of aquatic activities, with four swimming pools (including one wave pool), a lavish spa area and a 6-hectare lake for swimming and canoeing. You'll be spoilt for choice between relaxation (spa) and sports (fishing, golf, minigolf, skate park, fitness facilities), and your children will be kept amused with organized activities throughout the day. Every type of accommodation is available: spacious pitches for tents and caravans, chalets, cottages, tree houses, and – the latest arrival – 'explorer' and 'safari' lodges.

Yelloh! Village Mer et Soleil

⋀⋀⋀

LANGUEDOC-ROUSSILLON
Agde (34)
See page 222

Between the Rhone and the Mediterranean, this 8-hectare landscaped environment with its flat grassy or sandy terrain features mobile homes, chalets, furnished tents and simple pitches. Leisure activities involving water are a key feature at this site, with the sea just a kilometre away, an excellent aquatic area with an upstairs restaurant and, best of all for spa lovers, wonderful facilities over 650 square metres in size. In this haven of relaxation choose from such delightful options as 'Bitter Orange and Poppy', 'Volcanic Escape' or even 'Provençal Relaxation'. After treating yourself to a treatment, you will be ready for the evening activities that await.

L'Arche

LANGUEDOC-ROUSSILLON
Anduze (30)
See page 223

This seaside campsite seems a million miles from any urban or industrial setting. A charming and friendly welcome lends it a family atmosphere. Located at the foot of the Cevennes, it is the perfect place for a vacation in the countryside on a quiet site designed for relaxation. There isn't a great variety of properties to rent. Camping facilities predominate. Pleasant shady pitches overlook the river and the small sandy beach with rocks lying a little further on. The site's amenities include a pleasant indoor pool, while the hammam, sauna and jacuzzi complement the outdoor pool and water slides.

Albirondack Park

MIDI-PYRÉNÉES
Albi (81)
See page 282

Located near the historic city of Albi, a designated UNESCO World Heritage site, this campsite is in a hilly, shady location and provides pitches for tents, caravans and motor homes as well as chalets, mobile homes and even treehouses for the more adventurous. After a day of sightseeing or simply relaxing, you will find an on-site pool with a lovely terrace, a new indoor spa offering sauna, hammam and jacuzzi, and finally, for lunch or for dinner, a high-quality restaurant with American-style interior.

Sunêlia
Les Tropiques

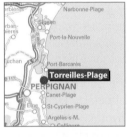

LANGUEDOC-ROUSSILLON
Torreilles-Plage (66)
See page 250

This 8-hectare site with its lush vegetation is an established resort with pitches under palm trees and mobile homes of various sizes, some of which have been adapted to accommodate disabled persons. Naturally, there is an aquatic area with several pools, one of which has a waterslide (with four tracks). Children and younger guests are catered for too and enjoy the giant inflatable giraffe. Adults can enjoy the numerous sports on offer (tennis, petanque, archery, etc.) and can take advantage of the spa facilities, which are open 7 days a week during the summer season.

Seasonova Village Vacances Le Domaine du Pré

PAYS-DE-LA-LOIRE
La Chapelle-Hermier (85)
See page 356

Situated beside Lake Jaunay, Domaine du Pré offers a concept of outdoor tourism that combines ecology, health and leisure. There are 82 chalets spread over 12 hectares of natural beauty, wholly dedicated to your relaxation and well-being. As well as enjoyable amenities such as an indoor pool and a heated lake for swimming, the resort has a fitness centre where massages, chromotherapy, colonic irrigation and rebirth relaxation are all available. The activities offered vary according to the season, but all revolve around similar themes combining nature and health.

Sunêlia Interlude

POITOU-CHARENTES
Le Bois-Plage-en-Ré (17)
See page 399

This really is Ile de Ré at its best. The huge campsite is set on slightly hilly terrain with dry vegetation reminiscent of that of the south of France. Its irregularly shaped plots seem to accentuate the feeling of an untamed landscape. Mobile homes clad in dark wood on terraces blend into the landscape perfectly. Some pitches for tents and caravans are also available. The site has excellent amenities including a brasserie, a restaurant, a supermarket and a beautiful pool. In summer the atmosphere buzzes with all the events and activities taking place throughout the day.

Sunêlia Le Fief

PAYS-DE-LA-LOIRE
St-Brévin-les-Pins (44)
See page 373

This village resort lies on the Côte de Jade between the sea and the forest. It covers a large flat grassy area. In addition to traditional camping facilities, high-quality mobile homes are also available. A dozen camp organizers ensure a lively atmosphere with colourful theme nights during which even children get to take part in musical extravaganzas. The area set aside for children is large and very well equipped. There is a 500-square metre aquatic area with rapids, lagoons and waterfalls, along with a wide variety of sports facilities, including archery and beach volleyball. And for those seeking tranquility and health, there is no better place to relax than the spa area with its jacuzzi and sauna.

L'Océan

POITOU-CHARENTES
La Couarde-sur-Mer (17)
See page 400

Although it was affected by Cyclone Xynthia, this campsite has made a spirited recovery. The management used the opportunity to refurbish and renew the rental accommodation and equipment to the latest standards. The result is a consistent, well-run site, with disabled access, offering a vast array of mobile homes, including an exclusive village made up of mobile homes with three bedrooms, superb bathrooms and a luxurious exclusive aquatic area with a large swimming pool under palm trees. The sports facilities include a multi-purpose sports ground, tennis courts and minigolf. And for those who like fishing, there is a small pond containing eels, bream and bass.

DéfiPlanet à Dienné

POITOU-CHARENTES
Dienné (86)
See page 398

In this beautiful area of 47 hectares you can choose between a small campsite, with all the modern comforts, in an environmentally friendly setting, and a range of unusual accommodation: prefab cube shelters (*carré d'étoiles*), 'gypsy' caravans, cabins and treehouses or yurts, etc. All the activities are organized with health in mind: there's a variety of sports, an equestrian centre, water aerobics, fitness trails, walking and biking. There are also zip wires, a climbing tower and fishing. If you just want to relax, you can use the jacuzzi and hammam. Finally, the restaurant offers 'designer menus' (for losing weight or to help with cardio-vascular problems) prepared by a doctor and a Michelin-starred chef.

Club Airotel Les Gros Joncs

POITOU-CHARENTES
St-Georges-d'Oléron (17)
See page 403

Backing onto the dunes that are lapped by the ocean, this campsite occupies a pleasant location with direct access to the beach via beautiful shady wild trails – a village hidden in the forest. The accommodation consists of mobile homes and cottages, five of which are accessible to people with reduced mobility. The site facilities offer disabled access, including to the pool. The amenities are also first rate, with a grocery store, a restaurant offering fine cuisine and a swimming pool, not to mention the spa with its counter-current pool and whirlpool. Most of all, it offers a charming and professional welcome.

Esterel Caravaning

PROVENCE-ALPES-
CÔTE-D'AZUR
Agay (83)
See page 418

At the heart of the Esterel massif, this is a very comfortable place to stay. The beautiful living space around which it is organized offers all the amenities you could ever want: a large grocery store, shop, excellent restaurant, bar with a cosy atmosphere and spa centre. The aquatic area may not be eye-catching, but it is fully equipped with covered swimming pools and paddling pools. There are other activities and a sports ground plus a ranch. You can stay in a mobile home or on one of the pitches in the hilly section of the site, shaded by pines. There are various clubs and activities to suit all ages and tastes, along with entertainment in the evenings.

© D. Ward / Gallery Stock / Photononstop

Yelloh! Village L'Étoile des Neiges

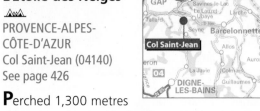

PROVENCE-ALPES-
CÔTE-D'AZUR
Col Saint-Jean (04140)
See page 426

Perched 1,300 metres above sea level, this family campsite is open in both winter and summer. Lying on a gentle green slope in the foothills of the Dormillouse massif, it has a panoramic outdoor pool, an indoor leisure pool and a beautiful indoor spa facility, including sauna, hammam and fitness suite. Most of the site consists of accommodation, offering a wide range of mobile homes and some beautiful cottages sheltered by pines. You can ski here in winter, using the nearby ski lifts.

Domaine de la Bergerie

PROVENCE-ALPES-
CÔTE-D'AZUR
Roquebrune-sur-Argens
(83)
See page 441

This site is located in a wonderful 60-hectare wooded park and its rental mobile homes are sparsely dotted around the entire complex, among cork oaks, shady pines and mimosa trees. Traditional camping pitches are situated in the lower section. Activities take place in the heart of the site and active holidaymakers will enjoy the water park, keep-fit and spa facilities, sports grounds, large open-air 600-seat amphitheatre for evening shows, clubs for kids, teenagers and adults and a disco. There are lovely places to relax and to eat.

Les Prairies de la Mer

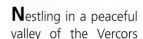

PROVENCE-ALPES-
CÔTE-D'AZUR
Grimaud (83)
See page 432

This site is notable for its direct access to a sandy beach and stunning views of St Tropez and its gulf. In addition to a standard range of accommodation and traditional campsite pitches, it also offers original accommodation in the shape of exotic wood-clad huts (*fares*). Some of these form an unusual village with small wooden bridges, water points, internal gardens and communal areas for relaxation. Other (very popular) huts line the beach and offer a unique view of the Gulf of St Tropez. Naturally, the site also possesses all the amenities you would expect, including spa facilities and leisure activities to suit all ages.

Yelloh! Village Au Joyeux Réveil

RHÔNE-ALPES
Autrans (38)
See page 455

Nestling in a peaceful valley of the Vercors mountains, this small campsite is 1,050 metres above sea level. It is run by Christine and Franck, and is a very family friendly. Just a short distance from the village of Autrans, the site offers a nice relaxing pool area, including three heated pools, one indoor pool for the more delicate and three small slides. The pitches, which boast thick grass, are quite spacious and provide some shade. Towards the rear of the site are tastefully furnished mobile homes. In summer, a lively team organizes entertainment and fun activities for children.

Sunêlia Domaine Les Ranchisses

RHÔNE-ALPES
Chassiers (07)
See page 461

The sound of cicadas, vines, olive trees… this stunning location is in the southern part of the Regional Natural Park of Monts d'Ardèche. At the entrance stands a restored Cévennes farmhouse, now home to the reception and restaurant. The extensive range of facilities and activities include a superb pool with a variety of slides, a wellness suite (offering massages and other treatments), a fitness club, a skate park and canoeing. The well-shaded and compact camping pitches are next to the river, while further up, on the other side of the road, another part of the site consists of cottages and modern accommodation, in the form of stylish 'Taos' mobile homes.

© L. Invernizzi Tettoni / Tips / Photononstop

Sunêlia Aluna Vacances

RHÔNE-ALPES
Ruoms (07)
See page 482

White oaks, vines and scrubland surround this family campsite, which has not been over-expanded. Part of the site consists of comfortable rental cottages, some of which are accessible to disabled persons, while the rest is, of course, dedicated to traditional camping pitches. The large pool facilities, featuring an artificial 'island', offer waterslides, waterfalls, a swimming area, a paddling pool and a solarium. And there's plenty to do at night too! There is a café-theatre, where cabaret and musicals and other entertainment are organized, as well as discos on some evenings.

Sunêlia Le Ranc Davaine

RHÔNE-ALPES
St-Alban-Auriolles (07)
See page 484

This village set in the scrubland really does offer all the shops and facilities you could ever need, including internet access. On the vast site, there is a choice of accommodation in chalets and cottages of varying sizes, all with private terraces, or on a shaded campsite. Most importantly, it has extensive aquatic facilities including a swimming area with two separate pools, waterfalls, a paddling pool, a whirlpool bath and a spa centre. There are clubs for younger children and of course, evening entertainment with shows, games and a disco.

Key

On the following pages you will find a region-by-region summary of localities with at least one site with the following facilities:

BRITTANY	Name of the region
Carnac	Name of the locality
🛶	Locality with at least one quiet and peaceful campsite
P	Town with at least one campsite open all year round
👪	Locality with at least one campsite suitable for families: child-friendly site including washing facilities for young children, playgrounds and activities monitored by professionals
🏊	Locality with at least one campsite with a water park
B	Locality with at least one selected site with a spa centre
🎭	Locality with at least one campsite offering entertainment/organized activities (sports, culture, leisure)

• For more details on specific sites, refer to the individual campsite entries

	Page	🦢	Permanent	👥	🎿	Spa centre	🎭
Saint-Alban-sur-Limagnole	246	🦢					🎭
Saint-Cyprien-Plage	246			👥			🎭
Saint-Georges-de-Lévéjac	247	🦢					
Saint-Hippolyte-du-Fort	247	🦢					
Saint-Jean-du-Gard	247	🦢		👥			🎭
Saint-Paul-le-Froid	248	🦢					
Saint-Victor-de-Malcap	248			👥			
Sainte-Enimie	248	🦢					
Sainte-Marie	249			👥			🎭
Sérignan	249			👥			🎭
Sérignan-Plage	249			👥		B	🎭
Sommières	250	🦢					
Torreilles-Plage	250			👥		B	🎭
Uzès	251	🦢		👥			
Valras-Plage	252			👥			🎭
Vernet-les-Bains	253	🦢					
Vers-Pont-du-Gard	253			👥			
Vias-Plage	253			👥	🎿	B	🎭
Villeneuve-lès-Avignon	256			👥			🎭
LIMOUSIN							
Argentat	259			👥			🎭
Aubazines	259	🦢		👥			🎭
Auriac	259	🦢					
Beaulieu-sur-Dordogne	260	🦢		👥			
Beynat	260	🦢					🎭
Bonnac-la-Côte	260	🦢					
Boussac-Bourg	260	🦢		👥			🎭
Chamberet	261	🦢					
Laguenne	263	🦢	P				
Liginiac	263	🦢					
Limoges	264			👥			
Lissac-sur-Couze	264	🦢		👥			
Magnac-Laval	264	🦢					
Neuvic	265	🦢		👥			🎭
Videix	267	🦢					
LORRAINE							
Bussang	271						🎭
Celles-sur-Plaine	272			👥			
Corcieux	272		P				🎭
Plombières-les-Bains	274		P				
Saint-Avold	275		P				
Sanchey	275		P				🎭
Saulxures-sur-Moselotte	276		P				
MIDI-PYRÉNÉES							
Agos-Vidalos	282			👥			🎭
Aigues-Vives	282	🦢					
Albi	282		P			B	
Alrance	282		P				
Arcizans-Avant	283	🦢	P				
Argelès-Gazost	283			👥			🎭
Arrens-Marsous	284		P				
Auch	284	🦢					
Aucun	284		P				
Augirein	285	🦢					
Aulus-les-Bains	285		P				

	Page	🦢	Permanent	👥	🎿	Spa centre	🎭
Ax-les-Thermes	285			👥			🎭
Ayzac-Ost	286		P				
Bagnères-de-Luchon	286		P	👥			
Barbotan-les-Thermes	287			👥			
Beaumont-de-Lomagne	287			👥			🎭
Le Bez	288	🦢					
Boisse-Penchot	288		P				
Bor-et-Bar	288	🦢					
Bourisp	288		P	👥			🎭
Brusque	289	🦢					🎭
Calmont	290		P				
Canet-de-Salars	290			👥			
Carlucet	290	🦢					
Carennac	290			👥			
Cayriech	292			👥			
Crayssac	293	🦢		👥			🎭
Creissels	294		P				
Damiatte	294			👥			
Duravel	294			👥			🎭
Entraygues-sur-Truyère	294	🦢					
Estang	295			👥			
Figeac	295						🎭
La Fouillade	296	🦢					
Gondrin	296			👥			
Lacam-d'Ourcet	297	🦢					
Lacave	298			👥			
Lau-Balagnas	298		P				🎭
Lectoure	298			👥			🎭
Loupiac	299			👥			
Luz-Saint-Sauveur	300		P	👥		B	🎭
Martres-Tolosane	301	🦢		👥			🎭
Mérens-les-Vals	301		P				
Millau	302			👥			
Mirandol-Bourgnounac	303	🦢					
Mirepoix	303	🦢					
Moissac	303			👥			
Monclar-de-Quercy	303	🦢					
Nages	304			👥			🎭
Nailloux	304		P				
Nant	304			👥			🎭
Padirac	305			👥			🎭
Payrac	306			👥			
Plaisance	306		P				
Pont-de-Salars	306			👥	🎿		🎭
Puybrun	307			👥			
Rieux-de-Pelleport	307	🦢	P				
Rivière-sur-Tarn	308			👥			🎭
Rocamadour	308	🦢		👥			
Rodez	308	🦢		👥			🎭
La Romieu	309	🦢		👥			🎭
Roquelaure	309			👥			🎭
Saint-Amans-des-Cots	309			👥			🎭
Saint-Antonin-Noble-Val	310			👥			
Saint-Cirq-Lapopie	310	🦢		👥			
Saint-Geniez-d'Olt	311	🦢		👥			🎭
Saint-Girons	311			👥			🎭

	Page	🛶	Permanent	👥	⛷	Spa centre	🎭
Saint-Jean-de-Monts	376	🛶		👥		B	🎭
Saint-Julien-des-Landes	379	🛶		👥		B	
Saint-Révérend	380						🎭
Saint-Vincent-sur-Jard	380						🎭
Sainte-Luce-sur-Loire	381		P				
Saumur	381			👥			🎭
La Selle-Craonnaise	381						🎭
Sillé-le-Guillaume	381	🛶					
Sillé-le-Philippe	381	🛶		👥			🎭
Talmont-Saint-Hilaire	382		P	👥			🎭
Tennie	382		P				
La Tranche-sur-Mer	382			👥			
La Turballe	383	🛶					
Varennes-sur-Loire	384			👥			🎭
Vendrennes	384		P				🎭
Villiers-Charlemagne	384		P				🎭
PICARDY							
Berny-Rivière	387		P	👥	⛷		🎭
Cayeux-sur-Mer	388			👥			
Le Crotoy	388	🛶	P				
Fort-Mahon-Plage	389			👥			
Moyenneville	389			👥			
Nampont-Saint-Martin	390						🎭
Le Nouvion-en-Thiérache	390	🛶					
Saint-Leu-d'Esserent	391	🛶					
Saint-Quentin-en-Tourmont	391	🛶					
Saint-Valery-sur-Somme	391			👥			🎭
Villers-sur-Authie	392			👥			🎭
POITOU-CHARENTES							
Angoulins	396					B	🎭
Châtelaillon-Plage	397	🛶		👥			🎭
Couhé	398			👥			🎭
Coulon	398			👥			
Dienné	398	🛶				B	🎭
Fouras	399		P	👥			🎭
Île de Ré	399	🛶		👥		B	🎭
Île d'Oléron	401	🛶		👥		B	🎭
Le Lindois	404	🛶	P				
Les Mathes	404			👥			🎭
Montbron	406	🛶		👥			🎭
La Palmyre	406	🛶		👥			🎭
Pressac	408	🛶					
Rochefort	408						
La Roche-Posay	408			👥			🎭
Ronce-les-Bains	409	🛶		👥			🎭
Royan	409			👥			🎭
Saint-Augustin-sur-Mer	409	🛶					
Saint-Cyr	410			👥			🎭
Saint-Georges-de-Didonne	410			👥			🎭
Saint-Georges-lès-Baillargeaux	410		P				🎭
Saint-Hilaire-la-Palud	410	🛶					
Saint-Just-Luzac	411			👥			🎭
Saint-Laurent-de-la-Prée	411			👥			🎭
Saint-Yrieix-sur-Charente	412	🛶					
Saujon	412			👥			
Vaux-sur-Mer	413						🎭
PROVENCE-ALPES-CÔTE-D'AZUR							
Agay	418			👥		B	🎭
Aix-en-Provence	419		P	👥			
Ancelle	419	🛶					
Apt	419	🛶					
Arles	420			👥			🎭
Baratier	420	🛶	P				🎭
Barret-sur-Méouge	421	🛶					
Beaumont-du-Ventoux	421	🛶	P				
Bonnieux	422	🛶					
Bormes-les-Mimosas	422	🛶	P	👥			🎭
Cadenet	423						🎭
Callas	423		P				
Carro	424	🛶					🎭
Castellane	424	🛶	P	👥			🎭
Cavalaire-sur-Mer	425	🛶					
Clamensane	426			👥			
La Colle-sur-Loup	426			👥			
Col-Saint-Jean	426			👥		B	🎭
La Couronne	427			👥			🎭
La Croix-Valmer	427			👥			🎭
Cros-de-Cagnes	427			👥			🎭
Cucuron	428	🛶					
Curbans	428						🎭
Embrun	428						🎭
Espinasses	429						🎭
Fréjus	429	🛶		👥		B	🎭
Giens	430	🛶					
Gréoux-les-Bains	431	🛶	P	👥		B	🎭
Grimaud	432	🛶		👥		B	🎭
Guillestre	432		P				
Hyères	433			👥			🎭
Isola	433		P				
La Londe-les-Maures	434		P				
Méolans-Revel	435			👥			🎭
Montpezat	436			👥			🎭
Moustiers-Sainte-Marie	436	🛶					
Murs	436	🛶					
Le Muy	436			👥			🎭
Nans-les-Pins	437			👥			
Névache	437	🛶					
Niozelles	437			👥			🎭
Orgon	437	🛶					
Pertuis	438			👥			🎭
Puget-sur-Argens	439			👥			
Puimichel	439	🛶					
Puyloubier	439	🛶					
Ramatuelle	439			👥		B	🎭
Régusse	440						🎭
La Roche-de-Rame	440		P				
La Roche-des-Arnauds	440		P				
Roquebrune-sur-Argens	441	🛶		👥		B	🎭
La Roque-d'Anthéron	441						🎭
Saint-Apollinaire	442	🛶					

	Page	🥾	Permanent	👥	⛷	Spa centre	🎭
Saint-Aygulf	442			👥			🎭
Saint-Laurent-du-Verdon	443	🥾		👥			
Saint-Mandrier-sur-Mer	443						🎭
Saint-Martin-d'Entraunes	443	🥾					
Saint-Paul-en-Forêt	444	🥾		👥			
Saint-Raphaël	444			👥			🎭
Sanary-sur-Mer	446			👥			
Serres	446	🥾		👥			
Seyne	446	🥾					
Taradeau	447		P				🎭
Vaison-la-Romaine	447			👥			🎭
Vence	448	🥾					
Veynes	448	🥾					
Villar-Loubière	448	🥾					
Villecroze	449			👥			
Villeneuve-Loubet-Plage	449		P				🎭
Volonne	450			👥			🎭
Volx	450	🥾					
RHÔNE-ALPES							
Les Abrets	454	🥾		👥			
Anse	455					B	
Aussois	455	🥾	P				
Autrans	455			👥		B	
Balbigny	455	🥾					
La Balme-de-Sillingy	456	🥾					
Beaufort	456	🥾					
Bénivay-Ollon	456	🥾					
Berrias-et-Casteljau	456			👥			
Bourdeaux	457					B	
Le Bourg-d'Oisans	457			👥			🎭
Bourget-du-Lac	458						🎭
Casteljau	459	🥾					
Chabeuil	460	🥾					🎭
Champdor	460		P				
Chassagnes	461	🥾					
Chassiers	461			👥		B	🎭
Châteauneuf-de-Galaure	461						🎭
Châteauneuf-sur-Isère	462			👥			🎭
Châtel	462			👥			🎭
Crest	463			👥			🎭
Dardilly	464		P				
Dieulefit	465	🥾					
Doussard	465			👥			🎭
Eclassan	466	🥾					
Excenevex	466						🎭
La Ferrière	466	🥾					
Gravières	468	🥾					
Gresse-en-Vercors	468	🥾					
Issarlès	469	🥾					
Joannas	469	🥾					
Lagorce	470	🥾					
Lalley	470	🥾					
Lanslevillard	470		P				
Larnas	470			👥			🎭
Lathuile	471			👥			🎭
Lépin-le-Lac	471	🥾					
Lescheraines	472	🥾					
Mars	472	🥾					
Les Mazes	473	🥾		👥			🎭
Menglon	474	🥾		👥			🎭
Montchavin	475		P				
Montrevel-en-Bresse	475			👥			🎭
Murs-et-Gélignieux	476		P				
Neydens	476						
Novalaise-Lac	476	🥾					
Les Ollières-sur-Eyrieux	477			👥			
Le Poët-Célard	478				⛷		
Poncins	478	🥾					
Pont-de-Vaux	478			👥			🎭
Pradons	479			👥			🎭
Privas	480			👥			
Recoubeau-Jansac	480					B	
Rosières	481	🥾					
Ruoms	482	🥾		👥		B	🎭
Sablières	483	🥾					
Saint-Agrève	483	🥾					
Saint-Alban-Auriolles	484			👥		B	🎭
Saint-Alban-de-Montbel	484			👥			
Saint-Christophe-en-Oisans	484	🥾					
Saint-Clair-du-Rhône	484	🥾					
Saint-Galmier	484			👥			🎭
Saint-Jorioz	487			👥			🎭
Saint-Laurent-les-Bains	488	🥾					
Saint-Martin-d'Ardèche	488			👥			
Saint-Maurice-d'Ardèche	489	🥾		👥			
Saint-Paul-de-Vézelin	489	🥾					
Sainte-Catherine	491	🥾					
Sallanches	491						🎭
La Salle-en-Beaumont	491	🥾					
Samoëns	492		P				🎭
Sampzon	492	🥾		👥			🎭
Séez	493		P				
Serrières-de-Briord	493						🎭
Sévrier	493						🎭
Taninges	494		P				
La Toussuire	494						🎭
Trept	494						🎭
Tulette	494	🥾					
Ucel	494			👥			🎭
Vagnas	495	🥾					
Vallon-Pont-d'Arc	495			👥		B	🎭
Vernioz	497	🥾					
Villars-les-Dombes	497			👥			
Vinsobres	497			👥			🎭
Vogüé	499			👥			🎭

ALSACE

R. Mattes / hemis.fr

Alsace is perhaps the most romantic of France's regions, a place of fairy-tale castles, gentle vine-clad hills and picturesque villages perched on rocky outcrops or nestling in lush, green valleys. From Colmar's 'Little Venice' with its flower-decked balconies, famous storks (the region's iconic emblem) and wonderful Unterlinden Museum, to the spectacular lights and tempting delights of Strasbourg's Christmas market, via the atmospheric half-timbered houses, reflected in the meandering River Ill, Alsace radiates an inviting warmth that even the winter temperatures cannot chill. The region is known for its wonderful scenery, traditional cuisine, local produce and excellent wine. Head to a brasserie and enjoy a regional beer in a lively atmosphere or relax in a local *winstub* (wine lounge), tucking into a steaming dish of *choucroute* (sauerkraut with smoked pork) and a generous slice of *Kugelhopf* cake, all washed down with a glass of fruity Sylvaner or Riesling. Alsace has something for everyone.

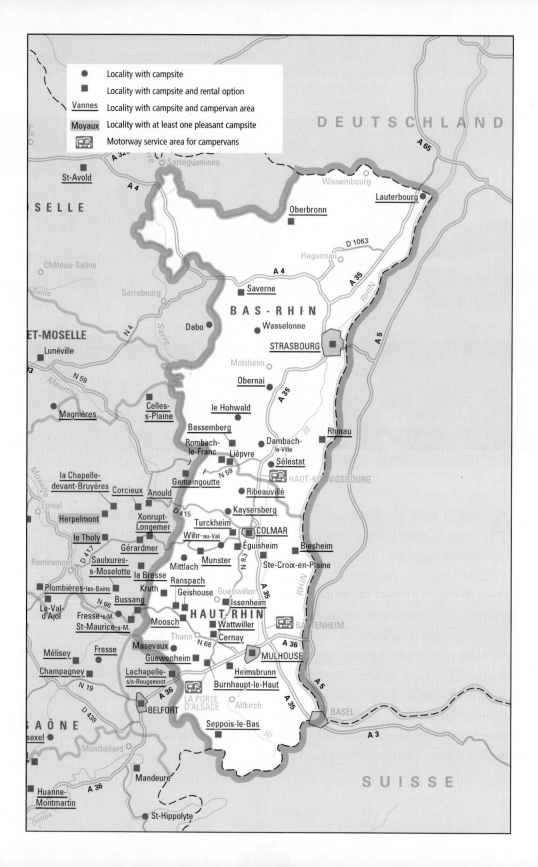

BASSEMBERG

67220 – Michelin map **315** H7 – pop. 268 – alt. 280
▶ Paris 432 – Barr 21 – St-Dié 35 – Sélestat 19

⛰ Campéole Le Giessen

✆ 03 88 58 98 14, www.camping-vosges.net

Address : route de Villé (take northeastern exit on the D 39; beside the Giessen river)

Opening times : from beginning April to end Sept.

4 ha (79 pitches) flat, grassy

Tariff : 11.70€ ✚✚ ⇔ 🔲 🄵 (10A) – Extra per person 10€
Rental rates : (from beginning April to end Sept.) ♿ (1 mobile home) – 35 🛏 – 20 🏠 – 8 canvas bungalows. Per night from 34 to 154€ – Per week from 238 to 1,078€ – Reservation fee 25€
🚰 AireService sani-station 5.20€ – 11 🔲 11.70€
A pretty site near a water park.

Surroundings : ≤ 🏞		
Leisure activities : 🍷 ⓘdaytime 🏄‍♂️🚲	**G**	Longitude : 7.28911
Facilities : ♿ ⚡ 🛁 🌂 🚾 🍴 🖼 refrigerators	**P**	Latitude : 48.33602
Nearby : 🍴 🏞 🏊 🎿 ⛷	**S**	

BIESHEIM

68600 – Michelin map **315** J8 – pop. 2 398 – alt. 189
▶ Paris 520 – Strasbourg 85 – Freiburg-im-Breisgau 37 – Basel 68

⛰ Tohapi L'Ile du Rhin

✆ 0825 00 20 30, www.tohapi.fr

Address : tourist area of l'Île du Rhin (5km east along the N 415, follow the signs for Fribourg)

Opening times : from end April to beginning Oct.

3 ha (220 pitches) lat, relatively flat, grassy

Tariff : (2015 price) 18€ ✚✚ ⇔ 🔲 🄵 (10A) – Extra per person 7€
Rental rates : (2015 price) (from end April to beginning Oct.) – 31 🛏. Per night from 31 to 102€ – Per week from 217 to 714€
🚰 local sani-station 3€
A pleasant site and setting between the Rhine and the Canal d'Alsace, on the Franco–German border.

Surroundings : ♀		
Leisure activities : ✘ 🏞 ⓘdaytime 🚲	**G**	Longitude : 7.57278
Facilities : ♿ ⚡ 🄲 🛁 🚾 🍴 launderette	**P**	Latitude : 48.02746
🏖 🖼	**S**	
Nearby : 🏞 🎿 ⛷ 🌊 water skiing		

BURNHAUPT-LE-HAUT

68520 – Michelin map **315** G10 – pop. 1 596 – alt. 300
▶ Paris 454 – Altkirch 16 – Belfort 32 – Mulhouse 17

⛰ Les Castors

✆ 03 89 48 78 58, www.camping-les-castors.fr

Address : 4 route de Guewenheim (2.5km northwest along the D 466)

Opening times : permanent

2.5 ha (135 pitches) flat, grassy

Tariff : 19,10€ ✚✚ ⇔ 🔲 🄵 (10A) – Extra per person 3,90€
Rental rates : permanent – 2 🛏 – 1 🏠. Per night from 80 to 90€ – Per week from 380 to 510€
🚰 local sani-station 4€ – 3 🔲 19.10€
A rural setting beside a river and a lake. Extensive green spaces.

Surroundings : ♀		
Leisure activities : 🍷✘ 🏄‍♂️ 🌊 🎣	**G**	Longitude : 7.12383
Facilities : ♿ ⚡ 🛁 🍴 launderette	**P**	Latitude : 47.77455
	S	

CERNAY

68700 – Michelin map **315** H10 – pop. 11 288 – alt. 275
▶ Paris 461 – Altkirch 26 – Belfort 39 – Colmar 37

⛺ Les Cigognes

✆ 03 89 75 56 97, www.camping-les-cigognes.com

Address : 16 rue René Guibert (take the exit following signs for Belfort then take a right turn after the bridge; beside the Thur river)

Opening times : from beginning April to end Sept.

3.5 ha (138 pitches) flat, grassy

Tariff : (2015 price) 18.50€ ✚✚ ⇔ 🔲 🄵 (10A) – Extra per person 4.90€ – Reservation fee 5€
Rental rates : (2015 price) (from beginning April to end Sept.) 🚫 – 4 🛏. Per night from 45 to 75€ – Per week from 280 to 480€ – Reservation fee 15€
🚰 local sani-station 6€
Pretty, green pitches situated within the town.

Surroundings : ♀		
Leisure activities : 🏞	**G**	Longitude : 7.16876
Facilities : ♿ ⚡ 🛁 🍴 🖼	**P**	Latitude : 47.80519
Nearby : 🍴 🏞 🎿 (open air in season)	**S**	

COLMAR

68000 – Michelin map **315** I8 – pop. 67 214 – alt. 194
▶ Paris 450 – Basel 68 – Freiburg 51 – Nancy 140

⛰ Indigo L'Ill

✆ 03 89 41 15 94, www.camping-indigo.com

Address : situated 2km east along the N 415, follow the signs for Fribourg; beside the Ill river

Opening times : from end March to beginning Jan.

2.2 ha (150 pitches) terraced, flat, grassy

Tariff : (2015 price) 22.60€ ✚✚ ⇔ 🔲 🄵 (10A) – Extra per person 4.80€ – Reservation fee 13€
Rental rates : (2015 price) (from end March to beginning Jan.) – 8 🛏 – 12 🏠 – 10 tent lodges. Per night from 41 to 97€ – Per week from 201 to 578€ – Reservation fee 13€
🚰 local sani-station 7€
A shaded site on the peaceful banks of the Ill river.

Surroundings : ♀♀		
Leisure activities : 🍷✘ 🏞 🏄‍♂️ 🎣	**G**	Longitude : 7.38676
Facilities : ♿ ⚡ 🛁 🍴 🖼 🏖 🍴	**P**	Latitude : 48.07838
	S	

DAMBACH-LA-VILLE

67650 – Michelin map **315** I7 – pop. 1 946 – alt. 210
▶ Paris 443 – Barr 17 – Obernai 24 – Saverne 61

⛺ L'Ours

✆ 03 88 92 46 09, camping-de-l-ours@orange.fr

Address : 2 rue du Stade (1.2km east along the D 210, follow the signs for Ebersheim and take road to the left)

1.8 ha (120 pitches) flat, grassy

A shaded setting in the heart of the countryside with an attractive view of the mountains.

Surroundings : ≤ ♀		
Facilities : ♿ ⚡ 🛁 🖼	**G**	Longitude : 7.44324
Nearby : 🏄‍♂️ 🍴 🏞	**P**	Latitude : 48.32274
	S	

ÉGUISHEIM

68420 – Michelin map **315** H8 – pop. 1 622 – alt. 210
▶ Paris 452 – Belfort 68 – Colmar 7 – Gérardmer 52

⚑ Des Trois Châteaux

✆ 03 89 23 19 39, www.camping-eguisheim.fr

Address : 10 rue du Bassin (to the west)

Opening times : from mid March to mid Dec.

2 ha (133 pitches) flat, relatively flat, gravel, grassy

Tariff : (2015 price) 14.80€ ✦✦ 🚙 🔲 🔌 (16A) – Extra per person 5€ – Reservation fee 10€

Rental rates : (from mid March to mid Dec.) – 22 🚐. Per night from 39 to 138€ – Per week from 272 to 636€ – Reservation fee 10€

The sanitary facilities are a little jaded, but in a pleasant location near a vineyard and the beautiful village of Eguisheim.

Surroundings : 🏞 ≤ 🌳
Facilities : 🚿 ⛲ 🚰 🏪

G P S Longitude : 7.29909
Latitude : 48.04274

Some campsites benefit from proximity to a municipal leisure centre.

GEISHOUSE

68690 – Michelin map **315** G9 – pop. 484 – alt. 730
▶ Paris 467 – Belfort 53 – Bussang 23 – Colmar 55

⚑ Au Relais du Grand Ballon

✆ 03 89 82 30 47, www.aurelaisdugrandballon.com – limited spaces for one-night stay

Address : 17 Grand-Rue (southern exit)

Opening times : permanent

0.3 ha (24 pitches) flat, grassy

Tariff : 22€ ✦✦ 🚙 🔲 🔌 (10A) – Extra per person 5.60€

Rental rates : permanent – 4 🏠. Per week from 329 to 432€

A small, pretty site in the heart of the mountains; a family atmosphere with a very busy restaurant.

Surroundings : 🏞 ☕ 🌳
Leisure activities : 🍽 ✗ 🏠 🏊
Facilities : 🚿 ⛲ 🏪 🏕 🚰 launderette

G P S Longitude : 7.05852
Latitude : 47.88056

GUEWENHEIM

68116 – Michelin map **315** G10 – pop. 1 256 – alt. 323
▶ Paris 458 – Altkirch 23 – Belfort 36 – Mulhouse 21

⚑ La Doller

✆ 03 89 82 56 90, www.campingdoller.com

Address : rue du Commandant Charpy (located 1km north along the D 34, follow the signs for Thann and take the road to the right; beside the Doller river)

0.8 ha (40 pitches) flat, grassy

Rentals : 6 🚐.

A family atmosphere in a green setting with flowers; a lovely dining room.

Surroundings : 🏞 🌳
Leisure activities : 🍽 🏠 🏊 🏊 🚣
Facilities : 🚿 ⛲ 🏪 🏕 🚰 🏪
Nearby : 🍴 ⛰

G P S Longitude : 7.09827
Latitude : 47.75597

HEIMSBRUNN

68990 – Michelin map **315** H10 – pop. 1 453 – alt. 280
▶ Paris 456 – Altkirch 14 – Basel 50 – Belfort 34

⚑ Parc la Chaumière

✆ 03 89 81 93 43, www.camping-lachaumiere.com – limited spaces for one-night stay

Address : 62 rue de Galfingue (take the southern exit along the D 19, follow the signs for Altkirch)

1 ha (53 pitches) flat, grassy, gravel

Rentals : 4 🚐.

🚐 local sani-station – 6 🔲

A convivial and family-orientated site, in a pleasant setting among trees and shrubs.

Surroundings : 🏞 ☕ 🌳
Leisure activities : 🏊 🏊 (small swimming pool)
Facilities : ⛲ 🏪 🚰 🏊

G P S Longitude : 7.22477
Latitude : 47.72242

LE HOHWALD

67140 – Michelin map **315** H6 – pop. 496 – alt. 570 – Winter sports : 600/1100 m
▶ Paris 430 – Lunéville 89 – Molsheim 33 – St-Dié 46

⚑ Municipal

✆ 03 88 08 30 90, lecamping.herrenhaus@orange.fr – alt. 615

Address : 28 rue du Herrenhaus (take the western exit along the D 425, follow the signs for Villé)

Opening times : from mid June to mid Sept.

2 ha (100 pitches) very uneven, terraced, fine gravel, flat, grassy

Tariff : (2015 price) ✦ 3.62€ 🚙 1.80€ 🔲 2.20€ – 🔌 (6A) 2.30€

A pleasant setting in the heart of the mountains among pines, spruces and beech trees.

Surroundings : 🌳
Leisure activities : 🏠 🏊 sports trail
Facilities : 🏪 🏊

G P S Longitude : 7.32328
Latitude : 48.4063

Routes nationales are main roads and their identifying numbers begin with N or RN. Routes départementales are generally quieter roads and begin with D or DN.

ISSENHEIM

68500 – Michelin map **315** H9 – pop. 3 418 – alt. 245
▶ Paris 487 – Strasbourg 98 – Colmar 24 – Mulhouse 22

⚑ Le Florival

✆ 03 89 74 20 47, www.camping-leflorival.com

Address : route de Soultz (2.5km southeast along the D 430, follow the signs for Mulhouse and take D 5 to the left, follow the signs for Issenheim)

Opening times : from beginning May to end Sept.

3.5 ha (73 pitches) flat, grassy, stony

Tariff : (2015 price) 17.80€ ✦✦ 🚙 🔲 🔌 (10A) – Extra per person 3.90€

Rental rates : (2015 price) (from beginning May to end Sept.) 🚿 (2 chalets) 🏊 – 20 🏠. Per night from 52 to 90€ – Per week from 270 to 584€ – Reservation fee 5€

🚐 6 🔲 17.80€ – 🚐 🔌 16.90€

In a pleasant setting at the edge of the woods. There's a swimming area with an Olympic-size pool nearby.

Surroundings : ≤ ☐
Leisure activities : 🏛 🏇
Facilities : & ⊶ 🏢 🛝 🕈 launderette
Nearby : 🏊 🛶 ⛷

GPS Longitude : 7.23879
Latitude : 47.90014

The information in the guide may have changed since going to press.

KAYSERSBERG

68240 – Michelin map **315** H8 – pop. 2 721 – alt. 242
▶ Paris 438 – Colmar 12 – Gérardmer 46 – Guebwiller 35

🏔 Municipal

✆ 03 89 47 14 47, www.camping-kaysersberg.fr ⚑
Address : rue des Acacias (take northwestern exit along the N 415, follow the signs for St-Dié and take a right turn)
Opening times : from beginning April to end Sept.
1.6 ha (115 pitches) flat, grassy
Tariff : (2015 price) 18.60€ ✦✦ 🚗 🔲 🔌 (8A) – Extra per person 4.30€
🚐 local sani-station
A charming site beside the La Weiss river.

Surroundings : ≤ ♀
Leisure activities : 🏛 🏇 ✕
Facilities : ⊶ 🛝 🏕 🕈 launderette

GPS Longitude : 7.25404
Latitude : 48.14887

KRUTH

68820 – Michelin map **315** F9 – pop. 1 029 – alt. 498
▶ Paris 453 – Colmar 63 – Épinal 68 – Gérardmer 31

🏔 Le Schlossberg

✆ 03 89 82 26 76, www.schlossberg.fr
Address : rue du Bourbaach (2.3km northwest along the D 13b, follow the signs for La Bresse and take turning to the left)
Opening times : from beginning April to beginning Oct.
5.2 ha (200 pitches) relatively flat, grassy, terraced
Tariff : (2015 price) ✦ 6€ 🚗 1.50€ 🔲 7€ – 🔌 (6A) 3€
Rental rates : (2015 price) permanent – 12 🏠. Per week from 335 to 699€
A pleasant location in the heart of the Parc des Ballons, close to the Magnificent Lac de Kruth. Cycle path at the entrance.

Surroundings : 🌄 ≤ ♀
Leisure activities : 🍸 🏇
Facilities : & ⊶ 🏢 🛝 🕈 launderette

GPS Longitude : 6.9546
Latitude : 47.94535

LAUTERBOURG

67630 – Michelin map **315** N3 – pop. 2 266 – alt. 115
▶ Paris 519 – Haguenau 40 – Karlsruhe 22 – Strasbourg 63

🏔 Municipal des Mouettes

✆ 03 88 54 68 60, camping-lauterbourg@wanadoo.fr – limited spaces for one-night stay
Address : located 1.5km southwest along the D 3 and take road to the left, 100m from a small lake (direct access)
2.7 ha (136 pitches) flat, grassy
🚐 local sani-station – 6 🔲

Extensive green spaces beside a large leisure and activity park.

Leisure activities : 🍸 ✕
Facilities : & ⊶ 🏢 🛝 🕈 🖫
Nearby : 🏇 🛶 ⛷ ◊

GPS Longitude : 8.1654
Latitude : 48.9708

LIEPVRE

68660 – Michelin map **315** H7 – pop. 1 751 – alt. 272
▶ Paris 428 – Colmar 35 – Ribeauvillé 27 – St-Dié-des-Vosges 31

🏔 Haut-Koenigsbourg

✆ 03 89 58 43 20, www.liepvre.fr/camping
Address : route de La Vancelle (900m east along the C 1 follow the signs for la Vancelle)
Opening times : from mid March to mid Oct.
1 ha (56 pitches) flat, relatively flat, grassy
Tariff : 16.20€ ✦✦ 🚗 🔲 🔌 (8A) – Extra per person 4€
Rental rates : (from mid March to mid Oct.) ⚑ – 6 🏠. Per night from 60 to 95€ – Per week from 310 to 480€
There's a centuries-old sequoia at the entrance; absolute peace in the middle of the countryside.

Surroundings : 🌄 ≤ ♀
Leisure activities : 🏛 🏇
Facilities : & ⊶ 🏢 🛝 🖫

GPS Longitude : 7.2903
Latitude : 48.27303

*To visit a town or region, use the **MICHELIN Green Guides**.*

MASEVAUX

68290 – Michelin map **315** F10 – pop. 3 278 – alt. 425
▶ Paris 440 – Altkirch 32 – Belfort 24 – Colmar 57

🏕 Le Masevaux

✆ 03 89 82 42 29, www.camping-masevaux.com
Address : 3 rue du Stade (beside the Doller river)
3.5 ha (133 pitches) flat, grassy
A pleasant wooded setting with flowers. Numerous walking trails begin at the site.

Surroundings : ♀♀
Leisure activities : 🍸 🏛 🏇 🎣
Facilities : & ⊶ 🏢 🛝 🕈 launderette
Nearby : 🏖 ✕ 🏊 🛶

GPS Longitude : 6.99093
Latitude : 47.77833

MITTLACH

68380 – Michelin map **315** G8 – pop. 323 – alt. 550
▶ Paris 467 – Colmar 28 – Gérardmer 42 – Guebwiller 44

🏕 Municipal Langenwasen

✆ 03 89 77 63 77, www.mittlach.fr – alt. 620
Address : chemin du Camping (3km southwest; beside a stream)
Opening times : from mid April to mid Oct.
3 ha (77 pitches) terrace, flat and relatively flat, gravelled, grassy
Tariff : (2015 price) ✦ 3.70€ 🚗 1.20€ 🔲 1.55€ – 🔌 (10A) 6.20€
A wooded site at the bottom of a peaceful valley.

Surroundings : 🌄 ≤ ☐ ♀
Leisure activities : 🏛 🏇
Facilities : ⊶ (July–Aug.) 🖫

GPS Longitude : 7.01867
Latitude : 47.98289

MOOSCH

68690 – Michelin map **315** G9 – pop. 1 764 – alt. 390
▶ Paris 463 – Colmar 51 – Gérardmer 42 – Mulhouse 28

⛰ La Mine d'Argent

✆ 03 89 82 30 66, www.camping-la-mine-argent.com – limited spaces for one-night stay

Address : rue de la Mine d'Argent (located 1.5km southwest along the r. de la Mairie; beside a stream)

2 ha (75 pitches) terraced, relatively flat, flat, grassy
Rentals : 4 🚐.
🚰 local sani-station
Situated on a lush, green undulating site in the mountains.

Surroundings : ⌖ ≤ ⚘
Leisure activities : 🏛 ⚓
Facilities : ⊶ 🚰 launderette

GPS Longitude : 7.03054
Latitude : 47.85102

MULHOUSE

68100 – Michelin map **315** I10 – pop. 111 156 – alt. 240
▶ Paris 465 – Basel 34 – Belfort 43 – Besançon 130

🏔 L'Ill

✆ 03 89 06 20 66, www.camping-de-lill.com

Address : 1 rue Pierre de Coubertin (to the southwest, along the A 36, take the exit for Dornach)

Opening times : from beginning April to end Sept.

5 ha (193 pitches) flat, grassy
Tariff : (2015 price) 21.20€ ✶✶ 🚐 🔌 (10A) – Extra per person 5.60€ – Reservation fee 5€

Rental rates : (2015 price) (from beginning April to end Sept.) 🚐 – 8 🚐 – 3 canvas bungalows. Per night from 19 to 90€ – Per week from 350 to 580€ – Reservation fee 15€
🚰 Eurorelais sani-station 6€ – 1 🔲 17.60€
In a wooded setting beside river arranged near Euro cycle route 6.

Surroundings : ⚘⚘
Leisure activities : 🏛 ⚓
Facilities : ⚓ ⊶ 🚰 🚿 ♨
Nearby : ⛷ 🖼 skating rink, mountain biking

GPS Longitude : 7.32283
Latitude : 47.73424

MUNSTER

68140 – Michelin map **315** G8 – pop. 4 889 – alt. 400
▶ Paris 458 – Colmar 19 – Gérardmer 34 – Guebwiller 40

⛰ Tohapi Le Parc de la Fecht

✆ 08 25 00 20 30, www.tohapi.fr

Address : route de Gunsbach (located 1km east along the D 10, follow the signs for Turckheim)

Opening times : from end April to beginning Sept.

4 ha (192 pitches) flat, grassy
Tariff : (2015 price) 16€ ✶✶ 🚐 🔌 (10A) – Extra per person 6€
Rental rates : (2015 price) (from end April to beginning Sept.) – 24 🚐. Per night from 32 to 48€
🚰 local sani-station 3€

Surroundings : ⚘⚘
Leisure activities : 🏛 🎣 ⚓ 🚲
Facilities : ⊶ 🔲 🚿 🖼
Nearby : ♨

GPS Longitude : 7.15102
Latitude : 48.04316

OBERBRONN

67110 – Michelin map **315** J3 – pop. 1 543 – alt. 260 – ⚓
▶ Paris 460 – Bitche 25 – Haguenau 24 – Saverne 36

🏔 Flower L'Oasis

✆ 03 88 09 71 96, www.opale-dmcc.fr

Address : 3 rue du Frohret (located 1.5km south along the D 28, follow the signs for Ingwiller and take the road to the left)

Opening times : permanent

2.5 ha (139 pitches) flat, relatively flat, stony, grassy
Tariff : 19.50€ ✶✶ 🚐 🔲 🔌 (10A) – Extra per person 3.50€ – Reservation fee 15€

Rental rates : (from beginning April to end Nov.) ⚓ (2 chalets) – 39 🚐. Per week from 160 to 610€ – Reservation fee 15€
🚰 local sani-station – 5 🔲 19.50€
On the edge of a forest, with a magnificent view over the mountain and the village of Oberbronn.

Surroundings : ⌖ ≤
Leisure activities : 🍽 🏛 🎣 ⚓ 🎿 ⛷ sports trail, spa centre
Facilities : ⚓ ⊶ 🚰 🚿 🖼 ♨
Nearby : ⛷

GPS Longitude : 7.60347
Latitude : 48.9286

OBERNAI

67210 – Michelin map **315** I6 – pop. 10 803 – alt. 185
▶ Paris 488 – Colmar 50 – Erstein 15 – Molsheim 12

🏔 Municipal le Vallon de l'Ehn

✆ 03 88 95 38 48, www.obernai.fr

Address : 1 rue de Berlin (take the western exit along the D 426, follow the signs for Ottrott, for caravans, recommended route via the bypass (rocade) south of the town)

Opening times : from mid March to end Dec.

3 ha (150 pitches) flat and relatively flat, grassy
Tariff : 21.90€ ✶✶ 🚐 🔲 🔌 (16A) – Extra per person 5.25€
🚰 Eurorelais sani-station 2€ – 30 🔲 21.90€
A restful site with a pretty view of Mont Sainte-Odile.

Surroundings : ≤ ⚘
Leisure activities : 🏛 🎣 ⛷
Facilities : ⚓ ⊶ 🚰 🚿 🖼 🚿 launderette
Nearby : ⚓ 🖼 ⛷ 🐎

GPS Longitude : 7.46715
Latitude : 48.46505

RANSPACH

68470 – Michelin map **315** G9 – pop. 852 – alt. 430
▶ Paris 459 – Belfort 54 – Bussang 15 – Gérardmer 38

🏔 Flower Les Bouleaux

✆ 03 89 82 64 70, www.alsace-camping.com

Address : 8 rue des Bouleaux (south of the town along the N 66)

Opening times : permanent

1.75 ha (75 pitches) flat, grassy
Tariff : 27€ ✶✶ 🚐 🔲 🔌 (6A) – Extra per person 6€ – Reservation fee 10€

Rental rates : permanent ⚓ (2 chalets) – 25 🚐. Per night from 50 to 110€ – Per week from 250 to 770€ – Reservation fee 10€
🚰 local sani-station 4€ – 5 🔲 27€

Extensive attractive green spaces in the shade of birch trees, but sanitary facilities are rather jaded.

Surroundings : ≤ ♀
Leisure activities : 🍷 ✕ 🛖 hammam ⛵
🚵 🏊 spa facilities, massages
Facilities : ⚕ ⛽ 🛁 ⛲ launderette

Longitude : 7.01037
Latitude : 47.88084

RHINAU

67860 – Michelin map **315** K7 – pop. 2 698 – alt. 158
▶ Paris 525 – Marckolsheim 26 – Molsheim 38 – Obernai 28

🏔 Ferme des Tuileries

🕾 03 88 74 60 45, www.fermedestuileries.com – ℞ 🚫
Address : 1 rue des Tuileries (take the northwestern exit, follow the signs for Benfeld)
Opening times : from beginning April to end Sept.
4 ha (150 pitches) flat, grassy
Tariff : (2015 price) 🚶 4 € ⛺ 🅿 4 € – ⚡ (6A) 3.20 €
Rental rates : (2015 price) (from beginning April to end Dec.) 🚫 – 5 🏠. Per night from 50 to 85 € – Per week from 320 to 600 €
🚉 local sani-station – 15 🅿
A well-equipped site scattered with fruit trees, next to a magnificent lake.

Surroundings : 🌳 ≤ ♀
Leisure activities : ✕ 🛖 ⛷ ⛵ 🚲 ✂ 🎣 ⛷
🏊 🛶 (lake) ⛷ 🎣
Facilities : ⛽ 🚽 ⛲ 🛁 ⛲ launderette ⛴

Longitude : 7.6986
Latitude : 48.32224

RIBEAUVILLÉ

68150 – Michelin map **315** H7 – pop. 4 798 – alt. 240
▶ Paris 439 – Colmar 16 – Gérardmer 56 – Mulhouse 60

🏔 Municipal Pierre-de-Coubertin

🕾 03 89 73 66 71, camping-alsace.com/camping-pierre-coubertin-ribeauville – ℞
Address : 23 rue de Landau (take the eastern exit along the D 106 then take the turning to the left)
Opening times : from mid March to mid Nov.
3.5 ha (208 pitches) flat, grassy
Tariff : 🚶 4.50 € ⛺ 🅿 5,50 € – ⚡ (16A) 3.70 €
🚉 local sani-station – 18 🅿
Pretty view of mountain, vineyards and château.

Surroundings : 🌳 ≤ ♀
Leisure activities : 🛖 ⛵ ✂
Facilities : ⚕ ⛽ ⛲ 🛁 ⛷ 🚿 ⛲ 🅿 🏊
Nearby : 🛶 ⛷ ⛷

Longitude : 7.336
Latitude : 48.195

ROMBACH-LE-FRANC

68660 – Michelin map **315** H7 – pop. 877 – alt. 290
▶ Paris 431 – Colmar 38 – Ribeauvillé 30 – St-Dié 34

🏔 Municipal les Bouleaux

🕾 03 89 58 41 56, www.valdargent.com/camping-rombach-les-bouleaux.htm – access difficult for caravans
Address : route de la Hingrie (located 1.5km to the northwest)
1.3 ha (38 pitches)

Rentals : – 5 🏠 .
Situated in a valley surrounded by pines and crossed by a stream.

Surroundings : 🌳 ♀
Leisure activities : 🛖 ⛵
Facilities : ⚕ ⛲ ⛲ launderette

Longitude : 7.2402
Latitude : 48.2877

STE-CROIX-EN-PLAINE

68127 – Michelin map **315** I8 – pop. 2 661 – alt. 192
▶ Paris 471 – Belfort 78 – Colmar 10 – Freiburg-im-Breisgau 49

🏔 Clair Vacances

🕾 03 89 49 27 28, www.clairvacances.com 🚫
Address : route de Herrlisheim (on the D1)
Opening times : from mid April to mid Oct.
4 ha (145 pitches) flat, grassy
Tariff : 26.50 € 🚶🚶 ⛺ 🅿 ⚡ (16A) – Extra per person 7.50 € – Reservation fee 10 €
Rental rates : (2015 price) (from mid April to mid Oct.) 🚫 – 13 🚐. Per night from 48 to 120 € – Per week from 332 to 852 € – Reservation fee 10 €
Attractive trees and shrubs decorate this peaceful site with plenty of charm.

Surroundings : 🔲
Leisure activities : 🛖 ⛵
Facilities : ⚕ ⛽ ⛲ 🛁 ⛲ launderette

Longitude : 7.35289
Latitude : 48.01454

Michelin classification:
🏔🏔🏔🏔🏔 *Extremely comfortable, equipped to a very high standard*
🏔🏔🏔🏔 *Very comfortable, equipped to a high standard*
🏔🏔🏔 *Comfortable and well equipped*
🏔🏔 *Reasonably comfortable*
🏔 *Satisfactory*

SAVERNE

67700 – Michelin map **315** I4 – pop. 12 046 – alt. 200
▶ Paris 450 – Lunéville 88 – St-Avold 89 – Sarreguemines 65

🏔 Seasonova Les Portes d'Alsace

🕾 03 88 91 35 65, www.camping-lesportesdalsace.com
Address : 40 rue du Père Libermann (1.3km southwest along the D 171)
Opening times : from beginning April to beginning Nov.
2.1 ha (145 pitches) flat, relatively flat, grassy
Tariff : (2015 price) 26 € 🚶🚶 ⛺ 🅿 ⚡ (4A) – Extra per person 6 € – Reservation fee 12 €
Rental rates : (2015 price) permanent 🚫 – 10 🚐. Per week from 300 to 790 € – Reservation fee 15 €
🚉 Flot Bleu sani-station 3 € – 15 🅿 10 €
A small rural oasis in an urban environment; a peaceful and well-appointed site.

Surroundings : ≤ ♀
Leisure activities : 🛖 ⛵ 🏊 (open air in season)
Facilities : ⚕ ⛽ ⛲ ⛷ ⛲ launderette
Nearby : ✂ 🐎

Longitude : 7.35539
Latitude : 48.73095

SÉLESTAT

67600 – Michelin map **315** I7 – pop. 19 332 – alt. 170
▶ Paris 441 – Colmar 24 – Gérardmer 65 – St-Dié 44

⚠ Municipal les Cigognes

✎ 03 88 92 03 98, www.selestat-haut-koenigsbourg.com

Address : 1 rue de la 1ère Division France Libre

Opening times : from beginning April to mid Oct.

0.7 ha (48 pitches) flat, grassy

Tariff : (2015 price) 17.85€ ✦✦ ⇌ 🔲 🔋 (10A) –
Extra per person 4.70€

🚾 Eurorelais sani-station 7€ – 20 🔲

A charming site 5 minutes from the town centre.

	GPS
Surroundings : ♀	Longitude : 7.44828
Leisure activities : 🎠🚴	Latitude : 48.25444
Facilities : ☞🗑🏛🍴🛍	
Nearby : 🍴🎣🏊	

For more information on visiting particular towns or regions, consult the relevant regional MICHELIN Green Guide. We also recommend you use the appropriate Michelin regional map to locate your selected campsite, to calculate distances and to work out the best route.

SEPPOIS-LE-BAS

68580 – Michelin map **315** H11 – pop. 1 164 – alt. 390
▶ Paris 454 – Altkirch 13 – Basel 42 – Belfort 38

⚠ Tohapi Les Lupins

✎ 03 89 25 65 37, www.tohapi.fr

Address : 1 ave de la Gare (take the northeastern exit along the D 17.2, follow the signs for Altkirch)

Opening times : from end May to beginning Sept.

3.5 ha (158 pitches) flat, grassy, terraced

Tariff : (2015 price) 17€ ✦✦ ⇌ 🔲 🔋 (16A) – Extra per person 4€ –
Reservation fee 10€

Rental rates : (2015 price) (from end May to beginning Sept.) 🅿 –
10 🏠. Per night from 25 to 100€ – Per week from 150 to 700€ –
Reservation fee 10€

🚾 10 🔲 17€

On the leafy site of the old station, very elongated location.

	GPS
Surroundings : 🐾♀	Longitude : 7.17893
Leisure activities : 🏛🎠🏊	Latitude : 47.53956
Facilities : ☞☞🔲🏛🍴🛍 launderette	
Nearby : 🍴	

STRASBOURG

67000 – Michelin map **315** K5 – pop. 271 708 – alt. 143
▶ Paris 488 – Stuttgart 160 – Baden-Baden 63 – Karlsruhe 87

⚠ Indigo Strasbourg 🚶

✎ 03 88 30 19 96, www.camping-indigo.com

Address : 9 rue de l'Auberge de Jeunesse

Opening times : permanent

3 ha (195 pitches) flat, grassy

Tariff : 32€ ✦✦ ⇌ 🔲 🔋 (10A) – Extra per person 5.70€ – Reservation fee 13€

Rental rates : permanent – 4 'gypsy' caravans – 12 🚐 –
35 🏠 – 12 tent lodges. Per night from 42 to 126€ – Per week from 294 to 882€ – Reservation fee 13€

🚾 local sani-station 9€

An urban site but quiet and with good shade.

	GPS
Surroundings : 🏞♀♀	Longitude : 7.71441
Leisure activities : 🍴🍴🏛🎣🏃🎠🚴🏊	Latitude : 48.57537
Facilities : ♿☞🏕🍴 launderette	

TURCKHEIM

68230 – Michelin map **315** H8 – pop. 3 747 – alt. 225
▶ Paris 471 – Colmar 7 – Gérardmer 47 – Munster 14

⚠ Le Médiéval

✎ 03 89 27 02 00, www.camping-turckheim.com

Address : quai de la Gare (to the west of the town, behind the stadium – access via the road between the level crossing and the bridge)

Opening times : from end March to mid Dec.

2.5 ha (117 pitches) flat, grassy

Tariff : 14.20€ ✦✦ ⇌ 🔲 🔋 (16A) – Extra per person 4.50€ – Reservation fee 10€

Rental rates : (2015 price) (from end March to mid Dec.) –
16 🚐. Per night from 40 to 124€ – Per week from 262 to 708€ – Reservation fee 10€

🚾 local sani-station 3€

Beside a small canal and near the Fecht river.

	GPS
Surroundings : 🏞♀	Longitude : 7.27144
Leisure activities : 🏛	Latitude : 48.08463
Facilities : ♿☞🔲🏛🍴 launderette	
Nearby : 🍴	

Key to rentals symbols :

12 🚐	*Number of mobile homes*
20 🏠	*Number of chalets*
6 🛏	*Number of rooms to rent*
Per night 30–50€	*Minimum/maximum rate per night*
Per week 300–1,000€	*Minimum/maximum rate per week*

WASSELONNE

67310 – Michelin map **315** I5 – pop. 5 562 – alt. 220
▶ Paris 464 – Haguenau 42 – Molsheim 15 – Saverne 15

⚠ Municipal

✎ 03 88 87 00 08, www.camping-wasselonne.com

Address : rue des Sapins (located 1km west along the D 224, follow the signs for Wangenbourg)

1.5 ha (100 pitches) terraced, grassy

Pretty green spaces within the grounds of a leisure centre.

	GPS
Surroundings : ⛰♀	Longitude : 7.44869
Leisure activities : 🎠🖼	Latitude : 48.63691
Facilities : ☞🍴 launderette 🚐	
Nearby : 🍴🍴🖼	

WATTWILLER

68700 – Michelin map **315** H10 – pop. 1 734 – alt. 356
▶ Paris 478 – Strasbourg 116 – Freiburg-im-Breisgau 81 – Basel 56

⛰ Les Sources ♦♦

✆ 03 89 75 44 94, www.campinglessources.com

Address : route des Crêtes

Opening times : from mid April to end Sept.

15 ha (200 pitches) terraced, grassy, stony

Tariff : 32 € ♦♦ ⇌ ▣ 🔌 (6A) – Extra per person 7 € – Reservation fee 10 €

Rental rates : (from mid April to end Sept.) – 60 🚍 – 20 🏠. Per night from 25 to 125 € – Per week from 175 to 875 € – Reservation fee 20 €

🚐 local sani-station 5 €

A pleasant wooded site, but the infrastructure and sanitary facilities are getting old.

Surroundings : 🐟 ⌂ 𝍌
Leisure activities : ▼ ✕ 🛋 ⛳daytime 🚴
🏇 ✂ 🏓 🎣 🛝 🛶
Facilities : ♿ ⚡ 🕤 ⚐ launderette ⛾ ⚒
Nearby : 🏇

Longitude : 7.16736
Latitude : 47.83675

WIHR-AU-VAL

68230 – Michelin map **315** H8 – pop. 1 237 – alt. 330
▶ Paris 463 – Colmar 14 – Gérardmer 38 – Guebwiller 35

⛰ La Route Verte

✆ 03 89 71 10 10, www.camping-routeverte.com

Address : 13 rue de la Gare (take the southern exit along the D 43, follow the signs for Soultzbach-les-Bains)

Opening times : from end April to end Sept.

1.2 ha (55 pitches) flat and relatively flat, grassy

Tariff : (2015 price) ♦ 3.15 €⇌ ▣ 4 € – 🔌 (10A) 6.45 € – Reservation fee 2 €

🚐 local sani-station 5 €

A small, lovely family-orientated site in the heart of a charming village surrounded by vineyards.

Surroundings : 🐟 ♀
Leisure activities : 🏇
Facilities : ♿ ⚡ 🕤 ⚐ 📷
Nearby : ▼ ✕

Longitude : 7.20513
Latitude : 48.05159

AQUITAINE

H. Lenain / hemis.fr

Welcome to Aquitaine, home to prehistoric remains, fortified towns and a mosaic of landscapes, as distinctive and welcoming as the hospitality and humour of its locals. A quick stop to buy *confit d'oie* (confit of goose) could lead to an invitation to look around the farm! Aquitaine has dense forests, imposing mountains and sweeping beaches; it is home to picturesque villages, bustling cities, large estates and imposing châteaux. No stay would be complete without visiting at least one of the renowned vineyards of Bordeaux. Then head over to the 'Silver Coast', with its many surfers, rugby fans and bullfighters, all raised on *gâteau Basque*, a cake made with almond flour, and *piment d'Espelette*, a rather spicy pepper. This rugged, sunlit land between the Pyrenees and the Atlantic remains fiercely proud of its identity. Spend a little time in a sleepy Basque village and you will soon discover the region's traditional colours of red, white and green proudly displayed.

AGEN

47000 – Michelin map **336** F4 – pop. 33 920 – alt. 50
▶ Paris 662 – Auch 74 – Bordeaux 141 – Pau 159

⛰ Le Moulin de Mellet

🖉 05 53 87 50 89. www.camping-moulin-mellet.com

Address : at St-Hilaire de Lusignan, route de Prayssas (head 8km northwest along the D 813 and take a right turn along the D 107)

Opening times : from beginning April to mid Oct.

5 ha/3.5 for camping (65 pitches) flat, grassy

Tariff : (2015 price) 27.60€ ★★ 🚗 ▣ ⚡ (10A) – Extra per person 6.45€

Rental rates : (2015 price) (from beginning April to mid Oct.) – 2 🚐 – 6 🏠. Per night from 55 to 130€ – Per week from 250 to 620€

🚮 local sani-station – 6 ▣ – 🚱11€

Choose pitches near the small stream, furthest from the road.

Surroundings : 🏞 ♨♨
Leisure activities : 🍽 ✕ 🏛 ⛵ 🎣 🦅 farm or petting farm
Facilities : ♿ ⛽ 🚿 🚻 ▣ 🧺
Nearby : 🛒

Longitude : 0.54188
Latitude : 44.2436

---

*To visit a town or region, use the **MICHELIN Green Guides**.*

AINHOA

64250 – Michelin map **342** C3 – pop. 672 – alt. 130
▶ Paris 791 – Bayonne 28 – Biarritz 29 – Cambo-les-Bains 11

⛰ Xokoan

🖉 05 59 29 90 26. www.camping-xokoan.com

Address : Dancharia district (head 2.5km southwest then take the left turn before the customs post, border with Spain)

Opening times : permanent

0.6 ha (30 pitches) relatively flat, flat, grassy

Tariff : 20€ ★★ 🚗 ▣ ⚡ (10A) – Extra per person 6€
Rental rates : permanent 🚫 – 2 🚐 – 6 🛏 – 12 gîtes. Per night from 90€ – Per week from 420€
🚮 AireService sani-station 6€ – 4 ▣ 10€

Situated alongside a stream that marks the border between France and Spain.

Surroundings : 🏞 ♨♨
Leisure activities : 🍽 ✕ 🏛
Facilities : ♿ ⛽ 🎱 🚿 🚻 launderette 🧺
Nearby : 🛒

Longitude : -1.50369
Latitude : 43.29139

⛰ Harazpy

🖉 05 59 29 89 38. www.camping-harazpy.com

Address : Gastelu-Gaïna district (to the northwest of the town, behind the church)

Opening times : from beginning March to beginning Nov.

1 ha (25 pitches), slightly sloping and flat, grassy

Tariff : 17.50€ ★★ 🚗 ▣ ⚡ (10A) – Extra per person 6€
🚮 AireService sani-station 6€ – 4 ▣ 17.50€

A delightful and tranquil meadow setting with a view of typical Basque countryside.

Surroundings : 🏞 ≤ ♨
Leisure activities : 🏛
Facilities : ♿ ⛽ 🚻 launderette

Longitude : -1.50172
Latitude : 43.3089

AIRE-SUR-L'ADOUR

40800 – Michelin map **335** J12 – pop. 6 275 – alt. 80
▶ Paris 722 – Auch 84 – Condom 68 – Dax 77

⛰ Les Ombrages de l'Adour

🖉 05 58 71 75 10. www.camping-adour-landes.com

Address : rue des Graviers (located near the bridge, behind the arenas; beside the Adour river)

Opening times : from mid April to mid Oct.

2 ha (100 pitches) flat, grassy

Tariff : (2015 price) 19€ ★★ 🚗 ▣ ⚡ (10A) – Extra per person 4.20€

Rental rates : (from mid April to mid Oct.) – 8 🚐 – 2 canvas bungalows. Per night from 40 to 69€ – Per week from 190 to 405€
🚮 AireService sani-station – 20 ▣ 19€

Situated near the town centre.

Surroundings : 🏞 ♨♨
Leisure activities : ⛵ 🎣 🛝 ⛲ (small swimming pool) 🎣
Facilities : ⛽ 🚿 🚻 launderette

Longitude : -0.25793
Latitude : 43.70257

ALLES-SUR-DORDOGNE

24480 – Michelin map **329** G6 – pop. 344 – alt. 70
▶ Paris 534 – Bergerac 36 – Le Bugue 12 – Les Eyzies-de-Tayac 22

⛰ Port de Limeuil

🖉 05 53 63 29 76. www.leportdelimeuil.com

Address : 3km northeast on the D 51e, near the bridge at Limeuil, where the Dordogne and the Vézère rivers meet

Opening times : from beginning May to end Sept.

7 ha/4 for camping (90 pitches)

Tariff : 34.20€ ★★ 🚗 ▣ ⚡ (10A) – Extra per person 7.60€ – Reservation fee 15€

Rental rates : (from beginning May to end Sept.) – 13 🚐 – 1 gîte. Per night from 50 to 100€ – Per week from 175 to 1,050€ – Reservation fee 15€
🚮 local sani-station – 14 ▣ 30.20€

Lots of green space; swimming possible where the Dordogne and Vézère rivers meet.

Surroundings : 🏞 ♨♨ ⛰
Leisure activities : 🍽 ✕ 🏛 ⛵ 🚲 🎿 🛝 🦅
Facilities : ♿ ⛽ 🚿 🚻 launderette 🚙 🧺

Longitude : 0.88599
Latitude : 44.87968

We have selected the best campsites in France with our usual care, listing those with the best facilities in the most pleasant surroundings.

ANGLET

64600 – Michelin map **342** C2 – pop. 37 661 – alt. 20
▶ Paris 773 – Bordeaux 187 – Pamplona 108 – Donostia-San Sebastián 51

⛰ Le Parme

🖉 05 59 23 03 00. www.campingdeparme.com

Address : 2 allée Etchecopar

Opening times : from end March to end Oct.

3.5 ha (187 pitches) grassy

Tariff : 47€ ★★ 🚗 ▣ ⚡ (6A) – Extra per person 7.50€ – Reservation fee 5€

Rental rates : (from end March to beginning Oct.) – 76 ⬛ – 14 ⬛ – 13 canvas bungalows. Per night from 35 to 155€ – Per week from 245 to 1,085€ – Reservation fee 15€

Surroundings : ⬛ 👥
Leisure activities : 🍷✗ ⬛ ⬛👥🏃🚣🏊🎿
multi-sports ground
Facilities : ♿⚷🚿 launderette ⬛
GPS Longitude : -1.53238
Latitude : 43.4643

ANGOISSE

24270 – Michelin map **329** H3 – pop. 610 – alt. 345
▶ Paris 445 – Bordeaux 180 – Périgueux 51 – Limoges 53

⛰ Rouffiac en Périgord

📞 0553526879. www.semitour.com – traditional camp. spaces also available

Address : Rouffiac leisure centre (4km southeast along the D 80, follow the signs for Payzac, 150m from a small lake (direct access)

Opening times : from beginning May to end Sept.

54 ha/6 for camping (78 pitches)

Tariff : (2015 price) 🧍5.50€ ⬛ 📶 8.40€ (16A)
Rental rates : (2015 price) permanent ♿ – 2 ⬛ – 44 ⬛. Per night from 83 to 165€ – Per week from 220 to 670€

🚰 local sani-station

In a green setting, part overlooking a well-equipped leisure centre. Some good-quality rental accommodation.

Surroundings : 🌳⬛ 👥
Leisure activities : ⬛ 🕐daytime 🏃🚴
Facilities : ♿⚷🚿 launderette
Nearby : 🍷✗ ⬛ (beach) 🎣 cable wakeboarding, pedalos, zip wiring
GPS Longitude : 1.16648
Latitude : 45.41449

*The classification (1 to 5 tents, **black** or red) that we award to selected sites in this guide is our own system. It should not be confused with the classification (1 to 5 stars) of official organisations.*

ANTONNE-ET-TRIGONANT

24420 – Michelin map **329** F4 – pop. 1 203 – alt. 106
▶ Paris 484 – Bordeaux 139 – Périgueux 10 – Limoges 91

⛰ Au Fil de l'Eau

📞 0553061788. www.campingaufildeleau.com

Address : at Antonne, 6 allée des Platanes (take the northeastern exit and follow the signs for Escoire to the right; beside the island, on the D 6)

Opening times : from mid April to mid Sept.

1.5 ha (50 pitches)

Tariff : (2015 price) 21.50€ ⬛⬛ 📶 (6A) – Extra per person 5€
Rental rates : (2015 price) (from mid April to mid Sept.) – 13 ⬛ – 4 canvas bungalows. Per night from 60 to 100€ – Per week from 300 to 700€

🚰 local sani-station 2€

Leafy site with plenty of green space; site extends to the river.

Surroundings : 🌳⬛ 👥
Leisure activities : ⬛ 🚣🏊🎿farm or petting farm 🐾
Facilities : ♿⚷🚿launderette ⬛
GPS Longitude : 0.83754
Latitude : 45.213

⛰ Huttopia Lanmary Forest Camp ⬛

📞 0553458863. www.huttopia.com

Address : Forest Camp ONF – RD 69

Opening times : from mid April to beginning Oct.

20 ha (140 pitches) very uneven, terraced, stony, gravelled

Tariff : (2015 price) 46.80€ ⬛⬛ 📶 (10A) –
Extra per person 7.50€ – Reservation fee 13€
Rental rates : (2015 price) (from mid April to beginning Oct.) – 21 ⬛ – 36 tent lodges. Per night from 47 to 180€ – Per week from 247 to 1,260€ – Reservation fee 13€

🚰 local sani-station 7€

Surroundings : 🌳👥
Leisure activities : 🍷✗ 👥🏃🚣🚴🎿
Facilities : ♿⚷🏖launderette ⬛
GPS Longitude : 0.82906
Latitude : 45.24033

ARAMITS

64570 – Michelin map **342** H4 – pop. 677 – alt. 293
▶ Paris 829 – Mauléon-Licharre 27 – Oloron-Ste-Marie 15 – Pau 49

⛰ Barétous-Pyrénées

📞 0559341221. www.camping-pyrenees.com

Address : Ripaude district (take the western exit along the D 918, follow the signs for Mauléon-Licharre; beside the Vert de Barlanes river)

Opening times : from beginning April to mid Oct.

2 ha (61 pitches) flat, grassy

Tariff : (2015 price) 29€ ⬛⬛ 📶 (10A) – Extra per person 6.50€ – Reservation fee 15€
Rental rates : (2015 price) (from end Dec. to mid Oct.) ♿ (chalet) – 10 ⬛ – 11 ⬛ – 3 canvas bungalows. Per night from 42 to 85€ – Per week from 250 to 610€ – Reservation fee 18€

🚰 local sani-station

Surroundings : ⬛👥
Leisure activities : 🍷✗ ⬛ ⬛ jacuzzi 🚣🚴🎿
Facilities : ♿⚷🅲🍴launderette ⬛
GPS Longitude : -0.73243
Latitude : 43.12135

This guide is updated regularly, so buy your new copy every year!

ARCACHON

33120 – Michelin map **335** D7 – pop. 12 153 – alt. 5
▶ Paris 651 – Bordeaux 73 – Mont-de-Marsan 125

⛰ Camping Club d'Arcachon ⬛

📞 0556832415. www.camping-arcachon.com

Address : 5 allée de la Galaxie

Opening times : permanent

6 ha (300 pitches) undulating, terraced, relatively flat, flat, sandy

Tariff : (2015 price) 🧍11€ ⬛ 9€ 📶 14€ – (8A) 5€ – Reservation fee 32€
Rental rates : (2015 price) (from mid Dec. to mid Nov.) – 4 'gypsy' caravans – 80 ⬛ – 4 ⬛. Per night from 56 to 169€ – Per week from 360 to 1,190€ – Reservation fee 32€

🚰 AireService sani-station 5€ – 50 📶 32.20€ – 🚐11.70€

Surroundings : 🌳⬛ 👥
Leisure activities : 🍷✗ ⬛ ⬛🏃 jacuzzi 🚣🚴
Facilities : ♿⚷🅲🍴⬛🚿launderette ⬛ refrigerated food storage facilities
GPS Longitude : -1.17667
Latitude : 44.65194

ARÈS

33740 – Michelin map **335** E6 – pop. 5 548 – alt. 6
▶ Paris 627 – Arcachon 47 – Bordeaux 48

▲▲▲ Les Goëlands

⌀ 05 56 82 55 64. www.goelands.com

Address : 64 avenue de la Libération (1.7km southeast, near lakes and 500m from the quayside)

Opening times : from beginning March to end Oct.

10 ha/6 for camping (400 pitches)

Tariff : (2015 price) 35€ ♣♣ ⇔ 🗉 ⍟ (6A) – Extra per person 9.50€ – Reservation fee 25.50€

Rental rates : (2015 price) (from beginning March to end Oct.) – 10 🚐. Per night from 45 to 132€ – Per week from 315 to 925€ – Reservation fee 25.50€

🛠 local sani-station

| Surroundings : |
| Leisure activities : ♈ ✕ 🖼 🗇 🏃 🛶 🚴 🏊 multi-sports ground |
| Facilities : ♿ ⚡ 🍴 launderette 🚗 🚿 |
| Nearby : 🏖 (pond) 🎣 ⚓ |

GPS
Longitude : -1.11979
Latitude : 44.75747

▲▲ La Cigale

⌀ 05 56 60 22 59. www.camping-lacigale-ares.com – limited spaces for one-night stay

Address : 53 rue du Général de Gaulle (take the northern exit)

Opening times : from end April to beginning Oct.

2.4 ha (75 pitches)

Tariff : (2015 price) 37.50€ ♣♣ ⇔ 🗉 ⍟ (10A) – Extra per person 8€ – Reservation fee 18€

Rental rates : (2015 price) (from beginning April to beginning Nov.) – 3 🚐 – 8 🏠 – 3 tent lodges. Per night from 40 to 130€ – Per week from 270 to 910€ – Reservation fee 20€

🛠 AireService sani-station – 🚐⍟19€

| Surroundings : |
| Leisure activities : ♈ ✕ 🖼 🛶 🏊 |
| Facilities : ♿ ⚡ 🍴 launderette 🚿 |

GPS
Longitude : -1.14188
Latitude : 44.77287

▲▲ Les Abberts

⌀ 05 56 60 26 80. www.lesabberts.com

Address : 17 rue des Abberts (take the northern exit then take the turning to the left)

Opening times : from beginning April to mid Sept.

2 ha (125 pitches)

Tariff : 38€ ♣♣ ⇔ 🗉 ⍟ (10A) – Extra per person 9.50€ – Reservation fee 17€

Rental rates : (from beginning April to end Sept.) 🚿 – 20 🚐 – 1 🏠. Per week from 300 to 980€ – Reservation fee 17€

| Surroundings : |
| Leisure activities : ♈ 🖼 🛶 🚴 🏊 |
| Facilities : ♿ ⚡ 🍴 launderette 🚿 |

GPS
Longitude : -1.1444
Latitude : 44.77163

⚠ Pasteur

⌀ 05 56 60 33 33. www.atlantic-vacances.com – limited spaces for one-night stay

Address : 1 rue du Pilote (take the southeastern exit, 300m from the quayside)

Opening times : from end March to mid Nov.

1 ha (50 pitches)

Tariff : ♣ 26€ ⇔ – ⍟ (6A) 4.50€ – Reservation fee 18€

Rental rates : (from end March to mid Nov.) – 16 🚐 – 14 🏠. Per week from 300 to 750€ – Reservation fee 18€

🛠 AireService sani-station – 17 🗉 15€ – 🚐 11€

Well-kept site in a residential area.

| Surroundings : |
| Leisure activities : 🛶 🚴 🏊 (small swimming pool) |
| Facilities : ♿ ⚡ 🚿 🍴 🔥 |

GPS
Longitude : -1.13681
Latitude : 44.76174

ATUR

24750 – Michelin map **329** F5 – pop. 1 744 – alt. 224
▶ Paris 499 – Bordeaux 134 – Périgueux 6 – Brive-la-Gaillarde 83

▲▲▲ Iris Parc Le Grand Dague ♠♠

⌀ 05 53 04 21 01. www.irisparc.com – limited spaces for one-night stay 🚿

Address : route du Grand Dague (3km southeast following signs for St-Laurent-sur-Manoire – if on southern diversion coming from Brive or Limoges, take the road towards Bergerac and take the road to the right)

Opening times : from end April to end Sept.

22 ha/12 for camping (420 pitches)

Tariff : (2015 price) 39€ ♣♣ ⇔ 🗉 ⍟ (10A) – Extra per person 8€ – Reservation fee 20€

Rental rates : (2015 price) (from end April to end Sept.) 🚿 ℗ – 278 🚐 – 92 tent lodges. Per night from 21 to 152€ – Per week from 105 to 1,064€ – Reservation fee 20€

🛠 sani-station 7€

A well-equipped indoor children's play area.

| Surroundings : |
| Leisure activities : ♈ ✕ 🖼 🗇 🏃 🛶 🚴 🏊 🏊 multi-sports ground |
| Facilities : ♿ ⚡ 🗉 🍴 🚗 🚿 🍴 launderette 🚗 🚿 |

GPS
Longitude : 0.77656
Latitude : 45.14816

Using the traditional Michelin classification method, the guide provides you with an easy, speedy reference for assessing the category of each site: 1 to 5 tents (see page 10).

AUDENGE

33980 – Michelin map **335** E6 – pop. 5 225 – alt. 12
▶ Paris 638 – Bordeaux 59 – Mont-de-Marsan 112

▲▲ Municipal Le Braou ♠♠

⌀ 05 56 26 90 03. www.camping-audenge.com

Address : 26 rue de Bordeaux

Opening times : from beginning April to end Sept.

5 ha (200 pitches) flat, grassy, sandy

Tariff : (2015 price) 30€ ♣♣ ⇔ 🗉 ⍟ (6A) – Extra per person 6€ – Reservation fee 25€

Rental rates : (2015 price) (from beginning April to end Sept.) 🚿 – 36 🚐 – 2 canvas bungalows. Per night from 54 to 130€ – Per week from 270 to 820€ – Reservation fee 25€

🛠 Eurorelais sani-station 5€ – 🚐 12.50€

| Surroundings : |
| Leisure activities : ♈ ✕ 🏃 🛶 🏊 |
| Facilities : ♿ ⚡ 🚿 🍴 launderette, refrigerated food storage facilities |

GPS
Longitude : -1.00444
Latitude : 44.68416

AZUR

40140 – Michelin map **335** D12 – pop. 575 – alt. 9
▶ Paris 730 – Bayonne 54 – Dax 25 – Mimizan 79

FranceLoc La Paillotte ⚑

✆ 05 58 48 12 12. www.paillotte.com – limited spaces for one-night stay ⌫

Address : 66 route des Campings (located 1.5km southwest; beside the Lac de Soustons)

Opening times : from mid April to end Sept.

7 ha (310 pitches)

Tariff : (2015 price) 40.50€ ✶✶ ⛟ ▣ (ℓ) (10A) – Extra per person 7€ – Reservation fee 26€

Rental rates : (2015 price) (from mid April to end Sept.) ♿ ⌫ – 2 'gypsy' caravans – 222 🛏 – 50 ⌂. Per night from 30 to 202€ – Per week from 210 to 1,414€ – Reservation fee 26€

An exotically decorated but pretty chalet village with a large water park, beside the lake.

Surroundings : ⚲ ≼ ▭ ♨♨ ⌂
Leisure activities : ♟ ✗ ⛱ ⛲ ⛏ ⚓ ◻
⛵ ⛷ ⏀ ⛸
Facilities : ♿ ⚮ ⛺ ⚱ ⚲ ☂ launderette
⛼ ⛽
Nearby : ⚵ ✗ ⛵ ⏀ pedalos

Longitude : -1.30875
Latitude : 43.78731

Azur Rivage ⚑

✆ 05 58 48 30 72. www.campingazurivage.com

Address : 720 route des Campings (situated 2km to the south, 100m from the lake at Soustons)

Opening times : from beginning June to mid Sept.

6.5 ha (250 pitches)

Tariff : (2015 price) 32.80€ ✶✶ ⛟ ▣ (ℓ) (10A) – Extra per person 7.30€ – Reservation fee 17€

Rental rates : (2015 price) (from beginning June to mid Sept.) ♿ – 62 🛏 – 2 canvas bungalows. Per night from 40 to 61€ – Per week from 555 to 995€ – Reservation fee 17€

🚿 local sani-station

Groups welcomed in a reserved section of the site.

Surroundings : ⚲ ▭ ♨♨
Leisure activities : ⚲ daytime ⛏ ⚓ ⛵ ⛷
⛸ multi-sports ground
Facilities : ♿ ⚮ ⛺ ⚱ ⚲ ⛽ refrigerated food storage facilities, refrigerators
Nearby : ⚵ ✗ ⏀ ⛵ pedalos

Longitude : -1.30461
Latitude : 43.78452

To visit a town or region, use the MICHELIN Green Guides.

BADEFOLS-SUR-DORDOGNE

24150 – Michelin map **329** F6 – pop. 211 – alt. 42
▶ Paris 542 – Bergerac 27 – Périgueux 54 – Sarlat-la-Canéda 47

Les Bö Bains

✆ 05 53 73 52 52. www.bo-bains.com – limited spaces for one-night stay

Address : route de Bergerac (take the western exit, along the D 29; beside the Dordogne)

Opening times : from beginning April to end Sept.

5 ha (97 pitches)

Tariff : (2015 price) 33€ ✶✶ ⛟ ▣ (ℓ) (9A) – Extra per person 9€ – Reservation fee 25€

Rental rates : (2015 price) (from beginning April to end Sept.) ♿ (1 mobile home) – 40 🛏 – 34 ⌂. Per night from 50 to 80€ – Per week from 250 to 999€ – Reservation fee 25€

🚿 local sani-station

Choose pitches furthest from the road along the Dordogne.

Surroundings : ≼ ▭ ♨♨
Leisure activities : ♟ ✗ ⛱ ⚲ nighttime ⛏
⛱ ⚓ ⛵ ⛷ ⛸ ◻
Facilities : ♿ ⚮ ⚱ ⚲ ☂ ⛽ launderette ⛼
Nearby : ✗

Longitude : 0.78541
Latitude : 44.84155

LA BASTIDE-CLAIRENCE

64240 – Michelin map **342** E4 – pop. 984 – alt. 50
▶ Paris 767 – Bayonne 26 – Hasparren 9 – Peyrehorade 29

Village Vacances Les Collines Iduki
(rental of apartments and maisonnettes only)

✆ 05 59 70 20 81. www.location-vacances-paysbasque.com

Address : Pont de Port

Opening times : permanent

2.5 ha very uneven, terraced

Rental rates : (2015 price) ♿ (1 apartment) – 6 ⌂ – 30 apartments. Per night from 65 to 214€ – Per week from 324 to 1,754€

Pretty Basque buildings and a good-quality restaurant.

Surroundings : ⚲ ≼ ♨♨
Leisure activities : ✗ ⛱ ⚓ ⛷
Facilities : ♿ ⚮ ℗ ⛼ ▦ ⛽ launderette
Nearby : ✗

Longitude : -1.25742
Latitude : 43.43324

The prices listed were supplied by the campsite owners in 2015 (if prices were not available, those from the previous year are given). The fees should be regarded as basic charges and may fluctuate with inflation.

BAUDREIX

64800 – Michelin map **342** K3 – pop. 537 – alt. 245
▶ Paris 791 – Argelès-Gazost 39 – Lourdes 26 – Oloron-Ste-Marie 48

Les Ôkiri

✆ 05 59 92 97 73. www.lesokiri.com – ⛺ ⌫

Address : avenue du Lac (at the leisure and activity park)

Opening times : from beginning April to end Sept.

20 ha/2 for camping (60 pitches) flat, grassy

Tariff : 20€ ✶✶ ⛟ ▣ (ℓ) (10A) – Extra per person 7.50€ – Reservation fee 10€

Rental rates : permanent ⌫ ℗ – 10 🛏 – 24 ⌂ – 5 canvas bungalows. Per night from 40 to 100€ – Per week from 200 to 715€ – Reservation fee 10€

Site is in a large leisure centre with comfortable wooden chalets and mobile homes with and without sanitary facilities.

Surroundings : ⚲ ▭ ♨♨ ⌂
Leisure activities : ♟ ✗ ⚓ ⚵ ⛵ (beach)
⛷ ⛸ pedalos ⚑ multi-sports ground
Facilities : ♿ ⚮ (July-Aug.) ▣ ⛽ launderette ⛼

Longitude : -0.26124
Latitude : 43.20439

BEAUVILLE

47470 – Michelin map **336** H4 – pop. 584 – alt. 208
▶ Paris 641 – Agen 26 – Moissac 32 – Montaigu-de-Quercy 16

⛰ Les 2 Lacs

✆ 05 53 95 45 41. www.les2lacs.info

Address : at Vallon de Gerbal (900m southeast along the D 122, follow the signs for Bourg de Visa)

Opening times : from beginning April to end Oct.

22 ha/2.5 for camping (80 pitches) open site, terrace, flat, grassy, wood, pond

Tariff : (2015 price) ☀ 5.60€ 🚗 📧 10.15€ – 🔌 (6A) 2.95€

Rental rates : (2015 price) (from beginning April to end Oct.) – 2 🛖 – 1 🏠 – 7 canvas bungalows. Per night from 30 to 150€ – Per week from 167 to 700€

Surroundings : 🏞 ⛵ 🎣	**G**	
Leisure activities : 🍷 ✗ 🛶 🎿 ⛱ (beach) 🛥 boats to hire 🎣	**P**	Longitude : 0.88819
Facilities : 🚿 ⛽ 🏕 🍴 launderette	**S**	Latitude : 44.27142

BÉLUS

40300 – Michelin map **335** E13 – pop. 605 – alt. 135
▶ Paris 749 – Bayonne 37 – Dax 18 – Orthez 36

⛰ La Comtesse

✆ 05 58 57 69 07. www.campinglacomtesse.com 🎣

Address : at Claquin (2.5km northwest along the D 75 and take turning to the right)

Opening times : from beginning April to end Sept.

6 ha (100 pitches) flat, grassy

Tariff : 20.50€ ☀☀ 🚗 📧 🔌 (10A) – Extra per person 3.95€ – Reservation fee 10€

Rental rates : (2015 price) permanent 🎣 – 16 🛖 – 2 canvas bungalows. Per night from €115 to 180€ – Per week from 200 to 810€ – Reservation fee 10€

In a pleasant wood of poplar trees, beside a lake.

Surroundings : 🏞 ⛵ 🎣	**G**	
Leisure activities : 🍷 ✗ 🛖 🎿 ⛱ 🎣	**P**	Longitude : -1.13075
Facilities : 🚿 ⛽ 🏕 🍴 launderette 🎣	**S**	Latitude : 43.60364

BELVÈS

24170 – Michelin map **329** H7 – pop. 1 432 – alt. 175
▶ Paris 553 – Bergerac 52 – Le Bugue 24 – Les Eyzies-de-Tayac 25

⛰ RCN Le Moulin de la Pique ♣⚡

✆ 05 53 29 01 15. www.rcn.fr

Address : at Moulin de la Pique (3km southeast along the D 710, follow the signs for Fumel; near the Nauze river, a lake and a millpond)

Opening times : from mid April to end Sept.

15 ha/6 for camping (219 pitches)

Tariff : 54.25€ ☀☀ 🚗 📧 🔌 (10A) – Extra per person 6.75€ – Reservation fee 19.95€

Rental rates : (from mid April to end Sept.) 🚿 – 62 🛖 – 3 apartments – 5 tent lodges. Per night from 36 to 193€ – Per week from 252 to 1,351€ – Reservation fee 19.95€

🚐 20 📧 15€

Surroundings : ⛵ 🎣	**G**	
Leisure activities : 🍷 ✗ 🛖 🎣 🎿 🚴 🎿 🏹 🎿 ⛱ 🎣	**P**	Longitude : 1.01438
Facilities : 🚿 ⛽ 🆒 🏕 🍴 🎣 launderette 🎣	**S**	Latitude : 44.76192

⛰ FranceLoc Les Hauts de Ratebout ♣⚡

✆ 05 53 29 02 10. www.camping-hauts-ratebout.fr – limited spaces for one-night stay

Address : at Ste-Foy-de-Belvès, Ratebout (7km southeast along the D 710. follow the signs for Fumel, D 54 and take turning to the left)

Opening times : from mid April to beginning Sept.

12 ha/6 for camping (220 pitches) open site, terraced, flat and relatively flat, grassy

Tariff : (2015 price) 43€ ☀☀ 🚗 📧 🔌 (10A) – Extra per person 7€ – Reservation fee 27€

Rental rates : (from mid April to beginning Sept.) 🚿 – 4 'gypsy' caravans - 168 🛖 – 12 tent lodges – 5 gîtes. Per night from 40 to 109€ – Per week from 161 to 1,316€ – Reservation fee 27€

Surroundings : 🏞 ⟨ 🎣	**G**	
Leisure activities : 🍷 ✗ 🛖 🎿 🏹 🎿 🎿 🎿 🏃 🎿 🎿 🎿 multi-sports ground	**P**	Longitude : 1.04529
Facilities : 🚿 ⛽ 🏕 🍴 🎿 🎿 🍴 launderette 🎿 🎣	**S**	Latitude : 44.74151

⛰ Flower Les Nauves ♣⚡

✆ 05 53 29 12 64. www.lesnauves.com

Address : at Le Bos Rouge (4.5km southwest along the D 53, follow the signs for Monpazier and turn left following the signs for Larzac)

Opening times : from beginning April to end Sept.

40 ha/5 for camping (100 pitches) relatively flat to hilly, grassy

Tariff : 24.90€ ☀☀ 🚗 📧 🔌 (8A) – Extra per person 5€

Rental rates : (from beginning April to end Sept.) – 30 🛖 – 4 🏠 – 4 canvas bungalows – 7 tent lodges. Per night from 44 to 104€ – Per week from 220 to 728€ – Reservation fee 15€

Surroundings : 🏞 ⛵ 🎣	**G**	
Leisure activities : 🍷 ✗ 🛖 🏹 🎿 🎿 farm or petting farm	**P**	Longitude : 0.98167
Facilities : 🚿 ⛽ 🏕 🍴 🎿 🆒 🎣	**S**	Latitude : 44.75306
Nearby : 🐎		

In order for the guide to remain wholly objective, the selection of campsites is made on an entirely independent basis.

BEYNAC-ET-CAZENAC

24220 – Michelin map **329** H6 – pop. 522 – alt. 75
▶ Paris 537 – Bergerac 62 – Brive-la-Gaillarde 63 – Fumel 60

⛰ Le Capeyrou

✆ 05 53 29 54 95. www.campinglecapeyrou.com

Address : route de Sarlat (take the eastern exit, along the D 57; beside the Dordogne river)

Opening times : from end April to end Sept.

4.5 ha (120 pitches) flat, grassy

Tariff : ☀ 7.25€ 🚗 📧 9€ – 🔌 (10A) 4.70€ – Reservation fee 10€

Rental rates : (from end April to end Sept.) 🎣 – 4 tent lodges. Per week from 290 to 720€ – Reservation fee 10€

🚐 local sani-station

Surroundings : ⟨ Château de Beynac 🎣	**G**	
Leisure activities : 🍷 🛖 🎿 ⛱ 🎿 🎿	**P**	Longitude : 1.14843
Facilities : 🚿 ⛽ 🎿 🍴 launderette	**S**	Latitude : 44.83828
Nearby : 🍴 ✗ 🎣 🎿 ⛱ (beach)		

BIARRITZ

64200 – Michelin map **342** C4 – pop. 25 397 – alt. 19
▶ Paris 772 – Bayonne 9 – Bordeaux 190 – Pau 122

⛰ Club Airotel Biarritz-Camping

✆ 05 59 23 00 12. www.biarritz-camping.fr ✄

Address : 28 rue Harcet

Opening times : from end March to beginning Oct.

3 ha (170 pitches) terraced, relatively flat, flat, grassy

Tariff : 47.50€ ✦✦ ⇌ 🔲 ⚡ (10A) – Extra per person 9€ – Reservation fee 20€

Rental rates : (2015 price) (from end Oct. to beginning Oct.) ✄ – 72 🚐 – 14 canvas bungalows. Per night from 60 to 265€ – Per week from 320 to 1,005€ – Reservation fee 20€

300m from the Cite de l'Ocean and 700m from the town.

Surroundings : ⚲⚲	
Leisure activities : ▼✕ jacuzzi ⇌ ⅃	**G P S** Longitude : -1.56685
Facilities : ⚹ ⌐ ⌂ ▯ launderette ⊿ ⟆	Latitude : 43.46199
Nearby : 🐎	

BIAS

40170 – Michelin map **335** D10 – pop. 736 – alt. 41
▶ Paris 706 – Castets 33 – Mimizan 7 – Morcenx 30

⛰ Municipal Le Tatiou ♟

Municipal Le Tatiou

✆ 05 58 09 04 76. www.campingletatiou.com

Address : route de Lespecier (situated 2km west)

Opening times : from beginning April to end Sept.

10 ha (501 pitches)

Tariff : (2015 price) 23.80€ ✦✦ ⇌ 🔲 ⚡ (10A) – Extra per person 6.20€ – Reservation fee 22€

Rental rates : (2015 price) (from beginning April to end Sept.) ⚹ – 8 🚐 – 5 canvas bungalows – 2 tent lodges. Per night from 15 to 102€ – Per week from 120 to 690€ – Reservation fee 22€

Lots of pitches for tents and caravans and a variety of options for different levels of comfort.

Surroundings : ⚲⚲	
Leisure activities : ▼✕ 🏠 ☑ 🏃 ⇌ 🚲 ✄⚲ ⅃	**G P S** Longitude : -1.24029
Facilities : ⚹ ⌐ ⌂ ▯ launderette ⊿ ⟆ refrigerated food storage facilities	Latitude : 44.14531

BIDART

64210 – Michelin map **342** C2 – pop. 6 117 – alt. 40
▶ Paris 783 – Bordeaux 196 – Pau 119 – Bayonne 13

⛰ Les Castels Le Ruisseau des Pyrénées

Le Ruisseau des Pyrénées

♟ (rental of mobile homes, chalets and canvas bungalows only)

✆ 05 59 41 94 50. www.camping-le-ruisseau.fr – traditional camping spaces also available

Address : rue Burruntz (situated 2km east; beside the Ouhabia river and a stream – divided into two separate areas)

Opening times : permanent

15 ha/7 for camping (440 pitches) terraced, flat, grassy

Rental rates : ⚹ (1 mobile home) – 200 🚐 – 7 🏠 – 4 tent lodges. Per night from 42 to 299€ – Per week from 294 to 2,093€

🚐 local sani-station – 14 🔲 22€

In two distinct sections with plenty of green space for activities or relaxation. Two water parks, one zen-style and one with slides.

Surroundings : ⚲ ⊏ ⚲⚲	
Leisure activities : ▼✕ 🏠 ☑ 🏃 ☖ 🌊 hammam, jacuzzi ⇌⚲ 🚲 ⚽ ☐ ⅃ ⇲ fitness trail, farm or petting farm, forest trail, multi-sports ground	**G P S** Longitude : -1.56835 Latitude : 43.43704
Facilities : ⚹ ⌐ ⌂ ▯ launderette ⊿ ⟆	
Nearby : 🐎	

⛰ Yelloh! Village Ilbarritz ♟

✆ 05 59 23 00 29. www.camping-ilbarritz.com

Address : avenue de Biarritz (situated 2km to the north)

Opening times : from beginning April to end Sept.

6 ha (374 pitches) terraced, flat and relatively flat, grassy, sandy

Tariff : (2015 price) 75€ ✦✦ ⇌ 🔲 ⚡ (10A) – Extra per person 9€

Rental rates : (2015 price) (from beginning April to end Sept.) ⚹ (1 mobile home) – 166 🚐 – 24 🏠. Per night from 88 to 268€ – Per week from 280 to 2,046€

The spacious entrance is attractive, with pretty buildings in the Basque style.

Surroundings : ⊏ ⚲⚲	
Leisure activities : ▼✕ 🏠 ☑ 🏃 jacuzzi ⇌ ☐ ⅃ ⚲ surfing, multi-sports ground	**G P S** Longitude : -1.57374 Latitude : 43.45315
Facilities : ⚹ ⌐ ▦ ▯ launderette ⟆ ⟆ refrigerated food storage facilities	
Nearby : ♪ disco	

⛰ Ur-Onea ♟

Ur-Onea

✆ 05 59 26 53 61. www.uronea.com

Address : rue de la Chapelle (300m east, 500m from the beach)

Opening times : from beginning April to end Sept.

5 ha (269 pitches) terraced, relatively flat, grassy, sandy

Tariff : 44€ ✦✦ ⇌ 🔲 ⚡ (10A) – Extra per person 8€ – Reservation fee 25€

Rental rates : (from beginning April to end Sept.) ✄ – 39 🚐 – 5 🏠. Per night from 41 to 146€ – Per week from 285 to 1,020€ – Reservation fee 35€

Surroundings : ⚲⚲	
Leisure activities : ▼✕ 🏠 🏃 ⇌ ☐ ⅃ multi-sports ground	**G P S** Longitude : -1.59035 Latitude : 43.43416
Facilities : ⚹ ⌐ ⌂ ▯ ✄ ▯ launderette ⟆ refrigerated food storage facilities	

Key to rentals symbols:

12 🚐	*Number of mobile homes*
20 🏠	*Number of chalets*
6 🛏	*Number of rooms to rent*
Per night 30–50€	*Minimum/maximum rate per night*
Per week 300–1,000€	*Minimum/maximum rate per week*

⛰ Sunêlia Berrua ♣♦

Sunêlia Berrua

☎ 05 59 54 96 66. www.berrua.com

Address : rue Berrua (500m east, follow the signs for Arbonne)

Opening times : from mid May to beginning Oct.

5 ha (261 pitches) terraced, relatively flat, grassy

Tariff : 49.30€ ♣♣ ⇔ 🔲 ⚡ (6A) – Extra per person 8.70€ – Reservation fee 36€

Rental rates : (from mid March to mid Oct.) – 140 🛖 – 10 🏠 – 5 tent lodges. Per night from 41 to 240€ – Per week from 300 to 1,680€ – Reservation fee 36€

🚐 AireService sani-station 3€

Surroundings : ⌂ ♀♀
Leisure activities : ⛲ ✕ 🎦 📺 ♣ hammam, jacuzzi 🚴 ♂ ⚽ 🏊 🛶 multi-sports ground
Facilities : ♿ ⊶ 🏕 ⍩ launderette 🏖 🏌
Nearby : surfing

GPS
Longitude : -1.58176
Latitude : 43.43824

The information in the guide may have changed since going to press.

⛰ Club Airotel Oyam ♣♦

☎ 05 59 54 91 61. www.camping-oyam.com

Address : chemin Oyhamburua (located 1km east along the follow the signs for Arbonne then take the turning to the right)

Opening times : from beginning April to end Sept.

7 ha (350 pitches)

Tariff : (2015 price) 44.30€ ♣♣ ⇔ 🔲 ⚡ (6A) – Extra per person 7.90€
Rental rates : (2015 price) (from beginning April to end Sept.) ♿ (1 mobile home) – 110 🛖 – 18 🏠 – 16 apartments – 5 tipis – 10 canvas bungalows – 27 tent lodges. Per night from 41 to 171€ – Per week from 182 to 1,197€

🚐 11 🔲 38€

Many and varied rental options; some attractive pitches for tents and caravans beside a water park surrounded by vegetation.

Surroundings : ⌂ ♀♀
Leisure activities : ⛲ ✕ 🎦 ♣ 🚴 🏊 🛶 multi-sports ground
Facilities : ♿ ⊶ 🏕 ⍩ launderette 🏌

GPS
Longitude : -1.58278
Latitude : 43.43501

⛰ Pavillon Royal

Pavillon Royal

☎ 05 59 23 00 54. www.pavillon-royal.com ⌖

Address : avenue du Prince de Galles (situated 2km to the north; beside the beach)

Opening times : from mid May to end Sept.

5 ha (303 pitches) terraced, flat, grassy

Tariff : 61€ ♣♣ ⇔ 🔲 ⚡ (10A) – Extra per person 14€ – Reservation fee 25€

Rental rates : (from mid May to end Sept.) ⌖ – 3 🏠. Per week from 492 to 1,106€ – Reservation fee 25€

🚐 local sani-station

In a secluded location, near a golf course, château and the ocean.

Surroundings : 🏞 ⇐ ⌂ ♀ ⛰
Leisure activities : ⛲ ✕ 🎦 📺 daytime 🎣 🚴 🏊 beauty treatments, surfing
Facilities : ♿ ⊶ 🅿 🏕 🏌 ⍩ launderette 🏖 🏌
Nearby : 🌙 nighttime 🎵 disco

GPS
Longitude : -1.57642
Latitude : 43.45469

⛰ Harrobia ♣♦

☎ 05 59 26 54 71. www.harrobia.fr

Address : rue Maurice Pierre (1.2km to the south, 400m from the beach)

Opening times : from beginning June to end Sept.

3 ha (145 pitches)

Tariff : (2015 price) 20€ ♣♣ ⇔ 🔲 ⚡ (10A) – Extra per person 4.50€
Rental rates : (2015 price) (from beginning April to end Oct.) – 126 🛖 – 2 🏠 – 4 apartments. Per night from 30 to 150€ – Per week from 200 to 1,050€ – Reservation fee 25€

Near the railway line, a mobile home park with just under 10 pitches for tents and caravans.

Surroundings : ⌂ ♀♀
Leisure activities : ⛲ ✕ 🎦 ♣ 🚴 🏊
Facilities : ♿ ⊶ 🏕 ⍩ launderette

GPS
Longitude : -1.59903
Latitude : 43.42773

BIGANOS

33380 – Michelin map **335** F7 – pop. 9 464 – alt. 16
▶ Paris 629 – Andernos-les-Bains 15 – Arcachon 27 – Bordeaux 47

⛰ Le Marache

☎ 05 57 70 61 19. www.marachevacances.com

Address : 25 rue Gambetta (take the northern exit along the D 3, follow the signs for Audenge and take turning to the right)

Opening times : from beginning April to end Sept.

2 ha (113 pitches)

Tariff : (2015 price) 6.50€ ♣ ⇔ 🔲 30.50€ – ⚡ (16A) 5.20€ – Reservation fee 15€
Rental rates : (2015 price) (from beginning April to end Sept.) – 35 🛖 – 3 🏠 – 6 canvas bungalows. Per week from 190 to 860€ – Reservation fee 20€

🚐 local sani-station 6.50€ – 6 🔲 19.50€

Surroundings : ⌂ ♀♀
Leisure activities : ⛲ ✕ 🎦 🏊 multi-sports ground
Facilities : ♿ ⊶ 🏕 ⍩ launderette 🏌

GPS
Longitude : -0.97943
Latitude : 44.65081

BIRON

24540 – Michelin map **329** G8 – pop. 182 – alt. 200
▶ Paris 583 – Beaumont 25 – Bergerac 46 – Fumel 20

⛰ FranceLoc Le Moulinal ♣♦

☎ 05 53 40 84 60. www.campings-franceloc.fr – limited spaces for one-night stay

Address : at Étang du Moulinal (4km to the south, follow the signs for Lacapelle-Biron then continue 2km following signs for Villeréal to the right)

Opening times : from beginning April to mid Sept.

10 ha/5 for camping (320 pitches) very uneven

Tariff : (2015 price) 38€ ♣♣ ⇔ 🔲 ⚡ (10A) – Extra per person 7€ – Reservation fee 27€

Rental rates : (2015 price) (from beginning April to mid Sept.) – 220 🚐 – 30 🏠 – 12 tent lodges. Per night from 45 to 213€ – Per week from 130 to 1,450€ – Reservation fee 27€

In a pleasant location beside a lake; surrounded by all kinds of trees and shrubs.

Surroundings : 🌳 ⌂ ♨♨
Leisure activities : ♟ ✗ 🍴 🎣 🏃 🏊 🚴
🏹 🎱 🏓 ⛵ (beach) 🏐 🎿 💦 multi-sports ground, entertainment room
Facilities : ♿ ⚓ 🛁 🍴 launderette 🧺 🚿

G P S Longitude : 0.87116
Latitude : 44.60031

🏔 **Village Vacances Castelwood**
(rental of chalets only)

℘ 05 53 57 96 08. www.castelwood.fr

Address : at Bois du Château-Les Fargues (located 1km south along the D 53, follow the signs for Lacapelle-Biron)

Opening times : permanent

1 ha

Rental rates : ♿ (1 chalet) – 15 🏠. Per night from 59 to 123€ – Per week from 310 to 861€

Luxury chalets nestling in the Périgord Pourpre (Purple Périgord) forest.

Surroundings : 🌳 ♨♨
Leisure activities : 🏃 🎿 🏹
Facilities : ⚓ 🏛 🍴 launderette

G P S Longitude : 0.87701
Latitude : 44.62495

BISCARROSSE

40600 – Michelin map **335** E8 – pop. 12 163 – alt. 22
▶ Paris 656 – Arcachon 40 – Bayonne 128 – Bordeaux 74

🏔 **Club Airotel Domaine de la Rive** ♁♂

℘ 05 58 78 12 33. www.larive.fr

Address : route de Bordeaux (8km northeast along the D 652, follow the signs for Sanguinet, then continue 2.2km along the turning to the left, beside the Étang de Cazaux – lake)

Opening times : from beginning April to end Aug.

15 ha (764 pitches)

Tariff : 62€ ⛺⛺ 🚗 🔌 🚿 (10A) – Extra per person 11.30€ – Reservation fee 30€

Rental rates : (from beginning April to end Aug.) ♿ (1 mobile home) 🏕 – 270 🚐 – 21 🏠. Per night from 63 to 325€ – Per week from 441 to 2,275€ – Reservation fee 30€

🚐 local sani-station

An impressive swimming pool area, partially covered. Plenty of activities and direct access to the beach.

Surroundings : 🌳 ⌂ ♨♨ 🏔
Leisure activities : ♟ ✗ 🍴 🎣 🏃 🏹 ⛵
(beach) 🏐 🎿 💦 water skiing, multi-sports ground, spa centre, entertainment room, skate park
Facilities : ♿ ⚓ 🛁 🚿 🍴 launderette 🧺 🚿 refrigerated food storage facilities

G P S Longitude : -1.1299
Latitude : 44.46022

Do not confuse:
🔺 *to* 🏔 : *MICHELIN classification with*
★ *to* ★★★★★ : *official classification*

🏔 **Mayotte Vacances** ♁♂

℘ 05 58 78 00 00. www.mayottevacances.com

Address : 368 chemin des Roseaux (6km north following signs for Sanguinet then turn left at Goubern and continue for 2.5km; 150m from the Étang de Cazaux (lake, direct access)

Opening times : from beginning April to end Sept.

15 ha (714 pitches)

Tariff : 57€ ⛺⛺ 🚗 🔌 🚿 (16A) – Extra per person 9.50€ – Reservation fee 30€

Rental rates : (from beginning April to end Sept.) – 322 🚐 – 3 🏠 – 21 canvas bungalows. Per night from 28 to 314€ – Per week from 196 to 2,198€ – Reservation fee 30€

Surroundings : 🌳 ⌂ ♨♨ 🏔
Leisure activities : ♟ ✗ 🍴 🎣 🏃 🎿 ⛵
hammam, jacuzzi 🏃 🚴 🏹 🎱 🎿 💦 🏊
fitness trail, forest, trail multi-sports ground, spa centre, entertainment room
Facilities : ♿ ⚓ 🛁 🚿 🍴 launderette 🛒 🚿 refrigerated food storage facilities

G P S Longitude : -1.1538
Latitude : 44.43488

🏔 **Bimbo** ♁♂

Bimbo

℘ 05 58 09 82 33. www.campingbimbo.fr – limited spaces for one-night stay

Address : 176 chemin de Bimbo (3.5km north following signs for Sanguinet and turn left towards Navarrosse)

Opening times : from beginning April to end Sept.

6 ha (177 pitches)

Tariff : (2015 price) 50€ ⛺⛺ 🚗 🔌 🚿 (6A) – Extra per person 8€ –

Reservation fee 25€

Rental rates : (2015 price) (from beginning April to mid Nov.) – 35 🚐 – 12 🏠 – 5 tent lodges. Per night from 27 to 168€ – Per week from 185 to 1,177€ – Reservation fee 25€

🚐 local sani-station

Surroundings : 🌳 ⌂ ♨♨
Leisure activities : ♟ ✗ 🍴 🏃 🎿 ⛵
jacuzzi 🏃 🚴 🏹 🎿 🏐 multi-sports ground
Facilities : ♿ ⚓ 🚿 🍴 launderette 🧺 🚿 refrigerated food storage facilities
Nearby : 🏇

G P S Longitude : -1.16137
Latitude : 44.42588

🏔 **Les Écureuils** ♁♂

℘ 05 58 09 80 00. www.ecureuils.fr – limited spaces for one-night stay

Address : 646 chemin de Navarrosse (4.2km north following signs for Sanguinet and turn left towards Navarrosse; 400m from the Étang de Cazaux (lake)

Opening times : from end April to mid Sept.

6 ha (183 pitches)

Tariff : 54€ ⛺⛺ 🚗 🔌 🚿 (10A) – Extra per person 8€ – Reservation fee 32€

Rental rates : (from end April to mid Sept.) 🏕 – 4 🚐 – 1 🏠 – 1 tent lodge. Per night from 50 to 158€ – Per week from 350 to 1,100€

🚐 AireService sani-station 3€

Family-friendly site; mostly mobile homes with owner-occupiers.

Surroundings : 🌳 ⌂ 🎣
Leisure activities : ♟ ✗ 🍴 🏃 jacuzzi 🏃
🚴 🏹 🎿 ⛵ (beach) 🏄
Facilities : ♿ ⚓ 🛁 🍴 launderette 🧺 🚿
Nearby : 🎣 🏊

G P S Longitude : -1.16765
Latitude : 44.42947

⛰ Campéole de Navarrosse ♠♣

📞 05 58 09 84 32. www.camping-navarrose.com

Address : 712 chemin de Navarrosse (5km to the north, follow the signs for Sanguinet and turn left towards Navarrosse; beside the Étang de Cazaux (lake)

Opening times : from end March to end Sept.

9 ha (500 pitches) open site

Tariff : 18€ ★★ ⇔ 🔲 🗓 (10A) – Extra per person 10€ – Reservation fee 25€

Rental rates : (from end March to end Sept.) ⅙ (1 mobile home) – 45 🚐 – 11 🏠 – 137 canvas bungalows. Per night from 33 to 214€ – Per week from 231 to 1,498€ – Reservation fee 25€

🚰 AireService sani-station

Surroundings : 🐟 ⌕⌕ ⛰ Leisure activities : 🍸 🍽 🎭 🎣 🏃 🚣 ✂ 🏹 🏊 Facilities : ⅙ ⊶ 🏕 🍴 launderette 🎣 Nearby : 🛒 🎠 💧 ⚓	**GPS** Longitude : -1.16765 Latitude : 44.42822

BISCARROSSE-PLAGE

40600 – Michelin map **335** E8

▶ Paris 669 – Bordeaux 91 – Mont-de-Marsan 100

⛰ Campéole le Vivier

📞 05 58 78 25 76. www.camping-biscarosse.info

Address : 681 rue du Tit (north of the resort, 700m from the beach)

Opening times : from beginning June to mid Sept.

17 ha (830 pitches)

Tariff : 17€ ★★ ⇔ 🔲 🗓 (10A) – Extra per person 10€ – Reservation fee 25€

Rental rates : (from beginning June to mid Sept.) ⅙ (1 mobile home) – 76 🚐 – 20 🏠 – 192 canvas bungalows. Per night from 33 to 214€ – Per week from 231 to 1,498€ – Reservation fee 25€

Surroundings : ⌕ ⌕⌕ Leisure activities : 🍸 🍽 🎭 🎣 🏃 🚣 🚲 🏹 🏊 multi-sports ground, entertainment room Facilities : ⅙ ⊶ 🍴 launderette 🎣 Nearby : 🏊	**GPS** Longitude : -1.24056 Latitude : 44.45938

⛰ Campéole Plage Sud ♠♣

📞 05 58 78 21 24. www.campeole.com/campeole/camping-plage-sud-landes.html

Address : 230 rue des Bécasses

Opening times : from beginning April to end Sept.

28 ha (1179 pitches) undulating, terraced, flat, sandy

Tariff : 19€ ★★ ⇔ 🔲 🗓 (10A) – Extra per person 10€ – Reservation fee 25€

Rental rates : (from beginning April to end Sept.) ⅙ – 125 🚐 – 72 🏠 – 245 canvas bungalows. Per night from 33 to 214€ – Per week from 231 to 1,498€ – Reservation fee 25€

🚰 AireService sani-station – 28 🔲

Surroundings : ⌕⌕ Leisure activities : 🍸 🍽 🎭 🎣 🏃 🚣 🚲 🏊 ⛵ forest trail, multi-sports ground, entertainment room Facilities : ⅙ ⊶ 🏕 🍴 launderette 🎣 Nearby : 🛒	**GPS** Longitude : -1.24575 Latitude : 44.4412

BLASIMON

33540 – Michelin map **335** K6 – pop. 866 – alt. 80

▶ Paris 607 – Bordeaux 47 – Mérignac 63 – Pessac 60

⛰ Le Lac

📞 05 56 71 59 62. www.gironde.fr/jcms/c_5115/les-domaines-de-hostens-et-blasim

Address : departmental field Volny Favory (at the leisure and activity park)

Opening times : from end April to end Oct.

50 ha/1 for camping (39 pitches) flat, grassy

Tariff : (2015 price) ★ 3€ ⇔ 🔲 12.50€ – 🗓 (15A) 3€

Rental rates : (2015 price) permanent – 9 🚐. Per night from 35 to 50€ – Per week from 210 to 300€

🚰 4 🔲 15€

Well marked-out pitches near the leisure centre.

Surroundings : 🐟 ⌕ ⌕ Leisure activities : 🎭 Facilities : ⅙ ⊶ 🚐 🖼 At the leisure/activities centre : 🍽 🎣 🚣 🏹 🏖 (beach) 🏊	**GPS** Longitude : -0.08757 Latitude : 44.75541

*We value your opinion and welcome your feedback.
Do email us at campingfrance@tp.michelin.com*

BORDEAUX

33000 – Michelin map **335** H5 – pop. 236 725 – alt. 4

▶ Paris 572 – Mont-de-Marsan 138 – Bayonne 191 – Arcachon 72

⛰ Village du Lac

📞 05 57 87 70 60. www.camping-bordeaux.com

Address : at Bordeaux Lac, Bruges, Bvld Jacques Chaban-Delmas – take exit 5 from the bypass: Parc des expositions

Opening times : permanent

13 ha/6 for camping (340 pitches) flat, grassy

Tariff : (2015 price) 33€ ★★ ⇔ 🔲 🗓 (10A) – Extra per person 9.50€

Rental rates : (2015 price) permanent ⅙ (1 mobile home) – 175 🚐. Per night from 40 to 150€ – Per week from 160 to 1,050€

🚰 local sani-station – 100 🔲 21€

Wooded setting with bus to the city centre.

Surroundings : ⌕⌕ Leisure activities : 🍸 🍽 🎭 🚣 🚲 🏊 multi-sports ground Facilities : ⅙ ⊶ 🏛 🚐 🎣 🍴 launderette 🏊 🎣 Nearby : 🏊 💧	**GPS** Longitude : -0.5827 Latitude : 44.89759

BRANTÔME

24310 – Michelin map **329** E3 – pop. 2 140 – alt. 104

▶ Paris 470 – Angoulême 58 – Limoges 83 – Nontron 23

⛰ Brantôme Peyrelevade ♠♣

📞 05 53 05 75 24. www.camping-dordogne.net

Address : avenue André Maurois (located 1km east along the D 78; beside the Dronne river)

Opening times : from beginning May to end Sept.

5 ha (150 pitches) flat, grassy

Tariff : (2015 price) 26€ ★★ ⇔ 🔲 🗓 (10A) – Extra per person 5€ – Reservation fee 10€

Rental rates : (2015 price) (from beginning May to end Sept.) – 18 🏠 – 5 tent lodges. Per night from 80 to 160€ – Per week from 195 to 735€ – Reservation fee 10€

🚐 Raclet sani-station – 10 ▣ 14.50€

Well-kept site with shade and a small beach with white sand at the edge of the Dronne river.

Surroundings : 🦢 ⌂ 🌳🌳
Leisure activities : 🍴 ✕ 🏸 ⛷ 🏖 ⛵
≋ (beach) 🎣
Facilities : ⚿ ⊶ ▥ 🛁 🚿 ♨ 🚽 launderette
🚿
Nearby : ✕

Longitude : 0.66043
Latitude : 45.36107

These symbols are used for a campsite that is exceptional in its category:

🏔🏔...🏔 *Particularly pleasant setting, quality and range of services available*

🦢🦢 *Tranquil, isolated site – quiet site, particularly at night*

⇐⇐ *Exceptional view – interesting or panoramic view*

LE BUGUE

24260 – Michelin map **329** G6 – pop. 2 800 – alt. 62
▶ Paris 522 – Bergerac 47 – Brive-la-Gaillarde 72 – Cahors 86

🏔 La Linotte ♟♟

✆ 05 53 04 50 01. www.vagues-oceanes.com – limited spaces for one-night stay

Address : route de Rouffignac (3.5km northeast along the D 710 following the signs for Périgueux and turn right onto D 32)

Opening times : from mid April to mid Sept.

13 ha/2.5 for camping (128 pitches) terraced, flat and relatively flat, grassy

Tariff : (2015 price) 40€ ✶✶ 🚗 ▣ 🗲 (5A) – Extra per person 8€
Rental rates : (2015 price) (from mid April to mid Sept.) – 2 'gypsy' caravans – 107 🏠 – 7 🏠. Per night from 35 to 163€ – Per week from 245 to 1,141€

🚐 5 ▣ 30€

A very undulating site with few pitches for tents and caravans.

Surroundings : 🦢 ⇐ ⌂ 🌳🌳
Leisure activities : 🍴 ✕ 🎣 🏸 jacuzzi ⛷
🏓 🛶 🏊 multi-sports ground
Facilities : ⚿ ⊶ 🛁 🚽 launderette 🚿

Longitude : 0.93659
Latitude : 44.93386

🏔 Les Trois Caupain

✆ 09 77 79 80 12. www.camping-des-trois-caupain.com
Address : allée Paul-Jean Souriau
Opening times : from beginning April to end Oct.
4 ha (160 pitches) flat, grassy
Tariff : 24.20€ ✶✶ 🚗 ▣ 🗲 (16A) – Extra per person 5.50€ – Reservation fee 5€
Rental rates : (from beginning April to end Oct.) – 38 🏠. Per night from 35 to 59€ – Per week from 159 to 700€ – Reservation fee 15€

🚐 local sani-station 5€ – 15 ▣ 9.90€ – 🚐 9.90€

Surroundings : 🦢 ⌂ 🌳
Leisure activities : ✕ ⛶ 🛶 multi-sports
ground
Facilities : ⚿ ⊶ 🛁 🚿 ♨ launderette 🚿
Nearby : 🎣 large aquarium

Longitude : 0.93178
Latitude : 44.90916

LE BUISSON-DE-CADOUIN

24480 – Michelin map **329** G6 – pop. 2 143 – alt. 63
▶ Paris 532 – Bergerac 38 – Périgueux 52 – Sarlat-la-Canéda 36

🏔 Domaine de Fromengal ♟♟

✆ 05 53 63 11 55. www.domaine-fromengal.com

Address : at La Combe de Cussac (6.5km southwest along the D 29, follow the signs for Lalinde, turn left onto D 2. follow the signs for Cadouin and take the road to the right)

Opening times : from mid April to end Sept.

22 ha/3 for camping (93 pitches) adjacent wood

Tariff : (2015 price) 36.50€ ✶✶ 🚗 ▣ 🗲 (10A) – Extra per person 9€ – Reservation fee 22€

Rental rates : (2015 price) permanent – 29 🏠 – 23 🏠 – 4 canvas bungalows. Per night from 44 to 180€ – Per week from 220 to 1,260€ – Reservation fee 22€

Undulating site with some high-quality rentals and plenty of space for relaxation and play

Surroundings : 🦢 ⌂ 🌳🌳
Leisure activities : ✕ 🏛 🏸 ⛷ 🚴 ✂
🏓 🛶
Facilities : ⚿ ⊶ ▥ 🛁 🚿 ♨ launderette 🚿

Longitude : 0.86006
Latitude : 44.82292

BUNUS

64120 – Michelin map **342** F3 – pop. 147 – alt. 186
▶ Paris 820 – Bayonne 61 – Hasparren 38 – Mauléon-Licharre 22

🏔 Inxauseta

✆ 05 59 37 81 49. www.inxauseta.fr

Address : in the town, near the church

Opening times : from mid June to mid Sept.

0.8 ha (40 pitches) relatively flat

Tariff : (2015 price) ✶ 4.60€ 🚗 ▣ 4.60€ – 🗲 (5A) 3.10€

Lovely sitting rooms in an old renovated Basque house where exhibitions are held (paintings, etc.).

Surroundings : 🦢 ⇐ 🌳🌳
Leisure activities : 🏛
Facilities : ⚿ ⊶ 🚽 ♨

Longitude : -1.06794
Latitude : 43.20974

CAMBO-LES-BAINS

64250 – Michelin map **342** D2 – pop. 6 466 – alt. 67 – ♨
▶ Paris 783 – Bayonne 20 – Biarritz 21 – Pau 115

🏔 Bixta Eder

✆ 05 59 29 94 23. www.campingbixtaeder.com

Address : 52 avenue d'Espagne (1.3km southwest along the D 918, follow the signs for St-Jean-de-Luz)

Opening times : from mid April to mid Oct.

1 ha (90 pitches) relatively flat, flat, grassy, gravelled

Tariff : 17.85€ ✶✶ 🚗 ▣ 🗲 (10A) – Extra per person 5€ – Reservation fee 15€

Rental rates : (from beginning April to beginning Nov.) – 19 🏠 – 3 🏠. Per night from 40 to 100€ – Per week from 225 to 640€ – Reservation fee 15€

A pleasant, small site with some well-appointed mobile homes.

Surroundings : ⌂ 🌳🌳
Leisure activities : 🏛
Facilities : ⚿ ♨ launderette 🚿
Nearby : ✕ 🛶

Longitude : -1.41448
Latitude : 43.35567

CAMPAGNE

24260 – Michelin map **329** G6 – pop. 367 – alt. 60
▶ Paris 542 – Bergerac 51 – Belvès 19 – Les Eyzies-de-Tayac 7

⛰ Le Val de la Marquise ♁♒

𝒫 05 53 54 74 10. www.levaldelamarquise.com

Address : at Le Moulin (500m east along the D 35, follow the signs for St-Cyprien)

Opening times : from end April to end Sept.

4 ha (104 pitches)

Tariff : 28€ ♦♦ ⇔ 🔲 (15A) – Extra per person 6.40€
Rental rates : (from end April to end Sept.) ⚡ – 18 🚐 – 8 🏠. Per night from 29 to 124€ – Per week from 203 to 868€ – Reservation fee 20€
🚉 AireService sani-station 12.90€
Elongated site near a pond for fishing. Choose sites furthest from the road.

Surroundings : ▭ 🎱🎱
Leisure activities : ✗ 🛖 🏃 🔫 🏹 🛶
Facilities : ♿ ⛱ 🏢 ♨ 🚽 launderette 🚿

	GPS
	Longitude : 0.9743
	Latitude : 44.90637

CARSAC-AILLAC

24200 – Michelin map **329** I6 – pop. 1 479 – alt. 80
▶ Paris 536 – Brive-la-Gaillarde 59 – Gourdon 18 – Sarlat-la-Canéda 9

⛰ Le Plein Air des Bories

𝒫 05 53 28 15 67. www.camping-desbories.com

Address : at Les Bories (1.3km south along the D 703, follow the signs for Vitrac and take road to the left; beside the Dordogne river)

Opening times : from end April to mid Sept.

3.5 ha (120 pitches)

Tariff : (2015 price) 27.60€ ♦♦ ⇔ 🔲 (16A) – Extra per person 6.50€ – Reservation fee 15€
Rental rates : (2015 price) (from end April to mid Sept.) – 38 🚐 – 4 canvas bungalows. Per night from 30 to 70€ – Per week from 180 to 730€ – Reservation fee 15€
Shady pitches with good-quality facilities, near the river.

Surroundings : 🏞 ▭ 🎱🎱 ⛰
Leisure activities : ♟ ✗ 🛖 🏃 🏹 (open air in season) 🛶 🚣
Facilities : ♿ ⛱ 🏢 ♨ 🚽 🔲 🚿

	GPS
	Longitude : 1.2684
	Latitude : 44.83299

⛰ Le Rocher de la Cave

𝒫 05 53 28 14 26. www.rocherdelacave.com

Address : at La Pommarède (1.7km south along the D 703, follow the signs for Vitrac and take road to the left; beside the Dordogne)

Opening times : from end April to end Sept.

5 ha (190 pitches) terraced, flat, grassy

Tariff : (2015 price) ♦ 6.80€ ⇔ 🔲 8.70€ – (16A) 4.20€
Rental rates : (2015 price) (from end April to end Sept.) – 23 🚐 – 5 🏠 – 9 canvas bungalows – 14 tent lodges. Per night from 30 to 115€ – Per week from 210 to 810€
Sunny and shady pitches near the Dordogne river with a variety of rentals.

Surroundings : 🏞 🎱🎱 ⛰
Leisure activities : ♟ ✗ 🏃 🏹 🏊 (beach) 🛶 🚣
Facilities : ♿ ⛱ 🏢 ♨ 🚽 launderette 🚿

	GPS
	Longitude : 1.26719
	Latitude : 44.82977

CASTELJALOUX

47700 – Michelin map **336** C4 – pop. 4 773 – alt. 52
▶ Paris 674 – Agen 55 – Langon 55 – Marmande 23

⛺ Village Vacances Castel Chalets du Lac
(rental of chalets only)

𝒫 05 53 93 07 45. www.castel-chalets.com

Address : route de Mont de Marsan, at the lake Clarens (2.5km southwest along the D 933, follow the signs for Mont-de-Marsan)

Opening times : permanent

4 ha

Rental rates : ♿ (1 chalet) – 25 🏠. Per night from 90 to 155€ – Per week from 285 to 690€
🚉 Eurorelais sani-station 15€ – 20 🔲 10€
A small chalet village beside the lake, opposite the very well-equipped leisure and activity park.

Surroundings : 🏞 ⛰ 🎱🎱 ⛰
Leisure activities : 🏃 🎣
Facilities : 🏢 🚽
Nearby : ♟ ✗ 🐎 forest trail, pedalos, paintballing, casino

	GPS
	Longitude : 0.0725
	Latitude : 44.29278

The information in the guide may have changed since going to press.

CASTELMORON-SUR-LOT

47260 – Michelin map **336** E3 – pop. 1 755 – alt. 49
▶ Paris 600 – Agen 33 – Bergerac 63 – Marmande 35

⛰ Village Vacances Port-Lalande – (rental of chalets only)

𝒫 04 68 37 65 65. www.grandbleu.fr

Address : located 1.5km southeast

4 ha flat, grassy

Situated beside the Lot river and a marina.

Surroundings : 🏞 ⛰ 🎱
Leisure activities : 🛖 🏃 🎣 🚠 hammam, jacuzzi 🛶 🎣 spa centre
Facilities : 🏢 🚽
Nearby : ✗ ⚓

	GPS
	Longitude : 0.50661
	Latitude : 44.38803

CASTELNAUD-LA-CHAPELLE

24250 – Michelin map **329** H7 – pop. 477 – alt. 140
▶ Paris 539 – Le Bugue 29 – Les Eyzies-de-Tayac 27 – Gourdon 25

⛰ Lou Castel ♁♒

𝒫 05 53 29 89 24. www.loucastel.com

Address : at Prente Garde (take the southern exit along the D 57 then continue 3.4km along the road to the château, for caravans, access is strongly recommended via Pont-de-Cause and the D 50, follow the signs for Veyrines-de-Domme)

5.5 ha/2.5 for camping (117 pitches) adjacent wood

Rentals : 2 'gypsy' caravans – 50 🚐 – 5 🏠 – 11 canvas bungalows – 3 tent lodges – 4 gîtes.
Situated in a pleasant wood of oak trees. Family-friendly.

Surroundings : 🏞 ▭ 🎱🎱🎱
Leisure activities : ♟ ✗ 🛖 🏃 🏹 🔫 🛶 🏊 multi-sports ground
Facilities : ♿ ⛱ ♨ 🔲 🚽 launderette 🚿

	GPS
	Longitude : 1.1315
	Latitude : 44.79755

⚿ Maisonneuve

✆ 05 53 29 51 29. www.campingmaisonneuve.com

Address : chemin de Maisonneuve (located 1km southeast along the D 57 and take road to the left; beside the Céou river)

Opening times : from beginning April to end Oct.

6 ha/3 for camping (140 pitches)

Tariff : ⋔ 7.70€ ⇌ 回 9.50€ – ▣ (10A) 5.50€ – Reservation fee 15€
Rental rates : (from beginning April to end Oct.) ⚒ – 10 ▦ – 2 tent lodges – 1 gîte. Per night from 56 to 64€ – Per week from 300 to 875€ – Reservation fee 15€
⛽ AireService sani-station

Based at an old renovated farmhouse and surrounded by flowers.

Surroundings : ≤ ⌑ ♤♤
Leisure activities : ⋔ ✗ ⌂ ⚲ ⚓ ⚒
Facilities : ㄠ �o-▪ ⊞ ♨ ♍ launderette ⚖

G	Longitude : 1.15822
P	
S	Latitude : 44.80482

CASTELS

24220 – Michelin map **329** H6 – pop. 647 – alt. 50
❿ Paris 551 – Bordeaux 181 – Montauban 145 – Brive-la-Gaillarde 73

⚿ Village Vacances La Noyeraie – (rental of chalets only)

✆ 05 53 31 24 43. www.chaletlanoyeraie.fr

Address : at Le Grelat (located 1km southeast along the D 703, follow the signs for Sarlat)

Opening times : from mid April to mid Nov.

1.5 ha flat, grassy
Rental rates : ℗ – 19 ⌂. Per night from 42 to 105€ – Per week from 240 to 950€ – Reservation fee 15€

Surroundings : ♤♤
Leisure activities : ⌂ ⚲ ⚓ (open air in season)
Facilities : o-▪ ℗ ⚐ ⊞ launderette

Do not confuse:
⚿ to ⚿⚿⚿ : *MICHELIN classification* with
★ to ★★★★★ : *official classification*

CÉNAC-ET-ST-JULIEN

24250 – Michelin map **329** I7 – pop. 1 218 – alt. 70
❿ Paris 537 – Le Bugue 34 – Gourdon 20 – Sarlat-la-Canéda 12

⚿ Le Pech de Caumont

✆ 05 53 28 21 63. www.pech-de-caumont.com

Address : situated 2km to the south

Opening times : from beginning April to end Sept.

2.2 ha (100 pitches) terraced, flat, grassy
Tariff : (2015 price) ⋔ 5.60€ ⇌ 回 7.20€ – ▣ (16A) 3.70€ – Reservation fee 12.50€
Rental rates : (2015 price) (from beginning April to end Sept.) ⚒ – 16 ▦ – 6 ⌂. Per night from 35 to 54€ – Per week from 200 to 690€

The site looks out over the Dordogne valley, opposite the village of Domme.

Surroundings : ⚏ ≤ ⌑ ♤♤
Leisure activities : ⋔ ✗ ⌂ ⚲ ⚓
Facilities : ㄠ o-▪ ⚐ ♨ ♍ launderette ⚖

G	Longitude : 1.20908
P	
S	Latitude : 44.78654

LA CHAPELLE-AUBAREIL

24290 – Michelin map **329** I5 – pop. 471 – alt. 230
❿ Paris 515 – Brive-la-Gaillarde 40 – Les Eyzies-de-Tayac 21 – Montignac 9

⚿ La Fage

✆ 05 53 50 76 50. www.camping-lafage.com

Address : at La Fage (1.2km northwest following signs for St-Amand-de-Coly, head towards D 704 and take road to the left)

Opening times : from mid April to mid Oct.

5 ha (92 pitches) terraced, relatively flat, flat, grassy
Tariff : (2015 price) 30€ ⋔ ⋔ ⇌ 回 ▣ (10A) – Extra per person 6.70€ – Reservation fee 10€
Rental rates : (2015 price) permanent – 17 ▦ – 4 ⌂. Per night from 40 to 68€ – Per week from 209 to 861€ – Reservation fee 10€

Lots of green space, ideal for relaxation and team games.

Surroundings : ⚏ ⌑ ♤♤
Leisure activities : ✗ ⌂ ⚲ ⚓ ⛾ (open air in season)
Facilities : ㄠ o-▪ ▣⚖ ⚐ ⚐ ♍ launderette ⚖

To visit a town or region, use the MICHELIN Green Guides.

CONTIS-PLAGE

40170 – Michelin map **335** D10
❿ Paris 714 – Bayonne 87 – Castets 32 – Dax 52

⚿ Yelloh! Village Lous Seurrots ⚑⚑

✆ 05 58 42 85 82. www.lous-seurrots.com

Address : 606 avenue de l'Océan (take the southeastern exit along the D 41, near the Courant de Contis (small river), 700m from the beach)

Opening times : from end March to end Sept.

14 ha (571 pitches) undulating, flat and relatively flat, grassy, sandy
Tariff : 53€ ⋔ ⋔ ⇌ 回 ▣ (10A) – Extra per person 8€
Rental rates : (from end March to end Sept.) ㄠ (1 chalet) – 240 ▦ – 110 ⌂. Per night from 35 to 239€ – Per week from 245 to 1,673€

Aquatic park beaches and a wonder view of the dune and ocean. Some high-quality rental options in the shade of a pine forest.

Surroundings : ⚏ ⌑ ♤♤
Leisure activities : ⋔ ✗ ⌂ ⛾ (open-air theatre) ⚵ ⛴ ⚓ ⚳ ✗ ⚲ ⚒ ⚴ multi-sports ground
Facilities : ㄠ o-▪ ⊞ ♍ launderette ⚖ ⚖ refrigerated food storage facilities
Nearby : ⚵ ⚱ surfing

G	Longitude : -1.31685
P	
S	Latitude : 44.08878

Key to rentals symbols:

12 ▦	*Number of mobile homes*
20 ⌂	*Number of chalets*
6 ⊨	*Number of rooms to rent*
Per night 30–50€	*Minimum/maximum rate per night*
Per week 300–1,000€	*Minimum/maximum rate per week*

COURBIAC

47370 – Michelin map **336** I3 – pop. 110 – alt. 145
▶ Paris 623 – Bordeaux 172 – Agen 46 – Montauban 59

� Le Pouchou

𝒸 06 42 83 37 62. www.camping-le-pouchou.com

Address : head 1.8km west following signs for Tournon-d'Agenais, take road to the left

Opening times : from beginning March to end Nov.

15 ha/2 for camping (30 pitches) open site, relatively flat, grassy

Tariff : (2015 price) 🛉 4.75€ ⇔ 🔲 7.30€ – [⚡] (10A) 4€

Rental rates : (2015 price) permanent ⚭ (1 chalet) – 1 ⛺ – 8 🏠 – 2 🛏. Per night from 55 to 88€ – Per week from 249 to 571€

🚿 Raclet sani-station 4€ – 2 🔲 13€ – 🚐 13€

Pleasant setting among undulating hills, beside a small lake.

Surroundings : 🏞 �‐ 🌳🌳	**G**
Leisure activities : 🍷 🏠 🚲 ⛵ 🎿 🛶 walking trails	**P** Longitude : 1.02293
Facilities : ⚭ 🔌 🚿 🛁 🍴 launderette	**S** Latitude : 44.37854

COUX-ET-BIGAROQUE

24220 – Michelin map **329** G7 – pop. 993 – alt. 85
▶ Paris 548 – Bergerac 44 – Le Bugue 14 – Les Eyzies-de-Tayac 17

⚘⚘ Les Valades 🏕🏕

𝒸 05 53 29 14 27. http://www.lesvalades.com

Address : at Les Valades (4km northwest along the D 703, follow the signs for Les Eyzies then take left turning)

Opening times : from beginning April to end Sept.

14 ha (85 pitches) very uneven, small lake, natural setting among trees and bushes

Tariff : (2015 price) 30€ 🛉🛉 ⇔ 🔲 [⚡] (10A) – Extra per person 7€ – Reservation fee 15€

Rental rates : (2015 price) (from beginning April to end Sept.) ⚭ (1 chalet) – 6 ⛺ – 19 🏠 – 4 tent lodges. Per week from 230 to 890€ – Reservation fee 15€

Shady pitches with comfortable rental options on an undulating site with lots of green space.

Surroundings : 🏞 �‐ 🔲 🌳🌳	**G**
Leisure activities : ✗ 🏠 🚣 ⛵ 🎿 ⛳ (beach) 🛶 🎣	**P** Longitude : 0.96367
Facilities : ⚭ 🔌 🔲🛁 – 10 private sanitary facilities (🚿 🚽 🛁 wc) 🍴 🍽 launderette 🛒	**S** Latitude : 44.8599

COUZE-ET-ST-FRONT

24150 – Michelin map **329** F7 – pop. 775 – alt. 45
▶ Paris 544 – Bergerac 21 – Lalinde 4 – Mussidan 46

⚘⚘ Les Moulins

𝒸 06 89 85 76 24. www.campingdesmoulins.com – limited spaces for one-night stay

Address : at Les Maury Bas (take the southeastern exit along the D 660, follow the signs for Beaumont and take a right turn, near the sports field; beside the Couze river)

Opening times : from mid March to mid Nov.

2.5 ha (50 pitches)

Tariff : 27€ 🛉🛉 ⇔ 🔲 [⚡] (10A) – Extra per person 7€ – Reservation fee 10€

Rental rates : (from mid March to mid Nov.) – 10 ⛺. Per night from 50 to 90€ – Per week from 250 to 500€ – Reservation fee 10€

🚿 local sani-station 5€ – 10 🔲 15€

In a green setting perched on a rocky spur opposite the village.

Surroundings : �‐ 🔲 🌳	**G**
Leisure activities : 🍷 🏠 🚣 🚲 ⛵ 🎿 🛶	**P** Longitude : 0.70448
Facilities : ⚭ 🔌 🍴 launderette	**S** Latitude : 44.82646

DAGLAN

24250 – Michelin map **329** I7 – pop. 555 – alt. 101
▶ Paris 547 – Cahors 48 – Fumel 40 – Gourdon 18

⚘⚘ La Peyrugue

𝒸 05 53 28 40 26. www.peyrugue.com

Address : at La Peyrugue (located 1.5km north along the D 57, follow the signs for St-Cybranet, 150m from the Céou river)

Opening times : from beginning April to end Sept.

5 ha/2.5 for camping (85 pitches) terraced, relatively flat, flat, grassy, stony, wood

Tariff : 🛉 8.20€ ⇔ 🔲 13€ – [⚡] (10A) 4.50€ – Reservation fee 15€

Rental rates : (from beginning April to end Sept.) ⚭ (2 chalets) – 10 🏠 – 1 gîte. Per night from 45 to 125€ – Per week from 315 to 875€ – Reservation fee 15€

Surroundings : 🏞 🌳🌳	**G**
Leisure activities : 🍷 ✗ 🏠 🎿	**P** Longitude : 1.18798
Facilities : ⚭ 🔌 🛁 🍴 launderette 🛒	**S** Latitude : 44.75267

DAX

40100 – Michelin map **335** E12 – pop. 21 003 – alt. 12 – ♨
▶ Paris 727 – Bayonne 54 – Biarritz 61 – Bordeaux 144

⚘⚘ Les Chênes 🏕🏕

𝒸 05 58 90 05 53. www.camping-les-chenes.fr

Address : allée du Bois de Boulogne (1.8km west of the town centre, in the Bois de Boulogne, 200m from the Adour river)

Opening times : from mid March to end Oct.

5 ha (230 pitches)

Tariff : 18.30€ 🛉🛉 ⇔ 🔲 [⚡] (10A) – Extra per person 6€ – Reservation fee 7.50€

Rental rates : (from mid March to end Oct.) ⚭ – 34 ⛺ – 20 🏠. Per week from 280 to 600€ – Reservation fee 7.50€

🚿 local sani-station – 20 🔲 25.40€

Surroundings : 🏞 🔲 🌳🌳	**G**
Leisure activities : 🏠 🚣 ⛵ 🚲 🛶	**P** Longitude : -1.07174
Facilities : ⚭ 🔌 🔲🛁 🛁 🍴 launderette 🏊	**S** Latitude : 43.71138
Nearby : 🎣	

⚘ Le Bascat

𝒸 05 58 56 16 68. www.campinglebascat.com

Address : rue de Jouandin (2.8km west from the town centre through the Bois de Boulogne, access from the Vieux Pont (left bank) and the avenue running along the banks of the Adour)

Opening times : from beginning March to mid Nov.

3.5 ha (160 pitches) terraced, flat, grassy, fine gravel

Tariff : 🛉 4.50€ ⇔ 🔲 9€ – [⚡] (6A) 2€ – Reservation fee 7€

Rental rates : (from mid March to mid Nov.) – 41 ⛺. Per night from 50 to 65€ – Per week from 300 to 375€ – Reservation fee 7€

🚿 local sani-station – 100 🔲 15.50€ – 🚐 12€

Surroundings : 🏞 🌳🌳	**G**
Leisure activities : 🏠	**P** Longitude : -1.07043
Facilities : ⚭ 🔌 🔲🍴 🛁 🍴 launderette 🛒	**S** Latitude : 43.70617

DOMME

24250 – Michelin map **329** I7 – pop. 989 – alt. 250
▶ Paris 538 – Cahors 51 – Fumel 50 – Gourdon 20

⚑ Village Vacances Les Ventoulines
   (rental of chalets only)

✆ 05 53 28 36 29. www.gites-dordogne-sarlat.fr

Address : at Les Ventoulines (3.6km to the southeast)

Opening times : permanent

3 ha open site, terraced

Rental rates : (2015 price) Ⓟ – 6 🚐 – 18 🏠 – 24 gîtes. Per night from 110 to 135 € – Per week from 460 to 1,183 €

Surroundings : 🐾 ♨	
Leisure activities : 🏛 🏋 🏊 ⛷	Longitude : 1.22587
Facilities : ⚕ ⊶ 🏢 ⛾ launderette	Latitude : 44.78408

⚑ Perpetuum 👥

✆ 05 53 28 35 18. www.campingleperpetuum.com

Address : head 2km south along the D 50 and take road to the right; beside the Dordogne river

Opening times : from beginning May to beginning Oct.

4.5 ha (120 pitches) flat, grassy

Tariff : 👤 8 € 🚐 3.50 € 🔲 8 € – 🔌 (10A) 5.20 € – Reservation fee 12 €
Rental rates : (from beginning May to beginning Oct.) 🏕 – 35 🚐. Per night from 62 to 82 € – Per week from 200 to 844 € – Reservation fee 12 €

🚰 Eurorelais sani-station – 🚙

Surroundings : 🐾 🗺 ♨	
Leisure activities : ✗ 🏛 🤸 🏋 🏊 ⛵ ♨	Longitude : 1.22065
multi-sports ground, entertainment room	Latitude : 44.81542
Facilities : ⚕ ⊶ 🚿 🏢 ⛾ launderette 🐾	

⚑ Village Vacances de la Combe – (rental of chalets only)

✆ 06 31 40 53 41. www.sarlat-gites-dordogne.com

Address : at Le Pradal (located 1.5km southeast)

Opening times : permanent

2 ha terraced, flat, grassy

Rental rates : ⚕ (1 chalet) Ⓟ – 12 🏠. Per night from 65 to 75 € – Per week from 350 to 825 € – Reservation fee 18 €

Surroundings : 🐾 ♨	
Leisure activities : 🏛 🏊 (open air in season)	Longitude : 1.22243
Facilities : ⊶ 🚿 🏢 ⛾ 🖼 🐾	Latitude : 44.8161

⚑ Le Bosquet

✆ 05 53 28 37 39. www.lebosquet.com

Address : at La Rivière (900m south of Vitrac-Port, along the D 46)

Opening times : from beginning April to beginning Oct.

1.5 ha (57 pitches)

Tariff : 22 € 👥 🚐 🔲 🔌 (10A) – Extra per person 5.20 € – Reservation fee 8 €
Rental rates : (from beginning April to beginning Oct.) – 12 🚐 – 8 canvas bungalows – 1 gîte. Per night from 36 to 75 € – Per week from 230 to 710 € – Reservation fee 8 €

🚰 local sani-station 10 € – 10 🔲 22 €

Surroundings : 🐾 🗺 ♨	
Leisure activities : ✗ 🏛 🏋 🏊	Longitude : 1.22555
Facilities : ⚕ ⊶ 🚿 ⛾ launderette 🐾	Latitude : 44.82185

⚑ Le Moulin de Caudon

✆ 05 53 31 03 69. www.campingdordogne.com

Address : at Caudon (6km northeast along the D 46e and the D 50, follow the signs for Groléjac; near the Dordogne – recommended route for caravans via Vitrac-Port)

Opening times : from mid May to mid Sept.

2 ha (60 pitches) flat, grassy

Tariff : (2015 price) 👤 4 € 🚐 3.30 € 🔲 3.30 € – 🔌 (10A) 3.30 €
Rental rates : (2015 price) (from mid May to mid Sept.) 🏕 – 4 🚐. Per week from 210 to 500 €

🚰 local sani-station – 🚙 🔌 13 €

Surroundings : 🗺 ♨	
Leisure activities : 🏛 🏋 🏊	Longitude : 1.24466
Facilities : ⚕ (season) 🚿 🖼 ⛾ 🖼	Latitude : 44.82061
Nearby : 🏊	

DOUVILLE

24140 – Michelin map **329** E6
▶ Paris 571 – Bordeaux 119 – Périgueux 29 – Agen 111

⚑ Orpheo Negro

✆ 05 53 82 96 58. www.orpheonegro.com

Address : at Les Trois Frères, RN 21

Opening times : from beginning April to end Oct.

11 ha/2.5 for camping (60 pitches) terraced, relatively flat, flat, grassy, stony

Tariff : 25.90 € 👥👥 🚐 🔲 🔌 (6A) – Extra per person 6 € – Reservation fee 50 €
Rental rates : (2015 price) (from beginning April to end Oct.) – 18 🚐 – 3 🏠. Per night from 63 to 73 € – Per week from 289 to 749 € – Reservation fee 99 €

🚰 local sani-station – 🚙 11 €

Site with bushes, overlooking the lake and pool.

Surroundings : 🐾 ⛰ ♨	
Leisure activities : 🍹 🤸 🏋 ⛵ 🏊 ⛷ ♨	Longitude : 0.61695
boats for hire, pedalos	Latitude : 45.02765
Facilities : ⚕ ⊶ 🚿 ⛾ 🖼 🐾	
Nearby : ✗	

We have selected the best campsites in France with our usual care, listing those with the best facilities in the most pleasant surroundings.

EYMET

24500 – Michelin map **329** D8 – pop. 2 563 – alt. 54
▶ Paris 560 – Bergerac 24 – Castillonnès 19 – Duras 22

⚑ Le Château

✆ 05 53 23 80 28. www.eymetcamping.com

Address : rue de la Sole (behind the château; beside the Dropt river)

Opening times : from end April to end Sept.

1.5 ha (66 pitches) flat, grassy, adjacent public garden

Tariff : 15 € 👥👥 🚐 🔲 🔌 (10A) – Extra per person 4 €

A pleasant location near the Dropt river, the municipal park and the chateau ramparts.

Surroundings : 🐾 🗺 ♨	
Leisure activities : 🚲 🎣 🛶	Longitude : 0.39584
Facilities : ⚕ ⊶ 🚿 ☑ ⛾ 🖼	Latitude : 44.66925

LES EYZIES-DE-TAYAC

24620 – Michelin map **329** H6 – pop. 839 – alt. 70
▶ Paris 536 – Brive-la-Gaillarde 62 – Fumel 62 – Lalinde 35

ᴍᴍ Tohapi Le Mas ♣♨

℘ 0825 00 20 30. www.campinglemas.com – limited spaces for one-night stay

Address : 7 km east along the D 47 follow the signs for Sarlat-la-Canéda then continue 2.5km following signs for Sireuil to the left

Opening times : from end April to mid Sept.

5 ha (137 pitches) terraced, flat, grassy, stony

Tariff : (2015 price) 45.40€ ✖✖ ⇋ 🅴 ⚡ (10A) –
Extra per person 8.70€ – Reservation fee 20€
Rental rates : (2015 price) (from end April to mid Sept.) – 117 🚐 –
10 tent lodges. Per week from 434 to 1,491€ – Reservation fee 20€

Surroundings : ⛵ ▭ ♋		
Leisure activities : 🍸✖ 🏛 ⛹ ⛷ ⤢ ⚐	**G**	Longitude : 1.0849
Facilities : ♿ ⛽ ♨ ⛺ launderette ♨ ⤵	**P S**	Latitude : 44.93675

ᴍᴍ La Rivière

℘ 05 53 06 97 14. www.larivielereyzies.com

Address : 3 route du Sorcier (located 1km northwest along the D 47, follow the signs for Périgueux and take the turning to the left after the bridge, 200m from the Vézère)

Opening times : from mid April to mid Oct.

7 ha/3 for camping (120 pitches) flat, grassy

Tariff : (2015 price) ✖ 7.20€ ⇋ 🅴 10.85€ – ⚡ (10A) 4.94€ –
Reservation fee 4€
Rental rates : (2015 price) (from mid April to mid Oct.) – 13 🚐 –
6 ⛺ – 1 tent lodge. Per night from 38 to 140€ – Per week from 174 to 976€ – Reservation fee 4€

🚐 local sani-station
Near the river close to a canoe centre.

Surroundings : ⛵ ▭ ♋		
Leisure activities : 🍸✖ 🏖 ⤢ ⚐	**G**	Longitude : 1.00582
Facilities : ♿ ⛽ ▥ ♨ ♨ ⛺ 🍴 launderette ♨ ⤵	**P S**	Latitude : 44.93732

⛺ La Ferme du Pelou

℘ 05 53 06 98 17. www.lafermedupelou.com

Address : at Le Pelou (4km northeast along the D 706, follow the signs for Montignac then take the turning to the right)

Opening times : from mid March to mid Nov.

1 ha (65 pitches)

Tariff : (2015 price) 15.34€ ✖✖ ⇋ 🅴 ⚡ (10A) –
Extra per person 4.20€
Rental rates : (from mid March to mid Nov.) – 3 🚐. Per night from 40 to 62€ – Per week from 310 to 480€

🚐 local sani-station
Farm site with animals and a great view of Tursac village.

Surroundings : ⛵ ▭ ♋		
Leisure activities : 🏛 ⤢	**G**	Longitude : 1.04472
Facilities : ♿ ⛽ ♨ 🍴 launderette	**P S**	Latitude : 44.95527

*The classification (1 to 5 tents, **black** or red) that we award to selected sites in this guide is our own system. It should not be confused with the classification (1 to 5 stars) of official organisations.*

FUMEL

47500 – Michelin map **336** H3 – pop. 5 186 – alt. 70
▶ Paris 594 – Agen 55 – Bergerac 64 – Cahors 48

ᴍᴍ Village Vacances Domaine de Guillalmes
(rental of chalets only)

℘ 05 53 71 01 99. www.domainedeguillalmes.com

Address : at La Gaillarde (3km east along the D 911, follow the signs for Cahors, at Condat exit follow right turn for 1km; beside the Lot river)

Opening times : from beginning April to end Oct.

3 ha flat, grassy

Rental rates : ♿ (1 chalet) – 18 🏡 – 2 gîtes. Per night from 60 to 80€ – Per week from 400 to 710€ – Reservation fee 10€
🚐 local sani-station 18€
Leafy and floral site with pitches near the Lot river.

Surroundings : ⛵ ♋		
Leisure activities : 🍸✖ 🏖 ⛴ ✂ ⤢ ⚐	**G**	Longitude : 1.00955
Facilities : ⛽ 🅿 ♨ ▥ 🍴 ▣ ⤵	**P S**	Latitude : 44.48343

ᴍᴍ Les Catalpas

℘ 05 53 71 11 99. www.les-catalpas.com

Address : at La Tour, chemin de la plaine de Condat (situated 2km east along the D 911, follow the signs for Cahors; at the Condat exit, follow the road to the right for 1.2km; beside the Lot river)

Opening times : from beginning April to end Oct.

2 ha (61 pitches) flat, grassy, hard surface areas

Tariff : 21.30€ ✖✖ ⇋ 🅴 ⚡ (10A) – Extra per person 5.50€
Rental rates : permanent – 6 🚐 – 3 🏡 – 2 canvas bungalows – 1 gîte. Per night from 35 to 55€ – Per week from 100 to 650€
🚐 6 🅴 13€
Cycle tourists welcome.

Surroundings : ⛵ ▭ ♋		
Leisure activities : ✖ 🏖 ⤢ ⚐	**G**	Longitude : 0.99737
Facilities : ⛽ ▥ ♨ ▣	**P S**	Latitude : 44.48916

Using the traditional Michelin classification method, the guide provides you with an easy, speedy reference for assessing the category of each site: 1 to 5 tents (see page 10).

GABARRET

40310 – Michelin map **335** L11 – pop. 1 270 – alt. 153
▶ Paris 715 – Agen 66 – Auch 76 – Bordeaux 140

⛺ Parc Municipal Touristique la Chêneraie

℘ 05 58 44 92 62. la-cheneraie@orange.fr

Address : take the eastern exit along the D 3, follow the signs for Castelnau-d'Auzan and take the road to the right

Opening times : from beginning March to end Oct.

0.7 ha (50 pitches) relatively flat, flat, grassy, sandy, fine gravel

Tariff : (2015 price) 11.94€ ✖✖ ⇋ 🅴 ⚡ (10A) – Extra per person 3€
Rental rates : permanent – 4 🚐 – 10 gîtes. Per night from 55 to 60€ – Per week from 170 to 290€
🚐 local sani-station

Surroundings : ⛵ ▭ ♋		
Leisure activities : 🏖 ⛴	**G**	Longitude : 0.01622
Facilities : ♿ ⛽ ♨ ▥ 🍴 ▣	**P S**	Latitude : 43.98361
Nearby : ⤢		

GRADIGNAN

33170 – Michelin map **335** H6 – pop. 23 386 – alt. 26
▶ Paris 592 – Bordeaux 9 – Lyon 550 – Nantes 336

⚠ Beausoleil

📞 05 56 89 17 66. www.camping-gradignan.com

Address : 371 cours du Général de Gaulle (on the bypass (rocade),
take exit 16 for Gradignan)

Opening times : permanent

0.5 ha (31 pitches) relatively flat, flat, grassy, fine gravel

Tariff : 20€ ♠♠ 🚐 🅔 (10A) – Extra per person 3.50€

Rental rates : permanent 🕸 – 4 🛖. Per week from 260 to 420€

There's a shuttle bus for the tram to Bordeaux.

Surroundings : 🗺 🌳🌳	
Facilities : 🕭 ⊙🔌 🛁 🏛 🚿 ♨ 🍴 launderette	**GPS** Longitude : -0.6278 Latitude : 44.75573

We have selected the best campsites in France with our usual care, listing those with the best facilities in the most pleasant surroundings.

GROLÉJAC

24250 – Michelin map **329** I7 – pop. 654 – alt. 67
▶ Paris 537 – Gourdon 14 – Périgueux 80 – Sarlat-la-Canéda 13

🏔 Les Granges ♠♣

📞 05 53 28 11 15. www.lesgranges-fr.com – limited spaces for one-night stay

Address : in the village

Opening times : from end April to mid Sept.

6 ha (188 pitches) terraced, flat and relatively flat, grassy

Tariff : 19.10€ ♠♠ 🚐 🅔 (6A) – Extra per person 5.70€ – Reservation fee 25€

Rental rates : (from end April to mid Sept.) 🕭 – 66 🛖 – 20 🏠 – 12 tent lodges. Per night from 41 to 116€ – Per week from 292 to 814€ – Reservation fee 25€

Leafy site with well marked-out terraced pitches and a variety of rental options.

Surroundings : 🌿 🗺 🌳🌳	
Leisure activities : 🍴 ✗ 🏛 🏓 ⛹ 🚴 🎣 🔥 🏊 🌊	
Facilities : 🕭 ⊙🔌 🛁 🚿 ♨ 🍴 launderette 🛒	**GPS** Longitude : 1.29117 Latitude : 44.81579
Nearby : 🏊	

🏔 Le Lac de Groléjac

📞 05 53 59 48 70. www.camping-dulac-dordogne.com

Address : at Le Roc Percé (situated 2km south along the D 704, D 50, follow the signs for Domme and turn left, following signs for Nabirat)

Opening times : from beginning May to mid Sept.

2 ha (96 pitches)

Tariff : 23.60€ ♠♠ 🚐 🅔 (10A) – Extra per person 5.80€ – Reservation fee 15€

Rental rates : permanent – 20 🛖 – 5 canvas bungalows. Per night from 35 to 55€ – Per week from 215 to 740€ – Reservation fee 15€

🚽 local sani-station – 🔌♨12€

Surroundings : 🌿 🗺 🌳🌳 ⛰	
Leisure activities : 🍴 ✗ 🏛 🏓 🎣 🌊	
Facilities : 🕭 ⊙🔌 🛁 🚿 ♨ 🍴 🔲 🛒	**GPS** Longitude : 1.29441 Latitude : 44.802
Nearby : 🦢 pedalos	

HAUTEFORT

24390 – Michelin map **329** H4 – pop. 1 086 – alt. 160
▶ Paris 466 – Bordeaux 190 – Périgueux 60 – Brive-la-Gaillarde 57

🏔 Village Vacances Les Sources – (rental of chalets only)

📞 05 53 51 96 56. www.dordogne-gite.fr

Address : at La Génèbre (2.6km south along the D 704 and the D 62E4)

Opening times : from beginning April to mid Nov.

30 ha/5 for camping undulating, pond

Rental rates : 🕭 🅿 – 15 gîtes. Per week from 280 to 1,680€

Some gites are 'semi-detached' but all with castle views. Farm animals.

Surroundings : 🌿 ≤ Château de Hautefort	
Leisure activities : 🍴 🏛 jacuzzi 🏓 🏊 🛷 🎿 paintballing, farm or petting farm	**GPS** Longitude : 1.12641 Latitude : 45.25085
Facilities : 🕭 ⊙🔌 🍴 launderette	

HENDAYE

64700 – Michelin map **342** B4 – pop. 14 412 – alt. 30
▶ Paris 799 – Biarritz 31 – Pau 143 – St-Jean-de-Luz 12

🏔 Eskualduna ♠♣

📞 05 59 20 04 64. www.camping-eskualduna.fr

Address : route de la Corniche (situated 2km east, rte da la Corniche; beside a stream)

Opening times : from beginning May to end Sept.

10 ha (330 pitches) undulating

Tariff : (2015 price) ♠ 10€ 🚐 6€ 🅔 9€ – 🔌 (10A) 6€ – Reservation fee 20€

Rental rates : (2015 price) (from mid April to mid Oct.) 🕭 (2 mobile homes) – 85 🛖 – 11 🏠. Per night from 65 to 110€ – Per week from 245 to 1,680€ – Reservation fee 20€

🚽 Eurorelais sani-station 5€ – 20 🅔 12€

Free shuttle service to the beach, choose the pitches away from the road.

Surroundings : 🌳🌳	
Leisure activities : 🍴 ✗ 🏛 🎲 🏓 🛷 🏊 multi-sports ground	
Facilities : 🕭 ⊙🔌 🛁 🚿 ♨ 🍴 launderette 🔲 🛒 refrigerators	**GPS** Longitude : -1.73925 Latitude : 43.37555

🏔 Club Airotel Ametza

📞 05 59 20 07 05. www.camping-ametza.com

Address : boulevard de l'Empereur (located 1km east)

Opening times : from mid April to end Sept.

4.5 ha (230 pitches) terraced, relatively flat, flat, grassy

Tariff : (2015 price) 40.50€ ♠♠ 🚐 🅔 (6A) – Extra per person 7.60€ – Reservation fee 15€

Rental rates : (2015 price) (from mid April to end Sept.) 🕭 (1 mobile home) 🕸 – 30 🛖 – 3 🏠 – 3 tent lodges. Per night from 30 to 50€ – Per week from 200 to 1,225€ – Reservation fee 15€

🚽 local sani-station

Pitches for tents and caravans are available, as well as owner-occupier and rental mobile homes.

Surroundings : 🗺 🌳🌳	
Leisure activities : 🍴 ✗ 🏛 🏓 🛷 🏓 🏊 🌊	
Facilities : 🕭 ⊙🔌 🍴 launderette 🔲 🛒	**GPS** Longitude : -1.75578 Latitude : 43.37285

🏔 Dorrondeguy

📞 05 59 20 26 16. www.camping-dorrondeguy.com

Address : rue de la Glacière

Opening times : permanent

4 ha (127 pitches) terrace, relatively flat, flat, grassy

Tariff : 29€ ♣♣ ⬅ 🔲 (8A) – Extra per person 7€ – Reservation fee 15€

Rental rates : permanent ♿ (1 mobile home) ✂ Ⓟ – 30 🚐 – 13 🏠 – 4 canvas bungalows. Per night from 40 to 120€ – Per week from 280 to 1,100€ – Reservation fee 20€

A pretty little chalet village.

Surroundings : 🐾 🚃 ⛰		
Leisure activities : 🍸 ✗ 🎲 🚣 🛶 Basque pelota walled court	**G**	Longitude : 1.74727
Facilities : ♿ ⚡ 🛁 🍴 launderette 🔧	**P** **S**	Latitude : 43.36867

HOURTIN

33990 – Michelin map **335** E3 – pop. 3 001 – alt. 18

▶ Paris 638 – Andernos-les-Bains 55 – Bordeaux 65 – Lesparre-Médoc 17

🏔 Les Castels Le Village Western 🏕

📞 05 56 09 10 60. www.village-western.com

Address : chemin de Bécassine (head 1.5km west along the av. du Lac and take road to the left, 500m from the lake (direct access)

Opening times : from mid April to end Sept.

17 ha/11 for camping (300 pitches) pond

Tariff : (2015 price) 37€ ♣♣ ⬅ 🔲 (10A) – Extra per person 8€ – Reservation fee 20€

Rental rates : (2015 price) (from mid April to end Oct.) ♿ – 91 🚐 – 4 🏠 – 12 tipis – 5 canvas bungalows – 5 tent lodges. Per night from 40 to 190€ – Per week from 182 to 1,330€ – Reservation fee 20€

🚐 local sani-station 2€ – 15 🔲 21€

Original Wild West décor, arranged around the riding centre.

Surroundings : 🐾 ⛰		
Leisure activities : 🍸 ✗ 🎲 🏊 🛶 🚴 🎿 🛝	**G**	Longitude : -1.07468
Facilities : ♿ ⚡ 🛁 🍴 launderette 🔧	**P** **S**	Latitude : 45.17935
Nearby : ✂ 🎣		

🏔 Les Ourmes 🏕

Les Ourmes

📞 05 56 09 12 76. www.lesourmes.com

Address : 90 avenue du Lac (located 1.5km west)

Opening times : from end April to end Sept.

7 ha (300 pitches)

Tariff : (2015 price) 35.70€ ♣♣ ⬅ 🔲 (10A) – Extra per person 7€ – Reservation fee 20€

Rental rates : (2015 price) (from end April to mid Sept.) ♿ – 37 🚐 – 2 tent lodges. Per night from 32 to 90€ – Per week from 142 to 815€ – Reservation fee 20€

🚐 local sani-station

Surroundings : 🐾 🚃 ⛰		
Leisure activities : 🍸 ✗ 🎲 🌙 nighttime 🏃 🚣 🎿	**G**	Longitude : -1.07584
Facilities : ♿ ⚡ (Jul–Aug) 🛁 🍴 launderette 🔧 refrigerated food storage facilities	**P** **S**	Latitude : 45.18204
Nearby : ✂ 🎣 🐴		

🏔 Aires Naturelles l'Acacia et le Lac

📞 05 56 73 80 80. www.campinglacacia.com

Address : route de Carcans (7km southwest along the D 3 and take the road to the right)

Opening times : from mid June to end Sept.

5 ha/2 for camping (50 pitches) adjacent pine trees

Tariff : 22€ ♣♣ ⬅ 🔲 (12A) – Extra per person 6€

All pitches are shady and peaceful.

Surroundings : 🐾 ⛰		
Leisure activities : 🎲 🛶 🚴	**G**	Longitude : -1.06361
Facilities : ⚡ 🛁 launderette	**P** **S**	Latitude : 45.13561

HOURTIN-PLAGE

33990 – Michelin map **335** D3

▶ Paris 556 – Andernos-les-Bains 66 – Bordeaux 76 – Lesparre-Médoc 26

🏔 Club Airotel La Côte d'Argent 🏕

Club Airotel La Côte d'Argent

📞 05 56 09 10 25. www.cca33.com

Address : 500m from the beach

Opening times : from mid May to mid Sept.

20 ha (870 pitches) undulating, terraced, flat, sandy

Tariff : 48€ ♣♣ ⬅ 🔲 (10A) – Extra per person 12€ – Reservation fee 35€

Rental rates : (from mid May to mid Sept.) ✂ – 252 🚐. Per night from 53 to 269€ – Per week from 212 to 1,883€ – Reservation fee 35€

🚐 150 🔲 62€

Undulating site in a pretty pine forest 500m from the sea with an aquatic park with plenty of activities.

Surroundings : 🐾 ⛰		
Leisure activities : 🍸 ✗ 🎲 🏊 🏃 🚣 🛶 🚴 🎿 🔲 🛝 🐴 multi-sports ground	**G**	Longitude : -1.16446
Facilities : ♿ ⚡ 🛁 🍴 launderette 🛒 refrigerated food storage facilities	**P** **S**	Latitude : 45.22259

LA HUME

33470 – Michelin map **335** E7

▶ Paris 645 – Bordeaux 59 – Mérignac 62 – Pessac 56

🏔 Municipal Le Verdalle

📞 05 56 66 12 62. www.campingdeverdalle.com

Address : 2 allée de l'Infante (continue north along the av. de la Plage and take the road to the right; beside the Bassin d'Arcachon, direct access to the beach)

Opening times : from beginning April to end Sept.

1.5 ha (108 pitches)

Tariff : (2015 price) 30€ ♣♣ ⬅ 🔲 (10A) – Extra per person 6.50€ – Reservation fee 12€

Rental rates : (2015 price) (from beginning April to end Sept.) ✂ – 2 🏠 – 8 canvas bungalows. Per night from 30 to 150€ – Per week from 210 to 850€ – Reservation fee 12€

🚐 local sani-station

Surroundings : 🐾 🚃 ⛰		
Facilities : ♿ ⚡ 🍴 launderette	**G** **P** **S**	Longitude : -1.11099
		Latitude : 44.64397

ITXASSOU

64250 – Michelin map **342** D3 – pop. 2 031 – alt. 39
▶ Paris 787 – Bayonne 24 – Biarritz 25 – Cambo-les-Bains 5

⚠ Hiriberria

✆ 05 59 29 98 09. www.hiriberria.com

Address : located 1km northwest along the D 918, follow the signs for Cambo-les-Bains and take the road to the right

Opening times : permanent

4 ha (228 pitches) terrace, relatively flat, flat, grassy, fine gravel

Tariff : (2015 price) 26€ ♣♣ ⇔ 🅴 ⚡ (10A) – Extra per person 7€

Rental rates : (2015 price) (from beginning March to end Nov.) – 12 🚐 – 22 🏠. Per night from 45 to 85€ – Per week from 255 to 695€

🚰 AireService sani-station 3.50€

A small, pretty chalet village. Choose the pitches furthest away from the road in preference.

Surroundings : ⬅ 🏕 ♨♨
Leisure activities : 🏖 ⛵ (open air in season)
Facilities : ♿ ⚊ 🏭 🍴 ♨ ⛽ ♨ launderette

Longitude : -1.40137
Latitude : 43.33887

In order for the guide to remain wholly objective, the selection of campsites is made on an entirely independent basis.

LABENNE-OCÉAN

40530 – Michelin map **335** C13
▶ Paris 763 – Bordeaux 185 – Mont-de-Marsan 98 – Pau 129

⚠ Yelloh! Village Sylvamar ♣♣

✆ 05 59 45 75 16. www.sylvamar.fr

Address : avenue de l'Océan (continue along the D 126, follow the signs for the beach, near Le Boudigau)

Opening times : from beginning March to mid Oct.

25 ha (750 pitches)

Tariff : 58€ ♣♣ ⇔ 🅴 ⚡ (16A) – Extra per person 9€

Rental rates : (from end March to mid Oct.) ♿ (2 chalets) – 377 🚐 – 100 🏠 – 1 cabin in the trees. Per night from 69 to 309€ – Per week from 1,113 to 2,163€

🚰 10 🅴 77€ – ♨ ⚡69€

A large water park with a covered paddling pool and play area; a range of luxury rental options.

Surroundings : ♨♨ 🏕 ♨♨
Leisure activities : 🍴 ✕ 🏖 ⛺(open-air theatre) ♨ ♨ ♨ hammam, jacuzzi ⛵ ♨♨ ✕ 🏊 🏊 ⛳ multi-sports ground, spa centre, entertainment room
Facilities : ♿ ⚊ 🍴 ♨ ⛽ ♨ launderette 🏪 🍴 refrigerated food storage facilities
Nearby : 🏇 🐾 wildlife park

Longitude : -1.45687
Latitude : 43.59532

⚠ Club Airotel Sud Land ♣♣

✆ 05 59 45 42 02. www.camping-sud-landes.com

Address : 60 avenue de l'Océan (along the D 126, follow the signs for the beach)

Opening times : from beginning April to end Oct.

4 ha (207 pitches)

Tariff : 45€ ♣♣ ⇔ 🅴 ⚡ (6A) – Extra per person 7€ – Reservation fee 25€

Rental rates : (from beginning April to end Oct.) – 23 🚐 – 35 🏠 – 3 apartments – 12 canvas bungalows. Per night from 45 to 70€ – Per week from 217 to 1,190€ – Reservation fee 25€

🚰 Eurorelais sani-station 5€

Choose pitches furthest from the road.

Surroundings : 🏕 ♨♨
Leisure activities : 🍴 ✕ ⛲daytime ♨ 🏊 ⛵ ♨♨ ✕ 🏊 multi-sports ground
Facilities : ♿ ⚊ 🏭 ⚊ 🍴 ♨ ⛽ ♨ launderette 🏪
Nearby : 🏖 🍴

Longitude : -1.45687
Latitude : 43.60229

⚠ Municipal Les Pins Bleus

✆ 05 59 45 41 13. www.lespinsbleus.com

Address : avenue de l'Océan (along the D 126, follow the signs for the beach; beside the Boudigau river)

Opening times : from beginning April to end Oct.

6.5 ha (120 pitches)

Tariff : (2015 price) 10€ ♣♣ ⇔ 🅴 ⚡ (6A) – Extra per person 6.40€ – Reservation fee 18.50€

Rental rates : (2015 price) (from beginning April to end Oct.) ♿ (1 chalet) – 15 🚐 – 22 🏠 – 10 canvas bungalows. Per night from 44 to 90€ – Per week from 240 to 645€ – Reservation fee 18.50€

🚰 local sani-station 9€ – 10 🅴 9€ – ♨ ⚡13€

A variety of quality rental options.

Surroundings : ♨♨ ♨♨
Leisure activities : 🍴 ✕ 🏖 ♨ ⛵ ♨♨ 🏊 🐟
Facilities : ⚊ ♨ launderette, refrigerated food storage facilities
Nearby : 🏖

Longitude : -1.45687
Latitude : 43.60229

There are several different types of sani-station ('borne' in French) – sanitation points providing fresh water and disposal points for grey water. See page 12 for further details.

LACANAU

33680 – Michelin map **335** E5 – pop. 4 412 – alt. 17
▶ Paris 625 – Bordeaux 47 – Mérignac 45 – Pessac 51

⚠ FranceLoc Talaris Vacances ♣♣

✆ 05 56 03 04 15. www.talaris-vacances.fr

Address : at the Moutchic (5km west along the D 6, follow the signs for Lacanau-Océan)

Opening times : from beginning April to mid Sept.

10 ha (476 pitches) flat, grassy, small lake

Tariff : (2015 price) 37€ ♣♣ ⇔ 🅴 ⚡ (10A) – Extra per person 7€

Rental rates : (2015 price) (from beginning April to mid Sept.) ♿ – 304 🚐 – 6 🏠 – 23 tent lodges. Per week from 147 to 1,309€ – Reservation fee 26€

🚰 local sani-station

In a pleasant wooded setting.

Surroundings : ♨♨ ♨♨♨
Leisure activities : 🍴 ✕ 🏖 ⛲ ♨ ⛵ ♨♨ ⛵ 🐟 ♨ 🏊 🏊 ⛳ multi-sports ground
Facilities : ♿ ⚊ ♨ ♨ launderette 🏪 🍴

Longitude : -1.11236
Latitude : 45.008

🏕 Le Tedey ♠♣

Le Tedey

📞 05 56 03 00 15. www.le-tedey.com 🏷

Address : at the Moutchic, route de Longarisse (3km south and take road to the left)

Opening times : from end April to mid Sept.

14 ha (680 pitches) adjacent wooded dunes

Tariff : (2015 price) 32.90€ ♦♦ 🚗 🅴 🄿 (6A) – Extra per person 6.40€ –

Reservation fee 20€

Rental rates : (2015 price) (from end April to mid Sept.) 🏷 – 38 🚐. Per week from 340 to 795€ – Reservation fee 20€

In a pleasant location beside the Lac de Lacanau, shaded by pine trees, but with poor sanitary facilities.

Surroundings : 🐟 🖵 ♨ ⛰
Leisure activities : 🍴 🎣 ⛹ 🚣 🚴 🎣 🐴 🏊
Facilities : ♿ ⊶ 🚿 🍴 launderette 🔲 🍽

GPS
Longitude : -1.13652
Latitude : 44.9875

A chambre d'hôte is a guesthouse or B & B-style accommodation.

LACANAU-OCÉAN

33680 – Michelin map **335** D4 – pop. 3 142
▶ Paris 636 – Andernos-les-Bains 38 – Arcachon 87 – Bordeaux 63

🏕 Yelloh! Village Les Grands Pins ♠♣

📞 05 56 03 20 77. www.lesgrandspins.com

Address : North Beach (north of the resort, 500m from the beach - direct access)

Opening times : from end April to mid Sept.

11 ha (570 pitches) terraced, undulating, sandy, stony

Tariff : 60€ ♦♦ 🚗 🅴 🄿 (10A) – Extra per person 9€

Rental rates : (from end April to mid Sept.) ♿ – 243 🚐. Per night from 35 to 305€ – Per week from 245 to 2,135€ 🚐 local sani-station 1€

Surroundings : 🐟 🖵 ♨
Leisure activities : 🍴 🍽 🎦 🏖 🚣 🎣 ⛵ hammam, jacuzzi ⛹ 🚴 🏊 🏊 fitness trail, multi-sports ground, spa centre
Facilities : ♿ ⊶ 🅿 🚻 🍴 launderette 🛒 🍽 refrigerated food storage facilities

GPS
Longitude : -1.19517
Latitude : 45.01088

🏕 Club Airotel L'Océan ♠♣

📞 05 56 03 24 45. www.airotel-ocean.com

Address : 24 rue du Repos (Plage Nord (North Beach)

Opening times : from beginning April to beginning Nov.

9 ha (550 pitches) terraced, undulating, sandy

Tariff : (2015 price) 58€ ♦♦ 🚗 🅴 🄿 (15A) – Extra per person 11€ – Reservation fee 28€

Rental rates : (2015 price) (from beginning April to beginning Nov.) 🏷 – 270 🚐. Per night from 60 to 250€ – Per week from 420 to 1,750€ – Reservation fee 28€
🚐 local sani-station – 30 🅴 60€

Surroundings : ♨
Leisure activities : 🍴 🍽 🎦 🏖 🚣 🎣 ⛵ hammam, jacuzzi ⛹ 🚴 🏊 🏊 disco, surfing, multi-sports ground, spa centre
Facilities : ♿ ⊶ 🚿 🏊 🍴 launderette 🛒 🍽 refrigerated food storage facilities

GPS
Longitude : -1.1928
Latitude : 45.00868

LAMONTJOIE

47310 – pop. 501 – alt. 130
▶ Paris 723 – Bordeaux 151 – Agen 21 – Toulouse 126

🏕 Sites et Paysages Le Saint-Louis

📞 05 53 99 59 38. www.camping-lamontjoie.fr

Address : Lac de Lamontjoie

Opening times : from mid April to mid Oct.

20 ha/2 for camping (80 pitches) terraced, flat, grassy

Tariff : 29.60€ ♦♦ 🚗 🅴 🄿 (10A) – Extra per person 6.40€ – Reservation fee 10€

Rental rates : (from mid April to mid Oct.) 🏷 – 2 🏠 – 3 🛏 – 2 cabins in the trees – 5 tent lodges – 2 gîtes. Per night from 54 to 120€ – Per week from 308 to 840€ – Reservation fee 10€
🚐 4 🅴 18.50€ – 🚐 11€

Surroundings : ♨
Leisure activities : 🍴 🍽 ⛹ 🚴 🏊 🎣 pedalos 🛶
Facilities : ♿ ⊶ 🚿 🍴 launderette 🍽

GPS
Longitude : 0.51733
Latitude : 44.07722

LAMONZIE-MONTASTRUC

24520 – Michelin map **329** E6 – pop. 632 – alt. 50
▶ Paris 587 – Bordeaux 131 – Périgueux 46 – Agen 103

🏕 L'Escapade ♠♣

📞 05 53 57 23 79. www.campinglescapade.com

Address : at Les Roussilloux (follow the signs for St-Alvère)

Opening times : from beginning April to mid Sept.

4.5 ha (107 pitches) very uneven

Tariff : (2015 price) 34€ ♦♦ 🚗 🅴 🄿 (10A) – Extra per person 8.50€ – Reservation fee 26€

Rental rates : (2015 price) (from beginning April to mid Sept.) – 67 🚐 – 10 🏠. Per night from 42 to 69€ – Per week from 217 to 980€ – Reservation fee 26€

Surroundings : 🐟 🖵 ♨
Leisure activities : 🍴 🍽 🎦 🏖 ⛵ hammam, jacuzzi ⛹ 🚴 🏊 🏊 donkey rides, multi-sports ground
Facilities : ♿ ⊶ 🚿 🍴 launderette 🍽

GPS
Longitude : 0.60793
Latitude : 44.88636

LANOUAILLE

24270 – Michelin map **329** H3 – pop. 989 – alt. 209
▶ Paris 446 – Brantôme 47 – Limoges 55 – Périgueux 46

🏕 Village Vacances Le Moulin de la Jarousse
(rental of chalets, yurts, cabins in the trees, gîtes only)

📞 05 53 52 37 91. www.location-en-dordogne.com

Address : at La Jarousse (continue 9km northeast along the D 704 to l'Hépital, then take right turn along the D 80)

Opening times : permanent

8 ha terraced, pond, forest

Rental rates : 8 🏠 – 7 yurts – 10 cabins in the trees – 3 gîtes. Per night from 45 to 140€ – Per week from 350 to 860€

In an unspoilt, wooded setting overlooking the lake.

Surroundings : 🐟 ≺ 🏔
Leisure activities : ⛹ 🚴 🏊 (open air in season) 🛶 pedalos, farm or petting farm 🐾
Facilities : ⊶ 🅿 🚻 🍴 🚰

GPS
Longitude : 1.18411
Latitude : 45.43694

LARRAU

64560 – Michelin map **342** G4 – pop. 204 – alt. 636
▶ Paris 840 – Bordeaux 254 – Pamplona 110 – Donostia-San Sebastián 142

⛰ Village Vacances Les Chalets d'Iraty
(rental of chalets only)

✆ 05 59 28 51 29. www.chalets-iraty.com – alt. 1 327

Address : the Col Bagargui (pass), (14km west along the D 19, follow the signs for St-Jean-Pied-de-Port)

Opening times : permanent

2,000 ha/4 for camping, undulating
Rental rates : (2015 price) **P** – 40 🏠. Per night from 40 to 70€ – Per week from 305 to 490€

Chalets located in the Iraty forest between the Bagargui and Hegui Xouri mountain passes.

Surroundings : 🐎 ♒︎
Leisure activities : 🚲 ✂️
Facilities : ⚲ 🎿 🚽 📷
Nearby : 🏖 🍹 🗡 🚣 🐎 cross-country skiing

Longitude : -1.03532
Latitude : 43.03638

LARUNS

64440 – Michelin map **342** J5 – pop. 1 326 – alt. 523
▶ Paris 811 – Argelès-Gazost 49 – Lourdes 51 – Oloron-Ste-Marie 34

⛰ Les Gaves

✆ 05 59 05 32 37. www.campingdesgaves.com – limited spaces for one-night stay

Address : Pon district (located 1.5km southeast of Larun, follow the signs for Le Col d'Aubisque and take the road to the left; beside the Gave d'Ossau river)

Opening times : permanent

2.4 ha (101 pitches) flat, grassy
Tariff : 31.20€ ♛ ♛ ⇔ 🔲 🔌 (10A) – Extra per person 7.80€ – Reservation fee 20€
Rental rates : permanent **P** – 13 🏚 – 11 🏠 – 5 apartments – 1 gîte. Per night from 77 to 143€ – Per week from 259 to 966€ – Reservation fee 20€
🚰 local sani-station – 20 🔲 25.20€ – 🚐 11€

A pleasant camping area, with varied rental options, but the rather jaded sanitary facilities are not of a high standard; many owner-occupier mobile homes.

Surroundings : ❄️ 🐎 ≤ ♒︎
Leisure activities : 🍹 🎱 🚣
Facilities : 🚽 🎿 🧺 🚰 launderette

Longitude : -0.41772
Latitude : 42.98306

LÈGE-CAP-FERRET

33950 – Michelin map **335** E6 – pop. 7 527 – alt. 9
▶ Paris 629 – Arcachon 65 – Belin-Beliet 56 – Bordeaux 50

⛰ La Prairie

✆ 05 56 60 09 75. www.campinglaprairie.com

Address : 93 avenue du Médoc (located 1km northeast along the D 3, follow the signs for Le Porge)

Opening times : from beginning March to end Oct.

2.5 ha (118 pitches)
Tariff : (2015 price) 21.80€ ♛ ♛ ⇔ 🔲 🔌 (10A) – Extra per person 4.10€

Rental rates : (2015 price) (from mid April to end Sept.) – 16 🏚 – 4 tent lodges. Per night from 40 to 108€ – Per week from 235 to 655€

🚰 local sani-station – 10 🔲 11.70€ – 🚐 9€

Surroundings : 🐟 ♒︎
Leisure activities : 🍹 🗡 🎱 🚣 🎿
Facilities : ⚲ 🚽 🎿 📷 🚿

Longitude : -1.13375
Latitude : 44.80271

LESCUN

64490 – Michelin map **342** I5 – pop. 178 – alt. 900
▶ Paris 846 – Lourdes 89 – Oloron-Ste-Marie 37 – Pau 70

⛰ Le Lauzart

✆ 05 59 34 51 77. www.camping-lescun.com

1 ha (55 pitches) flat and relatively flat

A magnificent mountain site, although with ageing sanitary facilities. Half board available.

Surroundings : 🐎 ≤ ♒︎
Leisure activities : 🎱
Facilities : ⚲ 🚽 🎿 🚽 🚿 📷

Longitude : -0.64217
Latitude : 42.92761

LIMEUIL

24510 – Michelin map **329** G6 – pop. 328 – alt. 65
▶ Paris 528 – Bergerac 43 – Brive-la-Gaillarde 78 – Périgueux 48

⛰ La Ferme des Poutiroux

✆ 05 53 63 31 62. www.poutiroux.com

Address : take the northwestern exit along the D 31, follow the signs for Trémolat then continue 1km along the road for Paunat to the right

Opening times : from beginning April to end Oct.

2.5 ha (50 pitches) terraced, relatively flat, flat, grassy
Tariff : (2015 price) ♛ 5.80€ ⇔ 🔲 6.40€ – 🔌 (6A) 4.20€ – Reservation fee 13€
Rental rates : (2015 price) (from beginning April to end Oct.) ♿ – 16 🏚. Per night from 28 to 89€ – Per week from 180 to 620€
🚰 AireService sani-station 3€ – 4 🔲 15€ – 🚐 🔌15€

Surroundings : 🐎 ≤ ♒︎
Leisure activities : 🍹 🎱 🚣 🎿
Facilities : ♿ 🚽 🚿 🧺 🚽

Longitude : 0.87946
Latitude : 44.89332

LINXE

40260 – Michelin map **335** D11 – pop. 1 236 – alt. 33
▶ Paris 712 – Castets 10 – Dax 31 – Mimizan 37

⛰ FranceLoc Domaine de Lila
(rental of mobile homes only)

✆ 05 58 43 96 25. www.franceloc.fr – limited spaces for one-night stay

Address : 190 route de Mixe (located 1.5km northwest along the D 42, follow the signs for St-Girons and take D 397, turning to the right)

Opening times : from beginning June to beginning Sept.

2 ha (241 pitches) flat, sandy
Rental rates : (2015 price) ♿ – 241 🏚. Per night from 42 to 168€ – Per week from 168 to 1,582€ – Reservation fee 27€

Surroundings : 🐎
Leisure activities : 🍹 🎱 🎪 🏃 🚣 🚲 🎿 🏊 (lake) ⛳ multi-sports ground
Facilities : ♿ 🚽 launderette

Longitude : -1.25758
Latitude : 43.93185

LIT-ET-MIXE

40170 – Michelin map **335** D10 – pop. 1 497 – alt. 13
▶ Paris 710 – Castets 21 – Dax 42 – Mimizan 22

⛺ Tohapi Les Vignes
(rental of mobile homes, chalets and canvas bungalows only)

✆ 05 58 42 85 60. www.tohapi.fr

Address : 2.7km southwest along the D 652 and take the D 88, to the right, follow the signs for Le Cap de l'Homy

Opening times : from beginning April to end Sept.

15 ha (490 pitches)

Rental rates : (2015 price) & (2 mobile homes) – 464 🚐 – 52 🏠 – 11 tent lodges. Per night from 24 to 234€ – Per week from 168 to 1,638€

Large holiday village with plenty of activities.

| Leisure activities : 🍽🍴🛶🎪(big top staging activities and shows) 🤸🏄🚲 🎯🎱🎿⛷multi-sports ground Facilities : &🚻🚿🍴launderette 🛒🚗 | **GPS** Longitude : -1.28275 Latitude : 44.02401 |

⛺ Municipal du Cap de l'Homy

✆ 05 58 42 83 47. www.camping-cap.com

Address : at Cap-de-l'Homy, 600 avenue de l'Océan (8km west along the D 652 and take D 88 to the right; 300m from the beach (direct access)

Opening times : from beginning May to end Sept.

10 ha (472 pitches) undulating, flat, sandy

Tariff : (2015 price) 33.20€ 👫 🚗 🔲 🔌 (6A) – Extra per person 7.50€ – Reservation fee 30€

Rental rates : (2015 price) (from beginning May to mid Sept.) 🚲 – 15 canvas bungalows. Per week from 233 to 763€ – Reservation fee 30€

🚐 AireService sani-station 6€ – 36 🔲 20€

In the shade of a pleasant pine wood.

| Surroundings : 🌲🎋 Leisure activities : 🛶🚲 Facilities : &🚻☑🚿🍴launderette, refrigerated food storage facilities Nearby : 🍖🍽🍴🏊surfing | **GPS** Longitude : -1.33435 Latitude : 44.03712 |

MARCILLAC-ST-QUENTIN

24200 – Michelin map **329** I6 – pop. 791 – alt. 235
▶ Paris 522 – Brive-la-Gaillarde 48 – Les Eyzies-de-Tayac 18 – Montignac 21

⛺ Les Tailladis

✆ 05 53 59 10 95. www.tailladis.com

Address : at Les Tailladis (situated 2km to the north, near the D 48; beside the Beune river and a lake)

Opening times : from mid March to end Oct.

25 ha/8 for camping (90 pitches) terraced, relatively flat, flat, grassy, stony

Tariff : (2015 price) 👤 6.85€ 🚗 🔲 7.85€ – 🔌 (10A) 4.20€ – Reservation fee 12.50€

Rental rates : (2015 price) (from mid March to end Oct.) – 3 🚐 – 4 🏠 – 2 tent lodges. Per night from 25 to 38€ – Per week from 450 to 615€ – Reservation fee 12.50€

| Surroundings : 🌲🏕🎋 Leisure activities : 🍽🍴🎿🎣 Facilities : &🚻🎛🚿🍴launderette 🖼🚗 | **GPS** Longitude : 1.18789 Latitude : 44.97465 |

MAULÉON-LICHARRE

64130 – Michelin map **342** G5 – pop. 3 205 – alt. 140
▶ Paris 802 – Oloron-Ste-Marie 31 – Orthez 39 – Pau 60

⛺ Aire Naturelle La Ferme Landran

✆ 05 59 28 19 55. www.ferme-landran-location.com

Address : at Ordiarp, Larréguy district (4.5km southwest along the D 918, follow the signs for St-Jean-Pied-de-Port then continue 1.5km along the road for Lambarre to the right)

Opening times : from mid April to end Sept.

1 ha (25 pitches) sloping, flat, grassy

Tariff : 15€ 👫 🚗 🔲 🔌 (6A) – Extra per person 3.10€

Rental rates : permanent – 2 🏠 – 1 gîte. Per night 60€ – Per week 380€

🚐 Eurorelais sani-station 3€

A farm campsite.

| Surroundings : 🌳⛰🎋 Leisure activities : 🛶🎣 Facilities : &🚻🚐🖼 | **GPS** Longitude : -0.93933 Latitude : 43.20185 |

⛺ Uhaitza – Le Saison

✆ 05 59 28 18 79. www.camping-uhaitza.com

Address : located 1.5km south along the D 918, follow the signs for Tardets-Sorholus; beside the Saison river

Opening times : from beginning April to mid Oct.

1 ha (50 pitches) terraced, flat, grassy

Tariff : 👤 6€ 🚗 3.10€ 🔲 5.80€ – 🔌 (10A) 5.20€ – Reservation fee 10€

Rental rates : (from beginning March to mid Nov.) 🚲 – 2 🚐 – 5 🏠. Per week from 307 to 617€ – Reservation fee 10€

🚐 local sani-station 5.25€ – 🚐 11€

Choose the pitches near the stream and further away from the road.

| Surroundings : 🌲🏕🎋 Leisure activities : 🍽🛶🎣🏊🎿 Facilities : &🚻🚗🚿🍴🏓🎿🍴launderette | **GPS** Longitude : -0.8972 Latitude : 43.20789 |

We have selected the best campsites in France with our usual care, listing those with the best facilities in the most pleasant surroundings.

MESSANGES

40660 – Michelin map **335** C12 – pop. 986 – alt. 8
▶ Paris 734 – Bayonne 45 – Castets 24 – Dax 33

⛺ Club Airotel Le Vieux Port

✆ 05 58 48 22 00. www.levieuxport.com

Address : route de la Plage Sud (2.5km southwest along the D 652, follow the signs for Vieux-Boucau-les-Bains then continue 800m along the road to the right; 500m from the beach, direct access)

Opening times : from mid March to end Sept.

40 ha/30 for camping (1546 pitches) undulating, flat, grassy, sandy

Tariff : 75€ 👫 🚗 🔲 🔌 (8A) – Extra per person 6€ – Reservation fee 40€

Rental rates : (from mid March to end Sept.) & (1 mobile home) 🚲 – 363 🚐 – 75 🏠 – 3 cabins in the trees. Per night from 75 to 165€ – Per week from 269 to 2,233€ – Reservation fee 40€

🚐 AireService sani-station

A spacious landscaped water park with plenty of shops and services at the entrance.

Surroundings : 🏕 ♨♨
Leisure activities : 🍴 ✕ 🎮 📺(cinema/theatre) 🚶 ♨ hammam, jacuzzi 🏊 🚴 🐴 multi-sports ground, spa centre
Facilities : ♿ ⚷ 🅿 ♨ 🚿 🍴 launderette 🛒 refrigerated food storage facilities

GPS	Longitude : -1.39995
	Latitude : 43.79773

⛰⛰⛰ Club Airotel Village Vacances Lou Pignada 👥

(rental of caravans, mobile homes and chalets only)

📞 05 58 48 22 00. www.loupignada.com
Address : route d'Azur (situated 2km south along the D 652, then continue 500m down road to the left)
Opening times : from mid March to end Sept.
8 ha (430 pitches)
Rental rates : ♿ (1 mobile home) 🅿 – 1 'gypsy' caravan – 120 🚐 – 25 🏠 – 3 cabins in the trees – 1 tent lodge. Per night from 59 to 279€ – Per week from 209 to 1,955€ – Reservation fee 40€
🚐 AireService sani-station – 🔌18€

Surroundings : 🏕 🛒 ♨♨
Leisure activities : 🍴 ✕ 📺 🚶 ♨ 🎯 hammam, jacuzzi 🏊 🚴 🐴 ✕ multi-sports ground, spa centre
Facilities : ♿ ⚷ 🅿 🚿 ♨ launderette refrigerated food storage facilities
Nearby : 🛒

GPS	Longitude : -1.38245
	Latitude : 43.79747

⛰ La Côte

📞 05 58 48 49 94. www.campinglacote.com
Address : chemin de la Côte (2.3km southwest along the D 652, follow the signs for Vieux-Boucau-les-Bains and take the road to the right)
Opening times : from beginning April to end Sept.
3.5 ha (151 pitches)
Tariff : 33.90€ ♣♣ 🚗 📺 🔌 (10A) – Extra per person 6.50€ – Reservation fee 20€
Rental rates : (from beginning April to end Sept.) 🐕 – 11 🚐 – 3 gîtes. Per night from 50 to 130€ – Per week from 250 to 865€ – Reservation fee 20€
🚐 local sani-station

Surroundings : 🏕 ♨♨
Leisure activities : 🎮 jacuzzi 🏊 🦺
Facilities : ♿ ⚷ 🚿 ♨ launderette, refrigerated food storage facilities
Nearby : 🛒

GPS	Longitude : -1.39171
	Latitude : 43.80035

⛰ Les Acacias 👥

📞 05 58 48 01 78. www.lesacacias.com
Address : 101 chemin du Houdin, Delest district (situated 2km south along the D 652, follow the signs for Vieux-Boucau-les-Bains then continue 1km along the turning to the left)
Opening times : from end March to end Oct.
1.7 ha (125 pitches)
Tariff : 26€ ♣♣ 🚗 📺 🔌 (10A) – Extra per person 5.10€ – Reservation fee 15€
Rental rates : (from end March to end Oct.) – 13 🚐 – 1 🏠. Per night from 55 to 65 – Per week from 245 to 740
🚐 local sani-station 9€ – 8 📺 21€

Good sanitary facilities and green spaces for sport and relaxation.

Surroundings : 🏕 🛒 ♀
Leisure activities : 🎮 🚶 🦺 🚴
Facilities : ♿ ⚷ 🏊 🚿 🍴 ♨ launderette, refrigerated food storage facilities
Nearby : 🛒

GPS	Longitude : -1.37567
	Latitude : 43.79757

MÉZOS

40170 – Michelin map **335** E10 – pop. 866 – alt. 23
▶ Paris 700 – Bordeaux 118 – Castets 24 – Mimizan 16

⛰⛰⛰ Club Airotel Le Village Tropical Sen Yan 👥

📞 05 58 42 60 05. www.sen-yan.com
Address : avenue de la Gare (located 1km east, follow the signs for Le Cout)
Opening times : from end April to mid Sept.
8 ha (574 pitches)
Tariff : (2015 price) 45.50€ ♣♣ 🚗 📺 🔌 (10A) – Extra per person 9€ – Reservation fee 26€
Rental rates : (2015 price) (from mid April to mid Sept.) 🐕 – 200 🚐 – 35 🏠. Per night from 55 to 195€ – Per week from 385 to 1,365€ – Reservation fee 26€

Tropical atmosphere around the pool with a professional team for activities and events.

Surroundings : 🏕 🛒 ♨♨
Leisure activities : 🍴 ✕ 🎮 📺 🚶 🦺 ♨ hammam, jacuzzi 🏊 🚴 🐴 ✕ 🦺 🏊 multi-sports ground, spa centre, entertainment room
Facilities : ♿ ⚷ 🏊 🚿 🍴 ♨ launderette 🏊 🚐

GPS	Longitude : -1.15657
	Latitude : 44.07164

Michelin classification:

⛰⛰⛰⛰	*Extremely comfortable, equipped to a very high standard*
⛰⛰⛰	*Very comfortable, equipped to a high standard*
⛰⛰	*Comfortable and well equipped*
⛰	*Reasonably comfortable*
⛺	*Satisfactory*

MIALET

24450 – Michelin map **329** G2 – pop. 665 – alt. 320
▶ Paris 436 – Limoges 49 – Nontron 23 – Périgueux 51

⛺ Village Vacances L'Étang de Vivale

(rental of chalets only)

📞 05 53 52 66 05. www.vivaledordogne.com
Address : 32 avenue de Nontron (700m west along the D 79; beside the lake)
Opening times : from end March to beginning Nov.
30 ha
Rental rates : 20 🏠. Per week from 390 to 820€

All the chalets have a view of the lake; perfect for fishing and relaxation.

Surroundings : 🏕 🐟 ♀
Leisure activities : 🍴 🎮 🏊 🚣 🦺
Facilities : ♿ ⚷ 🅿 ♨ 🚿

GPS	Longitude : 0.89788
	Latitude : 45.54793

MIMIZAN

40200 – Michelin map **335** D9 – pop. 7 000 – alt. 13
▶ Paris 692 – Arcachon 67 – Bayonne 109 – Bordeaux 109

⛰ Municipal du Lac

☎ 05 58 09 01 21. www.mimizanlac-camping.com

Address : avenue de Woolsack (situated 2km north along the D 87, follow the signs for Gastes; beside the Lac d'Aureilhan)

Opening times : from mid May to beginning Sept.

8 ha (459 pitches)

Tariff : (2015 price) 21.89€ ✶✶ ⬛ 🔲 🔲 (6A) – Extra per person 8.25€ – Reservation fee 21€

Rental rates : (2015 price) (from mid May to beginning Sept.) – 15 canvas bungalows. Per night from 26 to 60€ – Per week from 180 to 420€ – Reservation fee 21€

🚐 flot bleu sani-station 2€ – 21 🔲 18.44€

Pitches enjoy some shade under the pine trees near the lake.

Surroundings : 🎣⛰
Leisure activities : ✗ 🛶 🏖 (beach)
Facilities : 🚿 🔑 🛁 2 individual sanitary facilities (🔲 🚻 wc) launderette 🚗 refrigerated food storage facilities
Nearby : 🎣 pedalos
Longitude : -1.2299
Latitude : 44.21968

MIMIZAN-PLAGE

40200 – Michelin map **335** D9
▶ Paris 706 – Bordeaux 128 – Mont-de-Marsan 84

🏕 Club Airotel Marina-Landes 🛎

☎ 05 58 09 12 66. www.marinalandes.com

Address : 8 rue Marina (500m from La Plage du Sud (beach))

Opening times : from end April to mid Sept.

9 ha (502 pitches)

Tariff : (2015 price) 60€ ✶✶ ⬛ 🔲 🔲 (10A) – Extra per person 10€ – Reservation fee 35€

Rental rates : (2015 price) (from end April to mid Sept.) – 131 🏠 – 6 – 24 apartments – 10 canvas bungalows – 7 tent lodges. Per night from 39 to 83€ – Per week from 425 to 1 420€ – Reservation fee 35€

Lots of shade and a variety of rental options.

Surroundings : 🌲 🎣⛰
Leisure activities : 🍴 ✗ 🛶 🏖 🎯 🏇 🎣 🚴 🎿 ⛳ 🔲 🏊 multi-sports ground, entertainment room
Facilities : 🚿 🔑 🛁 🚻 launderette 🛒 🚗 refrigerated food storage facilities
Nearby : 🏇
Longitude : -1.2909
Latitude : 44.2043

🏕 Municipal de la Plage 🛎

☎ 05 58 09 00 32. www.mimizan-camping.com

Address : boulevard de l'Atlantique (northern suburb)

Opening times : from mid April to end Sept.

16 ha (608 pitches) undulating, flat, grassy, sandy

Tariff : (2015 price) 24€ ✶✶ ⬛ 🔲 🔲 (10A) – Extra per person 10€ – Reservation fee 21€

Rental rates : (2015 price) (from mid April to end Sept.) 🅿 – 36 🏠 – 15 🏡 – 4 tent lodges. Per night from 40 to 90€ – Per week from 180 to 800€ – Reservation fee 21€

🚐 50 🔲 18€

The campsite welcomes surfer groups.

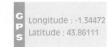

Surroundings : 🌲
Leisure activities : ✗ 🏖 🎯 🛶 climbing wall, multi-sports ground
Facilities : 🚿 🔑 🛁 🚻 launderette 🚗 refrigerated food storage facilities
Longitude : -1.28384
Latitude : 44.21719

MOLIETS ET MAA

40660 – Michelin map **335** C12 – pop. 1 024 – alt. 15
▶ Paris 732 – Bordeaux 154 – Mont-de-Marsan 86 – Pau 129

🏕 FranceLoc Landisland 🛎 (rental of mobile homes only)

☎ 05 58 47 13 78. http://www.camping-landisland.fr/

Address : 1010 rue des Templiers

24 ha/12 for camping (209 pitches) undulating, sandy
Rentals : 🚿 – 197 🏠 – 6 🏡 – 6 tent lodges.

Pleasant site in the middle of the Landes forest.

Surroundings : 🌲 🎣
Leisure activities : 🍴 ✗ 🛖 🏖 🎯 🏇 🛶 🚴 🎣 🎿 🔲 🏊 ⛳
Facilities : 🔑 🛁 🚗
Longitude : -1.34472
Latitude : 43.86111

MOLIETS-PLAGE

40660 – Michelin map **335** C11
▶ Paris 716 – Bordeaux 156 – Mont-de-Marsan 89 – Bayonne 67

🏕 Le Saint-Martin 🛎

☎ 05 58 48 52 30. www.camping-saint-martin.fr

Address : avenue de l'Océan (on the D 117. direct access to the beach)

Opening times : from beginning April to beginning Nov.

18 ha (673 pitches) undulating, flat and relatively flat, sandy

Tariff : (2015 price) 45.20€ ✶✶ ⬛ 🔲 🔲 (10A) – Extra per person 8.90€ – Reservation fee 35€

Rental rates : (2015 price) (from beginning April to beginning Nov.) – 14 🏠 – 137 🏡 – 16 tent lodges. Per week from 205 to 1 540€ – Reservation fee 35€

🚐 local sani-station – 45 🔲

Undulating site with viewing platform overlooking the ocean and forest. Direct access to the beach.

Surroundings : 🌲 🎣⛰
Leisure activities : 🍴 ✗ 🛖 🏖 🎯 🏇 🛶 🎣 🔲 🏊 multi-sports ground
Facilities : 🚿 🔑 🛁 🚽 🚻 launderette 🚗 refrigerated food storage facilities
Nearby : 🏇 🚴 ⛳ skate surfing
Longitude : -1.38731
Latitude : 43.85259

MONPAZIER

24540 – Michelin map **329** G7 – pop. 522 – alt. 180
▶ Paris 575 – Bergerac 47 – Fumel 26 – Périgueux 75

🏕 Le Moulin de David 🛎

☎ 05 53 22 65 25. www.moulindedavid.com

Address : 3km southwest along the D 2, follow the signs for Villeréal and take road to the left; beside a stream

Opening times : from beginning June to end Sept.

16 ha/4 for camping (160 pitches) terrace, flat, grassy, pond, wood

Tariff : 30€ ✶✶ ⬛ 🔲 🔲 (10A) – Extra per person 8€ – Reservation fee 18€

Rental rates : (from beginning June to end Sept.) – 57 ⊡ –
3 canvas bungalows – 7 tent lodges. Per night from 44 to 135€ –
Per week from 169 to 950€ – Reservation fee 18€

⊞ local sani-station – 4 ▣ 21€

Located partly in the forest around a renovated former farm-house with a cafe and gourmet restaurant.

Surroundings : 🌲 ⊏ 🌳🌳
Leisure activities : ❢ ✗ 🏠 ⏱🏃 ⚓ 🎿 ≋
(stream) ⚑
Facilities : ᒼ ⚬━ ᒼ ⚘ launderette 🚿 🚽

Longitude : 0.87873
Latitude : 44.65979

MONTIGNAC

24290 – Michelin map **329** H5 – pop. 2 851 – alt. 77
▶ Paris 513 – Brive-la-Gaillarde 39 – Périgueux 54 – Sarlat-la-Canéda 25

🏔 Le Moulin du Bieufond

☎ 05 53 51 83 95. www.bleufond.fr

Address : avenue Aristide Briand (500m south along the D 65, follow the signs for Sergeac; near the Vézère river)

Opening times : from beginning April to mid Oct.

1.3 ha (82 pitches) flat, grassy

Tariff : 29.10€ ❢❢ ⚓ ▣ (10A) – Extra per person 4.80€ –
Reservation fee 9€

Rental rates : (from beginning April to mid Oct.) ⚡ – 21 ⊡.
Per night from 120 to 145€ – Per week from 245 to 615€ –
Reservation fee 9€

The attractive pitches are situated beside an old mill.

Surroundings : 🌲 ⊏ 🌳🌳
Leisure activities : ✗ 🏠 ≋ jacuzzi ⚓ 🎿
Facilities : ᒼ ⚬━ ᒼ ⚘ ⚑ launderette
🚿
Nearby : ✗ 🎣

Longitude : 1.15864
Latitude : 45.05989

MONTPON-MÉNESTÉROL

24700 – Michelin map **329** B5 – pop. 5 535 – alt. 93
▶ Paris 532 – Bergerac 40 – Bordeaux 75 – Libourne 43

🏔 La Cigaline

☎ 05 53 80 22 16. www.lacigaline.fr

Address : 1 rue de la Paix (take the northern exit along the D 708, follow the signs for Ribérac and take the turning to the left before the bridge)

Opening times : from beginning April to end Sept.

2 ha (120 pitches) flat, grassy

Tariff : (2015 price) ❢ 4.60€ ⚓ ▣ 7.20€ (10A) – Reservation fee 12€

Rental rates : (2015 price) (from beginning April to end Sept.) –
12 ⊡ – 2 tent lodges. Per night from 45 to 81€ – Per week from 225 to 567€ – Reservation fee 12€

Snack bar with attractive terrace near the Isle river. Near the town centre.

Surroundings : ⊏ 🌳
Leisure activities : ❢ ✗ 🏠 ⚓ 🎣
Facilities : ᒼ ⚬━ ⚑ ⚘ 🚿 🚽
Nearby : ≋

Longitude : 0.15839
Latitude : 45.01217

NAVARRENX

64190 – Michelin map **342** H3 – pop. 1 104 – alt. 125
▶ Paris 787 – Oloron-Ste-Marie 23 – Orthez 22 – Pau 43

🏔 Beau Rivage

☎ 05 59 66 10 00. www.beaucamping.com

Address : allée des Marronniers (to the west of the town between the Gave d'Oloron (river) and the village ramparts)

Opening times : from end March to mid Oct.

2.5 ha (70 pitches) terraced, flat, grassy, fine gravel

Tariff : ❢ 6.20€ ⚓ ▣ 11.70€ – (10A) 3.80€

Rental rates : (from end March to mid Oct.) ᒼ (1 chalet) – 10 ⊡ –
3 studios. Per night from 65 to 125€ – Per week from 315 to 770€

⊞ local sani-station

By the Gave d'Oloron (rive) and the old village fortifications.

Surroundings : 🌲 ⊏ 🌳🌳
Leisure activities : 🏠 ⚓ 🎿
Facilities : ᒼ ⚬━ ⚑ ᒼ ⚘ ⚑ ⚘ launderette
Nearby : ✗ 🎣

Longitude : -0.76121
Latitude : 43.32003

LE NIZAN

33430 – Michelin map **335** J8 – pop. 423 – alt. 107
▶ Paris 635 – Agen 106 – Bordeaux 57 – Mont-de-Marsan 78

🏔 Village Vacances Domaine Ecôtelia

☎ 05 56 65 35 38. www.domaine-ecotelia.com

Address : 5 Tauzin

Opening times : permanent

10 ha/2.5 for camping (22 pitches)

Rental rates : permanent ⚡ – 3 'gypsy' caravans – 4 ⊡ –
4 yurts – 4 cabins in the trees – 5 tent lodges. Per night from
54 to 166€ – Per week from 278 to 996€

Unusual accommodation linking the five continents around an eco swimming pool.

Surroundings : 🌲 🌳
Leisure activities : ❢ 🏠 ⚓ 🎿
Facilities : ᒼ ⚬━ ⚑ ⚘ ▣

Longitude : -0.25778
Latitude : 44.47389

NONTRON

24300 – Michelin map **329** E2 – pop. 3 421 – alt. 260
▶ Paris 464 – Bordeaux 175 – Périgueux 49 – Angoulême 47

🏔 Camping de Nontron

☎ 05 53 56 02 04. www.campingdenontron.com

Address : at St-Martial-de-Valette (located 1km south on the D 675, follow the signs for Périgueux)

Opening times : permanent

2 ha (70 pitches) flat, grassy, beside river

Tariff : 18€ ❢❢ ⚓ ▣ (10A) – Extra per person 4€

Rental rates : permanent – 4 ⊡ – 1 ▭ – 6 studios. Per week from 230 to 590€

⊞ local sani-station

Beside a large indoor water park.

Surroundings : 🌲 ⊏ 🌳🌳
Leisure activities : 🏠 🎣
Facilities : ᒼ ⚬━ ⚑ ᒼ ⚘ ▣ 🚿
Nearby : ≋ hammam, jacuzzi 🏊 ⚑

Longitude : 0.65807
Latitude : 45.51951

ONDRES

40440 – Michelin map **335** C13 – pop. 4 479 – alt. 37
▶ Paris 761 – Bayonne 8 – Biarritz 15 – Dax 48

⚠ Du Lac

📞 05 59 45 28 45. www.camping-du-lac.fr

Address : 518 rue de Janin (2.2km north along the N 10 then take the D 26, follow the signs for Ondres-Plage then head towards Le Turc, road to the right; near a lake)

Opening times : from beginning April to beginning Oct.

3 ha (115 pitches) terraced, flat, grassy, sandy

Tariff : 43€ ★★ 🚗 🔲 ⚡ (10A) – Extra per person 7.50€ – Reservation fee 20€

Rental rates : (from beginning April to beginning Oct.) – 1 'gypsy' caravan – 33 🚃 – 3 🏠 – 7 canvas bungalows. Per night from 31 to 226€ – Per week from 217 to 1,582€ – Reservation fee 20€

🚐 Raclet sani-station

Pleasant site with varied rental options, some high quality.

Surroundings : 🌳 🏕 ♡♡
Leisure activities : ⛴ ✗ 🎣 ⛺ hammam 🏊 🚴
Facilities : 🚿 ⛽ 📶 ♨ 🍴 launderette 🔧
Nearby : 🎣

Longitude : -1.45249
Latitude : 43.56499

⚠ Lou Pignada ♣♣

📞 05 59 45 30 65. www.camping-loupignada.com

Address : 742 avenue de la Plage

Opening times : from beginning April to end Dec.

6.5 ha/4.5 for camping (214 pitches) flat, grassy, sandy

Tariff : (2015 price) 42€ ★★ 🚗 🔲 ⚡ (10A) – Extra per person 7€ – Reservation fee 20€

Rental rates : (2015 price) (from beginning April to end Dec.) – 40 🚃 – 30 🏠. Per week from 245 to 925€ – Reservation fee 20€

Lots of shade. Choose pitches furthest from the road and the railway track.

Surroundings : 🏕 ♡♡
Leisure activities : ⛴ ✗ ⛺ 🚴 🏊 multi-sports ground, entertainment room
Facilities : 🚿 ♨ launderette 🔧
Nearby : 🛒

Longitude : -1.46029
Latitude : 43.5695

This guide is updated regularly, so buy your new copy every year!

PARENTIS-EN-BORN

40160 – Michelin map **335** E8 – pop. 5 187 – alt. 32
▶ Paris 658 – Arcachon 43 – Bordeaux 76 – Mimizan 25

⚠ Yelloh! Village Au Lac de Biscarrosse ♣♣

📞 05 58 08 06 40. http://www.camping-lac-de-biscarrosse.com/fr/

Address : route de Lahitte

Opening times : from end March to end Sept.

14 ha (500 pitches) flat, sandy

Tariff : 53€ ★★ 🚗 🔲 ⚡ (20A) – Extra per person 7€

Rental rates : (from end March to end Sept.) 🚿 – 200 🚃. Per night from 39 to 259€ – Per week from 273 to 1,813€

🚐 Eurorelais sani-station 2€

New site with sunny pitches. A variety of high-quality rental options around pretty buildings.

Surroundings : 🌳 🏕
Leisure activities : ⛴ ✗ 🎣 ⛺ 🚴 🏊 🎿 hammam 🏊 🚴 ✗ 🎱 🏊 🏖 pedalos, multi-sports ground, spa centre, entertainment room
Facilities : 🚿 ⛽ 📶 ♨ 🍴 launderette 🔧 refrigerators
Nearby : 🏖 (beach) 🎣 🚣 ⚓

Longitude : -1.10139
Latitude : 44.35222

⚠ Le Pipiou ♣♣

📞 05 58 78 57 25. www.camping-pipiou.fr

Address : 382 route des Campings (2.5km west along the D 43 and take the turning to the right, 100m from the lake)

Opening times : from mid April to mid Oct.

9 ha (380 pitches) grassy

Tariff : 24€ ★★ 🚗 🔲 ⚡ (10A) – Extra per person 5.50€ – Reservation fee 15€

Rental rates : (from mid April to mid Oct.) – 35 🚃 – 3 canvas bungalows. Per week from 210 to 700€ – Reservation fee 15€

🚐 local sani-station

Shady or sunny pitches; many owner-occupier mobile homes.

Surroundings : 🌳 🏕 ♡♡
Leisure activities : ⛴ ✗ ⛺ 🏊 🚴 🏊 🎿 multi-sports ground
Facilities : 🚿 ⛽ 📶 ♨ 🍴 launderette 🔧
Nearby : 🏖 (beach) 🎣 🚣

Longitude : -1.10135
Latitude : 44.3457

⚠ L'Arbre d'Or

📞 05 58 78 41 56. www.arbre-dor.com

Address : 75 route du lac (located 1.5km west along the D 43)

Opening times : from beginning April to end Oct.

4 ha (200 pitches) flat, grassy, sandy

Tariff : 30.80€ ★★ 🚗 🔲 ⚡ (10A) – Extra per person 6.85€

Rental rates : (from beginning April to end Oct.) – 18 🚃 – 1 🏠 – 2 canvas bungalows. Per night from 60 to 115€ – Per week from 205 to 1,125€

🚐 local sani-station – 🚐 ⚡ 13€

Family atmosphere with covered and open-air swimming pools.

Surroundings : 🏕 ♡♡
Leisure activities : ⛴ ✗ 🎣 ⛺ 🏊 🏊 🎿 multi-sports ground
Facilities : 🚿 ⛽ 📶 🍴 launderette 🔧 refrigerators

Longitude : -1.09232
Latitude : 44.34615

PAUILLAC

33250 – Michelin map **335** G3 – pop. 5 135 – alt. 20
▶ Paris 625 – Arcachon 113 – Blaye 16 – Bordeaux 54

⚠ Municipal Les Gabarreys

📞 05 56 59 10 03. www.pauillac-medoc.com

Address : route de la Rivière (located 1km to the south, near the Gironde river)

Opening times : from end March to mid Oct.

1.6 ha (58 pitches)

Tariff : (2015 price) 22€ ★★ 🚗 🔲 ⚡ (10A) – Extra per person 5€ – Reservation fee 12€

Rental rates : (2015 price) (from end March to mid Oct.) &
(1 mobile home) – 7 ⟨⟩. Per night from 45 to 103€ – Per week
from 254 to 610€ – Reservation fee 12€

local sani-station 4.70€ – 40 ▣ 17.50€ – 14€

*There's an outdoor jacuzzi in an elevated position, with a
panoramic view of the Gironde river.*

Surroundings : 🐾 ⟶ 🌳	**G P S** Longitude : -0.74226
Leisure activities : 🏛 🏊 jacuzzi 🎿 ⛷	Latitude : 45.18517
Facilities : & ⟶ 🍴 launderette	

PETIT-PALAIS-ET-CORNEMPS

33570 – Michelin map **335** K5 – pop. 676 – alt. 35
▶ Paris 532 – Bergerac 51 – Castillon-la-Bataille 18 – Libourne 20

🏔 Club Airotel Le Pressoir

📞 0557697325. www.campinglepressoir.com

Address : at Queyrai (1.7km northwest along the D 21, follow the
signs for St-Médard-de-Guizières and take road to the left)

Opening times : permanent

2 ha (100 pitches)

Tariff : (2015 price) 29€ 🚶🚶 🚗 ▣ ⚡ (10A) – Extra per person 3€ –
Reservation fee 15€

Rental rates : (2015 price) permanent – 33 ⟨⟩ – 9 🏠 – 8 canvas
bungalows. Per night from 33 to 77€– Per week from 385 to 994€ –
Reservation fee 15€

local sani-station – 14 ▣ 16€ – 18€

*Surrounded by the grapes of Bordeaux vines with a renowned
restaurant.*

Surroundings : 🐾 < ⟶ 🌳	**G P S** Longitude : -0.06301
Leisure activities : 🍴 🍽 🏊 🎿 🚴 🌊	Latitude : 44.99693
Facilities : & ⟶ 🚰 🍴 launderette	

*This guide is not intended as a list of all the camping
sites in France; its aim is to provide a selection of the
best sites in each category.*

PEYRIGNAC

24210 – Michelin map **329** I5 – pop. 514 – alt. 200
▶ Paris 508 – Brive-la-Gaillarde 33 – Juillac 33 – Périgueux 44

🏔 La Garenne

📞 0553505773. www.lagarennedordogne.com

Address : at Le Combal (800m north of the village, near the stadium)

Opening times : permanent

4 ha/1.5 (70 pitches) terrace, flat, grassy, gravelled

Tariff : 21.50€ 🚶🚶 🚗 ▣ ⚡ (10A) – Extra per person 5€ – Reservation
fee 13.50€

Rental rates : permanent – 15 ⟨⟩ – 12 🏠. Per night
from 52 to 81€ – Per week from 207 to 766€ – Reservation fee
13.50€

3 ▣ 21.50€

*Among bushes with a view of the countryside from the pitches
near the pool.*

Surroundings : 🐾 🌿	
Leisure activities : 🍴 🍽 🏛 🏊 hammam, jacuzzi 🎿 ⛷	**G P S** Longitude : 1.1837
Facilities : & ⟶ 🚰 🌳 🚿 🍴 launderette	Latitude : 45.16175
Nearby : 🍽 🎣	

PEYRILLAC-ET-MILLAC

24370 – Michelin map **329** J6 – pop. 213 – alt. 88
▶ Paris 521 – Brive-la-Gaillarde 45 – Gourdon 23 – Sarlat-la-Canéda 22

🏔 Au P'tit Bonheur 👥

📞 0553297793. www.camping-auptitbonheur.com

Address : at Combe de Lafon (2.5km north along the follow the signs
for Le Bouscandier)

Opening times : from beginning April to end Sept.

2.8 ha (100 pitches) terraced, relatively flat, stony, grassy

Tariff : (2015 price) 22.70€ 🚶🚶 🚗 ▣ ⚡ (10A) –
Extra per person 5.65€ – Reservation fee 16€

Rental rates : (2015 price) (from beginning April to end Sept.) –
21 ⟨⟩ – 9 🏠 – 5 canvas bungalows – 2 tent lodges. Per
night from 36 to 108€ – Per week from 246 to 752€ – Reservation
fee 16€

local sani-station

Surroundings : 🐾 ⟶ 🌳	
Leisure activities : 🍴 🍽 🏛 🏊 🏃 🏊 jacuzzi 🎿 ⛷ 🌊	**G P S** Longitude : 1.40423
Facilities : & ⟶ 🌳 🚿 🍴 launderette 🧊 refrigerated food storage facilities	Latitude : 44.89934

PISSOS

40410 – Michelin map **335** G9 – pop. 1 315 – alt. 46
▶ Paris 657 – Arcachon 72 – Biscarrosse 34 – Bordeaux 75

🏔 Municipal de l'Arriu

📞 0558089038. www.pissos.fr –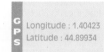

Address : 525 chemin de l'Arriu (1.2km east along the D 43, follow
the signs for Sore and take the road to the right, after the swimming
pool)

Opening times : from beginning July to mid Sept.

3 ha (74 pitches)

Tariff : 14€ 🚶🚶 🚗 ▣ ⚡ (12A) – Extra per person 3.50€

Surroundings : 🐾 🌳	
Facilities : & 🌳 🚿	**G P S** Longitude : -0.76944
Nearby : 🏛 🍴 🏊 🏊 🌊	Latitude : 44.305

PLAZAC

24580 – Michelin map **329** H5 – pop. 725 – alt. 110
▶ Paris 527 – Bergerac 65 – Brive-la-Gaillarde 53 – Périgueux 40

🏔 Le Lac 👥

📞 0553507586. www.campinglelac-dordogne.com

Address : at the lake (800m southeast along the D 45, follow the
signs for Thonac)

Opening times : from mid May to end Sept.

7 ha/2.5 for camping (115 pitches) terraced, flat and relatively flat,
grassy

Tariff : (2015 price) 🚶 6€ 🚗 ▣ 6€ – ⚡ (10A) 3.80€ – Reservation
fee 12€

Rental rates : (2015 price) (from mid May to end Sept.) &
(1 mobile home) – 40 ⟨⟩ – 4 🏠. Per night from 50 to 103€ –
Per week from 350 to 720€ – Reservation fee 12€

2 ▣ 21.80€

Surroundings : 🐾 ⟶ 🌳 🏔	
Leisure activities : 🍴 🍽 🏛 🏃 🎿 ⛷ 🌊 🔫 ⛷ 🌊 🏊 (pond) 🏹 multi-sports ground	**G P S** Longitude : 1.04778
Facilities : & ⟶ 🌳 🚿 🍴 launderette 🎿 🌳	Latitude : 45.03139

POMPORT

24240 – Michelin map **329** D7 – pop. 812 – alt. 120
▶ Paris 554 – Agen 89 – Bordeaux 92 – Périgueux 62

⛰ Pomport Beach ▲▪

📞 05 24 10 61 13. www.pomport-beach.com

Address : route de la Gardonnette

Opening times : from beginning June to mid Sept.

13 ha/5 for camping (199 pitches) terrace, flat, grassy, stony, wood

Tariff : 34 € ♦♦ 🚐 🔲 ⚡ (10A) – Extra per person 9 €

🚐 local sani-station 5 €

Surroundings : 🖼 ♀
Leisure activities : 🍽 ✕ 🎞 🕹 🏃 🚣 🚴 🎿 🏊 (beach) 🚣 pedalos 🏃 multi-sports ground
Facilities : 🚿 🍴 🚻 🧺 launderette 🚿

GPS Longitude : 0.41174
Latitude : 44.77135

PONT-DU-CASSE

47480 – Michelin map **336** G4 – pop. 4 305 – alt. 67
▶ Paris 658 – Bordeaux 147 – Toulouse 122 – Montauban 96

⛰ Village Vacances de Loisirs Darel
  (rental of chalets only)

📞 05 53 67 96 41. accueil@ville-pontducasse.fr

Address : at Darel (7km northeast along the D 656, follow the signs for Cahors and take a right turn towards St-Ferréol)

Opening times : permanent

34 ha/2 for camping undulating

Rental rates : 🚿 🅿 – 15 🏠. Per night from 53 € – Per week from 175 to 359 € – Reservation fee 27 €

A pleasant location surrounded by trees, near a large riding centre.

Surroundings : 🐾 ♒
Facilities : 🚿 🖩 🖼
Nearby : 🐎

GPS Longitude : 0.68536
Latitude : 44.21698

LE PORGE

33680 – Michelin map **335** E5 – pop. 2 428 – alt. 8
▶ Paris 624 – Andernos-les-Bains 18 – Bordeaux 47 – Lacanau-Océan 21

⛰ Municipal la Grigne ▲▪

📞 05 56 26 54 88. www.camping-leporge.fr

Address : 35 avenue de l'Océan (9.5km west along the D 107, 1km from Le Porge-Océan)

Opening times : from beginning April to end Sept.

30 ha (700 pitches) undulating, flat, sandy

Tariff : 33.20 € ♦♦ 🚐 🔲 ⚡ (10A) – Extra per person 6.80 € – Reservation fee 21 €

Rental rates : (from beginning April to end Sept.) 🚐 – 24 🏠 – 10 canvas bungalows. Per night from 50 to 142 € – Per week from 350 to 995 € – Reservation fee 21 €

🚐 20 🔲 33.20 €

Surroundings : ♀♀
Leisure activities : 🍽 ✕ 🎞 🕹 🏃 🚣 🚴 🎿 🏊
Facilities : 🚿 🍴 🚻 🧺 launderette 🚿
Nearby : forest trail

GPS Longitude : -1.20314
Latitude : 44.89363

PUJOLS

47300 – Michelin map **336** G3 – pop. 3 607 – alt. 180
▶ Paris 607 – Agen 28 – Bordeaux 145 – Cahors 73

⛰ Lot et Bastides ▲▪

📞 05 53 36 86 79. www.camping-lot-et-bastides.com

Address : rue Malbentre

Opening times : from end March to end Oct.

7 ha (117 pitches) flat, grassy, stony

Tariff : 21 € ♦♦ 🚐 🔲 ⚡ (16A) – Extra per person 5 €

Rental rates : (from end March to end Oct.) 🚿 – 14 🏠 – 12 🏠 – 4 tent lodges. Per night from 41 to 76 € – Per week from 161 to 756 €

🚐 Eurorelais sani-station 4 € – 🚐 11 €

Sunny pitches with a variety of rental options located below Pujols town.

Surroundings : 🐾 ← 🖼
Leisure activities : 🍽 ✕ 🕹 daytime 🏃 jacuzzi 🚣 🚴 🎿
Facilities : 🚿 🍴 🚻 🧺 launderette 🚿
Nearby : hammam 🖼 🏊

GPS Longitude : 0.68733
Latitude : 44.39564

The guide covers all 22 regions of France – see the map and list of regions on pages 4–5.

PYLA-SUR-MER

33115 – Michelin map **335** D7
▶ Paris 648 – Arcachon 8 – Biscarrosse 34 – Bordeaux 66

⛰ Yelloh! Village Panorama du Pyla ▲▪

📞 05 56 22 10 44. www.camping-panorama.com

Address : route de Biscarrosse (7km south along the D 218)

Opening times : from mid April to beginning Oct.

15 ha/10 for camping (450 pitches) very uneven, undulating, terraced, flat, sandy

Tariff : 49 € ♦♦ 🚐 🔲 ⚡ (10A) – Extra per person 9 €

Rental rates : (from mid April to beginning Oct.) 🚐 – 80 🏠 – 5 🏠 – 15 tent lodges. Per night from 34 to 165 € – Per week from 238 to 1,155 €

🚐 local sani-station

Access to the beach via a pedestrian path. Many pitches overlook the Banc d'Arguin nature reserve.

Surroundings : 🐾 ← 🖼 ♀♀
Leisure activities : 🍽 ✕ 🎞 🕹 🏃 🚣 🚴 🎿 🏊 hang-gliding skate park
Facilities : 🚿 🍴 🚻 🧺 launderette 🚐 🚿 refrigerated food storage facilities

GPS Longitude : -1.22502
Latitude : 44.57738

⛰ FranceLoc Le Petit Nice ▲▪

📞 05 56 22 74 03. www.petitnice.com

Address : route de Biscarrosse

Opening times : from beginning April to end Sept.

5 ha (225 pitches) very uneven, terraced, flat, sandy

Tariff : (2015 price) 40 € ♦♦ 🚐 🔲 ⚡ (8A) – Extra per person 7 € – Reservation fee 30 €

Rental rates : (2015 price) (from beginning April to end Sept.) – 4 'gypsy' caravans – 94 🏠 – 4 canvas bungalows – 10 tent lodges. Per night from 46 to 170 € – Per week from 182 to 1,386 € – Reservation fee 30 €

🚐 local sani-station

Situated at the foot of the Dune du Pyla with direct access to the beach.

Surroundings : ⛱ ≤ Banc d'Arguin National Park ♤♤
Leisure activities : ♈ ✕ 🏛 📷 🏃 ⛷ 🎿
multi-sports ground
Facilities : ♿ ⛲ ▥ ♨ 🍴 launderette ▦ 🚿
refrigerated food storage facilities
Nearby : paragliding

GPS Longitude : -1.22043
Latitude : 44.57274

⛰ Tohapi La Forêt 👥

☎ 0825002030. www.tohapi.fr

Address : 3 km to the south on the D 218, route de Biscarrosse (at the foot of the Dune du Pyla)

Opening times : from beginning April to end Sept.

8 ha (460 pitches) undulating, flat and relatively flat, sandy

Tariff : (2015 price) 16€ ♟♟ ⇔ 🔲 🔌 (10A) – Extra per person 7€

Rental rates : (2015 price) (from beginning April to end Sept.) ♿ (2 mobile homes) – 107 🏠 – 12 🏡 – 68 tent lodges. Per night from 16 to 64€

🚐 Eurorelais sani-station 5€
Situated at the foot of the Dune du Pyla.

Surroundings : ⛱ ≤ 🚐 ♤♤
Leisure activities : ♈ ✕ 🏛 📷 🏃 ⛷ 🚲 ✂
🏔 🎿 multi-sports ground
Facilities : ♿ ⛲ 🅿 ♨ 🍴 launderette ▦ 🚿
refrigerated food storage facilities

GPS Longitude : -1.20857
Latitude : 44.58542

RAUZAN

33420 – Michelin map **335** K6 – pop. 1 148 – alt. 69
▶ Paris 596 – Bergerac 57 – Bordeaux 39 – Langon 35

⛰ Le Vieux Château

Le Vieux Château

☎ 0557841538. www.vieuxchateau.fr

Address : take the northern exit follow the signs for St-Jean-de-Blaignac and take road to the left (1.2km)

Opening times : from beginning April to mid Oct.

2.5 ha (78 pitches) open site, relatively flat, flat, grassy

Tariff : 27.20€ ♟♟ ⇔ 🔲 🔌 (6A) – Extra per person 5€ – Reservation fee 8€

Rental rates : (from beginning April to mid Oct.) ✂ – 14 🏠 – 4 🏡 – 2 canvas bungalows. Per night from 43 to 123€ – Per week from 215 to 825€ – Reservation fee 8€

🚐 local sani-station – 1 🔲 22€
Situated beside a ruined 12th-century fortress, with a footpath to the village.

Surroundings : ⛱ ♤♤
Leisure activities : ♈ ✕ 🏛 jacuzzi 🎿
Facilities : ♿ ⛲ 🍴 launderette

GPS Longitude : -0.12715
Latitude : 44.78213

*For more information on visiting particular towns or regions, consult the relevant regional **MICHELIN Green Guide**. We also recommend you use the appropriate Michelin regional map to locate your selected campsite, to calculate distances and to work out the best route.*

RÉAUP

47170 – Michelin map **336** D5 – pop. 523 – alt. 168 – Leisure centre
▶ Paris 708 – Agen 46 – Aire-sur-l'Adour 64 – Condom 24

⛰ Le Lac de Lislebonne 👥

☎ 0553656528. www.camping-lac-lislebonne.com

Address : 3.2 km southeast on the D149, follow the signs or Mezin

15 ha/2 for camping (74 pitches) terraced, relatively flat, flat, grassy

Rentals : 11 🏠 – 18 🏡 – 7 canvas bungalows – 3 tent lodges.
Among bushes around a lake and its small sandy beach.

Surroundings : ⛱ 🚐 ♤♤ ⛵
Leisure activities : ♈ ✕ 🏛 🏃 ⛷ 🚲 🎿
⛵ (beach) ✂ 🍴 multi-sports ground
Facilities : ♿ ▥ 🚿 🎿 launderette 🚿
refrigerators

GPS Longitude : 0.20971
Latitude : 44.07325

This guide is not intended as a list of all the camping sites in France; its aim is to provide a selection of the best sites in each category.

RIVIÈRE-SAAS-ET-GOURBY

40180 – Michelin map **335** E12 – pop. 1 168 – alt. 50
▶ Paris 742 – Bordeaux 156 – Mont-de-Marsan 68 – Bayonne 44

⛰ Lou Bascou

☎ 0558975729. www.campingloubascou.fr – limited spaces for one-night stay

Address : 250 route de Houssat (to the northeast of the town)

Opening times : permanent

1 ha (41 pitches) flat, grassy

Tariff : 20€ ♟♟ ⇔ 🔲 🔌 (16A) – Extra per person 10€

Rental rates : permanent – 8 🏡. Per night from 64 to 120€ – Per week from 322 to 595€

🚐 local sani-station – 12 🔲 13€

Surroundings : ⛱ 🚐 ♤♤
Leisure activities : 🏛 entertainment room
Facilities : ♿ ⛲ 🅿 🍴 launderette
Nearby : ▦ ✂

GPS Longitude : -1.14971
Latitude : 43.68203

LA ROCHE-CHALAIS

24490 – Michelin map **329** B5 – pop. 2 857 – alt. 60
▶ Paris 510 – Bergerac 62 – Blaye 67 – Bordeaux 68

⛰ Municipal du Méridien

☎ 0553914065. www.larochechalais.com

Address : at Les Gerbes (located 1km west; beside the river)

Opening times : from mid April to end Sept.

3 ha (100 pitches) terrace, flat, grassy, small adjacent wood

Tariff : (2015 price) 11.68€ ♟♟ ⇔ 🔲 🔌 (10A) – Extra per person 2.50€

Rental rates : (2015 price) (from mid April to end Sept.) – 6 🏠 – 1 gîte. Per night from 55 to 60€ – Per week from 135 to 350€ – Reservation fee 15€

🚐 local sani-station – 10 🔲 9€ – 🚐 🔌9€
Leafy setting with a few pitches near the river.

Surroundings : ⛱ 🚐 ♤♤
Leisure activities : 🏛 🏃 🎿 ✂
Facilities : ♿ ⛲ 🅿 ♨ 🍴

GPS Longitude : -0.00207
Latitude : 45.14888

LA ROQUE-GAGEAC

24250 – Michelin map **329** I7 – pop. 416 – alt. 85
▶ Paris 535 – Brive-la-Gaillarde 71 – Cahors 53 – Fumel 52

⚠ Le Beau Rivage 🏕

📞 05 53 28 32 05. www.beaurivagedordogne.com

Address : at Le Gaillardou (4km east on the D 46; beside the Dordogne river)

Opening times : from end April to mid Sept.

8 ha (200 pitches) terraced, flat, grassy, sandy

Tariff : 27.80€ 🏕🏕 🚗 📺 🎇 (6A) – Extra per person 5.60€ – Reservation fee 20€

Rental rates : (from end April to end Sept.) – 45 🛖 – 4 tent lodges. Per night from 24 to 98€ – Per week from 173 to 689€ – Reservation fee 20€

Choose pitches near the Dorgogne river, furthest from the road.

Surroundings : 🌿🌳
Leisure activities : 🍷 ✗ 🎱 🎇nighttime 🏃
🛶 ✂ 🎿 🎯
Facilities : 🦽 🚰 🏕 🍴 launderette 🔀
Longitude : 1.21422
Latitude : 44.81587

In order for the guide to remain wholly objective, the selection of campsites is made on an entirely independent basis.

ROUFFIGNAC

24580 – Michelin map **329** G5 – pop. 1 552 – alt. 300
▶ Paris 531 – Bergerac 58 – Brive-la-Gaillarde 57 – Périgueux 32

⚠ L'Offrerie

📞 05 53 35 33 26. www.camping-ferme-offrerie.com

Address : at Le Grand Boisset (situated 2km south along the D 32, follow the signs for Les Grottes de Rouffignac and take a right turn)

3.5 ha (48 pitches) terraced, relatively flat, flat, grassy

Rentals : 19 🛖 – 10 canvas bungalows.

🚉 local sani-station – 1 📺

Leafy site with a variety of comfortable rental options.

Surroundings : 🌿🌳🌳
Leisure activities : ✗ 🎱 🎿 🎯 🎿farm or petting farm
Facilities : 🦽 🚰 🏕 🍴 launderette 🔀
Longitude : 0.97109
Latitude : 45.02775

⚠ La Nouvelle Croze

📞 05 53 05 38 90. www.lanouvellecroze.com

Address : 2.5km southeast along the D 31, follow the signs for Fleurac and take the road to the right

Opening times : from beginning June to end Sept.

1.3 ha (43 pitches) flat, grassy

Tariff : (2015 price) 22.70€ 🏕🏕 🚗 📺 🎇 (16A) – Extra per person 5.70€

Rental rates : (from beginning April to end Oct.) – 15 🛖 – 1 gîte. Per night from 45 to 80€ – Per week from 190 to 795€

🚉 local sani-station

Lots of green spaces for relaxation. Good quality rental options.

Surroundings : 🌿🌳🌳
Leisure activities : 🍷✗ 🎱 🎿 🎿
Facilities : 🦽 🚰 🏕 🚐 🍴 launderette
Longitude : 0.99783
Latitude : 45.02412

⚠ Bleu Soleil

📞 05 53 05 48 30. www.camping-bleusoleil.com

Address : at Domaine Touvent (located 1.5km north along the D 31, follow the signs for Thenon and take turning to the right)

Opening times : from beginning April to end Sept.

41 ha/7 for camping (110 pitches) terraced, relatively flat, flat, grassy

Tariff : (2015 price) 🏕 3€ 🚗 📺 5€ – 🎇 (10A) 3.90€

Rental rates : (2015 price) (from beginning April to end Sept.) – 22 🛖 – 2 canvas bungalows. Per night from 27 to 106€ – Per week from 320 to 745€.

Situated around a restored stone farmhouse with plenty of green space and a pretty view of the countryside.

Surroundings : 🌿 ⚘ 🌳🌳
Leisure activities : 🍷 ✗ 🎱 🎿 🎿 multi-sports ground
Facilities : 🦽 🚰 🏕 🍴 launderette 🔀 refrigerated food storage facilities
Longitude : 0.98586
Latitude : 45.05507

SABRES

40630 – Michelin map **335** G10 – pop. 1 200 – alt. 78
▶ Paris 676 – Arcachon 92 – Bayonne 111 – Bordeaux 94

⚠ Le Domaine de Peyricat

📞 05 58 07 51 88. www.vtf-vacances.com

Address : take the southern exit along the D 327, follow the signs for Luglon

Opening times : from end March to mid Sept.

20 ha/2 for camping (69 pitches)

Tariff : (2015 price) 23€ 🏕🏕 🚗 📺 🎇 (6A) – Extra per person 3€

Rental rates : (2015 price) (from end March to mid Sept.) 🎿 – 4 🛖 – 8 🛖. Per week from 319 to 779€

🚉 Eurorelais sani-station 5€

Lots of activities are available at the adjacent holiday village.

Surroundings : 🏕
Facilities : 🦽 🚰 🔀 ⊞ CC 🍴
At Village Vacances : launderette 🍷 ✗ 🎱
🏃 ⛵ ✂ 🎿
Longitude : -0.74235
Latitude : 44.144

ST-AMAND-DE-COLY

24290 – Michelin map **329** I5 – pop. 382 – alt. 180
▶ Paris 515 – Bordeaux 188 – Périgueux 58 – Cahors 104

⚠ Yelloh! Village Lascaux Vacances 🏕

📞 05 53 50 81 57. www.campinglascauxvacances.com

Address : at Les Malénies (located 1km south along the D 64, follow the signs for St-Geniès)

Opening times : from beginning May to mid Sept.

12 ha (150 pitches) very uneven, terraced, flat, stony

Tariff : 37€ 🏕🏕 🚗 📺 🎇 (10A) – Extra per person 7€

Rental rates : (from beginning May to mid Sept.) – 80 🛖 – 5 🛖 – 10 tent lodges. Per night from 35 to 125€ – Per week from 245 to 875€

🚉 local sani-station

Surroundings : 🌿 ⊑ 🌳🌳
Leisure activities : 🍷✗ 🎱 🎇🏃 🎿 🚴 🎿 🗺 🎿
🏊 multi-sports ground
Facilities : 🦽 🚰 🏕 🚐 🍴 launderette 🔀
Longitude : 1.24191
Latitude : 45.05461

ST-ANTOINE-D'AUBEROCHE

24330 – Michelin map **329** G5 – pop. 145 – alt. 152
▶ Paris 491 – Brive-la-Gaillarde 96 – Limoges 105 – Périgueux 24

⚠ La Pélonie

☏ 0553075578. www.lapelonie.com

Address : at La Pélonie (1.8km southwest towards Milhac-Gare, from Fossemagne, continue 6 km along the RN 89 and take the road to the right)

Opening times : from mid April to beginning Oct.

5 ha (96 pitches) terraced, wood

Tariff : ♣ 5.90€ ⇔ 6.90€ – ⚡ (10A) 3.90€ – Reservation fee 10€

Rental rates : (from mid April to beginning Oct.) – 25 ⌂. Per night from 82 to 95€ – Per week from 574 to 665€ – Reservation fee 10€

local sani-station – 5 回 18€

Surroundings : ⚘ ⌄ 〰
Leisure activities : ♟ ✕ 🎦 ⛵ ⚓ ♨
Facilities : ⚖ ⚬ 🚿 ♨ launderette 🛁

GPS	Longitude : 0.92845
	Latitude : 45.13135

ST-ANTOINE-DE-BREUILH

24230 – Michelin map **329** B6 – pop. 2 073 – alt. 18
▶ Paris 555 – Bergerac 30 – Duras 28 – Libourne 34

⚠ La Rivière Fleurie

☏ 0553248280. www.la-riviere-fleurie.com

Address : at St-Aulaye-de-Breuilh, 180 rue Théophile-Cart (3km southwest, 100m from the Dordogne river)

Opening times : from beginning April to end Sept.

2.5 ha (65 pitches) flat, grassy

Tariff : (2015 price) 28€ ♣♣ ⇔ 回 ⚡ (10A) – Extra per person 6.40€ – Reservation fee 5€

Rental rates : (2015 price) (from beginning April to end Sept.) – 21 ⌂ – 4 studios – 3 canvas bungalows. Per night from 35 to 80€ – Per week from 240 to 790€ – Reservation fee 8€

local sani-station – 🛥 ⚡28€

Surroundings : ⚘ ⌄ 〰
Leisure activities : ♟ ✕ 🎦 ⛵ ⚓
Facilities : ⚖ ⚬ 🅿 ♨ launderette 🛁
Nearby : ✕ 🛶

GPS	Longitude : 0.12235
	Latitude : 44.82879

ST-AULAYE

24410 – Michelin map **329** B4 – pop. 1 360 – alt. 61
▶ Paris 504 – Bergerac 56 – Blaye 79 – Bordeaux 81

⚠ Municipal de la Plage

☏ 0553906220. www.saint-aulaye.com

Address : Les Ponts (take the northern exit along the D 38, follow the signs for Aubeterre; beside the Dronne river)

Opening times : from beginning June to mid Sept.

1 ha (70 pitches) flat, grassy

Tariff : 13€ ♣♣ ⇔ 回 ⚡ (10A) – Extra per person 2€

Rental rates : (from beginning June to mid Sept.) – 11 ⌂ – 14 ⌂. Per week from 99 to 405€ – Reservation fee 20€

local sani-station 3€

Surroundings : ⌄ 〰
Leisure activities : 🎦 ⚓ 🚴 ✕ ♫ 🎣 ⚑
Facilities : ⚖ ⚬ 🅿 ♨ launderette
Nearby : ✕ 🛶 🛥 (beach) ⛷

GPS	Longitude : 0.13274
	Latitude : 45.20786

ST-AVIT-DE-VIALARD

24260 – Michelin map **329** G6 – pop. 145 – alt. 210
▶ Paris 520 – Bergerac 39 – Le Bugue 7 – Les Eyzies-de-Tayac 17

⚠ Les Castels St-Avit Loisirs ♣♣

☏ 0553026400. www.saint-avit-loisirs.com – limited spaces for one-night stay

Address : at Malefon (1.8km to the northwest)

Opening times : from end March to end Sept.

55 ha/15 for camping (400 pitches) terraced, natural setting among trees and bushes

Tariff : 49€ ♣♣ ⇔ 回 ⚡ (6A) – Extra per person 12.20€ – Reservation fee 19€

Rental rates : (from end March to end Sept.) – 40 ⌂ – 35 ⌂ – 30 🏠 – 15 apartments – 2 tent lodges – 1 gîte. Per night from 51 to 197€ – Per week from 357 to 1,379€ – Reservation fee 25€

local sani-station – 20 回 17€ – 🛥 ⚡17€

A spacious, undulating and wooded site boasting an impressive water park. New high-quality rental options.

Surroundings : ⚘ ⌄ ⌄ 〰
Leisure activities : ♟ ✕ 🎦 ⚿ ⛲ 🎿 jacuzzi ⚓ ⚓ 🎿 🏹 quad biking, multi-sports ground, entertainment room
Facilities : ⚖ ⚬ 🅿 ⛱ 🚿 ♨ launderette 🛁 🛁

GPS	Longitude : 0.84971
	Latitude : 44.95174

The prices listed were supplied by the campsite owners in 2015 (if prices were not available, those from the previous year are given). The fees should be regarded as basic charges and may fluctuate with inflation.

ST-CRÉPIN-ET-CARLUCET

24590 – Michelin map **329** I6 – pop. 493 – alt. 262
▶ Paris 514 – Brive-la-Gaillarde 40 – Les Eyzies-de-Tayac 29 – 8Montignac 21

⚠ Les Peneyrals ♣♣

☏ 0553288571. www.peneyrals.com

Address : at St Crépin (located 1km south along the D 56, follow the signs for Proissans)

Opening times : from mid May to mid Sept.

12 ha/8 for camping (250 pitches) very uneven, undulating, terraced, flat, grassy, stony, pond

Tariff : (2015 price) ♣ 10.20€ ⇔ 回 14.60€ – ⚡ (10A) 4.60€ – Reservation fee 20€

Rental rates : (2015 price) (from mid May to mid Sept.) ⚖ (1 chalet) – 40 ⌂ – 32 ⌂. Per night from 50 to 195€ – Per week from 350 to 1 365€ – Reservation fee 30€

flot bleu sani-station

Undulating site with shade between a lake reserved for fishing and a pretty water park.

Surroundings : ⚘ 〰
Leisure activities : ♟ ✕ 🎦 ⚿ ⚓ ⛵ 🚴 ✕ ♫ ⚓ 🎿 ⚑
Facilities : ⚖ ⚬ 🚽 🅿 ♨ launderette 🛁 🛁

GPS	Longitude : 1.27267
	Latitude : 44.95785

🔺 Village Vacances Les Gîtes de Combas
(rental of gîtes only)

📞 05 53 28 64 00. www.perigordgites.com

Address : at Les Combas (situated 2km south along the D 56, follow the signs for Proissans)

Opening times : permanent

4 ha

Rental rates : (2015 price) ♿ (1 gîte) Ⓟ – 22 🏠 – 22 gîtes. Per night from 100 to 200€ – Per week from 330 to 1,200€

A number of gîtes have been established in old farm buildings made of local stone.

Surroundings : 🐾 ♀
Leisure activities : 🏛 🛶 🏊 ⛵ 🚴 ✗ 🎣 ⛷
Facilities : ⊶ 🗑 🍴 🖼 🧺

| G P S | Longitude : 1.27718 |
| --- | Latitude : 44.94871 |

ST-CYBRANET

24250 – Michelin map **329** I7 – pop. 376 – alt. 78
▶ Paris 542 – Cahors 51 – Les Eyzies-de-Tayac 29 – Gourdon 21

🔺 Bel Ombrage

📞 05 53 28 34 14. www.belombrage.com

Address : on the D 50 (800m to the northwest; beside the Céou river)

Opening times : from beginning June to beginning Sept.

6 ha (180 pitches) flat, grassy

Tariff : ♦ 6.10€ �car 🔲 7.60€ – ⚡ (10A) 4.20€

Shady site with pitches for tents or caravans only. No rental accommodation.

Surroundings : 🐾 🎣 🏞 ⚠
Leisure activities : 🏛 🛶 ⛷
Facilities : ♿ ⊶ 🍴 launderette
Nearby : ✗

| G P S | Longitude : 1.16244 |
| --- | Latitude : 44.79082 |

Routes nationales are main roads and their identifying numbers begin with N or RN. Routes départementales are generally quieter roads and begin with D or DN.

ST-ÉMILION

33330 – Michelin map **335** K5 – pop. 2 005 – alt. 30
▶ Paris 584 – Bergerac 58 – Bordeaux 40 – Langon 49

🔺 Yelloh! Saint-Émilion 👥

📞 05 57 24 75 80. www.camping-saint-emilion.com

Address : at Les Combes (3km north along the D 122, follow the signs for Lussac and take turning to the right – caravans and camper vans are not permitted to pass through St-Émilion)

Opening times : from end April to end Sept.

4.5 ha (173 pitches) flat, grassy

Tariff : 40€ ♥♥ 🚗 🔲 ⚡ (10A) – Extra per person 7€

Rental rates : (from end April to end Sept.) – 48 🏠 – 1 'floating' chalet. Per night from 39 to 195€ – Per week from 273 to 1,365€
🚿 Eurorelais sani-station – 25 🔲 40€

There's a free shuttle bus to St-Émilion. High-quality and often unusual rental options.

Surroundings : 🐾 🗺 ♀♀
Leisure activities : ♥ ✗ 🏛 🏃 🛶 🚴 ⛷
🎿 ⛷ 🎣 pedalos
Facilities : ♿ ⊶ 🍴 launderette 🚿

| G P S | Longitude : -0.14241 |
| --- | Latitude : 44.91675 |

ST-ÉTIENNE-DE-BAIGORRY

64430 – Michelin map **342** D3 – pop. 1 618 – alt. 163
▶ Paris 820 – Bordeaux 241 – Pau 160 – Pamplona 69

🔺 Municipal l'Irouleguy

📞 05 59 37 43 96. mairie.baigorri@orange.fr

Address : Borciriette district (take the northeastern exit along the D 15, follow the signs for St-Jean-Pied-de-Port and take road to the left in front of the swimming pool and behind the Irouléguy wine co-operative; beside the Nive river)

Opening times : from mid March to end Nov.

1.5 ha (67 pitches) flat, grassy

Tariff : (2015 price) 12.20€ ♥♥ 🚗 🔲 ⚡ (6A) – Extra per person 3.10€
🚿 AireService sani-station

In a green setting, part stretching along the river.

Surroundings : ♀♀
Leisure activities : 🛶
Facilities : ♿ ⊶ 🚿 🍴 🖼
Nearby : 🛒 ♥ ✗ ⛷ ⛷

| G P S | Longitude : -1.33551 |
| --- | Latitude : 43.18386 |

The guide covers all 22 regions of France – see the map and list of regions on pages 4–5.

ST-ÉTIENNE-DE-VILLERÉAL

47210 – Michelin map **336** G2 – pop. 302 – alt. 130
▶ Paris 577 – Agen 59 – Bordeaux 129 – Périgueux 84

🔺 Les Ormes 👥

📞 05 53 36 60 26. www.campinglesormes.fr 🚭

Address : at Fauquié Haut

Opening times : from end April to end Sept.

4 ha (144 pitches) undulating, relatively flat, flat, grassy, stony, pond, wood

Tariff : ♦ 8€ 🚗 🔲 12€ – ⚡ (6A) 6€ – Reservation fee 20€

Rental rates : (from end April to end Sept.) 🚿 – 35 tent lodges. Per night from 42 to 142€ – Per week from 300 to 1,000€ – Reservation fee 20€

An unusual campsite with quirky rental options and a restaurant for children!

Surroundings : 🐾
Leisure activities : ♥ ✗ 🏛 🏃 🛶 🚴 ⛷
⛷ 🎿 farm or petting farm
Facilities : ♿ ⊶ 🚿 🍴 launderette 🚿

| G P S | Longitude : 0.76241 |
| --- | Latitude : 44.61017 |

ST-GENIÈS

24590 – Michelin map **329** I6 – pop. 941 – alt. 232
▶ Paris 515 – Brive-la-Gaillarde 41 – Les Eyzies-de-Tayac 29 – Montignac 13

🔺 Club Airotel La Bouquerie 👥

📞 05 53 28 98 22. www.labouquerie.com – limited spaces for one-night stay

Address : located 1.5km northwest along the D 704, follow the signs for Montignac and take the road to the right

Opening times : from mid April to beginning Sept.

8 ha/4 for camping (197 pitches) terraced, relatively flat, flat, grassy, stony, pond

Tariff : (2015 price) ♦ 9.50€ 🚗 🔲 14€ – ⚡ (10A) 4.20€ – Reservation fee 20€

Rental rates : (from mid April to beginning Sept.) &. (1 mobile homes) – 90 🏠 – 50 🏠. Per week from 320 to 2,190€ – Reservation fee 20€

Lovely pitches in the shade of oak trees. High-quality rentals near a small lake.

Surroundings : 🦢 🖻 🎣
Leisure activities : ♈ ✗ 🏠 🎲 🏃 🎿 🚣
🤾 🚲 🖼 🏊 ⛵ paintballing, multi-sports ground
Facilities : &. 🚿 🏢 🛁 – 3 individual sanitary facilities (🍳 ♨ wc) 🚰 launderette 🚮 🖾

GPS Longitude : 1.24594
Latitude : 44.99892

ST-GIRONS-PLAGE

40560 – Michelin map **335** C11
▶ Paris 728 – Bordeaux 142 – Mont-de-Marsan 79 – Bayonne 73

🔺 Eurosol 👥

🕿 05 58 47 90 14. www.camping-eurosol.com

Address : route de la Plage (350m from the beach)

Opening times : from mid May to mid Sept.

33 ha/18 for camping (510 pitches) undulating, relatively flat, flat, grassy, sandy

Tariff : 41€ ♈♈ 🚗 🔲 (10A) – Extra per person 7€ – Reservation fee 25€

Rental rates : (from mid May to mid Sept.) 🐾 Ⓟ – 110 🏠 – 29 🏠 – 6 tent lodges. Per night from 55 to 120€ – Per week from 335 to 1,295€ – Reservation fee 25€

🚐 local sani-station 23€ – 10 🔲 23€

Varied rental options and pretty pitches located under the pine trees.

Surroundings : 🦢 🎣
Leisure activities : ♈ ✗ 🏠 🎲 🏃 🎿 🚲 🤾
🖼 🏊 multi-sports ground
Facilities : &. 🚿 🛁 🖾 🚰 launderette 🖾🖾
Nearby : 🐎

GPS Longitude : -1.35162
Latitude : 43.95158

🔺 Campéole les Tourterelles 👥

Campéole les Tourterelles

🕿 05 58 47 93 12. www.camping-tourterelles.com

Address : route de la plage (5.2km west along the D 42, 300m from the ocean (direct access)

Opening times : from beginning April to end Sept.

18 ha (822 pitches) undulating, relatively flat, flat, sandy

Tariff : 19€ ♈♈ 🚗 🔲 (10A) – Extra per person 10€ – Reservation fee 25€

Rental rates : (from beginning April to end Sept.) &. (2 mobile homes) – 136 🏠 – 20 🏠 – 115 canvas bungalows. Per night from 34 to 214€ – Per week from 238 to 1,498€ – Reservation fee 25€

🚐 AireService sani-station – 49 🔲 14.50€ – 🛒 💧18.20€

Pitches beneath the pines. Welcomes groups of young surfers.

Surroundings : 🎣
Leisure activities : 🎲 🏃 🎿 🚲 🛴
multi-sports ground
Facilities : &. 🚿 🛁 🚰 launderette 🖾
refrigerated food storage facilities

GPS Longitude : -1.35691
Latitude : 43.95439

ST-JEAN-DE-LUZ

64500 – Michelin map **342** C2 – pop. 13 742 – alt. 3
▶ Paris 785 – Bayonne 24 – Biarritz 18 – Pau 129

🔺 Club Airotel Itsas Mendi

🕿 05 59 26 56 50. www.itsas-mendi.com

Address : Acotz district, chemin Duhartia (5km to the northeast, 500m from the beach)

Opening times : from end March to end Oct.

8.5 ha (475 pitches) terraced, flat and relatively flat, grassy

Tariff : (2015 price) 46.20€ ♈♈ 🚗 🔲 (10A) – Extra per person 7.90€ – Reservation fee 20€

Rental rates : (2015 price) (from end March to end Oct.) 🐾 – 156 🏠. Per night from 34 to 170€ – Per week from 238 to 1,190€ – Reservation fee 20€

🚐 local sani-station

In a green setting laid out on terraces, with half the pitches for mobile homes.

Surroundings : 🎣
Leisure activities : ♈ ✗ 🏠 🎲 🏃 🛶 jacuzzi
🎿 🤾 🖼 🏊 surfing school, multi-sports ground
Facilities : &. 🚿 🆒 🏢 🚰 launderette 🖾🖾
refrigerated food storage facilities

GPS Longitude : -1.61726
Latitude : 43.41347

🔺 Atlantica 👥

🕿 05 59 47 72 44. www.campingatlantica.com

Address : Acotz district, chemin Miquélénia (5km to the northeast, 500m from the beach)

Opening times : from beginning April to end Sept.

3.5 ha (200 pitches) terraced, flat, grassy

Tariff : (2015 price) 39.70€ ♈♈ 🚗 🔲 (6A) – Extra per person 8.20€ – Reservation fee 25€

Rental rates : (2015 price) (from beginning April to end Sept.) 🐾 – 100 🏠 – 12 tent lodges. Per night from 35 to 75€ – Per week from 360 to 1,150€ – Reservation fee 25€

Surroundings : 🖻 🎣
Leisure activities : ♈ ✗ 🏠 🏃 🛶 jacuzzi
🎿 🖼 🏊 multi-sports ground
Facilities : &. 🚿 🛁 🖾 🚰 🖼 🖾🖾
refrigerated food storage facilities

GPS Longitude : -1.61688
Latitude : 43.41525

🔺 Flower La Ferme Erromardie

🕿 05 59 26 34 26. www.camping-erromardie.com

Address : 40 chemin Erromardie (1.8km to the northeast, near the beach)

Opening times : from mid March to end Sept.

2 ha (176 pitches) flat, grassy

Tariff : 35€ ♈♈ 🚗 🔲 (16A) – Extra per person 6€ – Reservation fee 19€

Rental rates : permanent – 46 🏠. Per night from 39 to 150€ – Per week from 196 to 1,007€ – Reservation fee 19€

🚐 local sani-station 10€

Surroundings : 🦢 🖻 🎣
Leisure activities : ♈ ✗ 🏠 🛶 🖼
Facilities : &. 🚿 🛁 🚰 launderette 🖾 🖾

GPS Longitude : -1.64202
Latitude : 43.40564

▲▲ Inter-Plages

ℰ 05 59 26 56 94. www.campinginterplages.com

Address : Acotz district, 305 route des Plages (5km to the northeast, 150m from the beach (direct access)

Opening times : from beginning April to end Sept.

2.5 ha (91 pitches) relatively flat, flat, grassy

Tariff : (2015 price) 41€ ♥♥ ⇐ 🔲 🔌 (10A) – Extra per person 8€ – Reservation fee 20€

Rental rates : (2015 price) (from beginning April to end Sept.) ✂ – 21 🚐 – 5 🏠. Per night from 47 to 68 – Per week from 290 to 780 – Reservation fee 20€

🚰 local sani-station 4.50€

In an attractive location looking out over the sea.

Surroundings : ⤢ ⬅ ⊡ ♨♨		
Leisure activities : 🎣 ⛵ 🚲 ⛷	**G**	Longitude : -1.62667
Facilities : ♿ ⊶ 🚽 ⊞ ♨ ⚐ ♨ launderette	**P**	Latitude : 43.41527
Nearby : ⚒ ♈ ✕ 🚲 🔥 surfing	**S**	

▲ Merko-Lacarra

ℰ 05 59 26 56 76. http://www.merkolacarra.com

Address : Acotz district, 820 route des Plages (5km to the northeast, 150m from the beach d'Acotz)

Opening times : from end March to beginning Oct.

2 ha (123 pitches) terraced, relatively flat, flat, grassy

Tariff : (2015 price) 16€ ♥♥ ⇐ 🔲 🔌 (16A) – Extra per person 5€

🚰

A warm welcome, good-quality sanitary facilities and very close to the beach at Mayarco.

Leisure activities : ✕ ⛵		
Facilities : ♿ ⊶ 📶 ⊞ ♨ ⚐ ♨ launderette 🚲	**G**	Longitude : -1.62366
Nearby : ⚒ ♈ 🔥 surfing	**P**	Latitude : 43.41855
	S	

▲ Les Tamaris-Plage 👥

ℰ 05 59 26 55 90. www.tamaris-plage.com

Address : Acotz district, 720 route de Plages (5km to the northeast, 80m from the beach)

Opening times : from beginning April to end Oct.

1.5 ha (79 pitches)

Tariff : (2015 price) 34€ ♥♥ ⇐ 🔲 🔌 (7A) – Extra per person 11€ – Reservation fee 30€

Rental rates : (2015 price) (from beginning April to end Oct.) – 29 🚐 – 5 studios – 10 tent lodges. Per night from 45 to 70€ – Per week from 441 to 973€ – Reservation fee 30€

Surroundings : ⊡ ♀		
Leisure activities : 🎣 ⛵ ⛺ hammam, jacuzzi ⛵	**G**	Longitude : -1.62387
Facilities : ♿ ⊶ 📶 ♨ ⚐ ♨ launderette	**P**	Latitude : 43.41804
Nearby : ⚒ ♈ ✕ 🚲 🔥 surfing	**S**	

▲ Le Bord de mer

ℰ 05 59 26 24 61. www.camping-le-bord-de-mer.fr

Address : 71 chemin d'Erromardie (1.8km northeast)

Opening times : from beginning April to beginning Nov.

2 ha (78 pitches) terraced, relatively flat, flat, grassy

Tariff : (2015 price) 34€ ♥♥ ⇐ 🔲 🔌 (10A) – Extra per person 9€ – Reservation fee 85€

A small coastal footpath leads to the cliffs and the beach.

Surroundings : ⤢ the ocean and La Rhune mountain ⊡		
Leisure activities : ✕	**G**	Longitude : -1.64155
Facilities : ⊶ 🚽 ♨ ♨ launderette	**P**	Latitude : 43.40678
Nearby : ⚒ ♈ 🚲	**S**	

64220 – Michelin map **342** E4 – pop. 1 477 – alt. 159
▶ Paris 817 – Bayonne 54 – Biarritz 55 – Dax 105

▲▲▲ Narbaïtz Vacances

ℰ 05 59 37 10 13. www.camping-narbaitz.com

Address : at Ascarat (2.5km northwest along the D 918, follow the signs for Bayonne and take the turning to the left; 50m from the Nive river and beside a stream)

Opening times : from beginning April to mid Sept.

3.2 ha (140 pitches)

Tariff : (2015 price) 40.50€ ♥♥ ⇐ 🔲 🔌 (10A) – Extra per person 6.50€ – Reservation fee 20€

Rental rates : (2015 price) permanent ✂ – 12 🚐 – 3 🏠 – 3 gîtes. Per night from 60 to 70€ – Per week from 300 to 780€ – Reservation fee 20€

🚰 local sani-station

Lovely view of the Irouleguy vineyard. Choose pitches furthest from the road.

Surroundings : ⤢ ♨♨		
Leisure activities : 🎣 ⛵ ⛷ zip wiring	**G**	Longitude : -1.25911
Facilities : ♿ ⊶ ♨ ♨ ⚐ ♨ launderette 🚲	**P**	Latitude : 43.17835
Nearby : 🎣	**S**	

▲▲ Europ'Camping

ℰ 05 59 37 12 78. www.europ-camping.com

Address : at Ascarat (situated 2km northwest along the D 918, follow the signs for Bayonne and take road to the left)

Opening times : from beginning April to end Sept.

2 ha (110 pitches)

Tariff : 39€ ♥♥ ⇐ 🔲 🔌 (10A) – Extra per person 6.50€ – Reservation fee 22€

Rental rates : (from beginning April to end Sept.) – 45 🚐. Per night from 60 to 80€ – Per week from 270 to 780€ – Reservation fee 22€

Site has a lovely view of the Irouleguy vineyard with very well-maintained pitches.

Surroundings : ⤢ ♨♨		
Leisure activities : ♈ ✕ 🎣 ⛴ ⛷	**G**	Longitude : -1.25398
Facilities : ♿ ⊶ ♨ ⚐ ♨ launderette 🚲	**P**	Latitude : 43.17279
Nearby : 🎣	**S**	

24370 – Michelin map **329** J6 – pop. 613 – alt. 120
▶ Paris 528 – Brive-la-Gaillarde 51 – Gourdon 17 – Sarlat-la-Canéda 17

▲ Le Mondou

ℰ 05 53 29 70 37. www.camping-dordogne.info

Address : at Le Colombier (located 1km east along the D 50, follow the signs for Mareuil and take the road to the right)

Opening times : from beginning April to mid Oct.

1.2 ha (60 pitches)

Tariff : ♥ 5.75€ ⇐ 🔲 7.25€ – 🔌 (6A) 4€ – Reservation fee 5€

Rental rates : (from beginning April to mid Oct.) 🚿 – 4 ⛺ – 1 🏠 – 8 canvas bungalows. Per night from 28 to 84€ – Per week from 250 to 825€ – Reservation fee 5€

Surroundings : 🌳 ⌂ 🛝
Leisure activities : 🎱 ⛵🚴🎿
Facilities : 🚿 ⌛🍴🛝🍴 launderette ♨

G P S Longitude : 1.36691
Latitude : 44.86295

ST-JULIEN-EN-BORN

40170 – Michelin map **335** D10 – pop. 1 450 – alt. 22
▶ Paris 706 – Castets 23 – Dax 43 – Mimizan 18

⛰ Municipal la Lette Fleurie

📞 05 58 42 74 09. www.camping-municipal-plage.com

Address : at La Lette, route de l'Océan (4km northwest along the D 41, follow the signs for Contis-Plage)

Opening times : permanent

8.5 ha (457 pitches) undulating, flat, sandy

Tariff : (2015 price) 🧍 6€ – 🚗 2.50€ – 🔌 6.80€ – 🔋 (10A) 5.80€ – Reservation fee 15€

Pitches in the shade of pine trees with simple sanitary facilities.

Surroundings : 🌳 🛝
Leisure activities : 🎱 🍴 🛋 ⛵🎿
Facilities : 🚿 ⌛🛝🍴 launderette 🛝 ♨ refrigerated food storage facilities

G P S Longitude : -1.26173
Latitude : 44.08139

⛰ Municipal La Passerelle

📞 05 58 42 80 18. www.camping-municipal-bourg.com

Address : 811 route des Lacs

2 ha (123 pitches) flat, sandy, grassy

🚐 Raclet sani-station – 11 🔌

Surroundings : 🌳 🛝
Leisure activities : 🍴 ⛵
Facilities : 🚿 ⌛

G P S Longitude : -1.22951
Latitude : 44.06843

Routes nationales are main roads and their identifying numbers begin with N or RN. Routes départementales are generally quieter roads and begin with D or DN.

ST-JUSTIN

40240 – Michelin map **335** J11 – pop. 922 – alt. 90
▶ Paris 694 – Barbotan-les-Thermes 19 – Captieux 41 – Labrit 31

⛰ Le Pin

📞 05 58 44 88 91. www.campinglepin.com

Address : route de Roquefort (2.3km north on the D 626; beside a little lake)

Opening times : from mid April to mid Oct.

3 ha (80 pitches)

Tariff : 22€ 🧍🧍 🚗 🔌 🔋 (10A) – Extra per person 4.50€
Rental rates : (from mid April to mid Oct.) – 10 ⛺ – 10 🏠. Per night from 45 to 110€ – Per week from 260 to 800€

Choose the pitches with shade, furthest from the road and near a small fishing lake.

Surroundings : 🛝
Leisure activities : 🎱🍴 ⛵🎿🗨
Facilities : 🚿 ⌛🛝🍴 launderette ♨

G P S Longitude : -0.23468
Latitude : 44.00188

ST-LAURENT-MEDOC

33112 – Michelin map **335** G4 – pop. 4 054 – alt. 6
▶ Paris 603 – Bordeaux 45 – Mérignac 41 – Pessac 48

⛰ Le Paradis 👥

📞 05 56 59 42 15. www.leparadis-medoc.com

Address : at Fourthon (2.5km north along the D 1215, follow the signs for Lesparre)

Opening times : from beginning April to beginning Oct.

3 ha (70 pitches) flat, grassy

Tariff : (2015 price) 🧍 14€ – 🔌 (10A) 5€ – Reservation fee 15€

Rental rates : (from beginning April to beginning Oct.) ♿ 🚿 – 30 ⛺ – 4 🏠. Per night from 80 to 120€ – Per week from 224 to 890€ – Reservation fee 15€

A range of different rental options of varying standards and styles.

Surroundings : ⌂ 🛝
Leisure activities : 🎱🍴 ⛵⛳🏊 ▦ (open air in season) ⛷
Facilities : 🚿 ⌛🛝🍴 launderette ♨

G P S Longitude : -0.83995
Latitude : 45.17495

This guide is updated regularly, so buy your new copy every year!

ST-LÉON-SUR-VÉZÈRE

24290 – Michelin map **329** H5 – pop. 428 – alt. 70
▶ Paris 523 – Brive-la-Gaillarde 48 – Les Eyzies-de-Tayac 16 – Montignac 10

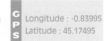 Le Paradis 👥

📞 05 53 50 72 64. www.le-paradis.fr

Address : at La Rebeyrolle (4km southwest along the D 706, follow the signs for Les Eyzies-de-Tayac; beside the Vézère)

Opening times : from end March to end Oct.

7 ha (200 pitches) flat, grassy

Tariff : (2015 price) 37€ 🧍🧍 🚗 🔌 🔋 (10A) – Extra per person 8.80€ – Reservation fee 20€

Rental rates : (2015 price) (from end March to end Oct.) ♿ – 42 ⛺ – 5 tent lodges – 3 gîtes. Per night from 49 to 194€ – Per week from 343 to 1,358€ – Reservation fee 20€

🚐 local sani-station 2€

Upmarket facilities based around an old renovated farmhouse.

Surroundings : 🌳 ⌂ 🛝
Leisure activities : 🎱🍴 🍴 🎣⛵🏖 hammam, jacuzzi ⛵🚴⛳🎿⛷🗨🎿 multi-sports ground, spa centre
Facilities : 🚿 ⌛🚰🛝🍴🗳🍴 launderette 🛝♨

G P S Longitude : 1.0712
Latitude : 45.00161

These symbols are used for a campsite that is exceptional in its category:

AAAA...A *Particularly pleasant setting, quality and range of services available*

🌳🌳 *Tranquil, isolated site – quiet site, particularly at night*

≼≼ *Exceptional view – interesting or panoramic view*

ST-MARTIN-DE-SEIGNANX

40390 – Michelin map **335** C13 – pop. 4 724 – alt. 57
▶ Paris 766 – Bayonne 11 – Capbreton 15 – Dax 42

⚲ Sites et Paysages Lou P'tit Poun ♠♠

☏ 05 59 56 55 79. www.louptitpoun.com

Address : 110 avenue du Quartier Neuf (4.7km southwest along the N 117, follow the signs for Bayonne and take road to the left)

Opening times : from mid June to beginning Sept.

6.5 ha (168 pitches) terraced, flat and relatively flat, grassy

Tariff : 36.90€ ✴✴ 🚗 🗉 🔌 (10A) – Extra per person 8.50€ – Reservation fee 30€

Rental rates : (from mid June to mid Sept.) – 10 🚐 – 16 🏠. Per night from 65 to 130€ – Per week from 679 to 905€ – Reservation fee 30€

🚐 local sani-station 7€ – 🔌 🔌16€

Pretty setting with trees and flowers.

Surroundings : 🗔 ♨♨
Leisure activities : 🏛 🏃 🏊 🗡
Facilities : 🔥 🔌 🖾 🏊 🚰 🍴 launderette 🚿

GPS Longitude : -1.41195
Latitude : 43.52437

Some information or pricing may have changed since the guide went to press. We recommend you check the price list online in advance or at the entrance to the campsite and enquire about possible restrictions.

ST-PAUL-LES-DAX

40990 – Michelin map **335** E12 – pop. 12 343 – alt. 21
▶ Paris 731 – Bordeaux 152 – Mont-de-Marsan 53 – Pau 89

⚲ Les Pins du Soleil ♠♠

☏ 05 58 91 37 91. www.pinsoleil.com

Address : route des Minières (5.8km northwest along the N 124, follow the signs for Bayonne and take the turning to the left along the D 459)

Opening times : from beginning April to end Oct.

6 ha (145 pitches)

Tariff : (2015 price) 25.88€ ✴✴ 🚗 🗉 🔌 (10A) – Extra per person 6.30€ – Reservation fee 10€

Rental rates : (2015 price) (from beginning April to end Oct.) 🔥 (1 chalet) – 42 🚐 – 10 🏠 – 4 canvas bungalows. Per night from 40 to 82€ – Per week from 278 to 795€ – Reservation fee 17€

🚐 AireService sani-station

Pitches with good shade and new and older rental options.

Surroundings : 🗔 ♨♨
Leisure activities : 🍷 🗡 🏛 🏃 🎣 jacuzzi 🏊 🗡
Facilities : 🔥 🔌 🖾 🖩 🏊 🚰 🍴 launderette 🚿

GPS Longitude : -1.09373
Latitude : 43.72029

⚲ L'Étang d'Ardy

☏ 05 58 97 57 74. www.camping-ardy.com

Address : allée d'Ardy (5.5km northwest along the N 124, follow the signs for Bayonne then take road to the left before the access road, continuing for 1.7km; beside a lake)

Opening times : from beginning April to mid Oct.

5 ha/3 for camping (102 pitches)

Tariff : 28€ ✴✴ 🚗 🗉 🔌 (10A) – Extra per person 6.50€

Rental rates : (from beginning April to end Oct.) – 24 🚐 – 7 🏠 – 1 tent lodge. Per night from 58 to 103€ – Per week from 272 to 659€

Shady pitches with simple private sanitary facilities around a large lake.

Surroundings : 🌲 🗔 ♨♨
Leisure activities : 🗡 🗡 🚣
Facilities : 🔥 🔌 – 53 private sanitary facilities (🚿 🚰 wc) 🏊 🚰 🍴 launderette 🚿

GPS Longitude : -1.12256
Latitude : 43.72643

⚠ Abesses

☏ 05 58 91 65 34. www.thermes-dax.com

Address : allée du Château (7.5km northwest following signs for Bayonne, D 16 to the right and take the Chemin d'Abesse)

4 ha (142 pitches) small lake

Rentals : 16 🚐 – 22 🏠 – 4 studios.

🚐 local sani-station – 40 🗉

Surroundings : 🌲 🗔 ♨♨
Leisure activities : 🏛
Facilities : 🔥 🔌 🖩 🏊 🚰 🍴 launderette
Nearby : 🎣

GPS Longitude : -1.09715
Latitude : 43.74216

In order for the guide to remain wholly objective, the selection of campsites is made on an entirely independent basis.

ST-PÉE-SUR-NIVELLE

64310 – Michelin map **342** C2 – pop. 5 550 – alt. 30
▶ Paris 785 – Bayonne 22 – Biarritz 17 – Cambo-les-Bains 17

⚲ Goyetchea ♠♠

☏ 05 59 54 19 59. www.camping-goyetchea.com

Address : Ibarron district (1.8km north along the D 855, follow the signs for Ahetze and take a right turn)

Opening times : from mid May to mid Sept.

3 ha (147 pitches) flat and relatively flat, grassy

Tariff : 29€ ✴✴ 🚗 🗉 🔌 (6A) – Extra per person 6€ – Reservation fee 13€

Rental rates : (from beginning May to mid Sept.) 🛖 – 2 'gypsy' caravans – 27 🚐 – 3 tent lodges. Per night from 38 to 57€ – Per week from 175 to 830€ – Reservation fee 13€

A view of pretty Basque houses and La Rhune (mountain).

Surroundings : 🌲 ⛰ ♨♨
Leisure activities : 🗡 🏛 🏃 🏊 🗡
Facilities : 🔥 🔌 🏊 🍴 launderette 🚿 refrigerators

GPS Longitude : -1.56683
Latitude : 43.36275

⚲ D'Ibarron

D'Ibarron

☏ 05 59 54 10 43. www.camping-ibarron. com

Address : Ibarron district (2km, take the western exit, on the D 918. follow the signs for St-Jean-de-Luz, near the Nivelle river)

Opening times : from end April to end Sept.

2.9 ha (142 pitches) flat, grassy

Tariff : (2015 price) 26.80€ ✴✴ 🚗 🗉 🔌 (6A) – Extra per person 5.40€ – Reservation fee 11€

Rental rates : (2015 price) (from beginning May to end Sept.) ✂ – 23 ⛺. Per night from 50 to 96€ – Per week from 230 to 670€ – Reservation fee 11€

⛽ local sani-station 5€ – 30 回 13.90€

Choose the pitches furthest away from the road.

Surroundings : ⌂ ♤♤	
Leisure activities : 🏠 ⛵ 🏊	**GPS** Longitude : -1.5749
Facilities : ♿ ⚷ ¶ launderette	Latitude : 43.3576
Nearby : 🛒 ¶ ✕ ⚓ 🚲	

ST-RÉMY

24700 – Michelin map **329** C6 – pop. 432 – alt. 80

▶ Paris 542 – Bergerac 33 – Libourne 46 – Montpon-Ménestérol 10

🏔 Les Cottages en Périgord – (rental of chalets only)

✆ 0553805946. www.cottagesenperigord.com

Address : at Les Pommiers (continue north following signs for Montpon-Ménestérol along the D 708)

Opening times : from mid Jan. to mid Dec.

7 ha/1 for camping flat, small lake, adjacent wood

Rental rates : ♿ (1 chalet) – 3 'gypsy' caravans – 8 🏠. Per night from 70 to 90 € – Per week from 250 to 680€ – Reservation fee 10€

Wooden chalets and 'gypsy' caravans are situated around a small lake.

Surroundings : 🌳 ⌂ ♧♧	
Leisure activities : 🏠 ♨ jacuzzi 🏊 ⚲	**GPS** Longitude : 0.16333
Facilities : ⚷ ▥ ¶ launderette	Latitude : 44.96024

To make the best possible use of this guide, please read pages 2–15 carefully.

ST-SAUD-LACOUSSIÈRE

24470 – Michelin map **329** F2 – pop. 864 – alt. 370

▶ Paris 443 – Brive-la-Gaillarde 105 – Châlus 23 – Limoges 57

🏔 Château Le Verdoyer 👥

✆ 0553569464. www.verdoyer.fr

Address : 2.5km northwest along the D 79, follow the signs for Nontron and take D 96, follow the signs for Abjat-sur-Bandiat; near lakes

Opening times : from end April to end Sept.

15 ha/5 for camping (186 pitches) terraced, undulating, relatively flat, flat, grassy, stony, pond

Tariff : 55€ ♟♟ 🚗 回 (10A) – Extra per person 7€ – Reservation fee 20€

Rental rates : (from end April to end Sept.) ♿ – 2 'gypsy' caravans – 25 ⛺ – 20 🏠 – 5 ⛺ – 2 tent lodges. Per night from 80 to 105€ – Per week from 240 to 735€ – Reservation fee 20€

⛽ local sani-station

Green setting around a chateau; bar, restaurant and plenty of activities.

Surroundings : 🌳 ⌂ ♨♨	
Leisure activities : ¶ ✕ 🏠 🎣 🏃 ⛵ 🚲 ✂ 🏊 🎣	
Facilities : ♿ ⚷ 🚿 – 14 private sanitary facilities (🛁 🚻 wc) ⚷ ¶ launderette 🚰 🧊 refrigerators	**GPS** Longitude : 0.79595 Latitude : 45.55133
Nearby : 🏖 (beach)	

ST-VINCENT-DE-COSSE

24220 – Michelin map **329** H6 – pop. 374 – alt. 80

▶ Paris 540 – Bergerac 61 – Brive-la-Gaillarde 65 – Fumel 58

🏔 Le Tiradou

✆ 0553303073. www.camping-le-tiradou.com

Address : at Larrit (500m southwest of the village; beside a stream)

Opening times : from end April to end Sept.

2 ha (66 pitches) flat, grassy

Tariff : ♟ 5€ 🚗 回 8€ – (6A) 4.50€ – Reservation fee 10€

Rental rates : (from end April to end Sept.) – 17 ⛺ – 5 🏠 – 2 tent lodges. Per night from 40 to 65€ – Per week from 210 to 750€ – Reservation fee 15€

⛽ 4 回 12.50€

Surroundings : ⌂ ♤♤	
Leisure activities : ✕ 🏠 ⛵ 🏊	**GPS** Longitude : 1.11268
Facilities : ♿ ⚷ 🅿 ¶ launderette ⚲	Latitude : 44.83747

STE-EULALIE-EN-BORN

40200 – Michelin map **335** D9 – pop. 1 116 – alt. 26

▶ Paris 673 – Arcachon 58 – Biscarrosse 98 – Mimizan 11

🏔 Les Bruyères

✆ 0558097336. www.camping-les-bruyeres.com

Address : 719 route de Laffont (2.5km north along the D 652)

Opening times : from beginning May to end Sept.

3 ha (177 pitches)

Tariff : (2015 price) 30.90€ ♟♟ 🚗 回 (10A) – Extra per person 8.40€ – Reservation fee 16€

Rental rates : (2015 price) (from beginning May to end Sept.) – 18 ⛺ – 1 🏠 – 3 yurts. Per night from 36 to 92€ – Per week from 224 to 756€ – Reservation fee 16€

Local home-made produce is available to taste and buy.

Surroundings : 🌳 ⌂ ♧♧	
Leisure activities : ¶ ✕ 🏠 ✂ 🏊	**GPS** Longitude : -1.17949
Facilities : ♿ ⚷ ⚷ ¶ launderette 🚰 ⚲	Latitude : 44.29387

STE-FOY-LA-GRANDE

33220 – Michelin map **335** M5 – pop. 2 544 – alt. 10

▶ Paris 555 – Bordeaux 71 – Langon 59 – Marmande 53

🏔 La Bastide

✆ 0557461384. www.camping-bastide.com

Address : at Pineuilh, allée du Camping (take northeastern exit along the D 130; beside the Dordogne river)

Opening times : from beginning April to end Oct.

1.2 ha (38 pitches) flat, grassy

Tariff : 25€ ♟♟ 🚗 回 (10A) – Extra per person 5.80€ – Reservation fee 10€

Rental rates : (from beginning April to mid Oct.) – 10 ⛺. Per night from 100 to 150€ – Per week from 230 to 695€ – Reservation fee 15€

Some pitches with shade. Ageing sanitary facilities.

Surroundings : 🌳 ⌂ ♤♤	
Leisure activities : 🏠 ⛵ 🏊	**GPS** Longitude : 0.22462
Facilities : ♿ ⚷ ¶ launderette	Latitude : 44.84403
Nearby : ⚲	

SALIES-DE-BÉARN

64270 – Michelin map **342** G4 – pop. 4 886 – alt. 50 – ⚓
▶ Paris 762 – Bayonne 60 – Dax 36 – Orthez 17

⚠ Mosqueros

🖉 05 59 38 12 94. camping2mosqueros@icloud.com

Address : avenue Al Cartero (take the western exit along the D 17, follow the signs for Bayonne, at the outdoor activity centre)

Opening times : permanent

0.7 ha (62 pitches)

Tariff : 18€ ♥♥ ⇔ 🗉 🗲 (10A) – Extra per person 4€

Rental rates : permanent – 3 🛖. Per night from 90 to 150€ – Per week from 280 to 400€

🚐 16 🗉 18€

A pleasant site next to the municipal sports centre. Rather poor and antiquated facilities.

Surroundings : 🌳 ♨♨	
Leisure activities : 🔲 multi-sports ground	**G P S**
Facilities : 🚻 🖙 🗑 🍽 launderette	Longitude : -0.93814
Nearby : 🍴 🚣	Latitude : 43.47643

A chambre d'hôte is a guesthouse or B & B-style accommodation.

SALIGNAC-EYVIGUES

24590 – Michelin map **329** I6 – pop. 1 141 – alt. 297
▶ Paris 509 – Brive-la-Gaillarde 34 – Cahors 84 – Périgueux 70

⚠ Flower Le Temps de Vivre

🖉 05 53 28 93 21. www.temps-de-vivre.com

Address : at Malmont (located 1.5km south along the D 61 and take the road to the right)

Opening times : from mid April to end Sept.

4.5 ha (50 pitches) terraced, relatively flat, flat, grassy, adjacent wood

Tariff : 29€ ♥♥ ⇔ 🗉 🗲 (10A) – Extra per person 5.50€ – Reservation fee 10€

Rental rates : (from beginning April to beginning Oct.) – 18 🛖 – 2 canvas bungalows – 2 tent lodges. Per night from 32 to 118€ – Per week from 160 to 826€ – Reservation fee 20€

🚐 5 🗉 11€ – 🗲 🗲 11€

Lots of green space for relaxation. High-quality rental options.

Surroundings : 🌳 🏞 ♨♨	
Leisure activities : 🍴 🍽 🔲 🚣	**G P S**
Facilities : 🚻 🖙 🍽 launderette	Longitude : 1.32817
	Latitude : 44.96355

SALLES

33770 – Michelin map **335** F7 – pop. 6 044 – alt. 23
▶ Paris 635 – Arcachon 36 – Bordeaux 56 – Mont-de-Marsan 88

⚠ Le Park du Val de l'Eyre ♨

🖉 05 56 88 47 03. www.camping-parcduvaldeleyre.com

Address : 8 route du Minoy (take the southwestern exit along the D 108e, follow the signs for Lugos; beside the Eyre river and a lake – from the A 63, take exit 21)

Opening times : from beginning April to beginning Nov.

13 ha/4 for camping (150 pitches) undulating, terraced, relatively flat, flat, grassy, sandy

Tariff : (2015 price) ♥ 9€ ⇔ 🗉 20€ 🗲 (32A) – Reservation fee 20€

Rental rates : (2015 price) (from beginning April to beginning Nov.) – 40 🛖 – 8 🛖 – 4 ⊨. Per week from 253 to 790€ – Reservation fee 20€

🚐 local sani-station – 🗲 🗲 21€

In a wooded setting near the Eyre river and a fishing lake.

Surroundings : 🌳 ♨♨	
Leisure activities : 🍴 🍽 🏠 🚣 jacuzzi 🚣 🎣 🛶 🏓 🛥	**G P S**
Facilities : 🚻 🖙 🗑 🍽 🏕 🍽 launderette 🧺	Longitude : -0.87399
Nearby : 🛒	Latitude : 44.54606

SALLES

47150 – Michelin map **336** H2 – pop. 314 – alt. 120
▶ Paris 588 – Agen 59 – Fumel 12 – Monflanquin 11

⚠ Des Bastides

🖉 05 53 40 83 09. www.campingdesbastides.com

Address : at Terre Rouge (located 1km to the northeast, follow the signs for Fumel, at junction of D 150 and D 162)

Opening times : from beginning April to end Sept.

6 ha/3 for camping (105 pitches) terraced, flat, grassy, wood

Tariff : 31.50€ ♥♥ ⇔ 🗉 🗲 (6A) – Extra per person 5.70€ – Reservation fee 18€

Rental rates : (from beginning April to end Sept.) 🏊 – 8 🛖 – 5 🛖 – 1 yurt – 2 canvas bungalows – 4 tent lodges. Per night from 39 to 139 v – Per week from 273 to 973€ – Reservation fee 20€

🚐 2 🗉 14€ – 🗲 🗲 14€

Surroundings : 🏞 ♨♨	
Leisure activities : 🍴 🍽 jacuzzi 🚣 🛶 🏓 multi-sports ground	**G P S**
Facilities : 🚻 🖙 🗑 🏕 – 2 private sanitary facilities (🛁 🚿 🚽 wc) 🍽 launderette 🧺	Longitude : 0.88161
	Latitude : 44.55263

This guide is updated regularly, so buy your new copy every year!

SANGUINET

40460 – Michelin map **335** E8 – pop. 3 133 – alt. 24
▶ Paris 643 – Arcachon 27 – Belin-Béliet 26 – Biscarrosse 120

⚠ Campéole Le lac de Sanguinet ♨

🖉 05 58 82 70 80. www.campeole.com

Address : rue de Pinton

Opening times : from beginning April to mid Sept.

9 ha (389 pitches) flat, grassy, sandy

Tariff : (2015 price) 31.10€ ♥♥ ⇔ 🗉 🗲 (10A) – Extra per person 9.90€ – Reservation fee 25€

Rental rates : (2015 price) (from beginning April to mid Sept.) 🚻 – 68 🛖 – 20 🛖 – 55 canvas bungalows. Per night from 24 to 159€ – Per week from 168 to 1,113€ – Reservation fee 25€

🚐 local sani-station 5€ – 🗲 🗲 19.30€

Several different rental options and pitches near the lake.

Surroundings : 🌳 ♨♨	
Leisure activities : 🍴 🍽 🔲 🎱 🚣 🎣 🛶	**G P S**
Facilities : 🚻 🖙 🏕 🍽 launderette 🧺	Longitude : -1.09278
Nearby : 🏖 (beach) 🛶 🦢 pedalos	Latitude : 44.48028

SARE

64310 – Michelin map **342** C3 – pop. 2 434 – alt. 70
▶ Paris 794 – Biarritz 26 – Cambo-les-Bains 19 – Pau 138

🔺 La Petite Rhune

☏ 05 59 54 23 97. www.lapetiterhune.com – limited spaces for one-night stay

Address : Lehenbiscaye district (situated 2km south along the road connecting D 406 and D 306)

Opening times : from mid June to mid Sept.

1.5 ha (39 pitches) terraced, relatively flat, flat, grassy

Tariff : (2015 price) 25.80€ ♦♦ ⇔ 🔲 🔋 (10A) – Extra per person 5.50€ – Reservation fee 10€

Rental rates : (2015 price) permanent 🛏 – 15 🏠 – 4 gîtes. Per night from 60 to 100€ – Per week from 230 to 670€ – Reservation fee 10€

A small village painted in the Basque colours!

Surroundings : 🛶 ≤ 🎠
Leisure activities : 🏛 🏄🏊 (small swimming pool), multi-sports ground
Facilities : 🦽 ⚡ 🚮🏚 🍴 launderette
Nearby : 🍷 🍴

G P S Longitude : -1.58771
Latitude : 43.30198

SARLAT-LA-CANÉDA

24200 – Michelin map **329** I6 – pop. 9 541 – alt. 145
▶ Paris 526 – Bergerac 74 – Brive-la-Gaillarde 52 – Cahors 60

🔺 La Palombière ♦♦

☏ 05 53 59 42 34. www.lapalombiere.fr – limited spaces for one-night stay

Address : at Ste-Nathalène, Galmier (9km northeast on the D 43 and take the turning to the left)

8.5 ha/4 for camping (177 pitches) terraced, relatively flat, flat, grassy, stony

Rentals : 59 🚐 – 10 🏠.

Pleasant oak grove with well marked-out pitches and luxury rental accommodation.

Surroundings : 🛶 ⬜ 🎠
Leisure activities : 🍷 🍴 🏛 🏃 👣 hammam 🏄🏊 🎯 launderette
Facilities : 🦽 ⚡ 🚮🏚 🍴 launderette 🏊🏄

G P S Longitude : 1.29157
Latitude : 44.90639

🔺 Les Castels Le Moulin du Roch ♦♦

☏ 05 53 59 20 27. www.moulin-du-roch.com 🛏

Address : at St-André d'Allas, on the D 47 (10km to the northwest, follow the signs for Les Eyzies; beside a stream)

Opening times : from mid May to mid Sept.

8 ha (200 pitches) open site, terraced, relatively flat, flat, grassy, small lake

Tariff : 40€ ♦♦ ⇔ 🔲 🔋 (10A) – Extra per person 10.50€ – Reservation fee 15€

Rental rates : (from mid May to mid Sept.) 🛏 – 55 🚐. Per night from 42 to 147€ – Reservation fee 15€

Pitches around a former mill, on the rocks or near a lake. Choose those furthest from the road.

Surroundings : ⬜ 🎠
Leisure activities : 🍷 🍴 🏛 🏃 👣 🏄🏊🎯
multi-sports ground
Facilities : 🦽 ⚡ 🖵🏚 🍴 launderette
🏊🏄

G P S Longitude : 1.11481
Latitude : 44.90843

🔺 La Châtaigneraie ♦♦

☏ 05 53 59 03 61. www.camping-lachataigneraie24.com

Address : at Prats de Carlux, La Garrigue Basse (10km east along the D 47, take turning ot the right)

Opening times : from end April to mid Sept.

9 ha (193 pitches) terraced, flat, grassy, sandy

Tariff : 33€ ♦♦ ⇔ 🔲 🔋 (10A) – Extra per person 8€ – Reservation fee 20€

Rental rates : (from end April to end Sept.) 🛏 – 61 🚐 – 11 🏠 – 3 gîtes. Per night from 44 to 130€ – Per week from 260 to 1,200€ – Reservation fee 20€

Pretty aquatic park surrounded by walls made o local stone. Lots of green space for sport and relaxation.

Surroundings : 🛶 ⬜ 🎠
Leisure activities : 🍷 🍴 🏛 🏃 👣 🏄🏊🎯
🏊🏄
Facilities : 🦽 ⚡ 🚮🏚 🍴 launderette
🏊🏄

G P S Longitude : 1.29871
Latitude : 44.90056

🔺 Domaine de Loisirs le Montant ♦♦

☏ 05 53 59 18 50. www.camping-sarlat.com

Address : at Négrelat (situated 2km southwest along the D 57, follow the signs for Bergerac then continue 2.3km along the road to the right)

Opening times : from beginning April to end Sept.

70 ha/8 for camping (135 pitches) very uneven, undulating, terraced, flat, grassy

Tariff : ♦ 8.90€ ⇔ 🔲 17.90€ – 🔋 (10A) 4.80€ – Reservation fee 19€

Rental rates : (from beginning April to end Sept.) – 26 🚐 – 26 🏠 – 2 gîtes. Per night from 52 to 161€ – Per week from 287 to 1,939€ – Reservation fee 18€

A range of luxury rental options in a naturally wooded and hilly setting.

Surroundings : 🛶 ≤ ⬜ 🎠
Leisure activities : 🍷 🍴 🏛 nighttime 👣 jacuzzi 🏄🏊 🔲🏊 multi-sports ground
Facilities : 🦽 ⚡ 🏚 🍴 launderette
🏊

G P S Longitude : 1.18903
Latitude : 44.86573

🔺 Indigo Sarlat - Les Périères ♦♦

☏ 05 53 59 05 84. www.camping-indigo.com

Address : rue Jean Gabin (located 1km to the northeast, by the exit from town)

Opening times : from end March to end Sept.

11 ha/5 for camping (195 pitches) very uneven, terraced, flat, grassy

Tariff : (2015 price) 36.90€ ♦♦ ⇔ 🔲 🔋 (10A) – Extra per person 7.50€ – Reservation fee 13€

Rental rates : (2015 price) (from end March to end Sept.) – 4 'gypsy' caravans – 20 🚐 – 15 🏠 – 34 tent lodges – 15 gîtes. Per night from 45 to 150€ – Per week from 221 to 1,050€ – Reservation fee 13€

🚐 local sani-station 7€

Surroundings : 🛶 ≤ 🎠
Leisure activities : 🍷 🍴 🏛 🏃 👣 🎯🏄
🔲🏊
Facilities : 🦽 ⚡ 🖵🏚 🍴 launderette
🏊

G P S Longitude : 1.22767
Latitude : 44.89357

▲▲ Domaine des Chênes Verts ▲▲

☏ 05 53 59 21 07. www.chenes-verts.com – limited spaces for one-night stay

Address : route de Sarlat et Souillac (8.5km southeast)

Opening times : from beginning April to end Sept.

8 ha (176 pitches) terraced, relatively flat, flat, grassy

Tariff : 29€ ★★ ⇔ 🔲 (6A) – Extra per person 7€ – Reservation fee 20€

Rental rates : (from beginning April to end Sept.) ⅊ – 72 🚐 – 31 🏠. Per week from 240 to 990€ – Reservation fee 20€

Pretty water and play park at the foot of a pretty building and high-quality chalets to rent.

Surroundings : ⬠ ⌂ ♨♨
Leisure activities : ♟ ✕ 🏠 ⛷ ⛴ ⛵ 🚴 ⛸ ⛱ farm or petting farm multi-sports ground
Facilities : ⛐ ⊶ 🏕 ⛱ ♨ launderette 🏳 ⛽
Longitude : 1.2972
Latitude : 44.86321

▲▲ Les Grottes de Roffy ▲▲

☏ 05 53 59 15 61. www.roffy.fr

Address : at Ste-Nathalène, at Roffy (8km east, along the D 47)

Opening times : from beginning May to mid Sept.

5 ha (165 pitches) open site, terraced, flat, grassy

Tariff : (2015 price) 16.50€ ★★ ⇔ 🔲 (8A) – Extra per person 4.50€ – Reservation fee 19€

Rental rates : (2015 price) (from beginning May to mid Sept.) – 50 🚐 – 2 apartments. Per night from 41 to 170€ – Per week from 280 to 1,000€

Surroundings : ⬠ ⌂ ♨♨
Leisure activities : ♟ ✕ 🏠 ⛷ ⛴ ⛵ ⛱
Facilities : ⛐ ⊶ ⛱ ⛲ ♨ launderette 🏳 ⛽
Longitude : 1.28211
Latitude : 44.90417

▲▲ Les Terrasses du Périgord

☏ 05 53 59 02 25. www.terrasses-du-perigord.com

Address : at Proissans, Pech d'Orance (2.8km to the northeast)

Opening times : from mid April to end Sept.

12 ha/5 for camping (85 pitches)

Tariff : 23.90€ ★★ ⇔ 🔲 (16A) – Extra per person 5.90€ – Reservation fee 8€

Rental rates : (from mid April to end Sept.) ⅊ – 9 🚐 – 9 🏠 – 2 tent lodges. Per week from 210 to 620€ – Reservation fee 10€

🚰 local sani-station 17.90€

Lots of shade and high-quality chalets.

Surroundings : ⬠ ← ⌂ ♨♨
Leisure activities : ✕ 🏠 jacuzzi ⛴ ⛰ ⛱ sports trail, zip wiring
Facilities : ⛐ ⊶ ⛱ ⛲ ♨ launderette 🏳 ⛽
Longitude : 1.23658
Latitude : 44.90617

▲▲ La Ferme de Villeneuve ▲▲

☏ 05 53 30 30 90. www.fermedevilleneuve.com

Address : at St-André-d'Allas, Villeneuve (8km northwest along the D 47, follow the signs for Les Eyzies-de-Tayac and take turning to the left)

Opening times : from beginning April to end Oct.

20 ha/2.5 for camping (100 pitches) natural setting among trees and bushes, lake

Tariff : (2015 price) ★ 7€ ⇔ 🔲 7.60€ – (10A) 4.25€ – Reservation fee 10€

Rental rates : (2015 price) (from beginning April to end Oct.) ⅊ – 2 'gypsy' caravans – 10 🚐 – 4 tipis – 3 canvas bungalows – 7 tent lodges – 1 gîte. Per night from 37 to 90€ – Per week from 290 to 739€ – Reservation fee 10€

🚰 AireService sani-station 2€ – 4 🔲 12€

A farm campsite.

Surroundings : ⬠ ← ⌂ ♨♨
Leisure activities : ♟ ✕ ⛷ ⛴ 🚴 ⛸
Facilities : ⛐ ⊶ ⛱ ♨ launderette ⛽
Nearby : cinema/activity centre
Longitude : 1.14051
Latitude : 44.90438

▲▲ Les Acacias

☏ 05 53 31 08 50. www.acacias.fr

Address : at the village of la Canéda, rue Louis de Champagne (6km southeast along the D 704 and take a right turn at the Leclerc hypermarket)

Opening times : from beginning April to end Sept.

4 ha (122 pitches) terraced, relatively flat, flat, grassy

Tariff : 26€ ★★ ⇔ 🔲 (10A) – Extra per person 6€ – Reservation fee 80€

Rental rates : (from beginning April to end Sept.) ⅊ – 20 🚐. Per night from 49 to 73€ – Per week from 240 to 730€

🚰 local sani-station 5€

In two distinct sections linked by a quiet road. Bus stop for Sarlat.

Surroundings : ← ⌂ ♨♨
Leisure activities : ♟ ⛴ 🚴 ⛱ multi-sports ground
Facilities : ⛐ ⊶ ⛱ ⛲ ⛱ ♨ launderette ⛽
Longitude : 1.23699
Latitude : 44.85711

For more information on visiting particular towns or regions, consult the relevant regional MICHELIN Green Guide. We also recommend you use the appropriate Michelin regional map to locate your selected campsite, to calculate distances and to work out the best route.

SAUBION

40230 – Michelin map **335** C12 – pop. 1 323 – alt. 17
▶ Paris 747 – Bordeaux 169 – Mont-de-Marsan 79 – Pau 106

▲▲ Club Airotel La Pomme de Pin

☏ 05 58 77 00 71. www.camping-lapommedepin.com

Address : 825 route de Seignosse (2km southeast along the D 652 and D 337)

Opening times : from mid March to beginning Oct.

5 ha (256 pitches)

Tariff : 39.50€ ★★ ⇔ 🔲 (6A) – Extra per person 9€ – Reservation fee 25€

Rental rates : (from mid March to beginning Oct.) – 48 🚐 – 24 canvas bungalows. Per night from 49 to 85€ – Per week from 180 to 1,190€ – Reservation fee 25€

🚰 Eurorelais sani-station

Choose pitches furthest from the road. Sanitary facilities are simple and ageing.

Surroundings : ⌂ ♨♨
Leisure activities : ♟ ✕ 🏠 jacuzzi ⛴ 🚴 ⛱ (open air in season)
Facilities : ⛐ ⊶ ⛘ ⛱ ♨ launderette 🏳 ⛽ refrigerators
Longitude : -1.35563
Latitude : 43.67608

SAUVETERRE-LA-LÉMANCE

47500 – Michelin map **336** I2 – pop. 587 – alt. 100
▶ Paris 572 – Agen 68 – Fumel 14 – Monflanquin 27

⚲ Flower Le Moulin du Périé

✆ 05 53 40 67 26. www.camping-moulin-perie.com

Address : at Moulin du Périé (3km east following signs for Loubejac;
beside a stream)

Opening times : from mid May to mid Sept.

4 ha (125 pitches) flat, grassy

Tariff : (2015 price) 31.25€ ✝✝ ⇔ 回 ⚡ (10A) –
Extra per person 7.30€ – Reservation fee 20€

Rental rates : (2015 price) (from mid May to mid Sept.) – 14 ⟨⟩ –
4 ⌂ – 12 canvas bungalows. Per night from 33 to 120€ –
Per week from 231 to 840€ – Reservation fee 35€

⟨⟩ local sani-station – 5 回 31.65€

Surroundings : 🐾 ⌂ 〰		Longitude : 1.04743
Leisure activities : ⛱ ✕ ⌂ 🚣 🚴 🏊 ⛵	**GPS**	Latitude : 44.5898
Facilities : 🚿 ⚬ 🅒 🚻 launderette 🧺		

SEIGNOSSE OCÉAN

40510 – Michelin map **335** C12
▶ Paris 763 – Bordeaux 184 – Mont-de-Marsan 89 – Pau 115

⚲ Océliances ♣

✆ 05 58 43 30 30. www.oceliances.com – limited spaces for one-night
stay

Address : avenue des Tucs (along the D 79e, 500m from the beach at
Les Bourdaines)

Opening times : from end March to end Oct.

13 ha (439 pitches) undulating, terraced, flat, sandy

Tariff : (2015 price) 39€ ✝✝ ⇔ 回 ⚡ (10A) – Extra per person 9€ –
Reservation fee 20€

Rental rates : (2015 price) (from end March to end Oct.) ⚡ –
190 ⟨⟩ – 44 ⌂ – 24 tent lodges. Per night from 46 to 162€ –
Per week from 392 to 1,708€ – Reservation fee 20€

Surroundings : 🐾 ♀		
Leisure activities : ⛱ ✕ ⌂ 🚣 🏊 🎣	**GPS**	Longitude : -1.43039
🚴 🏊 multi-sports ground, entertainment		Latitude : 43.69358
room		
Facilities : 🚿 ⚬ 🅒 🚻 launderette 🧺		
🧊 refrigerated food storage facilities		

SORDE-L'ABBAYE

40300 – Michelin map **335** E13 – pop. 646 – alt. 17
▶ Paris 758 – Bayonne 47 – Dax 27 – Oloron-Ste-Marie 63

⚲ Municipal la Galupe

✆ 05 58 73 18 13. mairie.sordelabbaye@wanadoo.fr

Address : 242 chemin du Camping (1.3km west along the D 29,
follow the signs for Peyrehorade, D 123 to the left and take the road
before the bridge; near the Gave d'Oloron – river)

Opening times : permanent

0.6 ha (28 pitches)

Tariff : (2015 price) ✝ 2.50€ ⇔ 回 4€ – ⚡ (9A) 2.50€

⟨⟩ sani-station

| Surroundings : 🐾 ⌂ ♀ | | Longitude : -1.06472 |
| Facilities : 🚿 ⚓ | **GPS** | Latitude : 43.53139 |

SOULAC-SUR-MER

33780 – Michelin map **335** E1 – pop. 2 711 – alt. 7
▶ Paris 515 – Bordeaux 99 – Lesparre-Médoc 31 – Royan 12

⚲ Les Lacs ♣

✆ 05 56 09 76 63. www.camping-les-lacs.com

Address : 126 route des Lacs (continue 3km east along the D 101)

Opening times : from beginning April to beginning Nov.

5 ha (228 pitches)

Tariff : 36.50€ ✝✝ ⇔ 回 ⚡ (10A) – Extra per person 6€

Rental rates : (2015 price) (from beginning April to beginning Nov.)
🚿 (1 mobile home) – 70 ⟨⟩ – 12 ⌂. Per night from 42 to 162€ –
Per week from 294 to 1,134€

⟨⟩ sani-station – 2 回 15€ – 🚐 ⚡ 14€

Organised coach excursions are available.

Surroundings : 🐾 ⌂ ♀♀		
Leisure activities : ⛱ ✕ ⌂ ⚐ 🏊 🚣 🏹 🏓	**GPS**	Longitude : -1.11932
🛶 🏊 multi-sports ground		Latitude : 45.48328
Facilities : 🚿 ⚬ 🅒 🚻 launderette		
🧊 🧺		
Nearby : 🐎		

⚲ Yelloh! Soulac sur Mer ♣

✆ 05 56 09 77 63. www.lelilhan.com

Address : 8 allée Michel de Montaigne (2.8km east along the D 101
E2 and D 101)

Opening times : from mid April to mid Sept.

4 ha (170 pitches)

Tariff : 46€ ✝✝ ⇔ 回 ⚡ (10A) – Extra per person 7€

Rental rates : (from mid April to mid Sept.) – 72 ⟨⟩ – 20 ⌂.
Per night from 39 to 254€ – Per week from 273 to 1,778€

⟨⟩ AireService sani-station

High-quality rental options in green setting.

Surroundings : 🐾 〰		
Leisure activities : ⛱ ✕ ⌂ ⚐ 🏃 ⛲ jacuzzi	**GPS**	Longitude : -1.11886
🚣 🚴 🏊 🛶 🏊		Latitude : 45.48563
Facilities : 🚿 ⚬ 🅒 🚻 launderette 🧺 🧊		

⚲ Sandaya Soulac Plage ♣

✆ 05 56 09 87 27. www.sandaya.fr

Address : at L'Amélie-sur-Mer

Opening times : from beginning April to mid Sept.

12 ha (507 pitches) undulating, terraced, flat, sandy, stony

Tariff : (2015 price) 46€ ✝✝ ⇔ 回 ⚡ (16A) – Extra per person 7.50€ –
Reservation fee 32€

Rental rates : (2015 price) (from beginning April to mid Sept.) –
209 ⟨⟩ – 15 tent lodges. Per night from 35 to 120€ – Per week
from 490 to 1,385€ – Reservation fee 32€

⟨⟩ local sani-station – 20 回 46€

Partly under a pine forest with some pitches near the beach.

Surroundings : 🐾 ⌂ ♀♀ ⛰		
Leisure activities : ⛱ ✕ ⌂ ⚐ 🏃 🚣 🚴	**GPS**	Longitude : -1.15055
🏊 🏊 🛶 multi-sports ground,		Latitude : 45.4825
entertainment room		
Facilities : 🚿 ⚬ 🅒 🚻 launderette 🧊 🧺		

To make the best possible use of this guide, please read
pages 2–15 carefully.

⚠ L'Océan

☎ 05 56 09 76 10. http://perso.wanadoo.fr/camping.ocean

Address : at L'Amélie-sur-Mer, 62 allée de la Négade (take the eastern exit along the D 101e 2 and take the D 101, 300m from the beach)

Opening times : from beginning June to mid Sept.

6 ha (300 pitches) flat, grassy, sandy, gravelled

Tariff : ♦ 6.50€ ⇔ 🔲 15€ – 🔌 (10A) 4.50€ – Reservation fee 20€

Surroundings : 🌊 ♀♀
Leisure activities : ♈ 🎫 🚲 ✂
Facilities : ♿ ⛽ 🚮 🚰 launderette 🏤 🔧
GPS Longitude : -1.14533 Latitude : 45.48043

SOUSTONS

40140 – Michelin map **335** D12 – pop. 7 240 – alt. 9
▷ Paris 732 – Biarritz 53 – Castets 23 – Dax 29

▲ Sunêlia Village Vacances Fram Nature
(rental of mobile homes, chalets and tent lodges only)

☎ 05 58 77 70 00. www.camping-nature-soustons.fr

Address : at Nicot-les-Pins, 63 avenue Port d'Albret (follow the signs for Les Lacs)

Opening times : from beginning April to end Sept.

14 ha (250 pitches) undulating

Rental rates : ♿ (1 mobile home) 🚫 Ⓟ – 200 🏠 – 12 🏠 – 37 tent lodges. Per night from 30 to 228€ – Per week from 210 to 1,596€

Organised excursions, an eco swimming pool and plenty of activities for children and teenagers.

Surroundings : 🌊 ♀
Leisure activities : ♈ ✗ 🎫 🎭(open-air theatre) 🛝 ♨ ⛵ hammam, jacuzzi 🏇 🚲 ✂ 🎮 🏊 multi-sports ground, spa centre, entertainment room
Facilities : 🚰 launderette 🏤 🔧
GPS Longitude : -1.35999 Latitude : 43.75593

▲ L'Airial

☎ 05 58 41 12 48. www.campinglairial.fr

Address : 67 avenue de Port d'Albret (situated 2km west along the D 652, follow the signs for Vieux-Boucau-les-Bains, 200m from the Étang de Soustons)

Opening times : from end March to beginning Oct.

13 ha (445 pitches) undulating, flat, sandy

Tariff : 35€ ♦♦ ⇔ 🔲 🔌 (10A) – Extra per person 7.50€ – Reservation fee 20€

Rental rates : (from end March to beginning Oct.) ♿ (2 mobile homes) 🚫 – 86 🏠 – 20 🏠 – 3 apartments. Per night from 85 to 165€ – Per week from 265 to 1,035€ – Reservation fee 20€

🏤 10 🔲 16€ – 🔌 8€

Surroundings : ♀
Leisure activities : ♈ ✗ 🎫 🎭 🛝 ⛵ 🚲 ✂ 🎮 🏊 multi-sports ground
Facilities : ♿ 🚰 🚮 launderette 🏤 🔧 refrigerated food storage facilities
GPS Longitude : -1.35195 Latitude : 43.75433

⚠ Village Vacances Le Dunéa

☎ 05 58 48 00 59. www.club-dunea.com

Address : at Souston-Plage, port d'Albret south 1 square de l'Herté (200m from the lake)

0.5 ha undulating, flat, sandy

Rentals : 20 gîtes.

Surroundings : 🌊 ♀
Leisure activities : 🎫 🏊
Facilities : 🚰 Ⓟ 🚰 🖥
Nearby : ✂ 🏇
GPS Longitude : -1.40065 Latitude : 43.7731

LE TEICH

33470 – Michelin map **335** E7 – pop. 6 485 – alt. 5
▷ Paris 633 – Arcachon 20 – Belin-Béliet 34 – Bordeaux 50

▲ Ker Helen 🚹🚺

☎ 05 56 66 03 79. www.kerhelen.com

Address : 119 avenue de la Côte d'Argent (situated 2km west along the D 650, follow the signs for Gujan-Mestras)

Opening times : from mid April to mid Oct.

4 ha (170 pitches) flat, grassy

Tariff : (2015 price) ♦ 5.50€ ⇔ 🔲 14.30€ – 🔌 (10A) 3.70€ – Reservation fee 18€

Rental rates : (from mid April to mid Oct.) ♿ (1 chalet) – 45 🏠 – 5 🏠 – 12 canvas bungalows – 4 tent lodges. Per night from 30 to 60€ – Per week from 180 to 990€ – Reservation fee 18€
🏤 local sani-station 10€

Surroundings : 🚮 ♀♀
Leisure activities : ♈ ✗ 🌙nighttime 🛝 🏇 🚲 🏊
Facilities : ♿ 🚰 🏤 🚮 🚰 launderette 🏤 🔧
GPS Longitude : -1.04284 Latitude : 44.63975

TERRASSON-LAVILLEDIEU

24120 – Michelin map **329** I5 – pop. 6 222 – alt. 90
▷ Paris 497 – Brive-la-Gaillarde 22 – Juillac 28 – Périgueux 53

▲ La Salvinie

☎ 05 53 50 06 11. www.camping-salvinie.fr

Address : at Bouillac Sud (take the southern exit along the D 63, follow the signs for Chavagnac then continue 3.4km, following signs for Condat; on the right after the bridge)

Opening times : from beginning April to end Sept.

2.5 ha (70 pitches) flat, grassy

Tariff : (2015 price) 22.40€ ♦♦ ⇔ 🔲 🔌 (10A) – Extra per person 5.80€

Rental rates : (2015 price) (from beginning April to end Sept.) – 12 🏠. Per night from 40 to 90€ – Per week from 250 to 820€
🏤 local sani-station – 🔌 11€

Surroundings : ⟨ 🚮 ♀♀
Leisure activities : ♈ 🎫 🏇 🏊
Facilities : ♿ 🚰 launderette
GPS Longitude : 1.26216 Latitude : 45.12069

▲ Village Vacances le Clos du Moulin
(rental of chalets only)

☎ 05 53 51 68 95. www.leclosdumoulin.com

Address : at Le Moulin de Bouch (6km west de Terrasson-Lavilledieu along the N 89, follow the signs for St-Lazare and take the D 62 following signs for Coly; beside the river)

1 ha flat, grassy
Rentals : Ⓟ – 14 🏠.

Surroundings : ♀
Leisure activities : ♈ ✗ 🚲 🏊
Facilities : ♿ 🚰 🖥 🚰
GPS Longitude : 1.26337 Latitude : 45.10288

LA TESTE-DE-BUCH

33260 – Michelin map **335** E7 – pop. 24 597 – alt. 5
▶ Paris 642 – Andernos-les-Bains 35 – Arcachon 5 – Belin-Béliet 44

🏔 **FranceLoc Village Vacances La Pinèda** 👥
(rental of mobile homes only)

📞 05 56 22 23 24. www.campinglapinede.net ou franceloc.fr

Address : route de Cazaux (11km south along the D 112; beside the Les Landes canal, 2.5km from Cazaux)

Opening times : from beginning April to mid Sept.

5 ha

Rental rates : (2015 price) ♿ (1 mobile home) – 184 🏠. Per night from 19 to 188€ – Per week from 133 to 1,316€ – Reservation fee 27€

Surroundings : 🐟 🏖 ⛳
Leisure activities : ♟ ✗ 🏠 ⛱ 🎣 🚴
🏊 🛶 multi-sports ground
Facilities : ♿ ⛽ 🏕 ㏗ launderette 🧺
Nearby : water skiing

Longitude : -1.15055
Latitude : 44.55516

THENON

24210 – Michelin map **329** H5 – pop. 1 283 – alt. 194
▶ Paris 515 – Brive-la-Gaillarde 41 – Excideuil 36 – Les Eyzies-de-Tayac 33

🏔 **Le Verdoyant**

📞 05 53 05 20 78. www.campingleverdoyant.fr

Address : route de Montignac-Lascaux (4km southeast along the D 67, near two lakes)

Opening times : from beginning April to end Sept.

9 ha/3 for camping (67 pitches) open site, terraced, flat, grassy, pond

Tariff : 21.20€ ♟♟ 🚗 🅿 🔌 (10A) – Extra per person 5.30€

Rental rates : (from beginning April to end Sept.) – 12 🏠 – 1 🏠 – 2 tent lodges. Per night from 65 to 122€ – Per week from 190 to 729€

🚉 local sani-station – 20 🅿 12.50€

Surroundings : ◁ ⛳
Leisure activities : ♟ ✗ ⛱ 🛶 🎣
Facilities : ♿ ⛽ 🏕 ㏗ 🧺 🧺

Longitude : 1.09102
Latitude : 45.11901

THIVIERS

24800 – Michelin map **329** G3 – pop. 3 121 – alt. 273
▶ Paris 449 – Brive-la-Gaillarde 81 – Limoges 62 – Nontron 33

🏔 **Le Repaire**

📞 05 53 52 69 75. www.camping-le-repaire.fr

Address : situated 2km southeast along the D 707, follow the signs for Lanouaille and take the road to the right

Opening times : from end March to beginning Nov.

10 ha/4.5 for camping (100 pitches) terrace, relatively flat, flat, grassy, adjacent wood

Tariff : ♟ 4€ 🚗 🅿 6€ – 🔌 (6A) 3€

Rental rates : permanent 🅿 – 1 🏠 – 9 🏠. Per night from 55 to 65€ – Per week from 200 to 550€

Attractive pitches set around a small lake.

Surroundings : 🏕 ⛳
Leisure activities : ♟ 🏠 ⛱ 🛶 🎣
Facilities : ♿ ⛽ launderette 🧺
Nearby : ✗

Longitude : 0.9321
Latitude : 45.41305

TOCANE-ST-APRE

24350 – Michelin map **329** D4 – pop. 1 679 – alt. 95
▶ Paris 498 – Brantôme 24 – Mussidan 33 – Périgueux 25

⛰ **Municipal le Pré Sec**

📞 05 53 90 40 60. www.campingdupresec.com

Address : north of the town along the D 103, follow the signs for Montagrier, near the stadium; beside the Dronne river

Opening times : from beginning May to end Sept.

1.8 ha (80 pitches)

Tariff : (2015 price) 11.16€ ♟♟ 🚗 🅿 🔌 (10A) – Extra per person 2€

Rental rates : (2015 price) permanent ♿ – 14 🏠. Per night from 30 to 43€ – Per week from 245 to 380€

🚉 Eurorelais sani-station 2€

Surroundings : 🐟 ⛳
Leisure activities : 🏠 🏊 (beach) 🎣
Facilities : ♿ ⛽ 🏕 ⛱ ㏗ 📮
Nearby : ⛱ ✗ 🏕

Longitude : 0.49685
Latitude : 45.25649

TOURNON-D AGENAIS

47370 – Michelin map **336** H3 – pop. 751 – alt. 156
▶ Paris 620 – Agen 42 – Cahors 44 – Montauban 63

🏔 **FranceLoc Ullule**

📞 05 53 40 90 12. www.camping-france-aquitaine-ullule.fr – limited spaces for one-night stay

Address : Pont Ramio, route de Fumel

Opening times : June to Sept.

12 ha (300 pitches) undulating, terraced, relatively flat, flat, grassy, stony, pond

Rental rates : (from beginning June to end Sept.) ♿ – 250 🏠. Per week from 175 to 980€

🚉 local sani-station

Surroundings : 🐟
Leisure activities : 🏠 🎣 ⛱ 🏊 🛶 🎣
Facilities : ♿ ⛽ ㏗ launderette
Nearby : ♟ ✗ 🐴

Longitude : 0.99955
Latitude : 44.40606

TURSAC

24620 – Michelin map **329** H6 – pop. 319 – alt. 75
▶ Paris 536 – Bordeaux 172 – Périgueux 48 – Brive-la-Gaillarde 57

🏔 **Le Vézère Périgord**

📞 05 53 06 96 31. www.levezereperigord.com

Address : 800m northeast along the D 706, follow the signs for Montignac and take the road to the right

Opening times : from end April to end Oct.

3.5 ha (99 pitches) terraced, relatively flat, flat, grassy, stony

Tariff : (2015 price) 27.80€ ♟♟ 🚗 🅿 🔌 (10A) – Extra per person 6.50€ – Reservation fee 1€

Rental rates : (2015 price) (from end April to end Oct.) – 25 🏠 – 3 canvas bungalows – 2 tent lodges. Per night from 36 to 50€ – Per week from 200 to 790€ – Reservation fee 1€

🚉 local sani-station

Surroundings : 🐟 ⛳
Leisure activities : ♟ ✗ 🏠 ⛱ 🚴 ✗ 🏊 🛶
Facilities : ♿ ⛽ 🆑 🏕 ㏗ launderette 🧺

Longitude : 1.04637
Latitude : 44.97599

URDOS

64490 – Michelin map **342** I5 – pop. 69 – alt. 780
▷ Paris 850 – Jaca 38 – Oloron-Ste-Marie 41 – Pau 75

⛰ La Via Natura Le Gave d'Aspe

☎ 05 59 34 88 26. www.campingaspe.com

Address : rue du Moulin de la Tourette (1.5km northwest along the N 134, take the road in front of the old station)

Opening times : from beginning May to end Sept.

1.5 ha (80 pitches) open site, relatively flat, flat, grassy

Tariff : 15.55 € ♣ ♣ ⇔ 回 ⁇ (6A) – Extra per person 3.95 €
Rental rates : permanent ⁇ – 2 ⌂ – 2 canvas bungalows.
Per night from 29 to 65 € – Per week from 200 to 399 €
⇱ Eurorelais sani-station 2 €

Pitches with good shade beside the Aspe mountain stream.

Surroundings :		G P S	Longitude : -0.55642
Leisure activities :			Latitude : 42.87719
Facilities :			

Some information or pricing may have changed since the guide went to press. We recommend you check the price list online in advance or at the entrance to the campsite and enquire about possible restrictions.

URRUGNE

64122 – Michelin map **342** B4 – pop. 8,427 – alt. 34
▷ Paris 791 – Bayonne 29 – Biarritz 23 – Hendaye 8

🏔 Sunêlia Col d'Ibardin 👥

Sunêlia Col d'Ibardin

☎ 05 59 54 31 21. www.col-ibardin.com

Address : route d'Olhette (4km south along the D 4, follow the signs for Ascain and Le Col d'Ibardin; beside a stream)

Opening times : from beginning April to end Sept.

8 ha (203 pitches) undulating, terraced, relatively flat, flat, grassy

Tariff : ⇔回 37 € – ⁇ (10A) 7 € –
Reservation fee 30 €
Rental rates : (from mid March to mid Nov.) ♿ (1 mobile home) ⁇ – 64 🚐 – 31 ⌂ – 5 tent lodges. Per night from 45 to 135 € – Per week from 315 to 945 € – Reservation fee 30 €
⇱ 1 回 31 €

In the middle of an oak forest; pitches beside a stream. Choose those furthest away from the road.

Surroundings :		G P S	Longitude : -1.68461
Leisure activities : multi-sports ground			Latitude : 43.33405
Facilities : launderette			

🏔 Larrouleta

☎ 05 59 47 37 84. www.larrouleta.com

Address : Socoa district, 210 route de Socoa (3km to the south)

Opening times : permanent

5 ha (327 pitches) flat, grassy

Tariff : (2015 price) 36 € ♣ ♣ ⇔ 回 ⁇ (10A) – Extra per person 8.50 €
⇱ AireService sani-station – 60 回 23 €

A very pleasant site surrounding a small lake (swimming). Choose the pitches away from the road.

Surroundings :		G P S	Longitude : -1.6859
Leisure activities : (open air in season) (beach) pedalos			Latitude : 43.37036
Facilities : launderette			

URT

64240 – Michelin map **342** E2 – pop. 2 183 – alt. 41
▷ Paris 757 – Bayonne 17 – Biarritz 24 – Cambo-les-Bains 28

🏔 Etche Zahar

☎ 05 59 56 27 36. www.etche-zahar.fr ⁇

Address : 175 allée de Mesplès (located 1km west along the D 257, towards Urcuit and take the turning to the left)

Opening times : from beginning March to mid Nov.

1.5 ha (47 pitches)

Tariff : ♣ 4.60 € ⇔ 3.20 € 回 12.40 € – ⁇ (10A) 3.85 € – Reservation fee 13 €
Rental rates : (from beginning March to mid Nov.) ♿ (2 chalets) ⁇ – 9 🚐 – 9 ⌂ – 4 canvas bungalows – 4 tent lodges. Per night from 31 to 98 € – Per week from 252 to 686 € – Reservation fee 13 €
⇱ 2 回 15 €

Leafy setting with a variety of rental options

Surroundings :		G P S	Longitude : -1.2973
Leisure activities :			Latitude : 43.4919
Facilities : launderette			

We value your opinion and welcome your feedback. Do email us at campingfrance@tp.michelin.com

VENDAYS-MONTALIVET

33930 – Michelin map **335** E2 – pop. 2,288 – alt. 9
▷ Paris 535 – Bordeaux 82 – Lesparre-Médoc 14 – Soulac-sur-Mer 21

🏔 Les Peupliers

☎ 05 56 41 70 44. www.camping-montalivet-lespeupliers.com

Address : 17 route de Sarnac

Opening times : from mid May to end Sept.

2.5 ha (116 pitches) flat, grassy

Tariff : 28 € ♣ ♣ ⇔ 回 ⁇ (6A) – Extra per person 5.20 €
Rental rates : (from beginning April to end Oct.) – 23 🚐 – 2 canvas bungalows. Per night from 26 to 110 € – Per week from 180 to 770 €

Pitches with shade and a variety of quality rental options.

Surroundings :		G P S	Longitude : -1.05694
Leisure activities :			Latitude : 45.35027
Facilities : launderette			

⛰ La Chesnays

☎ 05 56 41 72 74. www.camping-montalivet.com

Address : 8 route de Soulac, at Mayan

Opening times : from beginning May to mid Sept.

1.5 ha (59 pitches) flat, grassy

Tariff : 29.50 € ♣ ♣ ⇔ 回 ⁇ (6A) – Extra per person 5.90 € – Reservation fee 17 €

Rental rates : (from mid April to mid Sept.) ✈ – 4 🚐 – 3 🏠 – 2 canvas bungalows – 2 tent lodges. Per night from 44 to 107€ – Per week from 249 to 746€ – Reservation fee 17€

Surroundings : 🏕 ♤♤
Leisure activities : 🏖 🚣 🚴 ⛵
Facilities : & ⚬━ 🛁 🍴 🔳 refrigerators

GPS Longitude : -1.08262
Latitude : 45.37602

⚠ Le Mérin

📞 05 56 41 78 64. www.campinglemerin.com

Address : 7 route du Mérin (3.7km northwest along the D 102, follow the signs for Montalivet and take road to the left)

3.5 ha (165 pitches)
Rentals : 12 🚐 – 3 🏠 .

Surroundings : 🌿 🏕 ♤♤
Leisure activities : 🚣
Facilities : ⚬━ 🍴 🔳

GPS Longitude : -1.09932
Latitude : 45.36703

VENSAC

33590 – Michelin map **335** E2 – pop. 854 – alt. 5
▶ Paris 528 – Bordeaux 82 – Lesparre-Médoc 14 – Soulac-sur-Mer 18

⚑ Les Acacias

📞 05 56 09 58 81. www.les-acacias-du-medoc.fr

Address : 44 route de St-Vivien (located 1.5km northeast along the N 215, follow the signs for Verdon-sur-Mer and take the road to the right)

Opening times : from end March to end Oct.

3.5 ha (236 pitches)

Tariff : (2015 price) 30€ ♟♟ 🚗 🔳 ⚡ (6A) – Extra per person 5.20€
Rental rates : (2015 price) (from end March to end Oct.) – 60 🚐.
Per night from 49 to 130€ – Per week from 343 to 910€

Mostly shady pitches and high-quality rental accommodation.

Surroundings : 🌿 🏕 ♤♤
Leisure activities : 🍴 🍽 🏖 🌙nighttime 🚣 ⛵ ⛴
Facilities : & ⚬━ 🆑 🛁 🚿 🍴 launderette 🅿

GPS Longitude : -1.03252
Latitude : 45.40887

LE-VERDON-SUR-MER

33123 – Michelin map **335** E2 – pop. 1 334 – alt. 3
▶ Paris 514 – Bordeaux 100 – La Rochelle 80

⚑ Sunêlia La Pointe du Médoc ♠♠

📞 05 56 73 39 99. www.camping-lapointedumedoc.com

Address : 18 rue Ausone (follow signs for the Pointe de Grave – the tip of the Médoc Peninsula – along the D 1215 and turn right)

Opening times : from beginning April to mid Sept.

6.5 ha (260 pitches) terraced, flat, sandy

Tariff : 28€ ♟♟ 🚗 🔳 ⚡ (10A) – Extra per person 6€ – Reservation fee 10€
Rental rates : (from beginning April to mid Sept.) & (1 mobile home) – 119 🚐 – 31 🏠 – 2 tent lodges. Per night from 46 to 180€ – Per week from 322 to 1 260€ – Reservation fee 30€

🚏 47 🔳 18€

Surroundings : 🌿 🏕 ♤
Leisure activities : 🍴 🍽 🏖 🌙 🏹 hammam, jacuzzi 🚣 🚴 ⛵ ⛴ multi-sports ground, entertainment room
Facilities : & ⚬━ 🛁 🚿 🍴 launderette 🛒

GPS Longitude : -1.07965
Latitude : 45.54557

VÉZAC

24220 – Michelin map **329** I6 – pop. 617 – alt. 90
▶ Paris 535 – Bergerac 65 – Brive-la-Gaillarde 60 – Fumel 53

⚑ Les Deux Vallées

📞 05 53 29 53 55. www.campingles2vallees.com

Address : at La Gare (to the west, behind the old station; beside a small lake)

Opening times : from mid March to mid Oct.

2.5 ha (110 pitches) flat, grassy

Tariff : (2015 price) 30.60€ ♟♟ 🚗 🔳 ⚡ (10A) – Extra per person 7.70€ – Reservation fee 16€
Rental rates : (2015 price) (from mid March to end Oct.) – 19 🚐 – 8 tent lodges – 2 gîtes. Per night from 35 to 132 € – Reservation fee 16€

🚏 local sani-station – 4 🔳

An uninterrupted view of the Château de Beynac from some pitches.

Surroundings : 🌿 ⚘ 🏕 ♤♤
Leisure activities : 🍴 🍽 🏖 🚣 🚴 ⛵ ⛴
Facilities : & ⚬━ ▥ 🛁 🍴 launderette 🅿 refrigerators

GPS Longitude : 1.15844
Latitude : 44.83542

> **Key to rentals symbols:**
>
> 12 🚐   *Number of mobile homes*
> 20 🏠   *Number of chalets*
> 6 🛏   *Number of rooms to rent*
> Per night   *Minimum/maximum rate per night*
> 30–50€
> Per week   *Minimum/maximum rate per week*
> 300–1,000€

VIELLE-ST-GIRONS

40560 – Michelin map **335** D11 – pop. 1 160 – alt. 27
▶ Paris 719 – Castets 16 – Dax 37 – Mimizan 32

⚑ Sunêlia Le Col Vert ♠♠

Sunêlia Le Col Vert

📞 08 90 71 00 01. www.colvert.com

Address : 1548 route de l'Étang (5.5km south along the D 652; beside the Étang de Léon – lake)

Opening times : from beginning April to mid Sept.

24 ha (800 pitches)

Tariff : 40.20€ ♟♟ 🚗 🔳 ⚡ (6A) – Extra per person 7.60€ – Reservation fee 30€

Rental rates : (from beginning April to mid Sept.) & (1 mobile home) – 329 🚐 – 34 🏠 – 20 canvas bungalows – 18 tent lodges. Per night from 22 to 120€ – Per week from 154 to 1,036 € – Reservation fee 33€

🚏 local sani-station 3€ – 25 🔳 14€ – 🚐14€

Choose pitches near the lake. Free shuttle bus to St-Girons-Plage during season.

Surroundings : 🏕 ♤♤ ⛰
Leisure activities : 🍴 🍽 🏖 🌙 🏹 🎣 🎯 hammam, jacuzzi 🚣 🚴 🎾 ⛵ ⛴ ⛴ disco 🎿 multi-sports ground, spa centre
Facilities : & ⚬━ 🆑 🛁 – 10 private sanitary facilities (🚿 💧wc) 🛒 🚿 🍴 launderette 🛒 🅿 refrigerated food storage facilities
Nearby : 🏇 🚴 🐎 ⚓ boats to hire

GPS Longitude : -1.30946
Latitude : 43.90416

VIEUX-BOUCAU-LES-BAINS

40480 – Michelin map **335** C12 – pop. 1 577 – alt. 5
▶ Paris 740 – Bayonne 41 – Biarritz 48 – Castets 28

⚠ Municipal les Sablères

🔗 05 58 48 12 29. www.camping-les-sableres.com

Address : boulevard du Marensin (to the northwest, 250m from the beach (direct access)

Opening times : from end March to mid Oct.

11 ha (517 pitches)

Tariff : (2015 price) 24.10€ ♣♣ ⇌ 🖹 (⨍) (10A) – Extra per person 4.60€ – Reservation fee 20€

Rental rates : (2015 price) (from end March to mid Oct.) – 7 ⏚ – 11 🏠 – 2 tent lodges. Per night from 76 to 162€ – Per week from 190 to 896€ – Reservation fee 20€

Pitches near the sand dune have little shade.

Surroundings : ♀
Leisure activities : 🏊 multi-sports ground
Facilities : 🚿 ⚟ 🐕 🧺 launderette, refrigerated food storage facilities
Nearby : 🍺 🍴 ✕ 🍽

Longitude : -1.40596
Latitude : 43.79326

VILLERÉAL

47210 – Michelin map **336** G2 – pop. 1 286 – alt. 103
▶ Paris 566 – Agen 61 – Bergerac 35 – Cahors 76

⛰ Yelloh! Village Le Château de Fonrives ♣♣

🔗 05 53 36 63 38. www.campingchateaufonrives.com

Address : route d'Issigeac, at Rives (2.2km northwest along the D 207 and take the turning to the left, by the château)

Opening times : from mid April to mid Sept.

20 ha/10 for camping (370 pitches) terraced, relatively flat, flat, grassy, stony, pond, wood

Tariff : (2015 price) 18€ ♣♣ ⇌ 🖹 (⨍) (10A) – Extra per person 8€
Rental rates : (from mid April to mid Sept.) – 160 ⏚ – 22 🏠. Per night from 39 to 240 € – Per week from 273 to 1,680 €
⏚ 6 🖹 18€
Large green spaces surrounded by hazel trees; ideal for relaxation and sporting activities around the chateau.

Surroundings : 🌲 ⛱ ♀♀
Leisure activities : 🍺 ✕ 🎬 🎯 🏹 ♨ ⛵ jacuzzi 🏊 🚲 🍽 🎣 🏓 ⚾ sports trail
Facilities : 🚿 ⚟ 🐕 🧺 launderette ⚡ 🐕 tourist information

Longitude : 0.7314
Latitude : 44.65739

⛰ Sites et Paysages Fontaine du Roc

🔗 05 53 36 08 16. www.fontaineduroc.com

Address : at Dévillac (7.5km southeast along the D 255 and take the turning to the left)

Opening times : from beginning April to end Oct.

2 ha (60 pitches) flat, grassy

Tariff : ♣ 6€ ⇌ 🖹 8€ – (⨍) (10A) 4.50€
Rental rates : (from beginning April to end Oct.) 🚿 – 4 ⏚ – 3 🏠. Per night from 50 to 120 € – Per week from 350 to 665 €
⏚ local sani-station – 🚐 (⨍)11€

Pitches are well marked-out and have shade; a panoramic view of Biron chateau from the entrance.

Surroundings : 🌲 ⛱ ♀♀
Leisure activities : 🎬 🏹 ♨ jacuzzi 🏊 🎣
Facilities : 🚿 ⚟ 🐕 🧺 launderette

Longitude : 0.8187
Latitude : 44.61414

VITRAC

24200 – Michelin map **329** I7 – pop. 870 – alt. 150
▶ Paris 541 – Brive-la-Gaillarde 64 – Cahors 54 – Gourdon 23

⛰ Domaine Soleil Plage ♣♣

🔗 05 53 28 33 33. www.soleilplage.fr

Address : at Caudon (beside the Dordogne river)

Opening times : from beginning April to end Sept.

8 ha/5 for camping flat, grassy

Tariff : 40€ ♣♣ ⇌ 🖹 (⨍) (16A) – Extra per person 9€ – Reservation fee 39.50€

Rental rates : (from beginning April to end Sept.) 🅿 – 80 ⏚ – 20 🏠. Per night from 51 to 218 € – Per week from 330 to 1,490€ – Reservation fee 39.50€

⏚ AireService sani-station 3€ – 10 🖹 18€

Pitches near the river and luxury rentals around the lovely restored former farmhouse.

Surroundings : 🌲 ⛱ ♀♀
Leisure activities : 🍺 ✕ 🎬 🎯 🏹 🏊 🍽 🏓 🎣 ⚾ (beach) ♨ 🛶 🚣 multi-sports ground
Facilities : 🚿 ⚟ 🆑 🚻 🐕 🧺 launderette ⚡ 🐕

Longitude : 1.25374
Latitude : 44.82387

⛰ La Bouysse de Caudon

🔗 05 53 28 33 05. www.labouysse.com

Address : at Caudon (2.5km east, near the Dordogne river)

Opening times : from beginning April to mid Sept.

6 ha/3 for camping (160 pitches) flat, grassy, walnut trees

Tariff : (2015 price) ♣ 6.80€ ⇌ 🖹 8.70€ – (⨍) (10A) 4.90€ – Reservation fee 20€

Rental rates : (2015 price) (from beginning April to mid Sept.) 🚿 🅿 – 4 ⏚ – 9 🏠 – 4 apartments – 2 gîtes. Per week from 270 to 830 €

⏚ local sani-station 3€

Pitches near the Dordogne river enjoy lots of shade.

Surroundings : 🌲 ⛱ ♀♀
Leisure activities : 🍺 🏊 🍽 🎣 ⚾ (beach) 🛶 🚣
Facilities : 🚿 ⚟ 🐕 🧺 launderette ⚡ 🐕 refrigerators

Longitude : 1.25063
Latitude : 44.82357

Michelin classification:

⛰ Extremely comfortable, equipped to a very high standard
⛰ Very comfortable, equipped to a high standard
⛰ Comfortable and well equipped
⛰ Reasonably comfortable
⛰ Satisfactory

AUVERGNE

G. Labriet / Photononstop

Shhh! Don't wake the volcanoes. They are the giant sleeping beauties of the Auvergne, a stunning region at the heart of France. Dormant for several millennia, they form a natural barrier that keeps them secure from any encroachment by man. If you listen very carefully, you may just make out a distant rumble from Vulcania, the interactive and educational European Park of Volcanism, where you can learn all you could possibly want to know about volcanoes. The region's domes and peaks, sculpted by volcanic fire, are the source of countless mountain springs that cascade down the steep slopes into brooks, rivers and crystal-clear lakes. Renowned for the therapeutic qualities of its waters, the Auvergne has long played host to well-heeled visitors at its elegant spa resorts, but many find it simply impossible to follow doctor's orders when faced with the tempting aroma of an Auvergne country stew, a savoury *Pounti* cake or a full-bodied Cantal cheese!

ABREST

03200 – Michelin map **326** H6 – pop. 2 696 – alt. 290
▶ Paris 361 – Clermont-Ferrand 70 – Moulins 63 – Montluçon 94

🏕 La Croix St-Martin 👥

☎ 04 70 32 67 74. www.camping-vichy.com

Address : 99 avenue des Graviers (to the north, near the Allier)

Opening times : from beginning April to end Sept.

3 ha (89 pitches) flat, grassy

Tariff : (2015 price) ♣ 5.20€ ⇌ 🔲 6.30€ – 🔌 (10A) 3.70€ –
Reservation fee 5€

Rental rates : (2015 price) (from beginning April to end Sept.) –
20 🚐. Per night from 42 to 63€ – Per week from 480 to 620€ –
Reservation fee 5€

🚽 local sani-station 5€

*Shaded pitches beside a walking and cycling path that follows
the Allier river.*

Surroundings : 🌲 🚡 🎢
Leisure activities : 🎦 🏋 🛶 ⛴ 🏊 fitness
trail, bikepark 🚵
Facilities : 🚿 🔌 ♨ 🚻 launderette 🧺
Nearby : 🎣

Longitude : 3.44012
Latitude : 46.10819

ALLEYRAS

43580 – Michelin map **331** E4 – pop. 173 – alt. 779
▶ Paris 549 – Brioude 71 – Langogne 43 – Le Puy-en-Velay 32

🏕 Municipal Au Fil de l'Eau

☎ 04 71 57 56 86. www.camping-municipal.alleyras.fr – alt. 660

Address : Le Pont-d'Alleyras (2.5km to the northwest, direct access
to the Allier)

0.9 ha (60 pitches) flat and relatively flat
Rentals : 6 huts (without sanitary facilities).

Surroundings : 🌲 ⬅
Leisure activities : 🛶
Facilities : 🚿 🔌 launderette
Nearby : 🏊 🎣

Longitude : 3.67005
Latitude : 44.91786

*This guide is not intended as a list of all the camping
sites in France; its aim is to provide a selection of the
best sites in each category.*

AMBERT

63600 – Michelin map **326** J9 – pop. 6 962 – alt. 535
▶ Paris 438 – Brioude 63 – Clermont-Ferrand 77 – Montbrison 47

🏕 Municipal Les Trois Chênes

☎ 04 73 82 34 68. www.camping-ambert.com

Address : route du Puy (located 1.5km south along the D 906, follow
the signs for La Chaise-Dieu; near the Dore river)

Opening times : from end April to end Sept.

3 ha (120 pitches) flat, grassy

Tariff : 17.75€ ♣♣ ⇌ 🔲 🔌 (10A) – Extra per person 3.60€

Rental rates : permanent – 18 🏡. Per night from 80 to 173€ –
Per week from 275 to 715€

🚽 Raclet sani-station 2€ – 10 🔲 17.75€

*In a pleasant leafy setting but choose those pitches furthest
away from the road.*

Surroundings : ⬅ 🚡 🎢
Leisure activities : 🎦 🛶
Facilities : 🚿 🔌 ♨ 🚻 launderette
Nearby : 🏊 ♟ 🎣 🚣 🎿 🏄 🛶 🎣
fitness trail

Longitude : 3.7291
Latitude : 45.53953

ARNAC

15150 – Michelin map **330** B4 – pop. 148 – alt. 620
▶ Paris 541 – Argentat 38 – Aurillac 35 – Mauriac 36

🏕 Village Vacances La Gineste
(rental of mobile homes and chalets only)

☎ 04 71 62 91 90. www.village-vacances-cantal.com

Address : at La Gineste (3km northwest along the D 61, follow the
signs for Pleaux then continue 1.2km along the road to the right)

Opening times : permanent

3 ha terraced

Rental rates : 🅿 – 60 🚐 – 40 🏡. Per week from 340 to 625€
Reservation fee 15€

🚽 Eurorelais sani-station 2€ – 2 🔲

A pleasant location on a peninsula in the Lac de Enchanet.

Surroundings : 🌲 ⬅ 🚡 ♟
Leisure activities : ♟ 🍴 🎦 🎣 🛶 🎿 🏄
🏊 (beach) 🐎
Facilities : 🔌 🚻 🔲 🏊 🧺
Nearby : watersports centre

Longitude : 2.2121
Latitude : 45.08285

*The classification (1 to 5 tents, **black** or red) that we
award to selected sites in this guide is our own system.
It should not be confused with the classification
(1 to 5 stars) of official organisations.*

ARPAJON-SUR-CÈRE

15130 – Michelin map **330** C5 – pop. 6 009 – alt. 613
▶ Paris 559 – Argentat 56 – Aurillac 5 – Maurs 44

🏕 La Cère

☎ 04 71 64 55 07. www.camping.caba.fr

Address : south of the town, access via the D 920, opposite the Esso
service station; beside the river

Opening times : from beginning June to end Sept.

2 ha (78 pitches) flat, grassy

Tariff : (2015 price) 14.50€ ♣♣ ⇌ 🔲 🔌 (10A) –
Extra per person 4.70€

Rental rates : (2015 price) (from beginning June to end Sept.) –
10 🚐. Per week from 264 to 500€

A wooded setting and a well-kept site.

Surroundings : 🚡 ♟
Leisure activities : 🎦 🛶 🚲 🏊
Facilities : 🚿 🔌 🚻 🔲
Nearby : 🛒 ⚔

Longitude : 2.46246
Latitude : 44.89858

AURILLAC

15000 – Michelin map **330** C5 – pop. 28 207 – alt. 610
▶ Paris 557 – Brive-la-Gaillarde 98 – Clermont-Ferrand 158 – Montauban 174

⚠ Municipal l'Ombrade

✆ 04 71 48 28 87. www.camping.caba.fr

Address : head 1km north along the D 17 and take r. du Gué-Bouliaga to the right; on both sides of the Jordanne

Opening times : from mid June to mid Sept..

7.5 ha (200 pitches) flat, grassy

Tariff : (2015 price) 13 € ♣♣ ⇔ 🔲 🔌 (10A) – Extra per person 4.70 €
🚐 local sani-station – 35 🔲 12.10 €

Surroundings : 🌳🌳	
Leisure activities : 🏛 🚴	**G P S** Longitude : 2.4559
Facilities : 🔥 ⚡ 🌿 🚿 🍴 📶 🍽	Latitude : 44.93562
Nearby : 🛒	

AYDAT

63970 – Michelin map **326** E9 – pop. 2 122 – alt. 850
▶ Paris 438 – La Bourboule 33 – Clermont-Ferrand 21 – Issoire 38

⚠ Lac d'Aydat

✆ 04 73 79 38 09. www.camping-lac-aydat.com

Address : beside the lake, Foret du lot (head 2km northeast along the D 90 and take the road to the right; near the lake)

Opening times : from beginning April to end Sept.

7 ha (150 pitches) terraced, flat, grassy, stony

Tariff : (2015 price) ♣ 6 € ⇔ 2.50 € 🔲 16 € – 🔌 (15A) 6 € – Reservation fee 20 €
Rental rates : (2015 price) permanent 🔥 (1 chalet) – 53 🚐 – 17 🏠. Per night from 50 to 110 € – Per week from 350 to 770 € – Reservation fee 20 €
🚐 5 🔲 16 €

Situated beside a lake, on an undulating and very wooded site.

Surroundings : 🌊 🌳🌳	
Leisure activities : 🏛 ☑ 🏊 🎣	**G P S** Longitude : 2.98907
Facilities : 🔥 ⚡ 🌿 🍴 launderette	Latitude : 45.66903
Nearby : 🚣 📷 🚤 🚴 🏖 (beach) 🎿 🍴 forest trail	

BAGNOLS

63810 – Michelin map **326** C9 – pop. 496 – alt. 862
▶ Paris 483 – Bort-les-Orgues 19 – La Bourboule 23 – Bourg-Lastic 38

⚠ Municipal la Thialle

✆ 04 73 22 28 00. www.bagnols63.fr

Address : route de St-Donat (take southeastern exit along the D 25; beside the Thialle river)

Opening times : permanent

2.8 ha (70 pitches)

Tariff : 19 € ♣♣ ⇔ 🔲 🔌 (10A) – Extra per person 4.20 €
Rental rates : permanent 🔥 (1 mobile home) – 8 🏠. Per night from 40 to 57 € – Per week from 241 to 557 €
🚐 local sani-station – 6 🔲 13 €

Surroundings : 🌊 🏞 🌳	
Leisure activities : 🏛 🏊 🎣 🏓 🔲 (open air in season)	**G P S** Longitude : 2.63466
Facilities : 🔥 ⚡ (season) 🌿 📶 🍴 launderette	Latitude : 45.49758
Nearby : 🎿 🍴 🍽	

BELLERIVE-SUR-ALLIER

03700 – Michelin map **326** H6 – pop. 8 530 – alt. 340
▶ Paris 357 – Clermont-Ferrand 53 – Moulins 58 – Saint-Étienne 147

⛰ Club Airotel Beau Rivage et les Isles 👥

✆ 04 70 32 26 85. www.camping-beaurivage.com

Address : rue Claude Decloître

Opening times : from beginning April to mid Oct.

7 ha (143 pitches) flat, grassy, fine gravel

Tariff : (2015 price) 20 € ♣♣ ⇔ 🔲 🔌 (10A) – Extra per person 6 € – Reservation fee 5 €
Rental rates : (2015 price) (from beginning April to mid Oct.) 🔥 (1 mobile home) – 31 🚐 – 4 🏠 – 2 apartments. Per night from 38 to 75 € – Per week from 266 to 469 € – Reservation fee 15 €
🚐 local sani-station 10 €

The site is in two sections, with shaded pitches beside the Allier river, facing the Vichy parkland on the opposite bank.

Surroundings : 🌊 🏞 🌳🌳	
Leisure activities : 🍴 ✕ 🏛 ☑ 🏃 🏊 🎣 🚴 🔲 (open air in season) 🎿 pedalos, archery 🦋 entertainment room	**G P S** Longitude : 3.43192
Facilities : 🔥 ⚡ 📶 🌿 🚿 🍴 launderette	Latitude : 46.11482
Nearby : 🏊	

This guide is updated regularly, so buy your new copy every year!

BILLOM

63160 – Michelin map **326** H8 – pop. 4 637 – alt. 340
▶ Paris 437 – Clermont-Ferrand 28 – Cunlhat 30 – Issoire 31

⚠ Municipal le Colombier

✆ 04 73 68 91 50. www.billom.fr

Address : rue Carnot (To the northeast of the town, follow the signs for Lezoux)

1 ha (38 pitches)

Rentals : 12 🏠.

The well-marked out pitches are shaded and the chalet village has a pretty view.

Surroundings : 🌊 🏞 🌳🌳	
Leisure activities : 🏛 🏊	**G P S** Longitude : 3.3459
Facilities : 🔥 ⚡ 🍴 launderette	Latitude : 45.72839
Nearby : ✕ 🎿 🏊	

LA BOURBOULE

63150 – Michelin map **326** D9 – pop. 1 961 – alt. 880 – ♨
▶ Paris 469 – Aubusson 82 – Clermont-Ferrand 50 – Mauriac 71

⛰ Les Clarines

✆ 04 73 81 02 30. www.camping-les-clarines.com

Address : 1424 avenue du Maréchal Leclerc

Opening times : from mid Dec. to mid Oct.

3.75 ha (187 pitches) terraced, relatively flat, flat, grassy, fine gravel

Tariff : (2015 price) 21.70 € ♣♣ ⇔ 🔲 🔌 (10A) – Extra per person 4.85 €
Rental rates : (2015 price) (from mid Dec. to mid Oct.) – 30 🚐 – 1 gîte. Per night from 42 to 81 € – Per week from 252 to 686 €
🚐 local sani-station 5 € – 10 🔲 10 €

A free shuttle to the spa and a bus to the ski resorts.

Surroundings : ❄ ♤♤
Leisure activities : 🏠 🚣 ⛷ mountain bike trail
Facilities : ⊶ ▥ ♨ ⛺ launderette

GPS
Longitude : 2.76222
Latitude : 45.59463

🏔 Flower Les Vernières

📞 04 73 81 10 20. www.camping-la-bourboule.fr

Address : avenue du Maréchal de Lattre-de-Tassigny (take the eastern exit along the D 130, follow the signs for Le Mont-Dore; near the Dordogne)

Opening times : permanent

1.5 ha (174 pitches) terrace, flat, grassy

Tariff : 24€ ✹✹ 🚐 ▣ ⚡ (10A) – Extra per person 4.50€

Rental rates : permanent – 5 🏠 – 1 yurt – 6 tent lodges. Per night from 30 to 95€ – Per week from 190 to 640€

🚐 local sani-station – 30 ▣ 15€ – ⛟⚡15€

Very varied rental accommodation and plenty of green space. Choose the pitches furthest away from the road if possible.

Surroundings : 🖵 ♤♤
Leisure activities : ⛲ 🏠 🚶 ⛵ hammam 🚣
Facilities : ♿ ⊶ ▥ ⛺ launderette
Nearby : 🍴 🎣 ⛷

GPS
Longitude : 2.75285
Latitude : 45.58943

BRIOUDE

43100 – Michelin map **331** C2 – pop. 6 688 – alt. 427
▶ Paris 487 – Clermont-Ferrand 71 – Le Puy-en-Velay 59 – Aurillac 105

🏔 Aquadis Loisirs La Bageasse

📞 04 71 50 07 70. http://www.aquadis-loisirs.com/camping-la-bageasse/

Opening times : from beginning March to beginning Nov.

2.5 ha (49 pitches) terraced, flat, grassy

Tariff : 17.20€ ✹✹ 🚐 ▣ ⚡ (10A) – Extra per person 4.60€ – Reservation fee 10€

Rental rates : (from beginning March to beginning Nov.) ♿ (1 chalet) – 4 🚐 – 15 🏠. Per night from 60 to 78€ – Per week from 189 to 599€ – Reservation fee 20€

🚐 AireService sani-station – ⛟11€

A pleasant site near the river.

Surroundings : 🖵 ♤♤
Leisure activities : ⛲ 🍴
Facilities : ♿ ⊶ ▣ 🚿 ⛺ launderette
Nearby : 🎣

GPS
Longitude : 3.40479
Latitude : 45.28123

LA CHAISE-DIEU

43160 – Michelin map **331** E2 – pop. 730 – alt. 1 080
▶ Paris 503 – Ambert 29 – Brioude 35 – Issoire 59

🏔 Municipal les Prades

📞 04 71 00 07 88. lcdmairie@wanadoo.fr

Address : situated 2km northeast along the D 906, follow the signs for Ambert, near the small lake at La Tour (direct access)

Opening times : from beginning June to end Sept.

3 ha (100 pitches) relatively flat, grassy

Tariff : (2015 price) 11€ ✹✹ 🚐 ▣ ⚡ (10A) – Extra per person 3.50€

🚐 local sani-station – ⛟⚡15.50€

Surroundings : ♤♤
Leisure activities : 🚣
Facilities : ♿ ⊶ 🚿 ⛺ 🔲
Nearby : 🎿 🏊 🐎

GPS
Longitude : 3.70496
Latitude : 45.33321

CHAMBON-SUR-LAC

63790 – Michelin map **326** E9 – pop. 352 – alt. 885 – Winter sports : 1 150/1 760 m
▶ Paris 456 – Clermont-Ferrand 37 – Condat 39 – Issoire 32

🏔 Yelloh! Village Le Pré Bas ♤♟

Yelloh! Village Le Pré Bas

📞 04 73 88 63 04. www.campingauvergne.com

Address : near the lake (direct access)

Opening times : from end April to mid Sept.

3.8 ha (180 pitches)

Tariff : 38€ ✹✹ 🚐 ▣ ⚡ (6A) – Extra per person 7€

Rental rates : (from end April to mid Sept.) ♿ (1 mobile home) – 109 🚐 – 2 gîtes. Per night from 39 to 169€ – Per week from 273 to 1,183€

🚐 local sani-station – 30 ▣ 38€

Good activities for young children, some indoors.

Surroundings : 🏞 🖵 ♀
Leisure activities : ⛲ 🍴 🏠 🎮 🚶 ⛵ hammam, jacuzzi 🚣 🎣 🏊 spa centre, entertainment room
Facilities : ♿ ⊶ ▥ ⛺ launderette 🚿
Nearby : 🏊 (beach) 🚣 🦆 pedalos

GPS
Longitude : 2.91427
Latitude : 45.57516

🏔 Les Bombes

📞 04 73 88 64 03. www.camping-les-bombes.com

Address : chemin de Pétary (east of Chambon-sur-Lac, head towards Murol and take a right turn; beside the Couze de Chambon river)

Opening times : from mid April to mid Sept.

5 ha (150 pitches) flat, grassy

Tariff : ✹ 15.20€ 🚐 ▣ – ⚡ (10A) 4.70€ – Reservation fee 13€

Rental rates : (from mid April to mid Sept.) – 2 caravans – 3 🚐 – 15 🏠 – 3 canvas bungalows. Per night from 42 to 67€ – Per week from 185 to 740€ – Reservation fee 13€

🚐 Flot Bleu sani-station – 30 ▣ 7€

A variety of rental options with lots of green space, ideal for relaxation.

Surroundings : 🏞 ♀
Leisure activities : ⛲ 🍴 🏠 🚣 🚲 🎣 ⛷
Facilities : ♿ ⊶ 🚿 ⛺ launderette 🚿

GPS
Longitude : 2.90188
Latitude : 45.56994

Key to rentals symbols:

12 🚐	*Number of mobile homes*	
20 🏠	*Number of chalets*	
6 🛏	*Number of rooms to rent*	
Per night 30–50€	*Minimum/maximum rate per night*	
Per week 300–1,000€	*Minimum/maximum rate per week*	

⛰ Serrette

☎ 04 73 88 67 67. www.campingdeserrette.com – alt. 1.000

Address : 2.5km west along the D 996, follow the signs for Le Mont-Dore and take the D 636 (to the left), follow the signs for Chambon-des-Neiges

Opening times : from end April to mid Sept.

2 ha (75 pitches) terraced, flat and relatively flat, stony, grassy

Tariff : 25.10€ ♦♦ ⇔ 📧 ⚡ (10A) – Extra per person 5€ – Reservation fee 12€

Rental rates : (from end April to mid Sept.) ♿ (1 chalet) – 11 🚐 – 3 🏠. Per night from 35 to 65€ – Per week from 550 to 750€ – Reservation fee 12€

Surroundings : ⛵ ≼ Lac Chambon and the Château de Murol ♀	**G P S**	Longitude : 2.89105
Leisure activities : 🍴 ✕ 🏠 🛝 🖼 (open air in season)		Latitude : 45.57099
Facilities : ♿ ⊶ 🚽 launderette 🚿		

LE CHAMBON-SUR-LIGNON

43400 – Michelin map **331** H3 – pop. 2 690 – alt. 967

▶ Paris 573 – Annonay 48 – Lamastre 32 – Le Puy-en-Velay 45

⛰ Les Hirondelles

☎ 04 66 14 02 70. www.campingleshirondelles.fr – alt. 1 000

Address : route de la Suchère (located 1km south along the D 151 and turn left onto D 7)

Opening times : from mid June to beginning Sept.

1 ha (45 pitches) flat, grassy

Tariff : 15.95€ ♦♦ ⇔ 📧 ⚡ (6A) – Extra per person 4.50€

Rental rates : (from mid April to beginning Nov.) 🚿 – 4 🏠. Per night from 35 to 70€ – Per week from 240 to 485€

🚐 10 📧 15.95€

In a pleasant setting overlooking the village.

Surroundings : ⛵ ≼ ⊏ ♀♀	**G P S**	Longitude : 4.2986
Leisure activities : 🍴 🏠 🛝 🚣		Latitude : 45.05436
Facilities : ♿ ⊶ 🚿 🖼 🚿		
At the river : 🎣 ✕ 🖼 🚣 🐎 sports trail		

⛰ Le Lignon

☎ 04 71 59 72 86. contact@campingdulignon.com – alt. 1 000

Address : route du Stade (take the southwestern exit along the D 15, follow the signs for Mazet-sur-Voy and take a right turn before the bridge, near the river)

2 ha (130 pitches) flat, grassy
Rentals : 5 🚐.

Surroundings : ♀ ⛰	**G P S**	Longitude : 4.29686
Leisure activities : 🏠 🚣 🚲		Latitude : 45.05944
Facilities : ♿ ⊶ 🚽 🚿 🖼		
At the river : 🎣 ✕ 🖼 🚣 🐎 sports trail		

CHAMPAGNAC-LE-VIEUX

43440 – Michelin map **331** D1 – pop. 234 – alt. 880

▶ Paris 486 – Brioude 16 – La Chaise-Dieu 25 – Clermont-Ferrand 76

⛰ Le Chanterelle

☎ 04 71 76 34 00. www.champagnac.com

Address : Le Prat Barrat (1.4km north along the D 5, follow the signs for Auzon, and take the road to the right)

Opening times : from mid April to mid Oct.

4 ha (90 pitches) terraced, flat, grassy

Tariff : (2015 price) ♦ 4€ ⇔ 2.70€ 📧 6.20€ – ⚡ (10A) 10€

Rental rates : (2015 price) (from mid April to mid Oct.) – 4 🚐 – 20 🏠 – 8 canvas bungalows – 4 tent lodges. Per night from 40 to 114€ – Per week from 240 to 798€ – Reservation fee 16€

A lush, green site near a lake.

Surroundings : ⛵ ♀♀	**G P S**	Longitude : 3.50575
Leisure activities : 🛶 🚣 🚲		Latitude : 45.3657
Facilities : ♿ ⊶ 🖼 🚿 🚽 launderette		
Nearby : 🍴 ✕ 🚤 (beach) 🎣 🐎 fitness trail		

CHAMPS-SUR-TARENTAINE

15270 – Michelin map **330** D2 – pop. 1 035 – alt. 450

▶ Paris 500 – Aurillac 90 – Clermont-Ferrand 82 – Condat 24

⛰ Les Chalets de l'Eau Verte
(rental of rooms and chalets only)

☎ 04 71 78 78 78. www.auvergne-chalets.fr

Address : Le Jagounet

Opening times : permanent

8 ha relatively flat

Rental rates : 🅿 – 10 🏠 – 3 🛏. Per night from 42 to 116€ – Per week from 294 to 812€ – Reservation fee 10€

There is a 2-night minimum stay in low season.

Surroundings : ⛵	**G P S**	Longitude : 2.63853
Leisure activities : 🏠		Latitude : 45.40595
Facilities : ⊶ 🚽 🖼		
Nearby : ✕ 🚤 ♨ 🐎		

CHÂTELGUYON

63140 – Michelin map **326** F7 – pop. 6 223 – alt. 430 – ♨

▶ Paris 411 – Aubusson 93 – Clermont-Ferrand 21 – Gannat 31

⛰ Le Ranch des Volcans 👥

☎ 04 73 86 02 47. www.ranchdesvolcans.com

Address : route de la Piscine (take southeastern exit along the D 985, follow the signs for Riom)

Opening times : from mid March to end Oct.

4 ha (285 pitches)

Tariff : (2015 price) 25.50€ ♦♦ ⇔ 📧 ⚡ (10A) – Extra per person 4.50€

Rental rates : (from mid March to end Oct.) – 2 caravans – 35 🚐 – 2 🏠 – 3 tipis. Per night from 60 to 125€ – Per week from 250 to 660€ – Reservation fee 10€

🚐 22 📧 14.50€

Surroundings : ♀♀	**G P S**	Longitude : 3.07732
Leisure activities : 🍴 ✕ 🏠 🛝 🚶 🚣 🚲 ♨		Latitude : 45.91491
Facilities : ♿ ⊶ 🚿 🚽 launderette 🚿		

⛰ La Croze

☎ 04 73 86 08 27. www.campingcroze.com

Address : at St-Hippolyte, route de Mozac (located 1km southeast along the D 227, follow the signs for Riom)

3.7 ha (98 pitches) terraced, relatively flat, flat, grassy
Rentals : ♿ (1 chalet) – 17 🚐 – 9 🏠.

There is a shuttle bus to the spa centre.

Surroundings : ⛵ ♀♀	**G P S**	Longitude : 3.06083
Leisure activities : ✕ 🚣 🛝		Latitude : 45.90589
Facilities : ♿ ⊶ 🚿 🚽 launderette		

CHAUDES-AIGUES

15110 – Michelin map **330** G5 – pop. 940 – alt. 750 – ☘
▶ Paris 538 – Aurillac 94 – Entraygues-sur-Truyère 62 – Espalion 54

⚠ Le Château du Couffour

⌕ 04 71 23 57 08. www.camping-chaudes-aigues.fr – alt. 900

Address : at the stadium (situated 2km south along the D 921, follow the signs for Laguiole then take the road to the right)

2.5 ha (90 pitches) flat, grassy

Located high up, in the heart of the countryside.

Surroundings : ⊗ ≤ ♀
Leisure activities : 🏛 🚴
Facilities : ♿ ☕ ⊞ ⁱ 🚿
Nearby : 🚴 ⛵ climbing, casino

GPS Longitude : 3.00071
Latitude : 44.8449

COURNON-D'AUVERGNE

63800 – Michelin map **326** G8 – pop. 19 494 – alt. 380
▶ Paris 422 – Clermont-Ferrand 12 – Issoire 31 – Le Mont-Dore 54

⛰ Municipal le Pré des Laveuses

⌕ 04 73 84 81 30. www.cournon-auvergne.fr/camping

Address : rue des Laveuses (head 1.5km east via road to Billom and take the beach road to the left)

Opening times : from beginning April to mid Oct.

5 ha (145 pitches)

Tariff : (2015 price) 24.70€ ✚✚ ⊞ 🔌 (10A) –
Extra per person 5.70€

Rental rates : (2015 price) permanent ♿ (2 chalets) – 15 🚐 – 18 🏠 – 12 canvas bungalows. Per night from 54 to 115€ – Per week from 190 to 648€

🚿 Flot Bleu sani-station – 10 ▣

Near a small artificial lake and the Allier river.

Surroundings : ⊗ ♀♀ ⚠
Leisure activities : 🍴✕ 🏛 🚴 ✖ 🏊
Facilities : ♿ ☕ ⊞ ⛵ ⁱ launderette
Nearby : 🏇 🛶 🎣

GPS Longitude : 3.22271
Latitude : 45.74029

COURPIÈRE

63120 – Michelin map **326** I8 – pop. 4 514 – alt. 320
▶ Paris 399 – Ambert 40 – Clermont-Ferrand 50 – Issoire 53

⚠ Municipal les Taillades

⌕ 04 73 53 01 21. www.ville-courpiere.fr

Address : Les Taillades (take the southern exit along the D 906, follow the signs for Ambert, take the D 7 to the left, follow the signs for Aubusson-d'Auvergne and take the road to the right; by the swimming pool and near a stream)

Opening times : from mid June to end Aug.

0.5 ha (40 pitches) flat, grassy

Tariff : (2015 price) ✚ 2.60€ ⇦ 2.10€ ▣ 7€ – 🔌 (10A) 5€

Rental rates : (2015 price) (from mid June to end Aug.) – 3 🚐. Per night from 55 to 65€ – Per week from 300 to 375€ – Reservation fee 10€

The pitches are well marked out; free entry to the swimming pool.

Surroundings : ⊗ 🏕 ♀♀
Leisure activities : 🏊
Facilities : ♿ ☕ 🚿 ⁱ 🚿
Nearby : ✖

GPS Longitude : 3.5487
Latitude : 45.75354

DOMPIERRE-SUR-BESBRE

03290 – Michelin map **326** J3 – pop. 3 184 – alt. 234
▶ Paris 324 – Bourbon-Lancy 19 – Decize 46 – Digoin 27

⚠ Municipal Les Bords de Bresbre

⌕ 04 70 34 55 57. camping@mairie-dsb.fr

Address : La Madeleine (take the southeastern exit along the N 79, follow the signs for Digoin; near the Besbre river and not far from a lake)

Opening times : from mid May to mid Sept.

2 ha (70 pitches) flat, grassy

Tariff : (2015 price) ✚ 2.65€ ⇦ ▣ 2.15€ – 🔌 (10A) 2.45€

🚿 local sani-station 2€

By a large municipal stadium and 7km from the Le Pal animal and amusement park.

Surroundings : ⊗ 🏕 ♀♀
Leisure activities : 🚴 ✖ 🖼
Facilities : ☕ 🚾 ⊞ ⚓ ⁱ 🚿

GPS Longitude : 3.68289
Latitude : 46.51373

GANNAT

03800 – Michelin map **326** G6 – pop. 5 853 – alt. 345
▶ Paris 383 – Clermont-Ferrand 49 – Montluçon 78 – Moulins 58

⛰ Municipal Le Mont Libre

⌕ 04 70 90 12 16. www.camping-gannat.fr

Address : 10 route de la Batisse (located 1km south along the N 9 and take turning to the right)

Opening times : from beginning April to end Oct.

1.5 ha (70 pitches) terraced, flat, grassy

Tariff : (2015 price) 14.90€ ✚✚ ⇦ ▣ 🔌 (10A) –
Extra per person 2.70€

Rental rates : (2015 price) (from beginning April to end Oct.) – 13 🚐 – 13 🏠. Per night from 44 to 140€ – Per week from 245 to 438€

🚿 AireService sani-station 4.20€ – 6 ▣ 8.70€ – 🔋 🔌14.90€

Surroundings : ≤ 🏕 ♀
Leisure activities : 🏛 🚴 🏊 (small swimming pool)
Facilities : ♿ ☕ ⁱ launderette
Nearby : ✖

GPS Longitude : 3.19403
Latitude : 46.0916

ISLE-ET-BARDAIS

03360 – Michelin map **326** D2 – pop. 275 – alt. 285
▶ Paris 280 – Bourges 60 – Cérilly 9 – Montluçon 52

⛰ Les Écossais

⌕ 04 70 66 62 57. www.campingtroncais.com

Address : 1km south, follow signs for Chamignoux

Opening times : from beginning April to mid Oct.

2 ha (70 pitches) relatively flat, flat, grassy

Tariff : (2015 price) 13.60€ ✚✚ ⇦ ▣ 🔌 (10A) – Extra per person 3€ – Reservation fee 15€

Rental rates : (2015 price) (from beginning April to mid Oct.) – 2 🚐 – 7 gîtes. Per night from 50 to 67€ – Per week from 189 to 479€ – Reservation fee 15€

Beside the Lac de Pirot and at the edge of the Tronçais forest.

Surroundings : ⊗ ♀♀
Leisure activities : 🍴 🏛 🚴 ✖ 🏇
Facilities : ♿ ⁱ launderette
Nearby : 🛶 (beach) 🎣

GPS Longitude : 2.78814
Latitude : 46.68278

ISSOIRE

63500 – Michelin map **326** G9 – pop. 13 949 – alt. 400
▶ Paris 446 – Aurillac 121 – Clermont-Ferrand 36 – Le Puy-en-Velay 94

⚏ Château La Grange Fort

📞 0473710243. www.lagrangefort.eu

Address : 4km southeast along the D 996, follow the signs for la Chaise-Dieu then take a right turn, 3km along the D 34, follow the signs for Auzat-sur-Allier, from the A 75, take exit 13 towards Parentignat

Opening times : from beginning April to end Oct.

23 ha/4 for camping (120 pitches) relatively flat, flat, grassy, gravelled

Tariff : 🚶 6.25€ 🚗 3.50€ 🗐 26.95€ – 🔌 (6A) 3.50€ – Reservation fee 15€

Rental rates : (from beginning May to end Oct.) – 15 🛖 – 9 🏠 – 5 🛏 – 2 apartments – 4 canvas bungalows – 1 gîte. Per night from 72 to 132€ – Per week from 295 to 925€ – Reservation fee 17.50€

🚮 local sani-station – 10 🗐
The site is based near a picturesque medieval château, with some pitches overlooking the Allier river.

Surroundings : 🌄 ≤ 🗔 ♀
Leisure activities : 🍽 ✕ 🎦 ≋ jacuzzi 🏇
🚴 ✗ 🎳 🗑
Facilities : ♿ ⚡ 🅿 🍴 ♨ 🍴 launderette 🛁

GPS Longitude : 3.28501
Latitude : 45.50859

⚏ Municipal du Mas

📞 0473890359. www.camping-issoire.com

Address : rue du Docteur Bienfait (2.5km east along the D 9, follow the signs for Orbeil and take a right turn, 50m from a lake and 300m from the Allier river; from A 75 take exit 12)

Opening times : from beginning April to mid Nov.

3 ha (148 pitches) flat, grassy

Tariff : (2015 price) 🚶 17€ 🚗 🗐 – 🔌 (10A) 3.50€

Rental rates : (2015 price) (from beginning April to mid Nov.) ♿ (1 chalet) – 4 🛖 – 6 🏠 – 3 canvas bungalows. Per night from 34 to 87€ – Per week from 220 to 552€

🚮 Flot Bleu sani-station 4€
Situated near the Allier river and a fishing lake.

Surroundings : 🌄 ♀
Leisure activities : 🎦 🏇 🗑
Facilities : ♿ ⚡ 🍴 ♨ 🍴 launderette
Nearby : ✕ 🚴 ✗ 🏐 bowling

GPS Longitude : 3.27397
Latitude : 45.55108

To visit a town or region, use the MICHELIN Green Guides.

LANGEAC

43300 – Michelin map **331** C3 – pop. 4 004 – alt. 505
▶ Paris 513 – Clermont-Ferrand 97 – Le Puy-en-Velay 44 – Aurillac 134

⚏ Les Gorges de l'Allier

📞 0471770501. www.campinglangeac.com

Address : Domaine Le Pradeau (to the north on the D585, follow the signs for Brioude, near the Allier river)

Opening times : from beginning April to end Oct.

14 ha (214 pitches) flat, grassy

Tariff : (2015 price) 15.60€ 🚶🚶 🚗 🗐 🔌 (10A) – Extra per person 5.20€ – Reservation fee 15€

Rental rates : (2015 price) (from beginning April to end Oct.) ♿ (2 chalets) – 10 🛖 – 21 🏠 – 1 gîte. Per night from 102 to 120€ – Per week from 306 to 780€ – Reservation fee 15€

🚮 Flot Bleu sani-station 2.55€

Surroundings : 🌄 ≤ ♀
Leisure activities : 🍽 ✕ 🎦 ♨ 🏇 🎳 🗑
multi-sports ground, entertainment room
Facilities : ♿ ⚡ ♨ 🍴 launderette
Nearby : 🚣 🚴 ✗ 🗑

GPS Longitude : 3.50069
Latitude : 45.10389

LANOBRE

15270 – Michelin map **330** D2 – pop. 1 400 – alt. 650
▶ Paris 493 – Bort-les-Orgues 7 – La Bourboule 33 – Condat 30

⚏ Le Lac de la Siauve

📞 0471403185. www.camping-lac-siauve.fr – alt. 660

Address : rue du Camping (3km southwest along the D 922, follow the signs for Bort-les-Orgues and take turning to the right, 200m from the lake (direct access))

Opening times : from mid April to end Sept.

8 ha (220 pitches) terraced, flat, grassy

Tariff : 22€ 🚶🚶 🚗 🗐 🔌 (10A) – Extra per person 5.50€ – Reservation fee 12€

Rental rates : (2015 price) (from mid April to end Sept.) – 14 🛖 – 19 🏠. Per night from 40 to 70€ – Per week from 490 to 620€ – Reservation fee 12€

🚮 AireService sani-station 4€ – 10 🗐 14€

Surroundings : 🌄 ≤ ♀
Leisure activities : 🍽 🎦 ♨ daytime 🏇
🚴 🗑
Facilities : ♿ ⚡ ♨ 🍴 launderette
Nearby : 🏖 (beach) watersports centre

GPS Longitude : 2.50407
Latitude : 45.4306

For more information on visiting particular towns or regions, consult the relevant regional MICHELIN Green Guide. We also recommend you use the appropriate Michelin regional map to locate your selected campsite, to calculate distances and to work out the best route.

LAPALISSE

03120 – Michelin map **326** I5 – pop. 3 162 – alt. 280
▶ Paris 346 – Digoin 45 – Mâcon 122 – Moulins 50

⚏ Municipal La Route Bleue

📞 0470992631. www.lapalisse-tourisme.com

Address : rue des Vignes (take the southeastern exit along the N7)

Opening times : from beginning April to mid Sept.

0.8 ha (66 pitches) flat, grassy

Tariff : 🚶 2.50€ 🚗 1.85€ 🗐 1.90€ – 🔌 (10A) 2.45€

Rental rates : (from beginning April to end Sept.) ♿ – 2 🛖 – 6 🏠. Per night from 30 to 60€ – Per week from 150 to 380€

Beside the Besbre river with a small footpath linking the campsite with the town centre.

Surroundings : 🗔 ♀♀
Leisure activities : 🗑
Facilities : ♿ ⚡ 🍴 🗑
Nearby : ✗ fitness trail

GPS Longitude : 3.6395
Latitude : 46.2433

LAPEYROUSE

63700 – Michelin map **326** E5 – pop. 561 – alt. 510
▶ Paris 350 – Clermont-Ferrand 74 – Commentry 15 – Montmarault 14

⚠ Municipal les Marins

℘ 04 73 52 37 06. www.63lapeyrouse.free.fr

Address : Etang de la Loge (lake) (situated 2km southeast along the D 998, follow the signs for Echassières and turn right onto D 100, follow the signs for Durmignat)

Opening times : permanent

2 ha (68 pitches) flat, grassy

Tariff : (2015 price) 17.60 € ♦♦ ⊞ 🔌 (10A) – Extra per person 3.70 €

Rental rates : (2015 price) permanent – 5 🏠. Per week from 220 to 570 €

Hedges and shrubs mark out the pitches; near a small lake.

Surroundings : 🌿 ⊡
Leisure activities : 🏠 ⤢ 🎣
Facilities : ᵹ ⟞ 🚿 🗑
Nearby : 🍴 🍽 🏖 (beach)
GPS Longitude : 2.8837
Latitude : 46.22125

LEMPDES-SUR-ALLAGNON

43410 – Michelin map **331** B1 – pop. 1 324 – alt. 430
▶ Paris 472 – Clermont-Ferrand 56 – Le Puy-en-Velay 73 – Aurillac 102

⚠ Pont d'Allagnon

℘ 04 71 76 53 69. www.campingenauvergne.com

Address : rue René Filiol

Opening times : from end March to mid Oct.

2 ha (60 pitches) flat, grassy

Tariff : 20 € ♦♦ ⊞ 🔌 (10A) – Extra per person 4.55 €

Rental rates : permanent ᵹ (1 chalet) – 2 🚐 – 6 🏠 – 3 canvas bungalows. Per night from 33 to 62 € – Per week from 165 to 450 €

🚐 Eurorelais sani-station 2 €

Surroundings : 🌿 ⊡ ♀
Leisure activities : 🍴 🍽 🏠 ⤢ 🎣 🛶 multi-sports ground
Facilities : ᵹ ⟞ 🚿 🗑 launderette
Nearby : 🏊
GPS Longitude : 3.26624
Latitude : 45.38697

MAURIAC

15200 – Michelin map **330** B3 – pop. 3 854 – alt. 722
▶ Paris 490 – Aurillac 53 – Le Mont-Dore 77 – Riom-és-Montagnes 37

⚠⚠ Val St-Jean

℘ 04 71 67 31 13. www.tourismevalsaintjean.fr

Address : at the leisure centre (2.2km west along the D 681, follow the signs for Pleaux and turn right onto D 682, direct access to a small lake)

Opening times : from beginning May to mid Sept.

3.5 ha (100 pitches) terraced, flat, grassy

Tariff : (2015 price) 24.70 € ♦♦ ⊞ 🔌 (10A) – Extra per person 5.50 €

Rental rates : (2015 price) permanent ᵹ (1 chalet) – 20 🏠 – 2 tipis – 3 canvas bungalows – 2 gîtes. Per night from 45 to 70 € – Per week from 145 to 625 €

🚐 Eurorelais sani-station 2 € – 🔌 12 €

Beside a lake and close to the historic town.

Surroundings : 🌿 ⇜ ⊡ ♀
Leisure activities : 🏠 daytime 🏃
Facilities : ᵹ ⟞ 🚿 🗑 🍴 launderette
Nearby : 🛒 🍴 ⤢ 🚴 🎣 🛶 🏖 (beach)  pedalos
GPS Longitude : 2.31657
Latitude : 45.21835

MAURS

15600 – Michelin map **330** B6 – pop. 2 213 – alt. 290
▶ Paris 568 – Aurillac 43 – Entraygues-sur-Truyère 50 – Figeac 22

⚠⚠ Municipal le Vert

℘ 04 71 49 04 15. www.campinglevert-maurs.fr

Address : avenue du stade (800m southeast along the D 663, follow the signs for Décazeville; beside the Rance)

1.2 ha (44 pitches) flat, grassy

Rentals : 4 🏠

Surroundings : ⊡ ♀♀
Leisure activities : 🏠 ⤢ 🛶
Facilities : ᵹ ⟞ 🚿 🗑 🍴 🔌
Nearby : 🛒 🚴 🐎
GPS Longitude : 2.2064
Latitude : 44.70507

MONISTROL-D'ALLIER

43580 – Michelin map **331** D4 – pop. 219 – alt. 590
▶ Paris 535 – Brioude 58 – Langogne 56 – Le Puy-en-Velay 28

⚠ Municipal le Vivier

℘ 04 71 57 24 14. www.monistroldallier.com

Address : to the south, near the Allier (direct access)

Opening times : from mid April to mid Sept.

1 ha (48 pitches)

Tariff : 17.40 € ♦♦ ⊞ 🔌 (9A) – Extra per person 5.70 € – Reservation fee 5.20 €

Surroundings : ⇜ ♀
Leisure activities : 🏠
Facilities : ᵹ ⟞ 🗑 🍴
Nearby : 🍴 ⤢ 🍽 🎣 🛶 rafting and canyoning
GPS Longitude : 3.65348
Latitude : 44.96923

MONTAIGUT-LE-BLANC

63320 – Michelin map **326** F9 – pop. 717 – alt. 500
▶ Paris 443 – Clermont-Ferrand 33 – Issoire 17 – Pontgibaud 46

⚠ Le Pré

℘ 04 73 96 75 07. www.campinglepre.com

Address : place Amouroux (in the village)

Opening times : from beginning Feb. to mid Dec.

1.5 ha (100 pitches) flat, grassy

Tariff : 22.60 € ♦♦ ⊞ 🔌 (10A) – Extra per person 4.80 € – Reservation fee 8 €

Rental rates : permanent ᵹ (1 chalet) – 7 🏠. Per night from 45 to 50 € – Per week from 230 to 600 € – Reservation fee 8 €

🚐 local sani-station 2 € – 🔌 8 €

Beside the Couze de Chambon river with a view of the hilltop village.

Surroundings : 🌿 ⇜ ⊡ ♀♀
Leisure activities : 🏠 🛶
Facilities : ᵹ ⟞ 🗑 🍴 launderette refrigerators
Nearby : ⤢ 🍽 🎣 🛶
GPS Longitude : 3.09162
Latitude : 45.58482

LE MONT-DORE

63240 – Michelin map **326** D9 – pop. 1 391 – alt. 1 050 – ⚜ – Winter sports : 1 050/1 850 m
▶ Paris 462 – Aubusson 87 – Clermont-Ferrand 43 – Issoire 49

⚠ Municipal l'Esquiladou

✆ 04 73 65 23 74. www.mairie-mont-dore.fr

Address : at Queureuilh, route des Cascades (head along the D 996, following signs for Murat-le-Quaire and take turning to the right)

Opening times : from beginning April to mid Nov.

1.8 ha (100 pitches) terraced, flat, fine gravel

Tariff : ✶ 5€ ⬌ ▣ 5€ – (½) (10A) 4€

Rental rates : (from mid April to mid Nov.) – 17 🚐. Per night from 52 to 90€ – Per week from 285 to 550€

🚐 local sani-station

In a mountainous setting, green and wooded, near the village centre.

Surroundings : ⛰ ≼ 🏞	
Leisure activities : 🏛 jacuzzi 🛶 ⊠ (small swimming pool, open in season)	Longitude : 2.80162
Facilities : ⚹ ⛽ ▥ ⛲ launderette	Latitude : 45.58706

MURAT-LE-QUAIRE

63150 – Michelin map **326** D9 – pop. 476 – alt. 1 050
▶ Paris 478 – Clermont-Ferrand 45 – Aurillac 120 – Cournon d'Auvergne 60

⚠ Le Panoramique

✆ 04 73 81 18 79. www.campingpanoramique.fr – limited spaces for one-night stay

Address : 1.4km east along the D 219, follow the signs for Le Mont-Dore and take road to the left

Opening times : from beginning April to end Sept.

3 ha (85 pitches) very uneven, terraced, flat, grassy

Tariff : 18€ ✶✶ ⬌ ▣ (½) (10A) – Extra per person 6.40€

Rental rates : (from beginning April to end Sept.) – 16 🚐 – 16 🏠. Per night from 42 to 108€ – Per week from 220 to 809€

🚐 local sani-station 5€

Situated in an attractive, elevated location.

Surroundings : ⛰ ≼ Les Monts Dore and Dordogne valley	
Leisure activities : ♟ ✗ 🏛 🛶 ⊠ wildlife park	Longitude : 2.74779
Facilities : ⚹ ⛽ ▥ ⛲ ⛽ launderette	Latitude : 45.596

⚠ Municipal les Couderts

✆ 04 73 65 54 81. www.camping-couderts.e-monsite.com

Address : Les Couderts (take the northern exit; beside a stream)

Opening times : from mid May to mid Oct.

1.7 ha (62 pitches) terraced, relatively flat, flat, grassy

Tariff : (2015 price) 9.30€ ✶✶ ⬌ ▣ (½) (10A) – Extra per person 3€

Rental rates : (2015 price) permanent – 1 🚐 – 6 🏠. Per night from 52 to 85€ – Per week from 265 to 1,395€

🚐 local sani-station 9€

Surroundings : ⛰ ≼ 🏞 ⚲	
Leisure activities : 🛶 Finnish kota	Longitude : 2.73511
Facilities : ⚹ ▥ ⛲ launderette	Latitude : 45.59937
Nearby : ♟ ✗	

MUROL

63790 – Michelin map **326** E9 – pop. 546 – alt. 830
▶ Paris 456 – Besse-en-Chandesse 10 – Clermont-Ferrand 37 – Condat 37

⚠ Sunêlia La Ribeyre ♟♟

✆ 04 73 88 64 29. www.laribeyre.com

Address : at Jassat (1.2km to the south, follow the signs for Jassat; beside a stream)

Opening times : from end April to mid Sept.

13 ha (460 pitches)

Tariff : 43.50€ ✶✶ ⬌ ▣ (½) (10A) – Extra per person 8.30€ – Reservation fee 30€

Rental rates : (from end April to mid Sept.) ⚹ (1 mobile home) – 101 🚐. Per night from 38 to 214€ – Reservation fee 30€

A lovely water park and small lake for bathing and canoeing.

Surroundings : ⛰ ≼ ♨♨	
Leisure activities : ♟ ✗ 🏛 🎱 🕺 jacuzzi 🛶 ✗ ⊠ ⛱ (lake) ⛵ 🏊	Longitude : 2.93719
Facilities : ⚹ ⛽ ♨ 🌲 ⛲ launderette ⛱ ♨	Latitude : 45.56232
Nearby : 🎣	

⚠ Le Repos du Baladin

✆ 04 73 88 61 93. www.camping-auvergne-france.com

Address : Groire (located 1.5km east along the D 146, follow the signs for St-Diéry)

Opening times : from mid April to mid Sept.

1.6 ha (88 pitches) terraced, relatively flat, flat, grassy, rocks

Tariff : (2015 price) 24.85€ ✶✶ ⬌ ▣ (½) (10A) – Extra per person 5.35€ – Reservation fee 14€

Rental rates : (2015 price) (from mid April to mid Sept.) – 22 🚐 – 2 🏠. Per night from 49 to 65€ – Per week from 214 to 730€ – Reservation fee 14€

Surroundings : ≼ 🏞 ♨♨	
Leisure activities : ♟ ✗ 🏛 🛶 ⊠	Longitude : 2.95728
Facilities : ⚹ ⛽ ▥ ♨ ⛲ launderette ♨	Latitude : 45.57379

⚠ Les Fougères – Domaine du Marais

✆ 04 73 88 67 08. www.camping-auvergne-sancy.com

Address : at Pont du Marais (0.6km west along the D 996, follow signs for Chambon-Lac)

Opening times : from beginning May to mid Sept.

4 ha (135 pitches) very uneven, terraced, flat, grassy

Tariff : (2015 price) 25.70€ ✶✶ ⬌ ▣ (½) (10A) – Extra per person 5.40€ – Reservation fee 10€

Rental rates : (2015 price) (from beginning April to end Oct.) – 26 🚐 – 39 🏠 – 2 canvas bungalows. Per night from 36 to 97€ – Per week from 226 to 998€ – Reservation fee 10€

The site is in two sections on either side of the road.

Surroundings : 🏞 ♨♨	
Leisure activities : 🏛 ⛵ jacuzzi 🛶 ⊠	Longitude : 2.93056
Facilities : ⚹ ⛽ ♨ ⛲ launderette	Latitude : 45.57583
Nearby : ⛱ ✗ ♨ ⛱ (beach)	

The pitches of many campsites are marked out with low hedges of attractive bushes and shrubs.

NÉBOUZAT

63210 – Michelin map **326** E8 – pop. 774 – alt. 860
▶ Paris 434 – La Bourboule 34 – Clermont-Ferrand 20 – Pontgibaud 19

⛰ Les Dômes

𝒫 0473871406. www.les-domes.com – alt. 815

Address : Les Quatre Routes de Nébouzat (along the D 216, follow the signs for Rochefort-Montagne)

Opening times : from end April to beginning Oct.

1 ha (62 pitches) flat, grassy

Tariff : (2015 price) 25.10€ � ⚹⚹ ⇌ 🔲 🔋 (10A) – Extra per person 10.80€ – Reservation fee 10€

Rental rates : (2015 price) (from end April to beginning Oct.) 🦽 (1 chalet) – 10 ▥ – 5 🏠. Per night from 55 to 87€ – Per week from 387 to 716€ – Reservation fee 18€

🚐 local sani-station
The campsite is in green and well-kept surroundings.

Surroundings : ≤ 🞱🞱	
Leisure activities : 🖼 🖵 (open air in season)	**G** Longitude : 2.89028
Facilities : 🦽 ⚬⇌ 🛁 🚿 🚽 launderette	**P** Latitude : 45.72538
Nearby : 🍴 ✕	**S**

The guide covers all 22 regions of France – see the map and list of regions on pages 4–5.

NÉRIS-LES-BAINS

03310 – Michelin map **326** C5 – pop. 2 705 – alt. 364 – ⚘
▶ Paris 336 – Clermont-Ferrand 86 – Montluçon 9 – Moulins 73

⛰ Municipal du Lac

𝒫 0470032470. www.ville-neris-les-bains.fr

Address : rue Marx Dormoy (to the south along the D 155, follow the signs for Villebret)

Opening times : from mid March to mid Nov.

3.5 ha (129 pitches) terraced, flat and relatively flat, grassy, fine gravel

Tariff : (2015 price) 16.70€ ⚹⚹ ⇌ 🔲 🔋 (10A) – Extra per person 4.30€ – Reservation fee 20€

Rental rates : (2015 price) permanent 🦽 (1 chalet) – 14 🏠 – 2 🛏 – 7 apartments. Per night from 35 to 41€ – Per week from 225 to 515€

🚐 local sani-station 7.50€

Surroundings : 🞱 🞱🞱	
Leisure activities : 🍴 ✕ 🖼 ⛹ 🚣 🏊	**G** Longitude : 2.65174
Facilities : 🦽 🛁 🚽 launderette	**P** Latitude : 46.28702
Nearby : 🚴 ✕ 🎣 🎿 🖵 fitness trail	**S**

NEUSSARGUES-MOISSAC

15170 – Michelin map **330** F4 – pop. 959 – alt. 834
▶ Paris 509 – Aurillac 58 – Brioude 49 – Issoire 64

⛰ Municipal de la Prade

𝒫 0471205021. www.neussargues-moissac.fr

Address : route de Murat (take the western exit along the D 304, follow the signs for Murat ; beside the Alagnon)

Opening times : from mid May to mid Sept.

2 ha (22 pitches) terraced, flat, grassy, small wood

Tariff : 11.70€ ⚹⚹ ⇌ 🔲 🔋 (40A) – Extra per person 2.45€

Rental rates : permanent 🅟 – 8 ▥ – 6 🏠. Per night from 123 to 139€ – Per week from 199 to 439€
Situated on the banks of the river.

Surroundings : 🞱 ≤ ⇌ 🞱🞱	
Leisure activities : 🖼 🚣 🎣	**G** Longitude : 2.96695
Facilities : 🦽 ⚬⇌ 🛁 🚿 🚽 🚽 🖲	**P** Latitude : 45.12923
	S

NEUVÉGLISE

15260 – Michelin map **330** F5 – pop. 1 130 – alt. 938
▶ Paris 528 – Aurillac 78 – Entraygues-sur-Truyère 70 – Espalion 66

⛰ Flower Le Belvédère

𝒫 0471235050. www.campinglebelvedere.com – pitches accessed via steep slope, help moving caravans onto and off pitches avilable on request – alt. 670

Address : Lanau (6.5km south along the D 48, D 921, follow the signs for Chaudes-Aigues and take the Chemin de Gros to the right)

Opening times : from mid April to mid Oct.

5 ha (116 pitches) terraced, flat, grassy

Tariff : (2015 price) 29.50€ ⚹⚹ ⇌ 🔲 🔋 (15A) – Extra per person 6€ – Reservation fee 14€

Rental rates : (2015 price) (from mid April to mid Oct.) – 37 ▥ – 7 🏠 – 4 canvas bungalows – 4 tent lodges. Per night from 34 to 132€ – Per week from 170 to 924€ – Reservation fee 17€

🚐 AireService sani-station – 🅴 🔋15.90€
Situated in an attractive elevated location.

Surroundings : ≤ Gorges de la Truyère ⇌ 🞱	
Leisure activities : 🍴 ✕ 🖼 🎱 ⛹ 🛶 🖵	**G** Longitude : 3.00045
Facilities : 🦽 ⚬⇌ 🛁 🚿 🚽 🚽 launderette 🚿	**P** Latitude : 44.89534
	S

Using the traditional Michelin classification method, the guide provides you with an easy, speedy reference for assessing the category of each site: 1 to 5 tents (see page 10).

NONETTE

63340 – Michelin map **326** G10 – pop. 322 – alt. 480
▶ Paris 467 – Clermont-Ferrand 51 – Cournon-d'Auvergne 47 – Riom 66

⛰ Les Loges

𝒫 0473716582. www.lesloges.com

Address : 2km south along the D 722, follow the signs for Le Breuil-sur-Couze then 1km along the road near the bridge

Opening times : from end April to mid Sept.

4 ha (126 pitches) flat, grassy

Tariff : (2015 price) 17.60€ ⚹⚹ ⇌ 🔲 🔋 (6A) – Extra per person 4.60€ – Reservation fee 6€

Rental rates : (2015 price) (from end April to mid Sept.) – 24 ▥. Per night from 45 to 90€ – Per week from 150 to 600€ – Reservation fee 6€

There's plenty of green space for relaxation and some pitches are by the Allier river.

Surroundings : 🞱 ⇌ 🞱🞱	
Leisure activities : 🍴 ✕ 🖲 🚣 🏊 🛷 🏄	**G** Longitude : 3.27158
Facilities : 🦽 ⚬⇌ 🛁 🚽 launderette 🚿	**P** Latitude : 45.47367
	S

ORCET

63670 – Michelin map **326** G8 – pop. 2 729 – alt. 400
▶ Paris 424 – Billom 16 – Clermont-Ferrand 14 – Issoire 25

⚑ Clos Auroy

🖉 04 73 84 26 97. www.camping-le-clos-auroy.com

Address : 15 rue de la Narse (200m south of the town, near the Auzon river)

Opening times : permanent

3 ha (82 pitches) terrace, flat, grassy, fine gravel

Tariff : ✿ 6.50€ 🚗 🔌 14.50€ – ⚡ (10A) 5.10€ – Reservation fee 20€
Rental rates : (from beginning April to end Oct.) 🏕 –
9 🚐 – 2 tent lodges. Per night from 60 to 90€ – Per week from 250 to 750€ – Reservation fee 20€

🚐 Eurorelais sani-station 3€

The pitches are attractively marked out with shrubs.

Surroundings : 🏞 🌲🌲	**G** Longitude : 3.16912
Leisure activities : ✗ 🛶 jacuzzi ⚓ 🏊 ⛷	**P** Latitude : 45.70029
Facilities : 🚿 🚰 ▥ 🚻 launderette	**S**
Nearby : ✗	

ORLÉAT

63190 – Michelin map **326** H7 – pop. 2 010 – alt. 380
▶ Paris 440 – Clermont-Ferrand 34 – Roanne 76 – Vichy 38

⚑ Le Pont-Astier

🖉 04 73 53 64 40. www.camping-lepont-astier.cm

Address : at the leisure centre (5km east along the D 85, D 224 and take road to the left; beside the Dore river)

Opening times : from beginning March to end Nov.

2 ha (90 pitches) flat, grassy

Tariff : (2015 price) 17.60€ ✿✿ 🚗 🔌 ⚡ (16A) – Extra per person 5€ – Reservation fee 8€
Rental rates : (2015 price) (from beginning March to end Nov.) –
7 🚐. Per night from 60€ – Per week from 260 to 400€ – Reservation fee 8€

🚐 local sani-station

Some of the pitches (well marked out) look down on the Dore river.

Surroundings : 🏞 🏖 🌲🌲	**G** Longitude : 3.47664
Facilities : 🚿 🚰 🚻 launderette	**P** Latitude : 45.86813
Nearby : ✗✗	**S**

PAULHAGUET

43230 – Michelin map **331** D2 – pop. 959 – alt. 562
▶ Paris 495 – Brioude 18 – La Chaise-Dieu 24 – Langeac 15

⚑ La Fridière

🖉 04 71 76 65 54. www.campingfr.nl

Address : 6 route d'Esfacy (located to the southeast along the D 4; beside the Senouire river)

Opening times : from beginning April to end Sept.

3 ha (45 pitches) flat, grassy

Tariff : 19€ ✿✿ 🚗 🔌 ⚡ (16A) – Extra per person 1€

🚐 Eurorelais sani-station 3€

Surroundings : 🏖 🏞	**G** Longitude : 3.52
Leisure activities : 🍽 🛶 ⚓ 🏊	**P** Latitude : 45.199
Facilities : 🚿 🚰 ▥ 🚻 🏢	**S**

PERS

15290 – Michelin map **330** B5 – pop. 303 – alt. 570
▶ Paris 547 – Argentat 45 – Aurillac 25 – Maurs 24

⚑ Le Viaduc

🖉 04 71 64 70 08. www.camping-cantal.com

Address : Le Ribeyrès (5km northeast along the D 32 and take the D 61; beside the lake at St-Etienne-Cantalès)

Opening times : from mid April to mid Oct.

1 ha (54 pitches) terraced, flat, grassy

Tariff : (2015 price) 24€ ✿✿ 🚗 🔌 ⚡ (10A) – Extra per person 5.10€ – Reservation fee 14€
Rental rates : (2015 price) (from mid April to mid Oct.) – 8 🚐 –
1 🏠. Per night from 72 to 85€ – Per week from 299 to 575€ – Reservation fee 14€

🚐 local sani-station 6€

A pleasant location.

Surroundings : 🏖 ⛰ 🏞 🌲	**G** Longitude : 2.2556
Leisure activities : 🍽 🛶 ⚓ 🏊 🛶 🚣	**P** Latitude : 44.90602
Facilities : 🚿 🚰 🚻 launderette 🛒	**S**
Nearby : watersports centre	

PIERREFITTE-SUR-LOIRE

03470 – Michelin map **326** J3 – pop. 518 – alt. 228
▶ Paris 324 – Bourbon-Lancy 20 – Lapalisse 50 – Moulins 42

⚑ Municipal le Vernay

🖉 04 70 47 02 49. www.pierrefitte03.fr

Address : Le Vernay (Take the northwestern exit along the N 79, follow the signs for Dompierre, left onto D 295, follow the signs for Saligny-sur-Roudon then continue 900m along the road to the right after the bridge, 200m from the canal)

Opening times : from beginning April to mid Oct.

2 ha (52 pitches) flat, grassy, fine gravel

Tariff : ✿ 2.50€ 🚗 🔌 3.50€ – ⚡ (8A) 8€
Rental rates : (from mid April to end Sept.) 🚿 (3 mobile homes) –
12 🚐. Per night from 50 to 60€ – Per week from 200 to 300€ – Reservation fee 10€

🚐 local sani-station

Near a small lake, canal and cycle route.

Surroundings : 🏞	**G** Longitude : 3.80342
Leisure activities : 🚲 pedalos	**P** Latitude : 46.50857
Facilities : 🚿 🚰 (July-Aug.) 🏕 ▥ 🚻 🏢	**S**
Nearby : 🍽 ✗ ⚓ 🏊 🎯 🏖 (beach) 🎣 fitness trail	

PONTGIBAUD

63230 – Michelin map **326** E8 – pop. 745 – alt. 735
▶ Paris 432 – Aubusson 68 – Clermont-Ferrand 23 – Le Mont-Dore 37

⚑ Municipal de la Palle

🖉 04 73 88 96 99. ville-pontgibaud.fr

Address : route de la Miouze (500m southwest along the D 986, follow the signs for Rochefort-Montagne; beside the Sioule river)

Opening times : from mid April to end Sept.

4.5 ha (86 pitches) flat, grassy

Tariff : (2015 price) ✿ 5.20€ 🚗 🔌 5€ – ⚡ (12A) 4.50€

Rental rates : (2015 price) (from mid April to end Sept.) ♿ (1 chalet) – 6 ⌂. Per week from 280 to 520 €

🚐 AireService sani-station 5€

Choose the pitches furthest away from the road in preference.

Surroundings : 🔲 🌳		
Leisure activities : 🏠 🛶 🎣 🎿		G P S
Facilities : ♿ 🚿 🏕 ⛲ launderette		Longitude : 2.84516 Latitude : 45.82982
Nearby : 🍴 🍽		

PUY-GUILLAUME

63290 – Michelin map **326** H7 – pop. 2 631 – alt. 285
▶ Paris 374 – Clermont-Ferrand 53 – Lezoux 27 – Riom 35

⛺ Municipal de la Dore

🗺 0473 94 78 51. www.puy-guillaume.fr

Address : 86 rue Joseph-Claussat (take the western exit along the D 63, follow the signs for Randan and take a right turn before the bridge, near the river)

Opening times : from beginning June to beginning Sept.

3 ha (100 pitches) flat, grassy

Tariff : (2015 price) 🧍 3.95€ 🚗 ▣ 4.70€ – ⚡ (6A) 3.95€

Choose the pitches furthest away from the road in preference.

Surroundings : 🌳		
Leisure activities : 🏠 🛶 🎣 🎿		G P S
Facilities : ♿ 🚿 🏕 ⛲		Longitude : 3.46623 Latitude : 45.96223

The prices listed were supplied by the campsite owners in 2015 (if prices were not available, those from the previous year are given). The fees should be regarded as basic charges and may fluctuate with inflation.

ROYAT

63130 – Michelin map **326** F8 – pop. 4 431 – alt. 450 – ⚘
▶ Paris 423 – Aubusson 89 – La Bourboule 47 – Clermont-Ferrand 5

🏕 Indigo Royat 👥

🗺 0473 35 97 05. www.camping-indigo.com

Address : route de Gravenoire (situated 2km southeast along the D 941c, follow the signs for Le Mont-Dore and take a right turn D 5, follow the signs for Charade)

Opening times : from end March to beginning Nov.

7 ha (200 pitches) terraced, relatively flat, flat, grassy, fine gravel

Tariff : (2015 price) 32.10€ 🧍🧍 🚗 ▣ ⚡ (10A) –
Extra per person 6.60€ – Reservation fee 13€

Rental rates : (2015 price) (from end March to beginning Nov.) – 8 'gypsy' caravans – 23 ⌂ – 6 ⌂ – 15 tent lodges. Per night from 49 to 137€ – Per week from 240 to 959€ – Reservation fee 13€

🚐 local sani-station 7€

In a pleasantly leafy setting with shade and a variety of rental options; the pitches at the top of the site are very peaceful.

Surroundings : 🌳 🔲 🌳		
Leisure activities : 🍴 🍽 🏠 🎮 🤸 🛶 🚴 🎣 🎿		G P S
Facilities : ♿ 🚿 🏕 ⛲ launderette		Longitude : 3.05452 Latitude : 45.75868

RUYNES-EN-MARGERIDE

15320 – Michelin map **330** H4 – pop. 640 – alt. 920
▶ Paris 527 – Clermont-Ferrand 111 – Aurillac 86 – Le Puy-en-Velay 88

⛺ Révéa Le Petit Bois

🗺 0471 23 42 26. http://www.revea-camping.fr/fr/camping-le-petit-bois.html

Address : at Lesparot

Opening times : from end April to mid Sept.

4 ha (90 pitches) relatively flat, flat, grassy

Tariff : 18€ 🧍🧍 🚗 ▣ ⚡ (10A) – Extra per person 4€ – Reservation fee 10€

🚐 5 ▣ 18€

Located in a pleasant pine forest

Surroundings : 🌲 🌳		
Facilities : ♿ 🚿 ⛲ launderette		G P S
Nearby : 🚵 forest trail		Longitude : 3.21898 Latitude : 44.99899

SAIGNES

15240 – Michelin map **330** C2 – pop. 892 – alt. 480
▶ Paris 483 – Aurillac 78 – Clermont-Ferrand 91 – Mauriac 26

⛺ Municipal Bellevue

🗺 0471 40 68 40. www.saignes-mairie.fr

Address : take the northwestern exit, by the stadium

Opening times : from beginning July to end Aug.

1 ha (42 pitches) flat, grassy

Tariff : (2015 price) 🧍 2.35€ 🚗 1.25€ ▣ 1.45€ – ⚡ (16A) 2.55€

Rental rates : (2015 price) (from beginning July to end Aug.) – 3 ⌂. Per night from 40 to 50€ – Per week from 260 to 320€

Surroundings : 🌳 🔲 🌳		
Leisure activities : 🏠 🛶 🎣		G P S
Facilities : ♿ 🚿 🏕 📷		Longitude : 2.47416 Latitude : 45.33678
Nearby : 🍽 🎿		

ST-BONNET-TRONÇAIS

03360 – Michelin map **326** D3 – pop. 751 – alt. 224
▶ Paris 301 – Bourges 57 – Cérilly 12 – Montluçon 44

🏕 Centre de Tourisme de Champ Fossé

🗺 0470 06 11 30. www.campingstroncais.com

Address : place du Champ de Foire (700m southwest)

Opening times : from beginning April to mid Oct.

3 ha (110 pitches)

Tariff : (2015 price) 19.50€ 🧍🧍 🚗 ▣ ⚡ (10A) –
Extra per person 4.65€ – Reservation fee 15€

Rental rates : (2015 price) (from beginning April to mid Oct.) – 12 ⌂ – 10 gîtes. Per night from 50 to 124€ – Per week from 205 to 540€ – Reservation fee 15€

In an attractive location beside the Lac de St-Bonnet and a small leisure centre.

Surroundings : 🌲 🌳		
Leisure activities : 🍴 🏠 🎿		G P S
Facilities : 🚿 ⛲ launderette		Longitude : 2.68841 Latitude : 46.65687
Nearby : 🛶 🚴 🎣 🏖 (beach) 🎿 pedalos		

ST-DIDIER-EN-VELAY

43140 – Michelin map **331** H2 – pop. 3 313 – alt. 830
▶ Paris 538 – Annonay 49 – Monistrol-sur-Loire 11 – Le Puy-en-Velay 58

⚠ La Fressange

☏ 04 71 66 25 28. www.camping-lafressange.com

Address : 800m southeast along the D 45, follow the signs for St-Romain-Lachalm and take the turning to the left; beside a stream

Opening times : from end April to end Sept.

1.5 ha (72 pitches) relatively flat, grassy

Tariff : 25€ ⚬⚬ 🚗 🔌 (16A) – Extra per person 4€

Rental rates : (from mid April to mid Oct.) – 11 🏠 – 3 tent lodges. Per night from 50 to 117€ – Per week from 200 to 522€

A sunny site, on the side of a hill.

Surroundings : ⚘	**G**
Leisure activities : 🏇	**P** Longitude : 4.28302
Facilities : ⚅ 🗄 🚻 🍴	**S** Latitude : 45.30119
Nearby : 🍴 🎿 ⚓ sports trail	

ST-ÉLOY-LES-MINES

63700 – Michelin map **326** E6 – pop. 3 703 – alt. 490
▶ Paris 358 – Clermont-Ferrand 64 – Guéret 86 – Montluçon 31

⚠ Municipal la Poule d'Eau

☏ 04 73 85 45 47. www.sainteloylesmines.com

Address : rue de la Poule d'Eau (near lakes)

Opening times : from beginning June to end Sept.

1.8 ha (50 pitches)

Tariff : (2015 price) 11.20€ ⚬⚬ 🚗 🔌 (15A) – Extra per person 2.55€

🚐 local sani-station – 10 🔌 – 🔋 🔌 6.70€

Situated in a green setting beside two lakes.

Surroundings : ⚘	**G**
Leisure activities : 🏇 🛶	**P** Longitude : 2.83057
Facilities : ⚅ 🚻 🍴	**S** Latitude : 46.15064
Nearby : 🍴 🎿 ⚓ (beach) fitness trail, pedalos	

ST-GERMAIN-L'HERM

63630 – Michelin map **326** I10 – pop. 508 – alt. 1 050
▶ Paris 476 – Ambert 27 – Brioude 33 – Clermont-Ferrand 66

⚠⚠ St-Éloy

☏ 04 73 72 05 13. www.camping-le-saint-eloy.com

Address : route de la Chaise-Dieu (take the southeastern exit, on the D 999)

Opening times : from beginning May to end Sept.

3 ha (63 pitches) terraced, flat, grassy

Tariff : (2015 price) 15.50€ ⚬⚬ 🚗 🔌 (10A) – Extra per person 4.50€

Rental rates : permanent ⚅ (1 chalet) – 4 🚐 – 13 🏠. Per week from 237 to 527€

Good-quality chalet rentals and a pretty view over the village.

Surroundings : ⚘	**G**
Leisure activities : 🍴 🍴 🛁 jacuzzi 🏇 🚴 🛶	**P** Longitude : 3.54781
Facilities : ⚅ 🗄 🍴 launderette	**S** Latitude : 45.45653
Nearby : 🎿 🍴 ⚓	

ST-GÉRONS

15150 – Michelin map **330** B5 – pop. 209 – alt. 526
▶ Paris 538 – Argentat 35 – Aurillac 24 – Maurs 33

⚠⚠⚠ Les Rives du Lac

☏ 06 25 34 62 89. www.lesrivesdulac.fr

Address : 8.5km southeast along the follow the signs for Espinet; 300m from the lake at St-Étienne-Cantalès

Opening times : from mid March to mid Nov.

3 ha (100 pitches) relatively flat, flat, grassy

Tariff : 20€ ⚬⚬ 🚗 🔌 (10A) – Extra per person 4€ – Reservation fee 10€

Rental rates : (from mid March to mid Nov.) – 10 🚐. Per night from 60 to 70€ – Per week from 220 to 550€ – Reservation fee 16€

In a pleasant setting.

Surroundings : 🌊 🚤 〰	**G**
Leisure activities : 🍴 🏇 🛶 🚴	**P** Longitude : 2.23057
Facilities : ⚅ 🗄 🍴 launderette 🛒	**S** Latitude : 44.93523
Nearby : ✕ 🍴 ⚓ (beach) 🛶	

Do not confuse :
⚠ *to* ⚠⚠⚠ *: MICHELIN classification with*
★ *to* ★★★★★ *: official classification*

ST-GERVAIS-D'AUVERGNE

63390 – Michelin map **326** D6 – pop. 1 304 – alt. 725
▶ Paris 377 – Aubusson 72 – Clermont-Ferrand 55 – Gannat 41

⚠ Municipal de l'Étang Philippe

☏ 04 73 85 74 84. www.ville-stgervais-auvergne.fr

Address : Mazières (take the northern exit along the D 987, follow the signs for St-Éloy-les-Mines; near a small lake)

Opening times : from beginning April to end Sept.

3 ha (130 pitches)

Tariff : (2015 price) 10.90€ ⚬⚬ 🚗 🔌 (10A) – Extra per person 1.50€ – Reservation fee 20€

Rental rates : (2015 price) permanent ⚅ (1 chalet) – 11 🏠. Per night from 41 to 64€ – Per week from 290 to 450€

🚐 Eurorelais sani-station 2€ – 10 🔌 5€

Good-quality chalet rentals and an attractive view of the lake.

Surroundings : 🌊 🚤 ⚘ 〰	**G**
Leisure activities : 🏠	**P** Longitude : 2.81804
Facilities : ⚅ 🗄 🚻 🍴 🛒	**S** Latitude : 46.03688
Nearby : 🏇 🍴 ⚓ (beach) 🛶 fitness trail, skatepark	

ST-JACQUES-DES-BLATS

15800 – Michelin map **330** E4 – pop. 325 – alt. 990
▶ Paris 536 – Aurillac 32 – Brioude 76 – Issoire 91

⚠ des Blats

☏ 04 71 47 06 00. www.camping-des-blats.fr

Address : east of the village, follow the signs for Nierevèze, beside the Cère river

Opening times : from beginning May to end Sept.

1.5 ha (50 pitches) flat, grassy

Tariff : ⚬ 4.90€ 🚗 1.80€ 🔌 2.20€ – 🔌 (10A) 4.30€ – Reservation fee 4€

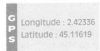

Rental rates : (from beginning May to end Sept.) 👤 (1 chalet) – 4 🏠 – 1 tent lodge. Per night from 85 to 105€ – Per week from 290 to 570€ – Reservation fee 8€

🚰 local sani-station 5€

Surroundings : ⟨ ⌐ 🎠

Leisure activities : ✗ 🖼 ☄ 🚲 🏊

Facilities : 👤 ⚬━ 🏛 ⚱ ☇ 🍴 launderette

Nearby : ✂ 🏕

Rental rates : (2015 price) permanent – 20 🏠 – 2 gîtes. Per night from 35 to 75€ – Per week from 175 to 505€

🚰 Eurorelais sani-station 2€ – 8 🔲

Surroundings : ⟨ ⌐

Leisure activities : 🖼 ☄ 🏊

Facilities : 👤 ⚬━ ⚱ ☇ ☄ ☇ 🍴 🔲

Nearby : ✂ 🏕 🛶

Longitude : 2.71345
Latitude : 45.05182

Longitude : 2.42336
Latitude : 45.11619

ST-JUST

15320 – Michelin map **330** H5 – pop. 206 – alt. 950
▶ Paris 531 – Chaudes-Aigues 29 – Ruynes-en-Margeride 22 – St-Chély-d'Apcher 16

🔺 Municipal

📞 0471737048. www.saintjust.com

Address : at the village (southeast; beside a stream – follow A 75: take exit 31 or 32)

Opening times : from beginning May to end Sept.

2 ha (60 pitches) flat and relatively flat

Tariff : 12.25€ 👫 ⚬ 🔲 🔌 (10A) – Extra per person 2.15€
Rental rates : permanent 👤 (1 mobile home) – 6 🚐 – 5 🏠 – 7 gîtes. Per week from 207 to 468€

🚰 local sani-station 2€ – 2 🔲 9.80€ – 🚐 🔌 9.80€

In the heart of the mountains; the site is crossed by a stream.

Surroundings : 🌳 ⛰
Leisure activities : 🖼
Facilities : 👤 ⚬━ ⚱ 🍴 launderette
Nearby : 🛶 🍴 ✗ ☄ ✂ 🛶

Longitude : 3.20938
Latitude : 44.88993

ST-MARTIN-CANTALES

15140 – Michelin map **330** B4 – pop. 177 – alt. 630
▶ Paris 546 – Clermont-Ferrand 135 – Le Puy-en-Velay 180 – Aurillac 34

🔺 Pont du Rouffet

📞 0471694276. www.campingpontdurouffet.com

Address : Pont du Rouffet

Opening times : from mid May to mid Sept.

1 ha (30 pitches) terraced, flat, grassy

Tariff : (2015 price) 18.20€ 👫 ⚬ 🔲 🔌 (6A) – Extra per person 3.50€
Rental rates : (2015 price) (from mid May to mid Sept.) 🚫 – 4 🚐. Per week from 245 to 415€

Surroundings : 🌳 ⟨ ⌐ 🎠
Leisure activities : 🖼 🏊 🚣 🏊
Facilities : 👤 ⚬━ ⚱ ☇ 🍴 🔲 refrigerators

Longitude : 2.2585
Latitude : 45.072

ST-MARTIN-VALMEROUX

15140 – Michelin map **330** C4 – pop. 856 – alt. 646
▶ Paris 510 – Aurillac 33 – Mauriac 21 – Murat 53

🔺 Municipal Le Moulin du Teinturier

📞 0471694312. mairie.saint-martin-valmeroux@wanadoo.fr

Address : 9 rue de Montjoly (take the western exit, on the D 37, follow the signs for Ste-Eulalie-Nozières; beside the Maronne)

Opening times : from mid June to mid Sept.

3 ha (100 pitches) flat, grassy

Tariff : (2015 price) 17.30€ 👫 ⚬ 🔲 🔌 (12A) – Extra per person 3.50€

ST-NECTAIRE

63710 – Michelin map **326** E9 – pop. 732 – alt. 700 – ⚓
▶ Paris 453 – Clermont-Ferrand 43 – Issoire 27 – Le Mont-Dore 24

🔺 Flower La Vallée Verte

📞 0473885268. www.valleeverte.com

Address : route des Granges (1.5km southeast along the D 996 and take a right turn)

Opening times : from mid April to mid Sept.

2.5 ha (91 pitches) terraced, flat, grassy

Tariff : 25.50€ 👫 ⚬ 🔲 🔌 (8A) – Extra per person 7€ – Reservation fee 9.50€
Rental rates : (from mid April to mid Sept.) – 9 🚐 – 5 🏠. Per night from 51 to 68€ – Per week from 282 to 810€ – Reservation fee 9.50€

🚰 local sani-station 5€ – 🚐 🔌 13€

Situated near a stream with a view of the sourrounding area.

Surroundings : 🌳 ⌐ 🎠
Leisure activities : 🍴 ✗ ☄ 🏊
Facilities : 👤 ⚬━ ☇ 🍴 launderette ☄
Nearby : 🏊

Longitude : 3.0008
Latitude : 45.575

🔺 Le Viginet

📞 0473885380. www.camping-viginet.com

Address : take southeastern exit along the D 996 then continue 600m along the road to the left (opposite the Ford garage)

2 ha (90 pitches) terraced, relatively flat, flat, grassy, stony

Rentals : 👤 (1 chalet) – 12 🏠 – 14 cabins.

Surroundings : 🌳 ⟨ ⌐ 🎠
Leisure activities : ☄ 🏊 (small swimming pool)
Facilities : 👤 ⚬━ ☇ 🍴 🔲 ☄ refrigerators
Nearby : ✂ fitness trail

Longitude : 3.00269
Latitude : 45.57945

🔺 La Clé des Champs

📞 0473885233. www.campingcledeschamps.com

Address : take southeastern exit along the D 996 and take D 642, follow the signs for Les Granges; beside a stream and 200m from the Couze de Chambon

Opening times : from beginning April to end Sept.

1 ha (64 pitches) terraced, flat, grassy

Tariff : (2015 price) 24€ 👫 ⚬ 🔲 🔌 (6A) – Extra per person 6.20€ – Reservation fee 9.50€
Rental rates : (2015 price) permanent – 18 🚐 – 10 🏠. Per night from 39 to 90€ – Per week from 195 to 850€ – Reservation fee 9.50€

🚰 Eurorelais sani-station 4€ – 4 🔲 12€
Good quality chalets to rent.

Surroundings : ⌐ 🎠
Leisure activities : 🍴 ✗ 🖼 ☄ 🏊 ☄ 🏊
Facilities : 👤 ⚬━ ☇ 🍴 launderette ☄

Longitude : 2.99934
Latitude : 45.57602

ST-PAULIEN

43350 – Michelin map **331** E3 – pop. 2 398 – alt. 795
▶ Paris 529 – La Chaise-Dieu 28 – Craponne-sur-Arzon 25 – Le Puy-en-Velay 14

⛰ Flower La Rochelambert

☎ 0471005402. www.camping-rochelambert.com

Address : route de Lanthenas (head 2.7km southwest along the D 13, follow the signs for Allègre and turn left onto D 25, follow the signs for Loudes; near the Borne (direct access))

Opening times : from beginning April to end Sept.

3 ha (100 pitches) flat, grassy

Tariff : 23.80€ � ★★ �car 🔲 (16A) – Extra per person 5€

Rental rates : (from beginning April to end Sept.) – 2 'gypsy' caravans – 12 🏠 – 2 canvas bungalows – 3 tent lodges. Per night from 61 to 106€ – Per week from 217 to 742€ – Reservation fee 13€

🚐 AireService sani-station 3€ – 🚐 🔲 18.50€

Surroundings : 🔲
Leisure activities : 🍴 🗙 ⛲ 🏊 🎿 ⛸
Facilities : ⛳ 🚿 🏕 🍽 launderette

GPS
Longitude : 3.81192
Latitude : 45.13547

ST-RÉMY-SUR-DUROLLE

63550 – Michelin map **326** I7 – pop. 1 847 – alt. 620
▶ Paris 395 – Chabreloche 13 – Clermont-Ferrand 55 – Thiers 7

⛰ Révéa Les Chanterelles

☎ 0473943171. www.camping-lac.fr

Address : 3km northeast along the D 201 and take the road to the right, take the A 72: exit 3

Opening times : from beginning April to mid Oct.

5 ha (150 pitches) terraced, very uneven, relatively flat, flat, grassy

Tariff : 20.90€ ★★ 🚗 🔲 (10A) – Extra per person 4€

Rental rates : (from beginning March to end Oct.) – 8 🏠 – 2 tent lodges. Per night from 42 to 87€ – Per week from 185 to 605€ – Reservation fee 10€

🚐 local sani-station – 4 🔲 16.50€

In a pleasant location on high ground, near a lake.

Surroundings : 🌊 ⋚ 🌳
Leisure activities : 🏛 🏊
Facilities : ⛳ 🚿 🏕
At the lake : 🎿 🍴 🗙 ✂ 🎣 🔫 🛶 ⛵ (beach) 🛷 🏓 squash

GPS
Longitude : 3.59918
Latitude : 45.90308

ST-SAUVES-D'AUVERGNE

63950 – Michelin map **326** D9 – pop. 1 133 – alt. 791
▶ Paris 458 – Clermont-Ferrand 49 – Limoges 181 – Tulle 104

⛰ Sites et Paysages Pont de la Dordogne

☎ 0473810192. www.auvergnecampingnature.com

Address : Le Pont district (0.8km south towards Tauve)

3 ha (56 pitches) flat, grassy, fine gravel

Rentals : ⛳ (1 chalet) – 5 'gypsy' caravans – 7 🏠 – 2 yurts – 6 cabins.

🚐 local sani-station – 20 🔲

Pont de la Dordogne

Situated beside a lake and near the Dorgogne river.

Surroundings : 🌊 🔲 🌳
Leisure activities : 🍴 🗙 🏛 hammam, jacuzzi ⛲ 🚴 🐎 🏊 farm or petting farm, freshwater paddling pool, archery
Facilities : ⛳ 🏕 🍽 🔥 🏠

GPS
Longitude : 2.69002
Latitude : 45.60281

STE-SIGOLÈNE

43600 – Michelin map **331** H2 – pop. 5 900 – alt. 808
▶ Paris 551 – Annonay 50 – Monistrol-sur-Loire 8 – Montfaucon-en-Velay 14

⛰ Vaubarlet 🏕👥

☎ 0471666495. www.vaubarlet.com – alt. 600

Address : head 6km southwest along the D 43, follow the signs for Grazac

Opening times : from end April to end Sept.

15 ha/3 for camping (131 pitches) flat, grassy

Tariff : 31€ ★★ 🚗 🔲 (16A) – Extra per person 4€ – Reservation fee 15€

Rental rates : (from end April to end Sept.) ⛳ (2 chalets) – 1 'gypsy' caravan – 19 🏠 – 5 🏠 – 3 canvas bungalows – 7 tent lodges. Per night from 50 to 100€ – Per week from 300 to 700€ – Reservation fee 30€

🚐 local sani-station 5€ – 🚐 🔲 14€

Situated in a green valley crossed by the Dunière river.

Surroundings : 🌊 ⋚ 🌳
Leisure activities : 🍴 🗙 🏛 ⏰daytime 🤸 ⛲ 🚴 🏊
Facilities : ⛳ 🚿 ♿ 🏕 – 2 private sanitary facilities (🏕 🚽 wc) 🍽 launderette ⛲

GPS
Longitude : 4.21254
Latitude : 45.21634

In order for the guide to remain wholly objective, the selection of campsites is made on an entirely independent basis.

SAUGUES

43170 – Michelin map **331** D4 – pop. 1 873 – alt. 960
▶ Paris 529 – Brioude 51 – Mende 72 – Le Puy-en-Velay 43

⛰ Municipal Sporting de la Seuge

☎ 0471778062. www.saugues.fr/tourisme/hebergements/camping

Address : avenue du Gévaudan (take the western exit along the D 589, follow the signs for Le Malzieu-Ville and take a right turn; beside the Seuge river and near two lakes and a pine forest)

Opening times : from beginning April to mid Nov.

3 ha (92 pitches) flat, grassy

Tariff : (2015 price) 10.60€ ★★ 🚗 🔲 (16A) – Extra per person 2.80€

Rental rates : (2015 price) (from beginning April to mid Nov.) – 14 🏠 – 1 gîte. Per night from 118€ – Per week from 187 to 390€

🚐 local sani-station – 3 🔲 7.50€

A natural pool (clean and filtered but no chemicals).

Surroundings : ⋚ 🌳
Leisure activities : 🏛 ⛲ ✂ 🏊 (fresh water) 🏊 multi-sports ground, entertainment room
Facilities : ⛳ 🏕 🍽 launderette
Nearby : 🍴 🏊 🛶 🐎 sports trail, pedalos

GPS
Longitude : 3.54073
Latitude : 44.95818

SAZERET

03390 – Michelin map **326** E4 – pop. 157 – alt. 370

▶ Paris 348 – Gannat 44 – Montluçon 34 – Montmarault 4

⚠ La Petite Valette

📞 04 70 07 64 57. www.valette.nl – access difficult in some places (track)

Address : 5.5km to the northeast, access via rte Les Deux-Chaises parallel to the N 79 and Chemin des Prugnes on the left - from the A 71, take exit 11.

4 ha (58 pitches) flat, grassy

Rentals : 8 🛏 – 5 🏠.

Facilities and activities based around a former traditional Bourbon farm.

Surroundings : 🐾 🏕 ⚘⚘
Leisure activities : ✗ 🖼 🚲 🎣 🪁
Facilities : ♿ 🚰 🏧 🍴 launderette

Longitude : 2.99231
Latitude : 46.3596

SINGLES

63690 – Michelin map **326** C9 – pop. 170 – alt. 737

▶ Paris 484 – Bort-les-Orgues 27 – La Bourboule 23 – Bourg-Lastic 20

⚠ Le Moulin de Serre 🏊

📞 04 73 21 16 06. www.moulindeserre.com

Address : 1.7km south of the Guinguette, along the D 73, follow the signs for Bort-les-Orgues; beside the Burande river

Opening times : from beginning April to mid Sept.

7 ha/2.6 for camping (99 pitches) flat, grassy

Tariff : 25.45€ ★★ 🚐 🔲 🔌 (10A) – Extra per person 5€ – Reservation fee 15€

Rental rates : (from beginning April to mid Sept.) ♿ (1 mobile home) – 23 🛏 – 12 canvas bungalows. Per night from 25 to 62€ – Per week from 175 to 742€ – Reservation fee 15€

🚐 local sani-station 4€ – 6 🔲 5€

In a green setting in a valley, near a small river.

Surroundings : 🐾 ≪ 🏕 ⚘⚘
Leisure activities : 🍴 ✗ 🖼 🏖 ♨ jacuzzi 🎣 🚲 🎣 🪁 🎣
Facilities : ♿ 🚰 🏧 🍴 launderette 🛁

We value your opinion and welcome your feedback. Do email us at campingfrance@tp.michelin.com

TAUVES

63690 – Michelin map **326** C9 – pop. 768 – alt. 820

▶ Paris 474 – Bort-les-Orgues 27 – La Bourboule 13 – Bourg-Lastic 29

⚠ Les Aurandeix

📞 04 73 21 14 06. www.camping-les-aurandeix.fr

Address : the stadium (east of the town)

Opening times : from mid April to end Sept.

2 ha (50 pitches) terraced, relatively flat, flat, grassy

Tariff : (2015 price) 24.45€ ★★ 🚐 🔲 🔌 (10A) – Extra per person 5.25€ – Reservation fee 10€

Rental rates : (2015 price) (from mid April to end Sept.) – 8 🛏. Per night from 55 to 135€ – Per week from 195 to 750€ – Reservation fee 19€

🚐 AireService sani-station 5€ – 🚐 10€

The pitches and rental accommodations are on terraces overlooking the swimming pool.

Surroundings : 🏕 ⚘
Leisure activities : 🖼 🎣 🎿 multi-sports ground
Facilities : ♿ 🚰 🔲 🏧 🍴 launderette
Nearby : 🚵 fitness trail

Longitude : 2.62473
Latitude : 45.56101

TREIGNAT

03380 – Michelin map **326** B4 – pop. 443 – alt. 450

▶ Paris 342 – Boussac 11 – Culan 27 – Gouzon 25

⚠ Municipal de l'Étang d'Herculat

📞 04 70 07 03 89. http://treignat-allier.weebly.com/

Address : 2.3km to the northeast, access via the road to the left, after the church

1.6 ha (35 pitches) open site, relatively flat to hilly, flat, grassy

In a pleasant location beside a large lake.

Surroundings : 🐾 🏕 ⚘
Leisure activities : 🖼 🎣 🪁
Facilities : ♿ 🏖 🍴

Longitude : 2.3673
Latitude : 46.35611

VIC-SUR-CÈRE

15800 – Michelin map **330** D5 – pop. 1 988 – alt. 678

▶ Paris 549 – Aurillac 19 – Murat 29

⚠⚠ Sites et Paysages La Pommeraie

📞 04 71 47 54 18. www.camping-la-pommeraie.com – alt. 750

Address : at Daïsses (2.5km southeast along the D 54. D 154 and take the road to the right)

Opening times : from beginning May to beginning Sept.

2.8 ha (100 pitches) terraced, flat, grassy

Tariff : (2015 price) 15€ ★★ 🚐 🔲 🔌 (10A) – Extra per person 5.50€ – Reservation fee 19€

Rental rates : (2015 price) (from beginning May to beginning Sept.) – 41 🛏 – 9 🏠 – 3 canvas bungalows. Per night from 50 to 149€ – Per week from 200 to 1,043€ – Reservation fee 19€

🚐 10 🔲 15€ – 🚐 🔌 15€

In an attractive elevated location.

Surroundings : 🐾 ≪ mountain peaks, Vallée de la Cère and small town of Vic-sur-Cère 🏕 ⚘
Leisure activities : 🍴 ✗ 🖼 ♨ nighttime 🎣 🍴 🎣 🎿 walking trails
Facilities : ♿ 🚰 🏧 🏖 🍴 launderette 🛁 🛁

Longitude : 2.63307
Latitude : 44.9711

These symbols are used for a campsite that is exceptional in its category:

⚠⚠ ... ⚠ *Particularly pleasant setting, quality and range of services available*

🐾🐾 *Tranquil, isolated site – quiet site, particularly at night*

≪ ≪ *Exceptional view – interesting or panoramic view*

⚠ Vic'Nature

📞 04 71 47 54 18. www.camping-la-pommeraie.com

Address : route de Salvanhac (beside the Cère river)

Opening times : from mid May to mid Sept.

3 ha (200 pitches) flat, grassy

Tariff : (2015 price) 17.10€ ★★ ⬛ ▣ ⚡ (6A) – Extra per person 4.30€ – Reservation fee 10€

Rental rates : (2015 price) (from beginning July to mid Sept.) – 4 🚐. Per night from 55 to 80€ – Per week from 280 to 465€ – Reservation fee 10€

🚐 50 ▣ 10.10€ – 🚿 10.10€

Surroundings : ⬅ 🌳🌳
Leisure activities : 🏓 🛥
Facilities : 🚿🚽🏛 launderette
Nearby : 🏊 🍴 🎣 🛶 🏊

G P S	Longitude : 2.62492
	Latitude : 44.97986

VOLVIC

63530 – Michelin map **326** F7 – pop. 4 409 – alt. 510
▶ Paris 419 – Clermont-Ferrand 14 – Moulins 99 – Saint-Étienne 160

⚠ Municipal Volvic Pierre et Sources

📞 04 73 33 50 16. www.camping-volvic.com

Address : rue de Chancelas (at the exit from the village, towards Châtel-Guyon)

Opening times : from beginning May to end Sept.

2 ha (68 pitches) relatively flat, flat, grassy

Tariff : (2015 price) 19€ ★★ ⬛ ▣ ⚡ (16A) – Extra per person 4.50€

Rental rates : (2015 price) permanent ♿ (1 chalet) – 10 🏠. Per night from 65 to 95€ – Per week from 250 to 560€

🚐 AireService sani-station 2€ – 5 ▣

The site has well marked-out pitches with a view of the Château de Tournoël.

Surroundings : ⬛
Leisure activities : 🏛
Facilities : ♿ 🚿🚽🚐🚽 launderette
Nearby : 🚴 🍴

G P S	Longitude : 3.04685
	Latitude : 45.87234

VOREY

43800 – Michelin map **331** F2 – pop. 1.428 – alt. 540
▶ Paris 544 – Ambert 53 – Craponne-sur-Arzon 18 – Le Puy en Velay 23

⛰ Pra de Mars

📞 04 71 03 40 86. http://www.leprademars.com

Address : le Chambon de Vorey

Opening times : from mid April to mid Oct.

3.6 ha (100 pitches) flat, grassy

Tariff : 20.60€ ★★ ⬛ ▣ ⚡ (5A) – Extra per person 3.95€

Rental rates : permanent – 7 🚐. Per night from 38 to 68€ – Per week from 250 to 450€

🚐 local sani-station 3€

Surroundings : 🌳 ⬅ ▱ 🌳
Leisure activities : 🍷 🍴 🏛 🛥 🚲 🍴 🎣 🛶 🏊 🏊
Facilities : ♿ 🚿🚽🚐🚽 🚽 launderette 🐾

G P S	Longitude : 3.9429
	Latitude : 45.20352

⛰ Les Moulettes

📞 04 71 03 70 48. www.camping-les-moulettes.fr

Address : chemin de Félines (to the west of the town centre; beside the Arzon river)

Opening times : from beginning May to mid Sept.

1.3 ha (45 pitches) flat, grassy

Tariff : (2015 price) ★ 6€ ⬛ ▣ 9€ – ⚡ (10A) 4€ – Reservation fee 8€

Rental rates : (2015 price) (from beginning May to end Sept.) 🏕 – 6 🚐 – 6 🏠. Per week from 250 to 600€ – Reservation fee 8€

🚐 local sani-station 2€ – 5 ▣ 2€

Surroundings : 🌳 ▱ 🌳🌳
Leisure activities : 🍷 🍴 🏛 🛥 🛶 🏊
Facilities : ♿ 🚿🚽🚐🚽 🚽 🖼
Nearby : 🍴 🏊

G P S	Longitude : 3.90363
	Latitude : 45.18637

To make the best possible use of this guide, please read pages 2–15 carefully.

BRITTANY

T. Deschamps / Photononstop

B rittany, or Breizh, as it is known to those lucky enough to live there, is a region of harsh granite coastlines, mysterious dolmens and menhirs, enchanted forests and pretty ports, dotted with colourful fishing boats. Its charm lies in its sea breeze, seafood and sea-faring history; in its varied landscapes, extensive coastline and delightful islands; in its gastronomy, music and traditional festivals. Its inhabitants were born – or so they claim – with a drop of salt water in their blood. Proud of the language handed down from their Celtic ancestors, today's Bretons nurture their identity with lively celebrations of folklore and customs. Naturally, such devotion to culture demands plenty of delicious and wholesome nourishment: sweet and savoury pancakes, thick slices of butter cake and mugs of cold cider. However, Brittany's gastronomic reputation doesn't end there and gourmets can feast on the oysters, lobster and crab for which it is famous. A visit to Brittany is a jigsaw of wonderful experiences.

MANCHE

Locality with campsite
Locality with campsite and rental option
Vannes — Locality with campsite and campervan area
Moyaux — Locality with at least one pleasant campsite
Motorway service area for campervans

Perros-Guirec
Primel-Trégastel
Trégastel
Plougrescant
Pleubian
Pleumeur-Bodou
Trébeurden
Trélévern
Paimpol
Brignogan-Plages
St-Pol-de-Léon
Plougasnou
Louannec
D 786
Plouguerneau
Roscoff
Trédrez
Lannion
Pontrieux
Plouézec
Plougoulm
St-Jean-du-Doigt
Plounévez-Lochrist
Carantec
Plestin-les-Grèves
Bégard
Lant
Lampaul-Ploudalmézeau
Landéda
N 12
Morlaix
Guingamp
D 767
Île d'Ouessant
Milizac
Plouigneau
N 12
St-Renan
Châtelaudren
Locmaria-Plouzané
BREST
Elorn
Sizun
Callac
le Conquet
Plougastel-Daoulas
Camaret-s-Mer
le Fret
FINISTÈRE
CÔTES-
Crozon
Morgat
Dinéault
N 165
Telgruc-s-Mer
D 887
Châteaulin
N 164
Pentrez-Plage
Ploéven
Plomodiern
Aulne
Tréboul
Kervel
Poullan-s-M.
Locronan
Odet
Île de Sein
Primelin
Plouhinec
D 765
Quimper
St-Yvi
Scaër
Priziac
Pontivy
Plozévet
Fouesnant
Tréguennec
la-Forêt-Fouesnant
Mousterlin
Arzano
D 765
Bénodet
Concarneau
Quimperlé
Plomeur
Moëlan-s-Mer
Pont-Scorff
N 24
Penmarch
Loctudy
Névez
Blavet
Treffiagat
Beg-Meil
le Pouldu
Guidel
LORIENT
N 165
Camors
Lesconil
Plobannalec-Lesconil
Raguenès-Plage
Ste-Anne d'Auray
Port-Manech
Île de Groix
Plouhinec
Ploemel
Plougoumelen
Belz
Erdeven
Crach
Baden
Plouharnel
Carnac-Plage
la Trinité
Arzor
Quiberon
St-Philibert
Locmariaquer
le Palais
OCÉAN ATLANTIQUE
Bangor
Belle-Île-en-Mer

ARRADON

56610 – Michelin map **308** O9 – pop. 5 301 – alt. 40
▶ Paris 467 – Auray 18 – Lorient 62 – Quiberon 49

▲▲▲ Sites et Paysages de Penboch

✆ 02 97 44 71 29. www.camping-penboch.fr

Address : 9 chemin de Penboch (situated 2km southeast following signs for Roguedas, 200m from the beach)

Opening times : from beginning April to end Sept.

4 ha (192 pitches)

Tariff : (2015 price) 39.80€ ✚✚ ⇌ 🅴 (10A) –
Extra per person 6.80€

Rental rates : (2015 price) (from beginning April to end Sept.) ᴋ –
55 🛖. Per night from 42 to 170€ – Per week from 280 to 1,190€ –
Reservation fee 20€

🚐 local sani-station 5€ – 🚽 (10A)14€

Green setting around a partially covered aquatic park; some pitches near beach.

Surroundings : 🚲 💬 ♀
Leisure activities : 🍹 🍽️ Jacuzzi 🏸 🎣 🖼️
🏊 ⛱️ multi-sports ground
Facilities : ᴋ ⚡ 🚿 – 4 private sanitary
facilities (🍳 ⚽ wc) 🧺 ♿ 🍴 launderette
refrigerators
Nearby : 🎣

Longitude : -2.80085
Latitude : 47.62217

▲▲ L'Allée

✆ 02 97 44 01 98. www.camping-allee.com

Address : L'Allée (located 1.5km west, follow the signs for
Le Moustoir and take the turning to the left)

Opening times : from beginning April to end Sept.

3 ha (148 pitches)

Tariff : (2015 price) ✚ 5.20€ ⇌ 2.30€ 🅴 9.85€ – 🅷 (10A) 4.70€
Rental rates : (2015 price) (from beginning April to end Sept.) ᴋ –
36 🛖 – 2 tent lodges. Per night from 90 to 110€ – Per week
from 210 to 730€ – Reservation fee 20€

🚐 AireService sani-station

Surroundings : 🚲 💬 ♀
Leisure activities : 🍽️ 🏸 🏊
Facilities : ᴋ ⚡ (July–Aug.) 🍴 launderette

Longitude : -2.8403
Latitude : 47.62189

ARZANO

29300 – Michelin map **308** K7 – pop. 1 403 – alt. 91
▶ Paris 508 – Carhaix-Plouguer 54 – Châteaulin 82 – Concarneau 40

▲▲▲ Les Castels Ty Nadan ▲▲

Ty Nadan

✆ 02 98 71 75 47. www.tynadan-vacances.fr

Address : at Locunolé, route d'Arzano
(3km west; beside the Ellé river)

Opening times : from beginning May
to beginning Sept.

20.5 ha/5 for camping (325 pitches)

Tariff : 49€ ✚✚ ⇌ 🅴 (10A) –
Extra per person 9.70€ – Reservation
fee 25€

Rental rates : (from beginning May to beginning Sept.) – 90 🛖 –
6 🏠 – 2 apartments – 5 canvas bungalows – 2 tent lodges –
1 gîte. Per night from 58 to 204€ – Per week from 406 to 1,428€ –
Reservation fee 30€

Partially indoor water park with lots of sports activities and leisure facillities, river swimming and canoeing.

Surroundings : 🚲 💬 ♀♀ ⚠
Leisure activities : 🍹 🍽️ 🍽️ 🏊 🧖 Jacuzzi
🏸 🚴 🎣 🏊 (beach) 🏊 🐎 farm
or petting farm, climbing wall, forest trail
🦋 entertainment room
Facilities : ᴋ ⚡ 🆒 – 4 private sanitary
facilities (🍳 ⚽ wc) 🧺 ♿ 🍴 launderette
🏊 🎣

Longitude : -3.47389
Latitude : 47.905

ARZON

56640 – Michelin map **308** N9 – pop. 2 132 – alt. 9
▶ Paris 487 – Auray 52 – Lorient 94 – Quiberon 81

▲ Municipal le Tindio

✆ 02 97 53 75 59. www.camping-arzon.fr

Address : 2 rue du Bilouris, at Kermers (800m to the northeast)

Opening times : from end March to beginning Nov.

5 ha (220 pitches)

Tariff : (2015 price) ✚ 4.40€ ⇌ 🅴 8.70€ – 🅷 (10A) 3.50€
Rental rates : (2015 price) (from end March to beginning Nov.)
ᴋ (3 chalets) – 18 🛖. Per week from 200 to 659€

🚐 local sani-station 2€ – 19 🅴 10€ – 🚽 10€

Surroundings : 🚲 ♀
Leisure activities : 🍽️ 🏸 🎣 multi-sports
ground
Facilities : ᴋ ⚡ 🍴 launderette

Longitude : -2.8828
Latitude : 47.55562

BADEN

56870 – Michelin map **308** N9 – pop. 4 077 – alt. 28
▶ Paris 473 – Auray 9 – Lorient 52 – Quiberon 40

▲▲▲▲ Yelloh! Vilage Mané Guernehué ▲▲

Mané Guernehué

✆ 02 97 57 02 06. www.camping-baden.com

Address : 52 rue Mané Er Groëz (located
1km southwest, follow the signs for
Mériadec and take a right turn)

Opening times : from beginning April
to beginning Nov.

18 ha/8 for camping (377 pitches)
undulating, terraced, flat and relatively
flat, grassy, pond, natural setting among
trees and bushes

Tariff : 50€ ✚✚ ⇌ 🅴 🅷 (10A) – Extra per person 8€
Rental rates : (from beginning April to beginning Nov.) ᴋ (1
mobile home) – 4 'gypsy' caravans – 162 🛖 – 19 🏠 – 1 studio –
2 tent lodges – 6 gîtes. Per night from 36 to 219€ – Per week from
252 to 1,533€

🚐 local sani-station 6.50€ – 🚽 (10A)16€

*An attractive indoor spa area and riding centre with ponies
and horses.*

Surroundings : 🚲 💬 ♀
Leisure activities : 🍹 🍽️ 🏊 🖼️ 🏊 🎣 🏋️ 🚴
hammam, jacuzzi 🏸 🚴 🖼️ 🏊 🎣 🐎
zip wiring, multi-sports ground, spa centre,
water park, entertainment room
Facilities : ᴋ ⚡ 🏢 🆒 – 8 private sanitary
facilities (🍳 ⚽ wc) 🧺 ♿ 🍴 launderette
🏊 🎣
Nearby : 🍴

Longitude : -2.92531
Latitude : 47.61418

BÉGARD

22140 – Michelin map **309** C3 – pop. 4 652 – alt. 142
▶ Paris 499 – Rennes 147 – St-Brieuc 51 – Quimper 132

⚑ Donant

📞 02 96 45 46 46. www.camping-donant-bretagne.com

Address : at Gwénézhan

Opening times : permanent

3 ha (91 pitches)

Tariff : (2015 price) ♦ 6.70€ ⇌ 2.30€ 🔲 3.40€ – (∮) (30A) 3€

Rental rates : (2015 price) permanent ♿ (1 chalet) – 15 🏠 –
12 ⊫ – 2 canvas bungalows – 1 gîte. Per night from 39 to 100€ –
Per week from 149 to 609€

🚐 local sani-station 6€ – 🚽 (∮)17.50€

Surroundings : ▱
Leisure activities : 🎦 🎱 🚣 entertainment
room
Facilities : ♿ 🚰 launderette
Nearby : ♟ ✗ 🛶 🔲 🛥 pedalos, leisure park

Longitude : -3.2837
Latitude : 48.61807

*The classification (1 to 5 tents, **black** or red) that we*
award to selected sites in this guide is our own system.
It should not be confused with the classification
(1 to 5 stars) of official organisations.

BEG-MEIL

29170 – Michelin map **308** H7
▶ Paris 562 – Rennes 211 – Quimper 23 – Brest 95

⚑ La Piscine ♦♦

📞 02 98 56 56 06. www.campingdelapiscine.com

Address : 51 Hent Kerleya (4km to the northwest)

3.8 ha (199 pitches) flat, grassy, small lake

Rentals : 30 🚐 – 4 🏠.

In a pleasant location close to the sea, situated beside an
enclosed lake

Surroundings : 🐾 ▱ ⛱
Leisure activities : 🎦 🏃 ⛵s hammam,
jacuzzi 🚣 🚲 🔲 🛥 🏹 mountain biking
Facilities : ♿ 🚰 🛁 🚿 🚰 launderette
🛥 🚿

Longitude : -4.01579
Latitude : 47.86671

⚑ Le Kervastard

📞 02 98 94 91 52. www.campinglekervastard.com

Address : 56 chemin de Kervastard (150m from the town)

Opening times : from beginning April to end Oct.

2 ha (122 pitches) flat, grassy

Tariff : 29.90€ ♦♦ ⇌ 🔲 (∮) (10A) – Extra per person 6.10€ –
Reservation fee 15€

Rental rates : (from beginning April to end Oct.) – 25 🚐.
Per week from 236 to 730€ – Reservation fee 15€

🚐 local sani-station 5€ – 5 🔲 13€ – 🚽 (∮)13€

In a pleasant setting with light shade, close to shops.

Surroundings : ▱ ⛱
Leisure activities : 🎦 🚣 🚲 🔲
Facilities : ♿ 🚰 🔲 🛁 🚰 launderette
Nearby : 🛥 ♟ ✗ 🐚

Longitude : -3.98825
Latitude : 47.86015

BELLE-ÎLE

56360 – Michelin map **308** – pop. 2 457 – alt. 7

Bangor 56360 – Michelin map **308** L11 – pop. 926 – alt. 45
▶ Paris 513 – Rennes 162 – Vannes 53

⚑ Le Kernest

📞 02 97 31 81 20. camping-kernest.com

Address : at Kernest

Opening times : from end March to beginning Oct.

2 ha (74 pitches) flat, grassy

Tariff : (2015 price) ♦ 3.50€ ⇌ 🔲 6.50€

Rental rates : (2015 price) (from end March to beginning Oct.) –
25 🚐 – 15 🏠 – 8 canvas bungalows – 14 tent lodges. Per week
from 205 to 728€

Surroundings : 🐾 ▱
Leisure activities : 🚣 🎾 multi-sports
ground
Facilities : ♿ 🏛 🚿

Longitude : -3.20076
Latitude : 47.31182

⚑ Municipal de Bangor

📞 02 97 31 89 75. http://www.bangor.fr/hebergements_camping.html

Address : 18 rue Pierre Cadre (to the west of the town)

Opening times : from beginning April to end Sept.

0.8 ha (75 pitches) relatively flat to hilly, grassy

Tariff : (2015 price) ♦ 3.30€ ⇌ 1.65€ 🔲 3€ – (∮) (10A) 2.70€ –
Reservation fee 15€

Rental rates : (2015 price) (from beginning April to end Sept.) –
6 🚐 – 16 ⊫. Per week from 290 to 592€

Surroundings : 🐾 ▱
Leisure activities : 🚣
Facilities : ♿ 🚰 🚰 launderette

Longitude : -3.19103
Latitude : 47.31453

Le Palais 56360 – Michelin map **308** M10 – pop. 2 545 – alt. 7
▶ Paris 508 – Rennes 157 – Vannes 48

⚑ Bordénéo

📞 02 97 31 88 96. www.bordeneo.com

Address : Bordénéo (1.7km northwest following signs for Port
Fouquet, 500m from the sea)

Opening times : from mid April to end Sept.

5.5 ha (202 pitches) flat, grassy

Tariff : (2015 price) ♦ 7.35€ ⇌ 2.70€ 🔲 11.35€ – (∮) (6A) 3.65€ –
Reservation fee 16€

Rental rates : (from beginning April to end Sept.) – 46 🚐 – 12 🏠 –
4 studios – 10 canvas bungalows. Per night from 65 to 135€ –
Per week from 310 to 930€ – Reservation fee 16€

Ornamental shrubs; partially covered aquatic park.

Surroundings : 🐾 ▱ ⛱⛱
Leisure activities : ♟ ✗ 🎦 🎱 nighttime
🚣 🚲 🎾 🔲 🛥
Facilities : ♿ 🚰 🛁 🚰 🚰 launderette 🛥 🚿

Longitude : -3.16711
Latitude : 47.35532

The prices listed were supplied by the campsite owners
in 2015 (if prices were not available, those from the
previous year are given). The fees should be regarded
as basic charges and may fluctuate with inflation.

⛰ L'Océan

📞 02 97 31 83 86. www.camping-ocean-belle-ile.com

Address : at Rosboscer (to the southwest of the town, 500m from the port)

Opening times : from beginning May to end Sept.

2.8 ha (108 pitches)

Tariff : (2015 price) 24.70 € ♦♦ ⇌ 🔲 🔌 (6A) – Extra per person 6 € – Reservation fee 5 €

Rental rates : (2015 price) (from beginning Feb. to mid Nov.) ♿ (1 mobile home) – 2 'gypsy' caravans – 17 🚐 – 36 🏠 – 3 tent lodges. Per night from 45 to 95 € – Per week from 309 to 669 € – Reservation fee 13 €

Surroundings : 🏞 🗭 ♤♤ Leisure activities : 🍴 ✕ 🏊 Facilities : ♿ o━ 🧺 launderette 🧹 Nearby : 🛒	**GPS** Longitude : -3.13996 Latitude : 47.53473

BELZ

56550 – Michelin map **308** L8 – pop. 3 476 – alt. 12
▶ Paris 494 – Rennes 143 – Vannes 34 – Lorient 25

⛰ Le Moulin des Oies

📞 02 97 55 53 26. www.lemoulindesoies.bzh

Address : 21 rue de la Côte

Opening times : from beginning April to end Sept.

1.9 ha (90 pitches) flat, grassy

Tariff : 21 € ♦♦ ⇌ 🔲 🔌 (6A) – Extra per person 5 € – Reservation fee 12 €

Rental rates : (from beginning April to end Sept.) – 18 🚐. Per week from 244 to 653 € – Reservation fee 12 €

🚐 sani-station – 🚌 🔌18 €

Situated beside the Ria d'Étel river. Large saltwater pool.

Surroundings : 🏞 🗭 ♤♤ Leisure activities : 🍴 ✕ 🏠 🚣 🌊 (seawater pool), multi-sports ground Facilities : ♿ o━ 🔲🏛 🧺 launderette 🧹	**GPS** Longitude : -3.17603 Latitude : 47.68045

BÉNODET

29950 – Michelin map **308** G7 – pop. 3 453
▶ Paris 563 – Concarneau 19 – Fouesnant 8 – Pont-l'Abbé 13

⛰ Sunêlia L'Escale St-Gilles ♠♠

📞 02 98 57 05 37. www.stgilles.fr – limited spaces for one-night stay 🚫

Address : corniche de la mer (located at La Pointe St-Gilles headland)

Opening times : from beginning May to mid Sept.

11 ha/7 for camping (467 pitches) flat, grassy

Tariff : 44 € ♦♦ ⇌ 🔲 🔌 (10A) – Extra per person 10 € – Reservation fee 35 €

Rental rates : (from beginning May to mid Sept.) ♿ (1 mobile home) 🚫 – 156 🚐 – 2 canvas bungalows. Per night from 39 to 191 €– Per week from 219 to 1,337 € – Reservation fee 35 €

An attractive location near the beach and ocean, with a moden and extensive water park. Option for full and half-board stays.

Surroundings : 🏞 🗭 ♤♤ Leisure activities : 🍴 ✕ 🏠 ⛳ 🏇 🎠 🛶 hammam, jacuzzi 🏄 🚴 ⛸ 🚣 🌊 🏓 spa centre, water park, entertainment room Facilities : ♿ o━ 🏛 🧺 🌡 🍴 launderette 🏊 🧹 Nearby : 🌊	**GPS** Longitude : -4.09669 Latitude : 47.86325

⛰ Le Letty ♠♠

📞 02 98 57 04 69. www.campingduletty.com

Address : impasse de Creisanguer

Opening times : from end June to beginning Sept.

10 ha (542 pitches) flat, grassy

Tariff : 47 € ♦♦ ⇌ 🔲 🔌 (10A) – Extra per person 11 € – Reservation fee 12 €

Rental rates : (2015 price) (from end June to beginning Sept.) 🚫 – 11 tent lodges. Per week from 340 to 720 €

🚐 AireService sani-station

An attractive location close to the beach with a spectacular view of the Mousterlin dunes. Plenty of places for tents and caravans. Extensive and exotic water park.

Surroundings : 🏞 ♤♤ 🏔 Leisure activities : 🍴 🏠 ⛳ 🏇 🎠 ⛸ hammam, jacuzzi 🏄 🚴 ✕ ⛸ 🚣 🌊 beauty treatments 🏊 entertainment room Facilities : ♿ o━ 🧺 🌡 🍴 launderette 🏊 🧹 Nearby : 🌊 🎿 🏔 🚣 ♭, squash	**GPS** Longitude : -4.08995 Latitude : 47.86537

⛰ Le Poulquer

📞 02 98 57 04 19. www.campingdupoulquer.com

Address : 23 rue du Poulquer (150m from the sea)

Opening times : from beginning May to end Sept.

3 ha (215 pitches)

Tariff : ♦ 7.30 € ⇌ 3.30 € 🔲 7.80 € – 🔌 (10A) 5.50 € – Reservation fee 20 €

Rental rates : permanent 🚫 – 33 🚐. Per night from 45 to 120 € – Per week from 300 to 850 € – Reservation fee 20 €

In a green and shady setting, with spacious pitches for tents.

Surroundings : 🗭 ♤♤ Leisure activities : 🍴 ✕ 🏠 🚴 🚣 🌊 🏓 entertainment room Facilities : ♿ o━ 🧺 🍴 launderette Nearby : 🌊 🎿 🏔 ♭	**GPS** Longitude : -4.09844 Latitude : 47.86794

BINIC

22520 – Michelin map **309** F3 – pop. 3 602 – alt. 35
▶ Paris 463 – Guingamp 37 – Lannion 69 – Paimpol 31

⛰ Le Panoramic

📞 02 96 73 60 43. www.lepanoramic.net

Address : rue Gasselin

Opening times : from beginning April to end Sept.

4 ha (150 pitches) terrace, relatively flat, flat, grassy

Tariff : 21 € ♦♦ ⇌ 🔲 🔌 (10A) – Extra per person 4 €

Rental rates : permanent ♿ – 1 'gypsy' caravan – 46 🚐 – 8 🏠 – 2 canvas bungalows. Per night from 69 to 99 € – Per week from 229 to 879 € – Reservation fee 10 €

Good aquatic park. Choose pitches away from road.

Surroundings : 🗭 ♤♤ Leisure activities : 🍴 ✕ 🏠 🚴 🚣 🌊 🏓 multi-sports ground Facilities : ♿ o━ 🏛 🍴 launderette	**GPS** Longitude : -2.82304 Latitude : 48.59098

⚠ Municipal des Fauvettes

Municipal des Fauvettes

℘ 02 96 73 60 83. www.ville-binic.fr

Address : rue des Fauvettes

Opening times : from end March to end Sept.

1 ha (88 pitches) terraced, flat and relatively flat, grassy

Tariff : (2015 price) 19.20€ ♣♣ ⇔ 🅴
🅷 (6A) – Extra per person 5€ –
Reservation fee 77€

Rental rates : (2015 price) (from end March to end Sept.) ⅍ 🕸 –
4 🚐 – 3 studios. Per night from 68 to 99€ – Per week from 262 to 419€

🚏 local sani-station – 🚐 🅷13€

Surroundings : ⅍ ≤ of the Baie de St-Brieuc ⚲
Leisure activities : 🏖🏃
Facilities : ⅍ ⛟ 🎳 🖧 🍽 🚿

GPS Longitude : -2.82122
Latitude : 48.60635

BRIGNOGAN-PLAGES

29890 – Michelin map **308** F3 – pop. 848 – alt. 17
▶ Paris 585 – Brest 41 – Carhaix-Plouguer 83 – Landerneau 27

⚠ La Côte des Légendes

℘ 02 98 83 41 65. www.campingcotedeslegendes.com

Address : rue Douar ar Pont (situated 2km to the northwest)

Opening times : from end March to mid Nov.

3.5 ha (147 pitches) flat, grassy, sandy

Tariff : (2015 price) 20.76€ ♣♣ ⇔ 🅴 🅷 (10A) –
Extra per person 4.85€

Rental rates : (2015 price) (from end March to mid Nov.) – 11 🚐 –
3 🏠 – 4 tent lodges. Per night from 36 to 131€ – Per week from 240 to 688€

🚏 local sani-station 3€ – 4 🅴 11.26€ – 🚐 🅷11.26€

Beside La Plage Des Crapauds (beach); an eco-friendly site.

Surroundings : ⅍ 🗆 ⚲ ♨
Leisure activities : 🏠🏃
Facilities : ⅍ ⛟ (July–Aug.) 🎳 🍽 🖧
Nearby : ♨

This guide is updated regularly, so buy your new copy every year!

GPS Longitude : -4.32928
Latitude : 48.67284

CALLAC

22160 – Michelin map **309** B4 – pop. 2 359 – alt. 172
▶ Paris 510 – Carhaix-Plouguer 22 – Guingamp 28 – Morlaix 41

⚠ Municipal Verte Vallée

℘ 02 96 45 58 50. 22commune025@mairie-callac.fr

Address : place Jean Auffret (take the western exit along the D 28, follow the signs for Morlaix and turn left onto avenue Ernest Renan; 50m from a small lake)

Opening times : from mid June to end Aug.

1 ha (60 pitches)

Tariff : (2015 price) ♣ 2.65€ ⇔ 1.30€ 🅴 2€ – 🅷 (10A) 2€

🚏 local sani-station 2€

Surroundings : ⅍ 🗆 ♨
Leisure activities : 🎱 🏃 🏄
Facilities : ⅍ ⛟ (July–Aug.) 🖼

CAMARET-SUR-MER

29570 – Michelin map **308** D5 – pop. 2 576 – alt. 4
▶ Paris 597 – Brest 4 – Châteaulin 45 – Crozon 11

⚠ Le Grand Large

℘ 02 98 27 91 41. www.campinglegrandlarge.com

Address : at Lambézen (3km northeast along the D 355 and take turning to the right; 400m from the beach)

2.8 ha (123 pitches) flat, relatively flat, grassy

Rentals : 27 🚐 – 3 🏠.

Looks out over the entrance to Brest's natural harbour, with a spectacular view from half of the pitches.

Surroundings : ⅍ ≤ the sea 🗆
Leisure activities : 🍽🏠🏃🏄 🏃
Facilities : ⅍ ⛟🎳 🖧 🍽 launderette 🧺🚿

GPS Longitude : -4.56472
Latitude : 48.28083

We have selected the best campsites in France with our usual care, listing those with the best facilities in the most pleasant surroundings.

CAMORS

56330 – Michelin map **308** M7 – pop. 2 788 – alt. 113
▶ Paris 472 – Auray 24 – Lorient 39 – Pontivy 31

⚠ Le Village Insolite

℘ 02 97 39 18 36. www.camping-levillageinsolite.com

Address : rue des Mésanges (located 1km west along the D 189, follow the signs for Lambel-Camors)

1 ha (34 pitches) flat, grassy, terraced

Rentals : 1 'gypsy' caravan – 2 🏠 – 1 yurt – 1 tipi.

🚏 local sani-station

Situated near lakes and a national forest.

Surroundings : ⅍ ⚲
Leisure activities : 🗓 (open air in season)
Facilities : ⅍ ⛟🎳 🖧 🍽 🖼
Nearby : 🌲 forest trail

GPS Longitude : -3.01304
Latitude : 47.84613

CANCALE

35260 – Michelin map **309** K2 – pop. 5 374 – alt. 50
▶ Paris 398 – Avranches 61 – Dinan 35 – Fougères 73

⚠ Le Bois Pastel

℘ 02 99 89 66 10. www.campingboispastel.fr

Address : 13 rue de la Corgnais (7km northwest along the D 201 coast road and take the turning to the left)

Opening times : from beginning April to end Sept.

5.2 ha (247 pitches) flat, grassy

Tariff : (2015 price) ♣ 4.90€ ⇔ 2€ 🅴 11€ – 🅷 (6A) 4€ – Reservation fee 15€

Rental rates : (2015 price) permanent – 20 🚐 – 6 canvas bungalows. Per week from 230 to 710€ – Reservation fee 15€

Pitches among greenery for tents and caravans, many of which are well shaded.

Surroundings : ⅍ ♨♨
Leisure activities : 🍽 🏃🏄 🗓 (open air in season), multi-sports ground
Facilities : ⅍ ⛟ 🍽 launderette 🧺🚿

GPS Longitude : -1.86861
Latitude : 48.68875

CARANTEC

29660 – Michelin map **308** H2 – pop. 3 249 – alt. 37
▶ Paris 552 – Brest 71 – Lannion 53 – Morlaix 14

⛰ Yelloh! Village Les Mouettes ☺♣

⚓ 02 98 67 02 46. www.les-mouettes.com – limited spaces for one-night stay

Address : 50 route de la Grande Grève (located 1.5km southwest following the signs for St-Pol-de-Léon and take right turn

Opening times : from beginning April to mid Sept.

4 ha (474 pitches) flat, grassy

Tariff : 52€ ♣♣ 🚗 🔲 (10A) – Extra per person 9€

Rental rates : (from beginning April to mid Sept.) ♿ Ⓟ – 242 🛖 – 34 🏠. Per night from 39 to 245€ – Per week from 273 to 1.715

A magnificent aquatic park with giant slides near the sea. High-quality rental options.

Surroundings : 🐾 ▭ ♀
Leisure activities : 🍽 ✗ 🎭 📷 🏃 🎣 jacuzzi 🚴 ✂ 🎿 🏊 library, spa centre, entertainment room
Facilities : ♿ ⚬▬ ⛴ ☂ ▽ ¶ launderette ♨
🐟

GPS
Longitude : -3.92802
Latitude : 48.65922

*To visit a town or region, use the **MICHELIN** Green Guides.*

CARNAC

56340 – Michelin map **308** M9 – pop. 4 362 – alt. 16
▶ Paris 490 – Auray 13 – Lorient 49 – Quiberon 19

⛰ Les Castels La Grande Métairie ☺♣

⚓ 02 97 52 24 01. www.lagrandemetairie.com – limited spaces for one-night stay

Address : route de Kerlescan (2.5km to the northeast)

Opening times : from beginning April to mid Sept.

15 ha/11 for camping (581 pitches) flat, relatively flat, grassy

Tariff : 66€ ♣♣ 🚗 🔲 (10A) – Extra per person 8.50€

Rental rates : (from beginning April to mid Sept.) ♿ (1 mobile home) – 8 'gypsy' caravans – 219 🛖 – 2 cabins in the trees. Per week from 273 to 1,883€

🚉 local sani-station

Located near the Kerloquet lake with a variety of high-quality rental options that can be quite near each other. Several tour operator-owned mobile homes.

Surroundings : ▭ ♀♀
Leisure activities : 🍽 ✗ 🎭 📷 (open-air theatre) 🏃 jacuzzi 🚴 🐎 ✂ 🎣 🎿 🏊 zip wiring, forest trail, farm or petting farm, skate park
Facilities : ♿ ⚬▬ ⛴ ☂ ▽ ¶ launderette ♨ 🐟
Nearby : 🐎

GPS
Longitude : -3.05975
Latitude : 47.59647

⛰ Le Moustoir ☺♣

⚓ 02 97 52 16 18. www.lemoustoir.com

Address : 71 route du Moustoir (situated 3km to the northeast)

Opening times : from beginning April to mid Sept.

5 ha (165 pitches) flat, relatively flat, grassy

Tariff : (2015 price) 24.40€ ♣♣ 🚗 🔲 (10A) – Extra per person 7.20€ – Reservation fee 8€

Rental rates : (2015 price) (from beginning April to mid Sept.) – 90 🛖 – 15 🏠 – 6 🛏. Per week from 225 to 1,180€ – Reservation fee 8€

🚉 local sani-station

Surroundings : ▭ ♀♀
Leisure activities : 🍽 ✗ 🎭 📷 🏃 🚴 🎿 🏊 farm or petting farm, multi-sports ground
Facilities : ♿ ⚬▬ ⛴ ☂ ▽ ¶ launderette ♨

GPS
Longitude : -3.06689
Latitude : 47.60829

⛰ Moulin de Kermaux ☺♣

⚓ 02 97 52 15 90. www.camping-moulinkermaux.com

Address : route de Kerlescan (2.5km to the northeast)

Opening times : from mid April to mid Sept.

3 ha (150 pitches) flat, relatively flat, grassy

Tariff : (2015 price) 38€ ♣♣ 🚗 🔲 (18A) – Extra per person 6.50€ – Reservation fee 18€

Rental rates : (2015 price) (from mid April to mid Sept.) ♿ – 70 🛖 – 3 canvas bungalows. Per night from 65 to 120€ – Per week from 258 to 934€ – Reservation fee 20€

🚉 Eurorelais sani-station

Surroundings : 🐾 ▭ ♀
Leisure activities : 🍽 ✗ 🎭 📷 🏃 🎣 jacuzzi 🚴 ✂ 🏊 (open air in season) 🎿 multi-sports ground
Facilities : ♿ ⚬▬ ⛴ ☂ ¶ launderette ♨
Nearby : 🐎

GPS
Longitude : -3.06523
Latitude : 47.59512

⛰ Le Lac ☺♣

⚓ 02 97 55 78 78. www.lelac-carnac.com

Address : Passage du Lac (6.3km to the northeast; beside the lake)

Opening times : from beginning May to end Sept.

2.5 ha (132 pitches) flat, grassy, terraced

Tariff : 14€ ♣♣ 🚗 🔲 (6A) – Extra per person 5€ – Reservation fee 8€

Rental rates : (2015 price) (from beginning May to end Sept.) – 3 'gypsy' caravans – 20 🛖 – 1 tipi – 5 tent lodges. Per week from 196 to 715€ – Reservation fee 8€

🚉 local sani-station – 🚐 10€

Surroundings : 🐾 ≤ ▭ ♀
Leisure activities : 🎭 🏃 🚴 🎿 🏊 multi-sports ground
Facilities : ♿ ⚬▬ ⛴ ¶ launderette ♨

GPS
Longitude : -3.02912
Latitude : 47.61117

⛰ Les Bruyères ☺♣

⚓ 02 97 52 30 57. www.camping-lesbruyeres.com

Address : at Kérogile (3km to the north)

Opening times : from beginning April to end Sept.

2 ha (115 pitches) flat, grassy

Tariff : (2015 price) ♣ 6.50€ 🚗 🔲 10.90€ – (10A) 4.80€ – Reservation fee 10€

Rental rates : (2015 price) (from beginning April to end Sept.) – 35 🛖 – 2 🏠 – 3 canvas bungalows – 2 tent lodges. Per night from 27 to 132€ – Per week from 189 to 924€ – Reservation fee 20€

🚉 local sani-station

Surroundings : 🐾 ♀♀
Leisure activities : 🎭 🏃 🚴 🐎 🏊 (open air in season), zip wiring, farm or petting farm
Facilities : ⚬▬ ☂ ¶ launderette
Nearby : bowling

GPS
Longitude : -3.08884
Latitude : 47.60437

⛰ Kérabus

☎ 02 97 52 24 90. www.camping-kerabus.com

Address : 13 allée des Alouettes (situated 2km to the northeast)

Opening times : from beginning April to end Sept.

1.4 ha (86 pitches) flat, grassy

Tariff : (2015 price) 20.50€ ♥♥ ⇌ 🔲 ⚡ (6A) – Extra per person 5.50€ – Reservation fee 8€

Rental rates : (2015 price) (from beginning April to end Sept.) – 14 🚐 – 1 tent lodge. Per night from 60 to 110€ – Per week from 180 to 670€ – Reservation fee 10€

🚱 Eurorelais sani-station 5€ – 🚐 8€

Surroundings : 🏊 ⛱ ♉
Leisure activities : ⛵ 🛶 multi-sports ground
Facilities : 🚿 🛁 🍴 launderette

Longitude : -3.07648	Latitude : 47.59641

⛰ Tohapi Le Domaine de Kermario
(rental of mobile homes and gîtes only)

☎ 08 25 00 20 30. www.tohapi.fr

Address : 1 chemin de Kerluir (situated 2km to the northeast)

Opening times : from mid April to end Sept.

4 ha flat, pond

Rental rates : (2015 price) 🅿 – 113 🚐 – 4 gîtes. Per night from 32 to 64€

Furnished gîtes in an old farmhouse that has been beautifully restored.

Surroundings : 🏊 ♉
Leisure activities : ✗ 🛶 🎣 🏋 ⛵ 🚴 🏓 🛶 multi-sports ground, entertainment room
Facilities : 🚿 🍴 launderette 🧺

Longitude : -3.06636	Latitude : 47.59521

CARNAC-PLAGE

56340 – Michelin map **308** M9
▶ Paris 494 – Rennes 143 – Vannes 34

⛰ Les Menhirs ♣♣

☎ 02 97 52 94 67. www.lesmenhirs.com – limited spaces for one-night stay

Address : allée Saint-Michel

Opening times : from mid April to end Sept.

6 ha (342 pitches) flat, grassy

Tariff : ♥ 8.85€ ⇌ 🔲 32.60€ – ⚡ (10A) 4.95€ – Reservation fee 20€

Rental rates : (from mid April to end Sept.) 🚱 (1 mobile home) 🏊 – 61 🚐 – 1 🏠. Per night from 45 to 164€ – Per week from 320 to 1,150€ – Reservation fee 20€

🚱 AireService sani-station

Situated 400m from the beach and the town centre.

Surroundings : 🏊 ⛱ ♉
Leisure activities : 🍴 🎯 🏋 🎣 🧖 jacuzzi ⛵ 🎿 🛶 multi-sports ground, entertainment room
Facilities : 🚿 🛁 🍴 launderette 🧺
Nearby : 🛒 🚴

Longitude : -3.06979	Latitude : 47.57683

This guide is not intended as a list of all the camping sites in France; its aim is to provide a selection of the best sites in each category.

⛰ Les Druides

☎ 02 97 52 08 18. www.camping-les-druides.com

Address : 55 chemin de Beaumer (To the east, in part of town called Beaumer, 500m from the beach)

Opening times : from mid April to beginning Sept.

2.5 ha (110 pitches)

Tariff : (2015 price) ♥ 6.80€ ⇌ 3.50€ 🔲 20.40€ – ⚡ (10A) 6.30€ – Reservation fee 20€

Rental rates : (2015 price) (from mid April to beginning Sept.) 🏊 – 17 🚐 – 3 apartments. Per week from 225 to 805€ – Reservation fee 20€

🚱 local sani-station

Surroundings : 🏊 ♉
Leisure activities : 🎣 ⛵ 🛶 multi-sports ground
Facilities : 🚿 🛁 🍴 launderette
Nearby : 🛒

Longitude : -3.05689	Latitude : 47.58012

⛺ Le Men-Du

☎ 02 97 52 04 23. www.camping-mendu.fr

Address : 22bis chemin de Beaumer (in suburb called Le Men-Du, 300m from the beach)

Opening times : from beginning April to beginning Oct.

1.5 ha (91 pitches) flat, relatively flat, grassy

Tariff : 28€ ♥♥ ⇌ 🔲 ⚡ (15A) – Extra per person 5€ – Reservation fee 15€

Rental rates : (from beginning April to beginning Oct.) 🚱 (1 mobile home) – 20 🚐. Per night from 105 to 140€ – Per week from 250 to 660€ – Reservation fee 15€

Surroundings : 🏊 ⛱ ♉
Leisure activities : ✗
Facilities : 🚿 🍴 launderette
Nearby : ✗

Longitude : -3.05522	Latitude : 47.57941

The Michelin classification (⛰⛰⛰ ... ⛺) is totally independent of the official star classification system awarded by the local prefecture or other official organisation.

LA CHAPELLE-AUX-FILTZMEENS

35190 – Michelin map **309** L4 – pop. 726 – alt. 40
▶ Paris 388 – Rennes 39 – Saint-Malo 42 – Fougères 83

⛰ Le Domaine du Logis

☎ 02 99 45 25 45. www.domainedulogis.com

Address : Le Logis (located 1.5km west on the D 13. follow the signs for St-Domineuc)

20 ha/6 for camping (188 pitches) flat, grassy

Rentals : 🚱 – 19 🚐.

In a lovely rural setting, based at a former traditional Breton farm complex.

Surroundings : 🏊 ⛱ ♉
Leisure activities : 🍴 ✗ 🛶 🏋 🎣 ⛵ 🚴 🛶 🛶 mountain biking
Facilities : 🚿 🍴 launderette 🧺
Nearby : 🎣

Longitude : -1.83566	Latitude : 48.38306

CHÂTEAUGIRON

35410 – Michelin map **309** M6 – pop. 6 450 – alt. 45
▶ Paris 336 – Angers 114 – Châteaubriant 45 – Fougères 56

⚐ Les Grands Bosquets

𝒫 02 99 37 89 02. www.tourisme-payschateaugiron.fr

Address : route d'Ossé (take the eastern exit along the D 34)

0.6 ha (33 pitches) flat, grassy

Situated beside a lake (suitable for bathing) in a rural setting.

Surroundings : ⚲⚲ Leisure activities : 🏖 (beach) 🎣 Nearby : 🛶 ✗	**GPS** Longitude : -1.49734 Latitude : 48.04983

CHÂTEAULIN

29150 – Michelin map **308** G5 – pop. 5 337 – alt. 10
▶ Paris 548 – Brest 49 – Douarnenez 27 – Châteauneuf-du-Faou 24

⚐ Le Rodaven

𝒫 02 98 86 32 93. www.campingderodaven.fr

Address : south of the town, beside the Aulne river (right bank)

Opening times : from beginning April to end Sept.

2.3 ha (94 pitches) flat, grassy

Tariff : 16.50€ ⚹⚹ ⛺ 🔲 (10A) – Extra per person 3.90€

Rental rates : (from beginning April to end Sept.) – 2 'gypsy' caravans – 7 🚐 – 3 tipis. Per night from 28 to 70€ – Per week from 130 to 590€

🚐 local sani-station 2€

Beside the Aulne river, attractive pitches for tents and caravans, with shops and restaurants nearby.

Surroundings : ⚲ Leisure activities : 🍹 🛶 🎣 Facilities : ♿ ⚷ 🔲 🚿 launderette 🧺 Nearby : 🛒 ✗ 🚲 ✗ 🎣 🖼 🛶 canoeing	**GPS** Longitude : -4.08995 Latitude : 48.19012

For more information on visiting particular towns or regions, consult the relevant regional MICHELIN Green Guide. We also recommend you use the appropriate Michelin regional map to locate your selected campsite, to calculate distances and to work out the best route.

CHÂTELAUDREN

22170 – Michelin map **309** E3 – pop. 1 047 – alt. 105
▶ Paris 469 – Guingamp 17 – Lannion 49 – St-Brieuc 18

⚐ Municipal de l'Étang

𝒫 02 96 74 10 38. www.chatelaudren.fr – ☞

Address : rue de la Gare (in the town; beside a large, beautiful lake)

Opening times : from beginning May to end Sept.

0.2 ha (17 pitches) flat, grassy

Tariff : (2015 price) ⚹ 3.20€ ⛺ 1.10€ 🔲 4.50€ – (10A) 3.50€

Near the town and opposite a lovely fishing lake.

Surroundings : 🌳 🏕 ⚲ Leisure activities : 🎣 Facilities : 🧺 Nearby : 🛶	**GPS** Longitude : -2.9709 Latitude : 48.53883

CHÂTILLON-EN-VENDELAIS

35210 – Michelin map **309** O5 – pop. 1 698 – alt. 133
▶ Paris 311 – Fougères 17 – Rennes 49 – Vitré 13

⚐ Le Lac

𝒫 06 03 33 64 35. www.chatillon-en-vendelais.fr

Address : rue des Rouxieres, at l'Épine (500m north along the D 108; beside the Étang de Châtillon)

0.6 ha (61 pitches) relatively flat, grassy

Rentals : 1 🏠.

In a pleasant natural setting by the lake (Étang de Chatillon).

Surroundings : 🌳 ← 🏕 ⚲⚲ ⛰ Leisure activities : 🎣 Facilities : 🚿 Nearby : 🍹 ✗ ✗	**GPS** Longitude : -1.18026 Latitude : 48.22909

To visit a town or region, use the MICHELIN Green Guides.

CHERRUEIX

35120 – Michelin map **309** L3 – pop. 1 141 – alt. 3
▶ Paris 377 – Cancale 20 – Dinard 32 – Dol-de-Bretagne 9

⚐ L'Aumône

𝒫 02 99 48 84 82. www.camping-de-laumone.com

Address : 0.5km south along the D 797

Opening times : from beginning April to beginning Nov.

1.6 ha (70 pitches) flat, grassy

Tariff : (2015 price) ⚹ 4€ ⛺ 🔲 9€ – (10A) 10€

Rental rates : (2015 price) permanent – 10 🚐 – 1 tipi – 1 canvas bungalow – 2 gîtes. Per night from 50 to 120€ – Per week from 230 to 590€ – Reservation fee 30€

Located behind a beautiful stone building in a leafy setting, with slightly old sanitary facilities.

Surroundings : ⚲ Leisure activities : 🍹 ✗ 🛶 🚲 🎣 Facilities : ⚷ 🚿 launderette	**GPS** Longitude : -1.71248 Latitude : 48.60172

CONCARNEAU

29900 – Michelin map **308** H7 – pop. 19 352 – alt. 4
▶ Paris 546 – Brest 96 – Lorient 49 – Quimper 22

⚐ Les Sables Blancs 👥

𝒫 02 98 97 16 44. www.camping-lessablesblancs.com

Address : rue des Fleurs (100m from the beach)

Opening times : from beginning April to end Oct.

3 ha (149 pitches) terraced, relatively flat, flat, grassy

Tariff : (2015 price) 31.30€ ⚹⚹ ⛺ 🔲 (10A) – Extra per person 7€

Rental rates : (2015 price) (from beginning April to end Oct.) – 41 🚐. Per night from 55 to 117€ – Per week from 285 to 819€

🚐 local sani-station

Situated close to the town centre and beaches, with a lovely view of the sea from some pitches.

Surroundings : 🌳 ← Concarneau bay 🏕 ⚲⚲ Leisure activities : 🍹 ✗ 🎮 ⚹⚹ jacuzzi 🛶 🏊 Facilities : ♿ ⚷ 🛁 🚿 launderette 🧺 Nearby : 🛶	**GPS** Longitude : -3.92836 Latitude : 47.88203

⛺ Les Prés Verts

📞 02 98 97 09 74. www.presverts.com

Address : Kernous-Plage (3km northwest along the coast road and take a left turn; 250m from the beach (direct access)

3 ha (142 pitches) relatively flat to hilly, flat, grassy

Rentals : 12 🛖.

Quiet and pleasant location, with a view over Concarneau bay from some pitches.

Surroundings : 🌿
Leisure activities : 🏛 🏊 ⛵
Facilities : ♿ 🚿 🍴 launderette

GPS Longitude : -3.93333
Latitude : 47.88333

LE CONQUET

29217 – Michelin map **308** C4 – pop. 2 635 – alt. 30
▶ Paris 619 – Brest 24 – Brignogan-Plages 59 – St-Pol-de-Léon 85

⛰ Les Blancs Sablons

📞 02 98 36 07 91. www.les-blancs-sablons.com

Address : Le Théven (5km northeast along the D 67 and take D 28, follow the signs for the beach at Les Blancs Sablons, 400m from the beach – passenger walkway to town)

Opening times : from beginning April to end Sept.

12 ha (360 pitches) flat, grassy, sandy

Tariff : (2015 price) 20.44€ 👫👫 ⚗ 🔌 (16A) –
Extra per person 4.50€ – Reservation fee 9€

Rental rates : (2015 price) (from beginning April to end Oct.) –
10 🛖 – 3 🏠. Per night from 45 to 77€ – Per week from 250 to 660€ – Reservation fee 9€

In a natural setting, bordering on the wild.

Surroundings : 🌿
Leisure activities : 🍴 🏊 ⛵
Facilities : ♿ 🚿 🍴 launderette

GPS Longitude : -4.76071
Latitude : 48.36687

A chambre d'hôte is a guesthouse or B & B-style accommodation.

CRACH

56950 – Michelin map **308** M9 – pop. 3 276 – alt. 35
▶ Paris 482 – Auray 6 – Lorient 46 – Quiberon 29

⛰ Flower Le Fort Espagnol

📞 02 97 55 14 88. www.fort-espagnol.com

Address : route du Fort Espagnol (800m east, follow the signs for La Rivière d'Auray)

Opening times : from beginning April to end Sept.

5 ha (209 pitches) relatively flat, flat, grassy

Tariff : (2015 price) 27€ 👫👫 ⚗ 🔌 (10A) – Extra per person 6.50€ – Reservation fee 26€

Rental rates : (2015 price) (from beginning April to end Sept.) – 3 'gypsy' caravans – 86 🛖 – 4 🏠 – 4 tent lodges. Per night from 21 to 131€ – Per week from 150 to 920€ – Reservation fee 26€

A variety of often high-quality rental options and a few pitches for tents and caravans.

Surroundings : 🌿
Leisure activities : 🍴✗🏛🏊🚲🏓⛵
Facilities : ♿ 🚿 🍴 launderette
Nearby : 🛒 ✖ 🎣

CROZON

29160 – Michelin map **308** E5 – pop. 7 697 – alt. 85
▶ Paris 587 – Brest 60 – Châteaulin 35 – Douarnenez 40

⛰ Les Pins

📞 06 60 54 40 09. www.camping-crozon-lespins.com

Address : route de Dinan (situated 2km southwest along the D 308 follow the signs for La Pointe de Dinan (headland)

Opening times : from mid May to mid Sept.

4 ha (155 pitches) open site, flat and relatively flat, grassy, sandy

Tariff : (2015 price) 👫 5€ ⚗ 🔌 9.50€ – 🔌 (10A) 3.95€

Rental rates : (2015 price) (from beginning April to end Oct.) ♿ (1 mobile home) – 12 🛖 – 13 🏠. Per night from 65€ – Per week from 330 to 690€

A very peaceful site under the pine trees, ideal for rest and relaxation.

Surroundings : 🌿 ♀♀
Leisure activities : 🏊 🏊 (small swimming pool)
Facilities : ♿ 🚿 🍴 🎮
Nearby : forest trail

GPS Longitude : -4.51462
Latitude : 48.24153

⛰ Plage de Goulien

📞 06 08 43 49 32. www.presquile-crozon.com

Address : Goullen beach (5km west along the D 308, follow signs for La Pointe de Dinan and take a right turn, 200m from the beach)

Opening times : from mid May to mid Sept.

3.5 ha (135 pitches) terraced, relatively flat, flat, grassy

Tariff : 👫 5.50€ ⚗ 🔌 9.80€ – 🔌 (10A) 4€

Rental rates : (from end April to mid Sept.) – 24 🛖 – 4 🏠. Per night from 65 to 95€ – Per week from 330 to 690€

Located near a sandy beach.

Surroundings : 🌿 ♀♀
Leisure activities : 🍴 🏛 🏊 🏓
Facilities : ♿ 🚿 🍴 launderette 🎮

GPS Longitude : -4.54437
Latitude : 48.23908

To make the best possible use of this guide, please read pages 2–15 carefully.

DINÉAULT

29150 – Michelin map **308** G5 – pop. 1 739 – alt. 160
▶ Paris 560 – Rennes 208 – Quimper 36 – Brest 54

⛺ Ty Provost

📞 02 98 86 29 23. www.typrovost.com

Address : 4km southeast along the C 1, follow the signs for Châteaulin and take road to the left

Opening times : from beginning June to mid Sept.

1.2 ha (44 pitches) terraced, flat and relatively flat, grassy

Tariff : 21.70€ 👫👫 ⚗ 🔌 (10A) – Extra per person 4.90€

Rental rates : permanent ♿ (2 chalets) – 5 🛖 – 7 🏠 – 2 gîtes. Per night from 49 to 79€ – Per week from 296 to 547€
🚉 local sani-station

In a lovely setting, based at an impressive traditional farm complex with a panoramic view of the meandering Aulne river.

Surroundings : 🌿 ≤ Aulne valley ♀
Leisure activities : 🍴 🏛 🏊
Facilities : ♿ 🚿 🍴 launderette

GPS Longitude : -4.12421
Latitude : 48.20706

DOL-DE-BRETAGNE

35120 – Michelin map **309** L3 – pop. 5 163 – alt. 20
▶ Paris 378 – Alençon 154 – Dinan 26 – Fougères 54

▲▲▲ Les Castels Domaine des Ormes

✆ 02 99 73 53 00. www.lesormes.com – limited spaces for one-night stay

Address : at Épiniac (7.5km south along the D 795, follow the signs for Combourg then take the road to the left)

Opening times : from beginning April to end Sept.

200 ha/40 for camping (630 pitches) flat, relatively flat, grassy, forest

Tariff : 65.40 € ✶✶ ⇌ ▣ ⚡ (10A) – Extra per person 8.70 € – Reservation fee 20 €

Rental rates : permanent – 1 'gypsy' caravan – 80 ⬚ – 28 ⬚ – 11 studios – 25 apartments – 26 cabins in the trees – 4 gîtes – Per night from 109 to 245 € – Per week from 520 to 1,830 € – Reservation fee 20 €

In the grounds of a 16th-century château, with wide open spaces and plenty of activities, including a partially covered water park.

Surroundings : 🐟 ≤ 🌳🌳
Leisure activities : ♈ ✗ 🏠 🛖 🏃 🎣 ≋ 🚣 🚴 ✂ 🏓 🎳 🎯 🏹 🐴 disco, climbing wall, forest trail, paintballing, zip wiring, golf course, driving range, multi-sports ground, entertainment room
Facilities : ♿ ⚬ ♈ launderette 🛒 🔧
G P S Longitude : -1.72722
Latitude : 48.49139

▲▲▲ Le Vieux Chêne

✆ 02 99 48 09 55. www.camping-vieuxchene.fr

Address : route de Pontorson (5km east, along the N 176. follow the signs for Pontorson, east of Baguer-Pican on the D 57. Advised route via the diversion, take exit Dol-de-Bretagne-Est and take D 80, D 576)

Opening times : from beginning May to mid Sept.

4 ha/2 for camping (213 pitches) flat, relatively flat, grassy

Tariff : 31 € ✶✶ ⇌ ▣ ⚡ (10A) – Extra per person 7.50 €

Rental rates : (from beginning April to mid Sept.) – 16 ⬚ – 18 ⬚. Per night from 44 to 117 € – Per week from 220 to 819 €
⬚ local sani-station 9 € – 2 ▣ 31 €

In a pleasant location beside two natural lakes, a perfect spot for fishing and relaxing.

Surroundings : 🐟 🌳🌳
Leisure activities : ♈ ✗ 🏠 🛖 ✂ 🏓 🎳 🎯 🚣
Facilities : ♿ ⚬ 🚿 🔧 🛒 🚰 ♈ launderette 🛒 🔧
G P S Longitude : -1.68361
Latitude : 48.54945

ERDEVEN

56410 – Michelin map **308** M9 – pop. 3 402 – alt. 18
▶ Paris 492 – Auray 15 – Carnac 10 – Lorient 28

▲ La Croëz-Villieu

✆ 02 97 55 90 43. www.la-croez-villieu.com – limited spaces for one-night stay

Address : at Kernogan, route de Kerhillio (located 1km southwest along the beach road at Kerhillio)

Opening times : from beginning May to end Sept.

3 ha (158 pitches) flat, grassy

Tariff : (2015 price) ✶ 6.90 € ⇌ ▣ 12.80 € – ⚡ (10A) 4.50 €

Rental rates : (2015 price) (from beginning April to mid Oct.) – 28 ⬚ – 2 tent lodges. Per week from 95 to 805 €
Choose the pitches furthest from the road.

Surroundings : 🔲 🌳
Leisure activities : ♈ ≋ hammam jacuzzi 🚴 ✂ 🏓 🎳 🚣
Facilities : ⚬ 🔧 ♈ launderette
Nearby : 🛒
G P S Longitude : -3.15838
Latitude : 47.63199

To make the best possible use of this guide, please read pages 2–15 carefully.

ERQUY

22430 – Michelin map **309** H3 – pop. 3 802 – alt. 12
▶ Paris 451 – Dinan 46 – Dinard 39 – Lamballe 21

▲▲▲ Sites et Paysages Bellevue ▲▲

✆ 02 96 72 33 04. http://campingbellevue.fr

Address : route de la Libération (5.5km southwest)

Opening times : from beginning April to mid Sept.

3.5 ha (160 pitches) flat, grassy

Tariff : 30 € ✶✶ ⇌ ▣ ⚡ (10A) – Extra per person 5.90 €

Rental rates : (from beginning April to end Sept.) ♿ (1 chalet) ✂ – 25 ⬚ – 5 ⬚ – 2 tent lodges. Per night from 45 to 112 € – Per week from 290 to 840 €
⬚ local sani-station – 🔧 ⚡ 17 €

The entrance is surrounded by flowers, and the pitches are surrounded by trees and shrubs.

Surroundings : 🔲 🌳🌳
Leisure activities : ♈ 🏠 🏃 🎣 🚣 ✂ 🎳 (open air in season), multi-sports ground
Facilities : ♿ ⚬ 🔧 ♈ launderette 🔧
Nearby : ✗
G P S Longitude : -2.48528
Latitude : 48.59444

▲▲▲ Le Vieux Moulin ▲▲

✆ 02 96 72 34 23. www.camping-vieux-moulin.com

Address : 14 rue des Moulins (situated 2km east)

Opening times : from mid April to beginning Sept.

2.5 ha (199 pitches) flat, grassy

Tariff : 41 € ✶✶ ⇌ ▣ ⚡ (10A) – Extra per person 7 €

Rental rates : (from mid April to beginning Sept.) – 70 ⬚. Per night from 48 to 155 € – Per week from 240 to 1,085 €

In a well-kept, green setting.

Surroundings : 🔲 🌳🌳
Leisure activities : ♈ ✗ 🏠 🛖 🏃 🎣 ≋ 🚣 ✂ 🎳 🎯 🏹 multi-sports ground
Facilities : ♿ ⚬ 🔧 🚰 🔧 ♈ launderette 🛒 🔧
Nearby : ✗ 🎯
G P S Longitude : -2.44222
Latitude : 48.63805

▲ Des Hautes Grées

✆ 02 96 72 34 78. www.camping-hautes-grees.com

Address : 123 rue St Michel, at Les Hopitaux (3.5km to the northeast, 400m from the St-Michel beach)

Opening times : permanent

3 ha (177 pitches) flat, grassy

Tariff : (2015 price) 26.65 € ✶✶ ⇌ ▣ ⚡ (10A) – Extra per person 5.65 € – Reservation fee 15 €

Rental rates : (2015 price) permanent – 35 🚐. Per night from 45 to 72€ – Per week from 290 to 780€ – Reservation fee 15€
🚻 local sani-station – 10 📧 14.65€ – 🚐 💧14.65€

Surroundings : 🏖 ☁ ♀
Leisure activities : ✗ 🏛 🎠 ⛵ hammam
🏇 🛶
Facilities : 🚿 ⛏ 🏕 🍴 launderette 🚮

GPS Longitude : -2.42491
Latitude : 48.64254

🏔 La Plage de St-Pabu et La Ville de Berneuf

📞 02 96 72 24 65. www.saintpabu.com

Address : at St-Pabu (at the St-Pabu beach, 4km southwest)

5.5 ha (435 pitches)

Rentals : 45 🚐.

🚻 local sani-station

Overlooks Erquy bay and the large St Pabu beach.

Surroundings : 🏖 < ☁ ⛰
Leisure activities : 🍸 🏛 🏄 🎠
Facilities : 🚿 ⛏ 🏕 🍴 launderette 🚮
Nearby : 💧 scuba diving, kite-surfing, sand yachting

GPS Longitude : -2.49459
Latitude : 48.60878

🏔 Les Roches

📞 02 96 73 23 90. www.camping-les-roches.com

Address : rue Pierre Vergos (3km southwest)

Opening times : from beginning April to end Sept.

3 ha (175 pitches) terraced, flat, grassy

Tariff : 🚶 4.10€ 🚐 3€ 📧 6.60€ – 💧 (10A) 3.30€

Rental rates : (from beginning April to beginning Nov.) – 18 🚐 – 1 tent lodge. Per night from 47 to 62€ – Per week from 270 to 670€

🚻 local sani-station

Surroundings : 🏖 ♀
Leisure activities : 🏛 🏄 🏊
Facilities : 🚿 ⛏ 🎣 🏕 🍴 launderette 🚮

GPS Longitude : -2.4769
Latitude : 48.6094

ÉTABLES-SUR-MER

22680 – Michelin map **309** E3 – pop. 3 091 – alt. 65
▶ Paris 467 – Guingamp 31 – Lannion 56 – St-Brieuc 19

🏔 L'Abri-Côtier

📞 02 96 70 61 57. www.camping-abricotier.fr

Address : 12 rue De Robien (located 1km north following signs for St-Quay-Portrieux and take the turning to the left)

Opening times : from beginning May to mid Sept.

3 ha (185 pitches) flat, relatively flat, grassy

Tariff : 🚶 5.80€ 🚐 📧 8€ – 💧 (10A) 4€

Rental rates : (from beginning May to mid Sept.) – 14 🚐 – 5 canvas bungalows. Per night from 40 to 100€ – Per week from 240 to 700€

🚻 local sani-station 2€

Surroundings : 🏖 ♀♀
Leisure activities : 🍸 jacuzzi 🏊
Facilities : 🚿 ⛏ 🎣 🏕 🚮 🚿 🍴 launderette 🚮 🚮
Nearby : ✂ 🏇

GPS Longitude : -2.83529
Latitude : 48.6354

FEINS

35440 – Michelin map **309** M5 – pop. 798 – alt. 104
▶ Paris 369 – Avranches 55 – Fougères 44 – Rennes 30

⛰ Domaine de Boulet

📞 02 99 69 63 23. www.pays-aubigne.fr/camping

Address : at Domaine de Boulet (situated 2km northeast along the D 91, follow the signs for Marcillé-Raoul and take road to the left)

Opening times : from beginning April to end Sept.

1.5 ha (62 pitches) flat, grassy

Tariff : (2015 price) 13€ 🚶🚶 🚐 📧 💧 (10A) – Extra per person 4.50€

Rental rates : (2015 price) (from beginning April to end Sept.) – 6 🏠. Per night from 20 to 95€ – Per week from 226 to 565€

In a pleasant location beside the Étang de Boulet (lake), with some unusual-style accommodation.

Surroundings : 🏖 < ☁ ♀ ⛰
Leisure activities : 🏛 🏄 🚲 ⛵
Facilities : 🚿 ⛏ (July-Aug.) 🏕 🍴 launderette, refrigerated food storage facilities
Nearby : ⛵ 💧 🏇 watersports centre

GPS Longitude : -1.63863
Latitude : 48.33845

LA FORÊT-FOUESNANT

29940 – Michelin map **308** H7 – pop. 3 299 – alt. 19
▶ Paris 553 – Rennes 202 – Quimper 18 – Brest 94

🏔 Club Airotel Kérantérec 🏕

📞 02 98 56 98 11. www.camping-keranterec.com

Address : at Kerleven (2.8km southeast)

Opening times : from beginning April to end Sept.

6.5 ha (265 pitches) very uneven, terraced, relatively flat, flat, grassy

Tariff : 15€ 🚶🚶 🚐 📧 💧 (10A) – Extra per person 7€

Rental rates : (from beginning April to end Sept.) – 55 🚐. Per night from 70 to 120€ – Per week from 250 to 1,000€

🚻 AireService sani-station – 🚐 💧16€

With special access to the beach, this site is set amid lovely surroundings and enjoys peace and tranquility.

Surroundings : 🏖 ☁ ♀ ⛰
Leisure activities : 🍸 ✗ 🏛 🏄 🧗 🏄 🚲 🍴 🎣 🏊 🏛 entertainment room
Facilities : 🚿 ⛏ 🏕 🚿 🍴 launderette

GPS Longitude : -3.95538
Latitude : 47.89903

Key to rentals symbols:

12 🚐	*Number of mobile homes*
20 🏠	*Number of chalets*
6 🛏	*Number of rooms to rent*
Per night 30–50€	*Minimum/maximum rate per night*
Per week 300–1,000€	*Minimum/maximum rate per week*

⚞⚞ Kerleven ♠♣

📞 02 98 56 98 83. www.campingdekerleven.com – limited spaces for one-night stay

Address : at Kerleven, 4 route de Port La Forêt, (situated 2km southeast, 200m from the beach)

Opening times : from mid May to end Sept.

4 ha (235 pitches)

Tariff : (2015 price) 33.20€ ♣♣ ⚐ 🔲 ⚡ (10A) – Extra per person 7.50€ – Reservation fee 10€

Rental rates : (2015 price) (from beginning April to end Sept.) ⚑ – 37 ⏢. Per night from 70 to 95€ – Per week from 250 to 805€ – Reservation fee 10€

🚐 Eurorelais sani-station 2€

In a pleasant location around a former Breton 'longère' farmhouse.

Surroundings : 🗔 ♀♀
Leisure activities : ♟ ✕ 🖼 ⑨ ⚛ ⚓ 🖼 🎿 ⚝
Facilities : ♿ ⚬ 🛁 ♈ launderette 🗑 🚿
Nearby : ♨

| | GPS | Longitude : -3.96788 |
| | | Latitude : 47.89807 |

⚞⚞ Les Saules ♠♣

📞 02 98 56 98 57. www.camping-les-saules.com

Address : at Kerléven, 54 route de la Plage (2.5km southeast; beside the beach at Kerléven (direct access)

Opening times : from beginning May to end Sept.

4 ha (235 pitches) flat, relatively flat, grassy

Tariff : 32.20€ ♣♣ ⚐ 🔲 ⚡ (6A) – Extra per person 7€ – Reservation fee 18€

Rental rates : (from beginning April to end Sept.) ♿ (1 mobile home) – 39 ⏢ – 1 apartment. Per night from 95 to 300€ – Per week from 199 to 990€ – Reservation fee 18€

Surroundings : 🗔 ♀ ⚠
Leisure activities : ♟ ✕ 🖼 ⚛ ⚓ 🎿 ⚝
Facilities : ⚬ 🛁 ♈ launderette 🗑
Nearby : ♨

| | GPS | Longitude : -3.9611 |
| | | Latitude : 47.899 |

⚞⚞ Manoir de Penn ar Ster

📞 02 98 56 97 75. www.camping-pennarster.com

Address : 2 chemin de Penn-Ar-Ster (take the northeastern exit, follow the signs for Quimper and take the turning to the left)

Opening times : from beginning March to mid Nov.

3 ha (97 pitches) terraced, flat, grassy

Tariff : 29€ ♣♣ ⚐ 🔲 ⚡ (10A) – Extra per person 7€ – Reservation fee 10€

Rental rates : (from mid March to mid Nov.) ♿ (2 chalets) – 8 ⏢ – 2 🏠 – 1 tent lodge. Per night from 45 to 100€ – Per week from 230 to 690€ – Reservation fee 15€

🚐 AireService sani-station 5€ – 5 🔲 17€

The site adjoins a pretty stone manor house with an adjacent garden.

Surroundings : 🗔 ♀♀
Leisure activities : 🖼 ✂ ♩
Facilities : ♿ ⚬ ▥ 🛁 🚿 ♈ launderette 🗑 🚿
Nearby : ♟ ✕

| | GPS | Longitude : -3.97977 |
| | | Latitude : 47.91215 |

⚞⚞ FranceLoc Le St-Laurent

📞 02 98 56 97 65. www.franceloc.fr

Address : at Kerleven (3km southeast, 500m from the large beach at Kerleven)

Opening times : from beginning April to end Sept.

5.4 ha (260 pitches) terraced, flat, grassy

Tariff : (2015 price) 19€ ♣♣ ⚐ 🔲 ⚡ (10A) – Extra per person 4.70€ – Reservation fee 27€

Rental rates : (2015 price) (from beginning April to end Sept.) ♿ (1 mobile home) – 215 ⏢. Per night from 33 to 119€ – Per week from 133 to 1,246€ – Reservation fee 27€

Some pitches have a view of the sea and the Îles de Glénan (islands). There is an impressive water park with water slides.

Surroundings : 🏖 🗔 ♀♀ ⚠
Leisure activities : ♟ ✕ ⑨ ⚛ ⚓ ✂ 🕹 🖼 🎿 ⚝ 🏓 multi-sports ground
Facilities : ♿ ⚬ 🛁 ♈ launderette 🗑
Nearby : ⚓ ♨

| | GPS | Longitude : -3.9547 |
| | | Latitude : 47.89623 |

FOUESNANT

29170 – Michelin map **308** G7 – pop. 9 356 – alt. 30
▶ Paris 555 – Carhaix-Plouguer 69 – Concarneau 11 – Quimper 16

⚞⚞ Sunêlia L'Atlantique ♠♣

📞 02 98 56 14 44. www.latlantique.fr – limited spaces for one-night stay ⚑

Address : 4.5km to the south, towards La Chapelle de Kerbader, 400m from the beach (direct access)

Opening times : from end April to beginning Sept.

10 ha (432 pitches) flat, grassy

Tariff : 46€ ♣♣ ⚐ 🔲 ⚡ (6A) – Extra per person 9€

Rental rates : (from end April to beginning Sept.) ♿ (1 mobile home) ⚑ – 172 ⏢ – 4 yurts – 14 canvas bungalows. Per night from 36 to 200€ – Per week from 252 to 1,400€

🚐 local sani-station – 12 🔲 46€

Equipped with a pretty swimming area and spa, this site has beach access via a lovely path across the Fouesnant marshland.

Surroundings : 🏖 🗔 ♀♀
Leisure activities : ♟ ✕ 🖼 ⑨ ⚛ 🎠 ⚘ hammam, jacuzzi ⚓ ✂ ♩ 🖼 🎿 ⚝ spa centre, entertainment room
Facilities : ♿ ⚬ ▥ 🛁 🚿 ♈ launderette 🗑 🚿

| | GPS | Longitude : -4.01854 |
| | | Latitude : 47.85487 |

A chambre d'hôte is a guesthouse or B & B-style accommodation.

FOUGÈRES

35300 – Michelin map **309** O4 – pop. 19 820 – alt. 115
▶ Paris 326 – Caen 148 – Le Mans 132 – Nantes 158

⚞ Municipal de Paron

📞 02 99 99 40 81. camping@fougeres.fr

Address : route de la Chapelle-Janson (located 1.5km east along the D 17, access recommended via the eastern bypass (rocade)

Opening times : from beginning May to mid Sept.

2.5 ha (90 pitches) relatively flat, flat, grassy

Tariff : (2015 price) ♣ 3.50€ ⚐ 2.80€ 🔲 6€ – ⚡ (10A) 4.20€

🚐 local sani-station – 21 🔲 6€

In a lovely setting among trees, a stone's throw from the medieval city of Fougères.

Surroundings : 🐾 🗗 ⚇⚇
Leisure activities : 🏄
Facilities : ⊙🛒 ℻ launderette
Nearby : 🍴 🖼 🐴 🛶

G P S Longitude : -1.18193
Latitude : 48.35371

LE FRET

29160 – Michelin map **308** D5
▶ Paris 591 – Rennes 239 – Quimper 56 – Brest 10

🔺 Gwel Kaër

🖉 02 98 27 61 06. www.camping-gwel-kaer.com

Address : 40 rue de Pen-An-Ero (take the southeastern exit along the D 55. follow the signs for Crozon; beside the sea)

Opening times : from beginning April to end Sept.

2.2 ha (98 pitches) terraced, flat and relatively flat, grassy

Tariff : 👤 4.70€ 🚗 2.50€ 🔲 4.50€ – 🔌 (10A) 3.80€

Rental rates : (from beginning April to end Sept.) 🚐 – 7 🛖. Per night from 45 to 65€ – Per week from 295 to 530€

℻ local sani-station

Surroundings : 🐾 ≤ ⚇ ⚠
Leisure activities : 🏄
Facilities : & ⊙🛒 (from mid Jun. to mid Sept.)
🛁 ℻ 🖼

G P S Longitude : -4.50237
Latitude : 48.28132

GUIDEL

56520 – Michelin map **308** K8 – pop. 10 174 – alt. 38
▶ Paris 511 – Nantes 178 – Quimper 60 – Rennes 162

🔺🔺 Les Jardins de Kergal 👥

🖉 02 97 05 98 18. www.camping-lorient.com

Address : route des Plages (3km southwest along the D 306, follow the signs for Guidel-Plages and take road to the left)

Opening times : from beginning April to mid Nov.

5 ha (200 pitches) flat, grassy

Tariff : (2015 price) 👤 9€ 🚗 3€ 🔲 10€ – 🔌 (16A) 4€ – Reservation fee 20€

Rental rates : (2015 price) (from beginning April to beginning Nov.) & (1 chalet) – 30 🛖 – 30 🏠. Per night from 65 to 160€ – Per week from 230 to 1,210€ – Reservation fee 20€

This is a pleasant wooded site.

Surroundings : 🐾 ⚇⚇
Leisure activities : 🍴 🍴 🏛 📷 🏃 🏄 🚴 🍴 🎯
🔲 🏊 ⛷ multi-sports ground
Facilities : & ⊙🛒 🛁 ℻ launderette 🚿 refrigerators
Nearby : 🐴 paintballing

G P S Longitude : -3.50734
Latitude : 47.77464

These symbols are used for a campsite that is exceptional in its category:

🔺🔺🔺...🔺 *Particularly pleasant setting, quality and range of services available*

🐾🐾 *Tranquil, isolated site – quiet site, particularly at night*

≤≤ *Exceptional view – interesting or panoramic view*

HILLION

22120 – Michelin map **309** F3 – pop. 3 786 – alt. 28
▶ Paris 445 – Rennes 94 – Saint-Brieuc 13 – Vannes 116

🔺🔺 Bellevue Mer

🖉 02 96 32 20 39. www.bellevuemer.com

Address : at Lerno (2.5 km north on the route de la Pointe des Guettes, 500 m from the beach)

Opening times : from beginning April to end Sept.

0.9 ha (55 pitches) terraced, flat, grassy

Tariff : 14.20€ 👤👤 🚗 🔲 🔌 (10A) – Extra per person 4.70€

Rental rates : (from beginning April to end Aug.) & 🚐 – 11 🛖. Per night from 80 to 130€ – Per week from 280 to 650€ – Reservation fee 10€

℻ local sani-station 3€ – 20 🔲 14.50€ – 🔌 11€

Pitches overlooking St Brieuc bay. Near the green trail and GR 34.

Surroundings : 🐾 ≤
Leisure activities : 🍴 🏄 🔲
Facilities : & ⊙🛒 🖼 ℻ launderette 🚿 refrigerated food storage facilities

G P S Longitude :
Latitude :

ÎLE-AUX-MOINES

56780 – Michelin map **308** N9 – pop. 601 – alt. 16
▶ Paris 483 – Rennes 132 – Vannes 15 – Lorient 59

🔺 Municipal du Vieux Moulin

🖉 02 97 26 30 68. www.mairie-ileauxmoines.fr 🚐

Address : at Le Vieux Moulin (take southeastern exit from town, follow the signs for La Pointe de Brouel (headland))

Opening times : from beginning April to mid Sept.

1 ha (44 pitches)

Tariff : (2015 price) 👤 7€ 🚗 🔲 🔌 (0A)

Site reserved for tents with no electricity supply (except for rental options). High-quality sanitary facilities.

Surroundings : 🐾 ⚇⚇
Leisure activities : 🏄
Facilities : ⊙🛒
Nearby : 🖼

G P S Longitude : -2.84514
Latitude : 47.59292

JOSSELIN

56120 – Michelin map **308** P7 – pop. 2 533 – alt. 58
▶ Paris 428 – Dinan 86 – Lorient 76 – Pontivy 35

🔺🔺 Domaine de Kerelly

🖉 02 97 22 22 20. www.camping-josselin.com

Address : at Le Bas de la Lande (2km west along the D 778 and take the D 724, follow the signs for Guégon to the left, 50m from the Oust river, take the western exit Guégon along the dual carriageway)

Opening times : from beginning April to beginning Oct.

2 ha (55 pitches) terraced, relatively flat, flat, grassy, wood

Tariff : 19.80€ 👤👤 🚗 🔲 🔌 (10A) – Extra per person 3€

Rental rates : (2015 price) (from beginning April to end Oct.) – 11 🛖. Per night from 40 to 100€ – Per week from 250 to 680€

℻ local sani-station – 5 🔲 14€

Near the Nantes to Brest canal. Touring cyclists welcome.

Surroundings : 🗗 ⚇⚇
Leisure activities : 🍴 🍴 🏛 🏄 🚴 ⛷
Facilities : & ⊙🛒 🛁 ℻ launderette 🚿
Nearby : 🐎 🛶

G P S Longitude : -2.57352
Latitude : 47.95239

JUGON-LES-LACS

22270 – Michelin map **309** I4 – pop. 1 683 – alt. 29
▶ Paris 417 – Lamballe 22 – Plancoët 16 – St-Brieuc 59

⚑ Au Bocage du Lac ♣♣

✆ 02 96 31 60 16. www.camping-location-bretagne.com

Address : rue du Bocage (located 1km southeast along the D 52, follow the signs for Mégrit)

Opening times : from beginning April to beginning Sept.

4 ha (183 pitches) flat, relatively flat, grassy

Tariff : (2015 price) 31.50€ ♣♣ ⇔ 回 ⚡ (10A) –
Extra per person 6.20€ – Reservation fee 18€

Rental rates : (2015 price) (from beginning March to beginning Sept.) – 8 ⌷⌷ – 36 🏠 – 1 cabin in the trees – 3 gîtes. Per night from 99 to 178€ – Per week from 303 to 850€ – Reservation fee 18€

🚽 Eurorelais sani-station 2.50€ – 2 回 6€ – ⛟ ⚡30€

Beside the large Étang de Jugon (lake), with a lovely indoor water park and play area.

Surroundings : 🐟 ⌂ ♨	
Leisure activities : 🍽 🎱 🎮 🏃 🚣 ♨ 🎳 🎿	
🎯 🦌 wildlife park	**G** Longitude : -2.31663
Facilities : 🚿 ⛲ 🏕 ⚒ launderette	**P** Latitude : 48.40165
Nearby : 🚲 🎾 🛶	**S**

KERVEL

29550 – Michelin map **308** F6
▶ Paris 586 – Rennes 234 – Quimper 24 – Brest 67

⚑ FranceLoc Domaine de Kervel ♣♣

✆ 02 98 92 51 54. www.kervel.fr

Address : at Kervel

Opening times : from mid April to mid Sept.

7 ha (316 pitches) flat, grassy

Tariff : (2015 price) 17€ ♣♣ ⇔ 回 ⚡ (10A) – Extra per person 4.70€ – Reservation fee 27€

Rental rates : (2015 price) (from mid April to mid Sept.) 🚿 (1 mobile home) – 159 ⌷⌷ – 3 🏠. Per night from 35 to 56€ – Per week from 140 to 224€ – Reservation fee 27€

Plenty of mobile homes around a partially indoor, substantial water park.

Surroundings : ♨	
Leisure activities : 🍽 🍴 🎱 🎮 🏃 🚣 🚲 🎾	
🏐 🎳 🎿🎯 multi-sports ground	**G** Longitude : -4.26737
Facilities : 🚿 ⛲ 🏕 ⚒ ♨ ⚒ launderette	**P** Latitude : 48.11617
🎱 🍳	**S**

KERVOYAL

56750 – Michelin map **308** P9
▶ Paris 471 – Rennes 124 – Vannes 30 – Lorient 87

⚑ Oasis

✆ 02 97 41 10 52. www.campingloasis.com

Address : rue Port Lestre (100m from the beach)

Opening times : from beginning April to end Sept.

3 ha (153 pitches) flat, grassy

Tariff : 23€ ♣♣ ⇔ 回 ⚡ (6A) – Extra per person 3.65€

🚽 Eurorelais sani-station

Surroundings : 🐟 ⌂ ♨	
Leisure activities : 🚣 🏃	**G** Longitude : -2.55013
Facilities : 🚿 ⛲ 🏕 ⚒ launderette	**P** Latitude : 47.51897
	S

LAMPAUL-PLOUDALMEZEAU

29830 – Michelin map **308** D3 – pop. 753 – alt. 24
▶ Paris 613 – Brest 27 – Brignogan-Plages 36 – Ploudalmézeau 4

⚑ Municipal des Dunes

✆ 02 98 48 14 29. lampaul-ploudalmezeau.mairie@wanadoo.fr

Address : at Le Vourc'h (700m north of the town, beside the sports field and 100m from the beach (direct access)

Opening times : from mid June to mid Sept.

1.5 ha (150 pitches) open site, flat, grassy, sandy, dunes

Tariff : (2015 price) ♣ 4.80€ ⇔ – ⚡ (12A) 2.70€

🚽 local sani-station 2€

A natural site among the dunes.

Surroundings : 🐟	
Leisure activities : 🎱	**G** Longitude : -4.65639
Facilities : 🚿 ⛲ (July–Aug.) 🎣 launderette	**P** Latitude : 48.56785
	S

LANDÉDA

29870 – Michelin map **308** D3 – pop. 3 620 – alt. 52
▶ Paris 604 – Brest 28 – Brignogan-Plages 25 – Ploudalmézeau 17

⚑ Les Abers ♣♣

✆ 02 98 04 93 35. www.camping-des-abers.com

Address : 51 Toull Tréaz (2.5km to the northwest; by the dunes at Ste-Marguerite)

Opening times : from beginning May to end Sept.

4.5 ha (180 pitches) dunes

Tariff : 21€ ♣♣ ⇔ 回 ⚡ (10A) – Extra per person 4.30€

Rental rates : (from beginning May to end Sept.) 🚿 (1 mobile home) – 22 ⌷⌷ – 1 studio – 1 apartment. Per week from 300 to 650€

🚽 local sani-station – 50 回 21€

In a pleasant location close to the beach, the site is well positioned among the dunes and has an information and map table at its centre.

Surroundings : 🐟 ⇐ 🏔	
Leisure activities : 🎱 🍴 🏃 🚣 🚲	**G** Longitude : -4.60306
Facilities : 🚿 ⛲ 🏕 ⚒ launderette 🎱	**P** Latitude : 48.59306
Nearby : 🍽 🍴	**S**

LANLOUP

22580 – Michelin map **309** E2 – pop. 272 – alt. 58
▶ Paris 484 – Guingamp 29 – Lannion 44 – St-Brieuc 36

⚑ Le Neptune

✆ 02 96 22 33 35. www.leneptune.com

Opening times : from beginning April to mid Oct.

2 ha (97 pitches) relatively flat, flat, grassy

Tariff : (2015 price) ♣ 6€ ⇔ 回 13€ – ⚡ (10A) 4€ – Reservation fee 10€

Rental rates : (2015 price) (from beginning April to mid Oct.) – 16 🏕 – 4 🚐 – 1 canvas bungalow. Per night from 26 to 159€ – Per week from 203 to 849€ – Reservation fee 10€

🚽 local sani-station 8€ – 10 📗 19€

Surroundings : 🏕 ♋♋
Leisure activities : 🍹 🎱 🚣 🏊 (open air in season), multi-sports ground
Facilities : ♿ ⚡ 📮♨ 🍴 launderette
Nearby : 🍴

G P S Longitude : -2.96704
Latitude : 48.71372

LANNION

22300 – Michelin map **309** B2 – pop. 19 847 – alt. 12
▶ Paris 516 – Brest 96 – Morlaix 42 – St-Brieuc 65

🏕 **Les Plages de Beg-Léguer**

📞 02 96 47 25 00. www.campingdesplages.com

Address : route de la Côte (6km west following signs for Trébeurden and take the turning to the left, 500m from the beach)

Opening times : from beginning May to end Sept.

5 ha (196 pitches) relatively flat, flat, grassy

Tariff : (2015 price) 🚶 7.80€ 🚐 📗 8.80€ – ⚡ (6A) 4€

Rental rates : (2015 price) (from beginning May to end Sept.) ♿ 🅿 – 35 🚐. Per night from 55 to 103 – Per week from 250 to 721

🚽 local sani-station

Surroundings : 🐾 🏕 ♋♋
Leisure activities : 🍹 🍴 🎱 🚣 🚴 🍴 🏊 🎿 multi-sports ground
Facilities : ♿ ⚡ ♨ 🍴 launderette ♨

G P S Longitude : -3.545
Latitude : 48.73834

🏕 **Les Alizés**

📞 02 96 47 28 58. www.camping-lesalizes.fr

Address : rue Champollion

Opening times : from beginning April to end Sept.

4.4 ha (184 pitches) flat, grassy

Tariff : (2015 price) 31.50€ 🚶🚶 🚐 📗 ⚡ (6A) – Extra per person 9€ – Reservation fee 17€

Rental rates : (2015 price) (from beginning April to end Sept.) – 102 🏕. Per week from 188 to 1,049€ – Reservation fee 17€

Surroundings : 🏕 ♋
Leisure activities : 🍹 🍴 🎱 🚴 🚣 🏊 🎿 multi-sports ground
Facilities : ♿ launderette ♨

G P S Longitude : -3.50611
Latitude : 48.75167

⚠ Municipal des 2 Rives

📞 02 96 46 31 40. www.ville-lannion.fr

Address : rue du Moulin du Duc (situated 2km southeast along the D 767, follow the signs for Guingamp and take the turning to the right after the Leclerc commercial centre)

2.3 ha (110 pitches) flat, grassy

Rentals : ♿ (1 chalet) – 14 🚐.

Surroundings : 🐾 ♋
Leisure activities : 🍹 🚣 🏊
Facilities : ♿ ⚡ ♨ 🚿 🍴 launderette
Nearby : 🛒 forest trail

G P S Longitude : -3.44584
Latitude : 48.72293

LANTIC

22410 – Michelin map **309** E3 – pop. 1 483 – alt. 50
▶ Paris 466 – Brest 139 – Lorient 133 – Rennes 116

🏕 **Les Étangs**

📞 02 96 71 95 47. www.campinglesetangs.com

Address : rue des Terres Neuvas, at Le Pont de la Motte (situated 2km east along the D 4, follow the signs for Binic, near two lakes)

Opening times : from mid April to end Sept.

1.5 ha (108 pitches) terrace, relatively flat, flat, grassy

Tariff : 21.40€ 🚶🚶 🚐 📗 ⚡ (10A) – Extra per person 4.70€

Rental rates : (from beginning April to end Sept.) – 10 🏕 – 1 🚐 – 3 canvas bungalows. Per night from 25 to 130€ – Per week from 140 to 700€

🚽 local sani-station – 🚐 ⚡14.40€

Leafy setting with different levels of quality in rental options.

Surroundings : ♋♋
Leisure activities : 🎱 🚣 🏊
Facilities : ♿ ⚡ ♨ 🍴 launderette
Nearby : 🎣

G P S Longitude : -2.86254
Latitude : 48.6068

LARMOR-BADEN

56870 – Michelin map **308** N9 – pop. 810 – alt. 10
▶ Paris 477 – Rennes 127 – Vannes 15 – Nantes 129

🏕 **Campéole Penn Marr** 👥

📞 02 97 57 49 90. http://www.camping-pennmar.com/

Address : 21 route de Port Blanc (5 km to the north on the D316A)

Opening times : from beginning April to end Sept.

6 ha (199 pitches) undulating, flat, grassy

Tariff : 13€ 🚶🚶 🚐 📗 ⚡ (10A) – Extra per person 10€ – Reservation fee 25€

Rental rates : (from beginning April to end Sept.) ♿ – 72 🏕 – 15 canvas bungalows – 30 tent lodges. Per night from 36 to 142€ – Per week from 252 to 994€ – Reservation fee 25€

🚽 raclet sani-station

Surroundings : 🐾 ♋♋
Leisure activities : 🍹 🌙 nighttime 🚴 🚣 🍴 🏊 multi-sports ground
Facilities : ♿ ⚡ 🚿 ♨ 🍴 launderette ♨ refrigerated food storage facilities

G P S Longitude : -2.87556
Latitude : 47.60694

🏕 **Le Diben**

📞 02 97 57 29 12. www.campinglediben.com

Address : at Le Diben

Opening times : from beginning May to mid Sept.

2.5 ha (118 pitches) relatively flat, flat, grassy

Tariff : 20.80€ 🚶🚶 🚐 📗 ⚡ (10A) – Extra per person 4.90€ – Reservation fee 5€

Rental rates : (from beginning May to mid Sept.) – 14 🏕 – 2 canvas bungalows – 4 gîtes. Per night from 50 to 90€ – Per week from 190 to 730€ – Reservation fee 5€

🚽 AireService sani-station – 8 📗 13.90€

Family atmosphere. Good shade for pitches.

Surroundings : 🐾 🏕 ♋♋
Leisure activities : 🍹 🎱 🚣 🚴 🏊
Facilities : ♿ ⚡ ♨ 🍴 launderette

G P S Longitude : -2.90556
Latitude : 47.59389

⚠ Ker Eden

🕿 02 97 57 05 23. www.camping-larmorbaden.com

Address : route d'Auray

Opening times : from mid May to mid Sept.

2 ha (100 pitches) flat, grassy

Tariff : (2015 price) ♦ 4.90€ – ⇔ 2.70€ – 🔲 5.20€ – (💡) (10A) 3.50€ – Reservation fee 20€

Rental rates : (2015 price) (from mid May to mid Sept.) – 10 [🛏] – 4 tent lodges. Per week from 210 to 710€ – Reservation fee 20€

🚐 local sani-station – 🌊 💡14€

Surroundings : 🐟 ≤ ♀ ⚤		
Leisure activities : 🏊	
Facilities : 🔥 ⚡☕🛏🍴 launderette		**G P S** Longitude : -2.90608 Latitude : 47.59389

LESCONIL

29740 – Michelin map **308** F8

▣ Paris 581 – Douarnenez 41 – Guilvinec 6 – Loctudy 7

🏔 Flower La Grande Plage

🕿 02 98 87 88 27. www.campinggrandeplage.com

Address : 71 rue Paul Langevin (located 1km west, follow the signs for Guilvinec, 300m from the beach (direct access)

Opening times : from beginning April to end Sept.

2.5 ha (120 pitches) flat, grassy, relatively flat

Tariff : 28€ ♦♦ ⇔ 🔲 (💡) (10A) – Extra per person 5.80€

Rentals : (from beginning April to end Sept.) – 5 canvas bungalows – 2 tent lodges.

🚐 local sani-station – 🌊 💡15€

A very pleasant site that has been renovated recently, with a pretty swimming pool and access to the beach at 200m.

Surroundings : ⌂ ♀♀		
Leisure activities : ♀ ✗ 🏠 🏊 🚲 ⛳		
Facilities : 🔥 ⚡☕🛏🍴 launderette 🛒		**G P S** Longitude : -4.22897 Latitude : 47.79804

⚠ Les Dunes

🕿 02 98 87 81 78. http://www.camping-desdunes.com

Address : 67 rue Paul Langevin (located 1km west, follow the signs for Guilvinec; 150m from the beach (direct access)

Opening times : from beginning April to end Sept.

2.8 ha (120 pitches) flat, grassy

Tariff : 25.30€ ♦♦ ⇔ 🔲 (💡) (16A) – Extra per person 4.90€

Rental rates : permanent 🌊 – 8 [🛏]. Per night from 60 to 110€ – Per week from 360 to 740€

🚐 local sani-station – 🌊 💡10€

A pleasant site, set back a little from the sea.

Surroundings : ⌂ ♀		
Leisure activities : 🏠 🏊		
Facilities : 🔥 ⚡🛏🍴 launderette		**G P S** Longitude : -4.22856 Latitude : 47.79716

⚠ Keralouet

🕿 02 98 82 23 05. www.campingkeralouet.com

Address : 11 rue Eric Tabarly (located 1km east on the Loctudy road)

Opening times : from beginning April to mid Sept.

1 ha (64 pitches) flat, grassy

Tariff : (2015 price) 22.25€ ♦♦ ⇔ 🔲 (💡) (10A) – Extra per person 4.80€

Rental rates : (2015 price) (from beginning April to mid Sept.) ♿ (1 chalet) – 9 [🛏] – 10 🏠 – 4 canvas bungalows – 2 tent lodges. Per night from 39 to 75€ – Per week from 205 to 659€

A well-kept and pleasant site, an interesting and restorative stop for touring cyclists.

Surroundings : ♀♀		
Leisure activities : 🏊 🚲 🏊		
Facilities : 🔥 ⚡☕🛏🍴 🖳		**G P S** Longitude : -4.20595 Latitude : 47.80424
Nearby : ◐		

LOCMARIA-PLOUZANÉ

29280 – Michelin map **308** D4 – pop. 4 837 – alt. 65

▣ Paris 610 – Brest 15 – Brignogan-Plages 50 – Ploudalmézeau 23

⚠ Municipal de Portez

🕿 02 98 48 49 85. http://www.locmaria-plouzane.fr/

Address : at Portez (3.5km southwest along the D 789 and follow the signs for the beach at Trégana; 200m from the beach)

Opening times : from mid May to mid Sept.

2 ha (110 pitches) open site, terraced, flat, grassy

Tariff : (2015 price) ♦ 4€ – ⇔ 🔲 5€ – (💡) (8A) 3€

Rental rates : (2015 price) permanent – 4 [🛏]. Per night from 36 to 70€ – Per week from 250 to 489€

🚐 AireService sani-station – 7 🔲 5€

Surroundings : 🐟 ≤ ⌂ ♀		
Leisure activities : 🏠 🏊		
Facilities : 🔥 ⚡ (15 Jun.–15 Sept.) 🛏🍴 launderette		**G P S** Longitude : -4.66344 Latitude : 48.3582
Nearby : ♀ ✗		

Michelin classification:

ᗰᗰᗰᗰ	*Extremely comfortable, equipped to a very high standard*
ᗰᗰᗰ	*Very comfortable, equipped to a high standard*
ᗰᗰ	*Comfortable and well equipped*
ᗰ	*Reasonably comfortable*
⚠	*Satisfactory*

LOCMARIAQUER

56740 – Michelin map **308** N9 – pop. 1 692 – alt. 5

▣ Paris 488 – Auray 13 – Quiberon 31 – La Trinité-sur-Mer 10

🏔 Lann-Brick

🕿 02 97 57 32 79. www.camping-lannbrick.com

Address : at Lann Brick - route de Kérinis (2.5km northwest following signs for Kérinis, 200m from the beach)

Opening times : from mid March to mid Oct.

1.2 ha (97 pitches) flat, grassy

Tariff : 28.10€ ♦♦ ⇔ 🔲 (💡) (10A) – Extra per person 5.50€ – Reservation fee 15€

Rental rates : (from mid March to end Oct.) ♿ – 22 [🛏] – 2 canvas bungalows. Per week from 180 to 770€ – Reservation fee 15€

🚐 local sani-station 3€ – 🌊 💡15€

Surroundings : ⌂ ♀		
Leisure activities : ♀ 🏠 🏊 🚲 🏊		**G P S** Longitude : -2.97436 Latitude : 47.57838
Facilities : 🔥 ⚡🛏🍴 launderette		

LOCRONAN

29180 – Michelin map **308** F6 – pop. 798 – alt. 105
▶ Paris 580 – Rennes 229 – Quimper 17

🏔 Le Locronan

𝒫 02 98 91 87 76. www.camping-locronan.fr

Address : rue de la Troménie

Opening times : from beginning April to end Sept.

2.6 ha (100 pitches) terraced, uneven, flat, grassy

Tariff : (2015 price) 23.92 € ✦✦ 🚐 📵 🔌 (10A) –
Extra per person 5.50 € – Reservation fee 5 €

Rental rates : (2015 price) (from beginning April to end Sept.) –
24 🛖 – 2 canvas bungalows. Per night from 39 to 130 € –
Per week from 195 to 835 € – Reservation fee 15 €

🚽 local sani-station

Situated right in the heart of the countryside.

Surroundings : 🌿 ≼ 🛤 ♨♨	**G** Longitude : -4.19918
Leisure activities : 🚴 🏊	**P** Latitude : 48.09582
Facilities : ♿ 🚿 🆔 🏕 🏳 launderette	**S**

We value your opinion and welcome your feedback.
Do email us at campingfrance@tp.michelin.com

LOCTUDY

29750 – Michelin map **308** F8 – pop. 4 207 – alt. 8
▶ Paris 578 – Bénodet 18 – Concarneau 35 – Pont-l'Abbé 6

🏔 Les Hortensias

𝒫 02 98 87 46 64. www.camping-loctudy.com

Address : 38 rue des Tulipes (3km southwest following signs for
Larvor, 500m from the beach at Lodonnec)

Opening times : from beginning April to end Sept.

1.5 ha (100 pitches) flat, grassy

Tariff : (2015 price) 25.40 € ✦✦ 🚐 📵 🔌 (10A) –
Extra per person 4.90 € – Reservation fee 11 €

Rental rates : (2015 price) (from beginning April to end Sept.) –
1 'gypsy' caravan – 22 🛖. Per night from 30 to 80 € – Per
week from 150 to 784 € – Reservation fee 11 €

🚽 local sani-station 5 €

*A good site for tents and caravans, set back a little from the
beach activities.*

Surroundings : 🌿 ♨♨	**G** Longitude : -4.1823
Leisure activities : 🍽 🚴 🚲 🏊	**P** Latitude : 47.81259
Facilities : ♿ 🚿 🏳 launderette 🔥 🐾	**S**
Nearby : ✗	

LOUANNEC

22700 – Michelin map **309** B2 – pop. 2 946 – alt. 53
▶ Paris 527 – Rennes 175 – St-Brieuc 77 – Lannion 10

🏔 Municipal Ernest Renan

𝒫 02 96 23 11 78. www.camping-louannec.fr

Address : located 1km west; beside the sea

Opening times : from beginning April to end Sept.

4 ha (265 pitches) open site, flat, grassy

Tariff : (2015 price) 18.30 € ✦✦ 🚐 📵 🔌 (16A) –
Extra per person 3.80 €

Rental rates : (2015 price) (from beginning April to end Sept.) –
14 🛖 – 2 canvas bungalows. Per week from 159 to 680 €

🚽 local sani-station 4.50 €

Surroundings : ≼ 🔺	
Leisure activities : 🍽 ✗ 🚤 🕐daytime 🚴	**G** Longitude : -3.42723
🏊 ♨	**P** Latitude : 48.79666
Facilities : ♿ 🚿 🏖 🏳 🏕 launderette	**S**
🔥 🐾	

LOUDEAC

22600 – Michelin map **309** – pop. 9 759 – alt. 155
▶ Paris 441 – Rennes 90 – Saint-Brieuc 44 – Vannes 66

🏔 Seasonova Aquarev

𝒫 02 96 26 21 92. www.camping-aquarev.com

Address : route de Rennes (near the leisure centre)

Opening times : from end March to end Oct.

3.1 ha (89 pitches) relatively flat, flat, grassy

Tariff : 19 € ✦✦ 🚐 📵 🔌 (10A) – Extra per person 5 € – Reservation
fee 15 €

Rental rates : (from end March to end Oct.) ♿ 🚫 – 7 🛖 – 9 🛏 –
1 gîte. Per night from 80 to 180 € – Per week from 295 to 695 € –
Reservation fee 15 €

🚽 AireService sani-station 5 € – 5 📵 10 € – 🔋 🔌14 €

Surroundings : ≼ 🛤	
Leisure activities : 🍽 🚤 🚲 🎣	**G** Longitude : -2.72889
Facilities : ♿ 🚿 🆔 🏳 launderette	**P** Latitude : 48.17778
Nearby : 🚴 🏸 ⛷ fitness trail	**S**

MARCILLÉ-ROBERT

35240 – Michelin map **309** N7 – pop. 929 – alt. 65
▶ Paris 333 – Bain-de-Bretagne 33 – Châteaubriant 30 – La Guerche-
de-Bretagne 11

🏔 Municipal de l'Étang

𝒫 06 02 08 60 22. camping.marcillerobert@yahoo.fr

Address : rue des Bas Gasts (take the southern exit along the D 32,
follow the signs for Arbrissel)

0.5 ha (22 pitches) terraced, flat, grassy, pond

Rentals : 1 🛖 – 1 🏠.

Surroundings : 🌿 ≼ 🛤 ♨♨	**G** Longitude : -1.36471
Facilities : ♿	**P** Latitude : 47.94768
Nearby : 🚴 🏸 🎣	**S**

MARTIGNÉ-FERCHAUD

35640 – Michelin map **309** O8 – pop. 2 650 – alt. 90
▶ Paris 340 – Bain-de-Bretagne 31 – Châteaubriant 15 – La Guerche-
de-Bretagne 16

🏔 Municipal du Bois Feuillet

𝒫 06 24 86 65 57. www.ville-martigne-ferchaud.fr

Address : at Étang de la Forge (lake, to the northwest of the town)

1.7 ha (50 pitches) terraced, flat, grassy

🚽 local sani-station

*Comfortable pitches in a pleasant setting with shade, at the
edge of a lake.*

Surroundings : 🌿 ≼ 🛤 ♨♨	
Leisure activities : 🏛	**G** Longitude : -1.31599
Facilities : ♿ 🚿 🏖 🏳 📵	**P** Latitude : 47.83385
Nearby : 🚴 🏸 ⛵ (beach) 🎣 ♨ pedalos	**S**

MATIGNON

22550 – Michelin map **309** I3 – pop. 1 647 – alt. 70
▶ Paris 425 – Dinan 30 – Dinard 23 – Lamballe 23

⚑ Le Vallon aux Merlettes

📞 02 96 80 37 99. www.campingdematignon.com

Address : 43 rue du Dr-Jobert (to the southwest along the D 13, follow the signs for Lamballe, by the stadium)

Opening times : from beginning April to end Sept.

3 ha (120 pitches) relatively flat, flat, grassy

Tariff : 19.50€ ♣ ♣ ⛺ 回 ⚡ (10A) – Extra per person 4.20€

Rental rates : (from beginning April to mid Sept.) – 6 🚐 – 3 tent lodges. Per night from 40 to 90€ – Per week from 220 to 560€

🚿 local sani-station 3.40€ – 3 回 19.50€

Surroundings : 🏞 ♀		
Leisure activities : ✗ 🛶 ▣	**G P S**	Longitude : -2.29607
Facilities : 🚿 ⊶ 🏠 ⚐ launderette 🧺		Latitude : 48.59168
Nearby : 🛒 ✗ 🎮		

The pitches of many campsites are marked out with low hedges of attractive bushes and shrubs.

MERDRIGNAC

22230 – Michelin map **309** H5 – pop. 2 916 – alt. 140
▶ Paris 411 – Dinan 47 – Josselin 33 – Lamballe 40

⚑ Val de Landrouet

📞 02 96 28 47 98. www.valdelandrouet.com

Address : 14 rue du Gouède (0.8km to the north, near the swimming pool and two lakes; at the leisure and activity park)

Opening times : from beginning May to end Sept.

15 ha/2 for camping (59 pitches) terraced, relatively flat, flat, grassy

Tariff : (2015 price) ♣ 4€ ⛺ 3€ 回 5€ – ⚡ (5A) 3€

Rental rates : (2015 price) (from beginning Jan. to mid Dec.) 🚿 (9 chalets) 🚙 – 4 🚐 – 9 🏠 – 16 studios – 14 gîtes. Per night from 38 to 98€ – Per week from 160 to 645€ – Reservation fee 15€

🚿 Eurorelais sani-station 3€ – 6 回 16€ – 🚰 ⚡12€

Surroundings : 🏞 ⛵ ♀♀		
Leisure activities : ⛳	**G P S**	Longitude : -2.41525
Facilities : 🚿 ⊶ 🏠 🏮		Latitude : 48.19843
Nearby : 🎣 🏄 ✗ 🎮 🏇 🛶 🚴		

MILIZAC

29290 – Michelin map **308** D4 – pop. 3 009 – alt. 89
▶ Paris 598 – Rennes 247 – Quimper 83

⚑ La Récré des 3 Curés

📞 02 98 07 92 17. www.larecredes3cures.fr

Address : situated at the Parc d'Attractions (leisure park)

Opening times : permanent

3 ha (100 pitches) flat, grassy

Tariff : (2015 price) 21€ ♣ ♣ ⛺ 回 ⚡ (16A) – Extra per person 7€

Rental rates : (2015 price) permanent 🚙 – 31 🚐 – 6 🏠. Per night from 103 to 201€ – Per week from 211 to 433€

🚿 local sani-station 21€ – 50 回 21€

Surroundings : ⛵ lake ♀		
Leisure activities : ⛳ 🛶 🎣 🏇 🚴	**G P S**	Longitude : -4.5294
Facilities : 🚿 ⊶ 🏠 ⚐ launderette		Latitude : 48.47377
Nearby : ✗ ▣ 🛶 🏇 amusement park		

MOËLAN-SUR-MER

29350 – Michelin map **308** J8 – pop. 6 956 – alt. 58
▶ Paris 523 – Carhaix-Plouguer 66 – Concarneau 27 – Lorient 27

△ L'Île Percée

📞 02 98 71 16 25. www.camping-ile-percee.fr

Address : plage de Trenez (5.8km west along the D 116, follow the signs for Kerfany-les-Pins, then continue 1.7km along the turning to the left)

1 ha (65 pitches) flat, grassy

Rentals : 4 🚐.

A pleasant site with a natural feel, at the edge of the coastal hiking path GR34. with pitches looking out over the ocean.

Surroundings : 🏞 < ♀ 🏞		
Leisure activities : ⛳ 🚲	**G P S**	Longitude : -3.70241
Facilities : 🚿 ⊶ 🏠 ⚐		Latitude : 47.78872
Nearby : ✗ 🏇 walking trails		

MONTERBLANC

56250 – Michelin map **308** O8 – pop. 3 139 – alt. 89
▶ Paris 453 – Nantes 122 – Rennes 102 – Vannes 14

⚑ Le Haras

Le Haras

📞 02 97 44 66 06. www.campingvannes.com

Address : at Kersimon (from Vannes, head north along the D 767 then take the D 778 E, behind Vannes-Meucon-Bretagne-Sud flying club)

Opening times : from mid March to mid Nov.

14 ha/2.5 for camping (140 pitches)

Tariff : (2015 price) 36€ ♣ ♣ ⛺ 回 ⚡ (16A) – Extra per person 5€ – Reservation fee 30€

Rental rates : (2015 price) (from beginning April to end Oct.) 🚿 (1 chalet) – 63 🚐 – 7 🏠. Per night from 50 to 180€ – Per week from 250 to 1,460€ – Reservation fee 30€

🚿 local sani-station – 10 回 17€

Surroundings : 🏞 ⛵ ♀♀		
Leisure activities : ⛳ ✗ 🛶 🕐daytime 🏊 🛁 hammam, jacuzzi 🎣 🚴 ✗ ▣ 🛶 🎮 farm or petting farm, multi-sports ground, spa centre	**G P S**	Longitude : -2.72795
Facilities : 🚿 ⊶ 🏮 🏠 🧺 ⚐ launderette, refrigerated food storage facilities		Latitude : 47.73035
Nearby : 🏇		

MORGAT

29160 – Michelin map **308** E5 – pop. 7 535
▶ Paris 590 – Rennes 238 – Quimper 55 – Brest 15

⚑ Les Bruyères

📞 02 98 26 14 87. www.camping-bruyeres-crozon.com

Address : at Le Bouis (located 1.5km along the D 25, follow the signs for Le Cap de la Chèvre and take road to the right)

Opening times : from beginning April to end Sept.

4 ha (130 pitches) flat, relatively flat, grassy

Tariff : (2015 price) ♣ 5.40€ ⛺ 回 8.20€ – ⚡ (6A) 3.60€

Rental rates : (2015 price) (from beginning April to end Sept.) ✍ – 18 🚐 – 2 tent lodges. Per night from 40 to 70 – Per week from 250 to 675

A natural setting with access to Morgat via a pedestrian path; the site includes a water park.

Surroundings : 🌳 ♀
Leisure activities : 🚣 ⛵ 🏊 ⛷
Facilities : ⊙🚿♨ ¶ launderette
Nearby : 🍴 ♀ ✕

G P S Longitude : -4.53183
Latitude : 48.22293

Rental rates : (from mid April to mid Sept.) – 9 🚐. Per night from 45 to 55 – Per week from 210 to 630 – Reservation fee 10€
🚐 local sani-station 5€

A lush, green and peaceful site, with access to the beach via a beautiful shaded footpath.

Surroundings : 🌳 � ♀
Leisure activities : 🚣
Facilities : ♿ ⊙🚿 (July–Aug.) ¶ launderette
Nearby : ♀ ✕

G P S Longitude : -3.77433
Latitude : 47.79598

MOUSTERLIN

29170 – Michelin map **308** G7
▶ Paris 563 – Rennes 212 – Quimper 22 – Brest 94

⛰ FranceLoc Le Grand Large ♣♣

🔗 02 98 56 04 06. www.franceloc.fr – limited spaces for one-night stay

Address : 48 route du Grand Large (near the beach)

Opening times : from mid April to beginning Sept.

5.8 ha (287 pitches) flat, grassy

Tariff : (2015 price) 35€ ♣♣ 🚐 🔌 (10A) – Extra per person 7€ – Reservation fee 27€
Rental rates : (2015 price) (from mid April to beginning Sept.) ♿ (1 mobile home) – 225 🚐. Per night from 33 to 114€ – Per week from 133 to 1,085€ – Reservation fee 27€

Numerous rental options arranged around a restaurant and a good water park, partially covered.

Surroundings : 🌳 ♀
Leisure activities : ♀ ✕ 🏛 🎣 🏃 🚣 🚴 ✕ ⛵ 🏊 ⛷ multi-sports ground
Facilities : ♿ ⊙🚿♨ 🚿 ¶ launderette ♨🚿

G P S Longitude : -4.0367
Latitude : 47.84809

⛰ Kost-Ar-Moor

🔗 02 98 56 04 16. www.camping-fouesnant.com

Address : 17 route du Grand Large (500m from the beach)

Opening times : from end April to mid Sept.

3.5 ha (177 pitches) flat, grassyTariff : 28€ ♣♣ 🚐 🔌 (10A) – Extra per person 5.90€ – Reservation fee 15€
Rental rates : (from mid April to mid Sept.) – 35 🚐 – 3 apartments. Per week from 220 to 780€ – Reservation fee 15€

A charming, tranquil setting beneath the shade of pine trees, ideal for tents and caravans.

Surroundings : 🌳 ♀♀
Leisure activities : ♀ ✕ 🏛 🚣 🚴 🏊
Facilities : ♿ ⊙🚿 ¶ launderette
Nearby : 💧

G P S Longitude : -4.03421
Latitude : 47.85106

NÉVEZ

29920 – Michelin map **308** I8 – pop. 2 718 – alt. 40
▶ Paris 541 – Concarneau 14 – Pont-Aven 8 – Quimper 40

⛰ Les Chaumières

🔗 02 98 06 73 06. www.camping-des-chaumieres.com

Address : 24 Hameau de Kerascoët (head 3km south along the D 77 towards Port Manec'h then take the turning to the right)

Opening times : from mid May to mid Sept.

3 ha (110 pitches) flat, grassy

Tariff : 22.40€ ♣♣ 🚐 🔌 (10A) – Extra per person 5.20€

NOYAL-MUZILLAC

56190 – Michelin map **308** Q9 – pop. 2 410 – alt. 52
▶ Paris 468 – Rennes 108 – Vannes 31 – Lorient 88

⛰ Moulin de Cadillac

🔗 02 97 67 03 47. www.camping-moulin-cadillac.com

Address : 4.5km northwest following signs for Berric

Opening times : from mid April to mid Sept.

7 ha (197 pitches) adjacent wood

Tariff : (2015 price) ♣ 6.20€ 🚐 🔌 14.50€ – (10A) 3.80€ – Reservation fee 10€
Rental rates : (2015 price) (from mid April to mid Sept.) – 66 🚐 – 6 🏠 – 4 canvas bungalows. Per night from 85 to 160€ – Per week from 240 to 790€ – Reservation fee 10€
🚐 local sani-station

Surroundings : 🌳 � ♀♀
Leisure activities : ♀ 🏛 🎣 🚣 ✕ 🎠 ⛵ 🏊 ⛷ 🏹 wildlife park, multi-sports ground, entertainment room
Facilities : ♿ ⊙🚿♨ ¶ launderette ♨

G P S Longitude : -2.50199
Latitude : 47.61412

For more information on visiting particular towns or regions, consult the relevant regional MICHELIN Green Guide. We also recommend you use the appropriate Michelin regional map to locate your selected campsite, to calculate distances and to work out the best route.

PAIMPOL

22500 – Michelin map **309** D2 – pop. 7 828 – alt. 15
▶ Paris 494 – Guingamp 29 – Lannion 33 – St-Brieuc 46

⛰ Municipal de Cruckin-Kérity

🔗 02 96 20 78 47. www.camping-paimpol.com

Address : at Kérity (head 2km southeast along the D 786, follow the signs for St-Quay-Portrieux, next to the stadium, 100m from the beach at Cruckin)

Opening times : from beginning April to beginning Oct.

2 ha (130 pitches) flat, grassy

Tariff : 20.90€ ♣♣ 🚐 🔌 (13A) – Extra per person 4.10€ – Reservation fee 20€
Rental rates : (from beginning April to beginning Oct.) – 5 canvas bungalows. Per week from 220 to 360€ – Reservation fee 90€
🚐 local sani-station 6.50€ – 10 🔌 10€

Surroundings : 🌳 � ♀
Leisure activities : 🏛
Facilities : ♿ ⊙🚿 ¶ launderette
Nearby : ✕

G P S Longitude : -3.02224
Latitude : 48.76972

PAIMPONT

35380 – Michelin map **309** I6 – pop. 1 641 – alt. 159
▶ Paris 390 – Dinan 60 – Ploërmel 26 – Redon 47

⛺ Municipal Paimpont Brocéliande

✆ 02 99 07 89 16. www.camping-paimpont-broceliande.com

Address : 2 rue du Chevalier Lancelot du Lac (take the northern exit along the D 773, near the lake)

Opening times : from beginning April to end Sept.

1.5 ha (90 pitches) flat, grassy

Tariff : (2015 price) ♣ 3.80€ ⇒ 1.90€ ▤ 3.45€ – ⚡ (5A) 3.70€

Rental rates : (2015 price) permanent ♿ (1 chalet) – 6 🏠.
Per night from 140 to 150€ – Per week from 260 to 490€

🚐 AireService sani-station 4€

A setting with only a little shade at the edge of the Forêt de Brocéliande (forest).

Leisure activities : 🎪 🏇	**GPS** Longitude : -2.17248
Facilities : ♿ ⚡ (July–Aug.) 🚽 launderette	Latitude : 48.02404
Nearby : 🏊 🍴	

PÉNESTIN

56760 – Michelin map **308** Q10 – pop. 1 867 – alt. 20
▶ Paris 458 – La Baule 29 – Nantes 84 – La Roche-Bernard 18

⛰ Les Îles ♣♣

✆ 02 99 90 30 24. www.camping-des-iles.fr

Address : at La Pointe du Bile, 119 route des Trois Îles (4.5km south along the D 201 to the right)

Opening times : from end March to beginning Nov.

3.5 ha (184 pitches) flat, grassy, pond

Tariff : 45€ ♣♣ ⇒ ▤ ⚡ (10A) – Extra per person 7€

Rental rates : permanent ♿ (1 chalet) – 100 🚐 – 5 🏠 – 2 tent lodges. Per night from 50 to 195€ – Per week from 250 to 1,340€

🚐 AireService sani-station 17€

Near beach in two distinct parts; high-quality rentals.

Surroundings : 🏖 🏕 ♀♀ ⛰	
Leisure activities : 🍸 🍴 🎪 🌙 nighttime 🏃 🏊 jacuzzi 🚴 🎾 🏊 multi-sports ground	**GPS** Longitude : -2.48426 Latitude : 47.44561
Facilities : ♿ ⚡ 🅒🅒 🚽 launderette 🏊 🍴	
Nearby : 🏇	

⛰ Le Cénic ♣♣

✆ 02 99 90 45 65. www.lecenic.com

Address : route de La Roche-Bernard (located 1.5km east along the D 34; beside a lake)

Opening times : from mid April to mid Sept.

5.5 ha (310 pitches)

Tariff : (2015 price) 35€ ♣♣ ⇒ ▤ ⚡ (10A) – Extra per person 7€ – Reservation fee 15€

Rental rates : (2015 price) (from mid April to mid Sept.) – 50 🚐 – 10 🏠. Per night from 95 to 130€ – Per week from 270 to 790€ – Reservation fee 15€

🚐 local sani-station 4€ – 30 ▤ 30€

Lots of indoor activities; covered aquatic park.

Surroundings : 🏕 ♀♀	
Leisure activities : 🍸 🎪 🌙 🏃 ⛱ hammam 🚴 🎾 🏊 ⛵ entertainment room	**GPS** Longitude : -2.45547 Latitude : 47.47889
Facilities : ♿ ⚡ 🚽 launderette	

PENMARCH

29760 – Michelin map **308** E8 – pop. 5 749 – alt. 7
▶ Paris 585 – Audierne 40 – Douarnenez 45 – Pont-l'Abbé 12

⛰ Yelloh! Village La Plage ♣♣

✆ 02 98 58 61 90. www.villagelaplage.com

Address : 241 Hent Maner ar Star (situated 100m from the beach (direct access)

Opening times : from beginning April to mid Sept.

14 ha (410 pitches)

Tariff : 48€ ♣♣ ⇒ ▤ ⚡ (10A) – Extra per person 8€

Rental rates : (from beginning April to mid Sept.) – 250 🚐 – 2 cabins in the trees – 10 canvas bungalows – 4 tent lodges. Per night from 35 to 245€ – Per week from 245 to 1,715€

Surroundings : ♀	
Leisure activities : 🍸 🍴 🎪 🌙 🏃 🏄 ⛱  🚴 🎾 🎣 🔫 🏊 ⛵ pedal go-carts, multi-sports ground	**GPS** Longitude : -4.31194 Latitude : 47.8035
Facilities : ♿ ⚡ 🚿 🚽 launderette 🏊 🍴	
Nearby : 🎣	

⛺ Municipal de Toul ar Ster

✆ 02 98 58 86 88. www.penmarch.fr/Office-de-Tourisme

Address : 110 rue Edmond Michelet (1.4km southeast following signs for Guilvinec along the coast and take turning to the right, 100m from the beach (direct access)

Opening times : from mid June to mid Sept.

3 ha (202 pitches) flat, grassy, sandy

Tariff : (2015 price) ♣ 3.50€ ⇒ 2.40€ ▤ 3.30€ – ⚡ (6A) 3€

🚐 local sani-station 2€ – 20 ▤ 14€

In a pleasant setting close to a sailing centre.

Surroundings : 🏄	
Leisure activities : 🎪 🏇	**GPS** Longitude : -4.33726 Latitude : 47.81246
Facilities : ♿ ⚡ (July–Aug.) 🚿 🚽 launderette	
Nearby : 🎣	

PENTREZ-PLAGE

29550 – Michelin map **308** F5
▶ Paris 566 – Brest 55 – Châteaulin 18 – Crozon 18

⛰ Homair Vacances Le Ker'Ys ♣♣

✆ 08 20 20 12 07. www.homair.com/camping/le-domaine-de-ker-ys – limited spaces for one-night stay

Address : chemin des Dunes (opposite the beach)

Opening times : from mid April to end Sept.

3.5 ha (190 pitches)

Tariff : (2015 price) 29.70€ ♣♣ ⇒ ▤ ⚡ (6A) – Extra per person 5.50€ – Reservation fee 49€

Rental rates : (2015 price) (from mid April to end Sept.) – 160 🚐. Per night from 17 to 130€ – Per week from 119 to 910€ – Reservation fee 49€

A good water park, lots of boating activities and the beach is nearby.

Surroundings : 🏕 ♀	
Leisure activities : 🎪 🌙 daytime 🏃 🎣 ⛱ jacuzzi 🚴 🎾 🏊	**GPS** Longitude : -4.30137 Latitude : 48.19249
Facilities : ♿ ⚡ 🚿 🚽 launderette	
Nearby : 🍸 🍴	

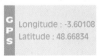

PERROS-GUIREC

22700 – Michelin map **309** B2 – pop. 7 375 – alt. 60
▶ Paris 527 – Lannion 12 – St-Brieuc 76 – Tréguier 19

⚠️ Yelloh! Village Le Ranolien ▲▲

📞 02 96 91 65 65. www.leranolien.fr

Address : at Ploumanac'h, boulevard du Sémaphore (located 1km southeast along the D 788, 200m from the sea)

Opening times : from beginning April to end Sept.

15 ha (525 pitches) undulating, flat and relatively flat, grassy, rocks

Tariff : 47 € ★★ 🚗 🅴 (🔌) (10A) – Extra per person 9 €

Rental rates : (from beginning April to end Sept.) – 5 'gypsy' caravans – 350 🛖 – 6 tent lodges. Per night from 39 to 239 € – Per week from 273 to 1,673 €

🚐 local sani-station – 8 🅴 15 € – 🚐 (🔌) 16 €

Quality spa, pool, and rental options in a beachside location.

Surroundings : ⊰ ⛱ ⚲
Leisure activities : 🍸 ✕ 🛶 🎣 🎳 🏓
🏄 hammam, jacuzzi 🛝 ♨ 🖼️ 🎿 ♒
disco, multi-sports ground, spa centre,
entertainment room
Facilities : ♿ ⚡ 🏛️ 🛁 🚿 launderette 🛒 ✂️
Longitude : -3.4747
Latitude : 48.82677

This guide is updated regularly, so buy your new copy every year!

PLÉNEUF-VAL-ANDRÉ

22370 – Michelin map **309** G3 – pop. 3 942 – alt. 52
▶ Paris 446 – Dinan 43 – Erquy 9 – Lamballe 16

⚠️ Campéole Les Monts Colleux ▲▲

📞 02 96 72 95 10. www.camping-montscolleux.com

Address : 26 rue Jean Lebrun (0.8km north east of the town)

Opening times : from beginning April to end Sept.

5 ha (180 pitches) terraced, flat, grassy

Tariff : 13 € ★★ 🚗 🅴 (🔌) (10A) – Extra per person 10 € – Reservation fee 25 €

Rental rates : (from beginning April to mid Sept.) ♿ (1 mobile home) – 43 🛖 – 23 🏠. Per night from 45 to 124 € – Per week from 315 to 868 € – Reservation fee 25 €

🚐 AireService sani-station

Surroundings : 🌿 ⊰
Leisure activities : 🛝 🎣 🏄 ♒
Facilities : ⚡ 🛁 🚿 launderette 🛒
Nearby : 🖼️
Longitude : -2.5508
Latitude : 48.5898

PLESTIN-LES-GRÈVES

22310 – Michelin map **309** A3 – pop. 3 644 – alt. 45
▶ Paris 528 – Brest 79 – Guingamp 46 – Lannion 18

⚠️ Municipal St-Efflam

📞 02 96 35 62 15. www.camping-municipal-bretagne.com

Address : at St-Efflam, place de Lan-Carré (3.5km to the northeast, follow the signs for St-Michel-en-Grève; 200m from the sea)

Opening times : from beginning April to beginning Oct.

4 ha (190 pitches) terraced, relatively flat, flat, grassy

Tariff : (2015 price) 18.40 € ★★ 🚗 🅴 (🔌) (10A) – Extra per person 3.80 €

Rental rates : (2015 price) (from beginning April to beginning Oct.)
♿ (1 mobile home) – 15 🛖 – 6 🏠. Per night from 40 to 90 € – Per week from 198 to 560 €

🚐 AireService sani-station 3 € – 10 🅴 17 €

Surroundings : 🌿 ⊰ ⚲
Leisure activities : 🍸 🖼️ 🛶 🖼️
Facilities : ♿ ⚡ (July-Aug.) 🛁 🚿 launderette
Nearby : ✕ ⚲
Longitude : -3.60108
Latitude : 48.66834

⚠️ Aire Naturelle Ker-Rolland

📞 02 96 35 08 37. www.camping-ker-rolland.com

Address : at Ker Rolland (2.2km southwest along the D 78, follow the signs for Morlaix and take the turning to the left, following signs for Plouégat-Guérand)

1.6 ha (22 pitches) flat, grassy

Rentals : 3 🛖.

🚐 local sani-station

A farm campsite with a market garden.

Surroundings : 🌿
Leisure activities : 🖼️
Facilities : ♿ ⚡ 🚿 🖼️
Longitude : -3.64337
Latitude : 48.64338

PLEUBIAN

22610 – Michelin map **309** D1 – pop. 2 577 – alt. 48
▶ Paris 506 – Lannion 31 – Paimpol 13 – St-Brieuc 58

⚠️ Port la Chaîne

📞 02 96 22 92 38. www.portlachaine.com

Address : situated 2km north along the D 20, follow the signs for Larmor-Pleubian and take turning to the left

4.9 ha (142 pitches) terraced, relatively flat, flat, grassy

Rentals : 42 🛖 – 3 canvas bungalows.

Surroundings : 🌿 ⚲⚲ 🏔️
Leisure activities : 🍸 🖼️ 🛶 🖼️ 🎿
Facilities : ♿ ⚡ 🛁 🚿 🛁 🚿 launderette
Longitude : -3.13284
Latitude : 48.85545

To make the best possible use of this guide, please read pages 2–15 carefully.

PLEUMEUR-BODOU

22560 – Michelin map **309** A2 – pop. 4 039 – alt. 94
▶ Paris 523 – Lannion 8 – Perros-Guirec 10 – St-Brieuc 72

⚠️ Le Port

📞 02 96 23 87 79. www.camping-du-port-22.com

Address : 3 chemin des Douaniers (6km to the north, to the south of Trégastel-Plage)

Opening times : from end March to end Oct.

2 ha (88 pitches) open site, flat and relatively flat, grassy, rocks

Tariff : ★ 6 € 🚗 4 € 🅴 20 € – (🔌) (15A) 4 € – Reservation fee 15 €

Rental rates : (from end March to end Oct.) – 34 🛖 – 6 🏠. Per night from 60 to 80 € – Per week from 260 to 790 € – Reservation fee 15 €

🚐 50 🅴 15 €

Surroundings : 🌿 ⊰ 🏔️
Leisure activities : 🍸 ✕ 🛶 🚣
Facilities : ♿ ⚡ 🛁 🚿 🚿 launderette
Longitude : -3.54278
Latitude : 48.81029

PLÉVEN

22130 – Michelin map **309** I4 – pop. 587 – alt. 80
▶ Paris 431 – Dinan 24 – Dinard 28 – St-Brieuc 38

⚠ Municipal

✆ 02 96 84 46 71. www.pleven.fr

Address : In the town

Opening times : from beginning April to mid Nov.

1 ha (40 pitches)

Tariff : ✝ 1.70€ 🚗 1€ 🅴 2€ – ⚡ (12A) 2.90€

In the town hall park with quality sanitary facilities.

Surroundings : 🌊 ♀♀
Facilities : ♿ ⊶🗓 ℉
Nearby : 🎣 ♀ ✕ ✂

GPS Longitude : -2.31911
Latitude : 48.48914

PLOBANNALEC-LESCONIL

29740 – Michelin map **308** F8 – pop. 3 326 – alt. 16
▶ Paris 578 – Audierne 38 – Douarnenez 38 – Pont-l'Abbé 6

🏔 Yelloh! Village L'Océan Breton 👥

✆ 02 98 82 23 89. www.oceanbreton.com – limited spaces for one-night stay

Address : route de Plobannalec, at Le Manoir de Kerlut (1.6km south along the D 102, follow the signs for Lesconil and take the road to the left)

Opening times : from beginning May to beginning Sept.

12 ha/8 for camping (240 pitches) flat, grassy Tariff : 54€ ✝✝ 🚗 🅴 ⚡ (16A) – Extra per person 8€

Rental rates : (from beginning May to beginning Sept.) – 180 🛖 – 1 🏠 – 3 yurts. Per night from 35 to 225€ – Per week from 245 to 1,575€

A very pleasant site, beside a fine water park; access to the beach via a free shuttle service.

Surroundings : 🌊 ♀
Leisure activities : ♀ ✕ 🎦 ⛳ 🎣 🏄 🕎 ⛵ forest trail, multi-sports ground
Facilities : ♿ ⊶ 🎏 ℉ launderette 🎣🚿

GPS Longitude : -4.22574
Latitude : 47.81167

PLOEMEL

56400 – Michelin map **308** M9 – pop. 2 508 – alt. 46
▶ Paris 485 – Auray 8 – Lorient 34 – Quiberon 23

🏔 St-Laurent 👥

✆ 02 97 56 85 90. www.camping-saint-laurent.fr

Address : at Kergonvo (2.5km to the northwest, follow the signs for Belz, near D 22 junction, take D 186)

Opening times : from beginning April to end Oct.

3 ha (90 pitches) flat, relatively flat, grassy

Tariff : (2015 price) 22.30€ ✝✝ 🚗 🅴 ⚡ (10A) – Extra per person 5.40€ – Reservation fee 10€

Rental rates : (2015 price) (from mid April to end Oct.) – 19 🛖 – 2 canvas bungalows – 6 tent lodges. Per night from 47 to 117€ – Per week from 332 to 821€ – Reservation fee 10€

🛖 local sani-station – 🔌 11€

Surroundings : 🍃 ♀♀
Leisure activities : 🎯 🏄 🎦
Facilities : ♿ ⊶ 🚿 ℉ launderette

GPS Longitude : -3.10013
Latitude : 47.66369

Village Vacances Dihan Évasion

✆ 02 97 56 88 27. www.dihan-evasion.org

Address : at Kerganiet (1km southwest on D 105, signs for Erdeven)

25 ha (23 pitches) undulating, wood

Rental rates : (2015 price) (from beginning March to beginning Nov.) 🚫 🅿 – 1 'gypsy' caravan – 4 yurts – 1 🛏 – 7 cabins in the trees. Per night from 68 to 158€ – Per week from 476 to 1,106€

Surroundings : 🌊 ♀♀
Leisure activities : 🎦 🧖 hammam 🏄 🚴
Facilities : ⊶ ℉

GPS Longitude : -3.07692
Latitude : 47.64647

⚠ Kergo

✆ 02 97 56 80 66. www.campingkergo.com

Address : situated 2km southeast along the D 186, follow the signs for La Trinité-sur-Mer and take the turning to the left

Opening times : from beginning May to beginning Nov.

2.5 ha (135 pitches) flat, relatively flat, grassy

Tariff : (2015 price) 19.40€ ✝✝ 🚗 🅴 ⚡ (10A) – Extra per person 4.30€

Rental rates : (2015 price) (from beginning April to beginning Nov.) – 12 🛖. Per night from 38 to 80€ – Per week from 245 to 565€ – Reservation fee 10€

🛖 AireService sani-station 6€ – 🔌 ⚡13€

Surroundings : 🌊 ♀♀
Leisure activities : 🎦 🧖 jacuzzi 🏄 🚴
Facilities : ♿ ⊶ 🚿 ℉ launderette

GPS Longitude : -3.05362
Latitude : 47.64403

PLOÉVEN

29550 – Michelin map **308** F6 – pop. 505 – alt. 60
▶ Paris 585 – Brest 64 – Châteaulin 15 – Crozon 25

⚠ La Mer

✆ 02 98 81 29 19. www.campingdelamer29.fr

Address : at Ty Anquer Plage (3km southwest, 300m from the beach)

1 ha (54 pitches) flat, grassy

Rentals : 1 🛖 – 6 canvas bungalows.

A charming small campsite where peace and tranquillity are guaranteed, 100m from an unspoilt beach.

Surroundings : 🌊 ♀
Facilities : ⊶ ℉ 🔳

GPS Longitude : -4.26796
Latitude : 48.14806

PLOMEUR

29120 – Michelin map **308** F7 – pop. 3 634 – alt. 33
▶ Paris 579 – Douarnenez 39 – Pont-l'Abbé 6 – Quimper 26

⚠ Aire Naturelle Kéraluic

✆ 02 98 82 10 22. www.keraluic.fr

Address : at Keraluic (4.3km northeast along the D 57, follow the signs for Plonéour-Lanvern)

Opening times : from mid April to mid Oct.

1 ha (25 pitches) flat, grassy

Tariff : 20.90€ ✝✝ 🚗 🅴 ⚡ (6A) – Extra per person 5.50€

Rental rates : permanent 🚫 – 2 🛏 – 3 studios – 1 apartment – 2 canvas bungalows. Per week from 395 to 450€

Old farmhouse buildings that have been attractively renovated; wide pitches for tents and caravans.

Surroundings : 🌊 ♀
Leisure activities : 🎦 🏄
Facilities : ♿ ⊶ 🚿 ℉ 🔳

GPS Longitude : -4.26624
Latitude : 47.86148

⚠ Lanven

📞 02 98 82 00 75. www.campinglanven.com

Address : at La Chapelle de Beuzec (3.5km northwest along the D 57, follow the signs for Plonéour-Lanvern then take the road to the left)

Opening times : from end March to mid Nov.

3.7 ha (132 pitches) flat, grassy

Tariff : 20€ ♦♦ 🚗 🗐 ⚡ (10A) – Extra per person 4.20€

Rental rates : (from end March to mid Nov.) – 7 🛖. Per night from 35 to 77€ – Per week from 245 to 539€

A pleasant setting in the heart of the countryside; around half the site is occupied by children's summer camps in July and August.

Surroundings : 🐾 ⛱ ♀
Leisure activities : ♈ ✗ 🛷
Facilities : ◉ 🚿 ⚑ launderette

GPS	Longitude : -4.30663
	Latitude : 47.8505

PLOMODIERN

29550 – Michelin map **308** F5 – pop. 2 182 – alt. 60
▶ Paris 559 – Brest 60 – Châteaulin 12 – Crozon 25

🏔 La Mer d'Iroise

📞 02 98 81 52 72. www.camping-iroise.fr

Address : plage de Pors-Ar-Vag (5km southwest, 100m from the beach)

Opening times : from beginning April to end Sept.

2.5 ha (132 pitches) terraced, flat and relatively flat, grassy

Tariff : ♦ 6.30€ 🚗 🗐 12.50€ – ⚡ (10A) 3.90€ – Reservation fee 16€

Rental rates : permanent – 2 'gypsy' caravans – 13 🛖 – 17 🏠. Per week from 265 to 765€ – Reservation fee 16€

🚰 local sani-station

A good camp site equipped to a high standard, with a fine view of the sea from some pitches.

Surroundings : 🐾 ≤ Baie de Douarnenez ♀
Leisure activities : ♈ 🏛 🛷 🌊 ⛷
Facilities : ♿ 🚿 🛁 🚿 ⚑ launderette 🛒
Nearby : ✗ watersports centre

GPS	Longitude : -4.29397
	Latitude : 48.17006

PLOUÉZEC

22470 – Michelin map **309** E2 – pop. 3 368 – alt. 100
▶ Paris 489 – Guingamp 28 – Lannion 39 – Paimpol 6

🏔 Le Cap de Bréhat

📞 02 96 20 64 28. www.cap-de-brehat.com

Address : rue de Port Lazo (2.3km northeast along the D 77, direct access to the beach)

Opening times : from beginning April to end Sept.

4 ha (149 pitches) very uneven, terraced, relatively flat, stony, grassy

Tariff : 29€ ♦♦ 🚗 🗐 ⚡ (10A) – Extra per person 6.20€ – Reservation fee 5€

Rental rates : (from beginning April to end Sept.) – 44 🛖 – 1 cabin in the trees – 3 canvas bungalows. Per night from 30 to 155€ – Per week from 210 to 1,085€ – Reservation fee 15€

Surroundings : 🐾 ≤ ⛱
Leisure activities : ♈ ✗ 🏛 🛷 🚲 🌊
Facilities : ♿ 🚿 🛁 🚿 ⚑ launderette

GPS	Longitude : -2.96311
	Latitude : 48.76

PLOUGASNOU

29630 – Michelin map **308** I2 – pop. 3 268 – alt. 55
▶ Paris 545 – Brest 76 – Guingamp 62 – Lannion 34

🏔 Flower Domaine de Mesqueau

📞 02 98 67 37 45. www.domaine-de-mesqueau.com

Address : 870 route de Mesqueau (3.5km south along the D 46, follow the signs for Morlaix then continue 800m along the turning to the left, 100m from a small lake (direct access)

7.5 ha (100 pitches) flat, grassy

Rentals : 🅿 – 40 🛖 – 4 canvas bungalows – 4 tent lodges.

Tranquil and spacious pitches in the heart of the countryside.

Surroundings : 🐾 ♀
Leisure activities : 🏛 🛷 🚲 ✗ 🌊
multi-sports ground
Facilities : 🚿 🛁 ⚑
Nearby : ✗ 🛷 🎣

GPS	Longitude : -3.78101
	Latitude : 48.66462

PLOUGASTEL-DAOULAS

29470 – Michelin map **308** E4 – pop. 13 304 – alt. 113
▶ Paris 596 – Brest 12 – Morlaix 60 – Quimper 64

🏔 St-Jean ♣

📞 02 98 40 32 90. www.campingsaintjean.com

Address : at St-Jean (4.6km northeast along the D 29 et N 165, take the exit for the Leclerc commercial centre)

Opening times : from beginning April to mid Sept.

203 ha (125 pitches)

Tariff : (2015 price) 22.50€ ♦♦ 🚗 🗐 ⚡ (10A) – Extra per person 5.50€

Rental rates : (2015 price) (from beginning April to mid Sept.) – 43 🛖. Per night from 70 to 100€ – Per week from 224 to 725€ – Reservation fee 20€

A pleasant site and location beside the estuary of the Elorn river, ideal for birdwatching.

Surroundings : 🐾 ♀ ⚓
Leisure activities : ♈ ✗ 🏛 🌙 nighttime 🏃
🛷 🚲 🌊 ⛷ multi-sports ground
Facilities : ♿ 🚿 🅲🅲 🛁 ⚑ launderette 🛒

GPS	Longitude : -4.35334
	Latitude : 48.40122

PLOUGOULM

29250 – Michelin map **308** G3 – pop. 1 805 – alt. 60
▶ Paris 560 – Brest 58 – Brignogan-Plages 27 – Morlaix 24

⚠ Municipal du Bois de la Palud

📞 02 98 29 81 82. www.plougoulm.bzh

Address : Creach ar Feunteun (900m west of the D 10-D 69 junction (Criossant de Plougoulm), following signs for Plouescat and take the road to the right)

Opening times : from mid June to beginning Sept.

0.7 ha (34 pitches) terraced, relatively flat, grassy

Tariff : (2015 price) 12.44€ ♦♦ 🚗 🗐 ⚡ (6A)

A lovely wooded setting, with some fine expanses of fields nearby,

Surroundings : 🐾 ≤ ⛱ ♀♀
Facilities : ♿ 🅲🅲 🛁
Nearby : 🛷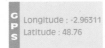

GPS	Longitude : -4.05323
	Latitude : 48.67236

PLOUGOUMELEN

56400 – Michelin map **308** N9 – pop. 2 378 – alt. 27
▶ Paris 471 – Auray 10 – Lorient 51 – Quiberon 39

⛺ La Via Natura Fontaine du Hallate

✆ 06 16 30 08 33. www.camping-morbihan.fr

Address : 8 chemin de Poul Fetan (3.2km southeast towards Ploeren and follow the signs for Baden to the right; at Hallate)

Opening times : from beginning April to end Oct.

3 ha (94 pitches) relatively flat, flat, grassy, pond

Tariff : 20.50€ ⚡🚗 🔌 (10A) – Extra per person 3.10€
Rental rates : (from beginning April to end Oct.) – 8 🛖 – 1 yurt. Per night from 70 to 100€ – Per week from 200 to 600€

Surroundings : 🏞 ≤ 🏕 🌳		GPS
Leisure activities : 🏊	Longitude : -2.8989
Facilities : ♿ ⛲ 🗑 ⛺ 🍴 launderette	Latitude : 47.6432

PLOUGRESCANT

22820 – Michelin map **309** C1 – pop. 1 347 – alt. 53
▶ Paris 516 – Lannion 26 – Perros-Guirec 23 – St-Brieuc 68

⛺ Le Varlen

✆ 02 96 92 52 15. www.levarlen.com

Address : 4 route de Pors Hir (2km to the northeast, follow the signs for Pors Hir, 200m from the sea)

1 ha (60 pitches) flat, grassy

Rentals : 13 🛖 – 2 studios – 1 canvas bungalow.
🚻 local sani-station

Surroundings : 🏞 🏕		GPS
Leisure activities : 🍴 ✕ 🏕 🏊	Longitude : -3.21873
Facilities : ♿ ⛲ 🍴 launderette 🐾	Latitude : 48.86078

⛺ Le Gouffre

✆ 02 96 92 02 95. www.camping-gouffre.com – limited spaces for one-night stay

Address : at Hent Crec'h Kermorvant (2.7km north following signs for La Pointe du Château (headland)

Opening times : from beginning April to end Sept.

3 ha (118 pitches) relatively flat, flat, grassy, pond

Tariff : 12.40€ ⚡🚗 🔌 (16A) – Extra per person 4€
Rental rates : (from beginning April to end Sept.) – 17 🛖. Per night from 55€ – Per week from 170 to 550€
🚻 local sani-station – 5 🔌 12.40€ – 🚐 12.40€

Surroundings : 🏞 🏕		GPS
Facilities : ♿ ⛲ (July–Aug.) 🍴 launderette	Longitude : -3.22749
	Latitude : 48.86081

PLOUGUERNEAU

29880 – Michelin map **308** D3 – pop. 6 411 – alt. 60
▶ Paris 604 – Brest 27 – Landerneau 33 – Morlaix 68

⛰ La Grève Blanche

✆ 02 98 04 70 35. www.campinggreveblanche.com

Address : at St-Michel (4km north along the D 32, follow the signs for St Michel and take a left turn; beside beach)

Opening times : from end March to mid Oct.

2.5 ha (100 pitches)

Tariff : (2015 price) ⚡ 3.80€ 🚗 1.70€ 🔌 5.10€ – 🔌 (10A) 2.95€

Rental rates : (2015 price) permanent – 2 'gypsy' caravans – 2 🛖 – 2 🛖 – 2 tipis – 2 canvas bungalows. Per night from 26 to 34€ – Per week from 245 to 530€
🚻 local sani-station – 25 🔌 14€ – 🚐 9€

A natural setting among rocks overlooking the beach.

Surroundings : ≤ the bay 🏔		GPS
Leisure activities : 🍴 🏊 🏕	Longitude : -4.523
Facilities : ♿ ⛲ 🗑 🍴	Latitude : 48.6305

⛺ Du Vougot

✆ 02 98 25 61 51. www.campingduvougot.com

Address : route de Prat Ledan (7.4km northeast along the D 13 and the D 10, follow the signs for Guisseny, then take the D 52; along the bank of the Vougot, 250m from the sea)

Opening times : from beginning April to mid Oct.

2.5 ha (55 pitches) flat, grassy, sandy

Tariff : ⚡ 4.80€ 🚗 2 🔌 8.50€ – 🔌 (10A) 3.80€ – Reservation fee 10€
Rental rates : (from beginning April to mid Oct.) – 14 🛖 – 1 canvas bungalow. Per night from 40 to 80€ – Per week from 200 to 640€ – Reservation fee 10€
🚻 local sani-station 4€ – 🚐 8€

A haven of peace in a well-preserved natural setting.

Surroundings : 🏞 🏕		GPS
Leisure activities : 🍴 🏊 🏕	Longitude : -4.45
Facilities : ⛲ 🍴 launderette	Latitude : 48.63132
Nearby : watersports centre	

PLOUHARNEL

56340 – Michelin map **308** M9 – pop. 2 000 – alt. 21
▶ Paris 490 – Auray 13 – Lorient 33 – Quiberon 15

⛰ Kersily

✆ 02 97 52 39 65. www.camping-kersily.com

Address : at Ste-Barbe (2.5km northwest along the D 781, follow the signs for Lorient)

Opening times : from beginning April to end Oct.

2.5 ha (120 pitches) relatively flat, flat, grassy

Tariff : (2015 price) ⚡ 6€ 🚗 🔌 10€ – 🔌 (10A) 4.40€ – Reservation fee 10€
Rental rates : (2015 price) (from beginning April to end Oct.) – 28 🛖. Per night from 54 to 75€ – Per week from 200 to 730€ – Reservation fee 10€
🚻 local sani-station 2€ – 🚐 20€

Surroundings : 🏞 🌳		GPS
Leisure activities : 🍴 ✕ 🏕 nighttime 🏊 🎿 📺 🛶 🏛 entertainment room	Longitude : -3.1316
Facilities : ♿ ⛲ ⛺ 🍴 launderette	Latitude : 47.61107

⛺ Les Goélands

✆ 02 97 52 31 92. www.camping-lesgoelands.com

Address : at Kergonan (located 1.5km east along the D 781, follow the signs for Carnac then continue 500m along the turning to the left)

1.6 ha (80 pitches) flat, grassy
Rentals : 2 🛖 – 2 🏠.

Surroundings : 🏞 🌳		GPS
Leisure activities : 🏕 🛶	Longitude : -3.09657
Facilities : ⛲ ⛺ 🍴 launderette	Latitude : 47.59461
Nearby : ✕	

PLOUHINEC

29780 – Michelin map **308** E6 – pop. 4 217 – alt. 101
▶ Paris 594 – Audierne 5 – Douarnenez 18 – Pont-l'Abbé 27

⛺ Kersiny-Plage

𝒫 02 98 70 82 44. www.kersinyplage.com

Address : 1 rue Nominoé (take the western exit along the D 784, follow the signs for Audierne then continue 1km south following signs for Kersiny, 100m from the beach (direct access)

Opening times : from mid May to mid Sept.

2 ha (70 pitches) terraced, relatively flat, grassy

Tariff : (2015 price) 19€ ♥♥ ⇔ 🗐 🖢 (10A) – Extra per person 5.90€ – Reservation fee 10€

Rental rates : (2015 price) (from mid May to mid Sept.) 🌂 – 4 🚐 – 3 🏠. Per week from 190 to 535€ – Reservation fee 10€
🚽 local sani-station

Surroundings : 🦢 ⪡ ocean ▭
Facilities : ⚲ 🖢 🖾
Nearby : ✂

| G P S | Longitude : -4.50819 |
| | Latitude : 48.00719 |

PLOUHINEC

56680 – Michelin map **308** L8 – pop. 4 922 – alt. 10
▶ Paris 503 – Auray 22 – Lorient 18 – Quiberon 30

🏔 Moténo 👥

𝒫 02 97 36 76 63. www.camping-le-moteno.com

Address : rue du Passage d'Étel (4.5km southeast along the D 781 and take a right turn, follow the signs for Le Magouër)

Opening times : from beginning April to end Sept.

4 ha (254 pitches) flat, grassy

Tariff : (2015 price) 35.50€ ♥♥ ⇔ 🗐 🖢 (10A) – Extra per person 6.99€ – Reservation fee 26€

Rental rates : (2015 price) (from beginning April to end Sept.) – 142 🚐 – 23 🏠. Per night from 27 to 155€ – Per week from 185 to 1,100€ – Reservation fee 26€

Surroundings : ▭ ℚ
Leisure activities : ♟ ✗ 🖾 ◔ ⚹ 🎣 jacuzzi ⚹ 🚲 🏊 ⛲ multi-sports ground, entertainment room
Facilities : ⚲ 🖢 🖾 🕱 launderette 🔧 🔧

| G P S | Longitude : -3.22127 |
| | Latitude : 47.66492 |

PLOUIGNEAU

29610 – Michelin map **308** I3 – pop. 4 685 – alt. 156
▶ Paris 526 – Brest 72 – Carhaix-Plouguer 43 – Guingamp 44

🏔 Aire Naturelle la Ferme de Croas Men

𝒫 02 98 79 11 50. http://ferme-de-croasmen.com

Address : at Croas Men (2.5km northwest along the D 712 and the D 64, follow the signs for Lanmeur then continue 4.7km following signs for Lanleya to the left, then follow the signs for Garlan)

Opening times : from beginning April to end Oct.

1 ha (25 pitches) flat, grassy, fruit trees

Tariff : (2015 price) ♥ 3.50€ ⇔ 🗐 8€ – 🖢 (6A) 3.50€

Rental rates : (2015 price) permanent – 2 'gypsy' caravans – 4 🚐 – 1 canvas bungalow – 2 tent lodges. Per night from 60 to 70€ – Per week from 350 to 550€
🚽 local sani-station

A working educational farm, with a museum of agricultural tools. A leafy setting for tents and caravans.

Surroundings : 🦢 ℚ
Leisure activities : 🖾 ⚹
Facilities : ⚲ 🖢 🕱 launderette
Nearby : 🐎 🐴

| G P S | Longitude : -3.73792 |
| | Latitude : 48.60465 |

PLOUNÉVEZ-LOCHRIST

29430 – Michelin map **308** F3 – pop. 2 398 – alt. 70
▶ Paris 576 – Brest 41 – Landerneau 24 – Landivisiau 22

⛺ Municipal Odé-Vras

𝒫 02 98 61 65 17. www.plounevez-lochrist.fr

Address : at Ode Vras (4.5km to the north, along the D 10, 300m from the Baie de Kernic (direct access)

Opening times : from beginning June to end Sept.

3 ha (135 pitches)

Tariff : (2015 price) 13.10€ ♥♥ ⇔ 🗐 🖢 (10A) – Extra per person 2.85€

Rental rates : (2015 price) (from beginning June to end Sept.) – 1 🚐. Per week from 270 to 345€

🚽 local sani-station 4€ – 🚐 8€

A site charmingly situated beside unspoilt sand dunes.

Surroundings : ▭ ℚ
Leisure activities : 🖾 ⚹
Facilities : 🖢 ⚹ 🕱 launderette

| G P S | Longitude : -4.23942 |
| | Latitude : 48.64564 |

Key to rentals symbols:

12 🚐	*Number of mobile homes*
20 🏠	*Number of chalets*
6 🛏	*Number of rooms to rent*
Per night 30–50€	*Minimum/maximum rate per night*
Per week 300–1,000€	*Minimum/maximum rate per week*

PLOZÉVET

29710 – Michelin map **308** E7 – pop. 2 988 – alt. 70
▶ Paris 588 – Audierne 11 – Douarnenez 19 – Pont-l'Abbé 22

🏔 Flower La Corniche 👥

𝒫 02 98 91 33 94. www.campinglacorniche.com

Address : chemin de la Corniche (take the southern exit along the coast road)

Opening times : from mid March to mid Nov.

2 ha (120 pitches) flat, grassy

Tariff : 24€ ♥♥ ⇔ 🗐 🖢 (10A) – Extra per person 4.90€ – Reservation fee 12€

Rental rates : (from beginning March to mid Nov.) – 16 🚐 – 9 🏠 – 6 tent lodges. Per night from 44 to 103€ – Per week from 245 to 721€ – Reservation fee 12€
🚽 local sani-station 4€

A haven of peace in the middle of the Baie d'Audierne (bay), 500m from the centre of the village.

Surroundings : 🦢 ℚ
Leisure activities : ♟ 🖾 ⚹ 🎣 🏊
Facilities : ⚲ 🖢 🖾 🔧 🕱 launderette

| G P S | Longitude : -4.4287 |
| | Latitude : 47.98237 |

PLURIEN

22240 – Michelin map **309** H3 – pop. 1 396 – alt. 48
▶ Paris 436 – Dinard 34 – Lamballe 25 – Plancoët 23

⚠ Les Salines

🔗 02 96 72 17 40. http://campinglessalines.fr

Address : rue du Lac, at Sables d'or-Les Pins (1.2km northwest along the D 34, follow the signs for Sables-d'Or-les-Pins; 500m from the sea)

Opening times : from beginning April to end Oct.

3 ha (150 pitches) terraced, flat, grassy

Tariff : (2015 price) 15.40€ ★★ 🚗 🗐 (½) (6A) – Extra per person 3.40€
Rental rates : (2015 price) (from beginning April to mid Nov.) – 8 🚐 – 5 yurts – 2 tent lodges. Per night from 38 to 97€ – Per week from 210 to 580€
🚐 local sani-station 2€ – 🛒 8.50€

Surroundings : ⪅ ♀	G P S	Longitude : -2.41396
Leisure activities : 🛶 🚲		Latitude : 48.63281
Facilities : 🚿 ⊶ 👕 🍴 launderette		
Nearby : 🐎		

A chambre d'hôte is a guesthouse or B & B-style accommodation.

PONTRIEUX

22260 – Michelin map **309** D2 – pop. 1 053 – alt. 13
▶ Paris 491 – Guingamp 18 – Lannion 27 – Morlaix 67

⚠ Traou-Mélédern

🔗 02 96 95 69 27. www.camping-pontrieux.com

Address : 400m south of the town; beside the Trieux river

Opening times : permanent

1 ha (50 pitches) flat, relatively flat, grassy

Tariff : (2015 price) ★ 4.30€ 🚗 🗐 5.40€ – (½) (10A) 3.30€
Rental rates : permanent – 1 🚐 – 2 gîtes. Per night from 60€ – Per week from 265 to 370€

Surroundings : 🏞 🗒 ♀♀	G P S	Longitude : -3.16355
Leisure activities : 🛶 🛥		Latitude : 48.6951
Facilities : 🚿 ⊶ 👕 🍴 🔲		
Nearby : marina		

PONT-SCORFF

56620 – Michelin map **308** K8 – pop. 3 167 – alt. 42
▶ Paris 509 – Auray 47 – Lorient 11 – Quiberon 56

⚠ La Via Natura Ty Nénez

🔗 02 97 32 51 16. www.lorient-camping.com

Address : route de Lorient (1.8km southwest along the D 6)

Opening times : permanent

2.5 ha (93 pitches) relatively flat, flat, grassy

Tariff : 22.80€ ★★ 🚗 🗐 (½) (16A) – Extra per person 5€
Rental rates : permanent 🚿 (1 mobile home) ⚡ – 18 🚐. Per night from 45 to 115€ – Per week from 250 to 770€
🚐 raclet sani-station 3€ – 7 🗐 10.60€ – 🛒 10.60€

Surroundings : 🏞 🗒 ♀♀	G P S	Longitude : -3.40361
Leisure activities : ♀ ✕ 🛶 🛥 🚲 🎯		Latitude : 47.82
Facilities : 🚿 ⊶ 👕 🍴 launderette 🎣		
Nearby : 🐟		

PORDIC

22590 – Michelin map **309** F3 – pop. 5 923 – alt. 97
▶ Paris 459 – Guingamp 33 – Lannion 65 – St-Brieuc 11

⛰ Les Madières

🔗 02 96 79 02 48. www.campinglesmadieres.com

Address : at Le Vau Madec (situated 2km northeast following signs for Binic and take a right turn)

Opening times : from beginning April to end Oct.

1.6 ha (93 pitches)

Tariff : (2015 price) 24.40€ ★★ 🚗 🗐 (½) (10A) – Extra per person 5.80€

Rental rates : (2015 price) (from beginning April to end Oct.) – 9 🚐. Per night from 45 to 60€ – Per week from 390 to 590€ – Reservation fee 10€
🚐 10 🗐 24.40€ – 🛒 (½)15€

A pleasant leafy setting, attractively shady; some pitches with a view of the sea and the port at St-Quay-Portrieux.

Surroundings : 🏞 🗒 ♀♀	G P S	Longitude : -2.80475
Leisure activities : ♀ ✕ 🛶		Latitude : 48.58266
Facilities : 🚿 ⊶ 🍴 launderette		

PORT-MANECH

29920 – Michelin map **308** I8
▶ Paris 545 – Carhaix-Plouguer 73 – Concarneau 18 – Pont-Aven 12

⛰ St-Nicolas

🔗 02 98 06 89 75. www.campinglesaintnicolas.com

Address : at Port-Manech, 8 Kergouliou (north of the town, 200m from the beach)

Opening times : from beginning May to mid Sept.

3 ha (180 pitches) terraced, relatively flat, flat, grassy

Tariff : (2015 price) 28.30€ ★★ 🚗 🗐 (½) (10A) – Extra per person 6.35€ – Reservation fee 7.50€
Rental rates : (2015 price) (from mid April to mid Sept.) – 27 🚐. Per week from 220 to 838€ – Reservation fee 7.50€

In two distinct parts, with ornamental flowers and bushes

Surroundings : 🏞 🗒 ♀♀	G P S	Longitude : -3.74541
Leisure activities : 🏓 🛶 🔲 🛥 ⛷		Latitude : 47.80512
Facilities : 🚿 ⊶ 🍴 launderette		
Nearby : 🏊 ♀ ✕ 🍷		

LE POULDU

29360 – Michelin map **308** J8
▶ Paris 521 – Concarneau 37 – Lorient 25 – Moëlan-sur-Mer 10

⛰ Les Embruns

🔗 02 98 39 91 07. www.camping-les-embruns.com

Address : rue du Philosophe-Alain (in the town, 350m from the beach)

Opening times : from end March to beginning Oct.

5.5 ha (176 pitches) fruit trees

Tariff : 42.50€ ★★ 🚗 🗐 (½) (16A) – Extra per person 8€ – Reservation fee 20€

Rental rates : (from end March to beginning Oct.) 🚿 (1 mobile home) – 35 🚐. Per night from 45 to 200 – Per week from 295 to 1.360 – Reservation fee 20€
🚐 local sani-station 6€ – 14 🗐 20€

Surroundings : ▱ ♤♤
Leisure activities : ♥ 🏠 ⅁ ◯ ⅄ ⛴ hammam
🚣🏊🚵 ☈ 🔲 (open air in season) ♨ wildlife
park, spa centre
Facilities : ♿ ⚬━ ▥ ♨ ⅄ ⚐ ⁂ launderette
Nearby : 🏊 ✗ ⛵ ✗ ⚓

G P S Longitude : -3.54696
Latitude : 47.76947

⚠ Keranquernat

✆ 02 98 39 92 32. www.camping.keranquernat.com

Address : Keranquernat (at the roundabout, take northeastern exit)

Opening times : from beginning April to beginning Sept.

1.5 ha (100 pitches)

Tariff : ♦ 4€ ⇔ ▣ 9€ – ⅍ (10A) 10€
Rental rates : (from beginning April to beginning Sept.) ⌇ –
10 ⊡. Per night from 40 to 85€ – Per week from 305 to 490€
⊟ local sani-station

In a pleasant setting shaded by apple trees and lots of flowers.

Surroundings : ⚘ ▱ ♤♤
Leisure activities : 🏠 ◯ 🚣🏊
Facilities : ♿ ⚬━ (July-Aug.) ♨ ⅄ ⁂
launderette
Nearby : 🏊 ✗ ✗ ⚓

G P S Longitude : -3.54332
Latitude : 47.7727

⚠ Locouarn

✆ 02 98 39 91 79. www.camping-locouarn.com

Address : situated 2km north along the D 49, follow the signs for Quimperlé

Opening times : permanent

2.5 ha (100 pitches) open site, relatively flat, flat, grassy

Tariff : ♦ 3.80€ ⇔ ▣ 6.90€ – ⅍ (10A) 4.20€
Rental rates : permanent – 13 ⊡. Per night from 50€ – Per week from 160 to 490€ – Reservation fee 5€

A pleasant site surrounded by fields.

Surroundings : ⚘ ⚓
Leisure activities : 🏊
Facilities : ♿ ⚬━ ♨ ⅄ ⚐ ⁂ launderette
Nearby : 🏊 ♥ ✗ 🐎

G P S Longitude : -3.54793
Latitude : 47.7855

⚠ Les Grands Sables

✆ 02 98 39 94 43. www.camping-lesgrandssables.com

Address : 22 rue Philosophe Alain (in the town, 200m from the beach)

Opening times : from mid April to mid Sept.

2.4 ha (128 pitches) terraced, flat and relatively flat, sandy, grassy

Tariff : (2015 price) 21.80€ ♦♦ ⇔ ▣ ⅍ (10A) –
Extra per person 5.20€ – Reservation fee 9€
Rental rates : (2015 price) (from mid April to mid Sept.) –
18 ⊡. Per night from 27 to 89€ – Per week from 220 to 620€ –
Reservation fee 9€
⊟ 40 ▣ 17.50€ – ⛽ 8.80€

In a green and leafy location with shade and a view of the pretty chapel of Notre-Dame-de-la-Paix.

Surroundings : ⚘ ⚓
Leisure activities : 🚣🏊
Facilities : ⚬━ ♨ ⅄ ⁂ launderette
Nearby : 🏊 ✗ ✗ ⚓

G P S Longitude : -3.54716
Latitude : 47.7683

⚠ Croas An Ter

✆ 02 98 39 94 19. www.campingcroasanter.com

Address : at Quelvez (located 1.5km north along the D49. follow the signs for Quimperlé)

Opening times : from beginning May to mid Sept.

3.5 ha (90 pitches) lat, hilly, grassy

Tariff : 16.80€ ♦♦ ⇔ ▣ ⅍ (6A) – Extra per person 3.90€
Rental rates : (from beginning May to mid Sept.) – 2 ⊡ – 2 tent lodges. Per night from 50 to 55€ – Per week from 210 to 440€

A site with good shade, integrated well in the natural surroundings; a perfect spot for touring cyclists.

Surroundings : ⚘ ▱ ♤♤
Leisure activities : ✗ 🚣🏊 🚵
Facilities : ♿ ⚬━ ♨ ⅄ ⁂ launderette
Nearby : ♥ ⛵

G P S Longitude : -3.54104
Latitude : 47.78515

POULLAN-SUR-MER

29100 – Michelin map **308** E6 – pop. 1 499 – alt. 79
▣ Paris 596 – Rennes 244 – Quimper 30 – Brest 80

⚞ Yelloh! Village La Baie de Douarnenez 🏖

✆ 02 98 74 26 39. www.camping-douarnenez.com

Address : 30 rue Luc Robet (600m east of the town along the D7)

Opening times : from end April to mid Sept.

5.7 ha (190 pitches) flat, grassy

Tariff : (2015 price) 44€ ♦♦ ⇔ ▣ ⅍ (6A) – Extra per person 7€
Rental rates : (2015 price) (from end April to mid Sept.) – 74 ⊡ –
20 ⌂ – 3 canvas bungalows – 6 tent lodges. Per week from 224 to 1,155€

Pitches beside a partially covered water park.

Surroundings : ⚘ ▱ ♤♤
Leisure activities : ♥ ✗ 🏠 ⅁ nighttime
🚣🏊🚵 ☈ 🔲 🏊 multi-sports
ground
Facilities : ♿ ⚬━ ♨ ⅄ ⚐ ⁂ launderette
🏊 ⛵

G P S Longitude : -4.40634
Latitude : 48.08162

To visit a town or region, use the MICHELIN Green Guides.

PRIMEL-TRÉGASTEL

29630 – Michelin map **308** I2
▣ Paris 554 – Rennes 198 – Quimper 105 – Brest 79

⚠ Municipal de la Mer

✆ 02 98 72 37 06. www.camping-plougasnou.fr

Address : 15 route de Karreg An Ty (4km north along the D 46)

Opening times : from beginning April to end Oct.

1 ha (63 pitches)

Tariff : (2015 price) ♦ 3.80€ ⇔ 1.30€ ▣ 7€ ⅍ (16A)
⊟ Eurorelais sani-station 3€

An exceptional location beside the sea, with an unrestricted view of the sea. Make sure tents are well secured as the site is exposed to the wind.

Surroundings : ⚘ ≼ Île de Batz and Roscoff ⛰
Leisure activities : 🏠 🚣🏊 🚵 ♨
Facilities : ♿ ⚬━ (July-Aug.) ⁂ launderette
Nearby : ♥ ✗

G P S Longitude : -3.81527
Latitude : 48.71477

PRIMELIN

29770 – Michelin map **308** D6 – pop. 742 – alt. 78
▶ Paris 605 – Audierne 7 – Douarnenez 28 – Quimper 44

⚲ Municipal de Kermalero

✆ 02 98 74 84 75. www.primelin.fr

Address : route de l'Océan (take the western exit towards the port)

Opening times : from beginning April to end Oct.

1 ha (75 pitches) flat, relatively flat, grassy

Tariff : (2015 price) 15€ ✷✷ ⇌ 🅴 🔌 (6A) – Extra per person 3.50€ – Reservation fee 10€

🚐 AireService sani-station 2€ – 6 🅴 3€

A simple but pleasant site beside the sea.

Surroundings : ⛱ ≼ 🏠		
Leisure activities : 🏛 🏃	**G**	Longitude : -4.61067
Facilities : ⚇ ⊶ (July–Aug.) 🚿 🚽 🍴 launderette	**P** **S**	Latitude : 48.02544
Nearby : 🍴		

PRIZIAC

56320 – Michelin map **308** K6 – pop. 1 046 – alt. 163
▶ Paris 498 – Concarneau 55 – Lorient 42 – Pontivy 39

⚲ Municipal Bel Air

✆ 02 97 34 61 26. www.priziac.com

Address : at l'Etang du Bel Air (lake, 500m north along the D 109 and take the turning to the left)

1.5 ha (60 pitches) relatively flat, flat, grassy

Rentals : 4 🛖.

🚐 local sani-station

Green setting and plenty of shade, near a small lake.

Surroundings : ⛱ ♨ ⛰		
Leisure activities : 🛶 boats for hire, pedalos	**G**	Longitude : -3.41418
Facilities : ⚇ launderette	**P** **S**	Latitude : 48.06155
Nearby : 🍹 🏃 🍴 ≊ (beach) 🎣 🚣 watersports centre		

QUIBERON

56170 – Michelin map **308** M10 – pop. 5 027 – alt. 10
▶ Paris 505 – Auray 28 – Concarneau 98 – Lorient 47

⚳⚳⚳ Do.Mi.Si.La.Mi. 👥

✆ 02 97 50 22 52. www.domisilami.com

Address : at St-Julien-Plage, 31 rue de la Vierge (600m to the north, 100m from the beach)

Opening times : from beginning April to end Sept.

4.4 ha (350 pitches)

Tariff : ✷ 5.50€ ⇌ 🅴 15.10€ – 🔌 (10A) 4.50€

Rental rates : (from beginning April to end Sept.) 🏕 – 80 🛖. Per night from 32 to 150€ – Per week from 192 to 900€

🚐 local sani-station 8€ – 10 🅴 18.60€

Leafy setting, near beach with a free shuttle bus to Quiberon.

Surroundings : ⛱ 🏠 ♨		
Leisure activities : 🍹 🍴 🛶 🏸 🏃 🚴 multi-sports ground	**G**	Longitude : -3.12045
Facilities : ⚇ ⊶ 🚿 🚽 🍴 launderette 🏪 🚗	**P** **S**	Latitude : 47.49937

⚳⚳⚳ Flower Le Bois d'Amour 👥

✆ 02 97 50 13 52. www.quiberon-camping.com

Opening times : from beginning April to end Sept.

4.6 ha (256 pitches)

Tariff : 41€ ✷✷ ⇌ 🅴 🔌 (6A) – Extra per person 6.50€ – Reservation fee 15€

Rental rates : (2015 price) (from beginning April to end Sept.) – 127 🛖 – 14 tent lodges. Per night from 47 to 156€ – Per week from 235 to 1,092€ – Reservation fee 20€

Surroundings : 🏠 ♨♨		
Leisure activities : 🍹 🍴 🛶 🏐 🏃 ⛵ 🚴 🍴 (open air in season)	**G**	Longitude : -3.10427
Facilities : ⚇ ⊶ 🚿 🍴 launderette 🏪 🚗	**P** **S**	Latitude : 47.47632
Nearby : 🍴 🐴 🚣		

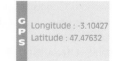

⚳⚳⚳ Les Joncs du Roch

✆ 02 97 50 24 37. www.lesjoncsduroch.com

Address : rue de l'Aérodrome (situated 2km southeast, 500m from the sea)

Opening times : from beginning April to end Sept.

2.3 ha (163 pitches) flat, grassy

Tariff : (2015 price) 35.50€ ✷✷ ⇌ 🅴 🔌 (10A) – Extra per person 7.20€ – Reservation fee 15€

Rental rates : (2015 price) (from beginning April to end Sept.) 🏕 – 25 🛖 – 2 canvas bungalows. Per week from 180 to 990€ – Reservation fee 15€

Surroundings : ⛱ 🏠 ♨		
Leisure activities : 🛶 🏃 🍴 (open air in season), multi-sports ground, entertainment room	**G**	Longitude : -3.10098
Facilities : ⚇ ⊶ 🚿 🚽 🍴 launderette	**P** **S**	Latitude : 47.47946
Nearby : 🍴 🚣 🐴		

⚲ Beauséjour

✆ 02 97 30 44 93. www.campingbeausejour.com

Address : At St Julien Plage, boulevard du Parco (800m to the north, 50m from the beach)

Opening times : from beginning April to end Sept.

2.4 ha (192 pitches) flat and relatively flat, grassy, sandy

Tariff : ✷ 4.50€ ⇌ 🅴 15€ – 🔌 (10A) 5.20€

Rental rates : (from beginning April to end Sept.) – 15 🛖. Per night from 60 to 100€ – Per week from 310 to 690€ – Reservation fee 18€

🚐 AireService sani-station 4€

Surroundings : ⛱ ♨		
Leisure activities : 🛶 🏃 multi-sports ground	**G**	Longitude : -3.12027
Facilities : ⚇ ⊶ (July–Aug.) 🚿 🚽 🍴 launderette	**P** **S**	Latitude : 47.5003
Nearby : 🛒 🍹 🍴 🚗		

These symbols are used for a campsite that is exceptional in its category :

⚳⚳⚳...⚲	*Particularly pleasant setting, quality and range of services available*
⛱⛱	*Tranquil, isolated site – quiet site, particularly at night*
≼≼	*Exceptional view – interesting or panoramic view*

QUIMPER

29000 – Michelin map **308** G7 – pop. 63 387 – alt. 41
▶ Paris 564 – Brest 73 – Lorient 67 – Rennes 215

⚑ Les Castels L'Orangerie de Lanniron ♙

✆ 02 98 90 62 02. www.lanniron.com

Address : allée de Lanniron (3km south along the ring road (périphérique), then take the exit towards Bénodet and a right turn; near the leisure centre at Creac'h Gwen)

Opening times : from mid March to mid Nov.

38 ha/6.5 for camping (235 pitches) flat, grassy

Tariff : (2015 price) ♦ 8.80 € ⇌ 圁 22.80 € – (₺) (10A) 5.90 € – Reservation fee 25 €
Rental rates : (2015 price) permanent – 35 ⟦⟧ – 12 studios – 2 tipis – 2 tent lodges – 5 gîtes. Per night from 60 to 161 € – Per week from 420 to 1,225 € – Reservation fee 25 €

⛽ AireService sani-station 5 € – 100 圁 29 € – ⛽ (₺)29 €

Surroundings : ⬜ ♡♡
Leisure activities : ♈ ✗ 🏠 ⛳ ⚡ jacuzzi
⚡⚡ 🚲 ✂ 🎣 🏊 ⛵ 9-hole golf course ⚡
Facilities : ♿ ⛤ 🛁 🚿 🚾 ⁂ launderette
🛁 🚱

| | | Longitude : -4.10338 |
| G P S | | Latitude : 47.97923 |

For more information on visiting particular towns or regions, consult the relevant regional MICHELIN Green Guide. We also recommend you use the appropriate Michelin regional map to locate your selected campsite, to calculate distances and to work out the best route.

QUIMPERLÉ

29300 – Michelin map **308** J7 – pop. 11 384 – alt. 30
▶ Paris 517 – Carhaix-Plouguer 57 – Concarneau 32 – Pontivy 76

⚑ Municipal de Kerbertrand

✆ 02 98 39 31 30. www.quimperle-tourisme.com

Address : 2 rue de Kermaria (located 1.5km west along the D 783, follow the signs for Concarneau and take the road to the right, after the stadium, opposite the Leclerc commercial centre)

1 ha (40 pitches) flat, grassy

Surroundings : ⬜ ♡♡
Leisure activities : 🏠 ⚡⚡
Facilities : ⛤
Nearby : ⛺ ✗ 🎣 🏊

| | | Longitude : -3.57044 |
| G P S | | Latitude : 47.872 |

RAGUENÈS-PLAGE

29920 – Michelin map **308** I8
▶ Paris 545 – Carhaix-Plouguer 73 – Concarneau 17 – Pont-Aven 12

⚑ Les Deux Fontaines ♙

✆ 02 98 06 81 91. www.les2fontaines.com

Address : at Feunten Vihan (1.3km north following signs for Névez and Trémorvezen)

Opening times : from end April to beginning Sept.

9 ha (270 pitches) flat, grassy

Tariff : 40.80 € ♦♦ ⇌ 圁 (₺) (10A) – Extra per person 7.40 € – Reservation fee 15 €

Rental rates : (from end April to beginning Sept.) – 47 ⟦⟧ – 7 🏠. Per night from 49 to 180 € – Per week from 199 to 1,260 € – Reservation fee 15 €

⛽ local sani-station 5 €

Surroundings : 🏊 ⬜ ♡♡
Leisure activities : ♈ ✗ 🏠 ⛳ ⚡ ⚡ ⚡ ✂ 🎣 🏊 ⛵ farm or petting farm, pool scuba diving
Facilities : ♿ ⛤ 🛁 🚿 🚾 ⁂ launderette 🛁 🚱

⚑ Club Airotel Le Raguenès-Plage ♙

Le Raguenès-Plage

✆ 02 98 06 80 69. www.camping-le-raguenes-plage.com

Address : 19 rue des Îles (400m from the beach, direct access)

Opening times : from mid April to end Sept.

6 ha (287 pitches) flat, grassy

Tariff : (2015 price) 39.50 € ♦♦ ⇌ 圁 (₺) (10A) – Extra per person 6.20 €

Rental rates : (2015 price) (from beginning April to end Sept.) – 66 ⟦⟧. Per night from 38 to 157 € – Per week from 265 to 1,099 €

⛽ AireService sani-station – 20 圁 17 €

In a pleasant setting, with an attractive water park.

Surroundings : ♡♡
Leisure activities : ♈ ✗ 🏠 ⛳ ⚡ ⚡ ⚡ 🚲 ✂ 🎣 🏊 ⛵
Facilities : ♿ ⛤ 🛁 🚿 🚾 ⁂ launderette 🛁 🚱

| | | Longitude : -3.80085 |
| G P S | | Latitude : 47.79373 |

⚑ Le Vieux Verger - Ty Noul

✆ 02 98 06 86 08. www.campingduvieuxverger.com

Address : 20 Kéroren (take the northern exit, follow the signs for Névez)

1.2 ha (42 pitches) flat, grassy

Rentals : 10 ⟦⟧ – 1 apartment.

A pretty water park; attractive pitches for tents and caravans.

Surroundings : ♡
Leisure activities : ⚡⚡ 🚲 🏊 ⛵
Facilities : ♿ ⛤ ⁂ 🛁

| | | Longitude : -3.79777 |
| G P S | | Latitude : 47.79663 |

⚑ L'Océan

✆ 02 98 06 87 13. www.camping-ocean.fr

Address : 15 impasse des Mouettes, at Kéroren (take the northern exit, follow the signs for Névez and take a right turn, 350m from the beach (direct access)

Opening times : from mid May to mid Sept.

2.2 ha (150 pitches)

Tariff : 29.50 € ♦♦ ⇌ 圁 (₺) (10A) – Extra per person 6.70 €
Rental rates : (from mid May to mid Sept.) ⚡ – 8 ⟦⟧. Per week from 330 to 610 €

⛽ Eurorelais sani-station

Quiet, peaceful pitches; a spacious site with flowers and a panoramic view of the ocean.

Surroundings : 🏊 ⚡ ⬜ ♡
Leisure activities : 🏠 ⚡⚡ 🏊 (open air in season)
Facilities : ♿ ⛤ 🛁 ⁂ launderette
Nearby : ✂ ⚓

| | | Longitude : -3.79789 |
| G P S | | Latitude : 47.79471 |

RENNES

35000 – Michelin map **309** L6 – pop. 206 604 – alt. 40
▶ Paris 349 – Angers 129 – Brest 246 – Caen 185

⚠ Municipal des Gayeulles

✆ 02 99 36 91 22. www.camping-rennes.com

Address : rue Professeur Maurice-Audin (take the northeastern exit towards the N 12, follow the signs for Fougères then take the av. des Gayeulles near a small lake)

Opening times : permanent

3 ha (178 pitches) flat, grassy

Tariff : (2015 price) ⚹ 4€ ⇐ 1.70€ 🅴 7.80€ – 🔌 (16A) 3.50€

🚐 Eurorelais sani-station 2€ – 30 🔋 15.60€

Situated in the middle of the immense wooded park at Les Gayeulles, in a natural setting shared with rabbits.

Surroundings : 🌿 ⊡ 🎴
Leisure activities : 🏊
Facilities : ₺ ⊶ (July–Aug.) 🅲🄲 🎆 ⚲ ⚶ launderette 🚿
Nearby : 🍴 ⚔ 🎣 🖼 🔲 (open air in season) skating rink, wildlife park

G P S
Longitude : -1.64772
Latitude : 48.13455

Some campsites benefit from proximity to a municipal leisure centre.

LA ROCHE-BERNARD

56130 – Michelin map **308** R9 – pop. 757 – alt. 38
▶ Paris 444 – Nantes 70 – Ploërmel 55 – Redon 28

⚠ Municipal le Pâtis

✆ 02 99 90 60 13. www.camping-larochebernard.com

Address : 3 chemin du Pâtis (to the west of the town towards the marina)

Opening times : from beginning April to mid Oct.

1 ha (63 pitches) flat, grassy

Tariff : (2015 price) 22.50€ ⚹⚹ ⇐ 🅴 🔌 (6A) – Extra per person 3.20€
Rental rates : (2015 price) (from beginning April to mid Oct.) – 2 🚐. Per night from 42 to 100€ – Per week from 215 to 590€

🚐 18 🅴 8.50€

Beside the Vilaine river, opposite the port.

Surroundings : 🌿 ⊡ 🎴
Leisure activities : 🎡
Facilities : ₺ ⊶ (July–Aug.) 🎆 ⚲ ⚶ launderette
Nearby : 🍷 ⚔ 🏊 ⚓ 💧

G P S
Longitude : -2.30523
Latitude : 47.51923

ROCHEFORT-EN-TERRE

56220 – Michelin map **308** Q8 – pop. 662 – alt. 40
▶ Paris 431 – Ploërmel 34 – Redon 26 – Rennes 82

⛰ Sites et Paysages Au Gré des Vents

✆ 02 97 43 37 52. www.campingaugredesvents.com

Address : 2 chemin de Bogeais (located 1km southwest along the D 774, follow the signs for Péaule and take the road to the right; 500m from a small lake)

Opening times : from beginning April to end Sept.

2.5 ha (85 pitches) terraced, relatively flat, flat, grassy

Tariff : (2015 price) 25.60€ ⚹⚹ ⇐ 🅴 🔌 (10A) – Extra per person 5.65€

Rental rates : (2015 price) (from beginning April to end Sept.) – 6 🚐 – 1 🏡 – 2 tent lodges. Per night from 58 to 83€ – Per week from 245 to 587€

🚐 local sani-station 4€ – 🔋🔌11€

Surroundings : 🌿 ⊡ 🎴
Leisure activities : 🍷 🏊 ⚔ 🖼 (open air in season)
Facilities : ₺ ⊶ 🎆 ⚶ launderette 🚿
Nearby : ⚔ 🏖 (beach) 🚣

G P S
Longitude : -2.34736
Latitude : 47.69587

LE ROC-ST-ANDRE

56460 – Michelin map **308** Q7 – pop. 941 – alt. 45
▶ Paris 426 – Nantes 121 – Rennes 75 – Vannes 41

⛰ Domaine du Roc

✆ 02 97 74 91 07. www.domaine-du-roc.com

Address : rue Beau Rivage

Opening times : from beginning April to end Oct.

2 ha (55 pitches) terrace, flat, grassy

Tariff : 19€ ⚹⚹ ⇐ 🅴 🔌 (10A) – Extra per person 4€
Rental rates : (from beginning April to end Oct.) – 9 🚐 – 6 🏡 – 2 cabins in the trees. Per night from 50 to 120€ – Per week from 260 to 640€

🚐 local sani-station – 🔋 14.25€

Surroundings : 🌿 ⪕ 🎴
Leisure activities : 🍷 🏊 ⚔ 🚴 🖼 (open air in season) 🚣 pedalos, forest trail ✈
Facilities : ₺ ⊶ ⚶
Nearby : ⚔

G P S
Longitude : -2.44606
Latitude : 47.86369

ROHAN

56580 – Michelin map **308** O6 – pop. 1 637 – alt. 55
▶ Paris 451 – Lorient 72 – Pontivy 17 – Quimperlé 86

⚠ Municipal le Val d'Oust

✆ 02 97 51 57 58. www.rohan.fr

Address : rue de St-Gouvry (take the northwestern exit)

Opening times : from beginning May to mid Sept.

1 ha (45 pitches) flat, grassy

Tariff : (2015 price) ⚹ 3.50€ ⇐ 1.50€ 🅴 2€ – 🔌 (16A) 3.40€

🚐 local sani-station

Surroundings : 🌿 🎴
Leisure activities : 🎡 🏊 ⚔ 🚣
Facilities : ₺ 🚿 ⚶ launderette
Nearby : 🍷 ⚔ 🏊 🏖 (beach) ⚓ sports trail

G P S
Longitude : -2.7504
Latitude : 48.07077

ROZ-SUR-COUESNON

35610 – Michelin map **309** M3 – pop. 1 034 – alt. 65
▶ Paris 365 – Rennes 82 – Caen 134 – St-Lô 99

⛰ Les Couesnons

✆ 02 99 80 26 86. www.lescouesnons.com

Address : l'Hopital (situated 2km southeast on the D 797)

Opening times : from beginning April to end Oct.

1 ha (50 pitches) flat, grassy

Tariff : (2015 price) 22€ ⚹⚹ ⇐ 🅴 🔌 (10A) – Extra per person 5.40€

Rental rates : (2015 price) (from beginning April to end Oct.) – 1 'gypsy' caravan – 8 ⌷⌷. Per night from 110 to 160€ – Per week from 310 to 770€

Choose the pitches furthest away from the road in preference.

Surroundings : ⌷ ♀♀
Leisure activities : ♥ ✕ ⌂
Facilities : ♿ ⊶ ⊞ ♨ ⌁ ⛲

GPS Longitude : -1.60904
     Latitude : 48.59597

ST-BRIAC-SUR-MER

35800 – Michelin map **309** J3 – pop. 1 955 – alt. 30
▶ Paris 411 – Dinan 24 – Dol-de-Bretagne 34 – Lamballe 41

⚠⚠⚠ Sea Green Émeraude

✆ 02 99 88 34 55. www.campingemeraude.com

Address : 7 chemin de la Souris

Opening times : from beginning April to beginning Nov.

3.2 ha (196 pitches)

Tariff : (2015 price) 40.50€ ♦♦ ⇔ ▣ ⚡ (6A) – Extra per person 8€ – Reservation fee 25€

Rental rates : (2015 price) (from beginning April to beginning Nov.) ♿ (1 mobile home) – 83 ⌷⌷ – 9 ⌂ – 10 canvas bungalows. Per week from 375 to 1,105€ – Reservation fee 25€

There's an attractive swimming area and restaurant, surrounded by palm trees.

Surroundings : ⚲ ⌷ ♀
Leisure activities : ♥ ✕ ⌂ ⚓ ⛵ ♂ ⚑ ⌁
entertainment room
Facilities : ♿ ⊶ ♨ ⌁ ⛲ launderette ⚒

GPS Longitude : -2.13012
     Latitude : 48.62735

There are several different types of sani-station ('borne' in French) – sanitation points providing fresh water and disposal points for grey water. See page 12 for further details.

ST-CAST-LE-GUILDO

22380 – Michelin map **309** I3 – pop. 3 500 – alt. 52
▶ Paris 427 – Avranches 91 – Dinan 32 – St-Brieuc 50

⚠⚠⚠⚠ Les Castels Le Château de Galinée ♠♠

✆ 02 96 41 10 56. www.chateaudegalinee.com

Address : rue de Galinée (7km to the south, access via the D 786, near the crossroads with the road to St-Cast-le-Guildo)

Opening times : from mid May to beginning Sept.

14 ha (273 pitches) flat, grassy

Tariff : ♦ 7.30€ ⇔ ▣ 21€ – ⚡ (10A) 6.20€ – Reservation fee 20€

Rental rates : (from mid April to beginning Sept.) ♿ ⚲ – 2 'gypsy' caravans – 46 ⌷⌷ – 4 ⌂ – 5 canvas bungalows. Per night from 45 to 165€ – Per week from 41 to 1,155€ – Reservation fee 20€

🚽 local sani-station

Surroundings : ⚲ ⌷ ♀♀
Leisure activities : ♥ ✕ ⌂ ⚓ ⛵ ⟆ ⚓ ⛵
✂ ⚑ ⌁ ⚞ ⚑ ⚲ zip wiring, multi-sports
ground, entertainment room
Facilities : ♿ ⊶ ⊞ ♨ – 4 private sanitary
facilities (⚞ ⚲ ⚾ wc) ⌁ ⛲ launderette
⚒ ⚒

GPS Longitude : -2.25725
     Latitude : 48.58403

⚠⚠ Le Châtelet ♠♠

✆ 02 96 41 96 33. www.lechatelet.com – limited spaces for one-night stay

Address : rue des Nouettes (located 1km west, 250m from the beach (direct access)

Opening times : from mid April to mid Sept.

9 ha/3.9 for camping (216 pitches) small lake

Tariff : (2015 price) ♦ 7.20€ ⇔ ▣ 22.50€ – ⚡ 5.20€ – Reservation fee 23€

Rental rates : (2015 price) (from mid April to mid Sept.) – 52 ⌷⌷ – 1 tipi – 6 tent lodges. Per week from 340 to 1,290€ – Reservation fee 23€

🚽 local sani-station

Surroundings : ⚲ ⟵ ⌷ ♀
Leisure activities : ♥ ✕ ⌂ ⚑ ♂ ⚓ ⛵ ⌁
(open air in season) ⚲
Facilities : ♿ ⊶ ⊞ ♨ ⌁ ⚒ ⛲ launderette
⚒ ⚒
Nearby : ⚲

GPS Longitude : -2.26959
     Latitude : 48.63773

⚠⚠ Les Blés d'Or

✆ 02 96 41 99 93. www.campinglesblesdor.fr

Address : rue Roger Roullier, at La Chapelle

Opening times : from beginning April to end Oct.

3.5 ha (161 pitches) open site, flat, grassy

Tariff : (2015 price) 22.90€ ♦♦ ⇔ ▣ ⚡ (10A) – Extra per person 4€

Rental rates : (2015 price) (from beginning April to end Oct.) ♿ – 11 ⌷⌷ – 8 ⌂. Per night from 45 to 65€ – Per week from 280 to 665€

🚽 AireService sani-station – 4 ▣ 10.50€

Surroundings : ⚲ ⌷ ♀♀
Leisure activities : ♥ ⌂ ⚓ ⛵ ⚑ spa centre
Facilities : ♿ ⊶ – 46 private sanitary facilities
(⚞ ⚲ ⚾ wc) ⛲ launderette
Nearby : ⚒ ⚒

GPS Longitude : -2.26181
     Latitude : 48.62746

ST-COULOMB

35350 – Michelin map **309** K2 – pop. 2 454 – alt. 35
▶ Paris 398 – Cancale 6 – Dinard 18 – Dol-de-Bretagne 21

⚠⚠ Le Tannée

✆ 02 99 89 41 20. www.campingdetannee.com – limited spaces for one-night stay

Address : at Tannée

Opening times : from beginning April to end Sept.

0.6 ha (30 pitches) flat and relatively flat

Tariff : (2015 price) 23.90€ ♦♦ ⇔ ▣ ⚡ (10A) – Extra per person 3€

Rental rates : (2015 price) (from beginning April to end Sept.) – 13 ⌷⌷. Per week from 235 to 670€ – Reservation fee 15€

Good-quality mobile home rentals with attractive terraces.

Surroundings : ⚲ ⌷
Leisure activities : hammam ♂ ⌁ (open air
in season)
Facilities : ♿ ⊶ ⚞ ⚞ ♨ ⛲ launderette

GPS Longitude : -1.889
     Latitude : 48.68655

Do not confuse:
⚠ to ⚠⚠⚠⚠ : MICHELIN classification with
★ to ★★★★★ : official classification

⚠ Duguesclin

📞 02 99 89 03 24. www.camping-duguesclin.com – limited spaces for one-night stay

Address : rue de Tannée (2.5km northeast along the D 355, follow the signs for Cancale and take turning to the left)

Opening times : from end March to beginning Nov.

0.9 ha (41 pitches)

Tariff : 21.90€ ♛♛ ⛺ 🔲 ⚡ (10A) – Extra per person 4.90€
Rental rates : (from end March to beginning Nov.) – 20 🚐 – 2 gîtes. Per week from 255 to 669€ – Reservation fee 15€

Only a few pitches for tents and caravans; a pretty vegetable garden is shared by campers.

Surroundings : 🏞 ⛱ 🌳	
Leisure activities : 🏛 ♨ hammam, jacuzzi 🚣 🚴	**G P S** Longitude : -1.89027 Latitude : 48.68628
Facilities : 🚿 ⊶ 🍽 🚽 💧 ♒ 🏢	

The Michelin classification (⚠⚠⚠ … ⚠) is totally independent of the official star classification system awarded by the local prefecture or other official organisation.

ST-GILDAS-DE-RHUYS

56730 – Michelin map **308** N9 – pop. 1 647 – alt. 10
▶ Paris 483 – Arzon 9 – Auray 48 – Sarzeau 7

⚠⚠⚠ Le Menhir ♣♣

📞 02 97 45 22 88. www.camping-bretagnesud.com

Address : route de Clos er Bé (3.5km north - recommended route via the D 780. follow the signs for Port-Navalo)

Opening times : from beginning May to mid Sept.

5 ha/3 for camping (176 pitches)

Tariff : ♛ 6.90€ ⛺ 🔲 16.80€ – ⚡ (6A) 4€ – Reservation fee 18.50€
Rental rates : (from mid April to mid Sept.) 🏕 – 49 🚐. Per night from 50 to 100€ – Per week from 200 to 980€ – Reservation fee 18.50€

Surroundings : 🏞 ⛱ 🌳🌳	
Leisure activities : 🍽 ✗ 🏛 🏃 🚣 🏕 🎣 🏊	**G P S** Longitude : -2.84781 Latitude : 47.52874
Facilities : 🚿 ⊶ 🍽 💧 launderette 🏊 🚣	

⚠⚠ Goh'Velin

📞 02 97 45 21 67. www.camping-gohvelin.fr

Address : 89 rue Guernevé (located 1.5km to the north, 300m from the beach)

Opening times : from beginning April to end Sept.

1 ha (88 pitches) flat, grassy

Tariff : 27.50€ ♛♛ ⛺ 🔲 ⚡ (16A) – Extra per person 5.50€ – Reservation fee 10€
Rental rates : (from beginning April to end Sept.) 🏕 – 18 🚐. Per night from 50 to 80€ – Per week from 260 to 780€ – Reservation fee 10€

Surroundings : 🏞 ⛱ 🌳🌳	
Leisure activities : ✗ 🏛 🚣 🏊	**G P S** Longitude : -2.84225 Latitude : 47.51144
Facilities : 🚿 ⊶ 🍽 💧 launderette	
Nearby : 💧	

ST-JEAN-DU-DOIGT

29630 – Michelin map **308** I2 – pop. 623 – alt. 15
▶ Paris 544 – Brest 77 – Guingamp 61 – Lannion 33

⚠ Municipal du Pont Ar Gler

📞 02 98 67 32 15. http://campingstj.jimdo.com/ – 🏪

Address : at Pont ar Gler (in the town)

Opening times : from mid June to end Aug.

1 ha (33 pitches) terraced, flat, grassy

Tariff : (2015 price) ♛ 3.40€ ⛺ 1.80€ 🔲 3.20€ – ⚡ (12A) 2.95€

A municipal site that is very green and natural, on the edge of a charming traditional village.

Surroundings : 🏞 ⛱ 🌳	
Leisure activities : 🏛 🚣	**G P S** Longitude : -3.77487 Latitude : 48.69405
Facilities : 🚿 🍽 ♒ 🏢	
Nearby : 🏊 🍷 ✗	

In order for the guide to remain wholly objective, the selection of campsites is made on an entirely independent basis.

ST-JOUAN-DES-GUÉRETS

35430 – Michelin map **309** K3 – pop. 2 699 – alt. 31
▶ Paris 396 – Rennes 63 – St-Helier 10 – St-Brieuc 85

⚠⚠⚠ Yelloh! Village Le P'tit Bois ♣♣

📞 02 99 21 14 30. www.ptitbois.com

Address : at La Chalandouze (access via the N 137)

Opening times : from beginning April to mid Sept.

6 ha (275 pitches) flat, grassy

Tariff : 49€ ♛♛ ⛺ 🔲 ⚡ (10A) – Extra per person 9€
Rental rates : (from beginning April to mid Sept.) – 180 🚐. Per night from 39 to 235€ – Per week from 273 to 1,645€
🚉 local sani-station 7€

A pleasant rural site with an extensive water park.

Surroundings : ⛱ 🌳	
Leisure activities : 🍷 ✗ 🏛 🎮 🏃 hammam, jacuzzi 🚣 🚴 🚴 🎣 🎳 🏊 multi-sports ground, entertainment room	**G P S** Longitude : -1.9869 Latitude : 48.60966
Facilities : 🚿 ⊶ 🍽 💧 launderette 🏊 🚣	

ST-LUNAIRE

35800 – Michelin map **309** J3 – pop. 2 309 – alt. 20
▶ Paris 410 – Rennes 76 – St-Helier 16 – St-Brieuc 83

⚠⚠ La Touesse

📞 02 99 46 61 13. www.campinglatouesse.com

Address : 171 rue Ville Géhan (situated 2km east along the D 786, follow the signs for Dinard; 400m from the beach)

Opening times : from beginning April to end Sept.

2.5 ha (141 pitches) flat, grassy

Tariff : (2015 price) 30.90€ ♛♛ ⛺ 🔲 ⚡ (10A) – Extra per person 5.80€ – Reservation fee 16€
Rental rates : (2015 price) (from beginning April to end Sept.) – 70 🚐 – 3 studios – 6 apartments – 1 gîte. Per night from 82 to 104€ – Per week from 574 to 728€ – Reservation fee 16€

🚉 local sani-station 7€

A pleasantly green site with access via a small path to Fourberie beach (700m).

Surroundings : 🌳🌿
Leisure activities : 🍸 🍴 🛋 ♨ jacuzzi 🏄
🛶 🎣 ⛱
Facilities : 🚿 ⛽ ▥ 🧺 🛁 ☂ 🚽 🍴 launderette
🧺 🚿
Nearby : 🐎

G P S Longitude : -2.08425
Latitude : 48.63086

ST-MALO

35400 – Michelin map **309** J3 – pop. 47 045 – alt. 5
▶ Paris 404 – Alençon 180 – Avranches 68 – Dinan 32

⚐ Domaine de la Ville Huchet 🏕👥

☏ 02 99 81 11 83. www.lavillehuchet.com

Address : route de la Passagère, at Quelmer (5km south along the D 301, follow the signs for Dinard and take turning for La Grassinais to the left in front of the Mercedes showroom)

Opening times : from mid April to mid Sept.

6 ha (198 pitches) flat, grassy

Tariff : (2015 price) 27.50€ 🏕🏕 🚗 ▣ 🔌 (16A) –
Extra per person 7.20€ – Reservation fee 18€

Rental rates : (2015 price) (from mid April to mid Sept.) 🚿 (1 mobile home) – 85 🚐 – 6 🏠 – 3 apartments. Per week from 280 to 1,015€ – Reservation fee 18€

🚽 local sani-station

A pleasant site based at a small château, with a pretty leisure pool.

Surroundings : 🌳 🌳🌿
Leisure activities : 🍸 🍴 🛋 🏃 🏄 🚴 m
🛶 🎣 ⛱ multi-sports ground
Facilities : 🚿 ⛽ ▥ 🛁 🍴 launderette 🧺 🚿

G P S Longitude : -1.98704
Latitude : 48.61545

Key to rentals symbols:

12 🚐	Number of mobile homes
20 🏠	Number of chalets
6 🛏	Number of rooms to rent
Per night 30–50€	Minimum/maximum rate per night
Per week 300–1,000€	Minimum/maximum rate per week

ST-MARCAN

35120 – Michelin map **309** M3 – pop. 455 – alt. 60
▶ Paris 370 – Dinan 42 – Dol-de-Bretagne 14 – Le Mont-St-Michel 17

⚐ Le Balcon de la Baie

☏ 02 99 80 22 95. www.lebalcondelabaie.com

Address : at Le Verger (500m southeast along the D 89, follow the signs for Pleine-Fougères and turn left after the cemetery)

Opening times : from beginning April to end Oct.

4 ha (80 pitches) flat, grassy

Tariff : 22.40€ 🏕🏕 🚗 ▣ 🔌 (6A) – Extra per person 5.40€
Rental rates : (from beginning April to end Oct.) – 12 🚐.
Per night from 55 to 105€ – Per week from 264 to 710€

Surroundings : 🏞 ⩽ Baie du Mont-St-Michel
🌿
Leisure activities : 🛋 🏄 🛶
Facilities : 🚿 ⛽ 🛁 🍴 launderette

G P S Longitude : -1.62929
Latitude : 48.58942

ST-PÈRE

35430 – Michelin map **309** K3 – pop. 2 289 – alt. 50
▶ Paris 392 – Cancale 14 – Dinard 15 – Dol-de-Bretagne 16

⚐ Bel Évent

☏ 02 99 58 83 79. www.camping-bel-event.com

Address : at Bellevent (located 1.5km southeast along the D 74, follow the signs for Châteauneuf and take the road to the right)

Opening times : from beginning April to mid Sept.

2.5 ha (120 pitches) flat, grassy

Tariff : (2015 price) 🏕 3.70€ 🚗 ▣ 9.30€ – 🔌 (10A) 2.20€

Rental rates : (2015 price) (from beginning April to mid Sept.) –
17 🚐 – 1 🏠. Per night from 65 to 140€ – Per week from 240 to 750€

Well-marked pitches and plenty of owner-occupier caravans.

Surroundings : 🌳 🌿
Leisure activities : 🍸 🛋 🏄 🏃 🛶 🎣
multi-sports ground
Facilities : 🚿 ⛽ 🛁 🍴 launderette

G P S Longitude : -1.91838
Latitude : 48.57347

ST-PHILIBERT

56470 – Michelin map **308** N9 – pop. 1 520 – alt. 15
▶ Paris 486 – Auray 11 – Locmariaquer 7 – Quiberon 27

⚐ Les Palmiers

☏ 02 97 55 01 17. www.campinglespalmiers.com

Address : at Kernivilit (situated 2km west, 500m from the river at Crach (sea)

Opening times : from beginning April to mid Oct.

3 ha (114 pitches) relatively flat, flat, grassy

Tariff : 26.40€ 🏕🏕 🚗 ▣ 🔌 (6A) – Extra per person 6.20€ –
Reservation fee 19.90€

Rental rates : (from beginning April to mid Oct.) – 44 🚐.
Per night from 60 to 85€ – Per week from 270 to 770€ –
Reservation fee 19.90€

🚽 10 ▣ 22.30€

Based around an old renovated farmhouse.

Surroundings : 🌿
Leisure activities : 🍸 🍴 🛋 🏄 🚴 🛶
entertainment room
Facilities : 🚿 ⛽ 🅒🅒 🛁 🍴 launderette
Nearby : 🍽

G P S Longitude : -3.01504
Latitude : 47.58831

⚐ L'Évasion

L'Évasion

☏ 02 97 55 04 90. www.campinglevasion.com

Address : at Le Congre (located 1km to the north)

Opening times : from beginning April to end Oct.

1.7 ha (87 pitches) flat, relatively flat, grassy

Tariff : (2015 price) 🏕 5.50€ 🚗
▣ 9.20€ – 🔌 (10A) 4.20€ – Reservation fee 20€

Rental rates : (2015 price) (from beginning April to end Oct.) –
33 🚐 – 2 canvas bungalows – 2 tent lodges. Per night from 35 to 75€ – Per week from 150 to 705€ – Reservation fee 20€

Surroundings : 🌳 🌳🌿
Leisure activities : 🛋 🏄 🛶
Facilities : 🚿 ⛽ 🛁 🍴 launderette

G P S Longitude : -2.99778
Latitude : 47.59591

ST-POL-DE-LÉON

29250 – Michelin map **308** H2 – pop. 7 043 – alt. 60
▶ Paris 557 – Brest 62 – Brignogan-Plages 31 – Morlaix 21

Ar Kleguer

📞 02 98 69 18 81. www.camping-ar-kleguer.com

Address : plage Ste-Anne (east of the town)

Opening times : from beginning April to end Sept.

5 ha (182 pitches)

Tariff : (2015 price) 30.45€ ★★ ⇔ 🗉 🚻 (10A) –
Extra per person 6.60€ – Reservation fee 18€
Rental rates : (2015 price) (from beginning April to end Sept.) –
45 🚐 – 4 🏠 – 3 gîtes. Per night from 50 to 125€ – Per week
from 330 to 855€ – Reservation fee 18€
🚐 Eurorelais sani-station

*A pleasant landscaped site near the sea, among rocks and
pines, with an educational farm for children.*

Surroundings : 🏖 ⇐ 🛖 🌳 ⛰
Leisure activities : 🍴 🎰 🎮 🎯 🚣 🎾 🖥
🛶 ⛵ farm or petting farm, multi-sports
ground
Facilities : 🚻 ⚡ 🛠 🖰 🚾 launderette
Longitude : -3.9677
Latitude : 48.6907

Le Trologot

📞 02 98 69 06 26. www.camping-trologot.com

Address : at Grève du Man (To the east, follow the signs for Îlot St-
Anne; near the beach)

Opening times : from beginning May to end Sept.

2 ha (100 pitches) flat, grassy

Tariff : 23.80€ ★★ ⇔ 🗉 🚻 (10A) – Extra per person 5.15€ –
Reservation fee 10€
Rental rates : (from mid April to end Sept.) – 15 🚐. Per week
from 280 to 700€ – Reservation fee 15€
🚐 Eurorelais sani-station

Near the sea and a pebble's throw from the large beach.

Surroundings : 🛖 🌳
Leisure activities : 🍴 🚣 🛶
Facilities : 🚻 ⚡ 🚾 🖰 launderette
Longitude : -3.9698
Latitude : 48.6935

*To make the best possible use of this guide, please read
pages 2–15 carefully.*

ST-RENAN

29290 – Michelin map **308** D4 – pop. 7 468 – alt. 50
▶ Paris 605 – Brest 14 – Brignogan-Plages 43 – Ploudalmézeau 14

Municipal de Lokournan

📞 02 98 84 37 67. www.saint-renan.fr

Address : route de l'Aber (take northwestern exit along the D 27 and
take the road to the right; near the stadium)

Opening times : from beginning June to mid Sept.

0.8 ha (70 pitches) flat, grassy, sandy

Tariff : (2015 price) ★ 3.40€ ⇔ 🗉 3.40€ – 🚻 (12A) 3.60€
🚐 local sani-station 2€ – 20 🗉 10.40€

In a well-shaded, natural setting near a small lake.

Surroundings : 🏖 🛖 🌳
Leisure activities : 🎰
Facilities : 🚻 ⚡ 🗑 🖰
Nearby : 🍴
Longitude : -4.62929
Latitude : 48.43991

ST-SAMSON-SUR-RANCE

22100 – Michelin map **309** J4 – pop. 1 514 – alt. 64
▶ Paris 401 – Rennes 57 – St-Brieuc 64 – St-Helier 34

Municipal Beauséjour

📞 02 96 39 53 27. www.beausejour-camping.com

Address : at La Hisse (3km east, along the D 57 and take the D 12 to
the right, 200m from the port - access via steep slope)

3 ha (112 pitches) flat, grassy
Rentals : 7 🚐 – 12 🏠 – 2 gîtes.

*Large pitches near a former stone farmhouse converted into
gites.*

Surroundings : 🏖
Leisure activities : 🎰 🚣
Facilities : 🚻 ⚡ 🖰 launderette
Nearby : 🍴 🔭 🐟
Longitude : -2.00889
Latitude : 48.48889

*Routes nationales are main roads and their identifying
numbers begin with N or RN. Routes départementales are
generally quieter roads and begin with D or DN.*

ST-YVI

29140 – Michelin map **308** H7 – pop. 2 755 – alt. 105
▶ Paris 563 – Rennes 212 – Quimper 17 – Vannes 119

Tohapi Le Bois de Pleuven

📞 08 25 00 20 30. www.tohapi.fr

Address : at Kerancolven

Opening times : from mid April to mid Sept.

17 ha/10 for camping (260 pitches) flat, grassy

Tariff : (2015 price) 16€ ★★ ⇔ 🗉 🚻 (10A) – Extra per person 5€
Rental rates : (2015 price) (from mid April to mid Sept.) – 147 🚐 –
17 tent lodges. Per night from 16 to 48€
🚐 local sani-station 3€

A natural, unspoilt setting among trees and bushes.

Surroundings : 🏖 🛖 🌲
Leisure activities : 🍴 🍽 🎰 🎮 🎯 🚴 🎾 🔭
🖥 🛶 🚣
Facilities : 🚻 ⚡ 🚾 🖰 launderette 🚐
Longitude : -3.97056
Latitude : 47.95028

STE-ANNE-D'AURAY

56400 – Michelin map **308** N8 – pop. 2 347 – alt. 42
▶ Paris 475 – Auray 7 – Hennebont 33 – Locminé 27

Municipal du Motten

📞 02 97 57 60 27. http://campingdumotten.wix.com/
campingsteannedauray

Address : allée des Pins (located 1km southwest along the D 17,
follow the signs for Auray and take r. du Parc to the right)

Opening times : from mid June to mid Sept.

1.5 ha (115 pitches) flat, grassy

Tariff : (2015 price) ★ 3.30€ ⇔ 2.30€ 🗉 2.90€ – 🚻 (10A) 3.60€

Surroundings : 🌳
Leisure activities : 🎰 🚣
Facilities : 🚻 ⚡ 🗑 🖰 🚾
Longitude : -2.96251
Latitude : 47.69831

SARZEAU

56370 – Michelin map **308** O9 – pop. 7 659 – alt. 30
▶ Paris 478 – Nantes 111 – Redon 62 – Vannes 23

⚞ Les Castels Manoir de Ker An Poul 👥

📞 02 97 67 33 30. www.manoirdekeranpoul.com – limited spaces for one-night stay

Address : 1 route de La Grée, Penvins

Opening times : from end March to end Sept.

5 ha (320 pitches) flat, grassy

Tariff : 35 € ✚✚ ⟺ ▣ ⚡ (10A) – Extra per person 7 € – Reservation fee 5 €

Rental rates : (from end March to end Sept.) – 2 'gypsy' caravans – 104 🚐 – 5 canvas bungalows. Per night from 29 to 127 € – Per week from 200 to 889 € – Reservation fee 15 €

Surroundings : ⌂ 🔱
Leisure activities : ⚐ ✗ 🏛 ⚅ 🏃 ⛷ 🚴
🏊 🛝 ⛷ multi-sports ground
Facilities : & ⚷ ⛺ 🍴 launderette 🏊 🛒 refrigerators
G P S Longitude : -2.68278 Latitude : 47.505

⚞ FranceLoc An Trest 👥

📞 02 97 41 79 60. www.franceloc.fr

Address : 1 chemin du Treste (2.5km to the south, follow the signs for Le Roaligen)

Opening times : from mid April to mid Sept.

5 ha (269 pitches) terraced, relatively flat, flat, grassy

Tariff : (2015 price) 33 € ✚✚ ⟺ ▣ ⚡ (16A) – Extra per person 7 €

Rental rates : (2015 price) (from mid April to mid Sept.) & (1 mobile home) – 186 🚐. Per night from 40 to 120 € – Per week from 150 to 1,100 €

A partially covered water park, with some impressive chutes.

Surroundings : 🏞 🔱
Leisure activities : ⚐ ✗ 🏛 ⚅ 🏃 ⛷ 🚴
🏊 🛝 ⛷
Facilities : & ⚷ ⛺ 🍴 launderette
G P S Longitude : -2.77208 Latitude : 47.50612

⚞ Lodge Club Presqu'Île de Rhuys 👥

📞 02 97 41 29 93. www.lodgeclub.fr

Address : at Le Bas Bohat (2.8km west)

15 ha/10 for camping (316 pitches) flat, grassy, adjacent forest
Rentals : 18 🚐 – 26 tent lodges.
🚐 local sani-station

Surroundings : 🏞 ⌂ 🔱
Leisure activities : ⚐ ✗ 🏛 🏃 ⛷ 🚴 🖾
🛝 ⛷ multi-sports ground
Facilities : & ⚷ ⛺ 🛒 ⚱ 🍴 launderette 🛒
Nearby : 🐎
G P S Longitude : -2.79722 Latitude : 47.5225

⚞ Ferme de Lann Hoedic

📞 02 97 48 01 73. www.camping-lannhoedic.fr

Address : rue Jean de La Fontaine

Opening times : from beginning April to end Oct.

3.6 ha (128 pitches) flat, relatively flat, grassy

Tariff : 23.40 € ✚✚ ⟺ ▣ ⚡ (10A) – Extra per person 5.20 € – Reservation fee 10 €

Rental rates : (from beginning April to end Oct.) 🚤 – 15 🚐. Per night from 70 to 100 € – Per week from 220 to 700 € – Reservation fee 14 €

🚐 local sani-station 11 € – 🛥 11 €

Surroundings : 🏞 🔱
Leisure activities : ⚐ 🕸 🏃 🚴 farm or petting farm
Facilities : & ⚷ ⚱ 🛒 🍴 launderette
G P S Longitude : -2.76139 Latitude : 47.50722

⚞ La Grée Penvins

📞 02 97 67 33 96. www.campinglagreepenvins.com – 🇫🇷

Address : 8 route de la Chapelle (9km southeast along the D 198)

Opening times : from beginning April to beginning Oct.

2.5 ha (111 pitches)

Tariff : 17.35 € ✚✚ ⟺ ▣ ⚡ (6A) – Extra per person 4 €

Rental rates : (from beginning April to beginning Oct.) 🚤 – 12 🚐. Per night from 83 to 119 € – Per week from 174 to 610 € – Reservation fee 12 €

Direct access to the beach at La Pointe de Penvins.

Surroundings : 🏞 🔱 ⛰
Facilities : & ⚷ 🛒 ⚱ launderette
Nearby : ⚐ ✗ ⚲
G P S Longitude : -2.68242 Latitude : 47.49665

SCAËR

29390 – Michelin map **308** I6 – pop. 5 244 – alt. 190
▶ Paris 544 – Carhaix-Plouguer 38 – Concarneau 29 – Quimper 35

⚞ Municipal de Kérisole

📞 02 98 57 60 91. www.ville-scaer.fr

Address : rue Louis Pasteur (take the eastern exit following signs for Le Faouët)

4 ha/2.3 for camping (83 pitches)
Rentals : 3 🚐.
🚐 sani-station

In a tranquil and pleasant setting among trees, near the new town library.

Surroundings : 🏞 ⚲
Leisure activities : 🏃
Facilities : & launderette
Nearby : 🚤 🛝 fitness trail
G P S Longitude : -3.69756 Latitude : 48.0278

SÉRENT

56460 – Michelin map **308** P8 – pop. 2 985 – alt. 80
▶ Paris 432 – Josselin 17 – Locminé 31 – Ploërmel 19

⚞ Municipal du Pont Salmon

📞 02 97 75 91 98. www.serent.fr

Address : 15 rue du Général de Gaulle (in the town, follow the signs for Ploërmel)

Opening times : from beginning April to mid Oct.

1 ha (30 pitches) flat, grassy

Tariff : (2015 price) 14.30 € ✚✚ ⟺ ▣ ⚡ (10A) – Extra per person 2.70 €

Rental rates : (2015 price) permanent & (1 chalet) – 4 🏠. Per night from 50 € – Per week from 255 to 450 €

🚐 AireService sani-station

Surroundings : ⌂ 🔱
Facilities : ⚷ 🛒 🏛 launderette
Nearby : 🚤 🛝 ⛷
G P S Longitude : -2.50191 Latitude : 47.82506

SIZUN

29450 – Michelin map **308** G4 – pop. 2 221 – alt. 112
▶ Paris 572 – Brest 37 – Carhaix-Plouguer 44 – Châteaulin 36

⚠ Municipal du Gollen

℘ 02 98 24 11 43. www.mairie-sizun.fr – ⚡

Address : at Le Gollen (located 1km south along the D 30, follow the signs for St-Cadou and take the turning to the left; beside the Elorn river)

Opening times : from beginning April to end Sept.

0.6 ha (29 pitches)

Tariff : (2015 price) ⚹ 3€ ⇦ 2€ ▣ 2.50€ – ⚡ (10A) 2.50€
🚽 Eurorelais sani-station 2€
Located on a large field near the Elorn river.

Surroundings : ⚲ ⚲		
Leisure activities : ⚲	**G**	Longitude : -4.07659
Facilities : ⚲ ⚲ ⚲ ⚲	**P**	Latitude : 48.4
Nearby : ⚲ ⚲	**S**	

Some campsites benefit from proximity to a municipal leisure centre.

SULNIAC

56250 – Michelin map **308** P8 – pop. 3 133 – alt. 125
▶ Paris 457 – Rennes 106 – Vannes 21 – Nantes 112

⚲ Village Vacances La Lande du Moulin
(rental of chalets, gîtes and mobile homes only)

℘ 02 97 53 29 39. www.la-lande-du-moulin.com

Address : at le Nounène (located 1.5km east along the D 104 and follow the signs for Theix)

12 ha undulating, terraced
Rentals : ⚲ (3 chalets) – 5 ▦ – 50 ⌂ – 17 gîtes.
Option available for full or half-board accommodation.

Surroundings : ⚲ ⚲		
Leisure activities : ⚲ ✕ ⚲ ⚲ ⚲ ⚲ ⚲	**G**	Longitude : -2.57028
⚲ ✕ ▣ ⚲ ⚲ pedalos, forest trail ⚲	**P**	Latitude : 47.66694
Facilities : ⚲ ▦ ⚲ launderette ⚲	**S**	

TADEN

22100 – Michelin map **309** J4 – pop. 2 340 – alt. 46
▶ Paris 404 – Rennes 71 – St-Brieuc 64 – St-Helier 34

⚲ Municipal de la Hallerais

℘ 02 96 39 15 93. http://www.camping-lahallerais.com

Address : 4 rue de la Robardais (to the southwest of the town)

Opening times : from mid March to mid Nov.

7 ha (225 pitches) terraced, relatively flat, flat, grassy, fine gravel

Tariff : (2015 price) 21.90€ ⚹⚹ ⇦ ▣ ⚡ (10A) –
Extra per person 4.57€
Rental rates : (2015 price) (from mid March to mid Nov.) ⚲ – 9 ▦ –
11 ⌂. Per night from 34 to 70€ – Per week from 177 to 476€
🚽 local sani-station – 7 ▣

Surroundings : ⚲ ⚲ ⚲ ⚲		
Leisure activities : ⚲ ✕ ⚲ ⚲ ⚲ ⚲ ⚲ ⚲		
multi-sports ground	**G**	Longitude : -2.0232
Facilities : ⚲ ⚲ ▦ ⚲ ⚲ ⚲ launderette ⚲	**P**	Latitude : 48.47181
⚲ ⚲	**S**	
Nearby : ⚲ ⚲ ⚲		

TAUPONT

56800 – Michelin map **308** Q7 – pop. 2 140 – alt. 81
▶ Paris 422 – Josselin 16 – Ploërmel 5 – Rohan 37

⚲ La Vallée du Ninian

℘ 02 97 93 53 01. www.camping-ninian.fr

Address : at Ville Bonne, le Rocher (take the northern exit along the D 8, follow the signs for la Trinité-Phoët, then continue 2.5km along the turning to the left, direct access to the river)

Opening times : from end March to end Sept.

2.7 ha (100 pitches) flat, grassy, fruit trees

Tariff : (2015 price) ⚹ 4.80€ ⇦ 2.60€ ▣ 6.90€ – ⚡ (10A) 4.80€ –
Reservation fee 10€
Rental rates : (2015 price) (from end March to end Sept.) – 12 ▦ –
2 canvas bungalows – 3 tent lodges. Per night from 40 to 90€ –
Per week from 180 to 680€ – Reservation fee 10€
🚽 Eurorelais sani-station – ⚲ ⚡14€
Evening events are organised, gathering around the bread oven or the apple press.

Surroundings : ⚲ ⚲ ⚲		
Leisure activities : ⚲ ⚲ ⚲ ⚲ ⚲	**G**	Longitude : -2.47
Facilities : ⚲ ⚲ ⚲ ⚲ ⚲ ⚲ launderette ⚲	**P**	Latitude : 47.96928
	S	

TELGRUC-SUR-MER

29560 – Michelin map **308** E5 – pop. 2 088 – alt. 90
▶ Paris 572 – Châteaulin 25 – Douarnenez 29 – Quimper 39

⚲ Armorique

℘ 02 98 27 77 33. www.campingarmorique.com

Address : 112 rue de la Plage (1.2km southwest following signs for Trez-Bellec-Plage)

Opening times : from beginning April to end Sept.

2.5 ha (98 pitches) terraced, relatively flat, flat, grassy

Tariff : (2015 price) 26.33€ ⚹⚹ ⇦ ▣ ⚡ (10A) –
Extra per person 5.50€
Rental rates : (2015 price) (from beginning April to end Sept.) –
30 ▦ – 4 ⌂. Per night from 58 to 88€ – Per week from
160 to 788€
🚽 Eurorelais sani-station
The site is on different levels, with attractive terraces.

Surroundings : ⚲ ⚲ ⚲ ⚲		
Leisure activities : ⚲ ✕ ⚲ ⚲ ⚲ ⚲	**G**	Longitude : -4.37085
Facilities : ⚲ ⚲ ⚲ ⚲ launderette ⚲	**P**	Latitude : 48.22531
	S	

To visit a town or region, use the MICHELIN Green Guides.

THEIX

56450 – Michelin map **308** P9 – pop. 6 765 – alt. 5
▶ Paris 464 – Ploërmel 51 – Redon 58 – La Roche-Bernard 33

⚲ Rhuys

℘ 02 97 54 14 77. http://www.campingderhuys.com

Address : rue Dugay Trouin, at Le Poteau Rouge (3.5km to the northwest, along the N 165; if coming from Vannes, take exit Sarzeau exit)

Opening times : from beginning April to end Oct.

2.7 ha (90 pitches) relatively flat, flat, grassy

Tariff : 25.15€ ⚹⚹ ⇦ ▣ ⚡ (10A) – Extra per person 5.65€ –
Reservation fee 15€

Rental rates : (2015 price) (from beginning April to end Oct.) – 21 🛖 – 2 tipis. Per night from 30 to 100€ – Per week from 200 to 700€ – Reservation fee 15€

🚐 15 ▣ 11€ – 🔋 11€

Surroundings : ♀	
Leisure activities : ⛵ 🚴 🎿 🏕 farm or petting farm	**G** Longitude : -2.69413
Facilities : ♿ ⊶ 🚿 🏖 🚰 ⛱ 🗄	**P** Latitude : 47.64108
Nearby : 🛒 ✕	**S**

TINTÉNIAC

35190 – Michelin map **309** K5 – pop. 3 304 – alt. 40
▶ Paris 377 – Avranches 70 – Dinan 28 – Dol-de-Bretagne 30

⛰ Domaine Les Peupliers

📞 02 99 45 49 75. www.domainelespeupliers.fr

Address : at the Domaine de la Besnelais (situated 2km southeast along the old road to Rennes; near lakes, along the N 137, take the exit for Tinténiac Sud)

Opening times : from beginning April to end Sept.

4 ha (93 pitches) flat, grassy

Tariff : (2015 price) 25.50€ ✶✶ ⇔ ▣ ⚡ (8A) – Extra per person 6€
Rental rates : (2015 price) (from mid March to end Oct.) – 4 🛖 – 2 🏠 – 2 tent lodges – 1 gîte. Per night from 25 to 70€ – Per week from 150 to 630€

🚐 Eurorelais sani-station – 5 ▣ 16€ – 🔋 ⚡ 16€

In a lovely setting and location near a natural lake.

Surroundings : ⊏ ♀	
Leisure activities : ⛵ 🏛 🚴 ✕ 🎿 🏕	**G** Longitude : -1.82167
Facilities : ♿ ⊶ 🏖 🚰 ⛱ launderette 🚗	**P** Latitude : 48.30917
	S

LE TOUR-DU-PARC

56370 – Michelin map **308** P9 – pop. 1 105
▶ Paris 476 – La Baule 62 – Redon 57 – St-Nazaire 81

⛰ Le Cadran Solaire

📞 02 97 67 30 40. www.campingcadransolaire.fr

Address : rue de Banastère (situated 2km south along the D 324, follow the signs for Sarzeau)

Opening times : from beginning April to end Sept.

2 ha (115 pitches) flat, grassy

Tariff : ✶ 4.60€ ⇔ ▣ 9.50€ – ⚡ (10A) 3.50€
Rental rates : (from beginning April to end Oct.) ✂ – 21 🛖. Per night from 40 to 60€ – Per week from 200 to 600€

🚐 20 ▣ 22.20€

Surroundings : ⛰ ⊏ ♀♀	
Leisure activities : 🏛 🚴 ✕	**G** Longitude : -2.65748
Facilities : ♿ ⊶ ⛏ 🚰 ⛱ launderette	**P** Latitude : 47.5208
	S

TRÉBEURDEN

22560 – Michelin map **309** A2 – pop. 3 714 – alt. 81
▶ Paris 525 – Lannion 10 – Perros-Guirec 14 – St-Brieuc 74

⛰ L'Espérance

📞 07 86 17 48 08. www.camping-esperance.com

Address : rue de Kéralégan (5km northwest along the D 788, follow the signs for Trégastel; near the sea)

Opening times : from beginning April to end Sept.

1 ha (56 pitches)

Tariff : ✶ 4.85€ ⇔ 3€ ▣ 5.10€ – ⚡ (10A) 3.75€ – Reservation fee 15€

Rental rates : (from beginning April to end Sept.) – 8 🛖. Per night from 58 to 80€ – Per week from 270 to 530€ – Reservation fee 20€

🚐 local sani-station

Surroundings : ≼ ⊏ ♀	
Leisure activities : ⛵	**G** Longitude : -3.55743
Facilities : ♿ ⊶ 🚜 ⛱ launderette	**P** Latitude : 48.79096
	S

TRÉBOUL

29100 – Michelin map **308** E6
▶ Paris 591 – Rennes 239 – Quimper 29 – Brest 75

⛰ Indigo Douarnenez le Bois d'Isis 👥

📞 02 98 74 05 67. www.camping-indigo.com

Address : avenue du Bois d'Isis

Opening times : from end April to end Sept.

3.2 ha (124 pitches) terraced, flat, grassy

Tariff : (2015 price) 27.10€ ✶✶ ⇔ ▣ ⚡ (13A) – Extra per person 4.90€ – Reservation fee 13€
Rental rates : (2015 price) (from end April to end Sept.) – 8 'gypsy' caravans – 42 tent lodges. Per night from 45 to 90€ – Per week from 221 to 630€ – Reservation fee 13€

🚐 local sani-station 7€

The pitches are in a natural wooded setting overlooking the Baie d'Douarnenez (bay).

Surroundings : ⛰ ≼ Douarnenez bay ♀♀	
Leisure activities : ⛵ 🏛 🏃 🚴 🎿	**G** Longitude : -4.3589
Facilities : ♿ ⊶ 🏖 🚰 ⛱ launderette	**P** Latitude : 48.10299
Nearby : 🏊 ✕ 🚗 🎣	**S**

⛰ Kerleyou

📞 02 98 74 13 03. www.camping-kerleyou.com

Address : 15 chemin de Kerleyou (located 1km to the west)

Opening times : from beginning April to end Sept.

3.5 ha (100 pitches)

Tariff : (2015 price) ✶ 5€ ⇔ 2€ ▣ 9€ – ⚡ (10A) 3.80€ – Reservation fee 12€
Rental rates : (2015 price) (from beginning April to end Sept.) ♿ (1 chalet) – 39 🛖 – 4 🏠. Per night from 40 to 107€ – Per week from 206 to 840€ – Reservation fee 15€

There are some lovely pitches for tents and caravans amid dolmens and menhirs.

Surroundings : ⛰ ⊏ ♀♀	
Leisure activities : ⛵ 🏛 🚴 🏐	**G** Longitude : -4.36198
Facilities : ♿ ⊶ ⛱ launderette 🚗	**P** Latitude : 48.09842
	S

Michelin classification:

⋀⋀⋀⋀	*Extremely comfortable, equipped to a very high standard*
⋀⋀⋀	*Very comfortable, equipped to a high standard*
⋀⋀	*Comfortable and well equipped*
⋀	*Reasonably comfortable*
△	*Satisfactory*

⛰ Trézulien

📞 02 98 74 12 30. www.camping-trezulien.com

Address : 14 route de Trézulien (via the r. Frédéric-Le-Guyader)

Opening times : from beginning April to end Sept.

5 ha (199 pitches) very uneven, terraced, relatively flat, flat, grassy

Tariff : (2015 price) ♦ 4.40€ ⇔ 2.80€ 🔲 5.50€ – ⚡ (10A) 3.80€

Rental rates : (2015 price) (from beginning April to mid Oct.) ⚿ (1 mobile home) – 14 ⛺ – 4 ⌂ – 1 tent lodge – 1 gîte. Per night from 40 to 82€ – Per week from 170 to 660€ – Reservation fee 13€

In a pleasant, partially wooded setting, with large pitches under poplar trees.

Surroundings : 🌳 ≤ ♀
Leisure activities : ♥ 🏠 🏄 ⛏ 🎣 ♨
Facilities : ⚿ ⚊ (season) ♛ launderette
Nearby : 🐎

Longitude : -4.34931
Latitude : 48.09311

TRÉDREZ

22300 – Michelin map **309** A2 – pop. 1 451 – alt. 78
▶ Paris 526 – Quimper 111 – Rennes 175 – Saint-Brieuc 79

⛰ Flower Les Capucines

📞 02 96 35 72 28. www.lescapucines.fr

Address : Route de la Voie Romaine, at Kervourdon (located 1.5km north following signs for Lannion and take road to the left)

Opening times : from end March to end Sept.

4 ha (106 pitches)

Tariff : 28.20€ ♦♦ ⇔ 🔲 ⚡ (10A) – Extra per person 5.80€ – Reservation fee 15€

Rental rates : (from end March to end Sept.) ⚿ (1 chalet) – 11 ⛺ – 5 ⌂ – 1 tent lodge. Per night from 55 to 174€ – Per week from 230 to 1,218€ – Reservation fee 15€

🚰 local sani-station 5€ – 🚐 ⚡15€

Surroundings : 🌳 ⊏ ♀♀
Leisure activities : ♥ ✗ 🏠 🏄 🎿 🖼 (open air in season), multi-sports ground
Facilities : ⚿ ⚊ 🛁 ♨ ♛ launderette 🚿

Longitude : -3.55694
Latitude : 48.69278

TREFFIAGAT

29730 – Michelin map **308** F8 – pop. 2 343 – alt. 20
▶ Paris 582 – Audierne 39 – Douarnenez 41 – Pont-l'Abbé 8

⛰ Les Ormes

📞 02 98 58 21 27. www.campingdesormesleguilvinec.fr

Address : at Kerlay (situated 2km to the south, follow the signs for Lesconil and take the turning to the right 400m from the beach (direct access)

Opening times : from beginning May to end Sept.

2 ha (76 pitches) flat, grassy

Tariff : (2015 price) ♦ 4.25€ ⇔ 2.55€ 🔲 4.25€ – ⚡ (6A) 3.60€ – Reservation fee 6.25€

Rental rates : (2015 price) (from beginning April to end Sept.) 🛖 – 2 ⌂. Per week from 315 to 465€

🚰 local sani-station – 4 🔲 15.30€

A small and attractive site in the countryside, not far from the sea.

Surroundings : 🌳 ⊏ ♀
Leisure activities : 🏄
Facilities : ⚊ 🛁 launderette
Nearby : ♨

Longitude : -4.25518
Latitude : 47.79666

TRÉGASTEL

22730 – Michelin map **309** B2 – pop. 2 435 – alt. 58
▶ Paris 526 – Lannion 11 – Perros-Guirec 9 – St-Brieuc 75

⛰ Tourony-Camping

📞 02 96 23 86 61. www.camping-tourony.com

Address : 105 rue de Poul Palud (1.8km east along the D 788. follow the signs for Perros-Guirec; 500m from the beach)

2 ha (100 pitches) flat, grassy

Rental rates : 17 ⛺ – 2 ⌂.

🚰 local sani-station – 10 🔲

Opposite the marina.

Surroundings : ♀
Leisure activities : ♥ ✗ 🏄
Facilities : ⚿ ⚊ 🛁 🚿 ♛ launderette
Nearby : 🛒

Longitude : -3.49131
Latitude : 48.82565

TRÉGUENNEC

29720 – Michelin map **308** F7 – pop. 348 – alt. 31
▶ Paris 582 – Audierne 27 – Douarnenez 27 – Pont-l'Abbé 11

⛰ Kerlaz

📞 02 98 87 76 79. www.kerlaz.com

Address : route de la mer (in the village, along the D 156)

Opening times : from beginning April to end Sept.

1.25 ha (65 pitches) flat, grassy

Tariff : 24.70€ ♦♦ ⇔ 🔲 ⚡ (10A) – Extra per person 4.40€ – Reservation fee 10€

Rental rates : (from beginning April to end Sept.) – 9 ⛺ – 5 ⌂ – 2 tent lodges. Per night from 53 to 95€ – Per week from 225 to 670€ – Reservation fee 10€

🚰 local sani-station

In a pleasant setting with little shade.

Surroundings : ♀
Leisure activities : ♥ 🏄 🚴 🖼 (open air in season)
Facilities : ⚿ ⚊ (July–Aug.) ♛ launderette
Nearby : 🏄 🐎

Longitude : -4.32848
Latitude : 47.89457

TRÉGUNC

29910 – Michelin map **308** H7 – pop. 6 785 – alt. 45
▶ Paris 543 – Concarneau 7 – Pont-Aven 9 – Quimper 29

⛰ La Pommeraie de l'Océan ♣♣

📞 02 98 50 02 73. www.campingdelapomeraie.com

Address : at Kerdalidec (6km south along the D 1. follow the signs for La Pointe de Trévignon (headland) and take the turning to the left following signs for St-Philibert)

Opening times : from beginning April to mid Sept.

7 ha (198 pitches) flat, grassy

Tariff : (2015 price) 41€ ♦♦ ⇔ 🔲 ⚡ (10A) – Reservation fee 16€

Rental rates : (2015 price) (from beginning April to mid Sept.) – 34 ⛺ – 5 tent lodges. Per week from 230€ to 1,310€ – Reservation fee 16€

A tranquil family site beside the sea, with a good aquatic and spa area.

Surroundings : ⊏ ♀
Leisure activities : ♥ ✗ 🏠 ⚃ 🏄 ⛸ jacuzzi 🏄 🚴 🖼 🎿 ♨ multi-sports ground, entertainment room
Facilities : ⚿ ⚊ 🛁 🚿 ♛ launderette 🚿

Longitude : -3.83698
Latitude : 47.80786

TRÉLÉVERN

22660 – Michelin map **309** B2 – pop. 1 390 – alt. 76
▶ Paris 524 – Lannion 13 – Perros-Guirec 9 – St-Brieuc 73

⚲ RCN Port-l'Épine

✆ 02 96 23 71 94. www.rcn.fr

Address : 10 Venelle de Pors Garo (1.5km northwest then take a road to the left; at Port-l'Épine)

3 ha (160 pitches) relatively flat, flat, grassy
Rental rates : 45 🚐.

Leafy site on the Port l'Epine peninsula, almost entirely surrounded by the sea.

	G P S	
Surroundings : ⚲ ⟨ Baie de Perros-Guirec ⌂ ♀ ⚘ Leisure activities : ♟ ✕ 🛶 🏊 Facilities : ♿ ⛽ 🚿 🚮 🚰 launderette 🧺		Longitude : -3.38594 Latitude : 48.8128

*We value your opinion and welcome your feedback.
Do email us at campingfrance@tp.michelin.com*

LA TRINITÉ-SUR-MER

56470 – Michelin map **308** M9 – pop. 1 622 – alt. 20
▶ Paris 488 – Auray 13 – Carnac 4 – Lorient 52

⚲ Kervilor

✆ 02 97 55 76 75. www.camping-kervilor.com

Address : route du Latz (1.6km to the north)

Opening times : from end March to mid Sept.

5 ha (250 pitches)
Tariff : (2015 price) ♟ 6.15€ 🚗 4.25€ ▣ 16€ – (⚡) (10A) 5.10€ – Reservation fee 18€
Rental rates : (2015 price) (from end March to mid Sept.) – 68 🚐. Per night from 108 to 223€ – Per week from 280 to 986€ – Reservation fee 18€

Leafy and peaceful site with a covered pool.

	G P S	
Surroundings : ⚲ ⌂ ♀♀ Leisure activities : ♟ 🛖 🏊 jacuzzi 🛶 🚲 ✕ 🏸 🏊 ⛵ multi-sports ground Facilities : ♿ ⛽ 🚿 🚰 launderette 🧺 🚲 refrigerators		Longitude : -3.03588 Latitude : 47.60168

⚲ APV Plijadur ♨♟

✆ 02 51 56 08 78. www.camping-apv.com

Address : 94 route de Carnac (1.3km northwest on the D 781)

Opening times : from beginning April to end Sept.

5 ha (218 pitches)
Tariff : (2015 price) 23.60€ ♟♟ 🚗 ▣ (⚡) (6A) – Extra per person 7.80€ – Reservation fee 28€
Rental rates : (2015 price) (from beginning April to end Sept.) – 127 🚐 – 2 apartments. Per night from 46 to 73€ – Per week from 294 to 973€ – Reservation fee 28€

🚉 AireService sani-station 15.80€

Choose pitches away from the road in preference, near the lake. Ageing sanitary facilities.

	G P S	
Surroundings : ⌂ ♀♀ Leisure activities : ♟ 🏊 🛖 🏊 🧖 jacuzzi 🛶 🚲 🏸 ⛵ 🎣 multi-sports ground Facilities : ♿ ⛽ 🚿 🚰 launderette 🧺 🚲		Longitude : -3.03667 Latitude : 47.58584

⚲ La Plage ♨♟

✆ 02 97 55 73 28. www.camping-plage.com

Address : plage de Kervillen (located 1km to the south, direct access to the beach)

Opening times : from beginning May to mid Sept.

3 ha (195 pitches)
Tariff : 45.90€ ♟♟ 🚗 ▣ (⚡) (6A) – Extra per person 6.20€ – Reservation fee 15€
Rental rates : (from beginning May to mid Sept.) – 40 🚐. Per night from 90 to 125€ – Per week from 255 to 940€ – Reservation fee 15€ 🚉 local sani-station 4.50€

	G P S	
Surroundings : ⚲ ⌂ ♀ ⚘ Leisure activities : 🛖 ☀ daytime 🧖 jacuzzi 🛶 🚲 🏊 🏊 Facilities : ♿ ⛽ 🚿 🚮 🚰 launderette Nearby : 🏊 ♟ ✕ 🏊 ✂ 🎣		Longitude : -3.02869 Latitude : 47.57562

⚲ La Baie ♨♟

✆ 02 97 55 73 42. www.camping-de-la-baie.net – limited spaces for one-night stay

Address : plage de Kervillen (located 1.5km to the south, 100m from the beach)

Opening times : from end April to mid Sept.

2.2 ha (170 pitches)
Tariff : (2015 price) ♟ 3.15€ 🚗 ▣ 12.90€ – (⚡) (10A) 3.70€ – Reservation fee 22€
Rental rates : (2015 price) (from end April to mid Sept.) – 42 🚐. Per night from 49 to 120€ – Per week from 256 to 994€ – Reservation fee 22€

	G P S	
Surroundings : ⚲ ⌂ ♀ Leisure activities : 🛖 ☀ daytime 🧖 🚲 🏊 ⛵ Facilities : ♿ ⛽ 🚿 🚮 🚰 launderette Nearby : 🏊 ♟ ✕ 🏊 ✂ 🎣		Longitude : -3.02789 Latitude : 47.57375

VANNES

56000 – Michelin map **308** O9 – pop. 52 683 – alt. 20
▶ Paris 459 – Quimper 122 – Rennes 110 – St-Brieuc 107

⚲ Flower Le Conleau ♨♟

✆ 02 97 63 13 88. www.vannes-camping.com

Address : at la Pointe de Conleau (to the south, towards the Parc du Golfe (leisure park), on the Avenue du Maréchal Juin)

Opening times : from beginning April to end Sept.

5 ha (250 pitches) terraced, relatively flat, flat, grassy, fine gravel
Tariff : (2015 price) 29€ ♟♟ 🚗 ▣ (⚡) (10A) – Extra per person 6€ – Reservation fee 15€
Rental rates : (2015 price) (from beginning April to end Sept.) ♿ – 70 🚐 – 8 🏠 – 3 canvas bungalows – 6 tent lodges. Per night from 44 to 120€ – Per week from 196 to 840€ – Reservation fee 20€

🚉 Eurorelais sani-station 5.50€ – 35 ▣ 12€

Pleasant location opposite the Golfe du Morbihan (gulf). A variety of good-quality rental options.

	G P S	
Surroundings : ⟨ ⌂ ♀♀ Leisure activities : ♟ ✕ 🛖 ☀ 🧖 🛶 🚲 ⛵ (open air in season) Facilities : ♿ ⛽ 🏛 🚰 launderette 🚲		Longitude : -2.77994 Latitude : 47.63326

BURGUNDY

H. Lenain / hemis.fr

A visit to Burgundy takes you back in time to an era when the influence of the mighty Burgundian dukes rivalled that of the kings of France. Stately castles and imposing abbeys still bear witness to a past golden age of ostentation and power. It is hard now to reproach the dukes too much for a flamboyance that has today made Dijon a world-renowned city of art, endowed with an exceptional architectural heritage. And who would dispute their claim to be the lords of the best wines in Christendom when wine lovers still flock to the region in search of the finest cellars and vintages? A dedication to time-honoured traditions remains at the heart of the cuisine of the region, from the pungent *Époisses* cheese to the delicious local gingerbread dripping with honey. After indulging yourself in such gourmet delights, what could be better than a delightful barge trip along the canals and rivers of the region to relax in peace amid the gloriously unspoilt countryside?

ANDRYES

89480 – Michelin map **319** D6 – pop. 471 – alt. 162
▶ Paris 204 – Auxerre 39 – Avallon 44 – Clamecy 10

⚲ Sites et Paysages Au Bois Joli

🕿 03 86 81 70 48. www.campingauboisjoli.fr

Address : 2 route de Villeprenoy (800m southwest)

Opening times : from beginning April to end Oct.

5 ha (100 pitches) sloping, flat, grassy

Tariff : 29.50€ ✭✭ ⇌ 🗉 🗐 (10A) – Extra per person 6€ – Reservation fee 9.50€

Rental rates : (from beginning April to mid Oct.) ⚡ – 6 🚐 – 1 tent lodge. Per night from 79 to 120€ – Per week from 325 to 750€ – Reservation fee 9.50€

🚰 Eurorelais sani-station 4.50€ – ⚓10€

A wooded campsite.

Surroundings : ⌂ ♀♀ Leisure activities : 🏛 ⚑ 🚲 ⚓ Facilities : ♿ ⌾ ⫿ ⚶ ⫥ 🍴 🗐 Nearby : ⚑ ✗	**GPS** Longitude : 3.47969 Latitude : 47.51655

ARNAY-LE-DUC

21230 – Michelin map **320** G7 – pop. 1 674 – alt. 375
▶ Paris 285 – Autun 28 – Beaune 36 – Chagny 38

⚲ Huttopia L'Étang de Fouché

🕿 03 80 90 02 23. www.huttopia.com

Address : rue du 8 mai 1945 (700m east along the D 17c, follow the signs for Longecourt)

Opening times : from mid April to mid Oct.

8 ha (209 pitches) flat, grassy

Tariff : (2015 price) 27€ ✭✭ ⇌ 🗉 🗐 (10A) – Extra per person 7€ – Reservation fee 13€

Rental rates : (2015 price) (from mid April to mid Oct.) – 26 🚐 – 19 🏠 – 6 canvas bungalows. Per night from 40 to 95€ – Per week from 168 to 805€

A pleasant location beside a lake.

Surroundings : ⌂ ⇐ ♀ ⛰ Leisure activities : 🍸 ✗ 🖼 ☺daytime ⛹ ⚑ 🚲 ⚓ pedalos Facilities : ♿ ⌾ ⫿ ⚶ ⫥ 🍴 launderette ⚶ ⚑ Nearby : ✗ ⚓ (beach) ⚓	**GPS** Longitude : 4.49802 Latitude : 47.13414

ASQUINS

89450 – Michelin map **319** F7 – pop. 324 – alt. 146
▶ Paris 219 – Dijon 123 – Auxerre 49 – Avallon 17

⚑ Municipal le Patis

🕿 03 86 33 30 80. www.asquins-sous-vezelay-camping-roulottes.com –

Address : route de Givry (500 m, after the bridge on the left)

Opening times : from end April to end Sept.

1 ha (33 pitches) flat, grassy

Tariff : 11.40€ ✭✭ ⇌ 🗉 🗐 (16A) – Extra per person 2€

Rental rates : permanent – 2 'gypsy' caravans. Per night from 75 to 95€ – Per week from 375 to 475€

Surroundings : ♀ Leisure activities : 🏛 ⚑ Facilities : ♿ ⫿ ⫿ ⫥ 🍴 🗐 Nearby : ⚓	**GPS** Longitude : 3.75899 Latitude : 47.48293

AUTUN

71400 – Michelin map **320** F8 – pop. 14 496 – alt. 326
▶ Paris 287 – Auxerre 128 – Avallon 78 – Chalon-sur-Saône 51

⚲ Aquadis Loisirs La Porte d'Arroux

🕿 03 85 52 10 82. http://www.aquadis-loisirs.com/camping-de-la-porte-d-arroux/

Address : rue du Traité d'Anvers, at Les Chaumottes (take the northern exit along the D 980, follow the signs for Saulieu, Arroux suburb; beside the Ternin river)

Opening times : from beginning March to beginning Nov.

2.8 ha (81 pitches) flat, grassy

Tariff : 19.80€ ✭✭ ⇌ 🗉 🗐 (10A) – Extra per person 3.80€ – Reservation fee 10€

Rental rates : (from beginning March to beginning Nov.) – 9 🚐. Per night from 65€ – Per week from 199 to 499€ – Reservation fee 20€

🚰 AireService sani-station – ⚓11€

Pretty, shady pitches beside the Ternin river.

Surroundings : ⌂ ♀♀ Leisure activities : 🍸 ✗ 🏛 ⚑ 🚲 ⚓ ⚑ Facilities : ♿ ⌾ ☒ 🗐 ⚑	**GPS** Longitude : 4.29358 Latitude : 46.96447

AUXERRE

89000 – Michelin map **319** E5 – pop. 36 702 – alt. 130
▶ Paris 166 – Bourges 144 – Chalon-sur-Saône 176 – Chaumont 143

⚲ Municipal

🕿 03 86 52 11 15. camping.mairie@auxerre.com

Address : 8 route de Vaux (to the southeast of the town, near the stadium, 150m from the Yonne river)

Opening times : from mid April to mid Sept.

4.5 ha (164 pitches) flat, grassy

Tariff : (2015 price) ✭ 4.37€ ⇌ 🗉 3.82€ – 🗐 (6A) 3.59€

🚰 local sani-station 3.36€

Surroundings : ♀ Leisure activities : 🏛 ⚑ 🚲 ⚓ Facilities : ♿ ⌾ ⫿ ⚶ launderette ⚑ Nearby : ✗ ⊠ ⚑ ⚓	**GPS** Longitude : 3.58703 Latitude : 47.7865

AVALLON

89200 – Michelin map **319** G7 – pop. 7 252 – alt. 250
▶ Paris 220 – Dijon 106 – Auxerre 55 – Autun 80

⚑ Municipal Sous Roches

🕿 03 86 34 10 39. www.campingsousroches.com

Address : route de Méluzien

Opening times : from beginning April to end Oct.

2.7 ha (98 pitches) terraced, flat, grassy

Tariff : (2015 price) 17€ ✭✭ ⇌ 🗉 🗐 (16A) – Extra per person 3.70€

Rental rates : (2015 price) (from beginning March to end Dec.) ♿ (1 chalet) ⚡ – 4 🏠 – 2 tent lodges. Per night from 45 to 90€ – Per week from 280 to 490€

🚰 local sani-station 5€

Surroundings : ⌂ Leisure activities : 🏛 ⚑ ⚓ Facilities : ♿ ⌾ ⫥ launderette ⚑	**GPS** Longitude : 3.91293 Latitude : 47.47993

BEAUNE

21200 – Michelin map **320** I7 – pop. 22 516 – alt. 220
▶ Paris 308 – Autun 49 – Auxerre 149 – Chalon-sur-Saône 29

⚠ Municipal les Cent Vignes

✆ 03 80 22 03 91. campinglescentvignes@mairie-beaune.fr

Address : 10 rue Auguste Dubois (take the northern exit along the r. du Faubourg-St-Nicolas and take D 18 to the left)

Opening times : from mid March to end Oct.

2 ha (116 pitches) flat, grassy

Tariff : (2015 price) 22.40€ ✶✶ ⇔ 🔲 ⚡ (16A) –
Extra per person 4.80€

Pitches attractively marked out and an entrance surrounded by flowers.

Surroundings : 🏕 ♀
Leisure activities : 🍹 ✕ 🎣 🏊 multi-sports ground
Facilities : 🚿 🔌 ⛲ 🗑 🍴 launderette 🧺

GPS Longitude : 4.8386
Latitude : 47.03285

This guide is updated regularly, so buy your new copy every year!

BOURBON-LANCY

71140 – Michelin map **320** C10 – pop. 5 275 – alt. 240 – ⚕
▶ Paris 308 – Autun 62 – Mâcon 110 – Montceau-les-Mines 55

⚠ Aquadis Loisirs Les Chalets du Breuil

✆ 03 85 89 20 98. http://www.aquadis-loisirs.com/camping-et-village-chalets-du-breuil/

Address : 11 rue des Eurimants (towards the southwestern exit, follow the signs for Digoin; by the swimming pool)

Opening times : from end March to end Oct.

2 ha (63 pitches) flat, grassy

Tariff : 18.60€ ✶✶ ⇔ 🔲 ⚡ (10A) – Extra per person 4.75€ – Reservation fee 10€

Rental rates : (from end March to end Oct.) 🚿 (1 chalet) – 4 🚐 –
22 🏠. Per night from 89€ – Per week from 277 to 599€ –
Reservation fee 20€

🚰 Flot Bleu sani-station 4€ – 🚐 11€

Camping around 200m from a small lake.

Surroundings : 🏕 ♀
Leisure activities : 🎣 🐎
Facilities : 🔌 ♿ 🗑 🚿 🍴 🧺
Nearby : 🍴 ✕ 🏊 🎿 🛶 (beach) 🎣 casino

GPS Longitude : 3.76646
Latitude : 46.62086

CHABLIS

89800 – Michelin map **319** F5 – pop. 2 383 – alt. 135
▶ Paris 181 – Dijon 138 – Orléans 172 – Troyes 76

⚠ Municipal du Serein

✆ 03 86 42 44 39. www.chablis.net

Address : quai Paul Louis Courier (600m west along the D 956, follow the signs for Tonnerre and take the road to the right after the bridge; beside the Serein river)

Opening times : from end May to mid Sept.

2 ha (43 pitches) flat, grassy

Tariff : (2015 price) ✶ 3€ ⇔ 🔲 6€ – ⚡ (6A) 2€

🚰 local sani-station

A green setting beside the Serein river.

Surroundings : 🏕 ♀
Leisure activities : 🏊
Facilities : 🚿 🔌 🗑 🍴
Nearby : 🚲

GPS Longitude : 3.80596
Latitude : 47.81368

CHAGNY

71150 – Michelin map **320** I8 – pop. 5 525 – alt. 215
▶ Paris 327 – Autun 44 – Beaune 15 – Chalon-sur-Saône 20

⚠ Le Pâquier Fané

✆ 03 85 87 21 42. www.campingchagny.com

Address : rue du Pâquier fané (to the west; beside the Dheune river)

Opening times : from beginning April to end Oct.

1.8 ha (85 pitches) flat, grassy

Tariff : 18.80€ ✶✶ ⇔ 🔲 ⚡ (16A) – Extra per person 3.20€

Rental rates : (from beginning April to end Oct.) – 6 🚐 –
4 🏠. Per night from 50 to 120€ – Per week from 350 to 840€ –
Reservation fee 15€

🚰 AireService sani-station – 16 🔲

Pleasant setting beside the Dheune.

Surroundings : 🏕 ♀
Leisure activities : 🏊
Facilities : 🚿 🔌 🍴 launderette 🧺
Nearby : 🚲 ✕ 🛶

GPS Longitude : 4.74574
Latitude : 46.91193

The guide covers all 22 regions of France – see the map and list of regions on pages 4–5.

CHAMBILLY

71110 – Michelin map **320** E12 – pop. 523 – alt. 249
▶ Paris 363 – Chauffailles 28 – Digoin 27 – Dompierre-sur-Besbre 55

⚠ La Motte aux Merles

✆ 03 85 25 37 67. campingpicard@yahoo.fr

Address : route de la Palisse (5km southwest along the D 990 and take road to the left)

Opening times : from beginning April to end Oct.

1 ha (25 pitches) flat, grassy

Tariff : ✶ 3.10€ ⇔ 🔲 4.20€ – ⚡ (8A) 2.40€

🚰 local sani-station – 3 🔲 4€

Surroundings : 🐾 ≼
Leisure activities : 🏊 🛶 (small swimming pool)
Facilities : 🚿 🔌 🗑 🍴 📺

GPS Longitude : 3.95755
Latitude : 46.26443

LA CHARITÉ-SUR-LOIRE

58400 – Michelin map **319** B8 – pop. 5 203 – alt. 170
▶ Paris 212 – Bourges 51 – Clamecy 54 – Cosne-sur-Loire 30

⚠ Municipal la Saulaie

✆ 03 86 70 00 83. www.lacharitesurloire-tourisme.com

Address : quai de La Saulaie (southwestern exit)

Opening times : from beginning April to end Sept.

1.7 ha (90 pitches) flat, grassy

Tariff : (2015 price) 17.60€ ✶✶ ⇔ 🔲 ⚡ (10A) –
Extra per person 4.20€

Rental rates : (2015 price) (from beginning April to end Sept.) ⅙ (1 'gypsy' caravan) ⚅ – 2 'gypsy' caravans – 1 canvas bungalow – 3 tent lodges. Per night from 20 to 89€ – Per week from 120 to 540€

Situated on the Île de la Saulaie (island), near the beach.

Surroundings : ♀
Leisure activities : 🏛 🐾
Facilities : ⅙ ⌇ 🚿 🚻 🍴
Nearby : ✕ 🎣

G P S Longitude : 3.00927
Latitude : 47.17879

CHAROLLES

71120 – Michelin map **320** F11 – pop. 2 807 – alt. 279
▶ Paris 374 – Autun 80 – Chalon-sur-Saône 67 – Mâcon 55

⚠ Municipal 👥

☎ 03 85 24 04 90. www.ville-charolles.fr

Address : route de Viry (take the northeastern exit, follow the signs for Mâcon and turn left onto the D 33)

Opening times : from beginning April to beginning Oct.

1 ha (50 pitches) flat, grassy

Tariff : (2015 price) 🧍 2.50€ ⇌ 2€ ▣ 4.20€ – ⚡ (6A) 2.50€
Rental rates : (2015 price) (from beginning March to mid Sept.) ⅙ (1 mobile home) ⚅ – 6 🚐. Per night from 55€ – Per week from 220 to 360€
🚐 Eurorelais sani-station 3€ – 10 ▣ 3€

A pleasant setting beside the Arconce river.

Surroundings : ⌇ ♀
Leisure activities : 🍴 🏃 🚣 🚲
Facilities : ⅙ ⌇ 🚿 🔥 🚻 🍴 ▣
Nearby : 🏛 🎣 🐾

G P S Longitude : 4.28209
Latitude : 46.43959

CHÂTEAU-CHINON

58120 – Michelin map **319** G9 – pop. 2 137 – alt. 510
▶ Paris 281 – Autun 39 – Avallon 60 – Clamecy 65

⚠ Municipal du Perthuy d'Oiseau

☎ 03 86 85 08 17. mairiechateauchinonville@wanadoo.fr

Address : rue du Perthuy d'Oiseau (take the southern exit along the D 27, follow the signs for Luzy and take a right turn)

1 ha (50 pitches) relatively flat to hilly, grassy

🚐 Flot Bleu sani-station
At the edge of a forest.

Surroundings : 🌳 ≤ ♀
Leisure activities : 🏛
Facilities : 🔥

G P S Longitude : 3.92613
Latitude : 47.05518

CHÂTILLON-SUR-SEINE

21400 – Michelin map **320** H2 – pop. 5 613 – alt. 219
▶ Paris 233 – Auxerre 85 – Avallon 75 – Chaumont 60

⚠ Municipal Louis-Rigoly

☎ 03 80 91 03 05. www.mairie-chatillon-sur-seine.fr

Address : esplanade St-Vorles (follow the signs for Langres)

Opening times : from beginning April to beginning Oct.

0.8 ha (46 pitches) flat and relatively flat, grassy, hard surface areas

Tariff : (2015 price) 🧍 4.20€ ⇌ 1.70€ ▣ 3.90€ – ⚡ (6A) 4.80€
Rental rates : (2015 price) (from beginning April to beginning Oct.) – 2 🚐. Per night from 48 to 63€ – Per week from 252 to 365€
🚐 local sani-station 4€

Situated on the shaded slopes of the town.

Surroundings : 🌳 ⌇ ♀
Leisure activities : 🏛
Facilities : ⅙ ⌇ 🚻 ▣
Nearby : 🍷 ✕ 🔥 🏊 🎣

G P S Longitude : 4.56969
Latitude : 47.87051

CHAUFFAILLES

71170 – Michelin map **320** G12 – pop. 3 939 – alt. 405
▶ Paris 404 – Charolles 32 – Lyon 77 – Mâcon 64

⛰ Municipal les Feuilles

☎ 03 85 26 48 12. www.chauffailles.com

Address : 18 rue de Châtillon (to the southwest along the r. du Chatillon)

4 ha (67 pitches) flat and relatively flat, grassy

Rentals : 2 🏠 – 14 canvas bungalows.

In a green setting beside the Botoret river.

Surroundings : ⌇ ♀
Leisure activities : 🏛 🚣 ✕ 🐾
Facilities : ⅙ ⌇ 🔥 🚻 ▣
Nearby : 🏊

G P S Longitude : 4.33817
Latitude : 46.20004

CLAMECY

58500 – Michelin map **319** E7 – pop. 4 238 – alt. 144
▶ Paris 208 – Auxerre 42 – Avallon 38 – Bourges 105

⚠ Le Pont Picot

☎ 03 86 27 05 97. clamecycamping@orange.fr

Address : rue de Chevroches (to the south; beside the Yonne and the Nivernais canal, recommended route via Beaugy)

Opening times : from beginning April to end Sept.

1 ha (90 pitches) flat, grassy

Tariff : (2015 price) 🧍 3€ ⇌ 3€ ▣ 7€ – ⚡ (6A) 9€
Rental rates : (2015 price) (from beginning April to end Sept.) – 7 🚐. Per night from 40 to 70€ – Per week from 250 to 400€
🚐 AireService sani-station 3€

A pleasant location on a small island.

Surroundings : 🌳 ≤ ♀
Leisure activities : 🐾
Facilities : ⅙ ⌇ 🚻 launderette

G P S Longitude : 3.52784
Latitude : 47.45203

CLUNY

71250 – Michelin map **320** H11 – pop. 4 624 – alt. 248
▶ Paris 384 – Chalon-sur-Saône 49 – Charolles 43 – Mâcon 25

⚠ Municipal St-Vital

☎ 03 85 59 08 34. www.cluny-camping.blogspot.com

Address : 30 rue des Griottons (take the eastern exit along the D 15, follow the signs for Azé)

Opening times : from mid April to mid Oct.

3 ha (174 pitches) flat, grassy

Tariff : (2015 price) 18.90€ 🧍🧍 ⇌ ▣ ⚡ (6A) – Extra per person 4.50€
Rental rates : (2015 price) (from mid April to mid Oct.) – 2 🏠. Per night from 65 to 96€ – Per week from 323 to 504€
🚐 AireService sani-station 5€

With a view of the old town of Cluny.

Surroundings : ≤ ♀
Leisure activities : 🚲
Facilities : ⅙ ⌇ 🏛 🚻 ▣
Nearby : ✕ 🎣 🏊 🐎

G P S Longitude : 4.66778
Latitude : 46.43088

CORMATIN

71460 – Michelin map **320** I10 – pop. 544 – alt. 212
▶ Paris 371 – Chalon-sur-Saône 37 – Mâcon 36 – Montceau-les-Mines 41

⚠ Le Hameau des Champs

☎ 03 85 50 76 71. www.le-hameau-des-champs.com

Address : take the northern exit along the D 981, follow the signs for Chalon-sur-Saône

Opening times : from beginning April to end Sept.

5.2 ha (50 pitches) flat, grassy

Tariff : (2015 price) ♣ 4€ ⇦ 🅴 6€ – 🗲 (13A) 3.50€
Rental rates : (2015 price) permanent ♿ (1) – 10 🏠. Per night from 65 to 88€ – Per week from 360 to 503€
🚻 local sani-station 3€
Situated 150m from a lake and the Givry-Cluny Voie Verte (cycle trail).

Surroundings : 🌿	
Leisure activities : 🍽 🏇 🚴	**G P S** Longitude : 4.68391
Facilities : ♿ ⚡ 🚿 🚽 🚰 🏢	Latitude : 46.54868
Nearby : 🏊 🍴 ✂ 🎣	

COUCHES

71490 – Michelin map **320** H8 – pop. 1 493 – alt. 320
▶ Paris 328 – Autun 26 – Beaune 31 – Le Creusot 16

⚠ La Gabrelle

☎ 03 85 45 59 49. www.lagabrelle.com

Address : 1.7km northwest along the D 978, follow the signs for Autun, near a small lake

1 ha (50 pitches) terraced, flat, grassy

🚻 local sani-station

Surroundings : 🏞	
Leisure activities : 🍽 🍴 🏠 🏇	**G P S** Longitude : 4.5588
Facilities : ♿ ⚡ 🚰	Latitude : 46.87586

We have selected the best campsites in France with our usual care, listing those with the best facilities in the most pleasant surroundings.

CRÊCHES-SUR-SAÔNE

71680 – Michelin map **320** I12 – pop. 2 838 – alt. 180
▶ Paris 398 – Bourg-en-Bresse 45 – Mâcon 9 – Villefranche-sur-Saône 30

⚠ Municipal Port d'Arciat

☎ 03 85 37 11 83. http://pagesperso-orange.fr/campingduportdarciat

Address : route du Port d'Arciat (located 1.5km east along the D 31, follow the signs for Pont de Veyle)

Opening times : from mid May to mid Sept.

5 ha (160 pitches) flat, grassy

Tariff : (2015 price) 16.65€ ♣♣ ⇦ 🅴 🗲 (6A) – Extra per person 4.35€
Beside the Saône river and near a small lake, direct access.

Surroundings : ♀	
Leisure activities : 🏇 🎣	**G P S** Longitude : 4.80581
Facilities : ♿ ⚡ 🚰 🏢	Latitude : 46.24037
Nearby : 🍷 🐎 🚤 🏊	

CRUX-LA-VILLE

58330 – Michelin map **319** E9 – pop. 410 – alt. 319
▶ Paris 248 – Autun 85 – Avallon 138 – La Charité-sur-Loire 45

⚠ Aquadis Loisirs Le Merle

☎ 03 86 58 38 42. http://www.aquadis-loisirs.com/camping-de-l-etang-du-merle/

Address : at Le Merle (4.5km southwest along the D 34, follow the signs for St-Saulge and turn right onto D 181, follow the signs for Ste-Marie; beside the lake)

Opening times : from end March to mid Oct.

2.6 ha (43 pitches) flat, grassy

Tariff : 17.30€ ♣♣ ⇦ 🅴 🗲 (10A) – Extra per person 3.80€ – Reservation fee 10€
Rental rates : (from end March to mid Oct.) – 11 🚐 – 5 🏠. Per night from 62 to 68€ – Per week from 189 to 599€ – Reservation fee 20€
🚻 local sani-station – 🚿 11€

Surroundings : 🌿 ♀♀ ⛰	
Leisure activities : 🍽 🏠 🏇 🎣 🛶	**G P S** Longitude : 3.52478
Facilities : ♿ ⚡ 🍽	Latitude : 47.1624
Nearby : pedalos	

The pitches of many campsites are marked out with low hedges of attractive bushes and shrubs.

DIGOIN

71160 – Michelin map **320** D11 – pop. 8 460 – alt. 232
▶ Paris 337 – Autun 69 – Charolles 26 – Moulins 57

⚠ La Chevrette

☎ 03 85 53 11 49. www.lachevrette.com

Address : rue de la Chevrette (take the western exit towards Moulins, towards the municipal swimming pool; near the Loire river)

Opening times : from beginning April to mid Oct.

1.6 ha (81 pitches) flat, grassy

Tariff : 19€ ♣♣ ⇦ 🅴 🗲 (10A) – Extra per person 4.90€
Rental rates : (from beginning April to mid Oct.) 🚿 – 2 🚐 – 2 🏠. Per night from 30 to 80€
🚻 local sani-station

Surroundings : 🏞 ♀	
Leisure activities : 🍴 🏠 🏊 (small swimming pool)	**G P S** Longitude : 3.96768
Facilities : ♿ ⚡ 🏢 🚿 🚽 🚰 launderette	Latitude : 46.47983
Nearby : 🚤 🚴 🎣	

DOMPIERRE-LES-ORMES

71520 – Michelin map **320** G11 – pop. 922 – alt. 480
▶ Paris 405 – Chauffailles 28 – Cluny 23 – Mâcon 35

⚠ Sites et Paysages Le Village des Meuniers

☎ 03 85 50 36 60. www.villagedesmeuniers.com

Address : 344 rue du Stade (take the northwestern exit along the D 41, follow the signs for La Clayette and take the road to the right, near the stadium)

Opening times : from beginning April to end Oct.

3 ha (113 pitches) terraced, flat, grassy

Tariff : 30€ ♣♣ ⇦ 🅴 🗲 (10A) – Extra per person 7€ – Reservation fee 15€

Rental rates : (from beginning April to end Oct.) ♿ (1) – 16 🚐 – 10 🏠 – 2 canvas bungalows – 2 tent lodges. Per night from 55 to 141€ – Per week from 275 to 987€ – Reservation fee 15€

🚾 local sani-station 5€ – 🚐14€

In an elevated, panoramic location.

Surroundings : 🌳 ⪉ 🏞
Leisure activities : 🍽 ✕ 🏞 🌙nighttime 🎠 🛝 🏇 ⛵
Facilities : ♿ ⚡ 🚿 🧺 🛁 🚰
Nearby : 🚴 ✂

GPS	Longitude : 4.47468
	Latitude : 46.36393

ÉPINAC

71360 – Michelin map **320** H8 – pop. 2 357 – alt. 340
▶ Paris 304 – Arnay-le-Duc 20 – Autun 19 – Chagny 29

⛺ Aquadis Loisirs Le Pont Vert

☎ 03 85 82 00 26. http://www.aquadis-loisirs.com/camping-du-pont-d-avignon/

Address : rue de la Piscine (take the southern exit along the D 43 and take the road to the right; beside the Drée river)

Opening times : from end April to beginning Oct.

2.9 ha (71 pitches) flat, grassy

Tariff : 16€ ✻✻ 🚐 🅿 🔌 (10A) – Extra per person 3.20€ – Reservation fee 10€

Rental rates : (from end April to beginning Oct.) – 12 🏠. Per night from 24 to 54€ – Per week from 99 to 249€ – Reservation fee 20€

🚾 local sani-station – 🚐11€

Surroundings : 🌳 🏞 🌿
Leisure activities : 🏞
Facilities : ♿ ⚡ 🧺 🚰
Nearby : 🍽 ✕ 🎠 🛝 🏞

GPS	Longitude : 4.50617
	Latitude : 46.98577

Do not confuse:
⚠ to ⛺⛺⛺ : *MICHELIN classification with*
★ *to* ★★★★★ : *official classification*

GIGNY-SUR-SAÔNE

71240 – Michelin map **320** J10 – pop. 522 – alt. 178
▶ Paris 355 – Chalon-sur-Saône 29 – Le Creusot 51 – Louhans 30

⛺⛺⛺ Les Castels Château de l'Épervière 👥

☎ 03 85 94 16 90. www.domaine-eperviere.com – limited spaces for one-night stay

Address : 6 rue du Château (located 1km to the south; at Épervière)

Opening times : from beginning April to end Sept.

7 ha (100 pitches) flat, grassy

Tariff : ✻ 9.50€ 🚐 🅿 16.50€ – 🔌 (10A) 5.60€ – Reservation fee 10€

Rental rates : (from beginning April to end Sept.) 🚐 – 5 🚐 – 3 gîtes. Per week from 459 to 899€ – Reservation fee 20€

🚾 local sani-station – 20 🅿 16.50€

A pleasant wooded park beside a lake. Burgundy wines can be tasted in the château's vaulted cellar.

Surroundings : 🌳 🏞 🌿🌿
Leisure activities : 🍽 ✕ 🏞 🏊 ⛵s jacuzzi 🎠 🛝 🏊 (pool) 🏊 paddling pool
Facilities : ♿ ⚡ 🚿 🧺 🛁 🚰 🚰
Nearby : ✂

GPS	Longitude : 4.94386
	Latitude : 46.65446

GUEUGNON

71130 – Michelin map **320** E10 – pop. 7 638 – alt. 243
▶ Paris 335 – Autun 53 – Bourbon-Lancy 27 – Digoin 16

⚠ Municipal de Chazey

☎ 03 85 85 56 90. www.ccpaysgueugnon.fr

Address : zone de Chazey (4km south along the D 994, follow the signs for Digoin and take the road to the right)

Opening times : permanent

1 ha (20 pitches) flat, grassy

Tariff : (2015 price) ✻ 2.75€ 🚐 🅿 5.40€ – 🔌 (16A) 4€

Rental rates : (2015 price) permanent – 3 🏠. Per night from 46 to 71€ – Per week from 212 to 323€

🚾 Eurorelais sani-station – 2 🅿

Near a small canal and two lakes.

Surroundings : 🌳 🏞
Leisure activities : 🏞 🎠
Facilities : ♿ 🧺 🛁 🚰
Nearby : 🎣

GPS	Longitude : 4.05386
	Latitude : 46.57077

Routes nationales are main roads and their identifying numbers begin with N or RN. Routes départementales are generally quieter roads and begin with D or DN.

L'ISLE-SUR-SEREIN

89440 – Michelin map **319** H6 – pop. 747 – alt. 190
▶ Paris 209 – Auxerre 50 – Avallon 17 – Montbard 36

⚠ Municipal le Parc du Château

☎ 03 86 33 93 50. www.isle-sur-serein.fr

Address : route d'Avallon (800m south along the D 86; by the stadium, 150m from the Serein river)

Opening times : from beginning April to mid Oct.

1 ha (30 pitches) flat, grassy

Tariff : (2015 price) 21€ ✻✻ 🚐 🅿 🔌 (6A) – Extra per person 2.30€

Rental rates : (2015 price) (from beginning April to beginning Oct.) 🚐 – 6 🚐. Per night from 40 to 45€ – Per week from 160 to 230€

🚾 local sani-station 5€ – 8 🅿 2€

Surroundings : 🌿
Facilities : ⚡ 🧺 🛁 🚰
Nearby : 🏇 ✂ sports trail

GPS	Longitude : 4.00542
	Latitude : 47.58119

ISSY-L'ÉVÊQUE

71760 – Michelin map **320** D9 – pop. 842 – alt. 310
▶ Paris 325 – Bourbon-Lancy 25 – Gueugnon 17 – Luzy 12

⛺⛺ L'Etang Neuf

☎ 03 85 24 96 05. camping-etangneuf@orange.fr

Address : rue de l'Étang (located 1km west along the D 42, follow the signs for Grury and take the road to the right)

6 ha/3 pitches (71 pitches) flat

Rentals : 2 🚐 – 6 🏠.

A pleasant location beside a lake and a wood.

Surroundings : 🌳 ⪉ 🏞
Leisure activities : 🍽 ✕ 🏞 🎠 🏊
Facilities : ♿ ⚡ 🧺 🚰
Nearby : 🛝 🏊 🎣 🏇

GPS	Longitude : 3.9602
	Latitude : 46.7078

LAIVES

71240 – Michelin map **320** J10 – pop. 997 – alt. 198
▶ Paris 355 – Chalon-sur-Saône 20 – Mâcon 48 – Montceau-les-Mines 49

🏔 Les Lacs de Laives - la Héronnière

🕿 03 85 44 98 85. www.camping-laheronniere.com

Address : route de la Ferté (4.2km north along the D 18, follow the signs for Buxy and take right turn)

Opening times : from mid March to beginning Nov.

1.5 ha (80 pitches) flat, grassy

Tariff : (2015 price) 26.80€ �pers ✶ 🚗 🔲 🔌 (15A) –
Extra per person 3.90€ – Reservation fee 5€

Rental rates : (2015 price) (from mid March to beginning Nov.) –
2 🚐 – 2 🏠. Per night from 59 to 74€ – Per week from 322 to 518€ – Reservation fee 10€

🚐 local sani-station 5€ – 9 🔲 16€

Situated close to the lakes at Laives.

Surroundings : 🌿 ⛱ ♨	
Leisure activities : 🚴 ⛵	GPS
Facilities : ♿ ⚡ 🚿 🏠	Longitude : 4.83426
Nearby : 🍷 ✕ 🛶	Latitude : 46.67448

LIGNY-LE-CHÂTEL

89144 – Michelin map **319** F4 – pop. 1 334 – alt. 130
▶ Paris 178 – Auxerre 22 – Sens 60 – Tonnerre 28

🏔 Municipal Parc de la Noue Marrou

🕿 03 86 47 56 99. www.tourisme-camping-municipal-de-la-noue-marrou.fr

Address : avenue de la Noue Marrou (take the southwestern exit along the D 8, follow the signs for Auxerre and take road to the left; beside the Serein)

2 ha (50 pitches) flat, grassy

🚐 local sani-station

On the edge of the Othe forest and the Serein river.

Surroundings : 🌿	
Leisure activities : 🍷 ⛵	GPS
Facilities : ♿ ⚡ 🚿 🏠	Longitude : 3.75274
Nearby : 🚣 🚴 ✕ 🛶	Latitude : 47.89597

LORMES

58140 – Michelin map **319** F8 – pop. 1 389 – alt. 420
▶ Paris 255 – Dijon 135 – Nevers 73 – Auxerre 76

🏔 L'Étang du Goulot

🕿 03 86 22 82 37. www.campingetangdugoulot.com

Address : 2 rue des Campeurs

Opening times : from mid April to end Sept.

2.5 ha (64 pitches) flat, grassy

Tariff : (2015 price) 16€ ✶ ✶ 🚗 🔲 🔌 (20A) – Extra per person 6€

Rental rates : (2015 price) (from beginning May to end Sept.) –
1 'gypsy' caravan – 2 🚐 – 2 yurts – 1 tipi – 2 canvas bungalows –
3 tent lodges – 3 gîtes. Per night from 55 to 95€ – Per week from 230 to 550€

🚐 local sani-station 3€

Surroundings : 🌿 ⛱ ♨	
Leisure activities : 🍷 ✕ 🏠 🚣 ⛵	GPS
Facilities : ♿ ⚡ 🚿 🏠	Longitude : 3.82297
Nearby : 🚣 🚴 ✂	Latitude : 47.28268

LOUHANS

71500 – Michelin map **320** L10 – pop. 6 451 – alt. 179
▶ Paris 373 – Bourg-en-Bresse 61 – Chalon-sur-Saône 38 – Dijon 85

🏔 Municipal

🕿 03 85 75 19 02. www.louhans-chateaurenaud.fr

Address : 10 chemin de La Chapellerie (located 1km southwest along the D 971, follow the signs for Tournus and take the D 12, following signs for Romenay, turn left after the stadium)

Opening times : from beginning April to end Sept.

1 ha (60 pitches) flat, grassy

Tariff : (2015 price) 15€ ✶ ✶ 🚗 🔲 🔌 (10A) – Extra per person 2.50€

Rental rates : (2015 price) (from beginning April to end Sept.) –
2 🚐. Per night from 70 to 90€ – Per week from 280 to 380€

🚐 25 🔲 6€

Green setting beside river.

Surroundings : ⛱ ♨	
Facilities : ♿ 🚿	GPS
Nearby : ✕ 🚣 ⛵	Longitude : 5.21714
	Latitude : 46.62436

LUZY

58170 – Michelin map **319** G11 – pop. 2 018 – alt. 275
▶ Paris 314 – Autun 34 – Château-Chinon 39 – Moulins 62

🏔 Club Airotel Château de Chigy 👥

🕿 03 86 30 10 80. www.chateaudechigy.com.fr

Address : at Tazilly (4km southwest along the D 973, follow the signs for Bourbon-Lancy then take the road to the left)

70 ha/15 pitches (135 pitches) flat, grassy

Rentals : 6 🚐 – 29 🏠 – 3 apartments – 6 gîtes.

A spacious site laid out around a château, with meadows, woods and lakes.

Surroundings : 🌿 ⛰	
Leisure activities : 🍷 ✕ 🏠 🎣 🏃 ⛵ 🐎 🎿	GPS
🚣 🛶 🎯 multi-sports ground	Longitude : 3.94445
Facilities : ♿ ⚡ 🚿 🏠 🧺	Latitude : 46.75716

In order for the guide to remain wholly objective, the selection of campsites is made on an entirely independent basis.

MACON

71000 – Michelin map **320** I12 – pop. 34 000 – alt. 175
▶ Paris 398 – Dijon 128 – Lyon 72 – Bourg-en-Bresse 37

🏔 Municipal

🕿 03 85 38 16 22. www.macon.fr/tourisme/camping – ♨

Address : at Sancé, 1 rue des Grandes Varennes

Opening times : from mid March to end Oct.

5 ha (266 pitches) flat, grassy

Tariff : (2015 price) 20.70€ ✶ ✶ 🚗 🔲 🔌 (10A) –
Extra per person 5.40€

🚐 Eurorelais sani-station 5€

Surroundings : ⛱ ♨	
Leisure activities : 🍷 ✕ 🏠 🚣 ⛵	GPS
Facilities : ♿ ⚡ 🚿 🏠 🚿 🏠 launderette 🚣 🚲	Longitude : 4.84372
Nearby : ⚓ marina	Latitude : 46.3301

MATOUR

71520 – Michelin map **320** G12 – pop. 1 095 – alt. 500
▶ Paris 405 – Chauffailles 22 – Cluny 24 – Mâcon 36

⛰ Flower Le Paluet

✆ 03 85 59 70 92. www.matour.com

Address : 2 rue de la Piscine (located to the west; follow the signs for la Clayette and take a left turn)

Opening times : from mid May to end Sept.

3 ha (73 pitches) flat and relatively flat

Tariff : 23.10€ ✚✚ ⛟ 回 ⚡ (10A) – Extra per person 5.10€ – Reservation fee 12€

Rental rates : (from mid March to mid Nov.) – 10 ☖ – 8 canvas bungalows – 2 gîtes. Per night from 35 to 113€ – Per week from 245 to 791€ – Reservation fee 25€

☖ local sani-station – 6 回

Situated beside a lake and near a leisure centre.

Surroundings : 🏞 🗓 ♀
Leisure activities : 🖼 🕙daytime ⛵ 🎣 🏌
🏊 🎿 🏹 multi-sports ground
Facilities : ♿ ⛽ (season) ♨ 🍴 launderette
G P S Longitude : 4.48232
Latitude : 46.30677

We value your opinion and welcome your feedback.
Do email us at campingfrance@tp.michelin.com

MEURSAULT

21190 – Michelin map **320** I8 – pop. 1 542 – alt. 243
▶ Paris 326 – Dijon 56 – Chalon-sur-Saône 28 – Le Creusot 40

⛺ La Grappe d'Or

✆ 03 80 21 22 48. www.camping-meursault.com

Address : 2 route de Volnay

Opening times : from mid April to mid Oct.

4.5 ha (130 pitches) terraced, flat, grassy

Tariff : 25€ ✚✚ ⛟ 回 ⚡ (10A) – Extra per person 4.20€ – Reservation fee 10€

Rental rates : (2015 price) (from mid April to end Sept.) – 19 ☖ – 3 ⊨ – 1 apartment – 1 gîte. Per night from 50 to 99 – Per week from 315 to 650 – Reservation fee 15€

☖ local sani-station 5€ – 10 回 16€

The site overlooks the old village of Mersault and vineyards.

Surroundings : ≤ ♀
Leisure activities : ✕ ⛵ 🚲 🎣 🎿 🏹
Facilities : ♿ ⛽ ♨ 🎿 🍴
G P S Longitude : 4.76987
Latitude : 46.98655

MIGENNES

89400 – Michelin map **319** E4 – pop. 7 360 – alt. 87
▶ Paris 162 – Dijon 169 – Auxerre 22 – Sens 46

⛰ Les Confluents

✆ 03 86 80 94 55. www.les-confluents.com

Address : allée Léo Lagrange (near the stadium)

Opening times : from beginning April to end Oct.

1.5 ha (61 pitches) flat, grassy

Tariff : (2015 price) 14.30€ ✚✚ ⛟ 回 ⚡ (10A) – Extra per person 4.50€

Rental rates : (2015 price) (from beginning April to end Oct.) – 12 ☖. Per night from 45 to 74€ – Per week from 365 to 500€

☖ AireService sani-station 3.35€ – 10 回 14.30€ – ⚡ ⚡14€

On the banks of the Yonne river.

Surroundings : 🗓 ♀
Leisure activities : 🖼 ⛵ 🚲 🏹
Facilities : ⛽ ♨ 🎿 🍴 🔥 🍴 🚿
Nearby : ✕ ✕ 🎣 watersports centre
G P S Longitude : 3.5095
Latitude : 47.95613

MONTBARD

21500 – Michelin map **320** G4 – pop. 5 527 – alt. 221
▶ Paris 240 – Autun 87 – Auxerre 81 – Dijon 81

⛰ Municipal les Treilles

✆ 03 80 92 69 50. www.montbard.com

Address : rue Michel Servet (along the D 980 diversion northwest of the town, near the swimming complex)

Opening times : from end March to end Oct.

2.5 ha (80 pitches) flat, grassy

Tariff : (2015 price) 19.30€ ✚✚ ⛟ 回 ⚡ (16A) – Extra per person 5.10€ – Reservation fee 4€

Rental rates : (2015 price) (from end March to end Oct.) – 2 ☖. Per night from 90 to 95€ – Per week from 255 to 555€ – Reservation fee 6€

☖ local sani-station 3.10€ – 6 回 19.30€ – ⚡11€

Attractive trees and shrubs surround some pitches.

Surroundings : ≤ 🗓 ♀
Leisure activities : 🖼 🕙daytime ⛵ multi-sports ground
Facilities : ♿ ⛽ ♨ 🎿 🍴 🔥
Nearby : ♨ hammam 🌐 🏊 🎿 ⛷
G P S Longitude : 4.33129
Latitude : 47.63111

Key to rentals symbols:

12 ☖ *Number of mobile homes*
20 ☖ *Number of chalets*
6 ⊨ *Number of rooms to rent*
Per night 30–50€ *Minimum/maximum rate per night*
Per week 300–1,000€ *Minimum/maximum rate per week*

MONTIGNY-EN-MORVAN

58120 – Michelin map **319** G9 – pop. 319 – alt. 350
▶ Paris 269 – Château-Chinon 13 – Corbigny 26 – Nevers 64

⛰ Municipal du Lac

✆ 03 86 84 71 77. www.montigny-en-morvan.fr

Address : Continue 2.3km northeast along the D 94, D 303 towards the dam at Pannecière-Chaumard and take the road to the right.

Opening times : from mid April to mid Oct.

2 ha (59 pitches) undulating, flat, grassy

Tariff : (2015 price) ✚ 2.80€ ⛟ 1.90€ – ⚡ (10A) 2.20€

In a pleasant location near a lake.

Surroundings : 🏞 ♀
Leisure activities : ⛵ 🏹
Facilities : ♿ ⛽ 🎿 ♨
Nearby : 🏊
G P S Longitude : 3.8735
Latitude : 47.15573

NEVERS

58000 – Michelin map **319** B10 – pop. 36 762 – alt. 194
▶ Paris 247 – Dijon 187 – Bourges 68 – Moulins 57

⚠ Aquadis Loisirs Nevers

✆ 03.86.36.40.75. http://www.aquadis-loisirs.com/camping-de-nevers/

Address : rue de la Jonction

Opening times : from beginning March to beginning Nov.

1.6 ha (73 pitches) terraced, flat, grassy

Tariff : 21.50€ ✚✚ 🚗 🗐 ⚡ (10A) – Extra per person 3.20€ –
Reservation fee 10€

Rental rates : (from beginning March to beginning Nov.) –
8 🚐. Per night from 62€ – Per week from 529€ – Reservation
fee 20€

🚰 AireService sani-station – 🚐11€
*Situated on the banks of the Loire river with a view of the
cathedral, Ducal Palace and the stone bridge.*

Surroundings : ⬔ ♀	**G** Longitude : 3.16095
Leisure activities : ♟ ✗ 🏠 🛝 🌊	**P**
Facilities : ᵹ ⚬ₒ 🗐 🛁 🚽 ↻ ⁿ launderette 🧺	**S** Latitude : 46.98222
Nearby : 🚲 🚴	

*These symbols are used for a campsite that is exceptional
in its category:*

🏔🏔...🏔 *Particularly pleasant setting, quality
and range of services available*

🦢🦢 *Tranquil, isolated site – quiet site,
particularly at night*

⬔⬔ *Exceptional view – interesting or panoramic
view*

NOLAY

21340 – Michelin map **320** H8 – pop. 1 510 – alt. 299
▶ Paris 316 – Autun 30 – Beaune 20 – Chalon-sur-Saône 34

⚠ Municipal les Chaumes du Mont

✆ 03 45 63 40 01. campingleschaumes@sfr.fr

Address : route de Couches (0.8km southwest along the D 33A,
follow the signs for Couches)

1.5 ha (70 pitches) terraced, relatively flat, flat, grassy
Situated near a lake.

Surroundings : ⬔ ♀ ⛰	**G** Longitude : 4.62457
Leisure activities : 🛝 🍴	**P**
Facilities : ᵹ ⚬ₒ 🗐	**S** Latitude : 46.94682

⚠ La Bruyère

✆ 03 80 21 87 59. www.bourgogne-sante-services.com

Address : rue de Moulin Larché (1.2km west along the D 973, follow
the signs for Autun and take road to the left)

Opening times : permanent

1.2 ha (22 pitches) flat, grassy

Tariff : 10.75€ ✚✚ 🚗 🗐 ⚡ (16A) – Extra per person 2.40€

🚰 Eurorelais sani-station

Surroundings : 🦢 ⬔	**G** Longitude : 4.62202
Leisure activities : 🏠	**P**
Facilities : ᵹ ⚬ₒ 🗐 ⁿ launderette	**S** Latitude : 46.95055

PALINGES

71430 – Michelin map **320** F10 – pop. 1 512 – alt. 274
▶ Paris 352 – Charolles 16 – Lapalisse 70 – Lyon 136

⚠ Le Lac

✆ 03 85 88 14 49. www.campingdulac.eu

Address : at Lac du Fourneau (located 1km northeast along the
D 128, rte de Génelard)

Opening times : from beginning April to end Oct.

1.5 ha (44 pitches) terraced, flat, grassy

Tariff : (2015 price) 23€ ✚✚ 🚗 🗐 ⚡ (10A) – Extra per person 4.10€

Rental rates : (2015 price) (from beginning April to end Oct.) ᵹ
(1) – 6 🚐 – 2 tent lodges. Per night from 30 to 165€ – Per week
from 185 to 750€

🚰 AireService sani-station – 6 🗐 23€
Near a small lake.

Surroundings : 🗺	**G** Longitude : 4.22521
Leisure activities : 🛝 🛝 🌊	**P**
Facilities : ᵹ ⚬ₒ 🛁 ⁿ 🖼 refrigerators	**S** Latitude : 46.56106
Nearby : 🚤 ✗ 🛥 (beach) 🌊	

*To make the best possible use of this guide, please read
pages 2–15 carefully.*

PARAY LE MONIAL

71600 – Michelin map **320** E11 – pop. 9 115 – alt. 245
▶ Paris 377 – Dijon 149 – Mâcon 66 – Moulins 69

🏔 Mambre

✆ 03 85 88 89 20. www.campingdemambre.com

Address : 19 rue du Gué Léger

Opening times : from beginning May to end Sept.

6 ha (161 pitches) flat, grassy

Tariff : (2015 price) ✱ 5€ 🚗 🗐 7.50€ – ⚡ (10A) 3.80€

Rental rates : (2015 price) (from mid May to mid Sept.) 🛶 –
20 🚐. Per night from 40 to 78€ – Per week from 240 to 468€

Surroundings : ♀♀	**G** Longitude : 4.10479
Leisure activities : 🍴 🛝 🚴 🌊	**P**
Facilities : ᵹ ⚬ₒ cc 🛁 ⁿ launderette 🛒	**S** Latitude : 46.45743
Nearby : ✗	

PRÉMERY

58700 – Michelin map **319** C8 – pop. 2 031 – alt. 237
▶ Paris 231 – La Charité-sur-Loire 28 – Château-Chinon 57
– Clamecy 41

⚠ Municipal

✆ 09 65 21 65 56. www.mairie-premery.fr rubrique camping

Address : chemin des Prés de la Ville (take the northeastern exit
along the D 977, follow the signs for Clamecy and take the road to
the right)

1.6 ha (50 pitches) flat and relatively flat

Rentals : 10 🚐.
Situated near the Nièvre river and a lake.

Leisure activities : 🚴 🛝 multi-sports ground	**G** Longitude : 3.33683
Facilities : ᵹ ⚬ₒ 🛁 ⁿ 🖼	**P**
Nearby : 🚤 🛝 ✗ 🛥	**S** Latitude : 47.1781

ST-GERMAIN-DU-BOIS

71330 – Michelin map **320** L9 – pop. 1 935 – alt. 210
▶ Paris 367 – Chalon-sur-Saône 33 – Dole 58 – Lons-le-Saunier 29

⚠ Municipal de l'Étang Titard

✆ 03 85 72 06 15. www.saintgermaindubois.fr

Address : route de Louhans (take the southern exit along the D 13)

Opening times : from beginning May to mid Sept.

1 ha (40 pitches) flat, grassy

Tariff : (2015 price) ✦ 2.30€ ⇔ 1.50€ ▣ 1.50€ – (10A) 2.50€
Rental rates : (2015 price) permanent ⅙ (1) ⌖ – 5 ⌂. Per night from 57 to 94€ – Per week from 294 to 420€

Situated near a lake.

Surroundings : ⌢	**G** Longitude : 5.24617
Leisure activities : ⌂	**P**
Facilities : ⅙ ⌖ ⌂ ⌂ ▣	**S** Latitude : 46.74635
Nearby : ✖ ▣ ⌂ ⌢ sports trail	

*The classification (1 to 5 tents, **black** or red) that we
award to selected sites in this guide is our own system.
It should not be confused with the classification
(1 to 5 stars) of official organisations.*

ST-HONORÉ-LES-BAINS

58360 – Michelin map **319** G10 – pop. 841 – alt. 300 – ⚕
▶ Paris 303 – Château-Chinon 28 – Luzy 22 – Moulins 69

⚠⚠ Camping et Gîtes des Bains

✆ 03 86 30 73 44. www.campinglesbains.com

Address : 15 avenue Jean Mermoz (take the western exit, follow the signs for Vandenesse)

Opening times : from end March to end Oct.

4.5 ha (130 pitches) flat, grassy

Tariff : 20€ ✦✦ ⇔ ▣ – (10A) – Extra per person 4.60€ – Reservation fee 8€
Rental rates : (from end March to end Oct.) – 4 ⌂ – 20 ⌂ – 3 apartments. Per night from 45 to 83€ – Per week from 200 to 578€ – Reservation fee 8€
⌖ local sani-station – 10 ▣ 13€

Surroundings : ⌢ ⌢	**G** Longitude : 3.82832
Leisure activities : ▾ ✖ ⌂ ⌂ ⌂ ⌂	**P**
Facilities : ⅙ ⌖ ⌂ ⌂ launderette	**S** Latitude : 46.90684
Nearby : ✖ ⌂	

⚠ Municipal Plateau du Gué

✆ 03 86 30 76 00. http://www.st-honore-les-bains.com/index.php?cat=campings

Address : 13 rue Eugène-Collin (in the village, 150m from the post office)

Opening times : from beginning April to end Oct.

1.2 ha (73 pitches) flat and relatively flat, grassy

Tariff : (2015 price) ✦ 3.30€ ⇔ ▣ 2.70€ – (10A) 3.80€
⌖ Eurorelais sani-station 2.30€ – 15 ▣ 2.70€

Surroundings : ⌢	**G** Longitude : 3.83918
Leisure activities : ⌂ ⌂	**P**
Facilities : ⅙ ⌖ ▣ ⌂ ⌂	**S** Latitude : 46.90376

ST-LÉGER-DE-FOUGERET

58120 – Michelin map **319** G9 – pop. 289 – alt. 500
▶ Paris 308 – Dijon 122 – Nevers 65 – Le Creusot 69

⚠ Sites et Paysages Étang de la Fougeraie

✆ 03 86 85 11 85. www.campingfougeraie.com

Address : at Hameau de champs (2.4km southeast along the D 157, follow the signs for Onlay)

Opening times : from beginning April to end Sept.

7 ha (60 pitches) flat, grassy

Tariff : 30€ ✦✦ ⇔ ▣ – (10A) – Extra per person 7.20€ – Reservation fee 9.50€
Rental rates : permanent – 5 ⌂ – 7 tent lodges. Per night from 45 to 100€ – Per week from 315 to 645€ – Reservation fee 17€
⌖ local sani-station – 3 ▣ 26€ – ⌂ 16€

In a rural setting beside a lake.

Surroundings : ⌢ ⌂	**G** Longitude : 3.90492
Leisure activities : ▾ ✖ ⌂ ⌂ ⌂	**P**
Facilities : ⅙ ⌖ ⌂ ⌂ launderette ⌂ refrigerators	**S** Latitude : 47.00616

ST-PÉREUSE

58110 – Michelin map **319** F9 – pop. 280 – alt. 355
▶ Paris 289 – Autun 54 – Château-Chinon 15 – Clamecy 57

⚠⚠⚠ Le Manoir de Bezolle

✆ 03 86 84 42 55. www.camping-bezolle.com

Address : to the southeast along the D 11, 300m from the D 978, follow the signs for Château-Chinon

8 ha/5 pitches (140 pitches) terraced, flat, grassy, small lakes
Rentals : 2 'gypsy' caravans – 4 ⌂ – 12 ⌂ – 2 yurts.
⌖ local sani-station

In the grounds of the manor house.

Surroundings : ⌢ ⌂ ⌂	**G** Longitude : 3.8158
Leisure activities : ▾ ✖ ⌂ ⌂ ⌂ ⌂ ⌂	**P**
Facilities : ⅙ ⌖ ▥ ⌂ ⌂ ⌂ launderette ⌂ ⌂	**S** Latitude : 47.05732

ST-POINT

71520 – Michelin map **320** H11 – pop. 341 – alt. 335
▶ Paris 396 – Beaune 90 – Cluny 14 – Mâcon 26

⚠ Lac de St-Point-Lamartine

✆ 03 85 50 52 31. www.campingsaintpoint.com

Address : take the southern exit along the D 22, follow the signs for Tramayes; beside a lake

Opening times : from beginning April to end Oct.

3 ha (102 pitches) flat and relatively flat, grassy

Tariff : ✦ 4€ ⇔ ▣ 5€ – (13A) 5€
Rental rates : (from beginning April to end Oct.) – 11 ⌂.
Per night from 45 to 50€ – Per week from 250 to 450€
⌖ local sani-station – 10 ▣ 10€ – ⌂ 12€

On the edge of a lake.

Surroundings : ⌢ ⌂ ⌂	**G** Longitude : 4.61175
Leisure activities : ⌂ ⌂ ⌂ ⌂	**P**
Facilities : ⅙ ⌖ ⌂ ⌂ ▣	**S** Latitude : 46.33703
Nearby : ▾ ✖ ⌂ ⌢ pedalos	

ST-SAUVEUR-EN-PUISAYE

89520 – Michelin map **319** C6 – pop. 946 – alt. 259
▶ Paris 174 – Dijon 184 – Moulins 146 – Tours 242

⛰ Parc des Joumiers

✆ 03 86 45 66 28. www.camping-motel-joumiers.com

Address : 2.3km northwest along the D 7 and take the road to the right

21 ha/7 pitches (100 pitches) flat and relatively flat, grassy

Rentals : 13 🚐 – 3 🏠 – 10 ⛺.

🚉 local sani-station – 2 🅴

Beside a lake.

Surroundings : 🏊 🚃 ⚴
Leisure activities : ✗ 🚣 🎣 🏹
Facilities : 🚿 ⛽ 🍴 ♨ 🚽 🍽 🗑
Nearby : boats to hire

GPS	Longitude : 3.19357
	Latitude : 47.63082

This guide is not intended as a list of all the camping sites in France; its aim is to provide a selection of the best sites in each category.

SALORNAY-SUR-GUYE

71250 – Michelin map **320** H10 – pop. 826 – alt. 210
▶ Paris 377 – Chalon-sur-Saône 51 – Cluny 12 – Paray-le-Monial 44

⛰ Municipal de la Clochette

✆ 03 85 59 90 11. www.salornay-sur-guye.fr

Address : place de la Clochette (in the village, access via the road in front of the post office)

Opening times : from end May to beginning Sept.

1 ha (60 pitches) flat, grassy

Tariff : 🧍 3.50€ 🚗 🅴 3€ – 🔌 (10A) 3€ – Reservation fee 5€

🚉 local sani-station 5€

Situated beside the Gande river.

Surroundings : 🚃 ⚴
Leisure activities : 🏹
Facilities : 🚿 🗑 🍴 ♨ 🗑
Nearby : 🚣 ✗

GPS	Longitude : 4.59907
	Latitude : 46.51659

SANTENAY

21590 – Michelin map **320** I8 – pop. 827 – alt. 225 – ♨
▶ Paris 330 – Autun 39 – Beaune 18 – Chalon-sur-Saône 25

⛰ Aquadis Loisirs Les Sources

✆ 03 80 20 66 55. www.aquadis-loisirs.com/camping-des-sources

Address : avenue des Sources (head 1km southwest following signs for Cheilly-les-Maranges, near the spa centre)

Opening times : from beginning April to end Oct.

3.1 ha (150 pitches) flat and relatively flat, grassy

Tariff : 18.20€ 🧍🧍 🚗 🅴 🔌 (10A) – Extra per person 3.40€ – Reservation fee 10€

Rental rates : (from beginning April to end Oct.) – 6 🚐. Per night from 62€ – Per week from 369 to 549€ – Reservation fee 10€

🚉 AireService sani-station – ⚓11€

Surroundings : ⩹ ⚴
Leisure activities : 🚣 ♨
Facilities : 🚿 ⛽ 🆑 🍴 🗑 🗑 🗑
Nearby : ✗ 🎣

GPS	Longitude : 4.6857
	Latitude : 46.90716

SAULIEU

21210 – Michelin map **320** F6 – pop. 2 574 – alt. 535
▶ Paris 248 – Autun 40 – Avallon 39 – Beaune 65

⛰ Aquadis Loisirs Saulieu

✆ 03 80 64 16 19. www.aquadis-loisirs.com/camping-de-saulieu

Address : located 1km northwest along the N 6, follow the signs for Paris; near a lake

Opening times : from beginning March to beginning Nov.

6 ha (100 pitches) flat and relatively flat, grassy

Tariff : 20.80€ 🧍🧍 🚗 🅴 🔌 (10A) – Extra per person 3.80€ – Reservation fee 10€

Rental rates : (from beginning March to beginning Nov.) – 6 🚐 – 6 🏠. Per night from 62 to 85€ – Per week from 199 to 639€ – Reservation fee 20€

🚉 AireService sani-station – ⚓11€

Leisure activities : 🍴 🚃 🚣 🚴 ✗ 🎣
Facilities : 🚿 ⛽ 🆑 🍴 🗑 🚽 🍽
GPS	Longitude : 4.22373
	Latitude : 47.28934

SAVIGNY-LÈS-BEAUNE

21420 – Michelin map **320** I7 – pop. 1 371 – alt. 237
▶ Paris 314 – Dijon 39 – Mâcon 93 – Lons-le-Saunier 109

⛰ Les Premiers Prés

✆ 03 80 26 15 06. www.camping-savigny-les-beaune.fr

Address : route de Bouilland (located 1km northwest along the D 2)

1.5 ha (88 pitches) flat and relatively flat

In a green setting beside a stream.

Surroundings : ⚴
Leisure activities : 🍴 🚣
Facilities : 🚿 ⛽ 🍽 🗑

GPS	Longitude : 4.82192
	Latitude : 47.06246

LES SETTONS

58230 – Michelin map **319** H8
▶ Paris 259 – Autun 41 – Avallon 44 – Château-Chinon 25

⛰ Plage du Midi

✆ 03 86 84 51 97. www.settons-camping.com

Address : on the right bank of Lac des Settons, Les Branlasses (2.5km southeast along the D 193 and take turning to the right)

4 ha (110 pitches) relatively flat

Rentals : 🚿 (1) – 2 'gypsy' caravans – 27 🏠 – 1 cabin in the trees.

Situated beside a lake.

Surroundings : ⩹ ⚴ ⚴
Leisure activities : 🍴 🚣 🖼 (open air in season)
Facilities : 🚿 ⛽ 🏕 🍽 launderette 🗑
Nearby : ✗ 🎣 🦆 pedalos

GPS	Longitude : 4.07056
	Latitude : 47.18578

⛰ Les Mésanges

✆ 03 86 84 55 77. www.campinglesmesanges.fr

Address : on the left bank of Lac des Settons, L'Huis-Gaumont (4km south along the D193, D 520, follow the signs for Planchez and turn left towards Chevigny, 200m from the lake)

Opening times : from mid May to mid Sept.

5 ha (100 pitches) relatively flat, flat, grassy

Tariff : (2015 price) 21€ 🧍🧍 🚗 🅴 🔌 (16A) – Extra per person 5.30€

local sani-station – 11€

in pleasant location beside a lake.

Surroundings :	
Leisure activities :	
Facilities : launderette	
Nearby :	

Longitude : 4.05385
Latitude : 47.18077

La Plage des Settons

03 86 84 51 99. www.camping-chalets-settons.com

Address : on the left bank of Lac des Settons (300m south of the dam)

Opening times : from beginning May to mid Sept.

2.6 ha (60 pitches) terraced, flat, grassy

Tariff : 19€ ★★ (10A) – Extra per person 7.50€

Rental rates : (from beginning April to mid Nov.) (2 chalets) – 14. Per night from 55 to 95€ – Per week from 366 to 665€

40 19€ – 12€

Pleasant pitches set out on terraces, opposite the lake.

Surroundings :	
Leisure activities : pedalos	
Facilities :	
Nearby :	

Longitude : 4.06132
Latitude : 47.18958

TONNERRE

89700 – Michelin map **319** G4 – pop. 5 246 – alt. 156
Paris 199 – Auxerre 38 – Montbard 45 – Troyes 60

La Cascade

03 86 55 15 44. www.revea-camping.fr/fr/accueil-camping-la-cascade.html

Address : avenue Aristide-Briand (take the northern exit along the D 905, follow the signs for Troyes and take D 944. towards the town centre; beside the Yonne canal)

Opening times : from beginning April to beginning Oct.

3 ha (107 pitches) flat, grassy

Tariff : 18€ ★★ (10A) – Extra per person 4€ – Reservation fee 10€

Rental rates : (from beginning April to mid Nov.) – 10. Per night from 70 to 90€ – Per week from 190 to 540€ – Reservation fee 25€

3 18€

Surroundings :	
Leisure activities :	
Facilities :	
Nearby :	

Longitude : 3.98415
Latitude : 47.8603

TOURNUS

71700 – Michelin map **320** J10 – pop. 5 884 – alt. 193
Paris 360 – Bourg-en-Bresse 70 – Chalon-sur-Saône 28 – Lons-le-Saunier 58

Camping de Tournus

03 85 51 16 58. www.camping-tournus.com

Address : 14 rue des Canes (located 1km north of the town; take the r. St-Laurent opposite the station, situated right next to the swimming pool and 150m from the Saône – direct access)

Opening times : from beginning April to end Sept.

2 ha (90 pitches) flat, grassy

Tariff : 26.90€ ★★ (10A) – Extra per person 6.20€

local sani-station – 26 26.90€ – 13€

Leisure activities :	
Facilities :	
Nearby :	

Longitude : 4.90932
Latitude : 46.57375

VANDENESSE-EN-AUXOIS

21320 – Michelin map **320** H6 – pop. 279 – alt. 360
Paris 275 – Arnay-le-Duc 16 – Autun 42 – Châteauneuf 3

Sunêlia Le Lac de Panthier

03 80 49 21 94. www.lac-de-panthier.com

Address : situated 2.5km northeast along the D 977bis; follow the road to Commarin and take turning to the left; near the lake

Opening times : from mid April to beginning Oct.

5.2 ha (210 pitches) terraced, flat, grassy

Tariff : (2015 price) 28€ ★★ (6A) – Extra per person 7€ – Reservation fee 15€

Rental rates : (2015 price) (from mid April to beginning Oct.) – 63. Per night from 43 to 148€ – Per week from 301 to 1,036€ – Reservation fee 30€

local sani-station 5€

Surroundings :	
Leisure activities :	
Facilities :	
Nearby :	

Longitude : 4.62507
Latitude : 47.24935

VARZY

58210 – Michelin map **319** D7 – pop. 1 329 – alt. 249
Paris 224 – La Charité-sur-Loire 37 – Clamecy 17 – Cosne-sur-Loire 43

Municipal du Moulin Naudin

03 86 29 43 12. mairievarzy@wanadoo.fr

Address : route de Corvol (located 1.5km north along the D 977)

Opening times : from mid May to end Sept.

3 ha (50 pitches) flat, grassy

Tariff : (2015 price) ★ 2.90€ 1.90€ 12€ – (5A) 2.30€

Situated near a small lake.

Surroundings :	
Leisure activities :	
Facilities :	
Nearby :	

Longitude : 3.38312
Latitude : 47.3722

Michelin classification:

Extremely comfortable, equipped to a very high standard

Very comfortable, equipped to a high standard

Comfortable and well equipped

Reasonably comfortable

Satisfactory

VENAREY-LES-LAUMES

21150 – Michelin map **320** G4 – pop. 2 981 – alt. 235
▶ Paris 259 – Avallon 54 – Dijon 66 – Montbard 15

⚠ Municipal Alésia

✆ 03 80 96 07 76. www.venareyleslaumes.fr

Address : rue du Dct Roux (take the western exit along the D 954,
follow the signs for Semur-en-Auxois and take a right turn before the
bridge; beside the Brenne and near a small lake)

Opening times : permanent

1.5 ha (67 pitches) flat, grassy

Tariff : (2015 price) 15.70€ ♥♥ ⇌ 🔲 🚻 (16A) –
Extra per person 3.50€ – Reservation fee 5€

Rental rates : (2015 price) permanent ♿ (1 chalet) – 5 🏠 –
1 🛏. Per night from 50 to 70€ – Per week from 300 to 400€ –
Reservation fee 5€

🚐 Eurorelais sani-station – 13 🔲 4€ – 🚿 🚻 11.70€

Surroundings : 🗂 🌳	
Leisure activities : 🏛 ⛵ 🎣	G
Facilities : ♿ ⚲ 🏢 🧺 🚿 🚻 🔲	P
Nearby : 🎿 🚣 (beach)	S

Longitude : 4.45151
Latitude : 47.54425

VERMENTON

89270 – Michelin map **319** F6 – pop. 1 183 – alt. 125
▶ Paris 190 – Auxerre 24 – Avallon 28 – Vézelay 28

⚠ Municipal les Coullemières

✆ 03 86 81 53 02. www.camping-vermenton.com

Address : at Les Coullemières (to the southwest of the town, behind
the station)

Opening times : from beginning April to end Sept.

1 ha (53 pitches) flat, grassy

Tariff : (2015 price) 15€ ♥♥ ⇌ 🔲 🚻 (6A) – Extra per person 3.50€

Rental rates : (2015 price) (from beginning April to end Sept.)
♿ (1) 🚫 – 6 🚐. Per night from 64 to 75€ – Per week
from 420 to 485€

🚐 3 🔲 15€

A pleasant setting near a wide stretch of the Cure river.

Surroundings : 🌳🌳⛰	
Leisure activities : 🏛 ⛵ 🚲 🎿	G
Facilities : ♿ ⚲ (season) 🏢 🚿 🔲	P
Nearby : 🐎 🚣 (beach) sports trail	S

Longitude : 3.73123
Latitude : 47.65843

VIGNOLES

21200 – Michelin map **320** J7 – pop. 810 – alt. 202
▶ Paris 317 – Dijon 40 – Chalon-sur-Saône 34 – Le Creusot 51

⚠ Les Bouleaux

✆ 03 80 22 26 88. camping-les-bouleaux@hotmail.fr

Address : 11 rue Jaune (located at Chevignerot; beside a stream)

Opening times : permanent

1.6 ha (46 pitches) flat, grassy

Tariff : (2015 price) ♥ 4.20€ ⇌ 2.30€ 🔲 3.70€ – 🚻 (6A) 3.90€

Surroundings : 🗂 🌳🌳	
Leisure activities : 🏛	G
Facilities : ♿ ⚲ 🏢 🧺 🏢 🚿 🚻	P
Nearby : 🎿 🏇	S

Longitude : 4.88298
Latitude : 47.02668

*Routes nationales are main roads and their identifying
numbers begin with N or RN. Routes départementales are
generally quieter roads and begin with D or DN.*

VINCELLES

89290 – Michelin map **319** E5 – pop. 841 – alt. 110
▶ Paris 180 – Auxerre 14 – Avallon 38 – Clamecy 39

⚠ Les Ceriselles ♣♣

✆ 03 86 42 50 47. www.campingceriselles.com

Address : route de Vincelottes (north of the village, along the D 38)

Opening times : from end March to end Sept.

1.5 ha (80 pitches) flat, grassy

Tariff : (2015 price) 20.40€ ♥♥ ⇌ 🔲 🚻 (10A) –
Extra per person 4.55€

Rental rates : (2015 price) (from end March to end Sept.)
♿ (1 chalet) – 18 🚐. Per night from 56 to 87€ – Per week
from 264 to 525€

Beside the Nivernais canal and 150m from the Yonne river.

Surroundings : 🐟 🌳	
Leisure activities : 🍴 ✕ 🏛 🏋 ⛵ 🚲 🎣	
(open air in season)	G
Facilities : ♿ ⚲ 🆑 🏢 🚿 🚻	P
launderette 🧺	S
Nearby : 🏊 🎿 ⚓ 🎣	

Longitude : 3.63536
Latitude : 47.70705

CENTRE

Ph. Body / hemis.fr

Sleeping Beauty is said to slumber still within the thick stone walls of one of the Loire's fairy-tale castles. Does she await that kiss in Chambord, Azay-le-Rideau, Chenonceau, or perhaps one of the many other wonderful châteaux that lie in wait for you? To list all the Centre's architectural wonders set in the most glorious of gardens would take far too long, but visitors can appreciate some of the Loire's treasures during a season of spectacular *son et lumière* (sound and light) shows. The landscape of the region has inspired a host of writers, from Pierre de Ronsard, the 16th-century 'Prince of Poets', to Balzac and Georges Sand. All succumbed to the charm and beauty of this valley of kings, with its untamed river and atmospheric woodlands. In order to savour the region's twin talents for storytelling and culinary arts to the full, enjoy a plate of delicious chicken stew before settling down to listen to your host's tales of werewolves and other local legends!

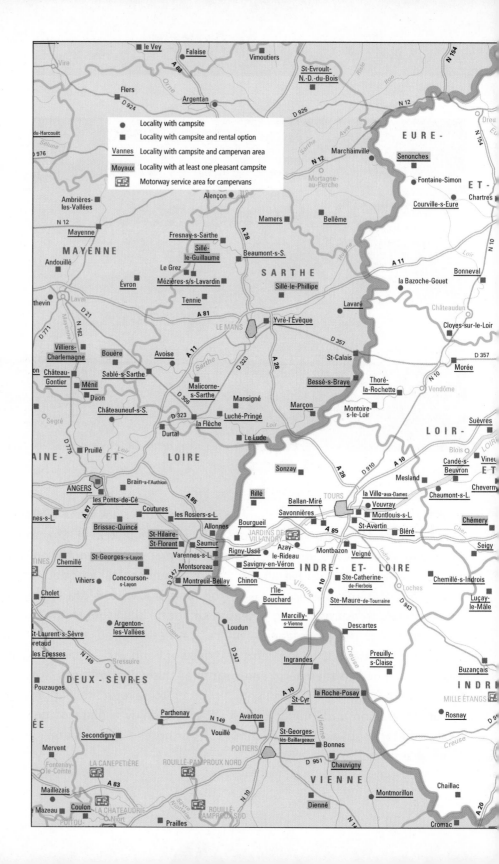

Locality with campsite

Locality with campsite and rental option

Vannes Locality with campsite and campervan area

Moyaux Locality with at least one pleasant campsite

Motorway service area for campervans

AUBIGNY-SUR-NÈRE

18700 – Michelin map **323** K2 – pop. 5 879 – alt. 180
▶ Paris 180 – Bourges 48 – Cosne-sur-Loire 41 – Gien 30

⚏ Les Étangs

✆ 02 48 58 02 37, www.camping-aubigny.com

Address : avenue du Parc des Sports (1.4km east along the D 923, near a lake – direct access)

Opening times : from mid March to end Oct.

3 ha (100 pitches) flat, grassy

Tariff : 17.50€ ✶✶ 🚗 🅴 ⚡ (10A) – Extra per person 4.50€ – Reservation fee 10€

Rental rates : (from beginning March to end Oct.) – 1 'gypsy' caravan – 10 🛖 – 6 🏠 – 2 canvas bungalows. Per night from 30 to 114€ – Per week from 150 to 798€ – Reservation fee 15€

The pitches are well shaded, some are situated on the lakeshore.

Surroundings : 🖵 ♀♀
Leisure activities : 🎣 ⚓ ⌑
Facilities : 🚿 ⚟ 🌡 ⚚ 🍴 launderette ⚒

Nearby : ✕ 🔲 ⚓

G P S Longitude : 2.46101
Latitude : 47.48574

AZAY-LE-RIDEAU

37190 – Michelin map **317** L5 – pop. 3 418 – alt. 51
▶ Paris 265 – Châtellerault 61 – Chinon 21 – Loches 58

⚏ Municipal le Sabot

✆ 02 47 45 42 72, www.azaylerideau.fr

Address : rue du Stade (take the eastern exit along the D 84, follow the signs for Artannes and take turning to the right)

Opening times : from beginning April to mid Oct.

6 ha (150 pitches) flat, grassy

Tariff : (2015 price) 18.50€ ✶✶ 🚗 🅴 ⚡ (8A) – Extra per person 3,80€

A pleasant location close to the château and beside the Indre river.

Surroundings : 🖎 ♀
Leisure activities : 🎣 ⚓ ⚓
Facilities : 🚿 ⚟ 🌡 🍴 launderette

Nearby : ⚋ 🚴 ✕ ⚓

G P S Longitude : 0.46963
Latitude : 47.25863

For more information on visiting particular towns or regions, consult the relevant regional MICHELIN Green Guide. We also recommend you use the appropriate Michelin regional map to locate your selected campsite, to calculate distances and to work out the best route.

BALLAN-MIRÉ

37510 – Michelin map **317** M4 – pop. 8 152 – alt. 88
▶ Paris 251 – Azay-le-Rideau 17 – Langeais 20 – Montbazon 13

⚏⚏ Club Airotel la Mignardière

✆ 02 47 73 31 00, www.mignardiere.com

Address : 22 avenue des Aubépines (2.5km northeast of the town, not far from the small lake at Joué-Ballan)

Opening times : from beginning April to mid Sept.

2.5 ha (177 pitches) flat, grassy, small adjacent wood

Tariff : 29.60€ ✶✶ 🚗 🅴 ⚡ (10A) – Extra per person 6€

Rental rates : (from beginning April to mid Sept.) – 4 'gypsy' caravans – 19 🛖 – 20 🏠. Per night from 42 to 165€ – Per week from 273 to 749€ – Reservation fee 15€

🚐 sani-station 5€

Surroundings : 🖵 ♀
Leisure activities : ✕ ⚓ ⚓ 🚴 ✕ 🔲 ⌑
Facilities : 🚿 ⚟ 🌡 ⚚ 🍴 🅿 🔲
Nearby : ♒ ⚓ ⚞ adventure park

G P S Longitude : 0.63402
Latitude : 47.35524

BARAIZE

36270 – Michelin map **323** F8 – pop. 313 – alt. 240
▶ Paris 318 – Orléans 192 – Châteauroux 47 – Guéret 86

⚏ Municipal Montcocu

✆ 02 54 25 34 28, syndicat.laceguzon@wanadoo.fr – for caravans – from the 'Montcocu' locality, 12% gradient for 1km

Address : at Montcocu (4.8km southeast along the D 913, follow the signs for Éguzon and take D 72, take left turn for Pont-de-Piles)

Opening times : from beginning June to end Sept.

1 ha (26 pitches) terraced, flat, grassy

Tariff : 10.90€ ✶✶ 🚗 🅴 ⚡ (8A) – Extra per person 2.35€

Rental rates : (2015 price) (from beginning May to end Oct.) – 4 🏠 – 4 canvas bungalows. Per night from 35 to 85€ – Per week from 144 to 450€

In a pleasant location and setting in the Creuse valley.

Surroundings : 🖎 🖵 ♀ ⛰
Leisure activities : ♒ ✕ 🎣 ⚓ ⚓ 🚴 ✈
Facilities : 🚿 ⚟ 🌡 🍴

G P S Longitude : 1.60023
Latitude : 46.47159

To visit a town or region, use the MICHELIN Green Guides.

LA BAZOCHE-GOUET

28330 – Michelin map **311** B7 – pop. 1 314 – alt. 185
▶ Paris 146 – Brou 18 – Chartres 61 – Châteaudun 33

⚏ Municipal la Rivière

✆ 02 37 49 36 49, commune-bazoche-gouet-28330@wanadoo.fr

Address : located 1.5km southwest along the D 927, follow the signs for la Chapelle-Guillaume and take road to the left

1.8 ha (30 pitches) flat, grassy

Rentals : 1 🛖.

Beside the Yerre river and close to some lakes.

Leisure activities : ⚓ 🚴 ✈
Facilities : 🚿 🔲
Nearby : ✕

G P S Longitude : 0.9689
Latitude : 48.129

BEAULIEU-SUR-LOIRE

45630 – Michelin map **318** N6 – pop. 1 794 – alt. 156
▶ Paris 170 – Aubigny-sur-Nère 36 – Briare 15 – Gien 27

⚏ Municipal Touristique du Canal

✆ 02 38 35 32 16, www.beaulieu-sur-loire.fr

Address : route de Bonny-sur-Loire (take the eastern exit along the D 926, near the canal)

0.6 ha (37 pitches) flat, grassy

Surroundings : 🖵 ♀
Facilities : 🚿 🌡
Nearby : ✕ ✈ ⚓

G P S Longitude : 2.8176
Latitude : 47.5435

BESSAIS-LE-FROMENTAL

18210 – Michelin map **323** M6 – pop. 313 – alt. 210
▶ Paris 300 – Orléans 172 – Bourges 51 – Moulins 66

🏔 Le Village de Goule

📞 02 48 60 82 66, www.levillagedegoule.com

Address : 1 route de Goule (4.7km southeast along the D 110 and D 110E)

120 ha/2 for camping (75 pitches) flat, grassy
Rentals : ♿ (1 chalet) – 15 🏠 – 1 yurt – 5 tipis – 5 canvas bungalows.
🚐 local sani-station
A leafy, green setting beside a lake offering various rental options.

Surroundings : 🐾 🏕 ♨️ ⛺	
Leisure activities : ✗ 🏠 🎣 ⛵ 🚣 ♨ pedalos 🛶	**G P S** Longitude : 2.79853 Latitude : 46.73515
Facilities : ♿ ⊶ 🚮 launderette	

Some information or pricing may have changed since the guide went to press. We recommend you check the price list online in advance or at the entrance to the campsite and enquire about possible restrictions.

BLÉRÉ

37150 – Michelin map **317** O5 – pop. 4 576 – alt. 59
▶ Paris 234 – Blois 48 – Château-Renault 36 – Loches 25

🏔 Municipal la Gâtine

📞 02 47 57 92 60, www.campingblereplage.com

Address : rue du Commandant-Lemaître

4 ha (270 pitches) flat, grassy
Rentals : 2 canvas bungalows.

Surroundings : 🐾 ≼ ♨️	
Leisure activities : 🍴 🏠 🤸	**G P S** Longitude : 0.9959 Latitude : 47.328
Facilities : ♿ ⊶ 🚮 🏕 🚿 🚽 launderette	
Nearby : 🚴 🎣 ✗ 🏊 🚣 ♨	

BONNEVAL

28800 – Michelin map **311** E6 – pop. 4 565 – alt. 128
▶ Paris 117 – Ablis 61 – Chartres 31 – Châteaudun 14

🏔 Le Bois Chièvre

📞 02 37 47 54 01, www.bonnevalaufilduloir.com – 🏮

Address : route de Vouvray (located 1.5km south following signs for Conie and take turning to the right; beside the Loir)

Opening times : from beginning April to mid Oct.

4.5 ha/2.5 for camping (104 pitches) relatively flat, flat, grassy, gravelled, adjacent wood

Tariff : (2015 price) 18€ ✶✶ 🚗 📶 💡 (10A) – Extra per person 5€
Rental rates : (2015 price) (from beginning April to mid Oct.) – 3 🏠. Per night from 60 to 82€ – Per week from 320 to 430€
🚐 local sani-station – 20 📶
A pleasant wood of oak trees overlooking the Loir river.

Surroundings : 🐾 🏕 ♨️	
Leisure activities : 🏠 🤸 🎣 🚣	**G P S** Longitude : 1.3864 Latitude : 48.1708
Facilities : ♿ ⊶ 🚮 🚿 🚽 🏕 📶 🚻	
Nearby : ✗ 🏊	

BOURGES

18000 – Michelin map **323** K4 – pop. 66 786 – alt. 153
▶ Paris 244 – Châteauroux 65 – Dijon 254 – Nevers 69

🏔 Municipal Robinson

📞 02 48 20 16 85, www.ville.bourges.fr

Address : 26 boulevard de l'Industrie (head towards the southern exit along the N 144, follow the signs for Montluçon and take the turning to the left, near the Lac d'Auron, take exit A 71 and follow the signs for Bourges Centre)

Opening times : from beginning April to end Oct.

2.2 ha (107 pitches)

Tariff : 17.40€ ✶✶ 🚗 📶 💡 (16A) – Extra per person 4.50€

Not far from the town centre (1.2km), in a green setting, but choose the pitches away from the road.

Surroundings : 🏕 ♨️	
Leisure activities : 🎣	**G P S** Longitude : 2.39488 Latitude : 47.07232
Facilities : ♿ ⊶ 🖼 🚮 🏕 🚿 🚽 🚻 launderette	
Nearby : ✗ 🎣 🏊	

A chambre d'hôte is a guesthouse or B & B-style accommodation.

BOURGUEIL

37140 – Michelin map **317** J5 – pop. 3 924 – alt. 42
▶ Paris 281 – Angers 81 – Chinon 16 – Saumur 23

🏔 Municipal de Bourgueil

📞 02 47 97 85 62, www.bourgueil.fr

Address : 31 avenue du Général de Gaulle (1.5 km south along the D 749, follow the signs for Chinon)

Opening times : from mid May to mid Sept.

2 ha (87 pitches) flat, grassy
Tariff : (2015 price) ✶ 2.25€ 🚗 📶 6.65€ – 💡 (16A) 2.50€
Rental rates : (2015 price) (from mid May to mid Sept.) – 2 🏠. Per week from 250€
🚐 local sani-station – 2 📶 6.65€
In a green setting with plenty of shade, near a lake.

Surroundings : 🏕 ♨	
Leisure activities : 🤸	**G P S** Longitude : 0.16684 Latitude : 47.27381
Facilities : ♿ ⊶ 🚻 🖥	
Nearby : 🛒 🍴 🎣 ✗ 🎣 🛶 ⛵ pedalos	

Key to rentals symbols:

12 🏠	*Number of mobile homes*
20 🏠	*Number of chalets*
6 🛏	*Number of rooms to rent*
Per night 30–50€	*Minimum/maximum rate per night*
Per week 300–1,000€	*Minimum/maximum rate per week*

BRACIEUX

41250 – Michelin map **318** G6 – pop. 1 256 – alt. 70
▶ Paris 185 – Blois 19 – Montrichard 39 – Orléans 64

⚠ Indigo Les Châteaux

✆ 02 54 46 41 84, www.camping-indigo.com

Address : 11 rue Roger-Brun (take the northern exit, follow the signs for Blois; beside the Beuvron)

Opening times : from end March to beginning Nov.

8 ha (350 pitches) flat, grassy

Tariff : (2015 price) 30,20€ ✿✿ ⇌ 🅔 🅗 (10A) –
Extra per person 6.35€ – Reservation fee 13€

Rental rates : (2015 price) (from end March to beginning Nov.)
⚑ (1 chalet) – 6 'gypsy' caravans – 30 🚐 – 6 🏠 – 26 tent lodges. Per night from 40 to 108€ – Per week from 224 to 719€ – Reservation fee 13€

🚏 local sani-station 7€

In a wooded setting comprised of different types of trees.

Surroundings : 🏞 ♤♤
Leisure activities : 🍽✗ 🎠 🛶 🚲 ✗ 🎣 ⛷
Facilities : ⚑ ⟲ ▾ launderette
GPS Longitude : 1.53821
Latitude : 47.55117

BRIARE

45250 – Michelin map **318** N6 – pop. 5 688 – alt. 135
▶ Paris 160 – Orléans 85 – Gien 11 – Montargis 50

⚠ Onlycamp Le Martinet

✆ 02 38 31 24 50, http://lemartinet.onlycamp.fr

Address : at Val Martinet (located 1km north via the town centre, between the Loire river and the canal)

Opening times : from beginning April to end Sept.

4.5 ha (160 pitches) flat, grassy

Tariff : (2015 price) 20.50€ ✿✿ ⇌ 🅔 🅗 (10A) –
Extra per person 4.40€

🚏 local sani-station 5€

Surroundings : 🏞 ♤♤
Leisure activities : 🎣
Facilities : ⚑ ⟲ ⊟ ▦ ⚷ ▾ 🖽
Nearby : ⛷ 🎣
GPS Longitude : 2.72441
Latitude : 47.64226

BUZANÇAIS

36500 – Michelin map **323** E5 – pop. 4 501 – alt. 111
▶ Paris 286 – Le Blanc 47 – Châteauroux 25 – Châtellerault 78

⚠ La Tête Noire

✆ 02 54 84 17 27, www.camping-latetenoire.com

Address : to the northwest along the r. des Ponts; beside the Indre river, near the stadium

Opening times : from beginning April to mid Oct.

2.5 ha (100 pitches) flat, grassy

Tariff : (2015 price) 15€ ✿✿ ⇌ 🅔 🅗 (16A) – Extra per person 4€

Rental rates : (2015 price) (from beginning April to mid Oct.) –
4 🚐 – 2 yurts. Per night from 45 to 60€ – Per week from 315 to 420€ – Reservation fee 10€

🚏 9 🅔 15€ – 🔌 🅗 11€

Surroundings : 🏞 ♤♤
Leisure activities : 🍽 🎠 ⥇ hammam 🎣
Facilities : ⚑ ⟲ ⟲🖽 ⚷ ▾ 🖽
Nearby : 🛶 ✗ ✗ ⛷
GPS Longitude : 1.41805
Latitude : 46.89285

CANDÉ-SUR-BEUVRON

41120 – Michelin map **318** E7 – pop. 1 462 – alt. 70
▶ Paris 199 – Blois 15 – Chaumont-sur-Loire 7 – Montrichard 21

⚠ La Grande Tortue

✆ 02 54 44 15 20, www.la-grande-tortue.com

Address : 3 route de Pontlevoy (500m south along the D 751, follow the signs for Chaumont-sus-Loire and take the turning to the left, follow the signs for La Pieuse, not far from the Beuvron river)

Opening times : from mid April to mid Sept.

5 ha (169 pitches) flat and relatively flat, grassy, sandy

Tariff : 42€ ✿✿ ⇌ 🅔 🅗 (10A) – Extra per person 10.50€ –
Reservation fee 12€

Rental rates : (from mid April to mid Sept.) ⚑ – 39 🚐 – 3 🏠.
Per night from 62 to 150€ – Per week from 290 to 930€ –
Reservation fee 12€

🚏 local sani-station 10€

Surroundings : 🏞 ⟷ ♤♤
Leisure activities : 🍽✗ 🎠 ⥇ 🛶 🚲 🎣
(open air in season) ⛷ water park
Facilities : ⚑ ⟲ ⟲🖽 ⚷ ▾ 🖽 ⛲ 🚿
GPS Longitude : 1.2583
Latitude : 47.48992

This guide is updated regularly, so buy your new copy every year!

CHAILLAC

36310 – Michelin map **323** D8 – pop. 1 136 – alt. 180
▶ Paris 333 – Argenton-sur-Creuse 35 – Le Blanc 34 – Magnac-Laval 34

⚠ Municipal les Vieux Chênes

✆ 02 54 25 61 39, www.chaillac36.fr

Address : allée des Vieux Chênes (southwest of the town, 500m from a lake)

2 ha (40 pitches)

Rentals : 3 🏠.

A green, well-kept site with flowers, close to the stadium and beside a lake.

Surroundings : 🏞 ⟷ ♤♤
Leisure activities : ⥇ 🎣 fitness trail
Facilities : ⟲ ▦ ⚷ 🖽
Nearby : ✗ ⥇ ⛷ pedalos
GPS Longitude : 1.29539
Latitude : 46.43224

CHARTRES

28000 – Michelin map **311** E5 – pop. 39 122 – alt. 142
▶ Paris 92 – Orléans 84 – Dreux 38 – Rambouillet 45

⚠ Les Bords de l'Eure

✆ 02 37 28 79 43, www.auxbordsdeleure.com

Address : 9 rue de Launay

4 ha (110 pitches) flat, grassy

Rentals : 2 'gypsy' caravans – 1 🚐.

In a pleasant wooded setting near the river.

Surroundings : ♤♤
Leisure activities : 🎠 ⥇ 🎣 pedalos
Facilities : ⚑ ⟲ ▦ ⚷ ▾ 🖽
Nearby : ✗ 🎣 sports trail
GPS Longitude : 1.4951
Latitude : 48.43265

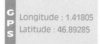

CHÂTEAUMEILLANT

18370 – Michelin map **323** J7 – pop. 2 082 – alt. 247
▸ Paris 313 – Aubusson 79 – Bourges 66 – La Châtre 19

⚠ Municipal l'Étang Merlin

📞 02 48 61 31 38, www.camping-etangmerlin.e-monsite.com

Address : route de Vicq (located 1km northwest along the D 70, follow the signs for Beddes and take D 80 to the left)

Opening times : from beginning May to end Sept.

1.5 ha (30 pitches) flat, grassy

Tariff : (2015 price) 11.50 € ★★ ⇔ ▣ ⚡ (10A) – Extra per person 3 €
Rental rates : (2015 price) permanent ♿ – 2 🚐 – 6 🏠 – 10 🛏. Per night from 28 to 50 € – Per week from 160 to 299 €

The chalets are in a pleasant setting beside the lake.

Surroundings : 🗔 ♨
Leisure activities : 🏕 🚣 🚴 🎣
Facilities : ♿ ⚡ 🪑 🚿 🍽 🔥
Nearby : 🍴 🏊

Longitude : 2.19034
Latitude : 46.56818

CHÂTEAUROUX

36000 – Michelin map **323** G6 – pop. 46 386 – alt. 155
▸ Paris 265 – Blois 101 – Bourges 65 – Châtellerault 98

⚠ Le Rochat Belle-Isle

📞 02 54 08 96 29, camping.lerochat@orange.fr

Address : 17 avenue du Parc de Loisirs (continue north along the av. de Paris and take turning to the left; beside the Indre river and 100m from a small lake)

Opening times : from end March to end Oct.

4 ha (205 pitches) flat, grassy

Tariff : 19.30 € ★★ ⇔ ▣ ⚡ (10A) – Extra per person 4.30 € – Reservation fee 10 €
Rental rates : (from end March to end Oct.) – 6 🚐. Per night from 68 € – Per week from 183 to 525 € – Reservation fee 20 €
🚉 Flot Bleu sani-station 5 € – 🚰 11 €
There's a free bus service nearby to the town centre.

Surroundings : 🗔 ♨♨
Leisure activities : 🏕 🚣 🚴
Facilities : ♿ ⚡ 🅲 📶 🚿 🪑 🍽 launderette
Nearby : 🍷 🍴 ✕ 🏊 🛶 🏄 bowling, fitness trail

Longitude : 1.69472
Latitude : 46.8236

CHÂTILLON-COLIGNY

45230 – Michelin map **318** O5 – pop. 1 962 – alt. 130
▸ Paris 140 – Auxerre 70 – Gien 26 – Joigny 48

⚠ Municipal de la Lancière

📞 06 16 09 30 26, lalanciere@wanadoo.fr – limited spaces for one-night stay

Address : route de la Lancière (south of the town, between the Loing river and the Briare canal)

1.9 ha (55 pitches) flat, grassy

Surroundings : 🗔 ♨♨
Leisure activities : 🚣 🏊 (small swimming pool)
Facilities : ⚡ launderette, refrigerated food storage facilities
Nearby : ⚓

Longitude : 2.84394
Latitude : 47.81816

CHAUMONT-SUR-LOIRE

41150 – Michelin map **318** E7 – pop. 1 037 – alt. 69
▸ Paris 201 – Amboise 21 – Blois 18 – Contres 24

⚠ Municipal Grosse Grève

📞 02 54 20 95 22, www.chaumont-sur-loire.fr –

Address : 81 rue du Maréchal de Lattre-de-Tassigny (take the eastern exit along the D 751, follow the signs for Blois and take the turning to the left, before the bridge; beside the Loire river)

Opening times : from end April to end Sept.

4 ha (150 pitches)

Tariff : (2015 price) ★ 3.10 € ⇔ 1 € ▣ 2.10 € – ⚡ (10A) 2.10 €
🚉 Eurorelais sani-station 2 €
Leisure activities : 🚣 🎣
Facilities : ♿ ⚡ 🍽 launderette
Nearby : 🏊 🚴

Longitude : 1.1999
Latitude : 47.48579

CHÉMERY

41700 – Michelin map **318** F7 – pop. 940 – alt. 90
▸ Paris 213 – Blois 32 – Montrichard 29 – Romorantin-Lanthenay 29

⚠ Le Gué

📞 06 14 84 11 34, www.camping-le-gue.com

Address : route de Couddes (to the west of the village; beside a stream)

Opening times : from beginning April to end Sept.

1.2 ha (50 pitches) flat, grassy

Tariff : (2015 price) 17.40 € ★★ ⇔ ▣ ⚡ (10A) – Extra per person 3.60 €
Rental rates : (2015 price) (from beginning April to end Sept.) 🏄 – 3 🚐. Per week from 470 to 599 €
🚉 local sani-station 3.50 €

Surroundings : 🌳 ♨
Leisure activities : 🏊
Facilities : ♿ ⚡ 🚿 🍽 🔥
Nearby : 🎣

Longitude : 1.47388
Latitude : 47.34562

CHEMILLÉ-SUR-INDROIS

37460 – Michelin map **317** P6 – pop. 221 – alt. 97
▸ Paris 244 – Châtillon-sur-Indre 25 – Loches 16 – Montrichard 27

⚠ Les Coteaux du Lac

📞 02 47 92 77 83, www.lescoteauxdulac.com

Address : at the leisure centre (to the southwest of the village)

Opening times : from end March to beginning Oct.

2 ha (72 pitches) flat, relatively flat, grassy

Tariff : 28 € ★★ ⇔ ▣ ⚡ (16A) – Extra per person 6.20 € – Reservation fee 14 €
Rental rates : (2015 price) (from end March to beginning Oct.) ♿ – 29 🏠 – 4 canvas bungalows. Per night from 50 to 154 € – Per week from 209 to 1,078 € – Reservation fee 14 €
🚉 local sani-station – 4 ▣ 13 € – 🚰 13 €
An attractive location near a lake.

Surroundings : ⟨
Leisure activities : 🚴 🏊
Facilities : ♿ ⚡ 🍽 🚿
Nearby : 🍷 ✕ 🚣 🎣 🛶 🚴 pedalos

Longitude : 1.15889
Latitude : 47.15772

CHEVERNY

41700 – Michelin map **318** F7 – pop. 939 – alt. 110
▶ Paris 194 – Blois 14 – Châteauroux 88 – Orléans 73

▲▲ Sites et Paysages Les Saules ♣♟

Les Saules

📞 02 54 79 90 01, www.camping-cheverny.com

Address : route de Contres (3km southeast along the D 102)

Opening times : from beginning April to mid Sept.

8 ha (164 pitches) flat, grassy

Tariff : 36€ ♥♥ ⇔ 🖭 🔌 (10A) – Extra per person 4.50€

Rental rates : (from beginning April to mid Sept.) 🚿 (1 chalet) – 11 🏠 – 4 tent lodges. Per night from 45 to 170€ – Per week from 294 to 798€

🚐 local sani-station – 🚌 14€

Surroundings : 🌳🌳
Leisure activities : 🎣🍴 🏠 ⚡ ⚡ 🚴🏃 🛶 🎿 🎯 sports trail
Facilities : 🛁 ⛲ 🚰 🍴 launderette 🔌 🚿

GPS Longitude : 1.45184 — Latitude : 47.47871

CHINON

37500 – Michelin map **317** K6 – pop. 7 986 – alt. 40
▶ Paris 285 – Châtellerault 51 – Poitiers 80 – Saumur 29

▲ Intercommunal de l'île Auger

📞 02 47 93 08 35, www.camping-chinon.com

Address : quai Danton

Opening times : from beginning April to end Oct.

4 ha (200 pitches) flat, grassy

Tariff : (2015 price) ♥ 3.10€ ⇔ 🖭 6.30€ – 🔌 (12A) 3.40€

Rental rates : (2015 price) (from beginning May to end Sept.) – 7 canvas bungalows – 2 tent lodges. Per night from 30 to 65€ – Per week from 180 to 390€

🚐 local sani-station 4.80€

In a pleasant location opposite the château and beside the Vienne river.

Surroundings : ≼ town and Château de Chinon ♀
Leisure activities : ⚡🛶
Facilities : 🛁 ⛲ (summer) 🚿 🍴 🔥
Nearby : 🍴🎣🍴🎿 🎯 🛶

GPS Longitude : 0.23654 — Latitude : 47.16379

CLOYES-SUR-LE-LOIR

28220 – Michelin map **311** D8 – pop. 2 692 – alt. 97
▶ Paris 143 – Blois 54 – Chartres 57 – Châteaudun 13

▲▲▲ Parc de Loisirs - Le Val Fleuri

📞 02 37 98 50 53, www.val-fleuri.fr – limited spaces for one-night stay

Address : route de Montigny (take the northern exit along the N 10, follow the signs for Chartres then turn left onto D 23)

Opening times : from mid March to mid Nov.

5 ha (196 pitches) flat, grassy

Tariff : (2015 price) 30.50€ ♥♥ ⇔ 🖭 🔌 (6A) – Extra per person 7.60€ – Reservation fee 16€

Rental rates : (2015 price) (from mid March to mid Nov.) – 10 🏚. Per week from 295 to 815€ – Reservation fee 22€

In a pleasant location beside the Loir river.

Surroundings : 🗒 ♀
Leisure activities : 🎣🍴 🏠 ⚡ 🚴🏃 🛶 🎿 🎿 pedalos 🚣
Facilities : 🛁 ⛲ 🚰 🚿 🍴 launderette 🔌 🚿
Nearby : 🍴 🎣

GPS Longitude : 1.2333 — Latitude : 48.0024

COURVILLE-SUR-EURE

28190 – Michelin map **311** D5 – pop. 2 776 – alt. 170
▶ Paris 111 – Bonneval 47 – Chartres 20 – Dreux 37

▲ Municipal les Bords de l'Eure

📞 02 37 23 76 38, www.courville-sur-eure.fr – 🏪

Address : rue Thiers (take the southern exit along the D 114)

Opening times : permanent

1.5 ha (56 pitches) flat, grassy

Tariff : (2015 price) ♥ 5.97€ ⇔ 🖭 4.62€ – 🔌 (6A) 3.96€

🚐 local sani-station – 12 🖭

A wooded setting on the banks of the river.

Surroundings : 🗒 ♀
Leisure activities : 🛶
Facilities : 🛁 ⛲ 🚰 🔥
Nearby : ⚡ 🎿

GPS Longitude : 1.2414 — Latitude : 48.4462

DESCARTES

37160 – Michelin map **317** N7 – pop. 3 817 – alt. 50
▶ Paris 292 – Châteauroux 94 – Châtellerault 24 – Chinon 51

▲ Municipal la Grosse Motte

📞 02 47 59 85 90, www.ville-descartes.fr

Address : allée Léo Lagrange (take the southern exit along the D 750, follow the signs for Le Blanc and take boulevard to the right; beside the Creuse river)

Opening times : from beginning May to end Sept.

1 ha (50 pitches) flat, grassy, undulating

Tariff : (2015 price) 10,50€ ♥♥ ⇔ 🖭 🔌 (10A) – Extra per person 3€

Rental rates : (2015 price) permanent – 8 🏠 – 1 gîte. Per week from 340 to 400€

🚐 4 🖭 12.50€

In a shady park next to a leisure centre and the municipal gardens.

Surroundings : 🎣 🗒 🌳🌳
Leisure activities : 🚴 🛶
Facilities : 🚿 🍴
Nearby : 🍴 ⚡ 🏃 🎿 🛶

GPS Longitude : 0.69715 — Latitude : 46.96961

ÉGUZON

36270 – Michelin map **323** F8 – pop. 1 362 – alt. 243
▶ Paris 319 – Argenton-sur-Creuse 20 – La Châtre 47 – Guéret 50

▲▲▲ Municipal du Lac Les Nugiras

📞 02 54 47 45 22, www.campingmunicipal-eguzon.com

Address : route de Messant (3km southeast along the D 36, follow the signs for the Lac de Chambon then continue 500m along the turning to the right; 450m from the lake)

Opening times : permanent

4 ha (180 pitches) terraced, relatively flat, flat, grassy, stony

Tariff : (2015 price) 13.70€ ♥♥ ⇔ 🖭 🔌 (10A) – Extra per person 3.49€

local sani-station 5.30€

A peaceful site laid out on terraces, near a well-equipped boating centre.

Surroundings : ≤ ♀
Leisure activities : ☕ 🍴 ⛵ ⛵ multi-sports ground
Facilities : ♿ ⌕ ▥ ♨ ⚲ ☂ 🍴 📷 ⚟
Nearby : 🚲 ≋ (beach) ⛷ ⚲ ♨ water skiing

Longitude : 1.604
Latitude : 46.433

FONTAINE-SIMON

28240 – Michelin map **311** C4 – pop. 870 – alt. 200
▷ Paris 117 – Chartres 40 – Dreux 40 – Évreux 66

⚠ Du Perche

☏ 02 37 81 88 11, www.campingduperche.com

Address : rue de la Ferrière (1.2km north following signs for Senonches and take turning to the left)

Opening times : permanent

5 ha (115 pitches) flat, grassy

Tariff : (2015 price) 30€ ⚭ ⚭ �car 🔲 ⚡ (6A) – Extra per person 4€
Rental rates : (2015 price) permanent ⚟ – 2 🏚 – 2 🏠. Per week from 340 to 900€
local sani-station – 7 🔲

Beside the Eure river and a lake.

Leisure activities : ⛷ ⚲
Facilities : ♿ ⌕ (July-Aug.) ☂ 🍴 📷
Nearby : 🍴 🔲 ≋ ⛷

Longitude : 1.0194
Latitude : 48.5132

GARGILESSE-DAMPIERRE

36190 – Michelin map **323** F7 – pop. 326 – alt. 220
▷ Paris 310 – Châteauroux 45 – Guéret 59 – Poitiers 113

⚠ La Chaumerette

☏ 02 54 47 84 22, www.gargilesse.fr

Address : at Le Moulin (1.4km southwest along the D 39, follow the signs for Argenton-sur-Creuse and take the road to the left leading to the Barrage de La Roche au Moine – dam)

Opening times : from beginning May to end Sept.

2.6 ha (72 pitches) flat, grassy

Tariff : (2015 price) ⚭ 1.90€ 🚗 🔲 6.60€ – ⚡ (10A) 4.80€
Rental rates : (2015 price) (from beginning March to end Nov.) – 8 🏠. Per night from 26 to 45€ – Per week from 175 to 300€

In a picturesque setting, part of the site is on an island in the Creuse river.

Surroundings : ≋ ♀♀
Leisure activities : 🍴 🍴 ⚲
Facilities : ♿ ⌕ 🍴

Longitude : 1.58346
Latitude : 46.5077

GIEN

45500 – Michelin map **318** M5 – pop. 15 161 – alt. 162
▷ Paris 149 – Auxerre 85 – Bourges 77 – Cosne-sur-Loire 46

⚠⚠ Les Bois du Bardelet ⚭

☏ 02 38 67 47 39, www.bardelet.com

Address : at Le Petit Bardelet, route de Bourges (5km southwest along the D 940 et 2km along the turning to the left – recommended route for vehicles coming from Gien, take the D 53, follow the signs for Poilly-lez-Gien and take first turning to the right)

Opening times : from beginning April to end Sept.

15 ha/8 for camping (260 pitches)

Tariff : 37.30€ ⚭ ⚭ 🚗 🔲 ⚡ (10A) – Extra per person 7.60€ – Reservation fee 9€

Rental rates : (from beginning April to end Sept.) ⚟ Ⓟ – 33 🏚 – 45 🏠. Per night from 52 to 160€ – Per week from 364 to 1,120€ – Reservation fee 9€

local sani-station – 25 🔲 27.80€ – ⚡12.50€

Surroundings : ≋ ♀♀
Leisure activities : 🍴 🍴 ♨ ⛷ ♬ ≋ jacuzzi
⛷ 🚲 ✂ ♬ 🔲 ⚲ ⚲ ♨
Facilities : ♿ ⌕ ▥ ☂ – 4 individual sanitary facilities (♨ ☂ wc) ☂ 🍴 launderette ⚟ ☂

LA GUERCHE-SUR-L'AUBOIS

18150 – Michelin map **323** N5 – pop. 3 395 – alt. 184
▷ Paris 242 – Bourges 48 – La Charité-sur-Loire 31 – Nevers 22

⚠ Municipal le Robinson

☏ 02 48 74 18 86, www.camping-robinson-la-guerche-sur-aubois.fr

Address : 2 rue de Couvache (1.4km southeast along the D 200, follow the signs for Apremont then take a right turn, 600m along the D 218 and take road to the left)

Opening times : permanent

1.5 ha (33 pitches)

Tariff : 15€ ⚭ ⚭ 🚗 🔲 ⚡ (16A) – Extra per person 2.50€
Rental rates : permanent – 6 🏠. Per night from €50 to 62 – Per week from 320 to 417€

local sani-station 1€ – 35 🔲 16€ – ⚡8€

A pleasant location beside a small lake, with very old chalets, some adjacent to each other.

Surroundings : ≋ ⛆ ♀♀
Leisure activities : 🔲 ⛷ 🚲 ⚲
Facilities : ♿ ⌕ 🍴 📷
Nearby : 🍴 ⛷ ♨ pedalos

Longitude : 2.95872
Latitude : 46.94029

The guide covers all 22 regions of France – see the map and list of regions on pages 4–5.

L'ÎLE-BOUCHARD

37220 – Michelin map **317** L6 – pop. 1 754 – alt. 41
▷ Paris 284 – Châteauroux 118 – Châtellerault 49 – Chinon 16

⚠ Les Bords de Vienne

☏ 02 47 95 23 59, info@campingbordsdevienne.com

Address : 4 allée du camping (near the quartier (district) of St-Gilles, upstream of the bridge over the Vienne, near the river)

Opening times : from beginning March to end Oct.

2 ha (90 pitches) flat, grassy

Tariff : (2015 price) 21,50€ ⚭ ⚭ 🚗 🔲 – Extra per person 5.20€
Rental rates : (2015 price) (from beginning March to end Oct.) – 1 gîte. Per week from 229 to 519€

Eurorelais sani-station 4€

Surroundings : ♀♀
Leisure activities : ⛷ ⚲
Facilities : ♿ ⌕ 🍴 📷
Nearby : 🛒 ✂

Longitude : 0.42833
Latitude : 47.12139

ISDES

45620 – Michelin map **318** K5 – pop. 612 – alt. 152
▶ Paris 174 – Bourges 75 – Gien 35 – Orléans 40

⚕ Municipal les Prés Bas

🖉 06 78 43 46 28, www.isdes.fr

Address : take the northeastern exit along the D 59, near a lake

Opening times : from beginning April to end Oct.

0.5 ha (20 pitches) flat, grassy

Tariff : (2015 price) 🛉 5€ 🚗 1.50€ 🗐 5€ 🔌 (6A)

🚿 Eurorelais sani-station 5€

Surroundings : 🏕	
Leisure activities : 🎣	**G P S** Longitude : 2.2565
Facilities : ⚙⚙⚙⚙⚙	Latitude : 47.6744
Nearby : 🎠🏹	

The pitches of many campsites are marked out with low hedges of attractive bushes and shrubs.

LORRIS

45260 – Michelin map **318** M4 – pop. 2 941 – alt. 126
▶ Paris 132 – Gien 27 – Montargis 23 – Orléans 55

⛰ L'Étang des Bois

🖉 02 38 92 32 00, www.canal-orleans.fr

Address : 6km west along the D 88, follow the signs for Châteauneuf-sur-Loire, near the lake at Les Bois

Opening times : from beginning April to end Sept.

3 ha (150 pitches) grassy

Tariff : (2015 price) 🛉 3.80€ 🚗 🗐 6.20€ – 🔌 (10A) 4.65€

Rental rates : (2015 price) (from beginning April to end Sept.) – 4 🛖. Per night from 52 to 67€ – Per week from 320 to 435€

A wooded setting in a pleasant location.

Surroundings : 🏕 ♨♨	
Leisure activities : 🏛 m	**G P S** Longitude : 2.44454
Facilities : ⚙⚙⚙⚙⚙⚙	Latitude : 47.87393
Nearby : 🍴 🏞 🏖 (beach) 🏇	

LUÇAY-LE-MÂLE

36360 – Michelin map **323** E4 – pop. 1 496 – alt. 160
▶ Paris 240 – Le Blanc 73 – Blois 60 – Châteauroux 43

⚕ Municipal la Foulquetière

🖉 02 54 40 43 31, www.lucaylemale.fr

Address : at La Foulquetière (3.8km southwest along the D 960, follow the signs for Loches, D 13, follow the signs for Ecueillé to the left and take the road to the right)

Opening times : from beginning April to mid Oct.

1.5 ha (30 pitches) flat and relatively flat, grassy

Tariff : (2015 price) 🛉 2€ 🚗 🗐 2€ – 🔌 (6A) 1.50€

Rental rates : permanent – 3 🛖 – 2 gîtes. Per night from 92€ – Per week from 275 to 345€

🚿 local sani-station 3€

80m from a small lake that is very popular with anglers.

Surroundings : 🏞 🏕 ♀	
Leisure activities : 🎣🏊	**G P S** Longitude : 1.40417
Facilities : ⚙⚙⚙⚙⚙	Latitude : 47.1109
Nearby : 🍴🍴 🏖🍴 🏖 (beach) 🚣 pedalos	

LUNERY

18400 – Michelin map **323** J5 – pop. 1 449 – alt. 150
▶ Paris 256 – Bourges 23 – Châteauroux 51 – Issoudun 28

⚕ Intercommunal de Lunery

🖉 02 48 68 07 38, www.cc-fercher.fr

Address : 6 rue de l'Abreuvoir

Opening times : from beginning May to mid Sept.

0.5 ha (37 pitches) flat, grassy

Tariff : (2015 price) 12€ 🛉🛉 🚗 🗐 🔌 (6A) – Extra per person 3€

🚿 local sani-station

Near the remains of an old windmill near the Cher river.

Surroundings : 🏞 🏕 ♨♨	
Leisure activities : 🏛🏊	**G P S** Longitude : 2.27038
Facilities : ⚙⚙⚙⚙	Latitude : 46.93658
Nearby : 🍴🍴🍴	

MARCILLY-SUR-VIENNE

37800 – Michelin map **317** M6 – pop. 559 – alt. 60
▶ Paris 280 – Azay-le-Rideau 32 – Chinon 30 – Châtellerault 29

⚕ Intercommunal la Croix de la Motte

🖉 02 47 65 20 38, www.cc-saintemauredetouraine.fr

Address : 1.2km north along the D 18, follow the signs for L'Ile-Bouchard and take turning to the right

Opening times : from mid June to mid Sept.

1.5 ha (61 pitches) flat, grassy

Tariff : (2015 price) 🛉 2,60€ 🚗 🗐 3,10€ – 🔌 (16A) 3.10€

Rental rates : (2015 price) (from beginning May to end Oct.) 🏊 – 2 🛖 – 1 canvas bungalow. Per night from 24 to 27€ – Per week from 155 to 325€

🚿 local sani-station 4.20€

Situated in pleasant, shaded surroundings near the Vienne river.

Surroundings : 🏞 🏕 ♀	
Leisure activities : 🏊🏊 🎣	**G P S** Longitude : 0.54337
Facilities : ⚙⚙⚙⚙⚙	Latitude : 47.05075

We have selected the best campsites in France with our usual care, listing those with the best facilities in the most pleasant surroundings.

MENNETOU-SUR-CHER

41320 – Michelin map **318** I8 – pop. 878 – alt. 100
▶ Paris 209 – Bourges 56 – Romorantin-Lanthenay 18 – Selles-sur-Cher 27

⚕ Municipal Val Rose

🖉 02 54 98 11 02, mairie.mennetou@wanadoo.fr

Address : rue de Val Rose (south of the town, to the right after the bridge over the canal, 100m from the Cher river)

Opening times : from mid May to mid Sept.

0.8 ha (50 pitches) flat, grassy

Tariff : 🛉 2.50€ 🚗 🗐 3.50€ – 🔌 (6A) 3€

🚿 Eurorelais sani-station 2€ – 🚐 🔌 8€

Surroundings : 🏕 ♀	
Facilities : ⚙⚙⚙	**G P S** Longitude : 1.86173
Nearby : 🍴 🏊 🎣	Latitude : 47.26937

MESLAND

41150 – Michelin map **318** D6 – pop. 547 – alt. 79
▶ Paris 205 – Amboise 19 – Blois 23 – Château-Renault 20

⚠ Yelloh! Village Parc du Val de Loire 👥

✆ 02 54 70 27 18, www.parcduvaldeloire.com

Address : 155 route de Fleuray (located 1.5km west)

Opening times : from beginning April to mid Sept.

15 ha (300 pitches) flat, relatively flat, grassy

Tariff : 18€ ♥ ♥ 🚐 🔲 ⚡ (10A) – Extra per person 6€

Rental rates : (from beginning April to mid Sept.) 🚲 – 130 🚲 – 20 🏕 – 2 canvas bungalows – 3 tent lodges. Per night from 30 to 141€ – Per week from 210 to 987€

In a wooded setting opposite a vineyard.

Surroundings : 🐟 📮 ᲲᲲ	**G**	Longitude : 1.10477
Leisure activities : ♀ ✕ 🎪 🏃 🎿 🚴 🎯 🎣 🏓 🎱 🎳	**P**	Latitude : 47.51001
Facilities : ♿ 🚿 🍽 🏧 🚰 📮 🚮	**S**	

Using the traditional Michelin classification method, the guide provides you with an easy, speedy reference for assessing the category of each site: 1 to 5 tents (see page 10).

MONTARGIS

45200 – Michelin map **318** N4 – pop. 15 020 – alt. 95
▶ Paris 109 – Auxerre 252 – Nemours 36 – Nevers 126

⚠ Municipal de la Forêt

✆ 02 38 98 00 20, www.agglo-montargoise.fr

Address : 38 avenue Louis-Maurice Chautemps (take the northern exit along the D 943 and continue 1km along the D 815, follow the signs for Paucourt)

Opening times : from beginning Feb. to end Nov.

5.5 ha (100 pitches) flat, grassy, stony, sandy

Tariff : (2015 price) ♥ 3.40€ 🚐 2.45€ 🔲 3.15€ – ⚡ (10A) 8€

🚲 Eurorelais sani-station 3.85€ – 🚿 ⚡ 8.30€

Surroundings : ᲲᲲᲲ	**G**	Longitude : 2.75102
Leisure activities : 🎪 🏃	**P**	Latitude : 48.00827
Facilities : ♿ 🚿 🏧 🚰 🚮 🍽	**S**	
Nearby : 🎱 🎿		

MONTBAZON

37250 – Michelin map **317** N5 – pop. 3 904 – alt. 59
▶ Paris 247 – Châtellerault 59 – Chinon 41 – Loches 33

⚠ La Grange Rouge

✆ 02 47 26 06 43, www.camping-montbazon.com

Address : route de Tours, RD 910 (after the bridge over the Indre; behind the tourist office and near the stadium)

2 ha (108 pitches) flat, grassy

Rentals : 15 🚲.

In a pleasant location beside the Indre river and near the town centre.

Surroundings : ᲲᲲ	**G**	Longitude : 0.7159
Leisure activities : ✕ 🎪 🏃 🎿	**P**	Latitude : 47.29049
Facilities : ♿ 🚿 🏧 🍽 📮	**S**	
Nearby : 🎱 🖼 ♿ sports trail		

MONTLOUIS-SUR-LOIRE

37270 – Michelin map **317** N4 – pop. 10 448 – alt. 60
▶ Paris 235 – Amboise 14 – Blois 49 – Château-Renault 32

⚠ Aquadis Loisirs Les Peupliers

✆ 02 47 50 81 90, http://www.aquadis-loisirs.com/camping-les-peupliers/

Address : located 1.5km west along the D 751, follow the signs for Tours, 100m from the Loire river

Opening times : from end March to end Oct.

6 ha (252 pitches) flat, grassy

Tariff : 18€ ♥ ♥ 🚐 🔲 ⚡ (10A) – Extra per person 3.85€ – Reservation fee 10€

Rental rates : (from end March to end Oct.) – 11 🚲. Per night from 62 to 80€ – Per week from 255 to 539€ – Reservation fee 20€

🚲 AireService sani-station – 🚿 11€

A pleasant wooded site.

Surroundings : 📮 ᲲᲲ	**G**	Longitude : 0.81144
Leisure activities : ♀ ✕ 🎪 🏃 🚴 🎯	**P**	Latitude : 47.39437
Facilities : ♿ 🚿 🔲 🍽 📮 🚮	**S**	
Nearby : 🎱 🎿 🎣		

MONTOIRE-SUR-LE-LOIR

41800 – Michelin map **318** C5 – pop. 4 081 – alt. 65
▶ Paris 186 – Blois 52 – Château-Renault 21 – La Flèche 81

⚠ Municipal les Reclusages

✆ 02 54 85 02 53, www.mairie-montoire.fr

Address : at Les Reclusages (southwestern exit, follow the signs for Tours and follow the signs for Lavardin to the left after the bridge)

Opening times : from beginning April to end Sept.

2 ha (120 pitches) flat, grassy

Tariff : ♥ 4.20€ 🚐 🔲 2.30€ – ⚡ (10A) 4.30€

Rental rates : permanent – 4 🚲. Per night from €69 to 100 – Per week from 236 to 377€

Beside the Loir river.

Surroundings : ᲲᲲ	**G**	Longitude : 0.86289
Leisure activities : 🎪 🎿	**P**	Latitude : 47.74788
Facilities : ♿ 🚿 🍽 📮	**S**	
Nearby : 🏃 🎱 🎿		

MORÉE

41160 – Michelin map **318** E4 – pop. 1 117 – alt. 96
▶ Paris 154 – Blois 42 – Châteaudun 24 – Orléans 58

⚠ Municipal de la Varenne

✆ 02 54 82 06 16, facebook : Camping de l'etang de la varenne

Address : chemin de la Varenne (to the west of the town; beside a small lake, recommended route via the D 19, follow the signs for St-Hilaire-la-Gravelle and take road to the left)

Opening times : from mid March to mid Nov.

0.8 ha (42 pitches) flat, grassy

Tariff : 14.50€ ♥ ♥ 🚐 🔲 ⚡ (10A) – Extra per person 4€

Rental rates : (from mid March to mid Nov.) – 2 🚲 – 2 🏕. Per night from 32 to 50€ – Per week from 180 to 400€

🚲 Flot Bleu sani-station 3€ – 🚿 ⚡ 11€

Surroundings : 🐟	**G**	Longitude : 1.23424
Leisure activities : ♀ ✕ 🏖 (beach) 🎿 🏊	**P**	Latitude : 47.9031
Facilities : ♿ 🚿 🚰 🍽 📮	**S**	
Nearby : 🏃		

MUIDES-SUR-LOIRE

41500 – Michelin map **318** G5 – pop. 1 350 – alt. 82
▶ Paris 169 – Beaugency 17 – Blois 20 – Chambord 9

▲▲▲ Château des Marais ▲▴

🔗 02 54 87 05 42, http://www.chateau-des-marais.com

Address : 27 rue de Chambord (to the southeast along the D 103, follow the signs for Crouy-sur-Cosson; for caravans, access via the D 112 and take D 103 to the right)

Opening times : from beginning May to mid Sept.

8 ha (299 pitches) flat, grassy

Tariff : 50€ ✦✦ ⚊ 🔲 🅿 (10A) – Extra per person 9€ – Reservation fee 15€

Rental rates : (from mid April to mid Sept.) 🏕 – 22 🚐 – 18 🏠 – 1 cabin in the trees. Per night from 68 to 176€ – Per week from 476 to 1,232€ – Reservation fee 15€

🚉 25 🔲 28€

In the pleasantly wooded grounds of a 17th-century château.

Surroundings : 🌲 ⛲ ♨♨
Leisure activities : 🍸 🍴 🎰 🎆 nighttime 🎿
♨ hammam 🏇 🚵 🎣 🛝 ⛳ 🏊
Facilities : ♿ ⚊ 🚿 🛁 🛗 🍴 launderette
🚽 🚰

Longitude : 1.52897
Latitude : 47.66585

▲ Municipal Bellevue

🔗 02 54 87 01 56, mairie.muides@wanadoo.fr – ⛺

Address : avenue de la Loire (north of the town along the D 112, follow the signs for Mer and take the turning to the left before the bridge; near the Loire)

Opening times : from mid April to mid Sept.

2.5 ha (100 pitches)

Tariff : 18,90€ ✦✦ ⚊ 🔲 🅿 (5A) – Extra per person 4.60€

🚉 local sani-station 10€

Facilities : ♿ ⚊ (June-Aug) 🍴 🔳
Nearby : 🏇 🏊 🍴

Longitude : 1.52607
Latitude : 47.67178

We value your opinion and welcome your feedback.
Do email us at campingfrance@tp.michelin.com

NEUNG-SUR-BEUVRON

41210 – Michelin map **318** H6 – pop. 1 223 – alt. 102
▶ Paris 183 – Beaugency 33 – Blois 39 – Lamotte-Beuvron 20

▲ Municipal de la Varenne

🔗 02 54 83 68 52, www.neung-sur-beuvron.fr

Address : 34 rue de Veillas (located 1km to the northeast, access via the turning to the left of the church; near the Beuvron)

Opening times : from beginning April to mid Oct.

4 ha (73 pitches) relatively flat, flat, grassy, sandy

Tariff : (2015 price) 12.20€ ✦✦ ⚊ 🔲 🅿 (10A) – Extra per person 2.80€

Rental rates : (2015 price) (from beginning April to mid Oct.) – 4 🚐. Per night from 57€ – Per week from 240 to 415€ – Reservation fee 60€

🚉 local sani-station

A pleasant wooded site.

Surroundings : 🌲 ⛲ ♨♨
Leisure activities : 🎰 🎣 🏊
Facilities : ♿ ⚊ 🍴 🔳

Longitude : 1.81507
Latitude : 47.53849

NEUVY-ST-SÉPULCHRE

36230 – Michelin map **323** G7 – pop. 1 690 – alt. 186
▶ Paris 295 – Argenton-sur-Creuse 24 – Châteauroux 29 – La Châtre 16

▲ Municipal les Frênes

🔗 02 54 30 82 51, www.campingdeneuvy.fr.nf

Address : route de l'Augère (take the western exit along the D 927, follow the signs for Argenton-sur-Creuse then continue 600m along the turning to the left and take the road to the right, 100m from a lake and the Bouzanne river)

Opening times : from mid June to mid Sept.

1 ha (35 pitches) flat, grassy

Tariff : (2015 price) 11,50€ ✦✦ ⚊ 🔲 🅿 (9A) – Extra per person 2€

Rental rates : (2015 price) permanent 🏕 – 2 🏠. Per night from 90€ – Per week from 240 to 270€

Surroundings : 🌲 ⛲ ♨
Leisure activities : 🏇 🏊
Facilities : ⚊ 🛁 🛗 🍴 launderette
Nearby : 🍸 🍴 🛝 🏊

Longitude : 1.7828
Latitude : 46.5903

Do not confuse:
▲ *to* ▲▲▲ *: MICHELIN classification with*
★ *to* ★★★★★ *: official classification*

NOUAN-LE-FUZELIER

41600 – Michelin map **318** J6 – pop. 2 439 – alt. 113
▶ Paris 177 – Blois 59 – Cosne-sur-Loire 74 – Gien 56

▲▲▲ La Grande Sologne ▲▴

🔗 02 54 88 70 22, www.campinggrandesologne.com

Address : rue des Peupliers (take the southern exit along the D 2020, then the road to the left opposite the station)

Opening times : from beginning April to mid Oct.

10 ha/4 for camping (180 pitches) flat, grassy

Tariff : (2015 price) ✦ 6.10€ ⚊ 🔲 🅿 (10A) 3.10€

Rental rates : (2015 price) (from beginning April to mid Oct.) – 10 🚐 – 4 canvas bungalows. Per night from 26 to 79€ – Per week from 182 to 700€

🚉 local sani-station

In a wooded setting beside a lake.

Surroundings : ♨♨
Leisure activities : 🎣 🎰 🎿 🏇 🚵 🛝 🏊
Facilities : ♿ ⚊ 🔳 🍴 🛗 🔳 🚿
Nearby : 🍸 🏊 🏊

Longitude : 2.03631
Latitude : 47.53337

OLIVET

45160 – Michelin map **318** I4 – pop. 19 806 – alt. 100
▶ Paris 137 – Orléans 4 – Blois 70 – Chartres 78

▲ Municipal

🔗 02 38 63 53 94, www.camping-olivet.org

Address : rue du Pont Bouchet (situated 2km southeast along the D 14, follow the signs for St-Cyr-en-Val)

Opening times : from beginning April to end Sept.

1 ha (46 pitches) flat, grassy

Tariff : (2015 price) 23.40€ ✦✦ ⚊ 🔲 🅿 (16A) – Extra per person 5€

🚉 10 🔲 19.80€

A pleasant location where the Loiret and Dhuy rivers meet.

Surroundings : 🖵 💆💆
Leisure activities : 🎣
Facilities : 🕭 ⚬━ 🏢 🛁 ⛌ 🍴 🖼️
Nearby : 🏊 🛶

GPS Longitude : 1.92543
Latitude : 47.85601

PIERREFITTE-SUR-SAULDRE

41300 – Michelin map **318** J6 – pop. 848 – alt. 125
▶ Paris 185 – Aubigny-sur-Nère 23 – Blois 73 – Bourges 55

🏕️ Les Alicourts 👥

℘ 02 54 88 63 34, www.lesalicourts.com

Address : Domaine des Alicourts (6km northeast along the D 126 and take the D 126b; beside a small lake)

Opening times : from end April to beginning Sept.

21 ha/10 for camping (420 pitches)

Tariff : 52€ ✚✚ 🚗 🔌 (6A) – Extra per person 12€
Rental rates : (from end April to beginning Sept.) 🕭 (3 chalets) 🏚️ – 200 🛖 – 70 🏠 – 8 cabins in the trees. Per night from 44 to 266€ – Per week from 308 to 1,862€

🚐 local sani-station

A pretty, partially enclosed swimming area, upmarket spa centre and good-quality rental options.

Surroundings : 💆 🖵 💆💆
Leisure activities : 🍴 🍽️ 🏛️ 🎏 🏊 🚴 🎿 🍸
hammam, jacuzzi 🏋️ 🚴 🎯 🏐 🏊 🍱 🏖️
🐠 (beach) 🛶 pedalos, spa centre, entertainment room, skate park
Facilities : 🕭 ⚬━ 🏢 🛁 ⛌ 🍴 🍴 launderette 🚿🚽

GPS Longitude : 2.191
Latitude : 47.54482

There are several different types of sani-station ('borne' in French) – sanitation points providing fresh water and disposal points for grey water. See page 12 for further details.

PREUILLY-SUR-CLAISE

37290 – Michelin map **317** 07 – pop. 1 075 – alt. 80
▶ Paris 299 – Le Blanc 31 – Châteauroux 64 – Châtellerault 35

🛖 Municipal

℘ 02 47 94 50 04, www.preuillysurclaise.fr

Address : to the southwest of the town; near the swimming pool, the Claise river and a small lake

Opening times : from beginning June to end Sept.

0.7 ha (36 pitches) flat, grassy

Tariff : (2015 price) ✚ 2.50€ 🚗 🔌 3€ – 🔌 (6A) 4€
Rental rates : (2015 price) (from beginning June to end Sept.) – 2 🛖 – 5 gîtes. Per night from 50 to 60€ – Per week from 200 to 250€

🚐 AireService sani-station – 5 🔌 10€
In a green setting In a leisure centre.

Surroundings : 🖵 💆
Leisure activities : 🎣
Facilities : ⚬━ 🚿 🍴 🖼️
Nearby : 🏋️ 🎯 🏊 🛶 sports trail

GPS Longitude : 0.92618
Latitude : 46.85305

RIGNY-USSÉ

37420 – Michelin map **317** K5 – pop. 521 – alt. 36
▶ Paris 285 – Orléans 161 – Tours 40 – Nantes 178

🛖 Municipal La Blardière

℘ 02 47 95 55 85, www.rigny-usse.fr

Address : 51 rue Principale

Opening times : from end May to end Sept.

1 ha (36 pitches)

Tariff : (2015 price) 18.50€ ✚✚ 🚗 🔌 🔌 (16A) – Extra per person 3€
🚐 AireService sani-station 2€

Surroundings : 💆 🖵 💆
Leisure activities : 🏋️
Facilities : 🕭🚿 🛁 ⛌
Nearby : 🏊 🍸 🍴 🎣

GPS Longitude : 0.3021
Latitude : 47.2547

RILLÉ

37340 – Michelin map **317** K4 – pop. 300 – alt. 82
▶ Paris 282 – Orléans 158 – Tours 47 – Nantes 160

🏕️ Huttopia Rillé

℘ 02 47 24 62 97, www.huttopia.com

Address : at the Lac de Rillé (situated 2km to the east along the D49)

Opening times : from beginning May to mid Oct.

5 ha (120 pitches) flat, grassy

Tariff : (2015 price) 35.50€ ✚✚ 🚗 🔌 🔌 (10A) –
Extra per person 8.40€ – Reservation fee 13€
Rental rates : (2015 price) (from beginning May to mid Oct.) – 10 'gypsy' caravans – 27 🏠 – 24 tent lodges. Per night from 49 to 169€ – Per week from 258 to 1,183€ – Reservation fee 13€

🚐 local sani-station 7€ – 24 🔌 28€

Surroundings : 💆💆
Leisure activities : 🍴 🍽️ 🏛️ daytime 🏋️
🚴 🎯 🏊 🎣 🎏
Facilities : 🕭 ⚬━ 🅿️ 🏢 launderette 🚿 🚿
Nearby : 🏇 pedalos

GPS Longitude : 0.33278
Latitude : 47.44584

ROMORANTIN-LANTHENAY

41200 – Michelin map **318** H7 – pop. 17 092 – alt. 93
▶ Paris 202 – Blois 42 – Bourges 74 – Châteauroux 72

🏕️ Tournefeuille

℘ 02 54 76 16 60, www.campingtournefeuille-sologne.com

Address : 32 rue des Lices (take the eastern exit, follow the signs for Salbris and then Long-Eaton; beside the Sauldre river)

1.5 ha (103 pitches) flat, grassy

Rentals : 🕭 – 6 🏠.
🚐 sani-station – 2 🔌

Surroundings : 💆 💆
Leisure activities : 🍴 🏛️ 🏋️ 🚴 🏊
Facilities : 🕭 ⚬━ 🏢 🛁 ⛌ 🍴 🖼️
Nearby : 🏇 🎯 🎰

GPS Longitude : 1.75586
Latitude : 47.35503

Some information or pricing may have changed since the guide went to press. We recommend you check the price list online in advance or at the entrance to the campsite and enquire about possible restrictions.

ROSNAY

36300 – Michelin map **323** D6 – pop. 615 – alt. 112
▶ Paris 307 – Argenton-sur-Creuse 31 – Le Blanc 16 – Châteauroux 44

⚠ Municipal Les Millots

🖉 0254385799, rosnay-mairie@wanadoo.fr

Address : route de St-Michel-en-Brenne (500m north along the D 44)

Opening times : from mid Feb. to mid Nov.

2 ha (36 pitches) flat, grassy

Tariff : (2015 price) ♀ 2€ ⬌ 2€ ▣ 3€ – ⚡ (10A) 2€
🚐 local sani-station – 15 ▣
A small, pleasant site near a lake.

Surroundings : 🐟 🎿	GPS
Leisure activities : ⛵ ✂ 🎣	Longitude : 1.21172
Facilities : 🗄 🏧 👶 🔥 🚿 🅿	Latitude : 46.70645

ST-AMAND-MONTROND

18200 – Michelin map **323** L6 – pop. 10 952 – alt. 160
▶ Paris 282 – Bourges 52 – Châteauroux 65 – Montluçon 56

⚠ Municipal de la Roche

🖉 0248960936, www.entreprisefrery.com

Address : chemin de la Roche

Opening times : from beginning April to end Sept.

4 ha (120 pitches)

Tariff : (2015 price) 17.10€ ♀♀ ⬌ ▣ ⚡ (6A) – Extra per person 3.30€

Rental rates : (2015 price) (from beginning April to end Sept.) – 3 canvas bungalows. Per night from 96€ – Per week from 161 to 230€

Attractive pitches in a green setting by a canal and the Cher river, but the sanitary facilities are rather old and basic.

Surroundings : 🐟 ☕ 🎿	GPS
Leisure activities : 🏛 ⛵ 🎣 ✂	Longitude : 2.49108
Facilities : ♿ 🚰 🏧 🚿 launderette	Latitude : 46.71816
Nearby : 🎣	

ST-AVERTIN

37550 – Michelin map **317** N4 – pop. 13 946 – alt. 49
▶ Paris 245 – Orléans 121 – Tours 7 – Blois 70

⚠ Onlycamp Tour Val de Loire

🖉 0247278747, http://valdeloire.onlycamp.fr

Address : 61 rue de Rochepinard (to the north along the left bank of the Cher river)

Opening times : from mid March to end Nov.

2 ha (90 pitches) flat, grassy

Tariff : (2015 price) 21.90€ ♀♀ ⬌ ▣ ⚡ (10A) – Extra per person 4.70€

Rental rates : (2015 price) (from mid March to end Nov.) – 12 🏠 – 2 tent lodges. Per night from 24 to 109€ – Per week from 167 to 654€

🚐 AireService sani-station 5€ – 10 ▣ 21,90€
Situated near a small lake.

Surroundings : ☕ 🎿	GPS
Leisure activities : 🎯	Longitude : 0.72296
Facilities : ♿ 🚰 🏧 👶 🚿 launderette	Latitude : 47.37064
Nearby : ⛵ ✂ 🎣 🎣 🛶	

ST-PÈRE-SUR-LOIRE

45600 – Michelin map **318** L5 – pop. 1 056 – alt. 115
▶ Paris 147 – Aubigny-sur-Nère 38 – Châteauneuf-sur-Loire 40 – Gien 25

⚠ Le Jardin de Sully

🖉 0238671084, www.camping-lejardindesully.fr

Address : 1 route de St-Benoit (to the west along the D 60, follow the signs for Châteauneuf-sur-Loire; near the river)

Opening times : permanent

2.7 ha (80 pitches)

Tariff : 21€ ♀♀ ⬌ ▣ ⚡ (10A) – Extra per person 5€ – Reservation fee 5€

Rental rates : permanent – 18 🚐 – 8 canvas bungalows. Per night from 37 to 100€ – Per week from 175 to 560€

🚐 AireService sani-station 2€ – 4 ▣ 15€ – 🚿 8€

Leisure activities : 🏛 ⛵	GPS
Facilities : ♿ 🚰 🏧 👶 🚿 🚿 launderette	Longitude : 2.36229
Nearby : ✂ 🚴	Latitude : 47.7718

ST-PLANTAIRE

36190 – Michelin map **323** G8 – pop. 549 – alt. 300
▶ Paris 339 – Orléans 214 – Châteauroux 68 – Limoges 95

⚠ Municipal de Fougères

🖉 0254472001, www.www.saint-plantaire.fr

Address : 19 plage de Fougères

Opening times : from beginning April to end Oct.

4.5 ha (150 pitches) flat, grassy

Tariff : (2015 price) ♀ 4.40€ ⬌ 1.70€ ▣ 12.30€ – ⚡ (10A) 3.90€

Rental rates : (2015 price) (from beginning March to end Dec.) ♿ – 5 🚐 – 13 🏠 – 4 canvas bungalows. Per night from 39 to 122€ – Per week from 152 to 620€

In a pleasant location beside the Lac de Chambon

Surroundings : ⛰ 🌲	GPS
Leisure activities : ♿ ⛵ ✂ 🎣 🏊 🚤 🎣	Longitude : 1.61952
Facilities : ♿ 🚰 🆒 🚿 launderette 🔥	Latitude : 46.42756
Nearby : ✕ 🚴 🛶 pedalos	

ST-SATUR

18300 – Michelin map **323** N2 – pop. 1 627 – alt. 155
▶ Paris 194 – Aubigny-sur-Nère 42 – Bourges 50 – Cosne-sur-Loire 12

⚠ Flower Les Portes de Sancerre

🖉 0248721088, www.camping-cher-sancerre.com

Address : quai de Loire (located 1km east along the D 2)

Opening times : from beginning April to mid Oct.

1 ha (87 pitches) flat, grassy

Tariff : (2015 price) 23.20€ ♀♀ ⬌ ▣ ⚡ (6A) – Extra per person 4.50€ – Reservation fee 10€

Rental rates : (2015 price) (from beginning April to mid Oct.) ♿ (1 mobile home) – 20 🚐 – 6 canvas bungalows. Per night from 22 to 111€ – Per week from 110 to 666€ – Reservation fee 20€

🚐 AireService sani-station 4€ – 8 ▣ 12.50€ – 🚿 ⚡ 12.70€

Surroundings : 🐟 ☕ 🎿	GPS
Leisure activities : 🏛 ✂	Longitude : 2.86671
Facilities : ♿ 🚰 🆒 👶 🚿 🚿 🅿	Latitude : 47.34251
Nearby : 🎯 🚴 🛶 🎣 🐴	

STE-CATHERINE-DE-FIERBOIS

37800 – Michelin map **317** M6 – pop. 657 – alt. 114
▶ Paris 263 – Azay-le-Rideau 25 – Chinon 37 – Ligueil 19

⋀⋀ Les Castels Parc de Fierbois 👥👤

Les Castels Parc de Fierbois

𝒫 02 47 65 43 35, www.fierbois.com
Address : Parc de Fierbois, 1.2km south of the village
Opening times : from beginning May to beginning Sept.
30 ha/12 for camping (420 pitches)
Tariff : 52€ 👫 🚐 🔲 🔌 (10A) – Extra per person 10€
Rental rates : (from beginning May to beginning Sept.) – 132 🛖 – 48 🛖 – 8 cabins in the trees – 8 gîtes. Per night from 45 to 210€ – Per week from 315 to 1,470€
🚮 AireService sani-station – 🔋🔌14€

A pleasant and spacious site with woods, lake and a water park.

Surroundings : 🏕 🏛 ⛰
Leisure activities : 🍽 🗽 🖼 🎣 ✏ 🏊 🚴
🔪 🎣 🗽 🗽 (beach) 🎿🪁
Facilities : 🚿 ⚡ 🗄 🎿 🍴 launderette 🗄
🗄 refrigerated food storage facilities
Nearby : adventure park

GPS Longitude : 0.6549
Latitude : 47.1486

STE-MAURE-DE-TOURAINE

37800 – Michelin map **317** M6 – pop. 4 072 – alt. 85
▶ Paris 273 – Le Blanc 71 – Châtellerault 39 – Chinon 32

⋀ Municipal de Marans

𝒫 02 47 65 44 93, camping@sainte-maure-de-touraine.fr
Address : rue de Toizelet (located 1.5km southeast along the D 760, follow the signs for Loches, and take the turning to the left; 150m from a small lake)
1 ha (66 pitches)
🚮 local sani-station

Leisure activities : 🚴 🔪 sports trail
Facilities : 🚿 ⚡ 🎿 🍴
Nearby : 🗽 🎣

GPS Longitude : 0.6252
Latitude : 47.10509

SALBRIS

41300 – Michelin map **318** J7 – pop. 5 682 – alt. 104
▶ Paris 187 – Aubigny-sur-Nère 32 – Blois 65 – Lamotte-Beuvron 21

⋀⋀ Le Sologne

𝒫 02 54 97 06 38, www.campingdesologne.fr
Address : 8 allée de la Sauldre (take northeastern exit along the D 55, follow the signs for Pierrefitte-sur-Sauldre; beside a lake and near the Sauldre river)
Opening times : from beginning April to end Sept.
2 ha (81 pitches) flat, grassy
Tariff : 20.65€ 👫 🚐 🔲 🔌 (10A) – Extra per person 5.10€
Rental rates : (2015 price) (from beginning April to end Sept.) 🍽 – 5 🛖 – 1 🛖. Per night from 65€ – Per week from 246 to 537€ – Reservation fee 15€
🚮 Eurorelais sani-station

Surroundings : 🏕 🌊
Leisure activities : 🍽 🗽 🖼 🗽 🎣
Facilities : 🚿 ⚡ 🎿 🍴 🔲
Nearby : 🛒 🔪 🖼🗽

GPS Longitude : 2.05522
Latitude : 47.43026

SAVIGNY-EN-VÉRON

37420 – Michelin map **317** J5 – pop. 1 447 – alt. 40
▶ Paris 292 – Chinon 9 – Langeais 27 – Saumur 20

⋀⋀ La Fritillaire

𝒫 02 47 58 03 79, www.camping-la-fritillaire.fr
Address : rue Basse (to the west of the town centre; 100m from a lake)
Opening times : from mid March to mid Oct.
2.5 ha (100 pitches) flat, grassy, adjacent wood
Tariff : (2015 price) 17.60€ 👫 🚐 🔲 🔌 (10A) – Extra per person 3€
Rental rates : (2015 price) permanent – 6 canvas bungalows. Per night from 43 to 65€ – Per week from 210 to 430€
🚮 local sani-station 4.50€ – 🔋12€

Surroundings : 🗽 🏕
Leisure activities : 🗽 🔪 🎣
Facilities : 🚿 ⚡ 🔲 🎿 🍴 🔲 🗄
Nearby : 🗽 🔪 🗽

GPS Longitude : 0.13937
Latitude : 47.20039

SAVONNIÈRES

37510 – Michelin map **317** M4 – pop. 3 041 – alt. 47
▶ Paris 263 – Orléans 139 – Tours 17 – Blois 88

⋀ Onlycamp Confluence

𝒫 02 47 50 00 25, www.onlycamp.fr
Address : route du Bray (take the northern exit from the town; beside Cher)
Opening times : from beginning April to end Sept.
flat, grassy
Tariff : (2015 price) 20.50€ 👫 🚐 🔲 🔌 (10A) – Extra per person 4.40€
Rental rates : (2015 price) (from beginning April to end Sept.) – 2 canvas bungalows – 4 tent lodges. Per night from 24 to 55€ – Per week from 168 to 385€
🚮 local sani-station 2€ – 10 🔲 20.50€

Beside the Cher river and a cycle path.

Surroundings : 🏕 🌊
Leisure activities : 🚴 🔪 🎣
Facilities : 🚿 ⚡ 🎿 🍴 🗄
Nearby : 🛒 🍽 🔪

GPS Longitude : 0.55006
Latitude : 47.34887

SEIGY

41110 – Michelin map **318** F8 – pop. 1 110 – alt. 160
▶ Paris 226 – Blois 43 – Châteauroux 63 – Tours 116519

⋀ Les Cochards

𝒫 02 54 75 15 59, www.campinglescochards.com
Address : 1 rue du Camping (1.8km to the northwest on D 4 and D 17)
Opening times : from beginning April to mid Oct.
4 ha (140 pitches) flat, grassy
Tariff : (2015 price) 29€ 👫 🚐 🔲 🔌 (10A) – Extra per person 5€
Rental rates : (from beginning April to mid Oct.) – 11 🛖 – 5 canvas bungalows. Per night from 39 to 68€ – Per week from 273 to 725€
🚮 local sani-station – 7 🔲

Surroundings : 🗽 🌊
Leisure activities : 🍽 🔪 🚴 🎣
Facilities : 🚿 ⚡ 🎿 launderette 🗄

GPS Longitude : 1.3889
Latitude : 47.2662

SENONCHES

28250 – Michelin map **311** C4 – pop. 3 186 – alt. 223
▶ Paris 115 – Chartres 38 – Dreux 38 – Mortagne-au-Perche 42

⚠ Huttopia Senonches ♣♣

🖉 02 37 37 81 40, www.huttopia.com

Address : Etang de Badouleau (lake), at end of ave de Badouleau

Opening times : from beginning May to beginning Oct.

10.5 ha (126 pitches)

Tariff : (2015 price) 39.30€ ♣♣ ⇔ 🗉 🗲 (10A) – Extra per person 7€ – Reservation fee 13€

Rental rates : (2015 price) (from beginning May to beginning Oct.)
🅿 – 20 🏠 – 16 tent lodges. Per night from 59 to 151€ – Per week from 372 to 952€ – Reservation fee 13€

🚐 local sani-station 7€ – 23 🗉 28.50€

Beside the lake and on the edge of the national forest at Senonches.

Surroundings : ♀♀ ⛰
Leisure activities : 🖿 ☺daytime ⚊ ⚊
⛫ ⚓
Facilities : ⚬┅🅿 🎠 ♨launderette ⚊
Nearby : 🍴 ✕ ✖ 🐎

| Longitude : 1.0435 |
| Latitude : 48.553 |

---

*To visit a town or region, use the **MICHELIN Green Guides**.*

SONZAY

37360 – Michelin map **317** L3 – pop. 1 298 – alt. 94
▶ Paris 257 – Château-la-Vallière 39 – Langeais 26 – Tours 25

⚠ L'Arada Parc ♣♣

🖉 02 47 24 72 69, www.laradaparc.com

Address : rue de la Baratière (take the western exit along the D 68, follow the signs for Souvigné and take a right turn)

Opening times : from end March to mid Oct.

1.7 ha (92 pitches)

Tariff : 40.50€ ♣♣ ⇔ 🗉 🗲 (10A) – Extra per person 6.10€
Rental rates : (from end March to mid Oct.) – 25 🖿 – 3 🏠 – 5 tent lodges. Per night from 46 to 102€ – Per week from 290 to 810€

Surroundings : ♨ 🗔
Leisure activities : 🍴 ✕ 🖿 ⚊ jacuzzi ⚓
⛫🎠⚊⚊
Facilities : ⚬┅🎠🗔🎠⚊⚊ ♨ ⚊launderette
Nearby : ✖ 🐟

| Longitude : 0.45069 |
| Latitude : 47.52615 |

SUÈVRES

41500 – Michelin map **318** F5 – pop. 1 481 – alt. 83
▶ Paris 170 – Beaugency 18 – Blois 15 – Chambord 16

⚠ Le Château de la Grenouillère ♣♣

🖉 02 54 87 80 37, www.camping-loire.com

Address : 3km northeast on the D 2152

Opening times : from mid April to mid Sept.

11 ha (250 pitches) flat, grassy

Tariff : (2015 price) 33€ ♣♣ ⇔ 🗉 🗲 (10A) – Extra per person 8€ – Reservation fee 10€

Rental rates : (2015 price) (from mid April to mid Sept.) ♨ – 140 🖿 – 20 🏠. Per night from 40 to 120€ – Per week from 300 to 870€ – Reservation fee 15€

🚐 local sani-station

In wooded parkland, with oak and apple trees.

Surroundings : 🗔 🎠
Leisure activities : 🍴 ✕ 🖿 ☺ ⚓ jacuzzi
⚊⛫🎠⚊⚊⚊ ⚊
Facilities : ⚬┅🎠⚊🎠 ⚊ ⚊ ⚊launderette
⚊⚊

| Longitude : 1.48512 |
| Latitude : 47.68688 |

THORÉ-LA-ROCHETTE

41100 – Michelin map **318** C5 – pop. 899 – alt. 75
▶ Paris 176 – Blois 42 – Château-Renault 25 – La Ferté-Bernard 58

⚠ Municipal la Bonne Aventure

Intercommunal la Bonne Aventure

🖉 02 54 72 00 59, www.camping-la-bonne-aventure.fr

Address : route de la Cunaille (head 1.7km north along the D 82, follow the signs for Lunay and take turning to the right; near the stadium; beside the Loir)

Opening times : from beginning May to end Sept.

2 ha (68 pitches) flat, grassy

Tariff : 13.50€ ♣♣ ⇔ 🗉 🗲 (6A) –
Extra per person 4.20€
Rental rates : permanent ♨ – 2 🖿. Per night from 53 to 79€ – Per week from 200 to 347€ – Reservation fee 86€

🚐 12 🗉 10,20€ – 🍴8€

Surroundings : ♨ ♀ ⛰
Leisure activities : 🖿 ⚓ ⛫ ✖ 🐟
Facilities : ⚬┅🎠 ⚊ ⚊
Nearby : ✕ 🏊

| Longitude : 0.95855 |
| Latitude : 47.80504 |

VALENÇAY

36600 – Michelin map **323** F4 – pop. 2 617 – alt. 140
▶ Paris 233 – Blois 59 – Bourges 73 – Châteauroux 42

⚠ Municipal les Chênes

🖉 02 54 00 03 92, commune@mairie-valencay.fr

Address : located 1km west on the D 960, follow the signs for Luçay-le-Mâle

Opening times : from beginning May to mid Sept.

5 ha (50 pitches) relatively flat, open site

Tariff : (2015 price) ♣ 4€ ⇔ 🗉 4,60€ – 🗲 (10A) 4.70€

🚐 local sani-station 4.20€

In a pleasant, green setting beside a lake.

Surroundings : 🗔 ♀♀
Leisure activities : ⚓ ⚊ 🐟
Facilities : ⚬┅🎠 ⚊
Nearby : 🍴 ✕ ✖

| Longitude : 1.55542 |
| Latitude : 47.15808 |

VATAN

36150 – Michelin map **323** G4 – pop. 2 059 – alt. 140
▶ Paris 235 – Blois 78 – Bourges 50 – Châteauroux 31

⚠ Municipal

🖉 02 54 49 91 37, www.vatan-en-berry.com

Address : rue du Collège (take the western exit along the D 2, follow the signs for Guilly and take the turning to the left)

Opening times : from mid April to mid Sept.

2.4 ha (55 pitches) flat, grassy

Tariff : 12€ ♣♣ ⇔ 🗉 🗲 (20A) – Extra per person 4.50€

Rental rates : (from beginning April to end Sept.) ✈ – 3 🏠. Per night from 50€ – Per week from 200 to 250€

🚐 local sani-station 5€

Situated beside a delightful lake.

Surroundings : ⌱ 🌳🌳
Leisure activities : 🛶⛵🏊
Facilities : 🚿🗑🚻🛁🌿📶🍴📞
Nearby : 🚴🏇🎣

GPS Longitude : 1.80601
Latitude : 47.07146

VEIGNÉ

37250 – Michelin map **317** N5 – pop. 6 055 – alt. 58
▶ Paris 252 – Orléans 128 – Tours 16 – Joué-lès-Tours 11

🏕 Onlycamp La Plage

☎ 02 47 34 95 39, www.onlycamp.fr

Address : route de Tours (take the northern exit along the D 50)

Opening times : from mid April to mid Sept.

2 ha (110 pitches) flat, grassy

Tariff : (2015 price) 20.50€ 🏕🏕 🚗 📧 ⚡ (10A) –
Extra per person 4.40€
Rental rates : (2015 price) (from mid April to mid Sept.) –
10 canvas bungalows. Per night from 45 to 65€ – Per week from 315 to 455€

🚐 local sani-station 2€

Surroundings : ♀
Leisure activities : 🍴✕🏛🤸🏃🎣
Facilities : 🚿🗑 (season) 🛁📞 launderette
Nearby : 🎣

GPS Longitude : 0.73464
Latitude : 47.28929

Key to rentals symbols :

12 🚐	*Number of mobile homes*
20 🏠	*Number of chalets*
6 🛏	*Number of rooms to rent*
Per night 30–50€	*Minimum/maximum rate per night*
Per week 300–1,000€	*Minimum/maximum rate per week*

LA VILLE-AUX-DAMES

37700 – Michelin map **317** N4 – pop. 4 889 – alt. 50
▶ Paris 244 – Orléans 120 – Tours 7 – Blois 53

🏕 Les Acacias

☎ 02 47 44 08 16, www.camplvad.com

Address : rue Berthe Morisot (to the northeast of the town, near the D 751)

Opening times : permanent

2.6 ha (90 pitches) flat, grassy

Tariff : (2015 price) 20€ 🏕🏕 🚗 📧 ⚡ (10A) – Extra per person 3.50€ –
Reservation fee 10€
Rental rates : (2015 price) permanent – 20 🚐. Per night from 60 to 110€ – Per week from 290 to 570€ – Reservation fee 10€

🚐 AireService sani-station 6€ – 10 📧 20€

Surroundings : 🌳🌳
Leisure activities : ✕🛶🚴🏇
Facilities : 🚿🗑📶📞 launderette
Nearby : 🍴🎣🛶 fitness trail

GPS Longitude : 0.7772
Latitude : 47.40224

VILLIERS-LE-MORHIER

28130 – Michelin map **311** F4 – pop. 1 338 – alt. 99
▶ Paris 83 – Orléans 108 – Chartres 24 – Versailles 61

🏔 Les Ilots de St-Val

Les Ilots de St-Val

☎ 02 37 82 71 30, www.campinglesilotsdestval.com – limited spaces for one-night stay

Address : at Le Haut Bourray (4.5km northwest along the D 983, follow the signs for Nogent-le-Roi then continue 1km along the D 1013, follow the signs for Neron to the left)
Opening times : from beginning Feb. to mid Dec.

10 ha/6 for camping (153 pitches) flat and relatively flat, grassy, stony

Tariff : 27€ 🏕🏕 🚗 📧 ⚡ (10A) – Extra per person 6€
Rental rates : (2015 price) (from beginning Feb. to mid Dec.)
✈ – 18 🚐 – 4 🏠. Per week from 266 to 434€

🚐 local sani-station

Surroundings : 🌳
Leisure activities : 🏛🛶🏇🎣
Facilities : 🚿🗝🗑🛁📶📞
Nearby : 🎣🏇

For more information on visiting particular towns or regions, consult the relevant regional MICHELIN Green Guide. We also recommend you use the appropriate Michelin regional map to locate your selected campsite, to calculate distances and to work out the best route.

VINEUIL

41350 – Michelin map **318** F6 – pop. 7 443 – alt. 73
▶ Paris 187 – Blois 6 – Orléans 63 – Tours 67

🏕 Onlycamp Le Val de Blois

☎ 02 54 78 82 05, www.valdeblois.onlycamp.fr

Address : RD 951 (at the leisure centre)

Opening times : from mid April to end Sept.

3 ha (120 pitches) flat, grassy

Tariff : (2015 price) 22,90€ 🏕🏕 🚗 📧 ⚡ (10A) – Extra per person 5€
Rental rates : (2015 price) (from mid April to end Sept.) – 5 🏠 – 5 yurts – 3 tent lodges. Per night from 24 to 80€ – Per week from 168 to 560€

🚐 local sani-station 5€

Surroundings : ♀
Leisure activities : 🛶🎣
Facilities : 🚿🗑📶🛁📶📞 launderette 🍴
Nearby : ✕🚴🎣🛶

GPS Longitude : 1.3744
Latitude : 47.6055

These symbols are used for a campsite that is exceptional in its category :

🏔🏔 ... 🏔 *Particularly pleasant setting, quality and range of services available*

🦢 🦢 *Tranquil, isolated site – quiet site, particularly at night*

≪ ≪ *Exceptional view – interesting or panoramic view*

VITRY-AUX-LOGES

45530 – Michelin map **318** K4 – pop. 1 826 – alt. 120
▶ Paris 111 – Bellegarde 17 – Châteauneuf-sur-Loire 11 – Malesherbes 48

⛰ Étang de la Vallée

℘ 06 10 53 35 37, www.campingdeletangdelavallee.fr

Address : at the leisure centre (3.3km to the northwest, 100m from the lake)

3,7 ha (180 pitches) flat, grassy

In a pleasant wooded setting near a leisure centre.

Surroundings : ⌑ ♀
Leisure activities : 🏇 ⌇
Facilities : 🚿 ⚬━ 🧺 ➰ 🕳 🔁
Nearby : 🍷 ✕ 🏖 (beach) 🛶 pedalos

Longitude : 2.28162
Latitude : 47.95868

We value your opinion and welcome your feedback.
Do email us at campingfrance@tp.michelin.com

VOUVRAY

37210 – Michelin map **317** N4 – pop. 3 076 – alt. 55
▶ Paris 240 – Amboise 18 – Château-Renault 25 – Chenonceaux 30

⛺ Onlycamp Le Bec de Cisse

℘ 02 47 35 55 32, www.vouvray.onlycamp.fr

Address : south of the town; beside the Cisse

Opening times : from beginning May to end Sept.

1,5 ha (41 pitches) flat, grassy

Tariff : (2015 price) 14,10€ ✶✶ 🚐 🗉 🔌 (10A) – Extra per person 3,80€

Rental rates : (2015 price) (from beginning May to end Sept.) – 1 tent lodge. Per night from 49€ – Per week from 308€

🚐 local sani-station 2€

Pitches with shade near the Cisse river.

Surroundings : ♀♀
Leisure activities : 🛶
Facilities : 🚿 ⚬━ 🧺 🛁 ➰ 🕳 🔁
Nearby : 🍷 ✕ 🍴 🛝 🏖 ⛴ Rochecorbon leisure park

Longitude : 0.79623
Latitude : 47.40871

CHAMPAGNE-ARDENNE

G. Labriet / Photononstop

It's easy to spot visitors heading to the Champagne-Ardenne region by the sparkle in their eyes and the look of pure anticipation and delight on their faces as they gaze out at endless vineyards. They are already picturing themselves sipping the famous delicacy that was once known as 'devil's wine' before a monk discovered the secret of its divine bubbles. As those lucky enough to taste the delights of Champagne continue their voyage, they will see the beautiful cathedral of Reims rise up ahead. They will drink in the sight of the delightful half-timbered houses of Troyes and savour the taste of *andouillettes* (chitterling sausages). Visitors can then explore the Ardennes forest by bike or by walking along its hiking trails. This ancient woodland paradise, bordered by the gentle river Meuse, has other delights as well: watch the graceful flight of the crane over a lake as smooth as glass, or succumb to the temptation of a plate of local wild boar.

Legend:
- Locality with campsite
- Locality with campsite and rental option
- *Vannes* Locality with campsite and campervan area
- Moyaux Locality with at least one pleasant campsite
- Motorway service area for campervans

BELGIQUE

LUXEME

Valenciennes

Cambrai

le Nouvion-
en-Thiérache

ST-QUENTIN

la Fère

Vervins

AISNE

Signy-l'Abbaye

CHARLEVILLE-MÉZIÈRES

ARDENNES

Buzancy

Rethel

Vouziers

CHAMP ROLAND

rny-Rivière

Soissons

REIMS

Verdun

Ste-Menehould

MEUSE

Jaulny

REIMS CHAMPAGNE SUD

Épernay

Charly-s-M.

CHÂLONS-EN-
CHAMPAGNE

Lac de
Madine

MARNE

Revigny-s-Ornain

Bar-le-Duc

Commercy

TOUL-
DOMMARTIN

Toul

A 31

Villey-le-Se

Sézanne

Vitry-le-François

Provins

St-Dizier

SOMMESOUS

Nogent-
sur-Seine

Lac du Der-
Chantecoq

Éclaron

Braucourt

Giffaumont-
Champaubert

Thonnance-
les-Moulins

Neufchâteau

Soulaines-Dhuys

Radonvilliers

TROYES
LE PLESSIS

Dienville

Lac de la
F. d'Orient

LORRAINE-SA

LORRAIN
LES RAP

TROYES

Bourg-
Ste-Marie

Bulgnéville

Vittel

Sens

VILLENEUVE-
L'ARCHEVÊQUE

VILLEROY

Mesnil-
St-Père

Bar-s-Aube

HAUTE-MARNE

Contrexéville

VAL-DE-

TROYES-
FRESNOY-LE-CHÂTEAU

AUBE

CHÂTEAUVILLAIN-
ORGES

Chaumont

Montigny-le-Roi

MONTIGNY-LE-ROI

Bourbonne-
les-Bains

Ervy-le-Châtel

Migennes

Bannes

YONNE

Ligny-le-Châtel

Auxerre

Chablis

Tonnerre

Châtillon-s-Seine

LANGRES-PERROGNEY

LANGRES-NOIDANT

Vincelles

Vermenton

l'Isle-s-Serein

Montbard

eur-en-Puisaye

Andryes

Asquins

Avallon

Venarey-les-Laumes

DIJON-BROGNON

BESANÇON-CHA

CÔTE-   D'OR

HAUT

Clamecy

Varzy

LA CHAPONNE

LE CHIEN

LES LOCHÈRES

BANNES

52360 – Michelin map 313 M6 – pop. 401 – alt. 388
▶ Paris 291 – Chaumont 35 – Dijon 86 – Langres 9

⚠ Hautoreille

✆ 03 25 84 83 40. www.campinghautoreille.com

Address : 6 rue du Boutonnier (take the southwestern exit along the D 74, follow the signs for Langres, then continue 700m along the road to the left)

Opening times : from beginning Jan. to end Nov.

3.5 ha (100 pitches) relatively flat, flat, grassy

Tariff : ♣ 5€ 🚐 🗉 5.50€ – 🔌 (10A) 3.50€

Surroundings : 🏊 ♀♀ Leisure activities : ♈ ✗ 🏛 🛶 Facilities : ♿ ⚿ 🖩 🛎 🍴 🖼	**GPS** Longitude : 5.39519 Latitude : 47.89508

BOURBONNE-LES-BAINS

52400 – Michelin map 313 O6 – pop. 2 255 – alt. 290 – ♨
▶ Paris 313 – Chaumont 55 – Dijon 124 – Langres 39

⚠ Le Montmorency

✆ 03 25 90 08 64. www.camping-montmorency.com

Address : rue du Stade (take the western exit following signs for Chaumont and take turning to the right; 100m from the stadium)

Opening times : from end March to beginning Nov.

2 ha (74 pitches)

Tariff : 18€ ♣♣ 🚐 🗉 🔌 (10A) – Extra per person 4.50€

Rental rates : (from end March to beginning Nov.) – 11 🛖 – 2 tent lodges. Per night from 35 to 55€ – Per week from 245 to 385€

🚽 Eurorelais sani-station – 10 🗉 14€

Surroundings : 🏊 ♀♀ Facilities : ⚿ 🖩 🛎 🍴 launderette Nearby : ✂ 🏊 (open air in season)	**GPS** Longitude : 5.74027 Latitude : 47.95742

The information in the guide may have changed since going to press.

BOURG-STE-MARIE

52150 – Michelin map 313 N4 – pop. 94 – alt. 329
▶ Paris 330 – Châlons-en-Champagne 153 – Chaumont 50 – Metz 142

⚠ Les Hirondelles

✆ 03 10 20 61 64. www.camping-les-hirondelles.eu

Address : at Romain-sur-Meuse, rue du Moulin de Dona (located 1.5km to the south, along the D 74, follow the signs for Montigny-le-Roi)

Opening times : from mid Feb. to beginning Dec.

4.6 ha (54 pitches)

Tariff : ♣ 4.50€ 🚐 🗉 5€ – 🔌 (10A) 3.80€

Rental rates : (from beginning Feb. to mid Dec.) – 7 🛖 – 2 🛏 – 1 gîte. Per night from 37 to 90€ – Per week from 231 to 385€

🚽 15 🗉 15€ – 🚐 🔌15€

Surroundings : 🏊 ♀♀ Leisure activities : 🏛 🛶 🚲 Facilities : ♿ ⚿ 🖩 🛎 🍴 launderette	**GPS** Longitude : 5.55533 Latitude : 48.17234

BRAUCOURT

52290 – Michelin map 313 I2
▶ Paris 220 – Bar-sur-Aube 39 – Brienne-le-Château 29 – Châlons-en-Champagne 69

⛰ La Presqu'île de Champaubert ♣♣

✆ 03 25 04 13 20. www.lescampingsduder.com

Address : 3km northwest along the D 153

Opening times : from beginning April to end Nov.

3.6 ha (200 pitches)

Tariff : (2015 price) 17€ ♣♣ 🚐 🗉 🔌 (10A) – Extra per person 5€

Rental rates : (2015 price) (from beginning April to end Nov.) – 47 🛖. Per night from 33 to 83€ – Per week from 230 to 581€

🚽 local sani-station

A pleasant location beside the Lac du Der-Chantecoq.

Surroundings : 🏊 ⬅ 🏛 ♀♀ ⛰ Leisure activities : ♈ ✗ 🏛 🎣 🤾 ⛵ ✂ 🛶 Facilities : ♿ ⚿ 🛎 🍴 launderette Nearby : 🏊 🛶 pedalos	**GPS** Longitude : 4.562 Latitude : 48.55413

*For more information on visiting particular towns or regions, consult the relevant regional **MICHELIN Green Guide**. We also recommend you use the appropriate Michelin regional map to locate your selected campsite, to calculate distances and to work out the best route.*

BUZANCY

08240 – Michelin map 306 L6 – pop. 372 – alt. 176
▶ Paris 228 – Châlons-en-Champagne 86 – Charleville-Mézières 58 – Metz 130

⚠ La Samaritaine

✆ 03 24 30 08 88. www.campinglasamaritaine.com

Address : 3 rue des Étangs (1.4km southwest along the road to the right near the leisure and activity park)

Opening times : from mid April to mid Sept.

2 ha (110 pitches) flat, grassy, stony

Tariff : (2015 price) ♣ 3.50€ 🚐 2.50€ 🗉 6.50€ – 🔌 (10A) 3.60€

Rental rates : (2015 price) (from mid April to mid Sept.) – 6 🛖 – 9 🛖. Per night from 48 to 67€ – Per week from 320 to 595€

🚽 local sani-station 3€ – 9 🗉 10€

Surroundings : 🏊 🏛 ♀ Leisure activities : 🏛 Facilities : ♿ ⚿ 🛎 🍴 🖼 Nearby : 🏊 (lake)	**GPS** Longitude : 4.9402 Latitude : 49.42365

Michelin classification:

 Extremely comfortable, equipped to a very high standard

Very comfortable, equipped to a high standard

Comfortable and well equipped

Reasonably comfortable

Satisfactory

CHÂLONS-EN-CHAMPAGNE

51000 – Michelin map **306** I9 – pop. 46 236 – alt. 83
▶ Paris 188 – Charleville-Mézières 101 – Metz 157 – Nancy 162

⛰ Aquadis Loisirs Châlons en Champagne

℘ 03 26 68 38 00. http://www.aquadis-loisirs.com/camping-de-chalons-en-champagne/

Address : rue de Plaisance (take the southeastern exit along the N 44, follow the signs for Vitry-le François and take the D 60, following signs for Sarry)

Opening times : from beginning March to beginning Nov.

3.5 ha (148 pitches) flat, grassy, gravel

Tariff : 22.90€ ✶✶ ⇦ 🖹 🗓 (10A) – Extra per person 5.50€ – Reservation fee 10€

Rental rates : (from beginning March to beginning Nov.) – 8 🚍. Per night from 70€ – Per week from 249 to 519€ – Reservation fee 20€

🚐 AireService sani-station – 🛒14€

An entrance decorated with flowers and a pleasant setting beside a lake.

Surroundings : ⌂ 🙾🙾
Leisure activities : ✗ 🏖 🛶 ✗ 🎣 ⌁
Facilities : 🛅 ⊶ 🅲🗍 🍴 🚿 ⛺ launderette

GPS Longitude : 4.38309
Latitude : 48.98582

CHARLEVILLE-MÉZIÈRES

08000 – Michelin map **306** K4 – pop. 49 975 – alt. 145
▶ Paris 233 – Châlons-en-Champagne 130 – Namur 149 – Arlon 120

⛰ Municipal du Mont Olympe

℘ 03 24 33 23 60. camping-charlevillemezieres@wanadoo.fr

Address : 174 rue des Paquis (in the town centre)

Opening times : from beginning April to end Sept.

2.7 ha (120 pitches) flat, grassy

Tariff : (2015 price) ✶ 3.80€ ⇦ 🖹 5.70€ – 🗓 (10A) 4.20€

🚐 Eurorelais sani-station – 10 🖹 12.40€

In a bend of the Meuse river, with pedestrian access to the town centre and the Rimbaud museum via a walkway.

Surroundings : 🙾 🙾🙾
Leisure activities : 🛶 🛶
Facilities : 🛅 ⊶ 🗍🖈 ⛺ 🚿 launderette
Nearby : 🍴✗ 🛋 🍴 hammam, jacuzzi 🎿 🏊 ⚓ marina

GPS Longitude : 4.72091
Latitude : 49.77914

DIENVILLE

10500 – Michelin map **313** H3 – pop. 828 – alt. 128
▶ Paris 209 – Bar-sur-Aube 20 – Bar-sur-Seine 33 – Brienne-le-Château 8

⛰ Le Tertre

℘ 03 25 92 26 50. www.campingdutertre.fr

Address : 1 route de Radonvilliers (take the western exit on the D 11)

Opening times : from mid March to mid Oct.

3.5 ha (155 pitches) flat, grassy, gravel

Tariff : ✶ 5€ ⇦ 🖹 10.20€ – 🗓 (10A) 4.20€ – Reservation fee 12€

Rental rates : permanent – 13 🏠 . Per night from 125 to 255€ – Per week from 200 to 550€ – Reservation fee 12€

Opposite the leisure and activity park's sailing centre.

Surroundings : ⌂
Leisure activities : 🍴✗ 🛶 🎿
Facilities : 🛅 ⊶🗍 🖈 ✗ 🚿 ⛺ 🖹
Nearby : 🎿 🚣 🛶 water skiing

GPS Longitude : 4.52737
Latitude : 48.34888

ÉCLARON

52290 – Michelin map **313** J2 – pop. 1 991 – alt. 132
▶ Paris 255 – Châlons-en-Champagne 71 – Chaumont 83 – Bar-le-Duc 37

⛰ Yelloh! en Champagne - Les Sources du Lac 👥

℘ 03 25 06 34 24. www.yellohvillage-en champagne.com – limited spaces for one-night stay

Address : RD 384 (situated 2km to the south, follow the signs for Montier-en-Der; beside the Lac du Der)

Opening times : from beginning April to mid Sept.

3 ha (120 pitches) flat, grassy, fine gravel

Tariff : 37€ ✶✶ ⇦ 🖹 🗓 (10A) – Extra per person 7€

Rental rates : (from beginning April to mid Sept.) – 3 'gypsy' caravans – 50 🚍. Per night from 30 to 165€ – Per week from 210 to 1,155€

🚐 30 🖹 19€

Choose the pitches furthest away from the road in preference.

Surroundings : ⌂ 🙾🙾
Leisure activities : 🍴🎲 🏃 🛶 🚲 🎿 🏹
multi-sports ground
Facilities : 🛅 ⊶ 🖈 🚿 ⛺ launderette 🖈

GPS Longitude : 4.84798
Latitude : 48.57179

ÉPERNAY

51200 – Michelin map **306** F8 – pop. 24 317 – alt. 75
▶ Paris 143 – Amiens 199 – Charleville-Mézières 113 – Meaux 96

⛰ Municipal

℘ 03 26 55 32 14. www.epernay.fr

Address : allée de Cumières (located 1.5km north along the D 301; beside the Marne river)

Opening times : from beginning May to end Sept.

2 ha (109 pitches) flat, grassy

Tariff : (2015 price) ✶ 5€ ⇦ 2.50€ 🖹 5€ – 🗓 (10A) 4€

🚐 Flot Bleu sani-station 2€

Surroundings : ⌂ 🙾🙾
Leisure activities : 🛶 🚲
Facilities : 🛅 ⊶ 🗍 🚿 launderette
Nearby : ⚓

GPS Longitude : 3.95026
Latitude : 49.05784

ERVY-LE-CHÂTEL

10130 – Michelin map **313** D5 – pop. 1 224 – alt. 160
▶ Paris 169 – Auxerre 48 – St-Florentin 18 – Sens 62

⛰ Municipal les Mottes

℘ 03 25 70 07 96. www.ervy-le-chatel.reseaudescommunes.fr/communes

Address : chemin des Mottes (1.8km east along the D 374, follow the signs for Auxon, D 92 and take the road to the right after the level crossing)

Opening times : from beginning May to end Sept.

0.7 ha (53 pitches) flat, grassy

Tariff : (2015 price) ✶ 3.50€ ⇦ 3€ 🖹 3€ – 🗓 (5A) 3.50€

The site is beside a small river and a wood.

Surroundings : 🙾
Leisure activities : 🏹
Facilities : 🛅 🗍 🚿 🖹

GPS Longitude : 3.91827
Latitude : 48.04069

GIFFAUMONT-CHAMPAUBERT

51290 – Michelin map **306** K11 – pop. 261 – alt. 130
▶ Paris 213 – Châlons-en-Champagne 67 – St-Dizier 25 – Bar-le-Duc 52

▲▲▲ Village Vacances Marina-Holyder
(rental of gîtes only)

✆ 03 26 72 84 04. www.marina-holyder.com

Address : rue de Champaubert (Presqu'Île de Rougemer (peninsula))

Opening times : permanent

2 ha, flat

Rental rates : (2015 price) Ⓟ – 43 gîtes. Per night from 89 to 149€ – Per week from 399 to 949€

Surroundings : 🌳 🍃
Leisure activities : 🍹 ✗ ⛲ ⛹ 🎣 ⛵ hammam jacuzzi ⛷ 🎿 🏐 🛶 🚶 forest trail
Facilities : 📶 🚿 launderette 🧺
Nearby : 🚲

GPS Longitude : 4.77328
Latitude : 48.54987

MESNIL-ST-PERE

10140 – Michelin map **313** G4 – pop. 415 – alt. 131
▶ Paris 209 – Châlons-en-Champagne 98 – Troyes 25 – Chaumont 79

▲▲ Le Lac d'Orient 👥

✆ 03 25 40 61 85. www.camping-lacdorient.com

Address : route du Lac

Opening times : from mid April to end Sept.

4 ha (199 pitches) flat, grassy

Tariff : 24.40€ 👥 🚗 📶 🔌 (10A) – Extra per person 8.50€ – Reservation fee 10€

Rental rates : (from mid April to end Sept.) 🌂 – 2 'gypsy' caravans – 22 🚐 – 2 🏠. Per night from 51 to 130€ – Per week from 348 to 910€ – Reservation fee 10€

🚐 local sani-station – 9 📶 16.40€

Surroundings : 🌳 🍃
Leisure activities : 🍹 🏕 ⛷ 🎣 ⛵ 🏐 🛶 multi-sports ground
Facilities : 🚿 🔌 📶 🚽 🧺 launderette 🍴 🥤
Nearby : 🎣 🐴

GPS Longitude : 4.34624
Latitude : 48.26297

MONTIGNY-LE-ROI

52140 – Michelin map **313** M6 – pop. 2 168 – alt. 404
▶ Paris 296 – Bourbonne-les-Bains 21 – Chaumont 35 – Langres 23

▲ Municipal du Château

✆ 03 25 87 38 93. www.campingduchateau.com

Address : rue Hubert Collot (access via the town centre and take the pedestrian path to the village)

Opening times : from mid April to end Sept.

6 ha/2 for camping (75 pitches) terraced, flat, grassy

Tariff : (2015 price) 👤 5.80€ 🚗 📶 5.80€ – 🔌 (10A) 4.80€

🚐 Raclet sani-station 2€

In a wooded park overlooking the Vallée de la Meuse.

Surroundings : ⛰ 🍃
Leisure activities : ⛷ 🏐
Facilities : 🚿 🔌 📶 🧺 🍴
Nearby : ✗

GPS Longitude : 5.4965
Latitude : 48.00068

RADONVILLIERS

10500 – Michelin map **313** H3 – pop. 384 – alt. 130
▶ Paris 206 – Bar-sur-Aube 22 – Bar-sur-Seine 35 – Brienne-le-Château 6

▲ Le Garillon

✆ 03 25 92 21 46. www.campinglegarillon.fr

Address : take the southwestern exit along the D 11, follow the signs for Piney and take turning to the right; beside a stream and 250m from the lake (top of dike, via steps)

Opening times : from beginning April to end Sept.

1 ha (55 pitches) flat, grassy

Tariff : (2015 price) 21€ 👥 🚗 📶 🔌 (16A) – Extra per person 4€

Rental rates : (2015 price) (from beginning April to end Sept.) – 10 🚐. Per night from 35 to 83€ – Per week from 210 to 498€

Leisure activities : 🛶
Facilities : 🚿 🔌 🍴
Nearby : ✗

GPS Longitude : 4.50206
Latitude : 48.3586

The Michelin classification (▲▲▲ … ▲) is totally independent of the official star classification system awarded by the local prefecture or other official organisation.

SÉZANNE

51120 – Michelin map **306** E10 – pop. 5 268 – alt. 137
▶ Paris 116 – Châlons-en-Champagne 59 – Meaux 78 – Melun 89

▲ Municipal

✆ 03 26 80 57 00. ville-sezanne.fr

Address : route de Launat (take the western exit along the D 373, follow the signs for Paris (near the N 4) then continue 700m along the road to the left and take turning to the right)

Opening times : from beginning April to end Sept.

1 ha (79 pitches) terrace, relatively flat, flat, grassy

Tariff : (2015 price) 11€ 👥 🚗 📶 🔌 (10A) – Extra per person 2.55€

Surroundings : 🍃
Leisure activities : ⛷ 🏐 🛶
Facilities : 🚿 🔌 🚽 📶 🖥
Nearby : ✗

GPS Longitude : 3.70212
Latitude : 48.72154

SIGNY-L'ABBAYE

08460 – Michelin map **306** I4 – pop. 1 365 – alt. 240
▶ Paris 208 – Charleville-Mézières 31 – Hirson 41 – Laon 74

▲ Municipal l'Abbaye

✆ 03 24 52 81 25. www.signy-abbaye.fr – 🚐

Address : rue de l'Abbaye (situated north, near the stadium, beside the Vaux river)

Opening times : from beginning May to end Sept.

1.2 ha (60 pitches) flat, grassy, fine gravel

Tariff : 👤 2€ 🚗 1.50€ 📶 1.70€ – 🔌 (15A) 3.20€

🚐 10 📶 10.50€

Surroundings : 🌳 🍃
Facilities : 🚽 🖥 📶
Nearby : ✗

GPS Longitude : 4.41967
Latitude : 49.70134

SOULAINES-DHUYS

10200 – Michelin map **313** I3 – pop. 311 – alt. 153
▶ Paris 228 – Bar-sur-Aube 18 – Brienne-le-Château 17 – Chaumont 48

⚠ La Croix Badeau

🖉 03 25 27 05 43. www.croix-badeau.com

Address : 6 rue de La Croix Badeau (to the northeast of the town, near the church)

Opening times : from beginning April to end Sept.

1 ha (39 pitches) relatively flat, gravel, grassy

Tariff : (2015 price) 19€ ✝✝ ⬅ 📧 ⚡ (10A) – Extra per person 3.80€
Rental rates : (2015 price) (from beginning April to end Sept.) – 1 🚎 . Per night from 50 to 70€ – Per week from 180 to 470€
🚰 local sani-station 2.50€ – 39 📧 19€

Surroundings : 🗺
Leisure activities : ▼ 🏛 🛶
Facilities : 👤 ⛽ 🎽 ♨ ♒ ♛
Nearby : 🏇 ✂

Longitude : 4.73846
Latitude : 48.37672

THONNANCE-LES-MOULINS

52230 – Michelin map **313** L3 – pop. 120 – alt. 282
▶ Paris 254 – Bar-le-Duc 64 – Chaumont 48 – Commercy 55

🏔 Les Castels La Forge de Sainte Marie 👥

🖉 03 25 94 42 00. www.laforgedesaintemarie.com

Address : route de Joinville (1.7km west along the D 427; beside the Rongeant river)

Opening times : from end April to mid Sept.

32 ha/3 for camping (133 pitches) terraced, relatively flat, flat, grassy, pond

Tariff : (2015 price) ✝ 10€ ⬅ 📧 19.50€ – ⚡ (10A) 6.50€

Rental rates : (2015 price) permanent – 45 🚎 – 15 gîtes. Per night from 60 to 150€ – Per week from 299 to 999€ – Reservation fee 15€

In a pleasant green setting beside an old restored forge.

Surroundings : 🐿 🗺 ♀
Leisure activities : ▼ ✕ 🏛 🎣 🏊 🛶 🚲 🗺 ♒
Facilities : 👤 ⛽ 🎽 ♨ ♒ ▼ launderette

Longitude : 5.27097
Latitude : 48.40629

TROYES

10000 – Michelin map **313** E4 – pop. 61 188 – alt. 113
▶ Paris 170 – Dijon 185 – Nancy 186

🏔 Municipal

🖉 03 25 81 02 64. www.troyescamping.net

Address : at Pont Sainte-Marie, 7 rue Roger Salengro (situated 2km to the northeast, follow the signs for Nancy)

Opening times : from beginning April to mid Oct.

3.8 ha (150 pitches) flat, grassy

Tariff : (2015 price) ✝ 6.50€ ⬅ 📧 9.70€ – ⚡ (10A) 3.50€
🚰 local sani-station 4€ – 15 📧

Near the bus stop for Troyes town centre and the factory shops of Pont-Ste-Marie.

Surroundings : ♀
Leisure activities : 🏛 🏊 🚲 ♒ 🛶
Facilities : 👤 ⛽ 🎽 launderette
Nearby : 🚣 ♒

Longitude : 4.09682
Latitude : 48.31112

In order for the guide to remain wholly objective, the selection of campsites is made on an entirely independent basis.

M. Rock / Cephas / Photononstop

Corsica emerges from the Mediterranean like a glinting jewel. It is indeed the 'Isle of Beauty'. Follow its twisting roads to ancient citadels, perched on the island's rocky flanks in spectacular cliff-top settings, and your efforts will be more than rewarded. Enjoy panoramic views and inhale the fragrance of wild rosemary as you make your way up the rugged hills, clad in *maquis* (Mediterranean shrubs and herbs). The sudden sight of a secluded chapel or timeless village, or indeed an unscheduled encounter with a herd of mountain sheep, are among the many lasting memories that those discovering Corsica on foot, by bike or in their cars take home with them. After exploring the wild interior of the island, plunge into the impossibly clear turquoise waters that surround it and recharge your solar batteries on its warm sandy beaches, dreaming of an *assiette de charcuterie* (pork platter) and traditional cheese. Corsica seduces the eyes and taste buds of every visitor.

Centuri

Pietracorbara

Marine de Farinole

Bastia

Lumio

Calvi

Moltifao

Castellare-
di-Casinca

HAUTE - CORSE

Calacuccia

Corte

Porto

Piana

Cargèse

Tiuccia

Vivario

Aléria

Casaglione

Calcatoggio

Ghisonaccia

CORSE

Ajaccio

DU

Solenzara

Zonza

Olmeto

Ste-Lucie-de-Porto-V.

Propriano

SUD

Pinarellu

Belvédère-
Campomoro

Sartène

Porto-Vecchio

Figari

Bonifacio

D 81
N 197
N 193
N 198
D 81
N 193
D 81
N 196
N 198

● Locality with campsite
■ Locality with campsite and rental option
Vannes Locality with campsite and campervan area
Moyaux Locality with at least one pleasant campsite
Motorway service area for campervans

AJACCIO

20000 – Michelin map **345** B8 – pop. 64 306
▶ Bastia 147 – Bonifacio 131 – Calvi 166 – Corte 80

⚠ Les Mimosas

✆ 04 95 20 99 85, www.camping-lesmimosas.com – ⚕ ✗

Address : route d'Alata (5km, take the northern exit along the D 61 and take the turning to the left, follow the signs for Les Milelli)

Opening times : from beginning April to mid Oct.

2.5 ha (70 pitches) terraced, flat, stony

Tariff : (2015 price) ✦ 6€ ⇌ 3€ ▣ 3€ – ⚡ (6A) 3€

Rental rates : (2015 price) permanent ✗ – 12 ☖ – 6 ☖ – 1 studio. Per week from 280 to 580€

☖ local sani-station 8€

The rental of mobile homes and chalets, with pleasant shade from eucalyptus trees.

Surroundings : ⌇ ♨	**GPS** Longitude : 8.73069
Facilities : ♿ ⚲ ⇌ ⚏ ⚑ launderette refrigerators	Latitude : 41.94066

We value your opinion and welcome your feedback.
Do email us at campingfrance@tp.michelin.com

ALÉRIA

20270 – Michelin map **345** G7 – pop. 1 996 – alt. 20
▶ Bastia 71 – Corte 50 – Vescovato 52

⚶ Marina d'Aléria ♨

✆ 04 95 57 01 42, www.marina-aleria.com

Address : Plage de Padulone (3km east of Cateraggio along the N 200; beside the Tavignano river)

Opening times : from end April to beginning Oct.

17 ha/7 for camping (335 pitches) flat, grassy, sandy

Tariff : 47.50€ ✦✦ ⇌ ▣ ⚡ (9A) – Extra per person 7.70€ – Reservation fee 25€

Rental rates : (from end April to beginning Oct.) ✗ ⓟ (mobile homes) – 151 ☖ – 31 ☖. Per week from 270 to 1,200€ – Reservation fee 25€

Shady and sunny pitches laid out alongside the beach.

Surroundings : ⌇ ≤ sea and mountain ♨ ▵	**GPS** Longitude : 9.55
Leisure activities : ⚑ ✗ ⛱ ☉daytime ⚡ ⚵ ⚷ ✗ ⚏	Latitude : 42.11139
Facilities : ♿ ⚲ ⚏ ⚑ launderette ⚏ ⚏ refrigerated food storage facilities	

BASTIA

20200 – Michelin map **345** F3 – pop. 43 545
▶ Ajaccio 148 – Bonifacio 171 – Calvi 92 – Corte 69

⚶ San Damiano

✆ 04 95 33 68 02, www.campingsandamiano.com

Address : Lido de la Marana (9km southeast along the N 193 and turn left onto the D 107)

Opening times : from beginning April to beginning Nov.

12 ha (320 pitches) flat, sandy

Tariff : 35.80€ ✦✦ ⇌ ▣ ⚡ (6A) – Extra per person 9.20€

Rental rates : (from beginning April to beginning Nov.) – 59 ☖ – 48 ☖. Per night from 49 to 188€ – Per week from 343 to 1,316€

☖ local sani-station

Some luxury chalets (some with with a sea view) and a bar-restaurant right next to the water.

Surroundings : ⌇ ⌇ ♨ ▵	**GPS** Longitude : 9.46718
Leisure activities : ⚑ ✗ ⛱ ⚵ ✗ ⚷ ⚏	Latitude : 42.63114
Facilities : ♿ ⚲ ⚏ ⚑ launderette ⚏ ⚏	
Nearby : ⚞ ♿	

BELVÉDÈRE-CAMPOMORO

20110 – Michelin map **345** B10 – pop. 135 – alt. 5
▶ Ajaccio 88 – Bonifacio 72 – Porto 82 – Sartène 24

⚠ La Vallée

✆ 04 95 74 21 20, www.campomoro-lavallee.com – ⚕ ✗

Address : at Campomoro (on the D 121, 400m from the beach)

Opening times : from beginning May to end Sept.

3.5 ha (199 pitches) terraced, flat and relatively flat, grassy, stony

Tariff : (2015 price) ✦ 9€ ⇌ 5€ ▣ 5€ – ⚡ (12A) 6€

Rental rates : (2015 price) (from beginning May to end Sept.) ✗ ⓟ – 12 ☖. Per week from 750 to 1,000€

A view of the sea and the Genoese tower from some pitches and chalets.

Surroundings : ⌇ ♨	**GPS** Longitude : 8.81625
Facilities : ♿ ⚲ ⚏ ⚏ ▣	Latitude : 41.62815
Nearby : ⚏	

*To visit a town or region, use the **MICHELIN Green Guides**.*

BONIFACIO

20169 – Michelin map **345** D11 – pop. 2 919 – alt. 55
▶ Ajaccio 132 – Corte 150 – Sartène 50

⚶ Pertamina Village - U-Farniente ♨

✆ 04 95 73 05 47, www.camping-pertamina.com

Address : at Canelli (5km northeast along the N 198, follow the signs for Porto-Vecchio – Bastia)

Opening times : from beginning April to end Oct.

20 ha/8 for camping (150 pitches) terraced, relatively flat, flat, stony

Tariff : 44€ ✦✦ ⇌ ▣ ⚡ (6A) – Extra per person 12€ – Reservation fee 26€

Rental rates : (from beginning April to end Oct.) ♿ (1 mobile home) – 23 ☖ – 67 ☖ – 6 apartments – 11 canvas bungalows. Per night from 50 to 250€ – Per week from 350 to 1,697€ – Reservation fee 26€

A pleasant, undulating site with plenty of shade and a variety of rental options, some of which are quite luxurious.

Surroundings : ⌇ ⌇ ♨	**GPS** Longitude : 9.17905
Leisure activities : ⚑ ✗ ⛱ ☉ ⚡ ⚑ jacuzzi ⚵ ✗ ⚏ ⚏	Latitude : 41.41825
Facilities : ♿ ⚲ ▣ ▥ ⚏ ⚑ launderette ⚏ ⚏ refrigerated food storage facilities	

The prices listed were supplied by the campsite owners in 2015 (if prices were not available, those from the previous year are given). The fees should be regarded as basic charges and may fluctuate with inflation.

▲▲▲ Rondinara

✆ 04 95 70 43 15, www.rondinara.fr

Address : at Suartone (18km northeast along the N 198, follow the signs for Porto-Vecchio and take D 158 to the right, follow the signs for La Pointe de la Rondinara (headland); 400m from the beach)

5 ha (120 pitches) terraced, relatively flat, flat, grassy, stony
Rentals : 36 .

Situated in the heart of the maquis (typical shrubland), with a swimming pool, a restaurant and a panoramic view of the sea and Sardinia.

Surroundings : 🏖 ≤ ⚲	**G P S**
Leisure activities : 🍷 ✗ 🏛 🛶 ⛵	Longitude : 9.26289
Facilities : ♿ ⚡ 🚿 🔒 ♨ 🚱 refrigerated food storage facilities	Latitude : 41.47322
Nearby : pedalos , bar-restaurant on the beach	

▲▲▲ Les Îles

✆ 04 95 73 11 89, www.camping-desiles.com

Address : route de Piantarella (4.5km east, follow the signs for Piantarella, towards the landing stage at Cavallo)

Opening times : from beginning April to end Sept.

8 ha (150 pitches) undulating, relatively flat, flat, grassy, stony
Tariff : (2015 price) 🧍 9.90€ ⛺ 5.20€ 🚗 7.90€ – [⚡] (6A) 3.90€
Rental rates : (2015 price) (from beginning April to mid Oct.) ♿ (1 mobile home) – 17  – 20 🏠. Per week from 364 to 994€

Some pitches have a panoramic view over to Sardinia and nearby islands.

Surroundings : 🏖 ≤ ⚲	**G P S**
Leisure activities : ✗ 🏛 🛶 ⛵ 🎿 🏐 🦆	Longitude : 9.21034
Facilities : ♿ ⚡ 🚿 🔒 ♨ 🚱	Latitude : 41.37818

▲▲▲ Campo-di-Liccia

✆ 04 95 73 03 09, www.campingdiliccia.com

Address : at Parmentil (5.2km northeast along the N 198, follow the signs for Porto-Vecchio)

5 ha (161 pitches) terrace, flat, stony
Rentals : 52  – 16 🏠.

🚽 Raclet sani-station

Centuries-old Holm oaks, eucalyptus and olive trees provide generous amounts of shade; a mobile home park of a good standard.

Surroundings : 🏖 ⚲	**G P S**
Leisure activities : 🍷 ✗ 🏛 🛶 ⛵	Longitude : 9.17893
Facilities : ♿ ⚡ 🚿 ♨ 🚱 refrigerated food storage facilities	Latitude : 41.41943

▲ Pian del Fosse

✆ 04 95 73 16 34, www.piandelfosse.com

Address : 3.8 km northeast along the D 58 – or 5km along the N 198 following the signs for Porto-Vecchio and take the D 60 following signs for Santa-Manza

Opening times : from mid April to mid Oct.

5.5 ha (100 pitches) terraced, flat and relatively flat, stony
Tariff : (2015 price) 🧍 8.50€ ⛺ 4.50€ 🚗 6.30€ – [⚡] (16A) 4.50€ – Reservation fee 15€

Rental rates : (2015 price) (from mid April to mid Sept.)  – 1  – 5 🏠 – 6 studios – 12 canvas bungalows. Per night from 45 to 135€ – Per week from 250 to 930€ – Reservation fee 15€

🚽 local sani-station

The pitches lie in the shade of mulberry or plane trees, pines and 400-year-old olive trees.

Surroundings : 🏖 🚃 ⚲	**G P S**
Leisure activities : ✗ 🛶	Longitude : 9.20083
Facilities : ♿ ⚡ 🅿 🚿 ♨ 🍴 launderette	Latitude : 41.39972
Nearby : 🐎	

CALACUCCIA

20224 – Michelin map **345** D5 – pop. 316 – alt. 830
▶ Ajaccio 107 – Bastia 76 – Porto-Vecchio 146 – Corte 27

▲ Acquaviva

✆ 04 95 48 00 08, www.acquaviva-fr.com

Address : 500m southwest along the D 84 and take road to the left, opposite the service station

Opening times : from mid April to mid Oct.

4 ha (50 pitches) flat and relatively flat, stony, grassy
Tariff : 🧍 7€ ⛺ 3€ 🚗 6€ – [⚡] (16A) 4€
🚽 2 🚗 22.40€

The site looks out over the lake with some shade; hotel-restaurant services are provided by the site owner.

Surroundings : 🏖 ≤ Lake and mountains ⚲	**G P S**
Leisure activities : 🏛 🛶	Longitude : 9.01049
Facilities : ♿ 🚳 🚿 ♨ 🍴	Latitude : 42.33341
Nearby : 🍷 ✗ 🏊 🦆	

The information in the guide may have changed since going to press.

CALCATOGGIO

20111 – Michelin map **345** B7 – pop. 522 – alt. 250
▶ Ajaccio 23 – Bastia 156

▲▲▲ La Liscia

✆ 04 95 52 20 65, www.la-liscia.com

Address : route de Tiuccia (5km northwest along the D 81; beside the river, in the Golfe de La Liscia (bay), 500m from the beach)

Opening times : from beginning May to end Sept.

3 ha (100 pitches) terraced, flat, grassy, stony
Tariff : (2015 price) 🧍 6.50€ ⛺ 3.50€ 🚗 4.80€ – [⚡] (10A) 4.50€ – Reservation fee 17€
Rental rates : (2015 price) (from beginning May to beginning Oct.)  – 7  – 1 🏠. Per night from 50 to 80€ – Per week from 450 to 820€

🚽 local sani-station

The site is partly laid out on well-shaded terraces, but choose the pitches furthest away from the road. Basic sanitary facilities.

Surroundings : ⚲	**G P S**
Leisure activities : 🍷 ✗ 🏛 🛶 🚲	Longitude : 8.75526
Facilities : ♿ ⚡ 🚿 🍴 launderette ♨ refrigerators	Latitude : 42.04678

CALVI

20260 – Michelin map **345** B4 – pop. 5 377
▶ Bastia 92 – Corte 88 – L'Ile-Rousse 25 – Porto 73

⚑ Les Castors

📞 04 95 65 13 30, www.camping-castors.fr – ⌂ ✕

Address : route de Piétramaggiore (located 1km south along the N 197 towards L'Île Rousse and follow the signs for Pietra-Major to the right)

Opening times : from beginning April to beginning Nov.

2 ha (105 pitches) flat, sandy, stony

Tariff : (2015 price) ♣ 12.50€ ⇌ 6€ 🅴 8€ – ⚡ (15A) 5.50€

Rental rates : (2015 price) (from beginning April to beginning Nov.) ✕ – 36 ⛺ – 28 studios – 9 apartments. Per night from 62 to 216 € – Per week from 371 to 1,295€ – Reservation fee 10€

🚮 Eurorelais sani-station

A site shaded by eucalpytus trees, with a variety of rental accommodation.

Surroundings : 🏞 ♨ ♨		
Leisure activities : 🍽 ✕ 🛶 🏊 🛝		**Longitude : 8.7561**
Facilities : ♿ ⛽ 🚿 🍴 🛒	**GPS**	**Latitude : 42.55735**

⚑ La Pinède ♟♟

📞 04 95 65 17 80, www.camping-calvi.com

Address : route de la Pinède (300m from the beach)

5 ha (262 pitches) flat, sandy, stony

Rentals : ♿ – 14 'gypsy' caravans – 20 ⛺ – 80 🏠.

Choose the pitches away from the road in preference.

Surroundings : ♨ ♨		
Leisure activities : 🍽 ✕ 🏛 🎯 🛶 🎾 ♜ 🏊 multi-sports ground		**Longitude : 8.76795**
Facilities : ♿ ⛽ 🚿 🍴 launderette 🛒 🚿 refrigerated food storage facilities	**GPS**	**Latitude : 42.55318**
Nearby : 🛒		

⚑ Bella Vista

📞 04 95 65 11 76, www.camping-bellavista.com

Address : route de Pietramaggiore (head 1.5km south along the N 197 towards l'Île Rousse and follow the signs for Pietra-Major to the right)

Opening times : from beginning April to end Sept.

6 ha/4 for camping (152 pitches) flat, relatively flat, sandy, stony

Tariff : (2015 price) ♣ 8.50€ ⇌ 4.50€ 🅴 4.50€ – ⚡ (10A) 4.50€

Rental rates : (2015 price) (from beginning April to end Oct.) ✕ – 21 ⛺ – 21 🏠. Per night from 80 to 90€ – Per week from 250 to 1,050€ – Reservation fee 15€

🚮 35 🅴 8€

In the shade of pine and eucalyptus trees, and oleanders.

Surroundings : 🏞 ♨ ♨		
Leisure activities : ✕ 🛶		**Longitude : 8.75334**
Facilities : ♿ ⛽ ⓟ 🚿 🍴 🚽 🛒 🚿	**GPS**	**Latitude : 42.55068**

The Michelin classification (⚑⚑⚑ ... ⛺) is totally independent of the official star classification system awarded by the local prefecture or other official organisation.

*For more information on visiting particular towns or regions, consult the relevant regional **MICHELIN Green Guide**. We also recommend you use the appropriate Michelin regional map to locate your selected campsite, to calculate distances and to work out the best route.*

⚑ Paradella

📞 04 95 65 00 97, www.camping-paradella.fr ✉ 20214 Calenzana

Address : route de la forêt de Bonifato (9.5km southeast along the N 197, follow the signs for l'Ile-Rousse and take the D 81 to the right, follow the signs for the airport and Bonifato)

Opening times : from beginning April to end Sept.

5 ha (150 pitches) flat, sandy, stony

Tariff : (2015 price) 28,60€ ♣♣ ⇌ 🅴 ⚡ (10A) – Extra per person 8.60€ – Reservation fee 10€

Rental rates : (2015 price) (from beginning April to end Sept.) ✕ – 2 ⛺ – 18 🏠. Per night from 63 to 120€ – Per week from 300 to 800€

🚮 local sani-station 5€

Choose the pitches away from the road in preference, sheltered by pines and eucalyptus trees.

Surroundings : 🌳 ♨ ♨		
Leisure activities : 🛶 🎾 🏊		**Longitude : 8.79166**
Facilities : ♿ ⛽ 🚿 🍴 🛒 🚿	**GPS**	**Latitude : 42.50237**
Nearby : 🐎		

⛺ Paduella

📞 04 95 65 06 16, www.campingpaduella.com

Address : route de Bastia (1.8km southeast along the N 197, follow the signs for l'Ile-Rousse; 400m from the beach)

Opening times : from beginning May to beginning Oct.

4,5 ha (160 pitches) flat, sandy, stony

Tariff : ♣ 8.80€ ⇌ 4€ 🅴 4€ – ⚡ (6A) 4€

Rental rates : (from beginning May to beginning Oct.) – 38 canvas bungalows. Per night from 55 to 85€ – Per week from 385 to 595€

🚮 local sani-station – 20 🅴 9.50€

Some pitches are well marked out in the shade of a beautiful pine wood.

Surroundings : ♨ ♨		
Leisure activities : 🍽 🛶		**Longitude : 8.76429**
Facilities : ♿ ⛽ 🚽 🚿 🍴 🛒 🚿	**GPS**	**Latitude : 42.55219**
Nearby : 🛒		

⛺ Dolce Vita

📞 04 95 65 05 99, www.dolce-vita.fr

Address : 4.5km southeast along the N 197, follow the signs for l'Ile-Rousse; at the mouth of the Figarella river, 200m from the sea

6 ha (200 pitches) flat, grassy, sandy, stony

Choose those pitches beside the sea, furthest from the road and the small Calvi–Ile-de-Rousee railway.

Surroundings : ♨♨♨		
Leisure activities : ✕ 🍴 🛶 🎾 🏄		**Longitude : 8.78972**
Facilities : ♿ ⛽ 🍴 launderette 🛒 🚿	**GPS**	**Latitude : 42.55582**
Nearby : ⚓		

CARGÈSE

20130 – Michelin map **345** A7 – pop. 1 117 – alt. 75
▶ Ajaccio 51 – Calvi 106 – Corte 119 – Piana 21

⛰ Torraccia

☏ 04 95 26 42 39, www.camping-torraccia.com

Address : at Bagghiuccia (4.5km north along the D 81, follow the signs for Porto)

Opening times : from beginning May to end Sept.

3 ha (90 pitches) terraced, flat, grassy, stony

Tariff : (2015 price) ⋆ 9.90€ ⇌ 4.50€ 🅴 4.50€ – 🔌 (10A) 4.50€ –
Reservation fee 18.50€
Rental rates : (2015 price) (from beginning May to end Sept.) –
25 🏠. Per week from 335 to 950€ – Reservation fee 18.50€

Choose the pitches furthest away from the road. Good sanitary facilities and some chalets have a panoramic view.

Surroundings : ≼ 🌳🌳 Leisure activities : 🍽 jacuzzi 🚣 🏊 Facilities : 🚿 ⊶ 🏕 🔥 🧺	**GPS** Longitude : 8.59797 Latitude : 42.16258

There are several different types of sani-station ('borne' in French) – sanitation points providing fresh water and disposal points for grey water. See page 12 for further details.

CASAGLIONE

20111 – Michelin map **345** B7 – pop. 365 – alt. 150
▶ Ajaccio 33 – Bastia 166

⛰ U Sommalu

☏ 04 95 52 24 21, www.usommalu-camping.fr

Address : route de Casaglione (3km northeast along the D 81, then right onto the D 25, 600m from La plage de Liamone (beach))

Opening times : from beginning April to end Sept.

4 ha (123 pitches) terraced, flat and relatively flat, stony, grassy

Tariff : ⋆ 8.50€ ⇌ 4€ 🅴 6€ – 🔌 (16A) 4.50€

Rental rates : (from beginning April to end Sept.) – 15 🚐 –
22 🏠 – 2 apartments. Per week from 385 to 840€ – Reservation fee 5€

🚉 local sani-station

Shady pitches arranged on terraces, some of which have a sea view.

Surroundings : 🌳🌳 Leisure activities : 🍽 🏠 🚣 🏊 Facilities : 🚿 ⊶ 🏕 🍴 launderette	**GPS** Longitude : 8.73126 Latitude : 42.07027

CASTELLARE-DI-CASINCA

20213 – Michelin map **345** F5 – pop. 557 – alt. 140
▶ Paris 943 – Ajaccio 136 – Bastia 31

⛰ Tohapi Domaine d'Anghione 👥
(rental of mobile homes and gîtes only)

☏ 04 95 36 50 22, www.tohapi.fr

Address : at Anghione (6km along the D 106)

Opening times : from beginning April to mid Oct.

40 ha/26 for camping flat, grassy, stony, sandy

Rental rates : (2015 price) – 95 🚐 – 240 gîtes. Per night from 48 to 64€

A holiday village close to the beach with plenty of green spaces.

Surroundings : 🌳 🌳🌳 ⛰ Leisure activities : 🍽 🍴 🏠 🎯 🚴 🏊 🎾 ⛵ 🔲 ⛳ multi-sports ground Facilities : 🚿 ⊶ 🏕 🍴 launderette 🧺 Nearby : 🐎	**GPS** Longitude : 9.52707 Latitude : 42.47547

CENTURI

20238 – Michelin map **345** F2 – pop. 221 – alt. 228
▶ Ajaccio 202 – Bastia 55

⛰ Isulottu

☏ 04 95 35 62 81, www.isulottu.fr

Address : at Marine de Mute (head along the D 35 following the signs for Morsiglia, 200m from the beach)

Opening times : from mid May to end Sept.

2,3 ha (150 pitches)

Tariff : ⋆ 7.60€ ⇌ 3.50€ 🅴 3.90€ – 🔌 (20A) 3.70€

🚉 local sani-station

Well-shaded pitches laid out across a series of small terraces, some of which have a view of the sea or the village.

Surroundings : 🌳 ≼ 🌳🌳 Leisure activities : 🍽 🚣 🏊 Facilities : 🚿 ⊶ 🏕 🍴 🔥 🧺 Nearby : scuba diving	**GPS** Longitude : 9.3515 Latitude : 42.96048

These symbols are used for a campsite that is exceptional in its category:

⛰⛰ ... ⛰   *Particularly pleasant setting, quality and range of services available*

🌳🌳   *Tranquil, isolated site – quiet site, particularly at night*

≼≼   *Exceptional view – interesting or panoramic view*

CORTE

20250 – Michelin map **345** D6 – pop. 6 744 – alt. 396
▶ Ajaccio 81 – Bastia 68

⛰ Aire Naturelle St-Pancrace

☏ 04 95 46 09 22, www.campingsaintpancrace.fr

Address : St-Pancrace district (located 1.5km north along the Cours Paoli and take road to the left after the Sous-Préfecture)

Opening times : from mid April to end Oct.

12 ha/1 for camping (25 pitches) relatively flat, grassy, stony

Tariff : ⋆ 6€ ⇌ 3€ 🅴 3€ – 🔌 (45A) 4€

A farm campsite with produce for sale: ewe's milk and tomme cheese, and a range of jams.

Surroundings : 🌳 ≼ 🌳🌳 Leisure activities : 🏠 Facilities : ⊶ 🔲 🏠	**GPS** Longitude : 9.14696 Latitude : 42.32026

FARINOLE (MARINA DE)

20253 – Michelin map **345** F3 – pop. 224 – alt. 250
▶ Bastia 20 – Rogliano 61 – St-Florent 13

⚠ A Stella

𝒫 04 95 37 14 37, www.campingastella.com

Address : Marine de Farinole (along the D 80; beside the sea)

3 ha (100 pitches) terraced, relatively flat, flat, grassy, stony

Rentals : 2 apartments.

Some sunny pitches are available with a sea view; close to a pebble beach.

Surroundings : 🏔 ≤ 🏘 ⚠ Leisure activities : 🏖 Facilities : o–ᴴ 🖥 🛒	**G P S** Longitude : 9.34259 Latitude : 42.72911

*For more information on visiting particular towns or regions, consult the relevant regional **MICHELIN Green Guide**. We also recommend you use the appropriate Michelin regional map to locate your selected campsite, to calculate distances and to work out the best route.*

FIGARI

20114 – Michelin map **345** D11 – pop. 1 217 – alt. 80
▶ Ajaccio 122 – Bonifacio 18 – Porto-Vecchio 20 – Sartène 39

⚠ U Moru

𝒫 04 95 71 23 40, www.u-moru.com

Address : 5km northeast along the D 859

Opening times : from mid June to mid Sept.

6 ha/4 for camping (100 pitches) flat and relatively flat, sandy

Tariff : ✴ 8.30€ 🚗 4€ 🔲 4.80€ – ⚡ (6A) 5€

Rental rates : (from mid June to mid Sept.) ♿ (1 mobile home) 🍴 – 12 🚐. Per week from 650 to 990€

The pitches are well shaded and the mobile home terraces are well equipped.

Surroundings : 🗀 🏘 Leisure activities : 🏖 Facilities : ♿ o–ᴴ 🛒 🖥 🛏 refrigerators	**G P S** Longitude : 9.16564 Latitude : 41.53096

GHISONACCIA

20240 – Michelin map **345** F7 – pop. 3 669 – alt. 25
▶ Bastia 85 – Aléria 14 – Ghisoni 27 – Venaco 56

⛰ Arinella-Bianca ▲▲

𝒫 04 95 56 04 78, www.arinellabianca.com

Address : route de la Mer (3.5km east along the D 144 then continue 700m along the road to the right)

Opening times : from mid April to mid Oct.

10 ha (416 pitches) flat, grassy, sandy

Tariff : 55€ ✴✴ 🚗 🔲 ⚡ (10A) – Extra per person 17€ – Reservation fee 50€

Rental rates : (from mid April to mid Oct.) ♿ – 177 🚐 – 56 🏠. Per night from 50 to 240€ – Per week from 285 to 1,900€ – Reservation fee 50€

🚐 Eurorelais sani-station 8€

A lovely spa area, with a pleasant Zen water park attached. Some luxurious rental accommodation beside the beach.

Surroundings : 🏘 ⚠ Leisure activities : 🍴 ✗ 🏖 🛶 🏃 🎿 ≋ hammam, jacuzzi 🏇 ✗ 🎿 tourist information, multi-sports ground, spa centre, water park Facilities : ♿ o–ᴴ 🖥 🛒 🛏 launderette 🛒 🛒 refrigerated food storage facilities Nearby : 🛒 ⚓	**G P S**  Longitude : 9.44331 Latitude : 41.9972

⛰ Homair Vacances Marina d'Erba Rossa ▲▲

𝒫 04 95 56 25 14, http://www.homair.com/

Address : route de la Mer (4km east along the D 144; beside the beach)

Opening times : from beginning April to mid Oct.

12 ha/8 for camping (588 pitches) flat, grassy

Tariff : (2015 price) 27€ ✴✴ 🚗 🔲 ⚡ (10A) – Extra per person 10.50€ – Reservation fee 10€

Rental rates : (from beginning April to mid Oct.) – 498 🚐. Per night from 29 to 226€ – Per week from 203 to 1,582€ – Reservation fee 25€

In a green and shaded setting, with a relaxation area close to the beach. There's an option for full-board or half-board stays.

Surroundings : 🗀 🏘 ⚠ Leisure activities : 🍴 ✗ 🏖 🛶 🏃 ≋ jacuzzi 🏇 ✗ 🛶 🎿 wildlife park, spa centre Facilities : ♿ o–ᴴ 🅿 🛒 🛏 launderette 🛒 🛒 refrigerated food storage facilities Nearby : ⚓ scuba diving	**G P S** 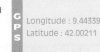 Longitude : 9.44339 Latitude : 42.00211

⛰ Sunêlia Village Vacances Perla Di Mare
(rental of mobile homes, gîtes and apartments only)

𝒫 04 95 56 53 10, www.perla.di.mare.fr

Address : Plage de Vignale

Opening times : permanent

10 ha (174 pitches) undulating

Rental rates : (2015 price) ♿ (2 mobile homes) – 100 🚐 – 4 studios – 50 apartments. Per night from 50 to 178€ – Per week from 350 to 1,246€ – Reservation fee 30€

A range of rental options with a relaxation area close to the beach.

Surroundings : 🏔 ⚓ ⚠ Leisure activities : 🍴 ✗ 🏖 🏃 hammam, jacuzzi 🏇 🚲 🎿 ⚓ archery, spa centre Facilities : o–ᴴ 🖥 🛒 launderette 🛒	**G P S** Longitude : 9.4558 Latitude : 42.00647

Key to rentals symbols:

12 🚐	*Number of mobile homes*
20 🏠	*Number of chalets*
6 🛏	*Number of rooms to rent*
Per night 30–50€	*Minimum/maximum rate per night*
Per week 300–1,000€	*Minimum/maximum rate per week*

LUMIO

20260 – Michelin map **345** B4 – pop. 1 250 – alt. 150
▶ Ajaccio 158 – Bastia 83 – Corte 77 – Calvi 10

🏔 Le Panoramic

𝒫 04 95 60 73 13, www.le-panoramic.com – ℞

Address : route de Lavatoggio (situated 2km northeast on the D 71, follow the signs for Belgodère)

Opening times : from beginning May to end Sept.

6 ha (108 pitches) very uneven, terraced, stony, sandy

Tariff : (2015 price) ⋆ 8.50€ ⟺ 3.50€ 🔲 7€ – ⚡ (6A) 4€
Rental rates : (2015 price) (from beginning May to end Sept.)
⚡ – 7 🚐. Per week from 380 to 950€

Some of the pitches have a panoramic view of the sea.

Surroundings : 🐾 ≤ ♎♎		
Leisure activities : ✗ 🛟	**G**	Longitude : 8.84805
Facilities : ⊶ 🏕 📷 🛁	**P S**	Latitude : 42.58973

The prices listed were supplied by the campsite owners in 2015 (if prices were not available, those from the previous year are given). The fees should be regarded as basic charges and may fluctuate with inflation.

MOLTIFAO

20218 – Michelin map **345** D5 – pop. 724 – alt. 420
▶ Ajaccio 113 – Bastia 58

🏔 E Canicce

𝒫 04 95 35 16 75, http://www.campingecanicce.com

Address : Vallée de l'Asco (3km south on the D 47; beside the Asco river)

Opening times : from beginning March to end Oct.

1 ha (25 pitches)

Tariff : 23€ ⋆⋆ ⟺ 🔲 ⚡ (10A) – Extra per person 6€
Rental rates : (from mid Jan. to mid Nov.) ⚡ – 3 🚐 – 3 gîtes.
Per night from 50 to 70€ – Per week from 550 to 720€

In the heart of the maquis (typical shrubland), at the foot of mountains and beside a stream.

Surroundings : 🐾 ≤ Monte Cinto and Scala		
di Santa Régina (gorge) ♎♎	**G**	Longitude : 9.13444
Leisure activities : ♤	**P**	Latitude : 42.47573
Facilities : ⊶ 🛁 🏕 📷	**S**	

OLMETO

20113 – Michelin map **345** C9 – pop. 1 230 – alt. 320
▶ Ajaccio 64 – Propriano 8 – Sartène 20

🏔 L'Esplanade

𝒫 04 95 76 05 03, www.camping-esplanade.com

Address : at Olmeto-Plage (1.6km along the D 157, 100m from the beach – direct access)

Opening times : from beginning April to end Oct.

4,5 ha (100 pitches) very uneven, terraced, flat and relatively flat, stony, rocks

Tariff : ⋆ 8.70€ ⟺ 4.50€ 🔲 4€ – ⚡ (10A) 5€ – Reservation fee 11€

Rental rates : (from beginning April to end Oct.) 🅿 (chalets) – 8 'gypsy' caravans – 42 🚐 – 14 🏠 – 2 canvas bungalows – 6 tent lodges. Per night from 58 to 165€ – Per week from 297 to 996€ – Reservation fee 11€

Choose the pitches furthest away from the road. There's a panoramic view from some chalets, a swimming pool and a restaurant.

Surroundings : 🛏 ♒♒		
Leisure activities : ✗ 🛟 🚤 🛟	**G**	Longitude : 8.88868
Facilities : ⚙ ⊶ 🏕 📷 🛁 🛒	**P S**	Latitude : 41.69562

Using the traditional Michelin classification method, the guide provides you with an easy, speedy reference for assessing the category of each site: 1 to 5 tents (see page 10).

PIANA

20115 – Michelin map **345** A6 – pop. 450 – alt. 420
▶ Ajaccio 72 – Calvi 85 – Évisa 33 – Porto 13

🏔 Plage d'Arone

𝒫 04 95 20 64 54 – ℞

Address : route Danièle Casanova (11.5km southwest along the D 824; 500m from the beach – direct access)

Opening times : from mid May to end Sept.

3.8 ha (125 pitches) terraced, open site, flat, grassy, stony

Tariff : ⋆ 9€ ⟺ 6€ 🔲 7€ – ⚡ (6A) 3€

Situated 500m from the beach in the maquis (typical shrubland), shaded by olive, eucalyptus, bay and other trees, and Mediterranean shrubs.

Surroundings : 🐾 ≤ ♎♎		
Facilities : ⚙ ⊶ 🏕 🛒 🛁 📷 🛁	**G**	Longitude : 8.58092
	P S	Latitude : 42.20843

PIETRACORBARA

20233 – Michelin map **345** F2 – pop. 573 – alt. 150
▶ Paris 967 – Ajaccio 170 – Bastia 21 – Biguglia 31

🏔 La Pietra

𝒫 04 95 35 27 49, www.la-pietra.com – ℞

Address : head 4km southeast along the D 232 and take road to the left; 500m from the beach

Opening times : from end March to beginning Nov.

3 ha (80 pitches) flat, grassy, stony

Tariff : ⋆ 9.95€ ⟺ 3.80€ – ⚡ (10A) 3.50€

Rental rates : (from end March to beginning Nov.) – 5 🏠.
Per night from 110 to 695€ – Per week from 600 to 4,800€

🚐 local sani-station

A well-maintained campsite with shaded, marked-out pitches or on a sunny meadow. Luxury rental options.

Surroundings : 🐾 ≤ 🛏 ♎♎		
Leisure activities : ✗ 🛟 🚤 🛴 🛟		
Facilities : ⚙ ⊶ 🛒 🛁 🏕 📷 🛁 refrigerated	**G**	Longitude : 9.4739
food storage facilities	**P S**	Latitude : 42.83939
Nearby : 🐎		

PINARELLU

20124 – Michelin map **345** F9
▶ Ajaccio 146 – Bonifacio 44 – Porto-Vecchio 16

⌂ California

✆ 04 95 71 49 24, www.camping-california.net ✉ 20144 Ste-Lucie-de-Porto-Vecchio

Address : at Pinarellu (800m south along the D 468 and 1.5km along the road to the left; beside the beach)

7 ha/5 for camping (100 pitches) undulating, flat, sandy, pond

Situated near lakes and the sea, an exclusive location in an unspoilt setting.

Surroundings : 🏞 🎣 ⛰
Leisure activities : ✗ ⛵ ✂
Facilities : ♿ ⛽ 🅿 🚽 🏪 ⛴ 🚿

GPS Longitude : 9.38084
Latitude : 41.66591

PORTO

20150 – Michelin map **345** B6 – pop. 544
▶ Ajaccio 84 – Calvi 73 – Corte 93 – Évisa 23

⌂⌂⌂ Les Oliviers

✆ 04 95 26 14 49, www.camping-oliviers-porto.com ✉ 20150 Ota ⚲

Address : Pont de Porto (at the bridge (just off the D 81, beside the Porto river, 100m from the town)

Opening times : from end March to beginning Nov.

5.4 ha (216 pitches) very uneven, terraced, flat, stony, rocks

Tariff : ♦ 10.90€ 🚗 4€ 🔲 7.50€ – (½) (10A) 5€ – Reservation fee 15€
Rental rates : (from end March to beginning Nov.) ⚲ – 6 'gypsy' caravans – 40 ⌂. Per night from 58 to 222€ – Per week from 320 to 1,590€ – Reservation fee 16€

Surroundings : 🏞 ⌂ 🎣
Leisure activities : 🍴 ✗ 🎯 🎠 ⛱ hammam ⛵ ⛴ ⚓ diving (sub aqua) school, spa centre
Facilities : ♿ ⛽ 🅿 🚿 🏪 launderette ⛴ refrigerated food storage facilities
Nearby : 🛒 🚲 🎣

GPS Longitude : 8.71005
Latitude : 42.26242

⌂⌂⌂ Sole e Vista

✆ 04 95 26 15 71, www.camping-sole-e-vista.com ✉ 20150 Ota

Address : in the village (main access via the supermarket car park – secondary access: head 1km east along the D 124, follow the signs for Ota, 150m from the Porto and the town)

Opening times : from beginning April to beginning Nov.

4 ha (170 pitches) very uneven, terraced, flat, stony, rocks

Tariff : (2015 price) ♦ 10€ 🚗 5€ 🔲 5€ – (½) (12A) 3.50€
Rental rates : (2015 price) (from beginning April to beginning Nov.) – 34 🏕 – 5 ⌂ – 5 tent lodges. Per night from 29 to 180€ – Per week from 200 to 1,350€
🚐 local sani-station – 15 🔲 9€

In a natural, wooded setting with pitches on numerous small terraces. There's a panoramic view of the sea and the mountains from the swimming pool and restaurant.

Surroundings : 🏞 ⌂ 🎣
Leisure activities : ✗ ⛵ ⛴
Facilities : ⛽ 🏪 launderette, refrigerators
Nearby : 🛒 ⚓ 🎣

GPS Longitude : 8.71114
Latitude : 42.26313

⌂⌂ Funtana a l'Ora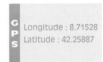

✆ 04 95 26 11 65, www.funtanaalora.com ✉ 20150 Ota

Address : route d'Évisa (1.4km southeast along the D 84, 200m from the Porto)

Opening times : from beginning April to beginning Nov.

2 ha (70 pitches) very uneven, terraced, flat and relatively flat, stony, rocks

Tariff : (2015 price) ♦ 9.40€ 🚗 4€ 🔲 4€ – (½) (10A) 4€ – Reservation fee 15€

Rental rates : (2015 price) (from beginning April to beginning Nov.) – 11 ⌂. Per night from 46 to 205€ – Per week from 290 to 1,300€ – Reservation fee 15€

🚐 local sani-station – 20 🔲 8€

Pitches with good amounts of shade on numerous small terraces, in a natural and unspoilt setting.

Surroundings : 🏞 ⌂ 🎣
Leisure activities : 🎯 ⛴ multi-sports ground
Facilities : ♿ ⛽ 🚿 🏪 launderette ⛴ refrigerated food storage facilities

GPS Longitude : 8.71528
Latitude : 42.25887

⌂ Casa del Torrente – (rental of chalets only)

✆ 04 95 22 45 14, www.casadeltorrente.com ✉ 20150 Ota

Address : route Evisa (located 1km southeast along the D 84; beside the Porto river – direct access)

Opening times : from beginning April to beginning Nov.

1.5 ha terraced

Rental rates : (2015 price) ⚲ – 12 ⌂ – 3 apartments. Per night from 46 to 205€ – Per week from 290 to 1,300€ – Reservation fee 15€

Gites suitable for large families and free access to the Funtana a l'Ora campsite services, 400m away, on the other side of the road.

Surroundings : 🏞 🎣
Leisure activities : ⛴
Facilities : ⛽ 🚿 🏪 🚿 🔑
Nearby : ⛴

GPS Longitude : 8.70824
Latitude : 42.26209

PORTO-VECCHIO

20137 – Michelin map **345** E10 – pop. 11 005 – alt. 40
▶ Ajaccio 141 – Bonifacio 28 – Corte 121 – Sartène 59

⌂⌂⌂ Golfo di Sogno

✆ 04 95 70 08 98, www.golfo-di-sogno.fr ⚲

Address : route de Cala-Rossa (6km northeast along the D 468)

Opening times : from beginning May to end Sept.

22 ha (650 pitches) flat, grassy, sandy

Tariff : 30€ ♦♦ 🚗 🔲 (½) (6A) – Extra per person 9.90€
Rental rates : (from beginning May to end Sept.) ⚲ – 12 🏕 – 61 ⌂ – 138 canvas bungalows – 12 gîtes. Per week from 290 to 2,240€

In a very pleasant pine wood beside the sea; a spacious site with a range of rental options of varying degrees of quality.

Surroundings : ⌂ 🎣 ⛰
Leisure activities : 🍴 ✗ 🎯 🎠 ✂ 🎣 🚣 watersports centre, multi-sports ground
Facilities : ⛽ 🚿 🚿 launderette 🛒 ⛴
Nearby : ⚓

GPS Longitude : 9.31297
Latitude : 41.62974

⛰ Pitrera

✆ 04 95 70 20 10, www.pitrera.com

Address : at La Trinité (head 5.8km north along the N 198, follow the signs for Bastia and take road to the right)

4 ha (95 pitches) very uneven, terraced, relatively flat, stony, rocks
Rentals : 1 🚐 – 56 🏠 – 1 yurt.

Well-shaded pitches, a lovely swimming pool area and a pan-oramic sea view from some chalets.

Surroundings : 💦
Leisure activities : ✗ ⚓ 🛶 ⛷
Facilities : ♿ ⚲ 🏕 🚇 🔋 ⚓

GPS Longitude : 9.29535
Latitude : 41.63461

⛰ U Pirellu

✆ 04 95 70 23 44, www.u-pirellu.com – acces to some pitches via a steep slope – 🏕 💦

Address : route de Palombaggia (located 9km to the east, at Piccovagia)

Opening times : from mid April to end Sept.

5 ha (150 pitches) very uneven, terraced, flat and relatively flat, grassy, stony

Tariff : (2015 price) 🚹 9.80€ 🚗 4€ 🔌 4.50€ – 📱 (6A) 4€
Rental rates : (2015 price) (from mid April to end Sept.) 💦 –
17 🏠. Per night from 65 to 220€ – Per week from 370 to 1,550€ –
Reservation fee 12€

Some chalets have a panoramic view of the sea and La Pointe de la Chiappa (headland).

Surroundings : 🐟 🚤 💦
Leisure activities : 🍴 ✗ ⚓ 🛶
Facilities : ♿ ⚲ 🅿 🏕 🚇 🔋 ⚓
Nearby : 🔥

GPS Longitude : 9.3322
Latitude : 41.58962

⛰ La Vetta

✆ 04 95 70 09 86, www.campinglavetta.com

Address : at La Trinité (5.5km north on N 198, follow the signs for Bastia)

8 ha (100 pitches) terraced, sloping, flat, grassy, stony, rocks
Rentals : 41 🚐 – 6 🏠.

In an unspoilt, natural setting with some high-quality rental accommodation. Try to pick pitches away from the road.

Surroundings : 💦
Leisure activities : ✗ ⚓ 🛶
Facilities : ♿ ⚲ 🏕 🚇 🔋

GPS Longitude : 9.29356
Latitude : 41.63285

⛰ Arutoli

✆ 04 95 70 12 73, www.arutoli.com

Address : route de l'Ospédale (situated 2km northwest along the D 368)

Opening times : from beginning April to end Oct.

4 ha (150 pitches) flat, relatively flat, rocky, stony

Tariff : 26.40€ 🚹🚹 🚗 🔌 📱 (6A) – Extra per person 7.85€
Rental rates : (from beginning April to end Oct.) – 30 🚐.
Per night from 53 to 150€ – Per week from 371 to 1,050€ –
Reservation fee 12€

🚐 local sani-station

Well-shaded pitches with a variety of rental options.

Surroundings : 💦
Leisure activities : ✗ 🏓 🛶
Facilities : ♿ ⚲ 🏕 🚇 🔋 ⚓
Nearby : 🐎

GPS Longitude : 9.26556
Latitude : 41.60186

⛰ Bella Vista

✆ 04 95 70 58 01, www.bella-vista.cc – 🏕

Address : route de Palombaggia (located 9.3km to the east, at Piccovagia)

Opening times : from beginning June to mid Sept.

2,5 ha (100 pitches) very uneven, terraced, flat, grassy, stony

Tariff : (2015 price) 🚹 8€ 🚗 3.50€ 🔌 5€ – 📱 (6A) 3.50€
Rental rates : (2015 price) (from beginning May to end Sept.) 💦 –
8 🏠. Per week from 420 to 910€ – Reservation fee 10€

Some chalets have a panoramic view of the sea and La Pointe de la Chiappa (headland).

Surroundings : 🐟 💦
Leisure activities : ✗ 🛶
Facilities : ♿ ⚲ 🏕 🚇 🔋

GPS Longitude : 9.3367
Latitude : 41.58672

⛰ Les Îlots d'Or

✆ 04 95 70 01 30, www.campinglesilotsdor.com

Address : route Pezza Cardo (head 6km northeast along the D 568 or the N 198, follow the signs for Bastia and take a right turn along the D 468 b before La Trinité)

4 ha (176 pitches) terraced, flat, grassy, flat, rocks
Rentals : 3 🚐 – 23 🏠.

Some pitches are virtually on top of the water!

Surroundings : 🐟 🚤 💦⚓
Leisure activities : ✗
Facilities : ♿ ⚲ 🏕 🚇 🔋
Nearby : 🚣

GPS Longitude : 9.30819
Latitude : 41.6275

⛰ Les Jardins du Golfe

✆ 04 95 70 46 92, www.a-stella.org

Address : route de Palombaggia (5.2km to the south)

4 ha (200 pitches) sloping, flat, grassy, sandy
Rentals : 9 🏠.

Surroundings : 💦
Leisure activities : 🍴 🛶 (small swimming pool)
Facilities : ⚲ 🏕 🔋
Nearby : 🚣

GPS Longitude : 9.2905
Latitude : 41.57353

PROPRIANO

20110 – Michelin map **345** C9 – pop. 3 292 – alt. 5
▶ Ajaccio 70 – Bastia 202 – Olbia 126 – Sassari 32

⛰ Village Vacances U Livanti – (rental of chalets only)

✆ 04 95 76 08 06, www.ulivanti.com

Address : at Portigliolo – route de Campomoro (8km south along the RN 196 and take D 121; in the Gulf of Le Valinco)

Opening times : from beginning April to beginning Nov.

6 ha terraced

Rental rates : 💦 🅿 – 15 🏠. Per night from 160 to 272€ –
Per week from 1 090 to 1,850€

A chalet village (standard varying from fairly basic to luxurious) on attractive terraces; a restaurant right by the water.

Surroundings : 🐟 🚤⚓
Leisure activities : 🍴 ✗ 🏃
Facilities : ⚲ 🏕 🔋
Nearby : 🚣 water skiing

GPS Longitude : 8.86912
Latitude : 41.64491

STE-LUCIE-DE-PORTO-VECCHIO

20144 – Michelin map **345** F9
▶ Ajaccio 142 – Porto-Vecchio 16

⚠ Homair Vacances Acqua E Sole ⚤
(rental of mobile homes and chalets only)

🕾 04 95 50 15 75, www.homair.com

Address : at Pianu Di Conca (located 1km northeast along the N 198; follow the signs for Solenzara and take road to the left)

Opening times : from beginning April to beginning Oct.

5 ha terraced, flat

Rental rates : ⚙ (1 mobile home) – 125 🚐. Per night from 25 to 47€ – Per week from 175 to 1,505€ – Reservation fee 25€
A selection of mobile homes and good-quality chalets.

Surroundings : 🗺 ⚘
Leisure activities : ♟ ✕ 🏘 ⚘ 🚣 ⛵
Facilities : ⌕ 🎦 🏛 🍴 launderette ⚗
Nearby : 🐴

⚠ Santa-Lucia ⚤

🕾 04 95 71 45 28, www.campingsantalucia.com

Address : on the RN 198 road (in the village)

3 ha (160 pitches)

Rentals : 21 🏠 – 22 canvas bungalows.
Well-shaded pitches with good sanitary facilities, and a charming small chalet village.

Surroundings : 🗺 🌳
Leisure activities : ✕ ⚘ 🚣 ⛵
Facilities : ⚙ ⌕ 🍴 🎦 ⚗
Nearby : 🛒

⚠ Fautea

🕾 04 95 71 41 51 – 🏕

Address : at Fautea, on the coast (5km northeast on the N 198, follow the signs for Solenzara)

Opening times : from beginning May to end Sept.

5 ha (100 pitches) terraced, stony

Tariff : (2015 price) ♣ 9.80€ ⚗ 2.10€ 🅴 3.90€ – ⚡ (3A) 4€
Choose the pitches on the small terraces with a panoramic sea view, furthest away from the road.

Surroundings : ≤ 🗺 🌳 ⚠
Leisure activities : 🚣
Facilities : ⚙ ⌕ 🔲 🛁 🍴 🎦 🚿
Nearby : ✕

To visit a town or region, use the MICHELIN Green Guides.

SOLENZARA

20145 – Michelin map **345** F8 – pop. 1 169
▶ Paris 1017 – Ajaccio 131 – Bastia 105

⚠ Homair Vacances Sole di Sari ⚤
(rental of mobile homes, chalets and tent lodges only)

🕾 04 95 57 07 70, www.soledisari.com

Address : route de Bavella (1.5km northwest along the D 268)

4 ha terraced

Rentals : ⚙ (1 mobile home) – 50 🚐 – 44 🏠 – 16 tent lodges.
An attractive site with some high-end rental options.

Surroundings : 🗺
Leisure activities : ✕ 🎦daytime ⚘ 🚣 ⛵ 🏊 ⛵
Facilities : ⚙ ⌕ 🏛 🛁 🍴 launderette ⚗

Longitude : 9.38396
Latitude : 41.86493

TIUCCIA

20111 – Michelin map **345** B7
▶ Ajaccio 30 – Cargèse 22 – Vico 22

⚠ Les Couchants

🕾 04 95 52 26 60, http://campinglescouchants.fr ✉ 20111 Casaglione

Address : route de Casaglione (4.9km north along the D 81 and turn right onto the D 25)

Opening times : from mid June to mid Sept.

5 ha (120 pitches) terraced, flat, grassy, stony

Tariff : ♣ 7€ ⚗ 3.50€ – ⚡ (6A) 5€
Rental rates : (from mid June to mid Sept.) – 8 🏠. Per night from 110 to 280€ – Per week from 770 to 924€
🚐 22 🅴 10.50€
Surrounded by attractive olive, eucalyptus and laurel trees.

Surroundings : 🗺 ≤ 🌳
Leisure activities : ♟ ✕ 🚣 ⛵
Facilities : ⚙ ⌕ 🔲 🛁 🎦 ⚗

Longitude : 8.74894
Latitude : 42.08114

VIVARIO

20219 – Michelin map **345** E6 – pop. 532 – alt. 850
▶ Bastia 89 – Aléria 49 – Corte 22 – Bocognano 22

⚠ Aire Naturelle le Soleil

🕾 04 95 47 21 16, http://www.camping-lesoleil.com/ – alt. 800

Address : at Tattone (6km southwest along the N 193, follow the signs for Ajaccio, near the small Tattone railway station)

Opening times : from beginning May to end Sept.

1 ha (25 pitches) terraced, flat, relatively flat, grassy

Tariff : 21€ ♣♣ ⚗ 🅴 ⚡ (10A) – Extra per person 7€
🚐 Eurorelais sani-station
Partly shaded by fruit trees, looking out over the mountains.

Surroundings : 🗺 ≤ 🌳
Leisure activities : ♟ ✕ 🏘
Facilities : ⚙ ⌕ 🔲 🍴 launderette, refrigerators
Nearby : 🚣

Longitude : 9.15186
Latitude : 42.1532

ZONZA

20124 – Michelin map **345** E9 – pop. 1 802 – alt. 780
▶ Ajaccio 93 – Porto-Vecchio 40 – Sartène 38 – Solenzara 40

⚠ Municipal

🕾 04 95 78 62 74, campingmunzonza@voila.fr

Address : route de Porto-Vecchio (3km southeast along the D 368)

2 ha (120 pitches) undulating, terraced, flat, stony

🚐 Flot Bleu sani-station
Situated in the shade of pretty pine trees, beside the river.

Surroundings : 🗺 🌳
Leisure activities : 🚣
Facilities : ⚙

Longitude : 9.19563
Latitude : 41.7504

Longitude : 9.35129
Latitude : 41.70328

Longitude : 9.3434
Latitude : 41.6966

Longitude : 9.40191
Latitude : 41.71557

FRANCHE-COMTÉ

H. Hughes / hemis.fr

Once upon a time in a land called Franche-Comté . . . many of France's tales and legends begin in the secret wilderness of this secluded region on the Swiss border. The high peaks and protected valleys of Jura, cloaked in fragrant conifers, cast a gentle charm over all who explore them. And an irresistible magic spell is woven by its cascading waterfalls, fascinating grottoes and mysterious lakes. The dark blue waters reflect the hills around them while forming a dramatic contrast with the lush green pastures. Nimble-fingered craftsmen transform the local wood into clocks, toys and pipes to the delight of all those who love and appreciate fine craftsmanship. Hungry travellers may want to savour the lovely hazelnut tang of Comté cheese but should beware the region's powerful gastronomic spell. The delicate smoked and salted meats, in which you can almost taste the pine and juniper, along with Franche-Comté's subtle but fruity wines, will have you coming back for more!

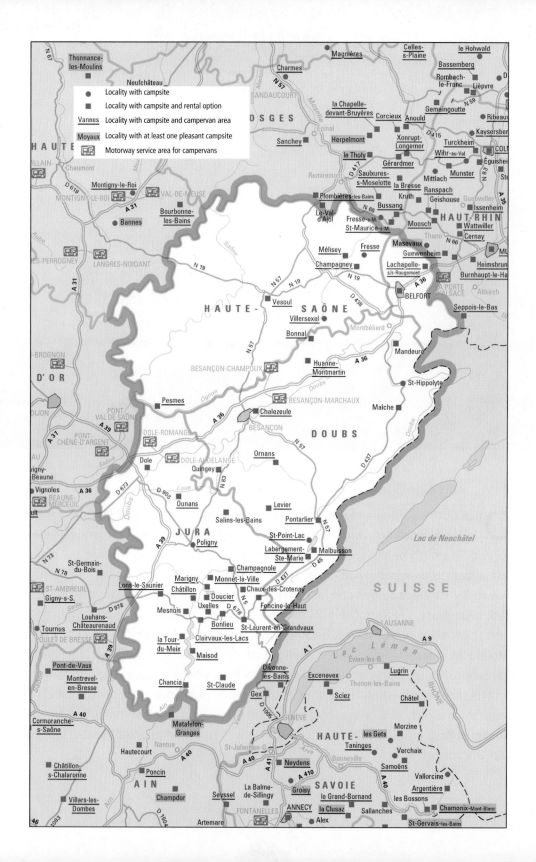

BELFORT

90000 – Michelin map **315** F11 – pop. 50 199 – alt. 360
▶ Paris 422 – Lure 33 – Luxeuil-les-Bains 52 – Montbéliard 23

⛰ L'Étang des Forges

✆ 03 84 22 54 92, www.camping-belfort.com

Address : rue du Général Béthouart (located 1.5km north along the D 13, follow the signs for Offemont and take a right turn – from the A 36, take exit 13)

Opening times : from beginning April to end Sept.

3.4 ha (90 pitches) flat, grassy, stony

Tariff : 27€ ✚✚ ⛟ 🔲 (10A) – Extra per person 5.50€ – Reservation fee 5€

Rental rates : (2015 price) (from beginning April to end Sept.) ⛵ (1 chalet) – 5 🚐 – 9 🏠 – 1 canvas bungalow. Per night from 40 to 120€ – Per week from 217 to 588€ – Reservation fee 15€

Smart and well-maintained campsite with a variety of trees.

Surroundings : ⩽ ♀
Leisure activities : 🍴 ✗ 🎲 ⛵ 🌳
Facilities : 🚿 ⟳ 🅲 🏧 🖥 ⛱ 🚰 launderette
Nearby : ♨

G P S Longitude : 6.86436 / Latitude : 47.65341

To visit a town or region, use the MICHELIN Green Guides.

BONLIEU

39130 – Michelin map **321** F7 – pop. 253 – alt. 785
▶ Paris 439 – Champagnole 23 – Lons-le-Saunier 32 – Morez 24

⛰ L'Abbaye

✆ 03 84 25 57 04, www.camping-abbaye.com

Address : 2 route du Lac (located 1.5km east along the N 78, follow the signs for St-Laurent-en-Grandvaux)

Opening times : from beginning May to end Sept.

3 ha (88 pitches) sloping, flat, grassy

Tariff : 20.80€ ✚✚ ⛟ 🔲 (10A) – Extra per person 4.80€
Rental rates : (from beginning May to end Sept.) ⛵ – 4 🚐 – 2 🛏 – 1 gîte. Per night from 52€ – Per week from 300 to 540€
flot bleu sani-station 9€

In an attracive location at the base of cliffs, not far from the Le Hérisson waterfall.

Surroundings : ⩾ ⩽ ☐
Leisure activities : 🍴 ✗ ⛵
Facilities : 🚿 ⟳ ⛱ 🚰 launderette ⛟
Nearby : 🐴 canoeing

G P S Longitude : 5.87562 / Latitude : 46.59199

BONNAL

25680 – Michelin map **321** I1 – pop. 21 – alt. 270
▶ Paris 392 – Besançon 47 – Belfort 51 – Épinal 106

⛰ Les Castels Le Val de Bonnal 👥

✆ 03 81 86 90 87, www.camping-valdebonnal.com

Address : 1 chemin du Moulin

Opening times : from beginning May to beginning Sept.

140 ha/15 for camping (280 pitches) flat, grassy

Tariff : 50.75€ ✚✚ ⛟ 🔲 (10A) – Extra per person 14.50€ – Reservation fee 20€

Rental rates : (from beginning May to beginning Sept.) ⛵ – 13 🚐 – 8 🏠 – 8 tent lodges. Per week from 375 to 1,375€ – Reservation fee 20€
local sani-station

In a pleasant location beside the Ognon river and near a lake.

Surroundings : ⩾ ☐ ♀
Leisure activities : 🍴 ✗ 🎲 🎆 nighttime 🏃 ⛵ 🚴 ⛵ 🏊 ⛵
Facilities : 🚿 ⟳ ⛱ 🚰 launderette 🅿 ⛟
Nearby : ≋ forest trail

G P S Longitude : 6.35619 / Latitude : 47.50734

CHALEZEULE

25220 – Michelin map **321** G3 – pop. 1 180 – alt. 252
▶ Paris 410 – Dijon 96 – Lyon 229 – Nancy 209

⛰ Municipal de la Plage

✆ 03 81 88 04 26, www.campingdebesancon.com

Address : 12 route de Belfort (4.5km northeast along the N 83; beside the Doubs river)

Opening times : from mid March to end Oct.

2.5 ha (152 pitches) terraced, flat, grassy

Tariff : (2015 price) ✚ 5.80€ ⛟ 🔲 7.95€ – (16A) 3.95€
Rental rates : (2015 price) (from mid March to end Oct.) – 8 🚐 – 2 canvas bungalows. Per night from 38 to 99€ – Per week from 252 to 665€
local sani-station 4€ – 10 🔲 20.65€

Particular attention has been paid to the floral decoration. A tram stop into the town centre is 500m away.

Surroundings : ♀♀
Leisure activities : ✗ ⛵
Facilities : 🚿 ⟳ 🖥 ⛱ 🚰 launderette
Nearby : ✂ 🎣 🏊 ⛵

G P S Longitude : 6.07103 / Latitude : 47.26445

*The classification (1 to 5 tents, **black** or red) that we award to selected sites in this guide is our own system. It should not be confused with the classification (1 to 5 stars) of official organisations.*

CHAMPAGNEY

70290 – Michelin map **314** H6 – pop. 3 728 – alt. 370
▶ Paris 413 – Besançon 115 – Vesoul 48

⛰ Domaine Des Ballastières

✆ 03 84 23 11 22, www.campingdesballastieres.com

Address : 20 rue du Pâquis

Opening times : from beginning April to end Oct.

5 ha (110 pitches) relatively flat, flat, grassy

Tariff : 17.50€ ✚✚ ⛟ 🔲 (16A) – Extra per person 3.70€ – Reservation fee 10€

Rental rates : (from beginning April to end Oct.) 🚿 (1 mobile home) – 10 🚐 – 8 tent lodges. Per night from 18 to 75€ – Per week from 90 to 610€ – Reservation fee 10€
Eurorelais sani-station – 10 🔲 10.50€

Situated beside a small lake.

Leisure activities : 🎲 🏃 ⛵ 🚴 🏊
Facilities : 🚿 ⟳ 🚰 launderette
Nearby : ≋ 🎣 🐴 pedalos

G P S Longitude : 6.67414 / Latitude : 47.70615

CHAMPAGNOLE

39300 – Michelin map **321** F6 – pop. 8 088 – alt. 541
▶ Paris 420 – Besançon 66 – Dole 68 – Genève 86

🏕 **Municipal de Boyse** 👥

📞 03 84 52 00 32, www.camping-boyse.com

Address : 20 rue Georges Vallerey (take the northwestern exit along the D 5, follow the signs for Lons-le-Saunier and take turning to the left)

Opening times : from beginning April to end Sept.

9 ha/7 for camping (240 pitches) relatively flat, flat, grassy

Tariff : 22.50€ ★★ 🚗 📧 🔌 (10A) – Extra per person 6€

Rental rates : (from beginning April to end Sept.) ♿ (2 chalets) – 27 🏠 – 2 tent lodges. Per night from 37 to 98€ – Per week from 260 to 680€

🚰 AireService sani-station 4€

A pretty site on a hillside, looking out over the Ain river from an elevation of 30m. Direct access along a road to the river.

Surroundings : 🌿 ♨️
Leisure activities : ✗ 🎣 🏃 ⛹ 🏛 🏊
Facilities : ♿ ⚡ 🚿 🍴 launderette 🧺
Nearby : 🍽 🎿 🎣 sports trail

Longitude : 5.89741
Latitude : 46.74643

This guide is updated regularly, so buy your new copy every year!

CHÂTILLON

39130 – Michelin map **321** E7 – pop. 131 – alt. 500
▶ Paris 421 – Champagnole 24 – Clairvaux-les-Lacs 15 – Lons-le-Saunier 19

🏕 **Le Domaine de l'Épinette** 👥

📞 03 84 25 71 44, www.domaine-epinette.com

Address : 15 rue de l'Epinette (1.3km south along the D 151)

7 ha (150 pitches) terraced, relatively flat, flat, grassy, stony

Rentals : 71 🚐 – 2 🏠 – 4 canvas bungalows.

🚰 local sani-station

The site is laid out on terraces on the side of a valley overlooking a river.

Surroundings : 🌿 ≤
Leisure activities : 🏛 🏃 ⛹ 🏊 🏓 ⛷
Facilities : ♿ ⚡ 🚿 launderette 🧺 🧺

Longitude : 5.72218
Latitude : 46.6513

CHAUX-DES-CROTENAY

39150 – pop. 412 – alt. 735
▶ Paris 440 – Besançon 88 – Lons-le-Saunier 48

🏕 Municipal du Bois Joli

📞 03 84 51 50 82, www.chaletsalesiajura.com

Address : 8 route de la Piscine

1 ha (42 pitches) flat, grassy

Rentals : ♿ (1 chalet) – 8 🏠.

There's an attractive view of the surrounding hills.

Surroundings : ≤ mountains
Leisure activities : 🏛 ⛹
Facilities : ♿ launderette
Nearby : 🎿 🍴 🚴 ⛷

Longitude : 5.96072
Latitude : 46.66307

CLAIRVAUX-LES-LACS

39130 – Michelin map **321** E7 – pop. 1 454 – alt. 540
▶ Paris 428 – Bourg-en-Bresse 94 – Champagnole 34 – Lons-le-Saunier 22

🏕 **Yelloh! Village Le Fayolan** 👥

📞 03 84 25 88 52, www.campinglefayolan.fr

Address : rue du Langard (1.2km southeast along the D 118)

Opening times : from beginning May to mid Sept.

17 ha/13 for camping (516 pitches) terraced, relatively flat, flat, grassy, pine trees

Tariff : 45€ ★★ 🚗 📧 🔌 (16A) – Extra per person 8€

Rental rates : permanent – 122 🚐 – 6 tent lodges. Per night from 55 to 213€ – Per week from 385 to 1,491€

🚰 AireService sani-station – 2 📧 19€

Situated beside a lake, with numerous services and leisure facilities.

Surroundings : ≤ 🏠 ♨️ ⛱
Leisure activities : 🍴 ✗ 🏛 📺 🏃 🎣 hammam ⛹ 🔲 🏊 🎿 ⛷ entertainment room
Facilities : ♿ ⚡ 🚿 🎿 📷 🍴 launderette 🧺 🧺
Nearby : 🎣 fitness trail

Longitude : 5.75
Latitude : 46.56667

🏕 Flower Le Grand Lac 👥

📞 03 84 25 22 14, www.odesia-clairvaux.com

Address : chemin du Langard (800m southeast along the D 118, follow the signs for Châtel-de-Joux and take the road to the right)

2.5 ha (191 pitches) terraced, relatively flat, flat, grassy

Situated beside the lake with a beautiful beach and an impressive diving board!

Surroundings : ≤ ♨️ ⛱
Leisure activities : 📺 🏃 ⛹ 🏊 🎿 (beach) 🎣 pedalos
Facilities : ♿ ⚡ 🚿 launderette
Nearby : 🍷

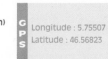

Longitude : 5.75507
Latitude : 46.56823

DOLE

39100 – Michelin map **321** C4 – pop. 24 906 – alt. 220
▶ Paris 363 – Besançon 55 – Chalon-sur-Saône 67 – Dijon 50

🏕 Le Pasquier

📞 03 84 72 02 61, www.camping-le-pasquier.com

Address : 18 chemin Victor et Georges Thévenot (to the southeast along the av. Jean-Jaurès)

Opening times : from mid March to mid Oct.

2 ha (120 pitches) flat, grassy, gravel

Tariff : 21.50€ ★★ 🚗 📧 🔌 (10A) – Extra per person 5€ – Reservation fee 15€

Rental rates : (from mid March to mid Oct.) – 8 🚐. Per night from 50 to 97€ – Reservation fee 15€

In a lush, green setting near the Doubs river, with a view of the Dole collegiate church.

Surroundings : ♨️
Leisure activities : 🍴 ✗ 📺 daytime ⛹ 🏊 (small swimming pool)
Facilities : ♿ ⚡ 🚿 🎿 📷 🍴 launderette
Nearby : 🎿 🎣

Longitude : 5.50357
Latitude : 47.08982

DOUCIER

39130 – Michelin map **321** E7 – pop. 300 – alt. 526
▶ Paris 427 – Champagnole 21 – Genève 99 – Lons-le-Saunier 25

⛰ Domaine de Chalain ♠♠

🕿 03 84 25 78 78, www.chalain.com

Address : 3km to the northeast

Opening times : from end April to mid Sept.

30 ha/18 for camping (712 pitches) flat, grassy, stony

Tariff : (2015 price) 41€ ♣♣ ⇔ 🔲 (10A) – Extra per person 7€ –
Reservation fee 10€

Rental rates : (2015 price) (from end April to mid Sept.) 🚐 –
55 🛖 – 35 🏠. Per night from 48 to 161€ – Per week
from 288 to 1,127€ – Reservation fee 10€

🚰 local sani-station 2€

*In an attractive location on a bay ringed by cliffs, between a
forest and the Lac de Chalain.*

Surroundings : ≼ ♀ ⚠
Leisure activities : ♈ ✗ 🖐 🏊 ⛵
hammam, jacuzzi ⚡🚲 ✗ 🎯 🔲 ⚡ ⚓
⚑ ⚓

Facilities : ♿ ⛶ ⛪ ♨ ♨ launderette
⚡ ♨ refrigerated food storage facilities

Longitude : 5.81395
Latitude : 46.66422

FONCINE-LE-HAUT

39460 – Michelin map **321** G7 – pop. 1 027 – alt. 790
▶ Paris 444 – Champagnole 24 – Clairvaux-les-Lacs 34 – Lons-le-Saunier 62

⛰ Les Chalets du Val de Saine (rental of chalets only)

🕿 03 84 51 93 11, www.camping-haut-jura.com – alt. 900 – traditional
camp. spaces also available

Address : take the southwestern exit along the D437, follow the
signs for St-Laurent-en-Grandvaux and take the turning to the left, by
the stadium; beside the Saine river

Opening times : permanent

1.2 ha flat

Rental rates : (2015 price) 🅿 – 19 🏠. Per night from 62 to 160€ –
Per week from 255 to 1,050€

🚰 AireService sani-station 3.50€

Surroundings : ⚑
Leisure activities : ⚓
Facilities : ⛶ ♨ launderette
Nearby : ⚡ ♈ ✗ ✗ ⚓

Longitude : 6.07253
Latitude : 46.65888

FRESSE

70270 – Michelin map **314** H6 – pop. 725 – alt. 472
▶ Paris 405 – Belfort 31 – Épinal 71 – Luxeuil-les-Bains 30

⛰ La Broche

🕿 677651055, www.camping-broche.com

Address : Le Volvet (take the western exit, follow the signs for
Melesey and then take road to the left)

Opening times : from beginning April to end Oct.

2 ha (50 pitches) terrace, relatively flat, flat, grassy

Tariff : ♣ 3€ ⇔ 🔲 3€ – (10A) 3€

🚰 local sani-station 5€

Situated in an undulating, wooded site beside a lake.

Surroundings : ⚑ ≼ ♀
Leisure activities : ⚓
Facilities : ♿ ⛶ ⛶ ♨ 🔲

Longitude : 6.65269
Latitude : 47.75587

HUANNE-MONTMARTIN

25680 – Michelin map **321** I2 – pop. 83 – alt. 310
▶ Paris 392 – Baume-les-Dames 14 – Besançon 37 – Montbéliard 52

⛰ Le Bois de Reveuge

🕿 03 81 84 38 60, www.campingduboisdereveuge.com

Address : route de Rougemont (1.1km north along the D 113)

Opening times : from end April to beginning Sept.

24 ha/15 for camping (320 pitches) terraced, flat, grassy, gravelled, wood

Tariff : (2015 price) 35€ ♣♣ ⇔ 🔲 (10A) – Extra per person 8.50€ –
Reservation fee 25€

Rental rates : (2015 price) (from end April to beginning Sept.) –
123 🛖 – 27 🏠. Per night from 49 to 199€ – Per week
from 294 to 1,393€ – Reservation fee 25€

🚰 local sani-station 20€ – 50 🔲 20€

The site is laid out beside two large lakes at the edge of a wood.

Surroundings : ⚑ ⛱ ♀♀
Leisure activities : ♈ ✗ 🖐 🏊 🎯 🏊 ⚓
⚡⚓ 🔲 ⚓ ⚓
Facilities : ♿ ⛪ ⚡ ♨ ♨ launderette ⚓

Longitude : 6.3447
Latitude : 47.44346

LABERGEMENT-STE-MARIE

25160 – Michelin map **321** H6 – pop. 1 040 – alt. 859
▶ Paris 454 – Champagnole 41 – Pontarlier 17 – St-Laurent-en-Grandvaux 41

⛰ Le Lac

🕿 03 81 69 31 24, www.camping-lac-remoray.com

Address : 10 rue du Lac (take the southwestern exit along the D 437,
follow the signs for Mouthe and take turning to the right)

Opening times : from mid May to mid Sept.

1.8 ha (80 pitches) terraced, relatively flat, flat, grassy

Tariff : ♣ 12€ ⇔ 17.20€ 🔲 17.20€ – (6A) 4€ – Reservation fee 10€
Rental rates : (from mid May to mid Sept.) – 4 🛖 – 4 🏠.
Per night from 43 to 100€ – Per week from 210 to 625€ –
Reservation fee 10€

🚰 local sani-station

Situated 300m from the Lac de Remoray.

Surroundings : ≼
Leisure activities : ♈ ✗ 🖐 🚲
Facilities : ♿ ⛶ ♨ ♨ launderette ⚓
Nearby : ✗ ⚓ ⚓

Longitude : 6.27563
Latitude : 46.77134

LACHAPELLE-SOUS-ROUGEMONT

90360 – Michelin map **315** G10 – pop. 549 – alt. 400
▶ Paris 442 – Belfort 16 – Basel 66 – Colmar 55

⛰ Flowert Le Lac de la Seigneurie

🕿 03 84 23 00 13, www.camping-lac-seigneurie.com

Address : 3 rue de la Seigneurie (3.2km north along the D 11, follow
the signs for Lauw)

4 ha (110 pitches) flat, grassy

Rentals : 2 🛖 – 4 🏠.

🚰 local sani-station

In a quiet rural location at the edge of a forest and near a lake.

Surroundings : ⚑ ⛱ ♀
Leisure activities : 🚣 ⚡ 🏊
Facilities : ♿ ⛪ ♨ launderette
Nearby : ✗ ⚓

Longitude : 7.01498
Latitude : 47.73613

LEVIER

25270 – Michelin map **321** G5 – pop. 1 949 – alt. 719
▶ Paris 443 – Besançon 45 – Champagnole 37 – Pontarlier 22

⚠ La Forêt

🖉 03 81 89 53 46, www.camping-dela-foret.com

Address : route de Septfontaines (located 1km northeast along the D 41)

Opening times : from beginning May to mid Sept.

4 ha/2.5 for camping (70 pitches) terraced, flat, grassy, relatively flat

Tariff : (2015 price) 23.70€ ✶✶ 🚐 🗉 (2) (10A) –
Extra per person 4.40€ – Reservation fee 10€
Rental rates : (2015 price) permanent – 1 'gypsy' caravan –
2 🚃 – 7 🏠. Per night from 40 to 152€ – Per week from 196 to 739€ – Reservation fee 10€
🚏 10 🗉 19.90€

Nestling at the edge of a forest in a very beautiful setting of fine trees and rocky outcrops.

Surroundings : 🏞 ♀♀	**G** Longitude : 6.13308
Leisure activities : 🏓 🚣 🚲 ⛷	**P**
Facilities : ৬ ⚡ 🛁 🏕 ੧ launderette	**S** Latitude : 46.95915
Nearby : sports trail	

LONS-LE-SAUNIER

39000 – Michelin map **321** D6 – pop. 17 907 – alt. 255 – ♨
▶ Paris 408 – Besançon 84 – Bourg-en-Bresse 73 – Chalon-sur-Saône 61

⚠⚠ La Marjorie

🖉 03 84 24 26 94, www.camping-marjorie.com

Address : 640 boulevard de l'Europe (to the northeast towards Besançon along the bd de Ceinture)

Opening times : from beginning April to end Oct.

9 ha/3 for camping (193 pitches) flat, grassy, stony, hard surface

Tariff : 23.40€ ✶✶ 🚐 🗉 (2) (10A) – Extra per person 6€ – Reservation fee 15€
Rental rates : (from end March to end Oct.) ৬ (1 chalet) – 4 🚃 – 15 🏠. Per night from 50 to 80€ – Per week from 240 to 590€ – Reservation fee 15€
🚏 local sani-station 4.50€ – 33 🗉 14€

Attractive trees and shrubs decorate the site; beside a stream.

Surroundings : 🌳 ♀♀	Longitude : 5.56855
Leisure activities : 🍸 🎣 🌙 nighttime 🏃	**G**
Facilities : ৬ ⚡ 🏛 🛁 🏕 ੧ launderette	**P**
🛶 🚣	**S** Latitude : 46.68422
Nearby : 🍴 🎣 🏊	

MAICHE

25120 – Michelin map **321** K3 – pop. 4 282 – alt. 777
▶ Paris 501 – Baume-les-Dames 69 – Besançon 74 – Montbéliard 43

⚠ Municipal St-Michel

🖉 03 81 64 12 56, www.mairie-maiche.fr

Address : 23 rue St-Michel (head 1.3km south on the D 422 before joining the D 464, follow the signs for Charquemont and take the D 437 heading for Pontarlier – recommended route via the D 437, follow the signs for Pontarlier)

Opening times : from beginning Dec. to mid Nov.

2 ha (70 pitches) terraced, wood, grassy, relatively flat

Tariff : (2015 price) ✶ 3.50€ 🚐 5€ – (2) (6A) 4.50€

Rental rates : (2015 price) (from beginning Dec. to mid Nov.) –
5 🏠 – 3 🛏 – 1 gîte. Per night from 60 to 80€ – Per week from 250 to 310€

Situated near an indoor water park.

Surroundings : ♀	**G** Longitude : 6.80109
Leisure activities : 🚣	**P**
Facilities : ৬ ⚡ 🏛 🛁	**S** Latitude : 47.24749
Nearby : 🚿 hammam, jacuzzi 🏊 ⛷ 🎣	

MAISOD

39260 – Michelin map **321** E8 – pop. 316 – alt. 520
▶ Paris 436 – Lons-le-Saunier 30 – Oyonnax 34 – St-Claude 29

⚠ Trelachaume

🖉 03 84 42 03 26, www.trelachaume.fr

Address : 50 route du Mont du Cerf (2.2km south along the D 301 and take turning to the right)

Opening times : from mid April to beginning Sept.

3 ha (180 pitches) relatively flat, stony, flat, grassy

Tariff : (2015 price) 20,50€ ✶✶ 🚐 🗉 (2) (10A) –
Extra per person 4.65€
Rental rates : (2015 price) (from mid April to mid Sept.) 🎿 –
5 'gypsy' caravans – 10 🚃 – 6 🏠 – 5 canvas bungalows.
Per night from 71 to 136€ – Per week from 205 to 682€
🚏 10 🗉 17€

Nestling in woods looking down over the Lac de Vouglans.

Surroundings : 🏞 ♀♀	**G** Longitude : 5.68875
Leisure activities : 🎣 🚣 cinema	**P**
Facilities : ৬ ⚡ 🛁 ੧ launderette	**S** Latitude : 46.46873

Do not confuse:

⚠ *to* ⚠⚠⚠ *: MICHELIN classification with*
★ *to* ★★★★★ *: official classification*

MALBUISSON

25160 – Michelin map **321** H6 – pop. 687 – alt. 900
▶ Paris 456 – Besançon 74 – Champagnole 42 – Pontarlier 16

⚠⚠ Les Fuvettes 👥

🖉 03 81 69 31 50, www.camping-fuvettes.com

Address : 24 route de la Plage et des Perrières (located 1km southwest)

Opening times : from beginning April to beginning Oct.

6 ha (306 pitches) flat, relatively flat, stony, grassy

Tariff : (2015 price) 26,90€ ✶✶ 🚐 🗉 (2) (10A) –
Extra per person 5.40€
Rental rates : (2015 price) (from beginning April to beginning Oct.)
৬ (1 mobile home) – 28 🚃 – 4 🏠 – 3 canvas bungalows – 4 tent lodges. Per night from 35 to 145€ – Per week from 239 to 929€ –
Reservation fee 15€
🚏 local sani-station 3€

Situated beside the Lac de St-Point, near a mini water activity park.

Surroundings : ⛰ ♀ ⚠	
Leisure activities : 🍸 🍴 🎣 🌙 🏃 🚣 🎿	**G** Longitude : 6.29391
🏊 ⛷ mini farm with ponies and alpacas	**P**
Facilities : ৬ ⚡ 🛁 ੧ launderette 🛶 🚣	**S** Latitude : 46.79232
Nearby : canoeing, pedalos	

MANDEURE

25350 – Michelin map **321** K2 – pop. 4 959 – alt. 336
▶ Paris 473 – Baume-les-Dames 41 – Maîche 34 – Sochaux 15

⚠ Municipal les Grands Ansanges

✆ 03 81 35 23 79, www.ville-mandeure.com ✖

Address : rue de l'Église (located to the northwest, take exit towards Pont-de-Roide; beside the Doubs)

Opening times : from beginning April to end Sept.

1.7 ha (96 pitches) flat, grassy

Tariff : (2015 price) ♦ 3.50€ ⛺ 3.50€ 🔲 3.50€ – 🔌 (10A) 5€

Rental rates : (2015 price) (from beginning April to end Sept.) – 4 canvas bungalows. Per week from 200 to 300€

A simple site but perfect for a one-night stay.

Surroundings : ♀
Leisure activities : 🍷 🏠 ⛵
Facilities : ⊶ 🏪 🄲🄲 🚿 launderette

Longitude : 6.80556
Latitude : 47.45557

MARIGNY

39130 – Michelin map **321** E6 – pop. 177 – alt. 519
▶ Paris 426 – Arbois 32 – Champagnole 17 – Doucier 5

🏔 FranceLoc La Pergola ♣♦

✆ 03 84 25 70 03, www.lapergola.com

Address : 1 rue des Vernois (800m to the south of the village)

Opening times : from beginning May to beginning Sept.

10 ha (350 pitches) terraced, flat, grassy, stony

Tariff : (2015 price) 47€ ♦♦ ⛺ 🔲 🔌 (12A) – Extra per person 8€ – Reservation fee 27€

Rental rates : (2015 price) (from beginning May to beginning Sept.) – 169 🏠. Per night from 42 to 194€ – Per week from 294 to 1,358€ – Reservation fee 27€

🚐 local sani-station

An attractive swimming pool area overlooks the Lac de Chalain; some high-quality mobile homes.

Surroundings : ⟨ 🏠 ♀ ⛰
Leisure activities : 🍷 🍽 🏠 ⛱ 🏊 🚴
🏊 ⛵ ⛵ ⚓
Facilities : ⬧ ⊶ 🏪 🚿 launderette
🏊 🚿

Longitude : 5.77984
Latitude : 46.67737

MÉLISEY

70270 – Michelin map **314** H6 – pop. 1 699 – alt. 330
▶ Paris 397 – Belfort 33 – Épinal 63 – Luxeuil-les-Bains 22

⚠ La Pierre

✆ 03 84 20 84 38, http://melisey.cchvo.org/index. – limited spaces for one-night stay – 🍴

Address : at Les Granges Baverey (2.7km north on the D 293, follow the signs for Mélay)

Opening times : from beginning May to end Sept.

1.5 ha (58 pitches) relatively flat, flat, grassy

Tariff : ♦ 3.20€ ⛺ 1.50€ 🔲 3.20€ – 🔌 (6A) 2.30€

Rental rates : permanent – 4 🏠. Per night from 90 to 220€ – Per week from 230 to 380€ – Reservation fee 19€

🚐 local sani-station 6€ – 8 🔲 10.60€

In a picturesque setting on a wooded site.

Surroundings : 🌳 🏠 ♀
Leisure activities : 🏠 🏊
Facilities : ⬧ 🏪 🔲

Longitude : 6.58101
Latitude : 47.77552

MESNOIS

39130 – Michelin map **321** E7 – pop. 202 – alt. 460
▶ Paris 431 – Besançon 90 – Lons 18 – Chalon 77

🏔 Sites et Paysages Beauregard

✆ 03 84 48 32 51, www.juracampingbeauregard.com

Address : 2 Grande-Rue (at the southern end of the hamlet of Mesnois)

Opening times : from end March to end Sept.

6 ha/4.5 for camping (192 pitches), terraced, grassy, relatively flat

Tariff : (2015 price) 30.80€ ♦♦ ⛺ 🔲 🔌 (6A) – Extra per person 5.70€ – Reservation fee 10€

Rental rates : (2015 price) (from beginning April to end Sept.) – 41 🏠 – 5 canvas bungalows. Per night from 45 to 118€ – Per week from 315 to 826€ – Reservation fee 10€

The site has a partially open-air water park.

Surroundings : ⟨ 🏠 ♀
Leisure activities : 🍷 🍽 🏠 ≋ hammam, jacuzzi ⛱ 🏸 ⛵ 🏊 ⚓
Facilities : ⬧ ⊶ 🏪 🚿 launderette ⚒

Longitude : 5.68878
Latitude : 46.60036

MONNET-LA-VILLE

39300 – Michelin map **321** E6 – pop. 372 – alt. 550
▶ Paris 421 – Arbois 28 – Champagnole 11 – Doucier 10

🏔 Sous Doriat

✆ 03 84 51 21 43, www.camping-sous-doriat.com

Address : 34 rue Marcel Hugon (take the northern exit along the D 27e, follow the signs for Ney)

Opening times : from beginning May to end Sept.

3 ha (110 pitches) flat, grassy

Tariff : 21€ ♦♦ ⛺ 🔲 🔌 (10A) – Extra per person 4.10€ – Reservation fee 10€

Rental rates : permanent – 17 🏠 – 5 🏠 – 4 canvas bungalows. Per night from 30 to 109€ – Per week from 210 to 763€ – Reservation fee 10€

🚐 flot bleu sani-station

A simple campsite with an unrestricted view of the Jura mountains.

Surroundings : ⟨ ♀
Leisure activities : 🏠 ⛱ 🏊 multi-sports area
Facilities : ⬧ ⊶ 🏪 🚿 launderette
Nearby : 🏊 🍷 🍽

Longitude : 5.79779
Latitude : 46.72143

⚠ Du Gît

✆ 03 84 51 21 17, www.campingdugit.com

Address : 7 chemin du Gît (located 1km southeast along the D 40, follow the signs for Mont-sur-Monnet and take the road to the right)

Opening times : from mid May to beginning Sept.

6 ha (60 pitches) flat, relatively flat, grassy

Tariff : 16.80€ ♦♦ ⛺ 🔲 🔌 (5A) – Extra per person 4€

Rental rates : permanent – 2 🏠. Per week from 250 to 450€

🚐 local sani-station 3€

A very simple campsite with poor sanitary facilities.

Surroundings : 🌳 ⟨
Leisure activities : 🏠 ⛱
Facilities : ⬧ ⊶ 🚿 🏊

Longitude : 5.79733
Latitude : 46.71234

ORNANS

25290 – Michelin map **321** G4 – pop. 4 152 – alt. 355

▶ Paris 428 – Baume-les-Dames 42 – Besançon 26 – Morteau 48

⚕ Domaine Le Chanet ♨

🖉 03 81 62 23 44, www.lechanet.com

Address : 9 chemin du Chanet (located 1.5km southwest along the D 241, follow the signs for Chassagne-St-Denis and take the road to the right; 100m from the Loue)

Opening times : from beginning April to beginning Oct.

1,4 ha (95 pitches) sloping, grassy, relatively flat

Tariff : (2015 price) 17€ ♟♟ 🚗 🔲 ⚡ (10A) – Extra per person 5.30€ – Reservation fee 7.50€

Rental rates : (2015 price) (from beginning April to beginning Oct.) – 21 🚐 – 3 gîtes. Per night from 70 to 125€ – Per week from 230 to 805€ – Reservation fee 15€

🚐 local sani-station 3.50€ – 4 🔲 14.50€

In the hills above the town, features an eco (no chemicals) swimming pool.

Surroundings : 🌿 ⪻ ♨♨
Leisure activities : ❢ ✕ 🎯 ♣ 🎠 ⛷
🏄 🎣
Facilities : ⅋ ⚤ ⛟ ♨ ¶ launderette
Nearby : 🚲 🎯 🎣

G P S Longitude : 6.12779
Latitude : 47.10164

⚕ Sites et Paysages La Roche d'Ully

🖉 03 81 57 17 79, www.camping-ornans.com

Address : allée de la Tour de Peilz

Opening times : from beginning April to mid Oct.

2 ha (125 pitches) flat, grassy

Tariff : 35€ ♟♟ 🚗 🔲 ⚡ (10A) – Extra per person 7.80€ – Reservation fee 7.50€

Rental rates : (from beginning April to mid Oct.) – 7 🚐 – 7 🏠 – 5 tipis – 5 tent lodges. Per night from 47 to 155€ – Per week from 220 to 980€ – Reservation fee 15€

🚐 local sani-station 3€ – 10 🔲 16€ – 🚐 14€

Surroundings : 🚐
Leisure activities : ❢ ✕ ♣ 🎯 🚲
Facilities : ⅋ ⚤ ⅏ ♨ ¶ 🚻 🔲 🐾
Nearby : ⛷ hammam, jacuzzi 🀄 🎣 🏄 🎣

G P S Longitude : 6.15807
Latitude : 47.10286

The guide covers all 22 regions of France – see the map and list of regions on pages 4–5.

OUNANS

39380 – Michelin map **321** D5 – pop. 371 – alt. 230

▶ Paris 383 – Arbois 16 – Arc-et-Senans 13 – Dole 23

⚕ Indigo La Plage Blanche ♨

🖉 03 84 37 69 63, www.la-plage-blanche.com

Address : 3 rue de la Plage (located 1.5km north along the D 71, follow the signs for Montbarey and take road to the left)

Opening times : from beginning May to end Sept.

7 ha (218 pitches) flat, grassy

Tariff : (2015 price) 29.50€ ♟♟ 🚗 🔲 ⚡ (10A) – Extra per person 5.50€ – Reservation fee 13€

Rental rates : (2015 price) (from beginning May to end Sept.) – 10 🚐 – 20 tent lodges. Per night from 39 to 105€ – Per week from 219 to 735€ – Reservation fee 13€

🚐 local sani-station 7€

The site is on the banks of the Loue river.

Surroundings : 🌿 ♀
Leisure activities : ❢ ✕ 🎯 ⊙ nighttime
🏃 ⛷ jacuzzi 🎯 🏄 🎠 multi-sports
ground
Facilities : ⅋ ⚤ ⛟ ♨ ¶ launderette 🐾 🌿
Nearby : 🚲

G P S Longitude : 5.66333
Latitude : 47.00276

⚕ Le Val d'Amour

🖉 03 84 37 61 89, www.levaldamour.com

Address : 1 rue du Val d'Amour (take the eastern exit along the D 472, towards Chamblay)

Opening times : from beginning April to end Sept.

3,7 ha (97 pitches) flat, grassy, fruit trees

Tariff : 24.60€ ♟♟ 🚗 🔲 ⚡ (10A) – Extra per person 6.50€ – Reservation fee 10€

Rental rates : (from beginning April to mid Oct.) – 14 🚐 – 6 🏠 – 9 canvas bungalows. Per night from 50 to 100€ – Per week from 190 to 700€ – Reservation fee 10€

🚐 local sani-station 2€

Pretty floral decoration.

Surroundings : 🌿 ♀♀
Leisure activities : ✕ ⊙ 🎯 🚲 🏄 🎣
mountain biking
Facilities : ⅋ ⚤ 🎯 ¶ launderette
Nearby : 🏄

G P S Longitude : 5.6733
Latitude : 46.99103

PESMES

70140 – Michelin map **314** B9 – pop. 1 111 – alt. 205

▶ Paris 387 – Besançon 52 – Vesoul 64 – Dijon 69

⚕ La Colombière

🖉 03 84 31 20 15, campinglacolombiere70140@orange.fr

Address : take the southern exit along the D 475, follow the signs for Dole; beside the Ognon river

Opening times : from beginning May to end Sept.

1 ha (70 pitches) flat, grassy

Tariff : (2015 price) 15€ ♟♟ 🚗 🔲 ⚡ (16A) – Extra per person 3€

Rental rates : (2015 price) (from beginning May to end Sept.) – 5 🚐 – 1 gîte. Per night from 35 to 90€ – Per week from 240 to 450€

🚐 flot bleu sani-station 2€ – 45 🔲 15€

Beside the river, not far from the centre of the village.

Surroundings : ♀
Leisure activities : 🎯 🏄 🎣
Facilities : ⅋ ⚤ 🎯 ⛟ ♨ ¶
Nearby : ❢ ✕ 🚲

G P S Longitude : 5.56392
Latitude : 47.27403

POLIGNY

39800 – Michelin map **321** E5 – pop. 4 229 – alt. 373

▶ Paris 397 – Besançon 57 – Dole 45 – Lons-le-Saunier 30

⚕ La Tulipe de Vigne

🖉 03 84 37 35 90, contact@camping-poligny.com

Address : route de Lons-le-Saunier

Opening times : from beginning May to mid Oct.

1.5 ha (87 pitches) flat, grassy

Tariff : (2015 price) 17€ ♟♟ 🚗 🔲 ⚡ (6A) – Extra per person 2.50€

🚐 local sani-station 3€
Situated at the exit from the town, ideal for a stopover.

Surroundings : ≤ ⚲
Leisure activities : 🏄
Facilities : 🚿 ⛺ 🍴

GPS Longitude : 5.70078
Latitude : 46.83424

PONTARLIER

25300 – Michelin map **321** I5 – pop. 18 267 – alt. 838
▶ Paris 462 – Basel 180 – Beaune 164 – Belfort 126

⚠ Le Larmont

📞 0381462333, www.camping-pontarlier.fr – alt. 880

Address : 2 chemin du Toulombief (to the southeast towards Lausanne, near the riding centre)

4 ha (75 pitches) terraced, gravel, flat, grassy

Rentals : 8 🏠.

🚐 Eurorelais sani-station – 20 🔳
Situated on a hillside with pitches that are well marked out.

Surroundings : 🌿 ≤ 🏡
Leisure activities : 🏄 🏄
Facilities : 🚿 ⚿ ▦ ⛺ 🍴 launderette
Nearby : 🏇 sports trail

GPS Longitude : 6.37349
Latitude : 46.90013

QUINGEY

25440 – Michelin map **321** F4 – pop. 1 300 – alt. 275
▶ Paris 397 – Baume-les-Dames 40 – Besançon 23 – Morteau 78

⚠ Municipal Les Promenades

📞 0381637401, www.campingquingey.fr

Address : at Les Promenades (take the southern exit, follow the signs for Lons-le-Saunier and take road to the right after the bridge)

Opening times : from beginning May to end Sept.

1.5 ha (75 pitches) flat, grassy, gravel

Tariff : (2015 price) 🚶 4.25€ 🚗 🔳 4€ – 🔌 (6A) 3€
Rental rates : (2015 price) (from beginning May to end Sept.) – 4 canvas bungalows. Per week from 200 to 350€

The site is on the bank of the Loue river, near the village centre and a water sports centre.

Surroundings : 🏡 ⚲⚲
Leisure activities : 🏄 🎿 🎣
Facilities : 🚿 ⚿ (July-Aug.) ⛺ 🍴 launderette
Nearby : 🏊 🍴 🚲

ST-CLAUDE

39200 – Michelin map **321** F8 – pop. 11 355 – alt. 450
▶ Paris 465 – Annecy 88 – Bourg-en-Bresse 90 – Genève 60

🏔 Flower Le Martinet

📞 0384450040, www.camping-saint-claude.fr

Address : 14 route du Martinet (situated 2km southeast following signs for Genève and take the D 290 to the right, where the Flumen and the Tacon rivers meet)

Opening times : from beginning April to end Sept.

2.9 ha (112 pitches)

Tariff : (2015 price) 20€ 🚶🚶 🚗 🔳 🔌 (10A) – Extra per person 4.50€ – Reservation fee 10€

Rental rates : (2015 price) (from beginning April to end Sept.)
– 8 🏠 – 1 tipi – 2 canvas bungalows. Per night from 41 to 96€
– Per week from 287 to 672€ – Reservation fee 10€
🚐 local sani-station – 24 🔳 20€
Nestling in a pleasant mountain setting beside a river.

Surroundings : ≤ ⚲⚲
Leisure activities : 🍴 🍴 🏡 🏄
Facilities : 🚿 ⚿ (July–Aug.) 🍴 launderette 🏊
Nearby : 🎿 🏊 🎣

GPS Longitude : 5.86953
Latitude : 46.37309

ST-HIPPOLYTE

25190 – Michelin map **321** K3 – pop. 917 – alt. 380
▶ Paris 490 – Basel 93 – Belfort 48 – Besançon 89

⚠ Les Grands Champs

📞 0381965453, www.ville.saint-hippolyte.fr

Address : located 1km northeast along the D 121, follow the signs for Montécheroux and take the road to the right, near the Doubs river (direct access)

2.2 ha (65 pitches) terraced, stony, grassy, relatively flat

A long, narrow site, with pitches on an incline leading down to the Doubs river.

Surroundings : 🌿 ≤ ⚲
Leisure activities : 🎣
Facilities : 🚿 ⚿ 🏊

GPS Longitude : 6.82332
Latitude : 47.32291

Key to rentals symbols:

12 🚐 *Number of mobile homes*
20 🏠 *Number of chalets*
6 🛏 *Number of rooms to rent*
Per night *Minimum/maximum rate per night*
30–50€
Per week *Minimum/maximum rate per week*
300–1,000€

ST-LAURENT-EN-GRANDVAUX

39150 – Michelin map **321** F7 – pop. 1 779 – alt. 904
▶ Paris 442 – Champagnole 22 – Lons-le-Saunier 45 – Morez 11

⚠ Municipal Champ de Mars

📞 0603610661, www.camping-saint-laurent-jura.fr

Address : 8 rue du Camping (take the eastern exit along the N 5)

Opening times : from mid Dec. to end Sept.

3 ha (133 pitches)

Tariff : 🚶 3.57€ 🚗 🔳 3.32€ – 🔌 (10A) 2.45€
Rental rates : (from mid Dec. to mid Nov.) 🚿 (2 chalets) – 10 🏠.
Per night from 120€ – Per week from 240 to 518€
🚐 12 🔳 10.46€ – 🛁 9.86€

Close to the snowshoe hiking trails and cross-country skiing pistes. Higher rates in winter.

Surroundings : ❄ ≤
Leisure activities : 🏡 🏄
Facilities : 🚿 ⚿ ▦ ⛺ 🍴 launderette

GPS Longitude : 5.96294
Latitude : 46.57616

ST-POINT-LAC

25160 – Michelin map **321** H6 – pop. 269 – alt. 860
▶ Paris 453 – Champagnole 39 – Pontarlier 13 – St-Laurent-en-Grandvaux 45

⚠ Municipal

✆ 03 81 69 61 64, www.camping-saintpointlac.fr

Address : 8 rue du Port (in the town)

Opening times : from beginning May to end Sept.

1,8 ha (84 pitches)

Tariff : 21€ ♛♛ 🚐 🗉 ⟨ℓ⟩ (16A) – Extra per person 4€
🚐 local sani-station 9€ – 30 🗉 9€
The campervan pitches are close to the campsite.

Surroundings : ≤ ⚠
Leisure activities : 🏠 ⛵ 🚲
Facilities : ♿ ⚗ ▥ ⓦ launderette ⚊
Nearby : 🏊 🎣 watersports centre

GPS
Longitude : 6.30336
Latitude : 46.81209

SALINS-LES-BAINS

39110 – Michelin map **321** F5 – pop. 2 987 – alt. 340 – ♨
▶ Paris 419 – Besançon 41 – Dole 43 – Lons-le-Saunier 52

⚠ Municipal

✆ 03 84 37 92 70, www.salinscamping.com

Address : place de la Gare (take the northern exit, following signs for Besançon)

1 ha (44 pitches) flat, gravel, grassy

Rentals : 1 🚐 – 1 studio.
Situated in a valley with a superb view of the citadel and surrounding mountains.

Surroundings : ≤ 🏠
Leisure activities : 🏠 ⛵ 🏊 (small swimming pool)
Facilities : ♿ ⚗ ⓦ ▦

GPS
Longitude : 5.87919
Latitude : 46.94625

LA TOUR-DU-MEIX

39270 – Michelin map **321** D7 – pop. 226 – alt. 470
▶ Paris 430 – Champagnole 42 – Lons-le-Saunier 24 – St-Claude 36

⚠ Surchauffant

Surchauffant

✆ 03 84 25 41 08, www.camping-surchauffant.fr

Address : at Le Pont de la Pyle (located 1km southeast along the D 470 and take road to the left, 150m from the Lac de Vouglans – direct access)

Opening times : from end April to mid Sept.

2.5 ha (200 pitches) lat, grassy, stony

Tariff : (2015 price) 26€ ♛♛ 🚐 🗉
⟨ℓ⟩ (10A) – Extra per person 6€
Rental rates : (2015 price) (from end April to mid Sept.)
⚡ – 24 🚐 – 24 🏠. Per night from 33 to 99€ – Per week from 198 to 693€
🚐 local sani-station 2€ – 15 🗉 9€

Surroundings : 🏞 ≤ ⚘
Leisure activities : ✗ 🏠 ⛵ 🚲 🏊
Facilities : ♿ ⚗ (July-Aug.) ⛱ ⚗ ⓦ launderette ⚊ refrigerated food storage facilities
Nearby : 🍷 🏊 (beach) 🎣

GPS
Longitude : 5.6742
Latitude : 46.52298

UXELLES

39130 – Michelin map **321** I2 – pop. 49 – alt. 598
▶ Paris 440 – Besançon 93 – Genève 86 – Lausanne 102

⚠⚠⚠ Village Vacances Odesia Les Crozats

(rental of chalets and rooms only)

✆ 03 84 25 51 43, www.odesia-lacs.com

Address : 1 rue Principale

Opening times : from mid Feb. to beginning Jan.

2 ha flat, grassy

Rental rates : (2015 price) ⚡ Ⓟ – 15 🏠 – 28 🛏. Per week from 299 to 799€
A small and pretty chalet village in the lake valley with an option for half-board accommodation.

Surroundings : ❄ 🏂
Leisure activities : 🍷 ✗ 🏠 ⊡ 🏃 🚡 hammam 🎣 🎬 cinema/activity centre
Facilities : ⚗ 🚿 ⓦ launderette ⚊

GPS
Longitude : 5.78836
Latitude : 46.60277

The pitches of many campsites are marked out with low hedges of attractive bushes and shrubs.

VESOUL

70000 – Michelin map **314** E7 – pop. 15 920 – alt. 221
▶ Paris 360 – Belfort 68 – Besançon 47 – Épinal 91

⚠⚠ International du Lac

✆ 03 84 76 22 86, www.camping-vesoul.com

Address : at Vaivre-et-Montoille, avenue des Rives du Lac (2.5km west)

Opening times : from beginning Jan. to end Dec.

4 ha (183 pitches) flat, grassy

Tariff : (2015 price) 19.20€ ♛♛ 🚐 🗉 ⟨ℓ⟩ (10A) – Extra per person 4.20€
Rental rates : permanent ♿ (1 mobile home) ⚡ – 8 🚐. Per night from 70 to 93€ – Per week from 320 to 559€
🚐 37 🗉 19.60€
Beside a wide lake.

Surroundings : 🏂 🏠 ⚘ 🎣
Leisure activities : 🏠 ⛵ 🏊 🎣
Facilities : ♿ ⚗ ▥ ⛱ ⚗ ⓦ launderette
Nearby : 🍷 ✗ 🏊 🏊 🏊

GPS
Longitude : 6.13084
Latitude : 47.63121

VILLERSEXEL

70110 – Michelin map **314** G7 – pop. 1 472 – alt. 287
▶ Paris 386 – Belfort 41 – Besançon 59 – Lure 18

⚠ Le Chapeau Chinois

✆ 03 84 63 40 60, www.camping-villersexel.com

Address : 92 rue du Chapeau Chinois (located 1km north along the D 486, follow the signs for Lure and take the road to the right after the bridge)

2 ha (80 pitches) flat, grassy
🚐 local sani-station – 2 🗉
Beside the Ognon river.

Surroundings : 🏂 ⚘
Leisure activities : 🏠 ⛵ 🏊 🏊
Facilities : ♿ ⚗ ⛱ ⓦ launderette
Nearby : ✗ 🛶

GPS
Longitude : 6.436
Latitude : 47.55814

ÎLE-DE-FRANCE

P. Escudero / hemis.fr

Paris, the 'City of Light' on the River Seine, lies at the heart of the Île-de-France. A chic and cosmopolitan capital, it is dominated by the iconic silhouette of the Eiffel Tower. Its former royal palace is now adorned with glass pyramids, a former railway station has been transformed into a magnificent museum and narrow streets lined with bohemian houses branch off from wide, formal, tree-lined boulevards. This is a city of endless contrasts: from busy department stores to elegant cafés, from the *bateaux-mouches* (restaurant boats) that glide along the majestic river at night to the sophisticated glamour of Parisian cabarets. But the region that lies beyond Paris has no intention of remaining in the capital's shadow; it is home to secluded châteaux, the magical world of Disneyland and the relaxed ambience of the summer cafés on the banks of the River Marne. And who could forget the magnificent splendour of Versailles, the most beautiful palace in the world?

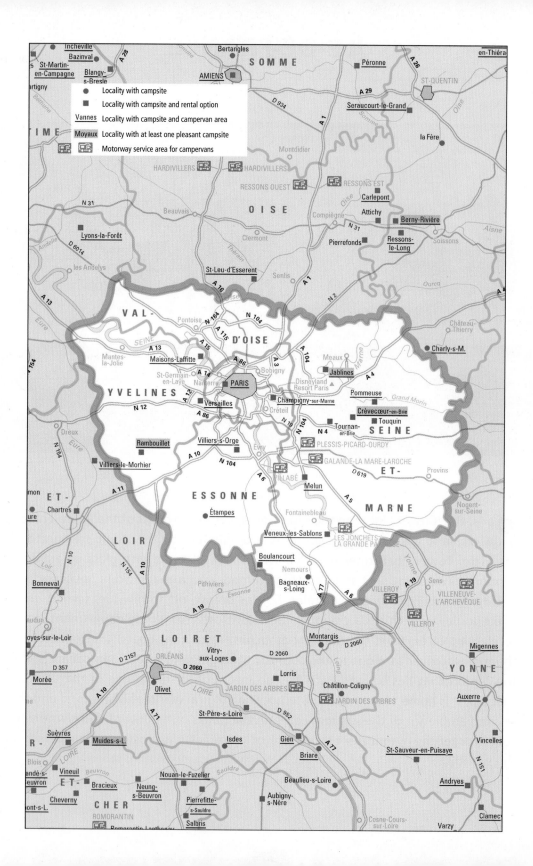

Legend:
- ● Locality with campsite
- ■ Locality with campsite and rental option
- <u>Vannes</u> Locality with campsite and campervan area
- Moyaux Locality with at least one pleasant campsite
- 🚐 🚐 Motorway service area for campervans

BAGNEAUX-SUR-LOING

77167 – Michelin map **312** F6 – pop. 1 686 – alt. 45
▶ Paris 84 – Fontainebleau 21 – Melun 39 – Montargis 30

⚠ Municipal de Pierre le Sault

🅟 01 64 29 97 51, www.camping-bagneaux-sur-loing.fr – limited spaces for one-night stay

Address : chemin des Grèves (to the northeast of the town, near the sports field, between the canal and the Loing river, 200m from a small lake)

Opening times : from beginning April to end Oct.

3 ha (160 pitches) flat, grassy, wood

Tariff : (2015 price) 13,80 € ★★ 🚗 🔲 ⓕ (10A) –
Extra per person 3.25 €

Located between a canal and the river, but in an industrial quarter.

Surroundings : 🗭 ♒♒
Leisure activities : 🏠 🏄 ✗
Facilities : ᚹ ⌒ 🚿 ⓕ 🍴 launderette
Nearby : 🐟

G P S Longitude : 2.70376
Latitude : 48.24069

BOULANCOURT

77760 – Michelin map **312** D6 – pop. 357 – alt. 79
▶ Paris 79 – Étampes 33 – Fontainebleau 28 – Melun 44

⚠ Île de Boulancourt

🅟 01 64 24 13 38, www.camping-iledeboulancourt.com – limited spaces for one-night stay

Address : 6 allée des Marronniers (to the south, follow the signs for Augerville-la-Rivière)

Opening times : permanent

5.5 ha (110 pitches) flat, grassy

Tariff : 14.70 € ★★ 🚗 🔲 ⓕ (6A) – Extra per person 4,85 €
Rental rates : permanent 🛏 – 4 'gypsy' caravans – 7 🚐 –
1 canvas bungalow. Per night from 29 to 150 € – Per week from 165 to 390 €
🚾 Eurorelais sani-station 4 € – 3 🔲 11 € – 🚐 11 €

In a pleasant wooded setting near a bend in the Essonne river.

Surroundings : 🐟 ♒♒
Leisure activities : 🏠 🏄 🐟
Facilities : ⌒ 🍴 ⓕ 🍴 📶

G P S Longitude : 2.435
Latitude : 48.25583

CHAMPIGNY-SUR-MARNE

94500 – Michelin map **312** E3 – pop. 75 090 – alt. 40
▶ Paris 13 – Créteil 10 – Amiens 150 – Bobigny 13

⚠ Homair Vacances Paris Est

🅟 01 43 97 43 97, www.campingchampigny.paris – reserved for residents outside the Île de France

Address : boulevard des Alliés

Opening times : permanent

3 ha (405 pitches) flat, grassy, gravelled, cement

Tariff : (2015 price) 23.90 € ★★ 🚗 🔲 ⓕ (10A) – Extra per person
5 € – Reservation fee 10 €
Rental rates : (2015 price) permanent – 350 🚐. Per night from 56 to 132 € – Per week from 392 to 924 € – Reservation fee 25 €
🚾 AireService sani-station 9.50 € – 15 🔲 22.50 € – 🚐 ⓕ 16.40 €

Beside the Marne river with a view of the Pavillon Baltard (19th-century concert hall).

Leisure activities : 🍷 ✗ jacuzzi 🚲
Facilities : ᚹ ⌒ 🆑 ⓕ 🔲 🏄 🍴 🍴 launderette
🏊 🐟
Nearby : 🐟

G P S Longitude : 2.47701
Latitude : 48.82958

CREVECOEUR-EN-BRIE

77610 – Michelin map **312** G3 – pop. 299 – alt. 116
▶ Paris 51 – Melun 36 – Boulogne-Billancourt 59 – Argenteuil 66

⚠ Caravaning des 4 Vents

🅟 01 64 07 41 11, www.caravaning-4vents.fr – limited spaces for one-night stay

Address : 22 rue de Beauregard (located 1km west following signs for la Houssaye and take turning to the left)

Opening times : from end March to end Oct.

9 ha (199 pitches) flat, grassy

Tariff : 30 € ★★ 🚗 🔲 ⓕ (6A) – Extra per person 6 €
Rental rates : (from end March to end Oct.) 🛏 – 5 🏠. Per night from 83 € – Per week from 560 €
🚾 local sani-station – 30 🔲 30 €

In a pleasant leafy setting with large, well marked out pitches.

Surroundings : 🐟 🗭 ♒
Leisure activities : 🏠 🏄 🐟
Facilities : ᚹ ⌒ 🚿 ⓕ 🏄 🍴 launderette
Nearby : ✗ 🐎

G P S Longitude : 2.89722
Latitude : 48.75065

These symbols are used for a campsite that is exceptional in its category:

🏔🏔🏔 ... 🏔 *Particularly pleasant setting, quality and range of services available*

🐥 🐥 *Tranquil, isolated site – quiet site, particularly at night*

≪ ≪ *Exceptional view – interesting or panoramic view*

ÉTAMPES

91150 – Michelin map **312** B5 – pop. 22 182 – alt. 80
▶ Paris 51 – Chartres 59 – Évry 35 – Fontainebleau 45

⚠ Le Vauvert

🅟 01 64 94 21 39, caravaning.levauvert@orange.fr – limited spaces for one-night stay

Address : route de Saclas (2.3km south along the D 49)

Opening times : from mid Jan. to mid Dec.

8 ha (230 pitches) flat, grassy

Tariff : 21 € ★★ 🚗 🔲 ⓕ (10A) – Extra per person 5.50 €
🚾 5 🔲 21 €

Fewer than 30 ptiches for tents and caravans next to 200 owner-occupier mobile homes.

Surroundings : 🗭 ♒
Leisure activities : 🍷 🏠 🏄 ✗
Facilities : ᚹ ⌒ 🚿 🏄 🍴 🍴
At the leisure/activities centre : 🏄 🏊 ⛷ 🐎
climbing

G P S Longitude : 2.14532
Latitude : 48.41215

JABLINES

77450 – Michelin map **312** F2 – pop. 629 – alt. 46
▶ Paris 44 – Meaux 14 – Melun 57

⚠ L' International

☏ 01 60 26 09 37, www.camping-jablines.com

Address : at the leisure centre (situated 2km southwest along the D 45, follow the signs for Annet-sur-Marne, 9km from the Disneyland-Paris park)

Opening times : from beginning April to beginning Nov.

300 ha/4 for camping (154 pitches) flat, grassy

Tariff : (2015 price) 31€ ★★ ⇌ 🔲 🚰 (10A) – Extra per person 8€ – Reservation fee 12€

Rental rates : (2015 price) (from beginning April to beginning Nov.) 🚲 – 11 🛖. Per night from 69 to 98€ – Per week from 590 to 690 €– Reservation fee 12€

🚐 Eurorelais sani-station 3€ – 150 🔲 31€

In an attractive location on a bend in the Marne river, next to a large leisure and activity centre.

Surroundings : 🐑 ⛱ ♤♤		
Leisure activities : 🏄	**G**	Longitude : 2.73437
Facilities : ♿ ⌾ cc 🎦 🌡 🍴 launderette 🧺	**P**	Latitude : 48.91367
At the leisure/activities centre : 🍴 ✗ 🎣 🚲 🎣 🎿 🏊 (fresh water) 🚣 🐴 cable wakeboarding	**S**	

MAISONS-LAFFITTE

78600 – Michelin map **311** I2 – pop. 22 717 – alt. 38
▶ Paris 23 – Versailles 24 – Pontoise 20 – Nanterre 13

⚘ Sandaya International

☏ 01 39 12 21 91, www.sandaya.fr

Address : 1 rue Johnson (on the Île de la Commune – island in the Seine river)

Opening times : from end March to beginning Nov.

6.5 ha (336 pitches) flat, grassy

Tariff : (2015 price) 38€ ★★ ⇌ 🔲 🚰 (10A) – Extra per person 7.50€ – Reservation fee 32€

Rental rates : (2015 price) (from end March to beginning Nov.) ♿ (1 mobile home) – 63 🛖 – 3 cabins in the trees. Per night from 88 to 153€ – Reservation fee 32€

🚐 local sani-station

On an island in the Seine river; part of the rental accommodation is booked on a hotel basis.

Surroundings : ⛱ 🌡		
Leisure activities : 🍴 ✗ 🎦 🏄 🎣	**G**	Longitude : 2.1458
Facilities : ♿ ⌾ 🎦 🌡 🍴 launderette 🧺 🚲	**P**	Latitude : 48.94156
Nearby : ✗	**S**	

MELUN

77000 – Michelin map **312** E4 – pop. 39 400 – alt. 43
▶ Paris 47 – Chartres 105 – Fontainebleau 18 – Meaux 55

⚘ La Belle Étoile

☏ 01 64 39 48 12, www.campinglabelleetoile.com

Address : 64bis quai Maréchal Joffre (to the southeast along the N 6, follow the signs for Fontainebleau (left bank)

Opening times : from beginning April to beginning Oct.

3.5 ha (180 pitches) flat, grassy

Tariff : ★ 7€ ⇌ 🔲 8€ – 🚰 (6A) 4€ – Reservation fee 8€

Rental rates : (from beginning April to beginning Oct.) ♿ 🚲 – 17 🛖 – 4 🛖 – 3 canvas bungalows. Per night from 40 to 130€ – Per week from 224 to 800€ – Reservation fee 8€

🚐 local sani-station 3€

In a very lush setting, right next to the Seine river.

Surroundings : 🐑 ♤♤		
Leisure activities : ✗ 🎦 🏄 🏊 (pool)	**G**	Longitude : 2.66765
Facilities : ♿ ⌾ cc 🎦 🌡 🍴 launderette 🧺	**P**	Latitude : 48.50929
Nearby : 🛁 hammam ✗ 🎦 🔲 🎿 🎣	**S**	

PARIS

75000 – pop. 2 234 105 – alt. 30
Au Bois de Boulogne – 75016

⚘⚘ Indigo Paris Bois de Boulogne

☏ 01 45 24 30 00, www.camping-indigo.com – reserved for residents outside the Île de France

Address : 2 allée du Bord de l'Eau (between the bridges at Suresnes and Puteaux; beside the Seine river)

Opening times : permanent

7 ha (410 pitches) grassy

Tariff : (2015 price) 41.80€ ★★ ⇌ 🔲 🚰 (10A) – Extra per person 8€ – Reservation fee 13€

Rental rates : (2015 price) permanent ♿ (1 mobile home) – 17 'gypsy' caravans – 58 🛖 – 6 tent lodges. Per night from 72 to 154€ – Per week from 454 to 970€ – Reservation fee 23€

🚐 local sani-station 9€

Choose the pitches along the Seine river, which are a little more peaceful. There's a bus for Porte Maillot, Paris (RER rail and metro station).

Surroundings : ⛱ ♤♤		
Leisure activities : 🍴 ✗ 🎦 🏄 🚲	**G**	Longitude : 2.23464
Facilities : ♿ ⌾ 🎦 🌡 🍴 launderette 🧺 🚲	**P**	Latitude : 48.86849

We value your opinion and welcome your feedback. Do email us at campingfrance@tp.michelin.com

POMMEUSE

77515 – Michelin map **312** H3 – pop. 2 756 – alt. 67
▶ Paris 58 – Château-Thierry 49 – Créteil 54 – Meaux 23

⚘⚘ Iris Parc Le Chêne Gris ♙♙

☏ 01 64 04 21 80, www.irisparc.com 🚲

Address : 24 place de la Gare (situated 2km southwest, behind Faremoutiers-Pommeuse train station)

Opening times : from end March to end Oct.

6 ha (350 pitches) terraced, flat, grassy, gravelled

Tariff : (2015 price) 44€ ★★ ⇌ 🔲 🚰 (10A) – Extra per person 6€ – Reservation fee 20€

Rental rates : (2015 price) (from end March to end Oct.) 🚲 – 218 🛖 – 79 canvas bungalows. Per night from 28 to 151€ – Per week from 140 to 1,057€ – Reservation fee 20€

🚐 sani-station 7€

There's a well-equipped indoor children's play area.

Surroundings : 🐑 ⛱ ♤♤		
Leisure activities : ✗ 🎦 🎮 🏃 🏄 🔲 🎿	**G**	Longitude : 2.99368
Facilities : ♿ ⌾ 🎦 🌡 🍴 launderette 🧺 🚲	**P**	Latitude : 48.80814

RAMBOUILLET

78120 – Michelin map **311** G4 – pop. 26 065 – alt. 160
▶ Paris 53 – Chartres 42 – Étampes 44 – Mantes-la-Jolie 50

⚍ Huttopia Rambouillet ⚍⚎

✆ 01 30 41 07 34, www.huttopia.com

Address : route du Château d'Eau (head 4km south along the N 10, follow the signs for Chartres)

Opening times : from end March to beginning Nov.

8 ha (116 pitches) flat, grassy, wood, gravel

Tariff : (2015 price) 36,60€ ✹✹ ⇔ 回 ⚡ (10A) –
Extra per person 8.30€ – Reservation fee 13€

Rental rates : (2015 price) (from end March to beginning Nov.)
Ⓟ – 10 'gypsy' caravans – 25 ⌂ – 40 tent lodges. Per night from 61 to 152€ – Per week from 385 to 852€ – Reservation fee 13€

⛽ local sani-station 7€

Situated beside a lake in the heart of Rambouillet forest, with an eco swimming pool.

Surroundings : ⛰ ⌂ ♨♨
Leisure activities : ⛶ ✕ ⛺ ⚐ ⚑ 🎿
Facilities : ♿ ⛽ 🏧 ⚒ ⚓ ⚗ launderette ⚘
Nearby : 🖼 ⚐ wildlife park

The information in the guide may have changed since going to press.

TOUQUIN

77131 – Michelin map **312** H3 – pop. 1 095 – alt. 112
▶ Paris 57 – Coulommiers 12 – Melun 36 – Montereau-Fault-Yonne 48

⚍ Les Étangs Fleuris

✆ 01 64 04 16 36, www.etangsfleuris.com

Address : route de La Couture (3km east)

Opening times : from beginning April to mid Sept.

9.4 ha (225 pitches) terraced relatively flat, flat, grassy

Tariff : 28€ ✹✹ ⇔ 回 ⚡ (10A) – Extra per person 6€
Rental rates : (from beginning April to mid Sept.) ⚓ – 14 ⛟.
Per night from 65 to 112€ – Per week from 290 to 672€

Some large sunny pitches, shade near the lakes, leafy setting.

Surroundings : ⛰ ⌂ ♨♨
Leisure activities : ⛶ ✕ ⛺ ⚐ ⚑ 🎿 ⚐ ⚑
multi-sports ground
Facilities : ♿ ⛽ 🏧 ⚗ ⚘ ⛽ launderette ⚘

TOURNAN-EN-BRIE

77220 – Michelin map **312** F3 – pop. 8 116 – alt. 102
▶ Paris 44 – Melun 29 – Amiens 176 – Créteil 38

⚍ FranceLoc Fredland – Parc de Combreux

✆ 01 64 07 96 44, www.campings-franceloc.fr

Address : 1.5 km, south of the town, off the D 10, route de Liverdy-en-Brie

Opening times : permanent

26 ha/7 for camping (189 pitches) flat, grassy

Tariff : (2015 price) 30€ ✹✹ ⇔ 回 ⚡ (6A) – Extra per person 7€ – Reservation fee 11€

Rental rates : (2015 price) permanent – 136 ⛟ – 142 ⌂ – 4 cabins in the trees. Per night from 39 to 205€ – Per week from 259 to 1,435€ – Reservation fee 27€

Situated 800m from the RER suburban rail station (25 minutes to Paris).

Surroundings : ⛰ ♨♨
Leisure activities : ⛶ ✕ ⚐ ⚑ 🖼 (small swimming pool) 🎿 ⚑ ⚘
Facilities : ♿ ⛽ 🏧 ⛽ launderette ⚗ ⚘

GPS Longitude : 2.76915
Latitude : 48.73517

VENEUX-LES-SABLONS

77250 – Michelin map **312** F5 – pop. 4 788 – alt. 76
▶ Paris 72 – Fontainebleau 9 – Melun 26 – Montereau-Fault-Yonne 14

⚍ Les Courtilles du Lido

✆ 01 60 70 46 05, http://www.les-courtilles-du-lido.fr

Address : chemin du Passeur (located 1.5km to the northeast)

Opening times : from end March to end Sept.

5 ha (180 pitches) flat, grassy, stony

Tariff : 19.50€ ✹✹ ⇔ 回 ⚡ (10A) – Extra per person 4€
Rental rates : (2015 price) (from end March to end Sept.) – 15 ⛟ – 2 canvas bungalows. Per night from 85 to 150€ – Per week from 251 to 689€

⛽ sani-station 4€ – ⚓ 16€

The pitches are very well shaded.

Surroundings : ⛰ ⌂ ♨♨
Leisure activities : ⛶ ✕ ⚐ ⚑ ⚐ 🎿
Facilities : ♿ ⛽ 🏧 launderette ⚘

GPS Longitude : 2.80194
Latitude : 48.38333

The Michelin classification (⚍⚍⚍ ... ⚍) is totally independent of the official star classification system awarded by the local prefecture or other official organisation.

VERSAILLES

78000 – Michelin map **311** I3 – pop. 86 477 – alt. 130
▶ Paris 29 – Chartres 80 – Fontainebleau 73 – Rambouillet 35

⚍ Huttopia Versailles

✆ 01 39 51 23 61, www.huttopia.com

Address : 31 rue Berthelot

Opening times : from end March to beginning Nov.

4.6 ha (180 pitches) terraced, relatively flat, flat, grassy

Tariff : (2015 price) 47,50€ ✹✹ ⇔ 回 ⚡ (10A) –
Extra per person 10.20€ – Reservation fee 13€

Rental rates : (2015 price) (from end March to beginning Nov.) ♿ (1 chalet) – 7 'gypsy' caravans – 26 ⌂ – 22 tent lodges. Per night from 70 to 145€ – Per week from 441 to 1,103€ – Reservation fee 13€

⛽ Flot Bleu sani-station 9€

The pitches are among trees and shrubs, close to the town.

Surroundings : ⛰ ♨♨♨
Leisure activities : ✕ ⚐ ⚑ 🚲 🎿
Facilities : ♿ ⛽ 🏧 ⚘ launderette

GPS Longitude : 2.15912
Latitude : 48.79441

VILLIERS-SUR-ORGE

91700 – Michelin map **312** C4 – pop. 3 896 – alt. 75
▶ Paris 25 – Chartres 71 – Dreux 89 – Évry 15

🏔 Le Beau Village de Paris

📞 01 60 16 17 86, www.campingaparis.com – limited spaces for one-night stay

Address : 1 voie des Prés (600m southeast via the town centre, 800m from St-Geneviève-des-Bois station – from A 6, take exit 6)

Opening times : permanent

2.5 ha (124 pitches) flat, grassy, fine gravel, hard surface

Tariff : 27.50€ ✝✝ 🚗 🔲 ⚡ (10A) – Extra per person 8.30€

Rental rates : permanent – 20 🚐 – 1 studio – 1 apartment. Per night from 55 to 140€ – Per week from 170 to 550€

🚐 Flot Bleu sani-station 5€ – 20 🔲 8.20€

In a green setting, slightly shady beside the Orge river, with proper pitches for campervans.

Surroundings : 🌿 🗐 ♀
Leisure activities : ♟ 🏛 🏇
Facilities : ♿ ⛽ 🏚 🍴 launderette
Nearby : 🏓 skate park

G P S Longitude : 2.30421
Latitude : 48.65511

Michelin classification:

🏔🏔🏔🏔	*Extremely comfortable, equipped to a very high standard*
🏔🏔🏔	*Very comfortable, equipped to a high standard*
🏔🏔🏔	*Comfortable and well equipped*
🏔🏔	*Reasonably comfortable*
🏔	*Satisfactory*

R. Mattes / hemis.fr

Languedoc-Roussillon is a kaleidoscope of landscapes, cultures and sensations. You will be seduced by the feverish rhythm of its festivals, the dizzying beauty of the Tarn gorges and the Pyrenees, the magical spell of its caves and stone statues, the seclusion of its cliff-top 'Citadels of Vertigo' with their panoramic views and the heady perfumes of its sun-drenched *garrigue*, the local scrubland fragrant with wild herbs. Admire the nonchalant flamingoes that thrive on its long stretches of salt flats, enjoy discovering the splendour of Carcassonne's medieval ramparts or explore the quiet waters of the Midi Canal and the harsh majesty of the Cévennes. Taking in so many different sights may exhaust some visitors, but remedies are close at hand: a plate of *aligot*, made from mashed potato, butter, cream, garlic and cheese, and a simmering *cassoulet*, the famously rich combination of duck, sausage, beans and herbs, followed by a slice of Roquefort cheese and a glass of ruby-red wine.

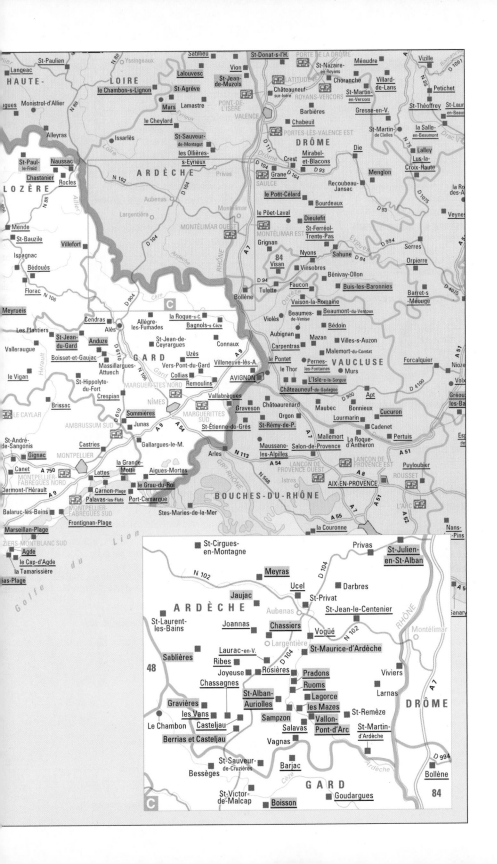

AGDE

34300 – Michelin map **339** F9 – pop. 24 031 – alt. 5
▶ Paris 754 – Béziers 24 – Lodève 60 – Millau 118

🏕 Yelloh! Village Mer et Soleil ▲▲

Yelloh! Village Mer et Soleil

📞 0467 94 21 14. www.camping-mer-soleil.com

Address : chemin de Notre Dame à Saint Martin, route de Rochelongue (3km to the south)

Opening times : from mid April to beginning Oct.

8 ha (477 pitches) flat, grassy, sandy

Tariff : 49€ ♣♣ ⊝ 🄴 🄗 (6A) – Extra per person 8€

Rental rates : (from mid April to beginning Oct.) ♿ (1 mobile home) ♨ – 212 🚐 – 5 🏠 – 42 canvas bungalows. Per night from 29 to 255€ – Per week from 203 to 1,785€

An impressive indoor spa area with some luxury mobile homes in a pedestrian zone.

Surroundings : 🌳 ⌂ ♀♀
Leisure activities : 🍴 ✕ 🖼 nighttime 🏃
🐟♒ jacuzzi 🚴 ❀ 🎯 🛝 spa centre
Facilities : ♿ ⛽ 🛁 🍴 launderette 🔲 🎣
Nearby : 🐎

GPS Longitude : 3.47812
Latitude : 43.28621

Some campsites benefit from proximity to a municipal leisure centre.

🏕 Village Vacances Les Pescalunes
(rental of chalets only)

📞 0467 01 37 06. www.grandbleu.fr

Address : route de Luxembourg (follow the signs for Le Cap-d'Agde)

Opening times : from beginning April to end Oct.

3 ha uneven, terraced

Rental rates : ♿ (2 chalets) 🅿 – 98 🏠. Per night from 75 to 110€ – Per week from 238 to 1,106€

A peaceful chalet village on the side of a hill, with a view of the surrounding area and the Cévennes mountains.

Surroundings : 🌳 ≤ ♀♀
Leisure activities : 🖼 🏃 ❀ 🛝
Facilities : ▥ 🍴 launderette

GPS Longitude : 3.50223
Latitude : 43.30109

🏕 Neptune ▲▲

Neptune

📞 0467 94 23 94. www.campingleneptune.com

Address : 46 boulevard du Saint-Christ (situated 2km to the south, near the Hérault river)

Opening times : from beginning April to beginning Oct.

2.1 ha (165 pitches) flat, grassy

Tariff : (2015 price) 38.40€ ♣♣ ⊝ 🄴 🄗 (10A) – Extra per person 8.40€ –
Reservation fee 30€

Rental rates : (2015 price) (from beginning April to beginning Oct.) – 20 🚐. Per night from 33 to 150€
– Per week from 231 to 1,050€ – Reservation fee 30€

🚽 local sani-station

Flowers and shrubs decorate the site; some high-quality mobile homes.

Surroundings : ⌂ ♀
Leisure activities : 🍴 ✕ 🏃 ❀ 🚴 🛝 multi-sports ground
Facilities : ♿ ⛽ 🛁 🗑 ♒ 🍴 launderette
Nearby : 🎣

GPS Longitude : 3.4581
Latitude : 43.29805

🏕 Les Romarins

📞 0467 94 18 59. www.romarins.com

Address : 6 route du Grau (3km to the south, near the Hérault river)

2 ha (120 pitches) flat, grassy, sandy

Rentals : 37 🚐 – 2 studios – 3 tent lodges.

🚽 Eurorelais sani-station

Surroundings : ⌂ ♀♀
Leisure activities : 🍴 ✕ 🖼 ❀ 🛝 multi-sports ground
Facilities : ♿ ⛽ 🛁 🍴 🖼

GPS Longitude : 3.4468
Latitude : 43.29131

🏕 Le Rochelongue ▲▲

📞 0467 21 25 51. www.camping-le-rochelongue.fr – limited spaces for one-night stay

Address : route de Rochelongue (4km to the south, 500m from the beach)

2 ha (107 pitches) flat, grassy, gravel

Rentals : 27 🚐.

Surroundings : ⌂ ♀♀
Leisure activities : 🍴 ✕ 🏃 ❀ 🛝
Facilities : ♿ ⛽ 🛁 🍴 launderette 🎣
Nearby : ✂ 🖼 🎣 🐎 watersports centre

GPS Longitude : 3.48139
Latitude : 43.27917

🏕 La Pépinière

📞 0467 94 10 94. www.campinglapepiniere.com

Address : 3 route du Grau

Opening times : from mid March to mid Oct.

3 ha (100 pitches) flat, grassy

Tariff : 31.50€ ♣♣ ⊝ 🄴 🄗 (10A) – Extra per person 7.50€ – Reservation fee 25€

Rental rates : (from mid April to end Sept.) – 31 🚐 – 2 tent lodges. Per night from 28 to 98€ – Per week from 206 to 626€ – Reservation fee 25€

🚽 local sani-station

A family-friendly site very near the Hérault river.

Surroundings : 🌳 ⌂
Leisure activities : 🍴 ✕ 🏃 ♒ ❀ 🛝
Facilities : ♿ ⛽ 🍴 🗑 🎣
Nearby : ⚓ 🎣

GPS Longitude : 3.45368
Latitude : 43.29488

Key to rentals symbols:

12 🚐	*Number of mobile homes*
20 🏠	*Number of chalets*
6 🛏	*Number of rooms to rent*
Per night 30–50€	*Minimum/maximum rate per night*
Per week 300–1,000€	*Minimum/maximum rate per week*

AIGUES-MORTES

30220 – Michelin map **339** K7 – pop. 8 116 – alt. 3
▶ Paris 745 – Arles 49 – Montpellier 38 – Nîmes 42

Yelloh! Village La Petite Camargue 🏕

✆ 04 66 53 98 98. www.yellohvillage-petite.camargue.com
Address : 3.5km west along the D 62, follow the signs for Montpellier
Opening times : from end April to mid Sept.
42 ha/10 for camping (553 pitches) flat, grassy, sandy
Tariff : 54 € ♣♣ 🚗 🔲 (16A) – Extra per person 9 €
Rental rates : (from end April to mid Sept.) – 299 🚐. Per night from 39 to 244 € – Per week from 273 to 1,708 €
🚐 local sani-station
Activities and services suitable for teenagers. A free shuttle service to the beaches.

Surroundings : 🌄 🏞 ♤♤
Leisure activities : ♈ ✕ 🎦 🗿 🏃 ⛷ 🚴 🎿
🛶 🏖 🐎 disco, multi-sports ground
Facilities : ♿ ⚬➙ 🏛 🏅 🍴 launderette 🚐 🚿

GPS Longitude : 4.15963
Latitude : 43.56376

ALET-LES-BAINS

11580 – Michelin map **344** E5 – pop. 436 – alt. 186
▶ Paris 786 – Montpellier 187 – Carcassonne 35 – Castelnaudary 49

Val d'Aleth

✆ 04 68 69 90 40. www.valdaleth.com
Address : in the village (D 2118 and take the right turning beside the Aude river)
Opening times : permanent
0.5 ha (37 pitches) flat grassy, stony
Tariff : (2015 price) 22 € ♣♣ 🚗 🔲 (10A) – Extra per person 4.95 €
Rental rates : permanent 🛖 – 4 🚐. Per night from 58 to 62 € – Per week from 365 to 390 €
🚐 local sani-station 16 € – 10 🔲 16 €
Well-shaded pitches near the river and a ruined château.

Surroundings : 🏞 ♤♤
Leisure activities : ⛷ 🛶
Facilities : ♿ ⚬➙ 🍴 launderette

GPS Longitude : 2.25564
Latitude : 42.99486

Some information or pricing may have changed since the guide went to press. We recommend you check the price list online in advance or at the entrance to the campsite and enquire about possible restrictions.

ALLÈGRE-LES-FUMADES

30500 – Michelin map **339** K3 – pop. 695 – alt. 135 – ⊹
▶ Paris 696 – Alès 16 – Barjac 102 – La Grand-Combe 28

FranceLoc Le Domaine des Fumades 🏕

✆ 04 66 24 80 78. www.domaine-des-fumades.com
Address : Les Fumade – Les Bains (access via the D 241)
Opening times : from mid April to mid Sept.
15 ha/6 for camping (253 pitches) relatively flat, flat, grassy, stony
Tariff : (2015 price) 38 € ♣♣ 🚗 🔲 (10A) – Extra per person 7 € – Reservation fee 27 €

Rental rates : (2015 price) (from mid April to mid Sept.) – 184 🚐 – 12 🏠 – 5 apartments – 8 canvas bungalows. Per night from 37 to 123 € – Per week from 147 to 1,316 € – Reservation fee 27 €
Beside the Alauzène river and close to the spa centre.

Surroundings : 🌄 🏞 ♤♤
Leisure activities : ♈ ✕ 🎦 🗿 🏃 ⛷ 🎿
🏕 🏖 ⛷ 🛶 cinema, multi-sports ground, entertainment room
Facilities : ♿ ⚬➙ 🏛 🏅 🍴 launderette 🚐 🚿
Nearby : 🐎

GPS Longitude : 4.22904
Latitude : 44.18484

In order for the guide to remain wholly objective, the selection of campsites is made on an entirely independent basis.

ANDUZE

30140 – Michelin map **339** I4 – pop. 3 303 – alt. 135
▶ Paris 718 – Alès 15 – Florac 68 – Lodève 84

L'Arche 🏕

✆ 04 66 61 74 08. www.camping-arche.fr
Address : 1105 chemin de Recoulin (situated 2km to the northwest; beside the Gardon river)
Opening times : from end March to end Sept.
5 ha (302 pitches) terraced, relatively flat, flat, grassy, sandy
Tariff : (2015 price) 45 € ♣♣ 🚗 🔲 (10A) – Extra per person 9.50 € – Reservation fee 15 €
Rental rates : (2015 price) (from end March to end Sept.) 🛖 – 20 🚐 – 16 🏠. Per week from 400 to 1,350 € – Reservation fee 15 €
🚐 Eurorelais sani-station 2 €

Surroundings : 🌄 ♈ 🏔
Leisure activities : ♈ ✕ 🎦 🗿 🏃 🏛
hammam ⛷ 🛶 🎿 🚴 multi-sports ground, spa centre
Facilities : ♿ ⚬➙ 🏛 🏅 🍴 🚿 launderette 🚐 🚿
Nearby : 🏪

GPS Longitude : 3.97284
Latitude : 44.06873

Cévennes-Provence 🏕

✆ 04 66 61 73 10. www.camping-cevennes-provence.fr
Address : at Corbès-Thoiras (by the Mas du Pont – old farmhouse beside the bridge; beside the Gardon de Mialet and near the Gardon de St-Jean rivers)
Opening times : from mid March to end Sept.
30 ha/15 for camping (242 pitches) very uneven, terraced, flat and relatively flat, grassy, stony
Tariff : 33 € ♣♣ 🚗 🔲 (10A) – Extra per person 9 € – Reservation fee 13 €
Rental rates : (from mid March to end Sept.) – 16 🏠. Per week from 360 to 700 €
🚐 local sani-station
Choose pitches near the river for swimming or higher up for the view over the valley.

Surroundings : 🌄 ← 🏞 ♤♤ 🏔
Leisure activities : ♈ ✕ 🎦 🏃 ⛷ 🎿 🚴
🍴
Facilities : ♿ ⚬➙ 🏛 🏅 🍴 launderette 🚐 🚿
Nearby : adventure park

GPS Longitude : 3.96643
Latitude : 44.07711

⛰ Les Fauvettes ♟♞

☎ 0466617223. www.lesfauvettes.fr

Address : route de St-Jean-du-Gard (1.7km to the northwest)

Opening times : from end April to end Sept.

7 ha/3 for camping (144 pitches) very uneven, terraced, flat and relatively flat, grassy

Tariff : 28€ ♟♟ ⛟ 🔲 (10A) – Extra per person 7€ – Reservation fee 18€

Rental rates : (from beginning April to end Nov.) – 20 🚐 – 20 🏠 – 1 canvas bungalow. Per night from 50 to 70€ – Per week from 209 to 790€ – Reservation fee 18€

🚐 20 🔲

Choose the pitches away from the road in preference.

Surroundings : 🛣 ♀
Leisure activities : ♟ ✗ ⛺ ♞♞ ⛷ ⟲ △ entertainment room
Facilities : ⚹ ⛎ ♨ ♒ 🔲 ⅌
Nearby : 🛒 🚲

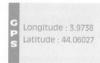
Longitude : 3.9738
Latitude : 44.06027

⛰ Le Bel Eté d'Anduze

☎ 0466617604. www.camping-bel-ete.com

Address : 1870 route de Nîmes (2.5km southeast)

Opening times : from beginning April to end Sept.

2.26 ha (97 pitches) flat, grassy

Tariff : (2015 price) 17€ ♟♟ ⛟ 🔲 ⚡ (16A) – Extra per person 4€ – Reservation fee 20€

Rental rates : (2015 price) (from beginning April to end Sept.) – 30 🚐. Per night from 50 to 70€ – Per week from 295 to 830€ – Reservation fee 20€

Choose the pitches near the Gardon river and away from the road in preference.

Surroundings : ♀♀
Leisure activities : ✗ ⛺ ♞♞ ⟲ △ multi-sports ground
Facilities : ⚹ ⛎ ♨ ♒ ⅌ ⅋ 🔲 ⅌ refrigerators
Nearby : 🍴 ⛵

Longitude : 3.99468
Latitude : 44.03827

This guide is not intended as a list of all the camping sites in France; its aim is to provide a selection of the best sites in each category.

ARGELÈS-SUR-MER

66700 – Michelin map **344** J7 – pop. 10 033 – alt. 19
▶ Paris 872 – Céret 28 – Perpignan 22 – Port-Vendres 9

Centre

⛰ Le Front de Mer ♟♞

☎ 0468810870. www.camping-front-mer.com

Address : avenue du Grau (250m from the beach)

Opening times : permanent

10 ha (588 pitches) flat, grassy

Tariff : 41.90€ ♟♟ ⛟ 🔲 ⚡ (6A) – Extra per person 7.40€ – Reservation fee 25€

Rental rates : permanent – 145 🚐. Per night from 50 to 70€ – Per week from 745 to 1,080€ – Reservation fee 25€

🚐 AireService sani-station 2€

A pretty water park and indoor spa area.

Surroundings : 🛣 ♀♀
Leisure activities : ♟ ✗ ⑭ ♞♞ ⛷ ⟲ hammam, jacuzzi ⟲ ⟲ ⛷ ⟲ △ multi-sports ground, spa centre
Facilities : ⚹ ⛎ ♨ ⅌ launderette ⚏ ⅌

Longitude : 3.04687
Latitude : 42.54684

⛰ Pujol

☎ 0468810025. www.campingdepujol.com

Address : avenue de la Rétirada 1939

Opening times : from end April to beginning Oct.

6.2 ha (312 pitches) flat, grassy, sandy

Tariff : 38€ ♟♟ ⛟ 🔲 ⚡ (6A) – Extra per person 8€ – Reservation fee 15€

Rental rates : (from end April to beginning Oct.) ⟳ – 50 🚐. Per night from 20 to 138€ – Per week from 140 to 966€ – Reservation fee 15€

Numerous pitches for tents or caravans, many with plenty of shade.

Surroundings : ♀♀
Leisure activities : ♟ ✗ ⑭ nighttime ⟲ ⟲ ⑭ ⟲ △
Facilities : ⚹ ⛎ ♨ ⅌ launderette ⚏ ⅌
Nearby : 🍴 ⛺

Longitude : 3.02768
Latitude : 42.55532

⛰ FranceLoc Paris-Roussillon ♟♞

☎ 0468811971. www.parisroussillon.com

Address : avenue de la Rétirada

Opening times : from mid April to mid Sept.

3.5 ha (210 pitches) flat, grassy

Tariff : (2015 price) 34€ ♟♟ ⛟ 🔲 ⚡ (10A) – Extra per person 7€ – Reservation fee 27€

Rental rates : (from mid April to mid Sept.) – 167 🚐. Per night from 33 to 93€ – Per week from 133 to 1,323€ – Reservation fee 27€

In a well-shaded setting with plenty of mobile homes, but also pitches for tents and caravans.

Surroundings : 🔅 ♀♀
Leisure activities : ♟ ✗ ⑭ ♞♞ ⟲ 🍴 🔲 ⟲ △
Facilities : ⚹ ⛎ ♨ ⅌ launderette ⅌
Nearby : ⛺

Longitude : 3.03117
Latitude : 42.55782

⛰ La Chapelle ♟♞

☎ 0468812814. www.camping-la-chapelle.com

Address : avenue du Général de Gaulle (400m from the beach)

Opening times : from end April to beginning Oct.

4.1 ha (270 pitches)

Tariff : 38.50€ ♟♟ ⛟ 🔲 ⚡ (10A) – Extra per person 13€ – Reservation fee 26€

Rental rates : (from end April to beginning Oct.) – 68 🚐. Per week from 229 to 1,329€ – Reservation fee 26€

🚐 Eurorelais sani-station 6€ – 8 🔲 18.50€

Some attractively shaded areas beneath plane trees.

Surroundings : 🛣 ♀♀♀
Leisure activities : ⛺ ♞♞ ⛷ ⟲ 🍴 ⑭ multi-sports ground
Facilities : ⚹ ⛎ ♨ ⅌ launderette
Nearby : 🚲 ♪

Longitude : 3.04214
Latitude : 42.55074

⚠ Europe

📞 04 68 81 08 10. www.camping-europe.net

Address : avenue du Général de Gaulle (500m from the beach)

Opening times : from beginning April to end Sept.

1.2 ha (91 pitches) flat, grassy

Tariff : 33 € ✦✦ ⊖ 🖳 🚽 (10A) – Extra per person 7.50 € – Reservation fee 20 €

Rental rates : (from beginning April to end Sept.) ♿ (1 mobile home) – 13 🚐. Per night from 50 to 100 € – Per week from 220 to 850 € – Reservation fee 20 €

🚐 local sani-station – 20 🖳 33 €

Attractively shaded in places by plane trees, with good sanitary facilities.

Surroundings : 🎋
Leisure activities : 🏊🎣
Facilities : ♿ ⊶ 🚿 🍴 launderette 🧺
Nearby : 🔥

Longitude : 3.04185
Latitude : 42.54987

⚠ Le Stade

📞 04 68 81 04 40. www.campingdustade.com

Address : 87 avenue du 8 Mai 1945 (also known as: rte de la Plage)

Opening times : from beginning April to beginning Oct.

2.4 ha (185 pitches) flat, grassy

Tariff : ⊖ 🖳 24.50 € – 🚽 (10A) 4.30 €

Rental rates : (from beginning April to beginning Oct.) 🐾 – 11 🚐. Per night from 32 to 42 € – Per week from 300 to 705 € – Reservation fee 10 €

Choose those pitches away from the road; the sanitary facilities are rather old.

Surroundings : 🎋
Leisure activities : 🏊
Facilities : ♿ ⊶ 🚿 🍴 launderette
Nearby : 🍴 🍽 🏊 🎣 🔥 🏊

Longitude : 3.03544
Latitude : 42.54774

⚠ La Massane

📞 04 68 81 06 85. www.camping-massane.com

Address : avenue Molière (opposite the 'Espace Jean Carrère')

Opening times : from beginning April to end Sept.

2.7 ha (184 pitches) flat, grassy

Tariff : 34 € ✦✦ ⊖ 🖳 🚽 (10A) – Extra per person 7 € – Reservation fee 15 €

Rental rates : (from beginning April to end Sept.) 🐾 – 23 🚐. Per night from 36 to 96 € – Per week from 252 to 670 € – Reservation fee 15 €

Rather old but well maintained sanitary facilities.

Surroundings : 🎋
Leisure activities : 🏠 🏊 🔥 🏊
Facilities : ♿ ⊶ 🚿 🍴 launderette
Nearby : 🍽

Longitude : 3.03115
Latitude : 42.55137

⚠ Comangès

📞 04 68 81 15 62. www.campingcomanges.com

Address : avenue du Général de Gaulle (300m from the beach)

Opening times : from end April to end Sept.

1.2 ha (90 pitches) flat, grassy

Tariff : 33.99 € ✦✦ ⊖ 🖳 🚽 (10A) – Extra per person 7.99 € – Reservation fee 20 €

Rental rates : (from end April to end Sept.) – 19 🏠. Per night from 34 to 123 € – Per week from 238 to 861 € – Reservation fee 20 €

🚐 local sani-station – 🚐 🚽 14.92 €

Surroundings : 🎋
Leisure activities : 🏊
Facilities : ♿ ⊶ 🚿 🍴 🖳
Nearby : 🚴 🍽 🔥 🎣

Longitude : 3.04423
Latitude : 42.55145

North

🏕 La Sirène et l'Hippocampe 👥

📞 04 68 81 04 61. www.camping-lasirene.fr

Address : route de Taxo

Opening times : from mid April to end Sept.

21 ha (903 pitches) flat, grassy, sandy

Tariff : 55 € ✦✦ ⊖ 🖳 🚽 (16A) – Extra per person 11 € – Reservation fee 20 €

Rental rates : (from mid April to end Sept.) ♿ (1 mobile home) – 640 🚐 – 20 🏠. Per night from 40 to 280 € – Per week from 280 to 1,960 € – Reservation fee 20 €

Surroundings : 🏞 🎋
Leisure activities : 🍴 🍽 🎬 🎣 🏊 🚴 🐎 disco, pub, scuba diving, multi-sports ground
Facilities : ♿ ⊶ 🚿 🏊 🚽 🍴 launderette 🧺

Longitude : 3.0326
Latitude : 42.57058

🏕 Club Airotel Le Soleil 👥

📞 04 68 81 14 48. www.camping-le-soleil.fr

Address : route du Littoral

Opening times : from beginning May to end Sept.

17 ha (844 pitches)

Tariff : 48.40 € ✦✦ ⊖ 🖳 🚽 (10A) – Extra per person 12.90 € – Reservation fee 25 €

Rental rates : permanent – 157 🚐. Per night from 25 to 193 € – Per week from 175 to 1,351 € – Reservation fee 25 €

🚐 local sani-station – 20 🖳 12 €

A lush, green setting with lots of shade, close to the beach.

Surroundings : 🏞 🎋 ⛱
Leisure activities : 🍴 🍽 🎬 🚴 🎣 🏊 🐎 disco
Facilities : ♿ ⊶ 🚿 🍴 launderette 🧺

Longitude : 3.04618
Latitude : 42.5744

🏕 Les Marsouins 👥

📞 04 68 81 14 81. www.lesmarsouins.cielavillage.fr

Address : avenue de la Rétirada

Opening times : from end April to beginning Oct.

10 ha (587 pitches) flat, grassy

Tariff : 46 € ✦✦ ⊖ 🖳 🚽 (5A) – Extra per person 10.30 € – Reservation fee 20 €

Rental rates : (from end April to beginning Oct.) ♿ (1 mobile home) – 203 🚐. Per night from 35 to 230 € – Per week from 212 to 1,610 € – Reservation fee 20 €

🚐 local sani-station 9 € – 6 🖳 16 €

Attractive pitches for tents and caravans in green and floral surroundings.

Surroundings : 🏞 🎋
Leisure activities : 🍴 🍽 🎬 🚴 🏊 🎣 🏊 scuba diving, multi-sports ground
Facilities : ♿ ⊶ 🚿 🏊 🚽 🍴 launderette 🧺
Nearby : 🐎

Longitude : 3.03471
Latitude : 42.56376

La Marende ♠♦

📞 04 68 81 12 09. www.marende.com

Address : avenue du Littoral (400m from the beach)

3 ha (208 pitches)

Rentals : 67 🛏️.

Good shade from pine and eucalyptus trees, but choose those pitches away from the road.

Surroundings : 🛣️ 🌳🌳
Leisure activities : 🍽️ ✕ 🎭 nighttime ⚡️
jacuzzi 🚴 🏊 🎿 multi-sports ground
Facilities : 🚿 ⚲ 🏧 🚽 laundrette 🚮 🛒
Nearby : ⚔️ 🐎

Longitude : 3.0422
Latitude : 42.57395

Club Airotel Les Galets ♠♦

📞 04 68 81 08 12. http://www.campinglesgalets.fr/ – limited spaces for one-night stay

Address : route de Taxo à la mer

Opening times : from beginning April to end Sept.

5 ha (232 pitches) flat, grassy

Tariff : 45.50€ ✶✶ �car 🔲 [⚡] (10A) – Extra per person 9.60€ – Reservation fee 30€

Rental rates : (from beginning April to end Sept.) 🚿 (2 mobile homes) – 170 🛏️ – 40 🏠. Per night from 30 to 185€ – Per week from 203 to 1,295€ – Reservation fee 30€

🚰 AireService sani-station 4€ – 2 🔲 10€

A family-friendly site with plenty of owner-occupier mobile homes, but few places for tents and caravans.

Surroundings : 🛣️ 🌳🌳
Leisure activities : 🍽️ ✕ 🎭 nighttime ⚡️
🚴 🎿 multi-sports ground
Facilities : 🚿 ⚲ 🏧 🚽 laundrette 🛒
Nearby : 🐎

Longitude : 3.0144
Latitude : 42.57249

Le Roussillonnais ♠♦

📞 04 68 81 10 42. www.leroussillonnais.com

Address : boulevard de la Mer

10 ha (690 pitches)

Rentals : 105 🛏️.

Close to a beach, well shaded, with plenty of pitches for tents and caravans; groups welcome.

Surroundings : 🌳🌳 ⛰️
Leisure activities : 🍽️ ✕ 🎭 🎭 ⚡️ 🚴 ✂️
multi-sports ground
Facilities : 🚿 ⚲ 🏧 🚽 laundrette 🛒 🛒
Nearby : 🐬 🐎

Longitude : 3.04367
Latitude : 42.56842

South

Les Castels Les Criques de Porteils ♠♦

📞 04 68 81 12 73. www.lescriques.com

Address : corniche de Collioure, RD 114

Opening times : from end March to end Oct.

4.5 ha (250 pitches) very uneven, terraced, relatively flat, flat, grassy, stony

Tariff : 54€ ✶✶ �car 🔲 [⚡] (10A) – Extra per person 13.50€ – Reservation fee 26€

Rental rates : (from end March to end Oct.) – 35 🛏️ – 10 canvas bungalows. Per week from 179 to 1,559€ – Reservation fee 26€

🚰 Eurorelais sani-station 6€ – 5 🔲 22€

Direct access to the beach via steep steps. A panoramic view of the bay one way and the Roussillon vineyards the other.

Surroundings : 🏖️ ⟨ Baie d'Argelès-sur-Mer
🛣️ 🌳🌳 ⛰️
Leisure activities : 🍽️ ✕ 🎭 🚴 🎣 🏊 🎿
scuba diving, multi-sports ground
Facilities : 🚿 ⚲ 🏧 🚽 🚽 laundrette 🚮 🛒
refrigerated food storage facilities

Longitude : 3.06778
Latitude : 42.53389

La Coste Rouge

📞 04 68 81 08 94. www.lacosterouge.com – limited spaces for one-night stay

Address : route de Collioure (3km southeast)

Opening times : from beginning April to end Sept.

3.7 ha (145 pitches) terrace, flat and relatively flat, grassy

Tariff : 36€ ✶✶ �car 🔲 [⚡] (6A) – Extra per person 6.10€ – Reservation fee 20€

Rental rates : (from beginning April to mid Sept.) – 30 🛏️ – 7 studios. Per night from 41 to 135€ – Per week from 287 to 945€ – Reservation fee 20€

🚰 Flot Bleu sani-station 15€

Away from the hustle and bustle of Argelès-sur-Mer, but access to the beaches via a free shuttle service.

Surroundings : 🛣️ 🌳🌳
Leisure activities : 🍽️ ✕ 🎭 🎣 🚴 🎿 🎿 🎿
Facilities : 🚿 ⚲ 🚽 🚽 laundrette 🚮 🛒
Nearby : 🚴 🐬 🐎 water skiing

Longitude : 3.05285
Latitude : 42.53301

ARLES-SUR-TECH

66150 – Michelin map **344** G8 – pop. 2 757 – alt. 280
▶ Paris 886 – Amélie-les-Bains-Palalda 4 – Perpignan 45 – Prats-de-Mollo-la-Preste 19

Le Vallespir

📞 04 68 39 90 00. http://www.campingvallespir.com/fr/index.html

Address : situated 2km to the northeast, follow the signs for Amélie-les-Bains-Palalda; beside the Tech river

Opening times : from mid March to mid Nov.

2.5 ha (141 pitches) flat, relatively flat, grassy

Tariff : (2015 price) 17.24€ ✶✶ �car 🔲 [⚡] (10A) – Extra per person 4.50€

Rental rates : (2015 price) (from mid March to mid Nov.) 🚿 (2 mobile homes) – 53 🛏️. Per night from 36 to 52€ – Per week from 219 to 791€

An attractive and sheltered site that always has plenty of pitches for tents and caravans.

Surroundings : 🛣️ 🌳🌳
Leisure activities : 🍽️ ✕ 🎭 🚴 ✂️ 🎿 🎿
Facilities : 🚿 ⚲ 🚽 🚽 laundrette

Longitude : 2.65306
Latitude : 42.46671

*For more information on visiting particular towns or regions, consult the relevant regional **MICHELIN** Green Guide. We also recommend you use the appropriate Michelin regional map to locate your selected campsite, to calculate distances and to work out the best route.*

BAGNOLS-SUR-CÈZE

30200 – Michelin map **339** M4 – pop. 18 105 – alt. 51
▶ Paris 653 – Alès 54 – Avignon 34 – Nîmes 56

⚠ Les Genêts d'Or

✆ 0466895867. www.camping-genets-dor.com ✍

Address : chemin de Carmignan (take the northern exit along the N 86 then continue 2km along the D 360 to the right; beside the Cèze river)

Opening times : from mid April to mid Sept.

8 ha/3.5 for camping (95 pitches) flat, grassy

Tariff : (2015 price) 27€ ✶✶ ⛺ 🅿 ⚡ (6A) – Extra per person 5.50€ – Reservation fee 10€

Rental rates : (2015 price) (from mid April to mid Sept.) ✍ – 8 🛖. Per week from 403 to 690€ – Reservation fee 10€

🚐 local sani-station 23€

There are well-shaded pitches beside the river.

Surroundings : ⚓⚓⛰
Leisure activities : 🍴✕⛵🎣⛵
Facilities : ♿ ⛽ 🏪 🏕🍴 launderette 🚿🧺
refrigerators

Longitude : 4.63694
Latitude : 44.17358

A chambre d'hôte is a guesthouse or B & B-style accommodation.

BALARUC-LES-BAINS

34540 – Michelin map **339** H8 – pop. 6 622 – alt. 3 – ♨
▶ Paris 781 – Agde 32 – Béziers 52 – Frontignan 8

⚠ Sites et Paysages Le Mas du Padre 🔆

Le Mas du Padre

✆ 0467485341. www.mas-du-padre.com

Address : 4 chemin du Mas du Padre (situated 2km northeast along the D 2e and take road to the right)

Opening times : from beginning April to end Oct.

1.8 ha (116 pitches) relatively flat, flat, grassy, fine gravel

Tariff : 39.10€ ✶✶ ⛺ 🅿 ⚡ (10A) – Extra per person 5.70€ – Reservation fee 13.50€

Rental rates : (from beginning April to end Oct.) ♿ (1 chalet) – 16 ✍ – 1 🛖. Per night from 174 to 397€ – Per week from 301 to 994€ – Reservation fee 21€

Pretty shrubs and flowers dotted around the site.

Surroundings : 🌳 ⚓⚓
Leisure activities : 🏓🎣⛵
Facilities : ♿ ⛽🍴🏊 refrigerators

Longitude : 3.6924
Latitude : 43.4522

⚠ Les Vignes

✆ 0467480493. www.camping-lesvignes.com – limited spaces for one-night stay

Address : 1 chemin des Vignes (1.7km northeast along the D 129, D 2e follow the signs for Sète and take road to the left)

2 ha (169 pitches)

Rentals : ♿ (1 mobile home) – 22 ✍ – 8 🛖.

Pitches are clearly marked out and on a gravel base, usually for people visiting the nearby spa (3 weeks).

Surroundings : ⚓⚓
Leisure activities : ✕🎣⛵
Facilities : ♿ ⛽🍴🏊

Longitude : 3.68806
Latitude : 43.45351

LE BARCARÈS

66420 – Michelin map **344** J6 – pop. 4 018 – alt. 3
▶ Paris 839 – Narbonne 56 – Perpignan 23 – Quillan 84

⚠ L'Oasis 🔆

✆ 0468861243. www.camping-oasis.com

Address : route de St-Laurent-de-la-Salanque (1.3km southwest along the D 90)

Opening times : from mid May to mid Sept.

10 ha (492 pitches) flat, grassy, sandy

Tariff : (2015 price) 40€ ✶✶ ⛺ 🅿 ⚡ (10A) – Extra per person 8.50€ – Reservation fee 29€

Rental rates : (2015 price) (from mid May to mid Sept.) – 218 ✍. Per night from 34 to 189€ – Per week from 238 to 1,323€ – Reservation fee 29€

Numerous mobile homes, but pitches for tents and caravans are always available.

Surroundings : 🗺⚓
Leisure activities : 🍴✕🏃⛵⛵🎣⛵🏊
Facilities : ♿ ⛽🏪🍴 launderette 🚿🧺

Longitude : 3.02462
Latitude : 42.77619

⚠ Sunêlia Le California 🔆

✆ 0468861608. www.camping-california.fr

Address : route de St-Laurent-de-la-Salanque (located 1.5km southwest along the D 90 – on the D 83, take exit 9: Canet-en-Roussillon)

Opening times : from beginning May to end Sept.

5 ha (265 pitches) flat, grassy, stony

Tariff : 49.50€ ✶✶ ⛺ 🅿 ⚡ (10A) – Extra per person 8€ – Reservation fee 35€

Rental rates : (from beginning May to end Sept.) ♿ (2 mobile homes) – 131 ✍ – 20 🛖 – 7 tent lodges. Per night from 32 to 173€ – Per week from 224 to 1,211€ – Reservation fee 35€

🚐 local sani-station 1€

The campsite has a large sports area.

Surroundings : 🗺⚓
Leisure activities : 🍴✕🏠🎣🏃⛵🏊 ⛵🏊
Facilities : ♿ ⛽🍴 launderette 🚿🧺
Nearby : 🛒

Longitude : 3.02346
Latitude : 42.77606

⚠ Yelloh! Village Le Pré Catalan 🔆

✆ 0468861260. www.precatalan.com

Address : route de St-Laurent-de-la-Salanque (located 1.5km southwest along the D 90, then continue 600m along the road to the right)

Opening times : from end April to mid Sept.

4 ha (250 pitches)

Tariff : 49€ ✶✶ ⛺ 🅿 ⚡ (10A) – Extra per person 8€

Rental rates : (from end April to mid Sept.) – 90 ✍. Per night from 30 to 219€ – Per week from 210 to 1,533€

A pleasant site with activities and services suitable for families with young children.

Surroundings : 🌳🗺⚓
Leisure activities : 🍴✕🏠🎣🏃⛵⛵
⛵ multi-sports ground
Facilities : ♿ ⛽🍴 launderette 🧺
Nearby : 🛒

Longitude : 3.02272
Latitude : 42.78086

▲▲▲ L'Europe

✆ 04 68 86 15 36. www.europe-camping.com – limited spaces for one-night stay

Address : route de St-Laurent-de-la-Salanque (situated 2km southwest along the D 90, 200m from the Agly river)

6 ha (360 pitches) flat, grassy
Rentals : 79 ⌂.

Choose the pitches away from the road. Good-quality rental options in mobile homes as well as some rather old bungalows.

Surroundings : 🏕 ♀	
Leisure activities : ♟ ✗ 🏠 ⛳ 🏋 🚤 ✂ 🛶 ⛷	G P S
Facilities : ♿ ⚡ – 339 private sanitary facilities (🚿 🚽 wc) 🔥 📶 ⛽ 🎱 🖲 🛁	Longitude : 3.02064 Latitude : 42.775

▲▲ Flower Le Soleil Bleu ▲▲

(rental of mobile homes and chalets only)

✆ 04 68 86 15 50. www.lesoleilbleu.com

Address : route de Saint Laurent, Mas de la Tourre (1.4km southwest along the D 90 follow the signs for St-Laurent-de-la-Salanque; 100m from the Agly river)

Opening times : from beginning April to end Oct.

3 ha (175 pitches) flat, grassy
Rental rates : (2015 price) ♿ (1 mobile home) – 175 ⌂. Per night from 45 to 199€ – Per week from 225 to 1,393€ – Reservation fee 30€

Choose the sites away from the road in preference.

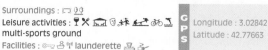

Surroundings : 🏕 ♀♀	
Leisure activities : ♟ ✗ 🏠 ⛳ 🏋 🚤 🚵 ⛷ multi-sports ground	G P S
Facilities : ⚡ ⛽ 📶 launderette 🛁 🐾	Longitude : 3.02842 Latitude : 42.77663

▲▲ FranceLoc Las Bousigues ▲▲

✆ 04 68 86 16 19. www.campings-franceloc.fr – limited spaces for one-night stay

Address : avenue des Corbières (900m west)

Opening times : from mid April to mid Sept.

3 ha (306 pitches) flat, sandy, stony

Tariff : (2015 price) 36€ ✸✸ 🚗 📧 ⚡ (10A) – Extra per person 7€ – Reservation fee 27€

Rental rates : (2015 price) (from mid April to mid Sept.) ♿ (2 mobile homes) – 181 ⌂ – 59 ⌂ – 2 tipis – 4 tent lodges. Per night from 37 to 107€ – Per week from 147 to 1,148€ – Reservation fee 27€

A very large children's play area and a range of rental options, but the bungalows are very old.

Surroundings : 🏕 ♀♀	
Leisure activities : ♟ ✗ 🏠 🏋 🚤 🎣 ⛷ multi-sports ground	G P S
Facilities : ♿ ⚡ ⛽ – 31 private sanitary facilities (🚿 🚽 wc) 📶 launderette 🐾	Longitude : 3.0254 Latitude : 42.7869
Nearby : 🌊	

▲▲ Cybele Vacances La Presqu'Île ▲▲

✆ 04 68 86 12 80. www.lapresquile.com – limited spaces for one-night stay

Address : rue de la Presquile (to the north, on the D 83 exit 12)

3.5 ha (163 pitches)

Rentals : 83 ⌂ – 29 ⌂ – 8 studios.

This site is surrounded by water on a peninsula and beside a lake. Some pitches are rather noisy; there is a swimming pool with a snack bar across the road.

Surroundings : 🏕 ♀♀	
Leisure activities : ♟ ✗ 🏠 🏋 jacuzzi 🚤 🚵 ✂ ⛷ ⛵ 🎣 multi-sports ground	G P S
Facilities : ♿ ⚡ ⛽ 📶 launderette 🛁 🐾	Longitude : 3.02672 Latitude : 42.80528
Nearby : ⚓	

BARJAC

30430 – Michelin map **339** L3 – pop. 1 546 – alt. 171
▶ Paris 666 – Alès 34 – Aubenas 45 – Pont-St-Esprit 33

▲▲▲ La Combe

✆ 04 66 24 51 21. www.campinglacombe.com

Address : at La Comb (3km west along the D 901, follow the signs for Les Vans and turn right onto the D 384)

Opening times : from beginning April to end Sept.

2.5 ha (100 pitches)

Tariff : 26.80€ ✸✸ 🚗 📧 ⚡ (6A) – Extra per person 9€ – Reservation fee 5€

Rental rates : (from beginning April to end Sept.) – 11 ⌂ – 4 ⌂ – 1 apartment – 4 canvas bungalows. Per night from 40 to 95€ – Per week from 270 to 660€ – Reservation fee 15€

🚐 Eurorelais sani-station 4.50€ – 🚐 12€

A peaceful, family-orientated site with plenty of shade.

Surroundings : 🌿 ♀♀	
Leisure activities : ♟ 🏠 🚤 ⛷	G P S
Facilities : ♿ ⚡ ⛽ 📶 🖲	Longitude : 4.34784 Latitude : 44.30917

There are several different types of sani-station ('borne' in French) – sanitation points providing fresh water and disposal points for grey water. See page 12 for further details.

BÉDOUÈS

48400 – Michelin map **330** J8 – pop. 291 – alt. 565
▶ Paris 624 – Alès 69 – Florac 5 – Mende 39

▲▲▲ Chon du Tarn

✆ 04 66 45 09 14. http://www.camping-chondutarn.com

Address : chemin du Chon du Tarn (take the northeastern exit, follow the signs for Cocurès)

Opening times : from beginning May to beginning Oct.

2 ha (100 pitches)

Tariff : ✸ 4.80€ 🚗 📧 4.80€ – ⚡ (6A) 2.40€

Rental rates : (from beginning May to end Sept.) ✂ – 3 ⌂. Per night from 30 to 35€ – Per week from 250 to 380€

🚐 local sani-station

In a pleasant setting with lots of green space beside the Tarn river.

Surroundings : 🌿 ♀	
Leisure activities : 🚤 🌊	G P S
Facilities : ♿ ⚡ 🔥 📶 launderette	Longitude : 3.60531 Latitude : 44.3446
Nearby : ♟ ✗ climbing	

BELCAIRE

11340 – Michelin map **344** C6 – pop. 440 – alt. 1 002
▶ Paris 810 – Ax-les-Thermes 26 – Axat 32 – Foix 54

⚠ Municipal la Mousquière

☎ 04 68 20 39 47. www.camping-pyrenees-cathare.fr – ⛺

Address : 4 chemin du Lac (take the western exit onto the D 613, follow the signs for Ax-les-Thermes, 150m from a small lake)

Opening times : from beginning June to end Sept.

0.6 ha (37 pitches)

Tariff : (2015 price) 17€ ★★ 🚐 🔲 [½] (8A) – Extra per person 3€

Rental rates : (2015 price) (from beginning Dec. to end Oct.) – 2 🚐 – 8 🏠. Per night from 60 to 85€ – Per week from 250 to 430€

An attractively shaded site with a pretty lake nearby.

Surroundings : 🔆
Leisure activities : 🎣
Facilities : 🚿 ⚡ 🧺 🚾 🍴 🔲
Nearby : 🏇 🍴 ⚾ 🏊 🚣 pedalos

GPS	Longitude : 1.95022	
	Latitude : 42.81637	

BESSÈGES

30160 – Michelin map **339** J3 – pop. 3 169 – alt. 170
▶ Paris 651 – Alès 32 – La Grand-Combe 20 – Les Vans 18

⛰ Les Drouilhèdes

☎ 04 66 25 04 80. www.campingcevennes.com

Address : situated 2km west along the D 17, follow the signs for Génolhac then continue 1km along the D 386 to the right; beside the Cèze river

Opening times : from beginning May to mid Sept.

2 ha (90 pitches)

Tariff : 32.20€ ★★ 🚐 🔲 [½] (6A) – Extra per person 5.70€ – Reservation fee 15.50€

Rental rates : (from beginning May to mid Sept.) – 6 🏠. Per week from 350 to 685€ – Reservation fee 15.50€

Surroundings : 🌿 ⛰
Leisure activities : 🍴 🏊 🎣 🚣
Facilities : 🚿 ⚡ 🧺 🍴 🔲

GPS	Longitude : 4.0678	
	Latitude : 44.29143	

BLAVIGNAC

48200 – Michelin map **330** H5 – pop. 236 – alt. 800
▶ Paris 542 – Montpellier 218 – Mende 58 – Clermont-Ferrand 126

⛰ Les Chalets de la Margeride   (rental of chalets only)

☎ 04 66 42 56 00. www.chalets-margeride.com

Address : at Chassagnes (4.5km northwest along the D 989. follow the signs for St-Chély-d'Apcher and take the D 4, following signs for La Garde – from the A 75: take exit 32)

Opening times : permanent

50 ha/2 for camping terraced

Rental rates : 🚿 (1 chalet) – 21 🏠. Per night from 99 to 170€ – Per week from 360 to 695€ – Reservation fee 9€

In an attractive panoramic location among the Margeride mountains.

Surroundings : 🌿 < Plateau de la Margeride
Leisure activities : 🏓 🚴 🔲 (open air in season)
Facilities : ⚡ 🧺 🍴 launderette

GPS	Longitude : 3.30631	
	Latitude : 44.87017	

BOISSET-ET-GAUJAC

30140 – Michelin map **339** J4 – pop. 2 302 – alt. 140
▶ Paris 722 – Montpellier 103 – Nîmes 53 – Alès 14

⛰⛰ Domaine de Gaujac 👥

☎ 04 66 61 67 57. www.domaine-de-gaujac.com

Address : 2406 chemin de la Madelaine

Opening times : permanent

10 ha/6.5 for camping (293 pitches) terraced, relatively flat, flat, grassy

Tariff : 40€ ★★ 🚐 🔲 [½] (10A) – Extra per person 8€ – Reservation fee 20€

Rental rates : (from beginning May to beginning Sept.) – 33 🚐 – 25 🏠. Per night from 42 to 100€ – Per week from 210 to 870€ – Reservation fee 20€

🚐 local sani-station 8€ – 8 🔲 8€

The lower pitches enjoy lots of shade, those on the terraces get plenty of sun.

Surroundings : 🌿
Leisure activities : 🍹 🍴 🎣 🏓 jacuzzi 🏊 🚴 🎾 🔲
Facilities : 🚿 ⚡ 🧺 🚾 🍴 launderette 🔲 🏊

Nearby : 🏊 🚣

GPS	Longitude : 4.02771	
	Latitude : 44.03471	

BOISSON

30500 – Michelin map **339** K3
▶ Paris 682 – Alès 19 – Barjac 17 – La Grand-Combe 28

⛰⛰ Les Castels Le Château de Boisson 👥

☎ 04 66 24 85 61. www.chateaudeboisson.com ✂

Address : off the D16, hameau de Boisson (Boisson hamlet)

Opening times : from beginning April to end Sept.

7.5 ha (165 pitches) very uneven, terraced, flat, grassy

Tariff : 44.90€ ★★ 🚐 🔲 [½] (10A) – Extra per person 10.50€ – Reservation fee 15€

Rental rates : (from beginning April to end Sept.) ✂ – 49 🚐 – 18 🏠 – 15 gîtes. Per night from 34 to 413€ – Per week from 238 to 2,891€ – Reservation fee 15€

🚐 local sani-station 20€

Attractive pitches near a restored Cévennes château, with a view over the Cévennes from some chalets.

Surroundings : 🌿 🏊
Leisure activities : 🍹 🍴 🍴 🏓 🏇 🎣 🚴 🏊 🎾
Facilities : 🚿 ⚡ 🧺 – 7 private sanitary facilities (🚿 🚽 wc) 🚾 🍴 launderette 🔲 refrigerators

GPS	Longitude : 4.25673	
	Latitude : 44.20966	

These symbols are used for a campsite that is exceptional in its category:

⛰⛰⛰…⚠ *Particularly pleasant setting, quality and range of services available*

🌿🌿 *Tranquil, isolated site – quiet site, particularly at night*

<⚓ *Exceptional view – interesting or panoramic view*

LE BOSC

34490 – Michelin map **339** F6 – pop. 1 046 – alt. 90
▶ Paris 706 – Montpellier 51 – Béziers 58 – Sète 68

⛰ Relais du Salagou – (rental of chalets only)

✆ 04 67 44 76 44. www.relais-du-salagou.com

Address : at Salelles, 8 rue des Terrasses (4.5km southeast along the D 140 – A 75, take exit 56)

12 ha/3 for camping flat
Rentals : ♿ (1 chalet) 🅿 – 28 🏠.

Surroundings : 🌳🌳
Leisure activities : 🍸 🛋 ≋ hammam, jacuzzi 🛶✂🏌🏊 fitness trail, spa centre
Facilities : 🚿 �🅿 🏧 🍴 launderette

GPS Longitude : 3.41539
Latitude : 43.68268

BRISSAC

34190 – Michelin map **339** H5 – pop. 615 – alt. 145
▶ Paris 732 – Ganges 7 – Montpellier 41 – St-Hippolyte-du-Fort 19

⛰ Le Val d'Hérault

✆ 04 67 73 72 29. www.camping-levaldherault.com

Address : avenue d'Issensac (4km south along the D 4, follow the signs for Causse-de-la-Selle, 250m from the Hérault river, direct access)

Opening times : from mid March to end Oct.

4 ha (135 pitches) terraced, flat and relatively flat, grassy, stony

Tariff : (2015 price) 29.60€ ✹✹ 🚗 🔲 (6A) – Extra per person 6.70€ – Reservation fee 10€

Rental rates : (2015 price) (from mid March to end Oct.) – 22 🛖 – 4 🏠 – 10 canvas bungalows. Per week from 445 to 910€ – Reservation fee 10€

🚐 local sani-station

Well-shaded pitches, some on small, individual terraces.

Surroundings : 🏊 🚐 🌳🌳
Leisure activities : 🍸 ✕ 🛋 🌙 nighttime 🛶🏊
Facilities : ♿ 🚿 🏧 🍴 📶 🔲
Nearby : ≋ (beach) climbing

GPS Longitude : 3.70433
Latitude : 43.84677

⛰ Le Domaine d'Anglas ♟

Le Domaine d'Anglas

✆ 04 67 73 70 18. www.camping-anglas.com

Address : 2km east along the D 108

Opening times : from beginning April to end Oct.

115 ha/5 for camping (101 pitches) terraced, flat, grassy, stony

Tariff : (2015 price) 33.90€ ✹✹ 🚗 🔲 (10A) – Extra per person 6.80€ – Reservation fee 17€

Rental rates : (2015 price) (from beginning April to end Oct.) – 4 'gypsy' caravans – 20 🛖 – 5 tent lodges – 1 gîte. Per night from 44 to 170 € – Per week from 230 to 840€ – Reservation fee 17€

🚐 local sani-station – 27 🔲 33.90€

Beside the Hérault river and in the heart of the winegrowing region; varied rental options and average sanitary facilities.

Surroundings : 🚐 🌳🌳
Leisure activities : 🚶‍♂️ 🛶 🚴 ≋ 🏊 zip wiring 🎣
Facilities : ♿ 🚿 🏧 🍴 launderette 🔲

GPS Longitude : 3.71615
Latitude : 43.87602

BROUSSES-ET-VILLARET

11390 – Michelin map **344** E2 – pop. 313 – alt. 412
▶ Paris 768 – Carcassonne 21 – Castelnaudary 36 – Foix 88

⛰ Le Martinet-Rouge Birdie

✆ 04 68 26 51 98. www.camping-martinet.com

Address : 500m south along the D 203 and take the road to the right, 200m from the Dure river

Opening times : from mid March to beginning Nov.

2.5 ha (63 pitches) undulating, flat, grassy, stony, rocks

Tariff : (2015 price) 35€ ✹✹ 🚗 🔲 (10A) – Extra per person 7.50€

Rental rates : (2015 price) (from mid March to mid Nov.) 🌳 – 14 🛖 – 3 🏠. Per night from 30 to 125€ – Per week from 245 to 875€

🚐 local sani-station – 🚐 (2)25€

A very pleasant site with pitches between the rocks and plenty of shade from small Holm oaks.

Surroundings : 🏊 🚐 🌳🌳
Leisure activities : 🍸 ✕ 🛋 🛶🏊 multi-sports ground
Facilities : ♿ 🚿 📶 🏧 🍴 launderette

GPS Longitude : 2.0381
Latitude : 43.33088

CANET

34800 – Michelin map **339** F7 – pop. 3 269 – alt. 42
▶ Paris 717 – Béziers 47 – Clermont-l'Hérault 6 – Gignac 10

⛰ Les Rivières

✆ 04 67 96 75 53. www.camping-lesrivieres.com

Address : route de la Sablière (1.8km north along the D 131e)

Opening times : from beginning April to mid Sept.

9 ha/5 for camping (110 pitches) flat, grassy, stony

Tariff : 31€ ✹✹ 🚗 🔲 (6A) – Extra per person 6.50€ – Reservation fee 12€

Rental rates : (from beginning April to mid Sept.) 🌳 – 15 🛖 – 8 🏠 – 3 canvas bungalows – 2 tent lodges – 2 gîtes. Per night from 80 to 130€ – Per week from 215 to 750€ – Reservation fee 12€

🚐 Flot Bleu sani-station 12€ – 7 🔲 12€ – 🚐 (2)10€

Plenty of space beside the Hérault river, where swimming is always an option.

Surroundings : 🏊 🚐 🌳🌳
Leisure activities : 🍸 ✕ 🛋 jacuzzi 🛶 🚴🏊⛵ climbing wall, multi-sports ground
Facilities : ♿ 🚿 🏧 🍴 🔲
Nearby : 🐎

GPS Longitude : 3.49229
Latitude : 43.61792

CANET-PLAGE

66140 – Michelin map **344** J6
▶ Paris 849 – Argelès-sur-Mer 20 – Le Boulou 35 – Canet-en-Roussillon 3

⛰ Yelloh! Village Le Brasilia ♟

Yelloh! Village Le Brasilia

✆ 04 68 80 23 82. www.brasilia.fr

Address : avenue des Anneaux du Roussillon (beside the Têt river; direct access to the beach)

Opening times : from end April to beginning Oct.

15 ha (735 pitches)

Tariff : 64.50€ ✹✹ 🚗 🔲 (10A) – Extra per person 9€ – Reservation fee 30€

Rental rates : (from end April to beginning Oct.) &. (2 mobile homes) – 132 ⌗. Per night from 48 to 285€ – Per week from 336 to 1,995€

⌗ local sani-station

Lush green pitches and plenty of shade, small landscaped mobile home areas and a variety of activities make this a real village club.

Surroundings : 🦌 🗔 🎯 ⛰
Leisure activities : 🍴 🗙 🏛 🎭 🏃 ✠ hammam, jacuzzi 🚣 🎿 disco, spa facilities, beauty treatments, massages, multi-sports ground
Facilities : &. ⊶ 🏢 ☕ 🚿 🚾 🍴 launderette 🛒 🛋
Nearby : 🐎 🐕

GPS
Longitude : 3.03392
Latitude : 42.69429

🏔 Mar Estang ♣♠

🕽 04 68 80 35 53. www.marestang.com

Address : route de Saint-Cyprien (1.5km south along the D 18a, near the lake and the beach)

Opening times : from mid April to mid Sept.

11 ha (600 pitches) flat, grassy

Tariff : (2015 price) 50€ ♦♦ 🚗 🔲 🕯 (6A) – Extra per person 13€ – Reservation fee 26€

Rental rates : (2015 price) (from mid April to mid Sept.) &. (1 mobile homes) 🅿 – 227 ⌗ – 32 canvas bungalows. Per night from 26 to 181€ – Per week from 177 to 1,267€ – Reservation fee 26€

⌗ Eurorelais sani-station – 8 🔲

Direct access to the beach via an underground passage; the pitches have some shade; activities for young people.

Surroundings : 🗔 🎯
Leisure activities : 🍴 🗙 🏛 🎭 (amphitheatre) 🏃 🧗 🚣 🚲 🎿 🏊 disco, multi-sports ground
Facilities : &. ⊶ ☕ 🍴 launderette 🛒 🛋

GPS
Longitude : 3.03256
Latitude : 42.67262

🏔 Les Fontaines

🕽 04 68 80 22 57. www.camping-les-fontaines.com

Address : 23 avenue de St-Nazaire

Opening times : from beginning May to mid Sept.

5.3 ha (160 pitches) flat, grassy, stony

Tariff : 37€ ♦♦ 🚗 🔲 🕯 (10A) – Extra per person 6.50€ – Reservation fee 15€

Rental rates : (2015 price) (from beginning May to mid Sept.) – 43 ⌗. Per night from 32 to 122€ – Per week from 224 to 854€ – Reservation fee 15€

⌗ local sani-station 6€

A natural site with slight or no shade; choose the pitches near the lake and away from the road in preference.

Surroundings : 🗔
Leisure activities : 🍴 🏛 🚣 🎿 wildlife park
Facilities : &. ⊶ (July-Aug.) ☕ 🚿 🍴 launderette

GPS
Longitude : 2.99892
Latitude : 42.68909

Les Fontaines

*We value your opinion and welcome your feedback.
Do email us at campingfrance@tp.michelin.com*

CANILHAC

48500 – Michelin map **330** G8 – pop. 138 – alt. 700
▶ Paris 593 – La Canourgue 8 – Marvejols 26 – Mende 52

🏔 Municipal la Vallée

🕽 04 66 32 91 14. http://www.camping-vallee-du-lot.com

Address : at Miège Rivière (12km north along the N 9, follow the signs for Marvejols, turn left onto the D 988, follow the signs for St-Geniez-d'Olt and take the road to the left – from the A 75, take exit 40 towards St-Laurent-d'Olt then continue 5km along the D 988)

Opening times : from mid June to mid Sept.

1 ha (50 pitches) flat, grassy

Tariff : (2015 price) 17€ ♦♦ 🚗 🔲 🕯 (16A) – Extra per person 3.50€

Rental rates : (2015 price) (from mid June to mid Sept.) – 3 ⌗ – 2 canvas bungalows. Per night from 25 to 50€ – Per week from 175 to 350€

⌗ local sani-station

In a small but lush green valley by the Lot river.

Surroundings : 🦌 ← 🗔 🎯
Leisure activities : 🏛 🚣 🎿 🏊 🚤
Facilities : &. ⊶ ☕ 🍴 📷
Nearby : 🗙

GPS
Longitude : 3.14892
Latitude : 44.4365

Key to rentals symbols:

12 ⌗ *Number of mobile homes*
20 🏠 *Number of chalets*
6 🛏 *Number of rooms to rent*
Per night 30–50€ *Minimum/maximum rate per night*
Per week 300–1,000€ *Minimum/maximum rate per week*

LA CANOURGUE

48500 – Michelin map **330** H8 – pop. 2 112 – alt. 563
▶ Paris 588 – Marvejols 21 – Mende 40 – Millau 53

🏔 Chalets et camping du golf

🕽 04 66 44 23 60. www.lozereleisure.com

Address : route des Gorges du Tarn (3.6km southeast along the D 988, follow the signs for Chanac, after the golf course; beside the Urugne river)

Opening times : from beginning May to mid Sept.

8 ha (72 pitches) grassy

Tariff : (2015 price) 14.50€ ♦♦ 🚗 🔲 🕯 (6A) – Extra per person 4€

Rental rates : (2015 price) (from end April to mid Sept.) – 14 🏠. Per night from 57€ – Per week from 199 to 624€

⌗ local sani-station

In a green setting, with chalets ranging from basic to more luxurious; very old sanitary facilities for tent and caravan pitches.

Surroundings : 🦌 🗔 🎯
Leisure activities : 🚣 🎿
Facilities : ⊶ 📮 🍴 launderette
Nearby : 🍴 🗙 golf

GPS
Longitude : 3.24072
Latitude : 44.40842

LE CAP-D'AGDE

34300 – Michelin map **339** G9
▶ Paris 767 – Montpellier 57 – Béziers 29 – Narbonne 59

⚠ La Clape

☎ 04 67 26 41 32. www.camping-laclape.com

Address : 2 rue du Gouverneur (near the beach, direct access)

Opening times : from beginning April to end Sept.

7 ha (450 pitches) flat, grassy, stony

Tariff : (2015 price) 42 € ♣♣ ⇐ ⊞ ⑭ (10A) – Extra per person 8.50 € – Reservation fee 27 €

Rental rates : (2015 price) (from beginning April to end Sept.) ৬ (1 chalet) ⚡ – 96 ⃞ – 24 ⌂ – 9 canvas bungalows. Per night from 40 to 140 € – Per week from 280 to 980 € – Reservation fee 27 €

🚐 Flot Bleu sani-station 12.50 €

Services and parking for campervans available off the site.

Surroundings : ⃞ ♡♡
Leisure activities : ♟ ✕ ⌂ ⛵ ⌇ multi-sports ground
Facilities : ৬ ⍾ ⊪ ♨ ⍭ launderette ⚓ ⚘ refrigerators
G P S Longitude : 3.5193 Latitude : 43.28534

CARCASSONNE

11000 – Michelin map **344** F3 – pop. 47 854 – alt. 110
▶ Paris 768 – Albi 110 – Béziers 90 – Narbonne 61

⚠ La Cité ♣♣

☎ 04 68 10 01 00. www.campingcitecarcassonne.com

Address : route de Saint-Hilaire (take the eastern exit along the N 113, follow the signs for Narbonne then continue 1.8km along the D 104, near a branch of the Aude river)

Opening times : from mid March to beginning Oct.

7 ha (200 pitches) flat, grassy

Tariff : 32.40 € ♣♣ ⇐ ⊞ ⑭ (10A) – Extra per person 9.10 €

Rental rates : (from end March to beginning Oct.) ৬ (2 mobile homes) – 26 ⃞. Per night from 60 to 140 € – Per week from 420 to 980 €

Situated very close to the old town of Carcassonne.

Surroundings : ⃞ ♡♡
Leisure activities : ♟ ✕ ⌂ ♡ ⛵ ⌇ multi-sports ground
Facilities : ৬ ⍾ ♨ ♨ launderette ⚘
G P S Longitude : 2.33716 Latitude : 43.19874

CARNON-PLAGE

34280 – Michelin map **339** I7
▶ Paris 758 – Aigues-Mortes 20 – Montpellier 20 – Nîmes 56

⚠ Les Saladelles

☎ 04 67 68 23 71. www.paysdelor.fr

Address : rue de l'Aigoual (head for Carnon-est, D 59, 100m from the beach)

Opening times : from beginning April to end Sept.

7.6 ha (340 pitches) flat, sandy

Tariff : (2015 price) 22.10 € ♣♣ ⇐ ⊞ ⑭ (10A) – Extra per person 4 € – Reservation fee 10 €

Rental rates : (2015 price) permanent ⚡ – 40 ⃞. Per week from 258 to 760 € – Reservation fee 10 €

🚐 local sani-station 13 € – 18 ⊞ 13 €

Choose the pitches away from the road in preference; parking for campervans nearby but off the site.

Surroundings : ♡♡
Leisure activities : ⛹ multi-sports ground
Facilities : ৬ ⍾ ⚘ ♨ ♨ ♨ ⍭
G P S Longitude : 3.99464 Latitude : 43.55079

CASTEIL

66820 – Michelin map **344** F7 – pop. 120 – alt. 780
▶ Paris 878 – Montpellier 215 – Perpignan 59 – Carcassonne 126

⚠ Domaine St-Martin

☎ 04 68 05 52 09. www.domainesaintmartin.com – help moving caravans onto and off pitches avilable on request

Address : 6 boulevard de la Cascade (take the northern exit along the D 116 and take the road to the right)

4.5 ha (60 pitches) very uneven, terraced, flat, stony, rocks
Rentals : 7 ⃞ – 6 tent lodges.

In a natural and unspoilt setting at the foot of the Massif du Canigou (mountains), near a waterfall.

Surroundings : ⚘ ⃞ ⣿
Leisure activities : ♟ ✕ ⌂ ⌇
Facilities : ৬ ⍾ ⊪ ♨ launderette
Nearby : ⚒
G P S Longitude : 2.39464 Latitude : 42.53296

CASTRIES

34160 – Michelin map **339** I6 – pop. 5 671 – alt. 70
▶ Paris 746 – Lunel 15 – Montpellier 19 – Nîmes 44

⚠ Le Fondespierre

☎ 04 67 91 20 03. www.campingfondespierre.com

Address : 277 chemin Pioch Viala (2.5km northeast along the N 110, follow the signs for Sommières and take turning to the left)

Opening times : permanent

3 ha (103 pitches) terraced, relatively flat, stony

Tariff : (2015 price) 33 € ♣♣ ⇐ ⊞ ⑭ (16A) – Extra per person 6 € – Reservation fee 15 €

Rental rates : (2015 price) permanent – 23 ⃞ – 2 ⌂ – 7 canvas bungalows. Per night from 88 to 220 € – Per week from 224 to 790 € – Reservation fee 15 €

🚐 AireService sani-station 4 €

Surroundings : ♡♡
Leisure activities : ⛵ ☸ ⌇
Facilities : ৬ ⍾ ♨ ♨ launderette
Nearby : ⚒
G P S Longitude : 3.99903 Latitude : 43.69125

CELLES

34700 – Michelin map **339** F7 – pop. 22 – alt. 140
▶ Paris 707 – Montpellier 55 – Nîmes 111 – Albi 190

⚠ Municipal les Vailhès

☎ 04 11 95 01 82. www.campinglesvailhes.fr

Address : situated 2km northeast along the D 148E4 follow the signs for Lodève – A75 take exit 54

Opening times : from beginning April to end Sept.

4 ha (246 pitches) terraced, flat, grassy

Tariff : (2015 price) ♣ 4.20 € ⇐ 4.65 € ⊞ 7.20 € – ⑭ (10A) 4.30 €

🚐 10 ⊞ 8 € – ⚓ 15.20 €

In an attractive location beside the Lac du Salagou.

Surroundings : 🏞 ⟨ ⌂ ♨ △
Leisure activities : 🎿 ⛵ 🛶
Facilities : 🔥 🚿 ⛽ 🍽 📷
Nearby : 🎣

GPS Longitude : 3.36012
Latitude : 43.66865

CENDRAS

30480 – Michelin map **339** J4 – pop. 1 930 – alt. 155
▶ Paris 694 – Montpellier 76 – Nîmes 50 – Avignon 76

▲▲▲ La Croix Clémentine

🔗 04 66 86 52 69. www.clementine.fr

Address : route de Mende, at La Fare (situated 2km northwest along the D 916 and turn left onto the D 32)

Opening times : from end March to mid Sept.

10 ha (250 pitches)

Tariff : 37 € ✦✦ 🚗 🔲 ⚡ (10A) – Extra per person 12 € – Reservation fee 12 €

Rental rates : (from end March to mid Sept.) – 20 🚐 – 20 🏠. Per night from 50 to 160 € – Per week from 300 to 950 € – Reservation fee 12 €

🚉 Eurorelais sani-station 16 € – 2 🔲 20 € – 🛒 ⚡8 €

In a pleasant wooded setting.

Surroundings : 🏞 ⌂ ♨
Leisure activities : 🍽 ✗ 🎪 nighttime
🎿 🚴 🏇 🏊 multi-sports ground
Facilities : 🔥 🚿 🏪 🍽 ⛽ 🍽 launderette
🍽 🧊 refrigerators
Nearby : 🐎 🎯

GPS Longitude : 4.04333
Latitude : 44.15167

LE CHAMBON

30450 – Michelin map **339** J3 – pop. 273 – alt. 260
▶ Paris 640 – Alès 31 – Florac 59 – Génolhac 10

▲ Municipal le Luech

🔗 04 66 61 51 32. mairie-du-chambon@wanadoo.fr

Address : at Palanquis (600m northwest along the D 29, follow the signs for Chamborigaud, at the junction with the D243A)

Opening times : from beginning July to end Aug.

0.5 ha (43 pitches) terraced, relatively flat, grassy, stony

Tariff : (2015 price) ✦ 2.40 € 🚗 1.68 € 🔲 3 € – ⚡ (4A) 3.52 €

Surroundings : ♨
Leisure activities : 🎣
Facilities : 🔥 🚿 🚽
Nearby : 🍴

GPS Longitude : 4.00317
Latitude : 44.30494

CHASTANIER

48300 – Michelin map **330** K6 – pop. 92 – alt. 1 090
▶ Paris 570 – Châteauneuf-de-Randon 17 – Langogne 10 – Marvejols 71

▲ La Via natura Le Pont de Braye

🔗 04 66 69 53 04. www.camping-lozere-naussac.fr

Address : Les Berges du Chapeauroux (located 1km west, near the junction of D 988 and D 34, by the bridge)

Opening times : from beginning May to mid Sept.

1.5 ha (35 pitches) terraced, flat, grassy

Tariff : (2015 price) 16.40 € ✦✦ 🚗 🔲 ⚡ (6A) – Extra per person 4.10 € – Reservation fee 7 €

Rental rates : (2015 price) (from beginning May to mid Sept.) – 3 yurts – 2 canvas bungalows – 2 tent lodges – 1 gîte. Per night from 55 € – Per week from 199 to 479 € – Reservation fee 7 €
🚉 local sani-station 2.50 € – 🛒 ⚡8 €

Beside the river; a variety of original rental options, simply equipped facilities.

Surroundings : 🏞 ♨
Leisure activities : 🍽 🏕 🎿 🚴 🎣
Facilities : 🔥 🚿 🏪 🍽 ⛽ 🍽 launderette 🍽
Nearby : ✗

GPS Longitude : 3.74755
Latitude : 44.72656

CLERMONT-L'HÉRAULT

34800 – Michelin map **339** F7 – pop. 7 627 – alt. 92
▶ Paris 718 – Béziers 46 – Lodève 24 – Montpellier 42

▲▲ Municipal Campotel Lac du Salagou

🔗 04 67 96 13 13. www.le-salagou.fr

Address : at Salagou lake (5km northwest along the D 156e 4, 300m from the lake)

Opening times : permanent

7.5 ha (388 pitches) terraced, relatively flat, flat, grassy, gravelled

Tariff : (2015 price) 19 € ✦✦ 🚗 🔲 ⚡ (10A) – Extra per person 3 € – Reservation fee 15 €

Rental rates : (2015 price) permanent 🔥 (1 mobile home) – 14 🚐 – 14 gîtes. Per night from 53 to 100 € – Per week from 385 to 680 € – Reservation fee 15 €

🚉 local sani-station 2 €

A pleasant location close to the lake and the sailing centre.

Surroundings : 🏞 ⟨ ⌂ ♨
Leisure activities : 🏕 🎿
Facilities : 🔥 🚿 🏪 🍽 ⛽ 🍽 📷 refrigerated food storage facilities
Nearby : 🍽 ✗ 🍽 🚴 ⛵ 🎣 🛶

GPS Longitude : 3.38957
Latitude : 43.6455

To make the best possible use of this guide, please read pages 2–15 carefully.

COLLIAS

30210 – Michelin map **339** L5 – pop. 1 002 – alt. 45
▶ Paris 694 – Alès 45 – Avignon 32 – Bagnols-sur-Cèze 35

▲▲ Le Barralet

🔗 04 66 22 84 52. www.barralet.fr

Address : 6 chemin du Grès (located 1km northeast along the D 3, follow the signs for Uzès and take the road to the right)

Opening times : from beginning April to end Sept.

2 ha (132 pitches) relatively flat, flat, grassy

Tariff : 27.30 € ✦✦ 🚗 🔲 ⚡ (6A) – Extra per person 6 € – Reservation fee 10 €

Rental rates : (from beginning April to end Sept.) – 36 🚐 – 9 🏠. Per night from 42 to 106 € – Per week from 210 to 770 € – Reservation fee 10 €

🚉 Eurorelais sani-station

There's panoramic view of the village and surrounding area from the swimming pool and the terrace of the bar.

Surroundings : 🏞 ⟨ ♨
Leisure activities : 🍽 ✗ 🎿 🏊 multi-sports ground
Facilities : 🔥 🚿 🍽 📷 🍽

GPS Longitude : 4.48718
Latitude : 43.95769

CONNAUX

30330 – Michelin map **339** M4 – pop. 1 583 – alt. 86
▶ Paris 661 – Avignon 32 – Alès 52 – Nîmes 48

⚑ Le Vieux Verger

🔗 04 66 82 91 62. www.campinglevieuxverger.com

Address : 526 avenue des Platanes (south of the town, 200m from the N 86)

Opening times : permanent

3 ha (60 pitches) terraced, flat, grassy, stony

Tariff : (2015 price) 23.90€ ♦♦ ⇔ 🗉 💈 (10A) –
Extra per person 4.80€ – Reservation fee 10€
Rental rates : (2015 price) permanent ⬦ – 11 ⬚ – 5 ⬚.
Per week from 309 to 760€ – Reservation fee 25€

There are more places for tents and caravans at the top of the site, and plenty of shade.

Surroundings : ⬚ ♀
Leisure activities : ✗ ⬚
Facilities : ⬚ ⬚ 🇨🇨 ⬚ ⬚
Nearby : ✗

G P S Longitude : 4.59108
Latitude : 44.08478

CRESPIAN

30260 – Michelin map **339** J5 – pop. 325 – alt. 80
▶ Paris 731 – Alès 32 – Anduze 27 – Nîmes 24

⚑ Le Mas de Reilhe 👥

🔗 04 66 77 82 12. www.camping-mas-de-reilhe.fr

Address : chemin du Mas de Reilhe (take the southern exit along the N 110)

Opening times : from end April to mid Sept.

2 ha (95 pitches)

Tariff : (2015 price) 31.90€ ♦♦ ⇔ 🗉 💈 (10A) –
Extra per person 7.40€ – Reservation fee 20€
Rental rates : (2015 price) (from end April to mid Sept.) – 15 ⬚ –
7 ⬚ – 4 tent lodges. Per night from 35 to 120€ – Per week from 245 to 840€ – Reservation fee 20€
⬚ local sani-station

Surroundings : ⬚ ♀♀
Leisure activities : ⬚ ✗ ⬚ ⬚ ⬚ ⬚ ⬚
multi-sports ground
Facilities : ⬚ 🇨🇨 ⬚ ⬚ ⬚ ⬚ ⬚ launderette ⬚
Nearby : ✗

G P S Longitude : 4.09676
Latitude : 43.88015

Some campsites benefit from proximity to a municipal leisure centre.

EGAT

66120 – Michelin map **344** D7 – pop. 453 – alt. 1 650
▶ Paris 856 – Andorra-la-Vella 70 – Ax-les-Thermes 53 – Bourg-Madame 15

⚑ Las Clotes

🔗 04 68 30 26 90. www.pro.pagesjaunes.fr/camping-las-clotes

Address : 400m north of the town; beside a small stream

Opening times : from mid Nov. to mid Oct.

2 ha (80 pitches) terraced, rocky, grassy

Tariff : 18€ ♦♦ ⇔ 🗉 💈 (6A) – Extra per person 5€
⬚ local sani-station

In an attractive elevated location, on the side of a rocky hill.

Surroundings : ⬚ < Sierra del Cadi and Puigmal (peak) ⬚ ♀♀
Leisure activities : ⬚
Facilities : ⬚ ⬚ ⬚ ⬚ ⬚ ⬚ ⬚

G P S Longitude : 2.01765
Latitude : 42.499

ERR

66800 – Michelin map **344** D8 – pop. 640 – alt. 1 350 – Winter sports : 1 850/2 520 m
▶ Paris 854 – Andorra-la-Vella 77 – Ax-les-Thermes 52 – Bourg-Madame 10

⚑ Le Puigmal

🔗 04 68 04 71 83. www.camping-le-puigmal.fr

Address : 30 route du Puigmal (along the D 33b; beside a stream)

Opening times : permanent

3.2 ha (125 pitches) relatively flat, flat, grassy

Tariff : 21.50€ ♦♦ ⇔ 🗉 💈 (6A) – Extra per person 5€
Rental rates : permanent – 10 ⬚. Per night from 65 to 85€ –
Per week from 360 to 475€

Surroundings : ⬚ ♀♀
Leisure activities : ⬚ ⬚
Facilities : ⬚ ⬚ ⬚ ⬚ launderette
Nearby : ⬚ ⬚

G P S Longitude : 2.03539
Latitude : 42.43751

⚑ Las Closas

🔗 04 68 04 71 42. www.camping-las-closas.com

Address : 1 place Saint-Génis (along the D 33b)

Opening times : permanent

2 ha (114 pitches) relatively flat, flat, grassy

Tariff : 23.60€ ♦♦ ⇔ 🗉 💈 (10A) – Extra per person 4.60€
Rental rates : permanent – 15 ⬚ – 1 apartment. Per night from 59 to 92€ – Per week from 378 to 539€
⬚ 7 🗉 15€

In the centre of the village close to the church; a pleasant site with good sanitary facilities.

Surroundings : ♀♀
Leisure activities : ⬚ ⬚
Facilities : ⬚ ⬚ ⬚ ⬚ ⬚ launderette
Nearby : ✗ ⬚ ⬚

G P S Longitude : 2.03138
Latitude : 42.44014

ESTAVAR

66800 – Michelin map **344** D8 – pop. 429 – alt. 1 200
▶ Paris 852 – Montpellier 247 – Perpignan 97

⚑ L'Enclave 👥

L'Enclave

🔗 04 68 04 72 27. www.camping.lenclave.com

Address : 2 rue Vinyals (take the eastern exit along the D 33; beside the Angoust river)

Opening times : from beginning Nov. to end Sept.

3.5 ha (175 pitches) terraced, flat and relatively flat, stony, grassy

Tariff : (2015 price) 33.50€ ♦♦ ⇔ 🗉 💈 (10A) – Extra per person 5.60€ – Reservation fee 10€

Rental rates : (2015 price) (from beginning Nov. to end Sept.) – 30 🚐. Per night from 30 to 120€ – Per week from 190 to 820 € – Reservation fee 10€

🚐 Eurorelais sani-station 6€ – 10 回 17€ – 🚱 (ᵇ)23.60€

An attractive shady area beside a stream with a lovely playground at the bottom of the site.

Surroundings : 🏊 ⌂ 🗻
Leisure activities : 🎬 🚴 ≋ jacuzzi 🏇
🍴 🏊 🚣 guided walks, entertainment room
Facilities : 🚿 🍴 🛒 🛁 🚽 🧺 launderette
Nearby : 🏊 🍷 🍴 🚣 🏇

GPS Longitude : 1.99813
Latitude : 42.4688

🏕 Yelloh! Village l'Escapade – (rental of chalets only)

📞 0466739739. www.lescapade.com

Address : cami del Segre (road 800m to the south of the village)

Opening times : permanent

5 ha flat, grassy

Rental rates : 🚿 (5 chalets) – 44 🏠. Per night from 35 to 155€ – Per week from 245 to 1,085€

A pretty village of luxurious genuine wooden chalets.

Surroundings : 🏊 🗻
Leisure activities : 🍷 🍴 🎬 🏇 multi-sports ground, entertainment room
Facilities : 🚿 🍴 🛒 🛁 🧺 launderette 🍴

GPS Longitude : 1.99921
Latitude : 42.46182

FLORAC

48400 – Michelin map **330** J9 – pop. 1 921 – alt. 542
▶ Paris 622 – Alès 65 – Mende 38 – Millau 84

🏕 Flower Le Pont du Tarn 🏕🚻

Flower Le Pont du Tarn

📞 0466451826. www.camping-florac.com

Address : route du Pont-de-Montvert (situated 2km north along the N 106, follow the signs for Mende and take the D 998 to the right, direct access to the Tarn river)

Opening times : from beginning April to beginning Nov.

3 ha (181 pitches) terraced, stoney, flat, grassy

Tariff : (2015 price) 30.20€ 🚹🚹 🚐 回 (ᵇ) (6A) – Extra per person 5.50€ – Reservation fee 12€

Rental rates : (2015 price) (from beginning April to beginning Nov.) – 22 🚐 – 6 canvas bungalows. Per week from 242 to 826€ – Reservation fee 12€

🚐 local sani-station 4.50€

Some pitches are beside the Tarn river, but choose those furthest from the road.

Surroundings : ≤ 🗻
Leisure activities : 🍷 🚴 🏇 🚣 ≋
Facilities : 🚿 🍴 🛒 🛁 🚽 🧺 launderette 🍴
Nearby : 🍴

GPS Longitude : 3.59013
Latitude : 44.33625

The prices listed were supplied by the campsite owners in 2015 (if prices were not available, those from the previous year are given). The fees should be regarded as basic charges and may fluctuate with inflation.

FONT-ROMEU

66120 – Michelin map **344** D7 – pop. 2 003 – alt. 1 800 – Winter sports : 🎿 🏂 🏊
▶ Paris 860 – Montpellier 245 – Perpignan 90 – Canillo 62

🏕 Huttopia Font Romeu 🏕🚻

📞 0468300932. www.huttopia.com – alt. 1 800

Address : route de Mont-Louis (RN 618)

Opening times : from mid June to mid Sept.

7 ha (175 pitches) relatively flat, flat, grassy

Tariff : (2015 price) 34.80€ 🚹🚹 🚐 回 (ᵇ) (10A) – Extra per person 7.70€ – Reservation fee 13€

Rental rates : (2015 price) (from mid June to mid Sept.) 🅿 – 34 🏠 – 24 tent lodges. Per night from 49 to 172€ – Per week from 258 to 1,204€ – Reservation fee 13€

🚐 local sani-station 7€

300m from the cable car station. High-quality rental options.

Surroundings : 🏊 ≤ Pyrénées 🗻
Leisure activities : 🍷 🍴 🎬 🍴 🏇 🚣
Facilities : 🍴 🅿 🛒 🛁 launderette 🍴

GPS Longitude : 2.04666
Latitude : 42.50628

FORMIGUÈRES

66210 – Michelin map **344** D7 – pop. 435 – alt. 1 500
▶ Paris 883 – Montpellier 248 – Perpignan 96

🏕 La Devèze

📞 0637597389. http://www.campingladeveze.com – alt. 1 600

Address : route de la Devèze

4 ha (117 pitches) terraced, flat, grassy, stony

Rentals : 1 'gypsy' caravan – 13 🚐 – 13 🏠 – 1 tipi – 4 tent lodges.

In a natural setting among pretty mountain pines. Horses and their riders welcome.

Surroundings : 🏊 ⌂ 🗻
Leisure activities : 🍴 🎬 🏇
Facilities : 🚿 🍴 🛒 🛁 🚽 🧺 launderette 🍴

GPS Longitude : 2.0922
Latitude : 42.61035

FRONTIGNAN-PLAGE

34110 – Michelin map **339** H8 – pop. 23 068 – alt. 2
▶ Paris 775 – Lodève 59 – Montpellier 26 – Sète 10

🏕 Sandaya Les Tamaris 🏕🚻

📞 0467434477. www.sandaya.fr

Address : 140 avenue d'Ingril (to the northeast along the D 60)

Opening times : from end March to mid Oct.

4 ha (250 pitches)

Tariff : (2015 price) 59€ 🚹🚹 🚐 回 (ᵇ) (10A) – Extra per person 10€ – Reservation fee 30€

Rental rates : (2015 price) (from end March to mid Oct.) – 99 🚐 – 24 🏠. Per night from 44 to 150€ – Per week from 308 to 1,710€ – Reservation fee 32€

🚐 local sani-station

In a pleasant setting close to the beach.

Surroundings : 🏊 ⌂ 🗻 ⛰
Leisure activities : 🍷 🍴 🎬 🍴 🚴 🏇 🚣
Facilities : 🚿 🍴 🛁 🚽 🧺 launderette 🏊
🍴 refrigerated food storage facilities

GPS Longitude : 3.80572
Latitude : 43.44993

FUILLA

66820 – Michelin map **344** F7 – pop. 372 – alt. 547
▶ Paris 902 – Font-Romeu-Odeillo-Via 42 – Perpignan 55 – Prades 9

⚠️ Le Rotja

✆ 04 68 96 52 75. www.camping-lerotja.com

Address : 34 avenue de la Rotja (in the village of Fuilla)

Opening times : from mid April to mid Oct.

1.6 ha (100 pitches) relatively flat, flat, grassy, stony, fruit trees

Tariff : (2015 price) 26.75€ ✸✸ 🚐 🗉 🔌 (32A) –
Extra per person 5.25€

Rental rates : (2015 price) (from mid April to mid Oct.) –
15 🛖 – 5 tent lodges. Per night from 80 to 102€ – Per week
from 450 to 615€

🚰 local sani-station – 🚐 🔌26.75€

Pitches laid out on terraces, some with shade.

Surroundings : 🏞️ ⛰️ 🛖 ♨️	**G** Longitude : 2.35883
Leisure activities : ✖ 🏊 (small swimming pool)	**P** Latitude : 42.56181
Facilities : 🚾 ⛽ 🆑🛖 📶 📮	**S**
Nearby : 🏊 🍷	

GALLARGUES-LE-MONTUEUX

30660 – Michelin map **339** K6 – pop. 3 257 – alt. 55
▶ Paris 727 – Aigues-Mortes 21 – Montpellier 39 – Nîmes 25

⚠️ Les Amandiers ♨️

✆ 04 66 35 28 02. www.camping-lesamandiers.fr

Address : 20 rue des stades (southwestern exit, follow the signs for Lunel)

Opening times : from beginning April to end Sept.

3 ha (150 pitches)

Tariff : 27€ ✸✸ 🚐 🗉 🔌 (16A) – Extra per person 6€ – Reservation
fee 21€

Rental rates : (from beginning April to end Sept.) 🏍️ – 100 🛖.
Per night from 24 to 140€ – Per week from 168 to 980€ –
Reservation fee 21€

*A swimming pool area with a spa and wellness centre: large
jacuzzi, counterflow swimming, bath with water jets.*

Surroundings : 🛖 ♨️	**G** Longitude : 4.16609
Leisure activities : 🍷 ✖ 🏠 🎣 🏃 🎮 🛶 hammam, jacuzzi 🏄 💆 🏊 spa centre	**P** Latitude : 43.71612
Facilities : 🚾 ⛽ 🛖 📶 launderette 🧺	**S**
Nearby : 🏊	

GIGNAC

34150 – Michelin map **339** G7 – pop. 5 271 – alt. 53
▶ Paris 719 – Béziers 58 – Clermont-l'Hérault 12 – Lodève 25

⚠️ Municipal la Meuse

✆ 04 67 57 92 97. www.ville-gignac.fr

Address : chemin de la Meuse (1.2km northeast along the D 32,
follow the signs for Aniane then take the road to the left, 200m from
the Hérault river and a water sports centre)

Opening times : from beginning May to mid Sept.

3.4 ha (100 pitches) flat, grassy

Tariff : (2015 price) ✸ 3€ 🚐 🗉 13.10€ – 🔌 (16A) 2.90€

Rental rates : (2015 price) (from beginning May to mid Sept.) 🏍️ –
9 🛖. Per night from 40 to 55€ – Per week from 270 to 460 € –
Reservation fee 7.53€

🚰 Eurorelais sani-station 3€

Pleasant, spacious, marked-out pitches with plenty of shade.

Surroundings : 🛖 ♨️	**G** Longitude : 3.55927
Leisure activities : ✖ 🎮	**P** Latitude : 43.662
Facilities : 🚾 ⛽ 📶 📮	**S**
Nearby : 🏊 🚴 fitness trail	

GOUDARGUES

30630 – Michelin map **339** L3 – pop. 1 032 – alt. 77
▶ Paris 667 – Alès 51 – Bagnols-sur-Cèze 17 – Barjac 20

⚠️ St-Michelet ♨️

✆ 04 66 82 24 99. www.lesaintmichelet.com

Address : route de Frigoulet (located 1km northwest along the
D 371; beside the Cèze river)

Opening times : from mid April to mid Sept.

4 ha (160 pitches) terrace, flat and relatively flat, grassy, stony

Tariff : (2015 price) 31.40€ ✸✸ 🚐 🗉 🔌 (10A) –
Extra per person 6.90€

Rental rates : (2015 price) (from mid April to mid Sept.) – 55 🛖 –
4 canvas bungalows. Per night from 46 to 69€ – Per week
from 300 to 665€

🚰 local sani-station

*The lower part of the site beside the Cèze river is for tents
and caravans and the upper part, where the swimming pool is
located, has mobile homes.*

Surroundings : 🏞️ 🛖 ♨️	**G** Longitude : 4.46271
Leisure activities : 🍷 ✖ 🏠 🏃 🏄 🛶 🏊 🚴	**P** Latitude : 44.22123
Facilities : 🚾 ⛽ 🛖 📶 📮	**S**

⚠️ Les Amarines 2

✆ 04 66 82 24 92. www.campinglesamarines.com

Address : at La Vérune Cornillon (located 1km northeast along the
D 23; beside the Cèze river)

Opening times : from beginning April to end Sept.

3.7 ha (120 pitches) flat, grassy

Tariff : 30€ ✸✸ 🚐 🗉 🔌 (10A) – Extra per person 6€ – Reservation
fee 15€

Rental rates : (from beginning April to end Sept.) – 22 🛖.
Per night from 50 to 70€ – Per week from 315 to 791€ –
Reservation fee 15€

*Beside the Cèze river, a linear site shaded by poplars and
surrounded by vineyards.*

Surroundings : 🛖 ♨️	**G** Longitude : 4.47924
Leisure activities : 🏠 🏄 🏊 🚴 🎣	**P** Latitude : 44.22047
Facilities : 🚾 ⛽ 🧺 🛖 🚿 🚽 📶 launderette, refrigerators	**S**

⚠️ La Grenouille

✆ 04 66 82 21 36. www.camping-la-grenouille.com

Address : avenue du Lavoir (near the Cèze river – direct access)

0.8 ha (50 pitches)

Rentals : 7 canvas bungalows.

🚰 Eurorelais sani-station

A small but very pleasant site with a stream running through it, located in the centre of the village.

Surroundings : 🏞 ⌂ ♤♤
Leisure activities : ⛵ ⛷ (small swimming pool) ⚲
Facilities : 🚿 ⌂ 🛒 ♨ 🖳 refrigerators
Nearby : ✗

Longitude : 4.46847
Latitude : 44.21468

LA GRANDE-MOTTE

34280 – Michelin map **339** J7 – pop. 8 391 – alt. 1
▶ Paris 747 – Aigues-Mortes 12 – Lunel 16 – Montpellier 28

🔺 Le Garden ♠♣

📞 0467565009. www.legarden.fr

Address : avenue de la Petite Motte (take the western exit along the D 59, 300m from the beach)

Opening times : from beginning April to beginning Oct.

3 ha (209 pitches) flat, grassy

Tariff : (2015 price) 44€ ♣♣ ⌂ 🖳 ⚡ (10A) – Extra per person 9.80€
Rental rates : (2015 price) (from beginning April to beginning Oct.) 🚿 (1 mobile home) – 122 🛏. Per night from 62 to 126€ – Per week from 315 to 980€ – Reservation fee 20€
Good sanitary facilities and upmarket rental options.

Surroundings : ⌂ ♤♤
Leisure activities : ⚑ ✗ 🏠 🏋 ⛷ ⛵
Facilities : 🚿 ⌂ 🖳 ♨ ♨ 🛒 launderette ⌂ ♨
Nearby : ♞ ♞

Longitude : 4.07235
Latitude : 43.56229

🔺 Les Cigales

📞 0467565085. www.paysdelor.fr

Address : allée des Pins (take the western exit along the D 59)

Opening times : from beginning April to end Sept.

2.5 ha (180 pitches) flat, grassy

Tariff : (2015 price) 24€ ♣♣ ⌂ 🖳 ⚡ (10A) – Extra per person 6.80€ – Reservation fee 10€
Rental rates : (2015 price) (from beginning April to end Sept.) – 20 🛏. Per night from 38 to 115€ – Per week from 220 to 710€ – Reservation fee 10€
🚉 local sani-station 16€
There is a large parking area for campervans adjoining the campsite.

Surroundings : ♤♤
Leisure activities : ⛵
Facilities : 🚿 ⌂ ♨ ♨ launderette
Nearby : ♞

Longitude : 4.07612
Latitude : 43.56722

LE GRAU-DU-ROI

34240 – Michelin map **339** J7 – pop. 7 995 – alt. 2
▶ Paris 751 – Aigues-Mortes 7 – Arles 55 – Lunel 22

🔺 FranceLoc Le Boucanet ♠♣

📞 0466514148. http://campingboucanet.franceloc.fr/ ⛱

Address : route de Carnon (situated 2km northwest of Le Grau-du-Roi (right bank) following signs for la Grande-Motte; beside beach)

Opening times : from beginning April to end Sept.

7.5 ha (462 pitches) flat, grassy

Tariff : (2015 price) 42€ ♣♣ ⌂ 🖳 ⚡ (6A) – Extra per person 9€ – Reservation fee 27€

Rental rates : (2015 price) (from beginning April to end Sept.) ⛱ – 2 'gypsy' caravans – 338 🛏. Per night from 65 to 257€ – Per week from 259 to 1,722€ – Reservation fee 27€
🚉 Eurorelais sani-station 4€ – 5 🖳 42€
In an exclusive location beside a beautiful beach.

Surroundings : ⌂ ♀ ⛰
Leisure activities : ▼ ✗ 🏠 🎡 🏋 ⛵ ☈
✗ 🖳 ⛷ ♤
Facilities : 🚿 ⌂ ♨ ♨ launderette 🛒 ♨
refrigerated food storage facilities
Nearby : ♞

Longitude : 4.10753
Latitude : 43.55428

ISPAGNAC

48320 – Michelin map **330** J8 – pop. 851 – alt. 518
▶ Paris 612 – Florac 11 – Mende 28 – Meyrueis 46

🔺 Municipal du Pré Morjal

📞 0466454357. www.campingdupremorjal.com

Address : chemin du Beldiou (take the western exit along the D 907bis, follow the signs for Millau and take road to the left; near the Tarn)

Opening times : from beginning April to beginning Nov.

2 ha (123 pitches) flat, grassy

Tariff : 18.50€ ♣♣ ⌂ 🖳 ⚡ (10A) – Extra per person 3.50€
Rental rates : (from end March to mid Nov.) – 8 🏠 – 8 canvas bungalows. Per night from 40 to 100€ – Per week from 175 to 595€
In a pleasant wooded setting at the entrance to the Tarn river gorges.

Surroundings : 🏞 ⌂ ♤♤
Leisure activities : 🏠 🏋 ☈ ⛷
Facilities : 🚿 ⌂ ♨ launderette
Nearby : ✗ ♞

Longitude : 3.53038
Latitude : 44.37223

We have selected the best campsites in France with our usual care, listing those with the best facilities in the most pleasant surroundings.

JUNAS

30250 – Michelin map **339** J6 – pop. 1 085 – alt. 75
▶ Paris 730 – Aigues-Mortes 30 – Aimargues 15 – Montpellier 42

🔺 Les Chênes

📞 0466809907. www.camping-les-chenes.com

Address : 95 chemin des Tuileries Basses (1.3km south along the D 140, follow the signs for Sommières and take road to the left)

Opening times : from mid April to mid Oct.

1.7 ha (90 pitches) terraced, flat and relatively flat, stony

Tariff : 22.10€ ♣♣ ⌂ 🖳 ⚡ (10A) – Extra per person 4.90€ – Reservation fee 12€

Rental rates : (from mid April to mid Oct.) ⛱ – 4 'gypsy' caravans – 13 🛏. Per week from 230 to 625€ – Reservation fee 12€

Attractively shaded by Holm oaks, with pitches laid out on terraces, some of which are marked out with low stone walls.

Surroundings : 🏞 ♤♤
Leisure activities : ⛵ ⛷
Facilities : 🚿 ⌂ ♨ ♨ 🖳

Longitude : 4.123
Latitude : 43.76921

⚠ L'Olivier

✆ 04 66 80 39 52. www.campinglolivier.fr

Address : 112 route de Congenies (take the eastern exit along the D 140 and take the road to the right)

Opening times : from beginning April to mid Oct.

1 ha (45 pitches) flat, relatively flat, rocky, grassy, stony

Tariff : (2015 price) 23.20€ ★★ ⇔ 🔲 🚿 (6A) – Extra per person 4.95€ – Reservation fee 10€

Rental rates : (2015 price) (from beginning April to mid Oct.) – 14 🛖 – 2 🏠 – 2 canvas bungalows. Per night from 52 to 72€ – Per week from 195 to 645€ – Reservation fee 10€

A family-friendly establishment in the shade of Holm oaks and near the village.

Surroundings : ⅃ 🎣
Leisure activities : 🏇 🚴 ⛓ 🌊
Facilities : ♿ ⊶ 🔌 🚿 🖼
GPS Longitude : 4.12489 Latitude : 43.77081

LANUÉJOLS

30750 – Michelin map **339** F4 – pop. 334 – alt. 905
▶ Paris 656 – Alès 109 – Mende 68 – Millau 35

⚠ Domaine de Pradines

✆ 04 67 82 73 85. www.domaine-de-pradines.com – alt. 800

Address : route de Millau, D28 (3.5km west along the D 28, follow the signs for Roujarie and take road to the left)

150 ha/30 for camping (75 pitches) relatively flat, flat, grassy

Rentals : 5 🛖 – 5 🏠 – 4 yurts – 4 apartments – 2 tipis – 2 canvas bungalows.

Right in the heart of the countryside, various rental options, extensive pitches, but only average and rather old sanitary facilities.

Surroundings : ⅃ ≤ 🎣
Leisure activities : ✗ 🍴 🏇 🎿 🌊
Facilities : ♿ ⊶ 🚿 launderette 🚮 🚿
GPS Longitude : 3.34722 Latitude : 44.13306

LAROQUE-DES-ALBÈRES

66740 – Michelin map **344** I7 – pop. 2 028 – alt. 100
▶ Paris 881 – Argelès-sur-Mer 11 – Le Boulou 14 – Collioure 18

⚠ Cybele Vacances Les Albères

✆ 04 68 89 23 64. www.camping-des-alberes.com

Address : route du Moulin de Cassagnes (take the northeastern exit along the D 2, follow the signs for Argelès-sur-Mer then continue 0.4km along the road to the right)

Opening times : from mid March to end Sept.

5 ha (300 pitches) very uneven, terraced, relatively flat, flat, grassy, stony

Tariff : 33€ ★★ ⇔ 🔲 🚿 (6A) – Extra per person 6€ – Reservation fee 30€

Rental rates : (from mid March to end Sept.) – 100 🛖 – 7 🏠 – 3 tent lodges. Per night from 24 to 96€ – Per week from 189 to 1,399€ – Reservation fee 25€

The pitches laid out on terraces have plenty of shade.

Surroundings : ⅃ ⅃ 🎣
Leisure activities : 🍴 ✗ 🏊 🏖 jacuzzi 🏇 🎿 🌊 ⛏ multi-sports ground
Facilities : ♿ ⊶ 🔌 🚿 🖼 🚮 🚿
GPS Longitude : 2.94418 Latitude : 42.52404

LATTES

34970 – Michelin map **339** I7 – pop. 15 804 – alt. 3
▶ Paris 766 – Montpellier 7 – Nîmes 54 – Béziers 68

🏔 Le Parc

✆ 04 67 65 85 67. www.leparccamping.com

Address : route de Mauguio (situated 2km northeast along the D 172)

Opening times : permanent

1.6 ha (100 pitches) flat, grassy, stony

Tariff : (2015 price) 29€ ★★ ⇔ 🔲 🚿 (10A) – Extra per person 6€ – Reservation fee 15€

Rental rates : (2015 price) permanent – 30 🛖 – 2 canvas bungalows. Per week from 220 to 760€ – Reservation fee 15€

🚐 local sani-station 5€

Close to the tramway (line 3) for Montpellier and Pérols or Lattes.

Surroundings : ⅃ 🎣
Leisure activities : 🏖 🏇 🌊
Facilities : ♿ ⊶ 🔌 🚿 launderette
Nearby : ✗
GPS Longitude : 3.92578 Latitude : 43.57622

LAURENS

34480 – Michelin map **339** E7 – pop. 1 349 – alt. 140
▶ Paris 736 – Bédarieux 14 – Béziers 22 – Clermont-l'Hérault 40

🏔 Sites et Paysages L'Oliveraie 🅰🔅

✆ 04 67 90 24 36. www.oliveraie.com

Address : 1600 chemin de Bédarieux (situated 2km north and take the road to the right)

Opening times : from beginning March to end Oct.

7 ha (110 pitches) terraced, relatively flat, flat, grassy, stony

Tariff : (2015 price) 33€ ★★ ⇔ 🔲 🚿 (10A) – Extra per person 6.50€ – Reservation fee 20€

Rental rates : (2015 price) (from beginning March to end Oct.) – 11 🛖 – 2 🏠 – 2 canvas bungalows. Per night from 42 to 90€ – Per week from 300 to 630€ – Reservation fee 20€

🚐 local sani-station

This shady site spreads out across terraces, with a swimming pool surrounded by olive trees.

Surroundings : ⅃ 🎣
Leisure activities : 🍴 ✗ 🌙 nighttime 🏃 ⛷
🏇 🚴 🎿 ⛏ 🏊 🐎
Facilities : ♿ ⊶ 🔌 🚿 🖼 🚮 🚿
GPS Longitude : 3.18571 Latitude : 43.53631

MARSEILLAN-PLAGE

34340 – Michelin map **339** G8
▶ Paris 765 – Montpellier 51 – Nîmes 100 – Carcassonne 114

🏔 Les Méditerranées – Beach Club Nouvelle Floride 🅰🔅

✆ 04 67 21 94 49. www. lesmediterranees.com

Address : 262 avenue des Campings

Opening times : from beginning April to end Sept.

7 ha (475 pitches) grassy

Tariff : 60€ ★★ ⇔ 🔲 🚿 (10A) – Extra per person 10€ – Reservation fee 30€

Beach Club Nouvelle Floride

Rental rates : (from beginning April to end Sept.) 🚐 – 160 🏠.
Per night from 40 to 280€ – Per week from 210 to 1,960€
– Reservation fee 30€

🚐 Eurorelais sani-station

In a pleasant location near the beach, with free access to the activities at the Les Méditerranées – Beach Garden campsite.

Surroundings : 🏞 🌳🌳⛰
Leisure activities : 🍴✗ 🏛 🌳🏃🏂 jacuzzi 🚣🏊 multi-sports ground, entertainment room
Facilities : 🚻 ⚡ 🛁 🚿 ▽ 🍴 launderette 🚿🚿
Nearby : 🎵 disco

GPS Longitude : 3.54243
Latitude : 43.30923

🏔 Les Méditerranées – Beach Garden 👥

Les Méditerranées - Beach Garden

☎ 04 67 21 92 83. www.lesmediterranees.com
Address : avenue des Campings
Opening times : from beginning April to end Sept.
14 ha (600 pitches) flat, grassy, sandy
Tariff : 58€ 👫 🚗 🔲 ⚡ (10A) – Extra per person 10€ – Reservation fee 30€

Rental rates : (from beginning April to end Sept.) 🚐 – 129 🏠.
Per night from 30 to 300€ – Per week from 210 to 2,100€ –
Reservation fee 30€

🚐 Eurorelais sani-station

Located close to the beach, with a panoramic restaurant and free access to the activities at the Les Méditerranées – Beach Club Nouvelle Floride campsite.

Surroundings : 🏞 🌳🌳⛰
Leisure activities : 🍴✗ 🏛 🌳🏃 hammam, jacuzzi 🚣🚲🏊 spa facilities, massages, multi-sports ground, spa centre
Facilities : 🚻 ⚡ 🛁 ▽ 🍴 launderette 🚿🚿
Nearby : 🛒

GPS Longitude : 3.538
Latitude : 43.3058

🏔 Les Méditerranées – Beach Club Charlemagne

Beach Club Charlemagne

☎ 04 67 21 92 49. www.lesmediterranees.com
Address : avenue des Campings (250m from the beach)
Opening times : from beginning April to end March
6.7 ha (480 pitches) flat, grassy, sandy
Tariff : 60€ 👫 🚗 🔲 ⚡ (10A) – Extra per person 10€ – Reservation fee 30€

Rental rates : (from beginning April to end Sept.) 🚐 – 173 🏠.
Per night from 40 to 280€ – Per week from 210 to 1,960€ –
Reservation fee 30€

🚐 Eurorelais sani-station

Free use of the services and facilities of two other sites Les Méditerranées – Beach Club, opposite and by the beach.

Surroundings : 🏞 🌳🌳
Leisure activities : 🍴✗ 🏛 🌳🚣 🏊 disco
Facilities : 🚻 ⚡ 🛁 ▽ 🍴 launderette 🎵
🚿🚿
Nearby : 🏃🏂

GPS Longitude : 3.54337
Latitude : 43.31052

🏔 Le Galet

☎ 04 67 21 95 61. www.camping-galet.com
Address : avenue des Campings (250m from the beach)
Opening times : from beginning April to end Sept.
3 ha (254 pitches) flat, grassy, sandy
Tariff : (2015 price) 43.50€ 👫 🚗 🔲 ⚡ (10A) – Extra per person 7€ – Reservation fee 25€
Rental rates : (2015 price) (from beginning April to end Nov.) – 67 🏠. Per night from 25 to 140€ – Per week from 175 to 970€ – Reservation fee 25€

A long, narrow site with a pretty water park at one end.

Surroundings : 🏞 🌳
Leisure activities : ✗ 🚣 🏊 🏂
Facilities : 🚻 ⚡ 🛁 🍴 launderette
Nearby : 🛒🍴🚿

GPS Longitude : 3.5421
Latitude : 43.31108

🏔 La Créole

☎ 04 67 21 92 69. www.campinglacreole.com
Address : 74 avenue des Campings
Opening times : from beginning April to mid Oct.
1.5 ha (110 pitches) flat, grassy, sandy
Tariff : (2015 price) 38€ 👫 🚗 🔲 ⚡ (10A) – Extra per person 7€ – Reservation fee 17€
Rental rates : (2015 price) (from beginning April to mid Oct.) 🚐 – 19 🏠. Per week from 200 to 790€ – Reservation fee 17€
🚐 local sani-station – 8 🔲 14€

Situated beside a beautiful beach of fine sand.

Surroundings : 🏞 🌳🌳⛰
Leisure activities : ✗ 🚣
Facilities : 🚻 ⚡ 🍴 🔲
Nearby : 🏊🍴🚿 🐎

GPS Longitude : 3.54375
Latitude : 43.31047

For more information on visiting particular towns or regions, consult the relevant regional MICHELIN Green Guide. We also recommend you use the appropriate Michelin regional map to locate your selected campsite, to calculate distances and to work out the best route.

MARVEJOLS

48100 – Michelin map **330** H7 – pop. 5 053 – alt. 650
▶ Paris 573 – Espalion 64 – Florac 50 – Mende 28

🏔 Village VAL V.V.F. et Camping de l'Europe

☎ 04 66 32 03 69. www.vvf-villages.fr
Address : at Le Colagnet (1.3km east along the D 999, D 1, follow the signs for Montrodat and take the road to the right; beside the Colagnet – from A 75, take exit 38)
3 ha (100 pitches) flat, grassy
Rentals : 9 🏠 – 41 apartments.

Well shaded pitches beside the river; basic gîtes available and chalets equipped to a higher standard.

Surroundings : 🏞 🌳🌳
Leisure activities : 🏛 🌳🚣 ✗ 🏊 multi-sports ground
Facilities : 🚻 🅿 🛁 ▽ 🍴 launderette
Nearby : 🛒

GPS Longitude : 3.30432
Latitude : 44.55075

MASSILLARGUES-ATTUECH

30140 – Michelin map **339** J4 – pop. 675 – alt. 156
▶ Paris 726 – Montpellier 56 – Nîmes 43 – Avignon 78

⚏ Le Fief d'Anduze ⚐⚐

⚲ 04 66 61 81 71. http://www.campinglefief.fr/

Address : at Attuech, 195 chemin du Plan d'Eau (located 1.5km to the north along the D 982, near a lake)

Opening times : from beginning April to end Sept.

5.5 ha (80 pitches) flat, grassy

Tariff : 26€ ✸✸ ⚗ 🅔 ⓗ (10A) – Extra per person 5.30€ – Reservation fee 10€

Rental rates : (from beginning April to end Sept.) – 18 ⌸. Per night from 54 to 88€ – Per week from 311 to 760€ – Reservation fee 10€

Well-shaded pitches but poor sanitary facilities.

Surroundings : 🌿 〰〰	
Leisure activities : ▼ ✗ ☷ ⚡ ⚑	
hammam, jacuzzi ⚓ ⚓ ⚊ multi-sports	**GPS** Longitude : 4.02576
ground	Latitude : 44.02946
Facilities : ⚿ ⚯ ⚒ ⚄ ⚑	
Nearby : ⚓	

MATEMALE

66210 – Michelin map **344** D7 – pop. 294 – alt. 1 514
▶ Paris 855 – Font-Romeu-Odeillo-Via 20 – Perpignan 92 – Prades 46

⚏ Le Lac

⚲ 04 68 30 94 49. www.camping-lac-matemale.com – alt. 1 540 – limited spaces for one-night stay

Address : 1.7km southwest along the D 52, follow the signs for Les Angles and take the turning to the left, 150m from the lake

Opening times : permanent

3.5 ha (110 pitches) undulating, wood, flat, relatively flat

Tariff : 20.80€ ✸✸ ⚗ 🅔 ⓗ (6A) – Extra per person 5.50€
Rental rates : permanent – 20 ⌸ – 5 ⌂. Per night from 60 to 70€ – Per week from 330 to 580€
⚑ local sani-station 2.50€

A pleasant mountain location in the shade of a pretty pine forest, direct access to the village along a pedestrian path.

Surroundings : 🌿 〰〰	
Leisure activities : ☷ ⚑ jacuzzi ⚓	**GPS** Longitude : 2.10673
Facilities : ⚿ ⚯ ⚒ ⚊ launderette	Latitude : 42.58164
Nearby : ▼ ✗ ⚲ ⚵ ⚑ ⚄ ⚊ ⚓ sports/	
activities centre at 800m	

MAUREILLAS-LAS-ILLAS

66480 – Michelin map **344** H8 – pop. 2 649 – alt. 130
▶ Paris 873 – Gerona 71 – Perpignan 31 – Port-Vendres 31

⚏ Les Bruyères

⚲ 04 68 83 26 64. www.camping-lesbruyeres66.fr

Address : route de Céret (1.2km west along the D 618)

Opening times : permanent

4 ha (106 pitches) very uneven, terraced, flat, grassy, stony

Tariff : 27.60€ ✸✸ ⚗ 🅔 ⓗ (10A) – Extra per person 5.80€ – Reservation fee 10€

Rental rates : permanent – 22 ⌸ – 4 ⌂. Per night from 60 to 130€ – Per week from 340 to 710€ – Reservation fee 10€

⚑ local sani-station 4€

In a pleasant wooded setting among cork oaks, but choose the pitches away from the road in preference.

Surroundings : ⚏ 〰〰	
Leisure activities : ☷ ⚑ ⚑	**GPS** Longitude : 2.79509
Facilities : ⚿ ⚯ ⚊ ⚄ ⚒ ⚑ ⚒	Latitude : 42.49249
Nearby : ⚞	

MENDE

48000 – Michelin map **330** J7 – pop. 12 285 – alt. 731
▶ Paris 584 – Clermont-Ferrand 174 – Florac 38 – Langogne 46

⚏ Tivoli

⚲ 04 66 65 31 10. www.campingtivoli.com

Address : chemin de Tivoli (situated 2km southwest along the N 88, follow the signs for Rodez and take the road to the right, opposite the shopping centre; beside the Lot river)

Opening times : permanent

1.8 ha (100 pitches) flat, grassy

Tariff : 24.90€ ✸✸ ⚗ 🅔 ⓗ (6A) – Extra per person 7€ – Reservation fee 25€

Rental rates : (from end April to end Sept.) ⚑ –18 ⌸. Per night from 60 to 80€ – Per week from 190 to 650€ – Reservation fee 25€
⚑ local sani-station

Below the road to Rodez and opposite a sports complex accessible by footbridge over the Lot river.

Surroundings : 〰〰	
Leisure activities : ☷ ⚓ ⚑	**GPS** Longitude : 3.45693
Facilities : ⚿ ⚯ ⚒ ⚒ ⚑ ⚒ ⚑	Latitude : 44.51268
Nearby : ⚵	

This guide is updated regularly, so buy your new copy every year!

MEYRUEIS

48150 – Michelin map **330** I9 – pop. 853 – alt. 698
▶ Paris 643 – Florac 36 – Mende 57 – Millau 43

⚏ Le Capelan

⚲ 04 66 45 60 50. www.campingcapelan.com

Address : route de Millau (located 1km northwest along the D 996; beside the Jonte river)

Opening times : from beginning May to mid May

2.8 ha (100 pitches) flat, grassy

Tariff : 32€ ✸✸ ⚗ 🅔 ⓗ (10A) – Extra per person 6.50€ – Reservation fee 16€

Rental rates : (from beginning May to mid Sept.) ⚑ – 44 ⌸. Per night from 40 to 121€ – Reservation fee 19€
⚑ local sani-station 5€ – ⚑ ⓗ12€

In a pleasant location in the steep valley of the Jonte river, with a path to the village and swimming pool across the road.

Surroundings : ⚞ ⚏ 〰〰	
Leisure activities : ▼ ☷ ⚑ ⚓ ⚑ ⚑	**GPS** Longitude : 3.4199
climbing	Latitude : 44.1859
Facilities : ⚿ ⚯ ⚄ – 3 private sanitary	
facilities (⚒ ⚒ wc) ⚊ ⚒ ⚒ launderette ⚊	

▲ Le Champ d'Ayres

☎ 04 66 45 60 51. www.campinglejardindescevennes.com

Address : route de la Brèze (500m east along the D 57, follow the signs for Campis, near the Brèze river)

Opening times : from end April to end Sept.

1.5 ha (91 pitches) relatively flat, grassy

Tariff : 30€ ✹✹ ⇌ 🖪 🄗 (10A) – Extra per person 5.90€ – Reservation fee 15€

Rental rates : (from end April to end Sept.) ✼ – 21 🚐 – 3 🏠. Per week from 190 to 740€ – Reservation fee 18€

🚽 local sani-station 5€ – 🔌🄗12€

A green and flowery setting.

Surroundings : ⋙ ⋖ ⊡ ♀
Leisure activities : 🍸 🖽 ♨ ⇲
Facilities : ♿ ⚬⊸ 🛁 ⁇ launderette
Nearby : ✂ 🐎

▲ La Via Natura La Cascade

☎ 04 66 45 45 45. www.camping-la-cascade.com

Address : at Salvinsac (3.8km northeast along the D 996, follow the signs for Florac and take the road to the right, near the Jonte river and a waterfall)

Opening times : from beginning April to end Sept.

1 ha (54 pitches) undulating, flat, grassy

Tariff : 15.70€ ✹✹ ⇌ 🖪 🄗 (16A) – Extra per person 3.30€

Rental rates : (from beginning April to end Sept.) – 13 🏠. Per night from 55 to 73€ – Per week from 280 to 665€

🚽 local sani-station 5€

In the Vallée de la Jonte, a site with a passion for nature and ecology.

Surroundings : ⋙ ⋖ ♀
Leisure activities : 🖽 ♨ ⇲
Facilities : ♿ ⚬⊸ 🛁 ⁇ ▣

Longitude : 3.45567
Latitude : 44.19645

▲ Le Pré de Charlet

☎ 04 66 45 63 65. www.camping-cevennes-meyrueis.com

Address : route de Florac (located 1km northeast along the D 996; beside the Jonte river)

2 ha (70 pitches) terraced, relatively flat, flat, grassy

Rentals : 6 🚐 – 3 canvas bungalows.

Situated below the road, with some pitches alongside the river with refurbished sanitary facilities.

Surroundings : ⋙ ♀♀
Leisure activities : 🖽 ♨ ⇲
Facilities : ♿ ⚬⊸ 🛁 ⁇ launderette
Nearby : ⇲

Longitude : 3.43831
Latitude : 44.18587

11250 – Michelin map **344** E4 – pop. 186 – alt. 210
▶ Paris 766 – Carcassonne 19 – Castelnaudary 41 – Limoux 15

▲▲▲ Yelloh! Village Domaine d'Arnauteille 👥

☎ 04 68 26 84 53. www.camping-arnauteille.com

Address : 2.2km southeast along the D 43

Opening times : from end April to mid Sept.

115 ha/12 for camping (198 pitches) very uneven, terraced, relatively flat, flat, grassy

Tariff : 40€ ✹✹ ⇌ 🖪 🄗 (10A) – Extra per person 8€

Rental rates : (from end April to mid Sept.) – 88 🚐 – 10 🏠. Per night from 39 to 227€ – Per week from 273 to 1,589€

🚽 local sani-station

On a sloping, spacious and pleasant site set on a hill, with both shaded and sunny pitches.

Surroundings : ⋙ ⋖ ⊡ ♀
Leisure activities : ✕ 🖽 ♨ ⛸ jacuzzi ⇲ 🏊 🐎 multi-sports ground, spa centre
Facilities : ♿ ⚬⊸ ▥ 🛁 ⁇ launderette ⇲ ⇲

Longitude : 2.26107
Latitude : 43.12431

11100 – Michelin map **344** J3 – pop. 51 227 – alt. 13
▶ Paris 787 – Béziers 28 – Carcassonne 61 – Montpellier 96

▲▲▲ Yelloh! Village Les Mimosas 👥

☎ 04 68 49 03 72. www.lesmimosas.com

Address : chaussée de Mandirac (10km to the south, after the suburb La Nautique)

Opening times : from mid March to end Oct.

9 ha (266 pitches) flat, grassy, stony, sandy

Tariff : 49€ ✹✹ ⇌ 🖪 🄗 (10A) – Extra per person 7€

Rental rates : (from end March to mid Oct.) – 113 🚐 – 4 studios. Per night from 39 to 222€ – Per week from 273 to 1,554€

Pitches nestling among Languedoc vineyards, with a welcoming wine bar for tastings.

Surroundings : ⋙ ⊡ ♀
Leisure activities : 🍸 ✕ 🖽 ♨ ⛸ 🎣 ⇲ 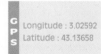 ⇲ 🚲 🏊 🐎 ⛸ 🎱 🏊 ⇲ multi-sports ground
Facilities : ♿ ⚬⊸ ⇲ ⇲ ⁇ launderette ⇲
Nearby : 🐎

Longitude : 3.02592
Latitude : 43.13658

▲▲▲ La Nautique

La Nautique

☎ 04 68 90 48 19. www.campinglanautique.com

Address : chemin de La Nautique (4km to the south; at Port La Nautique)

Opening times : from beginning March to end Oct.

16 ha (390 pitches)

Tariff : 46.50€ ✹✹ ⇌ 🖪 🄗 (10A) – Extra per person 8.60€

Rental rates : (from beginning March to end Oct.) ♿ (1 chalet, 4 mobile homes) – 120 🚐 – 6 canvas bungalows. Per night from 36 to 129€ – Per week from 216 to 903€

🚽 local sani-station

Beside the Etang de Bages and Etang de Sigean (coastal lagoons).

Surroundings : ⋖ ⊡ ♀
Leisure activities : 🍸 ✕ 🖽 ♨ ⇲ ⇲ 🚲 🏊 ✂ 🎱 🏊 ⇲ pedalos ⇌
Facilities : ♿ ⚬⊸ 390 private sanitary facilities ⇲ ⇲ wc) ⇲ ⁇ launderette ⇲ ⇲
Nearby : ⚓

Longitude : 3.00424
Latitude : 43.14703

Using the traditional Michelin classification method, the guide provides you with an easy, speedy reference for assessing the category of each site: 1 to 5 tents (see page 10).

NASBINALS

48260 – Michelin map **330** G7 – pop. 498 – alt. 1 180
▶ Paris 573 – Aumont-Aubrac 24 – Chaudes-Aigues 27 – Espalion 34

⚘ Municipal

𝒫 04 66 32 51 87. mairie.nasbinals@laposte.net – alt. 1 100

Address : route de Saint-Urcize (located 1km northwest along the D 12)

2 ha (75 pitches) flat, relatively flat, grassy

Surroundings : 🐾 ⋞ Leisure activities : 🏠 Facilities : ♿ ⛟ Nearby : 🐎	**GPS** Longitude : 3.04016 Latitude : 44.67022

NAUSSAC

48300 – Michelin map **330** L6 – pop. 206 – alt. 920
▶ Paris 575 – Grandrieu 26 – Langogne 3 – Mende 46

⚘ Les Terrasses du Lac

𝒫 04 66 69 29 62. www.naussac.com

Address : at Naussac lake (north of the town along the D 26, follow the signs for Saugues and take the turning to the left; 200m from the lake – direct access)

Opening times : from mid April to end Sept.

6 ha (180 pitches) terraced, relatively flat, flat, grassy

Tariff : 21.50€ ✶✶ ⛺ 🅴 (10A) – Extra per person 4.90€ – Reservation fee 10€

Rental rates : (from mid April to mid Oct.) – 2 🚐 – 6 🏠 – 17 🛏. Per night from 68 to 73€ – Per week from 325 to 675€ – Reservation fee 10€

🚻 local sani-station – 150 🅴 13.90€

All the pitches and rental accommodation benefit from a panoramic view of the 1,000-hectare lake.

Surroundings : 🐾 ⋞ Lac de Naussac Leisure activities : 🍽 ✕ 🎮 🏃 ✂ 🛶 Facilities : ♿ ⛟ 🍴 launderette 🐾 Nearby : 🏄 🚣 (beach) 🎣 💧	**GPS** Longitude : 3.83505 Latitude : 44.73478

PALAU-DEL-VIDRE

66690 – Michelin map **344** I7 – pop. 2 736 – alt. 26
▶ Paris 867 – Argelès-sur-Mer 8 – Le Boulou 16 – Collioure 15

⚘ Le Haras

𝒫 04 68 22 14 50. www.camping-le-haras.com

Address : 1 ter avenue Juliot Curie, Domaine Saint-Galdric (take the northeastern exit along the D 11)

Opening times : from beginning April to end Sept.

2.3 ha (131 pitches) flat, grassy

Tariff : 41€ ✶✶ ⛺ 🅴 (10A) – Extra per person 7€ – Reservation fee 20€

Rental rates : (from beginning April to end Sept.) – 14 🚐 – 1 canvas bungalow. Per night from 35 to 130€ – Per week from 245 to 910 v – Reservation fee 20€

🚻 local sani-station

The site is attractively shaded and has floral decoration.

Surroundings : 🌳 🎶 Leisure activities : 🍽 ✕ 🎮 🛶 🛶 Facilities : ♿ ⛟ 🚽 🍴 launderette 🐾	**GPS** Longitude : 2.96474 Latitude : 42.57575

PALAVAS-LES-FLOTS

34250 – Michelin map **339** I7 – pop. 5 996 – alt. 1
▶ Paris 765 – Montpellier 13 – Sète 41 – Lunel 33

⚘ Club Airotel Les Roquilles

𝒫 04 67 68 03 47. www.camping-les-roquilles.fr ✷

Address : 267 bis avenue Saint-Maurice (follow the signs for Carnon-Plage, 100m from the beach)

Opening times : from mid April to mid Sept.

15 ha (792 pitches) flat, grassy, gravel

Tariff : (2015 price) 45€ ✶✶ ⛺ 🅴 (6A) – Extra per person 7€ – Reservation fee 34€

Rental rates : (2015 price) (from mid April to mid Sept.) ♿ (1 mobile home) ✷ – 8 'gypsy' caravans – 100 🚐 – 50 🏠. Per night from 54 to 94€ – Per week from 275 to 1,325€ – Reservation fee 34€

🚻 local sani-station

Some pitches are beside the lake, which is occasionally visited by feeding flamingoes.

Surroundings : 🛶 ♨ Leisure activities : 🍽 ✕ 🎮 🎯 🏃 🏋 ✂ 🛶 ⛵ multi-sports ground Facilities : ♿ ⛟ 🚽 🖼 🔌 🐾	**GPS** Longitude : 3.96037 Latitude : 43.53851

⚘ Tohapi Palavas 👥

𝒫 08 25 00 20 30. www.tohapi.fr – limited spaces for one-night stay

Address : route de Maguelone (right bank)

Opening times : from beginning April to beginning Sept.

8 ha (438 pitches) flat, sandy, fine gravel

Tariff : (2015 price) 16€ ✶✶ ⛺ 🅴 (10A) – Extra per person 7€

Rental rates : (2015 price) (from beginning April to beginning Sept.) – 415 🚐. Per night from 32 to 64€

A mobile home village with some pitches for tents and caravans beside the sea.

Surroundings : 🛶 ⛰ Leisure activities : 🍽 ✕ 🎮 🎯 🏃 🏋 🚴 🛶 kite-surfing, multi-sports ground Facilities : ♿ ⛟ 🚽 🍴 launderette 🔌 🐾	**GPS** Longitude : 3.9095 Latitude : 43.51963

LES PLANTIERS

30122 – Michelin map **339** H4 – pop. 252 – alt. 400
▶ Paris 667 – Alès 48 – Florac 46 – Montpellier 85

⚘ Caylou

𝒫 04 66 83 92 85. www.camping-caylou.fr

Address : at Le Caylou (located 1km northeast along the D 20, follow the signs for Saumane; beside the Borgne river)

Opening times : from mid April to mid Oct.

4 ha (75 pitches) terraced, relatively flat, flat, grassy

Tariff : 18€ ✶✶ ⛺ 🅴 (12A) – Extra per person 5€

Rental rates : (from mid April to mid Oct.) – 4 🚐 – 2 gîtes. Per week from 280 to 410€

Good-quality gîtes and a nice bar terrace looking out over the valley.

Surroundings : 🛶 ⋞ 🌳 ♨ Leisure activities : 🍽 ✕ 🎮 🏋 🛶 ⛵ 🎣 entertainment room Facilities : ♿ ⛟ 🚽 🐾 🍴	**GPS** Longitude : 3.73101 Latitude : 44.12209

PORT-CAMARGUE

30240 – Michelin map **339** J7
▶ Paris 762 – Montpellier 36 – Nîmes 47 – Avignon 93

ᗰᗰ Yelloh! Village Les Petits Camarguais ᗩᒪ

✆ 04 66 51 16 16. www.yellohvillage-petits-camarguais.com – limited spaces for one-night stay ✀

Address : route de l'Espiguette

Opening times : from beginning April to beginning Nov.

10 ha (510 pitches) flat, grassy, sandy

Tariff : (2015 price) 52 € ♦♦ ⛻ 🔲 ⚡ (10A) – Extra per person 9 €
Rental rates : (2015 price) permanent ✀ – 482 🛏. Per night from 39 to 270 € – Per week from 273 to 1,890 €

Surroundings : 🗔 🌳
Leisure activities : ☂ ✗ 🏛 🎣 🏃 jacuzzi ⛴ 🚲 🏊 🎿 multi-sports ground, entertainment room
Facilities : ⛟ 🔌 🚿 🛁 🚻 launderette 🚮 🛒
Nearby : 🐎 🦌

Longitude : 4.14456
Latitude : 43.50472

ᗰᗰ Tohapi La Marine ᗩᒪ (rental of mobile homes only)

✆ 08 25 00 20 30. www.tohapi.fr

Address : 2196 route de l'Espiguette

Opening times : from mid April to end Sept.

5 ha flat, grassy, sandy
Rental rates : (2015 price) ⛟ (1 mobile home) – 292 🛏 – 15 tent lodges. Per night from 32 to 64 €

Choose the pitches away from the road in preference. There's a free shuttle service to the beaches

Surroundings : 🌳
Leisure activities : ☂ ✗ 🏛 🎣 🏃 🏊 🚲 🏊 🎿
Facilities : 🔌 🚿 🚻 launderette 🚮 🛒
Nearby : 🚣 🦌, casino

Longitude : 4.1457
Latitude : 43.5074

ᗰᗰ Abri de Camargue

✆ 04 66 51 54 83. www.abridecamargue.fr – limited spaces for one-night stay

Address : 320 route de l'Espiguette (near the Casino (gaming) and opposite the fairground)

4 ha (277 pitches)
Rentals : 93 🛏.
🛱 Eurorelais sani-station
There's a free shuttle service to the beaches.

Surroundings : 🗔 🌳
Leisure activities : ☂ ✗ 🎣 🏃 🏊 🔲 🎿 cinema, multi-sports ground
Facilities : 🔌 🚻 launderette 🚮 🛒
Nearby : 🚣 🦌 amusement park, casino

Longitude : 4.1488
Latitude : 43.52272

For more information on visiting particular towns or regions, consult the relevant regional MICHELIN Green Guide. We also recommend you use the appropriate Michelin regional map to locate your selected campsite, to calculate distances and to work out the best route.

These symbols are used for a campsite that is exceptional in its category:

ᗰᗰᗰ … ᗰ *Particularly pleasant setting, quality and range of services available*

🦢 🦢 *Tranquil, isolated site – quiet site, particularly at night*

≪ ≪ *Exceptional view – interesting or panoramic view*

PORTIRAGNES-PLAGE

34420 – Michelin map **339** F9
▶ Paris 768 – Montpellier 72 – Carcassonne 99 – Nîmes 121

ᗰᗰ Les Sablons ᗩᒪ

Les Sablons

✆ 04 67 90 90 55. www.les-sablons.com

Address : Avenue des Mûriers, Plage Est (east beach) on the D37

Opening times : from mid April to end Sept.

15 ha (800 pitches) flat, grassy, sandy, pond

Tariff : (2015 price) 57 € ♦♦ ⛻ 🔲 ⚡ (10A) – Extra per person 12 € – Reservation fee 25 €

Rental rates : (2015 price) (from mid April to end Sept.) – 210 🛏 – 85 🛏. Per night from 30 to 305 € – Per week from 240 to 2,002 € – Reservation fee 25 €

🛱 Eurorelais sani-station – 🛒 ⚡ 16 €
Situated close to the beach and a lake.

Surroundings : 🗔 🌳 ⛰
Leisure activities : ☂ ✗ 🏛 🎣 🏃 🏄 ⛵ 🚲 ✀ 🏊 🎿 disco
Facilities : ⛟ 🔌 🚿 🚻 launderette 🚮 🛒 refrigerated food storage facilities
Nearby : 🚣 🚤

Longitude : 3.36469
Latitude : 43.2788

ᗰᗰ Les Mimosas ᗩᒪ

Les Mimosas

✆ 04 67 90 92 92. www.mimosas.com – limited spaces for one-night stay

Address : at Port Cassafières, off the D37

Opening times : from end May to beginning Sept.

7 ha (400 pitches) flat, grassy

Tariff : 47 € ♦♦ ⛻ 🔲 ⚡ (6A) – Extra per person 11 € – Reservation fee 36 €

Rental rates : (from end May to beginning Sept.) ⛟ (1 mobile home) – 217 🛏 – 4 🛏 – 12 canvas bungalows. Per night from 35 to 268 € – Per week from 245 to 1,876 € – Reservation fee 36 €

🛱 Raclet sani-station 2 €
The site has a large water and play park.

Surroundings : 🗔 🌳
Leisure activities : ☂ ✗ 🏛 🎣 🏃 🏄 ⛵ ⛴ 🚲 🏊 🎿 multi-sports ground
Facilities : ⛟ 🔌 🚿 – 17 private sanitary facilities (🚿 🚽 wc) 🚻 launderette 🚮 🛒 refrigerated food storage facilities
Nearby : 🐎 ⚓

Longitude : 3.37305
Latitude : 43.2915

▲▲ L'Émeraude

𝒫 04 67 90 93 76. www.campinglemeraude.com

Address : located 1km north, follow the signs for Portiragnes

Opening times : from mid May to beginning Sept.

4.2 ha (280 pitches) flat, grassy, sandy

Tariff : (2015 price) ♣ 8€ 🚗 3€ 🔲 45€ – (½) (5A) 5€ – Reservation fee 25€

Rental rates : (2015 price) (from mid May to beginning Sept.) ⚡ – 170 🚐. Per night from 48 to 70€ – Per week from 210 to 1,136€ – Reservation fee 25€

The site has a pleasant water park.

Surroundings : ♡♡	
Leisure activities : ♥ ✗ 🏠 ⊙ 🏊 🛶 ⛵ multi-sports ground	**G P S** Longitude : 3.36199 Latitude : 43.28766
Facilities : 🚿 🌡 ⚑ 🅿 ▣ 🔥 – refrigerated food storage facilities	
Nearby : 🐎	

The prices listed were supplied by the campsite owners in 2015 (if prices were not available, those from the previous year are given). The fees should be regarded as basic charges and may fluctuate with inflation.

QUILLAN

11500 – Michelin map **344** E5 – pop. 3 352 – alt. 291

▶ Paris 797 – Andorra-la-Vella 113 – Ax-les-Thermes 55 – Carcassonne 52

▲▲ Village Vacances Domaine de l'Espinet
(rental of studios and maisonnettes only)

𝒫 04 68 20 88 88. www.lespinet.com

Address : located 1km north along the D 118

Opening times : permanent

25 ha flat, pond

Rental rates : (2015 price) ♿ Ⓟ – 24 studios. Per week from 448 to 2,135€

This is an upmarket, well-appointed holiday village.

Surroundings : ⚲ ≤ ♀	
Leisure activities : ♥ ✗ 🏠 🏓 ♪♪ ⚓ hammam, jacuzzi 🏊 ✗ ▣ ⛲ spa centre	**G P S** Longitude : 2.19776 Latitude : 42.89268
Facilities : 🚿 ⚑ launderette	

▲ Municipal la Sapinette

𝒫 04 68 20 13 52. www.villedequillan.fr

Address : 21 avenue René Delpech (0.8km west along the D 79, follow the signs for Ginoles)

Opening times : from beginning April to end Oct.

1.8 ha (90 pitches) terraced, relatively flat, flat, grassy

Tariff : (2015 price) 14€ ♣♣ 🚗 ▣ (½) (16A) – Extra per person 5.80€

Rental rates : (2015 price) (from beginning April to end Oct.) ⚡ – 26 🚐 – 26 🏠. Per night from 35€ – Per week from 250 to 730€

🚉 local sani-station 4€ – 6 ▣ 10€ – 🔌 (½)13€

The pitches are arranged on terraces with a modicum of shade.

Surroundings : ⚲ ≤ ♀	
Leisure activities : 🏠 🛶 ▣	**G P S** Longitude : 2.18445 Latitude : 42.87495
Facilities : 🚿 ⚑ 🅿 🌡 ⚑	

REMOULINS

30210 – Michelin map **339** M5 – pop. 2 405 – alt. 27

▶ Paris 685 – Alès 50 – Arles 37 – Avignon 23

▲▲ La Sousta 🚹

𝒫 04 66 37 12 80. www.lasousta.com

Address : avenue du Pont du Gard (situated 2km to the northwest, follow the signs for Le Pont du Gard, right bank)

Opening times : from beginning March to end Oct.

14 ha (300 pitches) undulating, relatively flat, flat, grassy, sandy

Tariff : 29.90€ ♣♣ 🚗 ▣ (½) (6A) – Extra per person 9€ – Reservation fee 15€

Rental rates : (from beginning March to end Oct.) – 60 🚐 – 4 🏠. Per night from 65 to 85€ – Per week from 252 to 875€ – Reservation fee 15€

🚉 local sani-station 2€

In a pleasant wooded setting beside the Gardon river, on the right bank near the Pont du Gard.

Surroundings : ⚲ ♨♨♨	
Leisure activities : ♥ ✗ ⊙ 🏓 🏊 🚲 ✗ 🛶	**G P S** Longitude : 4.54 Latitude : 43.94
Facilities : 🚿 🌡 🔲 ⚑ 🌡 launderette 🔥 ⚑	

▲ FranceLoc Domaine de La Soubeyranne 🚹

𝒫 04 66 37 03 21. www.soubeyranne.com

Address : 1110 route de Beaucaire (2.5km south along the N 86 and D 986, right bank)

Opening times : from mid April to mid Sept.

4 ha (200 pitches) flat, grassy, stony

Tariff : (2015 price) 38€ ♣♣ 🚗 ▣ (½) (6A) – Extra per person 7€ – Reservation fee 27€

The numerous mobile homes are well laid out and there's a very well equipped children's playground.

Surroundings : ⚲ 🏠 ♡♡	
Leisure activities : ♥ ✗ ⊙ 🏓 🏊 ✗ ⛲ ▣ 🛶 multi-sports ground	**G P S** Longitude : 4.56236 Latitude : 43.93031
Facilities : 🚿 🌡 launderette ⚑	

ROCLES

48300 – Michelin map **330** K6 – pop. 209 – alt. 1 085

▶ Paris 581 – Grandrieu 20 – Langogne 8 – Mende 44

▲ Rondin des Bois

𝒫 04 66 69 50 46. www.camping-rondin.com – alt. 1 000

Address : at Palhere (3km north following signs for Bessettes and take road for Vaysset to the right.)

Opening times : from beginning May to end Sept.

2 ha (78 pitches) terraced, relatively flat, flat, stony, rocks

Tariff : 18.50€ ♣♣ 🚗 ▣ (½) (10A) – Extra per person 4.80€ – Reservation fee 10€

Rental rates : (from beginning April to end Oct.) – 6 🚐 – 8 🏠. Per night from 48 to 95€ – Per week from 295 to 665€ – Reservation fee 10€

🚉 local sani-station – 10 ▣ 18.50€

Surroundings : ⚲ ≤ 🏠 ♀	
Leisure activities : ♥ ✗ 🏠 🏓 ⛷ ♪ forest trail	**G P S** Longitude : 3.78105 Latitude : 44.73814
Facilities : 🚿 🌡 launderette ⚑	
Nearby : 🚲 ♀	

ROQUEFEUIL

11340 – Michelin map **344** C6 – pop. 276 – alt. 900
▶ Paris 813 – Montpellier 226 – Carcassonne 78

▲▲ La Mare aux Fées

✆ 0468311137. www.pyrenees-camping.com

Address : rue de l'Église (in the village)

Opening times : from beginning Feb. to end Oct.

0.5 ha (23 pitches) terrace, flat, grassy

Tariff : 16€ ♣♣ ⬅ 🔲 🔌 (16A) – Extra per person 5€

Rental rates : (from beginning Feb. to end Oct.) ♿ (1 chalet) – 2 🛖 – 6 🏠. Per night from 65 to 100€ – Per week from 360 to 600€ – Reservation fee 9€

🚰 local sani-station 4€ – 11 🔲 19€

A well-kept site near the church bell tower.

Surroundings : 🌳 🔲 🎋		
Leisure activities : ✗ 🚲 🏊 (small swimming pool)	**G**	Longitude : 1.9952
Facilities : ♿ 🚰 🍴 🛁 🗑 🚿 🍴 🚰 📷	**P**	Latitude : 42.8193
Nearby : 🍴	**S**	

ROQUEFORT-DES-CORBIÈRES

11540 – Michelin map **344** I5 – pop. 947 – alt. 50
▶ Paris 813 – Montpellier 118 – Carcassonne 78 – Perpignan 45

▲ Gîtes La Capelle (rental of gîtes only)

✆ 0619509526. http://gitelacapelle.com

Address : 4 rue la Capelle (in the village)

Opening times : from end March to mid Dec.

0.3 ha flat

Rental rates : ⓟ – 31 🛏 – 13 gîtes. Per night from 90€ – Per week from 270 to 730€

A small group of 'semi-detached' gîtes located beside a swimming pool.

Surroundings : 🌳 🎋		
Leisure activities : 🏠 🏊	**G**	Longitude : 2.95345
Facilities : 🗑 🍴 🍴 📷	**P**	Latitude : 42.9897
	S	

There are several different types of sani-station ('borne' in French) – sanitation points providing fresh water and disposal points for grey water. See page 12 for further details.

LA ROQUE-SUR-CÈZE

30200 – Michelin map **339** M3 – pop. 173 – alt. 90
▶ Paris 663 – Alès 53 – Bagnols-sur-Cèze 13 – Bourg-St-Andéol 35

▲▲ Les Cascades

✆ 0466827297. www.campinglescascades.com

Address : route de Donnat (600m south along the D 166, direct access to the Cèze river)

Opening times : from beginning April to beginning Oct.

5 ha (118 pitches) terraced, flat and relatively flat, grassy

Tariff : 24€ ♣♣ ⬅ 🔲 🔌 (10A) – Extra per person 4.50€ – Reservation fee 15€

Rental rates : (from beginning April to beginning Oct.) – 53 🛖. Per night from 35 to 145€ – Per week from 171 to 1,015€ – Reservation fee 15€

🚰 local sani-station

The pitches arranged on terraces with lots of shade run down to a rocky river with a beach and a bathing area.

Surroundings : 🌳 🔲 🎋		
Leisure activities : 🍴 ✗ 🏊 🎯 🏊 🚣 (beach) 🛶 multi-sports ground	**G**	Longitude : 4.52
Facilities : ♿ 🚰 🍴 🛁 🗑 🚿 🍴 📷 🚰	**P**	Latitude : 44.19
	S	

LE ROZIER

48150 – Michelin map **330** H9 – pop. 145 – alt. 400
▶ Paris 632 – Florac 57 – Mende 63 – Millau 23

▲▲▲ Les Prades ♣♣

Les Prades

✆ 0565626209. www. campinglesprades.com

✉ 12720 Peyreleau

Address : on the D187 towards Le Rozier-Peyreleau, between the hamlets of La Cresse and Le Peyreleau

Opening times : from beginning May to mid Sept.

3.5 ha (150 pitches)

Tariff : 35€ ♣♣ ⬅ 🔲 🔌 (6A) – Extra per person 8€ – Reservation fee 15€

Rental rates : (from beginning May to mid Sept.) – 30 🛖 – 3 🛏 – 2 canvas bungalows. Per night from 40 to 60€ – Per week from 200 to 720€ – Reservation fee 15€

🚰 local sani-station – 6 🔲 18€

Below the road, some pitches beside the Tarn river with good sanitary facilities and an attractive small water park.

Surroundings : 🎋		
Leisure activities : 🍴 ✗ 🎯 🚣 🏊 🎣 🏊 🚣 🛶 🚲	**G**	Longitude : 3.17332
Facilities : ♿ 🚰 🍴 🛁 🚿 🍴 📷 🚰 🚰	**P**	Latitude : 44.1996
	S	

▲▲▲ Le St Pal et son Parc Longue Lègue

✆ 0565626446. www.campingsaintpal.com ✉ 12720 Mostuéjouls

Address : at La Muse-St Pal, route des Gorges du Tarn (located 1km northwest along the D 907, follow the signs for Millau; beside the Tarn)

Opening times : from beginning June to end Aug.

2 ha (105 pitches) flat, grassy

Tariff : 27.50€ ♣♣ ⬅ 🔲 🔌 (10A) – Extra per person 6€ – Reservation fee 18€

Rental rates : (from beginning June to end Aug.) – 21 🛖 – 7 canvas bungalows. Per night from 40 to 106€ – Per week from 217 to 742€ – Reservation fee 18€

Below the road, pitches partly alongside the Tarn river with a good standard of sanitary facilities.

Surroundings : 🎋 🏔		
Leisure activities : 🍴 ✗ 🏠 🏊 🛶 🚲	**G**	Longitude : 3.19822
Facilities : ♿ 🚰 🛁 🍴 launderette 🚰	**P**	Latitude : 44.19639
	S	

Do not confuse:

△ *to* ▲▲▲ : MICHELIN *classification with*

★ *to* ★★★★★ : *official classification*

ST-ALBAN-SUR-LIMAGNOLE

48120 – Michelin map **330** I6 – pop. 1 519 – alt. 950
▶ Paris 558 – Montpellier 214 – Mende 39 – Le Puy-en-Velay 76

⚑ Le Galier

☎ 04 66 31 58 80. www.campinglegalier.fr

Address : route de St-Chély-d'Apcher

Opening times : from beginning March to end Sept.

12 ha/3.5 for camping (77 pitches) terraced, flat, grassy, wood

Tariff : (2015 price) 19.40€ ✶✶ ⛟ 🅴 🅰 (6A) – Extra per person 4.60€ – Reservation fee 10€

Rental rates : (2015 price) (from beginning May to mid Sept.) 🚌 – 11 🛖. Per night from 100 to 140€ – Per week from 180 to 595€ – Reservation fee 25€

🚮 local sani-station

Some pitches are surrounded by trees and shrubs; the Limagnole river runs through the site.

Surroundings : 🌿 ⚲
Facilities : ♿ ⌒ 🏭 ♒

G P S Longitude : 3.37167
Latitude : 44.7752

ST-ANDRÉ-DE-SANGONIS

34725 – Michelin map **339** G7 – pop. 5 175 – alt. 65
▶ Paris 715 – Béziers 54 – Clermont-l'Hérault 8 – Gignac 5

⚑ Le Septimanien

☎ 04 67 57 84 23. www.camping-leseptimanien.com

Address : route de Cambous (located 1km southwest along the D 4, follow the signs for Brignac; beside a stream)

Opening times : from beginning May to mid Sept.

2.6 ha (86 pitches) terraced, flat, stony

Tariff : (2015 price) 26.50€ ✶✶ ⛟ 🅴 🅰 (10A) – Extra per person 4.60€ – Reservation fee 15€

Rental rates : (2015 price) (from beginning May to mid Sept.) – 10 🛖 – 9 🛖. Per week from 290 to 580€ – Reservation fee 15€

This is a peaceful, family-friendly site.

Surroundings : 🌿 ⛱ ⚲⚲
Leisure activities : ☂ ⚓ ⚒
Facilities : ♿ ⌒ ♒ 🗄

G P S Longitude : 3.49508
Latitude : 43.64066

Using the traditional Michelin classification method, the guide provides you with an easy, speedy reference for assessing the category of each site: 1 to 5 tents (see page 10).

ST-BAUZILE

48000 – Michelin map **330** J8 – pop. 579 – alt. 750
▶ Paris 598 – Chanac 19 – Florac 29 – Marvejols 30

⚑ Municipal les Berges de Bramont

☎ 04 66 47 05 97. www.saint-bauzile.fr – 🏠

Address : at Rouffiac (located 1.5km southwest along the D 41, N 106, follow the signs for Mende, near the Bramont river and the sports centre)

Opening times : from beginning July to mid Sept.

1.5 ha (50 pitches)

Tariff : 14.50€ ✶✶ ⛟ 🅴 🅰 (45A) – Extra per person 5€

Rental rates : (from beginning July to mid Sept.) – 4 🛖. Per week from 350€

In a leafy setting, with good-quality wooden chalets.

🚮 AireService sani-station 2.50€

Surroundings : ⛰ ⚲
Leisure activities : 🎮 ⚓
Facilities : ♿ 🛁 🏖 ♒ 🍴
Nearby : ☂ ✗ 🚲 ✂

G P S Longitude : 3.49428
Latitude : 44.47666

ST-CYPRIEN-PLAGE

66750 – Michelin map **344** J7
▶ Paris 870 – Montpellier 173 – Perpignan 21 – Carcassonne 135

⚑ Cala Gogo 👥

☎ 04 68 21 07 12. www.camping-le-calagogo.fr

Address : avenue Armand Lanoux – Les Capellans (4km to the south; beside the beach)

Opening times : from beginning May to end Sept.

11 ha (649 pitches) flat, grassy, stony, sandy

Tariff : 47.10€ ✶✶ ⛟ 🅴 🅰 (6A) – Extra per person 11.70€ – Reservation fee 25€

Rental rates : (from beginning May to end Sept.) ♿ (1 mobile home) – 117 🛖. Per night from 27 to 199€ – Per week from 189 to 1,393€ – Reservation fee 25€

🚮 local sani-station

The new rental accommodation is good quality, with a landscaped water park and direct access to the beach.

Surroundings : 🏖 ⚲ ⚠
Leisure activities : ☂ ✗ 🎮 🏊 ⚒ ✂ ⚓ disco
Facilities : ♿ ⌒ 🏭 🏖 ♒ 🍴 launderette 🛒 🏪

G P S Longitude : 3.03789
Latitude : 42.59998

This guide is not intended as a list of all the camping sites in France; its aim is to provide a selection of the best sites in each category.

ST-GENIS-DES-FONTAINES

66740 – Michelin map **344** I7 – pop. 2 792 – alt. 63
▶ Paris 878 – Argelès-sur-Mer 10 – Le Boulou 10 – Collioure 17

⚑ La Pinède

☎ 04 68 89 75 29. www.campinglapinede66.fr

Address : avenue des Albères (south of the town along the D 2)

Opening times : from end May to end Aug.

1 ha (71 pitches) flat, grassy

Tariff : (2015 price) 31.60€ ✶✶ ⛟ 🅴 🅰 (10A) – Extra per person 6.50€ – Reservation fee 19€

Rental rates : (from mid May to end Aug.) 🚌 – 10 🛖. Per night from 58 to 80€ – Per week from 400 to 550€ – Reservation fee 19€

Attractively shaded in places by pine trees; some of the rental mobile homes are a little old.

Surroundings : ⚲⚲
Leisure activities : ⚓
Facilities : ♿ ⌒ 🛁 🏖 🗄
Nearby : ✂

G P S Longitude : 2.9245
Latitude : 42.54093

ST-GEORGES-DE-LÉVÉJAC

48500 – Michelin map **330** H9 – pop. 259 – alt. 900
▶ Paris 603 – Florac 53 – Mende 45 – Millau 49

⚐ Cassaduc

☎ 04 66 48 85 80. www.camping-cassaduc.com

Address : route du Point Sublime (1.4km southeast)

Opening times : from beginning July to end Aug.

2.2 ha (75 pitches) terraced, relatively flat, flat, grassy, stony

Tariff : 20€ ✹✹ ⇌ 🅴 🄹 (16A) – Extra per person 6€

Rental rates : (from mid June to mid Sept.) – 2 🛏. Per night from 55 to 80€ – Per week from 350 to 495€

🛏 local sani-station 5€ – 6 🄴 16€

Situated 500m from the Point Sublime (elevated view point); the pitches are on terraces in the shade of a pretty pine wood.

Surroundings : ⛰ ◁ ♘
Leisure activities : 🎦 ≋ jacuzzi
Facilities : 🚿 ⚲ 🗑 🚾 🚻 🏐
Nearby : 🍷 🍴

G P S Longitude : 3.24282
Latitude : 44.31532

ST-GERMAIN-DU-TEIL

48340 – Michelin map **330** H8 – pop. 810 – alt. 760
▶ Paris 601 – Montpellier 166 – Mende 46 – Millau 58

⚑ Les Chalets du Plan d'Eau de Booz
(rental of chalets only)

☎ 04 66 48 48 48. www.lozere-resa.com

Address : near Booz lake (8km southeast along the D 52, turn onto the D 809, after the motorway)

5 ha flat, grassy, lake

Rentals : ♿ (1 chalet) – 43 🛖.

Wooden chalets in a leafy setting. Half board available.

Surroundings : ♘
Leisure activities : 🍷 🍴 🎦 ⛹ jacuzzi
⚓ ⤢ ⛵ pedalos ⚡
Facilities : ⚲ 🏛 🚻 launderette
Nearby : 🚵 forest trail

G P S Longitude : 3.19764
Latitude : 44.45787

ST-HIPPOLYTE-DU-FORT

30170 – Michelin map **339** I5 – pop. 3 803 – alt. 165
▶ Paris 703 – Alès 35 – Anduze 22 – Nîmes 48

⚑ Graniers

☎ 04 66 25 19 24. www.campingdegraniers.com

Address : head 4km northeast following signs for Uzès then take D 133, follow the signs for Monoblet and take the road to the right; beside a stream

Opening times : from beginning March to end Oct.

2 ha (50 pitches) terraced, relatively flat, wood, grassy

Tariff : 26.88€ ✹✹ ⇌ 🅴 🄹 (6A) – Extra per person 7€ – Reservation fee 8€

Rental rates : (from mid March to end Oct.) ⚡ – 6 🛏 – 3 canvas bungalows. Per night from 30 to 99€ – Per week from 180 to 690 € – Reservation fee 8€

This is a shady site with a range of both old and new rental accommodation.

Surroundings : ⛰ ♘
Leisure activities : 🍷 🍴 ⚓ 🚲 ⛵
Facilities : ♿ ⚲ 🚻 🏐 🌡

G P S Longitude : 3.88722
Latitude : 43.98084

ST-JEAN-DE-CEYRARGUES

30360 – Michelin map **339** K4 – pop. 158 – alt. 180
▶ Paris 700 – Alès 18 – Nîmes 33 – Uzès 21

⚑ Les Vistes

☎ 04 66 83 28 09. www.lesvistes.com

Address : 1 route des Vistes (500m south along the D 7)

6 ha/3 for camping (52 pitches) open site, relatively flat, flat, grassy, stony

Rentals : ♿ (1 chalet) – 12 🛖 – 5 canvas bungalows.

Situated in an attractive, panoramic location.

Surroundings : ◁ Mt Aigoual ♘
Leisure activities : 🎦 ⚓ ⛵
Facilities : ♿ ⚲ 🅿 ⛹ 🚻 🏐 refrigerators

G P S Longitude : 4.23016
Latitude : 44.04734

To make the best possible use of this guide, please read pages 2–15 carefully.

ST-JEAN-DU-GARD

30270 – Michelin map **339** I4 – pop. 2 687 – alt. 183
▶ Paris 675 – Alès 28 – Florac 54 – Lodève 91

⚑ Mas de la Cam ♟♟

☎ 04 66 85 12 02. http://www.camping-cevennes.info/

Address : route de Saint-André-de-Valborgne (3km northwest along the D 907; beside the Gardon de St-Jean)

Opening times : from end April to end Sept.

6 ha (200 pitches) terraced, relatively flat, grassy

Tariff : (2015 price) 39.90€ ✹✹ ⇌ 🅴 🄹 (10A) – Extra per person 9€ – Reservation fee 17€

Rental rates : (2015 price) (from end April to end Sept.) ⚡ – 6 gîtes. Per night from 55 to 91€ – Per week from 385 to 635€ – Reservation fee 17€

There's an attractive children's play area.

Surroundings : ⛰ ◁ 🛥 ♘
Leisure activities : 🍷 🍴 🎦 🎣 ⛹ ⚓ ⚒ ⛵
≋ ⚓ multi-sports ground
Facilities : ♿ ⚲ ⛹ 🏐 ⚓ ⚓

G P S Longitude : 3.85319
Latitude : 44.1123

⚑ Les Sources

☎ 04 66 85 38 03. www.camping-des-sources.fr

Address : route de Mialet (located 1km northeast along the D 983 and D 50)

Opening times : from mid March to end Sept.

3 ha (92 pitches) terraced, relatively flat, grassy

Tariff : 29€ ✹✹ ⇌ 🅴 🄹 (10A) – Extra per person 4.70€ – Reservation fee 15€

Rental rates : (from mid March to end Nov.) – 3 🛏 – 15 🛖 – 3 canvas bungalows. Per night from 50 to 98€ – Per week from 350 to 686€ – Reservation fee 20€

🛏 local sani-station 4€ – 12 🄴 16.50€ – 🚐 🄹 11.50€

The site enjoys a family atmosphere and has pitches that are well-shaded.

Surroundings : ⛰ ◁ 🛥 ♘
Leisure activities : 🍷 🍴 🎦 ⚓ ⛵
Facilities : ♿ ⚲ 🔗 🏛 ⛹ ⚓ 🚻
launderette ⚓

G P S Longitude : 3.89258
Latitude : 44.11393

⚠ La Forêt

🔗 04 66 85 37 00. www.campingalaforet.com

Address : route de Falguières (situated 2km north along the D 983, follow the signs for St-Étienne-Vallée-Française then continue 2km along the D 333)

Opening times : from mid May to mid Sept.

3 ha (65 pitches) terraced, flat, grassy, stony

Tariff : 34.80€ ✶✶ ⇌ 🅴 (🗲) (10A) – Extra per person 7.50€ – Reservation fee 5€

Rental rates : (from mid May to mid Sept.) 🦟 – 3 🏠. Per week from 300 to 600€ – Reservation fee 5€

At the edge of a spacious pine wood.

Surroundings : 🦢 ⟨ 🗔 ♨		
Leisure activities : 🛶 🏊		G P S	Longitude : 3.89072
Facilities : ⚬━ 🛁 🚿 🖫 🎣 refrigerators			Latitude : 44.12948

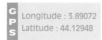

ST-PAUL-LE-FROID

48600 – Michelin map **330** J6 – pop. 147 – alt. 1 302 – Winter sports : 🎿
▶ Paris 582 – Montpellier 237 – Mende 54 – Le Puy-en-Velay 61

🏘 Village Vacances les Baraques des Bouviers
(rental of chalets, including Nordic-style chalets, only)

🔗 04 66 48 48 48. www.lesbouviers.com – alt. 1 418

Address : la Baraque des Bouviers (8.5km southeast along the D 58 and D 5, follow the signs for St-Alban-sur-Limagnole)

20 ha/2 for camping open site, terraced
Rentals : 🦽 – 14 🏠.

The chalets are well-spaced out across the Plateau de La Margeride, at the foot of cross-country ski pistes and snowshoe hiking trails.

Surroundings : 🦢 ⟨ ♨♨		
Leisure activities : 🏛		G P S	Longitude : 3.50574
Facilities : ⚬━ 🏚 🚿 🖫			Latitude : 44.76617
Nearby : 🍴 ✗ 🚲 climbing			

ST-VICTOR-DE-MALCAP

30500 – Michelin map **339** K3 – pop. 683 – alt. 140
▶ Paris 680 – Alès 23 – Barjac 15 – La Grand-Combe 25

🏘 Domaine de Labeiller 👥

🔗 04 66 24 15 27. www.labeiller.fr

Address : 1701 route de Barjac (located 1km southeast, access via the D 51, follow the signs for St-Jean-de-Maruéjols and take road to the left)

Opening times : from mid May to end Aug.

3 ha (132 pitches) terraced, flat, grassy, stony

Tariff : (2015 price) 37€ ✶✶ ⇌ 🅴 (🗲) (6A) – Extra per person 7€ – Reservation fee 15€

Rental rates : (2015 price) (from mid May to end Aug.) – 20 🚐. Per week from 250 to 910€ – Reservation fee 15€

Situated in a pleasant oak wood with an attractive swimming area.

Surroundings : 🦢 🗔 ♨♨		
Leisure activities : 🍴 ✗ 🛖 🧗 🛶 🏊 △ 🦢		G P S	Longitude : 4.22727
Facilities : 🦽 ⚬━ 🛁 🚿 🖫 launderette			Latitude : 44.24154
Nearby : 🍴			

STE-ÉNIMIE

48210 – Michelin map **330** I8 – pop. 525 – alt. 470
▶ Paris 612 – Florac 27 – Mende 28 – Meyrueis 30

🏘 Le Couderc

🔗 04 66 48 50 53. www.campingcouderc.fr

Address : route de Millau (situated 2km southwest along the D 907bis; beside the Tarn river)

Opening times : from beginning April to end Sept.

2.5 ha (130 pitches) terraced, flat, grassy, stony

Tariff : 29€ ✶✶ ⇌ 🅴 (🗲) (16A) – Extra per person 5€ – Reservation fee 15€

Rental rates : (from beginning April to end Sept.) – 7 🚐. Per night from 45 to 100€ – Per week from 250 to 695€ – Reservation fee 15€

🚐 Eurorelais sani-station 5€ – 40 🅴 29€

Situated below the road, with very well shaded pitches beside the Tarn river.

Surroundings : ♨♨ △		
Leisure activities : 🍴 🏊 🦢 🦅		G P S	Longitude : 3.39917
Facilities : 🦽 ⚬━ 🏚 🚿 🖫 launderette			Latitude : 44.35194

⚠ Yelloh! Village Nature et Rivière

🔗 04 66 48 57 36. www.camping-les-fayards.com

Address : route de Millau (3km southwest along the D 907bis; beside the Tarn river)

Opening times : from end April to beginning Sept.

2 ha (77 pitches) terraced, flat, grassy, stony

Tariff : 33€ ✶✶ ⇌ 🅴 (🗲) (16A) – Extra per person 7€

Rental rates : (from end April to beginning Sept.) 🦟 – 2 'gypsy' caravans – 15 🚐 – 4 🏠. Per night from 35 to 137€ – Per week from 245 to 959€

Situated below the road, with pitches on terraces beside the Tarn river.

Surroundings : 🦢 🗔 ♨♨		
Leisure activities : 🍴 🛶 🏊 🦢 🦅		G P S	Longitude : 3.39504
Facilities : 🦽 ⚬━ 🛁 🚿 launderette			Latitude : 44.34583

⚠ Le Site Locanoë

🔗 04 66 48 58 08. www.gorges-du-tarn.fr

Address : Castelbouc (7km southeast along the D 907b, follow the signs for Ispagnac then continue 500m to the right following signs for Castelbouc; beside the Tarn river)

Opening times : from mid April to mid Sept.

1 ha (60 pitches) open site, relatively flat, flat, grassy

Tariff : (2015 price) 18€ ✶✶ ⇌ 🅴 (🗲) (5A) – Extra per person 4€

Rental rates : (2015 price) (from mid May to mid Sept.) – 10 🚐 – 2 yurts – 2 tipis. Per week from 250 to 560€

Bordered by the river and opposite a small waterfall.

Surroundings : 🦢 🗔 ♨♨ △		
Leisure activities : 🦢 🦅		G P S	Longitude : 3.46571
Facilities : 🦽 ⚬━ 🚿 🖫			Latitude : 44.34423

*The classification (1 to 5 tents, **black** or red) that we award to selected sites in this guide is our own system. It should not be confused with the classification (1 to 5 stars) of official organisations.*

STE-MARIE

66470 – Michelin map **344** J6 – pop. 4 641 – alt. 4
▶ Paris 845 – Argelès-sur-Mer 24 – Le Boulou 37 – Perpignan 14

🏕 Le Palais de la Mer ♨♦

🖉 04 68 73 07 94. www.palaisdelamer.com

Address : avenue de Las Illes (600m north of the resort, 150m from the beach – direct access)

8 ha/3 for camping (181 pitches) flat, sandy

In a shaded setting, with laurel trees lining the paths.

Surroundings : 🗺 ♀♀		
Leisure activities : 🍴✕ 🎱nighttime ⚡🛶 hammam, jacuzzi 🛝 🎿 🏊 wildlife park	**G** **P** **S**	Longitude : 3.03307 Latitude : 42.74045
Facilities : 🚿 ⚬ᴙ ⛺ 🗑 ⚱ ⛲ 🚰 launderette 🗑 🧺		

🏕 Camp'Atlantique La Pergola

🖉 02 51 20 41 94. www.campinglapergola.com

Address : 21 avenue Frédéric Mistral (500m from the beach)

Opening times : from beginning April to end Sept.

3.5 ha (181 pitches) flat, sandy

Tariff : (2015 price) 38€ ♦♦ ⚓ 🔲 ⚡ (10A) – Extra per person 9€ – Reservation fee 25€

Rental rates : (2015 price) (from beginning April to end Sept.) – 120 🚐. Per night from 29 to 181€ – Per week from 203 to 1,267€ – Reservation fee 25€

Surroundings : ♀♀		
Leisure activities : ✕ 🏠 🛝 🏊	**G** **P** **S**	Longitude : 3.03315 Latitude : 42.72672
Facilities : 🚿 ⚬ᴙ ⛺ ⚱ 🚰 launderette 🧺 refrigerators		
Nearby : 🍴		

The prices listed were supplied by the campsite owners in 2015 (if prices were not available, those from the previous year are given). The fees should be regarded as basic charges and may fluctuate with inflation.

SÉRIGNAN

34410 – Michelin map **339** E9 – pop. 6 631 – alt. 7
▶ Paris 765 – Agde 22 – Béziers 11 – Narbonne 34

🏕 FranceLoc Le Domaine Les Vignes d'Or ♨♦
(rental of mobile homes and chalets only)

🖉 04 67 32 37 18. www.vignesdor.com

Address : chemin de l'Hermitage (3.5km to the south, take the side road located behind the Citroën garage)

Opening times : from beginning April to mid Sept.

4 ha (227 pitches) flat, grassy, stony

Rental rates : (2015 price) 🚹 (2 mobile homes) – 250 🚐 – 250 🏠. Per night from 20 to 188€ – Per week from 140 to 1,267€ – Reservation fee 27€

Surroundings : 🌊 🗺 ♀♀		
Leisure activities : 🍴✕ 🎱⚡🛶 🛝 🔲 🏊 🏊 multi-sports ground	**G** **P** **S**	Longitude : 3.2757 Latitude : 43.2593
Facilities : 🚿 ⚬ᴙ ⛺ 🔲 🧺		
Nearby : 🍴 🍴 🐎		

🏕 Le Paradis

🖉 04 67 32 24 03. www.camping-leparadis.com 🚲

Address : route de Valras-Plage (located 1.5km to the south)

Opening times : from beginning April to end Sept.

2.2 ha (129 pitches) flat, grassy

Tariff : (2015 price) 38€ ♦♦ ⚓ 🔲 ⚡ (10A) – Extra per person 6.50€ – Reservation fee 18€

Rental rates : (2015 price) (from beginning April to end Sept.) 🚲 – 20 🚐. Per night from 45€ – Per week from 170 to 650€ – Reservation fee 18€

🚉 local sani-station

A pleasant setting with flowers and large pitches.

Surroundings : 🗺 ♀♀		
Leisure activities : ✕ 🏠 🛝 🏊	**G** **P** **S**	Longitude : 3.28628 Latitude : 43.26829
Facilities : 🚿 ⚬ᴙ 🗄 ⚱ 🚰 launderette 🧺		
Nearby : 🛒		

🏕 Le Mas des Lavandes – (rental of mobile homes only)

🖉 04 67 39 75 88. www.masdeslavandes.fr

Address : chemin de la mer (D 19 follow the signs for Valras-Plage – from the A9 take exit Béziers-est)

Opening times : permanent

3.8 ha flat

Rental rates : 🚹 (1 mobile home) – 197 🚐. Per night from 40 to 160€ – Per week from 280 to 1,100 € – Reservation fee 22€

Luxury mobile homes, but choose those further away from the road in preference.

Surroundings : 🗺 ♀♀		
Leisure activities : 🍴✕ 🏠 ⚡🛶 🎿 🏊 🏊	**G** **P** **S**	Longitude : 3.2831 Latitude : 43.25732
Facilities : 🚿 ⚬ᴙ 🚰 🔲 🧺		
Nearby : 🛒		

SÉRIGNAN-PLAGE

34410 – Michelin map **339** E9
▶ Paris 769 – Montpellier 73 – Carcassonne 100

🏕 Yelloh! Village Le Sérignan Plage ♨♦

Yelloh! Village Le Sérignan Plage

🖉 04 67 32 35 33. www.leserignanplage.com

Address : at L'Orpellière (beside the beach, direct access)

Opening times : from end April to end Sept.

20 ha (1200 pitches) flat, grassy, sandy

Tariff : 62€ ♦♦ ⚓ 🔲 ⚡ (10A) –

Rental rates : (from end April to end Sept.) 🚲 – 440 🚐 – 18 🏠 – 5 tent lodges. Per night from 39 to 325€ – Per week from 273 to 2,275€

🚉 local sani-station

Natural, sunny pitches, close to the marsh; luxury rental options with plenty of shade close to the beach.

Surroundings : 🌊 🗺 ♀♀ 🏔		
Leisure activities : 🍴✕ 🏠 🎱⚡🛶 jacuzzi 🛝🚲🏊 🔲 🏊 spa centre (naturist in mornings), disco, multi-sports ground	**G** **P** **S**	Longitude : 3.3213 Latitude : 43.26401
Facilities : 🚿 ⚬ᴙ ⚱ 🚰 launderette 🛒 🧺		
Nearby : 💧 🐎		

▲▲ Yelloh! Village Aloha ▲▲

📞 0467397130. www.alohacamping.com

Address : chemin des Dunes

Opening times : from beginning May to mid Sept.

9.5 ha (444 pitches) flat, grassy, sandy

Tariff : 60€ ✝✝ ⇦ 🔲 (10A) – Extra per person 9€
Rental rates : (from beginning May to mid Sept.) 🅿 – 196 🚐 –
12 🏠. Per night from 49 to 169€ – Per week from 343 to 1,183€
🚽 local sani-station

The site lies on both sides of a path leading to the beach, with rental accommodation in a landscaped setting.

Surroundings : 🏊 ⛰ 🏞️ ⛰
Leisure activities : 🍷 🍴 🎬 🎮 🏃 ⛳ jacuzzi
🛶 🚴 🎯 🏓 🏊 ⛰ multi-sports ground
Facilities : 🚿 🔌 🏕️ 🧺 launderette 🛒 🚲
Nearby : 🐎 🐴

		GPS
		Longitude : 3.33941
		Latitude : 43.26745

▲▲ Domaine de Beauséjour ▲▲

📞 0467395093. www.camping-beausejour.com

Address : beside the beach

10 ha/6 for camping (380 pitches) flat, grassy, sandy
Rentals : 84 🚐 – 6 🏠.

There's a very pleasant spa centre, open all year round.

Surroundings : 🏊 ⛰ 🏞️ ⛰
Leisure activities : 🍷 🍴 🌙 nighttime 🏃
♨️ hammam, jacuzzi 🛶 🚴 disco,
watersports centre, spa centre
Facilities : 🚿 🔌 🏕️ 🧺 launderette 🛒 🚲

		GPS
		Longitude : 3.33692
		Latitude : 43.26711

▲▲ Le Clos Virgile ▲▲

📞 0467322064. www.leclosvirgile.com

Address : 500m from the beach

Opening times : from beginning May to mid Sept.

5 ha (300 pitches) flat, grassy, sandy

Tariff : (2015 price) 43€ ✝✝ ⇦ 🔲 (10A) – Extra per person 8€ –
Reservation fee 25€
Rental rates : (2015 price) (from beginning May to mid Sept.)
🏊 – 90 🚐 – 18 🏠. Per night from 28 to 141€ – Per week
from 199 to 990€ – Reservation fee 25€
🚽 Eurorelais sani-station 5€ – 49 🔲 12€
Shaded pitches.

Surroundings : ⛰ 🏞️
Leisure activities : 🍷 🍴 🎬 🎮 🏃 jacuzzi
🛶 🎯 🏊 ⛰ multi-sports ground
Facilities : 🚿 🔌 🏕️ 🧺 🛒 🚲
Nearby : 🐎 🐴

		GPS
		Longitude : 3.33152
		Latitude : 43.27204

30250 – Michelin map **339** J6 – pop. 4 496 – alt. 34
▶ Paris 734 – Alès 44 – Montpellier 35 – Nîmes 29

▲▲ Les Castels Le Domaine de Massereau

📞 0466531120. www.massereau.com

Address : 1990 route d'Aubais (Les Hauteurs de Sommières)

Opening times : from beginning April to end Oct.

90 ha/7.7 for camping (120 pitches) relatively flat, flat, grassy, stony

Tariff : 🟉 21.55€ ⇦ 6.50€ 🔲 52€ – 🔌 (16A) 8.90€ c Reservation fee 26€

Rental rates : (from beginning April to end Oct.) 🚿 – 35 🚐 –
24 🏠. Per night from 56 to 144€ – Per week from 336 to 1,509€ –
Reservation fee 26€ 🚽 Eurorelais sani-station 2€

Luxury rental options, in the middle of a wine-growing area, crossed by a cycle trail (Sommières –Nîmes).

Surroundings : 🏊 ⛰ 🏞️
Leisure activities : 🍷 🍴 ♨️ hammam, jacuzzi
🛶 🚴 🎯 🏓 🏊 ⛰ fitness trail, forest trail,
zip wiring, multi-sports ground
Facilities : 🚿 🔌 🏕️ 🧺 launderette 🛒 🚲
Nearby : 🏊

		GPS
		Longitude : 4.09735
		Latitude : 43.76574

▲ Municipal de Garanel

📞 0466803349. camping.garanel@sommieres.fr

Address : chemin Princesse (In the town, near the Vidourle river)

Opening times : from beginning April to end Sept.

7 ha (60 pitches) flat, sandy, stony

Tariff : (2015 price) 17.89€ ✝✝ ⇦ 🔲 🔌 (8A) – Extra per person 3.50€

Very close to sports arena and the town centre.

Surroundings : ⛰ 🏞️
Facilities : 🚿 🔌 🏕️ 🛒
Nearby : 🏊 🍷 🍴 🎮 🏊

		GPS
		Longitude : 4.08703
		Latitude : 43.78738

34300 – Michelin map **339** F9
▶ Paris 761 – Montpellier 62 – Béziers 24 – Narbonne 54

▲▲ La Tama

📞 0467947946. www.camping-latama.com

Address : 4 rue du Commandant Malet

Opening times : from mid April to mid Sept.

10 ha (700 pitches) undulating, flat and relatively flat, grassy, sandy

Tariff : (2015 price) 35.60€ ✝✝ ⇦ 🔲 🔌 (10A) –
Extra per person 8.50€ – Reservation fee 20€
Rental rates : (2015 price) (from mid April to mid Sept.) 🚿 (2
chalets) 🏊 – 60 🏠 – 30 tent lodges. Per night from 33 to 126€ –
Per week from 231 to 882€ – Reservation fee 27€

A pleasant location beside the sea, sheltered by pine trees.

Surroundings : 🏞️ ⛰
Leisure activities : 🛶 multi-sports ground
Facilities : 🚿 🔌 🏕️ 🧺 launderette,
refrigerated food storage facilities
Nearby : 🏊 🍷 🍴 🚲 🐬

		GPS
		Longitude : 3.44249
		Latitude : 43.28821

66440 – Michelin map **344** I6
▶ Paris 853 – Montpellier 157 – Perpignan 20 – Carcassonne 119

▲▲ Sunêlia Les Tropiques ▲▲

📞 0468280509. www.
campinglestropiques.com

Address : boulevard de la Plage (500m from the beach)

Opening times : from beginning April to beginning Oct.

8 ha (450 pitches) flat, sandy, stony

Tariff : 55€ ✝✝ ⇦ 🔲 🔌 (10A) –
Extra per person 10.50€ – Reservation fee 35€

Sunêlia Les Tropiques

Rental rates : (from beginning April to end Sept.) ♿ (2 mobile homes) – 250 🚐 – 2 canvas bungalows – 2 tent lodges. Per night from 42 to 226 € – Per week from 294 to 1,582 € – Reservation fee 35 €

🚽 local sani-station – 🔌 🚿18 €

The pitches are shady and there's a pleasant spa centre.

Surroundings : 🏕 ⛰⛰
Leisure activities : 🍴 ✕ 🏛 🎣 🏊 🎱 🏓 hammam, jacuzzi 🚴 🎾 🏊 ⛷ disco, multi-sports ground, spa centre
Facilities : ♿ ⛽ 🚿 🍴 launderette 🧺 🚿
Nearby : 🐴 🎣

Longitude : 3.02972
Latitude : 42.7675

⛰ Mar I Sol 🛖

📞 04 68 28 04 07. www.camping-marisol.com – limited spaces for one-night stay

Address : boulevard de la Plage (150m from the beach – direct access)

Opening times : from mid April to beginning Sept.

7 ha (377 pitches) flat, grassy, sandy

Tariff : 66 € 🚶🚶 🚗 🔌 🔋 (10A) – Extra per person 12 € – Reservation fee 49.50 €

Rental rates : (from end March to beginning Sept.) – 192 🚐 – 4 🛖. Per night from 29 to 398 € – Per week from 203 to 2,786 € – Reservation fee 49.50 €

A real village club with lots of activities and boasting a large water park.

Surroundings : 🏕 ⛰
Leisure activities : 🍴 ✕ 🏛 🎣 🏊 🎱 🏓 hammam, jacuzzi 🚴 🎾 🏊 ⛷ disco, multi-sports ground
Facilities : ♿ ⛽ 🚿 🍴 launderette 🧺 🚿
Nearby : 🎣

Longitude : 3.03327
Latitude : 42.76746

⛰ Le Calypso 🛖

📞 04 68 28 09 47. www.camping-calypso.com – limited spaces for one-night stay

Address : boulevard de la Plage

6 ha (308 pitches) flat, sandy, stony

Rentals : 80 🚐 – 28 🛖.

A pretty play and paddling pool area and private sanitary facilities for some pitches.

Surroundings : 🏕 ⛰⛰
Leisure activities : 🍴 ✕ 🏛 🎣 🏊 jacuzzi 🚴 🏊 ⛷ multi-sports ground
Facilities : ♿ ⛽ 🚿 – 9 private sanitary facilities (🚿 🚿 🚽 wc) 🍴 launderette 🧺 🚿 refrigerators
Nearby : 🎣 🐴

Longitude : 3.03043
Latitude : 42.77128

⛰ Homair Vacances La Palmeraie 🛖

📞 04 68 28 20 64. www.homair.com – limited spaces for one-night stay

Address : boulevard de la Plage

Opening times : from beginning April to end Sept.

4.5 ha (229 pitches) flat, grassy, sandy

Tariff : (2015 price) 17 € 🚶🚶 🚗 🔌 🔋 (10A) – Extra per person 2 € – Reservation fee 10 €

Rental rates : (from beginning April to end Sept.) – 206 🚐. Per night from 177 to 230 € – Per week from 119 to 1,610 € – Reservation fee 25 €

There's a good covering of shade for the mobile homes, but very few pitches for tents and caravans.

Surroundings : 🏕 ⛰⛰
Leisure activities : 🍴 ✕ 🏛 🌙 nighttime 🏊 🚴 🛴 multi-sports ground
Facilities : ♿ ⛽ 📶 🍴 launderette 🧺 🚿 refrigerated food storage facilities
Nearby : 🛒 🎾 🎣 🐴

Longitude : 3.02806
Latitude : 42.76361

11800 – Michelin map **344** F3 – pop. 5 416 – alt. 84
▶ Paris 776 – Carcassonne 8 – Conques-sur-Orbiel 9 – Lézignan-Corbières 28

⛰ A l'Ombre des Micocouliers

📞 04 68 78 61 75. www.campingmicocouliers.com

Address : chemin de la Lande

Opening times : from beginning April to end Sept.

1.5 ha (70 pitches) flat, grassy, sandy

Tariff : (2015 price) 24.50 € 🚶🚶 🚗 🔌 🔋 (16A) – Extra per person 5.80 €

Rental rates : (2015 price) (from beginning April to end Sept.) – 5 canvas bungalows. Per night from 30 to 50 € – Per week from 140 to 490 €

🚽 local sani-station 5 €

Situated beside the Aude river in the shade of hackberry trees, but with rather old sanitary facilities.

Surroundings : 🏕 ⛰⛰
Leisure activities : ✕ 🏛 🚴 🎣 🏊
Facilities : ♿ ⛽ 🚿 🍴 📶 🚿
Nearby : 🎾 🎾 🏊

Longitude : 2.44237
Latitude : 43.20682

30700 – Michelin map **339** L4 – pop. 8 339 – alt. 138
▶ Paris 682 – Alès 34 – Arles 52 – Avignon 38

⛰ Le Moulin Neuf 🛖

📞 04 66 22 17 21. www.le-moulin-neuf.fr

Address : at Saint-Quentin-La-Poterie (4.5km northeast along the D 982, follow the signs for Bagnols-sur-Cèze and take the D 5 to the left)

Opening times : from beginning April to end Sept.

5 ha (140 pitches) terraced, flat, grassy

Tariff : 24.50 € 🚶🚶 🚗 🔌 🔋 (5A) – Extra per person 6.70 € – Reservation fee 10 €

Rental rates : permanent – 30 🛖 – 30 gîtes. Per night from 45 to 100 € – Per week from 252 to 660 € – Reservation fee 10 €

🚽 local sani-station

The site is shaded by poplars, with rather old gîtes of modest comfort levels.

Surroundings : 🌳 🏕 ⛰⛰
Leisure activities : 🍴 ✕ 🏛 🏊 🚴 🎣 🏊
multi-sports ground
Facilities : ♿ ⛽ 🚿 🍴 📶 🧺 🚿
Nearby : 🐴

Longitude : 4.45569
Latitude : 44.0321

⛰ Le Mas de Rey

☎ 0466221827. www.campingmasderey.com

Address : route d'Anduze (3km southwest along the D 982)

Opening times : from end March to mid Oct.

5 ha/2.5 for camping (106 pitches) flat, grassy

Tariff : (2015 price) 32€ ♥♥ ⛟ 🔲 🔥 (10A) – Extra per person 8€ – Reservation fee 10€

Rental rates : (from end March to mid Oct.) ♿ (1 chalet) – 6 🏠 – 2 canvas bungalows – 2 tent lodges. Per night from 70 to 110€ – Per week from 375 to 900€ – Reservation fee 10€

Very peaceful pitches; good-quality wooden chalets beneath some lovely shade.

Surroundings : 🌿 🚐 ♎♎ Leisure activities : 🏛 ⛵ 🛶 Facilities : ♿ ⚬━ 🚿 🚰 📷 🔥	**G P S** Longitude : 4.38471 Latitude : 43.99806

VALLABRÈGUES

30300 – Michelin map **339** M5 – pop. 1 318 – alt. 8
▶ Paris 698 – Arles 26 – Avignon 22 – Beaucaire 9

⛰ Lou Vincen

☎ 0466592129. www.campinglouvincen.com

Address : to the west of the small town, 100m from the Rhône and a small lake

Opening times : from beginning April to end Oct.

1.4 ha (75 pitches) flat, grassy

Tariff : 27.85€ ♥♥ ⛟ 🔲 🔥 (6A) – Extra per person 8.20€ – Reservation fee 17€

Rental rates : (from mid April to mid Oct.) ⚋ – 10 🚐. Per week from 258 to 600€ – Reservation fee 18€

🔥 local sani-station

At the entrance to the town, on the left bank of the Rhône.

Surroundings : 🌿 🚐 ♎♎ Leisure activities : 🛶 Facilities : ⚬━ 🆒 🚰 🔥 Nearby : 🍴	**G P S** Longitude : 4.62546 Latitude : 43.85493

A chambre d'hôte is a guesthouse or B & B-style accommodation.

VALLERAUGUE

30570 – Michelin map **339** G4 – pop. 1 070 – alt. 346
▶ Paris 684 – Mende 100 – Millau 75 – Nîmes 86

⛰ Le Mourétou

☎ 0467822230. www.camping-mouretou.com

Address : route de l'Aigoual and on the right way (3km west on the D 986)

1 ha (33 pitches)

Rentals : 4 🚐 – 2 tent lodges – 2 gîtes.

The well-shaded pitches lie beside the Hérault river and a small lake.

Surroundings : 🚐 ♎♎ Leisure activities : 🎿 ⛵ 🛶 (small swimming pool) Facilities : 📷 🔥 Nearby : 🌊 (fresh water)	**G P S** Longitude : 3.60785 Latitude : 44.0871

VALRAS-PLAGE

34350 – Michelin map **339** E9 – pop. 4 649 – alt. 1
▶ Paris 767 – Agde 25 – Béziers 16 – Montpellier 76

⛰ Domaine de La Yole 🏖

☎ 0467373387. www.campinglayole.com

Address : situated 2km southwest, 500m from the beach

Opening times : from end April to mid Sept.

23 ha (1273 pitches) flat, grassy, sandy

Tariff : 56€ ♥♥ ⛟ 🔲 🔥 (5A) – Extra per person 9.95€ – Reservation fee 30€

Rental rates : (from end April to mid Sept.) 🅿 – 241 🚐 – 49 🏠 – 10 canvas bungalows – 10 tent lodges. Per night from 35 to 239€ – Per week from 175 to 1,673€ – Reservation fee 30€

🔥 local sani-station

Surroundings : 🚐 ♎♎ Leisure activities : 🍴 ✗ 🏛 🎮 🎿 ⛵ 🚴 🎾 🎣 🔲 🛶 ⚋ forest trail, multi-sports ground Facilities : ♿ ⚬━ 🚿 🚰 🔥 launderette 🛒 🔥 Nearby : 🐎	**G P S** Longitude : 3.27181 Latitude : 43.23639

⛰ La Plage et du Bord de Mer 🏖

☎ 0467373438. www.camping-plage-mediterranee.com ⚋

Address : route de Vendres (located 1.5km southwest; beside the sea)

Opening times : from end April to end Sept.

13 ha (655 pitches) flat, grassy, sandy

Tariff : 48€ ♥♥ ⛟ 🔲 🔥 (10A) – Extra per person 6€ – Reservation fee 30€

Rental rates : (from end April to end Sept.) ⚋ – 103 🚐 – 6 tent lodges. Per night from 40 to 190€ – Per week from 280 to 1,330€ – Reservation fee 30€

A good choice of pitches for tents and caravans, with sanitary facilities that are well maintained but a little old-fashioned.

Surroundings : 🚐 ♀ ⛰ Leisure activities : 🍴 ✗ 🎮 🎿 ⛵ 🚴 🎾 🎣 m 🛶 ⚋ multi-sports ground Facilities : ♿ ⚬━ 🚿 🚰 🔥 launderette 🛒 🔥 Nearby : 🚣 🐎	**G P S** Longitude : 3.26889 Latitude : 43.23559

⛰ Lou Village 🏖

☎ 0467373379. www.louvillage.com – limited spaces for one-night stay

Address : chemin des Montilles (2km southwest, 100m from the beach)

Opening times : from beginning May to mid Sept.

8 ha (470 pitches) flat, grassy, sandy, pond

Tariff : (2015 price) 54€ ♥♥ ⛟ 🔲 🔥 (10A) – Extra per person 9.80€ – Reservation fee 30€

Rental rates : (2015 price) (from beginning May to mid Sept.) ⚋ – 90 🚐 – 20 🏠. Per night from 40 to 200€ – Per week from 389 to 1,399€ – Reservation fee 30€

🔥 local sani-station

A water park and direct access to the beach are the plus points of the site.

Surroundings : ⊏⊐ ♀♀ ⚠
Leisure activities : ♈ ✗ ⌂ ☾nighttime ⅍
⚡⅍ ⚡ ⅍
Facilities : ⅊ ⊶ ♉ ♈ ⅃ ⅊ ⅊ ⅊
Nearby : ⅍ jet skis

G P S Longitude : 3.26046
Latitude : 43.23386

⚠⚠⚠ Le Méditerranée

✆ 04 67 37 34 29. www.camping-le-mediterranee.com

Address : route de Vendres (located 1.5km southwest, 200m from the beach)

4.5 ha (367 pitches) flat, grassy, sandy

Rentals : 65 ⏚ – 10 ⌂ – 5 mobile homes (without sanitary facilities).

The site is well shaded, with numerous pitches for tents and caravans.

Surroundings : ♀♀
Leisure activities : ♈ ✗ ⌂ ⚡⅍ ⅃ ⅍
multi-sports ground
Facilities : ⅊ ⊶ ♈ launderette ⅊ ⅊
refrigerators
Nearby : ⅊ ⚴ ✗ ♉ ⅍

G P S Longitude : 3.26848
Latitude : 43.23592

⚠⚠ Les Foulègues ♣♣

✆ 04 67 37 33 65. www.campinglesfoulegues.com

Address : at Grau-de-Vendres, avenue du Port (5km southwest, 400m from the beach)

Opening times : from mid April to end Sept.

5.3 ha (339 pitches) flat, grassy, sandy

Tariff : (2015 price) 51 € ♦♦ ⇔ ▣ ⚡ (6A) – Extra per person 8.80 € – Reservation fee 30 €

Rental rates : (2015 price) (from beginning May to mid Sept.) – 41 ⏚. Per week from 330 to 1,025 €– Reservation fee 30 €

A pleasant site with lots of shade and rather old chalet rental accommodation.

Surroundings : ⊏⊐ ♀♀
Leisure activities : ♈ ✗ ⌂ ☾nighttime ⅍
⚡⅍ ✗ ♏ ⅃ ⅍
Facilities : ⅊ ⊶ ⅊ ⅃ ♈ ♈ ▣ ⅊ ⅊
Nearby : ⅍

G P S Longitude : 3.24222
Latitude : 43.22575

Some campsites benefit from proximity to a municipal leisure centre.

VERNET-LES-BAINS

66820 – Michelin map **344** F7 – pop. 1 432 – alt. 650 – ♨
▷ Paris 904 – Mont-Louis 36 – Perpignan 57 – Prades 11

⚠⚠ L'Eau Vive

✆ 04 68 05 54 14. www.leauvive-camping.com

Address : chemin St Saturnin (take exit towards Sahorre then continue after the bridge 1.3km along the av. St-Saturnin to the right, near the Cady river)

Opening times : from beginning April to beginning Oct.

2 ha (90 pitches)

Tariff : (2015 price) 26.50 € ♦♦ ⇔ ▣ ⚡ (10A) – Extra per person 5 € – Reservation fee 15 €

Rental rates : (2015 price) (from beginning April to beginning Oct.)
⅊ (1 chalet) – 5 ⏚ – 10 ⌂. Per night from 50 to 65 € – Per week from 255 to 745 € – Reservation fee 15 €

In a pleasant location.

Surroundings : ⅍ ⋖ ♀
Leisure activities : ♈ ✗ jacuzzi ⚡⅍ ⅃
Facilities : ⅊ ⊶ ⅊ ⅃ ♈ ♈ ▣

G P S Longitude : 2.38342
Latitude : 42.5527

VERS-PONT-DU-GARD

30210 – Michelin map **339** M5 – pop. 1 696 – alt. 40
▷ Paris 698 – Montpellier 81 – Nîmes 26 – Avignon 27

⚠⚠ FranceLoc Gorges du Gardon ♣♣

✆ 04 66 22 81 81. www.franceloc.fr

Address : 762 chemin Barque-Vieille (to the south, D 981 and D 5; beside the Gardon/Gard river)

Opening times : from mid April to mid Sept.

4 ha (200 pitches) flat, grassy, sandy

Tariff : (2015 price) 37.20 € ♦♦ ⇔ ▣ (10A) –
Extra per person 7.60 € – Reservation fee 27 €

Rental rates : (2015 price) (from mid April to mid Sept.) ⅊ (1 mobile home) – 104 ⏚ – 4 ⌂. Per night from 21 to 103 € – Per week from 147 to 1,316 € – Reservation fee 27 €

The site has numerous mobile homes and pitches running down to the banks of the river.

Surroundings : ⅍ ⊏⊐ ♀♀
Leisure activities : ♈ ✗ ⅍ ⚡⅍ ⅃ ≍ ⅍
⅍ ♏
Facilities : ⅊ ⊶ ▣ ⅊ ♈ launderette ⅊
refrigerators

G P S Longitude : 4.51766
Latitude : 43.95599

For more information on visiting particular towns or regions, consult the relevant regional MICHELIN Green Guide. We also recommend you use the appropriate Michelin regional map to locate your selected campsite, to calculate distances and to work out the best route.

VIAS-PLAGE

34450 – Michelin map **339** F9 – pop. 5 386 – alt. 10
▷ Paris 752 – Agde 5 – Béziers 19 – Narbonne 46

⚠⚠⚠ Yelloh! Village Club Farret ♣♣

✆ 04 67 21 64 45. www.camping-farret.com

Address : chemin des Rosses (beside the beach)

Opening times : from beginning April to end Sept.

7 ha (437 pitches) flat, grassy, sandy

Tariff : 61 € ♦♦ ⇔ ▣ ⚡ (10A) – Extra per person 9 €

Rental rates : (from beginning April to end Sept.) ⅊ – 326 ⏚ – 64 ⌂ – 19 studios – 4 apartments. Per night from 30 to 320 € – Per week from 210 to 2,240 €

⏚ local sani-station

Surroundings : ⅍ ⊏⊐ ♀♀ ⚠
Leisure activities : ♈ ✗ ⌂ ▣ ⅍ ♏ ♏
⚴ ✗ ⅃ ♪ entertainment room
Facilities : ⅊ ⊶ ▣ ⅊ ⅃ ♈ ♈ launderette
⅊ ⅊
Nearby : ♏ ⅍

G P S Longitude : 3.419
Latitude : 43.2911

Sunêlia Domaine de la Dragonnière

Sunêlia Domaine de la Dragonnière

04 67 01 03 10. www.dragonniere.com – limited spaces for one-night stay

Address : off the RD 612 (5km west, follow the signs for Béziers)

Opening times : from end March to beginning Nov.

30 ha (980 pitches) flat, grassy, stony

Tariff : 75€ (10A) – Extra per person 13€ – Reservation fee 35€

Rental rates : (from end March to beginning Nov.) – 322 – 364 – 2 tent lodges. Per night from 35 to 329€ – Per week from 245 to 2,303€ – Reservation fee 35€

local sani-station

A wide range of accommodation options at different levels of comfort, with an upmarket spa centre and an Olympic-size swimming pool (50m).

Surroundings :

Leisure activities : hammam, jacuzzi multi-sports ground, spa centre

Facilities : – 38 private sanitary facilities (wc) launderette

GPS Longitude : 3.36335 Latitude : 43.3126

Le Napoléon

Le Napoléon

04 67 01 07 80. www.camping-napoleon.fr

Address : 1171 avenue de la Méditerranée (250m from the beach)

Opening times : from beginning April to end Sept.

3 ha (239 pitches) flat, grassy, sandy

Tariff : 23.70€ (10A) – Extra per person 6€ – Reservation fee 28€

Rental rates : (2015 price) (from beginning April to end Sept.) (1 mobile home) – 77 – 39 – 2 – 11 apartments – 5 tent lodges. Per night from 35 to 164€ – Reservation fee 28€

local sani-station 18€ – 10 23€ – 22€

Surroundings :

Leisure activities : hammam multi-sports ground

Facilities : launderette refrigerated food storage facilities

Nearby : disco, sports trail

GPS Longitude : 3.41661 Latitude : 43.29179

Méditerranée-Plage

04 67 90 99 07. www.mediterranee-plage.com

Address : Côté-Ouest (6km southwest along the D 137e2)

Opening times : from end March to end Sept.

9.6 ha (490 pitches) flat, grassy, sandy

Tariff : (2015 price) 47€ (6A) – Extra per person 8.90€ – Reservation fee 25€

Rental rates : (2015 price) permanent (1 mobile home) – 230 . Per week from 220 to 1,375€ – Reservation fee 25€

raclet sani-station

A pleasant setting beside the sea with high-quality facilities.

Surroundings :

Leisure activities : farm or petting farm, multi-sports ground

Facilities : launderette

GPS Longitude : 3.37106 Latitude : 43.28202

Les Flots Bleus

04 67 21 64 80. www.camping-flotsbleus.com

Address : Côté-Ouest (to the southwest; beside the beach)

Opening times : from end April to mid Sept.

5 ha (298 pitches) flat, grassy, stony

Tariff : (2015 price) 36€ (8A) – Extra per person 7€ – Reservation fee 22€

Rental rates : (2015 price) (from mid Dec. to end Sept.) – 110 – 25 – 4 gîtes. Per week from 190 to 930€ – Reservation fee 22€

local sani-station 5€ – 30 15€

Jointly run with the France Floride campsite next door.

Surroundings :

Leisure activities : nighttime multi-sports ground

Facilities : launderette

GPS Longitude : 3.4055 Latitude : 43.29

Cap Soleil

04 67 21 64 77. www.capsoleil.fr – limited spaces for one-night stay

Address : chemin de la Grande Cosse (Côte Ouest, 600m from the beach)

4.5 ha (288 pitches) flat, grassy

Rentals : (1 mobile home) – 100 .

local sani-station – 40

The covered swimming pool (uncovered in summer) is reserved for naturists in July and August.

Surroundings :

Leisure activities : (open air in season) multi-sports ground

Facilities : – 8 private sanitary facilities (wc) launderette refrigerators

Nearby :

GPS Longitude : 3.39953 Latitude : 43.29262

Californie Plage

04 67 21 64 69. www.californie-plage.fr

Address : chemin du Trou de Ragout (Côte Ouest, to the southwest along the D 137e and take road to the left; beside the sea)

Opening times : from mid April to end Sept.

5.8 ha (371 pitches) flat, grassy, sandy

Tariff : (2015 price) 46€ (10A) – Extra per person 8.75€ – Reservation fee 25€

Rental rates : (2015 price) (from mid April to end Sept.) – 121 . Per night from 32 to 173€ – Per week from 224 to 1,211€ – Reservation fee 25€

There's free admission to the water park at the Cap-Soleil campsite (opposite, 100m away).

Surroundings :

Leisure activities : multi-sports ground

Facilities : launderette refrigerators

Nearby :

GPS Longitude : 3.39843 Latitude : 43.29051

*The classification (1 to 5 tents, **black** or red) that we award to selected sites in this guide is our own system. It should not be confused with the classification (1 to 5 stars) of official organisations.*

⛰ L'Air Marin ♁♁

📞 0467216490. www.camping-air-marin.fr

Address : East Coast (Côte Est, behind the football pitch)

Opening times : from mid April to mid Sept.

5.5 ha (305 pitches) flat, grassy, sandy

Tariff : 45€ ✝✝ ⇔ 🔲 🔌 (6A) – Extra per person 9€ – Reservation fee 25€

Rental rates : (from mid April to mid Sept.) – 150 🚐 – 10 🏠. Per night from 34 to 191€ – Per week from 235 to 1,340€ – Reservation fee 25€

Surroundings : 🗆 🎔🎔
Leisure activities : ♟ ✕ 🎬 ⊙nighttime 🏹 🛶 🏊 🚣 ⚓boats for hire ∿ multi-sports ground
Facilities : ♿ ⚬⇥ 🚿 🌳 ♨ ⚐ launderette 🔧 🚰
Nearby : ⚓amusement park

G P S Longitude : 3.42129
Latitude : 43.30076

⛰ Tohapi Le Petit Mousse ♁♁
(rental of mobile homes only)

📞 0825002030. www.tohapi.fr

Address : route de la Grande Cosse

Opening times : from end April to mid Sept.

5.2 ha (365 pitches) flat, grassy, sandy

Rental rates : (2015 price) – 350 🚐. Per night from 32 to 64€

Surroundings : 🐟 🎔🎔⛰
Leisure activities : ♟ ✕ 🎬 ⊙ 🏹 🚣 🚴 ⚓
🔧 🛶
Facilities : ⚬⇥ 🌳 ⚐ launderette 🔧 🚰

G P S Longitude : 3.40147
Latitude : 43.28994

⛰ Hélios

📞 0467216366. www.camping-helios.com

Address : avenue des Pêcheurs (near the Libron, 250m from the beach)

Opening times : from end April to end Sept.

2.5 ha (215 pitches) flat, grassy, sandy

Tariff : 44€ ✝✝ ⇔ 🔲 🔌 (6A) – Extra per person 7€ – Reservation fee 10€

Rental rates : (2015 price) (from end April to end Sept.) – 27 🚐 – 6 🏠 – 4 canvas bungalows. Per night from 37 to 121€ – Per week from 160 to 850€ – Reservation fee 20€

Beside the Libron river, plenty of shade, with an attractive indoor spa area.

Surroundings : 🐟 🎔🎔
Leisure activities : ♟ ✕ 🎬 ≋ hammam, jacuzzi 🛶 🌳 ⚘ paddling pool, spa centre, water park
Facilities : ♿ ⚬⇥ 🌳 ⚐ 🍴 ⚐ 🔧 🚰

G P S Longitude : 3.40764
Latitude : 43.29115

LE VIGAN

30120 – Michelin map **339** G5 – pop. 3 959 – alt. 221
▶ Paris 707 – Alès 66 – Lodève 50 – Mende 108

⛰ Le Val de l'Arre

📞 0467810277. www.valdelarre.com

Address : at Roudoulouse, route du Pont de la Croix (2.5km east along the D 999, follow the rte de Ganges and take road to the right; beside the Arre)

Opening times : from beginning April to end Sept.

4 ha (173 pitches) terraced, relatively flat, flat, grassy

Tariff : 28€ ✝✝ ⇔ 🔲 🔌 (10A) – Extra per person 7.50€ – Reservation fee 15€

Rental rates : (2015 price) (from beginning April to end Sept.)
🚿 – 35 🚐 – 1 gîte. Per night from 40 to 95€ – Per week from 214 to 815€ – Reservation fee 15€

🚐 local sani-station 4€ – ⚓11€

In two separate sections on either side of the road with pitches for tents and caravans that are near the river and have plenty of shade.

Surroundings : 🎔🎔
Leisure activities : 🎬 🛶 🌳 ≋ 🏊
Facilities : ♿ ⚬⇥ 🌳 ⚐ launderette 🔧 🚰

G P S Longitude : 3.63751
Latitude : 43.99128

LES VIGNES

48210 – Michelin map **330** H9 – pop. 103 – alt. 410
▶ Paris 615 – Mende 52 – Meyrueis 33 – Le Rozier 12

⛰ Beldoire

📞 0466488279. www.camping-beldoire.com

Opening times : from mid May to mid Sept.

5 ha (142 pitches) terraced, flat, grassy, stony

Tariff : (2015 price) 27€ ✝✝ ⇔ 🔲 🔌 (6A) – Extra per person 5.50€ – Reservation fee 14€

Rental rates : (2015 price) (from mid April to mid Sept.) – 1 'gypsy' caravan – 8 🚐 – 15 canvas bungalows. Per night from 38 to 50€ – Per week from 239 to 649€

In two separate sections on both sides of the road with some pitches beside the Tarn river.

Surroundings : 🎔🎔⛰
Facilities : ♿ ⚬⇥ 🔧

G P S Longitude : 3.23445
Latitude : 44.28717

⛰ Village Vacances Castel de la Peyre
(rental of gîtes only)

📞 0466484848. www.lozere-resa.com

Address : located 1km south along the D 16

1 ha terraced

Rental rates : 10 gîtes.

A pretty village of small houses, with a view over the Vallée du Tarn.

Surroundings : 🐟 ≋
Leisure activities : 🎬 🌳
Facilities : ♿ 🏛 🔧 🖥

G P S Longitude : 3.2283
Latitude : 44.27292

⛰ La Blaquière

📞 0466485493. www.campinggorgesdutarn.fr

Address : 6km northeast along the D 907bis; beside the Tarn river

Opening times : from mid April to end Sept.

1 ha (79 pitches) terraced, stony, flat, grassy

Tariff : 23€ ✝✝ ⇔ 🔲 🔌 (10A) – Extra per person 6€

Rental rates : (from mid April to end Sept.) 🚿 – 2 'gypsy' caravans – 10 🚐 – 3 tent lodges. Per night from 35 to 65€ – Per week from 200 to 680€

🚐 5 🔲 13€

Below the road, beside the Tarn river, well-shaded pitches.

Surroundings : 🗆 🎔🎔⛰
Leisure activities : 🎬 🛶 🏊
Facilities : ♿ ⚬⇥ 🌳 ⚐ 🖥 🔧 🚰

G P S Longitude : 3.2685
Latitude : 44.3042

VILLEFORT

48800 – Michelin map **330** L8 – pop. 618 – alt. 600
▶ Paris 616 – Alès 52 – Aubenas 61 – Florac 63

⛰ La Palhère

✆ 04 66 46 80 63. www.campinglapalhere.com – alt. 750

Address : route du Mas de la Barque (4km southwest along the D 66; beside rapids)

Opening times : from mid April to end Oct.

1.8 ha (45 pitches) terraced, stony, grassy

Tariff : 16 € ♦♦ ⛺ 🔌 ⚡ (6A) – Extra per person 5 €

Rental rates : (from mid April to end Oct.) ⛺ – 3 'gypsy' caravans – 6 🚐 – 1 🏠 – 1 yurt – 2 tipis. Per night from 30 to 50 € – Per week from 210 to 715 €

Beside a pretty mountain stream with varied rental options.

Surroundings : ⛰ ≼ 🌳🌳
Leisure activities : ✗ ⛏ 🛶 ⤳
Facilities : ⚸ 🛁 🏪 🧺 🚿 🚻 🚮 ♿

Longitude : 3.91026
Latitude : 44.41862

⛰ Morangiés – Le Lac

✆ 04 66 46 81 27. www.camping-lac-cevennes.com – limited spaces for one-night stay

Address : at Morangiés (3.4km north along the D 901. follow the signs for Mende, take D 906. follow the signs for Prévenchère and take turning to the left down the road for Pourcharesses)

Opening times : from mid April to end Sept.

4 ha (75 pitches) terraced, gravel, grassy

Tariff : (2015 price) 18.20 € ♦♦ ⛺ 🔌 ⚡ (10A) – Extra per person 4.80 €

Rental rates : (2015 price) permanent – 32 🚐 – 19 🏠. Per night from 50 to 75 € – Per week from 148 to 765 €

An attractive location beside the lake; some of the infrastructure and rental options are a little old. 'Semi-detached' gîtes.

Surroundings : ⛰ ≼ 🛒 🌳🌳
Leisure activities : 🏊 🛶 ⛏
Facilities : ♿ ⚸ 🛁 🚿 🚻 🚮 ♿
Nearby : 🛶 ⤳ ⚓ ⛵

Longitude : 3.92812
Latitude : 44.46183

We value your opinion and welcome your feedback.
Do email us at campingfrance@tp.michelin.com

VILLEGLY

11600 – Michelin map **344** F3 – pop. 1 020 – alt. 130
▶ Paris 778 – Lézignan-Corbières 36 – Mazamet 46 – Carcassonne 14

⛰ Sites et Paysages Moulin de Ste-Anne

✆ 04 68 72 20 80. www.moulindesainteanne.com

Address : 2 chemin de Sainte-Anne (take the eastern exit along the D 435, follow the signs for Villarzel)

1.6 ha (60 pitches) terraced, relatively flat, flat, grassy
Rental rates : ♿ (1 chalet) – 15 🏠 – 2 tent lodges.
🚐 local sani-station

Attractive pitches and good-quality rental options, on shaded terraces.

Surroundings : 🛒 🌳🌳
Leisure activities : 🍸 ✗ 🏛 🛶 ⛏
multi-sports ground
Facilities : ♿ ⚸ 🏪 🛁 🚿 🚻 🚮 📶 ♿
Nearby : ✂

Longitude : 2.44347
Latitude : 43.28374

Some information or pricing may have changed since the guide went to press. We recommend you check the price list online in advance or at the entrance to the campsite and enquire about possible restrictions.

VILLENEUVE-LÈS-AVIGNON

30400 – Michelin map **339** N5 – pop. 12 463 – alt. 23
▶ Paris 678 – Avignon 8 – Nîmes 46 – Orange 28

⛰ Campéole L'Ile des Papes ♦♦

✆ 04 90 15 15 90. www.avignon-camping.com

Address : Barrage de Villeneuve (4.5km northeast along the D 980, follow the signs for Roquemaure and take D 780 to the right, between the Rhône and the canal)

Opening times : from end March to beginning Nov.

20 ha (210 pitches) flat, grassy, pond, stony

Tariff : 18 € ♦♦ ⛺ 🔌 ⚡ (10A) – Extra per person 10 € – Reservation fee 25 €

Rental rates : (from end March to beginning Nov.) – 117 🚐 – 15 🏠 – 61 canvas bungalows. Per night from 36 to 176 € – Per week from 252 to 1,232 € – Reservation fee 25 €

🚐 local sani-station

A spacious site, partially shaded, with a pretty play and paddling pool area.

Surroundings : ⛰ ≼ 🛒 🌳🌳
Leisure activities : 🍸 ✗ 🏛 🎦 nighttime 🏃
🛶 🚴 ⛏ ⤳ multi-sports ground
Facilities : ♿ ⚸ 🏪 🛁 🚻 launderette 🚮 ♿

Longitude : 4.81826
Latitude : 43.99383

⛺ VivaCamp La Laune

✆ 04 90 25 76 06. www.camping-villeneuvelezavignon.com

Address : chemin Saint Honore (to the northeast, access via the D 980, near the stadium and swimming pools)

Opening times : from end March to mid Oct.

2.3 ha (126 pitches) stony, flat, grassy

Tariff : 25 € ♦♦ ⛺ 🔌 ⚡ (10A) – Extra per person 5.50 € – Reservation fee 15 €

Rental rates : (from end March to mid Oct.) – 4 🚐 – 3 canvas bungalows. Per night from 40 to 90 € – Per week from 168 to 630 € – Reservation fee 25 €

Set among the town's sporting facilities, a well-shaded site with modest sanitary facilities.

Surroundings : 🛒 🌳🌳
Leisure activities : 🏛 🛶
Facilities : ♿ ⚸ 🚻 📶
Nearby : ✂ 🏊 ⛏

Longitude : 4.79711
Latitude : 43.96331

LIMOUSIN

N. Thibaut / Photononstop

L ife in Limousin is led at its own easy pace: weary Parisians wanting to reconnect with nature come to enjoy the joys of country life, inhale the bracing air of its high plateaus and wander through its woodlands in search of wild mushrooms and chestnuts. The region boasts hills and gorges and lush green meadows. The sight of cattle grazing happily or lambs frolicking in a spring meadow will rejuvenate the spirits of any jaded city dweller. Limousin is home to ancient village churches as well as imposing abbey churches and fortresses. In autumn, the forests are swathed in rich colours, forming a perfect backdrop to the granite and sandstone of the peaceful towns and villages, where ancestral crafts, such as Limoges enamels and porcelain and Aubusson tapestries, still blend the traditional with the best of the new. The food is wholesome – savoury bacon soup, Limousin stew and, as any proud local will tell you, the most tender, succulent beef in the world.

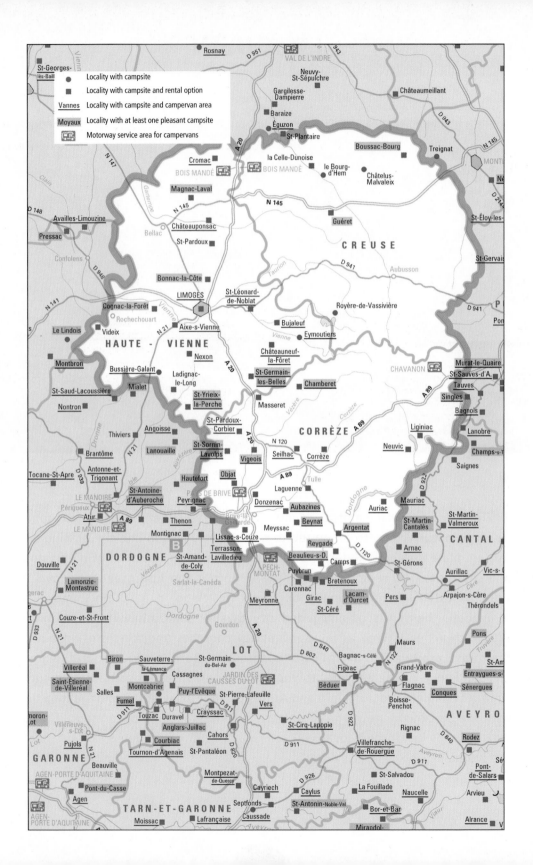

Locality with campsite
Locality with campsite and rental option
Vannes Locality with campsite and campervan area
Moyaux Locality with at least one pleasant campsite
Motorway service area for campervans

AIXE-SUR-VIENNE

87700 – Michelin map **325** D6 – pop. 5 464 – alt. 204
▶ Paris 400 – Châlus 21 – Confolens 60 – Limoges 14

⚠ Municipal les Grèves

☎ 05 55 70 12 98. www.mairie-aixesurvienne.fr

Address : rue Jean-Claude Papon (beside the Vienne river)

Opening times : from beginning June to end Sept.

3 ha (80 pitches) flat, grassy

Tariff : (2015 price) 15.70€ ♣♣ ⇔ 🔲 🏕 (10A) – Extra per person 4€
Rental rates : (2015 price) (from beginning April to end Oct.) 👍
(1 mobile home) – 3 🚏. Per night from 50 to 70€ – Per week
from 220 to 420€

🚐 AireService sani-station 4€

Surroundings : 🐾 ♨♨
Leisure activities : 🍸 🛖 🏊 🚣 🎣 🛶
Facilities : 👍 ⚲ 🛖 🚾 🔳
Nearby : 🖼

Longitude : 1.1149
Latitude : 45.8069

ARGENTAT

19400 – Michelin map **329** M5 – pop. 3 052 – alt. 183
▶ Paris 503 – Aurillac 54 – Brive-la-Gaillarde 45 – Mauriac 49

⚠ Le Gibanel

☎ 05 55 28 10 11. www.camping-gibanel.com

Address : 4.5km northeast along the D 18, follow the signs for
Égletons then take the road to the right

Opening times : from beginning June to end Aug.

60 ha/8.5 for camping (250 pitches) terraced, flat, grassy

Tariff : (2015 price) 31€ ♣♣ ⇔ 🔲 🏕 (10A) – Extra per person 6€ –
Reservation fee 10€
Rental rates : (2015 price) (from beginning June to end Aug.) –
10 🚏 – 2 apartments. Per week from 340 to 940€ – Reservation
fee 10€

In the grounds of a 16th-century château, beside a lake.

Surroundings : 🐾 ≤ ♨♨ ⚠
Leisure activities : 🍸 🛖 🏊daytime 🏊 🚣
🎣 🛶 multi-sports ground
Facilities : 👍 ⚲ 🛖 🚾 🏕 launderette 🔳 🚲

Longitude : 1.95852
Latitude : 45.1107

⚠ Au Soleil d'Oc ♣♣

☎ 05 55 28 84 84. www.campingsoleildoc.com

Address : at Monceaux-sur-Dordogne (4.5km southwest along the
D 12, follow the signs for Beaulieu then take the D 12e following signs
for Vergnolles and take road to the left after the bridge; beside the
Dordogne river)

Opening times : from mid April to mid Nov.

4 ha (120 pitches) terraced, flat, grassy

Tariff : 28.80€ ♣♣ ⇔ 🔲 🏕 (6A) – Extra per person 6.50€ –
Reservation fee 18€
Rental rates : (from mid April to mid Nov.) – 40 🚏 – 8 🏠 –
3 canvas bungalows – 1 tent lodge. Per night from 28 to 99€ –
Per week from 195 to 699€ – Reservation fee 18€

🚐 local sani-station – 🚐 🏕 12€

*Some very shady pitches, some of which are beside the
Dordogne river.*

Surroundings : 🐾 🚏 ♨♨ ⚠
Leisure activities : 🍸 🍴 🛖 🏊 🚣 🎣 🛶
🎣 🛶
Facilities : ⚲ 🚾 🏕 🛖 🚾 launderette 🚲

Longitude : 1.91836
Latitude : 45.07618

⛰ Le Vaurette ♣♣

☎ 05 55 28 09 67. www.vaurette.com

Address : Vaurette (9km southwest along the D 12, follow the signs
for Beaulieu; beside the Dordogne river)

4 ha (120 pitches) terraced, relatively flat, flat, grassy
Rentals : 2 🚏.

*Situated on the Dordogne river, with some pitches by the
water.*

Surroundings : 🐾 ♨♨ ⚠
Leisure activities : 🍸 🍴 🛖 🏊daytime. 🏊
🎣 🚣 🛶 entertainment room
Facilities : 👍 ⚲ 🛖 🚾 launderette 🔳

Longitude : 1.8825
Latitude : 45.04568

AUBAZINE

19190 – Michelin map **329** L4 – pop. 852 – alt. 345
▶ Paris 480 – Aurillac 86 – Brive-la-Gaillarde 14 – St-Céré 50

⛰ Campéole Le Coiroux ♣♣

☎ 05 55 27 21 96. www.camping-coiroux.com

Address : Coiroux tourist zone (5km east along the D 48, follow the
signs for Le Chastang, not far from a small lake and a leisure park)

Opening times : from beginning May to end Sept.

165 ha/6 for camping (174 pitches) relatively flat, flat, grassy, wood

Tariff : (2015 price) 13€ ♣♣ ⇔ 🔲 🏕 (10A) – Extra per person 10€ –
Reservation fee 25€
Rental rates : (from beginning May to end Sept.) 👍 (2 mobile
homes) – 45 🚏 – 10 🏠 – 27 canvas bungalows. Per night
from 28 to 200€ – Per week from 196 to 1,400€ – Reservation
fee 25€

🚐 local sani-station 3€

*In a setting with plenty of green spaces, large pitches and a
well-appointed activity centre.*

Surroundings : 🐾 🚏 ♨♨
Leisure activities : 🍸 🍴 🛖 🏊 🚣 🎣 🛶
multi-sports ground
Facilities : 👍 ⚲ 🛖 🚾 launderette 🔳 🚲
Nearby : 🎣 🚣 🏖 (beach) 🛶 forest trail,
climbing wall, golf (18 holes)

Longitude : 1.70739
Latitude : 45.18611

AURIAC

19220 – Michelin map **329** N4 – pop. 226 – alt. 608
▶ Paris 517 – Argentat 27 – Égletons 33 – Mauriac 23

⚠ Municipal

☎ 05 55 28 25 97. www.auriac.fr

Address : in the village (take the southeastern exit along the D 65,
follow the signs for St-Privat, near a lake and a wooded park)

Opening times : from beginning April to mid Nov.

1.7 ha (63 pitches) open site, relatively flat, grassy

Tariff : (2015 price) ♣ 3.95€ ⇔ 2€ 🔲 2€ – 🏕 (16A) 3.95€
Rental rates : (2015 price) (from beginning April to mid Nov.) –
8 🚏. Per night from 40 to 65€ – Per week from 230 to 405€

🚐 local sani-station – 🚐 🏕 10€

There's a view of the lake from some pitches.

Surroundings : 🐾 ≤ 🚏 ♨♨ ⚠
Leisure activities : 🛖 🏊
Facilities : ⚲ (mid July–mid Aug.) 🚾 🔳 🔳
Nearby : 🎣 🚣 🏖 (beach) 🛶 pedalos

Longitude : 2.14772
Latitude : 45.20206

BEAULIEU-SUR-DORDOGNE

19120 – Michelin map **329** M6 – pop. 1 283 – alt. 142
▶ Paris 513 – Aurillac 65 – Brive-la-Gaillarde 44 – Figeac 56

⋘ Indigo Les Îles ♣♣

🔗 05 55 91 02 65. www.campingdesiles.com

Address : boulevard Rodolphe de Turenne (east of the town centre)

Opening times : from beginning May to end Sept.

7 ha (185 pitches) flat, grassy

Tariff : (2015 price) 30.50€ ✶✶ ⇔ 🔲 🔌 (10A) –
Extra per person 7.70€ – Reservation fee 13€

Rental rates : (2015 price) (from beginning May to end Sept.) –
24 🔲 – 2 🏠 – 16 tent lodges. Per night from 39 to 138€ –
Per week from 219 to 966€ – Reservation fee 13€

🚐 local sani-station 7€

A picturesque site and setting on an island in the Dordogne river.

Surroundings : 🐟 ♀♀ ⚠
Leisure activities : 🍽 ✕ 🏠 ⚡ 🏊 ⅃ ⊠
Facilities : 🕭 ⊶ ▥ 🗑 ⸙ 🚰 launderette ⚇
Nearby : ✕

GPS	Longitude : 1.84049
	Latitude : 44.97968

BEYNAT

19190 – Michelin map **329** L5 – pop. 1 253 – alt. 420
▶ Paris 496 – Argentat 47 – Beaulieu-sur-Dordogne 23 – Brive-la-Gaillarde 21

⋘ Club Airotel Le Lac de Miel

🔗 05 55 85 50 66. www.camping-miel.com

Address : 4km east along the N 121, follow the signs for Argentat; beside a small lake

Opening times : from beginning May to mid Sept.

50 ha/9 for camping (180 pitches) undulating, relatively flat, grassy

Tariff : 28.80€ ✶✶ ⇔ 🔲 🔌 (6A) – Extra per person 6.50€ –
Reservation fee 18€

Rental rates : (from beginning May to end Sept.) – 2 'gypsy'
caravans – 80 🔲 – 10 🏠 – 3 canvas bungalows – 6 tent lodges
– 8 gîtes. Per night from 28 to 99€ – Per week from 195 to 693€ – Reservation fee 18€

🚐 local sani-station – 🚿 🔌12€

Surroundings : 🐟 ⋞♀♀ ⚠
Leisure activities : 🍽 ✕ 🏠 ⚡ ✕ 🏊 ⊠ ⊠
(open air in season) ⚇ 🐴 ⸙
Facilities : 🕭 ⊶ ⸙ 🚰 launderette
Nearby : ▨ (beach) pedalos, paintballing

GPS	Longitude : 1.77103
	Latitude : 45.13332

⋘ Village Vacances Chalets en France
Les Hameaux de Miel – (rental of chalets only)

🔗 05 55 84 34 48. www.hameauxdemiel.com

Address : at Miel, off the D921, 1.3km from the Etang de Miel (lake)

Opening times : permanent

12 ha very uneven, terraced

Rental rates : 🕭 (3 chalets) – 65 🏠. Per night from 49 to 125€ –
Per week from 149 to 749€

Surroundings : 🐟 ⋞♀
Leisure activities : 🍽 ✕ 🏠 ⚡ ⚡ ⊠ ⸙
multi-sports ground
Facilities : 🕭 ▥ 🚰 launderette
Nearby : ✕ ⸙ ▨ ⚇ 🐴 pedalos, paintballing

GPS	Longitude : 1.76141
	Latitude : 45.12932

BONNAC-LA-CÔTE

87270 – Michelin map **325** E5 – pop. 1 374 – alt. 428
▶ Paris 382 – Guéret 78 – Limoges 16 – Tulle 101

⋘ Les Castels Le Château de Leychoisier

Le Château de Leychoisier

🔗 05 55 39 93 43. www.leychoisier.com

Address : 1 route de Leychoisier (1km along the D 97, rte du 8 mai 1945)

Opening times : from mid April to mid Sept.

47 ha/4 for camping (80 pitches) relatively flat, flat, grassy

Tariff : 34€ ✶✶ ⇔ 🔲 🔌 (10A) –
Extra per person 9.50€

Rental rates : (from mid April to mid Sept.) ⸙ – 2 🏠. Per week from 400 to 600€

Situated in the grounds of the château.

Surroundings : 🐟 ♀♀
Leisure activities : 🍽 ✕ 🏠 ⊠
Facilities : 🕭 ⊶ ✉ ▥ ⸙ ⸙ 🚰 🍽 launderette ⚇

GPS	Longitude : 1.28973
	Latitude : 45.93337

LE BOURG-D'HEM

23220 – Michelin map **325** H3 – pop. 225 – alt. 320
▶ Paris 333 – Aigurande 20 – Le Grand-Bourg 28 – Guéret 21

⚠ Municipal

🔗 05 55 62 84 36. www.paysdunois.fr

Address : west along the D 48, follow the signs for Bussière-Dunoise and take the road to the right

0.33 ha (36 pitches) open site, terraced, flat, grassy

Basic sanitary facilities but a pleasant site where the Creuse river broadens out into a lake.

Surroundings : 🐟 ▱ ♀♀ ⚠
Leisure activities : 🐴
Facilities : 🕭 ⸙
Nearby : 🍷 ⚡ pedalos

GPS	Longitude : 1.82412
	Latitude : 46.29752

BOUSSAC-BOURG

23600 – Michelin map **325** K2 – pop. 787 – alt. 423
▶ Paris 334 – Aubusson 52 – La Châtre 37 – Guéret 43

⋘ Les Castels Le Château de Poinsouze ♣♣

🔗 05 55 65 02 21. www.camping-de-poinsouze.com ⚇

Address : route de La Châtre (2.8km north along the D 917)

Opening times : from mid May to mid Sept.

150 ha/22 for camping (145 pitches) relatively flat, grassy, pond

Tariff : 38€ ✶✶ ⇔ 🔲 🔌 (16A) – Extra per person 6.50€ – Reservation fee 15€

Rental rates : (from mid May to mid Sept.) ⚇ – 2 'gypsy' caravans –
22 🔲 – 2 🏠 – 2 gîtes. Per week from 240 to 710€ – Reservation fee 15€

A spacious site near a 16th-century château and its outbuildings, in a green setting with lots of flowers.

Surroundings : 🐟 ⋞▱♀
Leisure activities : 🍽 ✕ 🏠 ⚡ ⚡ 🚴 🏊 ⊠
🐴 pedalos, farm or petting farm ⚇
Facilities : 🕭 ⊶ ⸙ 🚰 🍽 launderette
⸙ ⚇

GPS	Longitude : 2.20472
	Latitude : 46.3725

BUJALEUF

87460 – Michelin map **325** G6 – pop. 881 – alt. 380
▶ Paris 423 – Bourganeuf 28 – Eymoutiers 14 – Limoges 35

⚠ Municipal du Lac

✆ 0555695004. www.bujaleuf.fr

Address : located 1km north along the D 16 and take the turning to the left, near the lake

Opening times : from mid May to end Sept.

2 ha (110 pitches) very uneven, terraced, flat, grassy

Tariff : 12.50€ ♣♣ ⇐ ▣ 🔌 (5A) – Extra per person 5€
Rentals : (2015 price) permanent – 10 gîtes.
🚐 local sani-station – 4 ▣
Wide terraces overlooking a lake.

Surroundings : 🐾 ♀
Leisure activities : 🚴
Facilities : 🕭🚿🆑🏛 ⁿ launderette
Nearby : 🍷 ✕ 🏊 (beach) 🎣

GPS Longitude : 1.6297
Latitude : 45.80166

BUSSIÈRE-GALANT

87230 – Michelin map **325** D7 – pop. 1 394 – alt. 410
▶ Paris 422 – Aixe-sur-Vienne 23 – Châlus 6 – Limoges 36

⚠ Municipal Espace Hermeline

✆ 0555788612. www.espace-hermeline.com

Address : avenue du Plan-d'eau (1.7km southwest along the D 20, follow the signs for La Coquille and take the road to the right, near the stadium and 100m from a small lake)

Opening times : from mid April to end Sept.

1 ha (23 pitches) terraced, relatively flat, grassy

Tariff : (2015 price) 13€ ♣♣ ⇐ ▣ 🔌 (16A) – Extra per person 5€
Rental rates : (2015 price) (from mid April to end Sept.) – 2 yurts.
Per night from 60 to 80€ – Per week from 420 to 560€
🚐 Eurorelais sani-station 2€
Based at a leisure and activity park.

Surroundings : 🐾 ⟨ 🛏 ♀♀
Facilities : 🕭 ⌒ⁿ 🏛 🏊 ⁿ
Nearby : ✕ 🏊 (beach) 🎣 forest trail, zip wiring, bike-rail, miniature railway

GPS Longitude : 1.03086
Latitude : 45.61364

CAMPS

19430 – Michelin map **329** M6 – pop. 246 – alt. 520
▶ Paris 520 – Argentat 17 – Aurillac 45 – Bretenoux 18

⚠ Municipal la Châtaigneraie

✆ 0555285315. www.correze-camping.fr

Address : in the village (to the west along the D 13 and take the road to the right)

Opening times : from beginning May to end Sept.

1 ha (23 pitches) gravelled, grassy, flat, relatively flat

Tariff : (2015 price) ♣ 2.50€ ⇐ ▣ 3€ – 🔌 (10A) 2.50€
Rental rates : (2015 price) permanent – 9 🏠. Per night from 40 to 80€ – Per week from 238 to 476€

Surroundings : 🐾 ⟨ ♀♀
Leisure activities : 🍷 ✕ 🏄
Facilities : 🕭 🚿ⁿ 🖼
Nearby : ✕ 🏊 (beach) 🎣

GPS Longitude : 1.98756
Latitude : 44.98368

LA CELLE-DUNOISE

23800 – Michelin map **325** H3 – pop. 607 – alt. 230
▶ Paris 329 – Aigurande 16 – Aubusson 63 – Dun-le-Palestel 11

⚠ Municipal de la Baignade

✆ 0555891077. www.lacelledunoise.fr

Address : east, along the D 48a, follow the signs for Le Bourg d'Hem, near the Creuse river (direct access)

1.4 ha (30 pitches) terraced, flat, grassy
Rentals : 3 🏠.

The reception and sanitary facilities are housed in a pretty stone building. A small steep path leads down to the river.

Surroundings : ♀♀
Leisure activities : 🛏 🎿
Facilities : 🕭 🚣 launderette
Nearby : 🍷 ✕ 🏊 🎣

GPS Longitude : 1.77583
Latitude : 46.30913

CHAMBERET

19370 – Michelin map **329** L2 – pop. 1 318 – alt. 450
▶ Paris 453 – Guéret 84 – Limoges 66 – Tulle 45

⛰ Village Vacances Les Chalets du Bois Combet
(rental of chalets only)

✆ 0555989683. www.chamberet.net – traditional camp. spaces also available

Address : 1.3km southwest along the D 132, follow the signs for Meilhards and take the road to the right, 100m from a small lake
Opening times : from beginning April to end Oct.

1 ha flat, grassy
Rental rates : 🕭 (1 chalet) 🅿 – 10 🚐 – 3 🏠. Per night from 45 to 72€ – Per week from 236 to 588€
🚐 Eurorelais sani-station – 8 ▣ 7€
A small and pretty chalet village overlooking the water park.

Surroundings : 🐾 ♀
Leisure activities : 🛏 🚣
Facilities : 🚿🆑ⁿ launderette
Nearby : 🎿 🏊 🏄 🎣 forest trail

GPS Longitude : 1.70994
Latitude : 45.57541

To visit a town or region, use the MICHELIN Green Guides.

CHÂTEAUNEUF-LA-FORÊT

87130 – Michelin map **325** G6 – pop. 1 641 – alt. 376
▶ Paris 424 – Eymoutiers 14 – Limoges 36 – St-Léonard-de-Noblat 19

⚠ Le Cheyenne

✆ 0555693929. www.camping-le-cheyenne.com

Address : avenue Michel Sinibaldi (800m west of the town centre, follow rte du Stade, 100m from a small lake)

Opening times : from beginning April to end Sept.

1 ha (45 pitches) flat, grassy

Tariff : 18.50€ ♣♣ ⇐ ▣ 🔌 (6A) – Extra per person 4€
Rental rates : (from beginning April to end Sept.) – 10 🚐 – 1 🏠. Per night from 60€ – Per week from 230 to 500€
🚐 AireService sani-station 4€

Surroundings : 🛏 ♀
Leisure activities : 🍷 ✕
Facilities : 🕭 ⌒ⁿ launderette
Nearby : 🏄 🎿 🏊 (beach) 🎣

GPS Longitude : 1.60127
Latitude : 45.71633

CHÂTEAUPONSAC

87290 – Michelin map **325** E4 – pop. 2 158 – alt. 290
▶ Paris 361 – Bélâbre 55 – Limoges 48 – Bellac 21

⛰ Aquadis Loisirs La Gartempe

📞 05 55 76 55 33. http://www.aquadis-loisirs.com/camping-de-la-gartempe/

Address : avenue de Ventenat (take the southwestern exit along the D 711, follow the signs for Nantiat; 200m from the river)

Opening times : from end April to beginning Oct.

1.5 ha (56 pitches) terraced, relatively flat, flat, grassy

Tariff : 16 € ♦♦ 🚗 🖭 (🗲) (16A) – Extra per person 3.70 € – Reservation fee 10 €

Rental rates : (from end April to beginning Oct.) – 2 🚐 – 13 🏠. Per night from 45 to 55 € – Per week from 179 to 469 € – Reservation fee 20 €

🚰 local sani-station – 🛒 11 €

The site is close to the church, the town and the lush, green river bank.

Surroundings : 🏞 ♀♀
Leisure activities : ♀ ✕ 🏠 🛶
Facilities : ♿ ⚡ ▦ ☔ launderette
Nearby : ♨ 🛶 🎣

GPS
Longitude : 1.27046
Latitude : 46.1318

CHÂTELUS-MALVALEIX

23270 – Michelin map **325** J3 – pop. 563 – alt. 410
▶ Paris 333 – Aigurande 25 – Aubusson 46 – Boussac 19

⛰ Municipal La Roussille

📞 05 55 80 70 31. www.chatelusmalvaleix.fr – 🍴

Address : 10 place de la Fontaine (to the west of the village)

Opening times : from beginning June to mid Sept.

0.5 ha (26 pitches) relatively flat, flat, grassy

Tariff : ♦ 6 € 🚗 – (🗲) (16A) 4 €

Basic sanitary facilities for the pitches but close to a good sports and leisure centre.

Surroundings : 🏞 ♀♀ ⛰
Leisure activities : 🏠 🚲 🎣
Facilities : ☔ launderette
Nearby : ♀ 🛶 ✕

GPS
Longitude : 2.01818
Latitude : 46.3031

COGNAC-LA-FORET

87310 – Michelin map **325** D5 – pop. 1 022 – alt. 410
▶ Paris 417 – Guéret 113 – Limoges 27 – Périgueux 87

⛰ Les Alouettes

📞 05 55 03 26 93. www.camping-des-alouettes.com

Address : at Les Alouettes (1km west along the D 10, follow signs for Rochechouart)

Opening times : from beginning April to end Sept.

5 ha (68 pitches) relatively flat, flat, grassy

Tariff : (2015 price) 21.50 € ♦♦ 🚗 🖭 (🗲) (10A) – Extra per person 4.75 €

Rental rates : (2015 price) (from beginning April to end Sept.) – 6 🚐 – 3 tent lodges. Per night from 59 to 84 € – Per week from 410 to 585 €

Surroundings : 🏞 🏞
Leisure activities : 🏠 🛶 🛶
Facilities : ♿ ⚡ 🛏 🖭

GPS
Longitude : 0.99678
Latitude : 45.82463

CORRÈZE

19800 – Michelin map **329** M3 – pop. 1 168 – alt. 455
▶ Paris 480 – Argentat 47 – Brive-la-Gaillarde 45 – Égletons 22

⛰ Municipal la Chapelle

📞 05 55 21 25 21. http://www.mairie-correze.fr/

Address : at La Chapelle (take the eastern exit along the D 143, follow the signs for Egletons and take a right turn, follow the signs for Bouysse – divided into two separate sections)

Opening times : from mid June to mid Sept.

3 ha (54 pitches) open site, terrace, relatively flat, flat, grassy, wood

Tariff : (2015 price) ♦ 2.65 € 🚗 1.40 € 🖭 2.50 € – (🗲) (5A) 2.50 €

Rental rates : (2015 price) (from mid April to end Oct.) – 3 🚐 – 1 gîte. Per week from 200 to 300 €

🚰 AireService sani-station – 10 🖭 – 🛒 (🗲) 8.50 €

The camping part of the site has a small road running through it; located beside the Corrèze river and near a small chapel.

Surroundings : 🏞 ♀♀
Leisure activities : 🏠 🛶 🎣
Facilities : ♿ ☔ 🖭
Nearby : 🛶

GPS
Longitude : 1.8798
Latitude : 45.37191

CROMAC

87160 – Michelin map **325** E2 – pop. 266 – alt. 224
▶ Paris 339 – Argenton-sur-Creuse 41 – Limoges 68 – Magnac-Laval 22

⛰ Lac de Mondon

Lac de Mondon

📞 05 55 76 93 34. www.campingdemondon.com

Address : at Les Forges de Mondon (situated 2km south along the D 105, follow the signs for St-Sulpice-les-Feuilles and take the D 60 – recommended route via the D 912)

Opening times : from mid April to end Sept.

2.8 ha (100 pitches) relatively flat, flat, grassy

Tariff : (2015 price) 14 € ♦♦ 🚗 🖭 (🗲) (10A) – Extra per person 4 €

Rental rates : (2015 price) permanent – 3 🚐. Per night from 42 to 68 € – Per week from 235 to 381 €

🚰 Eurorelais sani-station 2 €

A green setting with some pitches adjacent to a leisure centre.

Surroundings : 🏞 🏞 ♀♀
Leisure activities : ♀ ✕ 🏠 🚲 🎣 🎣
Facilities : ♿ ⚡ 🖭 🛏 ☔
Nearby : 🛶 ♨ 🛶 ⛱ pedalos

GPS
Longitude : 1.31153
Latitude : 46.3322

DONZENAC

19270 – Michelin map **329** K4 – pop. 2 492 – alt. 204
▶ Paris 469 – Brive-la-Gaillarde 11 – Limoges 81 – Tulle 27

⛰ La Rivière

📞 05 55 85 63 95. http://campinglariviere.jimdo.com

Address : route d'Ussac (1.6km south of the town, following the signs for Brive; beside the Maumont river)

Opening times : from beginning May to end Sept.

1.2 ha (60 pitches) flat, grassy

Tariff : (2015 price) ♦ 5.80 € 🚗 5.60 € 🖭 – (🗲) (10A) 4.20 €

Rental rates : (2015 price) (from beginning April to end Sept.) – 14 . Per week from 185 to 580€

🚐 Eurorelais sani-station

A pleasant, shaded grassy area, close to a small stream and the town's sports facilities.

Surroundings : 🗂 ♉️
Leisure activities : 🏖
Facilities : 👤 ☕ 🚾 🏢
Nearby : 🎿 🛶 🏊

G P S	Longitude : 1.52149
	Latitude : 45.21761

EYMOUTIERS

87120 – Michelin map **325** H6 – pop. 2 033 – alt. 417
▶ Paris 432 – Aubusson 55 – Guéret 62 – Limoges 44

⚠️ Municipal

📞 05 55 69 10 21. mairie-eymoutiers@wanadoo.fr – 🏪

Address : rue de St Pierre Château (situated 2km southeast along the D 940, follow the signs for Tulle and take road to the left)

Opening times : from beginning June to end Sept.

1 ha (33 pitches) open site, terraced, relatively flat, flat, grassy

Tariff : (2015 price) 6.50€ 👤👤 🚐 🅴 💧 (6A) – Extra per person 1.70€

🚐 local sani-station

In an elevated location, this is a small, simple site with no services.

Surroundings : 🏞 🗂 ♉️
Facilities : 👤🚐🗑

G P S	Longitude : 1.75296
	Latitude : 45.73161

GUÉRET

23000 – Michelin map **325** I3 – pop. 13 844 – alt. 457
▶ Paris 351 – Bourges 122 – Châteauroux 90 – Clermont-Ferrand 132

⚠️ Courtille

📞 05 55 81 92 24. www.camping-courtille.com

Address : route de Courtille (2.5km southwest along the D 914, follow the signs for Benevent and take road to the left)

Opening times : from beginning April to end Sept.

2.4 ha (70 pitches) flat, relatively flat, grassy

Tariff : 👤 3.10€ 🚐 2€ 🅴 8.30€ – 💧 (10A) 2.80€ – Reservation fee 5€
Rental rates : (from beginning April to end Sept.) – 4 – 1 🏠. Per week from 245 to 574€ – Reservation fee 10€

In a green and wooded location near a pretty lake and its activity centre.

Surroundings : 🏞 🗂 ♉️
Leisure activities : 🏖
Facilities : 👤 ☕ 🚾 launderette
Nearby : 🚲 🏖 (beach) 🎣 🚤 watersports centre

G P S	Longitude : 1.85823
	Latitude : 46.16093

LADIGNAC-LE-LONG

87500 – Michelin map **325** D7 – pop. 1 124 – alt. 334
▶ Paris 426 – Brive-la-Gaillarde 74 – Limoges 35 – Nontron 44

⚠️ Bel Air

📞 05 55 09 39 82. www.atouvert.com

Address : rue Bel'Air (located 1.5km north along the D 11, follow the signs for Nexon and take road to the left)

2.5 ha (100 pitches) terraced, flat, grassy

Rentals : 5 .

A wooded setting and pleasant location on the edge of a small lake.

Surroundings : 🏞 🗂 ♉️
Leisure activities : 🏖 🚲
Facilities : 👤 ☕ 🚾 launderette
Nearby : 🎣

G P S	Longitude : 1.11185
	Latitude : 45.59089

LAGUENNE

19150 – Michelin map **329** L4 – pop. 1 453 – alt. 205
▶ Paris 484 – Cahors 131 – Limoges 93 – Tulle 5

⚠️ Le Pré du Moulin

📞 05 55 26 21 96. www.lepredumoulin.com

Address : rue du Vieux Moulin (2km north)

Opening times : permanent

1.5 ha (22 pitches) terraced, flat, grassy

Tariff : 20€ 👤👤 🚐 🅴 💧 (6A) – Extra per person 5.50€ – Reservation fee 30€

Situated in a small clearing by the Corrèze river.

Surroundings : 🏞 🗂 ♉️
Leisure activities : 🏊 (small swimming pool) 🎣
Facilities : 👤 ☕ 🚾 🏢

G P S	Longitude : 1.78145
	Latitude : 45.24657

LIGINIAC

19160 – Michelin map **329** P3 – pop. 641 – alt. 665
▶ Paris 464 – Aurillac 83 – Bort-les-Orgues 24 – Clermont-Ferrand 107

⚠️ Municipal le Maury

📞 05 55 95 92 28. www.camping-du-maury.com

Address : 4.6km southwest following signs for the beach; beside the Lac de Triouzoune – recommended route via the D 20, follow the signs for Neuvic

2 ha (50 pitches) terraced, relatively flat, flat, grassy

Rentals : 12 gîtes – 10 cabins.

🚐 Eurorelais sani-station

The site is on a lovely undulating field that leads down to a lake.

Surroundings : 🏞 ♉️
Leisure activities : 🏖 🚣 🎿
Facilities : ☕ launderette
Nearby : 🍷 🍽 🚣 🏖 (beach), pedalos

G P S	Longitude : 2.30498
	Latitude : 45.39143

Key to rentals symbols:

12 🚐	*Number of mobile homes*
20 🏠	*Number of chalets*
6 🛏	*Number of rooms to rent*
Per night 30–50€	*Minimum/maximum rate per night*
Per week 300–1,000€	*Minimum/maximum rate per week*

LIMOGES

87000 – Michelin map **325** E6 – pop. 137 758 – alt. 300
▶ Paris 394 – Angoulême 104 – Guéret 90 – Tulle 90

⚠ Uzurat ▲▲

🔗 05 55 38 49 43. www.campinglimoges.fr

Address : 40 avenue d'Uzurat (Z.I. (industrial zone) north of Uzurat, near the Leclerc shopping centre)

Opening times : from mid March to end Oct.

2.5 ha (155 pitches) flat, grassy, gravelled

Tariff : (2015 price) 16.70€ ★★ 🚐 🔲 🔌 (10A) – Extra per person 3.70€
Rental rates : (2015 price) (from mid March to end Oct.) – 16 🚐.
Per night from 50 to 98€ – Per week from 245 to 815€
🚐 local sani-station
A well-shaded site near a shopping centre.

Surroundings : 🎍🎍	
Leisure activities : 🎣🖼. 🏄	**G** Longitude : 1.27577
Facilities : ☕ ⚡ 🍳 🍴 launderette	**P** Latitude : 45.87056
Nearby : 🏖 🍴 ✕ 🍽 🐎 forest trail	**S**

This guide is updated regularly, so buy your new copy every year!

LISSAC-SUR-COUZE

19600 – Michelin map **329** J5 – pop. 710 – alt. 170
▶ Paris 486 – Brive-la-Gaillarde 11 – Périgueux 68 – Sarlat-la-Canéda 42

⚠ La Prairie et gîtes de Lissac ▲▲

🔗 05 55 85 37 97. www.caussecorrezien.fr

Address : 1.4km southwest along the D 59 and take road to the left, near the Lac du Causse

Opening times : from beginning April to end Sept.

5 ha (120 pitches) terraced, flat, grassy, fine gravel

Tariff : 24€ ★★ 🚐 🔲 🔌 (16A) – Extra per person 5€
Rental rates : permanent – 20 🏠 – 14 tent lodges – 25 gîtes.
Per night from 51 to 155€ – Per week from 180 to 800€
🚐 Eurorelais sani-station 4€ – 6 🔲 12€
The gîtes village is 500m from the main site.

Surroundings : 🎍 ≤ the Lac du Causse 🏕 🎍🎍	
Leisure activities : 🍴 ✕ 🖼. 🏄 🏊 BMX track	**G** Longitude : 1.45465
Facilities : ☕ ⚡ 🍳 🍽 🍴 launderette 🧺	**P** Latitude : 45.10125
At the leisure/activities centre : 🚲 🛶 (beach) 🐎 🐴 pedalos	**S**

⚠ Village Vacances Les Hameaux du Perrier
(rental of chalets only)

🔗 05 55 84 34 48. www.terresdefrance.com

Address : at Le Perrier (off the D59)

Opening times : permanent

17 ha/10 for camping terraced

Rental rates : 60 🏠. Per night from 45 to 125€ – Per week from 149 to 749€
A large chalet village, accommodation of different standards.

Surroundings : 🎍 ≤ 🎍🎍	
Leisure activities : 🍴 ✕ 🏄 🏊 🏊	**G** Longitude : 1.43848
Facilities : ⚡ 🍳 🍴 launderette 🧺	**P** Latitude : 45.10029
Nearby : 🚲 🐎 🛶 ⛵ 🐴	**S**

MAGNAC-LAVAL

87190 – Michelin map **325** D3 – pop. 1 850 – alt. 231
▶ Paris 366 – Limoges 64 – Poitiers 86 – Guéret 62

⚠ Village Vacances Le Hameau de Gîtes des Pouyades

🔗 05 55 60 73 45. www.lelimousinsejoursvacances.com

Address : at Les Pouyades

Opening times : permanent (check website)

1.5 ha flat

Rental rates : (2015 price) (from end Jan. to end Dec.) – 12 🚐 – 12 gîtes. Per night from 72 to 127€ – Per week from 277 to 660€ – Reservation fee 16€
In a green setting beside a small, pretty lake.

Surroundings : 🎍 ≤ On the lake 🍃	
Leisure activities : 🖼 🚲 🏄 🏊	**G** Longitude : 1.19236
Facilities : ☕ 🍳 🍴 launderette	**P** Latitude : 46.20331
	S

MASSERET

19510 – Michelin map **329** K2 – pop. 675 – alt. 380
▶ Paris 432 – Guéret 132 – Limoges 45 – Tulle 48

⚠ Domaine des Forges

🔗 05 55 73 44 57. www.camping-domainedesforges.com

Address : 3km east along the D 20, follow the signs for Les Meilhards, near the exit from Masseret-Gare

Opening times : from beginning April to end Sept.

100 ha/2 for camping (80 pitches) open site, undulating, relatively flat, flat, grassy, fine gravel

Tariff : 18€ ★★ 🚐 🔲 🔌 (10A) – Extra per person 3€ – Reservation fee 5€
Rental rates : (from beginning April to end Sept.) – 4 🚐. Per night from 50 to 60€ – Per week from 230 to 440€ – Reservation fee 50€
In a pleasant wooded setting, looking out over a lake.

Surroundings : 🎍 ≤ the lake 🎍🎍	
Leisure activities : 🖼	**G** Longitude : 1.54908
Facilities : ☕ ⚡ 🍳 🔲	**P** Latitude : 45.54154
Nearby : 🍴 ✕ 🚲 🏄 🏊 🍽 🐴 🏊 (beach) 🐎	**S**

MEYSSAC

19500 – Michelin map **329** L5 – pop. 1 245 – alt. 220
▶ Paris 507 – Argentat 62 – Beaulieu-sur-Dordogne 21 – Brive-la-Gaillarde 23

⚠ Intercommunal Moulin de Valane

🔗 05 55 25 41 59. www.meyssac.fr

Address : located 1km to the northwest, follow the signs for Collonges-la-Rouge ; beside a stream

Opening times : from mid April to end Sept.

4 ha (115 pitches) terraced, relatively flat, flat, grassy

Tariff : (2015 price) 22€ ★★ 🚐 🔲 🔌 (10A) – Extra per person 4€
Rental rates : (2015 price) (from mid April to end Sept.) – 21 🚐. Per night from 50 to 60€ – Per week from 210 to 570€
Ageing sanitary facilities. The site welcomes groups and mini-camps for children.

Surroundings : 🏕 🎍🎍	
Leisure activities : ✕ 🖼 🏄 🚲 🍽 🏊 🏊	**G** Longitude : 1.66381
Facilities : ☕ ⚡ (July–Aug.) 🍴 launderette 🧺	**P** Latitude : 45.06102
	S

NEUVIC

19160 – Michelin map **329** O3 – pop. 1 868 – alt. 620
▶ Paris 465 – Aurillac 78 – Mauriac 25 – Tulle 56

⛰ Domaine de Mialaret

Domaine de Mialaret

✆ 05 55 46 02 50. www.lemialaret.com
Address : route d'Egleton (3km west along the D 991 and take a right turn)
Opening times : from end April to mid Oct.
44 ha/3 for camping (170 pitches) undulating, sloping, relatively flat, flat, grassy
Tariff : (2015 price) 34€ ♛♛ ⇌ 🅴 (10A) – Extra per person 9€
Rental rates : (2015 price) permanent – 31 🏠 – 25 tent lodges – 15 gîtes – hotel. Per night from 50 to 120€ – Per week from 350 to 840€ 🚐 Raclet sani-station

Surroundings : 🌊 🗙 ♒♒
Leisure activities : 🎣
Facilities : 🔥🏖

G P S Longitude : 2.22922
Latitude : 45.38216

⛰ Municipal du Lac

✆ 05 55 95 85 48. www.campingdulac-neuvic-correze.com
Address : route de la Plage (2.3km east along the D 20, follow the signs for Bort-les-Orgues and turn left onto the beach road; beside the Lac de la Triouzoune)
Opening times : from beginning March to end Nov.
5 ha (93 pitches) terraced, gravel, grassy
Tariff : 15€ ♛♛ ⇌ 🅴 (10A) – Extra per person 3.15€ – Reservation fee 16€
Rental rates : (from beginning March to end Nov.) – 12 🏠 – 15 gîtes. Per night from 42 to 49€ – Reservation fee 16€
🚐 AireService sani-station 1.50€ – 🚐8€
Some pitches for tents and caravans have a view of the Lac de la Triouzoune.

Surroundings : 🌊 🗙 ♒♒
Leisure activities : 🚣 ♒ 🎣
Facilities : 🔥 🍴 launderette
Nearby : 🍷 ✗ 🏖 (beach) ♒ ⚓ pedalos

G P S Longitude : 2.29207
Latitude : 45.3841

NEXON

87800 – Michelin map **325** E6 – pop. 2 457 – alt. 359
▶ Paris 412 – Châlus 20 – Limoges 22 – Nontron 53

⛰ Municipal de la Lande

✆ 05 55 58 35 44. www.camping-nexon.fr
Address : Etang de la Lande (lake, located 1km south following signs for St-Hilaire, access near the pl. de l'Hôtel-de-Ville)
Opening times : from beginning June to end Sept.
2 ha (60 pitches) terraced, relatively flat, grassy
Tariff : 10€ ♛♛ ⇌ 🅴 (10A) – Extra per person 3.20€
Rental rates : (2015 price) (from beginning April to beginning Nov.) – 6 🏠 – 9 tent lodges. Per night from 24 to 57€ – Per week from 114 to 485€ – Reservation fee 32€
🚐 local sani-station – 1 🅴
A well-shaded green site with views of the lake from some pitches.

Surroundings : 🗙 ♒♒
Leisure activities : 🚣 🚴
Facilities : 🔥 🍴 🚿 🍴 📷 🧺
Nearby : 🏖 🏖 (beach) pedalos

G P S Longitude : 1.17997
Latitude : 45.67078

OBJAT

19130 – Michelin map **329** J4 – pop. 3 605 – alt. 131
▶ Paris 495 – Limoges 106 – Tulle 46 – Brive-la-Gaillarde 20

⛰ Village Vacances Les Grands Prés
(rental of chalets only)

✆ 05 55 24 08 80. www.brive-tourisme.com
Address : Espace loisirs des Grands Prés (the Grands Prés leisure park)
Opening times : permanent
18 ha/4 for camping flat
Rental rates : (2015 price) – 20 🏠. Per night from 49 to 149€ – Per week from 245 to 505€
🚐 Eurorelais sani-station 7€
On a very large natural site with lots of activities.

Surroundings : 🌊 ⩽
Leisure activities : 🎣
Facilities : 🔥 🛖 launderette
Nearby : 🍷 ✗ 🏖 🚴 🎣 🏖 🛶 pedalos

G P S Longitude : 1.41069
Latitude : 45.26687

REYGADES

19430 – Michelin map **329** M5 – pop. 193 – alt. 460
▶ Paris 516 – Aurillac 56 – Brive-la-Gaillarde 56 – St-Céré 26

⛰ La Belle Étoile

✆ 05 55 28 50 08. www.campingbelle-etoile.fr
Address : at Lestrade (located 1km north off the D 41, follow the signs for Beaulieu-sur-Dordogne)
Opening times : from beginning June to end Sept.
5 ha/3 for camping (25 pitches) terraced, flat, grassy
Tariff : (2015 price) ♛ 4.15€ ⇌ 🅴 5.30€ – 🔥 (6A) 3.10€
Rental rates : (2015 price) permanent – 6 🏠 – 6 🏠 – 4 canvas bungalows. Per week from 195 to 640€
Peaceful, shaded pitches; rental accommodation of varying standards.

Surroundings : 🌊 ⩽ 🗙 ♒♒
Leisure activities : 🚣 🏖 🎣 (small swimming pool)
Facilities : 🔥 🚿 🏖 launderette 🏊

G P S Longitude : 1.90538
Latitude : 45.02405

ROYÈRE-DE-VASSIVIÈRE

23460 – Michelin map **325** I5 – pop. 563 – alt. 735
▶ Paris 412 – Bourganeuf 22 – Eymoutiers 25 – Felletin 29

⛰ Les Terrasses du Lac

✆ 05 55 64 76 77. www.campings.lelacdevassiviere.com
Address : at Vauveix (10km southwest along the D 3 and D 35, follow the signs for Eymoutiers; by the marina (direct access)
Opening times : from end March to beginning Nov.
4 ha (142 pitches) terraced, relatively flat, flat, grassy, gravelled
Tariff : (2015 price) 20.70€ ♛♛ ⇌ 🅴 (10A) – Extra per person 4.50€ – Reservation fee 15.20€
In a panoramic location looking over the lake and the marina.

Surroundings : ⩽ Lac de Vassivière 🗙 ♒♒
Leisure activities : 🚣 🏖 (beach) 🎣
Facilities : 🚿 (July-Aug.) 🍴 🛖 🏖 launderette
Nearby : 🏊 🍷 ✗ 🏖 ♒ ⚓ water skiing

G P S Longitude : 1.89526
Latitude : 45.78979

ST-GERMAIN-LES-BELLES

87380 – Michelin map **325** F7 – pop. 1 151 – alt. 432
▶ Paris 422 – Eymoutiers 33 – Limoges 34 – St-Léonard-de-Noblat 31

⚠ Le Montréal

⌖ 05 55 71 86 20. www.campingdemontreal.com

Address : rue du Petit Moulin (take the southeastern exit, follow the signs for La Porcherie; beside a small lake)

1 ha (60 pitches) terrace, relatively flat, flat, grassy
Rentals : 2 🚐 – 5 🏠 – 6 canvas bungalows.
🚽 local sani-station
Pitches that are well marked out, with a view of the lake.

Surroundings : ⅍ ← 🗐 ♀	
Leisure activities : 🏊	**G** Longitude : 1.5011
Facilities : ᵬ ⛬ ▥ 🍴 launderette	**P** Latitude : 45.61143
Nearby : ✗ 🚴 🏊 🍴 ☱ (beach) 🎣	**S**

ST-LÉONARD-DE-NOBLAT

87400 – Michelin map **325** F5 – pop. 4 665 – alt. 347
▶ Paris 407 – Aubusson 68 – Brive-la-Gaillarde 99 – Guéret 62

⚠ Municipal de Beaufort

⌖ 05 55 56 02 79. www.campingdebeaufort.fr

Address : at Beaufort (1.7km along the N 141, follow signs for Limoges, then 1.5km to the left following signs for Masleon)

Opening times : from mid May to mid Sept.

2 ha (98 pitches) relatively flat, flat, grassy

Tariff : (2015 price) 17.50€ ✶ ✶ 🚗 🔲 🔌 (15A) –
Extra per person 2.50€
Rental rates : (2015 price) (from mid April to end Oct.) – 10 🚐.
Per night from 35 to 65€ – Per week from 220 to 400€
🚽 AireService sani-station 3€
The pitches are marked out and shaded, beside the Vienne river.

Surroundings : 🗐 ♀♀	
Leisure activities : 🏠 🎣	**G** Longitude : 1.49211
Facilities : ᵬ ⛬ 🛁 ⚁ 🍴 launderette	**P** Latitude : 45.82276
Nearby : 🚴	**S**

ST-PARDOUX

87250 – Michelin map **325** E4 – pop. 536 – alt. 370
▶ Paris 366 – Bellac 25 – Limoges 33 – St-Junien 39

⚠ Aquadis Loisirs Le Freaudour

⌖ 05 55 76 57 22. http://www.aquadis-loisirs.com/camping-de-freaudour/

Address : at the leisure centre (1.2km to the south; beside the Lac de St-Pardoux)

Opening times : from beginning March to beginning Nov.

4.5 ha (107 pitches) relatively flat, flat, grassy

Tariff : 18.90€ ✶ ✶ 🚗 🔲 🔌 (10A) – Extra per person 5.30€ –
Reservation fee 10€
Rental rates : (from beginning March to beginning Nov.) – 20 🚐 –
10 🏠. Per night from 68 to 89€ – Per week from 189 to 599€ –
Reservation fee 20€
🚽 AireService sani-station – 🚐 14€

In a green and shady setting, beside the lake.

Surroundings : 🦢 🗐 ♀♀	
Leisure activities : 🍴 🏠 🏊 fitness trail, water skiing	**G** Longitude : 1.2788
Facilities : ᵬ ⛬ ▣🛁 ⚁ 🍴 launderette	**P** Latitude : 46.04931
Nearby : 🚴 ☱ (beach)	**S**

ST-PARDOUX-CORBIER

19210 – Michelin map **329** J3 – pop. 360 – alt. 404
▶ Paris 448 – Arnac-Pompadour 8 – Brive-la-Gaillarde 44 – St-Yrieix-la-Perche 27

⚠ Le Domaine Bleu ·

⌖ 05 55 73 59 89. www.ledomainebleu.eu

Address : take the eastern exit along the D 50, follow the signs for Vigeois and take the road to the right, near a lake

Opening times : from beginning July to beginning Sept.

1 ha (40 pitches) terraced, relatively flat, flat, grassy

Tariff : 16€ ✶ ✶ 🚗 🔲 🔌 (16A) – Extra per person 4€

Pitches on shaded terraces, overlooking a lake.

Surroundings : 🦢 🗐 ♀♀	
Leisure activities : 🎣	**G** Longitude : 1.45449
Facilities : ᵬ ⛬ 🗑🗹 ▥ ⚁ 🍴 launderette	**P** Latitude : 45.42973
Nearby : 🍴	**S**

ST-SORNIN-LAVOLPS

19230 – Michelin map **329** J3 – pop. 911 – alt. 400
▶ Paris 454 – Cahors 126 – Limoges 63 – Tulle 47

⚠ Les Étoiles

⌖ 05 55 73 01 27. www.camping-pompadour.com

Address : in the village

Opening times : from end March to end Oct.

1 ha (40 pitches) terraced, flat, grassy

Tariff : (2015 price) 15€ ✶ ✶ 🚗 🔲 🔌 (16A) – Extra per person 5€
Rental rates : (2015 price) (from end March to end Oct.) ᵬ (1 chalet) – 3 🚐 – 1 🏠 – 9 tent lodges. Per night from 55 to 100€ –
Per week from 199 to 600€
🚽 local sani-station 3€ – 🚐 11€
Located between the church and a small lake; 2km from the Pompadour horse racing course.

Surroundings : 🦢 ♀♀	
Leisure activities : 🏊	**G** Longitude : 1.38330
Facilities : ᵬ ⛬ ▥ 🍴 ⚁ 🔲	**P** Latitude : 45.377
Nearby : 🎣	**S**

ST-YRIEIX-LA-PERCHE

87500 – Michelin map **325** E7 – pop. 6 932 – alt. 360
▶ Paris 430 – Brive-la-Gaillarde 63 – Limoges 40 – Périgueux 63

⚠ Municipal d'Arfeuille

⌖ 05 55 75 08 75. camping@saint-yrieix.fr

Address : route du Viaduc (2.5km north following signs for Limoges and take the road to the left; beside a small lake)

Opening times : from beginning April to end Sept.

2 ha (76 pitches) terraced, flat, grassy

Tariff : (2015 price) 14.60€ ✶ ✶ 🚗 🔲 🔌 (10A) –
Extra per person 4.30€

Rental rates : (from beginning April to end Sept.) &. (1 chalet) –
11 🏠. Per night from 50 to 100€ – Per week from 230 to 510€
🚽 local sani-station – 🔌 ⚡11.60€
*A leafy green site, with shade and a panoramic view over a lake,
Simple and rather old sanitary facilities, but well maintained.*

Surroundings : 🌿 ⬱ 🗺 ♨♨
Leisure activities : 🎣 ⛷
Facilities : 🚿 ⚿ 🚻 launderette
Nearby : 🍷 ✗ 🚣 🏖 (beach) 🛶 pedalos

G P S Longitude : 1.20009
Latitude : 45.52791

---

*Some information or pricing may have changed since
the guide went to press. We recommend you check the
price list online in advance or at the entrance to the
campsite and enquire about possible restrictions.*

SEILHAC

19700 – Michelin map **329** L3 – pop. 1 721 – alt. 500
▶ Paris 461 – Aubusson 97 – Brive-la-Gaillarde 33 – Limoges 73

⚠ Le Lac de Bournazel

✆ 05 55 27 05 65. www.camping-lac-bournazel.com

Address : located 1.5km northwest along the N 120, follow the signs
for Uzerche then turn right after 1km

Opening times : from beginning April to end Sept.

6.5 ha (120 pitches) terraced, flat, grassy, gravelled

Tariff : (2015 price) 15.30€ ⚘⚘ 🚗 🅿 ⚡ (10A) –
Extra per person 4.80€ – Reservation fee 9€
Rental rates : (2015 price) (from beginning April to end Sept.) –
2 'gypsy' caravans – 10 🏠 – 2 tipis. Per night from 32 to
91€ – Per week from 224 to 637€ – Reservation fee 10€
🚽 local sani-station 4€ – 🔌11.90€
*In a pleasant leafy setting with plenty of shade; some pitches
under lime trees.*

Surroundings : 🌿 🗺 ♨♨
Leisure activities : 🍷 ✗ 🎣 🚣 🚲
Facilities : & ⚿ 🚻 launderette 🔧
Nearby : 🎯 🏖 🛶 🐎 fitness trail

G P S Longitude : 1.7022
Latitude : 45.37838

VIDEIX

87600 – Michelin map **325** B6 – pop. 234 – alt. 260
▶ Paris 443 – Angoulême 53 – Limoges 53 – Nontron 36

⚠⚠ Village Vacances Le Hameau de gîtes de Chassagne – (rental of chalets only)

✆ 05 55 48 83 39. www.tourisme-meteorite.com

Address : La Chassagne (head 1.7km north along the D 87, follow the
signs for Pressignac)

Opening times : permanent

3 ha flat, grassy
Rental rates : (2015 price) 🅿 – 16 🏠 – 16 gîtes. Per night
from 70 to 90€ – Per week from 245 to 480€

Surroundings : 🌿 ⬱ lake ⛰
Leisure activities : 🎣 ⛷
Facilities : & ⚿ 🚻 launderette
Nearby : 🍷 ✗ 🚣 🛶 ♨ pedalos

G P S Longitude : 0.71585
Latitude : 45.80106

VIGEOIS

19410 – Michelin map **329** K3 – pop. 1 194 – alt. 390
▶ Paris 457 – Limoges 68 – Tulle 32 – Brive-la-Gaillarde 41

⚠ Municipal du Lac de Pontcharal

✆ 05 55 98 90 86. www.vigeois.com

Address : at Pontcharal (situated 2km southeast along the D 7, follow
the signs for Brive, near the lake at Pontcharal)

Opening times : from beginning June to mid Sept.

32 ha/1.7 (85 pitches) terrace, undulating, relatively flat, flat, grassy

Tariff : ⚘ 3.90€ 🚗 🅿 4.80€ – ⚡ (15A) 4.30€
Rental rates : (from end March to end Oct.) – 7 🏠. Per night
from 75€ – Per week from 290 to 430€
🚽 Eurorelais sani-station 3€
A pleasant campsite situated beside a leisure centre.

Surroundings : 🌿 ♨♨ ⛰
Leisure activities : 🍷 ✗ 🏖 (beach) 🛶
Facilities : & ⚿ (July–Aug.) 🔥 🚻 🅿 🔧
Nearby : pedalos

G P S Longitude : 1.53806
Latitude : 45.36873

LORRAINE

Christian Legay / Mairie de Metz

If you want to do justice to the collage of stunning sights of Lorraine, a region that shares borders with Luxembourg, Germany and Belgium, don't forget to pack your walking boots. But before you head for the hills, make sure you leave enough time to discover the artistic heritage of Nancy and admire the lights and contemporary art gallery of historic Metz. Then embark upon the trail of tiny spa resorts and the famous centres of craftsmanship that produce the legendary Baccarat crystal, Longwy enamels and Lunéville porcelain. From there head to historic Domrémy and Colombey. The water, forests and wildlife of the Vosges regional park, nestling in the 'Valley of Lakes', will keep you entranced as you make your way down hillsides dotted with orchards bursting with plums. Stop for a little light refreshment in a *marcairerie* (traditional farmhouse inn) and sample the famous *quiche Lorraine* tarts, a slab of Munster cheese and a delicious kirsch-flavoured dessert.

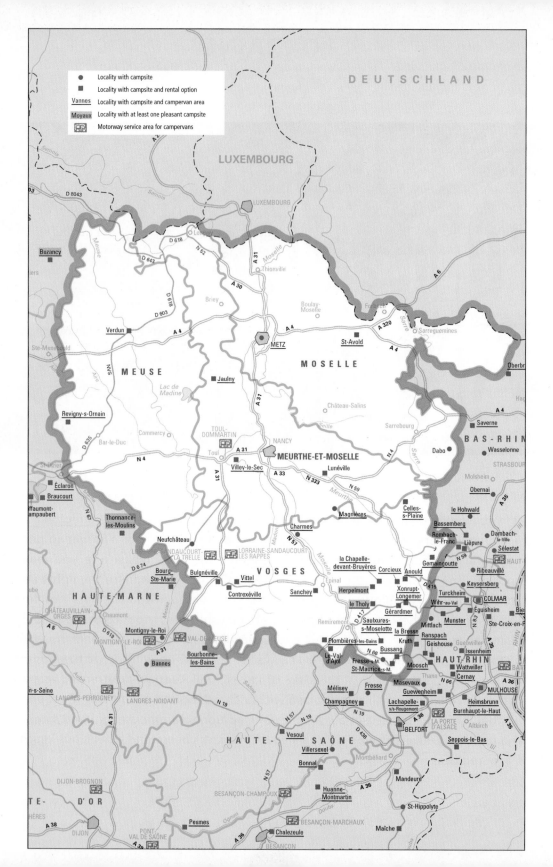

Locality with campsite
Locality with campsite and rental option
Vannes — Locality with campsite and campervan area
Moyaux — Locality with at least one pleasant campsite
Motorway service area for campervans

DEUTSCHLAND

LUXEMBOURG

LUXEMBOURG

Buzancy

D 8043

D 618

N 52

A 31

Thionville

Moselle

A 6

D 643

A 30

Briey

Boulay-Moselle

Sarre

A 320

Sarreguemines

Verdun

A 4

A 4

METZ

St-Avold

A 4

Oberbr

Ste-Menehould

MEUSE

MOSELLE

Lac de Madine

Jaulny

Château-Salins

Seille

Sarrebourg

A 4

Hag

Revigny-s-Ornain

Saverne

BAS-RHIN

Commercy

Bar-le-Duc

TOUL-DOMMARTIN

NANCY

Dabo

Wasselonne

N 4

A 31

MEURTHE-ET-MOSELLE

Sarre

STRASBOUR

St-Dizier

Toul

Villey-le-Sec

Lunéville

N 4

A 33

N 333

N 59

Molsheim

Éclaron

Braucourt

Meurthe

Obernai

A 35

iffaumont-ampaubert

N 67

Thonnance-les-Moulins

Magnières

Celles-s-Plaine

le Hohwald

Charmes

N 57

Bassemberg

Rombach-le-Franc

Dambach-la-Ville

Neufchâteau

LORRAINE-SANDAUCOURT
LES RAPPES

Liépvre

Sélestat

NDAUCOURT-
LA TRELLE

la Chapelle-devant-Bruyères

Corcieux

Gemaingoutte

HAUT-

D 674

Moselle

Anould

D 415

Ribeauvillé

Bourg-Ste-Marie

Bulgnéville

VOSGES

Vittel

Xonrupt-Longemer

Kaysersberg

HAUTE-MARNE

Contrexéville

Sanchey

Épinal

Herpelmont

le Tholy

Turckheim

Wihr-au-Val

COLMAR

CHÂTEAUVILLAIN-
ORGES

Chaumont

Gérardmer

Éguisheim

Bie

A 5

D 619

Montigny-le-Roi

VAL-DE-MEUSE

D 417

Remiremont

Saulxures-s-Moselotte

la Bresse

Mittlach

Munster

Ste-Croix-en-

MONTIGNY-LE-ROI

A 31

Plombières-les-Bains

Kruth

Ranspach

Geishouse

Guewiller

HAUT-RHIN

Bourbonne-les-Bains

Bussang

Issenheim

A 35

BA

Bannes

Le-Val-d'Ajol

N 66

Fresse-s-M.

St-Maurice-s-M.

Moosch

Thann

Wattwiller

Cernay

A 36

n-s-Seine

LANGRES-PERROGNEY

LANGRES-NOIDANT

N 19

Mélisey

Champagney

Fresse

Masevaux

Guewenheim

N 66

MULHOUSE

Lachapelle-s/s-Rougemont

Heimsbrunn

Burnhaupt-le-Haut

A 36

LA PORTE
D'ALSACE

DIJON-BROGNON

D'OR

N 57

N 19

A 36

BELFORT

Altkirch

A 35

HAUTE-

Vesoul

SAÔNE

Seppois-le-Bas

III

Villersexel

Montbéliard

Bonnal

Mandeure

A 36

BESANÇON-CHAMPOUX

Huanne-Montmartin

St-Hippolyte

ÔTE-

D'OR

PONT-
VAL DE SAÔNE

Pesmes

Ognon

BESANÇON-MARCHAUX

Doubs

Maîche

Chalezeule

A 36

A 38

DIJON

A 39

BESANÇON

ANOULD

88650 – Michelin map **314** J3 – pop. 3 336 – alt. 457
▶ Paris 430 – Colmar 43 – Épinal 45 – Gérardmer 15

⚓ Les Acacias

✆ 03 29 57 11 06, www.acaciascamp.com

Address : 191 rue Léonard de Vinci (take the western exit along the N 415, follow the signs for Colmar and take road to the right)

Opening times : from beginning Dec. to end Sept.

2.5 ha (84 pitches) terraced, flat, grassy

Tariff : (2015 price) 15.50€ ✸✸ ⟺ 🅴 🄰 (6A) – Extra per person 3.90€
Rental rates : (2015 price) (from beginning Dec. to end Sept.) – 2 'gypsy' caravans – 7 🛖 – 8 🏠. Per week from 250 to 565€
🚐 local sani-station – 6 🅴 10€ – 🔌 10€

Surroundings : 🔲 ♀
Leisure activities : 🍽 🏖 🛝 ⛷ (small swimming pool)
Facilities : 🚿 ⚭ (June–Sept.) 🛁 🏕 launderette
Nearby : walking trails

G P S	Longitude : 6.95786 Latitude : 48.18437

*The classification (1 to 5 tents, **black** or red) that we award to selected sites in this guide is our own system. It should not be confused with the classification (1 to 5 stars) of official organisations.*

LA BRESSE

88250 – Michelin map **314** J4 – pop. 4 732 – alt. 636 – Winter sports : 650/1 350 m
▶ Paris 437 – Colmar 52 – Épinal 52 – Gérardmer 13

⚓ Municipal le Haut des Bluches

✆ 03 29 25 64 80, www.hautdesbluches.com – alt. 708

Address : 5 route des Planches (head 3.2km east along the D 34, follow the signs for Le Col de la Schlucht; beside the Moselotte river)

Opening times : from mid Dec. to mid Nov.

4 ha (140 pitches) terraced, relatively flat, flat, grassy, rocks

Tariff : 20.30€ ✸✸ ⟺ 🅴 🄰 (13A) – Extra per person 3.40€ – Reservation fee 2€
Rental rates : (from mid Dec. to mid Nov.) 🚿 (2 chalets) – 6 🏠 – 13 🛏. Per night from 50 to 55€ – Per week from 360 to 646€ – Reservation fee 2€
🚐 local sani-station 3.30€ – 17 🅴 6.10€ – 🔌 8€
In a picturesque setting and crossed by a stream.

Surroundings : ❄ ◿
Leisure activities : 🍽 🍴 🏖 🛝 🎣 adventure park, multi-sports ground
Facilities : 🚿 ⚭ 🛁 🏕 ⛲ 🏕 launderette
Nearby : sports trail

G P S	Longitude : 6.91831 Latitude : 47.99878

⚓ Belle Hutte

✆ 03 29 25 49 75, www.camping-belle-hutte.com – alt. 900

Address : 1bis Vouille de Belle Hutte (head 9km northeast along the D 34, follow the signs for Le Col de la Schlucht; beside the Moselotte river)

Opening times : from mid Dec. to beginning Nov.

5 ha (125 pitches) terraced, stony, flat, grassy

Tariff : 30.60€ ✸✸ ⟺ 🅴 🄰 (10A) – Extra per person 8.30€ – Reservation fee 50€

Rental rates : (from mid Dec. to beginning Nov.) 🚿 (2 chalets) – 4 'gypsy' caravans – 20 🏠 – 2 apartments. Per night from 40 to 140€ – Per week from 200 to 1,000€ – Reservation fee 20€
Situated in a pleasant, wooded setting.

Surroundings : ❄ ◿ 🏞
Leisure activities : 🍽 🍴 🏖 🛝 ⛷ 🎣
Facilities : 🚿 ⚭ 🏕 🏕 launderette 🚿
Nearby : 🎿

BULGNÉVILLE

88140 – Michelin map **314** D3 – pop. 1 400 – alt. 350
▶ Paris 331 – Contrexéville 6 – Épinal 53 – Neufchâteau 22

⛰ Porte des Vosges

✆ 03 29 09 12 00, www.Camping-Portedesvosges.com

Address : at La Grande Tranchée (head 1.3km southeast along the D 164, follow the signs for Contrexéville and take D 14, follow the signs for Suriauville to the right)

Opening times : from beginning April to end Oct.

3.5 ha (100 pitches) relatively flat, gravelled, flat, grassy

Tariff : 19€ ✸✸ ⟺ 🅴 🄰 (6A) – Extra per person 4.60€
Rental rates : (from beginning April to end Oct.) – 1 🏠 – 3 tent lodges – 1 gîte. Per night from 25 to 50€ – Per week from 175 to 350€
🚐 local sani-station – 10 🅴 7.20€
In a rural setting.

Surroundings : ♀
Leisure activities : 🖼
Facilities : 🚿 ⚭ 🏕 🛁 🏕

G P S	Longitude : 5.84514 Latitude : 48.19529

Routes nationales are main roads and their identifying numbers begin with N or RN. Routes départementales are generally quieter roads and begin with D or DN.

BUSSANG

88540 – Michelin map **314** J5 – pop. 1 604 – alt. 605
▶ Paris 444 – Belfort 44 – Épinal 59 – Gérardmer 38

⚓ Sunêlia Domaine de Champé

✆ 03 29 61 61 51, www.domaine-de-champe.com

Address : 14 rue des Champs-Navets (located to the northeast, access via the turning to the left of the church)

Opening times : from mid March to end Nov.

3.5 ha (100 pitches) flat, grassy

Tariff : (2015 price) 34€ ✸✸ ⟺ 🅴 🄰 (6A) – Extra per person 6.50€ – Reservation fee 19€
Rental rates : (2015 price) permanent – 22 🛖 – 8 🏠. Per night from 70 to 170€ – Per week from 490 to 1,190€ – Reservation fee 19€
🚐 local sani-station
Situated beside the Moselle river and a stream.

Surroundings : ◿
Leisure activities : 🍽 🍴 🏖 🕐 daytime 🏃 🦶 ♨ hammam 🛝 ⛷ 🖼 🎣 multi-sports ground
Facilities : 🚿 ⚭ 🏕 🏕 launderette 🚿
Nearby : 🏊

CELLES-SUR-PLAINE

88110 – Michelin map **314** J2 – pop. 857 – alt. 318
▶ Paris 391 – Baccarat 23 – Blâmont 23 – Lunéville 49

⛰ Les Lacs ♣♨

🔗 0329412800, http://www.paysdeslacs.com/pole-hebergement/

Address : Place de la Gare (to the southwest of town)

Opening times : from beginning April to end Sept.

15 ha/4 for camping (135 pitches) flat, grassy, stony

Tariff : (2015 price) 24€ ♣♣ ⇔ 🔲 🔋 (10A) – Extra per person 7€ – Reservation fee 10€

Rental rates : (2015 price) (from beginning April to end Sept.) – 10 canvas bungalows – 20 gîtes. Per night from 90 to 125€ – Per week from 300 to 410€ – Reservation fee 16€

🚐 42 🔲 19€

Beside a river and close to a lake.

Surroundings : ⇐🛏	
Leisure activities : 🍷 🎯 🏃 🚣 ✂ 🎣 ⛳ 🏐	**G** **P** **S** Longitude : 6.94756 Latitude : 48.4557
Facilities : 🚿 🛒 🏧 🛁 � 🚽 🍴 launderette 🧺	
At the lake : 🚲 🛶 💧	

LA CHAPELLE-DEVANT-BRUYÈRES

88600 – Michelin map **314** I3 – pop. 621 – alt. 457
▶ Paris 416 – Épinal 31 – Gérardmer 22 – Rambervillers 26

⛰ Les Pinasses

🔗 0329585110, www.camping-les-pinasses.fr

Address : 215 route de Bruyères (located 1.2km to the northwest on the D 60)

Opening times : from end March to end Oct.

3 ha (139 pitches) flat, grassy, small lake

Tariff : 21€ ♣♣ ⇔ 🔲 🔋 (10A) – Extra per person 4€ – Reservation fee 15€

Rental rates : (from end March to end Oct.) – 2 🚐 – 18 🏠 – 5 tent lodges. Per night from 34 to 90€ – Per week from 238 to 670€ – Reservation fee 15€

🚐 local sani-station 3€ – 10 🔲 16€ – 🚐 12€

Surroundings : 🛏 ♨	
Leisure activities : ✗ 🏠 🚣 ✂ 🎣 🏐	**G** **P** **S** Longitude : 6.77411 Latitude : 48.18974
Facilities : 🚿 🛒 🛁 🚽 🍴 launderette	

CHARMES

88130 – Michelin map **314** F2 – pop. 4 613 – alt. 282
▶ Paris 381 – Mirecourt 17 – Nancy 43 – Neufchâteau 58

⛰ Les Îles

🔗 0329388771, campinglesilesdamiennazon@orange.fr

Address : 20 rue de l'Écluse (located 1km to the southwest along the D 157 and take road to the right; near the stadium)

Opening times : from beginning April to end Sept.

3.5 ha (67 pitches) flat, grassy

Tariff : (2015 price) 16.50€ ♣♣ ⇔ 🔲 🔋 (10A) – Extra per person 3.50€

🚐 local sani-station

In a pleasant setting between the Canal de l'Est and the Moselle river.

Leisure activities : 🚣 🚲 🏐	
Facilities : 🚿 🛒 🚮 🚽 🍴	**G** **P** **S** Longitude : 6.28668 Latitude : 48.37583
Nearby : ✂ 🏃	

CONTREXÉVILLE

88140 – Michelin map **314** D3 – pop. 3 440 – alt. 342 – ⚕
▶ Paris 337 – Épinal 47 – Langres 75 – Luxeuil 73

⛰ Le Tir aux Pigeons

🔗 0329081506, www.opale-dmcc.fr

Address : rue du 11 Septembre (located 1km southwest along the D 13, follow the signs for Suriauville)

Opening times : from beginning April to mid Oct.

1.8 ha (80 pitches) flat, grassy, gravel

Tariff : 19.50€ ♣♣ ⇔ 🔲 🔋 (10A) – Extra per person 3.50€ – Reservation fee 15€

Rental rates : (from beginning April to mid Oct.) – 5 🚐 – 5 🏠 – 4 canvas bungalows. Per week from 270 to 560€ – Reservation fee 15€

🚐 10 🔲 19.50€

Located at the edge of a wood.

Surroundings : 🐟 ♨♨	
Leisure activities : 🍷 🛏	**G** **P** **S** Longitude : 5.88517 Latitude : 48.18022
Facilities : 🚿 🛒 🛁 🚮 🚽 🍴 🔲	

CORCIEUX

88430 – Michelin map **314** J3 – pop. 1 668 – alt. 534
▶ Paris 424 – Épinal 39 – Gérardmer 15 – Remiremont 43

⛰ Yelloh! Village Le Domaine des Bans

🔗 0329516467, www.domaine-des-bans.fr

Address : 6 rue James Wiese (near the pl. Notre-Dame)

Opening times : permanent

15.7 ha (634 pitches) flat, grassy, stony

Tariff : 45€ ♣♣ ⇔ 🔲 🔋 (6A) – Extra per person 8€

Rental rates : permanent – 250 🚐 – 60 gîtes. Per night from 28 to 260€ – Per week from 196 to 1,820€

🚐 local sani-station 4€ – 16 🔲 12€ – 🚐 🔋12€

Pleasant setting, in two separate campsites (the des Bans site has 600 pitches, the la Tour site has 34 pitches); beside a small lake.

Surroundings : ⇐🛏 ♨	
Leisure activities : 🍷 ✗ 🏠 🎥 🏃 🚣 ✂ 🎣 🏊 ⛳ 🏐 disco	**G** **P** **S** Longitude : 6.87985 Latitude : 48.16867
Facilities : 🚿 🛒 🏧 🛁 🚽 🍴 launderette 🧺 🚐	
Nearby : 🐴	

⛰ Sites et paysages Au Clos de la Chaume

Clos de la Chaume

🔗 0329507676, www.camping-closdelachaume.com

Address : 21 rue d'Alsace

Opening times : from end April to end Sept.

4 ha (90 pitches) flat, grassy

Tariff : 26.10€ ♣♣ ⇔ 🔲 🔋 (10A) – Extra per person 6.50€ – Reservation fee 10€

Rental rates : (from beginning April to end Sept.) – 18 🚐 – 5 🏠 – 2 tent lodges. Per night from 54 to 117€ – Per week from 335 to 750€ – Reservation fee 15€

🚐 local sani-station 6€ – 10 🔲 12€ – 🚐 🔋11€

Surroundings : ♨	
Leisure activities : 🏠 🚣 🔲 🐴	**G** **P** **S** Longitude : 6.88383 Latitude : 48.17026
Facilities : 🚿 🛒 🛁 🚮 🚽 🍴 launderette	

DABO

57850 – Michelin map **307** O7 – pop. 2 636 – alt. 500
▶ Paris 453 – Baccarat 63 – Metz 127 – Phalsbourg 18

� Le Rocher

✆ 03 87 07 47 51, www.ot-dabo.fr

Address : route du Rocher (located 1.5km southeast along the D 45, at the junction with the road for Le Rocher)

Opening times : from end March to beginning Oct.

0.5 ha (42 pitches) relatively flat, flat, grassy

Tariff : (2015 price) 🚶 3.40€ 🚗 1.30€ 🔲 1.80€ – 🔌 (10A) 3.90€

Located in a pleasant forest of fir trees.

Surroundings : 🌳	**G**	Longitude : 7.25267
Leisure activities : 🏇	**P**	Latitude : 48.64844
Facilities : 🚰▥	**S**	

For more information on visiting particular towns or regions, consult the relevant regional MICHELIN Green Guide. We also recommend you use the appropriate Michelin regional map to locate your selected campsite, to calculate distances and to work out the best route.

FRESSE-SUR-MOSELLE

88160 – Michelin map **314** I5 – pop. 1 868 – alt. 515
▶ Paris 447 – Metz 178 – Épinal 54 – Mulhouse 56

⚲ Municipal Bon Accueil

✆ 03 29 25 08 98, campingaubonaccueil@orange.fr

Address : 36ter rue de Lorraine (take northwestern exit along the N 66, follow the signs for LeThillot; 80m from the Moselle river)

Opening times : from beginning April to end Oct.

0.6 ha (50 pitches) flat, grassy

Tariff : 🚶 2.78€ 🚗 1,63€ – 🔌 (16A) 2.90€

🚉 Eurorelais sani-station 3.49€

Surroundings : ⋖	**G**	Longitude : 6.78023
Leisure activities : 🏇	**P**	Latitude : 47.878
Facilities : 🚰	**S**	
Nearby : 🛒 ✂		

GEMAINGOUTTE

88520 – Michelin map **314** K3 – pop. 119 – alt. 446
▶ Paris 411 – Colmar 59 – Ribeauvillé 31 – St-Dié 14

⚲ Municipal le Violu

✆ 03 29 57 70 70, www.gemaingoutte.fr

Address : Pré Battant (take the western exit along the RD 59, follow the signs for St-Dié; beside a stream)

Opening times : from beginning May to end Oct.

1 ha (48 pitches) flat, grassy

Tariff : (2015 price) 🚶 2,50€ 🚗 1,70€ 🔲 1,80€ – 🔌 (6A) 2,20€

Rental rates : (2015 price) permanent – 2 🏠. Per night from 55€ – Per week from 220 to 425€

🚉 Raclet sani-station 2€ – 10 🔲 6€

Leisure activities : 🏇	**G**	Longitude : 7.08584
Facilities : 🔱🚰🏛	**P**	Latitude : 48.25361
	S	

GÉRARDMER

88400 – Michelin map **314** J4 – pop. 8 757 – alt. 669 – Winter sports : 660/1 350 m
▶ Paris 425 – Belfort 78 – Colmar 52 – Épinal 40

⚲ Les Sapins

✆ 03 29 63 15 01, www.camping-gerardmer.com

Address : 18 chemin de Sapois (located 1.5km southwest, 200m from the lake)

Opening times : from beginning April to mid Oct.

1.3 ha (70 pitches) flat, grassy, gravel

Tariff : 20.20€ 🚶🚶 🚗 🔲 🔌 (10A) – Extra per person 4.50€ – Reservation fee 8€

Rental rates : (from mid March to end Oct.) – 3 🏚. Per week from 290 to 550€ – Reservation fee 10€

🚉 local sani-station 2€

Surroundings : 🏞🌳	**G**	Longitude : 6.85614
Leisure activities : 🎣	**P**	Latitude : 48.0635
Facilities : 🔌🚰🍴	**S**	
Nearby : 🚣🐎		

⚲ Les Granges-Bas

✆ 03 29 63 12 03, www.lesgrangesbas.fr

Address : 116 chemin des Granges Bas (4km west along the D 417 then turn left at Costet-Beillard, follow road for 1km)

Opening times : from mid Dec. to mid Oct.

2 ha (100 pitches) flat, relatively flat, grassy

Tariff : 17€ 🚶🚶 🚗 🔲 🔌 (6A) – Extra per person 3,95€

Rental rates : (from mid Dec. to mid Oct.) – 12 🏚 – 2 apartments – 1 canvas bungalow – 1 tent lodge. Per week from 245 to 637€ – Reservation fee 10€

🚉 2 🔲 17€

Surroundings : 🏔⋖🏞	**G**	Longitude : 6.80653
Leisure activities : 🏛🏇✂	**P**	Latitude : 48.06927
Facilities : 🚰🍴 launderette	**S**	

The guide covers all 22 regions of France – see the map and list of regions on pages 4–5.

HERPELMONT

88600 – Michelin map **314** I3 – pop. 247 – alt. 480
▶ Paris 413 – Épinal 28 – Gérardmer 20 – Remiremont 33

⛰ Domaine des Messires

✆ 03 29 58 56 29, www.domainedesmessires.com

Address : rue des Messires (located 1.5km to the north)

Opening times : from end April to end Sept.

11 ha/2 for camping (100 pitches) flat, grassy

Tariff : (2015 price) 27€ 🚶🚶 🚗 🔲 🔌 (10A) – Extra per person 6.50€ – Reservation fee 12€

Rental rates : (2015 price) (from end April to end Sept.) 🏚 – 22 🏚. Per night from 45 to 100€ – Per week from 270 to 700€ – Reservation fee 12€

A pleasant site and setting beside a lake.

Surroundings : 🏞⋖ lake and mountain 🏞		Longitude : 6.74278
♨⚠		Latitude : 48.17854
Leisure activities : 🍴✖🏛🏇🎣🛶		
Facilities : 🔌🚰🚿🍴 launderette 🏛🛒		

JAULNY

54470 – Michelin map **307** G5 – pop. 262 – alt. 230
▶ Paris 310 – Commercy 41 – Metz 33 – Nancy 51

⚏ La Pelouse

✆ 03 83 81 91 67, www.campingdelapelouse.com – limited spaces for one-night stay

Address : chemin de Fey (500m south of the town, access located near the bridge)

Opening times : from beginning April to end Sept.

2.9 ha (100 pitches) relatively flat, flat, grassy

Tariff : (2015 price) 21.75€ ♛♛ ⇋ ▣ ⚡ (6A) – Extra per person 4.10€
Rental rates : (2015 price) permanent ♿ (2 chalets) – 5 ⌂.
Per night from 120€ – Per week from 340 to 432€
⛽ local sani-station 15€ – 🛒 11€
Situated on a small, wooded hill overlooking the river.

Surroundings : 🏞 ⌂ ♨
Leisure activities : ✕ ⌂ ⚓♨ ⚓
Facilities : ♿ ⚬⇋ ▣
Nearby : ⚓

Longitude : 5.88658
Latitude : 48.9705

LUNÉVILLE

54300 – Michelin map **307** J7 – pop. 19 937 – alt. 224
▶ Paris 347 – Épinal 69 – Metz 95 – Nancy 36

⚏ Les Bosquets

✆ 06 74 72 49 73, www.cc-lunevillois.fr

Address : chemin de la Ménagerie (head north towards Château-Salins and take a right turn; after the bridge over the Vézouze)

1 ha (36 pitches) terraced, flat, grassy

Rentals : 4 ⌂.

Situated close to the château grounds and gardens

Surroundings : ♨
Leisure activities : ⌂
Facilities : ♿ ⚬⇋ ⚓ ⚓ launderette
Nearby : ⚓ ✕ 🎯 📷

Longitude : 6.49886
Latitude : 48.59647

This guide is updated regularly, so buy your new copy every year!

MAGNIÈRES

54129 – Michelin map **307** K8 – pop. 341 – alt. 250
▶ Paris 365 – Baccarat 16 – Épinal 40 – Lunéville 22

⚏ Le Pré Fleury

✆ 03 83 72 34 73, http://campingdemagnieres.jimdo.com

Address : 18 rue de la Barre (500m west along the D 22, follow the signs for Bayon, 200m from the Mortagne river)

Opening times : from beginning April to end Sept.

1 ha (34 pitches) flat, relatively flat, grassy, fine gravel

Tariff : (2015 price) 14.50€ ♛♛ ⇋ ▣ ⚡ (10A) – Extra per person 3€

By the old railway station and beside a lake.

Surroundings : 🏞 ⌂
Leisure activities : ⌂ ⚓♨ ⚓ ⚓ draisines (handcars/rail cycling)
Facilities : ♿ ⚬⇋ ⚓ ⚓
Nearby : ✕

Longitude : 6.55735
Latitude : 48.44653

METZ

57000 – Michelin map **307** I4 – pop. 121 841 – alt. 173
▶ Paris 330 – Longuyon 80 – Pont-à-Mousson 31 – St-Avold 44

⚏ Municipal Metz-Plage

✆ 03 87 68 26 48, www.tourisme.mairie-metz.fr

Address : allée de Metz-Plage (to the north, between the Les Morts bridge and the bridge at Thionville; beside the Moselle – from A 31: take the exit for Metz-Nord Pontiffroy)

Opening times : from mid April to end Sept.

2.5 ha (150 pitches) flat, grassy, stony

Tariff : (2015 price) ♛ 3.10€ ⇋ 3.60€ ▣ 14€ – ⚡ (16A) 5.10€
⛽ 8 ▣

Surroundings : ♨
Leisure activities : ✕ ⚓♨ ⚓
Facilities : ♿ ⚬⇋ ⚓ ⚓ ⚓ launderette ⚓
Nearby : 📷

Longitude : 6.17058
Latitude : 49.12569

Some information or pricing may have changed since the guide went to press. We recommend you check the price list online in advance or at the entrance to the campsite and enquire about possible restrictions.

NEUFCHÂTEAU

88300 – Michelin map **314** C2 – pop. 7 040 – alt. 300
▶ Paris 321 – Chaumont 57 – Contrexéville 28 – Épinal 75

⚏ Intercommunal

✆ 03 29 94 19 03, http://www.bassin-neufchateau.fr/ – ⚐

Address : rue Georges Joecker (take the western exit, follow the signs for Chaumont and take a right turn, near the sports centre)

Opening times : from mid May to end Sept.

0.8 ha (50 pitches) flat, grassy

Tariff : (2015 price) ♛ 3€ ⇋ 2.80€ ▣ 3€ – ⚡ (16A) 4€

Surroundings : ♨
Facilities : ♿ ⚬⇋ ⚓ ⚓ ⚓
Nearby : 🎯 📷 📷 skateboarding

Longitude : 5.68605
Latitude : 48.35725

PLOMBIÈRES-LES-BAINS

88370 – Michelin map **314** G5 – pop. 1 869 – alt. 429 – ⚕
▶ Paris 378 – Belfort 79 – Épinal 38 – Gérardmer 43

⚏ L'Hermitage

✆ 03 29 30 01 87, www.hermitage-camping.com

Address : 54 rue du Boulot (located 1.5km northwest along the D 63, follow the signs for Xertigny then take the D 20, follow the signs for Ruaux)

Opening times : from beginning April to mid Oct.

1.4 ha (55 pitches) terraced, relatively flat, flat, grassy, gravelled

Tariff : 18.50€ ♛♛ ⇋ ▣ ⚡ (10A) – Extra per person 4.70€ – Reservation fee 10€

Rental rates : permanent – 3 ⌂ – 4 ⌂. Per week from 260 to 445€ – Reservation fee 10€
⛽ local sani-station 4€ – 25 ▣ 18.50€ – 🛒 ⚡16.65€

Surroundings : ♨
Leisure activities : ⌂ ⚓♨ ⚓
Facilities : ♿ ⚬⇋ ⚓ ⚓ ⚓

Longitude : 6.4431
Latitude : 47.96859

⌂ Le Fraiteux

✆ 03 29 66 00 71, www.camping-fraiteux.fr

Address : 81 rue du Camping (4km west along the D 20 and D 20e)

Opening times : permanent

0.8 ha (35 pitches) relatively flat, gravelled, flat, grassy

Tariff : 20€ ✦✦ ⌕ ▣ (4) (10A) – Extra per person 4,50€

Rental rates : permanent – 2 ⟏ – 4 ⌂. Per night from 100 to 120€ – Per week from 300 to 510€

⟏ local sani-station 4€ – 6 ▣ 12€

Surroundings : ⌇ ⌂ Leisure activities : ⌂ Facilities : ⊶ ⟟ ▥ ⟍ ♚ launderette	**G P S** Longitude : 6.41647 Latitude : 47.96573

REVIGNY-SUR-ORNAIN

55800 – Michelin map **307** A6 – pop. 3 145 – alt. 144

▶ Paris 239 – Bar-le-Duc 18 – St-Dizier 30 – Vitry-le-François 36

⌂ Municipal du Moulin des Gravières

✆ 03 29 78 73 34, www.ot-revigny-ornain.fr

Address : 1 rue du Stade (in the town towards southern exit, follow the signs for Vitry-le-François and turn right; 100m from the Ornain)

Opening times : from beginning April to end Sept.

1 ha (27 pitches) flat, grassy

Tariff : (2015 price) ✦ 2.10€ ⌕ ▣ 2.10€ – (4) (6A) 2.70€

Rental rates : (2015 price) (from beginning April to end Sept.) – 3 ⟏. Per night from 42 to 65€ – Per week from 193 to 224€

⟏ local sani-station 3€

In a pleasant setting beside a stream.

Surroundings : ⌇ ⌂ Leisure activities : ⌂ Facilities : ⅊ ⊶ ⟟ ▥ ♚ ▦ Nearby : ⌕ ▦ ⌂	**G P S** Longitude : 4.98373 Latitude : 48.82669

There are several different types of sani-station ('borne' in French) – sanitation points providing fresh water and disposal points for grey water. See page 12 for further details.

ST-AVOLD

57500 – Michelin map **307** L4 – pop. 16 298 – alt. 260

▶ Paris 372 – Haguenau 117 – Lunéville 77 – Metz 46

⌂ Le Felsberg

✆ 03 87 92 75 05, www.mairie-saint-avold.fr

Address : rue en Verrerie (to the north; near D the 603, opposite the Record service station – from A 4: take the exit for St-Avold Carling)

Opening times : permanent

1.2 ha (33 pitches) terraced, relatively flat, flat, grassy, stony

Tariff : ✦ 4€ ⌕ ▣ 6€ – (4) (10A) 5€

Rental rates : permanent ⌇ – 3 ⌂ – 15 ⌗. Per night from 55 to 65€ – Per week from 280 to 350€

⟏ local sani-station

On the the attractive wooded slopes of the town.

Surroundings : ⌇ ⌂ ⌂ Leisure activities : ⌶ ⌕ ⌂ ⌂ ⌂ Facilities : ⅊ ⊶ ⟟ ⌂ ⟍ ♚	**G P S** Longitude : 6.71579 Latitude : 49.11102

ST-MAURICE-SUR-MOSELLE

88560 – Michelin map **314** I5 – pop. 1 486 – alt. 560 – Winter sports : 550/1 250 m

▶ Paris 441 – Belfort 41 – Bussang 4 – Épinal 56

⌂ Les Deux Ballons

✆ 03 29 25 17 14, www.camping-deux-ballons.fr

Address : 17 rue du Stade (take the southwestern exit along the N 66, follow the signs for Le Thillot; beside a stream)

Opening times : from mid April to end Sept.

4 ha (160 pitches) teraced, flat, grassy

Tariff : 26€ ✦✦ ⌕ ▣ (4) (10A) – Extra per person 7.20€ – Reservation fee 15€

Rental rates : (from mid April to end Sept.) ⌇ – 7 ⌂. Per week from 390 to 1,600€

⟏ local sani-station

Surroundings : ⌇ ⌶ ⌕ Leisure activities : ⌶ ⌕ ⌂ ⌂ ⌂ ⌂ ⌂ ⌂ Facilities : ⅊ ⊶ ⟟ ⟟ ⌂ ♚ launderette ⌂ Nearby : ⌇ walking trails	**G P S** Longitude : 6.81124 Latitude : 47.8554

The prices listed were supplied by the campsite owners in 2015 (if prices were not available, those from the previous year are given). The fees should be regarded as basic charges and may fluctuate with inflation.

SANCHEY

88390 – Michelin map **314** G3 – pop. 789 – alt. 368

▶ Paris 390 – Metz 129 – Épinal 8 – Nancy 69

⌂ Le Lac de Bouzey

✆ 03 29 82 49 41, www.lacdebouzey.com

Address : 19 rue du Lac (to the south along the D 41)

Opening times : from end Jan. to beginning Jan.

3 ha (160 pitches) terraced, relatively flat, flat, grassy

Tariff : 37€ ✦✦ ⌕ ▣ (4) (10A) – Extra per person 11€ – Reservation fee 25€

Rental rates : (from end Jan to beginning Jan) – 34 ⟏. Per night from 70 to 180€ – Per week from 490 to 1,260€ – Reservation fee 25€ ⟏ Flot Bleu sani-station – 25 ▣ 37€

Situated by the lake; a pleasant reception area and leisure facillities.

Surroundings : ⌇ ⌂ ⌂ Leisure activities : ⌶ ⌕ ⌂ ⌂ ⌂ ⌂ disco ⌂ multi-sports ground, entertainment room Facilities : ⅊ ⊶ ⌂ ⟟ ⌂ ⌂ ⌂ ♚ launderette ⌂ ⌂	**G P S** Longitude : 6.3602 Latitude : 48.1667

Key to rentals symbols:

12 ⟏	*Number of mobile homes*
20 ⌂	*Number of chalets*
6 ⌗	*Number of rooms to rent*
Per night *30–50€*	*Minimum/maximum rate per night*
Per week *300–1,000€*	*Minimum/maximum rate per week*

SAULXURES-SUR-MOSELOTTE

88290 – Michelin map **314** I5 – pop. 2 782 – alt. 464
▶ Paris 431 – Épinal 46 – Gérardmer 24 – Luxeuil-les-Bains 53

⚠ Lac de la Moselotte

🕿 03 29 24 56 56, www.lac-moselotte.fr

Address : 336 route des Amias (located 1.5km west on the old D 43)

Opening times : permanent

23 ha/3 for camping (75 pitches) flat, grassy, stony

Tariff : 21.80€ ★★ ⛺ 回 (⁄) (10A) – Extra per person 5€

Rental rates : permanent – 10 🚐 – 20 🏠. Per night from 35 to 149€ – Per week from 195 to 895€ – Reservation fee 15€

🚻 local sani-station 3€

On a wooded site beside a lake and near a leisure and activity park.

Surroundings : ≤ 🗺 ♨
Leisure activities : 🍸 🖼 🏊 🚣 🚴 entertainment room
Facilities : ㅎ ⚡ 🗑 ♨ ♥ 🚾
At the leisure/activities centre : 🛶 ⚓ climbing

Longitude : 6.75236
Latitude : 47.95264

LE THOLY

88530 – Michelin map **314** I4 – pop. 1 589 – alt. 628
▶ Paris 414 – Bruyères 21 – Épinal 30 – Gérardmer 11

⚠ Noirrupt

🕿 03 29 61 81 27, www.jpvacances.com

Address : 15 chemin de l'Étang de Noirrupt (1.3km northwest along the D 11, follow the signs for Épinal and take road to the left)

Opening times : from beginning May to end Sept.

2.9 ha (70 pitches) terraced, stony, flat, grassy

Tariff : 27.10€ ★★ ⛺ 回 (⁄) (6A) – Extra per person 6.40€ – Reservation fee 13€

Rental rates : permanent 🚫 – 12 🏠. Per night from 52 to 75€ – Per week from 290 to 445€ – Reservation fee 13€

🚻 local sani-station

Surroundings : ≤ ♨
Leisure activities : 🍸 🖼 🛖 🚣 ⚔ 🦌
Facilities : ㅎ ⚡ 🗑 ♨ ♥ 🚾 launderette
Nearby : ⚓

Longitude : 6.72893
Latitude : 48.08881

To make the best possible use of this guide, please read pages 2–15 carefully.

LE VAL-D'AJOL

88340 – Michelin map **314** G5 – pop. 4 069 – alt. 380
▶ Paris 382 – Épinal 41 – Luxeuil-les-Bains 18 – Plombières-les-Bains 10

⚠ Municipal

🕿 03 29 66 55 17, mairie@valdajol.fr

Address : rue des Oeuvres (take the northwestern exit along the D 20, follow the signs for Plombières-les-Bains)

1 ha (46 pitches) flat, grassy
Rentals : ㅎ (1 chalet) – 2 🏠.

Surroundings : ≤ 🗺
Leisure activities : 🖼
Facilities : ㅎ ⚡ 🗑 ♨ ♥ 🚾
Nearby : ⚔ 🖼 ♨ ⚓

Longitude : 6.47586
Latitude : 47.92488

VERDUN

55100 – Michelin map **307** D4 – pop. 18 557 – alt. 198
▶ Paris 263 – Bar-le-Duc 56 – Châlons-en-Champagne 89 – Metz 78

⚠ Les Breuils

🕿 03 29 86 15 31, www.camping-lesbreuils.com

Address : 7 allée des Breuils (take the southwestern exit along the bypass (rocade) D 51 towards Paris and take road to the left)

Opening times : from mid March to mid Oct.

5.5 ha (162 pitches) terraced, relatively flat, flat, grassy, gravelled, wood

Tariff : 24€ ★★ ⛺ 回 (⁄) (6A) – Extra per person 6.70€ – Reservation fee 10€

Rental rates : (from mid March to mid Oct.) – 23 🚐. Per night from 65 to 90€ – Per week from 290 to 690€

🚻 Flot Bleu sani-station – 162 回 16€ – 🚿 (⁄)20.40€

In a rural setting beside a lake.

Surroundings : 🗺 ♨
Leisure activities : 🍸 🖼 🚣 🚴 ⚔ 🦌 ⚓ multi-sports ground
Facilities : ㅎ ⚡ 🗑 ♨ ♥ launderette 🚾

Longitude : 5.36598
Latitude : 49.15428

VILLEY-LE-SEC

54840 – Michelin map **307** G7 – pop. 415 – alt. 324
▶ Paris 302 – Lunéville 49 – Nancy 20 – Pont-à-Mousson 51

⚠ Camping de Villey-le-Sec

🕿 03 83 63 64 28, www.campingvilleylesec.com

Address : 34 rue de la Gare (situated 2km south along the D 909, follow the signs for Maron and take turning to the right)

Opening times : from beginning April to mid Oct.

2.5 ha (100 pitches) flat, grassy

Tariff : (2015 price) 22.60€ ★★ ⛺ 回 (⁄) (10A) – Extra per person 4€

Rental rates : (2015 price) (from beginning April to end Sept.) 🚫 – 4 🚐 – 1 🏠. Per week from 250 to 380€

🚻 local sani-station 5€

In a pleasant setting beside the Moselle river.

Surroundings : 🚣
Leisure activities : 🍸 🚣 ⚓ volleyball
Facilities : ㅎ ⚡ 🗑 ♥ 🚾 launderette 🚾 🚿

Longitude : 5.98559
Latitude : 48.6526

The Michelin classification (⚠⚠⚠… ⚠) is totally independent of the official star classification system awarded by the local prefecture or other official organisation.

VITTEL

88800 – Michelin map **314** D3 – pop. 5 434 – alt. 347
▶ Paris 342 – Belfort 129 – Épinal 43 – Chaumont 84

⚠ Aquadis Loisirs de Vittel

🕿 03 29 08 02 71, http://www.aquadis-loisirs.com/camping-de-vittel/

Address : 270 rue Claude Bassot (take the northeastern exit along the D 68, follow the signs for They-sous-Montfort)

Opening times : from end March to end Oct.

3.5 ha (120 pitches) flat, grassy, gravelled

Tariff : 17.20€ ★★ ⛺ 回 (⁄) (10A) – Extra per person 4.90€ – Reservation fee 10€

Rental rates : (from end March to end Oct.) – 12 ⟦🚐⟧. Per night from 65 to 70€ – Per week from 236 to 509€ – Reservation fee 20€ – 🛢 AireService sani-station – 🚽 11€

Surroundings : 🏕 ♀
Leisure activities : 🏛 ⛵
Facilities : ♿ ⚍ 🆑 �🏛 ᐟᐟ launderette

GPS Longitude : 5.95605
Latitude : 48.2082

To visit a town or region, use the MICHELIN Green Guides.

XONRUPT-LONGEMER

88400 – Michelin map **314** J4 – pop. 1 580 – alt. 714 – Winter sports : 750/1 300 m
▶ Paris 429 – Épinal 44 – Gérardmer 4 – Remiremont 32

⛺ La Vologne

✆ 03 29 60 87 23, http://camping-vosges-vologne.com

Address : 3030 route de Retournemer (4.5km southeast along the D 67a)

Opening times : from beginning May to end Sept.

2.5 ha (100 pitches) flat, grassy

Tariff : 🛉 3.60€ ⚌ 1,60€ 🅴 4.90€ – (🔌) (5A) 3.90€ – Reservation fee 15€

Rental rates : (from end April to end Sept.) – 3 🏠 – 1 yurt – 2 🛏 – 2 canvas bungalows – 1 gîte. Per night from 32 to 63€ – Per week from 254 to 588€ – Reservation fee 15€
On a wooded site beside the river.

Surroundings : ⋖
Leisure activities : 🏛 ⛵
Facilities : ♿ ⚍ 🔥 ᐟᐟ 📦
Nearby : 🍴

GPS Longitude : 6.96919
Latitude : 48.06245

⛺ Les Jonquilles

✆ 03 29 63 34 01, www.camping-jonquilles.com

Address : 2586 route du Lac (2.5km southeast)

Opening times : from mid April to beginning Oct.

4 ha (247 pitches) relatively flat, grassy

Tariff : 20.50€ 🛉🛉 ⚌ 🅴 (🔌) (10A) – Extra per person 3.80€ – Reservation fee 7€

🛢 local sani-station – 5 🅴 18.30€
In a pleasant location beside the lake.

Surroundings : ⋖ Lac de Longemer and wooded mountains ⛰
Leisure activities : 🍴 🏛 ⛵ 🎣
Facilities : ♿ ⚍ 🔥 ᐟᐟ launderette 📦 🚿

GPS Longitude : 6.94871
Latitude : 48.0677

MIDI-PYRÉNÉES

G. Bertolissio / hemis.fr

Lourdes may be famous for its many miracles and is visited by millions of pilgrims every year, but some would say that the whole of the Midi-Pyrénées has been uniquely blessed. France's leading agricultural region – larger in size than Belgium or Switzerland – offers sanctuary to a host of exceptional fauna and flora, including the wild bears that still roam the high peaks of the Pyrenees. At sunset, the towers of medieval cities and fortresses are bathed in the evening light. Forbidding Cathar castles are stained with a blood red glow, Albi is veiled in crimson and Toulouse is tinged a romantic pink. This list of the marvels of the region would not be complete without a mention of the Garonne Valley's thriving and fertile 'Garden of France', famous for its vegetables, fruit and wine. This land of milk and honey is rich in culinary traditions, and it would be a crime not to experience the delights of *foie gras* or a *confit de canard* (duck confit) before leaving.

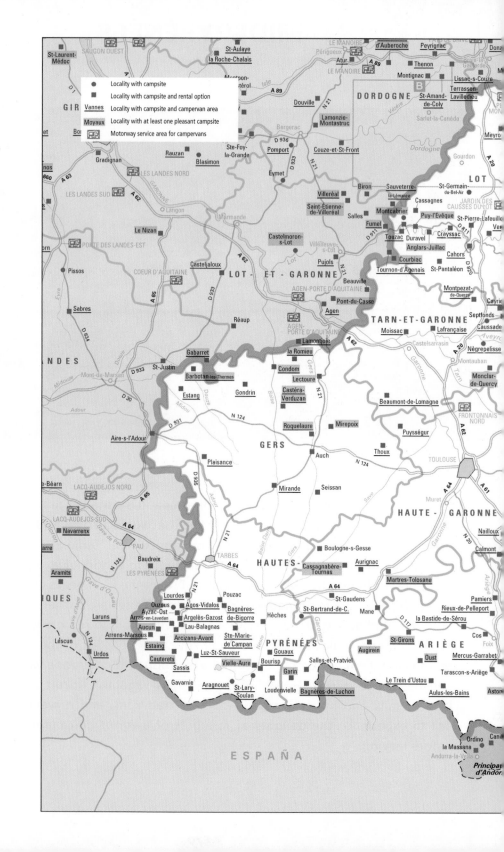

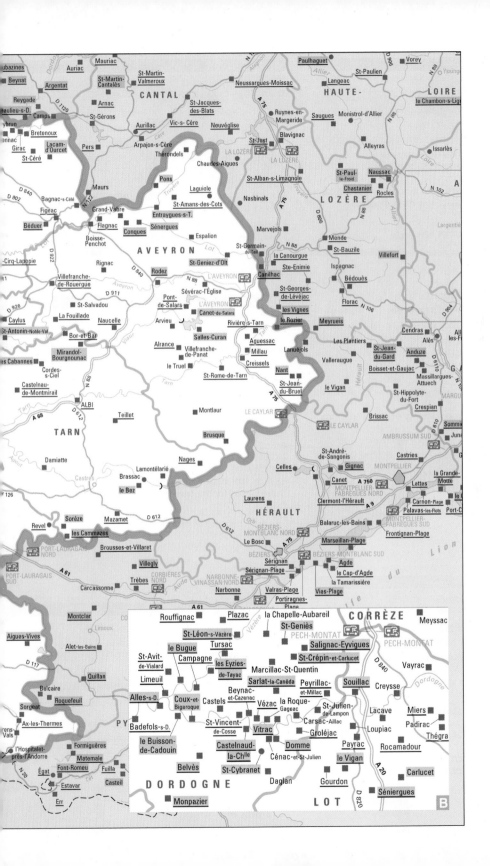

AGOS-VIDALOS

65400 – Michelin map **342** L4 – pop. 380 – alt. 450
▶ Paris 859 – Toulouse 185 – Tarbes 32 – Pau 51

⚲ Flower Le Soleil du Pibeste ♣♣

🔗 05 62 97 53 23. www.campingpibeste.com

Address : 16 avenue Lavedan (take the southern exit, along the N 21)

1.5 ha (80 pitches) terraced, relatively flat, flat, grassy

Rentals : ♿ (2 mobile homes) – 29 🏠 – 11 🏠.

🚐 local sani-station

Situated opposite the Pyrenees, with a good range of leisure facilities and services and a special area for camper vans.

Surroundings : ⩽ ♀ Leisure activities : ⧉ ✗ 🏠 ⨀daytime ⚡ jacuzzi ⬆ ⬆ multi-sports ground Facilities : ♿ ⚊ ⬛ ⬆ ⬆ ⬆ ⬆ launderette ⬆	**GPS** Longitude : -0.07081 Latitude : 43.03562

⚲ Club Airotel La Châtaigneraie

🔗 05 62 97 07 40. www.camping-chataigneraie.com

Address : 46 avenue du Lavedan (along the N 21; at Vidalos)

Opening times : from beginning Dec. to mid Oct.

1.5 ha (80 pitches) terraced, relatively flat, flat, grassy

Tariff : 30.50€ ♣♣ ⬅ 🔲 🔋 (6A) – Extra per person 6.40€ – Reservation fee 18€

Rental rates : permanent – 17 🏠 – 3 studios – 1 apartment. Per week from 225 to 705€

With the Pyrénées as a backdrop, a variety of rental accommodation and good sanitary facilities.

Surroundings : ⩽ ♀♀ Leisure activities : 🏠 ⬆ ⬆ ⬆ Facilities : ♿ ⚊ ⬛ ⬆ ⬆ launderette	**GPS** Longitude : -0.07534 Latitude : 43.03201

In order for the guide to remain wholly objective, the selection of campsites is made on an entirely independent basis.

AGUESSAC

12520 – Michelin map **338** K6 – pop. 872 – alt. 375
▶ Paris 635 – Toulouse 198 – Rodez 62 – Montpellier 129

⚲ La Via Natura Les Cerisiers

🔗 05 65 59 87 96. www.campinglescerisiers.com

Address : at Pailhas (3km north along the D 907, follow the signs for Gorges du Tarn – from the A 75 take exit 44-1)

Opening times : from beginning May to mid Sept.

2.5 ha (80 pitches) flat, grassy

Tariff : (2015 price) 17€ ♣♣ ⬅ 🔲 🔋 (6A) – Extra per person 5€
Rental rates : (from beginning May to mid Sept.) – 7 🏠 – 2 tent lodges. Per night from 40 to 60€ – Per week from 170 to 620€
🚐 local sani-station

A site allied to the LPO (French bird protection organization), with a bird sanctuary on the banks of the Tarn river.

Surroundings : 🌳 ⩽ ♀ Leisure activities : 🏠 ⬆ ⬆ Facilities : ♿ ⚊ ⬆ ⬛ Nearby : ⬆	**GPS** Longitude : 3.12053 Latitude : 44.16745

AIGUES VIVES

09600 – Michelin map **343** J7 – pop. 559 – alt. 425
▶ Paris 776 – Carcassonne 63 – Castelnaudary 46 – Foix 36

⚲ Sites et Paysages de La Serre

🔗 05 61 03 06 16. www.camping-la-serre.com

Address : 5 chemin de La Serre (to the west of the village)

6.5 ha (40 pitches) undulating, terraced, flat, grassy, fine gravel

Rentals : 6 🏠 – 8 🏠 – 1 cabin in the trees.

🚐 local sani-station

A spacious, undulating site with trees, some pitches have a view of the Pyrénées.

Surroundings : 🌳 ⬛ ♀♀ Leisure activities : 🏠 ⬆ ⬆ ⬆ ⬆ Facilities : ♿ ⚊ ⬆ ⬛	**GPS** Longitude : 1.87199 Latitude : 42.99741

ALBI

81000 – Michelin map **338** E7 – pop. 48 858 – alt. 174
▶ Paris 699 – Toulouse 77 – Montpellier 261 – Rodez 71

⚲ Albirondack Park

🔗 05 63 60 37 06. www.albirondack.fr

Address : 31 allée de la Piscine

Opening times : permanent

1.8 ha (84 pitches) terraced, flat, grassy, stony

Tariff : 35.70€ ♣♣ ⬅ 🔲 🔋 (10A) – Extra per person 7.50€ – Reservation fee 10€

Rental rates : permanent ♿ (1 chalet) ⬆ – 10 🏠 – 25 🏠 – 2 cabins in the trees. Per night from 50 to 150€ – Per week from 350 to 1,000€ – Reservation fee 10€

🚐 local sani-station – 5 🔲 16€

There's a bus for the town centre.

Surroundings : ⬛ ♀♀ Leisure activities : ⧉ ✗ 🛁 hammam, jacuzzi ⬆ spa centre Facilities : ♿ ⚊ ⬛ ⬛ ⬆ ⬆ launderette ⬆	**GPS** Longitude : 2.16397 Latitude : 43.93445

ALRANCE

12430 – Michelin map **338** I6 – pop. 404 – alt. 750
▶ Paris 664 – Albi 63 – Millau 52 – Rodez 37

⚲ Les Cantarelles

🔗 05 65 46 40 35. www.lescantarelles.com

Address : 3km south along the D 25; beside the Lac du Villefranche-de-Panat

Opening times : permanent

3.5 ha (165 pitches) relatively flat, flat, grassy

Tariff : 19€ ♣♣ ⬅ 🔲 🔋 (6A) – Extra per person 4.80€

Rental rates : (from beginning April to end Oct.) – 10 🏠. Per night from 50 to 64€ – Per week from 350 to 680€

🚐 local sani-station 6€

Surroundings : ⩽ ⬛ ♀ ⬆ Leisure activities : ⧉ ✗ 🏠 ⬆ ⬆ ⬆ ⬆ ⬆ pedalos ⬆ Facilities : ♿ ⚊ ⬆ ⬛ launderette	**GPS** Longitude : 2.68933 Latitude : 44.10669

ANGLARS-JUILLAC

46140 – Michelin map **337** D5 – pop. 331 – alt. 98
▶ Paris 590 – Cahors 26 – Gourdon 41 – Sarlat-la-Canéda 53

⚠ Base Nautique de Floiras

✆ 05 65 36 27 39. www.campingfloiras.com

Address : at Juillac, D8

Opening times : from beginning April to mid Oct.

1 ha (25 pitches) open site, flat, grassy

Tariff : ♟ 5.75€ ⇔ 🔲 12.50€ – 🔌 (10A) 4.25€ – Reservation fee 12€
Rental rates : (from end April to end Sept.) – 2 tent lodges.
Per week from 390 to 765 – Reservation fee 12€

All the pitches are opposite the Lot river.

Surroundings : 🏊 ♨♨
Leisure activities : ♟ ✗ 🎣 🚣
Facilities : 🚿 ⚟ 🍴 launderette

G P S   Longitude : 1.1987
        Latitude : 44.4872

ARAGNOUET

65170 – Michelin map **342** N8 – pop. 244 – alt. 1 100
▶ Paris 842 – Arreau 24 – Bagnères-de-Luchon 56 – Lannemezan 51

⚠ Fouga Pic de Bern

✆ 06 84 72 47 24. fouga.marc@orange.fr

Address : at Fabian (2.8km northeast along the D 118, follow the signs for St-Lary-Soulan, near the Neste-d'Avre – river)

Opening times : from beginning June to end Sept.

3 ha (80 pitches) open site, terraced, flat, grassy

Tariff : ♟ 3.50€ ⇔ 🔲 3.50€ – 🔌 (13A) 7€

🚉 local sani-station

Choose the meadow area, with both sun and shade, furthest away from the road.

Surroundings : 🏊 ≤ ♀
Leisure activities : ♟ ✗ 🎪
Facilities : 🚿 ⚟ 🍴 🎣

G P S   Longitude : 0.23608
        Latitude : 42.78853

ARCIZANS-AVANT

65400 – Michelin map **342** L5 – pop. 360 – alt. 640
▶ Paris 868 – Toulouse 194 – Tarbes 41 – Pau 61

🏔 Le Lac

✆ 05 62 97 01 88. www.camping-du-lac-pyrenees.com

Address : 29 chemin d'Azun (take the western exit, not far from the lake)

Opening times : from mid May to mid Sept.

2 ha (97 pitches) relatively flat

Tariff : 33.40€ ♟♟ ⇔ 🔲 🔌 (16A) – Extra per person 8.40€ – Reservation fee 25€
Rental rates : (2015 price) permanent – 14 🚐. Per night from 87 to 92€ – Per week from 315 to 795€ – Reservation fee 25€

🚉 local sani-station 18€

Many pitches have an uninterrupted view of the Pyrenees, the village and church.

Surroundings : 🏊 ≤ ♨♨
Leisure activities : 🎪 🚣 🚲 🚣 spa facilities
Facilities : 🚿 ⚟ 🍴 launderette 🎣
Nearby : 🎣

G P S   Longitude : -0.10803
        Latitude : 42.9857

🏔 Les Châtaigniers

✆ 05 62 97 94 77. www.camping-les-chataigniers.com

Address : 6 rue Cap Deth Vilatge

Opening times : permanent

3 ha (51 pitches) terraced, relatively flat, flat, grassy, wood

Tariff : 29.70€ ♟♟ ⇔ 🔲 🔌 (6A) – Extra per person 8€
Rental rates : permanent – 3 🏠. Per night from 40 to 80€ – Per week from 300 to 690€

Shaded pitches with a view of the valley and the village.

Surroundings : 🏊 ≤ ♨♨
Leisure activities : 🎪 🚣 🚣
Facilities : 🚿 ⚟ 🍴 launderette
Nearby : 🎣

G P S   Longitude : -0.10488
        Latitude : 42.98505

ARGELÈS-GAZOST

65400 – Michelin map **342** L6 – pop. 3 297 – alt. 462 – ⚓
▶ Paris 863 – Lourdes 13 – Pau 58 – Tarbes 32

🏔 Sunêlia Les Trois Vallées 👥

✆ 05 62 90 35 47. www.camping3vallees.com

Address : avenue des Pyrénées (take the northern exit)

Opening times : from beginning April to mid Oct.

11 ha (438 pitches) flat, grassy

Tariff : 49€ ♟♟ ⇔ 🔲 🔌 (10A) – Extra per person 14€ – Reservation fee 30€
Rental rates : (from beginning April to mid Oct.) 🚿 (2 mobile homes) – 250 🚐 – 4 canvas bungalows. Per night from 46 to 103€ – Per week from 455 to 1,638€ – Reservation fee 30€

🚉 local sani-station

A water park and shops with beautiful floral decoration and very well-appointed sanitary facilities.

Surroundings : 🏕 ♨♨
Leisure activities : ♟ ✗ 🎪 🎮 🏋 jacuzzi 🚣 🔲 🚣 🏊 disco, multi-sports ground, entertainment room
Facilities : 🚿 ⚟ 🍴 launderette 🎣
Nearby : 🛒 ✗ 🍴

G P S   Longitude : -0.09718
        Latitude : 43.0121

ARRAS-EN-LAVEDAN

65400 – Michelin map **342** L5 – pop. 527 – alt. 700
▶ Paris 868 – Toulouse 193 – Tarbes 40 – Pau 60

🏔 L'Idéal

✆ 05 62 97 03 13. www.camping-ideal-pyrenees.com – alt. 600

Address : route du Val d'Azun (300m northwest along the D 918, follow the signs for Argelès-Gazost)

Opening times : from beginning June to mid Sept.

2 ha (60 pitches) terraced, flat, grassy

Tariff : (2015 price) ♟ 4.50€ ⇔ 🔲 4.50€ – 🔌 (10A) 9.50€
Rental rates : (2015 price) permanent 🚿 – 2 🏠. Per night from 60€ – Per week from 290 to 550€

🚉 local sani-station 3€

A pleasant site, but choose the pitches the furthest away from the road.

Surroundings : ≤ ♨♨
Leisure activities : 🎪 🚣 🚣
Facilities : 🚿 ⚟ 🍴 launderette

G P S   Longitude : -0.11954
        Latitude : 42.99483

ARRENS-MARSOUS

65400 – Michelin map **342** K7 – pop. 741 – alt. 885
▶ Paris 875 – Argelès-Gazost 13 – Cauterets 29 – Laruns 37

⚠ La Hèche

✆ 05 62 97 02 64. www.campinglaheche.com – ℞

Address : 54 route d'Azun (800m east along the D 918, follow the signs for Argelès-Gazost and take the road to the right; beside the Gave d'Arrens – river)

Opening times : from mid June to mid Sept.

5 ha (166 pitches) flat, grassy

Tariff : (2015 price) 13.34€ ✶✶ ⇔ 🅴 (4A) – Extra per person 3.82€

Surroundings : ⌇ ≤ ♋♋
Leisure activities : 🎮 🏊
Facilities : & ⚲ ▦ 🚿 launderette
Nearby : 🏊 ✗ m 🚣

GPS Longitude : -0.20534
Latitude : 42.95847

⚠ Le Moulian

✆ 05 62 97 41 18. www.le-moulian.com

Address : 42 rue du Bourg (500m southeast of the village of Marsous)

Opening times : permanent

12 ha/4 for camping (75 pitches) flat, grassy

Tariff : 18.50€ ✶✶ ⇔ 🅴 (5A) – Extra per person 4.50€
Rental rates : permanent – 10 🚐 – 3 gîtes. Per night from 40 to 75€ – Per week from 250 to 500€
🚐 local sani-station 4€ – 2 🅴 9€ – 🚐 8€

The site is near a large equestrian centre with donkeys, ponies and horses.

Surroundings : ⌇ ≤ ♋♋
Leisure activities : ⛾ ✗ 🎮 🏊 🐎
Facilities : & ⚲ ⓒ 🚿 launderette 🚿
Nearby : 🏊 ✗ m 🚣

GPS Longitude : -0.19638
Latitude : 42.96232

Michelin classification:

⛰⛰⛰⛰ *Extremely comfortable, equipped to a very high standard*

⛰⛰⛰ *Very comfortable, equipped to a high standard*

⛰⛰ *Comfortable and well equipped*

⛰ *Reasonably comfortable*

⚠ *Satisfactory*

ARVIEU

12120 – Michelin map **338** H5 – pop. 861 – alt. 730
▶ Paris 663 – Albi 66 – Millau 59 – Rodez 31

⚠ Le Doumergal

✆ 05 65 74 24 92. www.camping-doumergal-aveyron.fr

Address : rue de la Rivière (west of the village; beside a stream)

1.5 ha (27 pitches) relatively flat, flat, grassy

Surroundings : ⌇ 🏠 ♀
Leisure activities : 🏊
Facilities : & ⚲ 🚿 ⚹
Nearby : ✗

GPS Longitude : 2.66014
Latitude : 44.19066

ASTON

09310 – Michelin map **343** I8 – pop. 219 – alt. 563
▶ Paris 788 – Andorra-la-Vella 78 – Ax-les-Thermes 20 – Foix 59

⛰ Le Pas de l'Ours

✆ 05 61 64 90 33. www.lepasdelours.fr

Address : at Les Gesquis (south of the town, near the rapids)

Opening times : from beginning June to beginning Sept.

3.5 ha (50 pitches)

Tariff : 27€ ✶✶ ⇔ 🅴 (6A) – Extra per person 7€ – Reservation fee 7€
Rental rates : (from mid Oct. to mid Sept.) – 27 🏠 – 4 gîtes. Per night from 70 to 85€ – Per week from 310 to 672€ – Reservation fee 7€

A pleasant site with rental options of a high standard.

Surroundings : ⌇ ≤ 🏠 ♋♋
Leisure activities : ⛾ 🏹 🚴 ✗ 🚣 entertainment room
Facilities : & ⚲ (July–Aug.) ⚹ launderette
Nearby : 🚣

GPS Longitude : 1.67181
Latitude : 42.77245

AUCH

32000 – Michelin map **336** F8 – pop. 21 792 – alt. 169
▶ Paris 713 – Agen 74 – Bordeaux 205 – Tarbes 74

⛰ Le Castagné

✆ 06 07 97 40 37. www.domainelecastagne.com

Address : chemin de Naréoux (4km east along the D 924, follow the signs for Toulouse and take a right turn.)

Opening times : from end May to beginning Oct.

70 ha/2 for camping (24 pitches) very uneven, stony

Tariff : 19€ ✶✶ ⇔ 🅴 (12A) – Extra per person 5€ – Reservation fee 20€
Rental rates : permanent – 4 🚐 – 9 🏠 – 4 🛏 – 9 gîtes. Per night from 80 to 130€ – Per week from 360 to 590€ – Reservation fee 20€

Surroundings : ⌇ ≤ ♋♋♋
Leisure activities : 🎮 🏹 jacuzzi 🏊 m 🚣 🏊 pedalos
Facilities : & ⚲ ⚹ 🚽

GPS Longitude : 0.6337
Latitude : 43.6483

AUCUN

65400 – Michelin map **342** K7 – pop. 261 – alt. 853
▶ Paris 872 – Argelès-Gazost 10 – Cauterets 26 – Lourdes 22

⚠ Azun Nature

✆ 05 62 97 45 05. www.camping-azun-nature.com

Address : 1 route des Poueyes (700m east along the D 918, follow the signs for Argeles-Gazost and take turning to the right, 300m from the Gave d'Azun – river)

Opening times : from beginning May to end Sept.

1 ha (43 pitches) flat, grassy

Tariff : (2015 price) 21.50€ ✶✶ ⇔ 🅴 (10A) – Extra per person 4.50€
Rental rates : permanent – 10 🏠. Per night from 50 to 90€ – Per week from 200 to 520€

A well-kept site with good quality rental options, open summer and winter.

Surroundings : ⌇ ≤ 🏠 ♀
Leisure activities : 🎮 🏊
Facilities : & ⚲ 🚿 ⚹ launderette
Nearby : 🚴 🚶 walking trails

GPS Longitude : -0.18796
Latitude : 42.97399

⛺ Lascrouts

📞 05 62 97 42 62. www.camping-lascrouts.com – limited spaces for one-night stay

Address : 2 route de Las Poueyes (700m east along the D 918, follow the signs for Argelès-Gazost and take turning to the right, 300m from the Gave d'Azun – river)

Opening times : permanent

4 ha (72 pitches) terrace, relatively flat, flat, grassy

Tariff : (2015 price) 14.50€ ♦♦ 🚗 📧 (6A) – Extra per person 3.50€
Rental rates : (2015 price) permanent – 3 🏠 – 15 🏠. Per night from 40 to 80€ – Per week from 240 to 510€ – Reservation fee 20€

A good choice of mobile homes and owner-occupier chalets, but very few pitches for tents or caravans.

Surroundings : 🌿 ≤
Leisure activities : 🎦 ≦ hammam, jacuzzi 🏊
Facilities : 🚾 🛒 🏢 ᵀ 📷
Nearby : paragliding

Longitude : -0.18612
Latitude : 42.97361

AUGIREIN

09800 – Michelin map **343** D7 – pop. 63 – alt. 629
🚩 Paris 788 – Aspet 22 – Castillon-en-Couserans 12 – St-Béat 30

⛺ La Vie en Vert

📞 05 61 96 82 66. www.lavieenvert.com

Address : east of the town; beside the Bouigane river

Opening times : from beginning June to end Sept.

0.3 ha (15 pitches) flat, grassy

Tariff : (2015 price) 22€ ♦♦ 🚗 📧 (10A) – Extra per person 5€
Rental rates : (2015 price) (from beginning June to end Sept.) 🏕 – 1 🛏 – 1 tipi. Per night from 50 to 55€ – Per week from 280 to 380€

Based around an old farmhouse made of local stone that has been painstakingly restored.

Surroundings : 🌿 🏞 ⚘
Leisure activities : 🎦 🏹
Facilities : 🚾 🛒 🏢 ᵀ 📷
Nearby : 🍷 ✕

This guide is updated regularly, so buy your new copy every year!

AULUS-LES-BAINS

09140 – Michelin map **343** G8 – pop. 221 – alt. 750 – ♨
🚩 Paris 807 – Foix 76 – Oust 17 – St-Girons 34

⛺ Le Coulédous

📞 05 61 66 43 56. www.camping-aulus-couledous.com

Address : route de Saint-Girons (take northwestern exit along the D 32, near the Garbet)

Opening times : permanent

1.6 ha (70 pitches)

Tariff : (2015 price) 21.50€ ♦♦ 🚗 📧 (10A) – Extra per person 4.70€
Rental rates : (2015 price) permanent – 18 🏠. Per night from 50 to 75€ – Per week from 220 to 510€
🚰 local sani-station – 10 📧 13€

In the middle of a park boasting some ancient trees, but the chalets and sanitary facilities are also rather old.

Surroundings : ≤ ⚘
Leisure activities : 🎦 🏊
Facilities : 🚾 🛒 🏢 ᵀ launderette
Nearby : ✕ 🎣 forest trail

Longitude : 1.33215
Latitude : 42.79394

AURIGNAC

31420 – Michelin map **343** D5 – pop. 1 187 – alt. 430
🚩 Paris 750 – Auch 71 – Bagnères-de-Luchon 69 – Pamiers 92

⛺ Les Petites Pyrénées

📞 05 61 87 06 91. fabrice.ramalingom@orange.fr

Address : route de Boussens (take the southeastern exit along the D 635, on the right, near the stadium – A64 take exit 21)

Opening times : from beginning April to end Oct.

0.9 ha (38 pitches) flat, grassy

Tariff : ♦ 6.50€ 🚗 📧 4.50€ – (15A) 3.50€
Rental rates : (from beginning April to end Oct.) – 3 🏠. Per night from 50 to 65€ – Per week from 250 to 360€
🚰 local sani-station – 2 📧 14.50€ – 🔌 (/)13.50€

A small, simple site, rather old sanitary facilities, free use of the municipal pool. Groups welcome.

Surroundings : 🏞 ⚘
Leisure activities : 🎦
Facilities : 🛒 🏢 ᵀ launderette
Nearby : ✕ 🏊 🐎

Longitude : 0.89132
Latitude : 43.21389

*The classification (1 to 5 tents, **black** or red) that we award to selected sites in this guide is our own system. It should not be confused with the classification (1 to 5 stars) of official organisations.*

AX-LES-THERMES

09110 – Michelin map **343** J8 – pop. 1 384 – alt. 720 – ♨
🚩 Paris 805 – Toulouse 129 – Foix 43 – Pamiers 62

🏔 Sunêlia Le Malazeou 🚹

📞 05 61 64 69 14. www.campingmalazeou.com

Address : off the RN 20, route de l'Espagne (situated at Savignac-les-Ormeaux, 1km to the northwest, follow the signs for Foix)

Opening times : from beginning Jan. to mid Nov.

6.5 ha (244 pitches) terraced, flat, grassy, stony

Tariff : 30.50€ ♦♦ 🚗 📧 (10A) – Extra per person 8€ – Reservation fee 30€
Rental rates : (from beginning Jan. to mid Nov.) – 21 🏠 – 31 🏠. Per night from 53 to 107€ – Per week from 371 to 749€ – Reservation fee 30€
🚰 local sani-station 5€

Plenty of shade, beside the Ariège river, but choose the pitches away from the road in preference.

Surroundings : ⚘
Leisure activities : 🍷 ✕ 🎦 nighttime 🏃 🎣 ≦ 🏊 🏹
Facilities : 🚾 🏢 ᵀ launderette

Longitude : 1.82538
Latitude : 42.72852

AYZAC-OST

65400 – Michelin map **342** L4 – pop. 399 – alt. 430
▶ Paris 862 – Toulouse 188 – Tarbes 35 – Pau 54

⚲ La Bergerie

🖉 05 62 97 59 99. www.camping-labergerie.com

Address : 8 chemin de la Bergerie (take the southern exit along the N 21 and take road to the left)

Opening times : permanent

2 ha (105 pitches) flat, grassy

Tariff : (2015 price) 31.20€ ✶✶ 🚗 🗉 🚾 (6A) – Extra per person 7.80€
Rental rates : (2015 price) permanent 🏕 – 13 🚠. Per night from 50 to 80€ – Per week from 350 to 805€

A pleasant, small, landscaped water park surrounded by a number of owner-occupier mobile homes.

Surroundings : ◁ 🏔🏔 Leisure activities : ▾ 🏊 🚣 🎣 ⛷ Facilities : ♿ ⚬🚻 🍴 🖥 Nearby : 🛒 🍴 🚴	**GPS** Longitude : -0.0961 Latitude : 43.01824

BAGNAC-SUR-CÉLÉ

46270 – Michelin map **337** I3 – pop. 1 562 – alt. 234
▶ Paris 593 – Cahors 83 – Decazeville 16 – Figeac 15

⚲ Les Berges du Célé

🖉 06 64 99 82 33. www.camping-sudouest.com

Address : at La Plaine (to the southeast of the town, behind the station; beside the Célé river)

1 ha (44 pitches) flat, grassy
Rentals : 5 🚠 – 2 canvas bungalows.

Surroundings : 🏔🏔 Leisure activities : 🚣 🎣 🏊 Facilities : ⚬🚻 🍴 🖥 Nearby : ✂🎨	**GPS** Longitude : 2.16009 Latitude : 44.66461

BAGNÈRES-DE-BIGORRE

65200 – Michelin map **342** M6 – pop. 8 040 – alt. 551 – ♨
▶ Paris 829 – Lourdes 24 – Pau 66 – St-Gaudens 65

⚲⚲ Le Monlôo

Le Monlôo

🖉 05 62 95 19 65. www.lemonloo.com

Address : 5 chemin de Monlôo (take the northeastern exit, along the D 938, follow the signs for Toulouse then take left turn 1.4km along the D 8, follow the signs for Tarbes and take the road to the right)

Opening times : from beginning Jan. to mid Dec.

4 ha (199 pitches)

Tariff : (2015 price) 21€ ✶✶ 🚗 🗉 🚾 (16A) – Extra per person 5€
Rental rates : (2015 price) (from mid Jan. to mid Dec.) – 20 🚠 – 9 🏠. Per night from 58 to 95€ – Per week from 275 to 790€
🚰 local sani-station 5€ 14€ – 🔌 14€

A range of good quality rental options with a small eco lake (no chemicals) and a pretty beach.

Surroundings : 🏖 ◁ 🏔🏔 Leisure activities : 🏊 🚣 🏊 🏄 (stretch of water) ⛷ Facilities : ♿ ⚬🚻 🍴 🖥 🍴 launderette	**GPS** Longitude : 0.15107 Latitude : 43.0817

Les Fruitiers

🖉 05 62 95 25 97. www.camping-les-fruitiers.com

Address : 8 rue Pierre Latécoère (rte de Toulouse)

Opening times : from beginning April to end Oct.

1.5 ha (88 pitches) flat, grassy

Tariff : (2015 price) ✶ 4.50€ 🚗 🗉 4.50€ – 🚾 (6A) 5€
Rental rates : (2015 price) (from beginning April to end Oct.) 🏕 – 2 🚠 – 3 studios. Per night from 50€ – Per week from 250 to 400€ 🚰 local sani-station 5.50€

Lovely shaded grass areas, but choose the pitches away from the road.

Surroundings : ◁ Pic du Midi (peak) 🏔🏔 Leisure activities : 🏊 🚣 Facilities : ⚬🚻 🍴 launderette Nearby : 🏊	**GPS** Longitude : 0.15746 Latitude : 43.07108

BAGNÈRES-DE-LUCHON

31110 – Michelin map **343** B8 – pop. 2 600 – alt. 630 – ♨ – Winter sports : at Superbagnères : 1 440/2 260 m
▶ Paris 814 – Bagnères-de-Bigorre 96 – St-Gaudens 48 – Tarbes 98

⚲⚲ Pradelongue

Pradelongue

🖉 05 61 79 86 44. www.camping-pradelongue.com

Address : at Moustajon (2km north along the D 125, near the Intermarché supermarket)

Opening times : from beginning April to end Sept.

4 ha (142 pitches) flat, grassy

Tariff : 27.60€ ✶✶ 🚗 🗉 🚾 (10A) – Extra per person 6.95€ – Reservation fee 13€
Rental rates : (from beginning April to end Sept.) 🏕 – 18 🚠. Per night from 60 to 97€ – Per week from 275 to 680€ – Reservation fee 13€
🚰 local sani-station 14€ – 7 🗉 14€ – 🔌 14€

Plenty of green spaces, perfect for team sports or just relaxing.

Surroundings : ◁ 🏕 🏔🏔 Leisure activities : 🏊 🚣 🏊 multi-sports ground Facilities : ♿ ⚬🚻 🖥 🍴 🍴 launderette Nearby : 🐎 🐎	**GPS** Longitude : 0.5981 Latitude : 42.81667

⚲⚲ Les Myrtilles 👥

🖉 05 61 79 89 89. www.camping-myrtilles.com

Address : at Moustajon (2.5km north along the D 125, beside a stream)

Opening times : permanent

2 ha (100 pitches) flat, grassy

Tariff : 19.80€ ✶✶ 🚗 🗉 🚾 (10A) – Extra per person 3.60€ – Reservation fee 14€
Rental rates : permanent – 20 🚠 – 7 🏕 – 3 canvas bungalows – 1 gîte. Per night from 35 to 63€ – Per week from 232 to 629€ – Reservation fee 14€
🚰 AireService sani-station 5€

A free shuttle to the thermal baths.

Surroundings : ◁ 🏕 🏔 Leisure activities : ▾ 🍴 🏊 🤸 🚣 🏊 Facilities : ♿ ⚬🚻 🖥 🍴 launderette 🚴 Nearby : 🐎	**GPS** Longitude : 0.59975 Latitude : 42.81663

🏕 Domaine Arôme Vanille ♣♣

📞 0561790038. www.camping-aromevanille.com

Address : Montauban-de-Luchon, route de Subercarrère, (located 1.5km east along the D 27)

Opening times : permanent

5 ha (194 pitches) flat and relatively flat, grassy

Tariff : 15.50€ ♥♥ ⇌ 🗐 🗓 (10A) – Extra per person 3.50€
Rental rates : permanent – 8 🛏 – 21 🏠. Per night from 45 to 75€ – Per week from 220 to 620€ – Reservation fee 10€
🚾 local sani-station
Pitches in both the shade and the sun.

Surroundings : 🌊 🏕 🎣	GPS	Longitude : 0.60814
Leisure activities : 🍴 ✕ 🏌 🎣 🚲		Latitude : 42.79496
Facilities : 🚿 🔌 🛁 🚽 🗐 🌿		

⛺ Au Fil de l'Oô

📞 0561793074. www.campingaufildeloo.com

Address : 37 avenue de Vénasque (1.5km south along the D 618)

2.5 ha (104 pitches) flat, grassy

Rentals : 8 🛏. 🚾 sani-station

Located by a stream with plenty of shade, but choose those pitches furthest away from the road.

Surroundings : 🛖 🏕	GPS	Longitude : 0.6003
Leisure activities : 🍴		Latitude : 42.77777
Facilities : 🚿 🔌 launderette 🌿		

BARBOTAN-LES-THERMES

32150 – Michelin map **336** B6 – ♨
▶ Paris 703 – Aire-sur-l'Adour 37 – Auch 75 – Condom 37

🏕 Le Lac de l'Uby ♣♣

📞 0562095391. www.camping-uby.com

Address : avenue du Lac (located 1.5km southwest, follow the signs for Cazaubon and take the turning to the left, at the leisure and activity park, beside the lake)

Opening times : from beginning April to mid Oct.

6 ha (286 pitches)

Tariff : 28€ ♥♥ ⇌ 🗐 🗓 (10A) – Extra per person 8€ – Reservation fee 8€
Rental rates : (from beginning April to mid Oct.) – 50 🛏 – 7 🏠. Per night from 34 to 107€ – Per week from 250 to 750€ – Reservation fee 8€ 🚾 local sani-station – 26 🗐 22€

Most pitches and rental options have a lovely view of the lake.

Surroundings : 🌊 ‹ 🏕 ⛰	GPS	Longitude : -0.04431
Leisure activities : 🍴 🏌 🎣 🚲 🛶 🎣 ⛵ multi-sports ground		Latitude : 43.93971
Facilities : 🚿 🔌 🛁 🚽 🌿 launderette 🌿 refrigerators		
Nearby : 🏖 🍴 🏊 (beach), pedalos		

LA BASTIDE DE SÉROU

09240 – Michelin map **343** G6 – pop. 959 – alt. 410
▶ Paris 779 – Foix 18 – Le Mas-d'Azil 17 – Pamiers 38

🏕 Flower L'Arize

📞 0561658151. www.camping-arize.com

Address : take the eastern exit along the D 117, follow the signs for Foix then continue 1.5km along the D 15, follow signs to Nescus to the right; beside the river

Opening times : from beginning April to end Oct.

7.5 ha/1.5 (90 pitches) flat, grassy

Tariff : 33€ ♥♥ ⇌ 🗐 🗓 (10A) – Extra per person 6.60€ – Reservation fee 13€
Rental rates : (from beginning April to end Oct.) – 16 🛏 – 4 🏠 – 3 canvas bungalows. Per night from 32 to 132€ – Per week from 224 to 924€ – Reservation fee 16€
🚾 local sani-station 4.50€ – 9 🗐 15.80€ – 🚐 🗓 15€

The site is crossed by a small stream that separates the shaded part from the sunny.

Surroundings : 🌊 🛖 🏕	GPS	Longitude : 1.44509
Leisure activities : 🍴 🎣 🚲 🛶 🎣		Latitude : 43.00168
Facilities : 🚿 🔌 🛁 🚽 🌿 🚽 launderette		
Nearby : ✕ 🏇		

⛺ Village Vacances Les Lambrilles
(rental of chalets only)

📞 0561645353. www.les-lambrilles.fr

Address : in the village; beside the Arize river

Opening times : permanent

1 ha flat, grassy

Rental rates : 24 🏠. Per night from 70 to 80€ – Per week from 320 to 620€ – Reservation fee 15€

'Semi-detached' chalets in pairs near a stream and a small fishing lake.

Surroundings : 🌊	GPS	Longitude : 1.42958
Leisure activities : 🍴 🎣 🎣 ⛵		Latitude : 43.00974
Facilities : 🚽 🌿 🗐		
Nearby : ✕ ⛳		

Routes nationales are main roads and their identifying numbers begin with N or RN. Routes départementales are generally quieter roads and begin with D or DN.

BEAUMONT-DE-LOMAGNE

82500 – Michelin map **337** B8 – pop. 3 809 – alt. 400
▶ Paris 662 – Agen 60 – Auch 51 – Castelsarrasin 27

🏕 Municipal Le Lomagnol ♣♣

📞 0563261200. www.village-de-loisirs.com

Address : avenue du Lac (800m east, access via the diversion; beside a small lake)

Opening times : from beginning April to end Oct.

6 ha/1.5 (100 pitches) flat, grassy

Tariff : 18€ ♥♥ ⇌ 🗐 🗓 (10A) – Extra per person 4€ – Reservation fee 15€
Rental rates : permanent ♿ (1 mobile home) 🅿 – 4 🛏 – 24 🏠. Per night from 60 to 80€ – Per week from 230 to 560€ – Reservation fee 15€
🚾 local sani-station 18€

The site spreads out beside the lake; there's the opportunity to take part in different water sports, but bathing is not permitted.

Surroundings : 🛖 🏕	GPS	Longitude : 0.99864
Leisure activities : 🍴 🌙 nighttime 🏌 ⛵ jacuzzi 🎣 🚲 ✕ 🛶 🎣 ⛵ pedalos 🏇		Latitude : 43.88295
Facilities : 🚿 🔌 🛁 🌿		
Nearby : ✕ fitness trail		

BÉDUER

46100 – Michelin map **337** H4 – pop. 730 – alt. 260
▶ Paris 572 – Cahors 63 – Figeac 9 – Villefranche-de-Rouergue 36

▲▲▲ La Via Natura Pech Ibert

✆ 05 65 40 05 85. www.camping-pech-ibert.com

Address : at Pech Ibert (located 1km northwest along the D 19, follow the signs for Cajarc and take turning to the right)

Opening times : from mid March to mid Oct.

1 ha (37 pitches) flat, grassy, stony, fine gravel

Tariff : ♗ 3.50€ ⇔ 1.40€ 🗐 3.50€ – 🔌 (6A) 3.50€ – Reservation fee 10€

Rental rates : (from mid March to mid Oct.) 🚐 – 1 'gypsy' caravan – 3 🛖 – 4 🏠 – 2 canvas bungalows. Per night from 15 to 40€ – Per week from 310 to 665€ – Reservation fee 15€

🚐 local sani-station 6€ – 2 🗐 10€ – 🔋10€
Some pitches are well shaded.

Surroundings : 🚣 🛶 ♀
Leisure activities : 🍷 🛖 🏇 🛝
Facilities : 🚿 🔌 ▥ 🌳 🕯 🌳 refrigerators
Nearby : 🍴

Longitude : 1.9375
Latitude : 44.57833

LE BEZ

81260 – Michelin map **338** G9 – pop. 803 – alt. 644
▶ Paris 745 – Albi 63 – Anglès 12 – Brassac 5

▲ Le Plô

✆ 05 63 74 00 82. www.leplo.com

Address : in the village (900m west along the D 30, follow the signs for Castres and take road to the left)

2.5 ha (60 pitches) terraced, relatively flat, grassy, wood

Rentals : 9 tent lodges.

Surroundings : 🚣 ♀♀
Leisure activities : 🛖 🏇 🛝
Facilities : 🚿 🔌 🕯 launderette

Longitude : 2.47064
Latitude : 43.60815

Do not confuse:
▲ to ▲▲▲ : *MICHELIN classification with*
★ to ★★★★★ : *official classification*

BOISSE-PENCHOT

12300 – Michelin map **338** F3 – pop. 539 – alt. 169
▶ Paris 594 – Toulouse 193 – Rodez 46 – Aurillac 65

▲ Le Roquelongue

✆ 05 65 63 39 67. www.camping-roquelongue.com

Address : at Boisse-Penchot (4.5km northwest along the D 963, D 21 and take the D 42, follow the signs for Boisse-Penchot, near the Lot river, direct access)

Opening times : permanent

3.5 ha (66 pitches) flat, grassy

Tariff : ♗ 4.65€ ⇔ 🗐 9€ – 🔌 (10A) 4.75€

Rental rates : permanent – 9 🛖 – 7 🏠. Per night from 38 to 101€ – Per week from 162 to 645€

Surroundings : 🚣 ♀♀
Leisure activities : 🍷 🍴 🏇 🛝 pedalos 🏊
Facilities : 🚿 🔌 🌳 🕯 🌳 🗐

Longitude : 2.22179
Latitude : 44.58224

BOR-ET-BAR

12270 – Michelin map **338** E5 – pop. 194 – alt. 250
▶ Paris 631 – Toulouse 109 – Rodez 61 – Albi 47

▲ Le Gourpassou

✆ 07 80 34 57 61. www.camping-legourpassou.com

Address : farm of Cessetière

Opening times : from beginning April to end Sept.

2.5 ha (39 pitches) flat, grassy

Tariff : (2015 price) ♗ 3.20€ ⇔ 1.50€ – 🔌 (6A) 3.20€

Rental rates : (2015 price) (from beginning April to end Sept.) – 7 🛖. Per night from 35 to 60€ – Per week from 210 to 410€

🚐 local sani-station – 2 🗐 13€
The campsite is based at a farm.

Surroundings : ≤ ♀
Leisure activities : 🛖 🛶
Facilities : 🔌 🌳 🌳 🕯

Longitude : 5.01096
Latitude : 47.32128

BOULOGNE-SUR-GESSE

31350 – Michelin map **343** B5 – pop. 1 612 – alt. 320
▶ Paris 735 – Auch 47 – Aurignac 24 – Castelnau-Magnoac 13

▲▲▲ Village Vacances Le Lac – (rental of chalets only)

✆ 05 61 88 20 54. www.ville-boulogne-sur-gesse.fr

Address : route du Lac (1.3km southeast along the D 633, follow the signs for Montréjeau and take turning to the left, 300m from the lake)

2 ha terraced

Rental rates : 🅿 – 24 🏠.

Surroundings : 🚣 ≤ on the lake ♀
Leisure activities : 🛖 🛶
Facilities : 🔌 ▥ 🗐
Nearby : 🍷 🍴 🍴 🏇 🏇 🏊 ♿ 🛝 🛶 pedalos

Longitude : 0.65712
Latitude : 43.28328

The guide covers all 22 regions of France – see the map and list of regions on pages 4–5.

BOURISP

65170 – Michelin map **342** O6 – pop. 147 – alt. 790
▶ Paris 828 – Toulouse 155 – Tarbes 70 – Lourdes 66

▲▲▲ Le Rioumajou 🏕

✆ 05 62 39 48 32. www.camping-le-rioumajou.com

Address : 1.3km northwest along the D 929, follow the signs for Arreau and take road to the left; beside the Neste d'Aure (river)

Opening times : permanent

5 ha (192 pitches) flat, grassy, fine gravel

Tariff : (2015 price) 26.48€ ♗♗ ⇔ 🗐 🔌 (10A) – Extra per person 6.80€ – Reservation fee 14€

Rental rates : (2015 price) permanent 🚐 – 5 🛖 – 6 canvas bungalows. Per night from 42 to 82€ – Per week from 290 to 570€ – Reservation fee 14€

🚐 eurorelais sani-station 4.20€ – 🔋 🔌14.88€
Plenty of green space in which to unwind, beside a stream.

Surroundings : ❄ 🚣 ≤ 🛏 ♀♀
Leisure activities : 🍷 🍴 🛖 🎣 ♿ 🚗 jacuzzi 🏇 🛝 🛶
Facilities : 🚿 🔌 ▥ 🌳 launderette 🚐

Longitude : 0.33943
Latitude : 42.83786

BRASSAC

81260 – Michelin map **338** G9 – pop. 1 396 – alt. 487
▶ Paris 747 – Albi 65 – Anglès 14 – Castres 26

⚠ Municipal de la Lande

🕾 05 63 74 09 11. www.brassac.fr

Address : by the sports centre (take the southwestern exit towards Castres and take a right turn after the bridge ; near the Agout river and crossed by a stream)

Opening times : from mid June to mid Sept.

1 ha (50 pitches) flat, grassy

Tariff : (2015 price) ♀ 2 € ⇌ 1.30 € 🔲 1.70 € – ⚡ (30A) 1.70 €

Surroundings : 🌊 ⚲⚲	**GPS** Longitude : 2.4952
Leisure activities : 🎦	Latitude : 43.63067
Facilities : 🚮⚐🗑	
Nearby : 🚴⚓🎿 🏊 🛶	

BRETENOUX

46130 – Michelin map **337** H2 – pop. 1 342 – alt. 136
▶ Paris 521 – Brive-la-Gaillarde 44 – Cahors 83 – Figeac 48

⚠ La Bourgnatelle

🕾 05 65 10 89 04. www.dordogne-vacances.fr

Address : rue de la Bourgnatelle (take the northwestern exit off the D803, turn left after the bridge, near the Cère river)

2.3 ha (135 pitches) flat, grassy

Rentals : 76 🛏 – 5 canvas bungalows.

🚐 local sani-station

Pitches beside the river. The sanitary facilities leave something to be desired.

Surroundings : 🌊 ⚲⚲⚠	**GPS** Longitude : 1.83772
Leisure activities : 🎦 🏖 🛶 🎿 ✈	Latitude : 44.91679
Facilities : 🚿 ⚲ 🍴 launderette 🚻	
Nearby : ✂	

BRUSQUE

12360 – Michelin map **338** J8 – pop. 309 – alt. 465
▶ Paris 698 – Albi 91 – Béziers 75 – Lacaune 30

⚠⚠ Village Vacances Val-VVF Le Domaine de Céras

🕾 05 65 49 50 66. www.vvfvillages.fr

Address : 1.6km south along the D 92, follow the signs for Arnac ; beside the Dourdou river and a small lake

Opening times : from beginning May to end Sept.

14 ha (160 pitches) undulating, flat, grassy

Tariff : (2015 price) 39.25 € ♀♀ ⇌ 🔲 ⚡ (10A) – Extra per person 3.90 € – Reservation fee 32 €

Rental rates : (2015 price) (from beginning May to end Sept.) 🚹 (3 apartments) – 19 🛖 – 48 apartments – 27 canvas bungalows. Per night from 42 to 140 € – Per week from 294 to 979 € – Reservation fee 32 €

Situated in a peaceful and secluded small green valley.

Surroundings : 🌊 ≤ ⚲⚲⚠	**GPS** Longitude : 2.95742
Leisure activities : 🍴 ✕ 🎦 🏖 🏖 ✖	Latitude : 43.75666
🏊 (fresh water) 🎿 fitness trail, multi-sports ground	
Facilities : ⚲ 🍴 launderette 🚻	

LES CABANNES

81170 – Michelin map **338** D6 – pop. 353 – alt. 200
▶ Paris 653 – Albi 27 – Montauban 57 – Rodez 80

⚠⚠ Le Garissou

Le Garissou

🕾 05 63 56 27 14. www.legarissou.fr

Address : 500m west of the village, along the D 600, follow the signs for Vindrac and take road to the left

Opening times : from mid March to mid Nov.

7 ha/4 for camping (72 pitches) terraced, flat, grassy, stony

Tariff : 19.90 € ♀♀ ⇌ 🔲 ⚡ (10A) – Extra per person 5 € – Reservation fee 9.90 €

Rental rates : (from mid March to mid Nov.) 🅿 – 30 🛖. Per night from 65 to 85 € – Per week from 260 to 655 € – Reservation fee 19.50 €

🚐 local sani-station 19.90 € – 🚐 11 €

Situated in an attractive elevated location.

Surroundings : 🌊 ≤ Cordes-sur-Ciel and valley 🏕 ⚲	**GPS** Longitude : 1.94247
Leisure activities : 🎦 🏖 🏖 🏊 🎿 multi-sports ground	Latitude : 44.06767
Facilities : 🚿 ⚲ CC 🚻 🍴 launderette	

Using the traditional Michelin classification method, the guide provides you with an easy, speedy reference for assessing the category of each site : 1 to 5 tents (see page 10).

CAHORS

46000 – Michelin map **337** E5 – pop. 19 948 – alt. 135
▶ Paris 575 – Agen 85 – Albi 110 – Bergerac 108

⚠⚠ Rivière de Cabessut

🕾 05 65 30 06 30. www.cabessut.com

Address : rue de la Rivière (3km south along the D 911 towards Rodez then take the road to the left, take quai Ludo-Rolles ; beside the Lot river)

Opening times : from beginning April to end Sept.

2 ha (113 pitches) flat, grassy

Tariff : ♀ 5.50 € ⇌ 🔲 9 € – ⚡ (10A) 2 €

Rental rates : (from beginning April to end Sept.) 🚹 – 8 🛏. Per night from 48 to 97 € – Per week from 340 to 680 €

🚐 local sani-station 4 €

Pitches that are well shaded in part, beside the Lot river.

Surroundings : 🏕 ⚲⚲	**GPS** Longitude : 1.44192
Leisure activities : 🎦 🏖 🏊 🎿 🛶	Latitude : 44.46364
Facilities : ⚲ 🚿 🚮 🏛 🗑 🍴 launderette	
Nearby : 🏊	

These symbols are used for a campsite that is exceptional in its category :

⚠⚠⚠...⚠	*Particularly pleasant setting, quality and range of services available*
🌊 🌊	*Tranquil, isolated site – quiet site, particularly at night*
≤ ≤	*Exceptional view – interesting or panoramic view*

CALMONT

31560 – Michelin map **343** H5 – pop. 2 177 – alt. 220
▶ Paris 724 – Toulouse 48 – Ordino 144 – Canillo 127

⚠ Le Mercier

✆ 05 34 48 81 31. www.camping-mercier.com ⚓

Address : 1 avenue de Pamiers (2.4km south along the D 11, follow the signs for Pamiers)

Opening times : permanent

0.6 ha (22 pitches) flat, grassy

Tariff : 21€ ♦♦ ⚛ 🔲 (5A) – Extra per person 5€
Rental rates : permanent ⚓ – 4 🚐. Per night from 45 to 75€ –
Per week from 270 to 450€
🚐 local sani-station 14€ – 3 🔲 14€ – 🛒 12.50€

A friendly welcome in a well-kept setting, with a variety of rental options.

Surroundings : 🌲 🗺 ♀
Leisure activities : 🛝
Facilities : 🚿 ⛽ 🔥 🍴 🎰

GPS
Longitude : 1.6334
Latitude : 43.2819

LES CAMMAZES

81540 – Michelin map **338** E10 – pop. 309 – alt. 610
▶ Paris 736 – Aurillac 241 – Castres 35 – Figeac 183

⚠ La Rigole

✆ 05 63 73 28 99. www.campingdelarigole.com

Address : route du Barrage, east of Les Cammazes (take the southern exit from the D 629 and road to the left)

Opening times : from mid April to end Sept.

3 ha (66 pitches) terrace, flat and relatively flat, grassy

Tariff : (2015 price) 30€ ♦♦ ⚛ 🔲 (8A) – Extra per person 6€ –
Reservation fee 5€
Rental rates : (2015 price) (from mid April to end Sept.) – 10 🚐 –
9 🏠. Per night from 39 to 120€ – Per week from 273 to 840€ –
Reservation fee 5€
🚐 3 🔲 13.80€

Surroundings : 🌲 🗺 ♀♀
Leisure activities : 🍴 🍽 🏊 🚲 🛝
Facilities : 🚿 ⛽ 🔥 🍴 launderette 🎰

GPS
Longitude : 2.08625
Latitude : 43.40787

The pitches of many campsites are marked out with low hedges of attractive bushes and shrubs.

CANET-DE-SALARS

12290 – Michelin map **338** I5 – pop. 416 – alt. 850
▶ Paris 654 – Pont-de-Salars 9 – Rodez 33 – St-Beauzély 28

⚠ Les Castels Le Caussanel ♣♣

Les Castels Le Caussanel

✆ 05 65 46 85 19. www.lecaussanel.com

Address : at the Lac de Pareloup (2.7km southeast along the D 538 and take a right turn)

Opening times : from beginning May to beginning Sept.

10 ha (228 pitches) terraced, flat, grassy

Tariff : 36.60€ ♦♦ ⚛ 🔲 (6A) –
Extra per person 7.90€ – Reservation fee 30€

Rental rates : (from beginning May to beginning Sept.) – 30 🚐 –
35 🏠. Per week from 363 to 917€ – Reservation fee 30€

Surroundings : 🌲 ◁ on the lake ♀ ⚠
Leisure activities : 🍴 🍽 🎬 📷 🏇 🏊 🚲 ⚽
🏊 🏖 ⛵ treetop adventure trail, pedalos 🎣
multi-sports ground, entertainment room
Facilities : 🚿 ⛽ 🔥 🔥 🍴 launderette 🎰 🌊

GPS
Longitude : 2.76651
Latitude : 44.21426

⚠ Soleil Levant

✆ 05 65 46 03 65. www.camping-soleil-levant.com

Address : at the Lac de Pareloup (3.7km southeast along the D 538 and D 993, follow the signs for Salles-Curan, to the left, before the bridge)

11 ha (206 pitches) terraced, flat, grassy

Rentals : 16 🚐.

In a pleasant location beside the Lac de Pareloup.

Surroundings : 🌲 ◁ ♀♀ ⚠
Leisure activities : 🍴 🎬 🏊 🏖 🎣
Facilities : 🚿 ⛽ 🔥 🔥 launderette
Nearby : 🚲 ⚓

GPS
Longitude : 2.77795
Latitude : 44.21551

CARENNAC

46110 – Michelin map **337** G2 – pop. 389 – alt. 123
▶ Paris 528 – Toulouse 183 – Cahors 81 – Limoges 139

⚠ L'Eau vive ♣♣

✆ 05 65 10 97 39. www.camping-lot-eauvive.com

Address : at Pré Nabots (1.3km southwest along the D 30)

Opening times : from beginning May to mid Oct.

2 ha (80 pitches) terraced, flat, grassy

Tariff : 24.80€ ♦♦ ⚛ 🔲 (6A) – Extra per person 6.50€ –
Reservation fee 18€
Rental rates : (from beginning May to mid Oct.) – 30 🚐 –
3 canvas bungalows. Per night from 34 to 118€ – Per week
from 238 to 826€ – Reservation fee 18€

Surroundings : 🗺 ♀♀
Leisure activities : 🍴 🍽 🎬 🏇 🏊 🏖 🛝 🎰
Facilities : 🚿 ⛽ 🔥 🍴 🎰 🌊

GPS
Longitude : 1.74105
Latitude : 44.9102

To visit a town or region, use the MICHELIN Green Guides.

CARLUCET

46500 – Michelin map **337** F3 – pop. 228 – alt. 322
▶ Paris 542 – Cahors 47 – Gourdon 26 – Labastide-Murat 11

⚠ Château de Lacomté

✆ 05 65 38 75 46. www.chateaulacomte.com

Address : at Lacomté (located 1.8km northwest of the town, by the castle)

12 ha/4 for camping (96 pitches) undulating, relatively flat, flat, grassy, wooded

Rentals : 4 🚐 – 5 🏠 – 1 gîte.

Reserved for adults (18 years +). Pitches among trees and bushes or more in the sun, in a large area of parkland.

Surroundings : 🌲 🗺 ♀♀
Leisure activities : 🍴 🍽 🎬 ⚽ 🛝
Facilities : 🚿 ⛽ 🎰 🔥 🍴 launderette 🌊

GPS
Longitude : 1.59692
Latitude : 44.72881

CASSAGNABÈRE-TOURNAS

31420 – Michelin map **343** C5 – pop. 415 – alt. 380
▶ Paris 758 – Auch 78 – Bagnères-de-Luchon 65 – Pamiers 101

⚠ La Via Natura Pré Fixe

☏ 05 61 98 71 00. www.camping-pre-fixe.com

Address : route de St-Gaudens (situated southwest of the town)

Opening times : from beginning May to end Sept.

1.2 ha (40 pitches) terraced, flat, grassy

Tariff : (2015 price) 24.80€ ✝✝ ⛟ 🅴 (½) (10A) –
Extra per person 6.20€
Rental rates : (2015 price) (from beginning April to mid Oct.)
⚡ – 6 🏠 – 2 tipis. Per night from 40 to 100€ – Per week
from 200 to 800€

*A pleasant site laid out in terraces, with a variety of upmarket
rental options and a small wine bar run by the owner.*

Surroundings : ⚲ ⛺ 〰〰
Leisure activities : 🍴 🎪 ⛹ 🏊
Facilities : & ⊶ 🚻 🖼 🛁
Nearby : 🍴

CASSAGNES

46700 – Michelin map **337** C4 – pop. 209 – alt. 185
▶ Paris 577 – Cahors 34 – Cazals 15 – Fumel 19

⚠ Le Carbet

☏ 05 65 36 61 79. www.camping-carbet.fr

Address : at La Barte (located 1.5km northwest along the D 673,
follow the signs for Fumel; near a lake)

Opening times : from mid April to mid Sept.

3 ha (29 pitches) open site, terraced, flat, grassy, stony

Tariff : ✝ 6.20€ ⛟ 🅴 5.60€ – (½) (6A) 3.20€ – Reservation fee 10€
Rental rates : (from mid April to mid Sept.) – 10 🚐 – 2 tent
lodges. Per week from 190 to 545€ – Reservation fee 10€

*Pitches among trees and shrubs, with a variety of rental ac-
commodation of different standards.*

Surroundings : ⛺ 〰〰
Leisure activities : 🍴 🗙 ⛹ 🏊
Facilities : ⊶ 🛁 🚻 launderette 🧺
Nearby : ⚓

---

*We value your opinion and welcome your feedback.
Do email us at campingfrance@tp.michelin.com*

CASTELNAU-DE-MONTMIRAL

81140 – Michelin map **338** C7 – pop. 950 – alt. 287
▶ Paris 645 – Albi 31 – Bruniquel 22 – Cordes-sur-Ciel 22

🏔 Le Chêne Vert

☏ 05 63 33 16 10. www.camping-du-chene-vert.com

Address : at Travers du Rieutort (head 3.5km northwest along the
D 964, follow the signs for Caussade, take D 1 and D 87, follow the
signs for Penne; on the left)

Opening times : from end April to mid Sept.

10 ha/2 for camping (130 pitches) undulating, terraced, relatively flat,
flat, grassy

Tariff : ✝ 11€ ⛟ 2€ – (½) (10A) 3.50€ – Reservation fee 8€

Rental rates : (from end April to mid Sept.) – 20 🚐 – 37 🏠 –
4 canvas bungalows. Per night from 40 to 85€ – Per week
from 364 to 672€ – Reservation fee 15€
🚰 local sani-station 9€ – 4 🅴 9€

Surroundings : ⚲ < ⛺ 〰〰
Leisure activities : 🍴 🗙 🎪 ⛹ 🏊
Facilities : & ⊶ 🚻 🖼 🛁 🧺
At the leisure/activities centre (800m) : 🗙
🎣 ⚓ (beach) 🏊

GPS
Longitude : 1.78947
Latitude : 43.97702

CASTÉRA-VERDUZAN

32410 – Michelin map **336** E7 – pop. 937 – alt. 114
▶ Paris 720 – Agen 61 – Auch 40 – Condom 20

🏔 La Plage de Verduzan

☏ 05 62 68 12 23. www.camping-castera.com

Address : 30 rue du Lac (north of the town; beside the Aulone river)

Opening times : from beginning May to end Sept.

2 ha (92 pitches) flat, grassy

Tariff : 24.60€ ✝✝ ⛟ 🅴 (½) (10A) – Extra per person 5€
Rental rates : (from beginning May to end Sept.) – 16 🚐.
Per night from 60€ – Per week from 250 to 545€
🚰 local sani-station 5€

Situated beside a lake; the pitches are well kept.

Surroundings : ⚲ ⛺ 〰〰
Leisure activities : 🎪
Facilities : & ⊶ 🛁 🚾 🚻 🖼
Nearby : 🗙 ⚓ (beach) 🏊 pedalos

GPS
Longitude : 0.43116
Latitude : 43.80817

Key to rentals symbols:

12 🚐	*Number of mobile homes*
20 🏠	*Number of chalets*
6 🛏	*Number of rooms to rent*
Per night *30–50€*	*Minimum/maximum rate per night*
Per week *300–1,000€*	*Minimum/maximum rate per week*

CAUSSADE

82300 – Michelin map **337** F7 – pop. 6 586 – alt. 109
▶ Paris 606 – Albi 70 – Cahors 38 – Montauban 28

⚠ Municipal la Piboulette

☏ 05 63 93 09 07. www.mairie-caussade.fr

Address : located 1km northeast along the D 17, follow the signs for
Puylaroque and take the turning to the left, by the stadium, 200m
from a lake

Opening times : from beginning May to end Sept.

1.5 ha (72 pitches) flat, grassy

Tariff : (2015 price) ✝ 3.50€ ⛟ 🅴 2€ – (½) (6A) 2€
🚰 Flot Bleu sani-station 4.50€ – 5 🅴 4.50€

*The shaded pitches are situated between the municipal sports
grounds.*

Surroundings : ⚲ 〰〰
Facilities : & ⊶ 🚾 🏚 🚻 🖼
Nearby : ⛹ 🗙 ⚓ fitness trail

GPS
Longitude : 1.54624
Latitude : 44.16877

CAUTERETS

65110 – Michelin map **342** L7 – pop. 1 118 – alt. 932 – ⚓ – Winter sports : 1 000/2 350 m
▶ Paris 880 – Argelès-Gazost 17 – Lourdes 30 – Pau 75

Les Glères

📞 0562925534. www.gleres.com

Address : 19 route de Pierrefitte (take the northern exit along the D 920; beside the Gave de Cauterets (river)

Opening times : from beginning Dec. to mid Oct.

1.2 ha (80 pitches) flat, grassy, gravel

Tariff : 20.65€ ✿✿ ⛺ 🖳 (6A) – Extra per person 4.95€ – Reservation fee 10.45€

Rental rates : (from beginning Dec. to mid Oct.) 🏠 – 16 🚐 – 8 🏠 – 1 apartment. Per night from 52 to 95€ – Per week from 245 to 655€

🚐 43 🖳 16.30€ – 🚐 16.30€

Good sanitary facilities, but slightly antiquated rental options for a location so close to the town centre.

Surroundings : ❄ ⛄ ☐ 🏊
Leisure activities : 🏠 ⛵ 🏊
Facilities : ♿ ☕ ⊞ 🛁 🚽 launderette
Nearby : 🍴 skating rink

GPS Longitude : -0.11275 | Latitude : 42.89625

Le Cabaliros

📞 0562925536. www.camping-cabaliros.com

Address : 93 avenue du Mamelon Vert (1.6 km north following signs for Lourdes, left across the bridge)

Opening times : from end May to beginning Oct.

2 ha (100 pitches) relatively flat to hilly, grassy

Tariff : 19.30€ ✿✿ ⛺ 🖳 (6A) – Extra per person 5.30€
Rental rates : permanent 🏠 – 6 🚐. Per night from 65 to 75€ – Per week from 280 to 590€

🚐 local sani-station 3€

Pitches in the shade or the sun, on a gentle slope leading down to the Gave de Pau (river).

Surroundings : 🏊 ⛄ 🏊
Leisure activities : 🏠 ⛵ 🏊
Facilities : ♿ ☕ 🛁 🚽 launderette

GPS Longitude : -0.10735 | Latitude : 42.90406

GR 10

📞 0620302585. www.gr10camping.com

Address : at Concé (2.8 km north along the D 920, follow the signs for Lourdes, near the Gave de Pau – river)

Opening times : from mid June to mid Sept.

1.5 ha (69 pitches) relatively flat, flat, grassy, rocks

Tariff : ✿ 7€ ⛺ 🖳 5€ – 🖳 (8A) 4€
Rental rates : permanent – 2 🚐 – 2 🏠 – 2 gîtes. Per night from 50 to 70€ – Per week from 390 to 690€

🚐 AireService sani-station 4€ – 7 🖳 15€ – 🚐 15€

A good departure point for many mountain activities.

Surroundings : 🏊 ⛄ ☐ ⛄
Leisure activities : 🏠 ⛵ 🍴 forest trail, rafting and canyoning, climbing
Facilities : ♿ ☕ ⊞ 🅿 ⊞ 🚽 launderette

GPS Longitude : -0.09892 | Latitude : 42.91107

Le Péguère

📞 0562925291. www.campingpeguere.com

Address : 31 route de Pierrefitte (located 1.5km north following signs for Lourdes; beside the Gave de Pau (river)

Opening times : from beginning April to end Sept.

3.5 ha (160 pitches) relatively flat, flat, grassy

Tariff : 15.66€ ✿✿ ⛺ 🖳 (10A) – Extra per person 4.48€
Rental rates : (from beginning April to end Sept.) 🏠 – 3 🚐 – 2 🏠. Per night from 45 to 55 – Per week from 180 to 445

🚐 local sani-station 2€

A site that lies between the road heading north from the town and the Gave de Cauterets (river).

Surroundings : ⛄ ⛄
Leisure activities : 🏠 🏊
Facilities : ♿ ☕ 🛁 🚽 launderette

GPS Longitude : -0.10683 | Latitude : 42.9024

CAYLUS

82160 – Michelin map **337** G6 – pop. 1 536 – alt. 228
▶ Paris 628 – Albi 60 – Cahors 59 – Montauban 50

La Bonnette

📞 0563657020. www.campingbonnette.com

Address : at Les Condamines (take the northeastern exit along the D 926, follow the signs for Villefranche-de-Rouergue and turn right onto the D 97, follow the signs for St-Antonin-Noble-Val)

Opening times : from mid March to beginning Oct.

1.5 ha (51 pitches) flat, grassy

Tariff : 23.70€ ✿✿ ⛺ 🖳 (10A) – Extra per person 6€
Rental rates : (from mid March to beginning Oct.) – 4 🚐 – 1 tent lodge. Per night from 45 to 100€ – Per week from 300 to 700€

🚐 local sani-station 5€

Situated beside the Bonnette river and near a lake.

Surroundings : ☐ ⛄
Leisure activities : 🍷 🍴 ⛵ 🏊
Facilities : ♿ ☕ 🅿 🛁 🚽 launderette
Nearby : 🏊

GPS Longitude : 1.77629 | Latitude : 44.23375

CAYRIECH

82240 – Michelin map **337** F6 – pop. 264 – alt. 140
▶ Paris 608 – Cahors 39 – Caussade 11 – Caylus 17

Le Clos de la Lère

📞 0563312041. www.camping-leclosdelalere.com

Address : at Clergue (take the southeastern exit along the D 9, follow the signs for Septfonds)

Opening times : from beginning March to mid Nov.

1 ha (55 pitches) flat, grassy

Tariff : 23.50€ ✿✿ ⛺ 🖳 (10A) – Extra per person 6€
Rental rates : (from beginning March to mid Nov.) – 7 🚐 – 6 🏠 – 1 tent lodge. Per night from 20 to 50€ – Per week from 160 to 751€ – Reservation fee 8€

🚐 eurorelais sani-station 3€ – 4 🖳 8€ – 🚐 10€

Attractive shrubs and flowers decorate the site.

Surroundings : 🏊 ☐ ⛄
Leisure activities : 🍷 🍴 🎯 ⛵ 🏊
Facilities : ♿ ☕ ⊞ 🛁 🚽 launderette 🏊
Nearby : 🍴

GPS Longitude : 1.61291 | Latitude : 44.21735

CONDOM

32100 – Michelin map **336** E6 – pop. 7 099 – alt. 81
▶ Paris 729 – Agen 41 – Auch 46 – Mont-de-Marsan 80

⚠ **Municipal L'Argenté**

🖉 05 62 28 17 32. www.condom.org/index.php/camping-municipal

Address : chemin de l'Argenté (2 km, southern exit from the D 931, follow the signs for Eauze; near the Baïse river)

Opening times : from beginning April to mid Sept.

2 ha (78 pitches) flat, grassy

Tariff : (2015 price) 🧍 3.60 € 🚗 5.14 € – 🔋 (10A) 3.80 €
Rental rates : (2015 price) (from beginning April to mid Oct.) 🔌
🦽 – 10 🏠. Per night from 77 to 99 € – Per week from 298 to 474 €
🚮 local sani-station
In a leafy, shaded setting, with good-quality wooden chalets.

Surroundings : 🏖🏞
Leisure activities : 🎣
Facilities : 🔌 ⚡️🍴🏕📶
Nearby : 🍷🍴 jacuzzi 🎿🎣⛷🚣

	Longitude : 0.36436
GPS	Latitude : 43.94802

CONQUES

12320 – Michelin map **338** G3 – pop. 280 – alt. 350
▶ Paris 601 – Aurillac 53 – Decazeville 26 – Espalion 42

⚠ **Beau Rivage**

🖉 05 65 69 82 23. www.campingconques.com – 🏕

Address : at Molinols (to the west of the town, along the D 901; beside the Dourdou river)

Opening times : from beginning April to end Sept.

1 ha (60 pitches) flat, grassy

Tariff : 🧍 5 € 🚗 4 € 📧 7.50 € – 🔋 (10A) 4.50 €
Rental rates : (from beginning April to end Sept.) – 12 🛖.
Per night from 49 to 69 € – Per week from 280 to 560 €
🚮 local sani-station 5 €
Situated on the river bank, just below the medieval village.

Surroundings : 🏞🏞
Leisure activities : 🍴 🚣 🏊
Facilities : 🔌 ⚡️ (season) 🍴 launderette 🧺

	Longitude : 2.39285
GPS	Latitude : 44.59891

CORDES-SUR-CIEL

81170 – Michelin map **338** D6 – pop. 1 006 – alt. 279
▶ Paris 655 – Albi 25 – Montauban 59 – Rodez 78

⛰ **Moulin de Julien**

🖉 05 63 56 11 10. www.campingmoulindejulien.com

Address : 1.5 km southeast along the D 922, follow the signs for Gaillac; beside a stream

Opening times : from beginning May to mid Sept.

9 ha (130 pitches) terraced, sloping, flat, grassy, pond

Tariff : (2015 price) 24.90 € 🧍🧍 🚗 📧 🔋 (5A) – Extra per person 7 € – Reservation fee 10 €
Rental rates : (2015 price) (from beginning May to mid Sept.) 🦽 – 3 🛖 – 5 🏠. Per week from 290 to 600 € – Reservation fee 10 €

Surroundings : 🏞
Leisure activities : 🍷 🏖 🚣🏊🎣⛷
Facilities : 🔌 ⚡️🏕🍴📶
Nearby : 🎿

	Longitude : 1.97628
GPS	Latitude : 44.05036

⚠ Camp Redon

🖉 05 63 56 14 64. www.campredon.com

Address : at Livers Cazelles (5km southeast along the D 600, follow the signs for Albi then continue 800m along the D 107, follow the signs for Virac to the left)

2 ha (40 pitches)
Rentals : 2 🛖 – 3 canvas bungalows – 4 tent lodges.

Surroundings : 🏖 ⬅🏠🏞
Leisure activities : 🏖 🚣🏊
Facilities : 🔌 🍴🏕

	Longitude : 2.01767
GPS	Latitude : 44.04318

COS

09000 – Michelin map **343** H7 – pop. 369 – alt. 486
▶ Paris 766 – La Bastide-de-Sérou 14 – Foix 5 – Pamiers 25

⚠ **Municipal**

🖉 06 71 18 10 38. www.camping-municipal-cos09.fr

Address : Le Rieutort (700m southwest on the D 61; beside a stream)

0.7 ha (32 pitches) open site, flat, grassy
Rentals : 3 🏠.

A small, shady site with basic and rather old sanitary facilities.

Surroundings : 🏖 🏞
Leisure activities : 🎣 🎿
Facilities : 🔌 ⚡️🏛🚣🍴📶
Nearby : 🚣🏊

	Longitude : 1.57332
GPS	Latitude : 42.97102

The information in the guide may have changed since going to press.

CRAYSSAC

46150 – Michelin map **337** D4 – pop. 695 – alt. 300
▶ Paris 582 – Agen 81 – Cahors 16 – Toulouse 129

⛰ **Campéole Les Reflets du Quercy**

🖉 05 65 30 00 27. www.camping-lot.info

Opening times : from end April to mid Sept.

4.5 ha (136 pitches) very uneven, terraced, relatively flat, flat, grassy, stony

Tariff : (2015 price) 16.10 € 🧍🧍 🚗 📧 🔋 (10A) – Extra per person 4.30 € – Reservation fee 25 €
Rental rates : (2015 price) (from end April to mid Sept.) – 28 🛖 – 26 🏠 – 27 canvas bungalows. Per night from 35 to 123 € – Per week from 245 to 861 € – Reservation fee 25 €
🚮 sani-station – 8 📧 16.10 €
Beneath the shade of attractive oak trees.

Surroundings : 🏖 🏠🏞
Facilities : 🔌 ⚡️🏕🍴

	Longitude : 1.32227
GPS	Latitude : 44.5099

For more information on visiting particular towns or regions, consult the relevant regional MICHELIN Green Guide. We also recommend you use the appropriate Michelin regional map to locate your selected campsite, to calculate distances and to work out the best route.

CREISSELS

12100 – Michelin map **338** K6 – pop. 1 487 – alt. 330
▶ Paris 646 – Toulouse 184 – Rodez 69 – Montpellier 115

⛰ St-Martin

☎ 05 65 60 31 83. www.campingsaintmartin.fr

Address : south of the town, near the Ruisseau de Saint-Martin (stream)

Opening times : permanent

3 ha (90 pitches) flat, grassy

Tariff : 19.50€ ★★ 🚗 🔲 – 🔋 (10A) 4€ – Extra per person 4€

Rental rates : (from beginning April to end Oct.) 🏚 – 8 🚐.
Per night from 40 to 70€ – Per week from 220 to 500€ –
Reservation fee 15€ 🚮 local sani-station 6€

Surroundings : 🐟 ⟨ 🛋 ♨
Leisure activities : 🛶 ⛵ 🏊
Facilities : 🔥 ⛗ 🚿 🍴 launderette
Nearby : 🍴

GPS Longitude : 3.04907
Latitude : 44.07461

CREYSSE

46600 – Michelin map **337** F2 – pop. 296 – alt. 110
▶ Paris 517 – Brive-la-Gaillarde 40 – Cahors 79 – Gourdon 40

⛰ Le Port

☎ 05 65 32 20 82. www.campingduport.com

Address : south of the village, near the château; beside the
Dordogne river

Opening times : from end April to end Sept.

3.5 ha (100 pitches) open site, flat, grassy

Tariff : 21.40€ ★★ 🚗 🔲 🔋 (10A) – Extra per person 6€ – Reservation
fee 10€

Rental rates : (2015 price) (from end April to end Sept.) – 6 🚐 –
4 canvas bungalows – 4 tent lodges. Per night from 27 to 81€ –
Per week from 190 to 650€ – Reservation fee 10€

Surroundings : 🐟 ♨ ⛰
Leisure activities : 🍴 🛶 ⛵ 🚲 🏊 🎣
climbing, rafting and canyoning ♨
Facilities : ⛗ 🚿 🍴 launderette

GPS Longitude : 1.59895
Latitude : 44.88545

DAMIATTE

81220 – Michelin map **338** D9 – pop. 931 – alt. 148
▶ Paris 698 – Castres 26 – Graulhet 16 – Lautrec 18

⛰ Sites et Paysages Le Plan d'Eau St-Charles ♣♦

☎ 05 63 70 66 07. www.campingplandeau.com

Address : La Cahuziere (take the exit following signs for Graulhet
then continue 1.2km along the turning to the left before the level
crossing)

Opening times : from mid May to beginning Sept.

7.5 ha/2 for camping (82 pitches)

Tariff : (2015 price) 23.50€ ★★ 🚗 🔲 🔋 (6A) – Extra per person
6.50€ – Reservation fee 17€

Rental rates : (from beginning April to end Oct.) – 22 🚐 – 16 🚐 –
7 canvas bungalows. Per night from 60 to 85€ – Per week
from 210 to 810€ – Reservation fee 17€

In an attractive location beside a small but pretty lake.

Surroundings : 🐟 ⟨ ♨ ⛰
Leisure activities : ✗ 🛶 🚣 ⛵ 🏊 🎣
Facilities : 🔥 ⛗ 🚿 🍴 🔲 🚐
Nearby : 🐎

GPS Longitude : 1.97011
Latitude : 43.66289

DURAVEL

46700 – Michelin map **337** C4 – pop. 957 – alt. 110
▶ Paris 610 – Toulouse 153 – Cahors 39 – Villeneuve-sur-Lot 37

⛰⛰ FranceLoc Le Domaine Duravel ♣♦

☎ 05 65 24 65 06. www.franceloc.fr

Address : route du Port-de-Vire (2.3km south along the D 58; beside
the Lot)

Opening times : from end April to mid Sept.

9 ha (290 pitches) flat, grassy

Tariff : (2015 price) 46€ ★★ 🚗 🔲 🔋 (10A) – Extra per person 7€

Rental rates : (2015 price) (from end April to end Sept.) – 136 🚐 –
24 🚐 – 7 canvas bungalows. Per night from 39 to 200€ –
Per week from 154 to 1,624€ – Reservation fee 27€

*In a wooded setting, with a variety of rental options and pri-
vate sanitary facilities for some VIP pitches.*

Surroundings : 🐟 🛋 ♨♨
Leisure activities : 🍷 ✗ 🛶 📷 🏋 ⛵ 🚲 🎣
🏊 🎣 ⚓ ♨ multi-sports ground
Facilities : 🔥 ⛗ ⛺ – 36 individual sanitary
facilities (🚿 🚽 🔲 wc) 🍴 launderette 🔲 🚐

GPS Longitude : 1.08201
Latitude : 44.49633

ENTRAYGUES-SUR-TRUYÈRE

12140 – Michelin map **338** H3 – pop. 1 224 – alt. 236
▶ Paris 600 – Aurillac 45 – Figeac 58 – Mende 128

⛰⛰ Le Val de Saures

☎ 05 65 44 56 92. www.camping-valdesaures.com

Address : chemin de Saures (1.6km south along the D 904, follow the
signs for Espeyrac, on the banks of the Lot river, direct access)

Opening times : from beginning May to end Sept.

4 ha (126 pitches) terraced, flat, grassy

Tariff : (2015 price) 23.50€ ★★ 🚗 🔲 🔋 (16A) –
Extra per person 4.20€ – Reservation fee 15€

Rental rates : (2015 price) (from mid April to end Sept.) –
11 🚐 – 5 tent lodges. Per night from 29 to 103€ – Per week
from 203 to 721€ – Reservation fee 20€

Surroundings : 🐟 ⟨ ♨♨
Leisure activities : 🛶 ⛵ 🎣
Facilities : 🔥 ⛗ ⛺ 🍴 launderette
Nearby : 🏊

GPS Longitude : 2.56352
Latitude : 44.64248

⛰ Le Lauradiol

☎ 05 65 44 53 95. http://camping-lelauradiol.jimdo.com/

Address : at Campouriez (5km northeast along the D 34, follow the
signs for St-Amans-des-Cots; beside the Selves river)

Opening times : from beginning July to end Aug.

1 ha (31 pitches) flat, grassy

Tariff : (2015 price) 17€ ★★ 🚗 🔲 🔋 (6A) – Extra per person 3€ –
Reservation fee 15€

Rental rates : (2015 price) (from beginning July to end Aug.) –
2 🚐. Per night from 29 to 73€ – Per week from 203 to 511€ –
Reservation fee 20€

*In a pleasant location at the bottom of a small valley, on the
banks of the river.*

Surroundings : 🐟 🛋 ♨♨
Leisure activities : 🛶 ⛵ ✗ 🏊 🎣
Facilities : 🔥 ⛗ (July–Aug.) 🚿 🍴 🔲

GPS Longitude : 2.58289
Latitude : 44.67768

ESPALION

12500 – Michelin map **338** I3 – pop. 4 409 – alt. 342
▶ Paris 592 – Aurillac 72 – Figeac 93 – Mende 101

⛰ Le Roc de l'Arche

📞 05 65 44 06 79. www.rocdelarche.com

Address : Le Foirail (to the east, Rue du Foirail via Ave. de la Gare, turn off to the left, after the sports grounds, beside the Lot river)

Opening times : from beginning May to beginning Sept.

2.5 ha (95 pitches) flat, grassy

Tariff : 24.80€ ♦♦ ⇔ 🔲 ⓥ (10A) – Extra per person 5.70€ – Reservation fee 15€

Rental rates : (from beginning May to beginning Sept.) – 20 🚐. Per week from 286 to 511€ – Reservation fee 15€

🚰 local sani-station 3€ – 5 🔲 8€ – 🚙 8€

Surroundings : 🗘 🏖
Leisure activities : 🎣 🚣 🚴 🏄
Facilities : 🚿 ⚏ 🆒 🔥 🚹 🔥
Nearby : 🛒 🍴 🚣

Longitude : 2.76959
Latitude : 44.52244

Some campsites benefit from proximity to a municipal leisure centre.

ESTAING

65400 – Michelin map **342** K7 – pop. 77 – alt. 970
▶ Paris 874 – Argelès-Gazost 12 – Arrens 7 – Laruns 43

⛰ La Via Natura Pyrénées Natura

📞 05 62 97 45 44. www.camping-pyrenees-natura.com – alt. 1 000

Address : route du Lac (north of the hamlet)

Opening times : from mid May to beginning Oct.

3 ha (65 pitches)

Tariff : 33.40€ ♦♦ ⇔ 🔲 ⓥ (10A) – Extra per person 6€

Rental rates : (from mid April to beginning Oct.) – 18 🚐. Per night from 50€ – Per week from 248 to 820€

🚰 local sani-station – 4 🔲 18.60€

Based at a 19th-century farm, with good-quality rental accommodation and sanitary facilities.

Surroundings : 🗘 ⛰ 🌲 🏖
Leisure activities : 🍴 🍽 🎣 ♨ jacuzzi 🚣 🏄
Facilities : 🚿 ⚏ 🔥 🔥 🚹 launderette 🔥

Longitude : -0.17725
Latitude : 42.94145

ESTANG

32240 – Michelin map **336** B6 – pop. 643 – alt. 120
▶ Paris 712 – Aire-sur-l'Adour 25 – Eauze 17 – Mont-de-Marsan 35

⛰ Les Lacs de Courtès 👥

📞 05 62 09 61 98. www.lacsdecourtes.com

Address : south of the town along the D 152, behind the church and beside a lake

Opening times : from mid April to mid Oct.

7 ha (136 pitches) terraced, relatively flat, flat, grassy

Tariff : (2015 price) ♦ 5.25€ ⇔ 🔲 14€ – ⓥ (10A) 3€ – Reservation fee 20€

Rental rates : (2015 price) permanent – 21 🏠 – 2 canvas bungalows – 22 gîtes. Per night from 48 to 450€ – Per week from 170 to 1,200€ – Reservation fee 20€

🚰 local sani-station 5€ – 8 🔲 13€ – 🚙 8€

Situated behind the church, beside a lake.

Surroundings : 🗘 🗎 🏖
Leisure activities : 🍴 🍽 🎣 🏃 jacuzzi 🚣 ⛵ 🚣 🏄 🦋 entertainment room
Facilities : 🚿 ⚏ 🆒 🔥 🚹 launderette 🔥

Longitude : -0.1025
Latitude : 43.86472

FIGEAC

46100 – Michelin map **337** I4 – pop. 9 847 – alt. 214
▶ Paris 578 – Aurillac 64 – Rodez 66 – Villefranche-de-Rouergue 36

⛰ Le Domaine du Surgié

📞 05 61 64 88 54. www.domainedusurgie.com

Address : at the Domaine du Surgié (1.2km to the east along the N 140, follow the signs for Rodez, beside the river and a small lake)

Opening times : from beginning April to end Sept.

2 ha (159 pitches) terraced, flat, grassy. gravelled

Tariff : 26€ ♦♦ ⇔ 🔲 ⓥ (10A) – Extra per person 7.50€

Rental rates : (from beginning March to end Oct.) 🏄 – 20 🚐 – 30 🏠 – 6 canvas bungalows. Per night from 29 to 114€ – Per week from 200 to 795€ – Reservation fee 21€

🚰 4 🔲 26€

The campsite is bordered by the Cele river and is next to a leisure complex.

Surroundings : 🏖
Leisure activities : 🎣 🗎 🏃 🏄
Facilities : 🚿 ⚏ 🚹 launderette
Nearby : 🍴 🍽 🚣 🚣 🚴 🏄 △ pedalos

Longitude : 2.05037
Latitude : 44.61031

There are several different types of sani-station ('borne' in French) – sanitation points providing fresh water and disposal points for grey water. See page 12 for further details.

FLAGNAC

12300 – Michelin map **338** F3 – pop. 972 – alt. 220
▶ Paris 603 – Conques 19 – Decazeville 5 – Figeac 25

⛰ Flower Le Port de Lacombe

📞 05 65 64 10 08. www.campingleportdelacombe.fr

Address : located 1km north along the D 963 and take road to the left; near a small lake and the Lot river (direct access)

Opening times : from mid April to mid Sept.

4 ha (97 pitches) flat, grassy

Tariff : 29.90€ ♦♦ ⇔ 🔲 ⓥ (10A) – Extra per person 5.50€ – Reservation fee 20€

Rental rates : (from mid April to mid Sept.) – 44 🚐. Per night from 50 to 132€ – Per week from 250 to 924€ – Reservation fee 20€

🚰 Flot Bleu sani-station 5€

Surroundings : 🗘 🗎 🏖
Leisure activities : 🍴 🍽 🎣 🚣 🚴 ⛵ △ 🏄
Facilities : 🚿 ⚏ 🚹 launderette
Nearby : 🍽 🐎 pedalos

Longitude : 2.23533
Latitude : 44.60819

LA FOUILLADE

12270 – Michelin map **338** E5 – pop. 1 113 – alt. 420
▶ Paris 624 – Toulouse 109 – Rodez 61 – Albi 52

⚠ Le Bosquet

🖉 06 63 95 30 65. www.campinglafouillade.fr

Address : rue des Genêts

Opening times : from beginning April to beginning Oct.

5 ha (76 pitches) terraced, flat, grassy

Tariff : 22€ ✶✶ ⬛ ▣ ⚡ (12A) – Extra per person 4€ – Reservation fee 8€

Rental rates : (from beginning April to beginning Oct.) ⚡ – 12 ▦ – 8 canvas bungalows – 1 gîte. Per week from 90 to 780€ – Reservation fee 8€

🚽 local sani-station 8€ – 10 ▣ 22€

Surroundings : 🐟 ⬳ 🎣
Leisure activities :
Facilities : ♿ ⚬ 🏕 ℡ launderette
Nearby : 🎿 🍴

GPS | Longitude : 2.03717
Latitude : 44.22635

GARIN

31110 – Michelin map **343** B8 – pop. 133 – alt. 1 100
▶ Paris 827 – Toulouse 153 – Tarbes 85 – Lourdes 84

⚠ Les Frênes – (rental of chalets only)

🖉 05 61 79 88 44. www.chalets-luchon-peyragudes.com – traditional camp. spaces also available

Address : at the eastern edge of the village, off the D 618, follow the signs for Bagnères-de-Luchon and take the turning to the left, D 76e towards Billière

Opening times : permanent

0.8 ha terraced

Tariff : 18.40€ ✶✶ ⬛ ▣ ⚡ (10A) – Extra per person 5€ – Reservation fee 15€

Rental rates : 🅿 – 9 🏠. Per night from 70 to 86€ – Per week from 212 to 729€

Rentals are available on a nightly basis outside school holidays.

Surroundings : 🐟 ⬳ ♀
Leisure activities : 🚴
Facilities : ⚬ 🏕 ℡ launderette
Nearby : 🎿 🍴

GPS | Longitude : 0.51976
Latitude : 42.80933

To make the best possible use of this guide, please read pages 2–15 carefully.

GAVARNIE

65120 – Michelin map **342** L8 – pop. 140 – alt. 1 350 – Winter sports : 1 350/2 400 m
▶ Paris 901 – Lourdes 52 – Luz-St-Sauveur 20 – Pau 96

⚠ Le Pain de Sucre

🖉 05 62 92 47 55. www.camping-gavarnie.com – alt. 1 273

Address : Couret district (3km north along the D 921, follow the signs for Luz-St-Sauveur; beside the Gave de Gavarnie – river)

Opening times : from mid Dec. to end Sept.

1.5 ha (54 pitches) open site, flat, grassy

Tariff : (2015 price) ✶ 4.80€ ⬛ ▣ 5€ – ⚡ (10A) 6.70€ – Reservation fee 5€

Rental rates : (2015 price) (from mid Dec. to end Sept.) ⚡ – 3 ▦ – 5 🏠. Per night from 34 to 60€ – Per week from 215 to 545€

A mountain setting beside a stream, with good-quality sanitary facilities.

Surroundings : ❄ ⬳ ♀♀
Leisure activities : ☕ 🍴 🚣 🎣
Facilities : ♿ ⚬ 🏕 ℡ launderette

GPS | Longitude : 0.00137
Latitude : 42.75983

GIRAC

46130 – Michelin map **337** G2 – pop. 379 – alt. 123
▶ Paris 522 – Beaulieu-sur-Dordogne 11 – Brive-la-Gaillarde 42 – Gramat 27

⚠ Les Chalets sur la Dordogne

🖉 05 65 10 93 33. www.camping-chalet-sur-dordogne.com

Address : Au Port (south off the D803; beside the Dordogne river)

Opening times : from mid April to end Sept.

2 ha (39 pitches) open site, flat, grassy, sandy

Tariff : (2015 price) 21.50€ ✶✶ ⬛ ▣ ⚡ (10A) – Extra per person 5.50€ – Reservation fee 8€

Rental rates : (2015 price) (from beginning March to end Sept.) – 8 ▦ – 3 🏠 – 1 canvas bungalow. Per night from 35 to 65€ – Per week from 169 to 609€ – Reservation fee 12€

🚽 local sani-station 3€ – 4 ▣ 6€ – 🚌 6€

Shaded pitches beside the river. The site welcomes groups and children.

Surroundings : 🐟 ⬳ ♀♀ 🌳
Leisure activities : ☕ 🍴 🚣 🎣
Facilities : ♿ ⚬ (June–Aug.) ℡ launderette 🛒

GPS | Longitude : 1.80501
Latitude : 44.91809

In order for the guide to remain wholly objective, the selection of campsites is made on an entirely independent basis.

GONDRIN

32330 – Michelin map **336** D6 – pop. 1 180 – alt. 174
▶ Paris 745 – Agen 58 – Auch 42 – Condom 17

⚠ Le Pardaillan ♨

🖉 05 62 29 16 69. www.camping-le-pardaillan.com

Address : 27 rue Pardaillan (in the small town)

Opening times : from mid April to mid Sept.

2.5 ha (115 pitches) terraced, pond, flat, grassy, gravelled

Tariff : 24€ ✶✶ ⬛ ▣ ⚡ (10A) – Extra per person 6.20€ – Reservation fee 15€

Rental rates : (from mid April to mid Sept.) ♿ – 25 ▦ – 25 🏠 – 5 canvas bungalows. Per week from 310 to 790€ – Reservation fee 15€

🚽 local sani-station – 4 ▣ 11€ – 🚌 ⚡ 11€

Surroundings : 🐟 ⬳ ♀♀
Leisure activities : ☕ 🍴 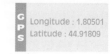 🏸 🚣 🚴 🎣
Facilities : ♿ ⚬ 🏕 🗑 ℡ launderette 🛒
Nearby : 🍴 ♒ (pool) ⛷ leisure park

GPS | Longitude : 0.23873
Latitude : 43.88165

GOUAUX

65240 – Michelin map **342** O5 – pop. 73 – alt. 923
▶ Paris 824 – Toulouse 151 – Tarbes 65 – Foix 149

� Le Ruisseau

✆ 05 62 39 95 49. www.camping-aure-pyrenees.com

Address : in the village

Opening times : from beginning April to beginning Oct.

2 ha (115 pitches) terraced, flat, grassy

Tariff : (2015 price) ✦ 4.80€ ⇔ 🚗 5.40€ – (≉) (6A) 4.90€ – Reservation fee 5€

Rental rates : (2015 price) (from beginning April to beginning Oct.) – 25 🚐. Per week from 199 to 585€ – Reservation fee 15€

🚏 local sani-station

Half of the pitches are occupied by rental or owner-occupier mobile homes.

Surroundings : ≼
Leisure activities : ✗
Facilities : ⅊ ⚊ 🛒 🏛 ⚒ ⛾ launderette ⚘

	GPS	
	Longitude : 0.36085	
	Latitude : 42.86423	

GOURDON

46300 – Michelin map **337** E3 – pop. 4 622 – alt. 250
▶ Paris 543 – Bergerac 91 – Brive-la-Gaillarde 66 – Cahors 44

� Le Paradis

✆ 05 65 41 65 01. www.campingleparadis.com

Address : at La Peyrugue (situated 2km southwest along the D 673, follow the signs for Fumel and take road to the left, near the Intermarché car park)

Opening times : from beginning May to mid Sept.

1 ha (25 pitches) open site, terraced, flat, grassy, wooded

Tariff : 17.10€ ✦✦ ⇔ 🚗 (≉) (6A) – Extra per person 5€

Rental rates : (from beginning May to mid Sept.) – 6 🚐 – 1 🏠. Per night from 40 to 55€ – Per week from 220 to 400€

🚏 4 🚗 17.10€ – ⛺ 14€

Some pitches lie among trees and shrubs, others are more in the sun.

Surroundings : ⚘ ♀♀
Leisure activities : 🏠 ⚒
Facilities : ⅊ ⚊ 🛒 ⛾ 🏛

	GPS	
	Longitude : 1.37397	
	Latitude : 44.72323	

GRAND-VABRE

12320 – Michelin map **338** G3 – pop. 406 – alt. 213
▶ Paris 615 – Aurillac 47 – Decazeville 18 – Espalion 50

⚑ Village Vacances Grand-Vabre Aventures et Nature
(rental of chalets only)

✆ 05 65 72 85 67. www.grand-vabre.com

Address : at Les Passes (located 1km southeast along the D 901, follow the signs for Conques; besides the Dourdou river)

Opening times : from beginning April to end Oct.

1.5 ha flat, grassy

Rental rates : ⅊ – 20 🏠 – 20 gîtes. Per night from 60 to 85€ – Per week from 310 to 675€

Surroundings : ♀♀
Leisure activities : 🏠 ⚑ ⚘ 🚲 ⚒ ⚑
Facilities : ⚊ 🏛 ⛾ launderette

	GPS	
	Longitude : 2.36297	
	Latitude : 44.62473	

HÈCHES

65250 – Michelin map **342** O6 – pop. 631 – alt. 690
▶ Paris 805 – Arreau 14 – Bagnères-de-Bigorre 35 – Bagnères-de-Luchon 47

⚑ La Bourie

✆ 05 62 98 73 19. www.camping-labourie.com

Address : at Rebouc (2km south along the D 929, follow the signs for Arreau and turn left onto the D 26, beside the Neste d'Aure river)

2 ha (122 pitches) flat, grassy

Rentals : 15 🚐.

On the site of an former factory, with many owner-occupiers.

Surroundings : ≼ ⛺ ♀♀
Leisure activities : ✗ 🏠 ⚒ ⚑
Facilities : ⅊ ⚊ 🏛 ⛾ 🏛

	GPS	
	Longitude : 0.37887	
	Latitude : 43.03815	

L'HOSPITALET-PRÈS-L'ANDORRE

09390 – Michelin map **343** I9 – pop. 91 – alt. 1 446
▶ Paris 822 – Andorra-la-Vella 40 – Ax-les-Thermes 19 – Bourg-Madame 26

⚑ Municipal La Porte des Cimes

✆ 05 61 05 21 10. www.laportedescimes.com – alt. 1 500

Address : 600m north along the N 20, follow the signs for Ax-les-Thermes and take turning to the right.

Opening times : from beginning June to end Oct.

1.5 ha (62 pitches) terraced, flat, grassy, fine gravel

Tariff : (2015 price) ✦ 3.50€ ⇔ 🚗 1€ 🚗 4€ – (≉) (10A) 6€

Choose the pitches furthest away from the road in preference.

Surroundings : ≼ ♀
Leisure activities : ✂
Facilities : ⅊ ⚊ (July–Aug.) 🏛 ⚒ ⚑ ⛾ launderette
Nearby : ⚒ ⚑

	GPS	
	Longitude : 1.80343	
	Latitude : 42.59135	

A chambre d'hôte is a guesthouse or B & B-style accommodation.

LACAM-D'OURCET

46190 – Michelin map **337** I2 – pop. 129 – alt. 520
▶ Paris 544 – Aurillac 51 – Cahors 92 – Figeac 38

⚑ Les Teuillères

✆ 05 65 11 90 55. www.lesteuilleres.com

Address : 4.8km southeast along the D 25, follow the signs for Sousceyrac and then Sénaillac-Latronquière, towards the Lac du Tolerme

Opening times : from beginning April to end Oct.

3 ha (30 pitches)

Tariff : (2015 price) ✦ 5.75€ ⇔ 🚗 6.75€ – (≉) (6A) 2.95€

Rental rates : (2015 price) (from beginning April to end Oct.) ✂ – 3 🛏 – 2 gîtes. Per week from 400 to 800€

The site is based around a pretty former farmhouse in local stone.

Surroundings : ⚘ ≼ ⛺ ♀♀
Leisure activities : ⚑ ⚒
Facilities : ⅊ ⚊ 🛒 ⛾ 🏛

	GPS	
	Longitude : 2.04086	
	Latitude : 44.8342	

LACAVE

46200 – Michelin map **337** F2 – pop. 284 – alt. 130
▶ Paris 528 – Brive-la-Gaillarde 51 – Cahors 58 – Gourdon 26

⛰ La Rivière ♣♣

✆ 05 65 37 02 04. www.campinglariviere.com

Address : at Le Bougayrou (2.5km northeast along the D 23, follow the signs for Martel and take road to the left; beside the Dordogne river)

Opening times : from beginning May to mid Sept.

2.5 ha (110 pitches) open site, flat, grassy, stony

Tariff : 25.95 € ♣♣ ⇔ 圓 ⚡ (10A) – Extra per person 6.65 € – Reservation fee 9.80 €

Rental rates : (from beginning May to mid Sept.) – 19 🚐. Per night from 83 to 113 € – Per week from 265 to 810 € – Reservation fee 9.80 €

This is a family-friendly site, with pitches overlooking the river.

Surroundings : 🌲 ♀♀
Leisure activities : ♈ ✕ 🎯 🚣 🏛 🎣 🚴
Facilities : ᴇ ☎ 🌳 ♒ launderette 🚿
GPS Longitude : 1.559
Latitude : 44.8613

LAFRANÇAISE

82130 – Michelin map **337** D7 – pop. 2 828 – alt. 183
▶ Paris 621 – Castelsarrasin 17 – Caussade 41 – Lauzerte 23

⛰ Le Lac

✆ 05 63 65 89 69. www.campings82.fr

Address : rue Jean Moulin (take the southeastern exit along the D 40, follow the signs for Montastruc and take the turning to the left, 250m from a small lake, direct access)

Opening times : from mid April to end Sept.

0.9 ha (41 pitches) terraced, relatively flat, flat, grassy, stony

Tariff : 20.80 € ♣♣ ⇔ 圓 ⚡ (8A) – Extra per person 9 €

Rental rates : (2015 price) (from mid April to end Sept.) ᴇ (1 gîte) – 19 🚐 – 1 🏠 – 11 gîtes. Per week from 370 to 605 €

🚏 Raclet sani-station 8 € – 4 圓 23 €

The campsite is situated among trees and shrubs, overlooking a small leisure and activity park.

Surroundings : 🌲 🚩 ♀♀♀
Leisure activities : 🚲 🏊
Facilities : ᴇ ☎ 🛁 🌳 ♒ 🧺
Nearby : ✕ 🚣 🎯 🏊 🚣 🌳 🎣 pedalos
GPS Longitude : 1.24675
Latitude : 44.1246

LAGUIOLE

12210 – Michelin map **338** J2 – pop. 1 267 – alt. 1 004 – Winter sports : 1 100/1 400 m
▶ Paris 571 – Aurillac 79 – Espalion 22 – Mende 83

⛺ Municipal les Monts d'Aubrac

✆ 05 65 44 39 72. http://www.campinglesmontsdaubraclaguiole.jimdo.com – alt. 1 050

Address : route de Rodez (take the southern exit along the D 921, follow the signs for Rodez then continue 600m along the turning to the left; by the stadium)

Opening times : from beginning May to mid Sept.

1.2 ha (57 pitches) relatively flat, flat, grassy

Tariff : (2015 price) 10 € ♣♣ ⇔ 圓 ⚡ (10A) – Extra per person 3 €

🚏 Flot Bleu sani-station 2 € – 🚐 ⚡ 10 €

Surroundings : 🌲 ⬗ ♀
Facilities : ᴇ ☎ ▥ 🛁 🔲
Nearby : ⚒ skateboarding
GPS Longitude : 2.85501
Latitude : 44.6815

LAMONTÉLARIÉ

81260 – Michelin map **338** H9 – pop. 62 – alt. 847
▶ Paris 736 – Toulouse 116 – Albi 83 – Castres 44

⛰ Rouquié

✆ 05 63 70 98 06. www.campingrouquie.fr

Address : on the edge of the Lac de la Raviège, off the D14E

Opening times : from beginning May to end Oct.

3 ha (97 pitches) very uneven, terraced, flat, grassy

Tariff : (2015 price) 24.50 € ♣♣ ⇔ 圓 ⚡ (10A) – Extra per person 4.80 € – Reservation fee 15 €

Rental rates : (2015 price) (from beginning April to end Oct.) ⚓ – 9 🚐 – 5 🏠. Per night from 57 to 72 € – Per week from 285 to 792 € – Reservation fee 15 €

Surroundings : 🌲 ⬗ ♀♀ ⛰
Leisure activities : ♈ ✕ 🎯 🚣 🎣 pedalos 🚴
Facilities : ᴇ ☎ 🌳 ♒ launderette 🚿
Nearby : ⚓
GPS Longitude : 2.60663
Latitude : 43.60038

LAU-BALAGNAS

65400 – Michelin map **342** L5 – pop. 499 – alt. 430
▶ Paris 864 – Toulouse 188 – Tarbes 36 – Pau 70

⛰ Le Lavedan

✆ 05 62 97 18 84. www.lavedan.com

Address : 44 route des Vallées (located 1km southeast)

Opening times : permanent

2 ha (108 pitches) flat, grassy

Tariff : 40.60 € ♣♣ ⇔ 圓 ⚡ (10A) – Extra per person 10.35 € – Reservation fee 25 €

Rental rates : permanent – 33 🚐 – 1 🏠. Per night from 50 to 99 € – Per week from 305 to 944 € – Reservation fee 25 €

Rental and owner-occupier mobile homes, and pitches for tents and caravans, best chosen away from the road.

Surroundings : ♀♀
Leisure activities : ♈ ✕ 🖼 🎯 🏊 (open air in season), entertainment room
Facilities : ᴇ ☎ ▥ 🛁 🌳 ♒ launderette 🚿
GPS Longitude : -0.08896
Latitude : 42.98818

LECTOURE

32700 – Michelin map **336** F6 – pop. 3 766 – alt. 155
▶ Paris 708 – Agen 39 – Auch 35 – Condom 26

⛰⛰ Yelloh! Village Le Lac des 3 Vallées ♣♣

✆ 05 62 68 82 33. www.lacdes3vallees.fr

Address : 2.4km southeast along the N 21, follow the signs for Auch, then continue 2.3km along the turning to the left beside the lake

Opening times : from beginning June to mid Sept.

40 ha (600 pitches) undulating, terraced, relatively flat, flat, grassy

Tariff : 50 € ♣♣ ⇔ 圓 ⚡ (10A) – Extra per person 9 €

Rental rates : (from beginning June to mid Sept.) – 300 –
23 canvas bungalows – 19 tent lodges. Per night from 37 to 199€ –
Per week from 259 to 1,393€

An undulating site with wide green spaces; numerous and varied good-quality rental options. A nice games room for young children.

Surroundings : 🐾 ⩽ ⌂ 🎠
Leisure activities : 🍽 ✗ 🏛 🎠 ⛷ ⛵
jacuzzi ⛸ ⚔ 🎯 ♨ 🏊 (beach) ⛱ disco,
pedalos 🚣 multi-sports ground, skate park
Facilities : ⚓ ⚮ 🚿 ⛺ ⚱ 🚽 launderette 🏪
🧊 refrigerators

G P S Longitude : 0.64533
Latitude : 43.91252

LOUDENVIELLE

65510 – Michelin map **342** O8 – pop. 308 – alt. 987
▶ Paris 833 – Arreau 15 – Bagnères-de-Luchon 27 – La Mongie 54

⛰ Pène Blanche

French Camps Pène Blanche

✆ 0562996885. www.peneblanche.com

Address : take the northwestern exit along the D 25, follow the signs for Génos; near the Neste de Louron (stream) and not far from a small lake

Opening times : from beginning April to end Oct.

4 ha (120 pitches) terraced, relatively flat, flat, grassy

Tariff : (2015 price) 16.50€ ✹✹ ⚓ 🔲 🔌 (10A) – Extra per person 4€
Rental rates : (2015 price) permanent – 18 – 3 tent lodges.
Per night from 33 to 104€ – Per week from 196 to 728€

A good choice of entertainment and water parks nearby.

Surroundings : 🐾 ⩽ 🌊
Facilities : ⚓ (July–Aug.) 🚿 🚽 launderette
Nearby : 🍽 ✗ ⚔ 🎯 ♨ 🏇 fitness centre,
paragliding

G P S Longitude : 0.40722
Latitude : 42.79611

This guide is updated regularly, so buy your new copy every year!

LOUPIAC

46350 – Michelin map **337** E3 – pop. 274 – alt. 230
▶ Paris 527 – Brive-la-Gaillarde 51 – Cahors 51 – Gourdon 16

⛰ Sites et Paysages Les Hirondelles 👫

✆ 0565376625. www.camping-leshirondelles.com

Address : at Al Pech (3km north following signs for Souillac and take road to the left; 200m from the N 20)

Opening times : from beginning April to beginning Sept.

2.5 ha (60 pitches) relatively flat, flat, grassy, stony

Tariff : 22.90€ ✹✹ ⚓ 🔲 🔌 (6A) – Extra per person 5.60€
Rental rates : (from beginning April to mid Sept.) ♿ (1 mobile home) 🚿 – 25 – 4 🏠 – 4 cabins in the trees – 5 tent lodges.
Per week from 243 to 778€

The pitches are among trees and shrubs, with a variety of rental accommodation of different standards.

Surroundings : ⌂ 🌳
Leisure activities : 🍽 ✗ 🏛 🎠 ⚔ 🎯 🏊
Facilities : ♿ ⚓ 🚿 🚽 launderette 🧊

G P S Longitude : 1.46455
Latitude : 44.82934

LOURDES

65100 – Michelin map **342** L6 – pop. 15 127 – alt. 420
▶ Paris 850 – Bayonne 147 – Pau 45 – St-Gaudens 86

⛰ Plein Soleil

✆ 670252310. www.camping-pleinsoleil.com

Address : 11 avenue du Monge (located 1km to the north)

Opening times : from end March to mid Oct.

0.5 ha (35 pitches) terraced, flat, grassy, fine gravel

Tariff : 23.20€ ✹✹ ⚓ 🔲 🔌 (13A) – Extra per person 5.30€
Rental rates : (from end March to mid Oct.) – 1 'gypsy' caravan –
2 – 7 🏠. Per night from 30 to 90€ – Per week from 200 to 650€

🚻 local sani-station 5€ – 16 🔲 15€ – 🚐 🔌18.30€

The site's pitches are laid out on terraces, with good sanitary facilities.

Surroundings : 🎠
Leisure activities : 🏛 ⚔ 🎯 🎱 (open air in season)
Facilities : ⚓ 🚿 🚽 ⚱ 🚽 launderette
Nearby : 🏪

G P S Longitude : -0.03646
Latitude : 43.11438

⛰ Sarsan

✆ 0562944309. www.lourdes-camping.com

Address : 4 avenue Jean Moulin (located 1.5km east via a diversion)

Opening times : from beginning April to mid Oct.

1.8 ha (67 pitches) relatively flat; flat, grassy

Tariff : (2015 price) 20.40€ ✹✹ ⚓ 🔲 🔌 (10A) –
Extra per person 5.20€
Rental rates : (from beginning April to mid Oct.) – 8 .
Per night from 50 to 80€ – Per week from 250 to 560€

🚻 local sani-station 3€

The swimming pool is in a shady grass area; choose the pitches furthest away from the road.

Surroundings : 🎠
Leisure activities : 🏛 ⚔ 🎯 🎱 (open air in season)
Facilities : ♿ ⚓ 🚿 🚽 🖥

G P S Longitude : -0.02744
Latitude : 43.10226

⛰ Le Moulin du Monge

✆ 0562942815. www.camping-lourdes.com

Address : 28 avenue Jean Moulin (1.3km to the north)

Opening times : from beginning April to beginning Oct.

1 ha (67 pitches) terrace, relatively flat, flat, grassy

Tariff : 23.50€ ✹✹ ⚓ 🔲 🔌 (6A) – Extra per person 5.90€
Rental rates : (from beginning April to beginning Oct.) – 12 –
1 🏠 – 2 🛏 – 1 gîte. Per night from 57 to 104€ – Per week from 399 to 728€

🚻 local sani-station 4€ – 12 🔲 14€

Lovely shady grass areas, but bear in mind the proximity of the road and the railway line.

Surroundings : 🎠
Leisure activities : 🏛 ⛷ ⚔ 🎯 🏊
Facilities : ♿ ⚓ 🚿 🚽 launderette 🧊

G P S Longitude : -0.03148
Latitude : 43.11575

The prices listed were supplied by the campsite owners in 2015 (if prices were not available, those from the previous year are given). The fees should be regarded as basic charges and may fluctuate with inflation.

⛰ Le Ruisseau Blanc

℘ 05 62 42 94 83. www.camping-lourdes-ruisseau-blanc.com

Address : at Anclades, route de Bagnères-de-Bigorre (1.5km east along the D 97, follow the signs for Jarret, caravans are recommended to take the D 937 towards Bagnère-de-Bigorre)

Opening times : from beginning April to mid Oct.

1.8 ha (102 pitches) flat, grassy

Tariff : (2015 price) ✝ 3€ ⇦ 🚗 3€ – 🔋 (6A) 3.80€

Rental rates : (2015 price) (from beginning April to mid Oct.) 🛖 – 3 🚐. Per week from 220 to 400€

🚐 local sani-station 4€ – 10 ▣

The site is on pleasant fields offering shade, but the sanitary facilities are very old.

Surroundings : 🌳 ⩽ ♤♤
Leisure activities : 🎣 🏇
Facilities : 🕭 ☛ 🛏 launderette

GPS Longitude : -0.01816
Latitude : 43.09531

LUZ-ST-SAUVEUR

65120 – Michelin map **342** L7 – pop. 1 014 – alt. 710 – 🔱 – Winter sports : 1 800/2 450 m

▶ Paris 882 – Argelès-Gazost 19 – Cauterets 24 – Lourdes 32

⛰ Club Airotel Pyrénées 🚶‍♂️

℘ 05 62 92 89 18. www.airotel-pyrenees.com

Address : Esquièze-Sère, 46 avenue du Barège (located 1km northwest along the D 921, follow the signs for Lourdes)

Opening times : from end Nov. to end Sept.

2.5 ha (146 pitches) terraced, relatively flat, flat, grassy

Tariff : 37€ ✝✝ ⇦ 🚗 ▣ 🔋 (10A) – Extra per person 8.50€ – Reservation fee 25€

Rental rates : (2015 price) (from end Nov. to end Sept.) 🛖 – 48 🚐 – 12 🏠. Per night from 103 to 200€ – Per week from 208 to 1,145€ – Reservation fee 25€

🚐 local sani-station 9€

A small pretty and well-equipped chalet village with several swimming pools, but choose pitches away from the road.

Surroundings : ❄ ⩽ ⬚ ♤♤
Leisure activities : 🎣 🏊 🛶 ♨ hammam, jacuzzi 🏇 🔲 ⛷ climbing wall, multi-sports ground, spa centre
Facilities : 🕭 ☛ 🛏 🍴 launderette ♨ 🌿

GPS Longitude : -0.01152
Latitude : 42.88014

⛰ International

℘ 05 62 92 82 02. www.international-camping.fr

Address : Esquièze-Sère, 50 avenue du Barège (1.3km northwest along the D 921, follow the signs for Lourdes)

Opening times : from mid May to end Sept.

4 ha (180 pitches) very uneven, terraced, flat, grassy

Tariff : (2015 price) 28€ ✝✝ ⇦ 🚗 ▣ 🔋 (10A) – Extra per person 6.90€ – Reservation fee 20€

Rental rates : (2015 price) (from mid May to end Sept.) 🛖 – 28 🚐 – 1 apartment. Per week from 220 to 800€ – Reservation fee 20€

Surroundings : ❄ ⩽ ⬚ ♤♤
Leisure activities : 🍴 🎣 jacuzzi 🏇 ♁ 🔲 (open air in season) ⛷ multi-sports ground
Facilities : 🕭 ☛ 🛏 launderette ♨

GPS Longitude : -0.01388
Latitude : 42.88322

⛰ Sites et Paysages Pyrénévasion

℘ 05 62 92 91 54. www.campingpyrenevasion.com – alt. 834

Address : at Sazos, route de Luz-Ardien (3.4km northwest along the D 921, follow the signs for Gavarnie and the D 12)

Opening times : from beginning April to end Oct.

3.5 ha (99 pitches) terraced, flat, grassy, rocks

Tariff : 35€ ✝✝ ⇦ 🚗 ▣ 🔋 (10A) – Extra per person 6.50€ – Reservation fee 10€

Rental rates : (from end Dec. to end Oct.) – 10 🚐 – 8 🏠 – 2 apartments. Per night from 45 to 115€ – Per week from 250 to 760€ – Reservation fee 12€

🚐 local sani-station 6€ – 🚐 14€

Surroundings : 🌳 ⩽ ♤♤
Leisure activities : 🍴 🍴 🎣 ♨ jacuzzi 🏇 🔲 ⛷ multi-sports ground
Facilities : 🕭 ☛ 🛏 ♨ 🌿 🍴 launderette 🌿

GPS Longitude : -0.02417
Latitude : 42.8831

⛰ Les Cascades

℘ 05 62 92 85 85. www.camping-luz.com

Address : rue Ste-Barbe (south of the town; beside rapids, recommended route via Gavarnie road)

Opening times : permanent

1.5 ha (77 pitches) terraced, relatively flat, flat, grassy, rocks

Tariff : 33€ ✝✝ ⇦ 🚗 ▣ 🔋 (10A) – Extra per person 6.50€

Rental rates : permanent – 18 🚐. Per night from 60 to 80€ – Per week from 280 to 700€

A very good standard of sanitary facilites for tents and caravans.

Surroundings : 🌳 ⩽ ♤♤
Leisure activities : 🍴 🍴 🎣 ♨ jacuzzi 🏇 ⛷
Facilities : 🕭 ☛ 🛏 🍴 launderette 🌿

GPS Longitude : -0.00292
Latitude : 42.86973

⛰ Le Bergons

℘ 05 62 92 90 77. www.camping-bergons.com

Address : route de Barèges (500m east along the D 918)

1 ha (74 pitches) terraced, flat, grassy

Rentals : 4 🚐 – 1 🏠 – 1 studio – 1 apartment.

Choose the pitches the furthest away from the road in preference.

Surroundings : ❄ ⩽ ♤♤
Leisure activities : 🎣 🏇
Facilities : 🕭 ☛ 🛏 launderette

GPS Longitude : 0.00281
Latitude : 42.87334

⛰ Toy

℘ 05 62 92 86 85. www.camping-toy.com

Address : 17 place du 8-Mai (town centre; beside the Bastan river)

Opening times : from beginning Dec. to end Sept.

1.2 ha (83 pitches) terraced, flat, grassy, stony

Tariff : ✝ 4.60€ ⇦ 🚗 ▣ 4.60€ – 🔋 (10A) 7.50€

🚐 local sani-station 13.80€

Beside a mountain stream, but in the centre of Luz, with shops close by.

Surroundings : 🌳 ⩽ ♤♤
Leisure activities : 🎣
Facilities : ☛ 🛏 🍴 launderette
Nearby : 🛒 🍴 🍴 ⛷

GPS Longitude : -0.00312
Latitude : 42.87328

MANE

31260 – Michelin map **343** D6 – pop. 998 – alt. 297
▶ Paris 753 – Aspet 19 – St-Gaudens 22 – St-Girons 22

⛰ Village Vacances de la Justale

✆ 05 61 90 68 18. www.village-vacances-mane.fr

Address : 2 allée de la Justale (500m southwest of the village, on the road near the town hall)

Opening times : from beginning April to end Oct.

3 ha (43 pitches) flat, grassy

Tariff : ♦ 2.90€ – 🚗 2.60€ – ⚡ (16A) 4.50€

Rental rates : permanent – 19 gîtes. Per night from 120 to 150€ – Per week from 250 to 450€

🚐 eurorelais sani-station – 26 🔲 17.90€ – 🛒 13.40€

A pleasant, leafy setting beside the Arbas river, with some basic, slightly old rental accommodation.

Surroundings : 🌲 🏞 ♈♈
Leisure activities : 🏠 🎯 🎣 🏊
Facilities : ♿ 🚿 🍴 ♈ launderette
Nearby : ✂ 🏇

GPS	Longitude : 0.94716
	Latitude : 43.07621

MARTRES-TOLOSANE

31220 – Michelin map **343** E5 – pop. 2 236 – alt. 268
▶ Paris 735 – Auch 80 – Auterive 48 – Bagnères-de-Luchon 81

⛰ Sites et Paysages Le Moulin 👥

Le Moulin

✆ 05 61 98 86 40. www.CampingLeMoulin.com

Address : at Le Moulin (head 1.5km southeast along the rte du Stade, take av. de St-Vidian and then the road to the left after the bridge; beside a stream and a canal, near the Garonne river – direct access)

Opening times : from mid March to beginning Oct.

6 ha/3 for camping (99 pitches) flat, grassy, stony

Tariff : (2015 price) 32.90€ ♦♦ 🚗 🔲 ⚡ (10A) – Extra per person 6€ – Reservation fee 9€

Rental rates : (2015 price) (from mid Jan. to mid Dec.) ♿ (1 chalet) – 2 'gypsy' caravans – 4 🛖 – 17 🏠 – 2 canvas bungalows – 2 tent lodges. Per night from 29 to 119€ – Per week from 252 to 959€ – Reservation fee 18€

🚐 local sani-station 18.90€ – 3 🔲 18.90€ – 🛒 14€

In a spacious green setting near the Garonne river and an old mill, with a range of good-quality rental accommodation.

Surroundings : 🌲 🏞 ♈♈
Leisure activities : ♈ ✕ 🏠 🍴 🏇 jacuzzi 🎣 ✂ 🏊 🎿 entertainment room
Facilities : ♿ 🚿 🍴 ♈ launderette 🌿

GPS	Longitude : 1.0181
	Latitude : 43.1905

MAZAMET

81200 – Michelin map **338** G10 – pop. 9 975 – alt. 241
▶ Paris 739 – Albi 64 – Béziers 90 – Carcassonne 50

⛰ Municipal la Lauze

✆ 05 63 61 24 69. www.camping-mazamet.com

Address : chemin de la Lauze (take the eastern exit along the N 112, follow the signs for Béziers and take a right turn)

1.7 ha (53 pitches) relatively flat, flat, grassy

Rentals : 5 🛖.
🚐 local sani-station – 11 🔲
Surroundings : 🌿 ♈♈
Leisure activities : 🏠 🎣 🏇
Facilities : ♿ 🚿 🍴 🎣 🌿 ♈ 🖥
Nearby : ✂ 🏊 🏇 sports trail

GPS	Longitude : 2.39148
	Latitude : 43.49692

MERCUS-GARRABET

09400 – Michelin map **343** H7 – pop. 1 153 – alt. 480
▶ Paris 772 – Ax-les-Thermes 32 – Foix 12 – Lavelanet 25

⛰ Le Lac

✆ 05 61 05 90 61. www.campingdulacmercus.com

Address : 1 promenade du Camping (800m south along the D 618, follow the signs for Tarascon and take a right turn at the level crossing)

Opening times : from beginning May to end Sept.

1.2 ha (50 pitches) terraced, flat, grassy

Tariff : (2015 price) 28€ ♦♦ 🚗 🔲 ⚡ (6A) – Extra per person 7.20€ – Reservation fee 15€

Rental rates : (2015 price) (from beginning April to end Sept.) – 11 🛖 – 16 🏠. Per week from 230 to 710€ – Reservation fee 15€

🚐 local sani-station 16€

Pitches and rental accommodation with plenty of shade beside the Ariège river.

Surroundings : ♈♈ ⛰
Leisure activities : 🏠 🏊 (small swimming pool) 🎣 🚣
Facilities : ♿ 🚿 🎣 🌿 ♈ 🖥

GPS	Longitude : 1.62252
	Latitude : 42.87154

Using the traditional Michelin classification method, the guide provides you with an easy, speedy reference for assessing the category of each site: 1 to 5 tents (see page 10).

MÉRENS-LES-VALS

09110 – Michelin map **343** J9 – pop. 185 – alt. 1 055
▶ Paris 812 – Ax-les-Thermes 10 – Axat 61 – Belcaire 36

⛰ Municipal de Ville de Bau

✆ 05 61 02 85 40. http://camping.merenslesvals.fr – alt. 1 100

Address : at Ville de Bau (located 1.5km southwest along the N 20, follow the signs for Andorra and take the road to the right; beside the Ariège)

Opening times : permanent

2 ha (70 pitches) flat, grassy, stony

Tariff : (2015 price) ♦ 3.70€ 🚗 🔲 3.80€ – ⚡ (10A) 5.50€ – Reservation fee 15€

Rental rates : (2015 price) permanent 🚐 – 3 🏠. Per night from 70 to 120€ – Per week from 280 to 600€

Beside the Ariège river. Choose the pitches further away from the road in preference.

Surroundings : ⛰ 🌿 ♈♈
Leisure activities : 🏠 🚣
Facilities : ♿ 🚿 🍴 🎣 🌿 ♈ launderette 🌿

GPS	Longitude : 1.83104
	Latitude : 42.64622

MEYRONNE

46200 – Michelin map **337** F2 – pop. 300 – alt. 130
▶ Paris 520 – Cahors 77 – Toulouse 180 – Tulle 74

⛰ La Plage

🔗 05 65 32 23 26. www.camping-laplage.com

Address : 1km south along the D 15 and D 23

Opening times : from beginning June to mid Sept.

1.8 ha (80 pitches) flat, grassy

Tariff : 19€ ✦✦ 🚗 📵 (½) (6A) – Extra per person 4.50€

Rental rates : (from beginning June to mid Sept.) – 10 canvas bungalows. Per night from 49 to 69€ – Per week from 200 to 550€
🚐 10 📵 15.50€

The shaded pitches lie near the Dordogne river, with a canoeing and kayaking centre.

Surroundings : 🏖 ♨♨
Leisure activities : 🛶 🎣 🏹 🛝
Facilities : 🚿 ⚬━ 🧺 🚻 🔌 🍴 refrigerators
GPS Longitude : 1.57732
Latitude : 44.87625

MIERS

46500 – Michelin map **337** G2 – pop. 435 – alt. 302
▶ Paris 526 – Brive-la-Gaillarde 49 – Cahors 69 – Rocamadour 12

⛰ Le Pigeonnier

🔗 05 65 33 71 95. www.campinglepigeonnier.com

Address : 700m east along the D 91, follow the signs for Padirac and take the road to the right behind the cemetery

Opening times : from beginning April to beginning Oct.

1 ha (45 pitches) terraced, relatively flat, flat, grassy

Tariff : (2015 price) ✦ 5.60€ 🚗 📵 6€ – (½) (16A) 3.70€ – Reservation fee 14€

Rental rates : (2015 price) (from beginning April to beginning Oct.) – 14 🚐. Per night from 50 to 74€ – Per week from 235 to 729€ – Reservation fee 14€
🚐 AireService sani-station 6€ – 6 📵 17.20€

Good-quality rental options, with a view of the village from some pitches.

Surroundings : 🏖 ☁ ♨♨
Leisure activities : 🏠 🛶 🎣 🏹
Facilities : 🚿 ⚬━ 🧺 🍴 launderette
GPS Longitude : 1.71028
Latitude : 44.85289

MILLAU

12100 – Michelin map **338** K6 – pop. 22 013 – alt. 372
▶ Paris 636 – Albi 106 – Alès 138 – Béziers 122

⛰ Club Airotel Les Rivages 👤👤

🔗 05 65 61 01 07. www.campinglesrivages.com

Address : 860 avenue de l'Aigoual (1.7km east along the D 991, follow the signs for Nant; beside the Dourbie river)

Opening times : from mid April to end Sept.

7 ha (314 pitches) flat, grassy

Tariff : (2015 price) 19.50€ ✦✦ 🚗 📵 (½) (10A) – Extra per person 8€ – Reservation fee 17€

Rental rates : (2015 price) (from mid April to end Sept.) – 40 🚐 – 12 canvas bungalows. Per night from 37 to 136€ – Per week from 250 to 952€ – Reservation fee 17€
🚐 local sani-station 5€

A pretty view over the wooded massif (mountains).

Surroundings : ♨♨ ⛰
Leisure activities : 🍴 ✗ 🏠 🎱 🏸 jacuzzi
🏊 🛶 🚣 🏹 🎣
Facilities : 🚿 ⚬━ 🧺 🚻 🔌 🍴 launderette
🚿 🍴
Nearby : hang-gliding
GPS Longitude : 3.09616
Latitude : 44.10161

⛰ Viaduc 👤👤

🔗 05 65 60 15 75. www.camping-du-viaduc.com

Address : 121 avenue de Millau-Plage (800m northeast along the D 991, follow the signs for Nant and turn left onto the D 187 following signs for Paulhe)

Opening times : from beginning April to end Sept.

5 ha (237 pitches) flat, grassy

Tariff : 37€ ✦✦ 🚗 📵 (½) (6A) – Extra per person 8€ – Reservation fee 18€

Rental rates : (from beginning April to end Sept.) – 39 🚐 – 6 canvas bungalows. Per night from 35 to 120€ – Per week from 245 to 840€ – Reservation fee 18€
🚐 local sani-station

Situated beside the Tarn river

Surroundings : ☁ ♨♨ ⛰
Leisure activities : 🍴 ✗ 🏠 🏸 🛶 🎣 🏹 🛝
Facilities : 🚿 ⚬━ 🧺 🚻 🔌 🍴 launderette
🚿 🍴
Nearby : 🛒 🚴 ✗ 🐴 paragliding
GPS Longitude : 3.08853
Latitude : 44.10578

⛰ Les Érables

🔗 05 65 59 15 13. www.campingleserables.fr

Address : avenue de Millau-Plage (900m northeast along the D 991, following signs for Nant and turn left onto D 187, follow the signs for Paulhe; beside the Tarn river)

Opening times : from beginning April to end Sept.

1.4 ha (78 pitches) flat, grassy

Tariff : 20€ ✦✦ 🚗 📵 (½) (10A) – Extra per person 4€ – Reservation fee 10€

Rental rates : (from beginning April to end Sept.) – 6 🚐. Per night from 41 to 80€ – Per week from 246 to 560€ – Reservation fee 10€

Surroundings : < ☁ ♨♨
Leisure activities : 🏠
Facilities : 🚿 ⚬━ 🍴 launderette
Nearby : 🛒 ✗ ⛵ 🛝
GPS Longitude : 3.08704
Latitude : 44.11022

MIRANDE

32300 – Michelin map **336** E8 – pop. 3 705 – alt. 173
▶ Paris 737 – Auch 25 – Mont-de-Marsan 98 – Tarbes 49

⛰ L'Île du Pont

🔗 05 62 66 64 11. www.groupevla.fr

Address : Le Batardeau (east of the town, on an island in the Grande Baïse river)

Opening times : from beginning April to end Sept.

10 ha/5 for camping (167 pitches) open site, flat, grassy

Tariff : 18.90€ ✦✦ 🚗 📵 (½) (6A) – Extra per person 6.30€ – Reservation fee 10€

Rental rates : permanent & (3 mobile homes) – 38 🚐 – 10 🏠.
Per night from 40 to 148€ – Per week from 239 to 1,036€ –
Reservation fee 22€

🚐 local sani-station – 10 📧

*A pleasant site on the Grande Baise island, with wide open
spaces and grass areas that are perfect for relaxation.*

Surroundings : 🌳 ♒♒
Leisure activities : 🏛 ⚡ 🚣 🎣
Facilities : & ⚡ 🍴 launderette
Nearby : 🚣 🏊

G P S Longitude : 0.40932
Latitude : 43.51376

MIRANDOL-BOURGNOUNAC

81190 – Michelin map **338** E6 – pop. 1 077 – alt. 393
▶ Paris 653 – Albi 29 – Rodez 51 – St-Affrique 79

⚠ Les Clots

📞 05 63 76 92 78. www.domainelesclots.com

Address : at Les Clots (5.5km north along the D 905, follow the
signs for Rieupeyroux and take road on the left; 500m from the Viaur
river – direct access)

Opening times : from beginning June to end Aug.

7 ha/4 for camping (62 pitches) very uneven, terraced, flat, grassy,
stony

Tariff : 37€ ⚡⚡ 🚐 📧 🔌 (6A) – Extra per person 6.70€
Rental rates : (from beginning June to end Aug.) – 5 🏠 –
3 canvas bungalows – 1 gîte. Per week from 340 to 965€

Surroundings : 🌳 ♒♒
Leisure activities : 🏛 🚣 🎿
Facilities : ⚡ 🍴 📧
Nearby : 🎣

G P S Longitude : 2.17881
Latitude : 44.17713

*These symbols are used for a campsite that is exceptional
in its category:*

🏔🏔...⚠ *Particularly pleasant setting, quality
and range of services available*

🌳🌳 *Tranquil, isolated site – quiet site,
particularly at night*

≪≪ *Exceptional view – interesting or panoramic
view*

MIREPOIX

32390 – Michelin map **336** G7 – pop. 204 – alt. 150
▶ Paris 696 – Auch 17 – Fleurance 13 – Gimont 25

⚠ Village Vacances Les Chalets des Mousquetaires
(rental of chalets only)

📞 05 62 64 33 66. www.chalets-mousquetaires.com

Address : at En Luquet (situated 2km southeast of the village)

Opening times : permanent

1 ha open site, pond, flat
Rental rates : & – 1 'gypsy' caravan – 11 🏠. Per night
from 45 to 84€ – Per week from 299 to 785€ – Reservation fee 20€

*Near a farm, the site looks out over the undulating coutryside
of the Gers.*

Surroundings : 🌳 ≪ ♒♒
Leisure activities : 🏛 🚣 🚴 🎣 🎿
Facilities : & ⚡ 🍴 📧
Nearby : 🎣

G P S Longitude : 0.69271
Latitude : 43.73682

MOISSAC

82200 – Michelin map **337** C7 – pop. 12 244 – alt. 76
▶ Paris 632 – Agen 57 – Auch 120 – Cahors 63

⚠ Municipal L'Île de Bidounet 👥

📞 05 63 32 52 52. www.camping-moissac.com

Address : St-Benoît (located 1km south along the N 113, follow the
signs for Castelsarrasin and turn left onto D 72)

Opening times : from beginning April to end Sept.

4.5 ha/2.5 for camping (109 pitches) flat, grassy

Tariff : (2015 price) 17.10€ ⚡⚡ 🚐 📧 🔌 (6A) – Extra per person 4.25€
Rental rates : (2015 price) (from beginning May to end Sept.)
🚐 – 12 canvas bungalows. Per night from 35 to 50€ – Per week
from 200 to 350€ – Reservation fee 15€

🚐 local sani-station – 6 📧 17.10€

In an attractive location on an island in the Tarn river.

Surroundings : 🌳 🚣 ♒♒
Leisure activities : 🍷 🏛 🚣 🎣 🎿
Facilities : & ⚡ 🍴 launderette
Nearby : watersports centre

G P S Longitude : 1.09005
Latitude : 44.09671

MONCLAR-DE-QUERCY

82230 – Michelin map **337** F8 – pop. 1 692 – alt. 178
▶ Paris 644 – Toulouse 73 – Montauban 22 – Albi 58

⚠ Village Vacances Les Hameaux des Lacs
(rental of chalets only)

📞 05 55 84 34 48. www.terresdefrance.com

Address : at the Les Lacs leisure centre

Opening times : permanent

5 ha very uneven, undulating, wood
Rental rates : 115 🏠. Per night from 45 to 125€ – Per week
from 149 to 799€

Surroundings : 🌳 ≪ ♒♒
Leisure activities : 🏛 🚣 🍴 🎿
multi-sports ground
Facilities : ⚡ 🍴 launderette
Nearby : 🚣 🏊 🏄 🎣 🦆 pedalos

G P S Longitude : 1.59544
Latitude : 43.96957

To visit a town or region, use the MICHELIN Green Guides.

MONTCABRIER

46700 – Michelin map **337** C4 – pop. 367 – alt. 191
▶ Paris 584 – Cahors 39 – Fumel 12 – Tournon-d'Agenais 24

⚠ Moulin de Laborde 🦆

📞 05 65 24 62 06. www.moulindelaborde.eu 🦆

Address : situated 2km northeast along the D 673, follow the signs
for Gourdon; beside the Thèze river

Opening times : from beginning May to beginning Sept.

4 ha (90 pitches) flat, grassy, small lake

Tariff : (2015 price) ⚡ 7.50€ 🚐 📧 10.80€ – 🔌 (10A) 4.50€

*Based around the buildings of an old mill; attractive, shaded
pitches.*

Surroundings : ♒♒
Leisure activities : 🍷 🍴 🏛 🚣 🎿 small
boating lake
Facilities : & ⚡ 🍴 📧 launderette 🚿

G P S Longitude : 1.08247
Latitude : 44.54819

MONTLAUR

12400 – Michelin map **338** I7 – pop. 664 – alt. 320
▶ Paris 686 – Toulouse 145 – Rodez 88 – Montpellier 138

⛰ Le Hameau des Genêts – (rental of gîtes only)

✆ 05 65 99 86 06. www.hameaudesgenets.com

Address : route de Briols, in the village

Opening times : from beginning April to end Oct.

2 ha flat

Rental rates : ⛓ (1 gîte) – 32 ⌂. Per night from 35 to 97 –
Per week from 245 to 679 € – Reservation fee 10 €

Free entry to see the animals on the site's mini-farm.

Surroundings : ⇦ ♀
Leisure activities : 🏠 🚲 ✂ 🔲 (open air in
season) 🌱 farm or petting farm
Facilities : ☛ 🛁 🍴 launderette
Nearby : 🏊 🚵

G P S	Longitude : 2.83404 Latitude : 43.87653

*The guide covers all 22 regions of France – see the map
and list of regions on pages 4–5.*

MONTPEZAT-DE-QUERCY

82270 – Michelin map **337** E6 – pop. 1 461 – alt. 275
▶ Paris 598 – Cahors 28 – Caussade 12 – Castelnau-Montratier 13

⛰ Révéa Le Faillal

✆ 05 63 02 07 08. http://www.revea-camping.fr/fr/accueil-camping-
le-faillal.html

Address : at the Le Faillal leisure centre (take the northern exit along
the D 20, follow the signs for Cahors and take the turning to the left)

Opening times : from beginning April to beginning Oct.

0.9 ha (69 pitches) terraced, grassy, stony

Tariff : 18 € ✚✚ 🚗 🔲 ⚡ (6A) – Extra per person 4 € – Reservation
fee 10 €

Rental rates : (from beginning April to beginning Nov.) Ⓟ –
22 ⌂. Per night from 55 to 90 € – Per week from 200 to 670 € –
Reservation fee 25 €

🚐 10 🔲 18 €

*Attrractive pitches for tents and caravans; some gîtes that are
a little old.*

Surroundings : ⇦ 🏞 ♀♀
Leisure activities : 🏠 🚵 🚲 🏕
Facilities : ☛ 🖵 🍴 🛁 🍴 🚿 📷
Nearby : ✂ 🔲

G P S	Longitude : 1.47725 Latitude : 44.24318

NAGES

81320 – Michelin map **338** I8 – pop. 340 – alt. 800
▶ Paris 717 – Brassac 36 – Lacaune 14 – Lamalou-les-Bains 45

⛰ Tohapi Rieu-Montagné ♣⚋

✆ 0825 00 20 30. www.tohapi.fr

Address : at the Lac du Laouzas leisure centre (4.5km south along the
D 62 and take turning to the left; 50m from the lake)

Opening times : from end April to mid Sept.

8.5 ha (179 pitches) terraced, grassy, stony

Tariff : (2015 price) 16 € ✚✚ 🚗 🔲 ⚡ (10A) – Extra per person 5 €

Rental rates : (2015 price) (from end April to mid Sept.) – 58 🚐 –
13 ⌂ – 20 tent lodges. Per night from 16 to 64 €

🚐 local sani-station 3 €

In an attractive elevated location.

Surroundings : 🏞 ⇦ Lac du Laouzas and
wooded mountains 🏞 ♀♀
Leisure activities : 🍴 ✗ 🏠 ⚬ daytime 🏃
🚵 🔲
Facilities : ☛ 🖵 🛁 🚿 🍴 launderette
🏖 🍴
Nearby : 🚲 ✂ 🏕 🌊 (beach) 🛶 🚵 pedalos

G P S	Longitude : 2.77806 Latitude : 43.64861

NAILLOUX

31560 – Michelin map **343** H4 – pop. 2 717 – alt. 285
▶ Paris 711 – Auterive 15 – Castelnaudary 42 – Foix 50

⛰ Le Lac de la Thésauque

✆ 05 61 81 34 67. www.campingthesauque.com

Address : 3.4km east along the D 622, follow the signs for
Villefranche-de-Lauragais, turn left onto D 25 and take road; 100m
from the lake

Opening times : permanent

6 ha (57 pitches) terraced, flat, grassy, stony

Tariff : 23.20 € ✚✚ 🚗 🔲 ⚡ (6A) – Extra per person 5.70 € –
Reservation fee 13 €

Rental rates : permanent ⛓ (1 mobile home) – 5 🚐 – 14 ⌂.
Per night from 38 to 89 € – Per week from 240 to 595 € –
Reservation fee 13 €

🚐 eurorelais sani-station 2.50 € – 10 🔲 6 € – 🚽 6 €

Situated near a lake with water activities.

Surroundings : 🏞 ♀♀
Leisure activities : 🍴 ✗ 🏠 🚵 ✂ 🏕 🔲 🌊
pedalos 🚵
Facilities : ⛓ ☛ 🖵 🍴 📷 🛁

G P S	Longitude : 1.64834 Latitude : 43.3554

Do not confuse:
⛰ *to* ⛰⛰⛰ *: MICHELIN classification with*
★ *to* ★★★★★ *: official classification*

NANT

12230 – Michelin map **338** L6 – pop. 919 – alt. 490
▶ Paris 669 – Le Caylar 21 – Millau 33 – Montpellier 92

⛰ RCN Le Val de Cantobre ♣⚋

✆ 05 65 58 43 00. www.rcn.fr

Address : Domaine de Vellas (4.5km north along the D 991, follow
the signs for Millau and take the road to the right; beside the
Dourbie river)

Opening times : from mid April to end Sept.

6 ha (216 pitches) very uneven, terraced, flat, grassy, stony, rocky

Tariff : 47.50 € ✚✚ 🚗 🔲 ⚡ (6A) – Extra per person 6.25 € –
Reservation fee 19.95 €

Rental rates : (from mid April to mid Oct.) – 29 🚐 – 9 ⌂.
Per night from 39 to 169 € – Per week from 234 to 1,183 € –
Reservation fee 19.95 €

🚐 local sani-station

*The site is based beside a 15th-century Caussenarde farm-
house.*

Surroundings : 🏞 ⇦ 🏞 ♀♀
Leisure activities : 🍴 ✗ 🏠 ⚬ 🏃 🚵 🏕 🔲
🏊 multi-sports ground
Facilities : ⛓ ☛ 🖵 🍴 🛁 🍴 launderette
🏖 🍴 refrigerated food storage facilities

G P S	Longitude : 3.30177 Latitude : 44.04554

Sites et Paysages Les 2 Vallées

▲ Sites et Paysages Les 2 Vallées

☏ 05 65 62 26 89. www.lesdeuxvallees.com

Address : route de l'Estrade Basse

Opening times : from mid April to mid Oct.

2 ha (80 pitches) flat, grassy

Tariff : 22€ ♥♥ ⇌ 🔲 (6A) – Extra per person 4€

Rental rates : (from mid April to mid Oct.) – 14 🚐 – 1 🏠 – 1 canvas bungalow. Per night from 25 to 62€ – Per week from 175 to 637€

🚽 local sani-station 5€ – 20 🔲 8€ – 🕳 8€

Surroundings : 🚣 ⛱ ♉♉
Leisure activities : ✗ 🏛 ⛵ ⚓ 🚲 ⛷ 🏊
Facilities : ♿ ⌗ ⛲ 🏕 🚿 ⛺ laundrette, refrigerators
Nearby : 🏇

G P S Longitude : 3.35457
Latitude : 44.0241

NAUCELLE

12800 – Michelin map **338** G5 – pop. 2 049 – alt. 490
▶ Paris 652 – Albi 46 – Millau 90 – Rodez 32

⛰ Flower Le Lac de Bonnefon

☏ 05 65 69 33 20. www.camping-du-lac-de-bonnefon.com

Address : take the southeastern exit along the D 997, follow the signs for Naucelle-Gare then continue 1.5km following signs for Crespin and turn left towards St-Just; 100m from the lake – direct access)

Opening times : from beginning April to mid Oct.

4.5 ha (112 pitches) terraced, flat, grassy

Tariff : 28.90€ ♥♥ ⇌ 🔲 (10A) – Extra per person 6€ – Reservation fee 10€

Rental rates : (from beginning April to mid Oct.) ♿ (1) – 8 🚐 – 15 🏠 – 15 canvas bungalows – 2 tent lodges. Per night from 38 to 140€ – Per week from 190 to 980€ – Reservation fee 15€

🚽 local sani-station 16.50€ – 4 🔲 16.50€

Surroundings : 🚣 ⛱ ♉♉
Leisure activities : 🍴 ✗ ⛵ 🎣 🏊 🛶
Facilities : ♿ ⌗ 🚿 🏕 🏊
Nearby : 🎿 🏇

G P S Longitude : 2.34867
Latitude : 44.18902

NÈGREPELISSE

82800 – Michelin map **337** F7 – pop. 5 056 – alt. 87
▶ Paris 614 – Bruniquel 13 – Caussade 11 – Gaillac 46

▲ Municipal le Colombier

☏ 05 63 64 20 34. www.ville-negrepelisse.fr

Address : the southwest part of the town, near the D 115

Opening times : from mid June to end Sept.

1 ha (53 pitches) terraced, flat, grassy

Tariff : 10.50€ ♥♥ ⇌ 🔲 (10A) – Extra per person 2€

🚽 local sani-station – 3 🔲 10.50€ – 🕳 9.50€

Surroundings : ♉♉
Facilities : ⌗ 🏕 🚿
Nearby : ⛵ 🏊

G P S Longitude : 1.51843
Latitude : 44.07286

OUST

09140 – Michelin map **343** F7 – pop. 545 – alt. 500
▶ Paris 792 – Aulus-les-Bains 17 – Castillon-en-Couserans 31 – Foix 61

⛰ Les Quatre Saisons

☏ 05 61 96 55 55. www.camping4saisons.com

Address : route d'Aulus-les-Bains (take southeastern exit along the D 32, near the Garbet)

Opening times : from beginning March to mid Nov.

3 ha (108 pitches) flat, grassy

Tariff : 18€ ♥♥ ⇌ 🔲 (10A) – Extra per person 5.70€ – Reservation fee 9.50€

Rental rates : (from beginning March to mid Nov.) – 21 🚐 – 3 🏠 – 6 ⛺ – 3 gîtes. Per night from 65 to 85€ – Per week from 405 to 770€ – Reservation fee 9.50€

🚽 local sani-station 16.50€ – 16 🔲 16.50€

Surroundings : ⛱ ♉♉
Leisure activities : 🍴 ✗ ⛵ 🎣 🏊
Facilities : ♿ ⌗ 🏕 laundrette 🚿
Nearby : 🎿 🏇

G P S Longitude : 1.22103
Latitude : 42.87215

OUZOUS

65400 – Michelin map **342** L4 – pop. 202 – alt. 550
▶ Paris 862 – Toulouse 188 – Tarbes 35 – Pau 55

▲ La Ferme du Plantier

☏ 05 62 97 58 01. b.capdevielle@laposte.net

Address : rue de l'Oulet (in the village, D 102)

0.6 ha (15 pitches) terraced, flat, grassy

Surroundings : 🚣 ⛰ mountains ♉
Leisure activities : ⛵
Facilities : ♿ ⌗ 🏕 📶

G P S Longitude : -0.1042
Latitude : 43.02958

Some information or pricing may have changed since the guide went to press. We recommend you check the price list online in advance or at the entrance to the campsite and enquire about possible restrictions.

PADIRAC

46500 – Michelin map **337** G2 – pop. 194 – alt. 360
▶ Paris 531 – Brive-la-Gaillarde 50 – Cahors 68 – Figeac 41

⛰ FranceLoc Roca D'Amour ▲▲

☏ 05 65 33 65 54. www.camping.franceloc.fr

Address : route du Gouffre (located 1.5km northeast along the D 90)

Opening times : from end April to mid Sept.

6 ha (248 pitches) terraced, relatively flat, flat, grassy, stony

Tariff : (2015 price) 27€ ♥♥ ⇌ 🔲 (9A) – Extra per person 7€ – Reservation fee 27€

Rental rates : (2015 price) (from end April to mid Sept.) ♿ (2 mobile homes) – 156 🚐 – 17 🏠 – 10 canvas bungalows – 4 tent lodges. Per night from 23 to 160€ – Per week from 161 to 1,120€ – Reservation fee 27€

Surroundings : 🚣 ⛱ ♉♉
Leisure activities : 🍴 ✗ 🏛 🎮 🏓 ⛵ 🎣 🏊 🛶 2 water parks, entertainment room
Facilities : ♿ ⌗ 🏕 laundrette 🍴 🚿

G P S Longitude : 1.74567
Latitude : 44.85125

PAMIERS

09100 – Michelin map **343** H6 – pop. 15 383 – alt. 280
▶ Paris 746 – Toulouse 70 – Carcassonne 77 – Castres 105

⚲ L' Apamée

✆ 05 61 60 09 09. http://www.vap-camping.fr/fr/camping-lapamee

Address : route de St-Girons (0.8km northwest along the D119)

Opening times : from beginning April to end Oct.

2 ha (80 pitches) flat, grassy

Tariff : 25.50€ ✦✦ 🚗 ▣ (10A) – Extra per person 9€
Rentals : (2015 price) (from beginning April to end Oct.) – 20 🛖 –
10 🏠 – 8 canvas bungalows.
🚉 local sani-station
*A shaded grassy area with a range of rental options, but choose
the pitches away from the road in preference.*

Surroundings : ♨♨		
Leisure activities : 🍷 ✕ 🚴🚴🚲 🏊 🎣	**G**	Longitude : 1.60205
Facilities : ♿ ⚲ cc ⛳ ☂ launderette	**P** **S**	Latitude : 43.1249

PAYRAC

46350 – Michelin map **337** E3 – pop. 670 – alt. 320
▶ Paris 530 – Bergerac 103 – Brive-la-Gaillarde 53 – Cahors 48

⚲ Yelloh! Village Les Pins ♙♙

✆ 05 65 37 96 32. www.les-pins-camping.com

Address : route de Toulouse, D 820 (take the exit south of Payrac)

Opening times : from mid April to mid Sept.

4 ha (137 pitches) terraced, relatively flat, flat, grassy

Tariff : 37€ ✦✦ 🚗 ▣ (10A) – Extra per person 7€
Rental rates : (from mid April to mid Sept.) – 55 🛖 – 3 🏠 –
5 canvas bungalows – 6 tent lodges. Per night from 29 to 149€ –
Per week from 203 to 1,043€.
🚉 AireService sani-station 5€ – 🚐 ⚡15€
*The campsite is in two separate parts. Choose those pitches
furthest away from the road.*

Surroundings : ♨♨♨		
Leisure activities : 🍷 ✕ 🏛 🚴🚴 🛶 jacuzzi	**G**	Longitude : 1.47214
🏋 🏊 🏊 multi-sports ground	**P**	Latitude : 44.78952
Facilities : ♿ ⚲ 🚿 ⛳ ☂ launderette ⛳	**S**	

PLAISANCE

32160 – Michelin map **336** – pop. 1 466 – alt. 131
▶ Paris 765 – Auch 56 – Bordeaux 186 – Tarbes 48

⚲ L'Arros

✆ 05 62 69 30 28. www.campingdelarros.com

Address : 21–37 allée des Ormeaux

Opening times : permanent

2 ha (50 pitches) flat, grassy

Tariff : ✦ 6€ 🚗 3.50€ ▣ – ⚡ (6A) 2€ – Reservation fee 5€
Rental rates : permanent – 3 🛖 – 25 🏠 – 4 canvas bungalows –
14 gîtes. Per night from 28 to 80€ – Per week from 196 to
749€ – Reservation fee 5€
🚉 local sani-station 10€ – 2 ▣ 10€

Surroundings : ♨♨♨		
Leisure activities : 🏛 🏋 🛶	**G**	Longitude : 0.05306
Facilities : ♿ ⚲ ☂ launderette	**P** **S**	Latitude : 43.6075
Nearby : 🚴 🏊 🚣 (fresh water)		

PONS

12140 – Michelin map **338** H2 – alt. 293
▶ Paris 588 – Aurillac 34 – Entraygues-sur-Truyère 11 – Montsalvy 12

⚲ Municipal de la Rivière

✆ 05 65 66 18 16. www.sainthippolyte.fr

Address : located 1km southeast of the town, along the D 526,
follow the signs for Entraygues-sur-Truyère; beside the Goul river

0.9 ha (46 pitches) flat, grassy

Rentals : 11 🏠.

Surroundings : 🏞 ⛵ ♨♨		
Leisure activities : 🏛 🏋 🎾 🏊 🎣	**G**	Longitude : 2.56363
Facilities : ♿ ⚲ ☂ ⛳ 🔲	**P** **S**	Latitude : 44.71119

PONT-DE-SALARS

12290 – Michelin map **338** I5 – pop. 1 606 – alt. 700
▶ Paris 651 – Albi 86 – Millau 47 – Rodez 25

⚲ Flower Les Terrasses du Lac ♙♙

✆ 05 65 46 88 18. www.campinglesterrasses.com

Address : route du Vibal (4km north along the D 523)

Opening times : from beginning April to end Sept.

6 ha (180 pitches) very uneven, terraced, flat, grassy

Tariff : (2015 price) 30.90€ ✦✦ 🚗 ▣ ⚡ (6A) – Extra per person 6€ –
Reservation fee 15€
Rental rates : (2015 price) (from beginning April to end Sept.) –
47 🛖 – 5 canvas bungalows. Per night from 46 to 129€ –
Per week from 196 to 903€ – Reservation fee 15€
🚉 local sani-station 24.50€ – 3 ▣ 24.50€
In an attractive location overlooking the lake.

Surroundings : 🏞 ⛵ ⛵ ♀		
Leisure activities : 🍷 ✕ 🏛 🎣 🚴🚴 🏋 🏊 🎣		
water park	**G**	Longitude : 2.73478
Facilities : ♿ ⚲ (July-Aug.) cc ⛳ ☂ ⛳ ☂	**P**	Latitude : 44.30473
launderette 🏊	**S**	
Nearby : 🍴 🚣 🏊 🐎		

*For more information on visiting particular towns or
regions, consult the relevant regional MICHELIN Green
Guide. We also recommend you use the appropriate
Michelin regional map to locate your selected campsite,
to calculate distances and to work out the best route.*

POUZAC

65200 – Michelin map **342** M4 – pop. 1 101 – alt. 505
▶ Paris 823 – Toulouse 149 – Tarbes 19 – Pau 60

⚲ Bigourdan

✆ 05 62 95 13 57. www.camping-bigourdan.com

Address : 79 avenue de la Mongie (on the D 935, between the
Renault garage and the Intermarché supermarket)

1 ha (48 pitches) flat, grassy

Rentals : 8 🛖.

Choose the pitches away from the road, if possible.

Surroundings : ♨♨		
Leisure activities : 🏛 🏋 🏊	**G**	Longitude : 0.13977
Facilities : ♿ ⚲ 🚿 ☂ launderette	**P** **S**	Latitude : 43.08036
Nearby : 🛒		

PUYBRUN

46130 – Michelin map **337** G2 – pop. 906 – alt. 146
▶ Paris 520 – Beaulieu-sur-Dordogne 12 – Brive-la-Gaillarde 39 – Cahors 86

⚠ La Sole ⚎

☎ 05 65 38 52 37. www.la-sole.com

Address : take the eastern exit, follow the signs for Bretenoux and take the road to the right after the service station

Opening times : from beginning April to end Oct.

2.3 ha (72 pitches) flat, grassy

Tariff : 22€ ⚎ ⚎ ▣ ⚡ (10A) – Extra per person 5.80€ – Reservation fee 15€

Rental rates : permanent – 10 🏠 – 17 canvas bungalows – 5 gîtes. Per night from 45 to 80€ – Per week from 170 to 689€ – Reservation fee 15€

Surroundings : ⚐ ⚐ ⚐
Leisure activities : ✗ ⚐ ⚐ jacuzzi ⚐ ⚐ multi-sports ground
Facilities : ⚐ ⚐ ⚐ ⚐ ⚐ ⚐

Longitude : 1.79432
Latitude : 44.91457

PUY-L'ÉVÊQUE

46700 – Michelin map **337** C4 – pop. 2 159 – alt. 130
▶ Paris 601 – Cahors 31 – Gourdon 41 – Sarlat-la-Canéda 52

⚠ Sites et Paysages L'Évasion

☎ 05 65 30 80 09. www.lotevasion.com

Address : at Martignac (3km northwest along the D 28, follow the signs for Villefranche-du-Périgord and take the road to the right)

Opening times : from mid April to end Oct.

8 ha/2 for camping (95 pitches) terraced, flat, grassy, stony

Tariff : (2015 price) ⚎ 11€ ⚎ ▣ – ⚡ (10A) 3.20€

Rental rates : (2015 price) (from mid April to end Oct.) ⚐ (1 chalet) – 8 🏠 – 29 🏠 – 9 canvas bungalows – 3 tent lodges. Per week from 300 to 940€ – Reservation fee 10€

A pretty water park, with chalets of various comfort standards set among trees, shrubs and bushes.

Surroundings : ⚐ ⚐ ⚐
Leisure activities : ⚐ ✗ ⚐ ⚐ ⚐ ⚐ ⚐ multi-sports ground
Facilities : ⚐ ⚐ ⚐ ⚐ launderette ⚐

Longitude : 1.12704
Latitude : 44.52546

PUYSSÉGUR

31480 – Michelin map **343** E2 – pop. 119 – alt. 265
▶ Paris 669 – Agen 83 – Auch 51 – Castelsarrasin 48

⚠ Namasté

☎ 05 61 85 77 84. http://www.camping-namaste.com

Address : take the northern exit along the D 1, follow the signs for Cox and take the road to the right

Opening times : from beginning May to end Sept.

10 ha/2 for camping (60 pitches) terraced, relatively flat, flat, grassy, pond, adjacent wood

Tariff : 30€ ⚎ ⚎ ⚎ ▣ ⚡ (10A) – Extra per person 8€ – Reservation fee 10€

Rental rates : (from end April to beginning Oct.) – 6 🏠 – 15 🏠. Per night from 95 to 120€ – Per week from 300 to 730€ – Reservation fee 15€

🏠 local sani-station 5€

The site also holds photographic exhibitions, sometimes outside, around the pitches.

Surroundings : ⚐ ⚐ ⚐
Leisure activities : ⚐ ⚐ ⚐ ⚐ ⚐ fitness trail
Facilities : ⚐ ⚐ ⚐ ⚐ ⚐ ⚐ ⚐ launderette ⚐

Longitude : 1.06134
Latitude : 43.75082

REVEL

31250 – Michelin map **343** K4 – pop. 9 253 – alt. 210
▶ Paris 727 – Carcassonne 46 – Castelnaudary 21 – Castres 28

⚠ Municipal du Moulin du Roy

☎ 05 61 83 32 47. www.mairie-revel.fr

Address : chemin de la Pergue (take southeastern exit along the D 1, follow the signs for Dourgne and take a right turn)

Opening times : from end May to beginning Sept.

1.2 ha (50 pitches) flat, grassy

Tariff : (2015 price) ⚎ 3.20€ ⚎ 2.30€ ▣ 2.70€ – ⚡ (6A) 3.50€
🏠 45 ▣ 11.50€

In a green setting, but choose pitches furthest away from the road.

Surroundings : ⚐ ⚐
Facilities : ⚐ ⚐ ⚐ ⚐ ⚐ ⚐
Nearby : ✗ ⚐ ⚐

Longitude : 2.01519
Latitude : 43.45464

RIEUX-DE-PELLEPORT

09120 – Michelin map **343** H6 – pop. 1 209 – alt. 333
▶ Paris 752 – Foix 13 – Pamiers 8 – St-Girons 47

⚠ Les Mijeannes

☎ 05 61 60 82 23. www.campinglesmijeannes.com

Address : route de Ferries (1.4km to the northeast, access via the D 311; beside a canal and near the Ariège river)

Opening times : permanent

10 ha/5 for camping (152 pitches) flat, grassy, stony

Tariff : ⚎ 5.90€ ⚎ ▣ 9.90€ – ⚡ (10A) 4.90€

Rental rates : permanent – 22 🏠 – 2 🏠. Per night from 42 to 73€ – Per week from 294 to 737€

🏠 AireService sani-station 4€ – ⚡ ⚡16€

Spacious, pleasant site with good shade, near the river.

Surroundings : ⚐ ⚐ ⚐ ⚐
Leisure activities : ⚐ ⚐ ⚐ ⚐ ⚐ ⚐ ⚐
Facilities : ⚐ ⚐ ⚐ launderette

Longitude : 1.62134
Latitude : 43.06293

RIGNAC

12390 – Michelin map **338** F4 – pop. 1 918 – alt. 500
▶ Paris 618 – Aurillac 86 – Figeac 40 – Rodez 27

⚠ La Peyrade

☎ 09 51 53 21 13. www.campinglapeyrade.fr

Address : south of the town, near a little lake

Opening times : from beginning June to mid Sept.

0.7 ha (36 pitches) terraced, flat, grassy

Tariff : 26€ ⚎ ⚎ ⚎ ▣ ⚡ (10A) – Extra per person 6€ – Reservation fee 20€

Rental rates : (from beginning June to mid Sept.) – 8 🏠. Per night from 45 to 81€ – Per week from 225 to 566€ – Reservation fee 20€

Surroundings : ⚐ ⚐ ⚐
Facilities : ⚐ ⚐ ⚐ ⚐ ⚐ ⚐ launderette
Nearby : ⚐ ⚐ ⚐ ✗ ⚐

Longitude : 2.28956
Latitude : 44.4058

RIVIÈRE-SUR-TARN

12640 – Michelin map **338** K5 – pop. 1 042 – alt. 380
▶ Paris 627 – Mende 70 – Millau 14 – Rodez 65

⚞ Flower Le Peyrelade ♟♟

🖉 05 65 62 62 54. www.campingpeyrelade.com

Address : route des Gorgers du Tarn (situated 2km east along the D 907, follow the signs for Florac; beside the Tarn river)

Opening times : from beginning May to mid Sept.

4 ha (190 pitches) terraced, flat, grassy

Tariff : 39€ ♟♟ ⇌ ▣ ⚡ (10A) – Extra per person 8€ – Reservation fee 19€

Rental rates : (from beginning May to mid Sept.) ⚟ – 45 ⟦⟧ – 8 tent lodges. Per night from 43 to 147€ – Per week from 196 to 1,029€ – Reservation fee 19€

⟦⟧ eurorelais sani-station

A pleasant site and setting at the entrance to the Tarn gorges.

Surroundings : ⋞ ♀		
Leisure activities : ♟ ✗ ▣ ⚟ ⚟ ⚟ ⚟ ⚟ ⚟	**G P S**	Longitude : 3.15807
Facilities : ⚟ ⚟ ⚟ ⚟ ⚟ ⚟ ⚟ ⚟ ⚟		Latitude : 44.18929
Nearby : ⚟ ⚟ forest trail		

⚞ Les Peupliers

🖉 05 65 59 85 17. www.campinglespeupliers.fr

Address : 11 rue de la Combe (take the southwestern exit follow the signs for Millau and take road to the left; beside the Tarn river)

Opening times : from beginning April to end Sept.

1.5 ha (115 pitches) flat, grassy

Tariff : (2015 price) 34€ ♟♟ ⇌ ▣ ⚡ (10A) – Extra per person 8€ – Reservation fee 20€

Rental rates : (2015 price) (from beginning April to end Sept.) – 17 ⟦⟧. Per night from 60 to 100€ – Per week from 300 to 920€ – Reservation fee 20€

⟦⟧ Raclet sani-station 5€

Surroundings : ⋞ ⟗ ♀		
Leisure activities : ♟ ✗ ⚟ ⚟ ⚟ ⚟ ⚟ ⚟ ⚟	**G P S**	Longitude : 3.12985
Facilities : ⚟ ⚟ ⚟ ⚟ ⚟ ⚟ launderette		Latitude : 44.18747

ROCAMADOUR

46500 – Michelin map **337** F3 – pop. 689 – alt. 279
▶ Paris 531 – Brive-la-Gaillarde 54 – Cahors 60 – Figeac 47

⚞ Padimadour ♟♟

🖉 05 65 33 72 11. www.padimadour.fr

Address : La Chataigneraie (7.7km northeast along the D 36, follow signs for Martel on D 840 and take a right turn)

Opening times : from end April to beginning Oct.

3.5 ha (52 pitches) terraced, relatively flat to hilly, flat, grassy

Tariff : 34.50€ ♟♟ ⇌ ▣ ⚡ (10A) – Extra per person 6.50€ – Reservation fee 14€

Rental rates : (from end April to beginning Oct.) ⚟ (1 mobile home) – 28 ⟦⟧. Per night from 63 to 141€ – Per week from 315 to 987€ – Reservation fee 14€

⟦⟧ local sani-station 4€ – 5 ▣ 17€ – ⚟⚡17€

New good-quality rental accommodation and sanitary facilities.

Surroundings : ⚟ ⟗ ♀		
Leisure activities : ✗ ▣ ⚟ ⚟ ⚟ ⚟	**G P S**	Longitude : 1.68617
Facilities : ⚟ ⚟ ⚟ ⚟ launderette ⚟		Latitude : 44.81765

⚞ Les Cigales

🖉 05 65 33 64 44. www.camping-cigales.com

Address : route de Gramat (take the eastern exit along the D 36 to Gramat)

Opening times : from beginning April to beginning Oct.

3 ha (100 pitches) flat, relatively flat, stony, grassy

Tariff : (2015 price) 26€ ♟♟ ⇌ ▣ ⚡ (10A) – Extra per person 9€

Rental rates : (2015 price) (from beginning April to beginning Oct.) – 2 'gypsy' caravans – 48 ⟦⟧ – 12 ⚟. Per night from 55 to 65€ – Per week from 229 to 835€

⟦⟧ local sani-station 5€

Pitches that are well shaded and good-quality rental options.

Surroundings : ⚟ ♀♀		
Leisure activities : ♟ ✗ ▣ ⚟ ⚟ ⚟	**G P S**	Longitude : 1.63221
Facilities : ⚟ ⚟ ⚟ ⚟ ⚟ ⚟ launderette ⚟ refrigerators		Latitude : 44.80549
Nearby : ⚟		

⚞ Le Roc

🖉 05 65 33 68 50. www.camping-leroc.com

Address : Pech-Alis (3km northeast along the D 673, follow the signs for Alvignac, 200m from the station)

Opening times : from beginning April to beginning Nov.

2 ha/0.5 (49 pitches)

Tariff : (2015 price) ♟ 6.20€ ⇌ ▣ 6.20€ – ⚡ (16A) 3.70€ – Reservation fee 10€

Rental rates : (2015 price) (from beginning April to beginning Nov.) – 4 ⟦⟧ – 8 ⚟. Per night from 99 to 150€ – Per week from 250 to 695€ – Reservation fee 14€

⟦⟧ local sani-station 5€ – 4 ▣ 13€ – ⚟⚡13€

Choose those pitches furthest away from the road.

Surroundings : ⟗ ♀♀		
Leisure activities : ✗ ⚟ ⚟	**G P S**	Longitude : 1.65379
Facilities : ⚟ ⚟ ⚟ ⚟ ⚟ ⚟ ⚟ ⚟		Latitude : 44.81947
Nearby : ⚟		

⚞ Le Paradis du Campeur ♟♟

🖉 05 65 33 63 28. www.leparadisducampeur.com

Address : L'Hospitalet (in the village)

1.7 ha (100 pitches)

⟦⟧ local sani-station

Choose those pitches furthest away from the road.

Surroundings : ♀♀		
Leisure activities : ⚟	**G P S**	Longitude : 1.62763
Facilities : ⚟ ⚟ launderette		Latitude : 44.80442
Nearby : ⚟ ♟ ✗		

RODEZ

12000 – Michelin map **338** H4 – pop. 24 358 – alt. 635
▶ Paris 623 – Albi 76 – Alès 187 – Aurillac 87

⚞ Village Vacances Domaine de Combelles ♟♟
(rental of mobile homes, chalets and canvas bungalows only)

🖉 05 65 78 29 53. www.camping-rodez.info

Address : Le Monastère, at the Domaine de Combelles (situated 2km southeast along the D 12, follow the signs for Ste-Radegonde, D 62, turn right towards Flavin and take road to the left)

120 ha/20 for camping undulating

Rentals : ♿ (2 chalets) – 30 🚐 – 35 🏠 – 27 canvas bungalows.

Plenty of activities for young and old, beside a large horse riding centre.

Surroundings : 🏊 ⟨ 🛏 ♤♤
Leisure activities : ♍ 🚣 🏊↟ 🚴 🏇 🚵 🎯
🛶 🐎 entertainment room
Facilities : ⟲ Ⓟ 🛁 🍴 launderette 🛒

GPS Longitude : 2.59147
Latitude : 44.33086

⛺ Municipal de Layoule

📞 0565670952. www.ville-rodez.com

Address : rue de la Chapelle (to the northeast of the town)

Opening times : from beginning May to end Sept.

2 ha (79 pitches) terraced, flat, grassy

Tariff : (2015 price) 10.80€ ✶✶ 🚗 🗉 🔌 (10A) –
Extra per person 4.40€
🚐 20 🗉 12€

In a pleasant, leafy setting with plenty of shade near the Aveyron river.

Surroundings : ⟨ 🛏 ♤♤
Leisure activities : 🛖 🚣
Facilities : ♿ ⟲ 🛁 🍴 🔲
Nearby : 🥾 walking trails

GPS Longitude : 2.58532
Latitude : 44.35367

LA ROMIEU

32480 – Michelin map **336** E6 – pop. 551 – alt. 188
▶ Paris 694 – Agen 32 – Auch 48 – Condom 12

⛰ Les Castels Le Camp de Florence ♙♙

📞 0562281558. www.lecampdeflorence.com

Address : route Astaffort (take the eastern exit from the town along the D 41)

Opening times : from beginning April to beginning Oct.

10 ha/4 for camping (197 pitches) terraced, flat, grassy

Tariff : (2015 price) 36€ ✶✶ 🚗 🗉 🔌 (10A) – Extra per person 8€
Rental rates : (2015 price) (from beginning April to beginning Oct.)
♿ (3 chalets) – 28 🚐 – 2 🏠 – 6 canvas bungalows. Per night from 50 to 160€ – Per week from 300 to 1,120€
🚐 local sani-station 5€ – 20 🗉 18€

Undulating and leafy site amid the fields of wheat, corn or sunflowers according to the season

Surroundings : 🏊 ⟨ 🛏 ♤♤
Leisure activities : ♍ ✗ 🛖 🏊↟ ↟ 🚣 🚴
🎯 🛶 wildlife park
Facilities : ♿ ⟲ 🛁 🍴 launderette 🛒

GPS Longitude : 0.50155
Latitude : 43.98303

ROQUELAURE

32810 – Michelin map **336** F7 – pop. 558 – alt. 206
▶ Paris 711 – Agen 67 – Auch 10 – Condom 39

⛰ Yelloh! Village Le Talouch ♙♙

📞 0562655243. www.camping-talouch.com

Address : at Cassou (3.5km north along the D 272, follow the signs for Mérens then take left turn D 148, follow the signs for Auch)

Opening times : from beginning April to mid Sept.

9 ha/5 for camping (147 pitches)

Tariff : 40€ ✶✶ 🚗 🗉 🔌 (10A) – Extra per person 8€

Rental rates : permanent – 17 🚐 – 32 🏠. Per night from 35 to 169€ – Per week from 245 to 1,183€
🚐 local sani-station 8€ – 3 🗉 15€

Surroundings : 🏊 🛏 ♤♤
Leisure activities : ♍ ✗ 🛖 🏊 ↟ 🛶
hammam, jacuzzi 🚣 🚴 🎯 🛶 🐎
Facilities : ♿ ⟲ 🛁 🍴 launderette 🛒

GPS Longitude : 0.56437
Latitude : 43.71284

ST-AMANS-DES-COTS

12460 – Michelin map **338** H2 – pop. 775 – alt. 735
▶ Paris 585 – Aurillac 54 – Entraygues-sur-Truyère 16 – Espalion 31

⛰ Tohapi Les Tours ♙♙

📞 0825002030. www.tohapi.fr – alt. 600

Address : at Les Tours (6km southeast along the D 97 and turn left onto D 599; beside the Lac de la Selves)

Opening times : from end April to end Sept.

15 ha (290 pitches) very uneven, terraced, flat, grassy

Tariff : (2015 price) 16€ ✶✶ 🚗 🗉 🔌 (10A) – Extra per person 6€
Rental rates : (2015 price) (from end April to end Sept.) – 152 🚐 –
55 tent lodges. Per night from 16 to 64€
🚐 local sani-station 3€

A pleasant site overlooking the lake.

Surroundings : 🏊 ⟨ 🛏 ♤♤ ⛰
Leisure activities : ♍ ✗ 🛖 🏊↟ ↟ 🚣 🚴 🎯
🛶 🐎 🥾 watersports centre
Facilities : ♿ ⟲ 🄲🄲 🛁 🍴 launderette
🐎 🛒

GPS Longitude : 2.68056
Latitude : 44.66803

⛰ La Romiguière

📞 0565444464. www.laromiguiere.com – alt. 600

Address : at the lake la Selve (8.5km southeast along the D 97 and turn left onto D 599; beside the Lac de la Selves)

Opening times : from mid April to mid Oct.

2 ha (62 pitches) terrace, flat, grassy

Tariff : 14.80€ ✶✶ 🚗 🗉 🔌 (10A) – Extra per person 4.50€
Rental rates : (from mid April to mid Oct.) – 19 🚐 – 4 canvas bungalows. Per night from 25 to 99€ – Per week from 175 to 693€ – Reservation fee 16€
🚐 local sani-station 2€ – 🛒 🔌14.80€

In a peaceful location beside a lake.

Surroundings : 🏊 ⟨ 🛏 ♤♤ ⛰
Leisure activities : ♍ ✗ 🛶 🥾 pedalos,
scuba diving 🏊
Facilities : ♿ ⟲ 🛁 🍴 launderette 🛒
Nearby : ⚓ water skiing

GPS Longitude : 2.70639
Latitude : 44.65528

Michelin classification:

⛰⛰⛰⛰ *Extremely comfortable, equipped to a very high standard*
⛰⛰⛰ *Very comfortable, equipped to a high standard*
⛰⛰⛰ *Comfortable and well equipped*
⛰⛰ *Reasonably comfortable*
⛰ *Satisfactory*

ST-ANTONIN-NOBLE-VAL

82140 – Michelin map **337** G7 – pop. 1 829 – alt. 125
▶ Paris 624 – Cahors 55 – Caussade 18 – Caylus 11

⛰ Sites et Paysages Les Trois Cantons ♣♦

✆ 05 63 31 98 57. www.3cantons.fr

Address : 7.7km northwest along the D 19, follow the signs for Caylus and take road to the left, after the little bridge over the Bonnette, between an area known as Tarau and the D 926, between Septfonds (6km) and Caylus (9km)

Opening times : from beginning May to end Sept.

15 ha/4 for camping (99 pitches)

Tariff : (2015 price) 30.20€ ♣♣ ⛟ ▣ ⚡ (10A) –
Extra per person 6.70€

Rental rates : (2015 price) (from mid May to end Sept.) – 15 🚐 –
2 🏠. Per night from 44 to 123€ – Per week from 308 to 860€

In a natural setting among trees, shrubs and bushes.

Surroundings : 🌿 ▱ ♨	**G** Longitude : 1.69612
Leisure activities : 🍷 🍴 🎪 🎯 🚣 🚴 ✂ 🧗 climbing wall	**P** **S** Latitude : 44.1933
Facilities : 🚿 ⚲ 🏕 🔥 🍴 refrigerators	

⛰ Flower Les Gorges de l'Aveyron ♣♦

✆ 05 63 30 69 76. www.camping-gorges-aveyron.com

Address : at Marsac bas

Opening times : from beginning May to end Sept.

3.8 ha (80 pitches) flat, grassy

Tariff : 32€ ♣♣ ⛟ ▣ ⚡ (10A) – Extra per person 7€ – Reservation fee 5€

Rental rates : (from beginning May to end Sept.) – 23 🚐 – 1 ⛺ – 10 tent lodges – 1 gîte. Per night from 43 to 128€ – Per week from 196 to 895€ – Reservation fee 15€

Pretty, well-shaded pitches, some beside the Aveyron river, with a variety of rental options.

Surroundings : 🌿 ♨	**G** Longitude : 1.77256
Leisure activities : 🍷 🏛 🎪 🎯 🚣 🎣	**P** **S** Latitude : 44.15211
Facilities : 🚿 ⚲ 🏕 🍴 launderette 🏖 🍴	

*To visit a town or region, use the **MICHELIN Green Guides**.*

ST-BERTRAND-DE-COMMINGES

31510 – Michelin map **343** B6 – pop. 259 – alt. 581
▶ Paris 783 – Bagnères-de-Luchon 33 – Lannemezan 23 – St-Gaudens 17

⛰ Es Pibous

✆ 05 61 88 31 42. www.es-pibous.fr

Address : chemin de St-Just (800m southeast along the D 26a, follow the signs for St-Béat and take road to the left)

Opening times : from beginning April to end Sept.

2 ha (80 pitches) flat, grassy

Tariff : (2015 price) ♣ 4.50€ ⛟ ▣ 4.50€ – ⚡ (6A) 4€

🚻 local sani-station 4€

Some pitches have a view over the Sainte-Marie cathedral.

Surroundings : 🌿 ≤ Cathédrale de St-Bertrand-de-Comminges ▱ ♨	**G** Longitude : 0.57799
Leisure activities : 🏛 🎯 🎣	**P** **S** Latitude : 43.02868
Facilities : 🚿 ⚲ 🏕 🔥	
Nearby : 🎣	

ST-CÉRÉ

46400 – Michelin map **337** H2 – pop. 3 563 – alt. 152
▶ Paris 531 – Aurillac 62 – Brive-la-Gaillarde 51 – Cahors 80

⛰ Le Soulhol

✆ 05 65 38 12 37. www.campinglesoulhol.com

Address : quai Salesses (take southeastern exit along the D 48; beside the Bave river)

Opening times : from beginning April to end Sept.

3.5 ha (120 pitches) flat, grassy, gravelled

Tariff : (2015 price) 21.40€ ♣♣ ⛟ ▣ ⚡ (10A) –
Extra per person 5.40€ – Reservation fee 10€

Rental rates : (2015 price) (from beginning April to end Sept.)
🏕 – 5 🚐 – 10 gîtes. Per week from 217 to 525€ – Reservation fee 10€

🚻 local sani-station 3€

Encircled by a stream, with a view of the château. Gîtes or somewhat ageing mobile homes to rent.

Surroundings : ≤ ♨	**G** Longitude : 1.89747
Leisure activities : 🏛 🎯 🚴 🎣 🎣	**P** **S** Latitude : 44.85791
Facilities : 🚿 ⚲ 🏕 launderette	
Nearby : 🍷 🍴 ✂	

In order for the guide to remain wholly objective, the selection of campsites is made on an entirely independent basis.

ST-CIRQ-LAPOPIE

46330 – Michelin map **337** G5 – pop. 217 – alt. 320
▶ Paris 574 – Cahors 26 – Figeac 44 – Villefranche-de-Rouergue 37

⛰ La Truffière ♣♦

✆ 05 65 30 20 22. www.camping-truffiere.com

Address : Pradines (3km south along the D 42, follow the signs for Concots)

Opening times : from beginning April to end Sept.

6 ha (96 pitches) terraced, flat, grassy, stony, natural setting among trees and bushes

Tariff : 22.80€ ♣♣ ⛟ ▣ ⚡ (6A) – Extra per person 6.20€

Rental rates : (from beginning April to end Sept.) – 13 🏠.
Per night from 70 to 90€ – Per week from 280 to 795€

🚻 local sani-station 5€ – 10 ▣ 6.20€

A pretty chalet village set among trees and shrubs, with some pitches enjoying a fine view of the Causse (limestone plateau).

Surroundings : 🌿 ≤ ♨	**G** Longitude : 1.6746
Leisure activities : 🍷 🍴 🏛 🎪 🎯 🎣	**P** **S** Latitude : 44.44842
Facilities : 🚿 ⚲ 🆒 🏕 🍴 launderette 🍴	

⛰ La Plage ♣♦

✆ 05 65 30 29 51. www.campingplage.com

Address : Porte Roques (1.4km northeast along the D 8, follow the signs for Tour-de-Faure, turn left before the bridge)

Opening times : from beginning April to end Sept.

3 ha (120 pitches) flat, grassy, stony

Tariff : ♣ 7€ ⛟ ▣ 16€ – ⚡ (10A) 5€ – Reservation fee 10€

Rental rates : (from beginning April to end Sept.) 🚿 (1 mobile home) – 10 🚐 – 12 🏠 – 5 tent lodges. Per night from 36 to 105€ – Per week from 252 to 740€ – Reservation fee 10€

🚻 eurorelais sani-station – 15 ▣ 17€ – 🔋 ⚡ 25€

Situated on the banks of the Lot river, at the foot of one of the prettiest villages in France.

Surroundings : 🐾 ◻ 🌳🌳
Leisure activities : ⛱ ✕ ⛹ 🚣⛵ 🏊 (beach) 🐎 🎣
Facilities : ♿ 🅿 🏢 ⛺ 🚿 🚽 🍳 launderette 🧺

G P S Longitude : 1.6812
Latitude : 44.46914

ST-GAUDENS

31800 – Michelin map **343** C6 – pop. 11 225 – alt. 405
▶ Paris 766 – Bagnères-de-Luchon 48 – Tarbes 68 – Toulouse 94

⚠ Municipal Belvédère des Pyrénées

☎ 05 62 00 16 03. www.st-gaudens.com

Address : rue des Chanteurs du Comminges (located 1km west along the N 117, towards Tarbes)

1 ha (83 pitches) flat, grassy, fine gravel

Rentals : 2 🚐

There's a panoramic view over the Pyrenees, but some pitches also look down on the road.

Surroundings : ≼ Pyrénées ◻ 🌳🌳
Facilities : ♿ 🅿 🏢 🍳 launderette
Nearby : 🛒 ⛱ ✕

G P S Longitude : 0.70814
Latitude : 43.11

ST-GENIEZ-D'OLT

12130 – Michelin map **338** J4 – pop. 2 068 – alt. 410
▶ Paris 612 – Espalion 28 – Florac 80 – Mende 68

🏕 Tohapi La Boissière ♨♨

☎ 08 25 00 20 30. www.tohapi.fr

Address : route de la Cascade (1.2km northeast along the D 988, follow the signs for St-Laurent-d'Olt and turn left following signs for Pomayrols; beside the Lot river)

Opening times : from mid April to mid Sept.

5 ha (220 pitches) terraced, flat, grassy

Tariff : (2015 price) 16€ ✿✿ �car 🔌 🔋 (10A) – Extra per person 4€
Rental rates : (2015 price) (from mid April to mid Sept.) ♿ (1 mobile home) – 45 🚐 – 19 🏠 – 19 tent lodges. Per night from 16 to 64€

In a pleasant wooded setting beside the Lot river.

Surroundings : 🐾 ◻ 🌳🌳
Leisure activities : ⛱ 🎪 🎮 ⛹ 🚣 🚴 🎿
🏊 🎣
Facilities : ♿ 🅿 📼 🍳 launderette, refrigerators
Nearby : 🐎

G P S Longitude : 2.98366
Latitude : 44.47011

🏕 Résidence Le Colombier - L'Aveyronnais du Nord
(rental of gîtes only)

☎ 05 65 71 52 88. http://location-chalet-aveyron.over-blog.com

Address : rue Rivié (located 1km northeast via D 988, follow the signs for St-Laurent-d'Olt and turn left following signs for Pomayrols; near the Lot)

3 ha flat

Rentals : 42 gîtes.

Surroundings : 🐾
Leisure activities : ⛹ 🚴 🎿
Facilities : 🅿 🏢 🍳 🔥
Nearby : 🎣

G P S Longitude : 2.97809
Latitude : 44.46893

🏔 Marmotel ♨♨

☎ 05 65 70 46 51. www.marmotel.com

Address : 18 place du Gal-de-Gaulle

Opening times : from end April to end Sept.

4 ha (173 pitches) flat, grassy

Tariff : (2015 price) 27€ ✿✿ 🚗 🔌 🔋 (10A) – Extra per person 6.50€ – Reservation fee 25€
Rental rates : (2015 price) (from end April to end Sept.) – 69 🚐 – 15 🏠. Per night from 35 to 50€ – Per week from 143 to 1,127€ – Reservation fee 25€

Surroundings : 🐾 ◻ 🌳🌳
Leisure activities : ⛱ ✕ 🎮 ⛹ 🚣 🎿 🏊 multi-sports ground, entertainment room
Facilities : ♿ 🅿 🚿 – 42 individual sanitary facilities (🚿 🍳 🚽 wc) 🧺 🍳 launderette 🧺
Nearby : 🛒

G P S Longitude : 2.9644
Latitude : 44.462

ST-GERMAIN-DU-BEL-AIR

46310 – Michelin map **337** E4 – pop. 518 – alt. 215
▶ Paris 551 – Cahors 28 – Cazals 20 – Fumel 52

⚠ Le Moulin Vieux

☎ 05 65 31 00 71. www.camping-moulin-vieux-lot.com

Address : to the northwest of the town; beside the Céou river

2 ha (90 pitches) flat, grassy

Rentals : 15 🏠.

The shaded pitches lie between the swimming pool and a small lake.

Surroundings : 🐾 🌳🌳
Leisure activities : 🎪 🚣 🎣
Facilities : 🅿 🍳 launderette
Nearby : 🎿

G P S Longitude : 1.43476
Latitude : 44.64986

ST-GIRONS

09200 – Michelin map **343** E7 – pop. 6 608 – alt. 398
▶ Paris 774 – Auch 123 – Foix 45 – St-Gaudens 43

🏕 Audinac ♨♨

☎ 05 61 66 44 50. www.camping-audinaclesbains.com

Address : at Audinac-les-Bains, au plan d'eau (head 4.5km northeast along the D 117, follow the signs for Foix and take D 627, follow the signs for Ste-Croix-Volvestre)

Opening times : from beginning April to mid Oct.

15 ha/6 for camping (115 pitches) small lake

Tariff : (2015 price) 21€ ✿✿ 🚗 🔌 🔋 (10A) – Extra per person 7€
Rental rates : (2015 price) (from beginning April to mid Oct.) ♿ (1 mobile home) – 22 🚐 – 12 🏠 – 20 tent lodges. Per week from 160 to 750€
🚐 local sani-station

Huge site with 3 small springs, a lake and a swimming pool in front of an old 19th-century building.

Surroundings : 🐾 🌳🌳
Leisure activities : ⛱ ✕ 🎪 🌙 nighttime ⛹
🚣 🚴 🎿 🏊 🎣 multi-sports ground
Facilities : ♿ 🅿 🏢 🍳 launderette 🧺
refrigerators

G P S Longitude : 1.18407
Latitude : 43.00705

ST-JEAN-DU-BRUEL

12230 – Michelin map **338** M6 – pop. 695 – alt. 520
▶ Paris 687 – Toulouse 295 – Rodez 128 – Millau 41

⛰ La Dourbie

☎ 05 65 46 06 40. www.camping-la-dourbie.com

Address : off the D999 (route de Nant)

Opening times : from mid April to end Sept.

2.5 ha (78 pitches) flat, grassy

Tariff : (2015 price) 24.50€ ★★ ⇔ 🔲 ⚡ (10A) – Extra per person 5€
Rental rates : (2015 price) (from mid April to end Sept.) – 14 🚐.
Per night from 35 to 45€ – Per week from 200 to 590€
🚐 local sani-station 4€ – 14 🔲 15€ – 🔋14€

A magnificent view over wooded hills.

Surroundings : 🖵 ♀	**G P S**	Longitude : 3.3466
Leisure activities : 🍴 ✕ ⚓ 🎿 🎣		Latitude : 44.02004
Facilities : ♿ ⊶ 🏢 🛁 🚽 🍴 🔳 🚿		

ST-LARY-SOULAN

65170 – Michelin map **342** N8 – pop. 946 – alt. 820 – Winter sports :
1 680/2 450 m
▶ Paris 830 – Arreau 12 – Auch 103 – Bagnères-de-Luchon 44

⛰ Municipal

☎ 05 62 39 41 58. www.saintlary-vacances.com

Address : rue Lalanne (in the village)

Opening times : from beginning Dec. to mid Sept.

1 ha (77 pitches) relatively flat, flat, grassy, stony

Tariff : (2015 price) 21.20€ ★★ ⇔ 🔲 ⚡ (6A) – Extra per person 5.90€
🚐 6 🔲 17.70€

A pleasant oasis of greenery in the centre of the village.

Surroundings : ❄ 🐟 ⩽ ♀♀	**G P S**	Longitude : 0.32282
Leisure activities : 🏛 ⚓		Latitude : 42.81548
Facilities : ♿ ⊶ 🏢 🛁 🚽 🍴 launderette		
Nearby : 🍴 🎿		

ST-PANTALÉON

46800 – Michelin map **337** D5 – pop. 239 – alt. 269
▶ Paris 597 – Cahors 22 – Castelnau-Montratier 18 – Montaigu-de-Quercy 28

⛰ Les Arcades

☎ 05 65 22 92 27. www.des-arcades.com

Address : Le Moulin de St. Martial (4.5km east on the D 653, follow
the signs for Cahors; beside the Barguelonnette river)

12 ha/2.6 for camping (80 pitches) open site, small lake

Tariff : ★ 7€ ⇔ 🔲 12€ – ⚡ (10A) 4.20€ – Reservation fee 17€
Rental rates : (from mid May to end Sept.) 🎿 – 11 🚐 – 2 tent
lodges. Per night from 70 to 146€ – Per week from 490 to
1,025€ – Reservation fee 17€

*There's a clubroom and small pub in a restored mill. Choose the
pitches furthest from the road.*

Surroundings : 🖵 ♀♀	**G P S**	Longitude : 1.30667
Leisure activities : 🍴 ✕ 🏛 🛝 ⚓ 🎿 🏔		Latitude : 44.36918
Facilities : ♿ ⊶ 🛁 🍴 🔳 🚿		

ST-PIERRE-LAFEUILLE

46090 – Michelin map **337** E4 – pop. 352 – alt. 350
▶ Paris 566 – Cahors 10 – Catus 14 – Labastide-Murat 23

⛰ Quercy-Vacances

☎ 05 65 36 87 15. www.quercy-vacances.com

Address : Mas de la Combe (located 1.5km northeast along the N 20,
follow the signs for Brive and take road to the left)

Opening times : from mid March to end Sept.

3 ha (80 pitches) flat, relatively flat, grassy

Tariff : (2015 price) ★ 5€ ⇔ 🔲 8€ – ⚡ (10A) 4.50€
Rental rates : (2015 price) (from end March to end Sept.) – 16 🚐 –
8 🏠 – 3 canvas bungalows. Per night from 35 to 95€ – Per week
from 210 to 630€

There's a variety of rental options, some of good quality.

Surroundings : 🐟 ♀♀	**G P S**	Longitude : 1.45925
Leisure activities : 🍴 ✕ 🏛 🛥 jacuzzi 🎿		Latitude : 44.53165
multi-sports ground		
Facilities : ♿ ⊶ 🛁 🍴 🔳 🚿		

ST-ROME-DE-TARN

12490 – Michelin map **338** J6 – pop. 853 – alt. 360
▶ Paris 655 – Millau 18 – Pont-de-Salars 42 – Rodez 66

⛰ La Cascade

☎ 05 65 62 56 59. www.camping-cascade-aveyron.com – pitches
accessed via steep slope, help moving caravans onto and off pitches
available on request

Address : route du Pont (300m north along the D 993, follow the
signs for Rodez; beside the Tarn river)

Opening times : permanent

4 ha (99 pitches) terraced, flat, grassy

Tariff : (2015 price) 19.50€ ★★ ⇔ 🔲 ⚡ (6A) – Extra per person 4€ –
Reservation fee 16€
Rental rates : (2015 price) permanent – 28 🚐 – 14 🏠 – 9 canvas
bungalows. Per night from 45 to 98€ – Per week from 200 to
530€ – Reservation fee 16€
🚐 Flot Bleu sani-station 6€

A terraced site on the side of a hill overlooking the Tarn river.

Surroundings : 🐟 ⩽ 🖵 ♀ ⛰	**G P S**	Longitude : 2.89947
Leisure activities : ✕ 🏛 ☕ ⚓ 🚴 🎣 🎿 🎣		Latitude : 44.05336
Facilities : ♿ ⊶ 🛁 🛁 🚽 🍴 launderette		
🚿 🚿		
Nearby : pedalos		

*A chambre d'hôte is a guesthouse or B & B-style
accommodation.*

ST-SALVADOU

12200 – Michelin map **338** E5 – pop. 410 – alt. 450
▶ Paris 619 – Toulouse 120 – Rodez 54 – Albi 63

⛰ Le Muret

☎ 05 65 81 80 69. www.campinglemuret.fr

Address : Le Muret, 3km south-east, beside a lake

Opening times : from beginning June to end Aug.

3 ha (44 pitches) flat, grassy

Tariff : 23€ ★★ ⇔ 🔲 ⚡ (16A) – Extra per person 4€

Rental rates : (from beginning June to end Aug.) – 4 🚐 – 5 🛏 – 4 tent lodges – 1 gîte. Per night from 38 to 84€ – Per week from 221 to 610€

Situated on the Le Muret estate with its 18th-century farm buildings.

Surroundings : 🐾 ⪜ 🗆 ⵚⵚ
Leisure activities : 🏛 🚣 🚴 🛶 🎣
multi-sports ground
Facilities : 🔥 ⚬━ 🔌 🍴 🗑 🎣

Nearby : 🏖 🐎 🥾

Longitude : 2.11563
Latitude : 44.26712

STE-MARIE-DE-CAMPAN

65710 – Michelin map **342** N5
▶ Paris 841 – Arreau 26 – Bagnères-de-Bigorre 13 – Luz-St-Sauveur 37

⛰ L'Orée des Monts

📞 05 62 91 83 98. www.camping-oree-des-monts.com – alt. 950

Address : at La Séoube (3km southeast along the D 918, follow the signs for Le Col d'Aspin; beside the Adour de Payolle river)

Opening times : permanent

1.8 ha (99 pitches) flat, relatively flat, grassy

Tariff : (2015 price) 26.40€ ✹✹ 🚐 🗉 ⑨ (10A) – Extra per person 5€ – Reservation fee 10€

Rental rates : (2015 price) permanent – 9 🚐. Per week from 175 to 630€ – Reservation fee 10€

🚾 local sani-station – 5 🗉 16.40€

A mountain site beside a stream.

Surroundings : ⪜ 🍴 ✕ 🏛 🚣 🎣 🛶
Leisure activities : 🍴 ✕ 🏛 🚣 🎣 🛶
Facilities : ⚬━ ᠁ 🔌 🍴 🗑 🎣

Longitude : 0.24522
Latitude : 42.96664

This guide is updated regularly, so buy your new copy every year!

SALLES-CURAN

12410 – Michelin map **338** I5 – pop. 1 067 – alt. 887
▶ Paris 650 – Albi 77 – Millau 39 – Rodez 40

⛰ Les Genêts 🔱👤

📞 05 65 46 35 34. www.camping-les-genets.fr – alt. 1 000

Address : at the Lac de Pareloup (5km northwest along the D 993 then take left turning along the D 577, follow the signs for Arvieu and continue 2km along the road to the right)

Opening times : from mid May to mid Sept.

3 ha (163 pitches) terraced, flat, grassy

Tariff : ✹ 8.30€ 🚗 4.20€ 🗉 42€ – ⑨ (10A) 2.60€ – Reservation fee 30€

Rental rates : (from mid May to mid Sept.) – 42 🚐 – 7 🏠 – 7 canvas bungalows. Per night from 37 to 128€ – Per week from 238 to 899€ – Reservation fee 30€

🚾 local sani-station

Beside the Lac de Pareloup.

Surroundings : 🐾 ⪜ 🗆 🛆 ⚓
Leisure activities : 🍴 ✕ 🎯 🚶 🚣 🚴 🛶 🎣
entertainment room
Facilities : 🔥 ⚬━ 🆑 🗑 🐾 🍴 launderette 🎣

Longitude : 2.76776
Latitude : 44.18963

⛰ Sites et Paysages Beau Rivage

📞 05 65 46 33 32. www.beau-rivage.fr – alt. 800

Address : route des Vernhes - lake Pareloup (3.5km north along the D 993, follow the signs for Pont-de-Salars and turn left onto D 243)

Opening times : from beginning May to end Sept.

2 ha (80 pitches) terraced, flat, grassy

Tariff : (2015 price) 35.90€ ✹✹ 🚐 🗉 ⑨ (10A) – Extra per person 5€ – Reservation fee 20€

Rental rates : (2015 price) (from mid April to mid Oct.) – 16 🚐 – 6 🏠 – 2 canvas bungalows – 2 tent lodges. Per night from 39 to 138€ – Per week from 195 to 798€ – Reservation fee 30€

🚾 local sani-station 15€ – 🔋 ⑨15€

In a pleasant location beside the Lac de Pareloup.

Surroundings : ⪜ 🗆 ⵚ 🛆
Leisure activities : 🍴 ✕ 🏛 🚣 🚴 🛶 🎣
Facilities : 🔥 ⚬━ 🔌 🍴 launderette 🎣
Nearby : 💧 forest trail

Longitude : 2.77585
Latitude : 44.20081

⛰ Parc du Charrouzech

📞 06 83 95 04 42. www.parducharrouzech.fr

Address : 5km northwest along the D 993 then take left turning along the D 577, follow the signs for Arvieu and continue 3.4km along the road to the right; near the Lac du Pareloup (direct access)

Opening times : from beginning July to end Aug.

3 ha (104 pitches) terraced, relatively flat, flat, grassy

Tariff : 30€ ✹✹ 🚐 🗉 ⑨ (5A) – Extra per person 4€

Rental rates : (from beginning July to end Aug.) – 20 🚐 – 30 canvas bungalows. Per week from 350 to 650€ – Reservation fee 30€

Situated with a view looking out over the lake.

Surroundings : 🐾 ⪜ 🗆 ⵚⵚ
Leisure activities : 🏛 🚶 🚣 🎯 🛶 🎣 🛶
Facilities : 🔥 ⚬━ 🛆 🚽 🍴 launderette

Longitude : 2.75659
Latitude : 44.1968

SALLES-ET-PRATVIEL

31110 – Michelin map **343** B8 – pop. 136 – alt. 625
▶ Paris 814 – Toulouse 141 – Tarbes 86 – Lourdes 105

⛰ Le Pyrénéen

📞 05 61 79 59 19. www.campinglepyreneen-luchon.com

Address : Les Sept Molles (600m south along the D 27 and a road; beside the Pique river)

Opening times : permanent

1.1 ha (75 pitches) flat, grassy

Tariff : (2015 price) 19.50€ ✹✹ 🚐 🗉 ⑨ (10A) – Extra per person 4.95€ – Reservation fee 15€

Rental rates : (2015 price) permanent 🔥 (1 mobile home) – 28 🚐. Per night from 45 to 95€ – Per week from 255 to 675€ – Reservation fee 15€

A free shuttle to the Bagnères-de-Luchon thermal baths.

Surroundings : ❄ 🐾 ⪜ 🗆 ⵚⵚ
Leisure activities : 🍴 ✕ 🏛 🚣
Facilities : 🔥 ⚬━ ᠁ 🔌 🍴 launderette
Nearby : 🐎

Longitude : 0.60637
Latitude : 42.8224

SASSIS

65120 – Michelin map **342** L5 – pop. 92 – alt. 700
▶ Paris 879 – Toulouse 206 – Tarbes 53 – Pau 72

⚠ Le Hounta

🖉 05 62 92 95 90. www.campinglehounta.com

Address : 600m south of Sassis, off the D 12

Opening times : permanent

2 ha (125 pitches) relatively flat, flat, grassy

Tariff : 18.90€ ★★ 🚐 🗉 [½] (6A) – Extra per person 4.20€ – Reservation fee 4.30€

Rental rates : permanent 🏕 – 16 🛖 – 1 🏠. Per night from 40 to 102€ – Per week from 197 to 605€ – Reservation fee 7.50€

🚐 local sani-station 5€

Choose those pitches near the small canal, furthest from the road.

Surroundings : ❄ 🦢 ⋖ ⍦	
Leisure activities : 🚣	**G P S** Longitude : -0.01491
Facilities : & ⌐ ▥ 🛁 🍴 launderette	Latitude : 42.87252
Nearby : 🍴	

SEISSAN

32260 – Michelin map **336** F9 – pop. 1 084 – alt. 182
▶ Paris 735 – Auch 19 – Tarbes 65 – Toulouse 84

⛰ Domaine Lacs de Gascogne

🖉 05 62 66 27 94. www.domainelacsdegascogne.eu – alt. 160

Address : rue du Lac, east of Seissan

14 ha (80 pitches) undulating, relatively flat, flat, grassy

Rentals : 21 🛖 – 2 🏠.

Pitches among trees and shrubs, with a view of the lakes.

Surroundings : 🦢 〰	
Leisure activities : 🍴 ✕ 🚗 🚣 🚲 🛶 🦢 🎣	**G P S** Longitude : 0.57972
Facilities : & launderette 🐾	Latitude : 43.49389

We have selected the best campsites in France with our usual care, listing those with the best facilities in the most pleasant surroundings.

SÉNERGUES

12320 – Michelin map **338** G3 – pop. 481 – alt. 525
▶ Paris 630 – Toulouse 197 – Rodez 50 – Aurillac 62

⚠ L'Étang du Camp

🖉 05 65 46 01 95. www.etangducamp.fr

Address : Le Camp (6km southwest along the D 242, follow the signs for St-Cyprien-sur-Dourdou; beside a lake)

Opening times : from beginning April to end Sept.

5 ha (60 pitches) flat and relatively flat, grassy

Tariff : 19.50€ ★★ 🚐 🗉 [½] (6A) – Extra per person 3.50€

Rental rates : (from beginning April to end Sept.) – 1 🛖 – 4 tipis. Per night from 34 to 62€ – Per week from 227 to 490€

Pretty decorative flowers and shrubs.

Surroundings : 🦢 🗔 ⍦	
Leisure activities : 🍴 ✕ 🚗 🚲 🦢	**G P S** Longitude : 2.46391
Facilities : & ⌐ 🛁 🍴 🗉	Latitude : 44.55837

SÉNIERGUES

46240 – Michelin map **337** F3 – pop. 136 – alt. 390
▶ Paris 540 – Cahors 45 – Figeac 46 – Fumel 69

⛰⛰ Flower Le Domaine de la Faurie

Domaine de la Faurie

🖉 05 65 21 14 36. www.camping-lafaurie.com

Address : at La Faurie (6km south along the D 10, follow the signs for Montfaucon then take the D 2, follow the signs for St-Germain-du-Bel-Air and take the road to the right; from the A 20, take exit 56)

Opening times : from beginning April to end Sept.

27 ha/5 for camping (84 pitches) relatively flat, flat, grassy, stony

Tariff : 38€ ★★ 🚐 🗉 [½] (10A) – Extra per person 7€

Rental rates : (from beginning April to end Sept.) 🅿 – 13 🛖 – 17 🏠 – 5 canvas bungalows – 2 tent lodges. Per night from 33 to 136€ – Per week from 198 to 973€

🚐 local sani-station 19.50€ – 🚐 [½]19.50€

On a 27-hectare wooded estate that looks out over the valley, with a shop selling local produce.

Surroundings : 🦢 ⋖ ⍦⍦	
Leisure activities : 🍴 ✕ 🚗 🚣 🚲 🛶	**G P S** Longitude : 1.53444
Facilities : & ⌐ 🗔 🛁 🍴 launderette 🐾	Latitude : 44.69175

SEPTFONDS

Michelin map **337** F6
▶ Paris 616 – Toulouse 87 – Montauban 33 – Cahors 44

⛰ Bois Redon

🖉 05 63 64 92 49. www.campingdeboisredon.com

Address : 10 chemin Redon (1.4km northwest)

Opening times : permanent

8 ha/2.5 for camping (40 pitches) sloping, relatively flat, grassy, stony

Tariff : 24.50€ ★★ 🚐 🗉 [½] (10A) – Extra per person 6€ – Reservation fee 10€

Rental rates : permanent – 4 🏠 – 4 tent lodges. Per night from 40 to 65€ – Per week from 260 to 695€ – Reservation fee 10€

This family-friendly campsite is laid out among trees and shrubs.

Surroundings : 🦢 〰	
Leisure activities : ✕ 🚗 🚣 🛶	**G P S** Longitude : 1.60492
Facilities : & ⌐ 🛒 ▥ 🍴 🗉	Latitude : 44.18285

SÉVÉRAC-L'ÉGLISE

12310 – Michelin map **338** J4 – pop. 412 – alt. 630
▶ Paris 625 – Espalion 26 – Mende 84 – Millau 58

⛰⛰ Yelloh! Village La Grange de Monteillac 👫

🖉 05 65 70 21 00. www.la-grange-de-monteillac.com

Address : chemin de Monteillac (take the northeastern exit along the D 28, follow the signs for Laissac, opposite the cemetery)

Opening times : from beginning May to mid Sept.

4.5 ha (104 pitches) terraced, flat, grassy

Tariff : 51€ ★★ 🚐 🗉 [½] (10A) – Extra per person 7€ – Reservation fee 15€

Rental rates : (2015 price) (from beginning May to mid Sept.) 🅿 – 15 🚐 – 22 🏠 – 9 canvas bungalows – 4 tent lodges. Per night from 45 to 159€ – Per week from 190 to 1,200€ – Reservation fee 15€

Pretty decorative flowers and shrubs dotted around the site.

Surroundings : 🗁 ♀
Leisure activities : 🍸 ✕ 🏖 🅖 🚶 🛶 🚴 ✂ 🛶
Facilities : 🕭 ⚷ (July–Aug.) 🅰 ♨ 🚿 launderette 🗄.

G P S Longitude : 2.85101
Latitude : 44.36434

SORÈZE

81540 – Michelin map **338** E10 – pop. 2 564 – alt. 272
▶ Paris 732 – Castelnaudary 26 – Castres 27 – Puylaurens 19

⛰ St-Martin

✆ 05 63 50 20 19. www.campingsaintmartin.com

Address : rue du 19 Mars 1962 at Les Vigariés (north of the town, access via the r. de la Mairie; by the stadium)

1 ha (54 pitches) relatively flat, flat, grassy
Rentals : 3 🚐 – 6 🏠.

Surroundings : 🏔 🗁 ♀♀
Leisure activities : 🛶 🛶
Facilities : 🕭 ⚷ 🚿 🚾
Nearby : ✕

G P S Longitude : 2.06594
Latitude : 43.45337

SORGEAT

09110 – Michelin map **343** J8 – pop. 95 – alt. 1 050
▶ Paris 808 – Ax-les-Thermes 6 – Axat 50 – Belcaire 23

⛰ Municipal La Prade

✆ 05 61 64 36 34. www.camping-ariege-sorgeat.fr – alt. 1 000 – limited spaces for one-night stay

Address : 800m north of the village

Opening times : from beginning March to end Oct.

2 ha (40 pitches) open site, terraced, flat, grassy

Tariff : (2015 price) 20€ 🚶🚶 🚗 🔲 🔌 (10A) – Extra per person 6€
Rental rates : (2015 price) (from beginning March to end Oct.) – 1 🚐. Per night from 50 to 65€ – Per week from 300 to 400€

A pleasant location, not far from the Bonascre Ax 3 Domaines ski resort.

Surroundings : 🏔 ⩽ Vallée d'Ax-les-Thermes 🗁 ♀♀
Leisure activities : 🏖
Facilities : 🕭 ▥ 🅰 ♨ 🚿 🚾

G P S Longitude : 1.85378
Latitude : 42.73322

SOUILLAC

46200 – Michelin map **337** E2 – pop. 3 864 – alt. 104
▶ Paris 516 – Brive-la-Gaillarde 39 – Cahors 68 – Figeac 74

🏔 Les Castels Le Domaine de la Paille Basse 🔱

✆ 05 65 37 85 48. www.lapaillebasse.com

Address : 6.5 km northwest along the D 15, follow the signs for Salignac-Eyvignes then continue 2km along the road to the right

Opening times : from beginning April to mid Sept.

80 ha/12 for camping (288 pitches) undulating, terraced, flat, grassy, stony

Tariff : 39€ 🚶🚶 🚗 🔲 🔌 (16A) – Extra per person 10€ – Reservation fee 20€

Rental rates : (from beginning April to mid Sept.) 🕭 (1 mobile home) – 71 🚐 – 2 tent lodges. Per week from 269 to 1,249€ – Reservation fee 20€
🚽 local sani-station – 🛁 🚾 14€

A spacious, undulating site with trees and bushes, based around a pretty restored hamlet built of local stone.

Surroundings : 🏔 🗁 〰
Leisure activities : 🍸 ✕ 🏖 🅖 🚶 🛶 🚴 ✂ 🛶 disco, farm or petting farm, entertainment room
Facilities : 🕭 ⚷ ▥ 🅰 ♨ 🚿 🚾 🍸 launderette 🗄 🚿

G P S Longitude : 1.44175
Latitude : 44.94482

🏔 Flower les Ondines 🔱

✆ 05 65 37 86 44. www.camping-lesondines.com

Address : at Les Ondines (located 1km southwest following signs for Sarlat and take road to the left; near the Dordogne river)

Opening times : from beginning May to end Sept.

5 ha (219 pitches) flat, grassy

Tariff : (2015 price) 27.50€ 🚶🚶 🚗 🔲 🔌 (6A) – Extra per person 5€ – Reservation fee 15€
Rental rates : (2015 price) (from beginning May to end Sept.) 🕭 (1 mobile home) – 47 🚐. Per night from 37 to 113€ – Per week from 223 to 811€ – Reservation fee 20€
🚽 local sani-station 4€ – 🛁 🚾 14.40€

Various good-quality rental options, on shaded or sunny pitches.

Surroundings : 🏔 ♀♀
Leisure activities : 🍸 ✕ 🅖 🚶 🛶 🏖 🛶
Facilities : 🕭 ⚷ 🅰 ♨ 🍸 launderette 🗄
Nearby : 🚴 ✂ 🎣 🚣 🏖 🐎 🌲 forest trail

G P S Longitude : 1.47604
Latitude : 44.89001

Routes nationales are main roads and their identifying numbers begin with N or RN. Routes départementales are generally quieter roads and begin with D or DN.

TARASCON-SUR-ARIÈGE

09400 – Michelin map **343** H7 – pop. 3 515 – alt. 474
▶ Paris 777 – Ax-les-Thermes 27 – Foix 18 – Lavelanet 30

🏔 Yelloh! Village Le Pré Lombard 🔱

✆ 05 61 05 61 94. www.prelombard.com

Address : located 1.5km southeast along the D 23; beside the Ariège

Opening times : from beginning March to beginning Oct.

4 ha (210 pitches) flat, grassy

Tariff : 41€ 🚶🚶 🚗 🔲 🔌 (10A) – Extra per person 8€
Rental rates : (from beginning March to beginning Oct.) – 60 🚐 – 19 🏠 – 9 canvas bungalows – 5 tent lodges. Per night from 31 to 184€ – Per week from 217 to 1,288€

Situated alongside the Ariège river with plenty of shade; a range of quality rental options.

Surroundings : 🏔 〰
Leisure activities : 🍸 ✕ 🏖 🅖 🚶 🛶 🚴 🛶 multi-sports ground
Facilities : 🕭 ⚷ ▥ 🅰 🍸 launderette 🗄
Nearby : 🛒

G P S Longitude : 1.61227
Latitude : 42.83984

TEILLET

81120 – Michelin map **338** G7 – pop. 462 – alt. 475
▶ Paris 717 – Albi 23 – Castres 43 – Lacaune 49

⚠ L'Entre Deux Lacs

⚲ 05 63 55 74 45. www.campingdutarn.com

Address : 29 rue du Baron de Solignac (take the southern exit along the D 81, follow the signs for Lacaune)

Opening times : from beginning April to end Sept.

4 ha (65 pitches) terraced, stony, flat, grassy

Tariff : (2015 price) 21.80€ ★★ ⛺ 🔲 🚿 (10A) –
Extra per person 4.70€ – Reservation fee 10€

Rental rates : (2015 price) (from beginning April to end Nov.)
🅿 – 17 🏠 – 2 canvas bungalows. Per night from 53 to 58€ –
Per week from 249 to 650€ – Reservation fee 10€

🚰 AireService sani-station 5€ – 🚐 11€

Surroundings : 🏖 🛶 〰	G
Leisure activities : 🍴✗ ⛴🛶 🏊	P Longitude : 2.34
Facilities : 🚿 🔌 🚰 📷	S Latitude : 43.83

THÉGRA

46500 – Michelin map **337** G3 – pop. 492 – alt. 330
▶ Paris 535 – Brive-la-Gaillarde 58 – Cahors 64 – Rocamadour 15

⚠ Sites et Paysages Le Ventoulou 👪

⚲ 05 65 33 67 01. www.camping-leventoulou.com

Address : 2.8km northeast along the D 14, follow the signs for Loubressac and take the D 60, follow the signs for Mayrinhac-Lentour to the right

Opening times : from beginning April to end Oct.

2 ha (66 pitches) terraced, flat, grassy

Tariff : 32€ ★★ ⛺ 🔲 🚿 (10A) – Extra per person 9€

Rental rates : (from beginning April to end Oct.) – 18 🚐 – 4 🏠 –
6 canvas bungalows – 1 tent lodge. Per night from 49 to 137€ –
Per week from 250 to 959€ – Reservation fee 18€

🚰 local sani-station 5€ – 🚐 12€

A pretty building in the local stone, with rental accommodation of different standards.

Surroundings : 🏖 〰	G
Leisure activities : 🍴✗ 🏛 🏊🛶 🏊 🎯	P Longitude : 1.77778
(open air in season) multi-sports ground	
Facilities : 🚿 🔌 🚰 🏊 🚿 🧺 launderette 🛁	S Latitude : 44.82603

THÉRONDELS

12600 – Michelin map **338** I1 – pop. 486 – alt. 965
▶ Paris 565 – Toulouse 234 – Rodez 87 – Aurillac 45

⚠ Flower La Source

⚲ 05 65 66 27 10. www.camping-la-source.com

Address : Presqu'Île de Laussac (peninsula in lake)

4.5 ha (62 pitches) terraced, flat, grassy
Rentals : 20 🚐 – 11 🏠 – 8 canvas bungalows.

A pleasant site situated beside the Lac de Sarrans.

Surroundings : 🏖 ⛵ 〰	G
Leisure activities : 🍴✗ 🏛 🏊🛶 🎯 🎣 🏊	P Longitude : 2.77143
🚤 🎣 pedalos 🏄 multi-sports ground	
Facilities : 🚿 🧺 launderette	S Latitude : 44.85381

THOUX

32430 – Michelin map **336** H7 – pop. 223 – alt. 145
▶ Paris 681 – Auch 40 – Cadours 13 – Gimont 14

⚠ Flower Lac de Thoux - Saint Cricq

⚲ 05 62 65 71 29. www.camping-lacdethoux.com

Address : at Lannes (head northeast along the D 654; beside the lake)

Opening times : from end April to beginning Oct.

5 ha (182 pitches) relatively flat, flat, grassy

Tariff : 33€ ★★ ⛺ 🔲 🚿 (10A) – Extra per person 8€ – Reservation fee 15€

Rental rates : (from end April to beginning Oct.) 🦽 – 41 🚐 –
12 canvas bungalows. Per night from 54 to 134€ – Per week
from 206 to 928€ – Reservation fee 15€

🚰 local sani-station – 2 🔲 14€

Surroundings : 〰 ⛰	G
Leisure activities : 🏊🛶 🛶	P Longitude : 1.00234
Facilities : 🦽 🔌 🚿 🧺 launderette	S Latitude : 43.68587
Nearby : 🏊 🍴✗ 🛁 jacuzzi 🏊🛶 🎯 🚤	
(beach) 🎣 🚣 pedalos	

TOUZAC

46700 – Michelin map **337** C5 – pop. 352 – alt. 75
▶ Paris 603 – Cahors 39 – Gourdon 51 – Sarlat-la-Canéda 63

⚠ Le Ch'Timi

⚲ 05 65 36 52 36. www.campinglechtimi.com

Address : La Roque (direct access to the Lot river, via steep steps)

Opening times : from beginning April to end Sept.

3.5 ha (79 pitches)

Tariff : 28€ ★★ ⛺ 🔲 🚿 (6A) – Extra per person 6.75€ – Reservation fee 10€

Rental rates : (from beginning April to end Sept.) – 1 'gypsy'
caravan – 1 🚐 – 6 🏠. Per night from 22 to 64€ – Per week from
154 to 695€ – Reservation fee 10€

🚰 local sani-station

There's a variety of rental options, some of high quality. Choose the pitches furthest away from the road.

Surroundings : 〰	G
Leisure activities : ✗ 🏊🛶 🚲 🏓 🏊 🎣	P Longitude : 1.06533
Facilities : 🔌 🚿 🚰 📷	S Latitude : 44.49889

The pitches of many campsites are marked out with low hedges of attractive bushes and shrubs.

LE TREIN D'USTOU

09140 – Michelin map **334** F8 – pop. 351 – alt. 739
▶ Paris 804 – Aulus-les-Bains 13 – Foix 73 – St-Girons 31

⚠ Le Montagnou

⚲ 05 61 66 94 97. www.lemontagnou.com

Address : route de Guzet (take northwestern exit along the D 8,
follow the signs for Seix, near the Alet)

Opening times : from beginning April to end Oct.

1.2 ha (40 pitches) flat, grassy

Tariff : (2015 price) 23.20€ ★★ ⛺ 🔲 🚿 (10A) –
Extra per person 5.50€

Rental rates : (2015 price) (from beginning April to end Oct.) – 2 'gypsy' caravans – 6 🚐 – 2 tent lodges. Per night from 30 to 90€ – Per week from 210 to 630€

🚽 local sani-station – 🛁 8€

Pleasant pine grove with pitches near the stream.

Surroundings : ♀	
Leisure activities : 🛶 🎣	**G** Longitude : 1.25618
Facilities : 🚿 ⚬━ 🏪 🚻 ♨ ♈ launderette 🧺	**P** Latitude : 42.81178
Nearby : 🍴	**S**

LE TRUEL

12430 – Michelin map **338** I6 – pop. 348 – alt. 290

▶ Paris 677 – Millau 40 – Pont-de-Salars 37 – Rodez 52

⚠ Municipal la Prade

☎ 05 65 46 41 46. camping.le.truel@orange.fr

Address : head east of the town along the D 31, turn left after the bridge; beside the Tarn river

Opening times : from mid June to mid Sept.

0.6 ha (28 pitches) flat, grassy

Tariff : (2015 price) 🧍 2€ ⇔ 🅿 6€ – (½) (6A) 2€

Rental rates : (2015 price) (from mid June to mid Sept.) – 3 🚐 – 5 🛏 – 1 gîte. Per week from 230€

The site is situated beneath the poplars beside the Tarn river.

Surroundings : ⬅ ⛺ ♀♀	
Leisure activities : 🛶 🚴 🎣	**G** Longitude : 2.76317
Facilities : 🚻 ♈ ⬛	**P** Latitude : 44.04937
Nearby : 🍴 ⚓ 🚣 pedalos	**S**

These symbols are used for a campsite that is exceptional in its category:

⛰⛰ ... ⚠ *Particularly pleasant setting, quality and range of services available*

🦢 🦢 *Tranquil, isolated site – quiet site, particularly at night*

⬅ ⬅ *Exceptional view – interesting or panoramic view*

VAYRAC

46110 – Michelin map **337** G2 – pop. 1 330 – alt. 139

▶ Paris 512 – Beaulieu-sur-Dordogne 17 – Brive-la-Gaillarde 32 – Cahors 89

⛰⛰ Chalets Mirandol Dordogne (rental of chalets only)

☎ 05 65 32 57 12. www.mirandol-dordogne.com

Address : at Vormes (2.3km south along the D 116, towards the leisure and activity park)

Opening times : from beginning April to end Sept.

2.6 ha open site, undulating, flat, grassy

Rental rates : (2015 price) 🅿 – 22 🏠. Per night from 40 to 70€ – Per week from 180 to 720€

A small village of chalets of various sizes, in a wooded setting.

Surroundings : 🦢 ♀♀	
Leisure activities : 🚣	**G** Longitude : 1.69771
Facilities : ⚬━ 🏪	**P** Latitude : 44.93657
Nearby : 🍸 🍴 🧺 🚣 🎣	**S**

⚠ Municipal la Palanquière

☎ 05 65 32 43 67. www.vayrac.fr

Address : at La Palanquière (located 1km south along the D 116, towards the leisure and activity park)

Opening times : from beginning June to mid Sept.

1 ha (33 pitches) flat, grassy

Tariff : 🧍 3.60€ ⇔ 🅿 3.60€ – (½) (10A) 3.70€

Set in a grassy area with tree shade. Campers have key access to the sanitary facilities.

Surroundings : 🦢 ♀♀	
Facilities : 🚿 🚻 ♈ ⬛	**G** Longitude : 1.70389
	P Latitude : 44.94464
	S

Some information or pricing may have changed since the guide went to press. We recommend you check the price list online in advance or at the entrance to the campsite and enquire about possible restrictions.

VERS

46090 – Michelin map **337** F5 – pop. 415 – alt. 132

▶ Paris 565 – Cahors 15 – Villefranche-de-Rouergue 55

⛰⛰ Village Vacances Domaine du Mas de Saboth
(rental of chalets and mobile homes only)

☎ 05 65 31 41 74. www.masdesaboth.com

Address : 1km west along the D 49

Opening times : from mid March to mid Dec.

20 ha terraced, grassy, stony

Rental rates : 🚿 (3 chalets) – 60 🚐 – 30 🏠. Per night from 55 to 110€ – Per week from 275 to 1,145€

A chalet and mobile home village surrounded by greenery, some of which enjoy a panoramic view over Le Causse (limestone plateau).

Surroundings : 🦢 ♀♀	
Leisure activities : 🍸 🍴 🛶 🎯 🏋 🏇 🚴	**G** Longitude : 1.54407
🍴 ⚓ 🚣 disco, ponies, entertainment room	**P** Latitude : 44.47792
Facilities : ⚬━ ♈ launderette 🧺	**S**

⛰⛰ La Chêneraie

☎ 05 65 31 40 29. www.cheneraie.com – limited spaces for one-night stay

Address : at Le Cuzoul (2.5km southwest along the D 653, follow the signs for Cahors and take the road to the right after the level crossing)

Opening times : from beginning May to end Sept.

2.6 ha (58 pitches) flat, grassy

Tariff : (2015 price) 28€ 🧍🧍 ⇔ 🅿 (½) (10A) – Extra per person 4€ – Reservation fee 9€

Rental rates : (2015 price) (from beginning April to mid Dec.) – 8 🚐. Per night from 50 to 100€ – Per week from 305 to 1,190€ – Reservation fee 9€

🚽 local sani-station 3€ – 2 🅿 19€

In a wooded setting with one section of the site for rentals and another for tents and caravans.

Surroundings : 🦢 ⛺ ♀♀♀	
Leisure activities : 🍸 🍴 🛶 jacuzzi 🏊	**G** Longitude : 1.54593
🍴 🚣	**P** Latitude : 44.47154
Facilities : 🚿 ⚬━ 🛁 ♈ ⬛ 🧺	**S**

VIELLE-AURE

65170 – Michelin map **342** N6 – pop. 355 – alt. 800
▶ Paris 828 – Toulouse 155 – Tarbes 70 – Lourdes 66

⚠ Le Lustou

✆ 0562394064. www.lustou.com

Address : 89 chemin d'Agos, (situated 2km northeast along the D 19, near the Neste-d'Aure (river) and a lake)

Opening times : permanent

2.8 ha (65 pitches) flat, grassy

Tariff : (2015 price) ★ 4.90€ ⇌ 🅴 5€ – (≴) (10A) 7.20€

Rental rates : (2015 price) (from beginning Dec. to end Sept.) ✁ – 5 ⎚ – 5 ⬜ – 1 gîte. Per night from 50 to 70€ – Per week from 325 to 490€

Surroundings : ❄ ≼ ♀♀
Leisure activities : ⍓ 🖼 ♨
Facilities : ⚹ ⛐ ⬛ ♨ ⚶ ♈ ♈ launderette
Nearby : ⚓ rafting and canyoning

G P S
Longitude : 0.33841
Latitude : 42.84492

LE VIGAN

46300 – Michelin map **337** E3 – pop. 1 457 – alt. 224
▶ Paris 537 – Cahors 43 – Gourdon 6 – Labastide-Murat 20

⚠ Le Rêve

✆ 0565412520. www.campinglereve.com

Address : at Revers (3.2km north along the D 673, follow the signs for Souillac then continue 2.8km along the road to the left)

Opening times : from mid May to mid Sept.

8 ha/2.5 for camping (60 pitches) relatively flat, flat, grassy, wooded

Tariff : 23.80€ ★★ ⇌ 🅴 (≴) (10A) – Extra per person 5.90€ – Reservation fee 5€

Rental rates : (from mid May to mid Sept.) – 4 ⌂. Per week from 260 to 595€ – Reservation fee 5€

🚲 local sani-station

Some pitches lie among trees and shrubs, others are more in the sun.

Surroundings : ☄ ⬚ ♀♀
Leisure activities : ⍓ ✗ ♨ ♨
Facilities : ⚹ ⛐ ♨ ♈ launderette ⚷

G P S
Longitude : 1.44183
Latitude : 44.77274

VILLEFRANCHE-DE-PANAT

12430 – Michelin map **338** I6 – pop. 771 – alt. 710
▶ Paris 676 – Toulouse 177 – Rodez 45 – Millau 46

⚠ Le Hameau des Lacs – (rental of chalets only)

✆ 0565658181. www.le-hameau-des-lacs.fr

Address : route de Rodez

Opening times : from mid June to mid Sept.

1 ha terraced, flat, grassy

Rental rates : 🅿 – 22 ⌂. Per night from 90 to 95€ – Per week from 285 to 660€ – Reservation fee 30€

Set in a large green meadow beside a lake.

Surroundings : ⬚ ≼ ♀
Leisure activities : ⍓ 🖼 ♨ ♨ ♨ multi-sports ground
Facilities : ⚹ ⛐ ⬛ ♈ launderette
Nearby : ⚮ (beach)

G P S
Longitude : 2.69457
Latitude : 44.09654

VILLEFRANCHE-DE-ROUERGUE

12200 – Michelin map **338** E4 – pop. 12 213 – alt. 230
▶ Paris 614 – Albi 68 – Cahors 61 – Montauban 80

⚠ Le Rouergue

✆ 0565451624. www.campingdurouergue.com

Address : 35bis avenue de Fondies (located 1.5km southwest along the D 47, follow the signs for Monteils)

Opening times : from beginning April to end Sept.

1.8 ha (93 pitches) flat, grassy

Tariff : 19€ ★★ ⇌ 🅴 (≴) (16A) – Extra per person 3.50€ – Reservation fee 3€

Rental rates : (from beginning April to end Sept.) – 6 ⎚ – 6 canvas bungalows. Per night from 28 to 80€ – Per week from 150 to 470€ – Reservation fee 3€

🚲 local sani-station 3€ – ⚓ 11€

Surroundings : ⬚ ♀♀
Leisure activities : ⍓ ♨
Facilities : ⚹ ⛐ ♨ ⚶ ♈ ♈ 🖼
Nearby : ⚮ jacuzzi ✗ 🖼 ◫ ♨

G P S
Longitude : 2.02615
Latitude : 44.3423

NORD-PAS-DE-CALAIS

P. Cheuve / Photononstop

A local saying claims that the hearts of the men of the north are warm enough to thaw the chilly climate. They certainly throw themselves body and soul into the traditional 'dance of the giants' at local fairs and carnivals. Giants are huge in this part of France, as are the street markets: several tonnes of *moules-frites* (mussels and chips) and countless litres of beer sustain around a million visitors to the Braderie, Lille's annual giant street market where people turn out their attics and sell their goods on the streets of the town. The influence of Flanders can be heard in the names of towns and people, seen in the wealth of Gothic architecture and tasted in such delicious regional dishes as beef in amber beer and *potjevleesch*, a terrine made with rabbit, chicken and veal. The sound of bells ringing from tall, slender belfries, neat rows of miners' houses and the distant silhouettes of windmills, all remind visitors that they are on the border with Belgium and within sight of the white cliffs of Dover.

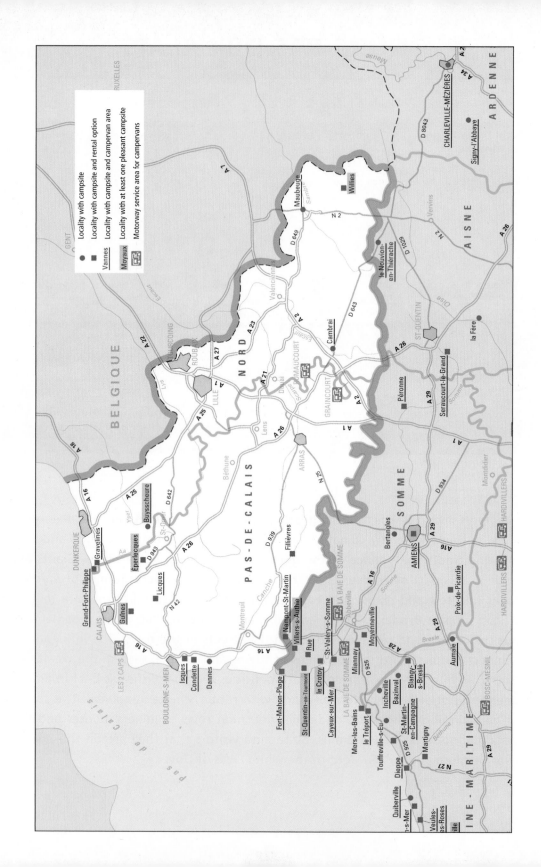

BUYSSCHEURE

59285 – Michelin map **302** B3 – pop. 510 – alt. 25
▶ Paris 269 – Béthune 44 – Calais 47 – Dunkerque 31

⚠ La Chaumière

✆ 03 28 43 03 57, www.campinglachaumiere.com

Address : 529 Langhemast Straete (in the village)

Opening times : from beginning April to end Oct.

1 ha (29 pitches) flat, grassy, stony, small lake

Tariff : 20€ ✶✶ ⇌ 🔲 [½] (6A) – Extra per person 8€

🚐 local sani-station – 20 🔲 20€

Surroundings : 🦊 ▭ ♀♀
Leisure activities : ▼ ✗ 🚣 ♒ ⌂ 🛶
Facilities : ⌷⊸🖍🗹🛁🕹 ⛲ ♈ 🔲

G P S Longitude : 2.33942
Latitude : 50.80166

*For more information on visiting particular towns or regions, consult the relevant regional **MICHELIN Green Guide**. We also recommend you use the appropriate Michelin regional map to locate your selected campsite, to calculate distances and to work out the best route.*

CAMBRAI

59400 – Michelin map **302** H6 – pop. 32 518 – alt. 53
▶ Paris 183 – Lille 67 – Amiens 100 – Namur 139

⚠ Municipal Les 3 Clochers

✆ 03 27 70 91 64, camping@mairie-cambrai.fr

Address : 77 rue Jean

Opening times : from beginning April to mid Oct.

1 ha (50 pitches) flat, grassy

Tariff : (2015 price) 14.50€ ✶✶ ⇌ 🔲 [½] (16A) – Extra per person 2€

🚐 50 🔲 12.50€

Tourist information about Cambrai available.

Surroundings : ▭ ♀
Facilities : 🚻 ⌷ 🖍 ▥ 🛁 ♈
Nearby : 🛒 ▼ ✗

G P S Longitude : 3.21476
Latitude : 50.17533

CONDETTE

62360 – Michelin map **301** C4 – pop. 2 575 – alt. 35
▶ Paris 254 – Boulogne-sur-Mer 10 – Calais 47 – Desvres 19

⚠ Caravaning du Château 👥

✆ 03 21 87 59 59, www.camping-caravaning-du-chateau.com

Address : 21 rue Nouvelle (take the southern exit along the D 119)

Opening times : from beginning April to end Oct.

1.2 ha (70 pitches) flat, grassy, gravelled

Tariff : (2015 price) 27.90€ ✶✶ ⇌ 🔲 [½] (10A) – Extra per person 6.30€

Rental rates : (from beginning April to end Oct.) – 2 🚐. Per night from 55 to 72€ – Per week from 385 to 690€

🚐 AireService sani-station 5€

Surroundings : ▭ ♀♀
Leisure activities : 🏃🚣
Facilities : 🚻 ⌷ ▥ 🛁 ♈ launderette, refrigerators
Nearby : ✗

G P S Longitude : 1.62557
Latitude : 50.64649

DANNES

62187 – Michelin map **301** C4 – pop. 1 303 – alt. 30
▶ Paris 242 – Lille 136 – Arras 133 – Amiens 114

⚠ Municipal Le Mont-St-Frieux

✆ 03 21 33 24 76, www.mairiededannes.fr

Address : rue de l'Eglise (in the small town)

1.5 ha (52 pitches) flat, grassy

Surroundings : ▭ ♀
Leisure activities : ⌂ 🚣 ⌀
Facilities : 🚻 ♈ launderette

G P S Longitude : 1.60997
Latitude : 50.58924

There are several different types of sani-station ('borne' in French) – sanitation points providing fresh water and disposal points for grey water. See page 12 for further details.

ÉPERLECQUES

62910 – Michelin map **301** G3 – pop. 3 162 – alt. 42
▶ Paris 271 – Lille 78 – Arras 86 – St-Omer 14

⛰ Château du Gandspette

✆ 03 21 93 43 93, www.chateau-gandspette.com

Address : 133 rue du Gandspette

Opening times : from beginning April to end Sept.

11 ha/4 for camping (167 pitches) relatively flat, grassy

Tariff : (2015 price) 25.80€ ✶✶ ⇌ 🔲 – Extra per person 6.20€

Rental rates : (2015 price) (from beginning April to end Sept.) ⚒ – 8 🚐. Per week from 278 to 625€

In the wooded grounds of the château.

Surroundings : 🦊 ♀
Leisure activities : ▼ ✗ ⌂ 🚣 ⚒ 🛶 multi-sports ground
Facilities : 🚻 ⌷ ▥🛁 ♈ launderette 🚿

G P S Longitude : 2.1789
Latitude : 50.81894

FILLIÈVRES

62770 – Michelin map **301** F6 – pop. 523 – alt. 46
▶ Paris 206 – Arras 52 – Béthune 46 – Hesdin 13

⛰ Les Trois Tilleuls

✆ 03 21 47 94 15, www.camping3tilleuls.com – limited spaces for one-night stay

Address : 28 rue de Frévent (take the southeastern exit along the D 340)

Opening times : from beginning April to mid Oct.

4.5 ha (120 pitches) open site, relatively flat

Tariff : (2015 price) ✶ 4,50€ ⇌ 3€ 🔲 3€ – [½] (10A) 4,50€

Rental rates : (2015 price) (from beginning April to mid Oct.) ♿ (1 mobile home) – 1 'gypsy' caravan – 10 🚐. Per night from 83 to 161€ – Per week from 219 to 762€

In the heart of the Vallée de la Canche.

Surroundings : ▭ ♀♀
Leisure activities : ⌂ 🎣 🚣 ⬚ (open air in season), multi-sports ground, entertainment room
Facilities : 🚻 ⌷ 🛁 ♈ launderette
Nearby : 🚿

G P S Longitude : 2.15952
Latitude : 50.31417

GRAND-FORT-PHILIPPE

59153 – Michelin map **302** A2 – pop. 5 491 – alt. 5
▶ Paris 289 – Calais 28 – Cassel 40 – Dunkerque 24

⚠ La Plage

✆ 03 28 65 31 95, www.camping-de-la-plage.info

Address : 115 rue du Maréchal Foch (to the northwest)

Opening times : permanent

1.5 ha (84 pitches) flat, grassy

Tariff : ✶ 5.23€ ➡ 2.11€ ▣ 4.12€ – 🔌 (10A) 3.95€ – Reservation fee 3.50€

Rental rates : permanent – 5 🏠 – 2 tent lodges. Per night from 46 to 116€ – Per week from 276 to 696€ – Reservation fee 3.50€

🚐 34 ▣ 11€ – 🔋🔌11€

Surroundings : 🔎
Leisure activities : 🛶
Facilities : 🚿 ⚞ 🏛 🚰 launderette

GPS Longitude : 2.09746 Latitude : 51.00264

GRAVELINES

59820 – Michelin map **302** A2 – pop. 11 499
▶ Paris 309 – Lille 94 – Arras 125 – Brugge 100

⚠ Les Dunes

✆ 03 28 23 09 80, www.camping-des-dunes.com

Address : at Petit-Fort-Philippe, rue Victor-Hugo (beside the beach)

Opening times : from beginning April to end Oct.

8 ha (304 pitches) flat, grassy, sandy

Tariff : ✶ 4.85€ ➡ 2.60€ ▣ 4.85€ – 🔌 (10A) 4.55€ – Reservation fee 3.50€

Rental rates : (from beginning April to end Oct.) – 25 🚐 – 5 🏠 – 5 tent lodges. Per night from 48 to 152€ – Per week from 154 to 767€ – Reservation fee 3.50€

🚐 raclet sani-station

Surroundings : 🐟 🔲
Facilities : 🚿 ⚞ 🏛 🚰 launderette

GPS Longitude : 2.11802 Latitude : 51.00754

GUÎNES

62340 – Michelin map **301** E2 – pop. 5 501 – alt. 5
▶ Paris 282 – Arras 102 – Boulogne-sur-Mer 29 – Calais 11

⛰ Les Castels La Bien Assise 👥

✆ 03 21 35 20 77, www.camping-la-bien-assise.com

Address : take the southwestern exit along the D 231, follow the signs for Marquise

Opening times : from beginning April to end Sept.

20 ha/12 for camping (198 pitches) flat, grassy, relatively flat, small lake

Tariff : 40€ ✶✶ ➡ ▣ 🔌 (10A) – Extra per person 9.50€ – Reservation fee 10€

Rental rates : (from beginning April to end Sept.) – 4 🚐 – 4 🏠. Per night from 100 to 170€ – Per week from 400 to 950€ – Reservation fee 10€

🚐 4 ▣ 40€

The outbuildings of the château house a hotel and haute cuisine restaurant.

Surroundings : 🐟 🔎
Leisure activities : 🍸 🍴 🏛 🏊 🛶 🚴 🎯 ⛳ (open air in season) ⛷
Facilities : 🚿 ⚞ 🏛 🍴 launderette 🧺 🚗

GPS Longitude : 1.85815 Latitude : 50.86631

ISQUES

62360 – Michelin map **301** C3 – pop. 1 173 – alt. 15
▶ Paris 247 – Lille 125 – Arras 122 – Calais 44

⚠ Les Cytises

✆ 03 21 31 11 10, www.campinglescytises.fr

Address : chemin Geoges Ducrocq (access via the N 1, near the stadium; from the A 16 take exit 28)

Opening times : from beginning April to mid Oct.

2.5 ha (100 pitches) terrace, flat, grassy

Tariff : (2015 price) 19.70€ ✶✶ ➡ ▣ 🔌 (6A) – Extra per person 4.60€

Rental rates : (2015 price) (from beginning April to mid Oct.) – 2 🚐. Per night from 60 to 80€ – Per week from 350 to 450€

🚐 local sani-station 3€

Surroundings : 🔲 🔎
Leisure activities : 🏛 🛶
Facilities : 🚿 ⚞ 🍴 launderette
Nearby : 🍴

GPS Longitude : 1.64332 Latitude : 50.67749

This guide is not intended as a list of all the camping sites in France; its aim is to provide a selection of the best sites in each category.

LICQUES

62850 – Michelin map **301** E3 – pop. 1 563 – alt. 81
▶ Paris 276 – Arras 97 – Boulogne-sur-Mer 31 – Calais 25

⛰ Pommiers des Trois Pays

✆ 03 21 35 02 02, www.pommiers-3pays.com

Address : 273 rue du Breuil

Opening times : from beginning April to end Oct.

2 ha (58 pitches) flat, grassy

Tariff : 28.90€ ✶✶ ➡ ▣ 🔌 (16A) – Extra per person 6.50€

Rental rates : (from beginning April to mid Oct.) 🚿 (1 chalet) – 9 🚐 – 9 🏠. Per night from 60 to 98€ – Per week from 290 to 670€

🚐 local sani-station 3€ – 2 ▣ 17.60€

Surroundings : 🐟 🔲 🌳
Leisure activities : 🍸 🍴 🏛 🛶 🔲 (open air in season)
Facilities : 🚿 ⚞ 🏛 🧺 🚗 🍴 launderette

GPS Longitude : 1.94776 Latitude : 50.77991

MAUBEUGE

59600 – Michelin map **302** L6 – pop. 31 970 – alt. 134
▶ Paris 242 – Charleville-Mézières 95 – Mons 21 – St-Quentin 114

⚠ Municipal du Clair de Lune

✆ 03 27 62 25 48, www.ville-maubeuge.fr

Address : 212 route de Mons (located 1.5km north along the N 2)

Opening times : from beginning April to end Sept.

2 ha (92 pitches) flat, grassy

Tariff : (2015 price) ✶ 3.61€ ➡ ▣ 3.52€ – 🔌 (10A) 4.51€

🚐 45 ▣

The site is decorated with flowers and shrubs.

Surroundings : 🔲 🌳
Leisure activities : 🛶
Facilities : 🚿 ⚞ 🏛 🍴

GPS Longitude : 3.9766 Latitude : 50.29573

WILLIES

59740 – Michelin map **302** M7 – pop. 165 – alt. 167
▶ Paris 225 – Avesnes-sur-Helpe 16 – Cambrai 69 – Charleroi 48

⚠ Val Joly

✆ 03 27 61 83 76, www.valjoly.com

Address : Eppé Sauvage, at the Val Joly water-sports centre (located 1.5km east along the D 133, 300m from the lake)

Opening times : from mid April to end Sept.

4 ha (180 pitches) relatively flat, flat, grassy

Tariff : (2015 price) ⚑ 4.95 € 🚗 🅴 7.50 € 🔌 (6A)

Rental rates : (2015 price) (from end March to end Sept.) – 30 🏠. Per week from 256 to 1,050 €

Located 1.5km from the tourist resort and the leisure and activity park.

Surroundings : 🦐 ♨
Leisure activities : 🎣 🏊 🎾
Facilities : ⚷ 🗄 CC ⛶ launderette ♨
Nearby : 🎣 ⚓

GPS
Longitude : 4.11518
Latitude : 50.12245

Michelin classification:

⚠⚠⚠⚠	Extremely comfortable, equipped to a very high standard
⚠⚠⚠	Very comfortable, equipped to a high standard
⚠⚠⚠	Comfortable and well equipped
⚠⚠	Reasonably comfortable
⚠	Satisfactory

Key to rentals symbols:

12 🚐	Number of mobile homes
20 🏠	Number of chalets
6 🛏	Number of rooms to rent
Per night 30–50€	Minimum/maximum rate per night
Per week 300–1,000€	Minimum/maximum rate per week

NORMANDY

B. Rieger / hemis.fr

Normandy has inspired many poets and artists, including Baudelaire, Turner and Monet. Today, it also offers rural relaxation and coastal rejuvenation. Take a walk along the coast to fill your lungs with sea air and admire the elegant resorts. You may need to catch your breath when you first see the medieval Benedictine abbey of Mont Saint-Michel rising up from the sands or glimpse the view over Étretat's white cliffs. No visitor could fail to be moved by the memory of the brave men who gave their lives on the Normandy beaches in World War II. Further inland, you will discover acres of neat, hedge-lined fields. Drink in the scent of apple blossom, admire the pretty half-timbered cottages and follow the River Seine as it meanders past medieval cities, impressive castles and venerable abbeys. No experience would be complete without savouring the region's culinary classics, including a plate of boat-fresh seafood, creamy Camembert, cider and Calvados, the famous apple brandy.

ALDERNEY

JERSEY

Îles Chausey

Omonville-la-Rogue
CHERBOURG-OCTEVILLE
Maupertus-s-M.

St-Vaast-la-Hougue

les Pieux
le Rozel
Surtainville
Baubigny
Barneville-Carteret
St-Sauveur-le-Vicomte
Ravenoville
Ste-Mère-Église
Ste-Marie-du-Mont
Isigny-s-M.
Surrain
Colleville-s-M.
Port-en-Bessin
Arromanches-les-Bⁱ
Courseulles-s-M.
Bernières-s-M.
St-Aubin-s-M.
Villers-s-M.
Luc-s-M.
Houlgate
Dives-s-M.

St-Jean-de-la-Rivière
Denneville
St-Germain-s-Ay
St-Symphorien-le-Valois
Carentan
Trévières
Bayeux
Merville-Franceville-Pl.
Martragny

A 13
D 613

N 13
D 2

N 13
N 174

St-Lô
CAEN
N 158

M A N C H E
Coutances

Agon-Coutainville

Annoville
Bréville-s-M.
Bréhal
Donville-les-B.
Granville
St-Pair-s-Mer

LA VALLÉE DE LA VIRE-GOUVET
Pont-Farcy
Thury-Harcourt
le Vey
Falaise

C A L V A D O S

D 971
D 999
Vire

D 973
D 924
A 84

Villedieu-les-Poêles
Brécey
Flers
Argentan

Genêts
Roz-sur-Couesnon
Courtils
Ducey
St-Hilaire-du-Harcouët
Bagnoles-de-l'O.

-le-Guildo
St-Lunaire
St-Malo
Cancale
St-Coulomb
St-Père
Cherrueix
Beauvoir
Les Biards

St-Briac-s-M.
St-Jouan-des-Guérets
St-Marcan
Pontorson

Pléven
St-Samson-s-R.
Taden
Dol-de-Bretagne
Jugon-les-Lacs

la Chapelle-aux-Filtzméens
Tinténiac
Feins

Fougères
Ambrières-les-Vallées
Alençon

LA DENTELLE D'ALENÇON

O R N E

Avranches
See
Sée
Séiune
D 976

N 176
N 176
N 175

Dinan

urien
ignon

Pléven

rignac

N 12
D 12

Châtillon-en-Vendelais
Mayenne
Andouillé
Fresnay-s-Sarthe
Sillé-le-Guillaume
Le Grez
Mézières-s/s-Lavardin

RENNES
Paimpont
Châteaugiron
St-Berthevin
Laval
Évron
Tennie

I L L E - E T - V I L A I N E
Marcillé-Robert
la Selle-Craonnaise
Villiers-Charlemagne
Bouère
Avoise

M A Y E N N E

N 24
N 157
A 81
D 21
A 81
A 11

N 137
D 771
N 162
D 175
A 84
D 137
D 766

Martigné-Ferchaud

AGON-COUTAINVILLE

50230 – Michelin map **303** C5 – pop. 2 826 – alt. 36
▶ Paris 348 – Barneville-Carteret 48 – Carentan 43 – Cherbourg 80

⚠ Municipal le Marais

℘ 02 33 47 05 20. http://www.agoncoutainville.fr

Address : boulevard Lebel-Jéhenne (take the northeastern exit, near the racecourse)

Opening times : from beginning July to end Aug.

2 ha (104 pitches) flat, grassy

Tariff : (2015 price) ✦ 4€ ⇌ 🅴 5.70€ – (½) (5A) 3.50€
🚐 Flot Bleu sani-station 6.80€

Surroundings : 🖵	
Leisure activities : 🏊	**G** Longitude : -1.59283
Facilities : ♿ ⚷	**P** Latitude : 49.04975
Nearby : 🍴 ✗ ⚓ ♨	**S**

⚠ Municipal le Martinet

℘ 02 33 47 05 20. www.agoncoutainville.fr

Address : boulevard Lebel-Jéhenne (take the northeastern exit, near the racecourse (hippodrome))

Opening times : from beginning April to end Oct.

1.5 ha (122 pitches) flat, grassy

Tariff : (2015 price) ✦ 4€ ⇌ 🅴 5.70€ – (½) (5A) 3.50€
🚐 Flot Bleu sani-station 6.80€

Surroundings : 🖵 ♀	
Leisure activities : 🏊	**G** Longitude : -1.59283
Facilities : ♿ ⚷ launderette	**P** Latitude : 49.04958
Nearby : 🍴 ✗ ⚓ ♨ 🐎	**S**

ALENÇON

61000 – Michelin map **310** J4 – pop. 27 325 – alt. 135
▶ Paris 190 – Chartres 119 – Évreux 119 – Laval 90

⚠ Municipal de Guéramé

℘ 02 33 26 34 95. camping.guerame@orange.fr

Address : 65 route de Guéramé (to the southwest along the ring road – périphérique)

1.5 ha (54 pitches) terraced, fine gravel, flat, grass

In a pleasant setting beside the Sarthe river.

Surroundings : 🖵 ♀	
Leisure activities : 🏛 🏊 ✗	**G** Longitude : 0.0728
Facilities : ♿ ⚷ 🏢 ⚱ ↻ launderette	**P** Latitude : 48.4259
Nearby : 🍴 🍷 🖳 ♨ 🐎	**S**

ANNOVILLE

50660 – Michelin map **303** C6 – pop. 619 – alt. 28
▶ Paris 348 – Barneville-Carteret 57 – Carentan 48 – Coutances 14

⚠ Municipal les Peupliers

℘ 02 33 47 67 73. www.camping-annoville.fr

Address : rue des Peupliers (3km southwest along the D 20 and take the road to the right, 500m from the beach)

Opening times : permanent

2 ha (100 pitches) flat, grassy, sandy

Tariff : (2015 price) ✦ 3.15€ ⇌ 🅴 3.55€ – (½) (6A) 6€

Rental rates : (2015 price) (from beginning April to end Sept.)
✈ – 6 🛏. Per night from 46 to 66€ – Per week from 257 to 462€

Surroundings : 🏊	
Leisure activities : 🏊 🚲 ♨	**G** Longitude : -1.55309
Facilities : ⚷ 📺 🖼 ⚱	**P** Latitude : 48.95767
	S

ARGENTAN

61200 – Michelin map **310** I2 – pop. 14 356 – alt. 160
▶ Paris 191 – Alençon 46 – Caen 59 – Dreux 115

⚠ Municipal de la Noë

℘ 02 33 36 05 69. www.argentan.fr/tourisme

Address : rue de la Noé, in the southern part of the town

Opening times : from beginning April to beginning Oct.

0.3 ha (23 pitches) flat, grassy

Tariff : (2015 price) ✦ 2.30€ ⇌ 2.10€ 🅴 2.60€ – (½) (10A) 2.70€
🚐 Raclet sani-station 2.20€

In a pleasant location near a park and a lake.

Surroundings : 🖵	
Leisure activities : 🏛	**G** Longitude : -0.01687
Facilities : ♿ ⚷ 🆗 launderette	**P** Latitude : 48.73995
Nearby : 🖳 🛝 ✗ fitness trail	**S**

ARROMANCHES-LES-BAINS

14117 – Michelin map **303** I3 – pop. 608 – alt. 15
▶ Paris 266 – Bayeux 11 – Caen 34 – St-Lô 46

⚠ Municipal

℘ 02 31 22 36 78. camping.arromanches@wanadoo.fr

Address : 9 avenue de Verdun, in the village

Opening times : from beginning April to beginning Nov.

1.5 ha (126 pitches) terraced, relatively flat, flat, grassy

Tariff : (2015 price) 17.90€ ✦✦ ⇌ 🅴 (½) (10A) –
Extra per person 4.10€

Rental rates : (2015 price) (from beginning April to beginning Nov.) – 6 🛏. Per night from 80 to 160€ – Per week from 365 to 420€

🚐 local sani-station – 10 🅴 18.10€

Surroundings : ♀	
Leisure activities : 🏊	**G** Longitude : -0.62642
Facilities : ♿ ⚷ (mid June–mid Sept.) 🆗 launderette	**P** Latitude : 49.3381
Nearby : ✗ 🖼 ♨ 🐎 🏹	**S**

AUMALE

76390 – Michelin map **304** K3 – pop. 2 405 – alt. 130
▶ Paris 136 – Amiens 48 – Beauvais 49 – Dieppe 69

⚠ Municipal le Grand Mail

℘ 02 35 93 40 50. www.aumale.com – ℞

Address : 6 Le Grand Mail, in the town

Opening times : from mid March to end Sept.

0.6 ha (40 pitches) flat, grassy

Tariff : (2015 price) ✦ 2.70€ ⇌ 2.70€ 🅴 2.70€ – (½) (10A) 2.70€
🚐 Flot Bleu sani-station 2€

On the side of a hill, on the slopes above the town.

Surroundings :
Facilities :

Longitude : 1.74202
Latitude : 49.76566

BAGNOLES-DE-L'ORNE

61140 – Michelin map **310** G3 – pop. 2 454 – alt. 140 –
▶ Paris 236 – Alençon 48 – Argentan 39 – Domfront 19

⚠ Municipal la Vée

✆ 02 33 37 87 45. www.campingbagnolesdelorne.com

Address : avenue du Président Coty (1.3km southwest, near Tessé-la-Madeleine, 30m from the river)

Opening times : from beginning March to mid Nov.

2.8 ha (250 pitches) relatively flat, flat, grassy

Tariff : 18.10€ ♥♥ ⚌ 🅿 (10A) – Extra per person 4.35€
Rental rates : (from beginning March to mid Nov.) – 14. Per night from 54 to 63€ – Per week from 342 to 420€
Flot Bleu sani-station 7.70€ – 51 🅿 18.10€ – 8.70€

Surroundings :
Leisure activities :
Facilities : launderette
Nearby : fitness trail

Longitude : -0.41982
Latitude : 48.54787

BARNEVILLE-CARTERET

50270 – Michelin map **303** B3 – pop. 2 282 – alt. 47
▶ Paris 356 – Caen 123 – Carentan 43 – Cherbourg 39

⚠ Les Bosquets

✆ 02 33 04 73 62. www.camping-lesbosquets.com

Address : rue du Capitaine Quenault (2.5km southwest following signs for Barneville-Plage and take turning to the left, 450m from the beach)

15 ha/6 for camping (331 pitches) very uneven, flat, grassy, sandy

In an unspoilt and natural setting among pine trees and sand dunes.

Surroundings :
Leisure activities :
Facilities : launderette
Nearby : sand yachting

Longitude : -1.76081
Latitude : 49.36587

⚠ La Gerfleur

✆ 02 33 04 38 41. www.lagerfleur.fr

Address : rue Guillaume-le-Conquérant (800m west along the D 903e, follow the signs for Carteret)

Opening times : from beginning April to end Oct.

2.3 ha (93 pitches) relatively flat, flat, grassy

Tariff : 22.64€ ♥♥ ⚌ 🅿 (6A) – Extra per person 5.50€
Rental rates : (from beginning April to end Oct.) – 5. Per night from 50 to 97€ – Per week from 320 to 590€
local sani-station 2€
Situated beside a small lake.

Surroundings :
Leisure activities :
Facilities : launderette
Nearby :

Longitude : -1.76435
Latitude : 49.38346

BAUBIGNY

50270 – Michelin map **303** B3 – pop. 154 – alt. 30
▶ Paris 361 – Barneville-Carteret 9 – Cherbourg 33 – Valognes 28

⚠ Bel Sito

✆ 02 33 04 32 74. www.bel-sito.com –

Address : north of the village

Opening times : from mid April to mid Sept.

6 ha/4 for camping (85 pitches) relatively flat to hilly, flat, grassy, sandy, dunes

Tariff : ♥ 8€ ⚌ 🅿 9.50€ – 🅿 (6A) 3.90€
Rental rates : (from beginning April to end Sept.) – 1 – 5. Per week from 400 to 880€

In a natural and unspoilt setting among sand dunes.

Surroundings :
Leisure activities :
Facilities : (July–Aug.) launderette

Longitude : -1.80513
Latitude : 49.42954

BAYEUX

14400 – Michelin map **303** H4 – pop. 13 348 – alt. 50
▶ Paris 265 – Caen 31 – Cherbourg 95 – Flers 69

⚠ Municipal

✆ 02 31 92 08 43. www.camping-bayeux.fr

Address : boulevard Eindhoven (off the D613, northern part of town)

Opening times : from beginning April to end Oct.

2.5 ha (140 pitches) flat, grassy

Tariff : (2015 price) ♥ 4.65€ ⚌ 2.12€ 🅿 9.71€ – 🅿 (5A) 4.12€
Rental rates : (2015 price) (from beginning April to end Oct.) – 10. Per night from 73 to 85€ – Per week from 309 to 630€
47 🅿 10€

Attractive shrubs and bushes decorate the site.

Surroundings :
Leisure activities :
Facilities : launderette
Nearby : (open air in season)

Longitude : -0.69774
Latitude : 49.28422

In order for the guide to remain wholly objective, the selection of campsites is made on an entirely independent basis.

BAZINVAL

76340 – Michelin map **304** J2 – pop. 350 – alt. 120
▶ Paris 165 – Abbeville 33 – Amiens 62 – Blangy-sur-Bresle 9

⚠ Municipal de la Forêt

✆ 02 32 97 04 01. bazinval2@wanadoo.fr

Address : 10 rue de Saulx (take the southwestern exit along the D 115 and take turning to the left, near the town hall)

Opening times : from beginning April to end Oct.

0.4 ha (20 pitches) open site, relatively flat, grassy

Tariff : ♥ 2.20€ ⚌ 2.20€ 🅿 2.20€ – 🅿 (10A) 4€
local sani-station 5€
Shrubs and bushes surround the pitches.

Surroundings :
Facilities :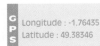

Longitude : 1.55136
Latitude : 49.95487

BEAUVOIR

50170 – Michelin map **303** C8 – pop. 419
▶ Paris 358 – Caen 125 – St-Lô 91 – Rennes 63

⚠ Aux Pommiers

✆ 02 33 60 11 36. www.camping-auxpommiers.com

Address : 28 route du Mont Saint Michel, off the D976

Opening times : from end March to mid Nov.

1.79 ha (107 pitches) flat, grassy

Tariff : (2015 price) ♦ 4.80€ ⇌ ▣ ⚡ (10A) 4.30€
Rental rates : (2015 price) (from end March to mid Nov.) – 1 'gypsy' caravan – 26 ⛺ – 4 🏠 – 4 ⛺ – 4 canvas bungalows.
local sani-station – 18.11€

Surroundings : ♀	
Leisure activities : ▦ 🚴 🏊	Longitude : -1.51264
Facilities : ⚡ – 2 private sanitary facilities (🚿 ♿ wc) 🍴 launderette	Latitude : 48.59618
Nearby : 🍴 🖼 🏇	

LE BEC-HELLOUIN

27800 – Michelin map **304** E6 – pop. 419 – alt. 101
▶ Paris 153 – Bernay 22 – Évreux 46 – Lisieux 46

⚠ Municipal St-Nicolas

✆ 02 32 44 83 55. www.campingsaintnicolas.fr

Address : 15 rue St-Nicolas (situated 2km east, along the D 39 and D 581, follow the signs for Malleville-sur-le-Bec and take road to the left)

Opening times : from mid March to mid Oct.

3 ha (90 pitches) flat, grassy

Tariff : (2015 price) 19.70€ ♦♦ ⇌ ▣ ⚡ (10A) – Extra per person 4.60€
Rental rates : (2015 price) (from mid March to mid Oct.) – 12 ⛺ – 3 🏠. Per night from 95 to 140€ – Per week from 210 to 610€
AireService sani-station 5€
A well-kept site with floral decoration.

Surroundings : 🌲 ♀	
Leisure activities : 🚴 🍴 library	Longitude : 0.72268
Facilities : ⚡ – cc 🍴 launderette	Latitude : 49.23586
Nearby : 🏇	

BELLÊME

61130 – Michelin map **310** M4 – pop. 1 547 – alt. 241
▶ Paris 168 – Alençon 42 – Chartres 76 – La Ferté-Bernard 23

⚠ Le Val

✆ 06 24 70 55 17. www.campingduperchebellemois.com

Address : take the western exit along the D 955, follow the signs for Mamers and take road to the left, near the swimming pool

Opening times : from mid April to mid Oct.

1.5 ha (50 pitches) terraced, relatively flat, flat, grassy

Tariff : 19.50€ ♦♦ ⇌ ▣ ⚡ (16A) – Extra per person 4.50€
Rental rates : (from mid April to mid Oct.) – 6 ⛺. Per week from 350 to 490€
local sani-station 4€ – 6 ▣ 11€ – 11€

Surroundings : 🌲 ▦ ♀	
Facilities : ⚡ 🚿 🍴	Longitude : 0.555
Nearby : 🍴 🏊	Latitude : 48.3747

BERNAY

27300 – Michelin map **304** D7 – pop. 10 285 – alt. 105
▶ Paris 155 – Argentan 69 – Évreux 49 – Le Havre 72

⚠ Municipal

✆ 02 32 43 30 47. www.bernay-tourisme.fr

Address : rue des Canadiens (situated 2km southwest along the N 138, follow the signs for Alençon and take turning to the left – recommended route via the diversion (déviation) and ZI Malouve)

Opening times : from beginning May to end Sept.

1 ha (50 pitches) flat, grassy

Tariff : (2015 price) 13.60€ ♦♦ ⇌ ▣ ⚡ (8A) – Extra per person 3.25€
Rental rates : (2015 price) permanent – 2 ⛺. Per night from 47€ – Per week from 296 to 374€
local sani-station 2.55€
A well-kept, lush and leafy campsite.

Surroundings : ▦ ♀	
Leisure activities : ▦ 🚴	Longitude : 0.58683
Facilities : ⚡ – 🚿 🍴 launderette	Latitude : 49.07879
Nearby : 🍴 🖼 🏊	

BERNIÈRES-SUR-MER

14990 – Michelin map **303** J4 – pop. 2 351
▶ Paris 253 – Caen 20 – Le Havre 114 – Hérouville-Saint-Clair 21

⚠ Le Havre de Bernières

✆ 02 31 96 67 09. www.camping-normandie.com

Address : chemin de Quintefeuille

6.5 ha (240 pitches) flat, grassy
Rentals : 32 ⛺.

Surroundings : ♀♀	
Leisure activities : 🍴 🍴 ▦ 🎱 🚴 🏊	Longitude : -0.42795
Facilities : ⚡ – ▦ 🍴 launderette	Latitude : 49.33245
Nearby : 🛒 🍴 🏖 🏊 (beach) 🎳 bowling	

Using the traditional Michelin classification method, the guide provides you with an easy, speedy reference for assessing the category of each site: 1 to 5 tents (see page 10).

LES BIARDS

50540 – Michelin map **303** E8 – alt. 495
▶ Paris 358 – Alençon 108 – Avranches 22 – Caen 126

⚠ Municipal La Mazure

✆ 02 33 89 19 50. www.lamazure.com

Address : at the Base de Loisirs/town leisure centre (2.3km southwest along the D 85e, on the banks of the lake at Vezins)

Opening times : from beginning May to end Sept.

3.5 ha/0.4 (28 pitches) terraced, flat, grassy

Tariff : ♦ 3.50€ ⇌ ▣ 6€ – ⚡ (6A) 3.50€
Rental rates : permanent – 3 🏠. Per night from 80 to 100€ – Per week from 420 to 500€

Surroundings : 🌲 🌲	
Leisure activities : 🍴 ▦ 🎱 🚴 🏊	Longitude : -1.2047
Facilities : ⚡ – 🚿 🍴 launderette	Latitude : 48.5734
At the leisure/activities centre : 🏇 electric boats	

BLANGY-LE-CHÂTEAU

14130 – Michelin map **303** N4 – pop. 678 – alt. 60
▶ Paris 197 – Caen 56 – Deauville 22 – Lisieux 16

⚠ Les Castels Le Brévedent ▲▲

✆ 02 31 64 72 88. www.campinglebrevedent.com

Address : route du Pin (3km southeast along the D 51, by the château; beside a lake)

6 ha/3.5 for camping (140 pitches) sloping, flat, grassy

Rentals : 8 ☐.

In the grounds of a 14th-century château that also features a lake.

Surroundings : 🐾 ≤ 🌲🌲
Leisure activities : ☂ 🛋 🕯nighttime 🎿
🛶🏊 : 🏊🏊
Facilities : ♿ ⚤ 🛁 🚰 launderette 🎨 🍴
Nearby : 🍴🐎

GPS
Longitude : 0.3045
Latitude : 49.2253

A chambre d'hôte is a guesthouse or B & B-style accommodation.

BLANGY-SUR-BRESLE

76340 – Michelin map **304** J2 – pop. 3 000 – alt. 70
▶ Paris 156 – Abbeville 29 – Amiens 56 – Dieppe 55

⚠ Aux Cygnes d'Opale

✆ 02 35 94 55 65. www.auxcygnesdopale.fr

Address : rue du Marais (southeast, between two lakes and 200m from the Bresle river; access via the r. du Maréchal-Leclerc, near the church)

Opening times : from beginning April to end Oct.

0.8 ha (57 pitches) flat, grassy

Tariff : (2015 price) 21€ ✚✚ �car 🔌 (10A) – Extra per person 3.50€

Rental rates : (2015 price) (from beginning April to end Oct.) – 10 ☐. Per night from 80 to 90€ – Per week from 390 to 600€

🚰 Eurorelais sani-station 2€ – 6 🔲 4€

Surroundings : 🌲🌲
Leisure activities : 🔲🏊
Facilities : ♿ ⚤ 🚰 🚰
Nearby : 🏊🏊 🍴 🎣

GPS
Longitude : 1.63638
Latitude : 49.93096

BOURG-ACHARD

27310 – Michelin map **304** E5 – pop. 2 948 – alt. 124
▶ Paris 141 – Bernay 39 – Évreux 62 – Le Havre 62

⚠ Le Clos Normand

✆ 02 32 56 34 84. www.leclosnormand.eu

Address : 235 route de Pont-Audemer (take the western exit)

Opening times : from mid April to end Sept.

1.4 ha (75 pitches) relatively flat, wood, flat, grassy

Tariff : (2015 price) 21€ ✚✚ 🚗 🔲 🔌 (6A) – Extra per person 5€

Rental rates : (2015 price) permanent 🏊 – 6 ☐. Per night from 70€ – Per week from 250 to 470€

🚰 local sani-station

In a green setting with lots of flowers.

Surroundings : 🌲 🌲
Leisure activities : ☂ 🛋 🏊🏊 🏊
Facilities : ⚤ 🚰 🔲 🍴

GPS
Longitude : 0.80765
Latitude : 49.35371

BRÉCEY

50370 – Michelin map **303** F7 – pop. 2 165 – alt. 75
▶ Paris 328 – Avranches 17 – Granville 42 – St-Hilaire-du-Harcouët 20

⚠ Intercommunal le Pont Roulland

✆ 02 33 48 60 60. www.camping-brecey.com

Address : Le Pont Roulland (1.1km east along the D 911, follow the signs for Cuves)

Opening times : from beginning April to end Sept.

1 ha (52 pitches) relatively flat, flat, grassy

Tariff : (2015 price) ✚ 2.90€ 🚗 🔲 3.90€ – 🔌 (6A) 2.90€

Rental rates : (from mid April to end Sept.) – 4 ☐. Per night from 39 to 57€

🚰 local sani-station 4.70€

In a rural setting near a small lake.

Surroundings : 🌲 🍴
Leisure activities : 🏊🏊 🔲 🎣
Facilities : ⚤ 🚰 🚰 🔲
Nearby : 🍴

GPS
Longitude : -1.15235
Latitude : 48.72184

BRÉHAL

50290 – Michelin map **303** C6 – pop. 3 017 – alt. 69
▶ Paris 345 – Caen 113 – St-Lô 48 – St-Malo 101

⚠ La Vanlée

✆ 02 33 61 63 80. www.camping-vanlee.com

Address : rue des Gabions (near the town golf course)

Opening times : from mid April to beginning Oct.

11 ha (466 pitches) undulating, sandy, flat, grassy

Tariff : (2015 price) 25.90€ ✚✚ 🚗 🔲 🔌 (10A) – Extra per person 5.80€ – Reservation fee 9€

🚰 local sani-station 4€ – 🚐18€

A pleasant campsite in an unspoilt setting beside the sea.

Surroundings : 🌲 ⛰
Leisure activities : ☂ 🛋 🕯🏊 multi-sports ground
Facilities : ♿ ⚤ 🚰 🚰 launderette 🧺

GPS
Longitude : -1.56474
Latitude : 48.90913

BRÉVILLE-SUR-MER

50290 – Michelin map **303** K4 – pop. 803 – alt. 70
▶ Paris 341 – Caen 108 – St-Lô 50 – St-Malo 95

⚠ La Route Blanche ▲▲

✆ 02 33 50 23 31. www.campinglarouteblanche.com

Address : 6 rue de La Route Blanche (located 1km northwest following signs for the beach, near the golf course)

Opening times : from beginning April to end Sept.

5.5 ha (273 pitches) flat, grassy, sandy

Tariff : (2015 price) 37.50€ ✚✚ 🚗 🔲 🔌 (10A) – Extra per person 7.50€ – Reservation fee 8€

Rental rates : (2015 price) (from beginning April to end Sept.) 🏊 – 40 ☐. Per week from 336 to 1,120€ – Reservation fee 8€

🚰 Eurorelais sani-station – 🚐14€

Surroundings : 🌲
Leisure activities : ✖ 🛋 🕯🎿 🏊🏊 🏊 🔲 multi-sports ground
Facilities : ♿ ⚤ 🔲 🚰 🚰 launderette 🎨
Nearby : 🍴 🐾 sports trail

GPS
Longitude : -1.56387
Latitude : 48.86966

331

CANY-BARVILLE

76450 – Michelin map **304** D3 – pop. 3 080 – alt. 25
▶ Paris 187 – Bolbec 34 – Dieppe 45 – Fécamp 21

⚠ Municipal

✆ 02 35 97 70 37. www.cany-barville.fr

Address : route de Barville (take the southern exit along the D 268, follow the signs for Yvetot, after the stadium)

Opening times : permanent

2.9 ha (100 pitches) flat, grassy, concrete surface areas

Tariff : (2015 price) ♥ 3.55€ – 🚗 1.80€ 🔲 2.40€ – (⌁) (10A) 3.55€
Rental rates : (2015 price) permanent ⧖ (2 mobile homes) ⚲ – 15 🏠. Per night from 60 to 80€ – Per week from 300 to 590€
🚐 62 🔲 12.45€
There are numerous pitches, some on a hard surface and some on grass.

Surroundings : 🏕 ⚲	
Leisure activities : 🖼 ⚓	G P S Longitude : 0.64231
Facilities : ⧖ ⛲ ▥ ♨ 🚾 ♈ launderette	Latitude : 49.7834

CARENTAN

50500 – Michelin map **303** E4 – pop. 6 056 – alt. 18
▶ Paris 308 – Avranches 89 – Caen 74 – Cherbourg 52

🏔 Flower Le Haut Dick

✆ 02 33 42 16 89. www.camping-lehautdick.com

Address : 30 chemin du Grand Bas Pays (beside the canal, near the swimming pool)

Opening times : from end March to end Sept.

2.5 ha (130 pitches) undulating, sandy, flat, grassy

Tariff : (2015 price) 27.50€ ♥♥ 🚗 🔲 (⌁) (10A) –
Extra per person 5.50€
Rental rates : (2015 price) (from end March to end Sept.) –
22 🚐 – 4 tent lodges. Per night from 45 to 107€ – Per week from 315 to 749€
🚐 local sani-station – 2 🔲 14€ – ♨ (⌁)11€
In a pleasant green setting.

Surroundings : 🏞 🏕 ⚲	
Leisure activities : ♈ ✗ 🖼 ⚓ ♭	G P S Longitude : -1.23917
Facilities : ⧖ ⛲ ♈	Latitude : 49.3087
Nearby : 🎿 🖼 🏊 🚣	

This guide is not intended as a list of all the camping sites in France; its aim is to provide a selection of the best sites in each category.

COLLEVILLE-SUR-MER

14710 – Michelin map **303** G3 – pop. 171 – alt. 42
▶ Paris 281 – Bayeux 18 – Caen 48 – Carentan 36

⚠ Le Robinson

✆ 02 31 22 45 19. www.campinglerobinson.com

Address : at the hamlet Cabourg (800m northeast along the D 514, follow the signs for Port-en-Bessin)

Opening times : from beginning April to end Sept.

1 ha (67 pitches) flat, grassy

Tariff : ♥ 6.45€ 🚗 2.85€ 🔲 6.25€ – (⌁) (10A) 4.80€ – Reservation fee 18€

Rental rates : (from beginning April to end Sept.) ⚲ – 22 🚐 –
2 🏠 – 1 canvas bungalow. Per night from 53 to 94€ – Per week from 298 to 799€ – Reservation fee 18€
🚐 Eurorelais sani-station

Surroundings : 🏕	
Leisure activities : ♈ ✗ ⚓ 🎣 🏊 🛶	G P S Longitude : -0.83497
Facilities : ⧖ ⛲ ♈ launderette	Latitude : 49.34968
Nearby : 🐎	

COURSEULLES-SUR-MER

14470 – Michelin map **303** J4 – pop. 4 185
▶ Paris 252 – Arromanches-les-Bains 14 – Bayeux 24 – Cabourg 41

🏔 Municipal le Champ de Course

✆ 02 31 37 99 26. www.campingcourseulles.com

Address : avenue de la Libération (in the northern part of the town)

7.5 ha (381 pitches) flat, grassy

Rentals : 26 🚐 – 4 🏠 – 2 tent lodges.
Situated close to the beach.

Surroundings : 🏕	
Leisure activities : 🖼 ⚓	G P S Longitude : -0.44606
Facilities : ⧖ ⛲ ♨ 🚾 ♈ launderette	Latitude : 49.33289
Nearby : ✗ 🎿 🎣 🚣 🐎	

COURTILS

50220 – Michelin map **303** D8 – pop. 245 – alt. 35
▶ Paris 349 – Avranches 13 – Fougères 43 – Pontorson 15

🏔 St-Michel

✆ 02 33 70 96 90. www.campingsaintmichel.com

Address : 35 route du Mont Saint Michel (take the western exit along the D 43)

Opening times : from end March to beginning Nov.

2.5 ha (100 pitches) flat, relatively flat, grassy

Tariff : 27€ ♥♥ 🚗 🔲 (⌁) (10A) – Extra per person 7.50€
Rental rates : (from end March to beginning Nov.) – 50 🚐.
Per night from 45 to 112€ – Per week from 525 to 805€
🚐 local sani-station 5€ – ♨ (⌁)16.70€

Surroundings : 🏕 ⚲	
Leisure activities : ✗ 🖼 ⚓ 🚴 🚣 wildlife park	G P S Longitude : -1.41611
Facilities : ⧖ ⛲ ♿ ▥ ♨ launderette ⚶	Latitude : 48.62829
Nearby : 🎿 🐎	

DENNEVILLE

50580 – Michelin map **303** C4 – pop. 539 – alt. 5
▶ Paris 347 – Barneville-Carteret 12 – Carentan 34 – St-Lô 53

🏔 L'Espérance

✆ 02 33 07 12 71. www.camping-esperance.fr – limited spaces for one-night stay

Address : 36 rue de la Gamburie (3.5km west along the D 137, 500m from the beach)

Opening times : from beginning April to end Sept.

3 ha (134 pitches) flat, grassy, sandy

Tariff : (2015 price) 31.50€ ♥♥ 🚗 🔲 (⌁) (10A) –
Extra per person 7.10€

Rental rates : (2015 price) (from beginning April to end Sept.) – 13 🏠. Per week from 330 to 730€

Surroundings : 🌊 ♀
Leisure activities : ▼ ✗ ☾nighttime 🏄
✗ 🔥 🏊 ♒
Facilities : ⚡ 🚰 launderette ♨ 🚿

GPS Longitude : -1.68832
Latitude : 49.30332

DIEPPE

76200 – Michelin map **304** G2 – pop. 32 670 – alt. 6
▶ Paris 197 – Abbeville 68 – Beauvais 107 – Caen 176

⚠ Vitamin'

📞 02 35 82 11 11. www.camping-vitamin.com – limited spaces for one-night stay

Address : 865 chemin des Vertus (3km south along the N 27, follow the signs for Rouen and take a right turn)

Opening times : from beginning March to beginning Oct.

5.3 ha (180 pitches) flat, grassy

Tariff : (2015 price) 26.40€ ♥♥ 🚗 🔲 ⚡ (10A)
Extra per person 6.40€ – Reservation fee 7€
Rental rates : (2015 price) (from end March to beginning Oct.) ♿ (1 mobile home) – 1 'gypsy' caravan – 39 🏠 – 4 🏡. Per night from 69€ – Per week from 349 to 719€ – Reservation fee 7€

There's an attractive indoor water park.

Surroundings : 🔲
Leisure activities : ▼ 🎪 🎣 ⛵ jacuzzi
🏄 🔲 🏊 🏓 multi-sports ground
Facilities : ♿ 🚰 🚿 launderette
Nearby : ✗ ✗ 🎿, squash

GPS Longitude : 1.07481
Latitude : 49.90054

⚠ La Source

📞 02 35 84 27 04. www.camping-la-source.fr – limited spaces for one-night stay

Address : 63 rue des Tisserands (3km southwest along the D 925, follow the signs for Le Havre then turn left onto D 153; at Petit-Appeville)

Opening times : from mid March to mid Oct.

2.5 ha (120 pitches) flat, grassy

Tariff : ♥ 6.70€ 🚗 2 🔲 9.10€ – ⚡ (10A) 4.50€ – Reservation fee 7€
Rental rates : (from mid March to mid Oct.) – 6 🏠. Per night from 100 to 140€ – Per week from 380 to 550€ – Reservation fee 15€

🚐 Eurorelais sani-station 2€ – 14 🔲 9.90€
The pitches are near the Scie river.

Leisure activities : ▼ 🎪 🏄 🚴 🏊 ♒
Facilities : ♿ 🚰 📶 🚿 launderette

GPS Longitude : 1.05732
Latitude : 49.89824

DIVES-SUR-MER

14160 – Michelin map **303** L4 – pop. 5 935 – alt. 3
▶ Paris 219 – Cabourg 2 – Caen 27 – Deauville 22

⚠ Le Golf

📞 02 31 24 73 09. www.campingdugolf.com – limited spaces for one-night stay

Address : route de Lisieux (take the eastern exit, D 45 for 3.5km)

Opening times : from beginning April to end Sept.

2.8 ha (155 pitches) flat, grassy

Tariff : 17.70€ ♥♥ 🚗 🔲 ⚡ (10A) – Extra per person 4.30€ – Reservation fee 5€

Rental rates : (2015 price) permanent – 15 🏠 – 1 canvas bungalow – 1 tent lodge. Per night from 44 to 77€ – Per week from 199 to 699€ – Reservation fee 15€

🚐 1 🔲 17.70€

Surroundings : 🔲 ♀
Leisure activities : ▼ 🏄 ♒
Facilities : ♿ 🚰 🚿 launderette

GPS Longitude : -0.0701
Latitude : 49.2792

DONVILLE-LES-BAINS

50350 – Michelin map **303** C6 – pop. 3 269 – alt. 40
▶ Paris 341 – Caen 112 – St-Lô 77

⚠ L'Ermitage

📞 02 33 50 09 01. www.camping-ermitage.com

Address : rue de l'Ermitage (located 1km north along the r. du Champ de Courses)

Opening times : from mid April to mid Oct.

5 ha (298 pitches) relatively flat, sandy, flat, grassy

Tariff : (2015 price) ♥ 5.73€ 🚗 2.26€ 🔲 8.84€ ⚡ (10A)

Situated near a beautiful beach of fine sand.

Surroundings : 🔲
Leisure activities : 🎪 ☀daytime 🏄
Facilities : ♿ 🚰 🚿 🏓 launderette
Nearby : ♨ ▼ ✗ 🚿 ✗ 🔲 (open air in season) ♒ 🎳 bowling

GPS Longitude : -1.58075
Latitude : 48.85212

DUCEY

50220 – Michelin map **303** E8 – pop. 2 465 – alt. 15
▶ Paris 348 – Avranches 11 – Fougères 41 – Rennes 80

⚠ Municipal la Sélune

📞 02 33 48 46 49. www.ducey-tourisme.com

Address : rue de Boishue (take the western exit along the N 176 and take the D 178, follow the signs for St-Aubin-de-Terregatte to the left; by the stadium)

0.42 ha (40 pitches) flat, grassy

The pitches are well marked out with hedges of thuja.

Surroundings : 🔲
Facilities : ♿ 🚿
Nearby : ✗ 🔲 🏊

GPS Longitude : -1.29452
Latitude : 48.61686

ÉTRÉHAM

14400 – Michelin map **303** H4 – pop. 271 – alt. 30
▶ Paris 276 – Bayeux 11 – Caen 42 – Carentan 40

⚠ Seasonova La Reine Mathilde

📞 02 31 21 76 55. www.camping-normandie-rm.fr

Address : Le Marais (located 1km west along the D 123 and take the road to the right)

Opening times : from beginning April to end Sept.

6.5 ha (115 pitches) flat, grassy

Tariff : (2015 price) 25€ ♥♥ 🚗 🔲 ⚡ (6A) – Extra per person 7€ – Reservation fee 15€
Rental rates : (2015 price) (from beginning April to end Sept.) – 6 🏠 – 6 🏡 – 2 canvas bungalows. Per week from 190 to 730€ – Reservation fee 15€

Surroundings : 🌊 🔲 ♀♀
Leisure activities : ▼ 🎪 🏄 🏊
Facilities : ♿ 🚰 🏓 🔲 🚿

GPS Longitude : -0.8025
Latitude : 49.33131

ÉTRETAT

76790 – Michelin map **304** B3 – pop. 1 502 – alt. 8
▶ Paris 206 – Bolbec 30 – Fécamp 16 – Le Havre 29

� Municipal

✆ 02 35 27 07 67. www.etretat.fr – **FR**

Address : 69 rue Guy de Maupassant (located 1km southeast along the D 39, follow the signs for Criquetot-l'Esneval)

Opening times : from beginning April to mid Oct.

1.2 ha (73 pitches) flat, grassy, gravelled

Tariff : (2015 price) ✱ 3.75€ ⊷ 4.80€ 🅴 4.80€ – 🔌 (6A) 6€

🚐 AireService sani-station 8€

Flowers surround the entrance and the whole site is very well kept; there's an adjacent service area for campervans.

Surroundings : ♀	
Leisure activities : 🎱 ⚓	**G** Longitude : 0.21557
Facilities : ⊶ 🎋 🍴 launderette	**P** Latitude : 49.70063
Nearby : 🍴 🎣	**S**

FALAISE

14700 – Michelin map **303** K6 – pop. 8 333 – alt. 132
▶ Paris 264 – Argentan 23 – Caen 36 – Flers 37

⚠ Municipal du Château

✆ 02 31 90 16 55. http://camping-falaise.com

Address : rue du Val d'Ante (to the west of the town, in the Val d'Ante)

Opening times : from beginning May to end Sept.

2 ha (66 pitches) terraced, flat, grassy, relatively flat

Tariff : 19.50€ ✱✱ ⊷ 🅴 🔌 (10A) – Extra per person 5.20€

🚐 35 🅴 15.20€

In a green setting in the grounds of the château.

Surroundings : ≼ Château Val de Meuse ♀	
Leisure activities : 🎱 ⚓ 🍴 library	**G** Longitude : -0.2052
Facilities : 🦽 ⊶ 🎋 🍴	**P** Latitude : 48.89563
Nearby : 🧗 climbing wall	**S**

To make the best possible use of this guide, please read pages 2–15 carefully.

FIQUEFLEUR-ÉQUAINVILLE

27210 – Michelin map **304** B5 – pop. 642 – alt. 17
▶ Paris 189 – Deauville 24 – Honfleur 7 – Lisieux 40

⚠ Sites et Paysages Domaine de La Catinière

✆ 02 32 57 63 51. www.camping-honfleur.com

Address : route de Honfleur (1km south of Fiquefleur along the D 22)

Opening times : from beginning April to mid Oct.

3.8 ha (130 pitches) flat, grassy

Tariff : 34€ ✱✱ ⊷ 🅴 🔌 (13A) – Extra per person 6€

Rental rates : (from beginning April to end June) – 24 🏠 – 1 gîte. Per night from 114 to 190€ – Per week from 290 to 850€

🚐 local sani-station – 🔌15€

A long site in a green setting, between two streams.

Surroundings : 🏕 ♀	
Leisure activities : 🍴 ✗ 🎱 ⚓ 🛝 🚣	**G** Longitude : 0.30382
Facilities : 🦽 ⊶ 🍴 launderette	**P** Latitude : 49.40161
	S

FLERS

61100 – Michelin map **310** F2 – pop. 15 592 – alt. 270
▶ Paris 234 – Alençon 73 – Argentan 42 – Caen 60

⚠ Le Pays de Flers

✆ 02 33 65 35 00. http://www.flers-agglomeration.fr/culture-sports-et-loisirs/heberg

Address : at La Fouquerie (1.7km east along the D 924, follow the signs for Argentan and take road to the left)

Opening times : from mid April to mid Oct.

1.5 ha (50 pitches) relatively flat, grassy

Tariff : (2015 price) 14€ ✱✱ ⊷ 🅴 🔌 (10A) – Extra per person 3.50€

Rental rates : (2015 price) permanent 🦽 (1 mobile home) – 3 🏠. Per week from 284 to 397

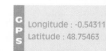

Surroundings : ♀	
Leisure activities : 🎱 ⚓ 🚲	**G** Longitude : -0.54311
Facilities : 🦽 ⊶ 🎋 🛝 🚿 launderette	**P** Latitude : 48.75463
Nearby : 🛶	**S**

GENÊTS

50530 – Michelin map **303** D7 – pop. 427 – alt. 2
▶ Paris 345 – Avranches 11 – Granville 24 – Le Mont-St-Michel 33

⚠ Les Coques d'Or

✆ 02 33 70 82 57. www.campinglescoquesdor.com

Address : 14 Le Bec d'Andaine (700m northwest along the D 35e1, follow the signs for Le Bec d'Andaine)

Opening times : from beginning April to end Sept.

4.7 ha (225 pitches) flat, grassy

Tariff : (2015 price) 23.30€ ✱✱ ⊷ 🅴 🔌 (10A) – Extra per person 6.20€

Rental rates : (2015 price) (from beginning April to end Sept.) – 32 🏠 – 2 🏠. Per night from 65 to 115€ – Per week from 310 to 820€

🚐 AireService sani-station 4€ – 20 🅴 5€ – 🔌10€

There's a pleasant indoor pool with a spa area.

Surroundings : 🏖 🏕 ♀	
Leisure activities : 🍴 ✗ 🎣 🏊 hammam, jacuzzi ⚓ 🚲 🖥 ⛳ multi-sports ground, spa centre	**G** Longitude : -1.48444
Facilities : 🦽 ⊶ 🛝 🍴 launderette 🧺	**P** Latitude : 48.68778
Nearby : 🏃 walking and horse-riding trail	**S**

GRANVILLE

50400 – Michelin map **303** C6 – pop. 12 847 – alt. 10
▶ Paris 342 – Avranches 27 – Caen 109 – Cherbourg 105

⚠ Les Castels Le Château de Lez-Eaux

✆ 02 33 51 66 09. www.lez-eaux.com

Address : St-Aubin-des-Préaux (7km southeast along the D 973, follow the signs for Avranches)

Opening times : from beginning April to mid Sept.

12 ha/8 for camping (229 pitches) relatively flat, flat, grassy

Tariff : 43.60€ ✱✱ ⊷ 🅴 🔌 (10A) – Extra per person 8.50€ – Reservation fee 8€

Rental rates : (from beginning April to mid Sept.) 🦽 (1 chalet) – 17 🏠 – 43 🏠 – 2 cabins in the trees. Per night from 99 to 385€ – Per week from 546 to 1,666€ – Reservation fee 8€

🚐 local sani-station 10€ – 8 🅴 51.50€

In the grounds of the château; an attractive swimming area.

Surroundings : 🌊 ♀
Leisure activities : 🍸 🏠 ⬚ 🏊 🚴 ✂ 🖼
🎣 🎿
Facilities : 🚿 ⛔ 🚻 🔲 🛁 ♿ 🍴
launderette 🧺
Nearby : 🚡 🐎

Longitude : -1.52461
Latitude : 48.79774

⛰ La Vague

🕿 0233502997. www.camping-la-vague.com

Address : 126 route de Voudrelin (2.5km southeast along the D 911, follow the signs for St-Pair and take the D 572 to the left; at St Nicolas-Plage)

2 ha (145 pitches)
Rentals : 7 🚐.

In a green setting that is pleasant and well kept.

Surroundings : ♀
Leisure activities : 🏠 🎣 m
Facilities : 🚿 ⛔ 🔲
Nearby : 🖼 (open air in season) 🐎

Longitude : -1.57317
Latitude : 48.82146

LE GROS-THEIL

27370 – Michelin map **304** F6 – pop. 931 – alt. 145
▶ Paris 136 – Bernay 30 – Elbeuf 16 – Évreux 34

⛰ Salverte

🕿 0232355134. www.camping-salverte.com – limited spaces for one-night stay

Address : 3km southwest along the D 26, follow the signs for Brionne and take road to the left

Opening times : permanent

17 ha/10 for camping (300 pitches) flat, grassy

Tariff : (2015 price) 21€ ⭑⭑ �car 🔲 ⚡ (6A) – Extra per person 7€
Rental rates : (2015 price) (from beginning April to end Oct.) – 4 🚐. Per night from 65 to 95€ – Per week from 390 to 510€

A pleasant wooded site.

Surroundings : 🌊 ♀♀
Leisure activities : 🍸 ✗ 🏠 🌿 ⛵ 🎣
🖼 m 🎿 library, entertainment room
Facilities : ⛔ 🔲 ♿ 🍴 launderette 🧺

Longitude : 0.84149
Latitude : 49.22619

HONFLEUR

14600 – Michelin map **303** N3 – pop. 8 163 – alt. 5
▶ Paris 195 – Caen 69 – Le Havre 27 – Lisieux 38

⛰ La Briquerie

🕿 0231892832. www.campinglabriquerie.com – limited spaces for one-night stay

Address : at Equemauville (follow the signs for Trouville, 3.5km southwest following signs for Pont-l'Évêque and right onto the D 62)

Opening times : from beginning April to end Sept.

11 ha (430 pitches) flat, grassy

Tariff : (2015 price) 34.70€ ⭑⭑ �car 🔲 ⚡ (10A) – Extra per person 9.30€
Rental rates : (2015 price) (from beginning April to end Sept.) – 13 🚐 – 11 🏠. Per week from 690€
🚐 30 🔲 35.70€ – 🔌 14€

The sanitary facilities are good quality, but a lot of the mobile homes belong to owner-occupiers.

Surroundings : ♀
Leisure activities : 🍸 ✗ 🏠 🎣 ⛵ jacuzzi
🎠 🏊 🔲 🎿 multi-sports ground
Facilities : 🚿 ⛔ 🚻 🔲 ♿ 🍴 🍴
launderette 🧺
Nearby : 🎿 ✂ 🐎

Longitude : 0.20826
Latitude : 49.39675

HOULGATE

14510 – Michelin map **303** L4 – pop. 1 988 – alt. 11
▶ Paris 214 – Caen 29 – Deauville 14 – Lisieux 33

⛰ Yelloh! Village La Vallée 👥

🕿 0231244069. www.campinglavallee.com

Address : 88 route de la Vallée (located 1km south along the D 24a, follow the signs for Lisieux and turn right onto the D 24)

Opening times : from beginning April to end Oct.

11 ha (350 pitches) terraced, relatively flat, flat, grassy

Tariff : 48€ ⭑⭑ �car 🔲 ⚡ (6A) – Extra per person 8€
Rental rates : (from beginning April to end Oct.) 🎿 – 100 🚐.
Per night from 39 to 149€ – Per week from 273 to 1,043€
🚐 AireService sani-station 2€ – 12 🔲 22€

In a pleasant setting beside some old Norman-style buildings.

Surroundings : ⛰ ♀
Leisure activities : 🍸 ✗ 🏠 🌿 🎠 🎣 🚴
✂ 🖼 🏊 🎿
Facilities : 🚿 ⛔ 🛁 ♿ 🍴 🍴 launderette
🎿 🧺
Nearby : 🖼 🐎

Longitude : -0.06733
Latitude : 49.29422

Some information or pricing may have changed since the guide went to press. We recommend you check the price list online in advance or at the entrance to the campsite and enquire about possible restrictions.

INCHEVILLE

76117 – Michelin map **304** I1 – pop. 1 357 – alt. 19
▶ Paris 169 – Abbeville 32 – Amiens 65 – Blangy-sur-Bresle 16

⛰ Municipal de l'Etang

🕿 0235503017. campingdeletang@orange.fr – limited spaces for one-night stay – 🚐

Address : rue Mozart (take the northeastern exit, follow the signs for Beauchamps and take right turn)

Opening times : from beginning March to end Oct.

2 ha (190 pitches) flat, grassy

Tariff : (2015 price) 13.80€ ⭑⭑ �car 🔲 ⚡ (16A) – Extra per person 2.75€
🚐 local sani-station 6€ – 2 🔲 13.80€
Situated near a fishing lake.

Surroundings : ♀
Leisure activities : 🏠 🎣
Facilities : 🚿 ⛔ 🔲 ♿ 🍴 🔲
Nearby : ✂ 🎿

Longitude : 1.50788
Latitude : 50.01238

ISIGNY-SUR-MER

14230 – Michelin map **303** F4 – pop. 2 782 – alt. 4
▶ Paris 298 – Bayeux 35 – Caen 64 – Carentan 14

⚲ Le Fanal

✆ 02 31 21 33 20. www.camping-normandie-fanal.fr

Address : rue du Fanal (west of the town, access via the town centre, near the sports field)

Opening times : from beginning April to end Sept.

6.5 ha/5.5 for camping (240 pitches) flat, grassy

Tariff : 17 € ✦✦ ⇔ 回 (½) (16A) – Extra per person 3.50 € – Reservation fee 11 €

Rental rates : (from beginning April to end Sept.) – 90 ⊡ – 10 ⌂ – 4 tent lodges. Per night from 34 to 76 € – Per week from 238 to 980 € – Reservation fee 22 €

In a pleasant, well-kept setting, beside a small lake.

Surroundings : ≋ ⚲	
Leisure activities : 🎱 ⅙ ⭢ ※ ▧	**G P S** Longitude : -1.10872
Facilities : ₺ ⌐ ⫿ ⚄ ∀ ⅋ launderette	Latitude : 49.31923
Nearby : ♨ ⌇ 𝄢 sports trail	

JUMIEGES

76480 – Michelin map **304** E5 – pop. 1 719 – alt. 25
▶ Paris 161 – Rouen 29 – Le Havre 82 – Caen 132

⚲ La Forêt

✆ 02 35 37 93 43. www.campinglaforet.com

Address : rue Mainberte, just off the D143, north of Jumièges

Opening times : from beginning April to end Oct.

2 ha (111 pitches) flat, grassy

Tariff : 28 € ✦✦ ⇔ 回 (½) (10A) – Extra per person 6 € – Reservation fee 5 €

Rental rates : (from beginning April to end Oct.) ⚓ – 16 ⊡ – 5 ⌂. Per night from 62 to 92 € – Per week from 372 to 644 € – Reservation fee 5 €

⊡ Raclet sani-station 6 €

Situated in the Brotonne Regional Park.

Surroundings : ≋ ⊡ ⚲	
Leisure activities : 🎱 ⭢ ▧ ⅃	**G P S** Longitude : 0.82883
Facilities : ₺ ⌐ ⅋ launderette	Latitude : 49.43485
Nearby : ※	

LISIEUX

14100 – Michelin map **303** N5 – pop. 21 826 – alt. 51
▶ Paris 169 – Caen 54 – Le Havre 66 – Hérouville-St-Clair 53

⚲ La Vallée

✆ 02 31 62 00 40. www.lisieux-tourisme.com

Address : 9 rue de la Vallée (take the northern exit along the D 48, follow the signs for Pont-l'Évêque)

Opening times : from beginning April to beginning Oct.

1 ha (75 pitches) flat, grassy, gravelled

Tariff : (2015 price) 13 € ✦✦ ⇔ 回 (½) (8A) – Extra per person 3.70 €

Rental rates : (2015 price) permanent – 5 ⊡. Per week from 250 to 399 € – Reservation fee 6 €

⊡ 30 回 13 €

Surroundings : ⚲	
Facilities : ₺ ⌐ ⊠ ⅋ launderette	**G P S** Longitude : 0.22068
Nearby : ※	Latitude : 49.16423

LES LOGES

76790 – Michelin map **304** B3 – pop. 1 155 – alt. 92
▶ Paris 205 – Rouen 83 – Le Havre 34 – Fécamp 10

⚲ Club Airotel L'Aiguille Creuse

✆ 02 35 29 52 10. www.campingaiguillecreuse.com

Address : 24 residence de l'Aiguille Creuse

Opening times : from beginning April to mid Sept.

3 ha (105 pitches) relatively flat, flat, grassy

Tariff : 28.50 € ✦✦ ⇔ 回 (½) (10A) – Extra per person 6 € – Reservation fee 7 €

Rental rates : (from mid April to mid Sept.) ⚓ – 21 ⊡. Per night from 38 to 113 € – Per week from 266 to 790 € – Reservation fee 15 €

⊡ local sani-station

Pleasant pitches with good-quality rental accommodation.

Surroundings : ⊡	
Leisure activities : ⅋ ⭢ ▧ (open air in season)	**G P S** Longitude : 0.27575
Facilities : ₺ ⌐ ⫿ ⅋ launderette	Latitude : 49.69884
Nearby : ※	

LOUVIERS

27400 – Michelin map **304** H6 – pop. 17 943 – alt. 15
▶ Paris 104 – Les Andelys 22 – Bernay 52 – Lisieux 75

⚲ Le Bel Air

✆ 02 32 40 10 77. www.camping-lebelair.fr – limited spaces for one-night stay

Address : route de la-Haye-Malherbe (3km west along the D 81)

Opening times : from mid March to mid Oct.

2.5 ha (92 pitches) flat, grassy

Tariff : ✦ 5.70 € ⇔ 回 6.90 € – (½) (10A) 4.90 €

Rental rates : (from mid March to mid Oct.) ⚓ – 1 ⊡ – 3 ⌂. Per night from 70 to 80 € – Per week from 472 to 582 €

⊡ 2 回 24 €

The site is set among trees with plenty of shade.

Surroundings : ⊡ ⚲⚲	
Leisure activities : 🎱 ⭢ ⅃	**G P S** Longitude : 1.1332
Facilities : ⌐ ⫿ ⅋ launderette	Latitude : 49.2152
Nearby : ※ ▨	

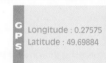
The prices listed were supplied by the campsite owners in 2015 (if prices were not available, those from the previous year are given). The fees should be regarded as basic charges and may fluctuate with inflation.

LUC-SUR-MER

14530 – Michelin map **303** J4 – pop. 3 133
▶ Paris 249 – Arromanches-les-Bains 23 – Bayeux 29 – Cabourg 28

⚲ Municipal la Capricieuse

✆ 02 31 97 34 43. www.campinglacapricieuse.com

Address : 2 rue Brummel (to the west, allée Brummel; 200m from the beach)

Opening times : from beginning April to end Sept.

4.6 ha (226 pitches) relatively flat, flat, grassy

Tariff : 23.65 € ✦✦ ⇔ 回 (½) (10A) – Extra per person 5.35 €

Rental rates : (from beginning April to end Oct.) 🚹 (1 mobile home) 🚲 – 18 🚐 – 10 🏠. Per week from 334 to 783€
🚽 local sani-station 5.20€

Surroundings : ⩽ ☐ ♀
Leisure activities : 🎣 ⤴ ✗ ≋ (beach), multi-sports ground
Facilities : ♿ ⊶ 🔥 ♨ ☷ ⊤ ᵞ launderette
Nearby : 🛒🚲🔥 🏊 🛶

GPS Longitude : -0.35781
Latitude : 49.3179

LYONS-LA-FORÊT

27480 – Michelin map **304** I5 – pop. 751 – alt. 88
▶ Paris 104 – Les Andelys 21 – Forges-les-Eaux 30 – Gisors 30

⚠ Municipal St-Paul

☎ 02 32 49 42 02. www.camping-saint-paul.fr – limited spaces for one-night stay

Address : 2 route Saint-Paul (to the northeast along the D 321, by the stadium; beside the Lieure river)

Opening times : from beginning April to end Oct.

3 ha (100 pitches) flat, grassy

Tariff : (2015 price) 20.50€ 🚹🚹 🚗 🚐 ▣ ⓗ (6A) – Extra per person 5.20€
Rental rates : (2015 price) (from beginning April to end Oct.) – 7 🏠. Per night from 60 to 85€ – Per week from 210 to 430€
🚽 local sani-station 3€ – 9 ▣ 16.50€ – 🚻 8€

Surroundings : ☐ ♀
Leisure activities : 🎣 ⤴ ⤳
Facilities : ♿ ⊶ 🔥 🍴 ☷ ☲ ⊤ ᵞ ⊞ 🔥
Nearby : ✗ 🔥 🏊 🐎 🐾

GPS Longitude : 1.47657
Latitude : 49.39869

MARCHAINVILLE

61290 – Michelin map **310** N3 – pop. 207 – alt. 235
▶ Paris 124 – L'Aigle 28 – Alençon 65 – Mortagne-au-Perche 28

⚠ Municipal les Fossés

☎ 02 33 73 65 80. mairiemarchainville@wanadoo.fr

Address : in northern part of the village, off the D 243

1 ha (17 pitches) relatively flat, flat, grassy

Surroundings : 🌿 ☐
Leisure activities : ✗
Facilities : ♿ ⤳

GPS Longitude : 0.8135
Latitude : 48.5861

We have selected the best campsites in France with our usual care, listing those with the best facilities in the most pleasant surroundings.

MARTIGNY

76880 – Michelin map **304** G2 – pop. 481 – alt. 24
▶ Paris 196 – Dieppe 10 – Fontaine-le-Dun 29 – Rouen 64

⚠ Les Deux Rivières

☎ 02 35 85 60 82. www.camping-2-rivieres.com – limited spaces for one-night stay

Address : off the D 154 (south of Arques-la-Bataille, off the rte de Dieppe)

Opening times : from end March to mid Oct.

3 ha (110 pitches) flat, grassy

Tariff : 18.50€ 🚹 🚹 🚗 ▣ ⓗ (10A) – Extra per person 4.20€

Rental rates : (from end March to mid Oct.) – 6 🚐. Per night from 85€ – Per week from 368 to 609€
In a pleasant location beside a river and lakes.

Surroundings : ⩽ extensive lakeland and the Château d'Arques ♀
Leisure activities : 🎣 ⤴ ⤳
Facilities : ♿ ⊶ 🔥 ᵞ launderette
Nearby : 🖾 🛶

GPS Longitude : 1.14417
Latitude : 49.87059

MARTRAGNY

14740 – Michelin map **303** I4 – pop. 367 – alt. 70
▶ Paris 257 – Bayeux 11 – Caen 23 – St-Lô 47

⚠⚠⚠ Les Castels Le Château de Martragny

☎ 02 31 80 21 40. www.chateau-martragny.com

Address : 52 Voie Communale Hameau de St-Léger (on the D 613, off the N 13 E 46, access via the village centre)

Opening times : from end May to end Aug.

13 ha/4 for camping (160 pitches) flat, grassy

Tariff : 🚹 9.50€ 🚐 ▣ 16.50€ – ⓗ (16A) 5€ – Reservation fee 10€
Rental rates : (from end May to end Aug.) – 5 🛏 – 4 tent lodges – 2 gîtes. Per week from 480 to 550€ – Reservation fee 10€
🚽 local sani-station – 4 ▣ 16.50€

B&B accommodation available in an 18th-century château.

Surroundings : 🌿 ♀♀
Leisure activities : 🍷 🎣 ⤴ ✗ ☲ ⤳
Facilities : ♿ ⊶ 🆒 ☷ ᵞ launderette ⊞ ⤳
Nearby : 🐾

GPS Longitude : -0.60532
Latitude : 49.24406

Some campsites benefit from proximity to a municipal leisure centre.

MAUPERTUS-SUR-MER

50330 – Michelin map **303** D2 – pop. 256 – alt. 119
▶ Paris 359 – Barfleur 21 – Cherbourg 13 – St-Lô 80

⚠⚠⚠ Les Castels l'Anse du Brick 🚹

l'Anse du Brick

☎ 02 33 54 33 57. www.anse-du-brick.com

Address : 18 Anse du Brick (to the northwest along the D 116. 200m from the beach, direct access via a walkway)

Opening times : from beginning April to mid Sept.

17 ha/7 for camping (189 pitches) very uneven, terraced, flat, grassy, stony, wood

Tariff : 44€ 🚹🚹 🚗 ▣ ⓗ (10A) – Extra per person 8.70€ – Reservation fee 8€
Rental rates : (from beginning April to mid Sept.) – 39 🚐 – 6 🏠 – 3 gîtes. Per night from 110€ – Per week from 406 to 910€ – Reservation fee 8€
🚽 local sani-station 8€

In a pleasantly leafy setting with plenty of shade, on an un-spoilt site.

Surroundings : 🌿 ⩽ ☐ ♀♀
Leisure activities : 🍷 🎣 🌐 ⛰ ⤴ 🚲 ✗ 🖾 🏊 ⤳
Facilities : ♿ ⊶ 🔥 ᵞ launderette ⤳
Nearby : ✗ 🖾 watersports centre

GPS Longitude : -1.49
Latitude : 49.66722

MERVILLE-FRANCEVILLE-PLAGE

14810 – Michelin map **303** K4 – pop. 1 991 – alt. 2
▶ Paris 225 – Arromanches-les-Bains 42 – Cabourg 7 – Caen 20

⚐ Les Peupliers

𝒫 02 31 24 05 07. www.camping-peupliers.com

Address : allée des Pins (2.5km east, a right turn off the rte de Cabourg; near Le Hôme)

Opening times : from beginning April to end Oct.

3.6 ha (164 pitches) flat, grassy

Tariff : (2015 price) 31.20€ ✦ ✦ 🚗 ▣ 🗲 (10A) –
Extra per person 8.10€

Rental rates : (from beginning April to end Oct.) – 1 'gypsy' caravan – 44 🛏 – 10 🏠. Per night from 92 to 160€ – Per week from 320 to 985€

🚿 local sani-station

Leisure activities : 🍸 🖼 🏓 🚣 ⛱
Facilities : ♿ ⚷ ▣ 🏛 🛁 ⚏ launderette
Nearby : 🎿 🏕 🛶 🐴 🎣

GPS	Longitude : -0.17011
	Latitude : 49.2829

⚐ Seasonova Le Point du Jour

𝒫 02 31 24 23 34. www.vacances-seasonova.com

Address : route de Cabourg (take the eastern exit along the D 514)

2.7 ha (140 pitches)
Rentals : 32 🛏.
🚿 local sani-station – 7 ▣

In an attractive location close to the beach.

Surroundings : 🏞 ⛰
Leisure activities : ✗ 🖼 🛁 jacuzzi 🚣
🖼 (open air in season)
Facilities : ♿ ⚷ 🏛 🛁 ⚏ launderette
Nearby : 🎿 🏕 🐴

GPS	Longitude : -0.19392
	Latitude : 49.2833

For more information on visiting particular towns or regions, consult the relevant regional MICHELIN Green Guide. We also recommend you use the appropriate Michelin regional map to locate your selected campsite, to calculate distances and to work out the best route.

MOYAUX

14590 – Michelin map **303** O4 – pop. 1 356 – alt. 160
▶ Paris 173 – Caen 64 – Deauville 31 – Lisieux 13

⚐ Le Colombier

𝒫 02 31 63 63 08. www.camping-lecolombier.com

Address : Le Val, 3km northeast along the D 143, follow the signs for Lieurey

Opening times : from beginning May to mid Sept.

15 ha/6 for camping (180 pitches) flat, grassy

Tariff : 38.70€ ✦ ✦ 🚗 ▣ 🗲 (12A) – Extra per person 8€
Rentals : (from beginning May to mid Sept.) – 2 gîtes.

The swimming pool is within the château's formal garden.

Surroundings : 🏞 ⚘
Leisure activities : 🍸 ✗ 🖼 🛁 🚣 🚴 🎿 🏕
⛱ library
Facilities : ♿ ⚷ 🛁 ⚏ launderette 🏪 🚰

GPS	Longitude : 0.3897
	Latitude : 49.2097

OMONVILLE-LA-ROGUE

50440 – Michelin map **303** A1 – pop. 534 – alt. 25
▶ Paris 377 – Caen 144 – St-Lô 99 – Cherbourg 24

⚐ Municipal du Hable

𝒫 02 33 52 86 15. www.omonvillelarogue.fr –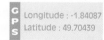

Address : 4 route de la Hague, in the village

Opening times : from beginning April to end Sept.

1 ha (60 pitches) flat, grassy, fine gravel

Tariff : (2015 price) ✦ 2.79€ 🚗 2.20€ ▣ 2.20€ – 🗲 (10A) 5.59€

Rental rates : (2015 price) permanent – 5 🏠. Per week from 260 to 357€

🚿 local sani-station 3.55€

Surroundings : 🐚
Facilities : ⚏ launderette
Nearby : 🎿 🎯 ⚓

GPS	Longitude : -1.84087
	Latitude : 49.70439

ORBEC

14290 – Michelin map **303** O5 – pop. 2 381 – alt. 110
▶ Paris 173 – L'Aigle 38 – Alençon 80 – Argentan 53

⚐ Les Capucins

𝒫 09 62 57 96 00. camping.sivom@orange.fr

Address : 13 avenue du Bois (located 1.5km northeast along the D 4, follow the signs for Bernay and take road to the left, by the stadium)

Opening times : from mid May to beginning Sept.

0.9 ha (35 pitches) flat, grassy

Tariff : (2015 price) ✦ 2.50€ 🚗 2€ ▣ 2€ – 🗲 (3A) 3€
🚿 20 ▣ 12€

In a green setting, a very well-kept site.

Surroundings : ⚘
Leisure activities : 🖼 🚣
Facilities : ⚷ 🗑 🛁 ⚏ launderette
Nearby : 🎿 🖼 🐴

GPS	Longitude : 0.40875
	Latitude : 49.02982

Using the traditional Michelin classification method, the guide provides you with an easy, speedy reference for assessing the category of each site: 1 to 5 tents (see page 10).

LES PIEUX

50340 – Michelin map **303** B2 – pop. 3 588 – alt. 104
▶ Paris 366 – Barneville-Carteret 18 – Cherbourg 22 – St-Lô 48

⚐ Le Grand Large

𝒫 02 33 52 40 75. www.legrandlarge.com

Address : 11 route du Grand Large (3km southwest along the D 117 and turn right onto the D 517, then continue 1km along the road to the left)

3.7 ha (236 pitches) flat, relatively flat, grassy, sandy
Rentals : 50 🛏.

In an attractive location among the dunes, near the Plage de Sciottot (beach).

Surroundings : 🐚 🏖 🏞 ⛰
Leisure activities : 🍸 🖼 🛁 jacuzzi 🚣 🎿
🖼 ⚏ paddling pool
Facilities : ♿ ⚷ 🏛 🛁 ⚏ launderette

GPS	Longitude : -1.8425
	Latitude : 49.49361

PONT-AUDEMER

27500 – Michelin map **304** D5 – pop. 8 599 – alt. 15
▶ Paris 165 – Rouen 58 – Évreux 91 – Le Havre 44

⛺ Flower Risle-Seine - Les Étangs

📞 02 32 42 46 65. http://www.camping-risle-seine.com

Address : 19 route des Étangs at Toutainville (2.5km east, turn left under the motorway bridge, near the water sports centre)

Opening times : from beginning April to end Oct.

2 ha (71 pitches) flat, grassy

Tariff : 22 € ✚✚ 🚗 🔲 (i) (10A) – Extra per person 4.20 € – Reservation fee 7 €
Rental rates : (from beginning April to end Dec.) & (1 mobile home) – 6 🚐 – 10 🏠 – 2 canvas bungalows. Per night from 52 to 78 € – Per week from 260 to 658 € – Reservation fee 15 €

A small chalet village on stilts overlooking the lake

Surroundings : ⌑ 🌳🌳
Leisure activities : 🏛 🚴‍♂️ 🚲
Facilities : & 🅾 🚿 🧺 launderette
Nearby : 🏊 ⛳ golf practice

Longitude : 0.48739
Latitude : 49.3666

PONT-FARCY

14380 – Michelin map **303** F6 – pop. 527 – alt. 72
▶ Paris 296 – Caen 63 – St-Lô 30 – Villedieu-les-Poêles 22

⛺ Municipal

📞 02 31 68 86 48. www.pont.farcy.fr

Address : route de Tessy (take the northern exit along the D 21, follow the signs for Tessy-sur-Vire)

Opening times : from beginning April to end Sept.

1.5 ha (60 pitches) flat, grassy

Tariff : (2015 price) 14.50 € ✚✚ 🚗 🔲 (i) (10A) –
Extra per person 2.50 €
Rental rates : (2015 price) (from beginning April to end Sept.) – 2 🚐. Per night from 45 € – Per week from 250 €

🚐 local sani-station

Situated beside the Vire river.

Leisure activities : 🏛 🚴‍♂️ 🎣
Facilities : & 🏕

Longitude : -1.0349
Latitude : 48.93899

The Michelin classification (⛰⛰⛰ … ⛺) is totally independent of the official star classification system awarded by the local prefecture or other official organisation.

PONTORSON

50170 – Michelin map **303** C8 – pop. 4 080 – alt. 15
▶ Paris 359 – Avranches 23 – Dinan 50 – Fougères 39

⛰⛰⛰ Haliotis ♣♣

📞 02 33 68 11 59. www.camping-haliotis-mont-saint-michel.com

Address : chemin des Soupirs (situated to the northwest along the D 19, follow the signs for Dol-de-Bretagne; near the Couesnon river)

Opening times : from beginning April to mid Nov.

8 ha/3.5 for camping (170 pitches) flat, grassy

Tariff : (2015 price) 20.50 € ✚✚ 🚗 🔲 (i) (16A) – Extra per person 6 € – Reservation fee 4 €

Rental rates : (from beginning April to mid Nov.) – 37 🚐 – 1 🏠 – 6 canvas bungalows. Per night from 35 to 110 € – Per week from 287 to 770 € – Reservation fee 4 €

🚐 local sani-station 4.50 € – 🚐 (i)20.50 €

Surroundings : ⌑ 🌳
Leisure activities : 🍴 🏛 🎯 daytime 🚶‍♂️ 🎣 jacuzzi 🏋️ 🚲 🎱 🏊 fitness trail, multi-sports ground
Facilities : 🅾 🔲 (cc) 🚿 – 12 private sanitary facilities (🚿 🚽 wc) 🏕 🧺 launderette
Nearby : 🏊 🎠 🎣 🐴

Longitude : -1.5145
Latitude : 48.55798

PORT-EN-BESSIN

14520 – Michelin map **303** H3 – pop. 2 141 – alt. 10
▶ Paris 277 – Caen 43 – Hérouville-St-Clair 45 – St-Lô 47

⛰⛰⛰ Port'Land ♣♣

📞 02 31 51 07 06. www.camping-portland.com

Address : chemin du Castel

Opening times : from beginning April to end Oct.

8.5 ha (256 pitches) flat, grassy

Tariff : (2015 price) 47 € ✚✚ 🚗 🔲 (i) (16A) – Extra per person 10 €
Rental rates : (2015 price) (from beginning April to end Oct.) – 99 🚐. Per night from 70 to 190 € – Per week from 490 to 1,330 €

🚐 Flot Bleu sani-station 5 € – 25 🔲 47 €

Pretty flowers and shrubs are dotted around several lakes.

Surroundings : 🎣 ⌑
Leisure activities : 🍴 🍴 🏛 🎯 🚶‍♂️ 🏋️ 🎱 🏊 🎣 fitness trail, multi-sports ground
Facilities : 🅾 🅾 🏕 🧺 launderette 🏊
Nearby : 🍴 ⛳

Longitude : -0.77044
Latitude : 49.34716

There are several different types of sani-station ('borne' in French) – sanitation points providing fresh water and disposal points for grey water. See page 12 for further details.

QUIBERVILLE

76860 – Michelin map **304** F2 – pop. 535 – alt. 50
▶ Paris 199 – Dieppe 18 – Fécamp 50 – Rouen 67

⛺ Municipal de la Plage

📞 02 35 83 01 04. www.campingplagequiberville.fr – limited spaces for one-night stay

Address : 123 rue de la Saane (at Quiberville-Plage, access via the D 127, follow the signs for Ouville-la-Rivière)

Opening times : from beginning April to end Oct.

2.5 ha (202 pitches) flat, grassy

Tariff : (2015 price) ✚ 6 € 🚗 🔲 11.45 € – (i) (10A) 5.50 €

🚐 local sani-station 3.90 € – 8 🔲 6 €

Situated 100m from the sea, on the other side of the road.

Surroundings : 🎣 ⌑
Leisure activities : 🏛 🚴‍♂️
Facilities : & 🅾 🚿 🧺 launderette
Nearby : 🍴 🍴 🎠 🎱 ⛳

Longitude : 0.92878
Latitude : 49.90507

RADON

61250 – Michelin map **310** J3 – pop. 1 042 – alt. 175
▶ Paris 200 – Caen 106 – Alençon 11 – Le Mans 67

⛰ Ferme des Noyers

📞 02 33 28 75 02. www.ecouves.net

Address : Les Noyers (off the D26)

Opening times : from beginning April to end Oct.

2 ha (43 pitches) flat, grassy

Tariff : 🚶 3.30€ 🚗 📧 6€ – 🔌 (16A) 3.80€

Rental rates : permanent – 1 'gypsy' caravan – 3 🏠 – 2 📐 – 1 apartment – 1 tent lodge – 1 gîte. Per night from 12 to 40€ – Per week from 170 to 390€

🚐 local sani-station 3€ – 6 📧 6€ – 🚌 🔌15.20€

Surroundings : 🌿
Leisure activities : 🎣 🏇 🪁
Facilities : 🚿 ⛽ 🛒 📶 🍴 🔥
Nearby : 🍴 🚣 (pond)

GPS Longitude : 0.0684
Latitude : 48.4957

RAVENOVILLE

50480 – Michelin map **303** E3 – pop. 261 – alt. 6
▶ Paris 328 – Barfleur 27 – Carentan 21 – Cherbourg 40

⛰ Le Cormoran ⚤

📞 02 33 41 33 94. www.lecormoran.com – limited spaces for one-night stay

Address : 2 rue du Cormoran (3.5km northeast along the D 421, follow the signs for Utah Beach)

Opening times : from beginning April to end Sept.

8 ha (256 pitches) flat, grassy, sandy

Tariff : 28€ 🚶🚶 🚗 📧 🔌 (10A) – Extra per person 5.50€ – Reservation fee 10€

Rental rates : (from beginning April to end Sept.) 🅿 – 1 'gypsy' caravan – 49 🏠. Per week from 301 to 1,092€ – Reservation fee 10€

🚐 local sani-station 5€ – 24 📧 12€ – 🚌 🔌17€

Lovely flowers and shrubs decorate this site near Utah beach.

Surroundings : 🏞
Leisure activities : 🍴 🏠 🎣 🏇 🏊 jacuzzi 🏇 🚲 🎯 🔲 🏊 farm or petting farm, radio controlled boats, multi-sports ground
Facilities : 🚿 ⛽ 📶 🔥 🍴 launderette 🧺 🚿
Nearby : 🏇

GPS Longitude : -1.23527
Latitude : 49.46658

The guide covers all 22 regions of France – see the map and list of regions on pages 4–5.

LE ROZEL

50340 – Michelin map **303** B3 – pop. 281 – alt. 21
▶ Paris 369 – Caen 135 – Cherbourg 26 – Rennes 197

⛰ Le Ranch

📞 02 33 10 07 10. www.camping-leranch.com

Address : at La Mielle (situated 2km southwest along the D 117 and take the D 62 to the right)

Opening times : from beginning April to end Sept.

4 ha (130 pitches) undulating, terrace, flat, grassy, sandy

Tariff : (2015 price) 39.50€ 🚶🚶 🚗 📧 🔌 (10A) – Extra per person 8.50€ – Reservation fee 5€

Rental rates : (2015 price) (from beginning April to end Sept.) – 21 🏠. Per week from 380 to 1,150€
Situated close to the beach.

Surroundings : 🏞 ⛰
Leisure activities : 🍴 🍽 🏠 🎣 🏊 🏇 🔲 🏊 🎯
Facilities : 🚿 ⛽ (July–Aug.) 📶 🔥 🚿 🍴 launderette
Nearby : 🏇 🚣 sand yachting

GPS Longitude : -1.84199
Latitude : 49.48013

ST-ARNOULT

14800 – Michelin map **303** M3 – pop. 1 193 – alt. 4
▶ Paris 198 – Caen 43 – Le Havre 41 – Rouen 90

⛰ La Vallée de Deauville ⚤

📞 02 31 88 58 17. www.camping-deauville.com – limited spaces for one-night stay

Address : avenue de la Vallée (located 1km south along the D 27, follow the signs for Varaville and take the D 275 following signs for Beaumont-en-Auge to the left; beside a stream and near a small lake)

Opening times : from beginning April to end Oct.

10 ha (411 pitches) flat, grassy

Tariff : (2015 price) 🚶 9.50€ 🚗 📧 12.50€ – 🔌 (10A) 4.20€ – Reservation fee 23€

Rental rates : permanent – 89 🏠. Per night from 98 to 120€ – Per week from 325 to 850€ – Reservation fee 23€

🚐 Eurorelais sani-station 10€

The site is laid out beside a pleasant lake.

Surroundings : 🏞 🌿
Leisure activities : 🍴 🏠 🎣 🏇 🏊 hammam, jacuzzi 🏇 🚲 🎯 🔲 🏊 🎣 multi-sports ground
Facilities : 🚿 📶 🔥 🍴 launderette 🧺 🚿
Nearby : 🛒 🍴 🎣 🏇 🚣 🏇

GPS Longitude : 0.0862
Latitude : 49.3287

The pitches of many campsites are marked out with low hedges of attractive bushes and shrubs.

ST-AUBIN-SUR-MER

14750 – Michelin map **303** J4 – pop. 2 048
▶ Paris 252 – Arromanches-les-Bains 19 – Bayeux 29 – Cabourg 32

⛰ Yelloh! Village Sandaya La Côte de Nacre ⚤

📞 02 31 97 14 45. http://www.sandaya.fr/web/FR/Campings/France/Normandie-1/La-Cote-de-Nacre/Apercu-1.htm – limited spaces for one-night stay

Address : 17 rue du Général Moulton (south of the town along the D 7b)

Opening times : from end March to mid Sept.

10 ha (350 pitches) flat, grassy

Tariff : 49€ 🚶🚶 🚗 📧 🔌 (10A) – Extra per person 9€

Rental rates : (from end March to mid Sept.) – 350 🏠. Per night from 60 to 199€ – Per week from 420 to 1,393€

🚐 local sani-station ,50€

There's a partially covered water park.

Leisure activities : 🍴 🏠 🎣 🏇 🏊 hammam, jacuzzi 🏇 🚲 🎯 🔲 🏊 multi-sports ground, spa centre
Facilities : 🚿 ⛽ 📶 🔥 🍴 launderette 🧺 🚿
Nearby : 🎯

GPS Longitude : -0.3946
Latitude : 49.3324

ST-AUBIN-SUR-MER

76740 – Michelin map **304** F2 – pop. 267 – alt. 15
▶ Paris 191 – Dieppe 21 – Fécamp 46 – Rouen 59

⛰ Municipal le Mesnil

📞 02 35 83 02 83. www.campinglemesnil.com

Address : route de Sotteville (situated 2km west along the D 68, follow the signs for Veules-les-Roses)

Opening times : from beginning April to end Oct.

2.2 ha (117 pitches) terraced, flat, grassy

Tariff : (2015 price) 26.80€ ✿✿ 🚐 🔲 [𝄞] (10A) –
Extra per person 5.55€

Rental rates : (2015 price) (from beginning April to end Oct.) ⌇ –
1 🏠. Per night from 44 to 74€ – Per week from 260 to 450€
🚰 local sani-station 5€ – 5 🔲 26.80€

The site is based around a former Norman farmhouse and its outbuildings with thatched roofs. Numerous old owner-occupier mobile homes.

Surroundings : ⌇ 🖵
Leisure activities : ✗ 🎦 ⛵
Facilities : ♿ ⚷ 🚿 ☕ ♨ launderette ≈

ST-ÉVROULT-NOTRE-DAME-DU-BOIS

61550 – Michelin map **310** L2 – pop. 452 – alt. 355
▶ Paris 153 – L'Aigle 14 – Alençon 56 – Argentan 42

⛰ Municipal des Saints-Pères

📞 06 78 33 04 94. catherine-motte@orange.fr

Address : in the southeast part of the village

Opening times : from beginning April to end Sept.

0.6 ha (27 pitches) terrace, flat, grassy, fine gravel, wood

Tariff : ✿ 3€ 🚐 1.50€ 🔲 4€ – [𝄞] (10A) 2.50€

Rental rates : permanent – 1 🏠. Per night from 30 to 40€ –
Per week from 250 to 350€
🚰 AireService sani-station 2€ – 3 🔲 6€ – 🚐 12€

Situated in a pleasant location, beside a lake.

Surroundings : ♀
Leisure activities : ⛵ ♨ 🏊 pedalos
Facilities : ♿ ⚷ 🏷 ♨ 🛒
Nearby : ≈ ✗ 🐎

ST-GEORGES-DU-VIÈVRE

27450 – Michelin map **304** D6 – pop. 720 – alt. 138
▶ Paris 161 – Bernay 21 – Évreux 54 – Lisieux 36

⛰ Municipal du Vièvre

📞 02 32 42 76 79. www.camping-eure-normandie.fr

Address : route de Noards (take the southwestern exit along the D 38)

Opening times : from beginning April to end Sept.

1.1 ha (50 pitches) flat, grassy

Tariff : (2015 price) ✿ 2.30€ 🚐 1.30€ 🔲 2.20€ – [𝄞] (5A) 2.20€
Rental rates : (2015 price) (from beginning April to end Sept.) –
2 🏠. Per week from 200 to 300€

Surroundings : ⌇ ⌇
Leisure activities : 🚲
Facilities : ♿ 🏷 🚲 ♨
Nearby : ✗ 🏊

ST-GERMAIN-SUR-AY

50430 – Michelin map **303** C4 – pop. 896 – alt. 5
▶ Paris 345 – Barneville-Carteret 26 – Carentan 35 – Coutances 27

🏔 Aux Grands Espaces

📞 02 33 07 10 14. www.auxgrandsespaces.com – limited spaces for one-night stay

Address : 6 rue du Camping (4km west along the D 306; at St-Germain-Plage)

Opening times : from mid April to mid Oct.

16 ha (580 pitches) very uneven, sandy, flat, grassy

Tariff : (2015 price) ✿ 5.50€ 🚐 🔲 6.90€ – [𝄞] (10A) 4.50€
Rental rates : (2015 price) (from mid April to mid Oct.) ⌇ –
20 🏠. Per week from 310 to 730€

Surroundings : ⌇ ⌇
Leisure activities : 🍽 🎦 ⛵ 🎾 🏓 🏊
Facilities : ⊶🗝 (July–Aug.) ♨ ♨ launderette ≋
Nearby : 🐎 sand yachting

ST-HILAIRE-DU-HARCOUËT

50600 – Michelin map **303** F8 – pop. 4 036 – alt. 70
▶ Paris 339 – Alençon 100 – Avranches 27 – Caen 102

⛰ Municipal de la Sélune

📞 02 33 49 43 74. www.st-hilaire.fr

Address : rue de Marly (700m northwest along the N 176, follow the signs for Avranches and take a right turn, near the river)

Opening times : from beginning April to end Sept.

1.9 ha (70 pitches) flat, grassy

Tariff : (2015 price) ✿ 2.35€ 🚐 1€ – [𝄞] (16A) 1.95€
Rental rates : (2015 price) (from beginning April to end Sept.) ⌇ –
2 'gypsy' caravans. Per night from 63 to 88€ – Per week from 251 to 451€
🚰 Eurorelais sani-station 3€ – 6 🔲 9.65€ – 🚐 9.65€

Leisure activities : 🎦 ⛵
Facilities : ♿ ⊶🗝 ♨ launderette
Nearby : ✗ 🎾 🎣 🏊 🏄

ST-JEAN-DE-LA-RIVIÈRE

50270 – Michelin map **303** B3 – pop. 355 – alt. 20
▶ Paris 351 – Caen 119 – St-Lô 63 – Cherbourg 40

🏔 Yelloh! Village Les Vikings

📞 02 33 53 84 13. www.camping-lesvikings.com

Address : 4 rue des Vikings (along the D 166 and take the road to the right)

Opening times : from beginning April to mid Sept.

6 ha (250 pitches) flat, grassy, sandy

Tariff : 48€ ✿✿ 🚐 🔲 [𝄞] (10A) – Extra per person 8€
Rental rates : (from beginning April to mid Sept.) ♿ (1 mobile home) – 87 🏠 – 2 tent lodges. Per night from 30 to 195€ –
Per week from 210 to 1,365€
🚰 local sani-station – 🔲 [𝄞] 43.20€

The entrance is decorated with flowers and small palm trees.

Surroundings : ⌇ ⌇
Leisure activities : 🍽 ✗ 🎦 🎲 ⛵ 🎰 🏊 🏄
multi-sports ground, entertainment room
Facilities : ♿ ⊶🗝 ♨ launderette ≈
Nearby : 🎾 ◊ 🐎 sand yachting

Longitude : 0.85204
Latitude : 49.88353

Longitude : 0.4663
Latitude : 48.7888

Longitude : 0.58064
Latitude : 49.2427

Longitude : -1.64089
Latitude : 49.23654

Longitude : -1.09765
Latitude : 48.58127

Longitude : -1.75293
Latitude : 49.36335

ST-MARTIN-EN-CAMPAGNE

76370 – Michelin map **304** H2 – pop. 1 319 – alt. 118
▶ Paris 209 – Dieppe 13 – Rouen 78 – Le Tréport 18

⚠️ Municipal les Goélands

🔗 02 35 83 82 90. www.camping-les-goelands.fr – limited spaces for one-night stay

Address : rue des Grèbes (situated 2km to the northwest, at St-Martin-Plage)

Opening times : from mid March to end Oct.

3 ha (140 pitches) terraced, flat and relatively flat, grassy

Tariff : (2015 price) 18.70€ ♥♥ ⇔ 🔲 🔌 (16A) –
Extra per person 4.20€
Rental rates : (2015 price) (from mid March to end Oct.) – 12 🚐.
Per week from 400 to 630€
🚮 5 🔲 14.50€

There's a view of the sea from some pitches and an excellent restaurant on site.

Surroundings : ⇐ 🗺️
Leisure activities : 🍽️ ✗ 🏠 🎱 🎯 multi-sports ground
Facilities : ⚙️ ⚡ 🏛️ 🛁 🚿 🚽 launderette 🎢 🔧

GPS
Longitude : 1.20425
Latitude : 49.96632

To visit a town or region, use the MICHELIN Green Guides.

ST-PAIR-SUR-MER

50380 – Michelin map **303** C7 – pop. 3 788 – alt. 30
▶ Paris 342 – Avranches 24 – Granville 4 – Villedieu-les-Poêles 29

⚠️ Angomesnil

🔗 02 33 61 85 87. www.angomesnil.com

Address : 891 route du Guigeois (head 4.9km southeast along the D 21, follow the signs for St-Michel-des-Loups and turn left onto D 154, following signs for St-Aubin-des-Préaux)

1.2 ha (45 pitches) flat, grassy
🚮 local sani-station

Surroundings : 🐑 🎯
Leisure activities : 🏠 🎯
Facilities : ⚙️ ⚡ 🛁

Nearby : 🎱 🎿 🏞️ (open air in season) 🚣 🐎 sports trail

GPS
Longitude : -1.5261
Latitude : 48.79065

ST-SAUVEUR-LE-VICOMTE

50390 – Michelin map **303** C3 – pop. 2 053 – alt. 30
▶ Paris 336 – Barneville-Carteret 20 – Cherbourg 37 – St-Lô 56

⚠️ Municipal du Vieux Château

🔗 02 33 41 72 04. www.saintsauveurlevicomte.stationverte.com

Address : avenue Division Leclerc (in the town; beside the Douve river)

Opening times : from mid June to mid Sept.

1 ha (57 pitches) flat, grassy

Tariff : (2015 price) 12€ ♥♥ ⇔ 🔲 🔌 (6A) – Extra per person 3€
🚮 local sani-station – 4 🔲
Situated in the grounds of the medieval château.

Leisure activities : 🏠
Facilities : ⚙️ 🎱 launderette
Nearby : 🎯 🎱

GPS
Longitude : -1.52779
Latitude : 49.38748

ST-SYMPHORIEN-LE-VALOIS

50250 – Michelin map **303** C4 – pop. 822 – alt. 35
▶ Paris 335 – Barneville-Carteret 19 – Carentan 25 – Cherbourg 47

⚠️ Club Airotel L'Étang des Haizes 👥

🔗 02 33 46 01 16. www.campingetangdeshaizes.com

Address : rue Cauticote (take the northern exit along the D 900, follow the signs for Valognes and turn left onto D 136 towards the village)

Opening times : from beginning April to beginning Oct.

4.5 ha (160 pitches) relatively flat, flat, grassy

Tariff : (2015 price) 37€ ♥♥ ⇔ 🔲 🔌 (10A) – Extra per person 8€
Rental rates : (2015 price) (from beginning April to beginning Oct.) ⚙️ (1 mobile home) 🎿 – 24 🚐 – 4 🏠 – 1 tipi – 2 tent lodges. Per night from 55 to 128€ – Per week from 327 to 896€
🚮 local sani-station
In a charming leafy setting beside a pretty lake.

Surroundings : 🗺️
Leisure activities : 🍽️ 🏠 🎱 🎯 🛷 🚲 🎣 🏊 🛶
Facilities : ⚙️ ⚡ 🛁 🚽 launderette

GPS
Longitude : -1.54482
Latitude : 49.29992

ST-VAAST-LA-HOUGUE

50550 – Michelin map **303** E2 – pop. 2 091 – alt. 4
▶ Paris 347 – Carentan 41 – Cherbourg 31 – St-Lô 68

⚠️ La Gallouette

🔗 02 33 54 20 57. www.lagallouette.com

Address : 10bis rue de la Gallouette (south of the town, 500m from the beach)

Opening times : from beginning April to end Sept.

2.3 ha (183 pitches) flat, grassy

Tariff : (2015 price) ♥ 6.80€ ⇔ 🔲 11.45€ – 🔌 (10A) 5€
Rental rates : (2015 price) (from beginning April to end Sept.) – 15 🚐 – 10 🏠. Per night from 73 to 110€ – Per week from 323 to 859€
🚮 local sani-station – 15 🔲 14.60€

Surroundings : 🗺️
Leisure activities : 🍽️ ✗ 🏠 🎱 🎯 🛷 multi-sports ground
Facilities : ⚙️ ⚡ 🛁 🚽 launderette
Nearby : 🎱 🚣 fitness trail

GPS
Longitude : -1.26873
Latitude : 49.5846

We value your opinion and welcome your feedback. Do email us at campingfrance@tp.michelin.com

---

ST-VALERY-EN-CAUX

76460 – Michelin map **304** E2 – pop. 4 463 – alt. 5
▶ Paris 190 – Bolbec 46 – Dieppe 35 – Fécamp 33

⚠️ Seasonova Etennemare

🔗 02 35 97 15 79. www.seasonova.com – limited spaces for one-night stay

Address : 21 rue du Hameau d'Etennemare (D68), south of St-valery

Opening times : from beginning April to beginning Nov.

4 ha (116 pitches) flat, grassy

Tariff : 26.50€ ♥♥ ⇔ 🔲 🔌 (10A) – Extra per person 4.50€ – Reservation fee 12€

Rental rates : permanent – 37 🏠 – 10 🏠. Per week from 345 to 750€ – Reservation fee 12€

Some owner-occupier mobile homes, with good-quality rental accommodation.

Surroundings : 🐾 🖵
Leisure activities : 🎱 🏊 (open air in season) 🏖
Facilities : 🔥 ⚷ 🗑 🏕 ☕ 🍴 launderette

GPS Longitude : 0.70378
Latitude : 49.85878

STE-MARIE-DU-MONT

50480 – Michelin map **303** E3 – pop. 761 – alt. 31
▶ Paris 318 – Barfleur 38 – Carentan 11 – Cherbourg 47

⚿ Flower Utah-Beach

☎ 02 33 71 53 69. www.camping-utahbeach.com – limited spaces for one-night stay

Address : La Madeleine (6km northeast along the D 913 and take D 421; 150m from the beach)

Opening times : permanent

5.5 ha (149 pitches) flat, relatively flat, grassy

Tariff : 30.50€ ✹ ✹ 🚗 🔟 🔌 (6A) – Extra per person 6€ – Reservation fee 20€

Rental rates : permanent – 8 🏠 – 10 🏠 – 2 tent lodges. Per night from 72 to 129€ – Per week from 196 to 903€ – Reservation fee 20€

🚻 local sani-station 12€ – 🔌 🔌16€

Surroundings : 🐾 🖵
Leisure activities : 🍴 🍽 🎱 ≋ jacuzzi 🏊 🎯 🎣 🏊 multi-sports ground, entertainment room
Facilities : 🔥 ⚷ 🗑 ☕ 🍴 launderette 🐕
Nearby : 🚲 sand yachting

GPS Longitude : -1.18028
Latitude : 49.42001

Routes nationales are main roads and their identifying numbers begin with N or RN. Routes départementales are generally quieter roads and begin with D or DN.

STE-MÈRE-ÉGLISE

50480 – Michelin map **303** E3 – pop. 1 643 – alt. 28
▶ Paris 321 – Bayeux 57 – Cherbourg 39 – St-Lô 42

⚿ Municipal

☎ 02 33 41 35 22. www.camping-sainte-mere.fr

Address : 6 rue Airborne (take the eastern exit along the D 17 and take a right turn; near the sports field)

Opening times : from beginning April to end Oct.

1.3 ha (70 pitches) flat, grassy

Tariff : (2015 price) ✹ 5€ 🚗 🔟 5€ – 🔌 (10A) 3€ – Reservation fee 9€

Rental rates : (2015 price) (from beginning April to end Oct.) – 3 🏠. Per night from 65 to 89€ – Per week from 350 to 590€ – Reservation fee 9€

🚻 AireService sani-station 1€ – 20 🔟 12€

Manufacture and sale on site of Sainte-Mere-Eglise craft beer.

Surroundings : 🐾
Leisure activities : 🎱 🏊 🎣 🚲 🎯 🏓 multi-sports ground
Facilities : ⚷ 🍴 launderette

GPS Longitude : -1.31018
Latitude : 49.41003

SURRAIN

14710 – Michelin map **303** G4 – pop. 159 – alt. 40
▶ Paris 278 – Cherbourg 83 – Rennes 187 – Rouen 167

⚿ La Roseraie d'Omaha

La Roseraie d'Omaha

☎ 02 31 21 17 71. www.camping-calvados-normandie.fr

Address : rue de l'église (take the southern exit along the D 208, follow the signs for Mandeville-en-Bessin)

Opening times : from mid March to end Sept.

3 ha (66 pitches) relatively flat, flat, grassy

Tariff : 20.10€ ✹ ✹ 🚗 🔟 🔌 (10A) – Extra per person 5.50€

Rental rates : permanent 🚐 – 20 🏠 – 10 🏠 – 1 gîte. Per night from 58 to 92€ – Per week from 299 to 760€

🚻 local sani-station – 🔌 🔌15€

Surroundings : 🖵 🌳
Leisure activities : 🍴 🎱 🚣 🚲 🎯 🏓 🏊 🏖
Facilities : 🔥 ⚷ 🏕 ☕ 🍴 launderette
Nearby : 🐴

GPS Longitude : -0.86443
Latitude : 49.32574

SURTAINVILLE

50270 – Michelin map **303** B3 – pop. 1 255 – alt. 12
▶ Paris 367 – Barneville-Carteret 12 – Cherbourg 29 – St-Lô 42

⚿ Municipal les Mielles

☎ 02 33 04 31 04. www.camping-municipal-normandie.com

Address : 80 route des Laguettes (head 1.5km west along the D 66 and follow the signs for the sea, 80m from the beach, direct access)

Opening times : permanent

25 ha (151 pitches) flat, grassy, sandy, fine gravel

Tariff : ✹ 3.90€ 🚗 🔟 3.90€ – 🔌 (4A) 3.60€ – Reservation fee 5€

Rental rates : permanent – 2 🏠. Per night from 65 – Per week from 240 to 407 – Reservation fee 5€

🚻 AireService sani-station 4.20€

Surroundings : 🐾 🖵
Leisure activities : 🎱 🚣
Facilities : 🔥 ⚷ 🗑 🏕 ☕ 🍴 launderette
Nearby : 🚣 sand yachting

GPS Longitude : -1.82881
Latitude : 49.46386

THURY-HARCOURT

14220 – Michelin map **303** J6 – pop. 1 968 – alt. 45
▶ Paris 257 – Caen 28 – Condé-sur-Noireau 20 – Falaise 27

⚿ Le Traspy

☎ 02 31 29 90 86. www.campingdutraspy.com

Address : rue du Pont Benoît (head east of the town along the bd du 30-Juin-1944 and take road to the left)

Opening times : from beginning April to mid Oct.

1.5 ha (78 pitches) terraced, flat, grassy

Tariff : (2015 price) ✹ 4.20€ 🚗 🔟 8.20€ – 🔌 (16A) 4.80€

Rental rates : (2015 price) (from beginning April to mid Oct.) – 6 🏠. Per night from 60 to 90€ – Per week from 400 to 600€

Beside the Traspy river and near a small lake.

Surroundings : 🖵 🌳
Leisure activities : 🍴 🎱 ≋ 🚣
Facilities : 🔥 ⚷ 🏕 ☕ 🍴 launderette 🏊 🐕
Nearby : 🚲 🎣 🏊 🏖 🎣 paragliding

GPS Longitude : -0.46913
Latitude : 48.98896

TOUFFREVILLE-SUR-EU

76910 – Michelin map **304** H2 – pop. 201 – alt. 45
▶ Paris 171 – Abbeville 46 – Amiens 101 – Blangy-sur-Nesle 35

⚠ Municipal Les Acacias

✆ 02 35 50 66 33. www.camping-acacias.fr – ℞

Address : at Les Prés du Thil (head 1km to the southeast along the D 226 and take D 454, following the signs for Guilmecourt)

Opening times : permanent

1 ha (50 pitches) flat, grassy

Tariff : (2015 price) ♣ 2.40€ ⇔ 1€ 🅴 2.70€ – 🔌 (10A) 5.50€

Near the old station buildings of Touffreville-Criel.

| Surroundings : 🐟 🚏 ♀ | | G | Longitude : 1.33537 |
| Facilities : ⅊ 📶 ⍦ | | P S | Latitude : 49.99531 |

TOUSSAINT

76400 – Michelin map **304** C3 – pop. 743 – alt. 105
▶ Paris 196 – Bolbec 24 – Fécamp 5 – Rouen 69

⚠ Municipal du Canada

✆ 02 35 29 78 34. www.commune-de-toussaint.fr – limited spaces for one-night stay

Address : rue de Rouen (500m northwest along the D 926, follow the signs for Fécamp and take road to the left)

Opening times : from mid March to mid Oct.

2.5 ha (100 pitches) flat, relatively flat, grassy

Tariff : 14.30€ ♣♣ ⇔ 🅴 🔌 (6A) – Extra per person 3.89€
Rental rates : (from mid March to mid Oct.) – 2 🛏 – 2 🏠. Per night from 36 to 64€ – Per week from 343 to 454€
🚐 Eurorelais sani-station 2.50€

Choose the pitches furthest from the road. Numerous old owner-occupier mobile homes.

Surroundings : 🚏 ♀		G	Longitude : 0.417
Facilities : ⅊ ⊶ 📶		P S	Latitude : 49.74008
Nearby : 🏊🏄 ✗			

This guide is not intended as a list of all the camping sites in France; its aim is to provide a selection of the best sites in each category.

LE TRÉPORT

76470 – Michelin map **304** I1 – pop. 5 416 – alt. 12
▶ Paris 180 – Abbeville 37 – Amiens 92 – Blangy-sur-Bresle 26

⛰ Municipal les Boucaniers

✆ 02 35 86 35 47. www.ville-le-treport.fr/camping

Address : rue Pierre Mendès-France (take the av. des Canadiens; near the stadium)

5.5 ha (243 pitches) flat, grassy

Rentals : ⅊ (1 chalet) – 50 🏠.
🚐 27 🅴
A pretty chalet village. Choose the pitches close to the entrance and furthest away from the nearby factory.

Surroundings : ♀		G	Longitude : 1.38882
Leisure activities : ♈ 🏛 🏄		P S	Latitude : 50.0577
Facilities : ⅊ ⊶ 📶 🛁 ⍦ launderette 🔧			
Nearby : ✗			

TRÉVIÈRES

14710 – Michelin map **303** G4 – pop. 938 – alt. 14
▶ Paris 283 – Bayeux 19 – Caen 49 – Carentan 31

⚠ Municipal Sous les Pommiers

✆ 02 31 92 89 24. www.ville-trevieres.fr

Address : rue du Pont de la Barre (take the northern exit along the D 30, follow the signs for Formigny; near a stream)

Opening times : from end March to end Sept.

1.2 ha (75 pitches) flat, grassy

Tariff : ♣ 3.50€ ⇔ 1.50€ 🅴 2.50€ – 🔌 (10A) 3.50€

Pitches in the shade of apple trees.

Surroundings : 🚏 ♀		G	Longitude : -0.90637
Leisure activities : 🏄		P S	Latitude : 49.3132
Facilities : ⅊ 🛁 🔧 ⍦			
Nearby : 🐎			

VEULES-LES-ROSES

76980 – Michelin map **304** E2 – pop. 561 – alt. 15
▶ Paris 188 – Dieppe 27 – Fontaine-le-Dun 8 – Rouen 57

⛰ Seasonova Les Mouettes

✆ 02 35 97 61 98. www.camping-lesmouettes-normandie.com

Address : avenue Jean-Moulin (take the eastern exit along the D 68, follow the signs for Sotteville-sur-Mer, 500m from the beach)

Opening times : from beginning April to end Oct.

3.6 ha (160 pitches) flat, grassy

Tariff : 28.30€ ♣♣ ⇔ 🅴 🔌 (6A) – Extra per person 5.60€ – Reservation fee 15€
Rental rates : (from beginning April to mid Oct.) 🏄 – 24 🛏 – 4 tent lodges. Per week from 195 to 860€ – Reservation fee 15€
🚐 16 🅴 10€

Attractive, marked-out pitches, 200m from the cliffs.

Surroundings : 🐟 🚏 ♀		G	Longitude : 0.80335
Leisure activities : 🏛 🎱 ⛱ jacuzzi 🏄 🚲 🎯		P S	Latitude : 49.87579
Facilities : ⅊ ⊶ 📶 🛁 ⍦ launderette			

LE VEY

14570 – Michelin map **303** J6 – pop. 87 – alt. 50
▶ Paris 269 – Caen 47 – Hérouville-St-Clair 46 – Flers 23

⛰ Les Rochers des Parcs

✆ 02 31 69 70 36. www.camping-normandie-clecy.fr

Address : at La Cour, south of the D133a, near the Orne river

Opening times : from end March to end Sept.

1.5 ha (90 pitches) relatively flat, flat, grassy

Tariff : (2015 price) ♣ 5.80€ ⇔ 2.95€ 🅴 6.50€ – 🔌 (10A) 3.90€ – Reservation fee 5€
Rental rates : (2015 price) (from end March to end Sept.) ⅊ – 11 🛏 – 6 canvas bungalows. Per night from 32 to 129€ – Per week from 280 to 578€ – Reservation fee 5€
🚐 local sani-station 2.50€ – 4 🅴 11€ – 🔋 11€

Surroundings : ♀ ⛰		G	Longitude : -0.47487
Leisure activities : 🏛 🏄 🚲 🐟 ✗		P S	Latitude : 48.91391
Facilities : ⅊ ⊶ 🆒 ⍦ launderette			
Nearby : ✗ 🐎 adventure park			

VILLEDIEU-LES-POÊLES

50800 – Michelin map **303** E6 – pop. 3 882 – alt. 105
▶ Paris 314 – Alençon 122 – Avranches 26 – Caen 82

⚲ Les Chevaliers

☎ 02 33 61 02 44. www.camping-deschevaliers.com

Opening times : from beginning April to end Sept.

1.4 ha (82 pitches) flat, grassy, fine gravel

Tariff : (2015 price) 27.90€ ♦♦ ⇔ 🗐 🗒 (6A) – Extra per person 5€

Rental rates : (2015 price) (from beginning April to end Sept.) –
21 . Per night from 46 to 109€ – Per week from 196 to 763€

⚲ Eurorelais sani-station

A pleasant, well-kept setting, beside the Sienne river.

Surroundings : ⚲ ⌂ ♀
Leisure activities : ✗ ⚲ ⚲ ♣ ✂ ⚲
multi-sports ground
Facilities : ⚲ ⟶ ♨ ⚲ launderette ⚲
Nearby : ⚲⚲

G P S Longitude : -1.21694
Latitude : 48.83639

VILLERS-SUR-MER

14640 – Michelin map **303** L4 – pop. 2 707 – alt. 10
▶ Paris 208 – Caen 35 – Deauville 8 – Le Havre 52

⚲ Bellevue

☎ 02 31 87 05 21. www.camping-bellevue.com – limited spaces for
one-night stay

Address : route de Dives (situated 2km southwest along the D 513.
follow the signs for Cabourg)

Opening times : from beginning April to beginning Oct.

5.5 ha (257 pitches) terraced, relatively flat, flat, grassy

Tariff : 31€ ♦♦ ⇔ 🗐 🗒 (10A) – Extra per person 8.50€ – Reservation
fee 10€

Rental rates : (from beginning April to mid Oct.) ⚲ – 40 ⌂.
Per week from 280 to 780€ – Reservation fee 10€

Situated overlooking the bay at Deauville.

Surroundings : ⚲ ⌂
Leisure activities : ♀ ⚲ ⚲nighttime ⚲
⚲ ⚲ ⚲
Facilities : ⚲ ⟶ ⚲ ⚲ ⚲ ⚲ launderette
Nearby : ⚲ ⚲ ✂ ⚲ ♨ ⚲ ⚲

G P S Longitude : -0.0195
Latitude : 49.3097

VIMOUTIERS

61120 – Michelin map **310** K1 – pop. 3 828 – alt. 95
▶ Paris 185 – L'Aigle 46 – Alençon 66 – Argentan 31

⚲ Municipal la Campière

☎ 02 33 39 18 86. www.mairie-vimoutiers.fr

Address : 14 boulevard Dentu (700m north, in the direction of
Lisieux, by the stadium; beside La Vie river)

Opening times : from beginning April to end Oct.

1 ha (40 pitches) flat, grassy

Tariff : (2015 price) 15.15€ ♦♦ ⇔ 🗐 🗒 (15A) –
Extra per person 3.55€

Rental rates : (2015 price) (from beginning April to end Oct.) –
4 . Per night from 59 to 64€ – Per week from 271 to 323€

*Norman-style buildings in a lush, green setting surrounded by
flowers.*

Surroundings : ⌂ ♀
Leisure activities : ⚲ ⚲ ✂
Facilities : ⚲ ⟶ ⚲⚲
Nearby : ⚲

G P S Longitude : 0.1966
Latitude : 48.9326

Key to rentals symbols:

12	*Number of mobile homes*	
20 ⌂	*Number of chalets*	
6 🛏	*Number of rooms to rent*	
Per night 30–50€	*Minimum/maximum rate per night*	
Per week 300–1,000€	*Minimum/maximum rate per week*	

B. Rieger / hemis.fr

The 'Garden of France' is renowned for its tranquil atmosphere, glorious châteaux, magnificent floral gardens and acres of orchards and vineyards. Enjoy a glass of light Loire wine accompanied by a plate of rillettes (pork pâté), *matelote d'anguilles* (eel stew) or a slice of goat's cheese, perfect partners in the gastronomic experience offered by the region. Continue downriver to Nantes, redolent today of the scent of spices first brought back from the New World. This is the home of the famous dry Muscadet wines. Further south, the Vendée region still echoes with the cries of 18th-century Royalists' before revolutionary fervour took hold. Explore the secrets of its salt marshes, relax in balmy seaside resorts or head for the spectacular attractions of the Puy du Fou amusement park. Simple country fare is the order of the day here, so make sure you sample a piping-hot plate of *chaudrée* (fish chowder) or a mouth-watering slice of fresh brioche.

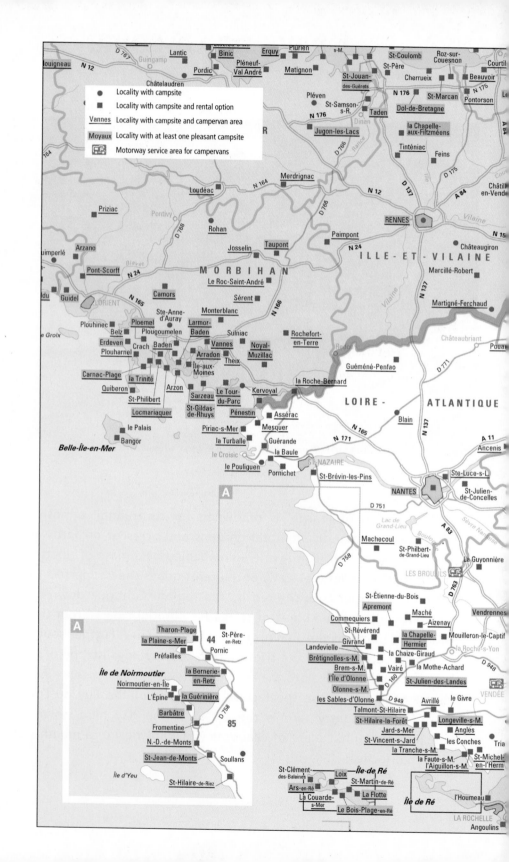

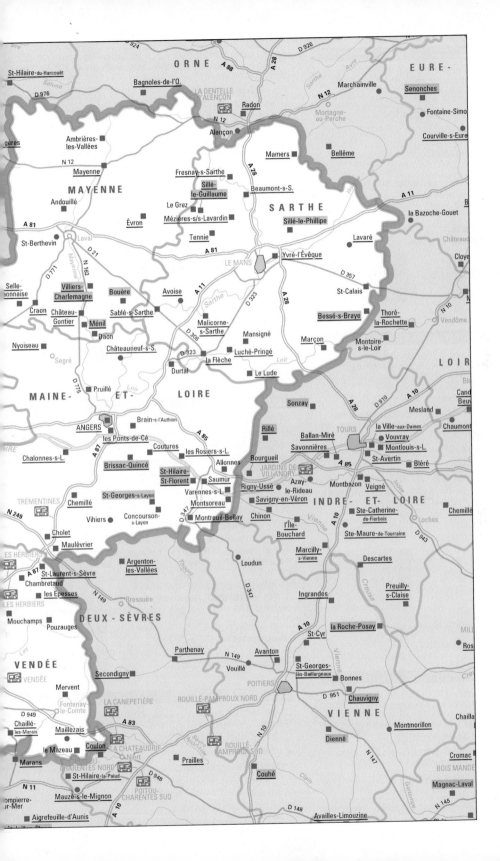

L'AIGUILLON-SUR-MER

85460 – Michelin map **316** I10 – pop. 2 310 – alt. 4
▶ Paris 458 – Luçon 20 – Niort 83 – La Rochelle 51

🏔 La Cléroca

𝒫 02 51 27 19 92. www.camping-la-cleroca.com ✘

Address : La Cleroca, 2.2km northwest along the D 44, follow the signs for Grues

Opening times : from beginning April to end Sept.

1.5 ha (66 pitches) flat, grassy

Tariff : 28€ ✸✸ 🚐 🅴 🔌 (10A) – Extra per person 5€
Rental rates : (from beginning April to end Sept.) ✘ – 1 yurt – 2 tent lodges – 1 gîte. Per night from 50€ – Per week from 180 to 460€

🚃 local sani-station 28€ – 🔋 9€
A lush, green setting and plenty of shade.

Surroundings : 🌳🌳
Leisure activities : 🏠 🛥 🚣 🏊
multi-sports ground
Facilities : 🚿 ⛽ 🔧 🍴 launderette

G P S Longitude : -1.31513
Latitude : 46.35003

AIZENAY

85190 – Michelin map **316** G7 – pop. 7 930 – alt. 62
▶ Paris 435 – Challans 26 – Nantes 60 – La Roche-sur-Yon 18

🏔 La Forêt

𝒫 02 51 34 78 12. www.camping-laforet.com

Address : 1 rue de la Clairière (located 1.5km southeast along the D 948, follow the signs for la Roche-sur-Yon and take road to the left, behind the commercial centre)

Opening times : from beginning April to end Sept.

2.5 ha (96 pitches) flat, grassy, wood

Tariff : (2015 price) 21.70€ ✸✸ 🚐 🅴 🔌 (6A) – Extra per person 3.40€
Rental rates : (2015 price) (from beginning April to end Sept.) – 14 🛖 – 1 🏠 – 2 canvas bungalows. Per night from 41 to 102€ – Per week from 322 to 767€

🚃 local sani-station 3€ – 🔋 11€
A pleasant site with plenty of shade.

Surroundings : 🌳🌳
Leisure activities : 🛥 🎣 🏊
Facilities : 🚿 ⛽ 🔧 🍴 launderette
Nearby : 🛒 🍴 ✗ 🚣 fitness trail

G P S Longitude : -1.58947
Latitude : 46.73427

This guide is updated regularly, so buy your new copy every year!

ALLONNES

49650 – Michelin map **317** J5 – pop. 2 979 – alt. 28
▶ Paris 292 – Angers 64 – Azay-le-Rideau 43 – Chinon 28

🏔 Club Airotel Le Pô Doré

𝒫 02 41 38 78 80. www.camping-lepodore.com

Address : 51 route du Pô (3.2km northwest along the D 10, follow the signs for Saumur and take road to the left)

Opening times : from mid March to mid Nov.

2 ha (90 pitches) flat, grassy

Tariff : 30.50€ ✸✸ 🚐 🅴 🔌 (10A) – Extra per person 6€ – Reservation fee 13€

Rental rates : (from mid March to beginning Nov.) – 20 🛖 – 2 🏠 – 2 canvas bungalows. Per week from 270 to 775€ – Reservation fee 13€

Surroundings : 🐟 🗑
Leisure activities : 🍴 ✗ 🏠 🛥 🎣 🏊
Facilities : 🚿 ⛽ 🔧 🍴 🍴 🔦 📮 🚿

G P S Longitude : -0.01244
Latitude : 47.29923

AMBRIÈRES-LES-VALLÉES

53300 – Michelin map **310** F4 – pop. 2 778 – alt. 144
▶ Paris 248 – Alençon 60 – Domfront 22 – Fougères 46

🏔 Flower Le Parc de Vaux

𝒫 02 43 04 90 25. www.parcdevaux.com

Address : 35 rue due Colvert (2km southeast along the D 23, follow the signs for Mayenne and take left turn, by the swimming pool)

Opening times : from beginning April to end Oct.

3.5 ha (112 pitches) terraced, fine gravel, flat, grassy

Tariff : (2015 price) 15.60€ ✸✸ 🚐 🅴 🔌 (10A) – Extra per person 5.20€
Rental rates : (2015 price) (from beginning April to end Oct.) 🚿 – 9 🛖 – 20 🏠 – 5 canvas bungalows. Per night from 25 to 45€ – Per week from 252 to 742€ – Reservation fee 10€

A pleasant wooded park beside the Varenne (small lake).

Surroundings : 🐟 🗑 🌳🌳
Leisure activities : 🏠 🚲
Facilities : 🚿 ⛽ 🅿 🔧 🍴 launderette
Nearby : 🚣 ✗ 🎣 🏊 🛥 🏇

G P S Longitude : -0.6171
Latitude : 48.39175

ANCENIS

44150 – Michelin map **316** I3 – pop. 7 543 – alt. 13
▶ Paris 347 – Angers 55 – Châteaubriant 48 – Cholet 49

🏔 L'Île Mouchet

𝒫 02 40 83 08 43. www.camping-estivance.com

Address : impasse de l'Île Mouchet (take the western exit along the bd Joubert and take the turning to the left, behind the municipal sports centre)

Opening times : permanent

3.5 ha (105 pitches) flat, grassy

Tariff : (2015 price) ✸ 🚐 🅴 11.20€ – 🔌 (16A) 16€
Rental rates : (2015 price) permanent – 7 🛖. Per night from 65 to 125€ – Per week from 280 to 575€ – Reservation fee 15€

🚃 local sani-station 5€ – 4 🔋 16.20€
A site established on lovely fields with plenty of shade, situated near the municipal stadium and the Loire river.

Surroundings : 🌳🌳
Leisure activities : 🏠 🛥 🏊 🛶
Facilities : 🚿 ⛽ (July–Aug.) 🍴 launderette
Nearby : ✗ 🚵 🚣 sports trail

G P S Longitude : -1.18707
Latitude : 47.36095

ANDOUILLÉ

53240 – Michelin map **310** E5 – pop. 2 300 – alt. 103
▶ Paris 282 – Fougères 42 – Laval 15 – Mayenne 23

🏔 Municipal le Pont

𝒫 02 43 01 18 10. www.ville-andouille.fr

Address : 5 allée des Isles (along the D 104, follow the signs for St-Germain-le-Fouilloux, right next to municipal gardens; beside the Ernée river)

Opening times : from mid April to mid Oct.

0.8 ha (30 pitches) flat, grassy

Tariff : (2015 price) ✸ 1.80€ 🚐 🅴 1.65€ – 🔌 (6A) 1.45€

Rental rates : (2015 price) permanent – 4 ⌂. Per night from 23 to 51€ – Per week from 220 to 378€

Surroundings : ⌱ ♀
Facilities : ⚒ ⚐ ⚏ ▦
Nearby : 🏃 **fitness trail**

Longitude : -0.78697
Latitude : 48.17604

ANGERS

49000 – Michelin map **317** F4 – pop. 147 305 – alt. 41
▶ Paris 294 – Caen 249 – Laval 79 – Le Mans 97

⛰ Lac de Maine ♣♣

📞 02 41 73 05 03. www.lacdemaine.fr

Address : avenue du Lac de Maine (4km southwest along the D 111, follow the signs for Pruniers, near the lake (direct access) and near the leisure and activity park)

Opening times : from end March to mid Oct.

4 ha (165 pitches) flat, grassy, fine gravel

Tariff : (2015 price) 28€ ✶✶ ⚗ 🅴 ⚡ (10A) – Extra per person 3.50€ – Reservation fee 2.10€

Rental rates : (2015 price) (from end March to mid Oct.) ⚒ (2 mobile homes) – 14 ⛺ – 3 ⌂ – 3 canvas bungalows. Per night from 42 to 101€ – Per week from 295 to 710€ – Reservation fee 2.10€

⛺ 70 🅴 19.70€ – ⚡ 17.70€
Public transport for the centre of Angers is just 300m away.

Surroundings : ⌱ ♀
Leisure activities : ♟ ✗ ⛱ 🏃 ⚓ 🚴 ⛴
spa facilities
Facilities : ⚒ ⚐ 🆑 ▥ ⚏ ⚒ ⚓ ⚏ ⚏ ▦ ⚏
Nearby : ✂ ⚓ ⚓ ♨ pedalos

We have selected the best campsites in France with our usual care, listing those with the best facilities in the most pleasant surroundings.

Longitude : -0.59654
Latitude : 47.45551

ANGLES

85750 – Michelin map **316** H9 – pop. 2 329 – alt. 10
▶ Paris 450 – Luçon 23 – La Mothe-Achard 38 – Niort 86

⛰ L'Atlantique ♣♣

📞 02 51 27 03 19. www.camping-atlantique.com

Address : 5bis rue du Chemin de Fer (in the town, take the exit for la Tranche-sur-Mer and take turning to the left)

Opening times : from end March to end Oct.

6.9 ha (363 pitches) flat, grassy, stony

Tariff : (2015 price) 31.90€ ✶✶ ⚗ 🅴 ⚡ (10A) –
Extra per person 7.80€ – Reservation fee 25€

Rental rates : (2015 price) (from end March to end Oct.) – 150 ⛺ – 15 ⌂. Per week from 149 to 795€ – Reservation fee 25€

The site is well laid out, although the sanitary facilities and some rental options are a bit old. There's a free shuttle service to the beaches.

Surroundings : ⌱ ♀♀
Leisure activities : ♟ ✗ ⛱ 🏃 ♨ ⛴
⚓ 🚴 ✂ ⚏ ⚏ entertainment room
Facilities : ⚒ ⚐ ⚏ ⚒ ⚏ ⚏ launderette ⚏
refrigerators

Longitude : -1.40552
Latitude : 46.40465

⛰ APV Moncalm ♣♣
(rental of mobile homes and chalets only)

📞 25156 0878. www.camping-apv.com

Address : rue du Chemin de Fer (in the town, take the exit for La Tranche-sur-Mer and take turning to the left)

Opening times : from beginning April to end Sept.

3 ha (200 pitches) flat, grassy, stony

Rental rates : (2015 price) – 85 ⛺ – 26 ⌂. Per night from 42 to 73 – Per week from 266 to 875€ – Reservation fee 28€

A mobile home park and chalets with an open-air play and paddling pool; free shuttle service to the beaches.

Surroundings : ⌱ ♀♀
Leisure activities : ♟ ✗ ⛱ 🏃 ⚓ ⛴
🚴 ⚏ ⚏ multi-sports ground
Facilities : ⚒ ⚐ ⚏ ⚏ launderette ⚏ ⚏

Longitude : -1.40548
Latitude : 46.40467

⛰ Flower Clos Cottet ♣♣

📞 02 51 28 90 72. www.camping-clos-cottet.com

Address : route de La Tranche-sur-Mer (2.2km to the south, near the D 747)

Opening times : from beginning April to end Sept.

4.5 ha (196 pitches) flat, grassy, small lake

Tariff : (2015 price) 30€ ✶✶ ⚗ 🅴 ⚡ (10A) – Extra per person 7€ – Reservation fee 25€

Rental rates : (2015 price) (from beginning April to end Sept.)
⚒ – 90 ⛺ – 9 ⌂. Per night from 49 to 159€ – Per week from 99 to 869€ – Reservation fee 25€

⛺ 4 🅴 31€
Based around a renovated farmhouse; mini-farm and free shuttle service to the beaches.

Surroundings : ⌱ ♀♀
Leisure activities : ♟ ✗ ⛱ 🏃 ♨ ⛴
hammam ⚏ ⚏ ⚏ ⚏ quad biking,
multi-sports ground, entertainment room
Facilities : ⚒ ⚐ ⚏ ⚏ launderette

Longitude : -1.40345
Latitude : 46.39248

APREMONT

85220 – Michelin map **316** F7 – pop. 1 546 – alt. 19
▶ Paris 448 – Challans 17 – Nantes 64 – La Roche-sur-Yon 30

⛰ Les Charmes

📞 02 51 54 48 08. www.campinglescharmes.com

Address : at Les Lilas (3.6km north along the D 21, follow the signs for Challans and take turning to the right, towards La Roussière)

Opening times : from beginning April to mid Sept.

1 ha (55 pitches) flat, grassy

Tariff : 24.30€ ✶✶ ⚗ 🅴 ⚡ (10A) – Extra per person 5.50€ – Reservation fee 16€

Rental rates : (from beginning March to end Oct.) ⚒ (1 mobile home) ⚒ – 12 ⛺ – 5 ⌂ – 2 canvas bungalows. Per night from 48 to 110€ – Per week from 162 to 712€ – Reservation fee 16€

A pleasant site with upmarket rental accommodation and a small wellness centre.

Surroundings : ⚏ ⌱ ♀♀
Leisure activities : ♟ ⛱ ⛴ jacuzzi ⚏
⚏ entertainment room
Facilities : ⚒ ⚐ ⚏ launderette

Longitude : -1.73397
Latitude : 46.77827

ASSÉRAC

44410 – Michelin map **316** B3 – pop. 1 773 – alt. 12
▶ Paris 454 – Nantes 79 – Rennes 108 – Vannes 48

⛰ Moulin de Leclis

📞 02 40 01 76 69. www.camping-leclis.com

Address : at Pont Mahé (situated 4km west along the D 82)

Opening times : from beginning April to mid Nov.

3.8 ha (180 pitches) flat, sandy, grassy

Tariff : (2015 price) 🚗🔌 16.10€ – 🔌 (10A) 4.50€ – Reservation fee 20€

Rental rates : (2015 price) (from beginning April to mid Nov.) ♿ (1 mobile home) – 31 🏠 – 31 🏕 – 1 canvas bungalow. Per night from 90 to 222€ – Per week from 238 to 1,204€ – Reservation fee 20€

🚐 local sani-station 4.70€ – 🚐 8€

In the bay at Pont-Mahé, with a view of La Pointe du Bile.

Surroundings : 🏖 🚲 ⛱ ⛰
Leisure activities : 🍴 ✕ 🛶 🖼 (open air in season) ⛱
Facilities : ♿ 🚿 🏧 🧺 🍴 launderette 🏖 🚲
Nearby : skate surfing

GPS — Longitude : -2.44795
Latitude : 47.44576

AVOISE

72430 – Michelin map **310** H7 – pop. 539 – alt. 112
▶ Paris 242 – La Flèche 28 – Le Mans 41 – Sablé-sur-Sarthe 11

⛰ L'Oeil dans le Rétro

📞 02 43 92 76 12. http://www.campingloeildansleretro.fr

Address : place des 2 Fonds (in the village, along the D 57)

Opening times : from beginning April to end Oct.

1.8 ha (54 pitches) flat, grassy

Tariff : (2015 price) 12.90€ 👫 🚗 🔌 (16A) – Extra per person 2.40€

🚐 local sani-station 3.50€

Situated beside the Sarthe river.

Surroundings : 🚲 ⛱
Leisure activities : 🍴 🛶 🚲
Facilities : ♿ 🚿 🧺 🍴
Nearby : 🏖 ✕ ⚓

GPS — Longitude : -0.20554
Latitude : 47.86545

AVRILLÉ

85440 – Michelin map **316** H9 – pop. 1 194 – alt. 45
▶ Paris 445 – Luçon 27 – La Rochelle 70 – La Roche-sur-Yon 27

⛰ FranceLoc Les Forges ▲▲

📞 02 51 22 38 85. www.campingdomainedesforges.com

Address : rue des Forges (take the northeastern exit along the D 19, follow the signs for Moutiers-les-Mauxfaits and take the turning to the left, 0.7km along the rue des Forges)

Opening times : from beginning April to mid Sept.

12 ha (295 pitches) flat, grassy, pond

Tariff : (2015 price) 34€ 👫 🚗 🔌 🔌 (16A) – Extra per person 7€ – Reservation fee 27€

Rental rates : (2015 price) (from beginning April to mid Sept.) ♿ (2 mobile homes) – 2 'gypsy' caravans – 194 🏠 – 2 🏕 – 15 canvas bungalows. Per night from 35 to 186€ – Per week from 140 to 1,771€ – Reservation fee 27€

🚐 local sani-station – 20 🔌 25.90€

Based around a small pretty château and a lake.

Surroundings : 🏖 🚲 ⛱
Leisure activities : 🍴 ✕ 🛶 🖼 🚴 🏃 ⛸ 🚣 🚲 ⛵ 🛶 ⛱ 🚲 🎣 cinema, multi-sports ground
Facilities : ♿ 🚿 🏧 🧺 🍴 launderette 🏖 🚲

GPS — Longitude : -1.49467
Latitude : 46.47587

⛰ Les Mancellières

📞 02 51 90 35 97. www.lesmancellieres.com

Address : 1300 route de Longeville (1.7km south along the D 105)

Opening times : from beginning April to mid Sept.

2.6 ha (133 pitches)

Tariff : (2015 price) 28.50€ 👫 🚗 🔌 🔌 (6A) – Extra per person 4.60€ – Reservation fee 20€

Rental rates : (2015 price) (from beginning April to mid Sept.) – 69 🏠 – 4 🏕. Per night from 40 to 115€ – Per week from 172 to 805€ – Reservation fee 20€

A pleasant, shady site with lots of green space.

Surroundings : 🚲 ⛱
Leisure activities : ✕ 🛶 jacuzzi 🚣 🖼 🚲 ⛱ multi-sports ground
Facilities : ♿ 🚿 🏕 🍴 launderette

GPS — Longitude : -1.48509
Latitude : 46.45608

LA BAULE

44500 – Michelin map **316** B4 – pop. 16 235 – alt. 31
▶ Paris 450 – Nantes 76 – Rennes 120 – St-Nazaire 19

⛰ Club Airotel La Roseraie ▲▲

📞 02 40 60 46 66. www.laroseraie.com

Address : 20 avenue Jean Sohier (take the northeastern exit for La Baule-Escoublac)

Opening times : from beginning April to end Sept.

5 ha (220 pitches) flat, grassy, sandy

Tariff : (2015 price) 41.20€ 👫 🚗 🔌 🔌 (10A) – Extra per person 8.30€ – Reservation fee 30€

Rental rates : (2015 price) (from beginning April to end Sept.) ♿ (1 mobile home) – 85 🏠 – 3 🏕. Per night from 67 to 184€ – Per week from 315 to 1,288€ – Reservation fee 30€

🚐 local sani-station – 3 🔌 35€

In a pleasant, green setting, but choose the pitches away from the road.

Surroundings : 🚲 ⛱
Leisure activities : 🍴 ✕ 🛶 🖼 🏃 🚣 jacuzzi 🚣 🚴 ✂ 🖼 (open air in season) ⛱ multi-sports ground, entertainment room
Facilities : ♿ 🚿 🏕 🧺 🍴 launderette 🚲

GPS — Longitude : -2.35776
Latitude : 47.29828

BEAUMONT-SUR-SARTHE

72170 – Michelin map **310** J5 – pop. 2 094 – alt. 76
▶ Paris 223 – Alençon 24 – La Ferté-Bernard 70 – Le Mans 29

⛰ Municipal du Val de Sarthe

📞 02 43 97 01 93. www.ville-beaumont-sur-sarthe.fr

Address : rue de l'Abreuvoir (in the southeast of the town)

Opening times : from beginning May to end Sept.

1 ha (73 pitches) flat, grassy

Tariff : (2015 price) 👤 2.55€ 🚗 2€ 🔌 2€ – 🔌 (10A) 3.70€

Rental rates : (2015 price) (from beginning May to end Sept.) –
2 canvas bungalows. Per night from 30 to 50€ – Per week
from 165 to 305€

🚐 local sani-station 4.95€

A pleasant site and setting beside the Sarthe river.

Surroundings : 🐿 🗔 ♀	**G** Longitude : 0.13384
Leisure activities : 🏠 ⚓	**P**
Facilities : 🚿 ⚭ ♨ 🅿	**S** Latitude : 48.2261
Nearby : 🛁	

LA BERNERIE-EN-RETZ

44760 – Michelin map **316** D5 – pop. 2 541 – alt. 24
▶ Paris 426 – Challans 40 – Nantes 46 – St-Nazaire 36

🔺 Les Écureuils ♨♨

✆ 02 40 82 76 95. www.camping-les-ecureuils.com

Address : 24 avenue Gilbert Burlot (take northeastern exit, follow
the signs for Nantes and take the turning to the left after the level
crossing, 350m from the sea)

Opening times : from beginning April to mid Sept.

5.3 ha (312 pitches) flat, relatively flat, grassy

Tariff : 47€ ♨♨ ⇔ 🔲 🅿 (10A) – Extra per person 8€ – Reservation fee 20€
Rental rates : (from beginning April to mid Sept.) ⚓ – 97 🛖 –
19 🛖 – 6 canvas bungalows. Per night from 33 to 59€ – Per week
from 231 to 910€ – Reservation fee 20€

🚐 local sani-station

*A pretty site with upmarket rental accommodation based
around the swimming and play area.*

Surroundings : 🐿 🗔 ♀	**G** Longitude : -2.03558
Leisure activities : 🍸 🏠 ☾nighttime 🏃	**P**
⚓ 🍴 🎿 🏊 multi-sports ground	Latitude : 47.08375
Facilities : 🚿 ⚭ 🅾 🏊 ♨ 🅿 launderette	**S**
🧊 refrigerators	
Nearby : 🎣	

*The guide covers all 22 regions of France – see the map
and list of regions on pages 4–5.*

BESSÉ-SUR-BRAYE

72310 – Michelin map **310** N7 – pop. 2 363 – alt. 72
▶ Paris 198 – La Ferté-Bernard 43 – Le Mans 57 – Tours 56

🔺 Val de Braye

✆ 02 43 35 31 13. www.campingduvaldebraye.com

Address : head southeast along the D 303, follow the signs for Pont
de Braye

Opening times : permanent

2 ha (78 pitches) flat, grassy

Tariff : 18.80€ ♨♨ ⇔ 🔲 🅿 (16A) – Extra per person 5€
Rental rates : permanent ⚓ (1 mobile home) – 420 🛖 – 4 tipis –
1 canvas bungalow. Per night from 30 to 65€ – Per week
from 160 to 420€

🚐 AireService sani-station 4€ – 🚐 🅿15€

*Beautiful trees and shrubs decorate this site beside the
Braye river.*

Surroundings : ♀	**G** Longitude : 0.75427
Leisure activities : 🏠 ⚓ 🐟	**P**
Facilities : 🚿 ⚭ (July–Aug.) 🅾 ♨ 🅿	**S** Latitude : 47.83119
Nearby : 🍴 🎿 🎣	

BLAIN

44130 – Michelin map **316** F3 – pop. 9 284 – alt. 23
▶ Paris 411 – Nantes 41 – Nort-sur-Erdre 22 – Nozay 16

🔺 Municipal le Château

✆ 02 40 79 11 00. www.ville-blain.fr

Address : rue Henri II de Rohan, at Le Gravier (take the southwestern
exit along the N 171, follow the signs for St-Nazaire and take the road
to the left, 250m from the Nantes–Brest canal)

Opening times : from beginning May to end Sept.

1 ha (44 pitches) flat, grassy

Tariff : (2015 price) 14.50€ ♨♨ ⇔ 🔲 🅿 (16A) –
Extra per person 2.80€

🚐 AireService sani-station – 4 🔲 9€ – 🚐 🅿12.30€

In a well-kept green setting, near a 14th-century château.

Surroundings : ♀♀	**G** Longitude : -1.76763
Leisure activities : 🏠 ⚓	**P**
Facilities : ⚓ (July–Aug.) 🅾🏊🅿	**S** Latitude : 47.46772
Nearby : 🍸 🍴 ⚓ ⚓	

BOUÈRE

53290 – Michelin map **310** G7 – pop. 1 027 – alt. 81
▶ Paris 273 – Nantes 146 – Laval 39 – Angers 70

🔺 Village Vacances Nature et Jardin
(rental of chalets only)

✆ 02 43 06 08 56. www.vacances-nature-jardin.fr

Address : rue Vierge Vacances (to the south, follow r. des Sencies and
take the road to the left)

Opening times : permanent

3 ha flat, grassy
Rental rates : (2015 price) ⚓ – 11 🛖. Per night from 77 to 92€ –
Per week from 219 to 428€ – Reservation fee 15€

Surroundings : 🐿 🗔	**G** Longitude : -0.47506
Leisure activities : 🏠 🐟	**P**
Facilities : 🅾 ♨ 🧊 refrigerators	**S** Latitude : 47.86306
Nearby : 🎿 🍴 ⚓ 🗔	

BRAIN-SUR-L'AUTHION

49800 – Michelin map **317** G4 – pop. 3 330 – alt. 22
▶ Paris 291 – Angers 16 – Baugé 28 – Doué-la-Fontaine 38

🔺 Port Caroline

✆ 02 41 80 42 18. www.campingduportcaroline.fr

Address : rue du Pont Caroline (take the southern exit along the
D 113. 100m from L'Authion)

Opening times : from beginning April to end Sept.

3.2 ha (121 pitches) flat, grassy

Tariff : 21€ ♨♨ ⇔ 🔲 🅿 (10A) – Extra per person 4.50€ – Reservation
fee 10€
Rental rates : (from beginning April to end Sept.) – 12 🛖 – 2 🛖 –
3 canvas bungalows – 4 tent lodges. Per night from 40 to 112€ –
Per week from 200 to 784€ – Reservation fee 10€

Surroundings : 🗔 ♀	**G** Longitude : -0.40855
Leisure activities : 🍴 🏠 ⚓ 🚲 🎿	**P**
Facilities : 🚿 ⚭ 🅾 🎱 ♨ 🅿 🧊	**S** Latitude : 47.44386
Nearby : 🎣 skateboarding	

BREM-SUR-MER

85470 – Michelin map **316** F8 – pop. 2 565 – alt. 13
▶ Paris 454 – Aizenay 26 – Challans 29 – La Roche-sur-Yon 34

⚠ Le Chaponnet ⚠

⌖ 02 51 90 55 56. www.le-chaponnet.com

Address : 16 rue du Chaponnet (to the west of the town)

Opening times : from beginning April to end Sept.

6 ha (357 pitches) flat, grassy

Tariff : 39.50€ ★★ 🚗 🖭 🔌 (10A) – Extra per person 7.80€

Rental rates : (from beginning April to end Sept.) ⚐ (1 mobile home) – 140 🚐 – 20 🏠. Per night from 29 to 117€ – Per week from 203 to 819€ – Reservation fee 15€

🚮 Eurorelais sani-station

In a green setting with flowers, with shade in places. A free shuttle service to the beaches.

Surroundings : 🏞 🗺 ♨
Leisure activities : ▼ ✕ 🎣 🌳 🏊 🦿 ⛵
🚴🏇✕ 🖭 🏊 ♨ multi-sports ground
Facilities : ⚐ ⌾ 🖭 🛁 🚿 ♨ launderette 🛒
Longitude : -1.83225
Latitude : 46.6043

⚠ Cybele Vacances L'Océan ⚠

⌖ 02 49 06 10 60. www.campingdelocean.fr

Address : rue des Gabelous (located 1km west, 600 from the beach)

Opening times : from beginning April to beginning Nov.

13 ha (566 pitches) flat, grassy, sandy

Tariff : 34€ ★★ 🚗 🖭 🔌 (6A) – Extra per person 6€ – Reservation fee 30€

Rental rates : (from beginning April to beginning Nov.) ⚐ (2 mobile homes) – 175 🚐 – 3 tent lodges. Per night from 25 to 93€ – Per week from 199 to 1,499€ – Reservation fee 30€

Surroundings : 🏞 🗺
Leisure activities : ▼ ✕ 🎣 🌳 🏊 🦿 🏊
🚴🖭 🏊 ♨ multi-sports ground
Facilities : ⚐ ⌾ 🖭 🛁 ♨ launderette 🛒 🛒
Nearby : ✕
Longitude : -1.83225
Latitude : 46.6043

⚠ Flower Le Brandais ⚠

⌖ 02 51 90 55 87. www.lebrandais.com – limited spaces for one-night stay

Address : rue du Sablais (take the northwestern exit along the D 38 and take turning to the left)

Opening times : from beginning April to end Oct.

2.3 ha (165 pitches) flat, relatively flat, grassy

Tariff : 28.50€ ★★ 🚗 🖭 🔌 (10A) – Extra per person 6€ – Reservation fee 18€

Rental rates : (from beginning April to end Oct.) ⚐ (1 mobile home) – 2 'gypsy' caravans – 60 🚐 – 4 canvas bungalows. Per night from 35 to 85€ – Per week from 271 to 875€ – Reservation fee 18€

🚮 local sani-station – 8 🖭 18€ – 🚐 🔌18€

In a residential area, with a range of rental options and some pitches for tents and caravans. Free shuttle service to the beaches.

Surroundings : 🏞 🗺 ♨
Leisure activities : ▼ 🎣 🌳 🏊 🚴🖭 🏊
Facilities : ⚐ ⌾ 🖭 🛁 ♨ launderette 🛒
Nearby : ✕
Longitude : -1.83949
Latitude : 46.60486

BRÉTIGNOLLES-SUR-MER

85470 – Michelin map **316** E8 – pop. 4 127 – alt. 14
▶ Paris 459 – Challans 30 – La Roche-sur-Yon 36 – Les Sables-d'Olonne 18

⚠ Les Vagues ⚠

⌖ 02 51 90 19 48. www.campinglesvagues.fr – limited spaces for one-night stay

Address : 20 boulevard du Nord (north along the D 38 towards St-Gilles-Croix-de-Vie)

Opening times : from beginning April to mid Oct.

4.5 ha (252 pitches) relatively flat, flat, grassy

Tariff : (2015 price) 18.50€ ★★ 🚗 🖭 🔌 (10A) – Extra per person 4€ – Reservation fee 20€

Rental rates : (2015 price) (from beginning April to end Sept.) – 22 🚐. Per night from 25 to 40€ – Per week from 250 to 795€ – Reservation fee 20€

🚮 70 🖭 18.50€

A pleasant site with shade, always pitches for tents and caravans.

Surroundings : 🗺 ♨♨
Leisure activities : ▼ ✕ 🎣 🌳 🦿 🖭 🏊
🏊 multi-sports ground
Facilities : ⚐ ⌾ 🛁 ♨ 🖭
Longitude : -1.85935
Latitude : 46.63012

⚠ Chadotel La Trevillière

⌖ 02 51 90 09 65. http://www.chadotel.com/fr/camping/vendee/bretignolles-sur-mer/camping-la-trevilliere

Address : rue de Bellevue (take the northern exit along the rte du Stade and take the turning to the left)

Opening times : from beginning April to end Sept.

3 ha (204 pitches) relatively flat, flat, grassy

Tariff : 32€ ★★ 🚗 🖭 🔌 (10A) – Extra per person 6€ – Reservation fee 25€

Rental rates : (from beginning April to end Sept.) ⚐ (1 mobile home) – 107 🚐 – 4 tent lodges. Per night from 22 to 132€ – Per week from 154 to 924€ – Reservation fee 25€

🚮 94 🖭

In a green setting, with plenty of shade in places.

Surroundings : 🏞 🗺 ♨
Leisure activities : ▼ ✕ 🦿 🏛 🖭 🏊 🏊
Facilities : ⚐ ⌾ 🛁 🚿 ♨ launderette 🛒
Longitude : -1.85822
Latitude : 46.63627

⚠ Le Marina

⌖ 02 51 33 83 17. www.le-marina.com

Address : rue de La Martinière (take the northwestern exit along the D 38, follow the signs for St-Gilles-Croix-de-Vie then take left turn 1km along the r. de la Martignière)

Opening times : from beginning April to end Sept.

2.7 ha (131 pitches) flat, grassy

Tariff : (2015 price) 24€ ★★ 🚗 🖭 🔌 (6A) – Extra per person 4.80€ – Reservation fee 15€

Rental rates : (2015 price) (from beginning April to end Sept.) – 6 🚐. Per week from 250 to 650€ – Reservation fee 15€

In a green setting in a residential area, but choose the pitches away from the road in preference.

Surroundings : 🗺 ♨♨
Leisure activities : 🎣 🏊
Facilities : ⚐ ⌾ 🚐 🛁 🚿 🖭
Longitude : -1.87185
Latitude : 46.63582

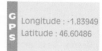

⚠ La Motine

🔗 02 51 90 04 42. www.lamotine.com

Address : 4 rue des Morinières (continue along the av. de la Plage and take a right turn)

Opening times : from beginning April to end Sept.

1.8 ha (103 pitches) relatively flat, grassy

Tariff : (2015 price) 28€ ✶✶ ⬤ 🅴 🅸 (10A) – Extra per person 5.50€ – Reservation fee 15€

Rental rates : (2015 price) permanent – 10 🚐. Per night from 100 to 160€ – Per week from 380 to 650€ – Reservation fee 15€

🚮 local sani-station 8€

Ornamental trees and shrubs surround the pitches; located in a residential area.

Surroundings : 🏡 ♀	
Leisure activities : 🖼	**GPS** Longitude : -1.8644
Facilities : 🚿 ⚲ 🛁 🌿 ⚑ 🍴 launderette	Latitude : 46.62745
Nearby : ♨	

⚠ Le Bon Accueil

🔗 02 51 90 15 92. https://sites.google.com/site/campinglebonaccueil

Address : 24 route de St-Gilles (1.2km northwest along the D 38)

3 ha (146 pitches) relatively flat, flat, grassy

Rentals : 7 🚐.

Few rental options, rather old sanitary facilities but well maintained.

Surroundings : ♀♀	
Leisure activities : 🚣 🖼	**GPS** Longitude : -1.86605
Facilities : 🚿 ⚲ 🍴 🖼	Latitude : 46.63625

BRISSAC-QUINCÉ

49320 – Michelin map **317** G4 – pop. 2 898 – alt. 65

▶ Paris 307 – Angers 18 – Cholet 62 – Doué-la-Fontaine 23

⛰ Sites et Paysages Domaine de l'Étang

Domaine de l'Étang

🔗 02 41 91 70 61. www.campingetang.com

Address : route de St-Mathurin (situated 2km northeast along the D 55, and take the road to the right; beside the Aubance river and near a lake)

Opening times : from end April to mid Sept.

3.5 ha (150 pitches) flat, grassy, small lake

Tariff : 35€ ✶✶ ⬤ 🅴 🅸 (16A) – Extra per person 6.80€ – Reservation fee 14€

Rental rates : (from end April to mid Sept.) 🚫 – 18 🚐 – 4 🏠 – 8 canvas bungalows – 4 tent lodges – 3 gîtes. Per night from 35 to 140€ – Per week from 215 to 890€ – Reservation fee 14€

🚮 local sani-station 14€ – 🚐 🅸16€

Spacious and comfortable pitches in the grounds of an old farmhouse.

Surroundings : 🐿 🏡	
Leisure activities : 🍴 🛏 🚴 🖼 (open air in season) 🏊	**GPS** Longitude : -0.43529
Facilities : 🚿 ⚲ ▥ 🛁 🍴 launderette 🖼	Latitude : 47.36082
Nearby : 🛒 🏞 leisure park	

CHAILLÉ-LES-MARAIS

85450 – Michelin map **316** J9 – pop. 1 902 – alt. 16

▶ Paris 446 – Fontenay-le-Comte 23 – Niort 57 – La Rochelle 34

⛰ L'Île Cariot

🔗 02 51 56 75 27. www.camping-chaille-les-marais.com

Address : rue du 8 Mai (south of the town)

Opening times : from beginning April to end Sept.

1.2 ha (50 pitches) flat, grassy

Tariff : 18.40€ ✶✶ ⬤ 🅴 🅸 (10A) – Extra per person 4.70€ – Reservation fee 8€

Rental rates : (from beginning April to end Sept.) – 5 🚐 – 5 🏠 – 2 canvas bungalows. Per night from 35 to 53€ – Per week from 170 to 540€ – Reservation fee 8€

🚮 local sani-station 3€ – 10 🅴 8€ – 🚐 8€

A very lush and leafy site, near a network of canals, ideal for canoeing.

Surroundings : 🏡 ♀♀	
Leisure activities : 🛶 🚣 🚴 🏊 🚡	**GPS** Longitude : -1.0209
Facilities : 🚿 ⚲ 🆒 🍴 launderette	Latitude : 46.3927
Nearby : 🍴	

LA CHAIZE-GIRAUD

85220 – Michelin map **316** F8 – pop. 878 – alt. 15

▶ Paris 453 – Challans 24 – La Roche-sur-Yon 32 – Les Sables-d'Olonne 21

⛰ Les Alouettes

🔗 02 51 22 96 21. www.lesalouettes.com – limited spaces for one-night stay

Address : route de Saint-Gilles (located 1km west along the D 12. follow the signs for St-Gilles-Croix-de-Vie)

3 ha (130 pitches) terraced, relatively flat, flat, grassy

Rentals : 66 🚐 – 19 🏠 – 5 canvas bungalows.

A mobile home and chalet park, with some pitches for tents and caravans.

Surroundings : 🏡 ♀	
Leisure activities : 🍴 🍴 🛏 🛁 jacuzzi 🚣 🖼 🏊	**GPS** Longitude : -1.83342
Facilities : 🚿 ⚲ 🛁 🍴 launderette	Latitude : 46.64832

CHALONNES-SUR-LOIRE

49290 – Michelin map **317** E4 – pop. 6 421 – alt. 25

▶ Paris 322 – Nantes 82 – Angers 26 – Cholet 40

⚠ Onlycamp Les Portes de La Loire

🔗 02 41 78 02 27. http://portesdelaloire.onlycamp.fr

Address : route de Rochefort (located 1km east along the D 751, follow the signs for Les Ponts-de-Cé; beside the Loire river and near a small lake)

3 ha (125 pitches) flat, grassy

Rentals : 5 canvas bungalows – 5 tent lodges.

Surroundings : ♀	
Leisure activities : 🛏 🚣	**GPS** Longitude : -0.74813
Facilities : 🚿 ⚲ 🍴 🖼	Latitude : 47.35132
Nearby : 🛒 🍴 🚴 🚫 ♨ 🏊	

CHAMBRETAUD

85500 – Michelin map **316** K6 – pop. 1 460 – alt. 214
▶ Paris 377 – Nantes 83 – La Roche-sur-Yon 56 – Cholet 21

⚠ Au Bois du Cé

📞 0251915432. www.camping-auboisduce.com ⌖

Address : route du Puy-du-Fou (located 1km to the south, on the D 27)

Opening times : from beginning April to end Sept.

5 ha (110 pitches) terraced, flat, grassy

Tariff : (2015 price) 23€ ✦✦ ⇌ 🔲 🄵 (16A) – Extra per person 3.50€
Rental rates : (2015 price) (from beginning April to end Sept.) ⌖ –
36 🚐 – 14 🏠 – 2 studios. Per night from 58 to 65€ – Per week from 320 to 800€

In a green setting laid out around swimming pools, with a range of upmarket rental options.

Surroundings : ⇐ 🗀
Leisure activities : 🍸 🎬 jacuzzi 🔲 🏊
Facilities : ⑁ ⚬━ ▥ ⚑ launderette
GPS Longitude : -0.95
Latitude : 46.915

*The classification (1 to 5 tents, **black** or red) that we award to selected sites in this guide is our own system. It should not be confused with the classification (1 to 5 stars) of official organisations.*

LA CHAPELLE-HERMIER

85220 – Michelin map **316** F7 – pop. 796 – alt. 58
▶ Paris 447 – Aizenay 13 – Challans 25 – La Roche-sur-Yon 29

⚠ Pin Parasol 👤👤

📞 0251346472. http://www.campingpinparasol.fr

Address : at Chateaulong (3.3km southwest along the D 42, follow the signs for L'Aiguillon-sur-Vie then continue 1km along the turning to the left)

Opening times : from end April to end Sept.

12 ha (379 pitches) terraced, relatively flat, flat, grassy

Tariff : (2015 price) 40.25€ ✦✦ ⇌ 🔲 🄵 (10A) –
Extra per person 8.10€ – Reservation fee 20€
Rental rates : (2015 price) (from mid April to mid Sept.) ⑁ (1 chalet) ⌖ – 84 🚐 – 21 🏠. Per week from 241 to 1,264 € – Reservation fee 25€

🚐 Eurorelais sani-station 5€

A swimming area with colourful play paddling-pool; near the Lac de Jaunay (direct access).

Surroundings : 🌿 ⇐ 🗀 ♀
Leisure activities : 🍸 🎬 🎮daytime 🏃 🏹
🍃 hammam 🛶 🚲 ✂ 🔲 🏊 ⛷multi-sports ground
Facilities : ⑁ ⚬━ ▥ 🔥 ⚑ launderette 🗜 🛁
Nearby : 🐟 pedalos
GPS Longitude : -1.75502
Latitude : 46.66647

⚠ Seasonova Village Vacances Le Domaine du Pré 👤👤
(rental of chalets only)

📞 0251080707. www.domainedupre.com

Address : at Bellevue (5km southwest along the D 42, follow the signs for L'Aiguillon-sur-Vie then continue along the turning to the left)

Opening times : from beginning March to end Oct.

11 ha terraced, flat, relatively flat

Rental rates : (2015 price) ⑁ (4 chalets) – 130 🚐 – 12 studios – 14 tent lodges. Per night from 56 to 156€ – Per week from 280 to 1,092€ – Reservation fee 10€

A chalet village beside a large spa and wellness centre.

Surroundings : 🌿 ⇐
Leisure activities : 🎬 🏃 🍃 hammam, jacuzzi 🛶 🔲 (small swimming pool) 🏊 multi-sports ground, spa centre
Facilities : ⑁ ⚬━ 🔥 ⚑ launderette 🗜 🛁
Nearby : 🐟 pedalos

GPS Longitude : -1.76769
Latitude : 46.66485

CHÂTEAU-GONTIER

53200 – Michelin map **310** E8 – pop. 11 532 – alt. 33
▶ Paris 288 – Angers 50 – Châteaubriant 56 – Laval 30

⚠ Le Parc

📞 0243073560. www.camping.parcchateaugontier.fr

Address : 15 route de Laval (800m north along the N 162 follow the signs for Laval; near the sports centre)

Opening times : permanent

2 ha (51 pitches) flat, relatively flat, grassy

Tariff : 17€ ✦✦ ⇌ 🔲 🄵 (10A) – Extra per person 4€
Rental rates : permanent ⑁ – 12 🏠. Per night from 35 to 65 – Per week from 195 to 380€

🚐 AireService sani-station

Shady pitches with a great variety of trees on the banks of the Mayenne river.

Leisure activities : 🎬 🚲 🐟
Facilities : ⚬━ ⚑
Nearby : 🔲 🏊 climbing wall

GPS Longitude : -0.6995
Latitude : 47.83866

CHÂTEAUNEUF-SUR-SARTHE

49330 – Michelin map **317** G2 – pop. 2 972 – alt. 20
▶ Paris 278 – Angers 31 – Château-Gontier 25 – La Flèche 33

⚠ Municipal du Port

📞 0241698202. www.chateauneufsursarthe.fr

Address : 14 place R. Le Fort (take the southeastern exit along the D 859, follow the signs for Durtal and take second road to the right after the bridge; beside the Sarthe river (mooring point)

1 ha (60 pitches) flat, grassy

🚐 local sani-station – 8 🔲

Surroundings : 🗀 ♀
Facilities : ⑁ 🔥
GPS Longitude : -0.48695
Latitude : 47.67749

CHEMILLÉ

49120 – Michelin map **317** E5 – pop. 6 967 – alt. 84
▶ Paris 331 – Angers 43 – Cholet 22 – Saumur 60

⚠ Coulvée

📞 0241303997. www.camping-coulvee-chemille.com

Address : route de Cholet (take the southern exit along the N 160, follow the signs for Cholet and take the road to the right; near a small lake)

Opening times : from beginning May to mid Sept.

2 ha (40 pitches) flat, grassy

Tariff : 15.20€ ✦✦ ⇌ 🔲 🄵 (11A) – Extra per person 3.50€

Rental rates : permanent 🚶 – 12 🏠. Per night from 72 to 92 € – Per week from 212 to 465 €
🚐 Eurorelais sani-station 3 € – 🚐 8 €

Surroundings : 🚫 ♨♨
Leisure activities : 🚲
Facilities : 🚶 ⚬⟷ 🚿🚻 🔺 ♨ ♨ ▯
Nearby : 🚴🏊

G P S Longitude : -0.7359
Latitude : 47.20308

CHOLET

49300 – Michelin map **317** D6 – pop. 54 121 – alt. 91
▶ Paris 353 – Ancenis 49 – Angers 64 – Nantes 60

⚠ FranceLoc Lac de Ribou 👥👤

✆ 02 41 49 74 30. www.franceloc.fr

Address : 5km southeast along the D 20. follow the signs for Maulevrier and turn right onto D 600

Opening times : from beginning April to end Sept.

10 ha (110 pitches) relatively flat, flat, grassy

Tariff : (2015 price) 27 € ✶✶ 🚗 ▯ (10A) – Extra per person 6 € – Reservation fee 17 €
Rental rates : (2015 price) (from beginning April to end Sept.) – 91 🏕 – 30 🏠 – 20 gîtes. Per night from 52 to 113 € – Per week from 154 to 987 € – Reservation fee 17 €
🚐 local sani-station 6 € – 🚐 8 €
Located 100m from the lake (direct access). In a landscaped park.

Surroundings : 🌲🚫
Leisure activities : 🍽️ ✗ 🏛 ⛲nighttime 🏃
🚴 ✗ 🎳 🏊 🏊
Facilities : 🚶 ⚬⟷ 🔲 🔺 ♨ ♨
launderette 🛒
Nearby : 🎠 🐎

We have selected the best campsites in France with our usual care, listing those with the best facilities in the most pleasant surroundings.

COMMEQUIERS

85220 – Michelin map **316** E7 – pop. 2 910 – alt. 19
▶ Paris 441 – Challans 13 – Nantes 63 – La Roche-sur-Yon 38

⚠ La Vie

✆ 02 51 54 90 04. www.campinglavie.com

Address : at Le Motteau (1.3km southeast along the D 82, follow the signs for Coëx and take road to the left)

Opening times : from beginning April to end Sept.

6 ha (110 pitches) flat, grassy, small lake

Tariff : (2015 price) 24 € ✶✶ 🚗 ▯ (6A) – Extra per person 4.50 € – Reservation fee 15 €
Rental rates : (2015 price) (from mid April to mid Sept.) – 18 🏕. Per night from 21 € – Per week from 310 to 608 € – Reservation fee 15 €
🚐 5 ▯ 15 €
A peaceful, rural setting; the site is able to accommodate groups and summer camps.

Surroundings : 🌲 ♨
Leisure activities : 🍽️ ✗ 🏛 🏊 🏊
Facilities : 🚶 ⚬⟷ 🔲🔺 ♨ launderette

G P S Longitude : -1.824
Latitude : 46.75902

⚠ Le Trèfle à 4 feuilles

✆ 02 51 54 87 54. www.campingletreflea4feuilles.com

Address : at La Jouère (3.3km southeast along the D 82, follow the signs for Coëx et 1.4km along the road to the left)

Opening times : from beginning April to end Sept.

1.8 ha (50 pitches) terraced, grassy, flat

Tariff : (2015 price) 13.20 € ✶✶ 🚗 ▯ (6A) – Extra per person 23 € – Reservation fee 8 €
Rental rates : (2015 price) (from beginning April to end Sept.) – 14 🏕. Per night from 60 to 8 € – Reservation fee 8 €
A farm campsite in the grounds of a grain farm with chickens, sheep, goats, a donkey....

Surroundings : 🌲 ♨♨
Leisure activities : 🍽️ 🏛 🚴 🏊 🎳
Facilities : 🚶 ⚬⟷ 🔲 ♨ launderette

G P S Longitude : -1.78507
Latitude : 46.75935

For more information on visiting particular towns or regions, consult the relevant regional MICHELIN Green Guide. We also recommend you use the appropriate Michelin regional map to locate your selected campsite, to calculate distances and to work out the best route.

LES CONCHES

85560 – Michelin map **316** H9
▶ Paris 465 – Nantes 109 – La Roche 37 – La Rochelle 63

⚠ Le Clos des Pins

✆ 02 51 90 31 69. www.campingclosdespins.com

Address : 1336 avenue du Docteur-Joussemet

Opening times : from beginning April to end Sept.

1.6 ha (94 pitches) undulating, sandy, flat

Tariff : 31 € ✶✶ 🚗 ▯ (6A) – Extra per person 7.50 €
Rental rates : (from beginning April to end Sept.) – 38 🏕 – 12 🏠. Per night from 60 to 299 € – Per week from 149 to 1,180 €
Some of the rental accommodatin is a little old, but there are also some luxury mobile homes.

Surroundings : 🚫 ♨♨
Leisure activities : 🍽️ 🏛 🚴 🚲 🏊 🎳
Facilities : 🚶 ⚬⟷ ♨ launderette
Nearby : 🏃

G P S Longitude : -1.48842
Latitude : 46.38856

⚠ Le Sous-Bois

✆ 02 51 33 36 90. lesousbois85@gmail.com

Address : at La Haute-Saligotière

Opening times : from beginning June to mid Sept.

1.7 ha (135 pitches) flat, sandy

Tariff : (2015 price) 23 € ✶✶ 🚗 ▯ (10A) – Extra per person 4 €
Rental rates : (2015 price) (from beginning June to end Sept.) – 4 🏕. Per week from 150 to 490 €
A simple, shady site with well-maintained but rather old facilities.

Surroundings : 🌲 🚫 ♨♨
Leisure activities : 🏛 🚴 ✗
Facilities : 🚶 ⚬⟷ 🔺 ♨ ▯

G P S Longitude : -1.48727
Latitude : 46.3956

CONCOURSON-SUR-LAYON

49700 – Michelin map **317** G5 – pop. 544 – alt. 55
▶ Paris 332 – Angers 44 – Cholet 45 – Saumur 25

▲▲ La Vallée des Vignes ♣♣

✆ 02 41 59 86 35. www.campingvdv.com

Address : at La Croix Patron (900m west along the D 960, follow the signs for Vihiers and take turning to the right after the bridge; beside the Layon river)

Opening times : from beginning April to end Sept.

3.5 ha (63 pitches) flat, grassy

Tariff : 30€ ♣♣ ⇔ 🅴 [½] (10A) – Extra per person 6€ – Reservation fee 10€

Rental rates : (from beginning April to end Sept.) – 4 🛏. Per night from 100 to 140€ – Per week from 260 to 620€ – Reservation fee 10€

Surroundings : 🏞		
Leisure activities : ¶♨️⚓️🚴♨️🛶		**G** Longitude : -0.34766
Facilities : ♿☎️🅿️🚿🚻🗑️		**P S** Latitude : 47.17394

A chambre d'hôte is a guesthouse or B & B-style accommodation.

COUTURES

49320 – Michelin map **317** G4 – pop. 530 – alt. 81
▶ Paris 303 – Angers 25 – Baugé 35 – Doué-la-Fontaine 23

▲▲▲ Yelloh! Village Parc de Montsabert

✆ 02 41 57 91 63. www.parcdemontsabert.com

Address : route de Montsabert (located 1.5km to the northeast, near the château at Montsabert)

Opening times : from beginning April to beginning Sept.

5 ha (157 pitches) flat, relatively flat, wood, stony, grassy

Tariff : 31€ ♣♣ ⇔ 🅴 [½] (10A) – Extra per person 7€

Rental rates : (from beginning April to beginning Sept.) – 3 'gypsy' caravans – 38 🛏 – 14 🛖 – 7 canvas bungalows. Per night from 30 to 147€ – Per week from 210 to 1,029€

🚐 sani-station – 2 🅴 16€ – 🚐 [½]16€

Situated in a pleasant wooded park.

Surroundings : 🏞 🏞		
Leisure activities : ✗ 🏛 ⚓️✂️🛶 (open air in season)		**G** Longitude : -0.34679
Facilities : ♿☎️🗑️🚿🚻🍴 launderette		**P S** Latitude : 47.37448

CRAON

53400 – Michelin map **310** D7 – pop. 4 590 – alt. 75
▶ Paris 309 – Fougères 70 – Laval 29 – Mayenne 60

▲ Municipal du Mûrier

✆ 02 43 06 96 33. www.ville-craon53.fr

Address : rue Alain Gerbault (800m east, follow the signs for Château-Gontier and take road to the left)

Opening times : permanent

1 ha (45 pitches) flat, grassy

Tariff : ♣ 3.50€ ⇔ 🅴 3.50€ – [½] (10A) 2.80€

Rental rates : permanent – 8 🛖. Per night from 39 to 73€ – Per week from 235 to 381€ – Reservation fee 16€

🚐 local sani-station 3€ – 🚐 8€

In a pleasant setting near a small lake.

Surroundings : 🏞 🏞		
Leisure activities : 🏛 ⚓️		**G** Longitude : -0.94398
Facilities : ♿🍴🗑️		**P S** Latitude : 47.84837
Nearby : 🛒¶✗✂️🏊🎣🛶🐴		

DAON

53200 – Michelin map **310** F8 – pop. 486 – alt. 42
▶ Paris 292 – Angers 46 – Château-Gontier 11 – Châteauneuf-sur-Sarthe 15

▲▲ Les Rivières

✆ 02 43 06 94 78. www.campingdaon.fr

Address : 1 rue du Port (take the western exit along the D 213, follow the signs for la Ricoullière and take a right turn before the bridge; near the Mayenne river)

Opening times : from beginning April to end Sept.

1.8 ha (98 pitches) flat, grassy

Tariff : (2015 price) 14€ ♣♣ ⇔ 🅴 [½] (10A) – Extra per person 4€

Rental rates : (2015 price) permanent ♿ – 10 🛖. Per week from 175 to 370€

Surroundings : 🏞 🏞		
Leisure activities : 🏛 🛶		**G** Longitude : -0.64059
Facilities : ♿☎️🍴🗑️		**P S** Latitude : 47.74996
Nearby : ¶✗⚓️🚴🎣🛶⚓ pedalos		

DURTAL

49430 – Michelin map **317** H2 – pop. 3 337 – alt. 39
▶ Paris 261 – Angers 38 – La Flèche 14 – Laval 66

▲▲ Les Portes de l'Anjou

✆ 02 41 76 31 80. www.lesportesdelanjou.com

Address : 9 rue du Camping (take northeastern exit following signs for la Flèche and take right turn)

Opening times : from end March to mid Oct.

3.5 ha (114 pitches) flat, grassy

Tariff : 19€ ♣♣ ⇔ 🅴 [½] (10A) – Extra per person 4.70€

Rental rates : (from end March to mid Oct.) – 11 🛏 – 9 canvas bungalows – 1 gîte. Per night from 27 to 97€ – Per week from 190 to 679€ – Reservation fee 10€

A pleasant site and setting along the Loir river.

Surroundings : 🏞 🏞		
Leisure activities : ¶✗🏛 ♨️⚓️🚴🛶		**G** Longitude : -0.23518
Facilities : ♿☎️🆑🍴🗑️		**P S** Latitude : 47.67136
Nearby : 🛶		

LES ÉPESSES

85590 – Michelin map **316** K6 – pop. 2 575 – alt. 214
▶ Paris 375 – Bressuire 38 – Chantonnay 29 – Cholet 24

▲▲▲ La Bretèche

✆ 02 51 57 33 34. www.campinglabreteche.com

Address : at Base de Loisirs/leisure centre (take northern exit along the D 752, follow signs for Cholet and take the road to the right)

Opening times : from beginning April to end Sept.

3 ha (164 pitches) relatively flat, flat, grassy

Tariff : (2015 price) 23.60€ ♣♣ ⇔ 🅴 [½] (10A) – Extra per person 4.80€ – Reservation fee 10€

Rental rates : (2015 price) (from beginning April to end Sept.) – 24 🏠 – 12 canvas bungalows – 4 tent lodges. Per night from 36 to 87€ – Per week from 210 to 750€ – Reservation fee 10€
🚐 local sani-station
Ornamental trees and shrubs decorate the site; 3km from Le Puy du Fou (history theme park).

Surroundings : 🐾 🛒 ⚲⚲
Leisure activities : 🍴✕ 🏕 ⚓ 🎿
Facilities : 🚿 🌡 🚰 launderette
Nearby : 🌊 amusement park

Longitude : -0.89925
Latitude : 46.88986

ÉVRON

53600 – Michelin map **310** G6 – pop. 7 099 – alt. 114
▶ Paris 250 – Alençon 58 – La Ferté-Bernard 98 – La Flèche 69

⛰ Municipal de la Zone Verte

℘ 02 43 01 65 36. www.camping-evron.fr

Address : boulevard du Maréchal Juin (take the western exit)

Opening times : permanent

3 ha (92 pitches) flat, relatively flat, fine gravel, grassy

Tariff : (2015 price) 11.30€ ✮✮ 🚗 🔲 [½] (10A) – Extra per person 2.30€
Rental rates : (2015 price) permanent – 11 🏠. Per night from 47 to 62€ – Per week from 158 to 287€
🚐 Eurorelais sani-station 2.10€ – 5 🔲

Surroundings : 🛒 ⚲
Leisure activities : 🏕 ⚓ m sports trail
Facilities : 🚿 🌡 🏖 🚰 launderette
Nearby : ✕ 🍴 🔲 🏊

Longitude : -0.41321
Latitude : 48.15073

These symbols are used for a campsite that is exceptional in its category:

🏔...🏔   *Particularly pleasant setting, quality and range of services available*

🐾🐾   *Tranquil, isolated site – quiet site, particularly at night*

≪≪   *Exceptional view – interesting or panoramic view*

LA FAUTE-SUR-MER

85460 – Michelin map **316** I9 – pop. 916 – alt. 4
▶ Paris 465 – Luçon 37 – Niort 106 – La Rochelle 71

⛰ APV Les Flots Bleus

℘ 02 51 27 11 11. www.camping-lesflotsbleus.com – limited spaces for one-night stay

Address : avenue des Chardons (located 1km southeast following signs for La Pointe d'Arçay (headland)

1.5 ha (104 pitches) flat, grassy, sandy
Rentals : 77 🚐 – 2 tent lodges.
Situated in a residential area, 200m from the beach.

Surroundings : 🛒 ⚲
Leisure activities : ✕ ⚓ 🔲 (open air in season)
Facilities : 🚿 🌡 🏖 🚰 launderette
Nearby : 🍷

Longitude : -1.31842
Latitude : 46.32508

LA FLÈCHE

72200 – Michelin map **310** I8 – pop. 15 228 – alt. 33
▶ Paris 244 – Angers 52 – Châteaubriant 106 – Laval 70

⛰ La Route d'Or

La Route d'Or

℘ 02 43 94 55 90. www.camping-lafleche.com

Address : allée du Camping (take the southern exit towards Saumur and take a right turn; beside the Loir river)

Opening times : from beginning March to end Oct.

4 ha (250 pitches) flat, grassy

Tariff : 16.69€ ✮✮ 🚗 🔲 [½] (10A) – Extra per person 3.52€ – Reservation fee 16€

Rental rates : (from beginning April to end Oct.) 🚿 – 10 🚐. Per night from 85 to 105€ – Per week from 199 to 555€
🚐 AireService sani-station – 20 🔲 16.69€

Surroundings : 🛒 ⚲
Leisure activities : 🏕 🚲 ✂ 🎿
Facilities : 🚿 🌡 🏖 🚰 🔲
Nearby : 🌊

Longitude : -0.07779
Latitude : 47.69509

The Michelin classification (🏔🏔🏔 ... 🏔) is totally independent of the official star classification system awarded by the local prefecture or other official organisation.

FRESNAY-SUR-SARTHE

72130 – Michelin map **310** J5 – pop. 2 198 – alt. 95
▶ Paris 235 – Alençon 22 – Laval 73 – Mamers 30

⛰ Municipal Sans Souci ♨♨

℘ 02 43 97 32 87. www.camping-fresnaysursarthe.fr

Address : rue du Haut Ary (located 1km west along the D 310, follow the signs for Sillé-le-Guillaume)

Opening times : from beginning April to end Oct.

2 ha (85 pitches) terraced, flat, grassy

Tariff : 13.31€ ✮✮ 🚗 🔲 [½] (10A) – Extra per person 2.50€
Rental rates : permanent 🚿 – 1 'gypsy' caravan – 6 🏠. Per week from 153 to 491€ – Reservation fee 60€
🚐 local sani-station 3.15€ – 39 🔲 9.30€
Attractive, marked-out pitches beside the Sarthe river.

Surroundings : 🐾 🛒
Leisure activities : 🏕 👫 ⚓ ✂
Facilities : 🚿 🌡 🏖 🚰 🔲 🔲
Nearby : 🛶 🏊 🌊

Longitude : 0.01589
Latitude : 48.28252

Michelin classification:

🏔🏔🏔🏔   *Extremely comfortable, equipped to a very high standard*
🏔🏔🏔   *Very comfortable, equipped to a high standard*
🏔🏔   *Comfortable and well equipped*
🏔   *Reasonably comfortable*
🏔   *Satisfactory*

FROMENTINE

85550 – Michelin map **316** D6
▶ Paris 455 – Nantes 69 – La Roche 72 – St-Nazaire 70

▲▲▲ Campéole La Grande Côte ♣♣

✆ 02 51 68 51 89. www.campeole.com

Address : route de la Grande Côte (situated 2km along the D 38b)

Opening times : from end April to mid Sept.

21 ha (810 pitches) terraced, flat, sandy

Tariff : 15€ ♣♣ ➾ 🔲 🎣 (10A) – Extra per person 10€ – Reservation fee 25€

Rental rates : (from end April to mid Sept.) ♿ (1 mobile home) – 85 🛏 – 36 🏠 – 115 canvas bungalows. Per night from 30 to 178€ – Per week from 210 to 1,246€ – Reservation fee 25€

🚿 local sani-station

Surroundings : ⚲⚲ ⛰ Leisure activities : 🍴 🏛 🎣 🏃 🛶 🚴 🛹 🏊 multi-sports ground Facilities : ♿ ☕ 🧺 launderette 🚿 🧍 Nearby : 🍴 🎣	**GPS** Longitude : -2.14732 Latitude : 46.88553

GIVRAND

85800 – Michelin map **316** E7 – pop. 1 946 – alt. 10
▶ Paris 460 – Nantes 79 – La Roche-sur-Yon 39

▲▲▲ FranceLoc Les Dauphins Bleus ♣♣
(rental of mobile homes and chalets only)

✆ 02 51 55 59 34. www.camping-franceloc.fr ⚡

Address : 16 rue du Rocher

Opening times : from mid April to mid Sept.

7 ha flat, grassy

Rental rates : (2015 price) ♿ (2 mobile homes) – 308 🛏 – 4 🏠. Per night from 39 to 133€ – Per week from 154 to 1,274€ – Reservation fee 27€

A mobile home village and chalets set beside a water park.

Surroundings : 🏊 ⚲ Leisure activities : 🍴 🍽 🏛 🎣 🏃 🛶 🚴 🎣 🏊 🔲 🏊 ⛲ cinema, multi-sports ground Facilities : ♿ ☕ 🧺 🧍 launderette 🚿 🧍	**GPS** Longitude : -1.89497 Latitude : 46.67292

▲▲ Chadotel Le Domaine de Beaulieu

✆ 02 51 55 59 46. http://www.chadotel.com/fr/camping/vendee/saint-gilles-croix-de-vie/camping-le-domaine-de-beaulieu – limited spaces for one-night stay

Address : rue du Parc (off the D 38, at Les Temples)

Opening times : from beginning April to end Sept.

8 ha (340 pitches) flat, grassy

Tariff : 32€ ♣♣ ➾ 🔲 🎣 (10A) – Extra per person 6€ – Reservation fee 25€

Rental rates : (from beginning April to end Sept.) – 148 🛏 – 6 🏠. Per night from 25 to 155€ – Per week from 175 to 1,085€ – Reservation fee 25€

🚿 local sani-station – 150 🔲 – 🚐 8€

In a partially shaded setting; ageing sanitary facilities.

Surroundings : 🏡 ⚲⚲ Leisure activities : 🍴 🍽 🏛 🌙 nighttime, jacuzzi 🏃 🚴 🎣 🏊 🏊 ⛲ multi-sports ground, entertainment room Facilities : ♿ ☕ 🧍 🧺 🧍 🔲 🚿 🧍	**GPS** Longitude : -1.90389 Latitude : 46.67056

LE GIVRE

85540 – Michelin map **316** H9 – pop. 424 – alt. 20
▶ Paris 446 – Luçon 20 – La Mothe-Achard 33 – Niort 88

▲ La Grisse

✆ 02 51 30 83 03. www.campinglagrisse.com

Address : at Le Givre (continue 2.5km south towards La Jonchère along the D 85)

Opening times : permanent

1 ha (79 pitches) flat, grassy

Tariff : ♣ 7.70€ ➾ 🔲 8.80€ – 🎣 (16A) 4.30€

Rental rates : permanent – 6 🛏 – 1 gîte. Per week from 199 to 674€

In the grounds of a farm (visits possible); one part of the site has plenty of shade.

Surroundings : 🏊 ⚲ Leisure activities : 🏃 Facilities : ♿ ☕ 🧍 🧺 launderette	**GPS** Longitude : -1.39815 Latitude : 46.44484

LE GREZ

72140 – Michelin map **310** I5 – pop. 390 – alt. 220
▶ Paris 235 – Caen 154 – Laval 57 – Le Mans 37

▲ Les Tournesols

✆ 02 43 20 12 69. www.campinglestournesols.com

Address : Le Landereau, off the D 304

Opening times : from beginning May to end Sept.

2.5 ha (75 pitches) flat, grassy

Tariff : 23€ ♣♣ ➾ 🔲 🎣 (6A) – Extra per person 5€ – Reservation fee 18€

Rental rates : (from beginning May to end Sept.) ⚡ – 1 🛏 – 11 canvas bungalows – 1 tent lodge. Per night from 35 to 65€ – Per week from 130 to 525€ – Reservation fee 18€

Leafy and peaceful site.

Surroundings : 🏊 ⚲ Leisure activities : 🍴 🏛 🏃 🏊 🏊 (small swimming pool) Facilities : ♿ ☕ ♿ 🧍 🧺 🧍 launderette	**GPS** Longitude : -0.1418 Latitude : 48.1893

The pitches of many campsites are marked out with low hedges of attractive bushes and shrubs.

GUÉMENÉ-PENFAO

44290 – Michelin map **316** F2 – pop. 4 951 – alt. 37
▶ Paris 408 – Bain-de-Bretagne 35 – Châteaubriant 39 – Nantes 59

▲▲▲ Flower L'Hermitage

✆ 02 40 79 23 48. www.campinglhermitage.com

Address : 46 avenue du Paradis (1.2km east following signs for Châteaubriant and take the road to the right, near the municipal swimming pool)

Opening times : from beginning April to end Oct.

2.5 ha (83 pitches) relatively flat, flat, grassy

Tariff : 22.50€ ♣♣ ➾ 🔲 🎣 (6A) – Extra per person 5€ – Reservation fee 13€

Rental rates : (from beginning April to end Oct.) – 10 🛏 – 2 🏠 – 3 canvas bungalows – 2 tent lodges – 1 gîte. Per night from 39 to 98€ – Per week from 196 to 686€ – Reservation fee 13€

🚿 local sani-station – 30 🔲 15€

A pleasant wooded campsite.

Surroundings : 🏞 ♀♀
Leisure activities : 🎣 🚣 🚲 🛴 (small swimming pool) 🏊
Facilities : 🚿🅿🛁🚻🍴 🖥
Nearby : 🚤 🍴 🎣 🤿 🐴

GPS Longitude : -1.81838
Latitude : 47.62572

GUÉRANDE

44350 – Michelin map **316** B4 – pop. 15 446 – alt. 54
▶ Paris 450 – La Baule 6 – Nantes 77 – St-Nazaire 20

🏕 Le Trémondec

📞 02 40 60 00 07. www.camping-tremondec.com

Address : 48 rue du Château Careil (north of La Baule)

2 ha (107 pitches) terraced, relatively flat, grassy
Rentals : 20 🚐 – 23 🏠.

Surroundings : 🏞 ♀
Leisure activities : 🍹 🏛 🚣 🚲
Facilities : 🚿 🛁 🍴 launderette 🐕
Nearby : 🍴

GPS Longitude : -2.40155
Latitude : 47.29792

LA GUYONNIÈRE

85600 – Michelin map **316** I6 – pop. 2 674 – alt. 63
▶ Paris 395 – Nantes 47 – La Roche-sur-Yon 48 – Angers 105

🏕 La Chausselière

📞 02 51 41 98 40. www.chausseliere.fr

Address : route des Herbiers (1.2km to the south; beside the Lac de La Chausselière)

Opening times : permanent

1 ha (51 pitches) flat, grassy

Tariff : 16€ ★★ 🚐 🔲 🔌 (16A) – Extra per person 4.50€ – Reservation fee 3€
Rental rates : permanent ♿ (1 chalet) – 1 'gypsy' caravan – 15 🚐 – 10 🏠 – 3 tent lodges. Per night from 37 to 120€ – Per week from 185 to 840€ – Reservation fee 5€

In a green setting beside the lake.

Surroundings : 🏞 🏞 ♀♀
Leisure activities : 🚣 🏊 multi-sports ground
Facilities : ♿ 🚿 🛁 🚻 🖥
Nearby : 🤿 🐟

GPS Longitude : -1.2457
Latitude : 46.95735

ÎLE DE NOIRMOUTIER

85 – Michelin map **316** – alt. 8

 85630 – Michelin map **316** C6 – pop. 1 802 – alt. 5
▶ Paris 453 – Challans 32 – Nantes 70 – Noirmoutier-en-l'Île 11

🏕 Original Camping Domaine Le Midi ⚑👥

📞 02 51 39 63 74. www.domaine-le-midi.com

Address : rue du Camping (continue 1km northwest along the D 948 and take road to the left)

Opening times : from beginning April to end Sept.

13 ha (419 pitches) undulating, flat and relatively flat, grassy, sandy

Tariff : (2015 price) 38€ ★★ 🚐 🔲 🔌 (16A) – Extra per person 8€ – Reservation fee 25€

Rental rates : (2015 price) (from beginning April to end Sept.) – 50 🚐 – 100 🏠 – 8 tipis – 15 canvas bungalows – 100 tent lodges. Per night from 44 to 120€ – Per week from 199 to 1,479€ – Reservation fee 25€

🚉 sani-station

Close to the beach; a range of rental options in a well laid out, natural site.

Surroundings : 🌊 ♀ ⛰
Leisure activities : ✖ 🎱 🏓 🎣 🚣 🍴 🎣 🏊 🎣 multi-sports ground, entertainment room
Facilities : ♿ 🚿 🛁 🍴 launderette 🐕
Nearby : 🚤 🚲

GPS Longitude : -2.18447
Latitude : 46.94531

L'Épine 85740 – Michelin map **316** C6 – pop. 1 727 – alt. 2
▶ Paris 466 – Nantes 79 – La Roche-sur-Yon 81

🏕 Original Camping La Bosse

📞 02 53 46 97 47. www.camping-de-la-bosse.com

Address : rue du Port

Opening times : from beginning April to end Sept.

10 ha (350 pitches)

Tariff : (2015 price) 24.90€ ★★ 🚐 🔲 🔌 (4A) – Extra per person 6.30€ – Reservation fee 21€

Rental rates : (2015 price) (from beginning April to end Sept.) – 5 tipis – 15 canvas bungalows – 8 tent lodges. Per night from 34 to 45€ – Per week from 169 to 516€ – Reservation fee 21€

Close to the beach in a natural, undulating setting.

Surroundings : ⊰ Port de Morin marina ♀ ⛰
Leisure activities : 🚣
Facilities : 🚿 🛁 launderette

GPS Longitude : -2.2833
Latitude : 46.98523

La Guérinière 85680 – Michelin map **316** C6 – pop. 1 488 – alt. 5
▶ Paris 460 – Challans 39 – Nantes 77 – Noirmoutier-en-l'Île 5

🏕 Domaine Les Moulins ⚑👥

📞 02 51 39 51 38. http://http://www.campingdelacourt.fr

Address : 54 rue des Moulins

Opening times : from beginning April to end Sept.

5.5 ha (175 pitches) dunes, flat, relatively flat, sandy, grassy

Tariff : (2015 price) 16.50€ ★★ 🚐 🔲 🔌 (16A) – Extra per person 4.50€ – Reservation fee 15€

Close to the beach, with a variety of unusual rental options – vehicles not permitted.

Surroundings : 🌊 🏞 ♀♀ ⛰
Leisure activities : 🍹 ✖ 🏛 🎱 daytime 🏓 🎣 hammam, jacuzzi 🚣 🎣 🏊 multi-sports ground, entertainment room
Facilities : ♿ 🚿 🅿 🏧 🍴 launderette 🐕
Nearby : 🚤

GPS Longitude : -2.217
Latitude : 46.96675

---

*For more information on visiting particular towns or regions, consult the relevant regional **MICHELIN Green Guide**. We also recommend you use the appropriate Michelin regional map to locate your selected campsite, to calculate distances and to work out the best route.*

⚠ Le Caravan'Île ♦♦

☎ 02 51 39 50 29. www.caravanile.com

Address : 1 rue de la Tresson (take the eastern exit along the D 948 and take a right turn before the roundabout)

8.5 ha (385 pitches) relatively flat, flat, grassy, sandy

Rentals : 95 🚐.

🚽 local sani-station – 49 🔲

Close to the beach (direct access via the steps through the dunes).

Surroundings : 🏖 ⛰
Leisure activities : ♈ ✗ 🏠 ☺ 🎯 🎣 jacuzzi 🚴 🎱 🔲 ⛵ multi-sports ground
Facilities : ♿ ⚡ 🚿 ☂ launderette 🧺 🚮
Longitude : -2.21674
Latitude : 46.96569

Noirmoutier-en-l'île 85330 – Michelin map **316** C5 – pop. 4 661 – alt. 8
▶ Paris 468 – Nantes 80 – St-Nazaire 82 – Vannes 160

⚠ Indigo Noirmoutier

☎ 02 51 39 06 24. www.camping-indigo.com

Address : 23 allée des Sableaux – Bois de la Chaize

Opening times : from mid April to beginning Oct.

12 ha (530 pitches) flat, grassy, sandy

Tariff : (2015 price) 29.70€ ♣♣ 🚗 🔲 ⚡ (10A) – Extra per person 5.80€ – Reservation fee 13€

Rental rates : (2015 price) (from mid April to beginning Oct.) – 100 tent lodges. Per night from 53 to 120€ – Per week from 260 to 840€ – Reservation fee 13€

🚽 local sani-station 7€

In an attractive location close to the La Plage des Sableaux beach.

Surroundings : 🏖 ⛰ ⛰
Leisure activities : ♈ ✗ 🏠 🚴
Facilities : ♿ ⚡ 🚿 ☂ launderette 🧺
Nearby : 🏇
Longitude : -2.2205
Latitude : 46.9966

⚠ Municipal le Clair Matin

☎ 02 51 39 05 56. www.noirmoutier-campings.fr

Address : rue des Sableaux (at Les Bois de la Chaize) near the Reserve Naturelle de Mullembourg

Opening times : from mid March to end Oct.

6.5 ha (276 pitches) flat, grassy, sandy

Tariff : (2015 price) 14.26€ ♣♣ 🚗 🔲 ⚡ (10A) – Extra per person 3.35€ – Reservation fee 9€

A site with open access to many natural areas.

Surroundings : 🏖 ⛰⛰
Leisure activities : ♿ 🎯 🚴
Facilities : ♿ ⚡ (summer) ☂ 🔲
Nearby : ♈ ✗ 🏇
Longitude : -2.2205
Latitude : 46.99567

L'ILE-D'OLONNE

85340 – Michelin map **316** F8 – pop. 2 668 – alt. 5
▶ Paris 455 – Nantes 100 – La Roche-sur-Yon 35 – Challans 37

⚠ Île aux Oiseaux ♦♦

☎ 02 51 90 89 96. www.ile-aux-oiseaux.fr – limited spaces for one-night stay

Address : rue du Pré Neuf (800m northeast along the D 87)

5 ha (215 pitches) flat, grassy

Rentals : 29 🚐.

In a pleasant setting, with very few places for tents or caravans.

Surroundings : 🏖 🔲 🎣
Leisure activities : 🏠 🎯 🚴 🎱 🔲 ⛵ multi-sports ground
Facilities : ♿ ⚡ 🚿 ☂ 🧺 ♈ launderette
Longitude : -1.77813
Latitude : 46.56624

To make the best possible use of this guide, please read pages 2–15 carefully.

JARD-SUR-MER

85520 – Michelin map **316** G9 – pop. 2 497 – alt. 14
▶ Paris 453 – Challans 62 – Luçon 36 – La Roche-sur-Yon 35

⚠ Chadotel L'Océano d'Or ♦♦

☎ 02 51 33 65 08. http://www.chadotel.com/fr/camping/vendee/jard-sur-mer/camping-loceano-dor

Address : 58 rue Georges Clemenceau (to the northeast of Jard sur Mer, along the D 21)

Opening times : from beginning April to end Sept.

8 ha (450 pitches) flat, grassy

Tariff : 34.50€ ♣♣ 🚗 🔲 ⚡ (10A) – Extra per person 6€ – Reservation fee 25€

Rental rates : (from beginning April to end Sept.) ♿ (1 chalet) – 285 🚐 – 15 🏠 – 4 gîtes. Per night from 29 to 160€ – Per week from 203 to 1,120€ – Reservation fee 25€

🚽 local sani-station – 150 🔲

A pretty site with classic and luxury rental accommodation in mobile homes and gîtes.

Surroundings : 🔲 🎣🎣
Leisure activities : ♈ 🏠 ☺ 🎯 🎣 🚴 🎱 ⛵ multi-sports ground, entertainment room
Facilities : ♿ ⚡ 🚿 ☂ 🧺 ♈ launderette 🚮 🧺
Longitude : -1.57195
Latitude : 46.42032

⚠ Club Airotel Le Curty's ♦♦
(rental of mobile homes and chalets only)

☎ 02 51 33 06 55. www.campinglecurtys.com

Address : rue de la Perpoise (north of Jard sur Mer)

8 ha (360 pitches) flat, grassy

Rentals : 191 🚐 – 20 🏠.

A mobile home park for rentals and owner-occupiers.

Surroundings : 🔲 🎣
Leisure activities : ♈ ✗ 🏠 ☺ 🎯 🚴 🎱 🔲 ⛵ multi-sports ground, entertainment room
Facilities : ♿ ⚡ 🚿 ☂ launderette 🧺
Nearby : 🎱 🏇
Longitude : -1.57825
Latitude : 46.42032

⚠ Chadotel La Pomme de Pin

☎ 75 75 75 75 75. www.chadotelzzzz.com – limited spaces for one-night stay ✂

Address : rue Vincent Auriol (southeast, 150m from the beach at Boisvinet)

Opening times : from beginning April to end Sept.

2 ha (150 pitches) flat, sandy

Tariff : (2015 price) 35.30€ ♣♣ 🚗 🔲 ⚡ (10A) – Extra per person 6€ – Reservation fee 24€

Rental rates : (2015 price) (from beginning Feb. to end Nov.) – 120 🛏️ – 30 🏠. Per night from 30 to 135€ – Per week from 210 to 940€ – Reservation fee 25€

Near the beach, numerous mobile homes based around a small (partially covered) water park.

Surroundings : 🏕️ 🌳
Leisure activities : 🍴 ✕ 🏛️ 🏊 🚴 🎯 🏓 🎣
Facilities : 🚿 ⚕️ 🔌 🛁 🚽 launderette 🧺 🚰

Longitude : -1.57264
Latitude : 46.41084

⛺ La Mouette Cendrée

📞 0251335904. www.mouettecendree.com

Address : chemin du Faux Prieur, at Les Malecots (take the northeastern exit along the D 19, follow the signs for St-Hilaire-la-Forêt)

Opening times : from beginning April to end Oct.

1.8 ha (101 pitches) flat, grassy

Tariff : 29.50€ 🚶🚶 🚗 🔌 (10A) – Extra per person 5€ – Reservation fee 18€

Rental rates : (from beginning April to end Oct.) ♿ (1 mobile home) – 24 🛏️ – 5 canvas bungalows. Per night from 35 to 50€ – Per week from 99 to 789€ – Reservation fee 18€

A leafy, green setting with rental mobile homes that are mostly modern.

Surroundings : 🏕️ 🌳🌳
Leisure activities : 🏊 🏓 🎯
Facilities : 🚿 ⚕️ 🔌 🧺

Longitude : -1.56702
Latitude : 46.42767

Michelin classification:

⛰️⛰️⛰️⛰️ *Extremely comfortable, equipped to a very high standard*
⛰️⛰️⛰️ *Very comfortable, equipped to a high standard*
⛰️⛰️ *Comfortable and well equipped*
⛰️ *Reasonably comfortable*
⛺ *Satisfactory*

LANDEVIEILLE

85220 – Michelin map **316** F8 – pop. 1 185 – alt. 37
▶ Paris 452 – Challans 25 – Nantes 83 – La Roche-sur-Yon 32

⛰️⛰️ L'Orée de l'Océan ♨️♨️

📞 0251229636. www.camping-oreedelocean.com

Address : rue du Capitaine de Mazenod (take the western exit, follow the signs for Brétignolles-sur-Mer)

Opening times : from end April to mid Sept.

2.8 ha (240 pitches) flat, relatively flat, grassy

Tariff : (2015 price) 32€ 🚶🚶 🚗 🔌 (6A) – Extra per person 6€ – Reservation fee 25€

Rental rates : (2015 price) (from beginning April to end Oct.) ♿ (1 mobile home) – 94 🛏️ – 18 canvas bungalows. Per night from 70 to 90€ – Per week from 210 to 910€ – Reservation fee 25€

A pretty, colourful play paddling pool area.

Surroundings : 🌊 🏕️ 🌳🌳
Leisure activities : 🍴 ✕ 🏛️ 🏖️ 🧗 🎿 🎱
🏊 🏓 🎯 multi-sports ground, entertainment room
Facilities : 🚿 ⚕️ 🛁 🚽 launderette
Nearby : ✂️

Longitude : -1.80635
Latitude : 46.64087

LAVARÉ

72390 – Michelin map **310** M6 – pop. 838 – alt. 122
▶ Paris 173 – Bonnétable 26 – Bouloire 14 – La Ferté-Bernard 19

⛺ Le Val de Braye

📞 0243719644. www.basedeloisirs-lavare.fr

Address : route de Vibraye (take the eastern exit along the D 302, at the leisure and activity park)

Opening times : permanent

0.3 ha (20 pitches) flat, grassy

Tariff : 🚶 2€ 🚗 1€ 🔌 – 🔌 (5A) 2€
🛏️ 16 🔌 2€

In an attractive location near a small lake.

Surroundings : 🌄 🏕️ 🌳
Leisure activities : 🏊 🎣
Facilities : ⚕️ 🛁 🚽
Nearby : ✕ 🍴 🚤 🎣 mountain biking

Longitude : 0.64522
Latitude : 48.05326

Some campsites benefit from proximity to a municipal leisure centre.

LONGEVILLE-SUR-MER

85560 – Michelin map **316** H9 – pop. 2 356 – alt. 10
▶ Paris 448 – Challans 74 – Luçon 29 – La Roche-sur-Yon 31

⛰️⛰️⛰️ MS Vacances Les Brunelles ♨️♨️

📞 0253817000. www.ms-vacances.com – limited spaces for one-night stay

Address : rue de La Parée (at Le Bouil, 1km to the south)

Opening times : from beginning April to end Sept.

13 ha (600 pitches) relatively flat, flat, grassy

Tariff : 48€ 🚶🚶 🚗 🔌 (10A) – Extra per person 13€ – Reservation fee 25€

Rental rates : (from beginning April to end Sept.) ♿ (1 mobile home) – 483 🛏️ – 10 🏠. Per night from 26 to 241€ – Per week from 182 to 1,687€ – Reservation fee 25€

🛏️ AireService sani-station

Surroundings : 🌊 🏕️ 🌳
Leisure activities : 🍴 ✕ 🏛️ 🏖️ 🧗 🏂 🛶 hammam, jacuzzi 🏊 🚴 ✂️ 🏓 🎯 🎱 multi-sports ground
Facilities : 🚿 ⚕️ 🔌 🛁 🚽 🚰 launderette 🧺 🚰
Nearby : 🎣

Longitude : -1.52191
Latitude : 46.41326

⛰️⛰️⛰️ Camp'Atlantique Le Petit Rocher ♨️♨️

📞 0251204194. www.campinglepetitrocher.com

Address : 1250 avenue du Dct Mathevet

Opening times : from beginning April to mid Sept.

5 ha (211 pitches) undulating, terraced, relatively flat, flat, grassy

Tariff : 32€ 🚶🚶 🚗 🔌 (10A) – Extra per person 9€ – Reservation fee 25€

Rental rates : permanent ♿ (1 mobile home) – 5 'gypsy' caravans – 143 🛏️ – 5 tent lodges. Per night from 30 to 175€ – Per week from 210 to 1,225€ – Reservation fee 25€

Surroundings : 🏕️ 🌳🌳
Leisure activities : ✕ 🏖️ 🧗 🏂 hammam, jacuzzi 🏊 🏓 🎯 multi-sports ground
Facilities : 🚿 ⚕️ 🛁 🚽 launderette
Nearby : 🧺 🍴 🚰

Longitude : -1.50727
Latitude : 46.40344

LUCHÉ-PRINGÉ

72800 – Michelin map **310** J8 – pop. 1 658 – alt. 34

▶ Paris 242 – Château-du-Loir 31 – Écommoy 24 – La Flèche 14

⚠ Municipal la Chabotière

🖉 06 74 78 39 97. www.lachabotiere.com

Address : place des Tilleuls (in the west of the small town)

Opening times : permanent

3 ha (75 pitches) terraced, flat, grassy

Tariff : 15.20€ ✦✦ ⇔ 🗉 ⚡ (10A) – Extra per person 4€ – Reservation fee 30€

Rental rates : permanent ♿ – 10 🏠 – 9 canvas bungalows. Per night from 33 to 92€ – Per week from 174 to 540€ – Reservation fee 75€

🚐 local sani-station 2€

In a leisure and activity park; beside the Loir river.

Surroundings : 🏊 ⛺ ♀	
Leisure activities : 🎣 🏄 🚴	**G** Longitude : 0.07364
Facilities : ♿ ⛽ (July–Aug.) 🅿 🏕 🍴 launderette	**P** Latitude : 47.70252
Nearby : 🏖 🍴 🎿 🛶 🐎 boats to hire	

LE LUDE

72800 – Michelin map **310** J9 – pop. 4 049 – alt. 48

▶ Paris 244 – Angers 63 – Chinon 63 – La Flèche 20

⚠ Municipal au Bord du Loir

🖉 02 43 94 67 70. www.camping-lelude.com

Address : route du Mans (0.8km northwest along the D 307, follow the signs for Le Mans)

Opening times : from beginning April to end Sept.

2.5 ha (113 pitches) flat, grassy

Tariff : (2015 price) 13€ ✦✦ ⇔ 🗉 ⚡ (10A) – Extra per person 5€

Rental rates : (2015 price) (from beginning April to end Sept.) 🏕 – 4 🚐 – 5 🏠 – 4 canvas bungalows. Per night from 30 to 75€ – Per week from 130 to 430€

🚐 Eurorelais sani-station 2€

In a rural setting beside the Loir river.

Surroundings : ♀	
Leisure activities : 🏓 🏄 🚴 🐎	**G** Longitude : 0.16247
Facilities : ♿ 🚿 🍴 🏕 🍴	**P** Latitude : 47.65119
Nearby : 🏖 🍴 🎿 🛶 🐎 pedalos	

MACHÉ

85190 – Michelin map **316** F7 – pop. 1 337 – alt. 42

▶ Paris 443 – Challans 22 – Nantes 59 – La Roche-sur-Yon 26

⚠ Le Val de Vie

🖉 02 51 60 21 02. www.campingvaldevie.fr

Address : 5 rue du Stade (take the exit for Apremont and take the road to the left; 400m from the lake)

Opening times : from mid April to end Sept.

2.5 ha (93 pitches) relatively flat, flat, grassy

Tariff : (2015 price) 23.90€ ✦✦ ⇔ 🗉 ⚡ (16A) – Extra per person 4€

Rental rates : (2015 price) (from beginning March to end Nov.) – 3 🚐 – 2 🏠. Per night from 30 to 55€ – Per week from 220 to 720€

🚐 local sani-station 2.50€ – 6 🗉 8.50€

Surroundings : 🏊 ⛺	
Leisure activities : 🎣 🏄 🐎	**G** Longitude : -1.68595
Facilities : ♿ ⛽ 🏕 🍴 🍴	**P** Latitude : 46.75305
Nearby : 🍴	

MACHECOUL

44270 – Michelin map **316** F6 – pop. 5 872 – alt. 5

▶ Paris 420 – Beauvoir-sur-Mer 23 – Nantes 39 – La Roche-sur-Yon 56

⚠ La Rabine

🖉 02 40 02 30 48. www.camping-la-rabine.com

Address : allée de la Rabine (take the southern exit along the D 95, follow the signs for Challans; beside the Falleron river)

Opening times : from beginning April to end Sept.

2.8 ha (131 pitches) flat, grassy

Tariff : (2015 price) 15€ ✦✦ ⇔ 🗉 ⚡ (13A) – Extra per person 4.10€

Rental rates : (2015 price) (from beginning April to end Sept.) – 1 'gypsy' caravan – 4 🚐 – 3 canvas bungalows. Per night from 45 to 70€ – Per week from 260 to 500€ – Reservation fee 15€

🚐 local sani-station 3.50€ – 4 🗉 11.30€

Very near the town centre, encircled by a small river.

Surroundings : ♀	
Leisure activities : 🎣 🐎	**G** Longitude : -1.81555
Facilities : ♿ ⛽ 🍴 launderette	**P** Latitude : 46.9887
Nearby : 🍴 🏖	

MAILLEZAIS

85420 – Michelin map **316** L9 – pop. 962 – alt. 6

▶ Paris 436 – Fontenay-le-Comte 15 – Niort 27 – La Rochelle 49

⚠ Municipal de l'Autize

🖉 06 43 19 14 90. www.maillezais.fr

Opening times : from beginning April to end Sept.

1 ha (40 pitches) flat, grassy

Tariff : (2015 price) 14.60€ ✦✦ ⇔ 🗉 ⚡ (13A) – Extra per person 2.60€

🚐 Raclet sani-station 2€

In a green setting at the exit from the village.

Surroundings : ⛺ ♀♀	
Leisure activities : 🏓	**G** Longitude : -0.73914
Facilities : ♿ ⛽ (July–Aug.) 🚿 🍴 🏕 🍴	**P** Latitude : 46.37133
Nearby : 🏄 🍴	

MALICORNE-SUR-SARTHE

72270 – Michelin map **310** I8 – pop. 1 962 – alt. 39

▶ Paris 236 – Château-Gontier 52 – La Flèche 16 – Le Mans 32

⚠ Municipal Port Ste Marie

🖉 02 43 94 80 14. www.ville-malicorne.fr

Address : northwest of the town, north of the Sarthe river, off the D 41

Opening times : from beginning April to end Sept.

1 ha (65 pitches) flat, grassy

Tariff : (2015 price) 11.25€ ✦✦ ⇔ 🗉 ⚡ (13A) – Extra per person 2.40€

Rental rates : (2015 price) (from beginning April to end Sept.) – 4 🚐 – 6 canvas bungalows. Per night from 49 to 127€ – Per week from 149 to 396€

🚐 local sani-station 4.15€ – 1 🔲 8.10€ – 🚐 8€

A pleasant site and setting near the Sarthe river.

Surroundings : ♀
Leisure activities : 🛶 🏊
Facilities : & (July–Aug.) 🏕 launderette
Nearby : 🚴 ✕ 🎾 🏹 🏊 🐴 pedalos

Longitude : -0.0893
Latitude : 47.81763

MAMERS

72600 – Michelin map **310** L4 – pop. 5 545 – alt. 128
▶ Paris 185 – Alençon 25 – Le Mans 51 – Mortagne-au-Perche 25

🏔 Municipal du Saosnois

📞 02 43 97 68 30. www.camping-mamers.fr

Address : continue 1km north following signs for Mortagne-au-Perche and take D 113 to the left, following signs for Contilly, near two lakes

Opening times : from mid April to end Sept.

1.5 ha (40 pitches) terraced, relatively flat, flat, grassy

Tariff : (2015 price) 15€ ✚✚ 🚐 🔲 (10A) – Extra per person 3€
Rental rates : (2015 price) (from mid April to end Sept.) – 3 🚐 – 5 canvas bungalows. Per night from 25 to 45€ – Per week from 150 to 330€

🚐 local sani-station – 8 🔲 7€

Surroundings : 🏞 ♀♀
Leisure activities : 🍽 🏊 (beach)
Facilities : 🔌 🔲 🏕 🏊 🚿
Nearby : 🚴 🎾 🏊 🐴

Longitude : 0.37303
Latitude : 48.35809

MANSIGNÉ

72510 – Michelin map **310** J8 – pop. 1 579 – alt. 80
▶ Paris 235 – Château-du-Loir 28 – La Flèche 21 – Le Lude 17

🏔 La Plage - Base de Loisirs

📞 02 43 46 14 17. www.basedeloisirsmansigne.fr

Address : rue du Plessis (take the northern exit along the D 31, follow the signs for La Suze-sur-Sarthe, 100m from a small lake)

3 ha (115 pitches) flat, grassy

Rentals : & – 8 🚐 – 20 🏠 – 8 canvas bungalows – 1 gîte.

🚐 Eurorelais sani-station – 15 🔲

Surroundings : ♀
Leisure activities : 🍽 🏞 🚴 🎾 🏊 🛶
Facilities : & 🔲 launderette
Nearby : ✕ 🏊 🏖 (beach) 🚣 🐟 pedalos, zip wiring

Longitude : 0.13284
Latitude : 47.75078

MARÇON

72340 – Michelin map **310** M8 – pop. 1 028 – alt. 59
▶ Paris 245 – Château-du-Loir 10 – Le Grand-Lucé 51 – Le Mans 52

🏔 Flower Le Lac des Varennes

📞 02 43 44 13 72. www.lacdesvarennes.com

Address : route de Port Gauthier (located 1km west along the D 61, near the leisure park)

Opening times : from beginning April to mid Oct.

5.5 ha (250 pitches) flat, grassy

Tariff : 20€ ✚✚ 🚐 🔲 (10A) – Extra per person 5.50€ – Reservation fee 10€

Rental rates : (from beginning April to mid Oct.) & – 25 🚐 – 5 canvas bungalows. Per night from 55 to 106€ – Per week from 195 to 742€ – Reservation fee 10€

🚐 local sani-station 4€ – 🚐 8€

In a pleasant setting beside a lake equipped for leisure activities.

Surroundings : ♀
Leisure activities : 🍽 ✕ 🏞 🏊 🚴 🏖 (beach) 🚣
Facilities : & 🔲 🏕 🔲 🏊 🚿
Nearby : 🎾 🏊 🐴 pedalos

Longitude : 0.4993
Latitude : 47.7125

MAULÉVRIER

49360 – Michelin map **317** E6 – pop. 2 855 – alt. 130
▶ Paris 366 – Angers 75 – Nantes 76 – La Roche-sur-Yon 80

🏔 Les Logis de L'Oumois

📞 06 26 93 93 45. www.logisdeloumois.com

Address : L'Oumois (southwest of the town, turn right off the D 20 heading south)

Opening times : permanent

30 ha/2 for camping (40 pitches) flat, grassy

Tariff : (2015 price) 14€ ✚✚ 🚐 🔲 (10A) – Extra per person 5€
Rental rates : (2015 price) permanent 🏠 – 10 🚐 – 2 🛏 – 2 gîtes. Per night from 60 to 130€ – Per week from 280 to 470€

🚐 local sani-station 14€

Surroundings : 🏞 ♀
Leisure activities : 🛶 🏊 🚣 🏊
Facilities : & 🔲 🔲 🏕 launderette

Longitude : -0.7592
Latitude : 46.9987

*For more information on visiting particular towns or regions, consult the relevant regional **MICHELIN Green Guide**. We also recommend you use the appropriate Michelin regional map to locate your selected campsite, to calculate distances and to work out the best route.*

MAYENNE

53100 – Michelin map **310** F5 – pop. 13 350 – alt. 124
▶ Paris 283 – Alençon 61 – Flers 56 – Fougères 47

🏔 Du Gué St-Léonard

📞 02 43 04 57 14. http://www.paysdemayenne-tourisme.fr

Address : rue du Gué St-Léonard (north of the town, via av. de Loré and turning to the right)

Opening times : from mid March to end Sept.

1.8 ha (70 pitches) flat, grassy

Tariff : (2015 price) 11.50€ ✚✚ 🚐 🔲 (16A) – Extra per person 4€
Rental rates : (2015 price) (from beginning March to end Oct.) – 6 🚐 – 1 canvas bungalow. Per week from 165 to 498€

🚐 5 🔲 11€ – 🚐 11€

In a pleasant setting beside the Mayenne river.

Surroundings : ♀♀
Leisure activities : ✕ 🏞 🛶 🚣
Facilities : & 🔲 🔲 🏕 launderette
Nearby : 🛒 🎾

Longitude : -0.61387
Latitude : 48.3142

LE MAZEAU

85420 – Michelin map **316** L9 – pop. 427 – alt. 8
🚩 Paris 435 – Fontenay-le-Comte 22 – Niort 21 – La Rochelle 53

⚠ Municipal le Relais du Pêcheur

🖉 02 51 52 93 23. www.mairielemazeau.fr

Address : route de la Sèvre (700m south of the town, near a canal)

Opening times : from beginning April to end Sept.

1 ha (54 pitches) flat, grassy

Tariff : (2015 price) 🧍 3.60 € 🚗 🔲 4.70 € – 🔌 (10A) 3.60 €
Rental rates : (from mid May to end Sept.) 🚿 – 3 canvas
bungalows. Per night from 32 to 52 € – Per week from 131 to 292 €

*A pleasant site and setting in the heart of the Venise Verte
('Green Venice').*

Surroundings : 🐟 🗔 ♨♨
Leisure activities : 🛖 🏄‍♂️
Facilities : 🚿 ⚓ (July–Aug.) 🧺 🖼
Nearby : 🎣

GPS	Longitude : -0.67535
	Latitude : 46.33052

MÉNIL

53200 – Michelin map **310** E8 – pop. 965 – alt. 32
🚩 Paris 297 – Angers 45 – Château-Gontier 7 – Châteauneuf-sur-
Sarthe 21

⚠ Municipal du Bac

🖉 02 43 70 24 54. www.camping.menil53.fr

Address : rue du Port (east of the village)

Opening times : from mid April to mid Sept.

0.5 ha (34 pitches) flat, grassy

Tariff : (2015 price) 11.50 € 🧍🧍 🚗 🔲 🔌 (10A) – Extra per person 4 €
Rental rates : (2015 price) permanent – 5 🏠. Per night
from 42 to 88 € – Per week from 163 to 350 € – Reservation fee 13 €
🚽 local sani-station 2 €

A pleasant site and setting near the Mayenne river.

Surroundings : 🐟 🗔 ♀
Leisure activities : ✗ 🏄‍♂️ 🚲 🛶 🏓
Facilities : 🚿 ⚓ 🚰
Nearby : pedalos

GPS	Longitude : -0.67319
	Latitude : 47.77494

*Some information or pricing may have changed since
the guide went to press. We recommend you check the
price list online in advance or at the entrance to the
campsite and enquire about possible restrictions.*

MERVENT

85200 – Michelin map **316** L8 – pop. 1 077 – alt. 85
🚩 Paris 426 – Bressuire 52 – Fontenay-le-Comte 12 – Parthenay 50

⚠ La Joletière

🖉 02 51 00 26 87. www.campinglajoletiere.fr

Address : 700m west along the D 99, north of the Vendée river

Opening times : from beginning April to end Oct.

1.3 ha (73 pitches) relatively flat, grassy

Tariff : 24 € 🧍🧍 🚗 🔲 🔌 (16A) – Extra per person 7 € – Reservation
fee 2 €

Rental rates : (from beginning April to end Oct.) – 1 'gypsy'
caravan – 20 🚐 – 4 🏠 – 3 canvas bungalows. Per night
from 54 to 113 € – Per week from 220 to 660 € – Reservation fee 2 €

*Expanses of greenery, on a gentle slope, with a range of rental
accommodation.*

Surroundings : 🐟 🗔 ♨♨
Leisure activities : ✗ 🛖 🏄‍♂️ 🚲 🖼 🎣
Facilities : 🚿 ⚓ 🧺 🚰 🖼
Nearby : 🍷

GPS	Longitude : -0.7691
	Latitude : 46.5214

MESQUER

44420 – Michelin map **316** B3 – pop. 1 710 – alt. 6
🚩 Paris 460 – La Baule 16 – Muzillac 32 – Pontchâteau 35

⚠ Soir d'Été 👥

🖉 02 40 42 57 26. www.camping-soirdete.com

Address : 401 rue de Bel Air (head 2km northwest along the D 352
and take turning to the left)

Opening times : from beginning April to end Sept.

1.5 ha (92 pitches) flat, relatively flat, sandy

Tariff : 34 € 🧍🧍 🚗 🔲 🔌 (6A) – Extra per person 6 €
Rental rates : (2015 price) (from beginning April to end Sept.) –
21 🚐 – 4 🏠. Per night from 60 to 80 € – Per week
from 270 to 789 €
🚽 local sani-station

In a shaded setting beside a salt marsh.

Surroundings : 🐟 🗔 ♨♨
Leisure activities : 🍷 ✗ 🛖 🏃 🏄‍♂️ 🚲 🖼
(open air in season), multi-sports ground
Facilities : 🚿 ⚓ 🏕 🚰 launderette 🧺
Nearby : 🏖 🎣

GPS	Longitude : -2.47575
	Latitude : 47.4064

⚠ Le Praderoi

🖉 02 40 42 66 72. http://www.camping-praderoi.com

Address : at Quimiac, 14 allée des Barges (2.5km to the northwest,
100m from the beach)

Opening times : from beginning April to end Sept.

0.4 ha (32 pitches) flat, grassy, sandy

Tariff : 25.50 € 🧍🧍 🚗 🔲 🔌 (10A) – Extra per person 4.50 €
Rental rates : (from beginning April to end Sept.) 🚿 – 2 'gypsy'
caravans – 5 🚐. Per night from 80 to 100 € – Per week
from 200 to 620 €

A small site, very peaceful and family-friendly.

Surroundings : 🐟 ♀
Leisure activities : 🏄‍♂️
Facilities : 🚿 ⚓ 🧺 🚰 launderette

GPS	Longitude : -2.48895
	Latitude : 47.40572

MÉZIÈRES-SOUS-LAVARDIN

72240 – Michelin map **310** J6 – pop. 634 – alt. 75
🚩 Paris 221 – Alençon 38 – La Ferté-Bernard 69 – Le Mans 25

⚠ Smile et Braudières

🖉 02 43 20 81 48. www.campingsmileetbraudieres.com – limited
spaces for one-night stay

Address : at Les Braudières (4.5km east along the back road to
St-Jean)

Opening times : permanent

1.7 ha (52 pitches) flat, relatively flat, grassy

Tariff : 20 € 🧍🧍 🚗 🔲 🔌 (5A) – Extra per person 5.50 €

Rental rates : permanent – 5 🚐 – 2 🏠 – 3 canvas bungalows.
Per night from 36 to 80€ – Per week from 252 to 560€
🚐 3 🅴 20€
Situated beside a small fishing lake.

Surroundings : 🌳 🗠 ♀
Leisure activities : ✗ jacuzzi ⚓ 🏊 🎣
Facilities : ᶒ ⟟

G P S Longitude : 0.06328
Latitude : 48.15758

MONTREUIL-BELLAY

49260 – Michelin map **317** I6 – pop. 4 041 – alt. 50
▶ Paris 335 – Angers 54 – Châtellerault 70 – Chinon 39

🏕 Flower Les Nobis d'Anjou 👥

📞 02 41 52 33 66. www.campinglesnobis.com

Address : rue Georges Girouy (take the northwestern exit, follow the signs for Angers and take the road to the left before the bridge)

3 ha (123 pitches) terraced, flat, grassy
Rentals : 16 🚐 – 2 canvas bungalows.
🚐 local sani-station
In a pleasant location on the banks of the Thouet river at the foot of a château.

Surroundings : 🗠 ♀♀
Leisure activities : ▼ ✗ 🏠 ⏱daytime 🏃
⚓ 🏊 🎣
Facilities : ᶒ ⟟ 🛁 ⓦ launderette
Nearby : pedalos

G P S Longitude : -0.15897
Latitude : 47.13204

MONTSOREAU

49730 – Michelin map **317** J5 – pop. 485 – alt. 77
▶ Paris 292 – Angers 75 – Châtellerault 65 – Chinon 18

🏕 L'Isle Verte

📞 02 41 51 76 60. www.campingisleverte.com

Address : avenue de la Loire (take the northwestern exit along the D 947, follow the signs for Saumur; beside the Loire river)

Opening times : from beginning April to mid Oct.

2.5 ha (105 pitches) flat, grassy

Tariff : 28.50€ ✶✶ 🚗 🅴 ⚡ (16A) – Extra per person 6€ – Reservation fee 10€
Rental rates : (from beginning April to mid Oct.) – 18 🚐 – 7 tent lodges. Per night from 45 to 125€ – Per week from 200 to 875€ – Reservation fee 15€
🚐 local sani-station

Surroundings : ⪕ ♀♀
Leisure activities : ✗ 🏠 ⚓ 🚲 🎣 🏊
Facilities : ᶒ ⟟ 🅶 🛁 ⓦ 🅱 ⚘

G P S Longitude : 0.05165
Latitude : 47.21861

LA MOTHE-ACHARD

85150 – Michelin map **316** G8 – pop. 2 524 – alt. 20
▶ Paris 439 – Aizenay 15 – Challans 40 – La Roche-sur-Yon 19

🏕 Le Pavillon

📞 02 51 05 63 46. www.camping-le-pavillon.com

Address : 175 avenue Georges Clemenceau (located 1.5km southwest, follow the signs for Les Sables-d'Olonne)

3.6 ha (117 pitches)

Rentals : 16 🚐 – 6 🏠 – 6 canvas bungalows.
In a green location with a range of mostly modern rental options.

Surroundings : ♀♀
Leisure activities : ▼ 🏠 ⚓ 🏊 🎣 🎣
multi-sports ground
Facilities : ᶒ ⟟ 🛁 ⓦ launderette

G P S Longitude : -1.66728
Latitude : 46.60653

MOUCHAMPS

85640 – Michelin map **316** J7 – pop. 2 600 – alt. 81
▶ Paris 394 – Cholet 40 – Fontenay-le-Comte 52 – Nantes 68

⚠ Le Hameau du Petit Lay

📞 02 51 66 25 72. www.lehameaudupetitlay.com

Address : at Chauvin (600m south along the D 113, follow the signs for St-Prouant)

0.4 ha (39 pitches) flat, grassy
Rentals : 15 🏠.

Surroundings : 🗠 ♀♀
Leisure activities : 🏠 🏃 ⚓ 🏊 (small swimming pool)
Facilities : ᶒ ⓦ 🅱
Nearby : 🎣

G P S Longitude : -1.05483
Latitude : 46.77585

These symbols are used for a campsite that is exceptional in its category:

🏔…⚠ *Particularly pleasant setting, quality and range of services available*

🐾🐾 *Tranquil, isolated site – quiet site, particularly at night*

⪕⪕ *Exceptional view – interesting or panoramic view*

MOUILLERON-LE-CAPTIF

85000 – Michelin map **316** h7 – pop. 4 511 – alt. 70
▶ Paris 421 – Challans 40 – La Mothe-Achard 22 – Nantes 63

🏕 L'Ambois

L'Ambois

📞 02 51 37 29 15. www.campingambois.com – limited spaces for one-night stay

Address : L'Ambois (take southeastern exit along the D 2, follow the signs for la Roche-sur-Yon, then continue 2.6km along the road to the right)

Opening times : permanent

1.75 ha (70 pitches) relatively flat, flat, grassy

Tariff : (2015 price) 17.90€ ✶✶ 🚗 🅴
⚡ (16A) – Extra per person 4.50€ – Reservation fee 12€
Rental rates : (2015 price) permanent – 40 🚐 – 18 🏠 – 2 studios – 1 gîte. Per night from 60 to 80€ – Per week from 178 to 612€ – Reservation fee 12€
In a rural setting with very few places for tents and caravans.

Surroundings : 🐾 🗠 ♀
Leisure activities : 🏠 jacuzzi ⚓ 🚲 🎯 🔲 (open air in season), farm or petting farm
Facilities : ᶒ ⟟ ⫟ 🛁 ⓦ launderette ⚘

G P S Longitude : -1.46092
Latitude : 46.69647

NANTES

44000 – Michelin map **316** G4 – pop. 282 047 – alt. 8
▶ Paris 381 – Angers 88 – Bordeaux 325 – Lyon 660

Nantes Camping

⚲ 02 40 74 47 94. www.nantes-camping.fr

Address : 21 boulevard du Petit Port (situated beside the Cens river)

Opening times : permanent

8 ha (151 pitches) relatively flat, flat, grassy, gravelled

Tariff : (2015 price) 34.90€ ✦✦ ⇌ 🅴 🅷 (16A) – Extra per person 6€ – Reservation fee 15€

Rental rates : (2015 price) permanent ⅋ (1 chalet) – 56 🛖 – 6 🏠 – 4 tent lodges. Per night from 41 to 159€ – Per week from 246 to 954€ – Reservation fee 25€

High-end rentals, free use of the Petit Port swimming pool (100m) and a tram stop for the town centre.

Surroundings : ⅋ ▱ ♨
Leisure activities : ♇ ✕ ⛵ 🚴 🏇
Facilities : ⅋ ⊶ ▥ ⚐ ☝ ⛩ launderette
Nearby : ▨ ⛸ skating rink

GPS Longitude : -1.5567
Latitude : 47.24346

To visit a town or region, use the MICHELIN Green Guides.

NOTRE-DAME-DE-MONTS

85690 – Michelin map **316** D6 – pop. 1 866 – alt. 6
▶ Paris 459 – Nantes 74 – La Roche-sur-Yon 72

L'Albizia

⚲ 02 28 11 28 50. www.campinglalbizia.com – limited spaces for one-night stay

Address : 52 rue de la Rive (1.9km to the north)

Opening times : from end Feb. to beginning Nov.

3.6 ha (153 pitches)

Tariff : (2015 price) 30€ ✦✦ ⇌ 🅴 🅷 (16A) – Extra per person 6€ – Reservation fee 14€

Rental rates : (from end Feb. to beginning Nov.) – 35 🛖. Per night from 83 to 99€ – Per week from 285 to 877€ – Reservation fee 14€

A pleasant campsite, but numerous owner-occupier mobile homes.

Surroundings : ▱
Leisure activities : ♇ ✕ 🌙 nighttime 🏃 ⛵ 🚴 🏇 ▨ 🏊 multi-sports ground
Facilities : ⅋ ⊶ ⛩ launderette

GPS Longitude : -2.12755
Latitude : 46.8503

Municipal de l'Orgatte

⚲ 02 51 58 84 31. www.notre-dame-de-monts.fr

Address : avenue Abbé Thibaud (1.2km north along the D 38, turn off to the left, 300m from the beach)

Opening times : from beginning April to end Sept.

4.5 ha (315 pitches) undulating, sandy

Tariff : (2015 price) 19.50€ ✦✦ ⇌ 🅴 🅷 (10A) – Extra per person 5.25€ – Reservation fee 10€

📷 local sani-station

In a pleasant location among hills shaded by a pine trees.

Surroundings : ⅋ ♨
Leisure activities : ⛵ multi-sports ground
Facilities : ⊶ ⛩ 🖼

GPS Longitude : -2.13882
Latitude : 46.83972

Le Pont d'Yeu

⚲ 02 51 58 83 76. www.camping-pontdyeu.com

Address : rue du Pont d'Yeu (located 1km south along the D 38, follow the signs for St-Jean-de-Monts, and take turning to the left)

Opening times : from beginning April to end Sept.

1.3 ha (90 pitches) flat, sandy

Tariff : (2015 price) 26.60€ ✦✦ ⇌ 🅴 🅷 (10A) – Extra per person 5€ – Reservation fee 10€

Rental rates : (2015 price) (from beginning April to end Sept.) – 28 🛖 – 2 🏠. Per night from 70€ – Per week from 230 to 700€

A peaceful, family atmosphere; half the pitches are for owner-occupied mobile homes.

Surroundings : ▱ ♨
Leisure activities : ⛵ ▨ (open air in season)
Facilities : ⅋ ⊶ ☝ ⛩ launderette

GPS Longitude : -2.13585
Latitude : 46.82052

NYOISEAU

49500 – Michelin map **317** D2 – pop. 1 305 – alt. 40
▶ Paris 316 – Ancenis 50 – Angers 47 – Châteaubriant 39

La Rivière

⚲ 02 41 92 26 77. www.campinglariviere.fr

Address : 1.2km southeast along the D 71, follow the signs for Segré and take turning to the left; beside the Oudon river

Opening times : from mid June to mid Sept.

1 ha (25 pitches) flat, grassy

Tariff : ✦ 3.30€ ⇌ 🅴 2.80€ – 🅷 (16A) 4€

Rental rates : (2015 price) (from mid June to mid Sept.) ⚹ – 1 🛖. Per night from 45€ – Per week from 300€

📷 local sani-station 4.50€

Surroundings : ⅋ ♨
Leisure activities : 🛶 ⛵ 🏇
Facilities : ⅋ (July–15 Sept.) ⛩
Nearby : 🚵 mountain biking

GPS Longitude : -0.90981
Latitude : 47.71216

Key to rentals symbols:

12 🛖	*Number of mobile homes*
20 🏠	*Number of chalets*
6 🛏	*Number of rooms to rent*
Per night 30–50€	*Minimum/maximum rate per night*
Per week 300–1,000€	*Minimum/maximum rate per week*

OLONNE-SUR-MER

85340 – Michelin map **316** F8 – pop. 13 279 – alt. 40
▶ Paris 458 – Nantes 102 – La Roche-sur-Yon 36 – La Rochelle 96

Sunêlia La Loubine ▲▲

⚲ 02 51 33 12 92. www.la-loubine.fr – limited spaces for one-night stay ⚹

Address : 1 route de la Mer (3km to the west)

Opening times : from beginning April to mid Sept.

8 ha (401 pitches) flat, grassy

Tariff : 41.90€ ✦✦ ⇌ 🅴 🅷 (6A) – Extra per person 7.50€ – Reservation fee 28€

Rental rates : (from beginning April to mid Sept.) ♿ (1 mobile home) ⚡ – 151 🚐 – 2 🏠 – 4 tent lodges. Per night from 29 to 162€ – Per week from 203 to 1,134€ – Reservation fee 28€

Based on a 16th-century Vendée farm, with a charming landscaped water and play park.

Surroundings : 🏕 ♨♨
Leisure activities : 🍴 ✕ 🎱 🌙nighttime 🤸 🎿 jacuzzi 🚣 🚲 ⛳ 🔲 🏊 💧 ⛷ multi-sports ground
Facilities : ♿ ⊶ 🛁 🍽 launderette 🔧 🚿
Nearby : 🐎

GPS Longitude : -1.80647
Latitude : 46.54595

�️ Le Moulin de la Salle 🔹

📞 02 51 95 99 10. www.moulindelasalle.com – limited spaces for one-night stay

Address : rue du Moulin de la Salle (2.7km to the west)

Opening times : from beginning April to mid Sept.

2.7 ha (216 pitches) flat, grassy

Tariff : (2015 price) 34.10€ 🚹🚺 🚐 🔲 (10A) –
Extra per person 5.20€ – Reservation fee 28€

Rental rates : (2015 price) (from beginning April to mid Sept.) –
136 🚐 – 7 🏠. Per night from 60 to 80€ – Per week from 220 to 850€ – Reservation fee 28€

Numerous mobile homes beside a pretty windmill, with very few pitches for tents and caravans.

Surroundings : 🏕 ♨
Leisure activities : 🍴 ✕ 🎱 🤸 🎿 🚣 🔲 🏊 💧 multi-sports ground, entertainment room
Facilities : ♿ ⊶ 🛁 🔧 🍽 launderette 🚿

GPS Longitude : -1.79217
Latitude : 46.53183

�️ Domaine de l'Orée 🔹

📞 02 51 33 10 59. www.l-oree.com

Address : 13 route des Amis de la Nature

Opening times : from mid April to mid Sept.

6 ha (320 pitches) flat, grassy

Tariff : (2015 price) 40.50€ 🚹🚺 🚐 🔲 (10A) – Extra per person 7€ –
Reservation fee 26€

Rental rates : (2015 price) (from mid April to mid Sept.) – 145 🚐 –
6 🏠. Per week from 265 to 1,160€ – Reservation fee 26€

Surroundings : 🏕 ♨
Leisure activities : 🍴 ✕ 🎱 🌙nighttime 🤸 🎿 jacuzzi 🚣 🚲 ⛳ 🔲 🏊 💧 multi-sports ground
Facilities : ♿ ⊶ 🛁 – 10 individual sanitary facilities (🚿 💧 🚽 wc) 🔧 🍽 launderette 🚿
Nearby : 🐎

GPS Longitude : -1.80827
Latitude : 46.5494

🔺 Nid d'Été

📞 02 51 95 34 38. www.leniddete.com

Address : 2 rue de la Vigne Verte (2.5km to the west)

Opening times : from beginning April to end Sept.

2 ha (199 pitches) flat, grassy

Tariff : (2015 price) 29.80€ 🚹🚺 🚐 🔲 (10A) –
Extra per person 5.30€ – Reservation fee 15€

Rental rates : (2015 price) (from beginning April to end Sept.) –
37 🚐 – 1 🏠. Per night from 90 to 169€ – Per week from 199 to 923€ – Reservation fee 15€

Surroundings : 🏞 🏕 ♨♨
Leisure activities : 🍴 ✕ 🎱 jacuzzi 🚣 🔲 (open air in season)
Facilities : ♿ ⊶ 🛁 🍽 launderette 🚿

GPS Longitude : -1.79393
Latitude : 46.53326

🔺 Flower Le Petit Paris 🔹

📞 02 51 22 04 44. www.campingpetitparis.com

Address : 41 rue du Petit-Versailles (located 5.5km southeast)

Opening times : from beginning April to end Sept.

3 ha (154 pitches) flat, grassy

Tariff : (2015 price) 18.50€ 🚹🚺 🚐 🔲 (10A) – Extra per person 3€ –
Reservation fee 18€

Rental rates : (2015 price) (from beginning April to mid Oct.)
⚡ – 4 'gypsy' caravans – 30 🚐. Per night from 44 to 140€ –
Per week from 220 to 980€ – Reservation fee 18€

A green setting with a range of rental options and one area reserved for tents and caravans.

Surroundings : 🏞 🏕 ♨♨
Leisure activities : 🍴 🎱 🤸 🚣 🚣 (open air in season) 💧 multi-sports ground
Facilities : ♿ ⊶ 🛁 🔧 🍽 launderette 🚿
Nearby : parachuting

GPS Longitude : -1.72041
Latitude : 46.47359

🔺 Les Fosses Rouges

📞 02 51 95 17 95. www.camping-lesfossesrouges.com

Address : 8 rue des Fosses Rouges, at la Pironnière (3km southeast)

3.5 ha (248 pitches) flat, grassy

Rentals : 13 🚐.

Situated in a residential area. Choose those pitches furthest away from the road.

Surroundings : 🏕 ♨♨
Leisure activities : 🍴 🚣 ⛳ 🔲 (open air in season)
Facilities : ♿ ⊶ 🛁 🍽 launderette 🚿

GPS Longitude : -1.74124
Latitude : 46.47956

🔺 Sauveterre

📞 02 51 33 10 58. www.campingsauveterre.com

Address : 3 route des Amis de la Nature (3km to the west)

3.2 ha (234 pitches) flat, grassy

Rentals : 23 🚐.

Surroundings : ♨♨
Leisure activities : ✕ 🏊 ⛷
Facilities : ♿ ⊶ 🍽 🔲 🚿
Nearby : 🐎

GPS Longitude : -1.80547
Latitude : 46.54697

Michelin classification:

🔺🔺🔺🔺 *Extremely comfortable, equipped to a very high standard*

🔺🔺🔺 *Very comfortable, equipped to a high standard*

🔺🔺🔺 *Comfortable and well equipped*

🔺🔺 *Reasonably comfortable*

🔺 *Satisfactory*

PIRIAC-SUR-MER

44420 – Michelin map **316** A3 – pop. 2 245 – alt. 7
▶ Paris 462 – La Baule 17 – Nantes 88 – La Roche-Bernard 33

⚞ Parc du Guibel ♟♞

⌖ 02 40 23 52 67. www.parcduguibel.com

Address : route de Kerdrien (3.5km east along the D 52, follow the signs for Mesquer and take turning to the left)

Opening times : from beginning April to end Sept.

14 ha (450 pitches) relatively flat, flat, grassy

Tariff : ♥ 6.50€ ⇦ 3.80€ ▣ 6.50€ – ⚡ (10A) 4.60€ – Reservation fee 18€

Rental rates : (from beginning April to end Sept.) – 90 ⟦⟧ – 34 ⟦⟧. Per night from 50 to 120€ – Per week from 266 to 840€ – Reservation fee 18€

⟱ local sani-station – ⚱11€

Surroundings : ⌇ ⩊
Leisure activities : ♟✗ ⌂ ⁂⛹⚵▨ ⛴⚲multi-sports ground
Facilities : ♿ ⚲⛺⚱⚛ ⁎launderette ⚲⚲
Nearby : ⛖⛏

G P S Longitude : -2.51024
Latitude : 47.3862

⚞ Armor Héol ♟♞

⌖ 02 40 23 57 80. www.camping-armor-heol.com

Address : at Kervin, route de Guérande (located 1km southeast along the D 333)

Opening times : from beginning April to mid Sept.

4.5 ha (270 pitches) flat, grassy, small lake

Tariff : (2015 price) 34€ ♥♥ ⇦ ▣ ⚡ (6A) – Extra per person 7.50€ – Reservation fee 20€

Rental rates : (2015 price) (from beginning April to mid Sept.) – 1 'gypsy' caravan – 58 ⟦⟧ – 22 ⟦⟧. Per night from 54 to 119€ – Per week from 275 to 835€ – Reservation fee 20€

Partially open-air swimming area and the luxury of 20 private sanitary facilities.

Surroundings : ▭ ⩊
Leisure activities : ♟✗ ⌂ ⛹⁂⛲⚵⚲⛴⚲multi-sports ground
Facilities : ♿ ⚲⛺– 20 individual sanitary facilities (⚱⚿ wc) ⁎launderette

G P S Longitude : -2.53563
Latitude : 47.3748

⚞ Mon Calme

⌖ 02 40 23 60 77. www.campingmoncalme.com

Address : rue de Norvoret (located 1km south following signs for La Turballe and take the turning to the left, 450m from the ocean)

Opening times : from beginning April to end Sept.

1.2 ha (88 pitches) flat, grassy

Tariff : 24.50€ ♥♥ ⇦ ▣ ⚡ (10A) – Extra per person 6.80€ – Reservation fee 18€

Rental rates : (from beginning April to end Sept.) – 20 ⟦⟧ – 12 studios. Per night from 48 to 68€ – Per week from 260 to 640€ – Reservation fee 18€

⟱ AireService sani-station 2€

Upmarket apartment hotels.

Surroundings : ⩊
Leisure activities : ✗ ⛲⛹⚵⚲
Facilities : ♿ ⚲⛺⁎
Nearby : ⛖⚵⚱

G P S Longitude : -2.54882
Latitude : 47.37208

LA PLAINE-SUR-MER

44770 – Michelin map **316** C5 – pop. 3 815 – alt. 26
▶ Paris 438 – Nantes 58 – Pornic 9 – St-Michel-Chef-Chef 7

⚞ Sites et Paysages La Tabardière ♟♞

⌖ 02 40 21 58 83. www.camping-la-tabardiere.com

Address : 2 route de la Tabardiere (3.5km east along the D 13, follow the signs for Pornic and take turning to the left)

Opening times : from beginning April to end Sept.

6 ha (270 pitches) terraced, flat, grassy

Tariff : 45€ ♥♥ ⇦ ▣ ⚡ (10A) – Extra per person 8.50€ – Reservation fee 25€

Rental rates : (from beginning April to end Sept.) ⚲ – 12 ⟦⟧ – 28 ⟦⟧. Per night from 40 to 129€ – Per week from 280 to 903€ – Reservation fee 25€

⟱ AireService sani-station 14€ – 5 ▣ 14€ – ⚱14€

Surroundings : ⚲ ⩊
Leisure activities : ♟⌂ ⁂⛲⛹▨(open air in season) ⚲⚲multi-sports ground
Facilities : ♿ ⚲⛺⚲⁎launderette ⚲⚲

G P S Longitude : -2.15313
Latitude : 47.14087

⚞ Le Ranch

⌖ 02 40 21 52 62. www.camping-le-ranch.com

Address : chemin des Hautes Raillères (3km northeast along the D 96)

Opening times : from beginning April to end Sept.

3 ha (183 pitches) flat, grassy

Tariff : (2015 price) 34.90€ ♥♥ ⇦ ▣ ⚡ (10A) – Extra per person 7€ – Reservation fee 17.50€

Rental rates : (2015 price) (from beginning April to end Oct.) ⚲ – 12 ⟦⟧ – 17 ⟦⟧. Per night from 59 to 119€ – Per week from 199 to 830€ – Reservation fee 17.50€

⟱ local sani-station

In a green setting with lots of flowers.

Surroundings : ⚲ ⩊
Leisure activities : ♟✗ ⌂ ⛲⚵⚲multi-sports ground, entertainment room
Facilities : ♿ ⚲⛺⁎launderette ⚲

G P S Longitude : -2.16292
Latitude : 47.15412

*The classification (1 to 5 tents, **black** or red) that we award to selected sites in this guide is our own system. It should not be confused with the classification (1 to 5 stars) of official organisations.*

LES PONTS-DE-CÉ

49130 – Michelin map **317** F4 – pop. 11 575 – alt. 25
▶ Paris 302 – Nantes 92 – Angers 7 – Cholet 57

⚞ Île du Château ♟♞

⌖ 06 59 08 15 09. www.camping-ileduchateau.fr

Address : avenue de la Boire Salée (on the Île du Château)

2.3 ha (135 pitches) flat, grassy

Rentals : 2 ⟦⟧ – 7 canvas bungalows – 1 gîte.

In a wooded setting near the Loire river and municipal gardens.

Surroundings : ▭ ⩊
Leisure activities : ✗ ⌂ ⁂⛲⛹⚵⚱
Facilities : ♿ ⚲⛺⚲⚛⁎▣
Nearby : ⚵⚲⚲

G P S Longitude : -0.53055
Latitude : 47.4244

PORNIC

44210 – Michelin map **316** D5 – pop. 14 052 – alt. 20
▶ Paris 429 – Nantes 49 – La Roche-sur-Yon 89 – Les Sables-d'Olonne 93

⚑ Club Airotel La Boutinardière ⚐⚑

✆ 02 40 82 05 68. www.camping-boutinardiere.com

Address : 23 rue de la Plage de la Boutinardiere (5km southeast along the D 13 and take turning to the right, 200m from the beach)

Opening times : from mid April to end Sept.

7.5 ha (400 pitches) relatively flat, flat, grassy

Tariff : 52€ ⚐⚑ ⇌ 🔲 🔌 (10A) – Extra per person 6.50€ – Reservation fee 25€

Rental rates : (from mid April to end Sept.) – 210 🚐 – 37 🏠 – 15 apartments – 4 tent lodges. Per night from 50 to 110€ – Per week from 203 to 1,300€ – Reservation fee 25€

A village club with a range of services, including a spa centre, and rental apartment equipped to a good standard.

Surroundings : 🌲 ⇌ ♨
Leisure activities : 🍴 ✕ 🏠 🎣 👫 🎿 hammam, jacuzzi ⇌ 🔲 multi-sports ground, spa centre
Facilities : 🚿 ☕ 🏕 🚰 🍴 launderette 🏊 ♨

GPS Longitude : -2.05222 Latitude : 47.09747

⚑ Yelloh! Village La Chênaie ⚐⚑

✆ 02 40 82 07 31. www.campinglachenaie.com

Address : 36 bis rue du Pâtisseau (east along the D 751, follow the signs for Nantes and take turning to the left)

Opening times : from end April to beginning Sept.

8 ha (305 pitches) terraced, relatively flat, flat, grassy

Tariff : 45€ ⚐⚑ ⇌ 🔲 🔌 (10A) – Extra per person 8€

Rental rates : (from mid April to beginning Sept.) – 93 🚐 – 3 tent lodges. Per night from 35 to 209€ – Per week from 245 to 1,463€

Extensive green spaces for relaxation; there is an enclosure with farm animals for the kids.

Surroundings : 🌲 ⇌ ♨
Leisure activities : 🍴 ✕ 🎣 👫 🎿 hammam, jacuzzi ⇌ 🚲 🔲 🏊 farm or petting farm, multi-sports ground, entertainment room
Facilities : 🚿 ☕ 🏕 🍴 launderette 🏊

GPS Longitude : -2.07196 Latitude : 47.1187

Routes nationales are main roads and their identifying numbers begin with N or RN. Routes départementales are generally quieter roads and begin with D or DN.

PORNICHET

44380 – Michelin map **316** B4 – pop. 10 466 – alt. 12
▶ Paris 449 – Nantes 74 – Vannes 84 – La Roche-sur-Yon 143

⚑ Les Forges

✆ 02 40 61 18 84. campinglesforges.com – limited spaces for one-night stay

Address : 98 route de la Villès-Blais, Les Forges district

Opening times : from beginning July to end Aug.

2 ha (130 pitches) terraced, flat, grassy

Tariff : (2015 price) 28.30€ ⚐⚑ ⇌ 🔲 🔌 (10A) – Extra per person 6.80€ – Reservation fee 30€

Rental rates : (2015 price) (from beginning July to end Aug.) – 25 🚐. Per night from 62 to 111€ – Per week from 434 to 777€ – Reservation fee 30€

There's a bus stop for the town centre.

Surroundings : ⇌ ♨
Leisure activities : 🏠 ⇌ 🔲 (open air in season), multi-sports ground
Facilities : 🚿 ☕ 🍴 launderette

GPS Longitude : -2.29379 Latitude : 47.26917

POUANCÉ

49420 – Michelin map **317** B2 – pop. 3 046 – alt. 56
▶ Paris 335 – Angers 67 – Laval 51 – Rennes 62

⚑ Municipal la Roche Martin

✆ 02 41 92 41 08. www.camping-pouance.fr

Address : 23 rue des Étangs

Opening times : permanent

1.5 ha (40 pitches) terraced, flat, grassy

Tariff : (2015 price) ⚐ 3€ ⇌ 1.50€ 🔲 1.50€ – 🔌 (6A) 6€

🚐 local sani-station 4€

Facilities : 🚿 ☕ 🏕 🍴 launderette
Nearby : 🍴 ✕ pedalos

GPS Longitude : -1.179 Latitude : 47.7487

A chambre d'hôte is a guesthouse or B & B-style accommodation.

LE POULIGUEN

44510 – Michelin map **316** B4 – pop. 4 977 – alt. 4
▶ Paris 453 – Guérande 8 – La Baule 4 – Nantes 80

⚑ Municipal les Mouettes

✆ 02 40 42 43 98. www.tourisme-lepouliguen.fr – 🅁

Address : 45 boulevard de l'Atlantique (to the west of the resort along the D 45, right next to the stadium)

Opening times : from mid March to mid Oct.

4.7 ha (220 pitches) flat, grassy, sandy, small lake

Tariff : (2015 price) 16€ ⚐⚑ ⇌ 🔲 🔌 (4A) – Extra per person 5€

🚐 Eurorelais sani-station 2€

Relatively near the town centre and the shops.

Surroundings : ⇌ ♨♨
Leisure activities : 🏠 ⇌
Facilities : 🚿 🏪 🏕 🍴 launderette
Nearby : ♨

GPS Longitude : -2.43942 Latitude : 47.27385

⚑ Municipal le Clein

✆ 02 40 42 43 99. www.lepouliguen.fr – 🅁

Address : 22 avenue de Kerdun

Opening times : from end March to beginning Oct.

1.5 ha (110 pitches) flat, grassy, sandy

Tariff : (2015 price) 20.20€ ⚐⚑ ⇌ 🔲 🔌 (10A) – Extra per person 5€

🚐 AireService sani-station 11.60€

Near the town centre and the beach, with a good parking area for campervans.

Surroundings : ♨♨
Leisure activities : ⇌
Facilities : 🚿 ☕ 🏪 🏕 🍴 launderette
Nearby : 🛒 ♨

GPS Longitude : -2.4301 Latitude : 47.27135

POUZAUGES

85700 – Michelin map **316** K7 – pop. 5 428 – alt. 225
▶ Paris 390 – Bressuire 30 – Chantonnay 22 – Cholet 42

🔺 Le Lac

🖉 02 51 91 37 55. www.campingpouzauges.com

Address : at the lake (located 1.5km west along the D 960 bis, follow the signs for Chantonnay and take the road to the right)

Opening times : permanent

1 ha (54 pitches) terrace, relatively flat, flat, grassy

Tariff : (2015 price) 19 € 🛉🛉 🚐 🗉 🗷 (10A) – Extra per person 5 € – Reservation fee 20 €

Rental rates : (2015 price) permanent – 6 🛏. – Reservation fee 40 €

The site is shaded by plane trees, 50m from the lake.

Surroundings : 🛱 ⚠
Leisure activities : ✗ 🎣
Facilities : 🕭 ⊶ 🏻 launderette
Nearby : 🍷 🎱 🥾

G P S	Longitude : -0.8532 Latitude : 46.78183

PRÉFAILLES

44770 – Michelin map **316** C5 – pop. 1 255 – alt. 10
▶ Paris 440 – Challans 56 – Machecoul 38 – Nantes 60

🔺 Éléovic

🖉 02 40 21 61 60. www.camping-eleovic.com

Address : route de la Pointe Saint-Gildas (located 1km west along the D 75)

3 ha (150 pitches) relatively flat, flat, grassy

Rentals : 60 🛖.

A site overlooking the ocean and picturesque creeks.

Surroundings : 🌊 ≤ ocean and île de Noirmoutier 🛱 🎱
Leisure activities : ✗ 🎣 🌙 nighttime 🏹 🏋️ 🏊 🚴 🗺 (open air in season), multi-sports ground
Facilities : 🕭 ⊶ 🏻 launderette 🚿

G P S	Longitude : -2.23151 Latitude : 47.13292

To visit a town or region, use the MICHELIN Green Guides.

PRUILLÉ

49220 – Michelin map **317** F3 – pop. 630 – alt. 30
▶ Paris 308 – Angers 22 – Candé 34 – Château-Gontier 33

🔺 Bac

🖉 02 41 32 67 29. www.campingdubac-pruille.com

Address : rue du Bac (north of the village; beside the Mayenne river – mooring point)

Opening times : permanent

1.2 ha (45 pitches) flat, grassy

Tariff : (2015 price) 8 € 🛉🛉 🚐 🗉 🗷 (3A) – Extra per person 2 €
Rental rates : (2015 price) permanent – 5 🛖. Per night from 45 to 50 € – Per week from 205 to 228 €

Surroundings : 🌊 🎱
Leisure activities : 🎣
Facilities : 🗑 🏻
Nearby : 🍷 ✗ pedalos

G P S	Longitude : -0.66474 Latitude : 47.57897

LES ROSIERS-SUR-LOIRE

49350 – Michelin map **317** H4 – pop. 2 348 – alt. 22
▶ Paris 304 – Angers 32 – Baugé 27 – Bressuire 66

🔼 Yelloh Village Les Voiles d'Anjou

🖉 02 41 51 94 33. www.camping-valdeloire.com

Address : 6 rue Sainte-Baudruche (take the northern exit along the D 59, follow the signs for Beaufort-en-Vallée, near the junction with the D 79)

Opening times : from beginning April to end Sept.

3.5 ha (110 pitches) flat, grassy

Tariff : 31 € 🛉🛉 🚐 🗉 🗷 (10A) – Extra per person 8 €

Rental rates : (from beginning April to end Sept.) – 2 'gypsy' caravans – 34 🛖 – 4 tent lodges. Per night from 29 to 147 € – Per week from 203 to 1,029 €

🚰 local sani-station – 5 🗉 16 €

In a pleasant leafy setting.

Surroundings : 🛱 🎱
Leisure activities : ✗ 🎣 🏋️ jacuzzi 🚴 🗺 🏊
Facilities : 🕭 ⊶ 🏻 🚿 🗑 🏻 🖼
Nearby : 🍴 🧗 🏔

G P S	Longitude : -0.22599 Latitude : 47.35821

LES SABLES-D'OLONNE

85100 – Michelin map **316** F8 – pop. 14 572 – alt. 4
▶ Paris 456 – Cholet 107 – Nantes 102 – Niort 115

🔼 Chadotel La Dune des Sables 🛎

🖉 02 51 32 31 21. http://www.chadotel.com/fr/camping/vendee/les-sables-dolonne/camping-la-dune-des-sables – limited spaces for one-night stay

Address : Le Paracou, chemin de la Bernardière (4km to the northwest, follow the signs for l'Aubraie)

Opening times : from beginning April to beginning Nov.

7.5 ha (290 pitches) undulating, terraced, flat, grassy, sandy

Tariff : 38.50 € 🛉🛉 🚐 🗉 🗷 (10A) – Extra per person 6 € – Reservation fee 25 €

Rental rates : (from beginning April to beginning Nov.) – 208 🛖 – 2 canvas bungalows. Per night from 25 to 160 € – Per week from 175 to 1,120 € – Reservation fee 25 €

🚰 local sani-station – 40 🗉

A mobile home park near the beach, overlooking the ocean, with very few pitches for tents or caravans.

Surroundings : 🌊 ≤ 🛱
Leisure activities : 🍷 ✗ 🎣 🌙 🏹 🏋️ 🚴 🍴 🧗 🏊 🏊
Facilities : 🕭 ⊶ 🚿 🗑 🏻 launderette 🏊 🚿

G P S	Longitude : -1.81931 Latitude : 46.51207

SABLÉ-SUR-SARTHE

72300 – Michelin map **310** G7 – pop. 12 399 – alt. 29
▶ Paris 252 – Angers 64 – La Flèche 27 – Laval 44

🔼 Municipal de l'Hippodrome 🛎

🖉 02 43 95 42 61. www.tourisme.sablesursarthe.fr

Address : allée du Québec (take the southern exit towards Angers and the turning to the left, next to the racecourse – hippodrome)

Opening times : from beginning April to mid Oct.

3 ha (74 pitches) flat, grassy

Tariff : (2015 price) 14.34 € 🛉🛉 🚐 🗉 🗷 (16A) – Extra per person 3.37 €

Rental rates : (2015 price) (from beginning April to mid Oct.) ♿ (1 chalet) ⚭ – 2 🚐 – 5 🏠. Per night from 70 to 95€ – Per week from 380 to 485€ – Reservation fee 2€
🚰 Flot Bleu sani-station 2€
Decorative trees and shrubs are dotted around the site; located beside the Sarthe river.

Surroundings : 🐟 🚃 ♋♋
Leisure activities : 🏛 🏊 🚣 ⛵ 🎣
Facilities : 👌 ⚭ 🚿 ♈ launderette
Nearby : 🍴 🖼 🔦 🐎

GPS Longitude : -0.33193
Latitude : 47.83136

ST-BERTHEVIN

53940 – Michelin map **310** E6 – pop. 7 097 – alt. 108
▶ Paris 289 – Nantes 128 – Laval 10 – Rennes 66

⛺ Municipal de Coupeau

📞 02 43 68 30 70. www.laval-tourisme.com

Address : rue Jean Cottereau, at the leisure centre (west of the town, 150m from the Vicoin river)

Opening times : from mid April to beginning Oct.

0.4 ha (32 pitches) terraced, flat, grassy

Tariff : (2015 price) ♦ 3.50€ ⇌ 2.20€ 🔲 2.50€ – ⚡ (10A) 2.50€
Situated looking out over a green and restful valley.

Surroundings : 🐟 🚃
Leisure activities : 🏛
Facilities : 👌 ♈
Nearby : 🍴 🖼 🏊 fitness trail

GPS Longitude : -0.83235
Latitude : 48.06431

Do not confuse:
⛺ to ⛺⛺⛺ : *MICHELIN classification with*
★ to ★★★★★ : *official classification*

ST-BRÉVIN-LES-PINS

44250 – Michelin map **316** C4 – pop. 12 133 – alt. 9
▶ Paris 438 – Challans 62 – Nantes 64 – Noirmoutier-en-l'Île 70

⛺⛺⛺ Sunêlia Le Fief 👥

Sunêlia Le Fief

📞 02 40 27 23 86. www.lefief.com

Address : 57 chemin du Fief (2.4km south following signs for Saint-Brévin-l'Océan and take turning to the left)

Opening times : from end March to end Sept.

7 ha (397 pitches) flat, grassy

Tariff : 50.50€ ♦♦ ⇌ 🔲 ⚡ (8A) – Extra per person 12€ – Reservation fee 35€

Rental rates : (from end March to end Sept.) ♿ (1 mobile home) – 205 🚐. Per night from 52 to 255€ – Reservation fee 35€
🚰 local sani-station – 2 🔲 50.50€
A superb spa centre and truly upmarket VIP rental village within a green area.

Surroundings : 🚃 ♋♋
Leisure activities : 🍴 🍴 🏛 🎮 🏊 🏸 🛝 hammam, jacuzzi 🚣 🚲 🎣 🖼 🏊 🎿 multi-sports ground, spa centre, entertainment room
Facilities : 👌 ⚭ 🚿 ♈ launderette 🚮 🛠

GPS Longitude : -2.16768
Latitude : 47.23465

⛺ La Courance

📞 02 40 27 22 91. www.campinglacourance.fr – limited spaces for one-night stay

Address : 110 avenue du Maréchal Foch

Opening times : permanent

2.4 ha (156 pitches) terraced, flat, sandy

Tariff : (2015 price) 18€ ♦♦ ⇌ 🔲 ⚡ (12A) – Extra per person 4.75€ – Reservation fee 25€

Rental rates : (2015 price) permanent ♿ (1 mobile home) – 1 'gypsy' caravan – 40 🚐 – 10 🏠 – 13 canvas bungalows. Per night from 61 to 93€ – Per week from 215 to 830€ – Reservation fee 25€
🚰 local sani-station 3€ – 🚐 11€
Beside the beach, with a view of the St-Nazaire bridge. A bathing area at 500m.

Surroundings : ♋♋
Leisure activities : 🍴 🍴 🎮 nighttime 🚣
Facilities : 👌 ⚭ 🚿 🏛 🚿 ♈ launderette
Nearby : 🍴 🖼

GPS Longitude : -2.1703
Latitude : 47.23786

⛺ Le Mindin

📞 02 40 27 46 41. www.camping-de-mindin.com – limited spaces for one-night stay

Address : 32 avenue du Bois (situated 2km to the north, near the ocean – direct access)

Opening times : permanent

1.7 ha (87 pitches) flat, grassy, sandy

Tariff : (2015 price) 27.75€ ♦♦ ⇌ 🔲 ⚡ (16A) – Extra per person 7.35€ – Reservation fee 25€

Rental rates : (2015 price) permanent – 34 🚐 – 3 canvas bungalows. Per night from 44 to 71€ – Per week from 215 to 830€ – Reservation fee 25€
🚰 local sani-station 3€ – 🚐 11€
Little pine grove close to the beach with view of the port and the bridge at St-Nazaire.

Surroundings : 🐟 🏊 ⛰
Leisure activities : 🍴 🍴 🏛 🖼
Facilities : 👌 ⚭ 🚮 🏛 🚿 ♈ 🚮

GPS Longitude : -2.16915
Latitude : 47.2648

Routes nationales are main roads and their identifying numbers begin with N or RN. Routes départementales are generally quieter roads and begin with D or DN.

ST-CALAIS

72120 – Michelin map **310** N7 – pop. 3 482 – alt. 155
▶ Paris 188 – Blois 65 – Chartres 102 – Châteaudun 58

⛺ Le Lac

📞 02 43 35 04 81. www.saint-calais.fr

Address : rue du Lac (take the northern exit along the D 249, follow the signs for Montaillé)

2 ha (85 pitches) flat, grassy

Rentals : 3 🚐 – 3 🏠.
Situated near a lake.

Surroundings : 🚃
Leisure activities : 🏛
Facilities : 👌 ⚭ 🚿 🚮 ♈
Nearby : 🛒 🍴 🏊 🎣

GPS Longitude : 0.74426
Latitude : 47.92688

ST-ÉTIENNE-DU-BOIS

85670 – Michelin map **316** G7 – pop. 1 901 – alt. 38
▶ Paris 427 – Aizenay 13 – Challans 26 – Nantes 49

⚠ Municipal la Petite Boulogne

✆ 0251345451. www.stetiennedubois-vendee.fr

Address : rue du Stade (south of the town along the D 81, follow the signs for Poiré-sur-Vie and take the road to the right; near the river and a lake)

Opening times : from beginning May to end Sept.

1.5 ha (35 pitches) terrace, flat and relatively flat, grassy

Tariff : (2015 price) 15.66€ ✦✦ 🚗 🗐 🔌 (8A) – Extra per person 3.51€
Rental rates : (2015 price) permanent – 2 🏕 – 5 🏠. Per night from 65€ – Per week from 266 to 348€

A footpath links the campsite to the town and a small chalet village set among shrubs and bushes.

Surroundings : 🌳 🛒 ⚲⚲	G
Leisure activities : 🏊 (small swimming pool)	P
Facilities : 🚿 (July–Aug.) 🧺 launderette	S
Nearby : 🚴 🍴 🛶	

Longitude : -1.59293
Latitude : 46.82925

ST-GEORGES-SUR-LAYON

49700 – Michelin map **317** G5 – pop. 769 – alt. 65
▶ Paris 328 – Angers 39 – Cholet 45 – Saumur 27

⚠ Les Grésillons

✆ 0241500232. camping.gresillon@wanadoo.fr

Address : chemin des Grésillons (800m south along the D 178, follow the signs for Concourson-sur-Layon and take the road to the right, near the river)

Opening times : from beginning April to end Sept.

1.5 ha (40 pitches) terraced, relatively flat, grassy

Tariff : 18.50€ ✦✦ 🚗 🗐 🔌 (10A) – Extra per person 4.30€
Rental rates : (from beginning April to end Sept.) – 12 canvas bungalows. Per night from 56 to 155€ – Per week from 157 to 435€

Surroundings : 🌳 ≼	G
Leisure activities : 🚴 🏊 (small swimming pool) 🛶	P
Facilities : 🚿 (July–Aug.) 🚽 🖼	S

Longitude : -0.37032
Latitude : 47.19324

ST-HILAIRE-DE-RIEZ

85270 – Michelin map **316** E7 – pop. 10 504 – alt. 8
▶ Paris 453 – Challans 18 – Noirmoutier-en-l'Île 48 – La Roche-sur-Yon 48

Le Pissot (4 km to the north)

🏕 Les Biches ♣♣

✆ 0251543882. www.campingdesbiches.com – limited spaces for one-night stay

Address : chemin de Petite Baisse (2km to the north of the town)

Opening times : from mid April to mid Sept.

13 ha/9 for camping (434 pitches) flat, grassy, sandy

Tariff : (2015 price) 37.75€ ✦✦ 🚗 🗐 🔌 (10A) –
Extra per person 8.75€ – Reservation fee 20€
Rental rates : (2015 price) (from mid April to mid Sept.) 🏕 –
200 🏕 – 60 🏠 – 7 studios. Per night from 35 to 143€ – Per week from 239 to 1,000€ – Reservation fee 20€

🏕 2 🗐 46.50€

A pleasant pine wood, with a range of rental accommodation, but very few places for tents and caravans.

Surroundings : 🌳 🛒 ⚲⚲	G
Leisure activities : 🍴 🍴 🏛 🎣 🚶 🎿 🏊 🚵 🚴 🎿 disco, multi-sports ground	P
Facilities : 🚿 🔌 🖼 🧺 🚽 launderette	S
🏧 refrigerators	

Longitude : -1.94445
Latitude : 46.74052

Les Demoiselles (10 km to the northwest)

🏔 Odalys Vitalys Les Demoiselles

✆ 0251581071. www.odalys-vacances.com – limited spaces for one-night stay

Address : avenue des Becs (9.5km to the northwest, along the D 123 and 300m from the beach)

Opening times : from mid April to end Sept.

13.7 ha (180 pitches) undulating, flat and relatively flat, grassy, sandy

Tariff : (2015 price) 25€ ✦✦ 🚗 🗐 🔌 (10A) – Extra per person 5.50€
Rental rates : (2015 price) permanent 🚿 (4 mobile homes) –
154 🏕. Per night from 70 to 135€ – Per week from 180 to 1,000€ –
Reservation fee 21€

🏕 25 🗐 25€

A mobile home park with plenty of shade and some pitches for tents and caravans.

Surroundings : 🌳 ⚲⚲	G
Leisure activities : 🎣 🚶 🚣 🚴 🏊 multi-sports ground	P
Facilities : 🚿 🔌 🧺 launderette	S
Nearby : 🍴 🛶	

Longitude : -2.04086
Latitude : 46.76815

La Fradinière (7 km to the northwest)

🏔 La Puerta del Sol ♣♣

✆ 0251491010. www.campinglapuertadelsol.com

Address : 7 chemin des Hommeaux (4.5km to the north of the town)

Opening times : from beginning April to end Sept.

4 ha (207 pitches) flat, grassy

Tariff : 36€ ✦✦ 🚗 🗐 🔌 (10A) – Extra per person 6.90€ – Reservation fee 22€

Rental rates : (from beginning April to end Sept.) 🚿
(1 chalet) – 100 🏕 – 30 🏠 – 4 canvas bungalows. Per night from 65 to 125€ – Per week from 455 to 875€ – Reservation fee 22€

🏕 local sani-station – 🚐 🔌36€

In a green setting with few pitches for tents and caravans, and rental accommodation of various standards.

Surroundings : 🌳 🛒 ⚲	G
Leisure activities : 🍴 🍴 🏛 🌙 nighttime 🚶 🎿 ♨ jacuzzi 🚣 🚴 🏊 🎿 multi-sports ground, entertainment room	P
Facilities : 🚿 🔌 🖼 🧺 🚽 launderette	S
🏧 refrigerators	

Longitude : -1.95887
Latitude : 46.76452

La Pège (6 km to the northwest)

🏔 Les Écureuils ♣♣

✆ 0251543371. www.camping-aux-ecureuils.com – limited spaces for one-night stay

Address : 98 avenue de la Pège (5.5km to the northwest, 200m from the beach)

4 ha (215 pitches) flat, grassy, sandy

Rentals : 19 🚐 – 2 🏠 .

Surroundings : 🏊 ⛵ ♨♨
Leisure activities : 🍴 ✕ 🎰 ⚑nighttime ⚡
♨ 🧖 hammam ⛹ ✕ 🎿 🎣
Facilities : ♿ ⚡🛁 🚻 launderette 🐾
Nearby : 🛒 🔥

GPS Longitude : -2.00897
Latitude : 46.74478

⛰ La Ningle

📞 02 51 54 07 11. www.campinglaningle.com

Address : 66 chemin des Roselières (situated 5.7km to the northwest)

Opening times : from beginning May to mid Sept.

3.2 ha (150 pitches) flat, grassy, small lake

Tariff : 34.90€ ♦♦ ⇔ ▣ ⒣ (10A) – Extra per person 5.50€ – Reservation fee 20€

Rental rates : (from beginning May to mid Sept.) – 27 🚐. Per night from 50 to 90 € – Per week from 345 to 825€ – Reservation fee 20€

A pleasantly leafy setting and a well-kept site.

Surroundings : 🏊 ⛵ ♀
Leisure activities : 🍴 🎰 ♨ ⛹ ✕ 🎿 🎣
Facilities : ♿ ⚡🛁 🚻 launderette
Nearby : 🛒 ✕ 🐾 🔥

GPS Longitude : -2.00473
Latitude : 46.7446

⛰ La Parée Préneau

📞 02 51 54 33 84. www.campinglapareepreneau.com

Address : 23 avenue de La Parée Préneau (3.5km to the northwest)

Opening times : from beginning April to end Sept.

3.6 ha (217 pitches)flat, grassy, sandy

Tariff : 29.90€ ♦♦ ⇔ ▣ ⒣ (6A) – Extra per person 5.90€ – Reservation fee 20€

Rental rates : (from beginning March to end Sept.) – 23 🚐 – 7 🏠 – 5 canvas bungalows. Per night from 59 to 109€ – Per week from 199 to 639€ – Reservation fee 20€

In a pleasant setting, but choose the pitches away from the road in preference.

Surroundings : ▢ ♀♀
Leisure activities : 🍴 🎰 ⚑nighttime ⚡
🚲 🎿 🎣 multi-sports ground
Facilities : ♿ ⚡🛁 🚻 launderette

GPS Longitude : -1.98488
Latitude : 46.74034

⛰ Le Bosquet

📞 02 51 54 34 61. www.lebosquet.fr

Address : 62 avenue de la Pège (5km to the northwest)

2 ha (115 pitches)flat, grassy, sandy
Rentals : 40 🚐 – 3 apartments.

Situated relatively close to the beach (250m).

Surroundings : ♀♀
Leisure activities : 🍴 ✕ 🎰 ⛹ 🎿 🎣
Facilities : ♿ ⚡🛁 launderette 🐾
Nearby : 🛒 🔥

GPS Longitude : -2.00326
Latitude : 46.74073

Some information or pricing may have changed since the guide went to press. We recommend you check the price list online in advance or at the entrance to the campsite and enquire about possible restrictions.

⛰ Le Romarin

📞 02 51 54 43 82. www.leromarin.fr

Address : rue des Martinets (3.8km to the northwest)

Opening times : from beginning April to end Sept.

4 ha/1.5 (97 pitches) undulating sandy, flat, grassy

Tariff : (2015 price) 28.50€ ♦♦ ⇔ ▣ ⒣ (10A) – Extra per person 4.30€ – Reservation fee 20€

Rental rates : (2015 price) (from beginning April to mid Sept.) 🚫 – 6 🚐. Per night from 50 to 90€ – Per week from 200 to 640€ – Reservation fee 20€

Mobile homes and some pitches for tents and caravans beneath the shade of a small pretty pine wood.

Surroundings : ▢ ♀♀
Leisure activities : ✕ ⛹ 🎿 multi-sports ground
Facilities : ♿ ⚡ (July-Aug.) 🚻 launderette 🐾

GPS Longitude : -1.98756
Latitude : 46.74243

⛰ La Pège

📞 02 51 54 34 52. www.campinglapege.com

Address : 67 avenue de la Pège (5km to the northwest)

1.8 ha (100 pitches) flat, grassy, sandy
Rentals : 20 🚐 – 1 🏠 .

Access to the beach (100m) along a small road leading directly to the lifeguard's station. Choose the pitches away from the road in preference

Surroundings : ▢ ♀
Leisure activities : ⛹ 🚲 🎿
Facilities : ♿ ⚡🛁 🚻 🎣
Nearby : 🛒 🍴 ✕ 🐾 🔥

GPS Longitude : -2.00545
Latitude : 46.7411

Key to rentals symbols:

12 🚐	*Number of mobile homes*
20 🏠	*Number of chalets*
6 🛏	*Number of rooms to rent*
Per night 30–50€	*Minimum/maximum rate per night*
Per week 300–1,000€	*Minimum/maximum rate per week*

Sion-sur-l'Océan (3 km to the west

⛰ Municipal de la Plage de Riez

📞 02 51 54 36 59. www.campingsainthilairederiez.com

Address : avenue des Mimosas (3km west, 200m from the beach)

9 ha (560 pitches) flat, sandy
Rentals : 66 🚐 – 1 🏠 – 10 canvas bungalows.
🚐 sani-station – 9 ▣

Shaded by a beautiful pine wood, with direct access to the beach.

Surroundings : 🏊 ▢ ♀♀♀
Leisure activities : 🍴 ✕ 🎰 ⚡ ⛹ 🚲 🎿 multi-sports ground
Facilities : ♿ ⚡🛁 🚻 launderette 🐾

GPS Longitude : -1.97941
Latitude : 46.72298

⌂ Municipal de la Plage de Sion

✆ 02 51 54 34 23. www.campingsainthilairederiez.com

Address : avenue de la Forêt (northwestern part of the town)

Opening times : from beginning April to end Oct.

3 ha (164 pitches) undulating, relatively flat, flat, grassy, sandy, gravelled

Tariff : (2015 price) 30€ ✦✦ ⟺ 圓 ⑷ (10A) – Extra per person 6.50€ – Reservation fee 19€

Rental rates : (2015 price) (from beginning April to end Oct.) ⚡ – 18 🚐 – 3 canvas bungalows. Per week from 185 to 762€ – Reservation fee 19€

🚰 AireService sani-station 4.50€ – 7 圓 17€

300m from the beach (direct access), surrounded by forest.

Surroundings : 🐾 ▭ 🞍	**G**	Longitude : -1.97246
Leisure activities : 🏠 🏄 🚲	**P**	Latitude : 46.71695
Facilities : ♿ ⊶ 🧺 launderette	**S**	

ST-HILAIRE-LA-FORÊT

85440 – Michelin map **316** G9 – pop. 611 – alt. 23
▶ Paris 449 – Challans 66 – Luçon 31 – La Roche-sur-Yon 31

⛰ La Grand' Métairie

✆ 02 51 33 32 38. www.la-grand-metairie.com – limited spaces for one-night stay

Address : 8 rue de La Vineuse en Plaine (north of the village along the D 70)

3.8 ha (172 pitches) flat, grassy
Rentals : 116 🚐 – 11 🏠.

Plenty of mobile homes set in a lush green space with lots of flowers.

Surroundings : 🐾 ▭ 🞍		**G**	Longitude : -1.52545
Leisure activities : 🍴 🍽 🎡 nighttime 🎿		**P**	Latitude : 46.44776
🛶 🚲 🎾 🏊 farm or petting farm		**S**	
Facilities : ♿ ⊶ 🧺 launderette			

⌂ Les Batardières

✆ 02 51 33 33 85. www.camping-lesbatardieres.com

Address : 2 rue des Batardières (continue west along the D 70 and take the turning to the left, following signs for Le Poteau)

Opening times : from beginning July to end Aug.

1.6 ha (75 pitches) flat, grassy

Tariff : 25€ ✦✦ ⟺ 圓 ⑷ (10A) – Extra per person 5€

Pretty, clearly marked-out pitches with lots of shade.

Surroundings : 🐾 ▭ 🞍	**G**	Longitude : -1.52934
Leisure activities : 🏠 🏄 🎾	**P**	Latitude : 46.44807
Facilities : ⊶ 🧺 cc 🧺 launderette	**S**	

ST-HILAIRE-ST-FLORENT

49400 – Michelin map **317** I5
▶ Paris 324 – Nantes 131 – Angers 45 – Tours 72

⛰ Indigo Chantepie ♨

✆ 02 41 67 95 34. www.campingchantepie.com

Address : route de Chantepie (5.5km northwest along the D 751, follow the signs for Gennes and take road to the left; at La Mimerolle)

Opening times : from beginning May to end Sept.

10 ha/5 for camping (160 pitches) flat, grassy

Tariff : (2015 price) 40€ ✦✦ ⟺ 圓 ⑷ (10A) – Extra per person 6.60€ – Reservation fee 13€

🚰 local sani-station 7€

Leafy site overlooking the Loire. Farm animals.

Surroundings : 🐾 ⟨ Loire Valley ▭ 🞍🞍	**G**	Longitude : -0.14305
Leisure activities : 🍴 🍽 🏠 🏄 🛶 🚲 🎿	**P**	Latitude : 47.2937
🏊 🎾	**S**	
Facilities : ♿ ⊶ 🧺 🍴 launderette 🧺 🞍		

ST-JEAN-DE-MONTS

85160 – Michelin map **316** D7 – pop. 8 037 – alt. 16
▶ Paris 451 – Cholet 123 – Nantes 73 – Noirmoutier-en-l'Île 34

Centre

⛰ Aux Coeurs Vendéens ♨

✆ 02 51 58 84 91. www.coeursvendeens.com

Address : 251 route de Notre-Dame-de-Monts (4km northwest on the D 38)

2 ha (117 pitches) flat, grassy, sandy
Rentals : 64 🚐 – 1 🏠.

Choose the pitches away from the road in preference.

Surroundings : ▭ 🞍🞍	**G**	Longitude : -2.11008
Leisure activities : 🍴 🍽 🏠 🏄 🎾	**P**	Latitude : 46.80988
hammam, jacuzzi 🛶 🚲 🏊 🏊 spa centre	**S**	
Facilities : ♿ ⊶ 🧺 🍴 launderette 🧺		
Nearby : 🧺		

⌂ Les Pins

✆ 02 51 58 17 42. www.camping-despins.fr

Address : 166 avenue Valentine (2.5km southeast on the D 123)

Opening times : from end May to end Sept.

1.2 ha (118 pitches) undulating, terraced, flat, sandy

Tariff : (2015 price) 28.60€ ✦✦ ⟺ 圓 ⑷ (10A) – Extra per person 8.40€ – Reservation fee 20€

Rental rates : (2015 price) (from end May to end Sept.) ⚡ – 14 🏠. Per week from 240 to 650€ – Reservation fee 20€

A very pleasant, undulating pine wood but the rental chalets are a little old.

Surroundings : ▭ 🞍	**G**	Longitude : -2.03894
Leisure activities : 🍴 🏠 🏄 🚲 🛴	**P**	Latitude : 46.78081
Facilities : ⊶ cc 🧺 🍴 🞍	**S**	
Nearby : 🧺 🞍		

North

⛰ Les Amiaux ♨

Les Amiaux

✆ 02 51 58 22 22. www.amiaux.fr

Address : 223 route de Notre-Dame (3.5km to the northwest, on the D 38)

Opening times : from beginning May to end Sept.

17 ha (543 pitches)

Tariff : ✦ 5.10€ ⟺ 圓 27.50€ ⑷ (10A) – Reservation fee 16€

Rental rates : (from beginning May to end Sept.) ⚡ – 32 🚐 – 4 apartments. Per night from 45 to 62€ – Per week from 322 to 940€ – Reservation fee 16€

Surroundings : ▭ 🞍	**G**	Longitude : -2.11517
Leisure activities : 🍴 🍽 🏠 🎡 🏄 🏄 🚲	**P**	Latitude : 46.81107
🎾 🏊 🏊 🞍 multi-sports ground	**S**	
Facilities : ♿ ⊶ 🧺 🍴 launderette		
🧺 🞍		

⚰ Le Bois Joly ♣♣

✆ 02 51 59 11 63. www.camping-lebois-joly.com

Address : 46 route de Notre-Dame-de-Monts (located 1km to the northwest; beside a brook)

Opening times : from beginning April to end Sept.

7.5 ha (356 pitches) flat, grassy, sandy

Tariff : (2015 price) 35€ ✿✿ ⇔ 回 ⓓ (10A) – Extra per person 6€ – Reservation fee 25€

Rental rates : (2015 price) (from beginning April to end Sept.) ⚒ (1 mobile home) ⚒ – 2 'gypsy' caravans – 102 ⏻ – 22 ⌂. Per week from 250 to 990€ – Reservation fee 25€

⚒ local sani-station – 5 回

The site has an attractive swimming area.

Surroundings : ⌁ ♀
Leisure activities : ♟ ✗ ⌂ ⚃ ⚶ ⛷ ⛵ jacuzzi ⚡ ⛷ ⚏ ⚎ multi-sports ground
Facilities : ♿ ⌕ ▥ ⚒ ⚶ ⚕ ⚑ launderette ⚒
Nearby : ⚷

GPS Longitude : -2.07417 / Latitude : 46.79918

⚰ Club Airotel Les Places Dorées ♣♣

✆ 02 51 59 02 93. www.placesdorees.com – limited spaces for one-night stay ⚒

Address : route de Notre-Dame-de-Monts (4km northwest on the D 38)

Opening times : from mid April to mid Sept.

5 ha (288 pitches) flat, grassy, sandy

Tariff : (2015 price) 38.80€ ✿✿ ⇔ 回 ⓓ (10A) – Extra per person 7.20€ – Reservation fee 25€

Rental rates : (2015 price) (from mid April to mid Sept.) ⚒ – 79 ⏻. Per week from 249 to 1,020€ – Reservation fee 25€

The site has an attractive swimming area.

Surroundings : ⌁ ♀♀
Leisure activities : ♟ ✗ ⚶ ⛷ ⛵ hammam, jacuzzi ⚡ ⚏ ⚎ multi-sports ground
Facilities : ♿ ⌕ ⚒ ⚑ launderette ⚒
Nearby : ⚑

GPS Longitude : -2.10997 / Latitude : 46.8097

⚰ APV Les Aventuriers de la Calypso ♣♣

✆ 251 56 08 78. www.camping-apv.com – limited spaces for one-night stay

Address : route de Notre-Dame-de-Monts, Les Tonnelles (4.6km to the northwest)

Opening times : from beginning April to end Sept.

4 ha (284 pitches) flat, grassy, sandy

Tariff : (2015 price) 33€ ✿✿ ⇔ 回 ⓓ (6A) – Extra per person 9.40€ – Reservation fee 28€

Rental rates : (2015 price) (from beginning April to end Sept.) – 155 ⏻ – 34 ⌂. Per night from 49 to 74€ – Per week from 908 to 987€ – Reservation fee 28€

⚒ AireService sani-station 20.30€

There are few pitches for tents or caravans and some rental accommodation is very old.

Surroundings : ⚶ ⌁ ♀
Leisure activities : ♟ ✗ ⌂ ⚃ nighttime ⚶ jacuzzi ⚡ ⚴ ⚕ ⚏ ⚎ multi-sports ground
Facilities : ♿ ⌕ ⚒ ⚶ ⚕ ⚑ launderette ⚒

GPS Longitude : -2.11533 / Latitude : 46.81232

⚰ Club Airotel l'Abri des Pins ♣♣

✆ 02 51 58 83 86. www.abridespins.com – limited spaces for one-night stay ⚒

Address : route de Notre-Dame-de-Monts (4km northwest on the D 38)

Opening times : from beginning April to mid Sept.

3 ha (209 pitches) flat, grassy, sandy

Tariff : 38.80€ ✿✿ ⇔ 回 ⓓ (10A) – Extra per person 7.20€

Rental rates : (2015 price) (from beginning April to mid Sept.) ⚒ – 79 ⏻. Per week from 273 to 1,020€

A pretty play and paddling pool area. Choose pitches away from the road in preference.

Surroundings : ⌁ ♀♀
Leisure activities : ♟ ✗ ⌂ ⚶ ⛷ hammam, jacuzzi ⚡ ⚴ ⚏ ⚎ ⚒
Facilities : ♿ ⌕ ⚒ ⚶ ⚕ ⚑ launderette ⚒
Nearby : ⚑

GPS Longitude : -2.10997 / Latitude : 46.8097

⚰ Le Vieux Ranch

✆ 02 51 58 86 58. www.levieuxranch.com

Address : chemin de la Parée du Jonc (4.3km to the northwest)

Opening times : from beginning April to end Sept.

5 ha (242 pitches) undulating, flat, grassy, sandy

Tariff : (2015 price) 32.95€ ✿✿ ⇔ 回 ⓓ (10A) – Extra per person 7€ – Reservation fee 16€

Rental rates : (2015 price) (from beginning April to end Sept.) ⚒ – 22 ⏻ – 8 ⌂. Per week from 230 to 880€ – Reservation fee 16€

A gently undulating, attractive location, 200m from the beach.

Surroundings : ⚶ ⌁ ♀♀
Leisure activities : ♟ ⌂ ⛷ ⚡ ⚴ ⚏ entertainment room
Facilities : ♿ ⌕ ⚒ ⚶ ⚕ ⚑ launderette
Nearby : ✗ ⚒

GPS Longitude : -2.11351 / Latitude : 46.80717

⚰ Flower Plein Sud ♣♣

✆ 02 51 59 10 40. www.campingpleinsud.com

Address : 246 route de Notre-Dame-de-Monts (4km to the northwest, on the D 38)

Opening times : from mid April to mid Sept.

2 ha (110 pitches) flat, grassy, sandy

Tariff : (2015 price) 32€ ✿✿ ⇔ 回 ⓓ (6A) – Extra per person 5€ – Reservation fee 20€

Rental rates : (2015 price) (from mid April to mid Sept.) ⚒ – 30 ⏻ – 2 canvas bungalows – 2 tent lodges. Per week from 294 to 791€ – Reservation fee 20€

A long, narrow site, with well marked-out pitches.

Surroundings : ⌁ ♀
Leisure activities : ♟ ⚶ ⚡ ⚴ ⚏ multi-sports ground
Facilities : ♿ ⌕ ⚒ ⚶ ⚕ ⚑ launderette

GPS Longitude : -2.11093 / Latitude : 46.8103

There are several different types of sani-station ('borne' in French) – sanitation points providing fresh water and disposal points for grey water. See page 12 for further details.

La Forêt

⚲ 02 51 58 84 63. www.hpa-laforet.com

Address : 190 chemin de la Rive (5.5km to the northwest, follow the signs for Notre-Dame-de-Monts and take turning to the left)

Opening times : from beginning May to end Sept.

1 ha (61 pitches) flat, grassy, sandy

Tariff : 36.50€ ✹✹ ⇔ 圓 ⚡ (10A) – Extra per person 5.50€ – Reservation fee 30€

Rental rates : (from beginning April to end Sept.) – 16 ⛺. Per night from 44 to 114€ – Per week from 309 to 799€ – Reservation fee 30€

🚽 local sani-station – 10 圓 17€

Attractive shrubs and bushes decorate this eco-friendly campsite.

Surroundings : ⌂ ♤♤
Leisure activities : ⌂ ⚓ ⚶ ⚡
Facilities : ♿ ⚬ ⚏ ⚌ ⚐ ⚑ ⚒
Longitude : -2.12993
Latitude : 46.81828

La Davière-Plage

⚲ 02 51 58 27 99. www.camping-daviereplage.com

Address : 197 route de Notre-Dame-de-Monts (3km to the northwest, on the D 38)

Opening times : from beginning May to end Sept.

3 ha (174 pitches) flat, grassy, sandy

Tariff : 28.80€ ✹✹ ⇔ 圓 ⚡ (10A) – Extra per person 6.25€ – Reservation fee 20€

Rental rates : (from beginning May to end Sept.) – 19 ⛺ – 6 canvas bungalows – 2 gîtes. Per night from 40 to 120€ – Per week from 250 to 815€ – Reservation fee 20€

🚽 local sani-station – 20 圓 15€ – ⚡15€

Surroundings : ⌂ ♤
Leisure activities : ✗ ⌂ ⚓ ⚶
Facilities : ♿ ⚬ (July–Aug.) ⚏ ⚐ launderette ⚌
Nearby : ⚱
Longitude : -2.10085
Latitude : 46.8054

South

La Yole ♿♨

⚲ 02 51 58 67 17. www.vendee-camping.eu – limited spaces for one-night stay

Address : chemin des Bosses, at Orouet (7km southeast)

Opening times : from beginning April to end Sept.

5 ha (369 pitches) flat, grassy, sandy

Tariff : 38.50€ ✹✹ ⇔ 圓 ⚡ (16A) – Extra per person 7.20€ – Reservation fee 29€

Rental rates : (from beginning April to end Sept.) ⚘ – 63 ⛺. Per night from 50 to 180€ – Per week from 270 to 1,250€ – Reservation fee 29€

🚽 50 圓 22€ – ⚡11€

In a green, well-kept setting, with lots of flowers and plenty of shade from a beautiful pine wood.

Surroundings : ⚶ ⌂ ♤♤
Leisure activities : ⚱ ✗ ⌂ ⚘ ⚶ jacuzzi
 ⚌ ⚐
Facilities : ♿ ⚬ ⚏ ⚐ launderette ⚌ ⚒
Longitude : -2.00728
Latitude : 46.75664

Les Jardins de l'Atlantique

⚲ 02 51 58 05 74. www.camping-jardins-atlantique.com – limited spaces for one-night stay ⚘

Address : 100 rue de la Caillauderie (5.5km to the northeast)

Opening times : from beginning April to end Sept.

5 ha (318 pitches) undulating, relatively flat, flat, sandy

Tariff : (2015 price) 22€ ✹✹ ⇔ 圓 ⚡ (6A) – Extra per person 6.10€ – Reservation fee 20€

Rental rates : (2015 price) (from beginning April to end Sept.) – 70 ⛺. Per night from 35 to 61€ – Per week from 200 to 755€ – Reservation fee 20€

Surroundings : ⌂ ♤♤
Leisure activities : ⚱ ✗ ⌂ ⚘ ⚶ hammam, jacuzzi ⚓ ⚶ ⚌ ⚐ multi-sports ground
Facilities : ♿ ⚬ ⚏ ⚐ launderette ⚌ ⚒
Longitude : -2.02751
Latitude : 46.76972

Le Both d'Orouet

⚲ 02 51 58 60 37. http://www.camping-lebothdorouet.com

Address : 77 avenue d'Orouët (6.7km southeast on the D 38, follow the signs for St-Hilaire-de-Riez, near a stream)

4.4 ha (200 pitches) flat, grassy, sandy

Rentals : 31 ⛺ – 19 ⛺ – 5 tent lodges.

🚽 local sani-station

In a green setting; there's a games room in an old barn attached to the farmhouse dating back to 1875.

Surroundings : ⌂ ♤♤
Leisure activities : ⌂ jacuzzi ⚓ ⚶ ⚌ multi-sports ground
Facilities : ♿ ⚬ ⚏ ⚐ launderette
Nearby : ⚱ ✗
Longitude : -1.99759
Latitude : 46.76495

Campéole les Sirènes

⚲ 02 51 58 01 31. http://vendee-camping.info

Address : avenue des Demoiselles (to the southeast, 500m from the beach)

Opening times : from beginning April to end Sept.

15 ha/5 for camping (470 pitches) undulating, flat, sandy

Tariff : 16€ ✹✹ ⇔ 圓 ⚡ (10A) – Extra per person 10€ – Reservation fee 25€

Rental rates : (from beginning April to end Sept.) ♿ (2 mobile homes) – 52 ⛺ – 40 ⛺ – 40 canvas bungalows. Per night from 30 to 146€ – Per week from 210 to 1,022€ – Reservation fee 25€

🚽 AireService sani-station

A pleasant, natural setting in Les Pays de Monts (regional pine forest), although the sanitary facilities are rather old.

Surroundings : ⚶ ♤♤
Leisure activities : ⚱ ⚶ ⚶ ⚶ multi-sports ground
Facilities : ♿ ⚬ ⚐ launderette
Nearby : ✗
Longitude : -2.0548
Latitude : 46.7799

We have selected the best campsites in France with our usual care, listing those with the best facilities in the most pleasant surroundings.

⚠ Le Logis

📞 0251586067. www.camping-saintjeandemonts.com – limited spaces for one-night stay ✂

Address : 4 chemin du Logis (4.3km southeast on the D 38, follow the signs for St-Gilles-Croix-de-Vie)

Opening times : from mid April to beginning Sept.

0.8 ha (44 pitches) terraced, flat, grassy

Tariff : (2015 price) 26.50€ ✦✦ ⛺ 🔲 (10A) – Extra per person 5€ – Reservation fee 16€

Rental rates : (2015 price) (from mid April to beginning Sept.) ✂ – 11 🏠 – 2 gîtes. Per week from 260 to 630€ – Reservation fee 16€

🚐 local sani-station – 🛒8€

Choose the pitches away from the road in preference.

Surroundings : 🏞
Leisure activities : 🏛 🏊 🏊(small swimming pool)
Facilities : 👤 🚿 🏠 📷
Nearby : 🍽 🍴 🏔

GPS Longitude : -2.01308
Latitude : 46.77953

ST-JULIEN-DE-CONCELLES

44450 – Michelin map **316** H4 – pop. 6 839 – alt. 24
▶ Paris 384 – Nantes 19 – Angers 89 – La Roche-sur-Yon 80

⛰ Le Chêne

📞 0240541200. www.campingduchene.fr

Address : 1 route du Lac (located 1.5km east along the D 37 (diversion), near the small lake)

Opening times : from beginning April to mid Oct.

2 ha (100 pitches) flat, grassy

Tariff : ✦ 5€ ⛺ 2.80€ 🔲 4.70€ – (10A) 3.90€
Rental rates : (2015 price) permanent – 26 🏠 – 4 canvas bungalows. Per night from 18 to 99€ – Per week from 296 to 624€

🚐 2 🔲 16.40€

In an attractive location, lots of green space; beside a lake.

Surroundings : 🏞 ♨♨
Leisure activities : 🍽 🏛 🏊 🎾 🏊(open air in season)
Facilities : 👤 🚿 🏠 🍴 launderette 🧺
Nearby : 🛶 🚣 pedalos

GPS Longitude : -1.37098
Latitude : 47.2492

This guide is not intended as a list of all the camping sites in France; its aim is to provide a selection of the best sites in each category.

ST-JULIEN-DES-LANDES

85150 – Michelin map **316** F8 – pop. 1 331 – alt. 59
▶ Paris 445 – Aizenay 17 – Challans 32 – La Roche-sur-Yon 24

⛰ Les Castels La Garangeoire ▲▲

📞 0251466539. www.camping-la-garangeoire.com

Address : La Garangeoire (2.8km north along the D 21, turn right)

Opening times : from beginning May to end Sept.

200 ha/10 for camping (356 pitches) undulating, terraced, flat, grassy

Tariff : 42.50€ ✦✦ ⛺ 🔲 (16A) – Extra per person 8.85€ – Reservation fee 25€

Rental rates : (2015 price) (from mid May to end Sept.) 👤 (1 mobile home) – 31 🏠 – 25 🏡. Per night from 42 to 198€ – Per week from 294 to 1,386€ – Reservation fee 25€

An extensive, charming site in the grounds of a château, with meadows, lakes and woodland.

Surroundings : 🏞 🏞 ♨♨
Leisure activities : 🍽 🏛 🏊 🎾 ⛳ jacuzzi 🏊 🚴 🎾 🏊 🏊 🛶 🐎 pedalos ✂ multi-sports ground
Facilities : 👤 🚿 – 4 individual sanitary facilities (🛁 🚿 wc) 🧺 🍴 launderette 🧺 refrigerators

GPS Longitude : -1.71359
Latitude : 46.66229

⛰ Sunêlia Village de La Guyonnière ▲▲

📞 0251466259. www.camping-guyonniere.com

Address : south of the Lac de Jaunay; head 2.4km northwest along the D 12, follow the signs for Landevieille then continue 1.2km along the road to the right

Opening times : from end April to mid Sept.

30 ha (294 pitches)

Tariff : 52€ ✦✦ ⛺ 🔲 (10A) – Extra per person 10€ – Reservation fee 20€

Rental rates : (from end April to mid Sept.) ✂ – 85 🏠 – 25 🏡 – 13 tent lodges. Per night from 37 to 299€ – Per week from 259 to 2,093€ – Reservation fee 20€

🚐 local sani-station 5€ – 5 🔲 22€ – 🛒 22€

A leafy, green location near the Lac de Jaunay.

Surroundings : 🏞 ♨
Leisure activities : 🍽 🏛 🏊 🎾 hammam, jacuzzi 🏊 🚴 🎾 🏊 🏊 🛶 🐎 farm or petting farm, multi-sports ground spa centre
Facilities : 👤 🚿 🔲 🍴 launderette 🧺

GPS Longitude : -1.74963
Latitude : 46.65258

⛰ Yelloh! Village Château La Forêt ▲▲

📞 0251466211. www.chateaulaforet.com

Address : 0.5 km northeast along the D 55 (La Lucillière), follow the signs for Martinet

Opening times : from end April to beginning Sept.

50 ha/5 for camping (209 pitches) flat, grassy, wood, pond

Tariff : 41€ ✦✦ ⛺ 🔲 (10A) – Extra per person 7€

Rental rates : (from end April to beginning Sept.) – 33 🏠 – 10 🏡 – 1 cabin in the trees – 2 canvas bungalows – 3 tent lodges. Per night from 30 to 205€ – Per week from 210 to 1,435€

In a wooded setting in the grounds of the château and its out-buildings.

Surroundings : 🏞 🏞 ♨♨
Leisure activities : 🍽 🍴 🏛 daytime 🏊 🏊 🚴 🎾 🏊 🏊 disco, zip wiring
Facilities : 👤 🚿 🏠 🧺 🍴 launderette 🧺

GPS Longitude : -1.71135
Latitude : 46.64182

These symbols are used for a campsite that is exceptional in its category:

⛰⛰...⛰ *Particularly pleasant setting, quality and range of services available*

🏞🏞 *Tranquil, isolated site – quiet site, particularly at night*

≪≪ *Exceptional view – interesting or panoramic view*

ST-LAURENT-SUR-SÈVRE

85290 – Michelin map **316** K6 – pop. 3 442 – alt. 121
▶ Paris 365 – Angers 76 – Bressuire 36 – Cholet 14

⚲ Le Rouge Gorge

✆ 02 51 67 86 39. www.camping-lerougegorge-vendee.com

Address : route de La Verrie (located 1km west along the D 111)

Opening times : from beginning April to end Sept.

2 ha (93 pitches) relatively flat, flat, grassy

Tariff : (2015 price) 23.10€ ✶✶ ⇔ 🔲 🔌 (13A) –
Extra per person 4.50€ – Reservation fee 6€

Rental rates : (2015 price) (from beginning April to end Sept.) –
13 🛖 – 13 🏕 – 4 tent lodges. Per night from 55 to 130€ –
Per week from 228 to 715€ – Reservation fee 10€

🚐 15 🔲 14.90€ – 🅿 17.91€

A pleasant setting with lots of green space and plenty of shade.

Surroundings : ☐ ♀♀	
Leisure activities : 🎣 🏊 zip wiring	**G P S** Longitude : -0.90307
Facilities : ♿ ⛽ 🚿 🧺 laundrette	Latitude : 46.95788
Nearby : 🎣	

ST-MICHEL-EN-L'HERM

85580 – Michelin map **316** I9 – pop. 2 129 – alt. 9
▶ Paris 453 – Luçon 15 – La Rochelle 46 – La Roche-sur-Yon 47

⚲ Les Mizottes

✆ 02 51 30 23 63. www.campinglesmizottes.fr

Address : 41 rue des Anciens Quais (800m southwest along the
D 746, follow the signs for l'Aiguillon-sur-Mer)

Opening times : from beginning April to end Sept.

3 ha (150 pitches) flat, grassy

Tariff : (2015 price) 30€ ✶✶ ⇔ 🔲 🔌 (6A) – Extra per person 6€ –
Reservation fee 20€

Rental rates : (2015 price) (from beginning April to end Sept.) ♿
(1 mobile home) – 20 🛖. Per night from 60 to 80€ – Per week
from 245 to 800€ – Reservation fee 20€

🚐 2 🔲 30€

High-quality services and leisure facillities.

Surroundings : 🌳 ☐ ♀	
Leisure activities : 🍴 ✗ 🎣 🚴 🏊 multi-sports ground, entertainment room	**G P S** Longitude : -1.25482
Facilities : ♿ ⛽ 🚿 laundrette	Latitude : 46.34943

ST-PÈRE-EN-RETZ

44320 – Michelin map **316** D4 – pop. 4 113 – alt. 14
▶ Paris 425 – Challans 54 – Nantes 45 – Pornic 13

⚲ Le Grand Fay

✆ 02 40 21 72 89. www.camping-grandfay.com

Address : rue du Grand Fay (take the eastern exit along the D 78,
follow the signs for Frossay then continue 500m down the turning
to the right)

1.2 ha (76 pitches) relatively flat, flat, grassy

Rentals : 5 🛖.

*In a quiet residential area, behind the municipal sports centre
and near a lake.*

Surroundings : ♀♀	
Leisure activities : 🎣 🏊	**G P S** Longitude : -2.03654
Facilities : ♿ ⛽ laundrette	Latitude : 47.20266
Nearby : 🍴 🎣	

ST-PHILBERT-DE-GRAND-LIEU

44310 – pop. 7 806 – alt. 10
▶ Paris 407 – Nantes 27 – La Roche-sur-Yon 57 – Angers 112

⚑ La Boulogne

✆ 02 40 78 88 79. www.camping-la-boulogne.com

Address : 1 avenue de Nantes

4.5 ha (180 pitches) flat, grassy

Rentals : 1 'gypsy' caravan – 10 🛖 – 10 canvas bungalows.

Beside the Boulogne river and near a pleasant lake.

Surroundings : ♀♀	
Leisure activities : 🎣 🎣	**G P S** Longitude : -1.64027
Facilities : ♿ ⛽ 🏛 🚿 laundrette	Latitude : 47.0419
Nearby : jacuzzi 🔲 🎣 🏊	

ST-RÉVÉREND

85220 – Michelin map **316** F7 – pop. 1 323 – alt. 19
▶ Paris 453 – Aizenay 20 – Challans 19 – La Roche-sur-Yon 36

⚲ Le Pont Rouge

✆ 02 51 54 68 50. www.camping-lepontrouge.com

Address : rue Georges Clemenceau (take the southwestern exit along
the D 94 and take the road to the right; beside a stream)

Opening times : from beginning April to mid Sept.

2.2 ha (73 pitches) relatively flat, flat, grassy

Tariff : 15€ ✶✶ ⇔ 🔲 🔌 (6A) – Extra per person 4€ – Reservation
fee 15€

Rental rates : (from beginning April to mid Sept.) – 17 🛖 – 1 🏕 –
5 canvas bungalows. Per night from 40 to 60€ – Per week
from 150 to 740€ – Reservation fee 15€

In a green, well-kept setting, with a range of rental options.

Surroundings : 🌳 ☐ ♀♀	
Leisure activities : 🍴 ✗ 🌙 nighttime 🎣 🏊	**G P S** Longitude : -1.83448
Facilities : ♿ ⛽ 🚿 laundrette	Latitude : 46.69366

ST-VINCENT-SUR-JARD

85520 – Michelin map **316** G9 – pop. 1 205 – alt. 10
▶ Paris 454 – Challans 64 – Luçon 34 – La Rochelle 70

⚲⚲ Chadotel La Bolée d'Air

✆ 02 51 90 36 05. http://www.chadotel.com/fr/camping/vendee/
saint-vincent-sur-jard/c

Address : route du Bouil (situated 2km east along the D 21 follow the
signs for Longeville and take a right turn)

Opening times : from beginning April to end Nov.

5.7 ha (280 pitches) flat, grassy

Tariff : 32€ ✶✶ ⇔ 🔲 🔌 (10A) – Extra per person 6€ – Reservation
fee 25€

Rental rates : (from beginning April to end Sept.) – 150 🛖.
Per night from 25 to 175€ – Per week from 235 to 875€ –
Reservation fee 25€

🚐 130 🔲

Choose the pitches away from the road in preference.

Surroundings : ☐ ♀♀	
Leisure activities : 🍴 🔲 🎰 🍴 🎣 🚴 ✂ 🎿 🔲 🏊 🏄 multi-sports ground	**G P S** Longitude : -1.52622
Facilities : ♿ ⛽ 🚿 🧺 🧺 laundrette 🚿	Latitude : 46.41978

380

STE-LUCE-SUR-LOIRE

44980 – Michelin map **316** H4 – pop. 11 679 – alt. 9
▶ Paris 378 – Nantes 7 – Angers 82 – Cholet 58

⚠ Belle Rivière

✆ 02 40 25 85 81. www.camping-belleriviere.com

Address : route des Perrières (situated 2km northeast along the D 68, follow the signs for Thouaré; at La Gicquelière, take turning to the right for 1km; direct access to a branch of the Loire river)

Opening times : permanent

3 ha (110 pitches) flat, grassy

Tariff : ♣ 4.65 € – ⇔ 2.30 € – 📧 5.35 € – (½) (10A) 4 €
Rental rates : permanent ✂ – 7 📠. Per night from 66 to 91 € – Per week from 354 to 572 € – Reservation fee 15 €
📠 local sani-station – 9 📧 20.95 €
A pleasant, leafy setting with a great variety of trees and shrubs. Bus stop for the town.

Surroundings : 📺 ♀♀
Leisure activities : ▲⊿ 🔥 (June–Aug.) 🎳 ♨ 🍴 launderette
Nearby : 🐎

G P S	Longitude : -1.45574 Latitude : 47.254

To make the best possible use of this guide, please read pages 2–15 carefully.

SAUMUR

49400 – Michelin map **317** I5 – pop. 28 070 – alt. 30
▶ Paris 300 – Angers 67 – Châtellerault 76 – Cholet 70

⛰ Flower L'Île d'Offard 👥

✆ 02 41 40 30 00. www.saumur-camping.com

Address : boulevard de Verden (access via the town centre, on an island in the Loire river)

Opening times : from mid March to end Oct.

4.5 ha (160 pitches) flat, grassy

Tariff : (2015 price) 35 € ♣♣ ⇔ 📧 (½) (10A) – Extra per person 7 €
Rental rates : (2015 price) (from mid March to end Oct.) – 50 📠 – 20 tent lodges. Per week from 350 to 945 €
📠 15 📧 – 🛥 (½)

Surroundings : ⊰ 📺 ♀
Leisure activities : 🍴 ✗ 🏛 ⊙daytime ⊀
☟ hammam, jacuzzi ▲⊿ 🎳 ♨ 🚲 🐴
Facilities : 🚻 ⊙ 🎳 ♨ 🍴 launderette ⊰
Nearby : 🍴

G P S	Longitude : -0.0656 Latitude : 47.26022

LA SELLE-CRAONNAISE

53800 – Michelin map **310** C7 – pop. 931 – alt. 71
▶ Paris 316 – Angers 68 – Châteaubriant 32 – Château-Gontier 29

⛰ Base de Loisirs de la Rincerie

✆ 02 43 06 17 52. http://www.la-rincerie.com

Address : 3.5km northwest along the D 111, D 150. follow the signs for Ballots and take turning to the left

Opening times : from beginning March to mid Oct.

120 ha/5 for camping (50 pitches) relatively flat, flat, grassy

Tariff : 11.85 € ♣♣ ⇔ 📧 (½) (10A) – Extra per person 3.35 €

Rental rates : (from beginning March to mid Oct.) ✂ – 1 📠 – 1 🏠 – 4 canvas bungalows. Per night from 51 to 66 € – Per week from 250 to 316 €
📠 Eurorelais sani-station 2 €
Near a small lake, with plenty of water-based activities.

Surroundings : 📺 ⊰
Leisure activities : ⊙daytime 🔥 🐴 cable wakeboarding
Facilities : 🚻 ⊙ 🎳 ♨ 🍴 📧
At the leisure/activities centre : 🐴 🚲 ♨ 🛥

G P S	Longitude : -1.06528 Latitude : 47.86631

SILLÉ-LE-GUILLAUME

72140 – Michelin map **310** I5 – pop. 2 361 – alt. 161
▶ Paris 230 – Alençon 39 – Laval 55 – Le Mans 35

⛰ Indigo Les Molières

✆ 02 43 20 16 12. www.camping-indigo.com

Address : at Sillé-Plage (head 2.5km north along the D 5, D 105, D 203 and take the road to the right)

Opening times : from beginning May to end Sept.

3.5 ha (163 pitches) flat, grassy

Tariff : (2015 price) 26.90 € ♣♣ ⇔ 📧 (½) (10A) – Extra per person 5.50 € – Reservation fee 13 €
Rental rates : (2015 price) (from beginning May to end Sept.) – 12 📠 – 25 tent lodges. Per night from 45 to 100 € – Per week from 221 to 700 € – Reservation fee 13 €
📠 local sani-station 7 €
Situated in the forest, near a small lake and two ponds.

Surroundings : 📺 ♀♀
Leisure activities : 🍴 🏛 ⊀ ▲⊿ 🚲 🎳 🛥
Facilities : 🚻 ⊙ ⊰
Nearby : 🍴 🛥 🐎 pedalos

G P S	Longitude : -0.12917 Latitude : 48.18333

The Michelin classification (⛰⛰⛰ … ⚠) is totally independent of the official star classification system awarded by the local prefecture or other official organisation.

SILLÉ-LE-PHILIPPE

72460 – Michelin map **310** L6 – pop. 1 091 – alt. 35
▶ Paris 195 – Beaumont-sur-Sarthe 25 – Bonnétable 11 – Connerré 15

⛰ Les Castels Le Château de Chanteloup 👥

✆ 02 43 27 51 07. www.chateau-de-chanteloup.com

Address : at Chanteloup (situated 2km southwest along the D 301, follow the signs for Le Mans)

Opening times : from beginning June to end Aug.

21 ha (110 pitches) relatively flat, flat, grassy, sandy, pond, natural setting among trees and bushes

Tariff : 41 € ♣♣ ⇔ 📧 (½) (10A) – Extra per person 10 €
Rental rates : (from beginning June to end Aug.) – 5 canvas bungalows – 5 gîtes. Per week from 610 to 750 €

Surroundings : 📺 ♀♀
Leisure activities : 🍴 ✗ 🏛 ⊙ ⊀ ▲⊿
🎳 ♨
Facilities : 🚻 ⊙ 🎳 🍴 launderette ⊰
Nearby : 🐎

G P S	Longitude : 0.34012 Latitude : 48.10461

SOULLANS

85300 – Michelin map **316** E7 – pop. 4 058 – alt. 12
▶ Paris 443 – Challans 7 – Noirmoutier-en-l'Île 46 – La Roche-sur-Yon 48

⚠ Municipal le Moulin Neuf

📞 02 51 68 00 24. camping-soullans@orange.fr

Address : rue Saint-Christophe (take the northern exit along the D 69, follow the signs for Challans and take the turning to the right)

Opening times : from mid June to mid Sept.

1.2 ha (80 pitches) flat, grassy

Tariff : (2015 price) 9.50€ ✶✶ ⛟ 🔲 🛠 (10A) – Extra per person 2.50€

Near the town, a small and peaceful site with clearly marked-out pitches but average sanitary facilities.

Surroundings : 🐟 🖵 ♀	**G**	Longitude : -1.89566
Facilities : 🚿 ⚡🛒 🔲	**P**	Latitude : 46.79817
Nearby : ✂	**S**	

TALMONT-ST-HILAIRE

85440 – Michelin map **316** G9 – pop. 6 829 – alt. 35
▶ Paris 448 – Challans 55 – Luçon 38 – La Roche-sur-Yon 30

⚠⚠ Yelloh! Village Le Littoral

📞 02 51 22 04 64. www.campinglelittoral.com

Address : at Le Porteau (9.5km southwest along the D 949, D 4a, after Querry-Pigeon, take right turn onto the D 129, follow the coast road to les Sables-d'Olonne; 100m from the ocean)

Opening times : from mid April to mid Sept.

9 ha (483 pitches) relatively flat, flat, grassy, sandy

Tariff : 18€ ✶✶ ⛟ 🔲 🛠 (10A) – Extra per person 6€
Rental rates : (from mid April to mid Sept.) 🚿 (1 mobile home) 🅿 – 224 🛏 – 19 🏠. Per night from 39 to 265€ – Per week from 273 to 1,855€
🚰 local sani-station

An attractive site with upmarket rental accommodation and a pedestrian-only area. Free shuttle to the beaches.

Surroundings : 🖵 ♀	**G**	Longitude : -1.70222
Leisure activities : 🍴 ✕ 🎦 🎮🛝 🦽 jacuzzi 🚲✂ 🎱 🏊 ⛷ multi-sports ground	**P**	Latitude : 46.45195
Facilities : 🚿 ⚡🛒 🚽🍴 🧺 🛠 launderette 🛁🚗	**S**	

⚠ Le Paradis 🏕

📞 02 51 22 22 36. www.camping-leparadis85.com

Address : rue de la Source (3.7km west along the D 949, follow the signs for Les Sables-d'Olonne, turn left onto the D 4a, follow the signs for Querry-Pigeon and take the road to the right)

Opening times : permanent

4.9 ha (148 pitches) terraced, relatively flat, flat, grassy, sandy

Tariff : 30€ ✶✶ ⛟ 🔲 🛠 (12A) – Extra per person 6€ – Reservation fee 25€
Rental rates : permanent – 54 🛏 – 9 🏠 – 10 canvas bungalows – 4 tent lodges. Per night from 25 to 45€ – Per week from 195 to 900€ – Reservation fee 25€

A sloping site, well shaded in parts, with a range of rental options.

Surroundings : 🐟 🖵 ♀♀	**G**	Longitude : -1.65491
Leisure activities : 🍴 ✕ nighttime 🎮🛝 🏊 (open air in season), multi-sports ground	**P**	Latitude : 46.46462
Facilities : 🚿 ⚡🛒 (July-Aug.) 🚽 🛠 launderette 🛁	**S**	

TENNIE

72240 – Michelin map **310** I6 – pop. 1 023 – alt. 100
▶ Paris 224 – Alençon 49 – Laval 69 – Le Mans 26

⚠ Municipal de la Vègre

📞 02 43 20 59 44. www.camping.tennie.fr – limited spaces for one-night stay

Address : rue Andrée Le Grou (take the western exit along the D 38, follow the signs for Ste-Suzanne)

Opening times : permanent

2 ha (80 pitches) flat, grassy

Tariff : (2015 price) ✶ 2.30€ ⛟ 1.60€ 🔲 1.90€ – 🛠 (6A) 3.30€
Rental rates : (2015 price) permanent 🚿 (1 chalet) – 2 🛏 – 5 🏠. Per night from 51 to 85€ – Per week from 340 to 442€
🚰 AireService sani-station 2€

A pleasant setting beside a river and a lake.

Surroundings : 🐟 🖵 ♀♀	**G**	Longitude : -0.07874
Leisure activities : 🍴 🎦 🦽 ✂ 🏊	**P**	Latitude : 48.10705
Facilities : 🚿 ⚡🛒 🚽 🛠 🔲	**S**	
Nearby : ✕ 🐟		

THARON-PLAGE

44730 – Michelin map **316** C5
▶ Paris 444 – Nantes 59 – St-Nazaire 25 – Vannes 94

⚠ La Riviera

📞 02 28 53 54 88. www.campinglariviera.com – limited spaces for one-night stay

Address : rue des Gâtineaux (east of the resort, along the D 96, follow the signs for St-Michel-Chef-Chef)

6 ha (250 pitches) terraced, flat, grassy, stony

Rentals : 2 🛏 – 5 🏠.

A mobile home village for owner-occupiers, but with some pitches for tents and caravans.

Surroundings : 🖵	**G**	Longitude : -2.15087
Leisure activities : 🍴 🎦 jacuzzi 🦽 🏊 multi-sports ground	**P**	Latitude : 47.16492
Facilities : 🚿 ⚡🛒 🎚 🛁 🛠 🔲	**S**	

LA TRANCHE-SUR-MER

85360 – Michelin map **316** H9 – pop. 2 715 – alt. 4
▶ Paris 459 – Luçon 31 – Niort 100 – La Rochelle 64

⚠⚠ Club Airotel Le Jard 🏕

📞 02 51 27 43 79. www.campingdujard.fr 🐾

Address : 123 boulevard de Lattre de Tassigny (at La Grière-Plage, 3.8km along the road to L'Aiguillon)

Opening times : from beginning May to mid Sept.

6 ha (350 pitches) flat, grassy

Tariff : (2015 price) 33€ ✶✶ ⛟ 🔲 🛠 (10A) – Extra per person 7€ – Reservation fee 25€
Rental rates : (2015 price) (from beginning May to mid Sept.) 🐾 – 60 🛏. Per night from 48 to 124€ – Per week from 195 to 865€ – Reservation fee 25€

A pleasant site with good sanitary facilities.

Surroundings : 🖵 ♀♀	**G**	Longitude : -1.38694
Leisure activities : 🍴 ✕ 🎦 🎮🛝 🦽 🛥 🦽✂ 🎱 🏊 ⛷	**P**	Latitude : 46.34788
Facilities : 🚿 ⚡🛒 🧺🛁 🛠 launderette 🛁🚗	**S**	

Les Préveils ⚑

📞 02 51 30 30 52. www.lespreveils.asso.fr

Address : avenue Sainte Anne (at La Grière-Plage, follow the signs for L'Aiguillon for 4.2km)

Opening times : from mid March to mid Oct.

4 ha (180 pitches) undulating, flat, grassy, sandy

Tariff : 22€ ⚑⚑ ⛟ 🔲 🔌 (10A) – Extra per person 7€ – Reservation fee 20€

Rental rates : (from mid March to end Sept.) ♿ (1 mobile home) – 50 🚐 – 5 🏠 – 6 ⛺ – 6 apartments – 5 canvas bungalows. Per night from 45 to 129€ – Per week from 320 to 900€ – Reservation fee 20€

A pleasant site 200m from the beach.

Surroundings : 🌳 ♨♨
Leisure activities : ✗ 🏠 🏃 ⛷ 🏄 jacuzzi ⛵ 🏊 multi-sports ground, entertainment room
Facilities : ♿ ⚡ 🚿 ⛽ 🚽 🍴 launderette 🧺

GPS Longitude : -1.3936
Latitude : 46.34398

Baie d'Aunis

📞 02 51 27 47 36. www.camping-baiedaunis.com 🚫

Address : 10 rue du Pertuis Breton (take the eastern exit, follow the signs for l'Aiguillon)

Opening times : from end April to mid Sept.

2.5 ha (149 pitches) flat, sandy

Tariff : (2015 price) 36€ ⚑⚑ ⛟ 🔲 🔌 (10A) – Extra per person 6.30€ – Reservation fee 30€

Rental rates : (2015 price) (from end April to mid Sept.) 🚫 – 10 🚐 – 9 🏠. Per week from 350 to 870€ – Reservation fee 30€

🚉 local sani-station

Situated 50m from the beach; choose the pitches away from the road.

Surroundings : 🌳 ♨♨
Leisure activities : 🍴 ✗ 🏠 ⛵ 🏊 multi-sports ground
Facilities : ♿ ⚡ 🏠 🚿 🍴 launderette 🧺
Nearby : 🍴 🎣 ♨

GPS Longitude : -1.4321
Latitude : 46.34602

This guide is not intended as a list of all the camping sites in France; its aim is to provide a selection of the best sites in each category.

85580 – Michelin map **316** I9 – pop. 1 011 – alt. 3
▶ Paris 446 – Fontenay-le-Comte 38 – Luçon 9 – Niort 71

Municipal

📞 02 51 56 11 53. www.triaize.fr

Address : rue du Stade (in the village)

Opening times : from mid June to end Aug.

2.7 ha (70 pitches) flat, grassy, stony, pond

Tariff : (2015 price) 12.90€ ⚑⚑ ⛟ 🔲 🔌 (6A) – Extra per person 2.70€

Surroundings : 🌳 🚪
Leisure activities : ⛵ 🏊
Facilities : ♿ 🚿 🔲
Nearby : 🍴

GPS Longitude : -1.20152
Latitude : 46.39515

44420 – Michelin map **316** A3 – pop. 4 515 – alt. 6
▶ Paris 457 – La Baule 13 – Guérande 7 – Nantes 84

Municipal les Chardons Bleus

📞 02 40 62 80 60. www.camping-laturballe.fr

Address : boulevard de La Grande Falaise (2.5km to the south)

5 ha (300 pitches) flat, grassy, sandy

Rental rates : ♿ (2 chalets) – 10 🏠.

For lovers of wide, open spaces, near the beach.

Surroundings : 🌳 🚪 ⛱
Leisure activities : 🍴 ✗ 🏠 ⛵ 🏊
Facilities : ♿ 🏠 🚿 🍴 launderette 🧺 🧺
Nearby : 🚴 🏃 fitness trail

GPS Longitude : -2.50048
Latitude : 47.32832

Parc Ste-Brigitte

📞 02 40 24 88 91. www.campingsaintebrigitte.com

Address : chemin des Routes (3km southeast, follow the signs for Guérande)

Opening times : from beginning April to end Sept.

10 ha/4 for camping (150 pitches) relatively flat, flat, grassy, pond

Tariff : ⚑ 6.90€ ⛟ 3.55€ 🔲 7.90€ – 🔌 (10A) 6.80€ – Reservation fee 16€

Rental rates : (2015 price) (from beginning April to end Sept.) – 18 🚐 – 2 gîtes. Per night from 57 to 83€ – Per week from 350 to 670€ – Reservation fee 16€

🚉 local sani-station

Pretty grounds and manor house; the ageing facilities are fortunately well maintained.

Surroundings : 🌳 ♨♨
Leisure activities : ✗ 🏠 ⛵ 🚴 🔲 (open air in season) 🏊
Facilities : ♿ ⚡ 🚿 🚽 🍴 launderette 🧺

GPS Longitude : -2.4717
Latitude : 47.34254

To visit a town or region, use the MICHELIN Green Guides.

85150 – Michelin map **316** F8 – pop. 1 474 – alt. 49
▶ Paris 448 – Challans 31 – La Mothe-Achard 9 – La Roche-sur-Yon 27

Le Roc

📞 02 51 33 71 89. www.campingleroc.com

Address : route de Brem-sur-Mer (located 1.5km northwest along the D 32. follow the signs for Landevieille and turn left towards Brem-sur-Mer)

Opening times : from beginning March to mid Nov.

1.4 ha (100 pitches) relatively flat, grassy

Tariff : (2015 price) 28€ ⚑⚑ ⛟ 🔲 🔌 (6A) – Extra per person 5€ – Reservation fee 20€

Rental rates : (2015 price) (from beginning March to mid Nov.) – 27 🚐 – 3 🏠 – 2 canvas bungalows. Per night from 50 to 90€ – Per week from 185 to 855€ – Reservation fee 20€

🚉 Eurorelais sani-station 10€ – 3 🔲 10€

A shaded setting, but choose the pitches away from the road.

Surroundings : 🚪 ♨
Leisure activities : 🍴 ✗ 🏃 ⛵ 🔲 (small swimming pool) 🏊
Facilities : ♿ ⚡ (July–Aug.) 🏠 🚿 🍴 launderette

GPS Longitude : -1.76785
Latitude : 46.60815

VARENNES-SUR-LOIRE

49730 – Michelin map **317** J5 – pop. 1 898 – alt. 27
▶ Paris 292 – Bourgueil 15 – Chinon 22 – Loudun 30

⚠️ Les Castels Domaine de la Brèche ♣♣

☏ 02 41 51 22 92. www.domainedelabreche.com

Address : 5 Impasse de la Brèche (6km west along the D 85, RD 952, follow the signs for Saumur, and take the road to the right; beside the lake)

Opening times : from beginning May to mid Sept.

14 ha/7 for camping (201 pitches) flat, grassy, sandy

Tariff : 44€ ♣♣ 🚗 🔲 🚽 (16A) – Extra per person 9€ – Reservation fee 10€

Rental rates : (from beginning May to mid Sept.) – 3 'gypsy' caravans – 38 🚐 – 1 cabin in the trees – 2 canvas bungalows. Per night from 33 to 203€ – Per week from 136 to 1,432€ – Reservation fee 10€

A pleasant site and setting beside a lake.

Surroundings : 🌿 🏕 ♨
Leisure activities : 🍽 🎠 🖥 🏃 🚣 🐎 🚴 ✂ 🧗 🏊 🛶 farm or petting farm, pitch & putt (18 holes), multi-sports ground
Facilities : 🚿 🍴 🏕 🚽 📶 🔌 🚮 🧺
Nearby : 🍴

G P S Longitude : 0.00213 Latitude : 47.24837

To visit a town or region, use the MICHELIN Green Guides.

VENDRENNES

85250 – Michelin map **316** J7 – pop. 1 447 – alt. 97
▶ Paris 392 – Nantes 65 – La Roche-sur-Yon 30 – Niort 95

⚠️ La Motte

☏ 02 51 63 59 67. www.camping-lamotte.com

Address : at La Motte (0.4km to the northeast, off the D160)

Opening times : permanent

3.5 ha (83 pitches) flat, grassy

Tariff : (2015 price) 20.60€ ♣♣ 🚗 🔲 🚽 (16A) – Extra per person 3.60€

Rental rates : (2015 price) permanent 🚫 – 33 🚐 – 3 🏠. Per night from 52 to 180€ – Per week from 225 to 1,030€

Green, floral setting arranged around a small ornamental lake.

Surroundings : 🌿 🏕
Leisure activities : 🍽 🍴 🏛 daytime 🚣
🛶 spa facilities, bowling
Facilities : 🚿 🍴 🏛 🚽 🧺 launderette 🐾

G P S Longitude : -1.11854 Latitude : 46.82587

VIHIERS

49310 – Michelin map **317** F6 – pop. 4 275 – alt. 100
▶ Paris 334 – Angers 45 – Cholet 29 – Saumur 40

⚠️ Municipal de la Vallée du Lys

☏ 02 41 75 00 14. www.vihiers.fr

Address : route du Voide (take the western exit along the D 960. follow the signs for Cholet then take the D 54 to the right, following signs for Valanjou; beside the Lys river)

0.3 ha (30 pitches) flat, grassy

Surroundings : 🌿 ♨
Leisure activities : 🏛 🚣 🏃
Facilities : 🚿

G P S Longitude : -0.54034 Latitude : 47.1471

VILLIERS-CHARLEMAGNE

53170 – Michelin map **310** E7 – pop. 1 052 – alt. 105
▶ Paris 277 – Angers 61 – Châteaubriant 61 – Château-Gontier 12

⚠️ Village Vacances Pêche

☏ 02 43 07 71 68. http://www.vacancesetpeche.fr

Address : Village des Haies (take the western exit along the D 4, follow the signs for Cossé-le-Vivien and take road to the left near the stadium)

Opening times : permanent

9 ha/1 campable (20 pitches) flat, grassy

Tariff : (2015 price) 17.70€ ♣♣ 🚗 🔲 🚽 (16A) – Extra per person 6.30€

Rental rates : permanent – 12 🏠. Per week from 200 to 595€ – Reservation fee 15€

🚮 AireService sani-station – 3 🔲 8.70€

Surroundings : 🌿 🌾 🏕 ♨
Leisure activities : 🏛 🖥 daytime 🚣 🏃 🚴
Facilities : 🚿 🔌 – 20 individual sanitary facilities (🚿 🚽 🚻 WC) 🛁 🍴 🧊 refrigerators
Nearby : 🍴 🎣

G P S Longitude : -0.68233 Latitude : 47.9208

Key to rentals symbols:

12 🚐	Number of mobile homes
20 🏠	Number of chalets
6 🛏	Number of rooms to rent
Per night 30–50€	Minimum/maximum rate per night
Per week 300–1,000€	Minimum/maximum rate per week

YVRÉ-L'ÉVÊQUE

72530 – Michelin map **310** K6 – pop. 4 412 – alt. 57
▶ Paris 204 – Nantes 194 – Le Mans 8 – Alençon 66

⚠️ Onlycamp Le Pont Romain

☏ 02 43 82 25 39. www.onlycamp.fr

Address : La Châtaigneraie, Allée des Ormeaux (exit the village via the the Roman bridge, then take the road to the left, continue for 200m)

Opening times : from mid March to mid Nov.

2.5 ha (70 pitches) flat, grassy

Tariff : (2015 price) 25.10€ ♣♣ 🚗 🔲 🚽 (16A) – Extra per person 5.40€

Rental rates : (2015 price) (from mid March to mid Nov.) 🅿 – 5 🚐 – 10 🏠 – 2 canvas bungalows – 5 tent lodges. Per night from 39 to 139€ – Per week from 270 to 970€

🚮 15 🔲 20€

Surroundings : ♨
Leisure activities : 🏛 🚣 🏃
Facilities : 🔌 🅿 🧺 🛁 🚽 🍴 launderette
Nearby : 🛶 🍴 🍴

G P S Longitude : 0.27972 Latitude : 48.01944

For more information on visiting particular towns or regions, consult the relevant regional MICHELIN Green Guide. We also recommend you use the appropriate Michelin regional map to locate your selected campsite, to calculate distances and to work out the best route.

H. Lenain / hemis.fr

A re you ready for an action-packed journey through Picardy's fair and historic lands? The region that gave Gaul – now France – her first Christian king, Clovis, is renowned for its wealthy Cistercian abbeys, splendid Gothic cathedrals and flamboyant town halls, along with deeply poignant reminders of two world wars. If you are in the mood to explore the countryside, take a boat trip through the floating gardens of Amiens or explore the botanical reserve of Marais de Cessière. Try a spot of birdwatching on the Somme estuary or at Marquenterre bird sanctuary. Spend time relaxing in unspoilt hills, woods, pastures and vineyards. Picardy has a rich culinary history, so where better to try *soupe aux hortillonages* (vegetable gardener's soup), the famous *agneau pré-salé* (lamb fattened on the salt marshes), a plate of smoked eel or duck pâté, or a dessert laced with Chantilly cream. 'Drink well, eat well and do nothing', to quote Lafleur, the famous 19th-century Amiens puppet.

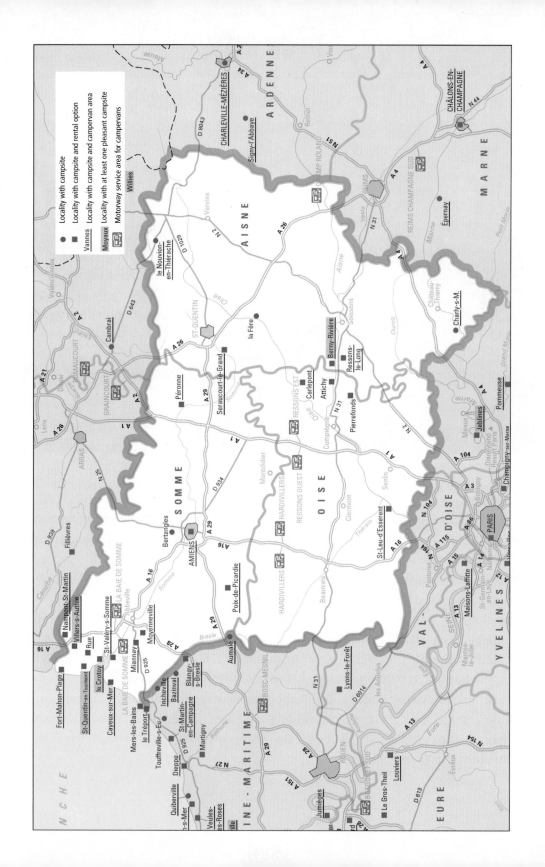

AMIENS

80000 – Michelin map **301** G8 – pop. 133 998 – alt. 34
▶ Paris 135 – Lille 122 – Beauvais 62 – Arras 74

▲ Sites et Paysages Le Parc des Cygnes

✆ 03 22 43 29 28, www.parcdescygnes.com

Address : 111 avenue des Cygnes (to the northeast, rue du Grand-Marais – from the bypass (rocade), take exit 40 for Amiens Longpré)

Opening times : from beginning April to mid Oct.

3,2 ha (145 pitches) flat, grassy, pond

Tariff : (2015 price) 27,70€ ✶✶ 🚗 🗐 🕴 (10A) –
Extra per person 6.70€ – Reservation fee 13.50€

Rental rates : (from beginning April to mid Oct.) – 9 🚐. Per night from 55 to 120€ – Per week from 300 to 700€ – Reservation fee 13.50€

🚱 local sani-station 4.20€ – 5 🗐 12.30€ – 🚐 14€
There's a bus to the town centre.

Surroundings : 🌳
Leisure activities : 🍸 ✗ 🏛 🚣 🚴 ⛸
Facilities : 👤 ⛽ 🗐 🛁 🛒 🚮 🍴 launderette
Nearby : 🎣

G P S	Longitude : 2.25918
	Latitude : 49.92118

ATTICHY

60350 – Michelin map **305** J4 – pop. 1 887 – alt. 73
▶ Paris 109 – Amiens 103 – Beauvais 80 – Laon 59

▲ L' Aigrette

✆ 03 44 42 15 97, www.campingdelaigrette.com

Address : 22 rue Fontaine Aubier

Opening times : from beginning March to end Nov.

1.3 ha (61 pitches) flat, grassy

Tariff : (2015 price) 20€ ✶✶ 🚗 🗐 🕴 (10A) – Extra per person 4€
Rental rates : (2015 price) permanent 🚲 – 1 🚐 – 4 tipis – 1 tent lodge. Per night from 60 to 110€ – Per week from 240 to 350€

Situated beside a large lake popular with swans and ducks.

Surroundings : 🌊 🗗 🌳🌳
Leisure activities : 🎣
Facilities : 👤 ⛽ 🗐 🛒 🚮 🍴 launderette
Nearby : ✗ 🚴 🛶

G P S	Longitude : 3.05295
	Latitude : 49.40667

BERNY-RIVIÈRE

02290 – Michelin map **306** A6 – pop. 604 – alt. 49
▶ Paris 100 – Compiègne 24 – Laon 55 – Noyon 28

▲▲▲ La Croix du Vieux Pont ▲▲

✆ 03 23 55 50 02, www.la-croix-du-vieux-pont.com – limited spaces for one-night stay

Address : rue de la Fabrique (located 1.5km south on the D 91, near Vic-sur-Aisne; beside the Aisne river)

Opening times : permanent

34 ha (660 pitches) flat, grassy, pond

Tariff : 40€ ✶✶ 🚗 🗐 🕴 (6A) – Extra per person 12.50€
Rental rates : (2015 price) (from beginning April to end Oct.) 👤 (mobile homes & chalets) 🚲 – 11 🏠 – 11 apartments – 1 cabin in the trees – 11 tent lodges. Per night from €
100 to 200 – Per week from 500 to 1,500€

🚱 local sani-station

A holiday village offering lots of activities, some indoor, in a pleasant setting by the Aisne river.

Surroundings : 🌊 🗗 🌳
Leisure activities : 🍸 ✗ 🏛 🕴 🚣 🛶 ⛸
jacuzzi 🚣 🚴 ✗ 🕴 🎱 🏊 (fresh water)
🏄 🎿 bowling, laser game,
pedalos, multi-sports ground, water park
Facilities : 👤 ⛽ 🗐 🛁 🛒 🚮 🍴 launderette
🚮🛒

G P S	Longitude : 3.1284
	Latitude : 49.40495

BERTANGLES

80260 – Michelin map **301** G8 – pop. 591 – alt. 95
▶ Paris 154 – Abbeville 44 – Amiens 11 – Bapaume 49

▲ Le Château

✆ 03 60 65 68 36, www.camping-bertangles.fr

Address : rue du Château (in the village)

Opening times : from end April to mid Sept.

0.7 ha (33 pitches) flat, grassy

Tariff : ✶ 4.60€ 🚗 2.90€ 🗐 4.60€ – 🕴 (5A) 4.20€

The site is in an orchard near the château

Surroundings : 🌊 🗗 🌳
Leisure activities : 🎠
Facilities : 👤 ⛽ 🗗 🍴

G P S	Longitude : 2.30131
	Latitude : 49.97167

This guide is updated regularly, so buy your new copy every year!

CARLEPONT

60170 – Michelin map **305** J3 – pop. 1 416 – alt. 59
▶ Paris 103 – Compiègne 19 – Ham 30 – Pierrefonds 21

▲ Les Araucarias

✆ 03 44 75 27 39, www.camping-les-araucarias.com – limited spaces for one-night stay

Address : 870 rue du Général Leclerc (take the southwestern exit along the D 130, follow the signs for Compiègne)

Opening times : from beginning April to end Oct.

1.2 ha (60 pitches) flat, relatively flat, grassy

Tariff : ✶ 3€ 🚗 2€ 🗐 4€ – 🕴 (12A) 3€
Rental rates : permanent – 16 🚐 – 4 🏠. Per night from 70 to 80 € – Per week from 280 to 380€

🚱 local sani-station 2€ – 2 🗐 15.50€

This site has a wide variety of vegetation around the camping area.

Surroundings : 🌊 🗗 🌳🌳
Leisure activities : 🎠
Facilities : 👤 ⛽ 🗗 🍴 launderette

G P S	Longitude : 3.01836
	Latitude : 49.50728

Key to rentals symbols:

12	*Number of mobile homes*
20 🏠	*Number of chalets*
6 🛏	*Number of rooms to rent*
Per night 30–50€	*Minimum/maximum rate per night*
Per week 300–1,000€	*Minimum/maximum rate per week*

CAYEUX-SUR-MER

80410 – Michelin map **301** B6 – pop. 2 813 – alt. 2
▶ Paris 217 – Abbeville 29 – Amiens 82 – Le Crotoy 26

Les Galets de la Mollière 👫

📞 03 22 26 61 85, www.campinglesgaletsdelamolliere.com

Address : at Mollière, rue Faidherbe (3.3km northeast along the D 102, coastal road)

6 ha (195 pitches)flat, relatively flat, grassy, sandy
Rentals : 39 🚐.
🚱 eurorelais sani-station – 40 🔲
Situated 100m from the beach and dunes

Surroundings : 🏕 🗺 ♀		G P S	Longitude : 1.52608
Leisure activities : 🍴 ✕ 🏛 🏃 🚣 ✂ 🛷			Latitude : 50.20275
Facilities : 🚿 ⚬ 🗑 🛏 🍴 launderette 🚰			

Le Bois de Pins

📞 03 22 26 71 04, www.campingleboisdepins.com – limited spaces for one-night stay

Address : at Brighton, avenue Guillaume-le-Conquérant (2km northeast along the D 102, coastal road)

4 ha (163 pitches) flat, grassy
🚱 local sani-station
Situated 400m from the beach and dunes, with numerous owner-occupier mobile homes.

Surroundings : 🏕 🗺 ♀		G P S	Longitude : 1.5169
Leisure activities : 🛶			Latitude : 50.1974
Facilities : 🚿 ⚬ 🗑 🛏 🍴 launderette			

CHARLY-SUR-MARNE

02310 – Michelin map **306** B9 – pop. 2 741 – alt. 63
▶ Paris 82 – Château-Thierry 14 – Coulommiers 33 – La Ferté-sous-Jouarre 16

Municipal des Illettes

📞 03 23 82 12 11, www.charly-sur-marne.fr

Address : route de Pavant (south of the town, 200m from the D 82 (recommended route)

Opening times : from beginning April to end Sept.

1.2 ha (43 pitches) flat, grassy, gravelled

Tariff : 17.50€ ♛♛ 🚗 🔲 ⚡ (10A) – Extra per person 4€
🚱 local sani-station

Surroundings : 🗺 ♀♀		G P S	Longitude : 3.28209
Leisure activities : 🛶			Latitude : 48.97369
Facilities : 🚿 ⚬ 🚻 🗑 🛏 🍴 launderette			
Nearby : 🛒 ✕ 🎯			

LE CROTOY

80550 – Michelin map **301** C6 – pop. 2 265 – alt. 1
▶ Paris 210 – Abbeville 22 – Amiens 75 – Berck-sur-Mer 29

Yelloh! Village Le Ridin

📞 03 22 27 03 22, www.campingleridin.com – limited spaces for one-night stay

Address : at Mayocq (3km north following signs for St-Quentin-en-Tourmont and take road to the right)

Opening times : permanent

4.5 ha (162 pitches) flat, grassy

Tariff : 34€ ♛♛ 🚗 🔲 ⚡ (10A) – Extra per person 8€

Rental rates : permanent – 37 🚐. Per night from 33 to 175€ – Per week from 231 to 1,225€
🚱 local sani-station – 🚐29€
The swimming pool area and restaurant are on the other side of the small road.

Surroundings : 🏕 🗺 ♀		G P S	Longitude : 1.63182
Leisure activities : 🍴 ✕ 🛶 🛁 jacuzzi 🚣 🚴 🛷			Latitude : 50.23905
Facilities : 🚿 ⚬ 🗑 🛏 🍴 launderette 🚰			

Flower Les Aubépines

📞 03 22 27 01 34, www.camping-lesaubepines.com – limited spaces for one-night stay

Address : at St-Firmin, 800 rue de la Maye (4km to the north, follow the signs for St-Quentin-en-Tourmont and take road to the left)

Opening times : from end March to beginning Nov.

2.5 ha (196 pitches) flat, grassy, sandy

Tariff : 32.50€ ♛♛ 🚗 🔲 ⚡ (10A) – Extra per person 6.50€ – Reservation fee 15€

Rental rates : (from end March to beginning Nov.) – 50 🚐. Per night from 52 to 160€ – Per week from 260 to 1,120€ – Reservation fee 15€
🚱 local sani-station 17€
Some of the rental accommodation is of a high standard and the area car-free.

Surroundings : 🏕 🗺 ♀		G P S	Longitude : 1.61139
Leisure activities : 🛶 🚣 🚴 🛷			Latitude : 50.24955
Facilities : 🚿 ⚬ 🗑 🛏 🍴 launderette			

Les Trois Sablières

📞 03 22 27 01 33, www.camping-les-trois-sablieres.com – limited spaces for one-night stay

Address : 1850 rue de la Maye (4km to the northwest, follow the signs for St-Quentin-en-Tourmont and take the road to the left, 400m from the beach)

Opening times : from mid April to beginning Nov.

1.5 ha (97 pitches) flat, grassy, sandy

Tariff : (2015 price) 29€ ♛♛ 🚗 🔲 ⚡ (6A) – Extra per person 6.80€
Rental rates : (from beginning April to beginning Nov.) 🚿 (1 mobile home) – 22 🚐 – 2 🏠 – 2 gîtes. Per night from 65 to 110€ – Per week from 300 to 742€
🚱 local sani-station 5€ – 🚐12€
In a green setting with flowers.

Surroundings : 🏕 🗺 ♀		G P S	Longitude : 1.59883
Leisure activities : 🍴 🛶 🛁 🛎 🚣 🛷			Latitude : 50.24825
Facilities : 🚿 ⚬ 🛏 🍴 launderette			

LA FÈRE

02800 – Michelin map **306** C5 – pop. 3 012 – alt. 54
▶ Paris 137 – Compiègne 59 – Laon 24 – Noyon 31

Municipal du Marais de la Fontaine

📞 03 23 56 82 94

Address : rue Vauban (via the town centre towards Tergnier and take a right turn at the sports centre; near a branch of the Oise river)

0.7 ha (26 pitches) flat, grassy

Surroundings : 🗺 ♀		G P S	Longitude : 3.36353
Facilities : 🚿 ⚬			Latitude : 49.6654
Nearby : ✕			

FORT-MAHON-PLAGE

80120 – Michelin map **301** C5 – pop. 1 311 – alt. 2
▶ Paris 225 – Abbeville 41 – Amiens 90 – Berck-sur-Mer 19

▲▲▲ Club Airotel Le Royon ▲▲

🕿 03 22 23 40 30, www.campingleroyon.com – limited spaces for one-night stay

Address : 1271 route de Quend (located 1km to the south)

Opening times : from end March to end Oct.

4 ha (376 pitches) flat, grassy, sandy

Tariff : 37€ ✸✸ ⇔ ▣ (*) (6A) – Extra per person 7€ – Reservation fee 12€

Rental rates : (from end March to end Oct.) – 85 ▭. Per night from 90 to 120€ – Per week from 300 to 790€ – Reservation fee 12€

▭ local sani-station 3€ – 8 ▣ 37€ – ▭ (*)18€

A pleasant campsite, but with numerous owner-occupier mobile homes.

Surroundings : ▭ ♀
Leisure activities : 🍷🏃🚣✂🎣 farm or petting farm, entertainment room
Facilities : ♿ ⚲ 🏛 ♨ ⛺ 🍴 launderette

G P S Longitude : 1.57963
Latitude : 50.33263

▲▲ Le Vert Gazon

🕿 03 22 23 37 69, www.camping-levertgazon.com – limited spaces for one-night stay

Address : 741 route de Quend

2.5 ha (130 pitches) flat, grassy

Rentals : ♿ (1 mobile home) – 1 'gypsy' caravan – 15 ▭ – 5 ⌂ – 5 gîtes.

▭ local sani-station – 5 ▣

A variety of rental accommodation of a good standard.

Surroundings : ▭
Leisure activities : 🍷 ⛱ 🚣 🚲 🛶
Facilities : ♿ ⚲ ⛺ 🍴 launderette

G P S Longitude : 1.57374
Latitude : 50.33438

The guide covers all 22 regions of France – see the map and list of regions on pages 4–5.

MERS-LES-BAINS

80350 – Michelin map **301** B7 – pop. 3 124 – alt. 3
▶ Paris 217 – Amiens 89 – Rouen 99 – Arras 130

▲▲ Flower Le Domaine du Rompval

🕿 02 35 84 43 21, www.campinglerompval.com

Address : at Blengues (situated 2km northeast of Mers-les-Bains)

Opening times : from end March to beginning Nov.

3 ha (132 pitches) flat, grassy

Tariff : 25.30€ ✸✸ ⇔ ▣ (*) (8A) – Extra per person 5€ – Reservation fee 6€

Rental rates : (from end March to beginning Nov.) – 29 ▭ – 6 studios – 2 canvas bungalows. Per night from 39 to 118€ – Per week from 195 to 826€ – Reservation fee 6€

Rental accommodation in unusual and colourful styles. Choose those pitches furthest away from the road in preference.

Surroundings : ▭ ♀
Leisure activities : 🍷 ⛱ 🚣 🚲 🖼 (open air in season)
Facilities : ♿ ⚲ 🆑 🏛 ⛺ 🍴 launderette

G P S Longitude : 1.4154
Latitude : 50.0773

MIANNAY

80132 – Michelin map **301** D7 – pop. 568 – alt. 15
▶ Paris 191 – Amiens 63 – Arras 104 – Rouen 109

▲▲ Sites et Paysages Le Clos Cacheleux

🕿 03 22 19 17 47, www.camping-lecloscacheleux.fr

Address : route de Bouillancourt-sous-Miannay

Opening times : from mid March to end Oct.

8 ha (119 pitches) relatively flat, flat, grassy

Tariff : 27.90€ ✸✸ ⇔ ▣ (*) (10A) – Extra per person 5.80€ – Reservation fee 12€

Rental rates : (from beginning April to end Oct.) – 5 cabins in the trees – 1 gîte. Per night from 85 to 160€ – Per week from 595 to 1,120€ – Reservation fee 12€

▭ 20 ▣ 27.90€ – ▭ 11€

Situated in the grounds of a working farm (crops and cattle).

Surroundings : ♨ ▭ ♀
Leisure activities : 🚣
Facilities : ♿ ⚲ ⛺ 🍴 launderette
Nearby : 🍷 🍴 ⛱ 🏃 🖼 (open air in season) activities at the Le Val de Trie, opposite

G P S Longitude : 1.71536
Latitude : 50.08646

These symbols are used for a campsite that is exceptional in its category:

▲▲▲...▲ *Particularly pleasant setting, quality and range of services available*

♨♨ *Tranquil, isolated site – quiet site, particularly at night*

≪≪ *Exceptional view – interesting or panoramic view*

MOYENNEVILLE

80870 – Michelin map **301** D7 – pop. 667 – alt. 92
▶ Paris 194 – Abbeville 9 – Amiens 59 – Blangy-sur-Bresle 22

▲▲▲ Le Val de Trie ▲▲

🕿 03 22 31 48 88, www.camping-levaldetrie.fr

Address : 1 rue des Sources at Bouillancourt-sous-Miannay (3km northwest along the D 86; beside a stream)

Opening times : from end March to beginning Oct.

2 ha (100 pitches) flat, grassy, small lake

Tariff : 27.90€ ✸✸ ⇔ ▣ (*) (10A) – Extra per person 5.80€ – Reservation fee 12€

Rental rates : (2015 price) (from end March to beginning Oct.) ♿ (1 chalet) – 20 ▭ – 5 ⌂ – 1 gîte. Per night from 49 to 157€ – Per week from 343 to 1,099€ – Reservation fee 12€

▭ 10 ▣ 27.90€

Surroundings : ♨ ▭ ♀♀
Leisure activities : 🍷 🍴 ⛱ 🏃 🚣 🖼 (open air in season)
Facilities : ♿ ⚲ 🆑 🏛 ⛺ 🍴 launderette

G P S Longitude : 1.71508
Latitude : 50.08552

*The classification (1 to 5 tents, **black** or red) that we award to selected sites in this guide is our own system. It should not be confused with the classification (1 to 5 stars) of official organisations.*

NAMPONT-ST-MARTIN

80120 – Michelin map **301** D5 – pop. 260 – alt. 10
▶ Paris 214 – Abbeville 30 – Amiens 79 – Boulogne-sur-Mer 52

🏔 La Ferme des Aulnes

🖉 0322292269, www.fermedesaulnes.com – limited spaces for one-night stay

Address : at Fresne, 1 rue du Marais (3km southwest along the D 85e, follow the signs for Villier-sur-Authie)

Opening times : from end March to beginning Nov.

4 ha (120 pitches) relatively flat, flat, grassy

Tariff : 27€ ★★ ⬌ 🖭 ⚡ (10A) – Extra per person 7€ – Reservation fee 10€

Rental rates : (from end March to beginning Nov.) – 17 🛖 – 1 🛖. Per night from 60 to 124€ – Per week from 399 to 824€ – Reservation fee 10€

🚽 local sani-station – 14 🖭 27€ – 🚐 ⚡ 20€

The setting is a traditional Picardy farm.

Surroundings : 🌳 🛋 ♀
Leisure activities : 🍴 ✕ 🛋 🎹 (piano bar)
🏋 ♨ jacuzzi 🏊 🎣 (open air in season), entertainment room
Facilities : ♿ ⚊ 🆑 ▦ 🚿 🚰 🚽 launderette 🐾

Longitude : 1.71201
Latitude : 50.33631

The pitches of many campsites are marked out with low hedges of attractive bushes and shrubs.

LE NOUVION-EN-THIÉRACHE

02170 – Michelin map **306** E2 – pop. 2 809 – alt. 185
▶ Paris 198 – Avesnes-sur-Helpe 20 – Le Cateau-Cambrésis 19 – Guise 21

⛺ Municipal du Lac de Condé

🖉 0323989858, www.camping-thierache.com

Address : promenade Henri d'Orléans (situated 2km south along the D 26 and take the road to the left)

Opening times : from beginning April to end Sept.

1.3 ha (56 pitches) flat and relatively flat

Tariff : (2015 price) 13.60€ ★★ ⬌ 🖭 ⚡ (8A) – Extra per person 3.60€
🚽 Eurorelais sani-station 2€ – 3 🖭 9.50€

On the edge of the forest, near a lake and a leisure park.

Surroundings : 🌳 🛋
Leisure activities : 🛋
Facilities : ♿ ⚊ 🖭
Nearby : 🍴 ✕ 🏊 🎣 🛶 🎿 bowling, mountain biking

Longitude : 3.78271
Latitude : 50.00561

PÉRONNE

80200 – Michelin map **301** K8 – pop. 7 981 – alt. 52
▶ Paris 141 – Amiens 58 – Arras 48 – Doullens 54

🏔 Port de Plaisance

🖉 0322841931, www.camping-plaisance.com

Address : head south from Peronne on the D 1017, following the signs for Paris; near the marina; by the Canal de la Somme

Opening times : from beginning March to end Oct.

2 ha (90 pitches) flat, grassy, fine gravel

Tariff : (2015 price) 30.10€ ★★ ⬌ 🖭 ⚡ (10A) – Extra per person 4€

Rental rates : (2015 price) (from beginning March to end Oct.)
🏄 – 4 🛖. Per night from 78€ – Per week from 287 to 513€
🚽 local sani-station – 🚐 ⚡ 21.80€

Surroundings : 🛋 ♀♀
Leisure activities : 🍴 🛋 🏊 🚴 🎿
Facilities : ♿ ⚊ ▦ 🚿 🚰 🚽 launderette
Nearby : 🎣 ⚓

Longitude : 2.93237
Latitude : 49.91786

PIERREFONDS

60350 – Michelin map **305** I4 – pop. 1 969 – alt. 81
▶ Paris 82 – Beauvais 78 – Compiègne 15 – Crépy-en-Valois 17

⛺ Municipal de Batigny

🖉 0344428083, www.lecoeurdelaforet.fr

Address : rue de l'Armistice (take northwestern exit along the D 973, follow the signs for Compiègne)

1 ha (60 pitches) terraced, flat, grassy

Rentals : 2 🛖.

Attractive trees and shrubs decorate the site.

Surroundings : 🛋 ♀♀
Leisure activities : 🏊
Facilities : ⚊ ▦ 🚿 🚰 🚽 🖭
Nearby : 🍴

Longitude : 2.97962
Latitude : 49.35194

POIX-DE-PICARDIE

80290 – Michelin map **301** E9 – pop. 2 388 – alt. 106
▶ Paris 133 – Abbeville 45 – Amiens 31 – Beauvais 46

⛺ Municipal le Bois des Pêcheurs

🖉 0322901171, www.ville-poix-de-picardie.fr – 🛉

Address : route de Verdun (take the western exit along the D 919, follow the signs for Formerie, beside a stream)

Opening times : from beginning April to end Sept.

2 ha (88 pitches) flat, grassy

Tariff : (2015 price) 18€ ★★ ⬌ 🖭 ⚡ (6A) – Extra per person 1.50€
Rental rates : (2015 price) (from beginning April to end Sept.) – 2 🛖. Per night from 100€ – Per week from 250 to 300€
🚽 Eurorelais sani-station 2€ – 4 🖭 8€

Some attractive, well marked-out pitches.

Surroundings : 🛋 ♀
Leisure activities : 🛋 🏊 🚴
Facilities : ♿ ⚊ 🚐 🚽 launderette
Nearby : 🍴 🏊

Longitude : 1.9743
Latitude : 49.75

*To visit a town or region, use the **MICHELIN Green Guides**.*

RESSONS-LE-LONG

02290 – Michelin map **306** A6 – pop. 756 – alt. 72
▶ Paris 97 – Compiègne 26 – Laon 53 – Noyon 31

🏔 La Halte de Mainville

🖉 0323742669, www.lahaltedemainville.com

Address : 18 rue du Routy (take the northeastern exit)

Opening times : from mid Jan. to mid Dec.

5 ha (155 pitches) flat, grassy, small lake

Tariff : 22€ ★★ ⬌ 🖭 ⚡ (8A) – Extra per person 4€

Rental rates : (from beginning April to end Oct.) – 2 ⟨image⟩ – 2 ⟨image⟩.
Per night from 125€ – Per week from 465€

⟨image⟩ local sani-station

Surroundings : ⟨icons⟩
Leisure activities : ⟨icons⟩
Facilities : ⟨icons⟩ launderette

G P S Longitude : 3.15186
Latitude : 49.39277

RUE

80120 – Michelin map **301** D6 – pop. 3 095 – alt. 9
▶ Paris 212 – Abbeville 28 – Amiens 77 – Berck-Plage 22

⚠ Les Oiseaux

🖉 03 22 25 73 44, www.campingbaiesomme.com – limited spaces for one-night stay – ⟨icon⟩

Address : 3.2km south along the D 940, follow the signs for Le Crotoy and take the Chemin de Favières to the left; near a stream

Opening times : from beginning Feb. to end Nov.

1.2 ha (71 pitches) flat, grassy

Tariff : 24€ ⟨icons⟩ (16A) – Extra per person 6€

Rental rates : (2015 price) (from mid April to mid Oct.) – 3 ⟨image⟩.
Per night from 70 to 180€ – Per week from 100 to 680€

⟨image⟩ local sani-station – 3 ⟨icon⟩ 18€ – ⟨icon⟩ 10€

Surroundings : ⟨icons⟩
Leisure activities : ⟨icon⟩
Facilities : ⟨icons⟩

G P S Longitude : 1.66872
Latitude : 50.25264

*The classification (1 to 5 tents, **black** or red) that we award to selected sites in this guide is our own system. It should not be confused with the classification (1 to 5 stars) of official organisations.*

ST-LEU-D'ESSERENT

60340 – Michelin map **305** F5 – pop. 4 708 – alt. 50
▶ Paris 57 – Beauvais 38 – Chantilly 7 – Creil 9

⛰ Campix

🖉 03 44 56 08 48, www.campingcampix.com

Address : rue Pasteur (take the northern exit off the D 12 just as you leave built-up area and come to open fields, and follow signs to campsite – winding road)

Opening times : from mid March to end Nov.

6 ha (160 pitches) undulating, terraced, flat, grassy, stony

Tariff : ⟨icon⟩ 7€ ⟨icon⟩ 7€ – ⟨icon⟩ (6A) 4€

Rental rates : (from beginning March to end Nov.) – 7 ⟨image⟩.
Per night from 85 to 115€ – Per week from 595 to 805€

⟨image⟩ Raclet sani-station 6€

In a shady former quarry overlooking the town and the Oise river.

Surroundings : ⟨icons⟩
Leisure activities : ⟨icons⟩
Facilities : ⟨icons⟩ launderette ⟨icon⟩

G P S Longitude : 2.42722
Latitude : 49.22492

The pitches of many campsites are marked out with low hedges of attractive bushes and shrubs.

ST-QUENTIN-EN-TOURMONT

80120 – Michelin map **301** C6 – pop. 305
▶ Paris 218 – Abbeville 29 – Amiens 83 – Berck-sur-Mer 24

⛰ Le Champ Neuf

🖉 03 22 25 07 94, www.camping-lechampneuf.com – limited spaces for one-night stay

Address : 8 rue du Champ Neuf

Opening times : from beginning April to end Oct.

8 ha/4.5 for camping (161 pitches) flat, grassy, wood

Tariff : (2015 price) 32€ ⟨icons⟩ (10A) – Extra per person 6.50€ – Reservation fee 10€

Rental rates : (2015 price) (from beginning April to end Oct.) – 35 ⟨image⟩ – 4 gîtes. Per night from 71 to 84€ – Reservation fee 10€

⟨image⟩ local sani-station

The site has a lovely indoor water park.

Surroundings : ⟨icons⟩
Leisure activities : ⟨icons⟩ jacuzzi ⟨icons⟩ fitness trail, multi-sports ground, entertainment room
Facilities : ⟨icons⟩ launderette
Nearby : ✕

G P S Longitude : 1.60153
Latitude : 50.26978

Michelin classification:

⛰⛰⛰⛰ *Extremely comfortable, equipped to a very high standard*

⛰⛰⛰ *Very comfortable, equipped to a high standard*

⛰⛰ *Comfortable and well equipped*

⛰ *Reasonably comfortable*

⛺ *Satisfactory*

ST-VALERY-SUR-SOMME

80230 – Michelin map **301** C6 – pop. 2 873 – alt. 27
▶ Paris 206 – Abbeville 18 – Amiens 71 – Blangy-sur-Bresle 45

⛰⛰⛰⛰ Club Airotel Le Walric

🖉 03 22 26 81 97, www.campinglewalric.com – limited spaces for one-night stay

Address : route d'Eu (west along the D 3)

Opening times : from beginning April to beginning Nov.

5.8 ha (263 pitches) flat, grassy, wood

Tariff : (2015 price) 36€ ⟨icons⟩ (6A) – Extra per person 7€ – Reservation fee 12€

Rental rates : (2015 price) (from beginning April to beginning Nov.) – 80 ⟨image⟩. Per night from 75 to 112€ – Per week from 287 to 784€ – Reservation fee 12€

⟨image⟩ Eurorelais sani-station

A pleasant site, but with numerous owner-occupier mobile homes and caravans.

Surroundings : ⟨icons⟩
Leisure activities : ⟨icons⟩ (open air in season)
Facilities : ⟨icons⟩ launderette
Nearby : ⟨icon⟩

G P S Longitude : 1.61791
Latitude : 50.1839

Using the traditional Michelin classification method, the guide provides you with an easy, speedy reference for assessing the category of each site: 1 to 5 tents (see page 10).

⩗⩗⩗ Les Castels Le Domaine de Drancourt ⚑⚑

𝒞 03 22 26 93 45, www.chateau-drancourt.com

Address : at Estréboeuf, at Drancourt (3.5km south along the D 48 and take a right turn after crossing the CD 940)

5 ha (326 pitches) flat and relatively flat, grassy

Rentals : 42 🛏 – 5 🏠.

🚉 local sani-station

On a pleasant site in the grounds of the château, with a partially covered water park.

Surroundings : 🦢 ⌁ ♀		
Leisure activities : 🍷 ✕ 🎦 🏃 ⚓ ♨ 🚴ₘ	**G**	Longitude : 1.63598
🏊 ⛴ ⛸ 🔥 ☛ 〽 🦺 launderette ⚒ 🚿	**P** **S**	Latitude : 50.15277
Facilities : ♿ ☛ 〽 🦺 launderette ⚒ 🚿		

SERAUCOURT-LE-GRAND

02790 – Michelin map **306** B4 – pop. 787 – alt. 102

▶ Paris 148 – Chauny 26 – Ham 16 – Péronne 28

⩗ Le Vivier aux Carpes

𝒞 03 23 60 50 10, www.camping-picardie.com

Address : 10 rue Charles Voyeux (north along the D 321, near the post office, 200m from the Somme)

Opening times : from end March to end Oct.

2 ha (60 pitches) flat, grassy

Tariff : 21.50€ ✶✶ 🚗 🔲 💧 (10A) – Extra per person 4.50€

Rental rates : (from end March to end Oct.) – 1 🛏 – 2 🏠. Per night from 77 to 89€ – Per week from 462 to 534€

🚉 local sani-station 4€

In a pleasant location near several lakes.

Surroundings : 🦢 ⌁ ♀♀		
Leisure activities : 🎦 🚣	**G**	Longitude : 3.21435
Facilities : ♿ ☛ 🗄 〽 🦺 launderette	**P** **S**	Latitude : 49.78272
Nearby : ⚒		

VILLERS-SUR-AUTHIE

80120 – Michelin map **301** D6 – pop. 411 – alt. 5

▶ Paris 215 – Abbeville 31 – Amiens 80 – Berck-sur-Mer 16

⩗⩗⩗ Sites et paysages Le Val d'Authie ⚑⚑

Sites et paysages Le Val d'Authie

𝒞 03 22 29 92 47, www.valdauthie.fr – limited spaces for one-night stay

Address : 20 route de Vercourt (on left heading south from village)

Opening times : from beginning April to end Sept.

7 ha/4 for camping (170 pitches) relatively flat, flat, grassy

Tariff : 34€ ✶✶ 🚗 🔲 💧 (10A) – Extra per person 6.50€

Rental rates : (from beginning April to end Sept.) – 24 🛏. Per night from 55 to 120€ – Per week from 365 to 840€

🚉 AireService sani-station 26€ – 6 🔲 26€ – 🛥 💧24,70€

Attractive shrubs and bushes decorate the site.

Surroundings : 🦢 ⌁ ♀♀		
Leisure activities : 🍷 ✕ 🎦 ☺ 🏃 ♨ 🛶 hammam, jacuzzi ⚓ 🚴 ✂ 🔲 (open air in season), fitness trail, multi-sports ground, entertainment room	**G** **P** **S**	Longitude : 1.69486 Latitude : 50.31356
Facilities : ♿ ☛ 🗄 〽 🦺 ☛ ⚒ 🚿 🎅 launderette		

Key to rentals symbols:

12 🛏	*Number of mobile homes*
20 🏠	*Number of chalets*
6 🛏	*Number of rooms to rent*
Per night 30–50€	*Minimum/maximum rate per night*
Per week 300–1,000€	*Minimum/maximum rate per week*

Spila Riccardo / Sime / Photononstop

Names such as Cognac, Angoulême or La Rochelle all echo through France's history, but there's just as much to appreciate in the Poitou-Charentes region today. Visit a thalassotherapy resort and allow the seawater to revive your spirits and tone aching muscles, or soak up the sun on the region's sandy beaches, where the scent of pine trees mingles with the fresh sea breezes. The best way to discover the region's attractive coastal islands is by bike; explore the country lanes lined with tiny blue and white cottages and colourful hollyhocks. Back on the mainland, take a trip on the canals of the marshy – and mercifully mosquito-free – Marais Poitevin, or 'Green Venice', with its poplar trees and green duckweed. You will have earned a drop of Cognac or a glass of the local apéritif, a fruity, ice-cold Pineau des Charentes. For a multimedia experience and a trip into the future of the moving image, head to Futuroscope, a hugely popular award-winning theme park located in Poitiers.

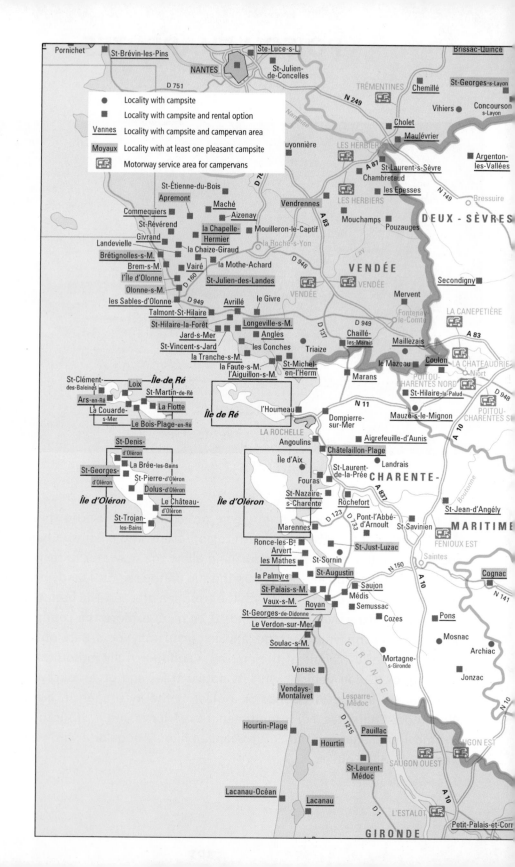

Pornichet   St-Brévin-les-Pins   Ste-Luce-s-L.   Brissac-Quince

NANTES   St-Julien-de-Concelles

D 751   TRÉMENTINES   Chemillé   St-Georges-s-Layon

Narbinaise   N 249   Vihiers   Concourson s-Layon

uyonnière   Cholet

LES HERBIER   Maulévrier

- Locality with campsite
- Locality with campsite and rental option

Vannes   Locality with campsite and campervan area

Moyaux   Locality with at least one pleasant campsite

Motorway service area for campervans

St-Étienne-du-Bois

Apremont

Commequiers   Maché

St-Révérend   Aizenay

Givrand   la Chapelle-Hermier   Mouilleron-le-Captif

Landevieille

Brétignolles-s-M.   la Chaize-Giraud

Brem-s-M.   Vairé   la Mothe-Achard

l'Île d'Olonne

Olonne-s-M.   St-Julien-des-Landes

les Sables-d'Olonne   D 949   Avrillé   le Givre

Talmont-St-Hilaire

St-Hilaire-la-Forêt   Longeville-s-M.

Jard-s-Mer   Angles

St-Vincent-s-Jard   les Conches   Triaize

la Tranche-s-M.   St-Michel-en-l'Herm

la Faute-s-M.

l'Aiguillon-s-M.

St-Clément-des-Baleines   Loix   Île de Ré

St-Martin-de-Ré

Ars-en-Ré   La Flotte

La Couarde-s-Mer   Île de Ré   l'Houmeau

Le Bois-Plage-en-Ré

St-Denis-d'Oléron   Angoulins

La Brée-les-Bains   Île d'Aix

St-Georges-d'Oléron   St-Pierre-d'Oléron   Fouras

Dolus-d'Oléron

Île d'Oléron   Le Château-d'Oléron   Île d'Oléron   St-Nazaire-s-Charente

St-Trojan-les-Bains   Rochefort

Marennes

Ronce-les-Bs   St-Just-Luzac

Arvert

les Mathes   St-Sornin

la Palmyre   St-Augustin

St-Palais-s-M.   Saujon

Vaux-s-M.   Royan   Médis

St-Georges-de-Didonne   Semussac

Le Verdon-sur-Mer   Cozes

Soulac-s-M.

Vensac

Vendays-Montalivet

Hourtin-Plage   Pauillac

Hourtin

St-Laurent-Médoc

Lacanau-Océan   Lacanau

VENDÉE   DEUX - SÈVRES

Vendrennes   Argenton-les-Vallées

Mouchamps   Pouzauges   Bressuire

la Roche-s-Yon   Secondigny

Mervent   LA CANEPETIÈRE

Fontenay-le-Comte   Maillezais

Chaillé-les-Marais   le Mazeau   Coulon   LA CHÂTEAUDRIE

Marans   Niort   POITOU-CHARENTES NORD

St-Hilaire-la-Palud   Mauzé-s-le-Mignon

Dompierre-sur-Mer   N 11   POITOU-CHARENTES S

LA ROCHELLE   Aigrefeuille-d'Aunis

Châtelaillon-Plage

St-Laurent-de-la-Prée   Landrais

CHARENTE-   St-Jean-d'Angély

MARITIME

FENIOUX EST   Saintes   Cognac

Pont-l'Abbé-d'Arnoult   St-Savinien

Pons   Mosnac

Archiac

Jonzac

Mortagne-s-Gironde

GIRONDE

L'ESTALÔT   Petit-Palais-et-Corr

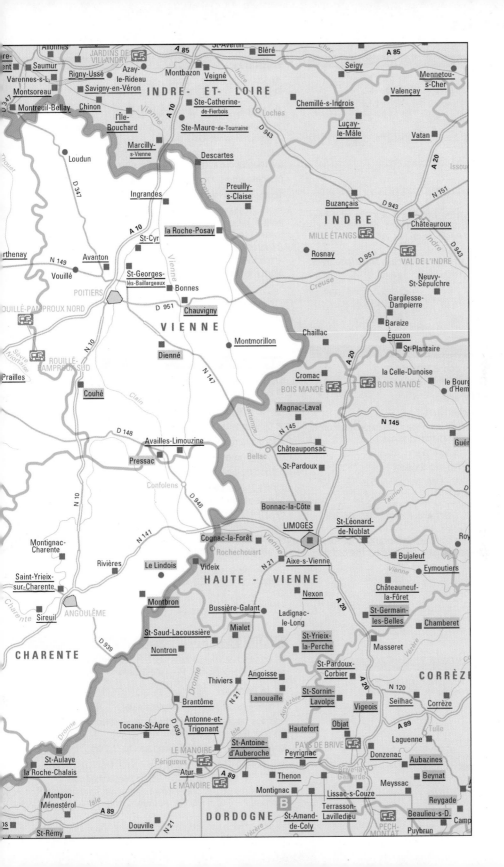

AIGREFEUILLE-D'AUNIS

17290 – Michelin map **324** E3 – pop. 3 682 – alt. 20
▶ Paris 457 – Niort 50 – Rochefort 22 – La Rochelle 25

⚶ La Taillée

✆ 05 46 35 50 88, www.lataillee.com

Address : 3 rue du Bois Gaillard (east of the town, near the swimming pool)

Opening times : from beginning April to end Oct.

2 ha (80 pitches) flat, grassy

Tariff : (2015 price) 18.90€ ✶ ✶ ⟶ 🔲 🔌 (6A) – Extra per person 4€ – Reservation fee 10€

Rental rates : (2015 price) (from beginning April to end Oct.) 🅿 – 28 🛖 – 8 canvas bungalows. Per night from 50 to 75€ – Per week from 315 to 695€ – Reservation fee 10€

🚐 local sani-station

A pleasant wooded setting among ancient ash and plane trees.

Surroundings : ⛲ ♤♤ Leisure activities : 🏛 🏊 m Facilities : ⅃ ⟶ ▥ ⅄ ⚲ launderette Nearby : 🏊	**G P S** Longitude : -0.92682 Latitude : 46.11514

ANGOULINS

17690 – Michelin map **324** D3 – pop. 3 720 – alt. 15
▶ Paris 481 – Poitiers 148 – La Rochelle 12 – Niort 73

⚶⚶ Les Chirats – La Platère

✆ 05 46 56 94 16, www.campingleschirats.fr

Address : rue du Chay (1.7km west along the r. des Salines and follow the signs for the customs post, 100m from the beach)

Opening times : from beginning April to end Sept.

4 ha (232 pitches) flat, relatively flat, stony, grassy

Tariff : 30.70€ ✶ ✶ ⟶ 🔲 🔌 (12A) – Extra per person 5.80€ – Reservation fee 20€

Rental rates : (from beginning April to end Sept.) – 35 🛖. Per night from 53 to 93€ – Per week from 363 to 733€ – Reservation fee 20€

A site in two sections, with a covered swimming pool for exclusive use of the spa in season; chalets a little on the old side.

Surroundings : ⌑ ♤♤ Leisure activities : 🍸 🏛 ▣ 🛁 ⛟ jacuzzi  m 🏊 (small swimming pool) 🏊 ⛷ spa centre Facilities : ⅃ ⟶ ⚲ ⚲ ⅄ 🍴 ▣ ⅃ Nearby : ♨ 🐎	**G P S** Longitude : -1.13076 Latitude : 46.104

ARCHIAC

17520 – Michelin map **324** I6 – pop. 812 – alt. 111
▶ Paris 514 – Angoulême 49 – Barbezieux 15 – Cognac 22

⚶ Municipal

✆ 05 46 49 10 46, archiacmairie@free.fr

Address : 7 rue des Voituriers

1 ha (44 pitches) terraced, flat, grassy

Close to the municipal sports complex.

Surroundings : ⛲ ⌑ ♤♤ Leisure activities : 🏛 Facilities : ▣ Nearby : 🎾 🏊 ⛷	**G P S** Longitude : -0.30467 Latitude : 45.52322

ARGENTON-LES-VALLEES

79150 – Michelin map **322** D3 – pop. 1 588
▶ Paris 367 – Poitiers 100 – Niort 89 – Nantes 102

⚶ Municipal Le Lac d'Hautibus

✆ 05 49 65 95 08, http://www.argentonlesvallees.fr/module-Contenus-viewpub-tid-2-pid

Address : rue de la Sablière (to the west of the town – access near the roundabout at the junction of the D 748 and D 759)

Opening times : from beginning April to end Sept.

1.5 ha (64 pitches) terraced, relatively flat, grassy

Tariff : (2015 price) 13.50€ ✶ ✶ ⟶ 🔲 🔌 (6A) – Extra per person 3.50€

Rental rates : (2015 price) permanent – 6 🛖. Per night from 41 to 66€ – Per week from 259 to 425€

🚐 AireService sani-station 2.60€ – 5 🔲 9€

Attractive pitches, marked out and with slight shade, 150 m from the lake to which there is direct access; a picturesque site.

Surroundings : ⟵ ⌑ ♧ Leisure activities : 🏛 Facilities : ⅃ ⟶ ⚲ launderette Nearby : 🎾 🏊 ⤳ boats to hire	**G P S** Longitude : -0.45164 Latitude : 46.98764

ARVERT

17530 – Michelin map **324** D5 – pop. 3 100 – alt. 20
▶ Paris 513 – Marennes 16 – Rochefort 37 – La Rochelle 74

⚶ Le Presqu'île

✆ 05 46 36 81 76, www.campinglepresquile.com

Address : 7 rue des Aigrettes (north of the town, 150m from the D 14)

Opening times : from beginning April to end Sept.

0.8 ha (60 pitches) flat, grassy

Tariff : 21.50€ ✶ ✶ ⟶ 🔲 🔌 (16A) – Extra per person 5€

Rental rates : permanent – 3 🛖 – 1 🛖. Per night from 40 to 60€ – Per week from 220 to 670€

🚐 local sani-station 13€

A pleasant site with good shade, but also many owner-occupied mobile homes.

Surroundings : ♤♤ Leisure activities : 🏛 🏊 Facilities : ⅃ ⟶ ▣ Nearby : 🎾	**G P S** Longitude : -1.12725 Latitude : 45.74526

AVAILLES-LIMOUZINE

86460 – Michelin map **322** J8 – pop. 1 314 – alt. 142
▶ Paris 410 – Confolens 14 – L'Isle-Jourdain 15 – Niort 100

⚶ le Parc

✆ 05 49 48 51 22, www.campingleparc.net

Address : at Les Places (take the eastern exit along the D 34, to the left after the bridge; beside the Vienne river)

Opening times : from beginning April to end Oct.

2.7 ha (102 pitches) flat, grassy

Tariff : 14€ ✶ ✶ ⟶ 🔲 🔌 (10A) – Extra per person 3.50€

Rental rates : (2015 price) (from beginning April to end Oct.) ⅃ (2 chalets) – 6 🛖 – 3 🛖. Per night from 44 to 59€ – Per week from 285 to 385€

🚐 AireService sani-station 2€ – 10 🔲 4€ – ⛟ 🔌 8€

A pleasant setting beside the Vienne river, with rental accommodation ranging from old to very old.

Surroundings : 🐾 ♈♈
Leisure activities : ♈ ✕ 🏠 🛥 🚲 pedalos
Facilities : ⚹ ⛌ cc 📶 ⛏ 🚰 🎏
Nearby : 🍴 🚣 🏊 pedalos

GPS Longitude : 0.65829
Latitude : 46.12401

AVANTON

86170 – Michelin map **322** H5 – pop. 1 819 – alt. 110
▶ Paris 337 – Poitiers 12 – Niort 84 – Châtellerault 37

⛰ Du Futur

☎ 05 49 54 09 67, www.camping-du-futur.com

Address : 9 rue des Bois (1.3km southwest along the D 757, follow the signs for Poitiers and take turning to the right after the level crossing)

Opening times : from beginning April to end Oct.

4 ha/1.5 (68 pitches) flat, grassy

Tariff : (2015 price) 23.70€ ♈♈ 🚗 🔲 🔌 (10A) –
Extra per person 3.80€ – Reservation fee 10€

Rental rates : (2015 price) (from beginning April to end Oct.) 🚫 –
1 'gypsy' caravan – 14 🛏. Per night from 60 to 100€ – Per week from 385 to 595€ – Reservation fee 15€

🚐 AireService sani-station 4.50€

Plenty of green spaces in which to relax, or play sports and games.

Surroundings : 🐾 🛏 ♈
Leisure activities : ♈ 🛥 🚣 🏊
Facilities : ⚹ ⛌ 🚰 launderette

GPS Longitude : 0.30192
Latitude : 46.65096

BONNES

86300 – Michelin map **322** J5 – pop. 1 688 – alt. 70
▶ Paris 331 – Châtellerault 25 – Chauvigny 7 – Poitiers 25

⛺ Municipal

☎ 05 49 56 44 34, www.campingbonnes86.fr

1.2 ha (56 pitches) open site, flat, grassy
Rentals : ⚹ (1 mobile home) – 6 gîtes.

Shady pitches beside the Vienne river and next to the municipal sports facilities.

Surroundings : 🐾 🛏 ♈♈
Leisure activities : 🏠 🛥 🚣
Facilities : ⚹ 🚰 launderette
Nearby : 🍴 🏊 🚣

GPS Longitude : 0.59856
Latitude : 46.60182

CHÂTELAILLON-PLAGE

17340 – Michelin map **324** D3 – pop. 6 081 – alt. 3
▶ Paris 482 – Niort 74 – Rochefort 22 – La Rochelle 19

⛰ Port Punay 👥

☎ 05 17 81 00 00, www.camping-port-punay.com

Address : Les Boucholeurs district, allée Bernard Moreau

Opening times : from beginning May to end Sept.

3 ha (157 pitches) flat, grassy

Tariff : (2015 price) 34,50€ ♈♈ 🚗 🔲 🔌 (10A) – Extra per person 7€ –
Reservation fee 18€

Rental rates : (2015 price) (from beginning May to end Sept.)
⚹ (1 mobile home) 🚫 – 36 🛏 – 4 tent lodges. Per night from 45 to 107€ – Per week from 295 to 980€ – Reservation fee 18€

Shady and sunny pitches, 200m from the beach and the port.

Surroundings : 🐾 🛏 ♈♈
Leisure activities : ♈ ✕ 🏠 🎣 🏃 🛥 🚲 🛴
Facilities : ⚹ ⛌ 🚰 launderette 🚻 🚿

GPS Longitude : -1.0846
Latitude : 46.05352

⛰ Club Airotel Village Corsaire des 2 Plages

☎ 05 46 56 27 53, www.2plages.com

Address : avenue d'Angoulins (follow the signs for La Rochelle; 300m from the beach)

Opening times : from beginning April to end Sept.

4.5 ha (265 pitches) flat, grassy

Tariff : 30€ ♈♈ 🚗 🔲 🔌 (10A) – Extra per person 7€ – Reservation fee 18€

Rental rates : permanent ⚹ (1 mobile home) – 115 🛏. Per night from 45 to 146€ – Per week from 300 to 1,024€

Choose the pitches away from the road and the railway line.

Surroundings : 🛏 ♈♈
Leisure activities : ♈ ✕ 🏠 🛥 🏊 multi-sports ground
Facilities : ⚹ ⛌ 🚰 🎏 launderette 🚻 🚿
Nearby : 🚲

GPS Longitude : -1.09344
Latitude : 46.08441

⛰ L'Océan

☎ 05 46 56 87 97, www.campingocean17.com

Address : avenue d'Angoulins (1.3km north along the D 202, follow the signs for La Rochelle and take a right turn)

3 ha (97 pitches) flat, grassy

🚐 local sani-station

A pretty, naturally filtered, landscaped lake.

Surroundings : 🐾 ♈♈
Leisure activities : 🏠 🛥 🏊 (lake), entertainment room
Facilities : ⚹ ⛌ 🚰 launderette

GPS Longitude : -1.09412
Latitude : 46.08818

CHAUVIGNY

86300 – Michelin map **322** J5 – pop. 6 848 – alt. 65
▶ Paris 333 – Bellac 64 – Le Blanc 36 – Châtellerault 30

⛺ Municipal de la Fontaine

☎ 05 49 46 31 94, www.chauvigny.fr

Address : rue de la Fontaine (take the northern exit along the D2, follow the signs for La Puye and take turning to the right; beside a stream)

Opening times : from beginning April to end Sept.

2.8 ha (104 pitches) flat, grassy, fine gravel

Tariff : (2015 price) ♈2.70€ 🚗 2€ 🔲 2€ – 🔌 (6A) 3.20€

Rental rates : (2015 price) permanent ⚹ – 1 🛏 – 4 🏠 – 5 studios. Per night from 18 to 23€ – Per week from 126 to 570€

🚐 local sani-station – 10 🔲 7€

The site adjoins some public gardens with a water feature.

Surroundings : ≤ Medieval city, several castles ♈♈
Leisure activities : 🏠 🛥
Facilities : ⚹ ⛌ 📶 🚰 🎏 launderette

GPS Longitude : 0.65349
Latitude : 46.57095

COGNAC

16100 – Michelin map **324** I5 – pop. 18 729 – alt. 25
▶ Paris 478 – Angoulême 45 – Bordeaux 120 – Libourne 116

⚲ Municipal

🖉 05 45 32 13 32, www.campingdecognac.com

Address : boulevard de Châtenay (2.3km north along the D 24, follow the signs for Boutiers; between the Charente and the Solençon rivers)

Opening times : from beginning May to mid Sept.

2 ha (160 pitches) flat, grassy

Tariff : (2015 price) ✶ 6 € ⇌ 2.50 € 🔲 6 € – ⚡ (6A) 3.40 €
Rental rates : (2015 price) (from beginning May to mid Sept.) ⚿ (1 mobile home) – 8 🛏 – 2 canvas bungalows. Per night from 30 to 50 € – Per week from 175 to 499 €
🚰 local sani-station

In an attractive parkland setting, well shaded in parts.

Surroundings : ▱ ΩΩ Leisure activities : ⚐ ⚑ ⚓ Facilities : ⚿ ⊶ ▥ (July-Aug.) ♨ ⚑ ▣ Nearby : ⚑ ✕	**G P S** Longitude : -0.30726 Latitude : 45.70926

COUHÉ

86700 – Michelin map **322** H7 – pop. 1 885 – alt. 140
▶ Paris 370 – Confolens 58 – Montmorillon 61 – Niort 65

⚲⚲⚲ Sites et Paysages Les Peupliers 👥

🖉 05 49 59 21 16, www.lespeupliers.fr

Address : avenue de Paris (situated 1km north, follow the signs for Poitiers; at Valence)

Opening times : from beginning May to end Sept.

16 ha/6 for camping (187 pitches) terraced, wood

Tariff : ✶ 8.50 € ⇌ 🔲 14 € – ⚡ (10A) 5 €
Rental rates : permanent ⚿ – 25 🛏 – 18 🏠. Per night from 105 to 175 € – Per week from 250 to 1,275 €
🚰 local sani-station – 6 🔲 14 € – 🚐 14 €

In a wooded setting with a picturesque river running through the site.

Surroundings : ⛰ ▱ ΩΩ Leisure activities : ⚑ ✕ ⛺ ⚐ ⚑ jacuzzi ⚐ ⚑ ⚓ ⚑ ⚓ ⚓ Facilities : ⚿ ⊶ ▥ ♨ – 4 private sanitary facilities (⚑ ⚑ ⚑ wc) ♨ ⚑ launderette ⚑ ⚑	**G P S** Longitude : 0.18222 Latitude : 46.31222

COULON

79510 – Michelin map **322** C7 – pop. 2 211 – alt. 6
▶ Paris 418 – Fontenay-le-Comte 25 – Niort 11 – La Rochelle 63

⚲ Flower La Venise Verte 👥

🖉 05 49 35 90 36, www.camping-laveniseverte.fr

Address : 178 route des Bords de Sèvre (2.2km southwest along the D 123, follow the signs for Vanneau; beside a canal and near the Sèvre Niortaise river)

Opening times : from beginning April to end Oct.

2.2 ha (120 pitches) flat, grassy

Tariff : 29.50 € ✶✶ ⇌ 🔲 ⚡ (10A) – Extra per person 7 €

Rental rates : (from beginning April to end Oct.) ⚿ – 27 🏠
Per night from 50 to 104 € – Per week from 250 to 875 € –
Reservation fee 10 € 🚰 AireService sani-station

A site that is making great ecological efforts.

Surroundings : ⛰ ΩΩ Leisure activities : ⚑ ✕ ⛺ ⚐ ⚑ ⚑ ⚓ ⚑ Facilities : ⚿ ⊶ ▥ ♨ ⚑ ⚑ ⚑ launderette ⚑ Nearby : ⚓	**G P S** Longitude : -0.60889 Latitude : 46.31444

COZES

17120 – Michelin map **324** E6 – pop. 1 973 – alt. 43
▶ Paris 494 – Marennes 41 – Mirambeau 35 – Pons 26

⚲ Municipal Le Sorlut

🖉 05 46 90 75 99, www.villedecozes.fr

Address : rue des Chênes (to the north, near the old station, behind the Champion supermarket)

1.4 ha (120 pitches) flat, grassy, near canal and river

Rentals : ⚿ (1 chalet) – 8 🏠.

Pleasantly shady pitches and comfortable chalets.

Surroundings : ⛰ ΩΩ Leisure activities : ⚑ Facilities : ⚿ ⊶ ⚑ ▣ Nearby : ⚑ ⚑ ⚑ ⚑	**G P S** Longitude : -0.83728 Latitude : 45.58649

DIENNE

86410 – Michelin map **322** J6 – pop. 508 – alt. 112
▶ Paris 362 – Poitiers 26 – Niort 107 – Limoges 107

⚲⚲⚲ DéfiPlanet à Dienné – (rental of chalets only)

🖉 05 49 45 87 63, www.defiplanet.com – traditional camping spaces also available

Address : at La Boquerie (off the RN 147)

Opening times : from beginning Feb. to beginning Jan.

47 ha (100 pitches) lake, forest

Rental rates : (2015 price) ⚿ ℗ – 22 'gypsy' caravans – 7 🏠 –
8 yurts – 26 cabins in the trees – 2 gîtes – 5 'mushroom'
houses - 5 'fairy' houses. Per night from 73 to 209 € – Per week
from 365 to 1,045 €
🚰 10 🔲

A vast wooded site, with lots of entertainment/activities.

Surroundings : ⛰ ΩΩ Leisure activities : ⚑ ✕ ⛺ ⚑ ⚑ ⚑ hammam, jacuzzi ⚑ ⚑ ⚑ ⚑ ⚑ ⚑ adventure park, horse riding centre, zip wiring, spa centre, entertainment room Facilities : ⚿ ⊶ ℗ ▥ ⚑ launderette ⚑	**G P S** Longitude : 0.56024 Latitude : 46.44614

DOMPIERRE-SUR-MER

17139 – Michelin map **324** H5 – pop. 5 337 – alt. 30
▶ Paris 465 – Poitiers 132 – La Rochelle 9 – La Roche-sur-Yon 84

⚲ Aire Naturelle Le Verger

🖉 05 46 34 91 00, www.
campingleverger17.com

Address : 27 rue Jean-Pierre Pigot (2km
northwest along the D 107)

Opening times : from mid June to
end Aug.

1.5 ha (25 pitches) flat, grassy

Tariff : ✶ 5 € ⇌ 🔲 7 € – ⚡ (8A) 5 €

Aire Naturelle Le Verger

Rental rates : (from mid June to end Aug.) 🚫 – 2 'gypsy' caravans – 1 tent lodge. Per week from 420 to 560€

Pitches in the shade of young apricot, cherry and apple trees.

Surroundings : 🐟 ♀
Facilities : ♿ ⚂ 🚽 🍴

Longitude : -1.05428
Latitude : 46.17787

FOURAS

17450 – Michelin map **324** D4 – pop. 4 092 – alt. 5
▶ Paris 485 – Châtelaillon-Plage 18 – Rochefort 15 – La Rochelle 34

Municipal le Cadoret ▲▲

📞 05 46 82 19 19, www.campings-fouras.com

Address : boulevard de Chaterny (north coast; beside the Anse de Fouras – bay, 100m from the beach)

Opening times : permanent

7,5 ha (498 pitches) flat, grassy, sandy

Tariff : (2015 price) 29.40€ ♟♟ �car 🔲 ⚡ (10A) –
Extra per person 6.10€ – Reservation fee 25€

Rental rates : (2015 price) (from beginning April to end Oct.)
♿ (2 mobile homes) – 23 🏚. Per week from 280 to 660€
– Reservation fee 25€

Beside the sea, near the sea fishing piers and the beautiful, wide beach 50m away.

Surroundings : 🏕 ♀♀
Leisure activities : 🍴✕ 🏠 🎱 🤸 🛶 🍧 🏊 ⛳
multi-sports ground
Facilities : ♿ ⚂ 🔲 🚿 🍴 launderette 🚿
Nearby : 🍴 🎯 🚣

Longitude : -1.08714
Latitude : 45.99296

L'HOUMEAU

17137 – Michelin map **324** C2 – pop. 2 073 – alt. 19
▶ Paris 478 – Poitiers 145 – La Rochelle 6 – Niort 83

Au Petit Port de l'Houmeau

📞 05 46 50 90 82, www.aupetitport.com

Address : rue des Sartières (take the northeastern exit along the D 106, follow the signs for Nieul-sur-Mer, via the ring road (périphérique) towards Île de Ré and take the exit for Lagord-l'Houmeau)

2 ha (132 pitches) flat, relatively flat, grassy
Rentals : ♿ (1 chalet) – 55 🏚 – 15 🏠.

The numerous rental options include some rather old chalets and newer mobile homes equipped to a good standard, clad in wood.

Surroundings : 🏕 ♀♀
Leisure activities : 🍴✕ 🏠 🚣 🚲
Facilities : ♿ ⚂ ⛺ 🍴 launderette 🚿
Nearby : 🍴 🎯

Longitude : -1.1883
Latitude : 46.19566

ÎLE-D'AIX

17123 – Michelin map **324** C3 – pop. 227 – alt. 10
▶ Paris 486 – Poitiers 152 – La Rochelle 31 – Niort 78

Le Fort de la Rade

📞 05 46 84 28 28, www.fortdelarade.ifrance.com

Address : situated at la Pointe Ste-Catherine, 300m from the beach at L'Anse de la Croix

3 ha (73 pitches) flat, grassy

Rentals : 5 tent lodges.

In the grounds of the Fort de la Rade, surrounded by fortified walls; reserved for tents.

Surroundings : 🐟
Leisure activities : ✕ 🏠 🏊 🚣
Facilities : ♿ ⚂ ✕ 🏠 🚿 no electrical hook-up
Nearby : 🚣 🍴 🚲 🤸

Longitude : -1.17657
Latitude : 46.00935

Routes nationales are main roads and their identifying numbers begin with N or RN. Routes départementales are generally quieter roads and begin with D or DN.

ÎLE DE RÉ

17 – Michelin map **324**

Ars-en-Ré 17590 – Michelin map **324** A2 – pop. 1 321 – alt. 4
▶ Paris 506 – Fontenay-le-Comte 85 – Luçon 75 – La Rochelle 34

Club Airotel le Cormoran ▲▲

📞 05 46 29 46 04, www.cormoran.com

Address : route de Radia (located 1km west)

Opening times : from beginning April to end Sept.

3 ha (142 pitches) flat, grassy

Tariff : (2015 price) 50,50€ ♟♟ 🚗 🔲 ⚡ (10A) –
Extra per person 11.80€ – Reservation fee 25€

Rental rates : (2015 price) (from beginning April to end Sept.) ♿
(1 mobile home) – 97 🏚 – 5 tent lodges. Per night
from 40 to 214€ – Per week from 230 to 1,498€ – Reservation
fee 35€

🏚 local sani-station 4€

An attractive site decorated with flowers, near vineyards, a forest and salt marshes.

Surroundings : 🐟 🏕 ♀
Leisure activities : 🍴✕ 🏠 🎱 🤸 🎣 🏊
🚣 🚲 🏊 🏊 multi-sports ground
Facilities : ♿ ⚂ 🚽 🔲 🚿 🍴 🍴
launderette 🚿

Longitude : -1.53026
Latitude : 46.21136

Le Bois-Plage-en-Ré 17580 – Michelin map **324** B2 – pop. 2 364 –
alt. 5
▶ Paris 494 – Fontenay-le-Comte 74 – Luçon 64 – La Rochelle 23

Sunêlia Interlude ▲▲

📞 05 46 09 18 22, www.interlude.fr

Address : 8 route de Gros Jonc (2.3km southeast)

Opening times : from beginning April to end Sept.

7.5 ha (387 pitches) undulating, flat, grassy, sandy

Tariff : 49€ ♟♟ 🚗 🔲 ⚡ (10A) – Extra per person 10€ – Reservation
fee 30€

Rental rates : (from beginning April to end Sept.) ♿ (1 mobile
home) – 194 🏚 – 5 tent lodges. Per night from 60 to 283€ –
Per week from 420 to 1,981€ – Reservation fee 30€

🏚 local sani-station 11€ – 7 🔲 11€ – 🚐 ⚡ 8€

150m from the beach.

Surroundings : 🐟 🏕 ♀
Leisure activities : 🍴✕ 🏠 🎱 🤸 🎣 🍧
hammam, jacuzzi 🚣 🚲 🏊 🏊 multi-
sports ground, spa centre
Facilities : ♿ ⚂ 🔲 🚿 ⛺ 🍴 launderette
🚿 🚿
Nearby : 🍴 🚣

Longitude : -1.3793
Latitude : 46.17472

Les Varennes

05 46 09 15 43, www.les-varennes.com

Address : at Raise Maritaise (1.7km southeast, 300m from the beach)

Opening times : from mid April to end Sept.

2.5 ha (145 pitches) flat, grassy

Tariff : (2015 price) 38.70€ ✶✶ 🚗 🔲 🔌 (10A) – Extra per person 8€ – Reservation fee 20€

Rental rates : (2015 price) (from beginning April to end Sept.) – 85 🛖. Per night from 61 to 118€ – Per week from 329 to 1,239€ – Reservation fee 20€

🚐 local sani-station 10€

Mobile homes and pitches in the shade of a lovely pine wood.

Surroundings : 🏞 🌳🌳		GPS
Leisure activities : 🏓 🚣 🚴🔲(open air in season)		Longitude : -1.38306
Facilities : ♿ ☎ 🏧 🚿 🍴 launderette 🚿		Latitude : 46.17829
Nearby : 🍴✂		

La Couarde-sur-Mer 17670 – Michelin map **324** B2 – pop. 1 248 – alt. 1
▶ Paris 497 – Fontenay-le-Comte 76 – Luçon 66 – La Rochelle 26

L'Océan ♣♣

05 46 29 87 70, www.campingocean.com

Address : 50 rue d'Ars (at La Passe)

Opening times : from beginning April to end Sept.

9 ha (338 pitches) flat, grassy

Tariff : 46€ ✶✶ 🚗 🔲 🔌 (10A) – Extra per person 13€ – Reservation fee 5€

Rental rates : (from beginning April to end Sept.) ♿ (1 mobile home) 🦀 – 172 🛖 – 10 tent lodges. Per night from 50 to 212€ – Per week from 350 to 1,484€ – Reservation fee 32€

🚐 AireService sani-station

Good-quality rental accommodation and a nice spa centre. Two natural salt-water pools at one end of the site, ideal for fishing.

Surroundings : 🏞 🛖 🌳🌳		GPS
Leisure activities : 🏓🍴🛶 🏊 🎣 hammam, jacuzzi 🚣🚴🎯🎱🦀🏊multi-sports ground, spa centre, entertainment room		Longitude : -1.46737
Facilities : ♿ ☎ 🔲🏧 🚿 🍴 launderette 🚿🚿		Latitude : 46.20447

La Tour des Prises

05 46 29 84 82, www.lesprises.com

Address : chemin de la Griffonerie (1.8km northwest along the D 735, turn off to the right)

Opening times : from beginning April to end Sept.

2.5 ha (140 pitches) flat, grassy

Tariff : (2015 price) 21.60€ ✶✶ 🚗 🔲 🔌 (16A) – Extra per person 5€

Rental rates : (from beginning April to end Sept.) – 60 🛖 – 3 canvas bungalows – 3 tent lodges. Per night from 40 to 255€ – Per week from 315 to 835€ – Reservation fee 20€

🚐 AireService sani-station 11€ – 30 🔲 16€ – 🚽 🔌12€

Enclosed by a pretty wall of local stone and surrounded by vines.

Surroundings : 🏞 🛖 🌳🌳		GPS
Leisure activities : 🛶 🚣🚴🔲(open air in season)		Longitude : -1.4447
Facilities : ♿ ☎ 🏧 🚿 🍴 launderette 🚿🚿		Latitude : 46.20473

La Flotte 17630 – Michelin map **324** C2 – pop. 2 918 – alt. 4
▶ Paris 489 – Fontenay-le-Comte 68 – Luçon 58 – La Rochelle 17

Camp'Atlantique Les Peupliers ♣♣

02 51 20 41 94, www.les-peupliers.com – limited spaces for one-night stay

Address : off the route de Rivedoux (RD 735) (1.3km east of La Flotte)

Opening times : from beginning April to beginning Nov.

4.5 ha (220 pitches) flat, grassy

Tariff : (2015 price) 36€ ✶✶ 🚗 🔲 🔌 (10A) – Extra per person 9€ – Reservation fee 25€

Rental rates : (2015 price) (from beginning April to beginning Nov.) ♿ (2 mobile homes) – 200 🛖. Per night from 47 to 222€ – Per week from 334 to 1,652€ – Reservation fee 25€

🚐 local sani-station

Located at the entrance to the village of La Flotte, with lots of mobile homes, some of which are for owner-occupiers, and a few tent or caravan pitches.

Surroundings : 🏞 🛖 🌳		GPS
Leisure activities : 🏓🍴🛶 🏊 🏃 🎣🏊 hammam, jacuzzi 🚣🚴🏊multi-sports ground, entertainment room		Longitude : -1.308
Facilities : ♿ ☎ 🚿 🍴 launderette 🚿		Latitude : 46.1846

La Grainetière ♣♣

05 46 09 68 86, www.la-grainetiere.com

Address : chemin des Essards (to the west of the town, follow the signs for Saint-Martin-de-Ré, recommended route via the D 735)

Opening times : from beginning April to beginning Oct.

2.3 ha (140 pitches) flat, sandy

Tariff : 45€ ✶✶ 🚗 🔲 🔌 (10A) – Extra per person 9€ – Reservation fee 15€

Rental rates : (from beginning April to beginning Oct.) – 3 'gypsy' caravans – 77 🛖. Per night from 70 to 115€ – Per week from 270 to 1,100€ – Reservation fee 15€

Choose the pitches furthest away from the road.

Surroundings : 🌳🌳		GPS
Leisure activities : 🍴 🛶 🏃 jacuzzi 🚣🚴🔲(open air in season), multi-sports ground		Longitude : -1.34412
Facilities : ♿ ☎ 🚿 🍴 launderette 🚿🚿		Latitude : 46.18747

Loix 17111 – Michelin map **324** B2 – pop. 731 – alt. 4
▶ Paris 505 – Fontenay-le-Comte 84 – Luçon 74 – La Rochelle 33

Flower Les Ilates ♣♣

05 46 29 05 43, www.camping-loix.com

Address : at Le Petit Boucheau, route du Grouin (take the eastern exit, 500m from the ocean)

Opening times : from beginning April to end Sept.

4,5 ha (228 pitches) flat, grassy

Tariff : (2015 price) 45€ ✶✶ 🚗 🔲 🔌 (10A) – Extra per person 9€ – Reservation fee 15€

Rental rates : (2015 price) (from beginning April to end Sept.) ♿ (2 chalets) – 112 🛖 – 28 🏠 – 4 canvas bungalows – 24 tent lodges. Per night from 85 to 169€ – Per week from 595 to 1,183€ – Reservation fee 20€

🚐 Eurorelais sani-station 4€ – 🚽 🔌18€

Rental options of varying degrees of comfort and design, sometimes unusual and suitable for large families.

Surroundings : 🐾 🖵 ♀
Leisure activities : ♈ ✕ 🏃 jacuzzi 🛥 🚲 ✂ 🛝
Facilities : 🚿 🔑 🍴 🛝 🚽 ♈ launderette 🚲

GPS Longitude : -1.42608
Latitude : 46.22756

St-Martin-de-Ré 17410 – Michelin map **324** B2 – pop. 2 585 – alt. 14
▶ Paris 493 – Fontenay-le-Comte 72 – Luçon 62 – La Rochelle 22

⛺ Municipal

📞 05 46 09 21 96, www.saint-martin-de-re.fr

Address : rue du Rempart (situated in the town)

3 ha (200 pitches) terraced, flat, grassy

Rentals : 21 🚐.

🚰 local sani-station

Set amidst the town's fortifications and close to the centre.

Surroundings : ♀♀
Leisure activities : ✕ 🎦 🛥
Facilities : 🚿 🔑 🛝 ♈ launderette

GPS Longitude : -1.36758
Latitude : 46.19921

ÎLE D'OLÉRON

17 – Michelin map **324**

La Brée-les-Bains 17840 – Michelin map **324** B3 – pop. 758 – alt. 5
▶ Paris 531 – Marennes 32 – Rochefort 53 – La Rochelle 90

⛰ Antioche d'Oléron

📞 05 46 47 92 00, www.camping-antiochedoleron.com

Address : route de Proires (located 1km northwest along the D 273 follow the signs for St Denis and take a right turn, 150m from the beach)

2.5 ha (129 pitches) flat, grassy

Rentals : 45 🚐.

Pitches in both the shade and full sun, and several luxurious mobile homes.

Surroundings : 🖵 ♀
Leisure activities : ✕ 🎦 jacuzzi 🛥 🛝 🛶
Facilities : 🚿 🔑 🛝 🛝 ♈ launderette 🚲
Nearby : 🍴

GPS Longitude : -1.35773
Latitude : 46.02033

Le Château-d'Oléron 17480 – Michelin map **324** C4 – pop. 3 930 – alt. 9
▶ Paris 507 – Marennes 12 – Rochefort 33 – La Rochelle 70

⛰ La Brande 👥

📞 05 46 47 62 37, www.camping-labrande.com

Address : route des Huîtres (2.5km to the northwest, 250m from the sea)

Opening times : from end March to beginning Nov.

4 ha (199 pitches) flat, grassy

Tariff : 44€ ✹✹ �car 🔌 🔥 (10A) – Extra per person 8.50€ – Reservation fee 20€

Rental rates : (from end March to beginning Nov.) 🚿 (4 chalets) – 40 🚐 – 40 🏠 – 1 tent lodge. Per night from 57 to 250€ – Per week from 279 to 1,250€ – Reservation fee 20€

🚰 local sani-station 7.50€ – 20 🔌 16€

Both shaded and sunny pitches are available.

Surroundings : ♀♀
Leisure activities : ♈ ✕ 🎦 🛝 🏃 🛥 hammam, jacuzzi 🛥 🚲 ✂ 🛶 🛝 (open air in season) 🛶 multi-sports ground
Facilities : 🚿 🔑 🛝 6 private sanitary facilities (🛝 🚿 wc) 🛝 ♈ launderette 🛝 🚲

GPS Longitude : -1.21607
Latitude : 45.90464

⛰ Fief-Melin

📞 05 46 47 60 85, www.campingfiefmelin.com

Address : rue des Alizés (1.7km west following signs for St-Pierre-d'Oléron then turn right and continue for 600m)

Opening times : from beginning May to end Sept.

2.2 ha (144 pitches) flat, grassy

Tariff : (2015 price) 32.40€ ✹✹ �car 🔌 🔥 (10A) – Extra per person 5.10€

Rental rates : (2015 price) (from beginning April to end Oct.) – 28 🚐. Per week from 255 to 740€

In a woodland setting on undulating land, close to the ocean.

Surroundings : 🐾 🖵 ♀
Leisure activities : 🎦 🛝 🛥 🚲 🛝 (open air in season), multi-sports ground
Facilities : 🔑 🛝 🛝

GPS Longitude : -1.21408
Latitude : 45.89371

Dolus-d'Oléron 17550 – Michelin map **324** C4 – pop. 3 176 – alt. 7
▶ Paris 511 – Marennes 17 – Rochefort 39 – La Rochelle 75

⛰ Ostréa

📞 05 46 47 62 36, www.camping-ostrea.com

Address : route des Huîtres (3.5km east)

Opening times : from end March to end Sept.

2 ha (110 pitches) flat, grassy

Tariff : 30.60€ ✹✹ �car 🔌 🔥 (6A) – Extra per person 8.55€ – Reservation fee 20€

Rental rates : (from end March to end Sept.) – 25 🚐. Per week from 320 to 740€ – Reservation fee 20€

🚰 Flot Bleu sani-station 5€

On the east coast, very close to the sea. Choose the pitches away from the road.

Surroundings : 🐾 ♀♀
Leisure activities : 🎦 🛥 🛝 (open air in season)
Facilities : 🚿 🔑 🛝 ♈ launderette 🛝 🚲

GPS Longitude : -1.22402
Latitude : 45.91299

⛰ Indigo Oléron Les Chênes Verts 👥

📞 05 46 75 32 88, www.camping-indigo.com

Address : 9 Passe de l'Écuissière (Côte Ouest – west side of the island – 3.2km southwest along the D 126)

Opening times : from beginning May to end Sept.

3 ha (120 pitches) undulating, flat, grassy

Tariff : (2015 price) 32.30€ ✹✹ �car 🔌 🔥 (10A) – Extra per person 6.20€ – Reservation fee 13€

Rental rates : (2015 price) (from beginning May to end Sept.) – 45 tent lodges. Per night from 51 to 99€ – Per week from 250 to 742€ – Reservation fee 13€

🚰 local sani-station 7€

Surroundings : 🐾 🍇
Leisure activities : ✕ 🌙 nighttime 🏃 🛥 🚲 archery
Facilities : 🚿 🔑 🛝 ♈ launderette 🚲

GPS Longitude : -1.27575
Latitude : 45.88727

⚠ La Perroche Leitner

☎ 05 46 75 37 33, www.oleron-camping.eu

Address : 18 rue du Renclos-de-la-Perroche (4km southwest, at La Perroche)

Opening times : from beginning April to end Sept.

1,5 ha (100 pitches) flat, grassy

Tariff : 30.20€ ✚✚ ⛟ 🔲 (♨) (6A) – Extra per person 7.50€ – Reservation fee 15€

Rental rates : (from beginning April to end Sept.) – 30 🚐 – 2 canvas bungalows – 3 tent lodges. Per night from 90 to 115€ – Per week from 150 to 740€ – Reservation fee 15€

🚱 Eurorelais sani-station 7€ – 🔋11€

In an attractive location close to the sea, with a choice of shady or sunny pitches.

Surroundings : 🐚 ♨♨
Leisure activities : 🏹🎯
Facilities : ♿ ⚬━ 🚿🍴 🖼
Nearby : 🍸 🍴

Longitude : -1.3031
Latitude : 45.9016

St-Denis-d'Oléron 17650 – Michelin map **324** B3 – pop. 1 336 – alt. 9

▶ Paris 527 – Marennes 33 – Rochefort 55 – La Rochelle 92

⛰ Village Vacances Les Hameaux des Marines

(rental of chalets only)

☎ 05 55 84 34 48, www.terresdefrance.com

Address : rue de Seulières (situated 300m from the beach)

Opening times : permanent

2.5 ha flat

Rental rates : ♿ (1 chalet) – 18 🏠. Per night from 59 to 160€ – Per week from 299 to 1,049€

A pleasant, small chalet village, all featuring lovely large covered terraces.

Surroundings : 🐚 ♨
Leisure activities : 🛶 🏹 🎯 🔲 (open air in season)
Facilities : ⚬🍴 🍴 launderette

Longitude : -1.39169
Latitude : 46.01354

⚠ Les Seulières

☎ 05 46 47 90 51, www.campinglesseulieres.com

Address : 1371 route des Seulières – Les Huttes (3.5km southwest, follow the signs for Chaucre; 400m from the beach)

Opening times : from beginning April to end Oct.

2.4 ha (120 pitches) flat, grassy

Tariff : 20€ ✚✚ ⛟ 🔲 (♨) (10A) – Extra per person 4€ – Reservation fee 15€

Rental rates : (2015 price) (from beginning April to end Oct.) – 10 🚐 – 8 🏠. Per night from 50 to 70€ – Per week from 300 to 700€ – Reservation fee 15€

🚱 local sani-station

Sunny or shaded pitches are available in a peaceful, fami-ly-friendly setting.

Surroundings : 🐚 ♨♨
Leisure activities : 🍸 🛶
Facilities : ♿ ⚬━🚿🍴 launderette
Nearby : 🍴

Longitude : -1.38512
Latitude : 46.0034

St-Georges-d'Oléron 17190 – Michelin map **324** C4 – pop. 3 497 – alt. 10

▶ Paris 527 – Marennes 27 – Rochefort 49 – La Rochelle 85

⛰ Camping-Club Verébleu ♨♨

Camping-Club Verébleu

☎ 05 46 76 57 70, www.verebleu.tm.fr 🏊

Address : at La Jousselinière (1.7km southeast along the D 273 and turn left, following signs for Sauzelle)

Opening times : from beginning June to mid Sept.

7.5 ha (324 pitches) flat, grassy

Tariff : (2015 price) 47€ ✚✚ ⛟ 🔲 (♨) (13A) – Extra per person 11.50€ – Reservation fee 25€

Rental rates : (2015 price) permanent ♿ (1 chalet) 🏊 – 76 🚐 – 59 🏠. Per week from 370 to 1,450€ – Reservation fee 25€

🚱 local sani-station 38€ – 160 🔲 38€

The site boasts a Fort Boyard-themed water park and play area.

Surroundings : 🐚 🗇 ♨♨
Leisure activities : 🎮 🏹 🛶 🚴 🏊 m 🎯 🛝 multi-sports ground
Facilities : ♿ ⚬━🔲🚿 🚽 🍴 launderette 🍴🍴

Longitude : -1.31759
Latitude : 45.97111

⛰ Domaine des 4 Vents

☎ 05 46 76 65 47, www.camping-oleron-4vents.com

Address : at La Jousselinière (2km southeast along the D 273 and turn left, following signs for Sauzelle)

Opening times : from mid April to mid Sept.

7 ha (300 pitches) flat, grassy

Tariff : (2015 price) ✚6.50€ ⛟ 3€ 🔲 13€ – (♨) (10A) 4€ – Reservation fee 30€

Rental rates : (2015 price) (from mid April to mid Sept.) – 90 🚐. Per night from 115 to 195€ – Per week from 250 to 950€ – Reservation fee 30€

🚱 local sani-station 4€ – 10 🔲 8€ – 🔋(♨)12€

Sunny or shaded pitches with a large number of owner-occupier mobile homes.

Surroundings : 🐚 🗇 ♨
Leisure activities : 🍴 🛶 🏹 🎯 🛝 🎮 multi-sports ground
Facilities : ♿ ⚬━ 🚿 🚽 🍴 launderette 🍴

Longitude : -1.31995
Latitude : 45.96973

⛰ La Campière ♨♨

☎ 05 46 76 72 25, www.la-campiere.com

Address : chemin de l'Achenau (5.4km southwest following signs for Chaucre and take road to the left)

Opening times : from mid April to end Sept.

1.7 ha (66 pitches) flat, grassy

Tariff : 39€ ✚✚ ⛟ 🔲 (♨) (10A) – Extra per person 8.80€ – Reservation fee 17€

Rental rates : (2015 price) (from beginning April to end Sept.) – 1 🚐 – 12 🏠 – 2 canvas bungalows – 5 tent lodges. Per week from 230 to 975€ – Reservation fee 19€

🚱 local sani-station

In a pleasant, leafy setting with a small wine bar where you can taste the local produce.

Surroundings : 🐚 ♨♨♨
Leisure activities : 🍸 🛶 🏹 🎯 🚴 (small swimming pool)
Facilities : ♿ ⚬━🚿🍴 launderette

Longitude : -1.38198
Latitude : 45.99108

West coast

⛰ Club Airotel Les Gros Joncs 👥

✆ 05 46 76 52 29, www.camping-les-gros-joncs.com – limited spaces for one-night stay

Address : 850 route de Ponthezière – Les Sables Vignier (5km southwest, 300m from the sea)

Opening times : from beginning April to mid Nov.

5 ha (253 pitches) terraced, flat, sandy

Tariff : 51.21€ ✶✶ 🚗 🔲 🔌 (16A) – Extra per person 13.30€ – Reservation fee 18€

Rental rates : (from beginning April to mid Nov.) ♿ (5 chalets) – 153 🏕 – 50 🏠. Per week from 890 to 1,506€ – Reservation fee 18€

A partially covered swimming area, good-quality rental options and some pitches for tents and caravans, but with old sanitary facilities.

Surroundings : 🏊 ⛺ 🎠
Leisure activities : 🍴 ✗ 🎱 🏓 🎣 hammam, jacuzzi 🛥 🚴 🏊 ⛷ ⛸ spa centre, entertainment room
Facilities : ♿ ⚡ 🛁 🚿 🍴 launderette 🏪 🔧

GPS Longitude : -1.379
Latitude : 45.95342

St-Pierre-d'Oléron 17310 – Michelin map **324** C4 – pop. 6 532 – alt. 8
▶ Paris 522 – Marennes 22 – Rochefort 44 – La Rochelle 80

⛰ Aqua 3 Masses

✆ 05 46 47 23 96, www.campingles3masses.com – limited spaces for one-night stay

Address : at Le Marais-Doux (4.3km southeast)

3 ha (130 pitches) flat, grassy
Rentals : ♿ (1 chalet) – 35 🏕 – 12 🏠.

In a pleasant setting with flowers; good-quality rental options.

Surroundings : 🏊 ⛺ 🎠
Leisure activities : ✗ 🏠 🛥 🚴 🏊 (open air in season) ⛷
Facilities : ♿ ⚡ 🛁 🍴 launderette 🔧

GPS Longitude : -1.29226
Latitude : 45.91815

St-Trojan-les-Bains 17370 – Michelin map **324** C4 – pop. 1 471 – alt. 5
▶ Paris 509 – Marennes 16 – Rochefort 38 – La Rochelle 74

⛰ Flower Saint-Trop'Park 👥

✆ 05 46 76 00 47, www.st-tro-park.com

Address : 36 avenue des Bris (located 1.5km southwest)

Opening times : from beginning April to mid Oct.

4 ha (208 pitches) undulating, flat, grassy, sandy

Tariff : 29.50€ ✶✶ 🚗 🔲 🔌 (10A) – Extra per person 9.70€ – Reservation fee 25€

Rental rates : (2015 price) (from beginning April to mid Oct.) 🏊 – 40 🏕 – 17 🏠 – 9 studios. Per night from 109€ – Per week from 265 to 689€ – Reservation fee 25€

An undulating site with shade and good-quality services.

Surroundings : 🏊 🎠
Leisure activities : 🍴 ✗ 🏠 🏓 🎣 ⛺ hammam, jacuzzi 🛥 🚴 🏊 multi-sports ground
Facilities : ♿ ⚡ 🛁 🚿 🍴 🔲 🏪 🔧
Nearby : 🍴

GPS Longitude : -1.2159
Latitude : 45.82958

⛰ Indigo Oléron Les Pins 👥

✆ 05 46 76 02 39, www.camping-indigo.com

Address : 11 avenue des Bris (to the southwest)

Opening times : from beginning May to mid Sept.

5 ha (160 pitches) undulating, flat, grassy, sandy

Tariff : (2015 price) 30.30€ ✶✶ 🚗 🔲 🔌 (10A) – Extra per person 5.90€ – Reservation fee 13€

Rental rates : (2015 price) (from beginning May to mid Sept.) – 56 tent lodges. Per night from 50 to 113€ – Per week from 245 to 791€ – Reservation fee 13€

🚉 local sani-station 7€

A natural setting, but choose the pitches away from the road.

Surroundings : 🏊🏊
Leisure activities : 🏓 🚴 🏊 ⛷
Facilities : ♿ ⚡ 🛁 🍴 launderette 🔧

GPS Longitude : -1.21413
Latitude : 45.83128

INGRANDES

86220 – Michelin map **322** J3 – pop. 1 784 – alt. 50
▶ Paris 305 – Châtellerault 7 – Descartes 18 – Poitiers 41

⛰ Les Castels Le Petit Trianon de Saint Ustre

✆ 05 49 02 61 47, www.petit-trianon.com

Address : 1 rue du Moulin de St-Ustre (3km to the northeast; at St-Ustre)

Opening times : from end April to beginning Sept.

4 ha (116 pitches) flat, relatively flat, grassy, wood

Tariff : 33.80€ ✶✶ 🚗 🔲 🔌 (10A) – Extra per person 8.60€ – Reservation fee 10€

Rental rates : (from end April to beginning Sept.) – 20 🏕 – 2 🏠 – 2 🏡 – 1 apartement – 1 cabin in the trees – 6 tipis – 1 gîte. Per night from 40 to 149€ – Per week from 224 to 1,043€ – Reservation fee 10€

🚉 local sani-station

A pleasant setting beside a small château, with a range of rental options.

Surroundings : 🏊 ⛷ ⛺ 🎠
Leisure activities : 🍴 🏠 jacuzzi 🛥 🏓 🎣 ⛷
Facilities : ♿ ⚡ 🛁 🍴 launderette 🔧
Nearby : ✗

GPS Longitude : 0.58653
Latitude : 46.88779

JONZAC

17500 – Michelin map **324** H7 – pop. 3 488 – alt. 40 – ♨
▶ Paris 512 – Angoulême 59 – Bordeaux 84 – Cognac 36

⛰ Les Castors

✆ 05 46 48 25 65, www.campingcastors.com

Address : 8 rue de Clavelaud (located 1.5km southwest along the D 19, follow the signs for Montendre and take the road to the right)

Opening times : from mid March to mid Nov.

3 ha (120 pitches) relatively flat, flat, grassy

Tariff : ✶5.70€ 🚗 🔲6.20€ – 🔌 (10A) 5.70€ – Reservation fee 8.50€

Rental rates : (from mid March to mid Nov.) – 60 🏕 – 6 🏠 – 1 canvas bungalow. Per night from 43 to 121€ – Per week from 245 to 663€ – Reservation fee 10€

The part of the site near the swimming pools is well shaded; another part is in the sun, with good-quality mobile homes.

Surroundings : ⛺ 🎠
Leisure activities : 🍴 🏠 jacuzzi 🛥 🚴 🏊 ⛷ multi-sports ground
Facilities : ♿ ⚡ 🚿 🍴 launderette 🔧

GPS Longitude : -0.44712
Latitude : 45.43009

LANDRAIS

17290 – Michelin map **324** E3 – pop. 680 – alt. 12
▶ Paris 455 – Niort 48 – Rochefort 23 – La Rochelle 32

⚠ le Pré Maréchat

🖉 05 46 27 73 69, landrais.e-monsite.com

Address : take northwestern exit along the D 112, follow the signs for Aigrefeuille-d'Aunis and take road to the left, 120m from a lake

Opening times : from mid June to mid Sept.

0.6 ha (37 pitches) flat, grassy

Tariff : (2015 price) ♠2.50€ ➡1.50€ 🔲 3€ – 🔌 (30A) 2€

Surroundings : 🏊 🖵 ♉♉
Leisure activities :
Facilities : 🚿 🚻

G P S	Longitude : -0.86536 Latitude : 46.06963

Nearby : 🎣

LE LINDOIS

16310 – Michelin map **324** N5 – pop. 343 – alt. 270
▶ Paris 453 – Angoulême 41 – Confolens 34 – Montbron 12

⚠ L'Étang

🖉 05 45 65 02 67, www.campingdeletang.com – 🅿️

Address : route de Rouzède (500m southwest along the D 112)

Opening times : permanent

10 ha/1.5 (29 pitches) relatively flat, grassy

Tariff : 23.50€ ♠♠ ➡ 🔲 🔌 (16A) – Extra per person 5€

In a pleasant unspoilt setting with trees, beside a lake.

Surroundings : 🏊 🖵 ♉♉
Leisure activities : 🍴 ✗ 🏖 (beach) 🎣
boats for hire
Facilities : 🚿 🚻

G P S	Longitude : 0.58555 Latitude : 45.73974

LOUDUN

86200 – Michelin map **322** G2 – pop. 7 089 – alt. 120
▶ Paris 311 – Angers 79 – Châtellerault 47 – Poitiers 55

⚠ Municipal de Beausoleil

🖉 05 49 98 15 38, www.ville-loudun.fr

Address : chemin de l'Étang (2.5km take the northern exit along the D 347, towards Angers and take road to the left after the level crossing; beside a stream and near a lake)

0.6 ha (33 pitches) terraced, flat, grassy

Good pitches that are well shaded and marked out.

Surroundings : 🖵 ♉♉
Leisure activities : 🛶
Facilities : 🚿 🏖

G P S	Longitude : 0.06175 Latitude : 47.00334

MARANS

17230 – Michelin map **324** E2 – pop. 4 623 – alt. 1
▶ Paris 461 – Fontenay-le-Comte 28 – Niort 56 – La Rochelle 24

⚠ Municipal du Bois Dinot

🖉 05 46 01 10 51, www.ville-marans.fr

Address : route de Nantes (500m north along the N 137, 80m from the Marans-La Rochelle canal)

7 ha/3 for camping (170 pitches) flat, grassy

Rentals : 🚶 (1 chalet) – 12 🏠 – 5 tent lodges.
🚐 local sani-station – 10 🔲

Surroundings : 🖵 ♉♉
Leisure activities : 🛶
Facilities : 🚿 🚻 🏖 🚰 launderette
Nearby : 🏄 🎣 pedalos

G P S	Longitude : -0.98945 Latitude : 46.31583

MARENNES

17320 – Michelin map **324** D5 – pop. 5 608 – alt. 10
▶ Paris 494 – Pons 61 – Rochefort 22 – Royan 31

⚠ Au Bon Air

🖉 05 46 85 02 40, www.aubonair.com

Address : 9 avenue Pierre Voyer (2.5km to the west; at Marennes-Plage)

Opening times : from beginning April to end Sept.

2.4 ha (126 pitches) flat, grassy, sandy

Tariff : 27.90€ ♠♠ ➡ 🔲 🔌 (16A) – Extra per person 4.10€ – Reservation fee 18€

Rental rates : (from beginning April to end Sept.) – 20 🚐 – 5 🏠. Per night from 42 to 77€ – Per week from 261 to 824€ – Reservation fee 18€

🚐 AireService sani-station 2€ – 🚿 🔌15€

Situated close to the beach (200m), pitches in the shade with some owner-occupier mobile homes.

Surroundings : 🖵 ♉♉
Leisure activities : 🍴 🎪 🛶 🏄
Facilities : 🚿 🚻 🏖 🚰 🚰 launderette

G P S	Longitude : -1.13442 Latitude : 45.81882

We have selected the best campsites in France with our usual care, listing those with the best facilities in the most pleasant surroundings.

LES MATHES

17570 – Michelin map **324** D5 – pop. 1 719 – alt. 10
▶ Paris 514 – Marennes 18 – Rochefort 40 – La Rochelle 76

⚠ La Pinède 🏠👤

🖉 05 46 22 45 13, www.campinglapinede.com – limited spaces for one-night stay 🐾

Address : 2103 route de la Fouasse (3km to the northwest)

Opening times : from beginning April to end Sept.

10 ha (472 pitches) flat and relatively flat, grassy

Tariff : (2015 price) 49€ ♠♠ ➡ 🔲 🔌 (10A) – Extra per person 9€

Rental rates : (2015 price) permanent 🚿 🐾 – 225 🚐 – 10 🏠. Per night from 91 to 263€ – Per week from 196 to 1,589€ – Reservation fee 20€

A large swimming area, partially covered, with several pitches for tents and caravans, but choose those furthest away from the road.

Surroundings : 🏊 🖵 ♉♉
Leisure activities : 🍴 ✗ 🎪 🎮 🎯 🏖 🏄 🏄
🚲 🏊 🛶 🏊 archery, multi-sports ground
Facilities : 🚿 🚻 🏖 – 4 private sanitary
facilities (🔥 🚿 🚽 WC) 🏖 🚰 🚰 launderette
🏊 🏖
Nearby : amusement park

G P S	Longitude : -1.17568 Latitude : 45.72784

⚠ L'Estanquet ♨♦

📞 05 46 22 47 32, www.campinglestanquet.com

Address : route de la Fouasse (3.5km to the northwest)

Opening times : from beginning April to end Sept.

6 ha (387 pitches) flat, sandy

Tariff : (2015 price) 40,50€ ♦♦ ⚘ ▣ ⚡ (10A) –
Extra per person 6.50€ – Reservation fee 20€

Rental rates : (2015 price) (from beginning April to end Sept.) –
155 🚐 – 10 🏠 – 20 canvas bungalows. Per night from 30 to
155€ – Per week from 159 to 1,085€ – Reservation fee 20€

*A good choice of mobile homes beside a water park; free use of
the covered swimming pool and play area at the Les Sables de
Cordouan campsite 200m away.*

Surroundings : 🛏 ♨♨
Leisure activities : ♟✗🚣 🏊🚴⚽🏊
🏊 multi-sports ground
Facilities : 🚻 ⚲ 🚿 ♨ 🚰 launderette
🏊🚸
Nearby : 🖼 amusement park

Longitude : -1.17661
Latitude : 45.73214

⚠ L'Orée du Bois ♨♦

📞 05 46 22 42 43, www.camping-oree-du-bois.fr – limited spaces for
one-night stay

Address : 225 route de la Bouverie (3.5km to the northwest, at La
Fouasse)

6 ha (429 pitches) flat, grassy

Rentals : 170 🚐.

*Tent and caravan pitches with refurbished private sanitary fa-
cilities; some luxury mobile homes.*

Surroundings : 🛏 ♨♨
Leisure activities : ♟✗ 🚣 🏊🚴⚽🏊
🏊🏊 multi-sports ground
Facilities : 🚻 ⚲ 🚿 – 40 private sanitary
facilities (🚿 🚽 🚽 wc) 🚰 launderette 🏊🚸

Longitude : -1.17905
Latitude : 45.72998

⚠ Les Sables de Cordouan

📞 05 32 09 04 08, www.campingsablesdecordouan.com – limited
spaces for one-night stay

Address : route de la Fouasse (situated 3.6km northwest)

Opening times : from beginning April to mid Oct.

3 ha (150 pitches) flat, grassy

Tariff : (2015 price) 40.50€ ♦♦ ⚘ ▣ ⚡ (10A) –
Extra per person 6.50€ – Reservation fee 20€

Rental rates : (2015 price) (from beginning April to mid Oct.) –
35 🚐. Per night from 32 to 164€ – Per week from 169 to 1,148€ –
Reservation fee 20€

*Campers can also make use of all the services and entertain-
ment provided at the Estanquet campsite (200m). Not many
pitches for tents and caravans.*

Surroundings : 🛏 ♨♨
Leisure activities : 🏊 🖼
Facilities : 🚻 ⚲ 🚰 launderette
Nearby : 🏊♟✗ 🏊🏊 amusement park

Longitude : -1.17563
Latitude : 45.73022

⚠ Monplaisir

📞 05 46 22 50 31, www.campingmonplaisirlesmathes.fr

Address : 26 avenue de La Palmyre (southwestern exit)

Opening times : from beginning April to end Sept.

2 ha (114 pitches) flat, grassy

Tariff : 26€ ♦♦ ⚘ ▣ ⚡ (10A) – Extra per person 7€
🚮 local sani-station 4€ – 10 ▣ 20€

Only pitches for tents and caravans, no rental accommodation.

Surroundings : ♨♨
Leisure activities : 🏊 🚣 🏊
Facilities : 🚻 ⚲ 🚿 🚰 launderette
Nearby : 🛒♟✗🚴🏊🚣🏊

Longitude : -1.15563
Latitude : 45.71541

MAUZÉ-SUR-LE-MIGNON
79210 – Michelin map **322** B7 – pop. 2 758 – alt. 30
▶ Paris 430 – Niort 23 – Rochefort 40 – La Rochelle 43

⚠ Municipal le Gué de la Rivière

📞 05 49 26 30 35, www.ville-mauze-mignon.fr – 🏮

Address : rue du Port (located 1km northwest along the D 101,
follow the signs for St-Hilaire-la-Palud and take the turning to the
left; between the Mignon river and the canal)

Opening times : from end May to beginning Sept.

1.5 ha (75 pitches) flat, grassy

Tariff : (2015 price) ♦2.70€ ⚘ ▣1.40€ – ⚡ (10A)3.70€
🚮 Flot Bleu sani-station 4€

*In a green setting, northwest of the town, near the Canal du
Mignon.*

Surroundings : 🏊 🛏 ♨♨
Leisure activities : 🏊
Facilities : 🚻 🖼

Longitude : -0.67959
Latitude : 46.19968

*Using the traditional Michelin classification method,
the guide provides you with an easy, speedy reference
for assessing the category of each site: 1 to 5 tents
(see page 10).*

MÉDIS
17600 – Michelin map **324** E6 – pop. 2 698 – alt. 29
▶ Paris 498 – Marennes 28 – Mirambeau 48 – Pons 39

⚠ Sites et Paysages Le Clos Fleuri

📞 05 46 05 62 17, www.le-clos-fleuri.com

Address : 8 impasse du Clos Fleuri (situated 2km southeast along the
D 117e 3)

Opening times : from beginning June to mid Sept.

3 ha (120 pitches) flat and relatively flat, grassy

Tariff : 39.50€ ♦♦ ⚘ ▣ ⚡ (10A) – Extra per person 9.50€ –
Reservation fee 20€

Rental rates : (from beginning June to mid Sept.) 🏊 – 4 🚐 –
10 🏠. Per week from 290 to 790€ – Reservation fee 20€

*A pleasant rural setting with ample shade from a great variety
of trees.*

Surroundings : 🏊 🛏 ♨♨
Leisure activities : ♟✗ 🏊 🍴 🏊🏊 🚣 🏊
Facilities : 🚻 ⚲ 🚿 🚰 launderette 🏊🚸

Longitude : -0.94633
Latitude : 45.63003

MONTBRON

16220 – Michelin map **324** N5 – pop. 2 161 – alt. 141
▶ Paris 460 – Angoulême 29 – Nontron 25 – Rochechouart 38

▲▲▲ Les Castels Les Gorges du Chambon ▲▲

🖉 05 45 70 71 70, www.camping-gorgesduchambon.com

Address : at Le Chambon (4.4km east along the D6, follow the signs for Piégut-Pluviers, then take left turn for 3.2km along the D 163, follow the signs for Ecuras and take the road to the right; 80m from the Tardoir river – direct access)

Opening times : from beginning May to mid May

28 ha/7 for camping (132 pitches) flat, grassy

Tariff : (2015 price) 34.10€ ♥♥ ⇄ 国 ⅓ (10A) – Extra per person 9.10€ – Reservation fee 15€

Rental rates : (2015 price) (from beginning May to mid Sept.) ⅙ (1 mobile home) – 17 🏚 – 8 🏠 – 5 canvas bungalows – 1 gîte. Per night from 40 to 100€ – Per week from 240 to 700€ – Reservation fee 20€

🚐 local sani-station – 🅿 ⅓16€

In a pretty, green woodland setting with old landscaped and renovated farmhouse.

Surroundings : 🐂 ◁ 🎣
Leisure activities : ♥ ✕ 🏠 🎱 🎿 🏹 🚴 ✂ 🎿 🏊 ≋ 🎣 multi-sports ground
Facilities : ⅙ ⊶ ⊞ ⅓ 🚰 launderette 🔧 🚗
Nearby : 🐎

GPS Longitude : 0.5593
Latitude : 45.65945

MONTIGNAC-CHARENTE

16330 – Michelin map **324** K5 – pop. 731 – alt. 50
▶ Paris 432 – Angoulême 17 – Cognac 42 – Rochechouart 66

▲ Municipal les Platanes

🖉 05 45 39 70 09, www.montignac-charente.fr

Address : 25 avenue de la Boixe (200m northwest along the D 115, follow the signs for Aigré)

Opening times : from beginning June to end Aug.

1.5 ha (100 pitches) flat, grassy

Tariff : (2015 price) ♥5.40€ ⇄ 国 – ⅓ (12A) 6.30€
Rental rates : (2015 price) (from beginning June to end Aug.) – 1 canvas bungalow. Per week from 300€ – Reservation fee 90€

Choose the shady pitches furthest away from the road.

Surroundings : 🎣
Leisure activities : 🏠
Facilities : ⅙ 🚰 🚰
Nearby : ≋ 🎣

GPS Longitude : 0.11797
Latitude : 45.78189

MONTMORILLON

86500 – Michelin map **322** L6 – pop. 6 410 – alt. 100
▶ Paris 354 – Bellac 43 – Le Blanc 32 – Chauvigny 27

▲ Municipal de l'Allochon

🖉 05 49 91 02 33, www.ville-montmorillon.fr

Address : 31 avenue Fernad-Tribot (take the southeastern exit along the D 54, follow the signs for Le Dorat; 50m from the Gartempe river, beside a stream)

Opening times : from beginning March to end Oct.

2 ha (75 pitches) open site, flat, grassy

Tariff : (2015 price) ♥1.85€ ⇄ 1€ 国 1€ – ⅓ (10A) 3.78€

🚐 local sani-station
Surroundings : 🎣
Leisure activities : 🏠 🎿
Facilities : ⅙ ⊶ ⊞ ⅓ 🚰 🔧
Nearby : 🏊 🎣 🎣

GPS Longitude : 0.87526
Latitude : 46.42038

MORTAGNE-SUR-GIRONDE

17120 – Michelin map **324** F7 – pop. 1 027 – alt. 51
▶ Paris 509 – Blaye 59 – Jonzac 30 – Pons 26

▲ Municipal Bel Air

🖉 06 42 01 17 62, www.mortagne-sur-gironde

Address : near the port

1 ha (20 pitches) terraced, flat, grassy

Several pitches have a fine view of the estuary and the marina.

Surroundings : 🐂 ◁ 🚤 🎣
Leisure activities : 🎿
Facilities : ⅙ 🚿 🚰 🚰

GPS Longitude : -0.79147
Latitude : 45.47974

*We value your opinion and welcome your feedback.
Do email us at campingfrance@tp.michelin.com*

MOSNAC

17240 – Michelin map **324** G6 – pop. 476 – alt. 23
▶ Paris 501 – Cognac 34 – Gémozac 20 – Jonzac 11

▲ Municipal les Bords de la Seugne

🖉 05 46 70 48 45, mosnac@mairie17.com

Address : 34 rue de la Seugne (in the village; beside the river)

0.9 ha (33 pitches) flat, grassy

A small campsite in the village, beside the pretty little church; very simple but very pleasant.

Surroundings : 🐂 ◁ the church 🏚 🎣
Leisure activities : 🎣
Facilities : ⊞ 🅿

GPS Longitude : -0.52293
Latitude : 45.5058

LA PALMYRE

17570 – Michelin map **324** C5
▶ Paris 524 – Poitiers 191 – La Rochelle 77 – Rochefort 46

▲▲▲ Village Siblu Bonne Anse Plage
(rental of mobile homes only)

🖉 05 46 22 40 90, www.siblu.fr/bonneanse

Address : avenue de la Coubre (situated 2km west along the D 25, 400m from the beach)

Opening times : from end May to mid Sept.

18 ha (613 pitches) undulating

Rental rates : (2015 price) 🛏 – 200 🏚. Per night from 59 to 227€ – Per week from 413 to 1,589€ – Reservation fee 15€

🚐 6 国

A mobile home park, the majority of which belong to owner-occupiers.

Surroundings : 🏚 🎣
Leisure activities : ♥ ✕ 🎱 🎿 🎣 🎿 🚴 🏓 🏊 🛝 climbing wall, multi-sports ground
Facilities : ⅙ ⊶ 🚰 launderette 🔧 🚗

GPS Longitude : -1.19983
Latitude : 45.69843

⚠ Yelloh! Village Parc de la Côte Sauvage ♣

🕿 05 46 22 40 18, www.yellohvillage-parcdelacotesauvage.com ✄

Address : La Coubre (3km west along the D 25)

Opening times : from beginning April to mid Sept.

14 ha (400 pitches) undulating, flat, relatively flat, grassy, sandy

Tariff : 51€ ♣♣ ⇔ 🗐 🕅 (10A) – Extra per person 9€

Rental rates : (from beginning April to mid Sept.) ✄ – 130 ⛺.
Per night from 42 to 235€ – Per week from 294 to 1,645€

🚽 local sani-station

A wooded setting very near the beach and the la Coubre lighthouse.

Surroundings : 🏖 ⛺ ♤♤
Leisure activities : 🍴 ✕ 🏛 🎣 ☙ 🎠
🚲 🏊 🛶 multi-sports ground
Facilities : 🚿 ☎ ▥ 🛢 🍴 launderette 🛒 🛒
Longitude : -1.22769
Latitude : 45.69584

⚠ Beausoleil

🕿 05 46 22 30 03, www.campingbeausoleil.com

Address : 20 avenue de la Coubre (take the northwestern exit, 500m from the beach)

Opening times : from beginning May to mid Sept.

4 ha (244 pitches) undulating, flat, grassy, sandy

Tariff : (2015 price) 34.80€ ♣♣ ⇔ 🗐 🕅 (10A) –
Extra per person 5.10€ – Reservation fee 18€

Rental rates : (2015 price) (from beginning April to mid Sept.) – 20 ⛺ –
4 canvas bungalows. Per night from 30 to 117€ – Per week from 210 to 820€ – Reservation fee 18.50€

A tranquil, family-friendly site with owner-occupiers and a further hundred or so pitches for tents or caravans.

Surroundings : ♤♤
Leisure activities : 🏛 🎣 🛶 (small swimming pool)
Facilities : 🚿 ☎ 🛢 🍴 launderette 🛒 🛒
Longitude : -1.18301
Latitude : 45.69242

79200 – Michelin map **322** E5 – pop. 10 338 – alt. 175
▶ Paris 377 – Bressuire 32 – Châtellerault 79 – Fontenay-le-Comte 69

⚠ Flower Le Bois Vert

🕿 05 49 64 78 43, www.camping-boisvert.com

Address : 14 rue Boisseau (take the southwestern exit follow the signs for La Roche-sur-Yon and take a right turn after the bridge over the Thouet; near a lake)

Opening times : from beginning April to end Oct.

2 ha (90 pitches) flat, grassy, gravelled

Tariff : 28€ ♣♣ ⇔ 🗐 🕅 (16A) – Extra per person 6.50€ – Reservation fee 10€

Rental rates : (from beginning April to end Oct.) 🚿 (1 mobile home) – 15 ⛺ – 4 🏠 – 4 canvas bungalows. Per night from 34 to 99€ – Per week from 305 to 693€ – Reservation fee 10€

🚽 AireService sani-station 9€ – 4 🗐 19.50€ – 🚐🕅17€

In a green setting with good-quality sanitary facilities.

Surroundings : 🏖 ⛺ ♤♤
Leisure activities : 🍴 ✕ 🏛 🏇🚲 🛶
Facilities : 🚿 ☎ ▥ 🛢 🍴 launderette 🛒
Nearby : 🏇 ✕ 🎣
Longitude : -0.2675
Latitude : 46.64194

17800 – Michelin map **324** G6 – pop. 4 446 – alt. 39
▶ Paris 493 – Blaye 64 – Bordeaux 97 – Cognac 24

⚠ Les Moulins de la Vergne

🕿 05 46 90 02 80, www.lesmoulinsdelavergne.coml

Address : 9 impasse du Moulin de la Vergne (situated 2km north along the D 234, towards Colombiers)

3 ha/1 for camping (51 pitches) flat, grassy

🚽 20 🗐

The bar-restaurant in the old mill has a pleasant terrace.

Surroundings : 🏖 ♧
Leisure activities : 🍴 ✕ 🏛 🛶 🎣
Facilities : ☎ 🍴 launderette 🛒
Longitude : -0.53906
Latitude : 45.59444

⚠ Municipal le Paradis

🕿 05 46 91 36 72, campingmunicipalpons@voila.fr

Address : avenue du Paradis (to the west near the swimming pool)

Opening times : from beginning May to end Sept.

1 ha (60 pitches) flat, grassy

Tariff : (2015 price) ♣3.50€ ⇔ 🗐 7€ – 🕅 (10A) 1€

🚽 Eurorelais sani-station 6€ – 4 🗐

A good expanse of grass and plenty of shade for this simple but very pleasant site.

Surroundings : ♤♤
Leisure activities : 🏛
Facilities : 🚿 ☎ 🛢 🍴 🖼
Nearby : 🛶 🏊
Longitude : -0.5553
Latitude : 45.57793

17250 – Michelin map **324** E5 – pop. 1 716 – alt. 20
▶ Paris 474 – Marennes 23 – Rochefort 19 – La Rochelle 59

⚠ Parc de la Garenne

🕿 05 46 97 01 46, www.lagarenne.net

Address : 24 avenue Bernard Chambenoit (take the southeastern exit along the D 125, follow the signs for Soulignonne)

2.7 ha (111 pitches) flat, grassy

Rentals : 30 ⛺ – 2 canvas bungalows.

Well shaded in part, some leisure activities and very simple sanitary facilities.

Surroundings : 🏖 ⛺ ♧
Leisure activities : 🏛 🏇 🚲 🎾 multi-sports ground
Facilities : 🚿 ☎ 🛢 🍴 launderette 🛒
Nearby : 🛶
Longitude : -0.87096
Latitude : 45.82729

Key to rentals symbols:

12 ⛺	*Number of mobile homes*	
20 🏠	*Number of chalets*	
6 🛏	*Number of rooms to rent*	
Per night 30–50€	*Minimum/maximum rate per night*	
Per week 300–1,000€	*Minimum/maximum rate per week*	

PRAILLES

79370 – Michelin map **322** E7 – pop. 666 – alt. 150
▶ Paris 394 – Melle 15 – Niort 23 – St-Maixent-l'École 13

⚠ Municipal Le Lambon

✆ 05 49 32 85 11, www.lelambon.com

Address : at Lambon lake (2.8km southeast)

Opening times : from beginning April to end Sept.

1 ha (50 pitches) terraced, sloping, relatively flat, grassy

Tariff : (2015 price) ♦4.50€ ⇌2.30€ 🔲 11€ – 🔌 (13A)2.30€
Rental rates : (2015 price) (from mid March to end Oct.) – 7 🚐 –
39 gîtes. Per night from 67 to 87€ – Per week from 156 to 378€
🚗 local sani-station

200m from the boating centre where a number of activities are offered.

Surroundings : 🐾 ♀♀ Facilities : ♿🏊 launderette Nearby : 🍴✕🏛🎣⛷🎿⛵ (beach) 🎣 sports trail	**GPS** Longitude : -0.20753 Latitude : 46.30055

PRESSAC

86460 – Michelin map **322** J8 – pop. 644 – alt. 162
▶ Paris 402 – Angoulême 76 – Limoges 73 – Poitiers 60

⚠ Le Village Flottant

✆ 05 86 16 02 25, www.village-flottant-pressac.com

Address : Etang du Ponteil (lake), northwest of the village

Opening times :

12 ha (21 pitches)

Rental rates : (from mid Feb. to end Dec.) ♿ 🎿. Per night
from 109 to 130€ – Per week from 599 to 715€

Unusual accommodation on a 7-hectare lake; food available in the restaurant or as picnic basket meals.

Leisure activities : 🍴✕🚲🎿🎣 boats for hire Facilities : ♿⚡🚿🍴🚰	**GPS** Longitude : 0.55299 Latitude : 46.12406

This guide is not intended as a list of all the camping sites in France; its aim is to provide a selection of the best sites in each category.

RIVIÈRES

16110 – Michelin map **324** M5 – pop. 1 833 – alt. 75
▶ Paris 445 – Poitiers 108 – Angoulême 26 – Limoges 84

⚠ des Flots

✆ 06 48 51 18 90, www.campinglesflots.16.hebergratuit.com

Address : 714 rue des Flots

1 ha (25 pitches) flat, grassy, stony
Rentals : 2 🚐.
🚗 Eurorelais sani-station – 5 🔲

Beside the river and close to the Château de La Rochefoucauld.

Surroundings : 🐾 ♀♀ Leisure activities : 🎣 Facilities : ♿🍴 Nearby : 🎿	**GPS** Longitude : 0.3809 Latitude : 45.74507

ROCHEFORT

17300 – Michelin map **324** E4 – pop. 25 317 – alt. 12 – ⚓
▶ Paris 475 – Limoges 221 – Niort 62 – La Rochelle 38

⚠ Le Bateau

✆ 05 46 99 41 00, www.campinglebateau.com

Address : rue des Pêcheurs d'Islande (near the Charente river, along
the western bypass (bd Bignon) and follow the signs for Port Neuf,
near the water park)

Opening times : from end March to beginning Nov.

5 ha/1.5 (133 pitches) flat, grassy stony

Tariff : (2015 price) 16€ ♦♦ ⇌ 🔲 🔌 (10A) – Extra per person 4€ –
Reservation fee 15€
Rental rates : (2015 price) (from end March to beginning Nov.) –
37 🚐. Per night from 57 to 111€ – Per week from 299 to 649€ –
Reservation fee 15€
🚗 49 🔲 14€

Many spa bathers in search of peace and quiet come to this site close to water.

Surroundings : 🐾🏕♀ Leisure activities : 🍴✕🏛🎣🎿🏊 Facilities : ♿⚡🏪🚿🚰🍴 launderette Nearby : 🎣	**GPS** Longitude : -0.9962 Latitude : 45.94834

⚠ Municipal Le Rayonnement

✆ 05 46 82 67 70, camping.municipal@ville-rochefort.fr

Address : 3 avenue de la Fosse aux Mâts (near the town centre)

Opening times : from beginning March to end Nov.

2 ha (138 pitches) flat, fine gravel, grassy

Tariff : 16.70€ ♦♦ ⇌ 🔲 🔌 (15A) – Extra per person 2.95€ –
Reservation fee 30€
Rental rates : (from beginning March to end Nov.) ♿ (1 mobile
home) – 19 🚐. Per week from 268 to 366€
🚗 AireService sani-station 3€

Shaded pitches near the town centre. A sani-station for campervans is available nearby.

Surroundings : 🏕♀♀ Leisure activities : 🏛🎣🚲 Facilities : ♿⚡🏪🚿🚰🍴 launderette	**GPS** Longitude : -0.95835 Latitude : 45.93

LA ROCHE-POSAY

86270 – Michelin map **322** K4 – pop. 1 556 – alt. 112 – ⚓
▶ Paris 325 – Le Blanc 29 – Châteauroux 76 – Châtellerault 23

⚠ Club Airotel La Roche-Posay Vacances ♦♦

✆ 05 49 86 21 23, www.larocheposay-vacances.com

Address : route de Lésigny (located 1.5km north along the D5, near
the racecourse; beside the Creuse river)

Opening times : from beginning April to end Sept.

7 ha (200 pitches) flat, relatively flat, grassy

Tariff : 36€ ♦♦ ⇌ 🔲 🔌 (10A) – Extra per person 6€
Rental rates : (from beginning April to end Sept.) – 83 🚐.
Per night from 47 to 142€ – Per week from 329 to 994€
🚗 local sani-station 6€ – 10 🔲 18€

Attractive pitches beside a partially covered water park.

Surroundings : 🐾🏕♀♀ Leisure activities : 🍴✕🏛🎣🏃🎿🚲 🎿🎿♣ Facilities : ♿⚡🏪🚿🍴 launderette 🎣 Nearby : 🏇	**GPS** Longitude : 0.80963 Latitude : 46.7991

RONCE-LES-BAINS

17390 – Michelin map **324** D5
▶ Paris 505 – Marennes 9 – Rochefort 31 – La Rochelle 68

⛺ La Clairière ♠♠

✆ 05 46 36 36 63, www.camping-la-clairiere.com – limited spaces for one-night stay

Address : rue du Bois de la Pesse (3.6km south along the D 25, follow the signs for Arvert and take turning to the right)

12 ha/4 for camping (292 pitches) undulating, flat, grassy, sandy
Rentals : 25 ⛺ – 8 🏠.

Plenty of space in a shady and undulating setting; verging on the wild in places.

Surroundings : 🐾 ♨♨
Leisure activities : 🍴 ✗ 🖼 ⓖ nighttime ✦✦
✦✦ 🚴🏊 🖼 🏊 ♨ massages
Facilities : 🚿 ⚌ – 10 private sanitary facilities (🍳 🚽 wc) 🍴 launderette 🖼 🖼
Nearby : 🐎

GPS Longitude : -1.16844
Latitude : 45.77502

⛺ Les Pins ♠♠

✆ 05 46 36 07 75, www.activ-loisirs.com – limited spaces for one-night stay

Address : 16 avenue Côte de Beauté (located 1km to the south)

Opening times : from beginning April to end Sept.

1.5 ha (89 pitches) flat, sandy

Tariff : (2015 price) 35.40€ ♣♣ 🚗 🖼 (16A) –
Extra per person 6.80€ – Reservation fee 20€
Rental rates : (2015 price) (from beginning April to end Sept.) –
36 ⛺ – 23 🏠 – 1 gîte. Per night from 99 to 153€ – Per week from 284 to 923€ – Reservation fee 20€

A variety of rental accommodation at different prices and standards.

Surroundings : ♨♨
Leisure activities : 🖼 ✦✦ ✦ 🚴🖼 (open air in season), entertainment room
Facilities : 🚿 ⚌ 🍴 launderette 🖼
Nearby : ✗🍴

GPS Longitude : -1.15862
Latitude : 45.78875

To visit a town or region, use the MICHELIN Green Guides.

ROYAN

17200 – Michelin map **324** D6 – pop. 18 259 – alt. 20
▶ Paris 504 – Bordeaux 121 – Périgueux 183 – Rochefort 40

⛺ Le Royan

✆ 05 46 39 09 06, www.le-royan.com

Opening times : from beginning April to mid Oct.

3.5 ha (194 pitches) relatively flat, grassy

Tariff : (2015 price) 28€ ♣♣ 🚗 🖼 (10A) – Extra per person 6.50€ – Reservation fee 20€
Rental rates : (2015 price) (from beginning April to mid Oct.) –
38 ⛺ – 13 🏠. Per night from 48 to 100€ – Per week from 305 to 905€ – Reservation fee 20€

Various rental options and degrees of comfort; pitches are well marked out, but choose those furthest away from the road.

Surroundings : 🖼 ♨♨
Leisure activities : 🍴 ✗ 🖼 ✦✦ 🏊 🖼
Facilities : 🚿 ⚌ 🖼 🖼 🍴 launderette
🖼 🖼

GPS Longitude : -1.04207
Latitude : 45.64456

⛺ Campéole Clairefontaine ♠♠

✆ 05 46 39 08 11, www.campingclairefontaine.com

Address : at Pontaillac, rue du Colonel Lachaux (400m from the beach)

Opening times : from beginning April to end Sept.

5 ha (246 pitches) flat, grassy

Tariff : 19€ ♣♣ 🚗 🖼 (10A) – Extra per person 10€ – Reservation fee 25€
Rental rates : (from beginning April to end Sept.) 🚿 (1 mobile home) – 33 ⛺ – 70 🏠 – 20 canvas bungalows. Per night from 36 to 214€ – Per week from 252 to 1,498€ – Reservation fee 25€
🖼 local sani-station

A pleasant, green site with a good games area; close to shops (300m).

Surroundings : 🐾 ♨♨
Leisure activities : 🍴 ✗ 🖼 ⓖ ✦✦ ✦ ✗ 🏊
multi-sports ground
Facilities : 🚿 ⚌ 🖼 🍴 launderette 🖼 🖼
Nearby :, casino

GPS Longitude : -1.04977
Latitude : 45.63094

⛺ Le Chant des Oiseaux

✆ 05 46 39 47 47, www.camping-royan-chantdesoiseaux.com

Address : 19 rue des Sansonnets (2.3km to the northwest)

Opening times : from beginning May to end Sept.

2.5 ha (150 pitches) flat, grassy

Tariff : (2015 price) 18€ ♣♣ 🚗 🖼 (10A) – Extra per person 4€
Rental rates : (2015 price) (from beginning April to end Sept.) 🏊 –
36 ⛺. Per week from 195 to 890€ – Reservation fee 16€
🖼 local sani-station – 3 🖼 18€ – 🖼 16€

High-quality rental options, some offering accommodation on a hotel-style basis.

Surroundings : 🐾 ♨♨
Leisure activities : ✗ 🖼 ⓖ nighttime ✦✦ 🏊
Facilities : 🚿 ⚌ 🖼 🍴 launderette 🖼

GPS Longitude : -1.02872
Latitude : 45.6466

ST-AUGUSTIN-SUR-MER

17570 – Michelin map **324** D5 – pop. 1 219 – alt. 10
▶ Paris 512 – Marennes 23 – Rochefort 44 – La Rochelle 81

⛺ Le Logis du Breuil

✆ 05 46 23 23 45, www.logis-du-breuil.com

Address : 36 rue du Centre (located to the southeast along the D 145, follow the signs for Royan)

Opening times : from beginning May to end Sept.

30 ha/8.5 for camping (390 pitches) undulating, flat, grassy, wood

Tariff : 34.25€ ♣♣ 🚗 🖼 (10A) – Extra per person 6.20€ – Reservation fee 10€
Rental rates : (from end April to end Sept.) – 9 ⛺ – 1 🏠 –
6 apartements. Per night from 60 to 130€ – Per week from 300 to 1,200€ – Reservation fee 20€
🖼 Raclet sani-station

On the edge of the Forêt de St-Augustin (forest), with vast green spaces and meadows; this site is ideal for both relaxation and ball games.

Surroundings : 🐾 ♨♨
Leisure activities : 🍴 ✗ 🖼 ✦✦ 🚴 ✗ 🏊
multi-sports ground
Facilities : 🚿 ⚌ 🖼 – 4 private sanitary facilities (🍳 🚽 wc) 🍴 launderette 🖼 🖼

GPS Longitude : -1.09612
Latitude : 45.67445

ST-CYR

86130 – Michelin map **322** I4 – pop. 1 024 – alt. 62
▶ Paris 321 – Poitiers 18 – Tours 85 – Joué 82

⚠ Lac de St-Cyr ⚠

✆ 05 49 62 57 22, www.campinglacdesaintcyr.com

Address : in St-Cyr park (1.5km northeast along the D4 and D82, follow the signs for Bonneuil-Matours)

Opening times : from end March to end Sept.

5.4 ha (198 pitches) flat, grassy

Tariff : 18€ ✴✴ 🚐 🗐 ⚡ (10A) – Extra per person 3€ – Reservation fee 15€

Rental rates : (from end March to end Sept.) ⚘ – 32 🏠 – 4 yurts – 3 canvas bungalows. Per night from 32 to 126€ – Per week from 224 to 882€ – Reservation fee 15€

🚉 Eurorelais sani-station – 15 🗐 18€ – 🚐 ⚡14€

In a green setting, with good shade, close to the lake and close to a leisure centre.

Surroundings : 🌳 🌲 🛶 ♨ ⛰
Leisure activities : ✗ 🏛 🗓 🏃 🏇 🏄 🚴 🎯 ⛱ 🎣
Facilities : ♿ 🚿 🎨 🛏 🚽 🍴 launderette 🛒 ♨
Nearby : 🍽 ⛱ 🛶 🦆 pedalos

Longitude : 0.44782
Latitude : 46.72056

ST-GEORGES-DE-DIDONNE

17110 – Michelin map **324** D6 – pop. 5 055 – alt. 7
▶ Paris 505 – Blaye 84 – Bordeaux 117 – Jonzac 56

⚠ Bois-Soleil ⚠

Bois-Soleil

✆ 546050594, www.bois-soleil.com ⚘

Address : 2 avenue de Suzac (situated to the south along the D 25, follow the signs for Meschers-sur-Gironde)

Opening times : from beginning April to beginning Oct.

10 ha (453 pitches) undulating, terraced, flat, grassy

Tariff : 48€ ✴✴ 🚐 🗐 ⚡ (10A) – Reservation fee 20€

Rental rates : (2015 price) (from beginning April to beginning Oct.) ⚘ – 81 🏠 – 15 studios. Per night from 45 to 350€ – Per week from 180 to 1,400€ – Reservation fee 30€

🚉 Eurorelais sani-station 5€

In three sections: one area with 200 owner-occupier mobile homes; one well shaded with some pitches close to the road; the third section more peaceful, with rental accommodation with terraces and a fine view of the ocean.

Surroundings : 🛶 ♨ ⛰
Leisure activities : 🍴 ✗ 🏛 🗓 🏃 🏇
hammam 🏄 🚴 🎯 ⛱ multi-sports ground
Facilities : ♿ 🚿 🎨 🛏 – 6 private sanitary facilities (🚿 💧 WC) 🛒 🚽 🍴 launderette 🛒 ♨
Nearby : 🐎

Longitude : -0.98629
Latitude : 45.58371

For more information on visiting particular towns or regions, consult the relevant regional MICHELIN Green Guide. We also recommend you use the appropriate Michelin regional map to locate your selected campsite, to calculate distances and to work out the best route.

ST-GEORGES-LÈS-BAILLARGEAUX

86130 – Michelin map **322** I4 – pop. 3 888 – alt. 100
▶ Paris 329 – Poitiers 12 – Joué 89 – Châtellerault 23

⚠ Le Futuriste

✆ 05 49 52 47 52, www.camping-le-futuriste.fr

Address : rue du Château (south of the town, access via the D 20)

Opening times : permanent

2 ha (112 pitches) flat, small lake

Tariff : 31.70€ ✴✴ 🚐 🗐 ⚡ (6A) – Extra per person 3.80€ – Reservation fee 15€

Rental rates : permanent ⚘ – 4 🏠 – 6 🏡. Per night from 67 to 135€ – Per week from 465 to 927€ – Reservation fee 15€

🚉 AireService sani-station 6€

A lovely green setting, with a fine view of Futuroscope theme park from the swimming pool.

Surroundings : ⚘ Futuroscope 🛶 ♨♨
Leisure activities : 🍴 ✗ 🏛 🗓 🏄 🖼 (open air in season) ⛱ ⚘ multi-sports ground
Facilities : ♿ 🚿 🎨 🛏 🛒 🚽 🍴 launderette 🛒

Longitude : 0.39543
Latitude : 46.66468

ST-HILAIRE-LA-PALUD

79210 – Michelin map **322** B7 – pop. 1 603 – alt. 15
▶ Paris 436 – Poitiers 104 – Niort 24 – La Rochelle 41

⚠ Le Lidon

✆ 05 49 35 33 64, www.le-lidon.com

Address : at Lidon (3km west along the D 3 follow the signs for Courçon and take road to the left, at the canoeing centre)

Opening times : from beginning April to mid Sept.

3 ha (140 pitches) flat, grassy

Tariff : 28€ ✴✴ 🚐 🗐 ⚡ (10A) – Extra per person 6.50€

Rental rates : (2015 price) (from beginning April to mid Sept.) – 1 'gypsy' caravan – 4 🏠 – 3 🏡 – 4 canvas bungalows – 9 tent lodges. Per night from 44 to 90€ – Per week from 150 to 700€ – Reservation fee 13.50€

🚉 local sani-station 4€

The reception, bar and restaurant are beside a small stream.

Surroundings : 🛶 ♨♨
Leisure activities : 🍴 ✗ 🏛 🚴 ⛱ ⚘ boats for hire 🦆
Facilities : ♿ 🚿 🎨 🛏 🚽 🍴 launderette 🛒

Longitude : -0.74324
Latitude : 46.28379

ST-JEAN-D'ANGÉLY

17400 – Michelin map **324** G4 – pop. 7 581 – alt. 25
▶ Paris 444 – Angoulême 70 – Cognac 35 – Niort 48

⚠ Val de Boutonne

✆ 05 46 32 26 16, www.campingcharentemartime17.com

Address : 56 quai de Bernouet (take the northwestern exit, follow the signs for La Rochelle, then take left turning onto Av. du Port (D 18)

Opening times : from beginning April to end Sept.

1,8 ha (99 pitches) flat, grassy

Tariff : 19.50€ ✴✴ 🚐 🗐 ⚡ (10A) – Extra per person 4.50€ – Reservation fee 5€

Rental rates : (from beginning April to end Sept.) ⚘ – 13 🏠 – 2 canvas bungalows. Per week from 250 to 630€ – Reservation fee 10€

🚉 local sani-station 18,50€ – 🚐 ⚡18,50€

A pleasant, simple site; only basic sanitary facilities, but not far from a good water sports centre.

Surroundings : 🏞 ⚲⚲
Leisure activities : 🏓 ⛹ 🚴 ⛵
Facilities : 👤 ⚲ 🚿 ☂ 🔧 ⚲ launderette
Nearby : 🍷 ✕ 🚹 🌊 🎣 watersports centre

G P S Longitude : -0.53638
Latitude : 45.94877

ST-JUST-LUZAC

17320 – Michelin map **324** D5 – pop. 1 838 – alt. 5
▶ Paris 502 – Rochefort 23 – La Rochelle 59 – Royan 26

⛰ Les Castels Séquoia Parc ♠♠

☎ 05 46 85 55 55, www.sequoiaparc.com
Address : at La Josephtrie (2.7km northwest along the D 728, follow the signs for Marennes and take the road to the right)
Opening times : from mid May to beginning Sept.
45 ha/28 for camping (460 pitches) flat, grassy
Tariff : (2015 price) 26 € ♟♟ 🚐 ▣
⚡ (10A) – Extra per person 8 € – Reservation fee 30 €
Rental rates : (from mid May to beginning Sept.) 👤 (1 mobile home) 🚲 – 360 🛏 – 40 🏠 – 2 tent lodges. Per night from 46 to 211 € – Per week from 322 to 1,477 €

An attractive swimming area near the outbuildings of a château, in a park featuring a variety of trees and flowers.

Surroundings : 🏞 🗔 ⚲⚲
Leisure activities : 🍷 ✕ 🎣 🥾 ⛹ 🚴 🎯
🏊 🚣 🐾 wildlife park, tourist information, multi-sports ground
Facilities : 👤 ⚲ 🚿 ☂ 🔧 ⚲ launderette
🍽 ⚲

G P S Longitude : -1.06046
Latitude : 45.81173

The information in the guide may have changed since going to press.

ST-LAURENT-DE-LA-PRÉE

17450 – Michelin map **324** D4 – pop. 1 814 – alt. 7
▶ Paris 483 – Rochefort 10 – La Rochelle 31

⛰ Domaine des Charmilles ♠♠

☎ 05 46 84 00 05, www.domainedescharmilles.com 🚲
Address : at Fouras, 1541 route de l'Océan (2.2km northwest along the D 214e 1, follow the signs for Fouras and turn right onto D 937, follow the signs for La Rochelle)
Opening times : from mid April to mid Sept.
5 ha (270 pitches) flat, grassy
Tariff : 35 € ♟♟ 🚐 ▣ ⚡ (10A) – Extra per person 6 € – Reservation fee 25 €
Rental rates : (from mid April to mid Sept.) 🚲 – 70 🛏 – 20 🏠 – 6 canvas bungalows. Per night from 45 to 100 € – Per week from 149 to 1,199 € – Reservation fee 25 €

There are also pitches for tents or caravans.

Surroundings : 🗔 ⚲⚲
Leisure activities : 🍷 🎣 🌙 nighttime ⛹
🥾 🚴 🚣 🏊 multi-sports ground
Facilities : 👤 ⚲ 🚿 ☂ 🔧 ⚲ launderette
🍽 ⚲

G P S Longitude : -1.05034
Latitude : 45.99052

⛰ Le Pré Vert ♠♠

☎ 05 46 84 89 40, www.camping-prevert.com
Address : rue du Petit Loir (2.3km northeast along the D 214, follow the signs for la Rochelle; at St-Pierre – take the expressway, Fouras exit)
3 ha (168 pitches) terraced, flat, grassy
Rentals : 50 🛏.
Plenty of mobile homes and a few pitches for tents and caravans beside a naturally filtered pool.

Surroundings : 🗔 ⚲⚲
Leisure activities : ✕ 🎣 🥾 ⛹ 🌊 (pool)
Facilities : 👤 ⚲ 🚿 ☂ 🔧 ⚲ launderette ⚲

G P S Longitude : -1.01917
Latitude : 45.99046

ST-NAZAIRE-SUR-CHARENTE

17780 – Michelin map **324** D4 – pop. 1 124 – alt. 14
▶ Paris 491 – Fouras 27 – Rochefort 13 – La Rochelle 49

⛰ L'Abri-Cotier

☎ 05 46 84 81 65, www.camping-la-rochelle.net
Address : 26 La Bernardière (located 1km southwest along the D 125e1)
Opening times : from beginning April to end Sept.
1.8 ha (100 pitches)
Tariff : (2015 price) 28,50 € ♟♟ 🚐 ▣ ⚡ (6A) – Extra per person 5.50 € – Reservation fee 20 €
Rental rates : (2015 price) (from beginning April to end Sept.) 👤 (1 mobile home) – 41 🛏 – 5 🏠. Per night from 70 to 115 € – Per week from 265 to 825 € – Reservation fee 20 €
🚐 local sani-station 5 € – ⚡ 8 €
Good shade, marked-out pitches and both new and slightly older rental accommodation.

Surroundings : 🏞 🗔 ⚲⚲
Leisure activities : 🍷 ✕ 🎣 🥾 🌊 (open air in season)
Facilities : 👤 ⚲ 🚿 🔧 launderette ⚲ refrigerators

G P S Longitude : -1.05856
Latitude : 45.93349

ST-PALAIS-SUR-MER

17420 – Michelin map **324** D6 – pop. 3 926 – alt. 5
▶ Paris 512 – La Rochelle 82 – Royan 6

⛰ Côte de Beauté

☎ 05 46 23 20 59, www.camping-cote-de-beaute.com
Address : 157 avenue de la Grande Côte (2.5km to the northwest, 50m from the sea)
Opening times : from mid April to end Sept.
1.7 ha (115 pitches) flat, grassy
Tariff : (2015 price) 33.50 € ♟♟ 🚐 ▣ ⚡ (6A) – Extra per person 5.20 € – Reservation fee 25 €
Rental rates : (2015 price) (from mid April to end Sept.) – 13 🛏 – 4 apartements – 4 canvas bungalows. Per night from 30 to 95 € – Per week from 160 to 665 € – Reservation fee 25 €
🚐 local sani-station
Some pitches above the road have a panoramic view of the ocean.

Surroundings : 🗔 ⚲
Leisure activities : 🏓 🎣
Facilities : 👤 ⚲ 🚿 🔧 🖼
Nearby : 🚣 🍷 ✕ ⚲

G P S Longitude : -1.1191
Latitude : 45.64973

ST-SAVINIEN

17350 – Michelin map **324** F4 – pop. 2 413 – alt. 18
▶ Paris 457 – Rochefort 28 – La Rochelle 62 – St-Jean-d'Angély 15

⚠ L'Île aux Loisirs

🖉 05 46 90 35 11, www.ilesauxloirs.com

Address : 102 rue de St-Savinien (500m west along the D 18, follow the signs for Pont-l'Abbé-d'Arnoult; between the Charente river and the canal, 200m from a small lake)

1.8 ha (82 pitches) flat, grassy
Rentals : 17 🚐.

Surroundings : 🗔 ♉♉
Leisure activities : ⛱ ✗ 🏊 🚲 ⚙
Facilities : ♿ ⌁ 🚿 🍴 launderette 🧺
Nearby : ✂ 🎣 ♨ 🏊 🚣 ⚓ sports trail

GPS
Longitude : -0.68427
Latitude : 45.87786

ST-SORNIN

17600 – Michelin map **324** E5 – pop. 303 – alt. 16
▶ Paris 495 – Marennes 13 – Rochefort 24 – La Rochelle 60

⚠ Le Valerick

🖉 05 46 85 15 95, www.camping-le-valerick.fr

Address : 1 La Mauvinière (1.3km northeast along the D 118, follow the signs for Pont-l'Abbé)

Opening times : from beginning April to end Sept.

1.5 ha (50 pitches) relatively flat, flat, grassy, wood

Tariff : 22.70€ ✱✱ �car 🔲 (6A) – Extra per person 5€

Rental rates : (from beginning April to end Sept.) 🏊 – 2 🚐. Per week from 330 to 650€

An undulating site, very well maintained, with basic sanitary facilities.

Surroundings : ♉
Leisure activities : ✗ 🏊
Facilities : ♿ ⌁ 🚿 🍴 🔲

GPS
Longitude : -0.96521
Latitude : 45.77446

*The classification (1 to 5 tents, **black** or red) that we award to selected sites in this guide is our own system. It should not be confused with the classification (1 to 5 stars) of official organisations.*

ST-YRIEIX-SUR-CHARENTE

16710 – Michelin map **324** K5 – pop. 7 025 – alt. 53
▶ Paris 451 – Poitiers 114 – Angoulême 7 – La Rochelle 142

⚠ du Plan d'Eau

Plan d'eau

🖉 05 45 92 14 64, www.campingduplandeau.fr

Address : 1 rue du Camping

Opening times : from beginning April to end Oct.

6 ha (148 pitches) flat, grassy, stony

Tariff : (2015 price) 19,85€ ✱✱ 🚐 🔲 (10A) – Extra per person 4.70€

Rental rates : (2015 price) (from beginning April to end Oct.) ♿ (1 mobile home) – 17 🚐. Per night from 37 to 105€ – Per week from 204 to 661€

🚻 AireService sani-station 2.50€ – 14 🔲 8€ – 🚐8€

Located near Angoulême town centre with a bus stop for trips to town.

Surroundings : 🏊 🗔
Leisure activities : ⛱ 🏊 🚲 ✗ multi-sports ground
Facilities : ♿ 🎱 🚿 🍴 launderette
Nearby : 🚡 hammam, jacuzzi 🔲 🏖 (beach) 🏊 🚣 ♨ watersports centre

GPS
Longitude : 0.13808
Latitude : 45.67652

SAUJON

17600 – Michelin map **324** E5 – pop. 6 636 – alt. 7
▶ Paris 499 – Poitiers 165 – La Rochelle 71 – Saintes 28

⚠ Flower Lac de Saujon 👥

Flower Lac de Saujon

🖉 05 46 06 82 99, www.campingsaujon.com

Address : voie des Tourterelles

Opening times : from beginning March to mid Oct.

3.7 ha (150 pitches) flat, grassy

Tariff : (2015 price) 23€ ✱✱ 🚐 🔲 (10A) – Extra per person 5.50€ – Reservation fee 19€

Rental rates : (2015 price) (from beginning March to end Oct.) 🏊 – 38 🚐 – 4 🏠 – 4 canvas bungalows. Per night from 40 to 92€ – Per week from 200 to 714€ – Reservation fee 19€

🚻 local sani-station 5€ – 18 🔲 12€ – 🚐8€

A pleasant site beside a large lake; a high standard of rental accommodation.

Surroundings : 🏊
Leisure activities : ⛱ ✗ 🏊 🏊 🚲
Facilities : ♿ ⌁ 🚿 🍴 🚿 🍴 launderette 🏊 🧺
Nearby : 🎣 🔲 🏊 🚣 ♨ 🐎 fitness trail

GPS
Longitude : -0.93848
Latitude : 45.68282

SECONDIGNY

79130 – Michelin map **322** D5 – pop. 1 773 – alt. 177
▶ Paris 391 – Bressuire 27 – Champdeniers 15 – Coulonges-sur-l'Autize 22

⚠ Le Moulin des Effres

🖉 05 49 95 61 97, www.camping-lemoulindeseffres.com

Address : take the southern exit along the D 748, follow the signs for Niort and take road to the left, near a lake

Opening times : from beginning April to mid Sept.

2 ha (90 pitches) relatively flat, flat, grassy

Tariff : (2015 price) 22€ ✱✱ 🚐 🔲 (10A) – Extra per person 5€ – Reservation fee 10€

Rental rates : (2015 price) (from beginning April to mid Sept.) – 23 🚐 – 5 🏠 – 3 tipis – 2 tent lodges. Per night from 43 to 64€ – Per week from 100 to 707€ – Reservation fee 20€

🚻 local sani-station 5€ – 6 🔲 17€

The pitches are well marked out and shady.

Surroundings : 🏊 🗔 ♉♉
Leisure activities : ⛱ 🏊 🚲 🏊 ✗
Facilities : ♿ ⌁ (June–Aug.) 🏊 🍴 launderette
Nearby : ⛱ ✗ ✂ 🎣 🚣 pedalos

GPS
Longitude : -0.41418
Latitude : 46.60421

SEMUSSAC

17120 – Michelin map **324** E6 – pop. 1 998 – alt. 36

▶ Paris 520 – Poitiers 187 – La Rochelle 85 – Angoulême 111

⚠ Le 2 B

☏ 05 46 05 95 16, www.camping-2b.com

Address : 9 chemin des Bardonneries (3.8km east along the D 730, follow the signs for St-Georges-de-Didonne)

Opening times : from beginning April to end Sept.

1,8 ha (93 pitches) relatively flat, flat, grassy

Tariff : (2015 price) 25€ ★★ ⇔ 🅔 🔌 (10A) – Extra per person 5€ – Reservation fee 14€

Rental rates : (2015 price) (from beginning April to end Sept.) – 20 🚐 – 10 tent lodges. Per night from 37 to 97€ – Per week from 217 to 680€ – Reservation fee 14€

Choose the pitches away from the road if possible.

Surroundings : 🔲 ♀♀
Leisure activities : 🍴 ✕ 🏠 🚣 🕯 🏊 ⚲
Facilities : 🚿 ⚬ 🚻 ⚐ launderette

Longitude : -0.94793
Latitude : 45.6041

In order for the guide to remain wholly objective, the selection of campsites is made on an entirely independent basis.

SIREUIL

16440 – Michelin map **324** K6 – pop. 1 189 – alt. 26

▶ Paris 460 – Angoulême 16 – Barbezieux 24 – Cognac 35

⚠ Nizour

☏ 05 45 90 56 27, www.campingdunizour.com

Address : 2 route de la Charente (located 1.5km southeast along the D7, follow the signs for Blanzac, turn left before the bridge; 120m from the Charente – direct access)

Opening times : from beginning May to end Sept.

1,6 ha (56 pitches) flat, grassy

Tariff : 21,95€ ★★ ⇔ 🅔 🔌 (6A) – Extra per person 5.20€ – Reservation fee 8€

Rental rates : (from mid May to mid Sept.) – 5 🚐 – 1 🏠. Per night from 115 to 160€ – Per week from 362 to 537€ – Reservation fee 8€

🚽 local sani-station 5€ – 1 🅔 12€

Choose the pitches further away from the road in preference.

Surroundings : 🔲 ♀♀
Leisure activities : 🍴 🏠 🚣 🚲 🏊 ⚲
Facilities : 🚿 ⚬ 🛁 launderette
Nearby : 🎣 ⚓

Longitude : 0.02418
Latitude : 45.60688

VAUX-SUR-MER

17640 – Michelin map **324** D6 – pop. 3 835 – alt. 12

▶ Paris 514 – Poitiers 181 – La Rochelle 75 – Rochefort 44

⚠ Le Nauzan-Plage

☏ 05 46 38 29 13, www.campinglenauzanplage.com

Address : 39 avenue de Nauzan-Plage (500m from the beach)

Opening times : from beginning May to end Sept.

3,9 ha (239 pitches) flat, grassy

Tariff : 24€ ★★ ⇔ 🅔 🔌 (10A) – Extra per person 4€ – Reservation fee 20€

Rental rates : (from beginning May to end Sept.) – 41 🚐. Per night from 35 to 162€ – Per week from 245 to 1,134€ – Reservation fee 20€

🚽 local sani-station 8€ – 2 🅔 8€

The site is beside a pretty park, crossed by a stream.

Surroundings : 🔲 ♀
Leisure activities : 🍴 ✕ 🏠 ⊙daytime 🚣 🏊
Facilities : 🚿 ⚬ 🛁 ⚐ launderette 🅿 🛁
Nearby : 🍴 🎣 🎣

Longitude : -1.07196
Latitude : 45.64295

⚠ Le Val-Vert

☏ 05 46 38 25 51, www.val-vert.com

Address : 108 avenue Fréderic Garnier (to the southwest of the town)

Opening times : from mid April to end Sept.

3 ha (181 pitches) terraced, flat, grassy, stony

Tariff : 39,20€ ★★ ⇔ 🅔 🔌 (10A) – Extra per person 8€ – Reservation fee 16€

Rental rates : (from mid April to end Sept.) – 35 🚐 – 28 🏠. Per week from 250 to 823€ – Reservation fee 16€

🚽 local sani-station

Beside a pretty park, lake and stream.

Surroundings : 🔲 ♀♀
Leisure activities : ✕ 🏠 🚣 🚲 🏊
Facilities : 🚿 ⚬ 🅔 🛁 ⚐ launderette 🛁
Nearby : 🍴 🎣 🎣

Longitude : -1.06299
Latitude : 45.64357

VOUILLÉ

86190 – Michelin map **322** G5 – pop. 3 498 – alt. 118

▶ Paris 345 – Châtellerault 46 – Parthenay 34 – Poitiers 18

⚠ Municipal

☏ 05 49 51 90 10, www.vouille86.fr

Address : chemin de la Piscine (in the town; beside the Auxance)

Opening times : from beginning June to mid Sept.

0,5 ha (48 pitches) flat, grassy

Tariff : (2015 price) ★3.80€ ⇔ 5€ 🅔 5€ – 🔌 (10A) 5€

The shaded, marked-out pitches are beside an imposing building housing the reception (camping-pool) and sanitary facilities.

Surroundings : 🦢 🔲 ♀♀
Leisure activities : 🚣 🏊 ⚲
Facilities : 🚿 🅿
Nearby : ✕

Longitude : 0.16417
Latitude : 46.64016

These symbols are used for a campsite that is exceptional in its category:

⚠⚠...⚠ *Particularly pleasant setting, quality and range of services available*

🦢 🦢 *Tranquil, isolated site – quiet site, particularly at night*

≪ ≪ *Exceptional view – interesting or panoramic view*

PROVENCE-ALPES-CÔTE D'AZUR

B. Jaubert / age fotostock

A new day dawns in sun-drenched Provence. As the fishmongers tell jokes, chat and sell their freshly-caught fish under clear blue skies, you cannot help but fall in love with the relaxed, happy-go-lucky spirit of Marseilles. In the countryside beyond, the sun casts its first amber rays across the ochre walls of a hilltop village and over the glorious fields of lavender in the valley below. The steady chirping of the cicadas is interrupted only by the gentle sound of sheep bells ringing in the hills. Slow down to the gentle pace of the villagers and join them as they gather within the refreshingly cool walls of a local café. However, by 2pm you may begin to wonder where everyone has gone. On hot afternoons, most people exercise their traditional right to a siesta, even those who frequent the chic beaches of St Tropez and in the seaside cabins of the Camargue. Fear not, it will soon be time to wake up and prepare for a serious game of *pétanque* and a chilled glass of pastis.

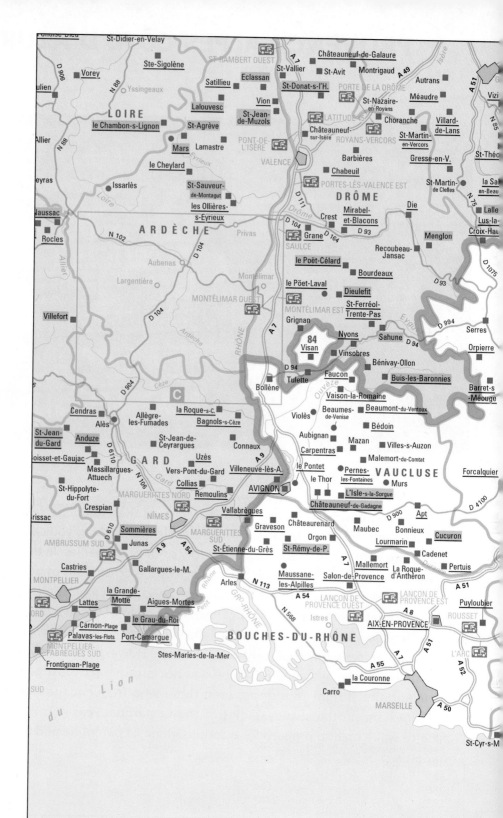

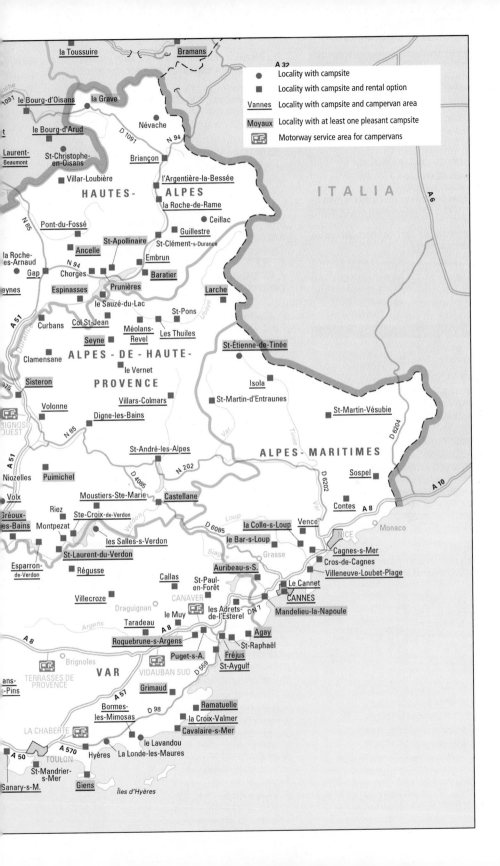

Locality with campsite

Locality with campsite and rental option

Vannes Locality with campsite and campervan area

Moyaux Locality with at least one pleasant campsite

Motorway service area for campervans

LES ADRETS-DE-L'ESTEREL

83600 – Michelin map **340** P4 – pop. 2 063 – alt. 295
▶ Paris 881 – Cannes 26 – Draguignan 44 – Fréjus 17

🏔 Les Philippons

✆ 04 94 40 90 67. www.lesphilippons.com

Address : 378 route de l'Argentière (head 3km east along the D 237)

Opening times : from beginning April to end Sept.

5 ha (120 pitches) very uneven, terraced, flat, grassy, stony

Tariff : (2015 price) 33.60€ ★★ 🚗 ▣ ⚡ (10A) –
Extra per person 6.50€ – Reservation fee 20€

Rental rates : (2015 price) (from beginning April to end Sept.) –
13 🏠. Per night from 39 to 123€ – Per week from 273 to 861€ –
Reservation fee 30€

In two sections, in a Mediterranean setting, beneath olive, eucalyptus, cor-oaks and mimosa trees.

Surroundings : 🐾 ⟵ 🏞 ⛰
Leisure activities : ▯ ✕ 🛶 🏊
Facilities : 🔌 🛁 🍴 launderette 🚿
refrigerators

G P S Longitude : 6.84002
Latitude : 43.52876

AGAY

83530 – Michelin map **340** Q5 – alt. 20
▶ Paris 880 – Cannes 34 – Draguignan 43 – Fréjus 12

🏔🏔 Esterel Caravaning 🔆

Esterel Caravaning

✆ 04 94 82 03 28. www.esterel-caravaning.fr

Address : avenue des Golfs (situated 4km to the northwest)

Opening times : from end March to end Sept.

15 ha (495 pitches) terraced, relatively flat, flat, grassy, stony

Tariff : 60€ ★★ 🚗 ▣ ⚡ (16A) – Extra per person 12€ – Reservation fee 40€

Rental rates : (from end March to end Sept.) – 331 🏠. Per night from 24 to 460€ – Per week from 168 to 3,220€ – Reservation fee 40€

🚰 local sani-station 10€ – 🚿8€

There's an indoor pool for children and nursery, and luxury pitches with private jacuzzi, kitchenette and sanitary facilities.

Surroundings : 🐾 🏞 ⛰
Leisure activities : ▯ ✕ 🛶 🏄 🏊 🚴 ⛳ 🎣 ⛸ 🏊 🛶 🎿 disco, squash, multi-sports ground, spa centre, skate park
Facilities : 🔌 🛁 🍴 – 18 individual sanitary facilities (🚿 wc) launderette

G P S Longitude : 6.83256
Latitude : 43.45419

🏔🏔 Campéole Le Dramont 🔆

✆ 04 94 82 07 68. www.camping-mer.com

Address : 986 boulevard de la 36ème Division du Texas

Opening times : from beginning April to end Sept.

6.5 ha (374 pitches) undulating, flat, sandy, stony

Tariff : 26€ ★★ 🚗 ▣ ⚡ (10A) – Extra per person 10€ – Reservation fee 25€

Rental rates : (from beginning April to end Sept.) – 67 🏠 – 21 🏠 – 65 canvas bungalows. Per night from 42 to 231€ – Per week from 294 to 1,617€ – Reservation fee 25€

🚰 Raclet sani-station 7.50€

In a pleasant wood of pine trees, with pitches near the sea and rental accommodation of different standards.

Surroundings : 🐾 ⛰ ⚓
Leisure activities : ▯ ✕ 🛶 ⛳ 🏄 🏊 🛶 🎿 scuba diving, multi-sports ground
Facilities : 🔌 🛁 🍴 launderette 🚿

G P S Longitude : 6.84835
Latitude : 43.41782

🏔 Village Vacances Vallée du Paradis 🔆

(rental of mobile homes only)

✆ 04 94 82 16 00. www.camping-vallee-du-paradis.fr

Address : avenue du Gratadis (located 1km to the northwest; beside the Agay river)

Opening times : from mid March to mid Oct.

3 ha flat

Rental rates : 198 🏠. Per night from 45 to 232€ – Per week from 315 to 1,624€

A mobile home village beside the Agay river, bordered by a pontoon walkway.

Surroundings : ⟵ 🏞 ⚓
Leisure activities : ▯ ✕ 🛶 ⛳ 🏄 🎣 ⛸ 🛶 🎿 🏊
Facilities : 🔌 🛁 🍴 launderette 🚿
Nearby : ⚓

G P S Longitude : 6.85285
Latitude : 43.43546

🏔 Les Rives de l'Agay

✆ 04 94 82 02 74. www.lesrivesdelagay.com

Address : 575 avenue du Gratadis (700m to the northwest; beside the Agay and 500m from the beach)

Opening times : from mid March to beginning Nov.

2 ha (171 pitches) flat, grassy, sandy

Tariff : (2015 price) 48.60€ ★★ 🚗 ▣ ⚡ (6A) – Extra per person 8€ – Reservation fee 20€

Rental rates : (2015 price) (from mid March to beginning Nov.) – 43 🏠. Per night from 39 to 54€ – Per week from 349 to 1,009€ – Reservation fee 20€

Bordered by the river, with a pontoon walkway

Surroundings : 🏞 ⚓
Leisure activities : ✕ 🛶 🎣 🏊 scuba diving
Facilities : 🔌 🛁 🍴 🚿 launderette 🚿
Nearby : ⚓

G P S Longitude : 6.85263
Latitude : 43.43408

🏕 Agay-Soleil

✆ 04 94 82 00 79. www.agay-soleil.com

Address : 1152 boulevard de la Plage (700m east on the D 559, follow the signs for Cannes)

Opening times : from end March to beginning Nov.

0.7 ha (53 pitches) terraced, relatively flat, flat, sandy

Tariff : (2015 price) 35.50€ ★★ 🚗 ▣ ⚡ (10A) – Extra per person 6.50€ – Reservation fee 20€

Rental rates : (2015 price) permanent – 7 🏠 – 2 🏠 – 2 apartments. Per night from 60 to 120€ – Per week from 350 to 775€

🚰 local sani-station 10€

Surroundings : ⟵ 🏞 ⚓ ⛰
Leisure activities : ▯ ✕ 🛶
Facilities : 🔌 🛁 🍴 🚿

Nearby : watersports centre

G P S Longitude : 6.86822
Latitude : 43.43333

⛺ Royal-Camping

✆ 04 94 82 00 20. www.royalcamping.net

Address : rue Louise Robinson (located 1.5km west along the D 559, follow the signs for St Raphael and take turning to the left)

Opening times : from mid Feb. to mid Nov.

0.6 ha (45 pitches) flat, grassy, gravelled

Tariff : 36.50€ ✶✶ ⛘ ▣ Ⓗ (6A) – Extra per person 7€ – Reservation fee 20€

Rental rates : (from mid March to mid Nov.) – 9 ⛺. Per night from 50 to 100€ – Per week from 320 to 780€ – Reservation fee 20€

Surroundings : ♤♤ ⛰
Leisure activities : ⛱
Facilities : ⚷⬚⛴⛊
Nearby : ▨⛴♈✕⛾

GPS Longitude : 6.85707
Latitude : 43.42027

AIX-EN-PROVENCE

13100 – Michelin map **340** H4 – pop. 141 895 – alt. 206
▶ Paris 752 – Aubagne 39 – Avignon 82 – Manosque 57

🏔 Chantecler ♟♛

✆ 04 42 26 12 98. www.campingchantecler.com

Address : 41 avenue du Val-Saint-André (2.5km southeast, access via Cours Gambetta – from the A8, take exit 31 for Aix – Val-St-André)

Opening times : permanent

8 ha (240 pitches) undulating, terraced, flat, grassy, stony

Tariff : (2015 price) 28.10€ ✶✶ ⛘ ▣ Ⓗ (10A) –
Extra per person 7.50€

Rental rates : (2015 price) permanent ⛺ – 42 ⛺ – 10 ⌂.
Per night from 134 to 240 – Per week from 434 to 807

⛽ sani-station 5€

There's a view of Mont Ste-Victoire from some pitches.

Surroundings : ▱ ♤♤
Leisure activities : ♈✕⛱✸⛴⛴
Facilities : ⚷⚷⛴⛊⛊ launderette ⚓

GPS Longitude : 5.47416
Latitude : 43.51522

ANCELLE

05260 – Michelin map **334** F5 – pop. 854 – alt. 1 340 – Winter sports : 1 350/1 807 m
▶ Paris 665 – Gap 17 – Grenoble 103 – Orcières 18

🏔 Les Auches

✆ 04 92 50 80 28. www.lesauches.com

Address : Les Auches (take the northern exit following signs for Pont du Fossé and take turning to the right)

Opening times : from beginning April to end Oct.

2 ha (67 pitches) terraced, relatively flat, grassy

Tariff : (2015 price) 24.40€ ✶✶ ⛘ ▣ Ⓗ (6A) – Extra per person 4.80€
Rental rates : (2015 price) permanent ⚷ ⛺ – 12 ⛺ – 11 ⌂ –
2 studios – 1 apartment – 2 canvas bungalows. Per week from 259 to 686€ – Reservation fee 15€

⛽ local sani-station 15€

Surroundings : ⛰ ♤♤
Leisure activities : ✕⛱✸ jacuzzi ⛴⛴
Facilities : ⚷⚷⛴⛊ launderette

GPS Longitude : 6.21075
Latitude : 44.62435

APT

84400 – Michelin map **332** F10 – pop. 11 405 – alt. 250
▶ Paris 728 – Aix-en-Provence 56 – Avignon 54 – Carpentras 49

🏔 Le Lubéron

✆ 04 90 04 85 40. www.campingleluberon.com

Address : avenue de Saignon (situated 2km southeast along the D 48)

Opening times : from beginning April to end Sept.

5 ha (110 pitches) terraced, flat and relatively flat, grassy, fine gravel

Tariff : (2015 price) 21€ ✶✶ ⛘ ▣ Ⓗ (6A) – Extra per person 3.60€ –
Reservation fee 18€

Rental rates : (2015 price) (from beginning April to end Sept.) –
9 ⛺ – 19 ⌂ – 6 tent lodges – 2 gîtes. Per night from 33 to 106€ –
Per week from 231 to 740€ – Reservation fee 18€

⛽ local sani-station 2€ – ⛴15.49€

Surroundings : ⛰ ⛰♤♤
Leisure activities : ♈✕⛴⛴⛴
Facilities : ⚷⚷⛴⛊⛊ launderette

GPS Longitude : 5.41327
Latitude : 43.86632

⛺ Les Cèdres

✆ 04 90 74 14 61. www.camping-les-cedres.fr

Address : 63 Impasse de la Fantaisie (take northwestern exit off the D 22 towards Rustrel)

Opening times : from mid Feb. to mid Nov.

1.8 ha (75 pitches) terraced, flat and slightly flat, grassy, gravelled

Tariff : (2015 price) ✶ 2.90€ ⛘ 2.20€ ▣ 4€ – Ⓗ (10A) 3.60€
Rental rates : (2015 price) (from mid June to mid Sept.) – 4 canvas bungalows. Per night from 35 to 42 – Per week from 240 to 280

⛽ local sani-station 4€

Surroundings : ♀
Leisure activities : ⛱ ⛴ climbing wall
Facilities : ⚷⚷⛴⛊ ▣ refrigerators
Nearby : ⛴

GPS Longitude : 5.4013
Latitude : 43.87765

L'ARGENTIÈRE-LA-BESSÉE

05120 – Michelin map **334** H4 – pop. 2 328 – alt. 1 024
▶ Paris 696 – Briançon 17 – Embrun 33 – Gap 74

⛺ Municipal Les Écrins

✆ 04 92 23 03 38. www.camping-les-ecrins.com

Address : avenue Pierre Sainte (head 2.3km south along the N 94, follow the signs for Gap, and take D 104 to the right)

Opening times : from mid April to mid Sept.

3 ha (71 pitches) flat, grassy, stony

Tariff : (2015 price) 18.80€ ✶✶ ⛘ ▣ Ⓗ (10A) –
Extra per person 5.20€ – Reservation fee 3€

Rental rates : (2015 price) (from mid May to mid Sept.) – 4 canvas bungalows. Per night from 40 to 65€ – Per week from 220 to 445€

⛽ AireService sani-station 2€ – 1 ▣ 10€ – ⛴Ⓗ17€

A young and sporty crowd comes here for the numerous whitewater activities.

Surroundings : ⛰ ▱♀
Leisure activities : ⛱ ⛴✂⛴
Facilities : ⚷⚷⛴⛊⛊⚓
Nearby : ⛴⛴⛴ (river), rafting and canyoning

GPS Longitude : 6.55823
Latitude : 44.77687

ARLES

13200 – Michelin map **340** C3 – pop. 52 439 – alt. 13
▶ Paris 719 – Aix-en-Provence 77 – Avignon 37 – Cavaillon 44
West : 14 km via N 572 rte de St-Gilles and D 37 on the left

⚠️ Crin Blanc ♣♣

📞 04 66 87 48 78. www.camping-crin-blanc.com

Address : southwest of Saliers hamlet, off the D 37)

Opening times : from beginning April to end Sept.

4.5 ha (170 pitches)

Tariff : 19€ ★★ ⇌ 🗐 (6) (10A) – Extra per person 5.50€ – Reservation fee 10€

Rental rates : (from beginning April to end Sept.) – 120 🚐. Per night from 60 to 85€ – Per week from 150 to 920€ – Reservation fee 19€

Surroundings : 🗺	
Leisure activities : 🍹 🗙 🏠 🎣 🏃 ⚓ 🛶 🛶	**G P S**
Facilities : ♿ ☕ 🛁 🚿 🚽 🍴 launderette 🖰 🚿	Longitude : 4.47392
Nearby : 🐎	Latitude : 43.66149

AUBIGNAN

84810 – Michelin map **332** D9 – pop. 4 861 – alt. 65
▶ Paris 675 – Avignon 31 – Carpentras 7 – Orange 21

⚠️ Le Brégoux

📞 04 90 62 62 50. www.camping-lebregoux.fr

Address : 410 chemin du Vas (800m southeast along the D 55, follow the signs for Caromb and take road to the right.)

Opening times : from beginning March to end Oct.

3.5 ha (170 pitches) flat, grassy

Tariff : ★ 4.20€ ⇌ 🗐 4.10€ – (6) (10A) 4.10€

Rental rates : (from mid March to end Oct.) – 5 🚐. Per week from 340 to 575€

Surroundings : 🌿	
Leisure activities : 🏠 ⚓ 🛶 🎾	**G P S**
Facilities : ☕ 🗄 🚿 🍴 launderette	Longitude : 5.03609
	Latitude : 44.09808

AURIBEAU-SUR-SIAGNE

06810 – Michelin map **341** C6 – pop. 2 945 – alt. 85
▶ Paris 900 – Cannes 15 – Draguignan 62 – Grasse 9

⚠️ Le Parc des Monges

📞 04 93 60 91 71. www.parcdesmonges.com

Address : 635 chemin du Gabre (head 1.4km northwest along the D 509, follow the signs for Tanneron)

Opening times : from end April to end Sept.

1.3 ha (55 pitches) terraced, flat, grassy, stony

Tariff : ★ 6.10€ ⇌ 4€ 🗐 32€ – (6) (10A) 6.50€

Rental rates : (from end April to end Sept.) 🎾 – 7 🚐 – 8 🏠. Per week from 300 to 800€

🚐 local sani-station 7€ – 🛁 (6)18€

Beside the Siagne river, with pitches marked out by oleanders.

Surroundings : 🌿 🗺	
Leisure activities : jacuzzi 🛶	**G P S**
Facilities : ♿ ☕ 🗄 🛁 🚿 🚽 🍴 🖰	Longitude : 6.90252
Nearby : 🍹 🗙 ⚓ 🛶	Latitude : 43.60659

AVIGNON

84000 – Michelin map **332** B10 – pop. 89 592 – alt. 21
▶ Paris 682 – Aix-en-Provence 82 – Arles 37 – Marseille 98

⚠️ Aquadis Loisirs Le Pont d'Avignon

📞 04 90 80 63 50. http://www.aquadis-loisirs.com/camping-du-pont-d-avignon

Address : 10 chemin de la Barthelasse (take northwestern exit, follow the signs for Villeneuve-lès-Avignon across the Édouard-Daladier bridge and take a right turn, on the Île-de-la-Barthelasse)

Opening times : from end Feb. to end Nov.

8 ha (300 pitches) flat, grassy, gravelled

Tariff : 31€ ★★ ⇌ 🗐 (6) (10A) – Extra per person 5.80€ – Reservation fee 10€

Rental rates : (from end Feb. to end Nov.) – 10 🚐 – 14 canvas bungalows. Per night from 35 to 58€ – Per week from 200 to 840€ – Reservation fee 20€

🚐 AireService sani-station 5€ – 35 🗐 15€

Surroundings : 🗺 🌳	
Leisure activities : 🍹 🗙 🏠 ⚓ 🎾 🛶	**G P S**
Facilities : ♿ ☕ 🗄 🍴 launderette 🖰 🚿	Longitude : 4.7971
	Latitude : 43.95331

BARATIER

05200 – Michelin map **334** G4 – pop. 511 – alt. 855
▶ Paris 704 – Marseille 214 – Gap 39 – Digne 90

⚠️ Les Airelles

📞 04 92 43 11 57. www.lesairelles.com

Address : route des Orres (1.2km southeast along the D 40, follow the signs for Les Orres and take turning to the right)

Opening times : from mid June to mid Sept.

5 ha/4 for camping (130 pitches) terraced, flat and relatively flat, grassy, stony

Tariff : (2015 price) ★ 7.30€ ⇌ 🗐 8.50€ – (6) (10A) 5€

Rental rates : (2015 price) (from mid June to mid Sept.) – 8 'gypsy' caravans – 16 🚐 – 32 🏠 – 5 tent lodges. Per night from 80 to 200€ – Per week from 320 to 895€

Surroundings : 🌿 ≤ 🌳	
Leisure activities : 🍹 🗙 🏠 🎣 daytime ⚓ 🛶 multi-sports ground	**G P S**
Facilities : ♿ ☕ 🛁 🍴 launderette	Longitude : 6.50164
	Latitude : 44.5291

⚠️ Le Verger

📞 06 81 93 06 15. www.campingleverger.fr – limited spaces for one-night stay

Address : chemin de Jouglar (take the western exit; recommended route for caravans is via the village)

Opening times : permanent

4.3 ha/2.5 for camping (110 pitches) terraced, relatively flat, flat, grassy, stony

Tariff : 19€ ★★ ⇌ 🗐 (6) (10A) – Extra per person 6€ – Reservation fee 14€

Rentals : permanent – 14 gîtes.

Surroundings : 🌿 🗺 🌳	
Leisure activities : 🍹 🗙 🏠 🛶	**G P S**
Facilities : ☕ 🗄 🛁 🍴	Longitude : 6.49143
Nearby : 🎾 🏇 🛶	Latitude : 44.5374

⚠ **Les Deux Bois**

☏ 04 92 43 54 14. www.camping-les2bois.com

Address : route de Pra Fouran (access to the town along the D 204)

Opening times : from mid May to end Sept.

2.5 ha (100 pitches) terraced, sloping, flat, grassy, stony

Tariff : (2015 price) 23.10€ ♣♣ ⇔ 🔲 ⚡ (10A) –
Extra per person 5.70€ – Reservation fee 15€

Rental rates : (2015 price) permanent 🅿 – 4 ⛺. Per night
from 79 to 95€ – Per week from 390 to 670€

🚐 local sani-station

High-quality mobile home accommodation; open all year.

Surroundings : 🌳 🎿	**G**	Longitude : 6.49207
Leisure activities : 🍴✗ 🚴⛷	**P**	Latitude : 44.53837
Facilities : ⚐ ⚐ 🏛 🚿 🏠 🚐	**S**	
Nearby : ✗ 🏇		

⚠ **Les Grillons**

☏ 04 92 43 32 75. www.lesgrillons.com

Address : route de la Madeleine (located 1km north along the D 40,
D 340 and take road to the left)

Opening times : from mid May to mid Sept.

1.5 ha (95 pitches) relatively flat, grassy, stony

Tariff : (2015 price) 23.10€ ♣♣ ⇔ 🔲 ⚡ (16A) –
Extra per person 5.80€ – Reservation fee 10€

Rental rates : (2015 price) (from mid May to mid Sept.) – 16 ⛺ –
3 ⛺ – 3 tent lodges. Per night from 59 to 89€ – Per week
from 280 to 724€ – Reservation fee 13€

Surroundings : 🌳 🎿	**G**	Longitude : 6.49755
Leisure activities : ✗ ⛷	**P**	Latitude : 44.54689
Facilities : ⚐ ⚐ 🏠 🚿 launderette	**S**	

Michelin classification:

⚠⚠⚠⚠ *Extremely comfortable, equipped to a very high
standard*

⚠⚠⚠ *Very comfortable, equipped to a high standard*

⚠⚠ *Comfortable and well equipped*

⚠ *Reasonably comfortable*

⚠ *Satisfactory*

BARRET-SUR-MÉOUGE

05300 – Michelin map **334** C7 – pop. 220 – alt. 640
▶ Paris 700 – Laragne-Montéglin 14 – Sault 46 – Séderon 21

⚠ **Les Gorges de la Méouge**

☏ 04 92 65 08 47. www.camping-meouge.com

Address : at Le Serre (take the eastern exit along the D 942, follow
the signs for Laragne-Montéglin and take the road to the right, near
the Méouge river)

3 ha (115 pitches) flat, grassy

Rentals : 13 ⛺.

🚐 local sani-station

Surroundings : 🌳 🎿	**G**	Longitude : 5.73822
Leisure activities : 🎠 ⛷	**P**	Latitude : 44.26078
Facilities : ⚐ ⚐ 🏠 🚿 🔧 🚿 🔲	**S**	

LE BAR-SUR-LOUP

06620 – Michelin map **341** C5 – pop. 2 805 – alt. 320
▶ Paris 916 – Cannes 22 – Grasse 10 – Nice 31

⚠ **Les Gorges du Loup**

☏ 04 93 42 45 06. www.lesgorgesduloup.com

Address : 965 chemin des Vergers (1km northeast along the D 2210)

Opening times : from beginning April to end Sept.

1.6 ha (70 pitches) very uneven, terraced, flat, grassy, stony

Tariff : (2015 price) 28.60€ ♣♣ ⇔ 🔲 ⚡ (6A) – Extra per person 6€ –
Reservation fee 15€

Rental rates : (2015 price) (from beginning April to end Sept.) –
5 ⛺ – 10 ⛺ – 1 apartment. Per week from 370 to 750€ –
Reservation fee 15€

*Small terraces, many shaded by centuries-old olive trees, with
some pitches enjoying a view of the Gorges du Loup.*

Surroundings : 🌳 ← 🏕 🎿	**G**	Longitude : 6.99527
Leisure activities : 🏠 🚴⛷	**P**	Latitude : 43.70183
Facilities : ⚐ ⚐ 🅿 🚿 🔧 🚿 🚐	**S**	

BEAUMES-DE-VENISE

84190 – Michelin map **332** D9 – pop. 2 283 – alt. 100
▶ Paris 666 – Avignon 34 – Nyons 39 – Orange 23

⚠ **Municipal de Roquefiguier**

☏ 04 90 62 95 07. www.mairie-de-beaumes-de-venise – ▣

Address : route de Lafare (take the northern exit along the D 90,
follow the signs for Malaucène and take a right turn; beside the
Salette river)

Opening times : from beginning March to end Oct.

1.5 ha (63 pitches) terraced, relatively flat, grassy, stony

Tariff : (2015 price) ♣ 2.95€ ⇔ 2€ 🔲 3.56€ – ⚡ (16A) 3.40€

Surroundings : ← 🏕 🎿	**G**	Longitude : 5.03448
Leisure activities : 🚴⛷ 🏇	**P**	Latitude : 44.12244
Facilities : ⚐ ⚐ 🏠 🚿 🔲 refrigerators	**S**	
Nearby : ✗		

BEAUMONT-DU-VENTOUX

84340 – Michelin map **332** E8 – pop. 317 – alt. 360
▶ Paris 676 – Avignon 48 – Carpentras 21 – Nyons 28

⚠ **Mont-Serein**

☏ 04 90 60 49 16. www.camping-ventoux.com – alt. 1 400

Address : at the Mont-Serein ski resort (20km east along the D 974
and take the D 164a, r. du Mont-Ventoux via Malaucène)

Opening times : permanent

1.2 ha (60 pitches) flat, stony, grassy

Tariff : ♣ 9€ ⇔ 🔲 – ⚡ (16A) 5€

Rental rates : permanent – 8 ⛺ – 3 cabins in the trees. Per night
from 16€ – Per week from 112 to 650€

🚐 30 🔲 9€

In an attractive elevated location.

Surroundings : 🌳 ← Mont Ventoux and the Alps 🏕	**G**	Longitude : 5.25898
Leisure activities : 🏠 ♨ jacuzzi	**P**	Latitude : 44.1811
Facilities : ⚐ 🏛 🚿 🔧 🔲 🚿	**S**	

BÉDOIN

84410 – Michelin map **332** E9 – pop. 3 132 – alt. 295
▶ Paris 692 – Avignon 43 – Carpentras 16 – Vaison-la-Romaine 21

⚠ Municipal la Pinède

✆ 04 90 65 61 03. camping.municipal@bedoin.fr

Address : chemin des Sablières (take the western exit following signs for Crillon-le-Brave and take the road to the right, next to the municipal swimming pool)

Opening times : from mid March to end Oct.

6 ha (121 pitches) terraced, stony, grassy

Tariff : (2015 price) 15€ ✶✶ ⮞ 🔲 🚰 (16A) – Extra per person 3.40€

Rental rates : (2015 price) (from mid March to end Oct.) – 3 🏠. Per week from 290 to 470€

🚗 10 🔲 15€

Surroundings : 🟡🟡	
Facilities : 🚻 ⛲ 🚿 🍽 🔲	**Longitude :** 5.17261
Nearby : 🍴 🛶	**Latitude :** 44.12486

To visit a town or region, use the MICHELIN Green Guides.

BOLLÈNE

84500 – Michelin map **332** B8 – pop. 13 885 – alt. 40
▶ Paris 634 – Avignon 53 – Montélimar 34 – Nyons 35

⚠ La Simioune

✆ 04 90 63 17 91. www.la-simioune.fr

Address : Guffiage district (5km northeast following signs for Lambisque – access on the D 8 along the old road to Suze-la-Rousse following the Lez – and take road to the left)

Opening times : from beginning March to end Nov.

2 ha (80 pitches) terraced, flat, sandy

Tariff : 23.50€ ✶✶ ⮞ 🔲 🚰 (10A) – Extra per person 5€

Rental rates : (from beginning March to end Nov.) 🚐 – 8 🛖 – 3 🏠. Per night from 50 to 90€ – Per week from 200 to 800€

Pitches in both sun and shade in a pine forest.

Surroundings : 🌄 🟡🟡	
Leisure activities : 🍴 🛶 🐴	**Longitude :** 4.74848
Facilities : 🚻 ⛲ 🚿 🍽 🔲 🛒	**Latitude :** 44.28203

BONNIEUX

84480 – Michelin map **332** E11 – pop. 1 424 – alt. 400
▶ Paris 721 – Aix-en-Provence 49 – Apt 12 – Cavaillon 27

⚠ Le Vallon

✆ 04 90 75 86 14. www.campinglevallon.com

Address : route de Ménerbes (take the southern exit along the D 3 and turn off left)

Opening times : from mid March to mid Oct.

1.3 ha (80 pitches) terraced, flat, grassy, stony, wood

Tariff : 24€ ✶✶ ⮞ 🔲 🚰 (10A) – Extra per person 4.50€ – Reservation fee 10€

Rental rates : permanent 🚐 – 1 'gypsy' caravan – 1 🛖 – 3 yurts – 5 canvas bungalows. Per night from 55 to 70€ – Per week from 350 to 395€

Surroundings : 🌄 🔲 🟡	
Facilities : ⛲ 🚿 🍽 🔲	**Longitude :** 5.22838
Nearby : 🏇 🍴	**Latitude :** 43.81881

BORMES-LES-MIMOSAS

83230 – Michelin map **340** N7 – pop. 7 321 – alt. 180
▶ Paris 871 – Fréjus 57 – Hyères 21 – Le Lavandou 4

⚠ Le Camp du Domaine 👥

✆ 04 94 71 03 12. www.campdudomaine.com

Address : at La Favière, 2581 route de Bénat (situated 2km to the south, near the port)

Opening times : from mid March to end Oct.

38 ha (1300 pitches) very uneven, terraced, flat, stony, rocks

Tariff : (2015 price) 54€ ✶✶ ⮞ 🔲 🚰 (16A) – Extra per person 12€ – Reservation fee 27€

Rental rates : (2015 price) (from mid March to end Oct.) 🚐 – 50 🛖 – 125 🏠. Per night from 140€ – Per week from 567 to 1,330€ – Reservation fee 27€

🚗 local sani-station – 150 🔲 35€

An exclusive site on an undulating, wooded peninsula close to the beach. Excursions organised out of season

Surroundings : 🌄 🔲 🟡🟡 ⛰	
Leisure activities : 🍴 🍴 🎦 🗖 🏕 🛶 🚴 🎣 🏓 🐾 multi-sports ground	
Facilities : 🚻 ⛲ ⛲ 🚿 🛒 🚰 🍽 launderette ⛲ 🛒 refrigerated food storage facilities	**Longitude :** 6.35129 **Latitude :** 43.11788
Nearby : 🛶 ⚓ pedalos, water skiing	

⚠ Manjastre

✆ 04 94 71 03 28. www.campingmanjastre.com 🚐

Address : 150 chemin des Girolles (5km northwest on the N 98, follow the signs for Cogolin)

Opening times : permanent

3.5 ha (120 pitches) terraced, flat and relatively flat, stony

Tariff : 36.50€ ✶✶ ⮞ 🔲 🚰 (10A) – Extra per person 6.90€ – Reservation fee 15.50€

🚗 local sani-station 6.50€ – 8 🔲 18.50€

An attractive arrangement of terraces among mimosas and cork oaks.

Surroundings : 🌄 🔲 🟡🟡	
Leisure activities : 🍴 🍴 🏕 🛶 🛶	
Facilities : 🚻 ⛲ 🔲 📼 🎦 🚿 🍽 🚰 launderette 🛒	**Longitude :** 6.32153 **Latitude :** 43.16258

We have selected the best campsites in France with our usual care, listing those with the best facilities in the most pleasant surroundings.

BRIANÇON

05100 – Michelin map **334** H2 – pop. 11 574 – alt. 1 321 – Winter sports : 1 200/2 800 m
▶ Paris 681 – Digne-les-Bains 145 – Embrun 48 – Grenoble 89

⚠ Les 5 Vallées

✆ 04 92 21 06 27. www.camping5vallees.com

Address : at St-Blaise (situated 2km south along the N 94)

Opening times : from end May to end Sept.

5 ha (180 pitches) flat, grassy, stony

Tariff : (2015 price) ✶ 7.90€ ⮞ 2.90€ 🔲 4.90€ – 🚰 (10A) 4.70€

Rental rates : (2015 price) (from mid Dec. to end Sept.) – 31 🚐.
Per night from 60 to 112€ – Per week from 614 to 785€ –
Reservation fee 60€

🚐 Eurorelais sani-station 5€

Surroundings : 🏖
Leisure activities : 🏛 🚴 🎣
Facilities : ♿ ⚡ 🚿 🍴 launderette 🔌 🚰
Nearby : 🎣

GPS Longitude : 6.69323
Latitude : 45.11898

CADENET

84160 – Michelin map **332** F11 – pop. 4 061 – alt. 170
▶ Paris 734 – Aix-en-Provence 33 – Apt 23 – Avignon 63

⛰ Homair Vacances Val de Durance

📞 0490683775. www.homair.com

Address : 570 avenue du Club Hippique (2.7km southwest along the
D 943, follow the signs for Aix, turn right onto D 59 and take road to
the left)

10 ha/2.4 for camping (232 pitches) flat, grassy, stony

Rentals : 220 🚐.

Located beside a lake and 300m from the Durance river.

Surroundings : 🏖 ← 🚐
Leisure activities : 🍴 🍽 🏛 daytime 🎿
🚴 🎣 multi-sports ground
Facilities : ♿ ⚡ 🚿 🚻 🍴 🔌 🚰

GPS Longitude : 5.35515
Latitude : 43.71957

Key to rentals symbols:

12 🚐   *Number of mobile homes*
20 🏠   *Number of chalets*
6 🛏   *Number of rooms to rent*
*Per night
30–50€*   *Minimum/maximum rate per night*
*Per week
300–1,000€*   *Minimum/maximum rate per week*

CAGNES-SUR-MER

06800 – Michelin map **341** D6 – pop. 48 024 – alt. 20
▶ Paris 915 – Antibes 11 – Cannes 21 – Grasse 25

⛰ La Rivière

📞 0493206227. www.campinglariviere06.fr

Address : 168 chemin des Salles (3.5km to the north; beside the
Cagne river)

Opening times : from beginning April to end Sept.

1.2 ha (90 pitches) flat, grassy, gravel

Tariff : 26.50€ ✚✚ 🚗 回 (6A) – Extra per person 4€

Rental rates : (from beginning April to end Sept.) 🚫 – 4 🚐.
Per week from 240 to 430€

The campsite has few mobile homes.

Surroundings : 🏖 🚐
Leisure activities : ✗ 🏛 🚴 🎣
Facilities : ♿ ⚡ 🚿 🚻 🍴 🔌 🚰

GPS Longitude : 7.14283
Latitude : 43.69581

⛺ Le Colombier

📞 0493731277. www.campinglecolombier.com 🚫

Address : 35 chemin Sainte Colombe (head 2km north along the
route de Vence, left off this road)

Opening times : from beginning April to end Sept.

0.5 ha (33 pitches) flat and relatively flat, grassy, gravelled

Tariff : 32€ ✚✚ 🚗 回 (6A) – Extra per person 6€ – Reservation
fee 8€

Rentals : (from beginning April to end Sept.) 🚫 – 1 studio.

🚐 local sani-station

*The sanitary facilities are rather old and weak. The swimming
pool is on the other side of the road.*

Surroundings : 🏖 🚐 🌳
Leisure activities : 🏛 🎣 (small swimming
pool)
Facilities : ♿ ⚡ 🚿 🍴 launderette
refrigerators

GPS Longitude : 7.13893
Latitude : 43.67107

CALLAS

83830 – Michelin map **340** O4 – pop. 1 813 – alt. 398
▶ Paris 872 – Castellane 51 – Draguignan 14 – Toulon 94

⛰ Les Blimouses

📞 0494478341. www.campinglesblimouses.com

Address : Les Blimouses (3km south along the D 25 and take D 225,
follow the signs for Draguignan)

Opening times : permanent

6 ha (170 pitches) terraced, flat and relatively flat, grassy, stony

Tariff : 31€ ✚✚ 🚗 回 (10A) – Extra per person 4€ – Reservation
fee 20€

Rental rates : (from beginning March to mid Dec.) – 35 🚐 –
7 🏠. Per night from 65 to 80€ – Per week from 250 to 890€ –
Reservation fee 20€

🚐 AireService sani-station 8€ – 2 回 16€ – 🚗8€

Shaded pitches with many owner-occupiers.

Surroundings : 🏖 🚐 🌳
Leisure activities : ✗ 🚴 🎣 🎿
Facilities : ♿ ⚡ 🚿 🍴 🔌 🚰

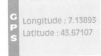
G P S Longitude : 6.53242
Latitude : 43.57456

CANNES

06400 – Michelin map **341** D6 – pop. 73 372 – alt. 2
▶ Paris 898 – Aix-en-Provence 149 – Marseille 160 – Nice 33

⛰ Le Parc Bellevue

📞 0493472897. www.parcbellevue.com

Address : at La Bocca, 67 avenue Maurice Chevalier (to the north,
near the municipal stadium)

Opening times : from beginning April to end Sept.

5 ha (250 pitches) very uneven, terraced, flat, grassy, gravelled

Tariff : 30€ ✚✚ 🚗 回 (6A) – Extra per person 4.25€

Rental rates : (from beginning April to end Sept.) – 50 🚐.
Per week from 255 to 765€

🚐 local sani-station – 80 回 26€

*In a shaded setting, but choose the pitches away from the road
in preference.*

Surroundings : 🚐 🌳
Leisure activities : ✗ 🏛 🚴 🎣
Facilities : ♿ ⚡ 🚿 🍴 🚰

G P S Longitude : 6.96042
Latitude : 43.55617

LE CANNET

06110 – Michelin map **341** C6 – pop. 41 725 – alt. 80
▶ Paris 909 – Marseille 180 – Nice 39 – Monaco 54

⚠ Le Ranch

🔗 04 93 46 00 11. www.leranchcamping.fr

Address : at Aubarède, chemin St. Joseph (located 1.5km northwest along the D 9 then take bd. de l'Esterel to the right)

Opening times : from mid April to mid Oct.

2 ha (128 pitches) terraced, relatively flat, flat, grassy, stony

Tariff : (2015 price) ∗ 7 € ⇔ 3 € 🔲 22 € ⚡ (6A) – Reservation fee 15 €
Rental rates : (2015 price) (from mid April to mid Oct.) – 2 'gypsy' caravans – 15 🛖 – 5 🏠 – 2 ⌂ – 1 studio. Per week from 250 to 730 € – Reservation fee 15 €

🚐 AireService sani-station 5 €

In an urban zone; choose pitches furthest away from the road.

Surroundings : 🏕 ♨♨	**G** Longitude : 6.97698
Leisure activities : 🏊 ⚓ 🔲 (open air in season)	**P** Latitude : 43.56508
Facilities : ♿ 🚿 ∭ 🔥 🍴 launderette 🧺	**S**

CARPENTRAS

84200 – Michelin map **332** D9 – pop. 29 271 – alt. 102
▶ Paris 679 – Avignon 30 – Cavaillon 28 – Orange 24

⚠ Flower Municipal Lou Comtadou

🔗 04 90 67 03 16. www.campingloucomtadou.com

Address : 881 avenue Pierre de Coubertin (located 1.5km southeast along the D 4, follow the signs for St-Didier and take turning to the right, near the sports centre)

Opening times : from beginning March to end Oct.

1 ha (99 pitches) flat, grassy, stony, small lake

Tariff : (2015 price) 17.50 € ∗∗ ⇔ 🔲 ⚡ (6A) – Extra per person 4.50 € – Reservation fee 10 €
Rental rates : (2015 price) (from beginning March to end Oct.) – 24 🛖 – 2 canvas bungalows – 3 tent lodges. Per night from 33 to 124 € – Per week from 165 to 868 € – Reservation fee 15 €

🚐 local sani-station

Surroundings : 🏕 ♨♨	**G** Longitude : 5.05429
Leisure activities : 🏊 ⚓	**P** Latitude : 44.04417
Facilities : ♿ 🚿 🔥 🧺 🍴 🔲	**S**
Nearby : 🎿 🏊	

CARRO

13500 – Michelin map **340** F6
▶ Paris 787 – Marseille 44 – Aix-en-Provence 51 – Martigues 13

⚠ Yelloh! Village Les Chalets de la Mer

(rental of chalets only)

🔗 04 42 80 73 46. www.semovim-martigues.com

Address : rue de la Tramontane

3 ha flat

Rentals : ♿ (8 chalets) – 78 🏠.

Around 20 of the chalets offer accommodation on a hotel-style basis, with half board available.

Surroundings : 🌊 🏕 ♨♨	**G** Longitude : 5.04117
Leisure activities : 🍴 ✕ 🔲 🏙 nighttime 🏃 🎰 🍹 ⚓ 🏊	**P** Latitude : 43.33291
Facilities : 🚿 🍴 launderette 🧺	**S**

CASTELLANE

04120 – Michelin map **334** H9 – pop. 1 553 – alt. 730
▶ Paris 797 – Digne-les-Bains 54 – Draguignan 59 – Grasse 64

⚠ Les Castels Le Domaine du Verdon 👥

🔗 04 92 83 61 29. www.camp-du-verdon.com

Address : at Domaine de la Salaou (2km southwest along the D 952, follow signs for Moustier-Ste-Marie)

Opening times : from mid May to mid Sept.

9 ha (500 pitches) flat, grassy

Tariff : 49 € ∗∗ ⇔ 🔲 ⚡ (16A) – Extra per person 14 € – Reservation fee 20 €
Rental rates : (from mid May to mid Sept.) ♿ (1 mobile home) – 150 🛖. Per night from 52 to 159 € – Per week from 364 to 1,113 € – Reservation fee 20 €

🚐 Flot Bleu sani-station

The rental options are good, but the sanitary facilities for tents and caravans are basic or even delapidated.

Surroundings : 🏕 ♨♨	
Leisure activities : 🍹 ✕ 🔲 🏙 🏃 ⚓ 🚲 🏊 🎣 🏊 🎿 entertainment room	**G** Longitude : 6.49402
Facilities : ♿ 🚿 🔥 🍴 launderette 🧺 🧺 refrigerated food storage facilities	**P** Latitude : 43.83895
Nearby : rafting and canyoning	**S**

⚠ RCN Les Collines de Castellane 👥

🔗 04 92 83 68 96. www.rcn.fr/collinesdecastellane – pitches accessed via steep slope, help moving caravans onto and off pitches avilable on request – alt. 1 000

Address : route de Grasse (7km southeast along the N 85; at La Garde)

7 ha (200 pitches) terraced, relatively flat, stony, flat, grassy, wood

Rentals : 36 🛖 – 4 🏠 – 4 tent lodges.

Surroundings : 🌄 < 🏕 ♨♨	
Leisure activities : 🍹 ✕ 🔲 🏃 ⚓ 🎿 ✂ 🎰 🏊 🏊 forest trail	**G** Longitude : 6.56994
Facilities : ♿ 🚿 🔥 🧺 🌳 🍴 launderette 🧺 🧺 refrigerators	**P** Latitude : 43.8244
	S

⚠ Calme et Nature La Colle

🔗 04 92 83 61 57. www.campingcastellane.com

Address : La Colle (2.5km southwest along the D 952, follow the signs for Moustiers-Ste-Marie and take a right turn – GR 4)

Opening times : permanent

3 ha/1.5 (41 pitches) very uneven, terraced, flat and relatively flat, grassy, stony

Tariff : 24 € ∗∗ ⇔ 🔲 ⚡ (10A) – Extra per person 6 €
Rental rates : (2015 price) permanent – 12 🛖 – 2 🏠. Per night from 43 to 48 € – Per week from 580 €

The site is laid out in terraces and is crossed by a small stream.

Surroundings : 🌄 🏕 ♨♨	**G** Longitude : 6.49312
Leisure activities : 🍹 ✕ 🐴 small petting zoo	**P** Latitude : 43.83864
Facilities : ♿ 🚿 🌳 🍴 🔲	**S**

The Michelin classification (⚠⚠⚠ ... ⚠) is totally independent of the official star classification system awarded by the local prefecture or other official organisation.

⚞ Notre-Dame

☏ 04 92 83 63 02. www.camping-notredame.com

Address : route des Gorges du Verdon (500m southwest along the D 952, follow the signs for Moustiers-Ste-Marie; beside a stream)

Opening times : from beginning April to mid Oct.

0.6 ha (44 pitches) flat, grassy

Tariff : 24.50€ ✶✶ 🚗 ▤ ⚡ (6A) – Extra per person 6.10€ – Reservation fee 9€

Rental rates : (from beginning April to mid Oct.) ⚓ – 11 🚐. Per night from 47 to 99€ – Per week from 330 to 630€

🚽 local sani-station 6€ – 6 ▤ 13€ – ♨ 11€

Located at the entrance to the village, near the road.

Surroundings : 💧💧	
Leisure activities : 🎣	**GPS** Longitude : 6.50425
Facilities : ♿ ⚡ 🚿 🕎 launderette	Latitude : 43.84545

Nearby : adventure park

This guide is not intended as a list of all the camping sites in France; its aim is to provide a selection of the best sites in each category.

CAVALAIRE-SUR-MER

83240 – Michelin map **340** O6 – pop. 6 731 – alt. 2
▶ Paris 880 – Draguignan 55 – Fréjus 41 – Le Lavandou 21

⚞ Cros de Mouton

☏ 04 94 64 10 87. www.crosdemouton.com – pitches accessed via steep slope, help moving caravans onto and off pitches avilable on request

Address : chemin du Cros de Mouton (located 1.5km to the northwest)

Opening times : from mid March to end Oct.

5 ha (199 pitches) very uneven, terraced, flat, stony

Tariff : (2015 price) ♦ 9.80€ 🚗 ▤ 9.80€ – ⚡ (10A) 5.40€ – Reservation fee 20€

Rental rates : (2015 price) (from mid March to end Oct.) – 65 🚐 – 9 🏠. Per night from 85 to 130€ – Per week from 720 to 1,060€ – Reservation fee 20€

Pitches on a hill with a panoramic view of the sea from some of them and from the restaurant terrace.

Surroundings : 💧 ⬕ Baie de Cavalaire ⬚ 💧💧	
Leisure activities : 🍴 ✗ 🛁 jacuzzi 🏄 🏊 ⛷	**GPS** Longitude : 6.51662
Facilities : ♿ ⚡ 🚿 🕎 ▤ 🏊	Latitude : 43.18243

CEILLAC

05600 – Michelin map **334** I4 – pop. 307 – alt. 1 640 – Winter sports : 1 700/2 500 m
▶ Paris 729 – Briançon 50 – Gap 75 – Guillestre 14

⚞ Les Mélèzes

☏ 04 92 45 21 93. www.campingdeceillac.com

Address : at La Rua des Reynauds (1.8km southeast)

Opening times : from beginning June to beginning Sept.

3 ha (100 pitches) very uneven, terraced, relatively flat, stony, grassy

Tariff : ♦ 6.80€ 🚗 ▤ 7.20€ – ⚡ (10A) 5€

A pleasant campsite and location, beside the Mélezet river.

Surroundings : 💧 ⬕ 💧	
Leisure activities : 🏄	**GPS** Longitude : 6.78843
Facilities : ⚡ 🏊 🚿 🕎 ▤	Latitude : 44.65389

CHÂTEAUNEUF-DE-GADAGNE

84470 – Michelin map **332** C10 – pop. 3 249 – alt. 90
▶ Paris 701 – Marseille 95 – Avignon 14 – Nîmes 58

⚞ Le Fontisson

☏ 04 90 22 59 77. www.campingfontisson.com

Address : 1125 route d'Avignon (D 901) (western side of Chateauneuf-de-Gadagne)

Opening times : from beginning April to beginning Oct.

2 ha (55 pitches) relatively flat, grassy, stony

Tariff : (2015 price) 28.30€ ✶✶ 🚗 ▤ ⚡ (10A) – Extra per person 7.50€ – Reservation fee 10€

Rental rates : (2015 price) (from beginning April to beginning Oct.) – 19 🚐 – 4 canvas bungalows. Per night from 100 to 195€ – Per week from 190 to 860€ – Reservation fee 15€

🚽 local sani-station 23€

Surroundings : 💧 ⬚ 💧💧	
Leisure activities : 🏠 🏄 ✗ 🎿 🏊 multi-sports ground	**GPS** Longitude : 4.93297
Facilities : ♿ ⚡ 🏊 🕎 ▤	Latitude : 43.92846

CHÂTEAURENARD

13160 – Michelin map **340** E2 – pop. 14 971 – alt. 37
▶ Paris 692 – Avignon 10 – Carpentras 37 – Cavaillon 23

⚞ La Roquette

☏ 04 90 94 46 81. www.camping-la-roquette.com

Address : 745 avenue Jean-Mermoz (located 1.5km east along the D 28, follow the signs for Noves and take a right turn, near the swimming pool – from A 7 take exit Avignon-Sud)

Opening times : from beginning April to mid Oct.

2 ha (74 pitches) flat, grassy

Tariff : ♦ 7€ 🚗 2€ ▤ 22€ – ⚡ (10A) 4€ – Reservation fee 12€

Rental rates : (from beginning April to mid Oct.) – 14 🚐. Per night from 38 to 120€ – Per week from 267 to 845€ – Reservation fee 12€

Surroundings : ⬚ 💧	
Leisure activities : 🍴 ✗ 🏄 🏊	**GPS** Longitude : 4.87017
Facilities : ♿ ⚡ 🏊 🕎 ▤	Latitude : 43.88328

CHORGES

05230 – Michelin map **334** F5 – pop. 2 567 – alt. 864
▶ Paris 676 – Embrun 23 – Gap 18 – Savines-le-Lac 12

⚞ Municipal

☏ 04 92 50 67 72. www.baiestmichel.com

Address : baie St-Michel (4.5km southeast along the N 9, follow the signs for Briançon, 200m from the lake at Serre-Ponçon)

Opening times : from mid May to mid Sept.

2 ha (110 pitches) terraced, flat, grassy, stony

Tariff : (2015 price) 20.50€ ✶✶ 🚗 ▤ ⚡ (16A) – Extra per person 5.10€

Rental rates : (2015 price) (from mid April to end Sept.) ♿ (1 chalet) – 10 🏠. Per night from 57 to 85€ – Per week from 320 to 625€

Surroundings : 💧 ⬕ 💧	
Leisure activities : 🛁 🏄 🏊 (lake)	**GPS** Longitude : 6.32379
Facilities : ♿ ⚡ 🕎	Latitude : 44.5283

Nearby : 🍷 ✗ 🚣 🎣 🦆 pedalos

CLAMENSANE

04250 – Michelin map **334** E7 – pop. 166 – alt. 694
▶ Paris 720 – Avignon 180 – Grenoble 158 – Marseille 152

🏕 Le Clot du Jay en Provence ♣♨

🔗 04 92 68 35 32. www.clotdujay.com

Address : route de Bayons (located 1km east along the D 1, follow the signs for Bayons, near the Sasse river)

Opening times : from mid April to end Sept.

6 ha/3 for camping (50 pitches) very uneven, terraced, flat, grassy, stony

Tariff : 25.50€ ♦♦ 🚐 🔳 🔌 (10A) – Extra per person 4€ – Reservation fee 9€

Rental rates : (from mid April to mid Sept.) – 8 🚍 – 12 🏠.
Per night from 42 to 80€ – Per week from 290 to 840€ –
Reservation fee 9€

Choose the pitches at the edge of the Forêt Domaniale du Grand Vallon (forest), furthest away from the road.

Surroundings : 🖵 ♨♨
Leisure activities : ♟ ✗ ✦ ⚁ ⏛ 🛝
Facilities : ♿ ☛ 🛁 🍴 🔲 🐾

GPS Longitude : 6.0845
Latitude : 44.3226

LA COLLE-SUR-LOUP

06480 – Michelin map **341** D5 – pop. 7 640 – alt. 90
▶ Paris 919 – Antibes 15 – Cagnes-sur-Mer 7 – Cannes 26

🏕 Sites et Paysages Les Pinèdes ♣♨

🔗 04 93 32 98 94. www.lespinedes.com

Address : route du Pont de Pierre (located 1.5km west along the D 6, follow the signs for Grasse, 50m from the Loup river)

Opening times : from end March to end Sept.

3.8 ha (149 pitches) very uneven, terraced, flat, grassy, fine gravel

Tariff : 46€ ♦♦ 🚐 🔳 🔌 (10A) – Extra per person 6.50€ – Reservation fee 20€

Rental rates : (from beginning April to end Sept.) – 35 🚍 –
5 🏠. Per night from 50 to 160€ – Per week from 300 to 1,280€ –
Reservation fee 20€

🚰 local sani-station 6€ – ⛽15€

The campsite is laid out across shaded terraces, with good-quality rental accommodation.

Surroundings : 🖵 ♨♨
Leisure activities : ♟ ✗ ✦ ⚁ ⏛ 🛝
multi-sports ground
Facilities : ☛ 🛁 🍴 🔲 launderette 🐾
refrigerated food storage facilities
Nearby : ≈ 🐎 leisure park

GPS Longitude : 7.08337
Latitude : 43.68177

🏕 Flower Le Vallon Rouge

🔗 04 93 32 86 12. www.auvallonrouge.com – limited spaces for one-night stay

Address : route de Gréolières (3.5km west along the D 6, follow signs for Grasse)

3 ha (103 pitches) terraced, flat, grassy, sandy, fine gravel

Rentals : 45 🚍 – 19 🏠 – 7 canvas bungalows.

🚰 Eurorelais sani-station

Choose the pitches beside the Loup river, furthest away from the road.

Surroundings : 🖄 🖵 ♨♨
Leisure activities : ✗ 🎣 ✦ ⚁ ≈ multi-sports ground
Facilities : ♿ ☛ 🛁 🍴 launderette 🐾
GPS Longitude : 7.07324
Latitude : 43.68452

Key to rentals symbols:

12 🚍	*Number of mobile homes*	
20 🏠	*Number of chalets*	
6 🛏	*Number of rooms to rent*	
Per night 30–50€	*Minimum/maximum rate per night*	
Per week 300–1,000€	*Minimum/maximum rate per week*	

COL-ST-JEAN

04340 – Michelin map **334** G6 – alt. 1 333 – Winter sports : 1 300/2 500 m
▶ Paris 709 – Barcelonnette 34 – Savines-le-Lac 31 – Seyne 10

🏕 Yelloh! Village L'Étoile des Neiges ♣♨

🔗 04 92 35 07 08. www.etoile-des-neiges.com – alt. 1 300

Address : at the Col St-Jean ski resort (800m south along the D 207 and turn right onto the D 307)

Opening times : from beginning May to mid Sept.

3 ha (150 pitches) terraced, flat, grassy, stony

Tariff : 39€ ♦♦ 🚐 🔳 🔌 (6A) – Extra per person 8€

Rental rates : (2015 price) (from beginning May to mid Sept.) ⌇
🅿 – 68 🚍 – 26 🏠 – 1 🛏. Per night from 37 to 175€ – Per week from 273 to 1,225€

🚰 local sani-station 8€

Various rental options, including some high-quality chalets.

Surroundings : 🖄 ← 🖵 ♨♨
Leisure activities : ♟ ✗ 🎣 ⊕ ✦ 🎿 🛷
hammam, jacuzzi ✦ ✂ 🔲 ⏛ multi-sports ground, spa centre
Facilities : ♿ ☛ ▥ 🛁 🍴 🍽 🍴 launderette 🐾
Nearby : 🚣 🚴 adventure park

GPS Longitude : 6.348
Latitude : 44.40927

CONTES

06390 – Michelin map **341** E5 – pop. 7 095 – alt. 250
▶ Paris 954 – Marseille 208 – Monaco 30 – Nice 19

🏕 La Ferme Riola

🔗 04 93 79 03 02. www.campinglafermeriola.com

Address : 5309 route de Sclos

Opening times : from beginning April to end Sept.

3 ha (25 pitches) terraced, flat, grassy, stony

Tariff : 23.50€ ♦♦ 🚐 🔳 🔌 (6A) – Extra per person 10€

Rental rates : permanent ⌇ – 6 🏠 – 2 studios – 4 gîtes.
Per week from 250 to 650€

🚰 4 🔳 11€

There is a small museum of agricultural tools and local olive oil is for sale.

Surroundings : 🖄 ♨♨
Leisure activities : 🎣 ✦ 🎿
Facilities : ♿ ☛ 🚿 🍴 🔲
GPS Longitude : 7.34379
Latitude : 43.8152

LA COURONNE

13500 – Michelin map **340** F5

▶ Paris 786 – Marseille 42 – Aix-en-Provence 49 – Martigues 11

⚠️ Le Mas ♙♙

℘ 04 42 80 70 34. www.camping-le-mas.com – limited spaces for one-night stay

Address : chemin de Sainte Croix (4km southeast along the D 49, follow the signs for Sausset-les-Pins and take a right turn; near the beach at Ste-Croix)

Opening times : from mid March to end Oct.

5.5 ha (300 pitches) terraced, flat, grassy, stony

Tariff : (2015 price) 46€ ♙♙ ⇘ 🖼 🔋 (6A) – Extra per person 9€ – Reservation fee 20€

Rental rates : (2015 price) (from mid March to end Oct.) 🛇 – 160 ⛺ – 46 🏠. Per week from 224 to 1,491€ – Reservation fee 20€

🚐 Raclet sani-station

Some pitches have a sea view.

Surroundings : 🌊 ♙♙
Leisure activities : 🍷✗ 🎦 🎱 ⛳️ 🏄 🚣 ⛵
multi-sports ground
Facilities : 🚿 ⚬ 🛁 🍴 launderette ♙
Nearby : 🛶

GPS
Longitude : 5.07349
Latitude : 43.33168

⚠️ Yelloh! Village La Côte Bleue

℘ 04 42 42 81 00. www.semovim-martigues.com

Address : chemin de la Batterie

Opening times : from beginning April to end Sept.

6 ha (200 pitches) terraced, flat, stony, sandy

Tariff : 49€ ♙♙ ⇘ 🖼 🔋 (10A) – Extra per person 8€

Rental rates : (2015 price) (from mid April to end Sept.) ♿ (1 mobile home) – 80 ⛺. Per night from 39 to 241€ – Per week from 273 to 1,687€

🚐 local sani-station

Surroundings : 🌊 ♙♙
Leisure activities : ✗ 🎦 🎱 ⛳️ 🏄 🚣 ⛵
Facilities : ♿ ⚬ 🍴 launderette 🛶 ♙

GPS
Longitude : 5.05639
Latitude : 43.33067

⚠️ Flower Le Marius

℘ 04 42 80 70 29. www.camping-marius.com

Address : plage de la Saulce (3km southeast along the D 49)

Opening times : from mid April to mid Oct.

2 ha (113 pitches) flat, grassy, gravelled

Tariff : 39€ ♙♙ ⇘ 🖼 🔋 (6A) – Extra per person 9€

Rental rates : permanent ♿ (2 chalets) – 54 🏠 – 16 tipis. Per night from 35 to 220€ – Per week from 245 to 1,540€

Surroundings : 🌊 ♙♙
Leisure activities : 🍷✗ 🛁 hammam, jacuzzi 🏄 🏊 massages 🎣
Facilities : ♿ ⚬ 🛁 🍴 launderette ♙

GPS
Longitude : 5.06744
Latitude : 43.33512

*The classification (1 to 5 tents, **black** or red) that we award to selected sites in this guide is our own system. It should not be confused with the classification (1 to 5 stars) of official organisations.*

⚠️ Les Mouettes

℘ 04 42 80 70 01. www.campinglesmouettes.com – limited spaces for one-night stay

Address : 16 chemin de la Quiétude (4km southeast along the D 49, follow the signs for Sausset, along the r. du Tamaris, near the beach at Ste-Croix)

Opening times : from end March to end Sept.

2 ha (131 pitches) terrace, flat, stony

Tariff : (2015 price) 31€ ♙♙ ⇘ 🖼 🔋 (6A) – Extra per person 8€ – Reservation fee 8€

Rental rates : (2015 price) permanent – 30 ⛺ – 20 🏠. Per night from 43 to 78€ – Per week from 190 to 880€ – Reservation fee 8€

Some pitches enjoy a sea view.

Surroundings : 🌊 ♙♙
Leisure activities : 🍷✗
Facilities : ♿ ⚬ 🛁 🍴 launderette
Nearby : 🛶

GPS
Longitude : 5.07618
Latitude : 43.33024

LA CROIX-VALMER

83420 – Michelin map **340** O6 – pop. 3 351 – alt. 120

▶ Paris 873 – Brignoles 70 – Draguignan 48 – Fréjus 35

⚠️ Sélection Camping ♙♙

℘ 04 94 55 10 30. www.selectioncamping.com 🛇

Address : 12 boulevard de la Mer (2.5km southwest along the D 559, follow the signs for Cavalaire and take road to the right at the roundabout)

Opening times : from mid March to mid Oct.

4 ha (185 pitches) terraced, flat, grassy, stony

Tariff : (2015 price) 45€ ♙♙ ⇘ 🖼 🔋 (10A) – Reservation fee 32€

Rental rates : (2015 price) (from mid March to mid Oct.) 🛇 – 60 ⛺ – 15 gîtes. Per night from 64 to 180€ – Per week from 445 to 1,290€ – Reservation fee 32€

🚐 local sani-station

On shaded terraces under eucalyptus, mimosa and other Mediterranean trees.

Surroundings : 🌊 🎦 ♙♙
Leisure activities : 🍷✗ 🎱 daytime 🏄 🚣 ⛵ multi-sports ground, entertainment room
Facilities : ♿ ⚬ 🎱 🍴 launderette 🛶 ♙

GPS
Longitude : 6.55501
Latitude : 43.19439

CROS-DE-CAGNES

06800 – Michelin map **341** D6

▶ Paris 923 – Marseille 194 – Nice 12 – Antibes 11

⚠️ Homair Vacances Green Park ♙♙

℘ 04 93 07 09 96. www.homair.com – limited spaces for one-night stay

Address : 159 bis chemin du Vallon des Vaux (3.8km to the north)

5 ha (156 pitches) very uneven, terraced, flat, grassy, fine gravel

Rentals : ♿ (2 chalets) – 63 ⛺ – 55 🏠.

A bus serves the beach. A mobile home and chalet village; some pitches for tents but not for caravans.

Surroundings : 🌊 🎦 ♙♙
Leisure activities : 🍷✗ 🎦 🎱 ⛳️ 🏄 🚣 🚴 ⛵ multi-sports ground
Facilities : ♿ ⚬ 🛁 🍴 launderette 🛶 ♙
Nearby : 🎾 ⛳️ golf practice

GPS
Longitude : 7.1569
Latitude : 43.68904

⛰ Le Val Fleuri

⚓ 04 93 31 21 74. www.campingvalfleuri.fr

Address : 139 chemin du Vallon des Vaux (3.5km to the north)

1.5 ha (87 pitches) very uneven, terraced, flat, grassy, stony

Rentals : 11 🛖 – 1 studio – 1 apartment.

Surroundings : 🐾 🗗 ♀♀
Leisure activities : ♈ 🛶 🛷
Facilities : ♿ ⚲ 🏢 🍴 🖼
Nearby : ✂ golf practice

GPS Longitude : 7.15577
Latitude : 43.68745

For more information on visiting particular towns or regions, consult the relevant regional MICHELIN Green Guide. We also recommend you use the appropriate Michelin regional map to locate your selected campsite, to calculate distances and to work out the best route.

CUCURON

84160 – Michelin map **332** F11 – pop. 1 844 – alt. 350
▶ Paris 739 – Aix-en-Provence 34 – Apt 25 – Cadenet 9

⚠ Le Moulin à Vent

⚓ 04 90 77 25 77. www.le-moulin-a-vent.com

Address : chemin de Gastoule (located 1.5km south along the D 182; follow the signs for Villelaure then continue 800m along the turning to the left)

Opening times : from beginning April to beginning Oct.

2.2 ha (80 pitches) terraced, relatively flat, flat, stony

Tariff : 20€ ♈♈ 🚗 🔲 ⚡ (10A) – Extra per person 5.10€

Rental rates : (from beginning April to beginning Oct.) ✍ – 1 🛖 – 4 🛖. Per night from 69 to 75€ – Per week from 435 to 565€

🚽 local sani-station 5€

This campsite is surrounded by vineyards.

Surroundings : 🐾 ‹ 🗗 ♀♀
Leisure activities : 🏓 ⚏ 🛷
Facilities : ♿ ⚲ 🍴 🖼 🧊 refrigerators

GPS Longitude : 5.44484
Latitude : 43.75641

CURBANS

05110 – Michelin map **334** E6 – pop. 418 – alt. 650
▶ Paris 717 – Marseille 171 – Digne-les-Bains 78 – Gap 20

⛰ Le Lac

⚓ 04 92 54 23 10. www.au-camping-du-lac.com – limited spaces for one-night stay

Address : at Le Fangeas

Opening times : from beginning April to end Oct.

5.2 ha (140 pitches) flat, relatively flat, grassy

Tariff : (2015 price) 28.20€ ♈♈ 🚗 🔲 ⚡ (10A) – Extra per person 6€ – Reservation fee 14€

Rental rates : (2015 price) permanent – 53 🛖. Per night from 37 to 122€ – Per week from 259 to 860€ – Reservation fee 14€

This site has an Hautes-Alpes post code (05), but is actually located in the Alpes-de-Haute-Provence (04).

Surroundings : ‹ ♀
Leisure activities : ♈ ✕ ⚙nighttime ✂ 🛶 🛷
⚏ multi-sports ground
Facilities : ⚲ 🍴 launderette 🧊

GPS Longitude : 6.0299
Latitude : 44.42452

DIGNE-LES-BAINS

04000 – Michelin map **334** F8 – pop. 17 172 – alt. 608 – ⚑
▶ Paris 744 – Aix-en-Provence 109 – Antibes 140 – Avignon 167

⛰ Les Eaux Chaudes

⚓ 04 92 32 31 04. www.campingleseauxchaudes.com

Opening times : from mid April to mid Oct.

3.7 ha (90 pitches)

Tariff : 19.50€ ♈♈ 🚗 🔲 ⚡ (4A) – Extra per person 6€ – Reservation fee 15€

Rental rates : (from beginning April to end Oct.) – 54 🛖 – 4 🛖. Per night from 49 to 133€ – Per week from 343 to 931€ – Reservation fee 18€

🚽 Eurorelais sani-station 5€

Beside a stream, with both new and older rental options, equipped to varying standards.

Surroundings : ♀♀
Leisure activities : 🏓 🛷 🛶
Facilities : ♿ ⚲ 🏢 🛷 🍴 launderette

GPS Longitude : 6.2507
Latitude : 44.08656

EMBRUN

05200 – Michelin map **334** G5 – pop. 6 188 – alt. 871
▶ Paris 706 – Barcelonnette 55 – Briançon 48 – Digne-les-Bains 97

⛰ Municipal de la Clapière

⚓ 04 92 43 01 83. www.camping-embrun-clapiere.com

Address : avenue du Lac (2.5km southwest along the N 94, follow the signs for Gap and take a right turn; at the leisure and activity park)

6.5 ha (291 pitches) terraced, flat, grassy, fine gravel

Rentals : 6 🛖 – 14 🛖.

🚽 local sani-station

There's a nice leisure and activity centre with direct access in season.

Surroundings : ♀♀
Leisure activities : 🏓 ⚙nighttime 🛷
Facilities : ♿ ⚲ ⛺ 🍴 launderette
Nearby : 🛒 🏓 ♈ ✕ 🛶 ✂ 🎣 ▣ 📼 (lake) 🛷 🛶
🦆 pedalos

GPS Longitude : 6.47875
Latitude : 44.55075

ESPARRON-DU-VERDON

04800 – Michelin map **334** D10 – pop. 433 – alt. 397
▶ Paris 795 – Barjols 31 – Digne-les-Bains 58 – Gréoux-les-Bains 13

⛰ Le Soleil

Le Soleil

⚓ 04 92 77 13 78. www.camping-le-soleil.com ✍

Opening times : from mid April to beginning Oct.

2 ha (100 pitches) very uneven, terraced, stony, fine gravel

Tariff : ♈ 7.50€ 🚗 🔲 10€ – ⚡ (6A) 3.70€ – Reservation fee 15€

Rental rates : (from mid April to beginning Oct.) ✍ – 12 🛖 – 2 canvas bungalows. Per night from 30 to 88€ – Per week from 120 to 650€ – Reservation fee 20€

🚽 local sani-station 5€ – 🚿 28.70€

In a pleasant setting beside a lake.

Surroundings : 🐾 🗗 ♀♀ ▲
Leisure activities : ♈ ✕ ♀♀ 🛷 ✍
Facilities : ♿ ⚲ 🅿 🍴 🖼 🛷 🧊
Nearby : 🦆 pedalos

GPS Longitude : 5.97062
Latitude : 43.73439

ESPINASSES

05190 – Michelin map **334** F6 – pop. 665 – alt. 630
▶ Paris 689 – Chorges 19 – Gap 25 – Le Lauzet-Ubaye 23

🏕 La Viste

✆ 04 92 54 43 39. www.laviste.fr – alt. 900

Address : Le Belvédère de Serre-Ponçon (head 5.5km northeast along the D 900b, take the D 3 following signs for Chorges and turn left onto D 103)

Opening times : from mid May to mid Sept.

4.5 ha/2.5 for camping (170 pitches) terraced, undulating, flat, grassy, stony

Tariff : (2015 price) ♦ 7.60€ ⇔ 🅴 7.60€ – (5A) 4€ – Reservation fee 15€

Rental rates : (2015 price) (from mid May to mid Sept.) – 10 ⟐ – 30 ⟐. Per night from 51 to 142€ – Per week from 355 to 990€ – Reservation fee 15€

In an attractive location overlooking the Lac de Serre-Ponçon.

Surroundings : ⋟ ≼ mountains, lake and Barrage de Serre-Ponçon (dam) ⟐⟐
Leisure activities : ♈ ✕ ☺daytime ⚓ ⟐
Facilities : ⟐ ⟐ launderette ⟐ ⟐
Nearby : ≋ (fresh water) ⚓ water skiing
Longitude : 6.26832
Latitude : 44.47613

FAUCON

84110 – Michelin map **332** D8 – pop. 414 – alt. 350
▶ Paris 677 – Marseille 152 – Avignon 59 – Montélimar 68

🏕 L'Ayguette

✆ 04 90 46 40 35. www.ayguette.com

Address : northwest of the village (take the eastern exit off the D 938, follow the signs for Nyons and continue 4.1 km to the right along the D 71, follow the signs for St-Romains-Viennois then take the D 86)

Opening times : from mid April to end Sept.

2.8 ha (100 pitches) undulating, flat, grassy, stony

Tariff : 33€ ♦♦ ⇔ 🅴 (10A) – Extra per person 6.50€
Rental rates : (from mid April to end Sept.) – 24 ⟐. Per night from 36 to 102€ – Per week from 252 to 714€
⟐ local sani-station – 15 🅴 33€
In a natural setting.

Surroundings : ⋟ ⟐ ⟐⟐
Leisure activities : ✕ ⚓ ⟐
Facilities : ⟐ ⟐ ⟐ ⟐
Longitude : 5.12933
Latitude : 44.26215

FORCALQUIER

04300 – Michelin map **334** C9 – pop. 4 640 – alt. 550
▶ Paris 747 – Aix-en-Provence 80 – Apt 42 – Digne-les-Bains 50

🏕 Indigo Forcalquier

✆ 04 92 75 27 94. www.camping-indigo.com

Address : route de Sigonce (take the eastern exit on D 16)

Opening times : from beginning May to end Sept.

2.9 ha (130 pitches) terraced, relatively flat, flat, grassy, stony

Tariff : (2015 price) 29.30€ ♦♦ ⇔ 🅴 (10A) – Extra per person 6.60€ – Reservation fee 13€

Rental rates : (2015 price) (from beginning May to end Sept.) 🅿 – 25 ⟐ – 4 ⟐ – 30 tent lodges. Per night from 48 to 119€ – Per week from 236 to 833€ – Reservation fee 13€
⟐ local sani-station 7€
There are numerous and varied rental options.

Surroundings : ⟐ ⟐⟐
Leisure activities : ✕ ⟐ ⚓ ⚓ ⚲ ⟐
Facilities : ⟐ ⟐ ⟐ ⟐ ⟐ ⟐ ⟐
Nearby : ✂
Longitude : 5.78723
Latitude : 43.96218

FRÉJUS

83600 – Michelin map **340** P5 – pop. 52 203 – alt. 20
▶ Paris 868 – Brignoles 64 – Cannes 40 – Draguignan 31

🏕 La Baume - La Palmeraie 🔔

✆ 04 94 19 88 88. www.labaume-lapalmeraie.com – limited spaces for one-night stay

Address : 3775 rue des Combattants d'Afrique du Nord (4.5km north along the D 4; follow the signs for Bagnols-en-Forêt)

Opening times : from end March to beginning Oct.

26 ha/20 for camping (780 pitches) relatively flat, flat, stony, sandy

Tariff : 55€ ♦♦ ⇔ 🅴 (6A) – Extra per person 15€ – Reservation fee 33€

Rental rates : (from end March to beginning Oct.) ⟐ (11 gîtes) – 183 ⟐ – 182 ⟐. Per night from 40 to 290€ – Per week from 280 to 2,030€ – Reservation fee 23€

There are two swimming areas, one partially covered, and a variety of rental accommodation. Choose the pitches furthest from the road.

Surroundings : ⟐ ⟐⟐
Leisure activities : ♈ ✕ ⟐ ☺(open-air theatre) ⚓ ⚲ hammam, jacuzzi ⚓ ⚓ ✂ ⟐ ⚓ ⟐ disco, skate park
Facilities : ⟐ ⟐ ⟐ ⟐ ⟐ ⟐ launderette ⟐ ⟐
Longitude : 6.72319
Latitude : 43.46655

🏕 Yelloh! Village Domaine du Colombier 🔔

✆ 04 94 51 56 01. www.domaine-du-colombier.com – limited spaces for one-night stay

Address : 1052 rue des Combattants d'Afrique du Nord (situated 2km north along the D 4; follow the signs for Bagnols-en-Forêt)

Opening times : from end March to mid Oct.

10 ha (400 pitches) very uneven, terraced, undulating, flat, grassy

Tariff : 59€ ♦♦ ⇔ 🅴 (16A) – Extra per person 9€
Rental rates : (from end March to mid Oct.) – 344 ⟐ – 39 ⟐. Per night from 39 to 419€ – Per week from 273 to 2,933€
⟐ local sani-station

A themed mobile home village, some high quality, with a partially covered spa area. Choose the pitches furthest from the road.

Surroundings : ⋟ ≼ ⟐
Leisure activities : ♈ ✕ ⟐ ☺ ⚓ ⚲ hammam, jacuzzi ⚓ ⚓ ⟐ ⟐ disco, spa centre, entertainment room
Facilities : ⟐ ⟐ ⟐ ⟐ ⟐ ⟐ launderette ⟐ ⟐
Longitude : 6.72688
Latitude : 43.44588

⚠️ Sunêlia Holiday Green

📞 04 94 19 88 30. www.holidaygreen.com – limited spaces for one-night stay

Address : 1900 RD 4 (road number) (north of the town)

Opening times : from end March to end Sept.

15 ha (640 pitches) very uneven, terraced, flat, grassy, stony

Tariff : 62€ ⚥ 🚗 🔲 (16A) – Extra per person 10€ – Reservation fee 40€

Rental rates : (from end March to end Sept.) 🚲 (1 mobile home) – 310 🛖 – 20 🏠. Per night from 45 to 370€ – Per week from 315 to 2,590€ – Reservation fee 40€

There's an attractive, partially-covered swimming area. Choose the pitches furthest from the road.

Surroundings : 🏖 🗺 🕗
Leisure activities : 🍴 🗙 🏛 🕗 🏃 hammam, jacuzzi 🚴 🖼 🔲 🏊 disco, multi-sports ground, spa centre
Facilities : 🚻 🚰 🏠 🍴 launderette 🗑 🚿

	GPS
	Longitude : 6.71683
	Latitude : 43.48481

⚠️ La Pierre Verte 🧑‍🤝‍🧑

📞 04 94 40 88 30. www.campinglapierreverte.com

Address : 1880 RD 4 (road number) (6.5km north of the town, follow the signs for Bagnols-en-Forêt and take a right turn)

Opening times : from beginning April to end Sept.

28 ha/15 for camping (450 pitches) very uneven, terraced, flat, grassy, stony, rocks

Tariff : 47€ ⚥ 🚗 🔲 (10A) – Extra per person 11€ – Reservation fee 25€

Rental rates : (from beginning April to end Sept.) – 180 🛖. Per night from 60 to 200€ – Per week from 280 to 1,400€ – Reservation fee 25€

This spacious site is on two small hills, with pitches in the peace and quiet.

Surroundings : 🏖 🗺 🕗
Leisure activities : 🍴 🗙 🏛 🕗 🏃 🏹 🎣 🏊 multi-sports ground
Facilities : 🚻 🚰 🏠 🚿 🍴 launderette 🗑 🚿

	GPS
	Longitude : 6.72054
	Latitude : 43.48382

⚠️ La Plage d'Argens

📞 04 94 51 14 97. www.laplagedargens.fr

Address : 541 RD 559 (road number) (3km south of the town via the N 98, direct access to the beach)

Opening times : from beginning April to beginning Oct.

7 ha (436 pitches) flat, grassy, sandy

Tariff : (2015 price) 42€ ⚥ 🚗 🔲 (5A) – Extra per person 8€ – Reservation fee 30€

Rental rates : (2015 price) (from beginning April to mid Oct.) – 141 🛖 – 8 tent lodges. Per night from 33 to 228€ – Reservation fee 30€

🚉 local sani-station 9€ – 4 🔲 23€

Situated beside the Argens river, with direct access to the beach. Choose the pitches away from the road.

Surroundings : 🕗
Leisure activities : 🍴 🗙 🏛 🚣 🚴 🏊 scuba diving, multi-sports ground
Facilities : 🚻 🚰 🏠 🍴 launderette 🗑 🚿 refrigerators

	GPS
	Longitude : 6.72489
	Latitude : 43.4087

⚠️ Les Pins Parasols

📞 04 94 40 88 43. www.lespinsparasols.com

Address : 3360 rue des Combattants d'Afrique du Nord (4km north along the D 4, follow the signs for Bagnols-en-Forêt)

Opening times : from beginning April to end Sept.

4.5 ha (200 pitches) terraced, undulating, flat, grassy, stony

Tariff : 34.10€ ⚥ 🚗 🔲 (6A) – Extra per person 6.80€

Rental rates : (from beginning April to end Sept.) 🚲 – 15 🛖. Per night from 199 to 820€ – Per week from 199 to 820€

Some pitches have private sanitary facilities, on a spacious site among shady pine trees.

Surroundings : 🗺 🕗
Leisure activities : 🗙 🏛 🚣 🏊 🏊
Facilities : 🚻 🚰 🏠 🏠 – 48 private sanitary facilities (🏠 🚿 🛁 wc) 🍴 🏠 🚿 🚿

	GPS
	Longitude : 6.7253
	Latitude : 43.464

GAP

05000 – Michelin map **334** E5 – pop. 39 243 – alt. 735
▶ Paris 665 – Avignon 209 – Grenoble 103 – Sisteron 52

⚠️ Alpes-Dauphiné

📞 04 92 51 29 95. www.alpesdauphine.com – alt. 850

Address : route Napoléon (3km north along the N 85, follow the signs for Grenoble)

Opening times : from mid April to mid Oct.

10 ha/6 for camping (185 pitches)

Tariff : (2015 price) 26.20€ ⚥ 🚗 🔲 (6A) – Extra per person 5.80€ – Reservation fee 20€

Rental rates : (2015 price) (from mid April to mid Oct.) – 40 🛖 – 15 🏠 – 3 gîtes. Per night from 50 to 95€ – Per week from 285 to 780€ – Reservation fee 20€

🚉 local sani-station 6€ – 5 🔲 17€

Surroundings : 🕗
Leisure activities : 🍴 🗙 🏛 jacuzzi 🚣 🏊
Facilities : 🚻 🚰 🏠 🏠 🚿 🍴 launderette 🚿

	GPS
	Longitude : 6.08255
	Latitude : 44.58022

GIENS

83400 – Michelin map **340** L7
▶ Paris 869 – Marseille 93 – Toulon 29 – La Seyne-sur-Mer 37

⚠️ La Presqu'île de Giens 🧑‍🤝‍🧑

📞 04 94 58 22 86. www.camping-giens.com

Address : 153 route de la Madrague

Opening times : from end March to beginning Oct.

7 ha (427 pitches) very uneven, terraced, flat, grassy, stony

Tariff : (2015 price) 35.40€ ⚥ 🚗 🔲 (15A) – Extra per person 8.80€ – Reservation fee 19€

Rental rates : (2015 price) (from end March to beginning Oct.) – 64 🛖 – 30 🏠. Per night from 47 to 177€ – Per week from 329 to 1,239€ – Reservation fee 19€

🚉 local sani-station 2€ – 🔌 21.33€

Numerous small terraces and good-quality sanitary facilities.

Surroundings : 🗺 🕗
Leisure activities : 🍴 🗙 🏛 🕗 daytime 🏃 🚣
Facilities : 🚰 cc 🏠 🍴 launderette 🗑 🚿

	GPS
	Longitude : 6.14332
	Latitude : 43.04084

⚠ La Tour Fondue

☏ 04 94 58 22 86. www.camping-latourfondue.com – ℝ

Address : avenue des Arbanais

Opening times : from beginning April to beginning Nov.

2 ha (146 pitches) terraced, relatively flat, flat, grassy

Tariff : (2015 price) 33.40€ ✷✷ ⇋ 🔲 (12) (15A) –
Extra per person 8.80€

Rental rates : (2015 price) (from beginning April to beginning Nov.) –
21 🛏. Per night from 55 to 129€ – Per week from 385 to 903€ –
Reservation fee 19€

🚐 local sani-station 16.90€ – 🚐 20.16€

*Pitches at the end of the Giens peninsula, looking towards the
Ile de Porquerolles.*

Surroundings : 🏞 ⛱ ♨♨ ⛰	**GPS** Longitude : 6.15569
Leisure activities : ☂ ✕	Latitude : 43.02971
Facilities : ⊶ 🖉 launderette 🏖 🐾	
Nearby : scuba diving	

⚠ Olbia

☏ 04 94 58 21 96. www.camping-olbia.com

Address : 545 avenue René de Knyff (near La Madrague harbour)

Opening times : from end March to end Sept.

1.5 ha (100 pitches) terraced, relatively flat, flat, stony, fine gravel

Tariff : (2015 price) 34.40€ ✷✷ ⇋ 🔲 (12) (6A) – Extra per person
7.20€ – Reservation fee 19€

*Pitches beneath the shade of eucalyptus, maritime pines and
palm trees.*

Surroundings : 🏞 ⛱ ♨♨	**GPS** Longitude : 6.10325
Leisure activities : ☂ ✕ 🏄 🛶	Latitude : 43.03966
Facilities : ᕯ ⊶ 🖉 🏖 🐾	

LA GRAVE

05320 – Michelin map **334** F2 – pop. 493 – alt. 1 526 – Winter sports :
1 450/3 250 m

▶ Paris 642 – Briançon 38 – Gap 126 – Grenoble 80

⚠ La Meije

☏ 06 08 54 30 84. www.camping-delameije.com

Address : head east towards Briançon along the D 1091; beside the
Romanche river

Opening times : from beginning May to end Sept.

2.5 ha (50 pitches) terrace, flat and relatively flat, grassy

Tariff : 19.60€ ✷✷ ⇋ 🔲 (12) (6A) – Extra per person 3€

The site has a magnificent view of the La Grave glacier

Surroundings : 🏞 ⛰ ♨♨	**GPS** Longitude : 6.30911
Leisure activities : ✂ 🏖 🛶 🐟	Latitude : 45.04526
Facilities : ᕯ ⊶ 🖉 🖉 🖉	
Nearby : 🚣 rafting and canyoning	

⚠ Le Gravelotte

☏ 04 76 79 93 14. www.camping-le-gravelotte.com

Address : southwest of the village (1.2km west along the D 1091,
follow the signs for Grenoble and take road to the left; beside the
Meije river)

Opening times : from mid June to end Sept.

4 ha (75 pitches) flat, grassy

Tariff : 17.60€ ✷✷ ⇋ 🔲 (12) (10A) – Extra per person 3.70€

---

*An attractive location at the foot of the mountains and beside
the Romanche river.*

Surroundings : ⛰ ♀	**GPS** Longitude : 6.29697
Leisure activities : ☂ 🏖 🐾	Latitude : 45.04328
Facilities : ᕯ ⊶ 🖉 🖉	

*The information in the guide may have changed since
going to press.*

GRAVESON

13690 – Michelin map **340** D2 – pop. 3 875 – alt. 14

▶ Paris 696 – Arles 25 – Avignon 14 – Cavaillon 30

⚠ Les Micocouliers

Les Micocouliers

☏ 04 90 95 81 49. www.lesmicocouliers.fr

Address : 445 route de Cassoulen
(1.2km southeast along the D 28, follow
the signs for Châteaurenard and turn
right onto D 5, follow the signs for
Maillane)

Opening times : from mid March to
mid Oct.

3.5 ha (118 pitches) flat, grassy

Tariff : ✷ 8.80€ ⇋ 3€ 🔲 9.40€ –
(12) (8A) 5.90€ – Reservation fee 10€

Rental rates : (from mid March to mid Oct.) – 6 🛏. Per
night from 65 to 110€ – Per week from 430 to 760€ – Reservation
fee 20€

🚐 local sani-station 6€

Surroundings : ⛱ ♀	**GPS** Longitude : 4.78111
Leisure activities : 🏖 🛶	Latitude : 43.84389
Facilities : ᕯ ⊶ 🖉 🖉	

GRÉOUX-LES-BAINS

04800 – Michelin map **334** D10 – pop. 2 510 – alt. 386 – ♨

▶ Paris 783 – Aix-en-Provence 55 – Brignoles 52 – Digne-les-Bains 69

⚠ Yelloh! Village le Verdon Parc 👥

Yelloh! Village le Verdon Parc

☏ 04 92 78 08 08. www.
campingverdonparc.fr 🐾

Address : Domaine de la Paludette
(600m south along the D 8, follow the
signs for St-Pierre and take the turning
to the left after the bridge; beside the
Verdon river)

Opening times : from end March to
beginning Nov.

8 ha (324 pitches) terraced, flat, grassy, stony, gravelled

Tariff : 43€ ✷✷ ⇋ 🔲 (12) (16A) – Extra per person 7€

Rental rates : (from end March to beginning Nov.) ᕯ (2 mobile
homes) 🐾 – 42 🛏 – 54 🏠 – 29 tent lodges. Per night
from 29 to 241€ – Per week from 203 to 1,687€

🚐 AireService sani-station

The site is beside the Verdon river and a small, equipped beach.

Surroundings : 🏞 ⛱ ♨♨	**GPS** Longitude : 5.89407
Leisure activities : ☂ ✕ 🎭 🎬 🎯 🚣 🚴 🏄 🏊 🛶 🐟 multi-sports ground	Latitude : 43.75188
Facilities : ᕯ ⊶ 🏪 🖉 🖉 launderette 🏖 🐾 refrigerators	

⚲ La Pinède

✆ 04 92 78 05 47. www.camping-lapinede-04.com

Address : route de Saint-Pierre (located 1.5km south along the D 8, 200m from the Verdon river)

Opening times : from beginning March to end Nov.

3 ha (166 pitches) terraced, flat and relatively flat, stony, fine gravel

Tariff : (2015 price) 25.70€ ★★ ⊷ 🅴 (⚡) (10A) – Extra per person 3.30€

Rental rates : (2015 price) (from beginning March to end Nov.) – 56 ⛺. Per week from 34 to 107€

🚐 local sani-station 4.50€

Attractive, shaded terraces and good sanitary facilities.

Surroundings : 🦌 ◁ 🏕 ♨♨	
Leisure activities : 🍷 🗙 🏠 🚣 🏊 multi-sports ground	**G P S**
Facilities : 👤 ⊶ 🆒 🎼 👕 launderette	Longitude : 5.88294
Nearby : 🎣	Latitude : 43.74848

⚲ Verseau

✆ 04 92 77 67 10. www.camping-le-verseau.com

Address : 113 chemin Gaspard de Besse (1.2km south along the D 8, follow the signs for St-Pierre and take the road to the right, near the Verdon river)

Opening times : from beginning March to end Nov.

2.5 ha (120 pitches) flat and relatively flat, grassy, stony

Tariff : ★ 5€ ⊷ 4€ 🅴 23€ – (⚡) (16A) 3.90€

Rental rates : (from beginning March to end Nov.) 👤 (1 chalet) – 50 ⛺ – 13 🏠. Per night from 40 to 102€ – Per week from 280 to 710€

🚐 60 🅴 14.90€

Close to the Verdon river and the dam.

Surroundings : 🦌 ◁ 🏕 ♨♨	
Leisure activities : 🍷 🏠 🚣 🏊 entertainment room	**G P S**
Facilities : 👤 ⊶ 🎼 ♨ 🚿 👕 🔳 refrigerators	Longitude : 5.88199
Nearby : 🏊 🎣	Latitude : 43.75152

There are several different types of sani-station ('borne' in French) – sanitation points providing fresh water and disposal points for grey water. See page 12 for further details.

83310 – Michelin map **340** O6 – pop. 4 309 – alt. 105
▶ Paris 861 – Brignoles 58 – Fréjus 32 – Le Lavandou 32

⚲ Les Prairies de la Mer ♠♠

✆ 04 94 79 09 09. www.riviera-villages.com

Address : at Saint-Pons-les-Mûres, off the D 559 (RN 98)

Opening times : from beginning April to mid Oct.

30 ha (1400 pitches)open site, flat, sandy

Tariff : (2015 price) 63€ ★★ ⊷ 🅴 (⚡) (6A) – Extra per person 6€

Rental rates : (2015 price) (from beginning April to mid Oct.) ℗ – 150 ⛺ – 150 🏠. Per night from 52 to 499€ – Per week from 365 to 3,085€

🚐 local sani-station

A vast complex divided into several villages: tents and caravanes, owner-occupiers, classic mobile homes classiques and luxury rental options (some opposite the beach).

Surroundings : 🦌 ◁ St Tropez and the gulf 🏕 ♨♨ 🛶	
Leisure activities : 🍷 🗙 🏠 👦 🏊 🎿 🚣 hammam, jacuzzi 🚣 🚴 ✂ 🛶 disco, concierge services, scuba diving, multi-sports ground, spa centre	**G P S**
Facilities : 👤 ⊶ 🎼 ♨ 🚿 👕 launderette 🛒 🚿	Longitude : 6.58241
	Latitude : 43.28086

⚲ Domaine des Naïades ♠♠

✆ 04 94 55 67 80. www.lesnaiades.com – limited spaces for one-night stay

Address : at Saint-Pons-les-Mûres (RN 98 and take a left turn)

Opening times : from beginning April to beginning Oct.

27 ha/14 for camping (470 pitches) very uneven, terraced, flat, grassy, sandy

Tariff : (2015 price) 65.20€ ★★ ⊷ 🅴 (⚡) (10A) – Extra per person 8.50€

Rental rates : (2015 price) (from beginning April to beginning Oct.) – 126 ⛺. Per night from 50 to 265€ – Per week from 350 to 1,855€

🚐 local sani-station 2.50€

A long-shaped site, part of which is very quiet and peaceful and with luxury rentals.

Surroundings : 🦌 ◁ 🏕 ♨♨	
Leisure activities : 🍷 🗙 👦 🏊 🚣 🚴 🛶 🎿	**G P S**
Facilities : 👤 ⊶ 🎼 ♨ 👕 launderette 🛒 🚿	Longitude : 6.57937
	Latitude : 43.28517

Michelin classification:

⚲⚲⚲⚲ *Extremely comfortable, equipped to a very high standard*

⚲⚲⚲ *Very comfortable, equipped to a high standard*

⚲⚲⚲ *Comfortable and well equipped*

⚲⚲ *Reasonably comfortable*

⚲ *Satisfactory*

05600 – Michelin map **334** H5 – pop. 2 308 – alt. 1 000
▶ Paris 715 – Barcelonnette 51 – Briançon 36 – Digne-les-Bains 114

⚲ Parc Le Villard

✆ 04 92 45 06 54. www.camping-levillard.com

Address : route des campings, at Le Villard (situated 2km west along the D 902a, follow the signs for Gap; beside the Chagne river)

Opening times : permanent

3.2 ha (120 pitches) flat and relatively flat, grassy, stony

Tariff : 22€ ★★ ⊷ 🅴 (⚡) (10A) – Extra per person 6€ – Reservation fee 8€

Rental rates : permanent – 17 ⛺ – 6 🏠 – 4 canvas bungalows. Per night from 50 to 80€ – Per week from 295 to 790€ – Reservation fee 8€

The site occupies both sides of a small road.

Surroundings : ◁ ♀	
Leisure activities : 🗙 🏠 🚣 ✂ 👦 🚣 🏊	**G P S**
Facilities : 👤 ⊶ ♨ 👕 launderette 🚿 refrigerators	Longitude : 6.62687
	Latitude : 44.65895

🏔 St-James-les-Pins

🖉 04 92 45 08 24. www.lesaintjames.com

Address : route des Campings (head 1.5km west following signs for Risoul and take turning to the right)

Opening times : permanent

2.5 ha (100 pitches) flat, relatively flat, stony, grassy

Tariff : (2015 price) 19.15€ ♠♠ 🚗 ▣ 🔌 (10A) – Extra per person 3.60€

Rental rates : (2015 price) permanent – 10 🚐 – 13 🏠 – 10 🛏. Per night from 54 to 100 v – Per week from 320 to 660€

🚱 local sani-station 4.60€ – 5 ▣ 20€

The site is crossed by the Chagne rapids.

Surroundings : ❄ 🌳🌳
Leisure activities : 🛶 ⛹ 🎣 multi-sports ground
Facilities : 🚿 🔌 🍽 launderette
Nearby : 🛶 ⛷

GPS Longitude : 6.63293
Latitude : 44.65685

🏔 La Rochette

🖉 04 92 45 02 15. www.campingguillestre.com

Address : route des Campings (head 1km west following signs for Risoul and take turning to the right)

Opening times : from mid May to end Sept.

4 ha (190 pitches) flat and relatively flat, stony, grassy

Tariff : (2015 price) 20.40€ ♠♠ 🚗 ▣ 🔌 (6A) – Extra per person 4€ – Reservation fee 9€

🚱 local sani-station – 🚐 11€

Surroundings : ‹ 🌳🌳
Leisure activities : 🛶 ⛹ 🎣
Facilities : 🚿 🔌 🍽 launderette 🛁
Nearby : ✕ 🛁 🛶 ⛷

GPS Longitude : 6.63845
Latitude : 44.65895

To visit a town or region, use the MICHELIN Green Guides.

HYÈRES

83400 – Michelin map **340** L7 – pop. 54 686 – alt. 40
▶ Paris 851 – Aix-en-Provence 102 – Cannes 123 – Draguignan 78

🏔 Les Palmiers – 👥 (rental of mobile homes only)

🖉 04 94 66 39 66. www.camping-les-palmiers.fr

Address : rue du Ceinturon, at L'Ayguade

Opening times : from end March to beginning Nov.

5.5 ha

Rental rates : 348 🚐. Per night from 42 to 231€ – Per week from 294 to 1,617€ – Reservation fee 20€

Numerous mobile homes in an attractive setting beside a water park.

Surroundings : 🌊 🌳🌳
Leisure activities : 🍽✕ 🛶 nighttime 🏓 🎣 hammam ⛹ 🚴 🎣 🛶
Facilities : 🚿 🔌 🍽 launderette 🛁

GPS Longitude : 6.16725
Latitude : 43.10344

🏔 Le Ceinturon 3

🖉 04 94 66 32 65. www.ceinturon3.fr – 🏧

Address : 2 rue des Saraniers (5km southeast, 100m from the sea)

Opening times : from mid March to end Sept.

2.5 ha (200 pitches) flat, grassy, sandy

Tariff : 33.70€ ♠♠ 🚗 ▣ 🔌 (10A) – Extra per person 6.25€

Rental rates : (from mid March to end Sept.) 🚿 (1 mobile home) 🐾 – 1 🚐 – 40 🏠. Per night from 50 to 65€ – Per week from 330 to 825€ – Reservation fee 16€

Pitches in the shade with good-quality sanitary facilities.

Surroundings : 🌊 🌳🌳
Leisure activities : 🍽✕ ⛹ 🏊 multi-sports ground
Facilities : 🚿 🔌 📷 🍽 launderette 🛁 🛁
Nearby : ✂

GPS Longitude : 6.16962
Latitude : 43.10109

L'ISLE-SUR-LA-SORGUE

84800 – Michelin map **332** D10 – pop. 18 936 – alt. 57
▶ Paris 693 – Apt 34 – Avignon 23 – Carpentras 18

🏔 Club Airotel La Sorguette

Club Airotel La Sorguette

🖉 04 90 38 05 71. www.camping-sorguette.com

Address : 871 route d'Apt (located 1.5km southeast along the N 100; near the Sorgue)

Opening times : from mid March to mid Oct.

2.5 ha (164 pitches) flat, grassy, stony

Tariff : 29.50€ ♠♠ 🚗 ▣ 🔌 (10A) – Extra per person 8.50€ – Reservation fee 20€

Rental rates : (from mid March to mid Oct.) 🚿 (1 mobile home) – 30 🚐 – 3 yurts – 1 tipi – 3 tent lodges. Per night from 46 to 124€ – Per week from 287 to 833€ – Reservation fee 20€

🚱 local sani-station 7€

Surroundings : 🌳
Leisure activities : ✕ 🛶 🏓 ⛹ 🚴 🎣
Facilities : 🚿 🔌 🍽 launderette 🛁 🛁 refrigerated food storage facilities

GPS Longitude : 5.07192
Latitude : 43.9146

ISOLA

06420 – Michelin map **341** D2 – pop. 748 – alt. 873
▶ Paris 897 – Marseille 246 – Nice 76 – Cuneo 79

🏔 Le Lac des Neiges

🖉 04 93 02 18 16. www.princiland.fr – alt. 875

Address : route de St-Etienne-de-Tinée (located 1km north of the village along the D 2205)

Opening times : permanent

3 ha (98 pitches) flat, grassy, stony

Tariff : (2015 price) 26€ ♠♠ 🚗 ▣ 🔌 (10A) – Extra per person 10€

Rental rates : (2015 price) permanent – 13 🚐 – 2 gîtes. Per night from 31 to 110€ – Per week from 350 to 500€

🚱 local sani-station

The site is in two sections, which are slightly apart from each other.

Surroundings : 🌲 🌳
Leisure activities : 🍽✕ 🛶 ⛹ 🏓
Facilities : 🚿 🔌 📷 🛁 🛁 🍽 🛁 🛁
Nearby : ✂

GPS Longitude : 7.03912
Latitude : 44.18898

To make the best possible use of this guide, please read pages 2–15 carefully.

LARCHE

04530 – Michelin map **334** J6 – pop. 74 – alt. 1 691
▶ Paris 760 – Barcelonnette 28 – Briançon 81 – Cuneo 70

⚠ Domaine des Marmottes

✆ 04 92 84 33 64. www.camping-marmottes.fr

Address : Malboisset (800m southeast down a turning to the right; beside the Ubayette river)

Opening times : from beginning June to end Sept.

2 ha (52 pitches) open site, flat, grassy

Tariff : (2015 price) ⚲ 8€ ⚌ ▤ – ⚡ (10A) 3.50€

Rental rates : (2015 price) (from beginning June to end Sept.) – 2 🏠. Per night from 60 to 80€ – Per week from 300 to 400€
🚐 local sani-station 3€

Near a pretty waterfall; the site is well-equipped for walkers.

Surroundings : 🌲 ⛰ ⌂ 🌳🌳	
Leisure activities : ✗	**G** Longitude : 6.85257
Facilities : 🚿 ⛟ 🛒 🍴 launderette	**P** Latitude : 44.44615
Nearby : 🍷	**S**

The Michelin classification (⚠⚠⚠ … ⚠) is totally independent of the official star classification system awarded by the local prefecture or other official organisation.

LE LAVANDOU

83980 – Michelin map **340** N7 – pop. 5 747 – alt. 1
▶ Paris 873 – Cannes 102 – Draguignan 75 – Fréjus 61

⚠ Beau Séjour

✆ 04 94 71 25 30. www.campingbeausejourvar.com

Address : at la Grande Bastide (located 1.5km to the southwest)

1.5 ha (135 pitches) flat, gravel

Attractive and shaded marked-out pitches. Choose those furthest from the road.

Surroundings : ⌂ 🌳🌳	
Leisure activities : 🍷 ✗	**G** Longitude : 6.35165
Facilities : 🚿 ⛟ 🍴 ▣ 🚿	**P** Latitude : 43.13497
Nearby : 🏊	**S**

LA LONDE-LES-MAURES

83250 – Michelin map **340** M7 – pop. 9 910 – alt. 24
▶ Paris 861 – Bormes-les-Mimosas 11 – Cuers 31 – Hyères 10

⚠ Les Moulières

✆ 04 94 01 53 21. www.campinglesmoulieres.com

Address : 15 chemin de la Garenne, at Le Puits de Magne (situated 2.5km southeast; follow the signs for Port-de-Miramar and take turning to the right)

Opening times : from beginning April to mid Sept.

3 ha (250 pitches) flat, grassy

Tariff : (2015 price) 31€ ⚲⚲ ⚌ ▤ ⚡ (6A) – Extra per person 8.50€ – Reservation fee 10€

Surroundings : 🌲 ♀	
Leisure activities : 🍷 ✗ 🏊 ⛳ fitness trail, multi-sports ground	**G** Longitude : 6.23526
Facilities : 🚿 ⛟ 🍴 ▣ 🚿	**P** Latitude : 43.12236
	S

LOURMARIN

84160 – Michelin map **332** F11 – pop. 1 000 – alt. 224
▶ Paris 732 – Aix-en-Provence 37 – Apt 19 – Cavaillon 73

⚠ Les Hautes Prairies

✆ 04 90 68 02 89. www.campinghautesprairies.com

Address : route de Vaugines (700m east along the D 56)

Opening times : from mid April to end Sept.

3.6 ha (158 pitches) flat and relatively flat, grassy, stony

Tariff : (2015 price) 37€ ⚲⚲ ⚌ ▤ ⚡ (6A) – Extra per person 7.70€
Rental rates : (2015 price) (from mid April to end Sept.) – 1 'gypsy' caravan – 20 🏕 – 16 🏠 – 6 ⛺. Per night from 50 to 175€ – Per week from 195 to 990€ 🚐 Eurorelais sani-station 5€

Surroundings : ⌂ ♀	
Leisure activities : 🍷 ✗ 🏊 🏊	**G** Longitude : 5.37291
Facilities : 🚿 ⛟ 🛒 🍴 ▣ 🚿	**P** Latitude : 43.76784
	S

MALEMORT-DU-COMTAT

84570 – Michelin map **332** D9 – pop. 1 461 – alt. 208
▶ Paris 688 – Avignon 33 – Carpentras 11 – Malaucène 22

⚠ Font Neuve

Font Neuve

✆ 04 90 69 90 00. www.campingfontneuve.com

Address : Font-Neuve district (1.6km southeast along the D 5, follow the signs for Méthanis and take road to the left)

Opening times : from beginning April to end Sept.

1.5 ha (54 pitches) terraced, relatively flat, flat, grassy, stony

Tariff : (2015 price) 22.80€ ⚲⚲ ⚌ ▤ ⚡ (6A) – Extra per person 5€
Rental rates : (from beginning April to end Sept.) – 4 🏕 – 4 🏠. Per night from 80 to 200€ – Per week from 300 to 720€ – Reservation fee 10€

Surroundings : 🌲 ⛰ ⌂ 🌳🌳	
Leisure activities : ✗ 🏊 ⛳ 🏊	**G** Longitude : 5.17098
Facilities : 🚿 ⛟ 🛒 🍴 ▣ 🚿	**P** Latitude : 44.0142
	S

MALLEMORT

13370 – Michelin map **340** G3 – pop. 5 925 – alt. 120
▶ Paris 716 – Aix-en-Provence 34 – Apt 38 – Cavaillon 20

⚠ Durance Luberon

✆ 04 90 59 13 36. www.campingduranceluberon.com – for caravans, access via town centre not advised, acces via N 7 and D 561. signs for Charleval

Address : at the Domaine du Vergon (2.8km southeast along the D 23, 200m from the canal, towards the power station – from the A 7 take exits 26 and 7)

Opening times : from beginning April to end Sept.

4 ha (110 pitches) flat, grassy

Tariff : (2015 price) 23.50€ ⚲⚲ ⚌ ▤ ⚡ (10A) – Extra per person 5€ – Reservation fee 15€

Rental rates : (2015 price) (from beginning April to end Sept.) – 8 🏕. Per night from 57 to 74€ – Per week from 390 to 750€ – Reservation fee 15€ 🚐 local sani-station 5€

Surroundings : 🌲 ⌂ 🌳🌳	
Leisure activities : ✗ 🏊 🏊	**G** Longitude : 5.20492
Facilities : 🚿 ⛟ 🍴🍴 🏊 🍴 ▣ 🚿	**P** Latitude : 43.72091
Nearby : 🏇	**S**

MANDELIEU-LA-NAPOULE

06210 – Michelin map **341** C6 – pop. 21 764 – alt. 4
▶ Paris 890 – Brignoles 86 – Cannes 9 – Draguignan 53

⚑ Les Cigales

☎ 04 93 49 23 53. www.lescigales.com

Address : 505 avenue de la Mer (at Mandelieu)

Opening times : from mid Feb. to mid Nov.

1 ha (62 pitches) flat, grassy, gravel

Tariff : (2015 price) ☗ 8.60€ ⇌ 5€ ▣ 35€ – ⚡ (6A) 6€ – Reservation fee 25€

Rental rates : (2015 price) (from mid March to beginning Nov.) – 22 ⌂. Per night from 70 to 175€ – Per week from 415 to 1,050€ – Reservation fee 25€

A green 'oasis' in the town; beside the Siagne river, equipped with a small decking area.

Surroundings : ⌂ ⌗ ᴼᴼ
Leisure activities : ⚔ ⤳
Facilities : ⚙ ⛽ ▥ ♨ ⚐ ☂ ⚑ launderette
Nearby : ⛾ ✗ ⚒ ⚲ ⚓

| | Longitude : 6.9424 |
| GPS | Latitude : 43.53883 |

⚑ Les Pruniers - Les Bungalows du Golfe

☎ 04 93 49 99 23. www.bungalow-camping.com

Address : 118 rue de la Pinéa (via the av. de la Mer)

Opening times : from mid Feb. to end Oct.

0.8 ha (64 pitches) flat, grassy, gravel

Tariff : (2015 price) 37.40€ ☗☗ ⇌ ▣ ⚡ (10A) – Extra per person 5.20€

Rental rates : (2015 price) (from mid Feb. to end Oct.) – 36 studios. Per night from 40 to 98€ – Per week from 285 to 685€

⛽ 🚐 9.40€

The site has a swimming pool beside the Siagne river.

Surroundings : ⌂ ⌗ ᴼᴼ
Leisure activities : ⚔ ⤳
Facilities : ⛽ ♨ ⚐
Nearby : ⛾ ✗ ⚓

| | Longitude : 6.94349 |
| GPS | Latitude : 43.53503 |

Some campsites benefit from proximity to a municipal leisure centre.

MAUBEC

84660 – Michelin map **332** D10 – pop. 1 877 – alt. 120
▶ Paris 706 – Aix-en-Provence 68 – Apt 25 – Avignon 32

⚑ Municipal Les Royères du Prieuré

☎ 04 90 76 50 34. www.campingmaubec-luberon.com

Address : 52 chemin de la Combe St-Pierre (south of the town)

Opening times : from beginning April to mid Oct.

1 ha (93 pitches) terraced, flat, grassy, stony

Tariff : (2015 price) ☗ 3.50€ ⇌ 2.30€ ▣ 2.30€ – ⚡ (10A) 4.70€ – Reservation fee 10€

Rental rates : (2015 price) (from beginning April to mid Oct.) ⚘ – 3 ⌂. Per night from 70 to 80€ – Per week from 375 to 520€ – Reservation fee 10€

Lovely terraces with plenty of shade.

Surroundings : ⌂ < ᴼᴼ
Facilities : ⛽ ♨ ▥

| | Longitude : 5.1326 |
| GPS | Latitude : 43.84032 |

MAUSSANE-LES-ALPILLES

13520 – Michelin map **340** D3 – pop. 2 076 – alt. 32
▶ Paris 712 – Arles 20 – Avignon 30 – Marseille 81

⚑ Municipal les Romarins

☎ 04 90 54 33 60. www.maussane.com

Address : avenue des Alpilles (take the northern exit along the D 5, follow the signs for St-Rémy)

Opening times : from mid March to end Nov.

3 ha (145 pitches) flat, grassy, stony

Tariff : (2015 price) 25.70€ ☗☗ ⇌ ▣ ⚡ (6A) – Extra per person 6€

⛽ local sani-station

Note that the reception is at the tourist office (Maison du Tourisme).

Surroundings : ⌗ ᴼᴼ
Leisure activities : ⚐ ⚔ ✗
Facilities : ⚙ ⛽ ⚐ ☂ ♨ launderette
Nearby : ⤳

| | Longitude : 4.8093 |
| GPS | Latitude : 43.72104 |

MAZAN

84380 – Michelin map **332** D9 – pop. 5 641 – alt. 100
▶ Paris 684 – Avignon 35 – Carpentras 9 – Cavaillon 30

⛰ Le Ventoux

☎ 04 90 69 70 94. www.camping-le-ventoux.com

Address : 1348 chemin de la Combe (3km north along the D 70, follow the signs for Caromb then take the road to the left, follow the signs for Carpentras, recommended route via D 974)

0.7 ha (49 pitches) flat, grassy, stony

Rentals : 16 ⌂.

Surroundings : ⌂ < Mont Ventoux ᴼᴼ
Leisure activities : ⛾ ✗ ⚔ ⤳
Facilities : ⚙ ⛽ ▥ ♨ launderette ⚐

| | Longitude : 5.11378 |
| GPS | Latitude : 44.0805 |

MÉOLANS-REVEL

04340 – Michelin map **334** H6 – pop. 333 – alt. 1 080
▶ Paris 787 – Marseille 216 – Digne-les-Bains 74 – Gap 64

⛰ Le Rioclar ♊

☎ 04 92 81 10 32. www.rioclar.fr – alt. 1 073

Address : D 900 (located 1.5km east, follow the signs for Barcelonnette, near the Ubaye et a small lake)

Opening times : from mid May to beginning Sept.

8 ha (200 pitches) terraced, flat, grassy, stony

Tariff : 25€ ☗☗ ⇌ ▣ ⚡ (10A) – Extra per person 6€ – Reservation fee 18€

Rental rates : (from mid May to beginning Sept.) – 26 ⌂ – 3 ⌂. Per night from 60 to 100€ – Per week from 420 to 700€ – Reservation fee 18€

The owners go to great lengths to ensure the setting remains 'natural'; mobile homes with large verandah/patio areas.

Surroundings : ⌂ ⌗ ᴼᴼ
Leisure activities : ⛾ ✗ ⚐ ⚑ ⛹ ⚔ ⚲
⚐ ⤳ rafting and canyoning ⚘ multi-sports ground
Facilities : ⚙ ⛽ ⚐ ♨ launderette ⚒ ⚐
Nearby : ≋ (lake)

| | Longitude : 6.53172 |
| GPS | Latitude : 44.39928 |

▲▲▲ Domaine Loisirs de l'Ubaye

📞 04 92 81 01 96. www.loisirsubaye.com – alt. 1 073

Address : on the D 900 (3km east, follow the signs for Barcelonnette, beside the Ubaye river)

Opening times : from mid May to mid Oct.

9.5 ha (267 pitches) terraced, flat, grassy, stony

Tariff : 28.50€ ✳✳ ⇔ ▣ ⚡ (10A) – Extra per person 6.50€ – Reservation fee 15€

Rental rates : (from mid Feb. to mid Oct.) – 17 🛏 – 19 🏚 – 5 🛏. Per night from 100 to 200€ – Per week from 310 to 810€ – Reservation fee 15€ 🚽 local sani-station

Choose those pitches that look out over the river, or are near it, in preference.

Surroundings : 🌳 ⌂ ♨♨
Leisure activities : ✗ 🎦 ⏰daytime 🚣
🚴🛶 ⚓
Facilities : ♿ ⚡ 🏧 🛁 🚿 ♨ 🚻 launderette
🛶 🚐
Nearby : rafting and canyoning

GPS Longitude : 6.54638
Latitude : 44.39645

MONTPEZAT

04500 – Michelin map **334** E10
▶ Paris 806 – Digne-les-Bains 54 – Gréoux-les-Bains 23 – Manosque 37

▲▲▲ Tohapi Côteau de la Marine �</br>

📞 08 25 00 20 30. www.tohapi.fr

Address : at Vauvert, route de Baudinard (situated 2km southeast)

Opening times : from mid April to mid Sept.

12 ha (251 pitches) very uneven, terraced, gravelled, stony

Tariff : (2015 price) 16€ ✳✳ ⇔ ▣ ⚡ (10A) – Extra per person 4€
Rental rates : (2015 price) (from mid April to mid Sept.) – 186 🛏 – 58 tent lodges. Per night from 32 to 64€

Some pitches enjoy a view of the Verdon river.

Surroundings : 🌳 ⌂ ♨♨
Leisure activities : 🍸 ✗ ⏰ 🚴 ⚓ 🏓 🚣 ⚓
pedalos, electric boats ♨
Facilities : ♿ ⚡ 🛁 🚿 ♨ 🚻 launderette 🛶 🚐

GPS Longitude : 6.09818
Latitude : 43.74765

MOUSTIERS-STE-MARIE

04360 – Michelin map **334** F9 – pop. 718 – alt. 631
▶ Paris 783 – Aix-en-Provence 90 – Castellane 45 – Digne-les-Bains 47

▲▲▲ St-Jean

📞 04 92 74 66 85. www.camping-st-jean.fr

Address : St-Jean district (located 1km southwest along the D 952, follow the signs for Riez; beside the Maïre river)

Opening times : from end March to mid Oct.

1.6 ha (125 pitches) flat, relatively flat, grassy

Tariff : 24.40€ ✳✳ ⇔ ▣ ⚡ (10A) – Extra per person 6.40€ – Reservation fee 10€

Rental rates : (2015 price) (from end March to mid Oct.) – 14 🛏 – 2 canvas bungalows. Per night from 40 to 55€ – Per week from 259 to 630€ – Reservation fee 10€ 🚽 local sani-station 4€

Situated beside a river and boasting high-quality sanitary facilities.

Surroundings : 🌳 ♨♨
Leisure activities : 🍸 ⚓ 🏓
Facilities : ♿ ⚡ 🛁 🚿 🚻 🔥 refrigerated food storage facilities

GPS Longitude : 6.21496
Latitude : 43.84366

▲ Le Vieux Colombier

📞 04 92 74 61 89. caminglevieuxcolombier.com

Address : St-Michel district (800m to the south)

Opening times : from end April to mid Sept.

2.7 ha (70 pitches) very uneven, terraced, relatively flat, grassy, stony

Tariff : (2015 price) 23.30€ ✳✳ ⇔ ▣ ⚡ (6A) – Extra per person 6.10€ – Reservation fee 9€

Rental rates : (2015 price) (from end April to mid Sept.) – 14 🛏. Per night from 44 to 58€ – Per week from 270 to 630€ – Reservation fee 9€

🚽 local sani-station 7€

Situated on peaceful terraces, with some well marked-out pitches.

Surroundings : 🌳 ← ⌂ ♨♨
Leisure activities : 🎦
Facilities : ♿ ⚡ 🚻 launderette 🚐
Nearby : ✗ 🍴

GPS Longitude : 6.22166
Latitude : 43.83956

▲ Manaysse

📞 04 92 74 66 71. www.camping-manaysse.com

Address : Manaysse district (900m southwest along the D 952, follow the signs for Riez)

Opening times : from beginning April to end Oct.

1.6 ha (97 pitches) terraced, sloping, flat, grassy, gravelled

Tariff : (2015 price) 15.50€ ✳✳ ⇔ ▣ ⚡ (10A) – Extra per person 3.90€

🚽 local sani-station – 50 ▣ 11.50€

Some pitches overlook the village.

Surroundings : 🌳 ♨♨
Leisure activities : 🎦 ♨
Facilities : ♿ ⚡ 🛁 🚿 🚻 🔥

GPS Longitude : 6.21494
Latitude : 43.84452

MURS

84220 – Michelin map **332** E10 – pop. 428 – alt. 510
▶ Paris 704 – Apt 17 – Avignon 48 – Carpentras 26

▲ Municipal des Chalottes

📞 04 90 72 63 08. www.communedemurs-vaucluse.fr

Address : take the southern exit along the D 4, follow the signs for Apt then continue 1.8km to the right, after the VVF holiday village

4 ha (50 pitches) very uneven, relatively flat to hilly, stony

A wooded setting in a pleasant location.

Surroundings : 🌳 ← 🌳
Leisure activities : ⚓
Facilities : ♿ 🚻

GPS Longitude : 5.22749
Latitude : 43.93864

LE MUY

83490 – Michelin map **340** O5 – pop. 8 983 – alt. 27
▶ Paris 853 – Les Arcs 9 – Draguignan 14 – Fréjus 17

▲▲▲ Les Cigales �

📞 04 94 45 12 08. www.camping-les-cigales-sud.fr

Address : 4 chemin de Jas de la Paro (3km southwest, access via the junction with the A 8 and take the road to the right before the toll road)

Opening times : from mid March to mid Oct.

22 ha (437 pitches) very uneven, terraced, flat, grassy, stony, rocks

Tariff : ✳ 5.50€ ⇔ 4.50€ ▣ 22€ – ⚡ (10A) 6.20€

Rental rates : (from mid March to mid Oct.) – 263 🚐 – 53 🏠.
Per night from 43 to 220€ – Per week from 301 to 1,540€

In an undulating setting with pitches in both sun and shade.

Surroundings : 🏕 ♤♤
Leisure activities : 🍴 ✕ 🎱 🎯 🏇 jacuzzi 💺 ⚔
🛶 forest trail, multi-sports ground
Facilities : & ⚡ 🚐 🍴 launderette 🚿 🏊
refrigerators
GPS · Longitude : 6.54355 · Latitude : 43.46225

🏔 RCN Le Domaine de la Noguière ♣♣

📞 04 94 45 13 78. www.rcn.fr

Address : 1617 route de Fréjus

Opening times : from mid March to end Oct.

11 ha (350 pitches) undulating, flat, stony, grassy

Tariff : 53.95€ ✻✻ 🚐 🖹 🔌 (6A) – Extra per person 7€ – Reservation
fee 19.95€

Rental rates : (from mid March to end Oct.) – 37 🚐 – 25 canvas
bungalows – 3 tent lodges. Per night from 25 to 198€ – Per week
from 256 to 1,386€ – Reservation fee 19.95€

*Pitches in both sun and shade, with good quality rental op-
tions and a small lake for relaxing.*

Surroundings : ⩽ 🏕 ♤♤
Leisure activities : 🍴 ✕ 🎱 🎯 🏇 💺 ⚔ 🛶 🛶
🏊 🛶 multi-sports ground
Facilities : & ⚡ 🔌 🍴 launderette 🚿 🏊
GPS · Longitude : 6.59222 · Latitude : 43.46828

*For more information on visiting particular towns or
regions, consult the relevant regional MICHELIN Green
Guide. We also recommend you use the appropriate
Michelin regional map to locate your selected campsite,
to calculate distances and to work out the best route.*

83860 – Michelin map **340** J5 – pop. 4 123 – alt. 380
▶ Paris 794 – Aix-en-Provence 44 – Brignoles 26 – Marseille 42

🏔 Tohapi Domaine de La Sainte Baume ♣♣

📞 04 94 78 92 68. www.saintebaume.com – limited spaces for one-
night stay

Address : Delvieux Sud district (900m north along the D 80 and take a
right turn, from the A 8: take exit St-Maximin-la-Ste-Baume)

Opening times : from beginning April to end Sept.

8 ha (250 pitches) relatively flat, flat, grassy, stony

Tariff : (2015 price) 39€ ✻✻ 🚐 🖹 🔌 (10A) – Extra per person 11€ –
Reservation fee 20€

Rental rates : (2015 price) (from beginning April to end Sept.) –
200 🚐. Per night from 40 to 92€ – Per week from 224 to 1,316€ –
Reservation fee 20€

🚐 local sani-station

The pitches are well shaded and laid out beside a water park.

Surroundings : 🏊 🏕 ♤♤
Leisure activities : 🍴 ✕ 🎱 🎯 🏇 jacuzzi
💺 ⚔ 🚴 ✂ 🏊 multi-sports ground,
entertainment room
Facilities : & ⚡ 🔌 🏊 🍴 launderette
🚿 🏊
Nearby : 🏇
GPS · Longitude : 5.78808 · Latitude : 43.37664

05100 – Michelin map **334** H2 – pop. 339 – alt. 1 640 – Winter sports :
1 400/2 000 m
▶ Paris 693 – Bardonècchia 18 – Briançon 21

⛰ Fontcouverte

📞 04 92 21 38 21. www.camping-fontcouverte-névache-alpes – access
difficult for caravans – alt. 1 860 – 🏕

Address : 1 lot. de l'Aiguille Rouge (6.2km northwest along the
D 301t, Vallée de la Clarée)

Opening times : from beginning June to mid Sept.

2 ha (100 pitches) terraced, relatively flat, flat, grassy, stony

Tariff : ✻ 3€ 🚐 1.80€ 🖹 3.20€

*In a pleasant location at the end of a valley and beside a moun-
tain stream.*

Surroundings : 🏊 ⩽ ♤♤
Leisure activities : 🛶
Facilities : & ⚡ 🚐 🚿
Nearby : ✕
GPS · Longitude : 6.69323 · Latitude : 45.11898

04300 – Michelin map **334** D9 – pop. 237 – alt. 450
▶ Paris 745 – Digne-les-Bains 49 – Forcalquier 7 – Gréoux-les-
Bains 33

🏔 Sites et Paysages Moulin de Ventre ♣♣

📞 04 92 78 63 31. www.moulin-de-ventre.com

Address : 2.5km east along the N 100, follow the signs for La
Brillanne

28 ha/3 for camping (124 pitches) terraced, flat and relatively flat,
grassy

Rentals : 12 🚐 – 5 🏠 – 2 apartments – 2 tent lodges.

Situated beside the Lauzon river and a small lake.

Surroundings : 🏊 🏕 ♤♤
Leisure activities : 🍴 ✕ 🎱 🕐 daytime
(July-Aug.) 🏇 💺 ⚔ 🏊 🛶 pedalos
Facilities : & ⚡ 🍴 🏊 🍴 launderette 🚿
GPS · Longitude : 5.86798 · Latitude : 43.9333

13660 – Michelin map **340** F3 – pop. 3 055 – alt. 90
▶ Paris 709 – Marseille 72 – Avignon 29 – Nîmes 98

🏔 La Vallée Heureuse

📞 04 90 44 17 13. www.valleeheureuse.com

Address : Lavau district (situated 2km to the south, follow the signs
for Sénas then take left turning along the D 73D)

Opening times : from beginning April to end Oct.

8 ha (80 pitches) terraced, gravelled, flat, grassy

Tariff : (2015 price) 16.50€ ✻✻ 🚐 🖹 🔌 (10A) – Extra per person 5€

Rental rates : (2015 price) (from beginning April to end Oct.) –
10 🚐 – 2 gîtes. Per night from 54 to 87€ – Per week
from 735 to 840€

In a lovely natural setting.

Surroundings : 🏊 ⩽ 🏕 ♤♤
Leisure activities : 🎱 💺 ⚔ 🏊
Facilities : & ⚡ 🔌 🍴 launderette,
refrigerated food storage facilities
Nearby : ✕ 🏊 🛶
GPS · Longitude : 5.03956 · Latitude : 43.7817

ORPIERRE

05700 – Michelin map **334** C7 – pop. 326 – alt. 682
▶ Paris 689 – Château-Arnoux 47 – Digne-les-Bains 72 – Gap 55

⚠ Les Princes d'Orange

✆ 04 92 66 22 53. www.campingorpierre.com

Address : at Le Flonsaine (300m south of the village, 150m from the Céans river)

Opening times : from beginning April to end Oct.

20 ha/4 for camping (120 pitches) very uneven, terraced, flat, grassy, stony

Tariff : (2015 price) 41€ ✿✿ ⇔ 🗐 (10A) – Extra per person 10.80€ – Reservation fee 10€

Rental rates : (2015 price) (from beginning April to end Oct.) – 36 🚐 – 2 tent lodges. Per night from 68 to 120€ – Per week from 322 to 896€ – Reservation fee 12€

🚐 AireService sani-station 4€ – 🚿 🗐 13.50€

Surroundings : ⟋ ≼ Orpierre and the mountains 🎯🎯	G	
Leisure activities : 🍴✗ 🏠 ⚡ 🕹	P	Longitude : 5.69652
Facilities : 🚿 ⚬ 🚽 🎽 launderette	S	Latitude : 44.31077
Nearby : ⛹		

This guide is not intended as a list of all the camping sites in France; its aim is to provide a selection of the best sites in each category.

PERNES-LES-FONTAINES

84210 – Michelin map **332** D10 – pop. 10 454 – alt. 75
▶ Paris 685 – Apt 43 – Avignon 23 – Carpentras 6

⚠ Municipal de la Coucourelle

✆ 04 90 66 45 55. camping@perneslesfontaines.fr

Address : 391 avenue René Char (located 1km east along the D 28, follow the signs for St-Didier, at the sports centre)

Opening times : from beginning April to end Sept.

1 ha (40 pitches) flat, grassy

Tariff : (2015 price) 15.50€ ✿✿ ⇔ 🗐 (10A) – Extra per person 4€
🚐 local sani-station

A leafy, green setting with bushes and shrubs.

Surroundings : ⟋ 🏠 🎯	G	
Leisure activities : ⚡	P	Longitude : 5.0677
Facilities : 🚿 ⚬ 🎽 🚽 🖥	S	Latitude : 43.99967
Nearby : ✗ 🕹		

PERTUIS

84120 – Michelin map **332** G11 – pop. 18 706 – alt. 246
▶ Paris 747 – Aix-en-Provence 23 – Apt 36 – Avignon 76

⚠⚠⚠ Franceloc Domaine les Pinèdes du Luberon ▲▲

✆ 04 90 79 10 98. www.campings-franceloc.fr/accueil-camping-les_pinedes_du_luberon

Address : avenue Pierre Augier (situated 2km east along the D 973)

Opening times : from mid March to mid Oct.

5 ha (220 pitches) terraced, flat, grassy, stony

Tariff : (2015 price) 46€ ✿✿ ⇔ 🗐 (10A) – Extra per person 7€ – Reservation fee 27€

Rental rates : (2015 price) (from mid March to mid Oct.) 🚿 (1 mobile home) – 140 🚐 – 6 🏠 – 8 canvas bungalows. Per night from 19 to 203€ – Per week from 133 to 1,421€ – Reservation fee 27€

🚐 AireService sani-station 6€

Surroundings : 🏠 🎯🎯	G	
Leisure activities : 🍴✗ 🏠 🖥 🕹 ⚡ 🕹		
🏊 ⚡	P	Longitude : 5.5253
Facilities : 🚿 ⚬ 🖥 🎽 🚽 🎽 launderette	S	Latitude : 43.68979
Nearby : ✗		

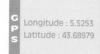

PONT-DU-FOSSÉ

05260 – Michelin map **334** F4 – pop. 980
▶ Paris 673 – Marseille 204 – Gap 24 – Grenoble 102

⚠ Le Diamant

✆ 04 92 55 91 25. www.campingdiamant.com

Address : at Pont du Fossé (800m southwest along the D 944, follow the signs for Gap)

Opening times : from beginning May to end Sept.

4 ha (100 pitches) flat, grassy

Tariff : (2015 price) 23.60€ ✿✿ ⇔ 🗐 (10A) – Extra per person 4.80€

Rental rates : (from beginning May to mid Sept.) – 16 🚐. Per night from 35 to 80€ – Per week from 250 to 550€

🚐 local sani-station 21.60€ – 10 🗐 21.60€
Situated beside the Drac river.

Surroundings : 🎯🎯	G	
Leisure activities : 🏠 ⚡ ⛹ 🎣 climbing wall	P	Longitude : 6.2197
Facilities : 🚿 ⚬ 🎽 🚽 🎽 launderette 🏠	S	Latitude : 44.66535

LE PONTET

84130 – Michelin map **332** C10 – pop. 16 891 – alt. 40
▶ Paris 688 – Marseille 100 – Avignon 5 – Aix 83

⚠ Le Grand Bois

✆ 04 90 31 37 44. www.campinglegrandbois.fr

Address : 1340 chemin du Grand Bois (3km northeast along the D 62, follow the signs for Vedène and take turning to the left, at La Tapy, from the A 7 take the Avignon-Nord exit)

Opening times : from mid May to mid Sept.

1.5 ha (100 pitches) flat, grassy

Tariff : 25€ ✿✿ ⇔ 🗐 (5A) – Extra per person 6€
🚐 local sani-station 4€
A pleasant wooded site.

Surroundings : 🏠 🎯🎯	G	
Leisure activities : 🏠 🕹	P	Longitude : 4.8836
Facilities : 🚿 ⚬ 🎽 🚽 🎽 🖥	S	Latitude : 43.97455

PRUNIÈRES

05230 – Michelin map **334** F5 – pop. 287 – alt. 1 018
▶ Paris 681 – Briançon 68 – Gap 23 – Grenoble 119

⚠⚠⚠ Le Roustou

✆ 04 92 50 62 63. www.campingleroustou.com

Address : 4km south along the N 94 (coastal road, south of village)

11 ha/6 for camping (180 pitches) terraced, undulating, relatively flat, flat, grassy, fine gravel

Rentals : 26 ⌂ – 1 gîte.

Surroundings : ⬚ ⬚ ⬚ ⬚ ⬚
Leisure activities : 🍸 ✗ 🏛 ⬚ ⬚ ⬚ ⬚
Facilities : ⬚ ⬚ ⬚ ⬚ ⬚ ⬚
Nearby : ⚓

GPS — Longitude : 6.34111
Latitude : 44.5225

PUGET-SUR-ARGENS

83480 – Michelin map **340** P5 – pop. 6 722 – alt. 17
▶ Paris 863 – Les Arcs 21 – Cannes 41 – Draguignan 26

⋀⋀⋀ Yelloh! Village La Bastiane ⚊⚊

☎ 04 94 55 55 94. www.labastiane.com

Address : 1056 chemin de Suvière (2.50km to the north)

Opening times : from mid April to mid Oct.

4 ha (180 pitches) terraced, flat, grassy, stony

Tariff : 52€ 🚶🚶 ⬚ 🔲 ⬚ (10A) – Extra per person 8€
Rental rates : (from mid April to mid Oct.) – 100 ⬚ – 6 ⌂ –
18 canvas bungalows. Per night from 30 to 247€ – Per week
from 210 to 1,729€

The site offers pleasant shade under pine trees.

Surroundings : ⬚ ⬚ ⬚
Leisure activities : 🍸 ✗ 🏛 ⬚ ⬚ ⬚ ⬚
⬚ disco, multi-sports ground
Facilities : ⬚ ⬚ ⬚ ⬚ ⬚ launderette ⬚
Nearby : 🏇

GPS — Longitude : 6.67837
Latitude : 43.46975

PUIMICHEL

04700 – Michelin map **334** E9 – pop. 253 – alt. 723
▶ Paris 737 – Avignon 140 – Grenoble 175 – Marseille 112

⋀ Les Matherons

☎ 04 92 79 60 10. www.campinglesmatherons.com

Address : on the D 12 (northern part of the village)

Opening times : from mid April to end Sept.

70 ha/4 for camping (27 pitches) terraced, relatively flat, flat, grassy, stony

Tariff : 🚶 5.50€ ⬚ 🔲 9€ – ⬚ (3A) 3.50€
Rental rates : permanent – 2 ⬚. Per night from 290 to 550€

In a wild and unspoilt setting, in the heart of woodland. Vehicles are not permitted.

Surroundings : ⬚ ⬚
Leisure activities : ⬚
Facilities : ⬚ ⬚ ⬚ ⬚ ⬚ ⬚

GPS — Longitude : 6.00763
Latitude : 43.96035

PUYLOUBIER

13114 – Michelin map **340** J4 – pop. 1 798 – alt. 380
▶ Paris 775 – Aix-en-Provence 26 – Rians 38 – St-Maximin-la-Ste-Baume 19

⋀ Municipal Cézanne

☎ 04 42 66 36 33. www.le-cezanne.com

Address : chemin Philippe Noclercq (take the eastern exit along the D 57, by the stadium)

Opening times : from mid March to mid Nov.

1 ha (50 pitches) terraced, relatively flat, grassy, stony

Tariff : 🚶 6€ ⬚ 2.20€ 🔲 3.10€ – ⬚ (6A) 3.20€

Rental rates : (from beginning March to end Nov.) – 2 'gypsy' caravans – 4 ⬚ – 2 gîtes. Per night from 50 to 80€ – Per week from 250 to 480€

⬚ local sani-station 3€ – 2 🔲 12€ – ⬚ ⬚ 12€
Situated at the foot of Mont Ste-Victoire.

Surroundings : ⬚ ⬚
Leisure activities : ⬚
Facilities : ⬚ ⬚ ⬚

GPS — Longitude : 5.68227
Latitude : 43.527

RAMATUELLE

83350 – Michelin map **340** O6 – pop. 2 240 – alt. 136
▶ Paris 873 – Fréjus 35 – Hyères 52 – Le Lavandou 34

⋀⋀⋀ Yelloh! Village les Tournels ⚊⚊

☎ 04 94 55 90 90. www.tournels.com

Address : route de Camarat

Opening times : from end March to end Oct.

20 ha (890 pitches) very uneven, terraced, flat, grassy, stony

Tariff : 67€ 🚶🚶 ⬚ 🔲 ⬚ (10A) – Extra per person 8€
Rental rates : (from mid March to end Oct.) ⬚ (2 mobile homes) –
304 ⬚ – 50 ⌂. Per night from 69 to 331€ – Per week
from 483 to 2,317€

⬚ Flot Bleu sani-station 5€
On a shaded hillside with a lovely covered aquatic centre; some pitches have a fine view of Pampelonne beach.

Surroundings : ⬚ ⬚ ⬚ ⬚ ⬚
Leisure activities : 🍸 ✗ 🏛 ⬚ (amphitheatre)
⬚ ⬚ ⬚ hammam, jacuzzi ⬚ ⬚ ⬚ ⬚
⬚ ⬚ disco, multi-sports ground, spa centre
Facilities : ⬚ ⬚ ⬚ ⬚ ⬚ ⬚ ⬚ launderette
⬚ refrigerated food storage facilities

GPS — Longitude : 6.65112
Latitude : 43.20537

⋀⋀⋀ Village Vacances La Toison d'Or ⚊⚊
(rental of mobile homes only)

☎ 04 94 79 83 54. www.riviera-villages.com

Address : route des Tamaris (Plage de Pampelonne – beach)

Opening times : from mid March to beginning Oct.

5 ha (500 pitches) open site, flat, grassy, sandy

Rental rates : (2015 price) – 220 ⬚. Per night from 44 to 310€ –
Per week from 490 to 2,170€

Several mobile home villages with themed decoration, very popular.

Surroundings : ⬚ ⬚ ⬚
Leisure activities : 🍸 ✗ 🏛 ⬚ ⬚ ⬚ ⬚
hammam, jacuzzi ⬚ ⬚ concierge
services, spa centre
Facilities : ⬚ ⬚ ⬚ launderette ⬚ ⬚
Nearby : ⬚

GPS — Longitude : 6.66007
Latitude : 43.23884

These symbols are used for a campsite that is exceptional in its category:
⋀⋀⋀ … ⋀ *Particularly pleasant setting, quality and range of services available*
⬚ ⬚ *Tranquil, isolated site – quiet site, particularly at night*
⬚ ⬚ *Exceptional view – interesting or panoramic view*

⚠️ Campéole la Croix du Sud ♠️

📞 04 94 55 51 23. https://www.campeole.com/campeole/camping-la-croix-du-sud-var.html#content – limited spaces for one-night stay

Address : route des Plages (D61, then D93 heading east out of town)

Opening times : from end March to beginning Oct.

3 ha (120 pitches) terraced, flat, grassy, stony, sandy

Tariff : 24€ ✚✚ ⇔ 🔲 (10A) – Extra per person 10€ – Reservation fee 25€

Rental rates : (from end March to beginning Oct.) – 17 🏠 – 11 🏚 – 30 canvas bungalows. Per night from 34 to 214€ – Per week from 238 to 1,498€ – Reservation fee 25€

In the heart of wine country, with pitches in the shade of pine trees.

Surroundings : 🌿 ♨️ Leisure activities : 🍴✕ 🏸 🎣 🚴 🛶 Facilities : 🚿 🔌 🚰 📷	**GPS** Longitude : 6.64104 Latitude : 43.21426

RÉGUSSE

83630 – Michelin map **340** L4 – pop. 2 067 – alt. 545
▶ Paris 838 – Marseille 113 – Toulon 94 – Digne-les-Bains 75

⚠️ Homair Vacances Les Lacs du Verdon

📞 04 94 70 17 95. www.homair.com

Address : Domaine de Roquelande

Opening times : from beginning April to end Sept.

17 ha (444 pitches) fine gravel

Tariff : (2015 price) 15.50€ ✚✚ ⇔ 🔲 (10A) – Extra per person 1.50€ – Reservation fee 10€

Rental rates : (from beginning April to end Sept.) – 359 🏠 – 10 tent lodges. Per night from 15 to 168€ – Per week from 105 to 1,176€ – Reservation fee 25€

🏕 6 🔲 25€

The site is in two sections, lying either side of a small road.

Surroundings : 🌿 🚽 ♨️ Leisure activities : 🍴✕ 🏛 🏸 🎣 🚴 ✂️ 🏊 🛶 multi-sports area Facilities : 🐴 🔌 📷 🚰 launderette 🌊 Nearby : 🐎	**GPS** Longitude : 6.15073 Latitude : 43.66041

RIEZ

04500 – Michelin map **334** E10 – pop. 1 783 – alt. 520
▶ Paris 792 – Marseille 105 – Digne-les-Bains 41 – Draguignan 64

⚠️ Rose de Provence

📞 04 92 77 75 45. www.rose-de-provence.com

Address : rue Edouard Dauphin

Opening times : from mid April to beginning Oct.

1 ha (81 pitches) terrace, flat, grassy, gravelled

Tariff : (2015 price) 21.90€ ✚✚ ⇔ 🔲 (6A) – Extra per person 6.10€ – Reservation fee 10€

Rental rates : (2015 price) (from beginning April to mid Oct.) – 7 🏠 – 2 🏚 – 2 canvas bungalows. Per night from 38 to 69€ – Per week from 210 to 637€ – Reservation fee 15€

A variety of rental accommodation of good quality.

Surroundings : 🌿 🚽 ♨️ Leisure activities : 🎣 Facilities : 🚿 🔌 🚰 📷 refrigerated food storage facilities Nearby : 🐎 ✂️	**GPS** Longitude : 6.09922 Latitude : 43.81307

LA ROCHE-DE-RAME

05310 – Michelin map **334** H4 – pop. 830 – alt. 1 000
▶ Paris 701 – Briançon 22 – Embrun 27 – Gap 68

⚠️ Le Verger

📞 04 92 20 92 23. www.campingleverger.com

Address : at Les Gillis (head 1.2km northwest along the N 94, follow the signs for Briançon)

Opening times : permanent

1.6 ha (50 pitches) terraced, relatively flat, grassy

Tariff : (2015 price) 20.50€ ✚✚ ⇔ 🔲 (10A) – Extra per person 5.50€ – Reservation fee 30€

Rental rates : (2015 price) (from beginning May to beginning June) – 6 🏠 – 1 🏚 – 1 gîte. Per night from 50 to 72€ – Per week from 400 to 510€ – Reservation fee 90€

🏕 local sani-station 4€

Pitches in the shade of cherry and apricot trees.

Surroundings : 🌿 ≤ ♨️ Leisure activities : 🏛 🎣 Facilities : 🚿 🔌 🚰 🏛 🛁 🚰 launderette	**GPS** Longitude : 6.57951 Latitude : 44.7581

⚠️ Municipal du Lac

📞 06 82 04 70 71. www.camping-du-lac-05.fr

Address : heading south on the N94 from the village, left turn

Opening times : from beginning May to end Sept.

1 ha (81 pitches) terraced, relatively flat, grassy

Tariff : (2015 price) 20.60€ ✚✚ ⇔ 🔲 (10A) – Extra per person 4.90€

Rental rates : (2015 price) (from beginning May to end Sept.) – 3 🏚 – 1 tent lodge. Per night from 55 to 110€ – Per week from 370 to 700€

🏕 local sani-station – 15 🔲

Surroundings : ≤ ♨️ Leisure activities : 🍴 Facilities : 🚿 🔌 🚰 🚰 📷 Nearby : ✕ 🎣 🏊 (lake) 🚣 pedalos	**GPS** Longitude : 6.58145 Latitude : 44.74673

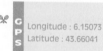

Using the traditional Michelin classification method, the guide provides you with an easy, speedy reference for assessing the category of each site: 1 to 5 tents (see page 10).

LA ROCHE DES ARNAUDS

05400 – Michelin map **334** D5 – pop. 1 372 – alt. 945
▶ Paris 672 – Corps 49 – Gap 15 – St-Étienne-en-Dévoluy 33

⚠️ Au Blanc Manteau

📞 04 92 57 82 56. www.campingaublancmanteau.fr – alt. 900 – 🏪

Address : route de Ceuze (1.3km southwest along the D 18; beside some rapids)

Opening times : permanent

4 ha (40 pitches) flat, grassy, stony

Tariff : (2015 price) 18€ ✚✚ ⇔ 🔲 (10A) – Extra per person 4.50€

Surroundings : ❄️ 🌿 ♨️ Leisure activities : 🍴 🏛 🎣 🚴 ✂️ 🏊 Facilities : 🚿 🔌 🚰 🏛 🛁 🚰 📷 🌊	**GPS** Longitude : 5.95085 Latitude : 44.54962

ROQUEBRUNE-SUR-ARGENS

83520 – Michelin map **340** O5 – pop. 12 708 – alt. 13
▶ Paris 862 – Les Arcs 18 – Cannes 49 – Draguignan 23

⁂ Domaine de la Bergerie ⚏

🕿 04 98 11 45 45. www.domainelabergerie.com
Address : Vallée du Fournel – route du Col de Bougnon (head 8km southeast along the D 7, follow the signs for St-Aygulf and turn right onto D 8; beside some lakes)
Opening times : from end April to mid Oct.
60 ha (700 pitches) very uneven, terraced, flat, grassy, stony
Tariff : 44.50€ ✸✸ 🚗 🔟 (10A) – Extra per person 12.20€ – Reservation fee 25€
Rental rates : (from beginning March to end Oct.) – 500 🛖. Per night from 68 to 188€ – Per week from 476 to 1,319€

Attractive pitches, partly on a wooded hill.

Surroundings : 🏞 ⌂ ♨
Leisure activities : 🍴 ✕ 🎣 🎦 (open-air theatre) 🏃 🛶 🚣 hammam, jacuzzi 🏹 🚲 ⚽ 🐎 🎱 🏊 ♨ disco, paintballing, farm or petting farm, ponies, multi-sports ground, spa centre, entertainment room
Facilities : 🚿 ⚐ 🚽 🔥 ♨ launderette 🛒 🏧

⁂ Les Pêcheurs ⚏

🕿 04 94 45 71 25. www.camping-les-pecheurs.com
Address : 700m northwest on the D 7, north of the Argens river
Opening times : from beginning April to end Sept.
3.3 ha (190 pitches) flat, grassy
Tariff : (2015 price) 18.20€ ✸✸ 🚗 🔟 🔥 (10A) – Extra per person 4.20€ – Reservation fee 25€
Rental rates : (2015 price) (from beginning April to end Sept.) – 47 🛖 – 20 🛖 – 20 canvas bungalows. Per night from 49 to 87€ – Per week from 294 to 1,330€ – Reservation fee 25€
🚐 AireService sani-station

An open spa area, with access via a tunnel to a small boating centre on the other side of the road.

Surroundings : 🏞 ⌂ 🎋
Leisure activities : 🍴 ✕ 🎣 🎦 daytime 🏃 🚣 jacuzzi 🏹 🎱 🏊 🚣 multi-sports ground
Facilities : 🚿 ⚐ 🔥 ♨ launderette 🛒 🏧
Nearby : 🏖 watersports centre, pedalos

⁂ Lei Suves

🕿 04 94 45 43 95. www.lei-suves.com – limited spaces for one-night stay
Address : Le Blavet district (head 4km north along the D 7 and take underpass under A 8)
Opening times : from beginning April to mid Oct.
7 ha (309 pitches) terraced, flat, grassy, stony
Tariff : 52.75€ ✸✸ 🚗 🔟 🔥 (6A) – Extra per person 11.30€ – Reservation fee 25€
Rental rates : (from beginning April to mid Oct.) 🎿 – 30 🛖. Per week from 395 to 1,070€ – Reservation fee 25€

In a pleasant wooded setting, with pines and cork oaks.

Surroundings : 🏞 ⌂ ♨
Leisure activities : 🍴 ✕ 🎦 (open air theatre) 🏃 🏹 ⚽ 🏊 multi-sports ground
Facilities : 🚿 ⚐ 🔥 ♨ launderette 🛒 🏧

⛺ Moulin des Iscles

🕿 04 94 45 70 74. www.campingdesiscles.com
Address : chemin du Moulin des Iscles (head 1.8km east along the D 7, follow the signs for St-Aygulf and take road to the left)
Opening times : from beginning April to end Sept.
1.5 ha (90 pitches) flat, grassy
Tariff : 🚗 🔟 23.90€ – 🔥 (6A) 3.90€ – Reservation fee 15€
Rental rates : (2015 price) (from beginning April to end Sept.) 🚿 (1 mobile home) – 6 🛖 – 1 🏠 – 5 apartments. Per night from 100€ – Per week from 700 to 780€ – Reservation fee 15€

A peaceful site beside the Argens river.

Surroundings : 🏞 ♨
Leisure activities : ✕ 🎣 🚲 🏹 🚣
Facilities : 🚿 ⚐ 🔟 🏛 🔥 🔥 ♨ 🌳 launderette 🛒 🏧

Longitude : 6.65784
Latitude : 43.44497

Do not confuse:
⛺ to ⁂ : *MICHELIN classification with*
★ to ★★★★★ : *official classification*

LA ROQUE-D'ANTHÉRON

13640 – Michelin map **340** G3 – pop. 5 143 – alt. 183
▶ Paris 726 – Aix-en-Provence 29 – Cavaillon 34 – Manosque 60

⁂ Tohapi Les Iscles – (rental of mobile homes only)

🕿 08 25 00 20 30. www.tohapi.fr
Address : at La Durance (head 3km south along the D 23)
Opening times : from mid April to mid Sept.
10 ha (269 pitches) flat, grassy, stony
Rental rates : (2015 price) – 270 🛖. Per night from 32 to 64€

Surroundings : 🏞 ♨
Leisure activities : 🍴 ✕ 🎦 🏃 🏹 ⚽ 🏊 🏖 (river) 🚣 🚣 🚣
Facilities : ⚐ ♨ launderette 🛒 🏧

Longitude : 5.32099
Latitude : 43.72819

ST-ANDRÉ-LES-ALPES

04170 – Michelin map **334** H9 – pop. 930 – alt. 914
▶ Paris 786 – Castellane 20 – Colmars 28 – Digne-les-Bains 43

⛺ Municipal les Iscles

🕿 04 92 89 02 29. www.camping-les-iscles.com – alt. 894
Address : chemin des Iscles (located 1km south along the N 202, follow the signs for Annot and take the turning to the left, 300m from the Verdon river)
Opening times : from beginning April to end Oct.
2.5 ha (200 pitches) flat, grassy, stony
Tariff : (2015 price) 15.10€ ✸✸ 🚗 🔟 🔥 (10A) – Extra per person 4.30€
Rental rates : (from beginning April to end Oct.) 🚿 (1 mobile home) – 16 🛖. Per night from 30 to 50€ – Per week from 210 to 525€
🚐 160 🔟 16€

Ssituated in a pleasant pine wood.

Surroundings : 🏞 ♨
Leisure activities : 🎣 🏹
Facilities : 🚿 ⚐ 🔥 ♨ launderette
Nearby : ⚽ 🏃 sports trail

Longitude : 6.50844
Latitude : 43.9612

ST-APOLLINAIRE

05160 – Michelin map **334** G5 – pop. 117 – alt. 1 285
▶ Paris 684 – Embrun 19 – Gap 27 – Mont-Dauphin 37

⚠ Campéole Le Clos du Lac

✆ 04 92 44 27 43. www.camping-closdulac.com – access difficult for caravans and campervans – alt. 1 450

Address : route des Lacs (2.3km northwest along the D 509; 50m from the small lake at St-Apollinaire)

Opening times : from mid June to mid Sept.

2 ha (68 pitches) terraced, relatively flat, grassy

Tariff : 13€ ★★ ⊕ 🔲 ⚡ (10A) – Extra per person 10€ – Reservation fee 25€

Rental rates : (from mid June to mid Sept.) – 18 🛖. Per night from 47 to 102€ – Per week from 329 to 714€ – Reservation fee 25€

In an attractive elevated location.

Surroundings : 🏞 ⩽ Lac de Serre-Ponçon and mountains ♀
Leisure activities : 🛶 jacuzzi 🛥
Facilities : 🚿 ⛲ 🔗 🚮
Nearby : 🍴 ✕ 🚿 ⛺ ≅ (lake) 🎣
Longitude : 6.34642
Latitude : 44.56127

ST-AYGULF

83370 – Michelin map **340** P5
▶ Paris 872 – Brignoles 69 – Draguignan 35 – Fréjus 6

⚠ L'Étoile d'Argens 👥

✆ 04 94 81 01 41. www.etoiledargens.com

Address : chemin des Étangs (5km northwest along the D 7, follow the signs for Roquebrune-sur-Argens and turn right onto the D 8; beside the Argens river)

Opening times : from beginning April to end Sept.

11 ha (493 pitches) flat, grassy

Tariff : 64€ ★★ ⊕ 🔲 ⚡ (10A) – Extra per person 10€ – Reservation fee 25€

Rental rates : (from beginning April to end Sept.) 🏠 – 107 🛖. Per night from 40 to 250€ – Per week from 280 to 1,750€ – Reservation fee 35€
🛖 100 🔲 64€

Pretty, spacious pitches with shade. There's a river shuttle service to the beaches (duration: 30 min).

Surroundings : 🏞 ⬜ ♀♀
Leisure activities : 🍴 ✕ 🎮 🏋 jacuzzi 🛥 🚴 🎯 ⛱ 🛶 disco, multi-sports ground
Facilities : 🛗 🚿 🔢 🔗 🚮 ⛺ 🔗 launderette ⛲ 🚿
Nearby : ⚓ scuba diving
Longitude : 6.70562
Latitude : 43.41596

⚠ Sandaya La Résidence du Campeur

✆ 04 94 81 01 59. www.sandaya.fr

Address : 189 Les Grands Châteaux-de-Villepey (3km northwest along the D 7, follow the signs for Roquebrune-sur-Argens)

Opening times : from mid April to beginning Oct.

10 ha (451 pitches) flat, gravelled, stony

Tariff : (2015 price) 44€ ★★ ⊕ 🔲 ⚡ (10A) – Extra per person 7.50€

Rental rates : (2015 price) permanent – 265 🛖 – 20 🏠 – 20 tent lodges. Per night from 42 to 127€ – Per week from 720 to 1,730€ – Reservation fee 32€
🛖 130 🔲 68€

A variety of good-quality rental accommodation with private sanitary facilities for each pitch.

Surroundings : 🏞 ⬜ ♀♀
Leisure activities : 🍴 ✕ 🎮 🎯 🏋 🛥 🚴
🎾 ⛱ 🛶 ⛴ multi-sports ground
Facilities : 🚿 – 451 individual sanitary facilities (🔲 ⛲ 🔗 wc) ⛺ 🚿 ⛲ launderette 🚿 🚿
Longitude : 6.70875
Latitude : 43.40867

⚠⚠⚠ Au Paradis des Campeurs

✆ 04 94 96 93 55. www.paradis-des-campeurs.com

Address : at La Gaillarde-Plage (2.5km south along the N 98, follow the signs for Ste-Maxime)

Opening times : from beginning April to beginning Oct.

6 ha/3.5 for camping (180 pitches)

Tariff : (2015 price) 32€ ★★ ⊕ 🔲 ⚡ (6A) – Extra per person 6€ – Reservation fee 30€

Rental rates : (2015 price) (from beginning April to beginning Oct.) 🛗 (1 mobile home) – 17 🛖. Per week from 290 to 770€
🛖 local sani-station

Some pitches have a sea view and direct access to the beach via a tunnel. Choose those pitches furthest away from the road.

Surroundings : ⬜ ♀♀
Leisure activities : 🍴 ✕ 🎮 🛥
Facilities : 🛗 🚿 📮 ⛲ 🔗 ⛺ 🚿 ⛲ launderette 🚿 🚿
Nearby : disco
Longitude : 6.71235
Latitude : 43.366

ST-CLÉMENT-SUR-DURANCE

05600 – Michelin map **334** H5 – pop. 285 – alt. 872
▶ Paris 715 – L'Argentière-la-Bessée 21 – Embrun 13 – Gap 54

⚠ Les Mille Vents

✆ 04 92 45 10 90. www.camping-les-mille-vents.com

Address : route de St-André (located 1km east along the N 94, follow the signs for Briançon and take D 994d to the right after the bridge and the white water sports centre)

3.5 ha (100 pitches) terrace, flat, grassy

Rentals : 3 🏠.

Situated beside the river.

Surroundings : ⩽ ♀
Leisure activities : 🛥 🛶
Facilities : 🛗 🚿 ⛲ 🔗 🚮
Nearby : ✕ rafting and canyoning
Longitude : 6.6618
Latitude : 44.66362

ST-CYR-SUR-MER

83270 – Michelin map **340** J6 – pop. 11 865 – alt. 10
▶ Paris 810 – Bandol 8 – Brignoles 70 – La Ciotat 10

⚠⚠⚠ Le Clos Ste-Thérèse

✆ 04 94 32 12 21. www.clos-therese.com – pitches accessed via steep slope, help moving caravans onto and off pitches avilable on request – limited spaces for one-night stay

Address : route de Bandol (3.5km south of the town along the D 559)

Opening times : from beginning April to end Sept.

4 ha (123 pitches) very uneven, terraced, flat, grassy, stony

Tariff : (2015 price) 33.70€ ★★ ⊕ 🔲 ⚡ (10A) – Extra per person 7€ – Reservation fee 24€

Rental rates : (2015 price) (from beginning April to end Sept.) – 5 🚐 – 25 🏠 – 5 canvas bungalows. Per night from 44 to 72€ – Per week from 252 to 1,260€

Choose those pitches furthest away from the road.

Surroundings : 🏕 ♉♉
Leisure activities : 🍽 🏛 🚣 ⛵
Facilities : &. ⚡ 🗑 🚿 🚻 🖾 ⚓

Longitude : 5.72951
Latitude : 43.15955

ST-ÉTIENNE-DE-TINÉE

06660 – Michelin map **341** C2 – pop. 1 311 – alt. 1 147
▶ Paris 788 – Grenoble 226 – Marseille 262 – Nice 90

⚠ Municipal du Plan d'Eau

✆ 04 93 02 41 57. www.campingduplandeau.com

Address : route du col de la Bonette (500m north of the town)

Opening times : from beginning June to end Sept.

0.5 ha (23 pitches) terraced, flat, stony

Tariff : (2015 price) ♦ 3€ 🚗 🖾 7€ ⚡ (13A)
🚉 local sani-station 3€ – 6 🖾 13.40€

Situated beside the Tinée river, overlooking a small, pretty lake; pitches for tents only. Electricity hook-ups for campervans only at the site entrance.

Surroundings : 🏊 ♉ 🏕
Leisure activities : 🏛 🏖 (beach) 🎣 ⚓
Facilities : ⚡ 🅿 🗛 🚻
Nearby : fitness trail

Longitude : 6.92299
Latitude : 44.25858

ST-ÉTIENNE-DU-GRÈS

13103 – Michelin map **340** D3 – pop. 2 202 – alt. 7
▶ Paris 706 – Arles 16 – Avignon 24 – Les Baux-de-Provence 15

⚠ Municipal du Grès

✆ 04 90 49 00 03. www.campingalpilles.com

Address : avenue du Dr-Barberin (take the northwestern exit along the D 99, follow the signs for Tarascon; near the stadium, 50m from the Vigueira)

Opening times : from beginning Jan. to end Nov.

0.6 ha (40 pitches) flat, grassy, stony

Tariff : (2015 price) 18€ ♦♦ 🚗 🖾 ⚡ (16A) – Extra per person 3.50€
🚉 local sani-station 4€ – 6 🖾 18€

Surroundings : 🏕 ♉♉
Facilities : ⚡ 🚿 🗑 🚻 🖾 🚻 launderette

Longitude : 4.71772
Latitude : 43.78628

ST-LAURENT-DU-VERDON

04500 – Michelin map **334** E10 – pop. 92 – alt. 468
▶ Paris 797 – Marseille 118 – Digne-les-Bains 59 – Avignon 166

⚠ La Farigoulette 👥

✆ 04 92 74 41 62. www.lafarigoulette.cielavillage.fr

Address : Lac du St Laurent (located 1km north follow signs along the C 1 for Montpezat, near the lake)

Opening times : from end April to beginning Oct.

14 ha (219 pitches) relatively flat, grassy, stony

Tariff : 32€ ♦♦ 🚗 🖾 ⚡ (10A) – Extra per person 10.30€ – Reservation fee 18€

Rental rates : (from end April to beginning Oct.) – 120 🚐 – 10 tent lodges. Per night from 29 to 230€ – Per week from 203 to 1,610€ – Reservation fee 25.50€

🚉 local sani-station 5€

The site nestles in a pretty pine forest that stretches down to the banks of the lake.

Surroundings : 🏊 🏕 ♉♉
Leisure activities : 🍽 🎬 daytime 🏃 🚣 ⛵
🏖 pedalos, electric boats 🚴 multi-sports ground
Facilities : ⚡ 🚿 🚻 launderette 🖾 ⚓

Longitude : 6.0777
Latitude : 43.73407

ST-MANDRIER-SUR-MER

83430 – Michelin map **340** K7 – pop. 5 773 – alt. 1
▶ Paris 836 – Bandol 20 – Le Beausset 22 – Hyères 30

🏔 Homair Vacances La Presqu'île
(rental of mobile homes only)

✆ 04 94 30 74 70. www.homair.com

Address : Residence Pin Rolland (2.5km west, D 18 and follow the signs for La Pointe de Marégau (headland), near the marina)

Opening times : from beginning April to end Sept.

2.5 ha very uneven, terraced

Rental rates : 125 🚐. Per night from 24 to 199€ – Per week from 168 to 1,393€ – Reservation fee 25€

Choose the pitches in the shade of eucalyptus trees and furthest away from the road.

Surroundings : ♉♉♉
Leisure activities : 🍽 🍴 🎬 🏃 🚣 🚴 ⛵
Facilities : &. ⚡ 🗛 🚻 🖾 ⚓
Nearby : 🍴

Longitude : 5.90577
Latitude : 43.07655

We have selected the best campsites in France with our usual care, listing those with the best facilities in the most pleasant surroundings.

ST-MARTIN-D'ENTRAUNES

06470 – Michelin map **341** B3 – pop. 83 – alt. 1 050
▶ Paris 778 – Annot 39 – Barcelonnette 50 – Puget-Théniers 44

🏔 Le Prieuré

✆ 04 93 05 54 99. www.le-prieure.com – alt. 1 070 🚫

Address : route des Blancs (located 1km east along the D 2202, follow the signs for Guillaumes then continue 1.8km along road to the left, after the bridge over the Var)

Opening times : from beginning May to end Sept.

12 ha/1.5 (35 pitches) terraced, relatively flat, flat, grassy

Tariff : ♦ 5€ 🚗 🖾 8€ – ⚡ (10A) 3.50€ – Reservation fee 10€

Rental rates : (2015 price) permanent 🚫 – 5 🏠 – 4 canvas bungalows – 1 tent lodge – 9 gîtes. Per night from 45 to 95€ – Per week from 315 to 660€ – Reservation fee 10€

Situated in a mountain location, with simple but varied rental accommodation.

Surroundings : 🏊 ♉ 🏕 ♉♉
Leisure activities : 🍴 🏛 🚣 ⛵ (small swimming pool)
Facilities : ⚡ 🗑 🚻 🖾 ⚓

Longitude : 6.76283
Latitude : 44.14895

ST-MARTIN-VESUBIE

06450 – Michelin map **341** E3 – pop. 1 325 – alt. 1 000
▶ Paris 899 – Marseille 235 – Nice 65 – Cuneo 140

⛺ À la Ferme St-Joseph

✆ 06 70 51 90 14. www.camping-alafermestjoseph.com

Address : southeast of the town along the D 2565 follow the signs for Roquebillière, near Saint-Martin-Vésubie

Opening times : from end April to end Sept.

0.6 ha (50 pitches) sloping, flat, grassy

Tariff : 25.20€ ✶✶ ⇔ 🔲 ⚡ (6A) – Extra per person 4.90€ – Reservation fee 10€

Rentals : (from end April to end Sept.) 🚫 – 3 🛏.
🚮 local sani-station

The site has shaded terraces, often beneath pear trees.

Surroundings : 🌿 ≤ 🌳	**G** Longitude : 7.25711
Facilities : 🚿 (July–Aug.) 🗑 ♨ 🖳	**P** Latitude : 44.06469
Nearby : ✕ 🎿	**S**

ST-PAUL-EN-FORÊT

83440 – Michelin map **340** P4 – pop. 1 616 – alt. 310
▶ Paris 884 – Cannes 46 – Draguignan 27 – Fayence 10

⛰ Le Parc 🛂

✆ 04 94 76 15 35. www.campingleparc.com

Address : 408 Quartier Trestaure (3km north along the D 4, follow the signs for Fayence then take road to the right)

Opening times : from beginning April to end Sept.

3 ha (110 pitches) terraced, flat, grassy, stony

Tariff : 35€ ✶✶ ⇔ 🔲 ⚡ (10A) – Extra per person 7€ – Reservation fee 20€

Rental rates : (from beginning April to mid Oct.) – 10 🚐 – 4 🏠. Per night from 45 to 70€ – Per week from 170 to 800€ – Reservation fee 20€

Pitches that are well shaded and peaceful.

Surroundings : 🌿 🎇	**G** Longitude : 6.68979
Leisure activities : ✕ 🏕 🎯 🛶 ✂ ♨ 🎿	**P** Latitude : 43.58445
Facilities : 🚿 🖳 🔲 ♨ launderette 🗑	**S**

ST-PONS

04400 – Michelin map **334** H6 – pop. 742 – alt. 1 157
▶ Paris 797 – Marseille 227 – Digne-les-Bains 84 – Gap 74

⛰ Village Vacances Le Loup Blanc du Riou
(rental of chalets only)

✆ 04 92 81 44 97. www.leloupblanc.com

Address : 1km southwest, near Ubaye aerodrome

Opening times : permanent

2 ha terraced, flat

Rental rates : 🚫 (1 chalet) – 7 🏠. Per night from 60 to 90€ – Per week from 295 to 780€

In the shade of a pine wood, a village of chalets for rent with some owner-occupiers.

Surroundings : 🌿 ≤ 🎇	**G** Longitude : 6.6122
Leisure activities : 🏕 🛶 🎿	**P** Latitude : 44.39107
Facilities : 🚿 🅿 ♨ launderette	**S**
Nearby : ✕ ♨ 🚵 adventure park	

ST-RAPHAËL

83700 – Michelin map **340** P5 – pop. 34 269
▶ Paris 870 – Aix-en-Provence 121 – Cannes 42 – Fréjus 4

⛺⛺ Les Castels Douce Quiétude 🛂

Les Castels Douce Quiétude

✆ 04 94 44 30 00. www.douce-quietude.com – limited spaces for one-night stay

Address : 3435 boulevard Jacques Baudino (take northeastern exit towards Valescure then continue 3km – from the A 8, take exit 38)

Opening times : from beginning April to mid Oct.

10 ha (440 pitches) terraced, undulating, flat, grassy, stony

Tariff : 62€ ✶✶ ⇔ 🔲 ⚡ (16A) – Extra per person 11.50€ – Reservation fee 30€

Rental rates : (from beginning April to mid Oct.) – 239 🚐. Per night from 45 to 288€ – Per week from 252 to 2,016€ – Reservation fee 30€

Some pitches and high-quality rental options. Shuttle buses for the beaches.

Surroundings : 🌿 🏞 🎇	
Leisure activities : 🍴 ✕ 🎯 🏕 🎯 🛶 🎠 hammam, jacuzzi 🚴 ✂ 🎿 🛶 disco, covered paddling pool, multi-sports ground	**G** Longitude : 6.80587
Facilities : 🚿 🔲 – 6 individual sanitary facilities (🚿 wc) 🗑 ♨ launderette 🗑	**P** Latitude : 43.44734
	S

ST-RÉMY-DE-PROVENCE

13210 – Michelin map **340** D3 – pop. 10 458 – alt. 59
▶ Paris 702 – Arles 25 – Avignon 20 – Marseille 89

⛰ Monplaisir

✆ 04 90 92 22 70. www.camping-monplaisir.fr

Address : chemin de Monplaisir (800m northwest along the D 5, follow the signs for Maillane and take road to the left)

Opening times : from beginning March to end Oct.

2.8 ha (140 pitches) flat, grassy, stony

Tariff : (2015 price) 34.50€ ✶✶ ⇔ 🔲 ⚡ (10A) – Extra per person 8.50€ – Reservation fee 18€

Rental rates : (2015 price) (from beginning March to end Oct.) 🚫 – 12 🚐. Per week from 360 to 790€
🚮 local sani-station

A pleasant site with flowers, located beside a Provençal mas (traditional house).

Surroundings : 🌿 🏞 🎇	
Leisure activities : 🍴 ✕ 🏕 🛶 🎿	**G** Longitude : 4.8729
Facilities : 🚿 🖳 🔲 ♨ launderette 🗑 🗑	**P** Latitude : 43.78417
Nearby : 🐴	**S**

⛰ Pégomas

✆ 04 90 92 01 21. www.campingpegomas.com

Address : 3 avenue Jean Moulin (take the eastern exit along the D 99a, follow the signs for Cavaillon and take the turning to the left, at intersection of the Chemin de Pégomas et av. Jean-Moulin (towards D 30, follow the signs for Noves)

Opening times : from mid March to mid Oct.

2 ha (105 pitches) flat, grassy

Tariff : 30.20€ ✶✶ ⇔ 🔲 ⚡ (6A) – Extra per person 8€ – Reservation fee 17€

Rental rates : (from end March to mid Oct.) ⚭ – 6 ⬚ – 4 canvas bungalows. Per night from 40 to 113€ – Per week from 280 to 790€

⬚ local sani-station

Surroundings : ⬚ ♋♋	
Leisure activities : ♟ ♨⬚ ⬚	**G P S**
Facilities : ⬚ ⬚ ⬚ ⬚ ⬚ launderette, refrigerated food storage facilities	Longitude : 4.84099 Latitude : 43.78838
Nearby : ✕	

STE-CROIX-DU-VERDON

04500 – Michelin map **334** E10 – pop. 124 – alt. 530
▶ Paris 780 – Brignoles 59 – Castellane 59 – Digne-les-Bains 51

⚠ Municipal les Roches

✆ 04 92 77 78 99. www.blog4ever.com

Address : route du Lac (located 1km northeast of the village, 50m from the lake at Ste-Croix – caravans are not permitted through village)

Opening times : from beginning April to end Sept.

6 ha (199 pitches) terraced, undulating, flat, grassy, fine gravel

Tariff : (2015 price) 19.80€ ♣♣ ⬚ 🔲 🔌 (10A) – Extra per person 4.10€ – Reservation fee 30€

Rental rates : (2015 price) (from mid April to mid Sept.) ⚭ – 6 ⬚.

⬚ AireService sani-station

The pitches enjoy the shade of olive and almond trees and some have a view of the lake or the village.

Surroundings : ⬚ ≶♋♋	
Facilities : ⬚ ⬚ ⬚ ⬚ launderette, refrigerated food storage facilities	**G P S** Longitude : 6.15381 Latitude : 43.76043
Nearby : ✕ ⬚ ◊ pedalos	

A chambre d'hôte is a guesthouse or B & B-style accommodation.

STES-MARIES-DE-LA-MER

13460 – Michelin map **340** B5 – pop. 2 308 – alt. 1
▶ Paris 761 – Aigues-Mortes 31 – Arles 40 – Marseille 131

⋀⋀ Sunêlia Le Clos du Rhône

✆ 04 90 97 85 99. www.camping-leclos.fr

Address : route d'Aigues-Mortes (head 2km west along the D 38 and take the turning to the left)

Opening times : from end March to beginning Nov.

7 ha (376 pitches) flat, sandy, stony

Tariff : 32.20€ ♣♣ ⬚ 🔲 🔌 (16A) – Extra per person 9€

Rental rates : permanent ⬚ (1 mobile home) – 104 ⬚ – 14 tent lodges. Per night from 28 to 108€ – Per week from 170 to 1,220€

Situated near the Petit Rhône river and the beach.

Surroundings : ♀⚠	
Leisure activities : ✕ ⬚ ⬚ ⬚	**G P S**
Facilities : ⬚ ⬚ ⬚ ⬚ ⬚ launderette ⬚ ⬚ refrigerated food storage facilities	Longitude : 4.40231 Latitude : 43.44996
Nearby : ⬚ boat trips on the Rhône	

LES SALLES-SUR-VERDON

83630 – Michelin map **340** M3 – pop. 231 – alt. 440
▶ Paris 790 – Brignoles 57 – Digne-les-Bains 60 – Draguignan 49

⋀⋀ Les Pins

✆ 04 98 10 23 80. www.campinglespins.com

Address : take the southern exit along the D 71 then continue 1.2km along the road to the right; 100m from the Lac de Ste-Croix

Opening times : from beginning April to mid Oct.

3 ha/2 for camping (104 pitches) terraced, very uneven, flat, grassy, stony

Tariff : (2015 price) ♣ 6.30€ ⬚ 🔲 13€ 🔌 (6A) – Reservation fee 25€

⬚ local sani-station

In an attractive, shaded setting, adjoining a small pine wood, with direct access to the village.

Surroundings : ⬚ ⬚ ♋♋	
Leisure activities : ⬚ ♨⬚	**G P S**
Facilities : ⬚ ⬚ ⬚ ⬚ ⬚ launderette, refrigerated food storage facilities	Longitude : 6.2084 Latitude : 43.77603
Nearby : ⬚ ⬚ ◊ fitness trail	

⋀⋀ La Source

✆ 04 94 70 20 40. www.camping-la-source.eu

Address : chemin du Lac (southern exit along the D 71, then 1km along the road to the right, 100 m from Lac de Ste-Croix, direct access for pedestrians from the village)

Opening times : from end April to beginning Oct.

2 ha (89 pitches) terraced, very uneven, relatively flat, flat, stony, fine gravel

Tariff : (2015 price) 25.70€ ♣♣ ⬚ 🔲 🔌 (10A) – Extra per person 7€

⬚ local sani-station 25.70€

The site is close to the Lac de Sainte-Croix and the village.

Surroundings : ⬚ ⬚ ♋♋	
Leisure activities : ✕ ⬚ ♨⬚	**G P S**
Facilities : ⬚ ⬚ ⬚ ⬚ ⬚ ⬚ launderette ⬚	Longitude : 6.20737 Latitude : 43.77547
Nearby : ⬚ ⬚ ◊ fitness trail	

SALON-DE-PROVENCE

13300 – Michelin map **340** F4 – pop. 42 440 – alt. 80
▶ Paris 720 – Aix-en-Provence 37 – Arles 46 – Avignon 50

⚠ Nostradamus

✆ 04 90 56 08 36. www.camping-nostradamus.com

Address : route d'Eyguières (5.8km northwest along the D 17 and turn left onto D 72D)

Opening times : from beginning March to end Oct.

2.7 ha (83 pitches) flat, grassy

Tariff : 27.50€ ♣♣ ⬚ 🔲 🔌 (6A) – Extra per person 6.50€ – Reservation fee 20€

Rental rates : permanent – 20 ⬚ – 3 gîtes. Per night from 54 to 182€ – Per week from 317 to 962€ – Reservation fee 20€

⬚ local sani-station 4.50€ – 10 🔲 18.40€

Situated beside a canal.

Surroundings : ⬚ ⬚ ♋♋♋	
Leisure activities : ⬚ ♨⬚ ⬚	**G P S**
Facilities : ⬚ ⬚ ⬚ ⬚ ⬚ launderette	Longitude : 5.06229 Latitude : 43.68401

SANARY-SUR-MER

83110 – Michelin map **340** J7 – pop. 16 806 – alt. 1
▶ Paris 824 – Aix-en-Provence 75 – La Ciotat 23 – Marseille 55

⚏⚏⚏ Campasun Parc Mogador ⚏⚏

⌖ 04 94 74 53 16. www.campasun.eu

Address : 167 chemin de Beaucours

Opening times : from beginning March to end Dec.

3 ha (160 pitches) terraced, flat, grassy, stony

Tariff : (2015 price) 48.50€ ⚏⚏ ⚏ ▣ ⚏ (10A) –
Extra per person 9.70€ – Reservation fee 25€

Rental rates : (2015 price) (from beginning March to end Dec.) –
65 ⚏ – 5 ⚏. Per night from 47 to 77€ – Per week
from 230 to 1,140€ – Reservation fee 25€

⚏ Eurorelais sani-station 5€

In a peaceful residential area, with some rental accommoda-
tion and good-quality sanitary facilities.

Surroundings : ⚏ ⚏ ⚏⚏ Leisure activities : ⚏ ⚏ ⚏ ⚏ ⚏ ⚏ ⚏ bowling Facilities : ⚏ ⚏ ⚏ ⚏ ⚏ ⚏ launderette ⚏	**GPS** Longitude : 5.78777 Latitude : 43.12367

⚏⚏⚏ Campasun Mas de Pierredon ⚏⚏

⌖ 04 94 74 25 02. www.campasun.eu

Address : 652 chemin Raoul Coletta (3km to the north, follow the
signs for Ollioules and take the turning to the left after the motorway
bridge)

6 ha/2.5 for camping (120 pitches) very uneven, terraced, flat, grassy,
stony

Rentals : 45 ⚏ – 10 ⚏.

⚏ Eurorelais sani-station

The pitches at the top of the site are more impacted by the
noise of the motorway.

Surroundings : ⚏ ⚏⚏ Leisure activities : ⚏ ⚏ ⚏ ⚏ ⚏ ⚏ ⚏ ⚏ ⚏ Facilities : ⚏ ⚏ ⚏ – 12 individual sanitary facilities (⚏ ⚏ WC) ⚏ ⚏ ⚏ ⚏ ⚏	**GPS** Longitude : 5.81452 Latitude : 43.13159

LE SAUZÉ-DU-LAC

05160 – Michelin map **334** F6 – pop. 129 – alt. 1 052
▶ Paris 697 – Barcelonette 35 – Digne-les-Bains 74 – Gap 40

⚏⚏ La Palatrière

⌖ 04 92 44 20 98. www.lapalatriere.com

Address : at Orbanne (off the D 954)

Opening times : from beginning May to end Sept.

3 ha (30 pitches) terraced, flat, grassy, stony

Tariff : (2015 price) 24.50€ ⚏⚏ ⚏ ▣ ⚏ (10A) – Extra per person 7€ –
Reservation fee 8€

Rental rates : (2015 price) (from beginning April to end Sept.) –
6 ⚏ – 10 ⚏. Per night from 55 to 98€ – Per week
from 298 to 800€ – Reservation fee 8€

An attractive location overlooking the Lac de Serre-Ponçon.

Surroundings : ⚏ ⚏ Lac de Serre-Ponçon and the mountains ⚏⚏ Leisure activities : ⚏ ⚏ ⚏ jacuzzi ⚏ ⚏ Facilities : ⚏ ⚏ ⚏ ▣	**GPS** Longitude : 6.34543 Latitude : 44.49909

SERRES

05700 – Michelin map **334** C6 – pop. 1 308 – alt. 670
▶ Paris 670 – Die 68 – Gap 41 – Manosque 89

⚏⚏ Flower Domaine des Deux Soleils ⚏⚏

⌖ 04 92 67 01 33. www.domaine-2soleils.com – alt. 800

Address : avenue Des Pins – La Flamenche (800m southeast along
the N 75, follow the signs for Sisteron then continue 1km along the
turning to the left; at Super-Serres)

Opening times : from mid April to end Sept.

26 ha/12 for camping (72 pitches) terraced, flat, grassy, stony

Tariff : 27€ ⚏ ⚏ ⚏ ▣ ⚏ (6A) – Extra per person 4.50€ – Reservation
fee 15€

Rental rates : (from mid April to end Sept.) – 4 ⚏ – 18 ⚏ –
4 tent lodges. Per night from 38 to 310€ – Per week
from 190 to 756€ – Reservation fee 15€

Many pitches are set among trees and bushes in a natural and
unspoilt setting.

Surroundings : ⚏ ⚏ ⚏ Leisure activities : ⚏ ⚏ ⚏ ⚏ multi- sports ground Facilities : ⚏ ⚏ ⚏ ⚏ ▣ ⚏	**GPS** Longitude : 5.72767 Latitude : 44.4203

SEYNE

04140 – Michelin map **334** G6 – pop. 1 434 – alt. 1 200
▶ Paris 719 – Barcelonnette 43 – Digne-les-Bains 43 – Gap 54

⚏⚏ Les Prairies

⌖ 04 92 35 10 21. www.campinglesprairies.com

Address : at Haute Gréyère, chemin Charcherie (located 1km south
along the D 7, follow the signs for Auzet and take road to the left;
beside the Blanche river)

Opening times : from beginning May to mid Sept.

3.6 ha (100 pitches) open site, flat, grassy, stony

Tariff : (2015 price) 21€ ⚏⚏ ⚏ ▣ ⚏ (10A) – Extra per person 6€ –
Reservation fee 16€

Rental rates : (2015 price) (from beginning May to mid Sept.) –
8 ⚏ – 8 ⚏. Per night from 50 to 80€ – Per week from 265 to 695€
– Reservation fee 16€

⚏ local sani-station 20€

In a pleasant setting, partially wooded, beside a stream.

Surroundings : ⚏ ⚏ ⚏ ⚏⚏ Leisure activities : ⚏ ⚏ ⚏ ⚏ ⚏ Facilities : ⚏ ⚏ ⚏ ⚏ ⚏ launderette ⚏ Nearby : ⚏ ⚏	**GPS** Longitude : 6.35972 Latitude : 44.34262

SISTERON

04200 – Michelin map **334** D7 – pop. 7 427 – alt. 490
▶ Paris 704 – Barcelonnette 100 – Digne-les-Bains 40 – Gap 52

⚏⚏ Municipal des Prés-Hauts

⌖ 04 92 61 19 69. www.sisteron.fr

Address : 44 chemin des Prés Hauts (3km north following signs for
Gap and take D 951 to the right, follow the signs for La Motte-du-
Caire, near the Durance river)

Opening times : from beginning April to end Sept.

4 ha (145 pitches) flat, slightly sloping, grassy

Tariff : (2015 price) 25.70€ ⚏⚏ ⚏ ▣ ⚏ (10A) – Extra per person 4€

Rental rates : (2015 price) (from beginning May to end Sept.)
⚲ – 10 🚐. Per week from 330 to 610€ 🚐 24 ▣ 21.50€

There's a shuttle bus for the town centre.

Surroundings : ⛰ ≤ 🏕 ♨
Leisure activities : 🎣 🚵 🏊 🎯
Facilities : ⛟ ⚡ 🏛 🛁 🚿 🍴 🍽

G P S   Longitude : 5.93645
       Latitude : 44.21432

SOSPEL

06380 – Michelin map **341** F4 – pop. 3 523 – alt. 360
▶ Paris 967 – Breil-sur-Roya 21 – L'Escarène 22 – Lantosque 42

⛺ Domaine Ste-Madeleine

📞 04 93 04 10 48. www.camping-sainte-madeleine.com
Address : route de Moulinet (4.5km northwest along the D 2566, follow the signs for Le Col de Turini)
Opening times : from beginning April to end Sept.
3 ha (90 pitches) very uneven, terraced, stony, grassy
Tariff : 29.50€ ⭐⭐ 🚗 ▣ ⚡ (10A) – Extra per person 5€
Rental rates : (from beginning April to end Sept.) ⚲ – 3 🚐 – 10 🏠 – 1 apartment. Per night from 55 to 85€ – Per week from 320 to 620€
🚐 local sani-station 4€

The pitches are on shaded terrances beneath olive trees, but the rental and sanitary facilities are old.

Surroundings : ⛰ ≤ ♨
Leisure activities : 🏊
Facilities : ⛟ ⚡ 🚿 🍴 🍽

G P S   Longitude : 7.41575
       Latitude : 43.8967

TARADEAU

83460 – Michelin map **340** N5 – pop. 1 694 – alt. 74
▶ Paris 853 – Marseille 107 – Toulon 66 – Monaco 111

⛺ La Vallée de Taradeau

📞 04 94 73 09 14. www.campingdetaradeau.com
Address : chemin de la Musardière (towards Vidauban, D 73)
Opening times : permanent
1.5 ha (80 pitches) flat, stony, gravelled
Tariff : (2015 price) 19.90€ ⭐⭐ 🚗 ▣ ⚡ (10A) – Extra per person 5€
Rental rates : (2015 price) permanent – 30 🚐 – 13 🏠 – 6 canvas bungalows. Per night from 40 to 150€ – Per week from 259 to 1,149€ – Reservation fee 18€
🚐 local sani-station – 🚐 8€

There are various rental options, including some of good quality.

Surroundings : ⛰ 🏕 ♨♨
Leisure activities : 🍴 ✗ 🎣 🎯 ≈ hammam, jacuzzi 🚵 🏊 spa facilities
Facilities : ⚡ 🍴 launderette 🛒

G P S   Longitude : 6.42755
       Latitude : 43.44118

LE THOR

84250 – Michelin map **332** C10 – pop. 8 099 – alt. 50
▶ Paris 688 – Avignon 18 – Carpentras 16 – Cavaillon 14

⛺ FranceLoc Domaine Le Jantou

📞 04 90 33 90 07. www.franceloc.fr
Address : 535 chemin des Coudelières (head 1.2km west via the northern exit towards Bédarrides; direct access to the Sorgue, recommended route via the D 1 (bypass)
Opening times : from mid April to mid Sept.
6 ha/4 for camping (195 pitches) flat, grassy
Tariff : (2015 price) 20€ ⭐⭐ 🚗 ▣ ⚡ (6A) – Extra per person 4.70€ – Reservation fee 11€

Rental rates : (2015 price) (from mid April to mid Sept.) – 9 'gypsy' caravans – 162 🚐 – 6 canvas bungalows. Per night from 30 to 75€ – Per week from 119 to 1,197€ – Reservation fee 27€

Surroundings : ⛰ ♨♨
Leisure activities : 🎣 🚵 🎯 🏊 🎯 🛶
Facilities : ⛟ ⚡ 🏛 🛁 🚿 🍴 launderette 🛒 refrigerators
Nearby : 🛒

G P S   Longitude : 4.98282
       Latitude : 43.92969

LES THUILES

04400 – Michelin map **334** H6 – pop. 374 – alt. 1 130
▶ Paris 752 – Marseille 221 – Digne-les-Bains 82 – Gap 62

⛰ Le Fontarache

📞 04 92 81 90 42. www.camping-fontarache.fr – alt. 1 108
Address : at Les Thuiles Basses (take the eastern exit out of the town, D 900, follow the signs for Barcelonnette)
6 ha (150 pitches) open site, grassy
Rentals : 16 🚐 – 2 🏠.
🚐 local sani-station

Choose the pitches furthest away from the river in preference.

Surroundings : ⛰ ≤ ♨♨
Leisure activities : 🍴 ✗ 🏊 multi-sports ground
Facilities : ⛟ ⚡ 🛁 🍴 launderette
Nearby : 🚵 ✗ 🛒 🛶 (river) rafting and canyoning

G P S   Longitude : 6.57537
       Latitude : 44.3924

Using the traditional Michelin classification method, the guide provides you with an easy, speedy reference for assessing the category of each site: 1 to 5 tents (see page 10).

VAISON-LA-ROMAINE

84110 – Michelin map **332** D8 – pop. 6 153 – alt. 193
▶ Paris 664 – Avignon 51 – Carpentras 27 – Montélimar 64

⛺ FranceLoc Le Carpe Diem 👥

📞 04 90 36 02 02. www.camping-carpe-diem.com
Address : route de St-Marcellin (situated 2km southeast at the intersection of the D 938 (rte de Malaucène) and the D 151)
Opening times : from mid April to end Oct.
10 ha/6.5 for camping (232 pitches) terraced, relatively flat, flat, grassy
Tariff : (2015 price) 40€ ⭐⭐ 🚗 ▣ ⚡ (10A) – Extra per person 7€ – Reservation fee 11€
Rental rates : (2015 price) (from mid April to end Oct.) – 233 🚐 – 8 🏠 – 1 cabin in the trees – 3 tent lodges. Per night from 40 to 155€ – Per week from 147 to 1,316€ – Reservation fee 27€
🚐 local sani-station

A reconstruction of an amphitheatre beside the swimming pool.

Surroundings : ⛰ 🏕 ♨♨
Leisure activities : 🍴 ✗ 🎣 🎯 🏊 🚵 🎯 🏊 🏊 🎯
Facilities : ⛟ ⚡ 🔳 🛁 🍴 🚿 🛒 refrigerated food storage facilities

G P S   Longitude : 5.08945
       Latitude : 44.23424

⚠️ Le Soleil de Provence

📞 04 90 46 46 00. www.camping-soleil-de-provence.fr

Address : Trameiller district (3.5km northeast along the D 938, follow the signs for Nyons)

Opening times : from mid March to end Oct.

4 ha (153 pitches) terraced, relatively flat, flat, grassy, stony

Tariff : 34.40€ ✸✸ 🚗 🔲 🐕 (10A) – Extra per person 8.35€ – Reservation fee 10€

Rental rates : (from mid March to end Oct.) 🏖 – 26 🚐 – 26 🏠. Per week from 250 to 890€ – Reservation fee 10€

🚐 Eurorelais sani-station 2€

Surroundings : ⩽ Ventoux and mountains of Nyons 🏕️ ♨️ Leisure activities : 🎏 🛶 🎣 ⛷️ Facilities : ♿ ⛽ 🏪 🛒 📶 ♨️ 🍴 📺	**GPS** Longitude : 5.10616 Latitude : 44.26838

⛰️ Théâtre Romain

Théâtre Romain

📞 04 90 28 78 66. www.camping-theatre.com

Address : Les Arts district – chemin du Brusquet (to the northeast of the town, recommended route via the bypass – rocade)

Opening times : from mid March to beginning Nov.

1.2 ha (75 pitches) flat, grassy, fine gravel

Tariff : 29.90€ ✸✸ 🚗 🔲 🐕 (10A) – Extra per person 8€ – Reservation fee 11€

Rental rates : (from mid March to beginning Nov.) – 9 🚐. Per week from 220 to 680€ – Reservation fee 11€

🚐 local sani-station 5€ – 🚐 14€

Surroundings : 🏕️ ♨️ Leisure activities : 🎏 🛶 🎣 (small swimming pool) Facilities : ♿ ⛽ ♨️ 🛒 🍴 📺 Nearby : 🍽️	**GPS** Longitude : 5.07843 Latitude : 44.24505

VENCE

06140 – Michelin map **341** D5 – pop. 19 183 – alt. 325
▶ Paris 923 – Antibes 20 – Cannes 30 – Grasse 24

⛰️ Domaine de la Bergerie

📞 04 93 58 09 36. www.camping-domainedelabergerie.com

Address : 1330 chemin de la Sine (4km west along the D 2210, follow the signs for Grasse and take road to the left)

Opening times : from mid March to mid Oct.

30 ha/13 for camping (450 pitches) terraced, flat, grassy, stony

Tariff : (2015 price) 34€ ✸✸ 🚗 🔲 🐕 (5A) – Extra per person 5.40€ – Reservation fee 15€

Rental rates : (2015 price) (from end March to mid Oct.) 🏖 – 6 cabins and 2 chalets (without sanitary facilities). Per night from 32 to 42€ – Reservation fee 15€

🚐 local sani-station 5€

A very pleasant natural setting at an old, attractively restored sheepfarm.

Surroundings : 🏖️ 🏕️ 🎆 Leisure activities : 🍴 🍽️ 🛶 🎣 🎣 Facilities : ♿ ⛽ 🛒 🛒 🛒 🔧 launderette 🏕️ 🛒 Nearby : sports trail	**GPS** Longitude : 7.08981 Latitude : 43.71253

LE VERNET

04140 – Michelin map **334** G7 – pop. 123 – alt. 1 200
▶ Paris 729 – Digne-les-Bains 32 – La Javie 16 – Gap 68

⚠️ Lou Passavous

📞 04 92 35 14 67. www.loupassavous.com

Address : route Roussimal (800m north of the village, on the D90 following signs for Roussimal, turn right onto Les Souquets; beside the Bès river and a lake)

Opening times : from beginning May to beginning Sept.

1.5 ha (60 pitches) open site, relatively flat, flat, grassy, stony

Tariff : (2015 price) ✸ 5.50€ 🚗 2€ 🔲 21.50€ – 🐕 (6A) 4€ – Reservation fee 14€

Rental rates : (2015 price) (from beginning May to beginning Sept.) 🏖 – 4 🚐 – 4 tent lodges. Per night from 70€ – Per week from 475 to 650€ – Reservation fee 14€

In a green setting, crossed by a small stream.

Surroundings : 🏖️ ⩽ ♨️♨️ Leisure activities : 🍴 🍽️ 🛶 Facilities : ♿ ⛽ 🛒 ♨️ 📺 🛒 Nearby : 🍽️ 🎣 🎣	**GPS** Longitude : 6.39139 Latitude : 44.28194

VEYNES

05400 – Michelin map **334** C5 – pop. 3 166 – alt. 827
▶ Paris 660 – Aspres-sur-Buëch 9 – Gap 25 – Sisteron 51

⚠️ Les Prés

📞 04 92 57 26 22. www.camping-les-pres.com – alt. 960

Address : at Le Petit Vaux (3.4km northeast along the D 994 follow the signs for Gap, then continue 5.5km along the D 937 following signs for Superdevoluy and take road to the left via the bridge over the Béoux)

Opening times : from beginning May to end Sept.

0.35 ha (22 pitches) flat, slightly sloping, grassy

Tariff : (2015 price) 14.50€ ✸✸ 🚗 🔲 🐕 (10A) – Extra per person 4€

Rental rates : (2015 price) (from mid April to end Oct.) – 4 🚐 – 3 canvas bungalows. Per night from 15 to 100€ – Per week from 180 to 480€

🚐 local sani-station – 🚐 8€

Surroundings : 🏖️ ⩽ ♨️ Facilities : ♿ ⛽ 🍴 📺	**GPS** Longitude : 5.84995 Latitude : 44.58842

To make the best possible use of this guide, please read pages 2–15 carefully.

VILLAR-LOUBIÈRE

05800 – Michelin map **334** E4 – pop. 48 – alt. 1 026
▶ Paris 648 – La Chapelle-en-Valgaudémar 5 – Corps 22 – Gap 43

⚠️ Municipal Les Gravières

📞 04 92 55 35 35. http://www.eauvivepassion.fr/camping-villar-loubiere.html

Address : Les Gravières (700m east following signs for La Chapelle-en-Valgaudémar and take road to the right)

Opening times : from mid June to mid Sept.

2 ha (50 pitches) flat, grassy, stony, wood

Tariff : (2015 price) ✸ 2.90€ 🚗 3.30€ 🔲 3.70€ – 🐕 (2A) 4.40€ – Reservation fee 10€

Rentals : (2015 price) permanent ✄ – 1 'gypsy' caravan.
An ideal spot for fans of whitewater sports.

Surroundings : ♒ ⩻ ♉♉
Leisure activities : 🏠 ✀ ✄ rafting and canyoning
Facilities : ♿ ⚲ (July–Aug.) ♨ 🔥

VILLARS-COLMARS

04370 – Michelin map **334** H7 – pop. 246 – alt. 1 225
▶ Paris 774 – Annot 37 – Barcelonnette 46 – Colmars 3

🏔 Le Haut-Verdon

📞 04 92 83 40 09. www.lehautverdon.com – access via Col d'Allos strictly not advised
Address : 0.6km south of the village on the D 908, follow the signs for Castellane
Opening times : from beginning May to end Sept.
3.5 ha (109 pitches) open site, flat, stony
Tariff : 28€ ♦♦ ⇔ 🔳 🚰 (10A) – Extra per person 5€ – Reservation fee 15€
Rental rates : permanent – 7 🚐 – 4 🏠. Per night from 45 to 70€ – Per week from 320 to 700€ – Reservation fee 15€
🚿 local sani-station 4€
Choose the pitches near the Verdon river in preference.

For more information on visiting particular towns or regions, consult the relevant regional MICHELIN Green Guide. We also recommend you use the appropriate Michelin regional map to locate your selected campsite, to calculate distances and to work out the best route.

VILLECROZE

83690 – Michelin map **340** M4 – pop. 1 128 – alt. 300
▶ Paris 835 – Aups 8 – Brignoles 38 – Draguignan 21

🏔 Le Ruou ♦♦

📞 04 94 70 67 70. www.leruou.com – limited spaces for one-night stay
Address : 309 road RD 560 (5.4km southeast along the D 251, follow the signs for Barbebelle and take D 560, follow the signs for Flayosc, recommended route via the D 560)
Opening times : from beginning June to mid Sept.
4.3 ha (134 pitches) very uneven, terraced, flat, grassy
Tariff : (2015 price) 40€ ♦♦ ⇔ 🔳 🚰 (10A) – Extra per person 7€ – Reservation fee 25€
Rental rates : (2015 price) permanent – 53 🚐 – 19 🏠 – 12 canvas bungalows. Per night from 36 to 154€ – Per week from 252 to 1,078€ – Reservation fee 25€
🚿 local sani-station 5€
The pitches are arranged on terraces under pine trees, with a view from some over the water park.

Surroundings : ♉♉
Leisure activities : ♟ ✗ 🏠 🎯 ⛹ 🏊 🛝
Facilities : ♿ ⚲ 🛁 ♨ launderette 🍴

Longitude : 6.29795
Latitude : 43.55542

VILLENEUVE-LOUBET-PLAGE

06270 – Michelin map **341**
▶ Paris 919 – Marseille 191 – Nice 24 – Monaco 38

🏔 La Vieille Ferme

📞 04 93 33 41 44. www.vieilleferme.com
Address : 296 boulevard des Groules (2.8km south along the N 7, follow the signs for Antibes and take a right turn)
Opening times : permanent
2.9 ha (153 pitches) terraced, flat, grassy, fine gravel
Tariff : 42€ ♦♦ ⇔ 🔳 🚰 (10A) – Extra per person 6€ – Reservation fee 28€
Rental rates : permanent – 32 🏠. Per night from 55 to 80€ – Per week from 365 to 960€ – Reservation fee 28€

Surroundings : 🛏 ♉♉
Leisure activities : 🏠 ☀daytime, jacuzzi ⛹ 🛝 (open air in season)
Facilities : ♿ ⚲ ▦ 🛁 ♨ 🍴 launderette 🗄 refrigerated food storage facilities

Longitude : 7.12579
Latitude : 43.61967

🏔 Parc des Maurettes

📞 04 93 20 91 91. www.parcdesmaurettes.com
Address : 730 avenue du Dr Lefèbvre (along the N 7)
Opening times : from beginning Jan. to mid Nov.
2 ha (108 pitches) terraced, flat, grassy, gravelled, stony
Tariff : (2015 price) 39.50€ ♦♦ ⇔ 🔳 🚰 (16A) – Extra per person 6€ – Reservation fee 26€
Rental rates : (from beginning Jan. to mid Nov.) – 14 🏠 – 2 🚐 – 3 studios. Per night from 69 to 84€ – Per week from 728 to 838€ – Reservation fee 26€
🚿 local sani-station 6€ – 5 🔳 25.50€.
Situated in an urban zone, with good shade and a pleasant spa and relaxation area

Surroundings : 🛏 ♉♉
Leisure activities : 🏠 ☕ jacuzzi ⛹
Facilities : ♿ ⚲ 🅿 ▦ 🛁 ♨ launderette
Nearby : 🍴

Longitude : 7.12964
Latitude : 43.63111

🏔 L'Hippodrome

📞 04 93 20 02 00. www.camping-hippodrome.com
Address : 5 avenue des Rives (400m from the beach, behind the Géant Casino commercial centre)
Opening times : permanent
0.8 ha (57 pitches) flat, grassy, fine gravel
Tariff : 36€ ♦♦ ⇔ 🔳 🚰 (10A) – Extra per person 5.50€ – Reservation fee 20€
Rentals : permanent ✄ – 15 studios – Reservation fee 20€
🚿 Flot Bleu sani-station
Situated in an urban zone, the site is in two sections.

Surroundings : 🛏 ♉♉
Leisure activities : 🏠 ⛹ 🛝 (open air in season)
Facilities : ♿ ⚲ 🛗 ▦ 🛁 ♨ launderette, refrigerators
Nearby : 🍴 ✗

Longitude : 7.13771
Latitude : 43.64199

*We value your opinion and welcome your feedback.
Do email us at campingfrance@tp.michelin.com*

VILLES-SUR-AUZON

84570 – Michelin map **332** E9 – pop. 1 296 – alt. 255
▶ Paris 694 – Avignon 45 – Carpentras 19 – Malaucène 24

🏔 Les Verguettes

📞 04 90 61 88 18. www.provence-camping.com

Address : route de Carpentras (take the western exit along the D 942)

2 ha (88 pitches) terraced, relatively flat, flat, grassy, stony

Rentals : 8 🛖.

Surroundings : 🐾 ≤ Mont Ventoux 🛒 🔎
Leisure activities : 🍴 ✂ 🎣 🛝
Facilities : 👤 🚿 🏛 🚯 🔧 🍴 🔲 🛒
refrigerators

G P S Longitude : 5.22834
Latitude : 44.05686

VIOLÈS

84150 – Michelin map **332** C9 – pop. 1 546 – alt. 94
▶ Paris 659 – Avignon 34 – Carpentras 21 – Nyons 33

🏔 Les Favards

📞 04 90 70 90 93. www.favards.com

Address : route d'Orange (1.2km west along the D 67)

Opening times : from mid April to beginning Oct.

20 ha/1.5 (49 pitches) flat, grassy

Tariff : 👤 6.50 € 🚗 📧 5.60 € – 🔌 (10A) 3.70 €

Situated in the grounds of a vineyard.

Surroundings : 🐾 ≤ 🛒 🔎
Leisure activities : 🍴 🛝
Facilities : 👤 🚿 🍴 🏛 refrigerated food
storage facilities

G P S Longitude : 4.93528
Latitude : 44.16229

VISAN

84820 – Michelin map **332** C8 – pop. 1 956 – alt. 218
▶ Paris 652 – Avignon 57 – Bollène 19 – Nyons 20

🏔 L'Hérein

📞 04 90 41 95 99. www.campingvisan.com

Address : route de Bouchet (located 1km west along the D 161, follow the signs for Bouchet; near a stream)

Opening times : from beginning April to mid Oct.

3.3 ha (75 pitches) flat, grassy, stony

Tariff : 17 € 👤👤 🚗 📧 🔌 (10A) – Extra per person 4.50 € – Reservation fee 10 €

Rental rates : (from beginning April to mid Oct.) – 5 🛖. Per night from 45 to 75 € – Per week from 285 to 630 € – Reservation fee 10 €

🚉 local sani-station 11.50 € – 8 📧 11.50 € – 🚐 11.50 €

Surroundings : 🐾 🛒 🔎
Leisure activities : ✂ 🛶 🚣 🎣 🛝
Facilities : 👤 🚿 🅿 🏛 🚯 🔧 🍴 🔲 🛒

G P S Longitude : 4.93601
Latitude : 44.31236

VOLONNE

04290 – Michelin map **334** E8 – pop. 1 658 – alt. 450
▶ Paris 718 – Château-Arnoux-St-Aubin 4 – Digne-les-Bains 29 – Forcalquier 33

🏔🏔 Sunêlia L'Hippocampe 👥

📞 04 92 33 50 00. www.l-hippocampe.com

Address : route Napoléon (500m southeast along the D 4)

Opening times : from beginning April to end Sept.

8 ha (447 pitches) flat, grassy, fruit trees

Tariff : 46 € 👤👤 🚗 📧 🔌 (10A) – Extra per person 8 € – Reservation fee 30 €

Rental rates : (from beginning April to end Sept.) – 214 🛖 – 30 🏠 – 16 canvas bungalows. Per night from 42 to 246 € – Per week from 294 to 1,722 € – Reservation fee 30 €

🚉 local sani-station 5 € – 9 📧 22 € – 🚐 🔌28 €

Situated beside the Durance river; various rental options and some luxury mobile homes and chalets.

Surroundings : 🐾 ≤ 🔎
Leisure activities : 🍴 ✂ 🎣 🎱 🛝 🚣 🚴 ✂ 🛝 🏊 🎣 disco, pedalos ⛵ multi-sports ground, entertainment room
Facilities : 👤 🚿 🚯 🔧 🍴 launderette 🚐 🛒

G P S Longitude : 6.0173
Latitude : 44.1054

VOLX

04130 – Michelin map **334** D9 – pop. 2 953 – alt. 350
▶ Paris 748 – Digne-les-Bains 51 – Forcalquier 15 – Gréoux-les-Bains 22

🏔 La Vandelle

📞 04 86 56 67 83. www.camping-lavandelle.com

Address : avenue de la Vandelle (1.3km southwest of the town)

2 ha (50 pitches) terraced, flat, grassy, wood

🚉 local sani-station

Part of the site is situated among trees, very quiet and peaceful.

Surroundings : 🐾 🔎
Leisure activities : 🛝
Facilities : 👤 🚿 🍴 🏛

G P S Longitude : 5.83162
Latitude : 43.869

Michelin classification:

🏔🏔🏔🏔 *Extremely comfortable, equipped to a very high standard*

🏔🏔🏔 *Very comfortable, equipped to a high standard*

🏔🏔🏔 *Comfortable and well equipped*

🏔🏔 *Reasonably comfortable*

🏔 *Satisfactory*

RHÔNE-ALPES

G. Labriet / Photononstop

Rhône-Alpes is a region of contrasts and a cultural crossroads. Its lofty peaks are a snow-covered paradise for skiers, climbers and hikers, drawn by the beauty of its shimmering glaciers and tranquil lakes; stylish Chamonix and Courchevel set the tone and the pace in cool Alpine chic. Descend from the roof of Europe, past herds of cattle on the mountain pastures and into the bustle of the Rhône valley. From Roman roads to speedy TGVs, playing host to the main arteries between north and south has forged the region's reputation for economic drive. Holidaymakers may rush through Rhône-Alpes in summer but those in the know linger to enjoy its culinary specialities. The region boasts a host of Michelin-starred restaurants: three-starred trendsetters and the legendary neighbourhood *bouchons* (small, family-run bistros) of Lyon, capital of this gastronomic paradise, make it a compulsory stop. Enjoy a Bresse chicken, cheese and sausages from Lyon and a glass of Côtes du Rhône.

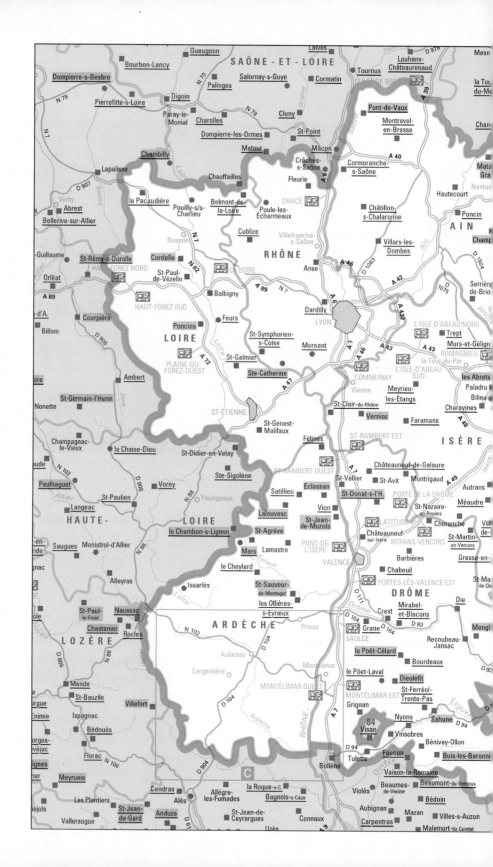

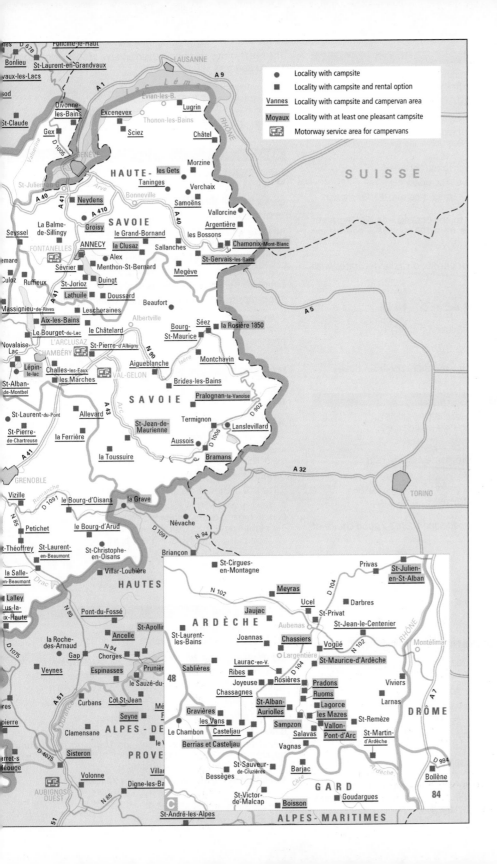

LES ABRETS

38490 – Michelin map **333** G4 – pop. 3 186 – alt. 398
▶ Paris 514 – Aix-les-Bains 45 – Belley 31 – Chambéry 38

⏘ Le Coin Tranquille ♠♣

𝒫 04 76 32 13 48. www.coin-tranquille.com

Address : 6 chemin des Vignes (head 2.3km east along the N 6, follow the signs for Le Pont-de-Beauvoisin and take turning to the left)

Opening times : from end March to end Oct.

4 ha (196 pitches) flat and relatively flat, grassy

Tariff : 39€ ♦♦ ⇔ 🔲 🔋 (10A) – Extra per person 8€ – Reservation fee 16€

Rental rates : (from end May to end Oct.) 🅿 – 14 🏠. Per night from 87 to 111€ – Per week from 399 to 889€ – Reservation fee 31€

🚽 local sani-station
Some lovely, well marked-out pitches, on a site decorated with flowers.

Surroundings : ⬚ ⬚ 🎣 ⬚⬚
Leisure activities : 🍽 ✕ 🏠 🎿 ⛷ 🚴 multi-sports ground
Facilities : ♿ ⚯ 🔲 ⬚ ⁱⁱ launderette 🚿 ⬚
G P S Longitude : 5.6084
Latitude : 45.54139

To visit a town or region, use the MICHELIN Green Guides.

AIGUEBLANCHE

73260 – Michelin map **333** M4 – pop. 3 129 – alt. 461
▶ Paris 641 – Lyon 174 – Chambéry 74 – Albertville 25

⚠ Marie-France

𝒫 06 09 47 32 30. www.campingresidencesmariefrance.fr

Address : 453 avenue de Savoie

0.5 ha (30 pitches) terraced, flat, grassy
Rentals : 20 studios – 10 apartments.
🚽 local sani-station – 10 🔲

The pitches have plenty of shade and there's a good choice of rental accommodation.

Surroundings : ⬚ ⬚ ⬚⬚
Leisure activities : 🏠 ⬚
Facilities : ♿ ⚯ ⁱⁱ 🔲
At the leisure/activities centre : 🍽 ✕ ⬚
🎿 ✕ ⬚ 🎣 ⬚ ⬚ sports trail
G P S Longitude : 6.489
Latitude : 45.50717

AIX-LES-BAINS

73100 – Michelin map **333** I3 – pop. 26 819 – alt. 200 – ⚘
▶ Paris 539 – Annecy 34 – Bourg-en-Bresse 115 – Chambéry 18

⏘ International du Sierroz

𝒫 04 79 61 89 89. www.camping-sierroz.com

Address : boulevard Robert Barrier (2.5km to the northwest)

Opening times : from end March to end Oct.

5 ha (255 pitches)

Tariff : (2015 price) ♦ 4.90€ ⇔ 🔲 9.40€ – 🔋 (10A) 5.60€ – Reservation fee 3.50€

Rental rates : (2015 price) (from end March to end Oct.) ♿ (1 mobile home) – 34 🏠 – 4 tent lodges. Per week from 289 to 689€ – Reservation fee 3.50€
🚽 local sani-station 5€

The site is in two sections with an annexe at 500m, close to the Lac du Bourget.

Surroundings : ⬚ ⬚⬚
Leisure activities : 🍽 ✕ 🏠 🎿 ⬚
Facilities : ♿ ⚯ 🔲 🎿 ⬚ ⁱⁱ launderette ⬚
Nearby : ⬚ ⬚ ⬚

G P S Longitude : 5.88628
Latitude : 45.70104

ALEX

74290 – Michelin map **328** K5 – pop. 980 – alt. 589
▶ Paris 545 – Albertville 42 – Annecy 12 – La Clusaz 20

⚠ La Ferme des Ferrières

𝒫 04 50 02 87 09. www.camping-des-ferrieres.com

Address : located 1.5km west along the D 909, follow the signs for Annecy and take road to the right

Opening times : from beginning June to end Sept.

5 ha (200 pitches) relatively flat, flat, grassy

Tariff : (2015 price) 17.50€ ♦♦ ⇔ 🔲 🔋 (5A) – Extra per person 3€

The campsite is on an attractive, shaded field, at a working farm.

Surroundings : ⬚ ⬚⬚
Leisure activities : 🍽 🏠 🎿
Facilities : ♿ ⚯ ⬚ 🎿 ⬚
G P S Longitude : 6.22346
Latitude : 45.89015

ALLEVARD

38580 – Michelin map **333** J5 – pop. 3 768 – alt. 470 – ⚘
▶ Paris 593 – Albertville 50 – Chambéry 33 – Grenoble 40

⏘ Clair Matin

𝒫 04 76 97 55 19. www.camping-clair-matin.com

Address : 20 rue des Pommiers (take the southwestern exit along the D 525, follow the signs for Grenoble)

Opening times : from end April to mid Oct.

5.5 ha (200 pitches) terraced, relatively flat, flat, grassy

Tariff : ♦ 3.78€ ⇔ 🔲 14.35€ – 🔋 (10A) 5.80€ – Reservation fee 8€

Rental rates : (from beginning May to mid Oct.) – 33 🏠. Per night from 212 to 820€ – Reservation fee 14€
🚽 local sani-station 3€ – 5 🔲 11€ – ⬚ 8€

Surroundings : ⬚ ⬚⬚
Leisure activities : ✕ 🏠 🎿
Facilities : ♿ ⚯ 🎿 ⬚ ⁱⁱ launderette
G P S Longitude : 6.06591
Latitude : 45.38869

ANNECY

74000 – Michelin map **328** J5 – pop. 51 012 – alt. 448
▶ Paris 544 – Chambéry 51 – Genève 42 – Lyon 138

⏘ Municipal Le Belvédère

𝒫 04 50 45 48 30. www.annecy.fr

Address : 8 route du Semnoz (to the south along the D 41)

Opening times : from end March to mid Oct.

3 ha (102 pitches) terraced, flat, grassy, gravelled

Tariff : (2015 price) 27€ ♦♦ ⇔ 🔲 🔋 (16A) – Extra per person 6.30€

Rental rates : (2015 price) (from end March to mid Oct.) ♿ (10 chalets) – 12 🏠. Per night from 75 to 96€ – Per week from 400 to 700€ 🚽 local sani-station

A pretty little chalet village adjacent to a forest.

Surroundings : ⬚ ⬚⬚
Leisure activities : 🍽 ✕ 🏠 🎿 ⬚
Facilities : ♿ ⚯ 🔲 🎿 ⬚ ⁱⁱ launderette
G P S Longitude : 6.13237
Latitude : 45.89025

ANSE

69480 – Michelin map **327** H4 – pop. 5 604 – alt. 170
▶ Paris 436 – L'Arbresle 17 – Bourg-en-Bresse 57 – Lyon 27

⋀⋀⋀ Les Portes du Beaujolais

℘ 0474671287. www.camping-beaujolais.com

Address : 495 avenue Jean Vacher (take the southeastern exit, follow the signs for Lyon and 600m along the road turn left before the bridge)

Opening times : from beginning March to end Oct.

7.5 ha (198 pitches) flat, grassy

Tariff : 29.50€ ♥♥ ⇔ 回 ⚡ (16A) – Extra per person 5.20€
Rental rates : permanent – 35 ⟮⟯ – 30 ⟮⟯. Per night from 69 to 129€ – Per week from 299 to 1,190€ – Reservation fee 10€

Situated at the point where the Azergues and Saône rivers meet.

Surroundings : ⌂ ♀
Leisure activities : ♈ ✕ ⌂ ≅ hammam, jacuzzi ⚓ ⚙ 🔥 ⟍ ⟍ spa centre
Facilities : & ☛ ▥ ☂ ⤳ ⍲ 🗑 ⤵
Nearby : ⟍

Longitude : 4.72616
Latitude : 45.94106

We have selected the best campsites in France with our usual care, listing those with the best facilities in the most pleasant surroundings.

ARGENTIÈRE

74400 – Michelin map **328** O5 – alt. 1 252
▶ Paris 619 – Annecy 106 – Chamonix-Mont-Blanc 10 – Vallorcine 10

⋀ Le Glacier d'Argentière

℘ 0450541736. www.campingchamonix.com – ⽊

Address : 161 chemin des Chosalets (located 1km south following signs for Chamonix, 200m from the Arve river)

Opening times : from mid May to end Sept.

1 ha (80 pitches) flat, grassy

Tariff : ♥ 5.60€ ⇔ 2€ 回 5.10€ – ⚡ (10A) 4.50€
Rental rates : (from mid May to end Sept.) – 1 apartment – 1 canvas bungalow – 2 tent lodges. Per night from 35 to 45€ – Per week from 210 to 270€
⟮⟯ local sani-station 10€ – 18 回 17.70€

Surroundings : ⋖ ♀
Leisure activities : ✕ ⌂
Facilities : & ☛ (July-Aug.) ⤳ ⍲ launderette

Longitude : 6.92363
Latitude : 45.9747

ARTEMARE

01510 – Michelin map **328** H5 – pop. 1 112 – alt. 245
▶ Paris 506 – Aix-les-Bains 33 – Ambérieu-en-Bugey 47 – Belley 18

⋀⋀ Sites et Paysages Le Vaugrais

℘ 0479873734. www.camping-le-vaugrais.fr

Address : at Cerveyrieu, 2 chemin le Vaugrais (700m west along the D 69d, follow the signs for Belmont, beside the Séran river)

1 ha (33 pitches) flat, grassy

Surroundings : ⋖ ⌂ ♀
Leisure activities : ♈ ⌂ ⚓ ⚙ ⟍ ⟍
Facilities : & ☛ ▥ ⤳ ⍲ ⤳ 🗑

Longitude : 5.68383
Latitude : 45.87465

AUSSOIS

73500 – Michelin map **333** N6 – pop. 677 – alt. 1 489
▶ Paris 670 – Albertville 97 – Chambéry 110 – Lanslebourg-Mont-Cenis 17

⋀ Municipal la Buidonnière

℘ 0479203558. www.camping-aussois.com

Address : route de Cottériat (take the southern exit along the D 215, follow the signs for Modane and take road to the left)

Opening times : permanent

4 ha (160 pitches) terraced, relatively flat, grassy, stony

Tariff : (2015 price) ♥ 6.90€ ⇔ 回 – ⚡ (10A) 6€
⟮⟯ Eurorelais sani-station 2€

Panoramic views and numerous owner-occupier caravans.

Surroundings : ❋ ⟍ ⋖ Parc de la Vanoise
⌂ ♀
Leisure activities : ⌂ ⚓ ✕ 🔥 ≅ (pool) sports trail
Facilities : & ☛ ▥ ☂ ⍲ launderette

Longitude : 6.74586
Latitude : 45.22432

AUTRANS

38880 – Michelin map **333** G6 – pop. 1 676 – alt. 1 050 – Winter sports : 1 050/1 650 m
▶ Paris 586 – Grenoble 36 – Romans-sur-Isère 58 – St-Marcellin 47

⋀⋀⋀ Yelloh! Village au Joyeux Réveil ♟♟

℘ 0476953344. www.camping-au-joyeux-reveil.fr

Address : at Le Château (take the northeastern exit following signs for Montaud and take a right turn)

Opening times : from beginning May to mid Sept.

1.5 ha (100 pitches) flat, grassy

Tariff : 18€ ♥♥ ⇔ 回 ⚡ (6A) – Extra per person 6€ – Reservation fee 30€
Rental rates : (from beginning May to mid Sept.) – 36 ⟮⟯. Per night from 35 to 185€ – Per week from 245 to 1,295€

Some luxury rental accommodation.

Surroundings : ⋖
Leisure activities : ✕ ⌂ 🔥 ≅ hammam, jacuzzi ⚓ ⟍ ⟍ spa centre
Facilities : & ☛ ▥ ⍲ 🗑 ⤵

Longitude : 5.54844
Latitude : 45.17555

BALBIGNY

42510 – Michelin map **327** E5 – pop. 2 809 – alt. 331
▶ Paris 423 – Feurs 10 – Noirétable 44 – Roanne 29

⋀⋀ La Route Bleue

℘ 0477272497. http://www.campingdelaroutebleue.com

Address : at Pralery (2.8km northwest along the N 82 and turn left onto the D 56, follow the signs for St-Georges-de-Baroille)

Opening times : from mid March to end Oct.

2 ha (100 pitches) relatively flat, flat, grassy

Tariff : (2015 price) 16.30€ ♥♥ ⇔ 回 ⚡ (16A) – Extra per person 4€
Rental rates : (2015 price) (from beginning April to end Sept.) – 2 ⟮⟯. Per night from 50 to 80€ – Per week from 270 to 540€

In a pleasant location beside the Loire river.

Surroundings : ⟍ ♀
Leisure activities : ♈ ✕ ⌂ ⟍ ⟍
Facilities : & ☛ ⍲ launderette

Longitude : 4.15725
Latitude : 45.82719

LA BALME-DE-SILLINGY

74330 – Michelin map **328** J5 – pop. 4 891 – alt. 480
▶ Paris 524 – Dijon 250 – Grenoble 111 – Lons-le-Saunier 136

⚲ La Caille

✆ 04 50 68 85 21. www.domainedelacaille.com

Address : 18 chemin de la Caille (4km north on the N 508 towards Frangy and take road to the right)

Opening times : from end April to mid Sept.

4 ha/1 campable (50 pitches) relatively flat, flat, grassy

Tariff : (2015 price) 29€ ♥♥ ⇛ 🔲 🔌 (10A) – Extra per person 6€
Rental rates : (2015 price) permanent 🅿 – 8 🚐 – 13 🏠 – 7 🛏 – 2 gîtes. Per night from 70 to 160€ – Per week from 290 to 740€ – Reservation fee 20€

Surroundings : ⚲ 🗻 ♀
Leisure activities : 🍹 🍴 🏛 ⛷ 🎿
Facilities : ⅙ o•ー 🚻 launderette 🔧

GPS Longitude : 6.03609
Latitude : 45.97828

BARBIÈRES

26300 – Michelin map **332** D4 – pop. 771 – alt. 426
▶ Paris 586 – Lyon 124 – Valence 23 – Grenoble 79

⚲ Flower Le Gallo-Romain

✆ 04 75 47 44 07. www.legalloromain.net

Address : route du Col de Tourniol (1.2km southeast along the D 101; beside the Barberolle river)

3 ha (62 pitches) terrace, flat and relatively flat, grassy, stony
Rentals : 14 🚐.

Surroundings : ⚲ ← 🗻 ♀♀
Leisure activities : 🍹 🍴 🏛 🎿 🐟
Facilities : ⅙ o•ー 🏢 🔥 🚻 launderette 🔧 refrigerators

GPS Longitude : 5.15092
Latitude : 44.94456

BEAUFORT

73270 – Michelin map **333** M3 – pop. 2 206 – alt. 750
▶ Paris 601 – Albertville 21 – Chambéry 72 – Megève 37

⚲ Municipal Domelin

✆ 04 79 38 33 88. www.mairie-beaufort73.com

Address : north of the village (off the RD 925)

2 ha (100 pitches) relatively flat, flat, grassy

This pretty grassy site is in partial shade, but one of the sanitary blocks is not of a high standard.

Surroundings : ⚲ ← ♀
Facilities : ⅙ o•ー launderette

GPS Longitude : 6.56403
Latitude : 45.7218

BELMONT-DE-LA-LOIRE

42670 – Michelin map **327** F3 – pop. 1 515 – alt. 525
▶ Paris 405 – Chauffailles 6 – Roanne 35 – St-Étienne 108

⚲ Municipal les Écureuils

✆ 04 77 63 72 25. www.belmontdelaloire.fr

Address : at the lake leisure center (1.4km west along the D 4, follow the signs for Charlieu and take road to the left, 300m from the lake)

Opening times : from beginning May to end Aug.

0.6 ha (28 pitches) terraced, relatively flat to hilly, grassy, gravelled

Tariff : (2015 price) ♥ 2.40€ ⇛ 1.25€ 🔲 1.50€ – 🔌 (5A) 2.50€

Rental rates : (2015 price) permanent – 9 🏠. Per night from 45 to 79€ – Per week from 260 to 466€
🚽 local sani-station

Situated beside a leisure and activity park.

Surroundings : ⚲ 🗻
Leisure activities : ⛷
Facilities : 🚿 🚻 📷
Nearby : 🍴 🎣

GPS Longitude : 4.33819
Latitude : 46.1662

BENIVAY-OLLON

26170 – Michelin map **332** E8 – pop. 66 – alt. 450
▶ Paris 689 – Lyon 227 – Valence 126 – Avignon 71

⚲ Domaine de l'Écluse

✆ 04 75 28 07 32. www.campecluse.com

Address : at Barastrage (1km south on the D 347)

Opening times : from beginning May to mid Sept.

4 ha (75 pitches) undulating, terraced, flat, grassy, stony, fine gravel

Tariff : (2015 price) 31.50€ ♥♥ ⇛ 🔲 🔌 (6A) – Extra per person 7€ – Reservation fee 30€

Rental rates : (2015 price) (from end April to mid Sept.) ⅙ – 12 🚐 – 12 🏠 – 2 gîtes. Per night from 95 to 150€ – Per week from 301 to 812€ – Reservation fee 30€

Shaded by cherry trees, surrounded by vineyards and beside a stream.

Surroundings : ⚲ ← 🗻 ♀♀
Leisure activities : 🍹 🍴 🏛 ⛷ 🎿 🐟 🏹
Facilities : ⅙ o•ー 🚮 🔥 🚻 📷

GPS Longitude : 5.18545
Latitude : 44.30298

For more information on visiting particular towns or regions, consult the relevant regional MICHELIN Green Guide. We also recommend you use the appropriate Michelin regional map to locate your selected campsite, to calculate distances and to work out the best route.

BERRIAS-ET-CASTELJAU

07460 – Michelin map **331** H7 – pop. 643 – alt. 126
▶ Paris 668 – Aubenas 40 – Largentière 29 – St-Ambroix 18

⚲ La Source ≗

✆ 04 75 39 39 13. www.camping-source-ardeche.com

Address : La Rouvière (situated 1.5km northeast, follow the signs for Casteljau)

Opening times : from end April to mid Sept.

2.5 ha (93 pitches) flat, grassy, stony

Tariff : (2015 price) 26.50€ ♥♥ ⇛ 🔲 🔌 (6A) – Extra per person 7.20€
Rental rates : (2015 price) (from end April to mid Sept.) – 22 🚐 – 4 🏠 – 1 tent lodge. Per week from 260 to 895€

Various rental options with chalets of a good standard, a pleasant swimming pool area on a site bordered by a stream, Le Gravierou.

Surroundings : ⚲ 🗻 ♀♀
Leisure activities : 🍴 🏛 🤸 ⛷ 🎿 spa facilities, farm or petting farm
Facilities : ⅙ o•ー 🚮 📷 🔥 🚻 📷 🔧

GPS Longitude : 4.20646
Latitude : 44.37725

⛰ Les Cigales

☎ 0475393033. www.camping-cigales-ardeche.com

Address : La Rouvière (1km to the northeast, follow the signs for Casteljau)

Opening times : from beginning April to end Sept.

3 ha (110 pitches) terraced, relatively flat, flat, grassy

Tariff : 29€ ✚✚ ⬅ 🔲 🔌 (10A) – Extra per person 6€

Rental rates : (from beginning April to end Sept.) – 23 🚐 – 7 🏠 – 1 apartment – 3 gîtes. Per night from 60€ – Per week from 250 to 610€

Shaded pitches on terraces, with a pleasant swimming pool.

Surroundings : 🌳 ♨♨ Leisure activities : 🍽 🎪 ⛵ 🎯 🏊 Facilities : 🚿 ⛽ 🚐🏕🏪 🍴 🛒🍴	**G P S** Longitude : 4.21133 Latitude : 44.37829

BILIEU

38850 – Michelin map **333** G5 – pop. 1 232 – alt. 580
▶ Paris 526 – Belley 44 – Chambéry 47 – Grenoble 38

⛺ Municipal Bord du Lac

☎ 0476066700. http://campingleborddulac.fr – limited spaces for one-night stay

Address : le Petit Bilieu (1.9km west, follow the signs for Charavines, recommended route via the D 50d and D 90)

1.3 ha (81 pitches) terraced, flat, grassy, fine gravel

Surroundings : 🌳 ⛰ ♨♨ △ Leisure activities : 🎣 Facilities : 🚿 ⛽ 🏪 🍴 Nearby : ⚓	**G P S** Longitude : 5.5312 Latitude : 45.44615

*The classification (1 to 5 tents, **black** or red) that we award to selected sites in this guide is our own system. It should not be confused with the classification (1 to 5 stars) of official organisations.*

BOURDEAUX

26460 – Michelin map **332** D6 – pop. 621 – alt. 426
▶ Paris 608 – Crest 24 – Montélimar 42 – Nyons 40

⛰ Yelloh! Village Les Bois du Châtelas

☎ 0475006080. www.chatelas.com

Address : route de Dieulefit (1.4km southwest along the D 538)

Opening times : from beginning April to mid Sept.

17 ha/7 for camping (80 pitches) terraced, relatively flat, stony, grassy

Tariff : 52€ ✚✚ ⬅ 🔲 🔌 (10A) – Extra per person 8€

Rental rates : (from beginning April to mid Sept.) – 59 🚐 – 25 🏠 – 3 tipis – 8 canvas bungalows – 1 gîte. Per night from 41 to 215€ – Per week from 287 to 1,505€

🚐 AireService sani-station 1€ – 🔌17€

The site boasts a panoramic view from the chalets and restaurant.

Surroundings : 🌳 ⛰ Leisure activities : 🍽 🎪 ⛵ hammam, jacuzzi 🎯 🚴 🏊 🏊 multi-sports ground, spa centre Facilities : 🚿 ⛽ 🏪 🏕 🍴 🛒 🍴 Nearby : 🐾 🐎	**G P S** Longitude : 5.12783 Latitude : 44.57832

LE BOURG-D'ARUD

38520 – Michelin map **333** J8
▶ Paris 628 – L'Alpe-d'Huez 25 – Le Bourg-d'Oisans 15 – Les Deux-Alpes 29

⛰ Le Champ du Moulin

☎ 0476800738. www.champ-du-moulin.com

Address : take the western exit along the D 530

Opening times : from mid Dec. to end April

1.5 ha (80 pitches) open site, flat, grassy, stony

Tariff : 30€ ✚✚ ⬅ 🔲 🔌 (10A) – Extra per person 6.40€ – Reservation fee 17€

Rental rates : (from mid Dec. to end April) – 4 🚐 – 10 🏠 – 4 apartments – 2 canvas bungalows. Per night from 43 to 102€ – Per week from 301 to 714€ – Reservation fee 17€

🚐 local sani-station – 12 🔲 24€ – 🔌11€

The site is surrounded by the Oisans mountains and beside the Vénéon river.

Surroundings : ❄ 🌳 ♨ Leisure activities : 🍽 🍽 🎪 🛶 🎣 Facilities : 🚿 ⛽ 🏕 🍴 🛒🍴 At the leisure/activities centre : 🎯 🏊 🚣 🏊 rafting and canyoning	**G P S** Longitude : 6.11986 Latitude : 44.98596

LE BOURG-D'OISANS

38520 – Michelin map **333** J7 – pop. 3 381 – alt. 720
▶ Paris 614 – Briançon 66 – Gap 95 – Grenoble 52

⛰ Les Castels Le Château de Rochetaillée 🧍‍♂️

☎ 0476110440. www.camping-le-chateau.fr

Address : chemin de Bouthéon, Rochetaillée (north of the town, off the D 1091)

Opening times : from mid May to mid Sept.

2.6 ha (135 pitches) flat, grassy

Tariff : 44.40€ ✚✚ ⬅ 🔲 🔌 (10A) – Extra per person 9.90€ – Reservation fee 10€

Rental rates : (from mid May to mid Sept.) – 50 🚐 – 1 🏠 – 3 🛏. Per night from 35 to 125€ – Per week from 250 to 1,010€ – Reservation fee 10€

🚐 local sani-station – 5 🔲 44.40€

Surroundings : ⛰ 🏠 ♨♨ Leisure activities : 🍽 🍽 🎪 🎮 🚴 🏇 🎣 hammam, jacuzzi 🎯 🧗 🏊 climbing wall Facilities : 🚿 ⛽ 🏕 🍴 🛒 🍴 launderette 🛒 🍴	**G P S** Longitude : 6.00512 Latitude : 45.11543

⛰ Sites et Paysages À la Rencontre du Soleil

☎ 0476791222. www.alarencontredusoleil.com

Address : route de l'Alpe d'Huez (1.7km to the northeast)

Opening times : from mid April to end Sept.

1.6 ha (73 pitches) flat, grassy

Tariff : 43€ ✚✚ ⬅ 🔲 🔌 (10A) – Extra per person 8.70€ – Reservation fee 20€

Rental rates : (from mid April to end Oct.) – 🅿 – 4 'gypsy' caravans – 12 🚐 – 11 🏠 – 1 apartment. Per night from 60 to 160€ – Per week from 230 to 1,125€ – Reservation fee 20€

🚐 50 🔲 36€ – 🔌16€

Surroundings : ⛰ 🏠 ♨♨ Leisure activities : 🍽 🎪 🎯 🏊 (open air in season), multi-sports ground Facilities : ⛽ 🏕 🍴 launderette 🛒 Nearby : 🛒	**G P S** Longitude : 6.03716 Latitude : 45.06296

⛰ RCN Belledonne

𝄞 0476800718. www.rcn-belledonne.fr

Address : at Rochetaillée

3.5 ha (180 pitches) flat, grassy

Rentals : 24 🚐.

The whole site is very green and floral.

Surroundings : ≤ 🎄	GPS
Leisure activities : ♈ ✕ 🏠 🎥 ♨ hammam 🏋 🚴 ⛵ ✳ sports trail	Longitude : 6.01095
Facilities : ♿ ⚡ 🏢 ♨ launderette 🚮	Latitude : 45.11331

⛰ Le Colporteur 👪

𝄞 0476791144. www.camping-colporteur.com

Address : Le Mas du Plan (south of the town, access via r. de la Piscine)

3.3 ha (135 pitches) flat, grassy

Rentals : 4 'gypsy' caravans – 4 🚐 – 30 🏠.

Located beside a small river.

Surroundings : 🌊 ≤ 🎄	GPS
Leisure activities : ♈ ✕ 🏠 🏃 ⛷	Longitude : 6.03546
Facilities : ♿ ⚡ ♨ 🏢	Latitude : 45.0527
Nearby : 🎿 ⛷ ✳	

⚠ La Cascade

𝄞 0476800242. www.lacascadesarenne.com

Address : route d'Huez (off the D211, 1.5km to the northeast, follow the signs for L'Alpe-d'Huez, near the Sarennes river)

Opening times : from mid Dec. to end Sept.

2.4 ha (140 pitches) flat, grassy, stony

Tariff : (2015 price) 36.50€ ✱ ✱ 🚗 🔲 ⚡ (16A) – Extra per person 9.20€

Rental rates : (2015 price) (from mid Dec. to end Sept.) – 18 🏠. Per night from 58 to 110€ – Per week from 364 to 945€

🚐 15 🔲 36.50€ – 🚐⚡36.50€

Surroundings : ❄ ≤ 🎄	GPS
Leisure activities : 🏠 🏃 ✳	Longitude : 6.03988
Facilities : ⚡ 🏢 ♨ 🏢	Latitude : 45.06446
Nearby : 🎿	

To visit a town or region, use the MICHELIN Green Guides.

BOURGET-DU-LAC

73370 – Michelin map **333** I4 – pop. 4 277 – alt. 240
▶ Paris 531 – Aix-les-Bains 10 – Annecy 44 – Chambéry 13

⛰ International l'Île aux Cygnes

𝄞 0479250176. www.campingileauxcygnes.fr

Address : 501 boulevard E. Coudurier (located 1km to the north; beside the lake)

Opening times : from mid April to beginning Oct.

2.5 ha (267 pitches) flat, gravelled, grassy

Tariff : (2015 price) 23.70€ ✱ ✱ 🚗 🔲 ⚡ (6A) – Extra per person 5.30€ – Reservation fee 10€

Rental rates : (2015 price) (from mid April to beginning Oct.) ♿ (1 mobile home) 🌱 – 6 🚐 – 4 🏠. Per night from 73 to 113€ – Per week from 277 to 796€ – Reservation fee 10€

🚐 local sani-station 6.20€ – 🚐⚡12.60€

The campervan pitches are at the entrance to the campsite.

Surroundings : 🌊 ≤ 🎄 ⚠	GPS
Leisure activities : ✕ 🏠 🕐daytime 🏋 🚴 🏖 (beach) 🎣	Longitude : 5.86308
Facilities : ⚡ ♿ 🏢 ♨ 🏢 launderette 🚮	Latitude : 45.65307
Nearby : ✂ 🏊 ⚓	

BOURG-ST-MAURICE

73700 – Michelin map **333** N4 – pop. 7 650 – alt. 850 – Winter sports : at Les Arcs : 1 600/3 226 m
▶ Paris 635 – Albertville 54 – Aosta 79 – Chambéry 103

⛰ Indigo Le Versoyen

𝄞 0479070345. http://www.camping-bourgsaintmaurice.com/

Address : off the route des Arcs (RD 119) (take the northeastern exit along the N 90, follow the signs for Séez then continue 500m along the turning to the right, near some rapids)

Opening times : from mid June to mid Sept.

3.5 ha (153 pitches) surfaced road

Tariff : (2015 price) 22.70€ ✱ ✱ 🚗 🔲 ⚡ (10A) – Extra per person 5.70€ – Reservation fee 13€

Rental rates : (2015 price) (from mid June to mid Sept.) – 4 'gypsy' caravans – 8 🚐 – 8 tent lodges. Per night from 39 to 112€ – Per week from 192 to 784€ – Reservation fee 13€

🚐 local sani-station 4.50€ – 24 🔲 15.50€

There's a free shuttle service to the funicular railway.

Surroundings : ❄ 🌊 ≤ 🎄	GPS
Leisure activities : 🏠 🏋	Longitude : 6.78373
Facilities : ⚡ 🏢 launderette	Latitude : 45.6221
At the leisure/activities park : ✂ 🏄 🔲 ✳ ♞ sports trail	

This guide is not intended as a list of all the camping sites in France; its aim is to provide a selection of the best sites in each category.

BRAMANS

73500 – Michelin map **333** N6 – pop. 388 – alt. 1 200
▶ Paris 673 – Albertville 100 – Briançon 71 – Chambéry 113

⛰ Le Val d'Ambin

𝄞 0479050305. www.camping-bramansvanoise.com

Address : 602 route de l'Eglise (700m northeast – access is recommended via Le Verney, on the N6)

Opening times : from mid April to end Oct.

6 ha (166 pitches) open site, undulating, terraced, flat, grassy, pond

Tariff : ✱ 3.50€ 🚗 1.95€ 🔲 3.50€ – ⚡ (6A) 4.10€

Rental rates : permanent ♿ (1 chalet) – 1 'gypsy' caravan – 10 🏠 – 5 canvas bungalows – 3 tent lodges. Per night from 23 to 129 € – Per week from 139 to 679€

🚐 Eurorelais sani-station 2€ – 🚐⚡14€

In a lovely situation not far from an old church; good-quality rental options.

Surroundings : 🌊 ≤ 🎄	GPS
Leisure activities : 🏠 🏋 ✳ 🎣	Longitude : 6.78144
Facilities : ♿ ⚡ 🏢 🚮 ♨ launderette	Latitude : 45.22787
Nearby : ♈ ✕	

BRIDES-LES-BAINS

73570 – Michelin map **333** M5 – pop. 560 – alt. 580
▶ Paris 612 – Albertville 32 – Annecy 77 – Chambéry 81

⚠ La Piat

✆ 0479552274. www.camping-brideslesbains.com

Address : avenue du Comte Greyfié de Bellecombe

Opening times : from mid April to mid Oct.

2 ha (80 pitches) terraced, flat, grassy

Tariff : 16.70€ ✚✚ 🚗 🔲 🔌 (10A) – Extra per person 3.50€

Rental rates : (from beginning April to mid Oct.) – 2 'gypsy' caravans – 5 🚐. Per night from 39 to 82€ – Per week from 238 to 496€

🚰 local sani-station 4€

Located on terraces with little shade, near the town centre.

Surroundings : 🏔 ♀	**G** Longitude : 6.56172
Facilities : 🚿 ⛲ 📷 🛁 🍴 launderette	**P** Latitude : 45.453
	S

BUIS-LES-BARONNIES

26170 – Michelin map **332** E8 – pop. 2 291 – alt. 365
▶ Paris 685 – Carpentras 39 – Nyons 29 – Orange 50

⛰ La Fontaine d'Annibal

✆ 0475280312. www.vacances-baronnies.com

Address : route de Séderon (located 1km to the north, road to the left just after the bridge over the Ouvèze.)

Opening times : from beginning April to mid Oct.

(50 pitches) terraced, stony, grassy, relatively flat

Tariff : 19.70€ ✚✚ 🚗 🔲 🔌 (10A) – Extra per person 4.20€

Rental rates : (from beginning April to mid Oct.) 🚿 – 3 🚐 – 8 🏠 – 36 🛏 – 8 apartments – 4 canvas bungalows. Per night from 51 to 104€ – Per week from 296 to 799€

Surroundings : 🛏 ♀	**G** Longitude : 5.28187
Leisure activities : 🏓 🏊	**P** Latitude : 44.28438
Facilities : 🚿 ⛲ 📷 🛁 🍴 launderette	**S**
Nearby : 🛒 🍴 🎣	

⚠ La Via Natura Les Éphélides

✆ 0475281015. www.ephelides.com

Address : Tuves district (1.4km southwest along av. de Rieuchaud)

2 ha (40 pitches) flat, grassy, stony

Rentals : 1 'gypsy' caravan – 6 🚐 – 5 🏠.

The site is shaded by cherry trees, near the Ouvèze river, and welcomes horses and their riders.

Surroundings : 🏔 ≤ ♀	**G** Longitude : 5.26793
Leisure activities : 🏊 🏄 🏓	**P** Latitude : 44.21875
Facilities : 🚿 ⛲ 🛁 📷	**S**
Nearby : 🍴 🐎 skateboarding	

⚠ Domaine de la Gautière

✆ 0475280268. www.camping-lagautiere.com

Address : at La Gautière (5km southwest along the D 5, then take a right turn)

Opening times : from end March to mid Nov.

6 ha/3 for camping (40 pitches) terraced, relatively flat, grassy, stony

Tariff : ✚ 6.80€ 🚗 🔲 7€ – 🔌 (10A) 5€ – Reservation fee 10€

Rental rates : (from end March to mid Nov.) – 6 🚐 – 4 🏠. Per night from 170 to 225€ – Per week from 340 to 800€ – Reservation fee 15€

🚰 local sani-station 4€ – 🚐 10€

The site is largely shaded by olive trees.

Surroundings : 🏔 ≤ ♀	**G** Longitude : 5.24258
Leisure activities : 🏓 🏄 🏊	**P** Latitude : 44.2517
Facilities : 🚿 ⛲ 🛁 🍴 📷	**S**

CASTELJAU

07460 – Michelin map **331** H7
▶ Paris 665 – Aubenas 38 – Largentière 28 – Privas 69

⛰ La Rouveyrolle

✆ 0475390067. www.campingrouveyrolle.fr – limited spaces for one-night stay

Address : La Rouveyrolle (east of the village, off the D252, near the Chassezac river)

Opening times : from beginning April to end Sept.

3 ha (100 pitches)

Tariff : 35€ ✚✚ 🚗 🔲 🔌 (6A) – Extra per person 9.50€ – Reservation fee 25€

Rental rates : (from beginning April to end Sept.) – 75 🚐. Per night from 81 to 148€ – Reservation fee 25€

🚰 3 🔲 35€

A spacious site in a natural setting beside the river. A range of large and luxury mobile homes, but also some rather old sanitary facilities.

Surroundings : 🏔 🚐 ♀♀	**G** Longitude : 4.22222
Leisure activities : 🍴 🍽 🏠 🏄 🎣 jacuzzi 🏊 🏓 🏊	**P** Latitude : 44.39583
Facilities : 🚿 ⛲ 🍴 launderette 🛁 🍴	**S**

⛰ Bel Air – (rental of mobile homes only)

✆ 0475393639. www.camping-belair-ardeche.com

Address : at Les Tournaires (500m to the north, follow the signs for Chaulet-Plage)

Opening times : from beginning April to end Oct.

1.5 ha (60 pitches) flat and relatively flat, grassy

Rental rates : 45 🚐. Per night from 40 to 150€ – Per week from 190 to 990€

🚰 sani-station 25€

A mobile home park, some very well equipped and some owner-occupiers, sometimes a little too close together.

Surroundings : 🏔 ♀♀	**G** Longitude : 4.21574
Leisure activities : 🍴 🍽 🏠 🏄 🏊	**P** Latitude : 44.4006
Facilities : 🚿 ⛲ 🛁 🍴 📷 🍴	**S**
Nearby : 🏊 🎣	

⚠ Chaulet Plage

✆ 0475393027. www.chaulet-plage.com

Address : Terres du Moulin (600m to the north, follow the signs for Chaulet-Plage)

1.5 ha (62 pitches) terraced, stony grassy, flat

Rentals : 6 🏠 – 6 apartments – military tents.

Pitches on terraces that descend to the snackbar beside the Chassezac river.

Surroundings : 🏔 ♀♀	**G** Longitude : 4.21528
Leisure activities : 🍴 🍽 🏊 🎣 🏄	**P** Latitude : 44.40453
Facilities : 🚿 ⛲ 🛁 🍴 launderette 🛁 🍴	**S**

⛺ Le Pousadou

☎ 04 75 39 04 05. www.pousadou.fr

Address : reception is at the vineyard Domaine de Cassagnole, off the D252, northwest of the town

Opening times : from end April to end Sept.

23 ha/1.7 (52 pitches) flat, grassy

Tariff : (2015 price) 24.50€ ✶✶ ⇔ 🖵 🗲 (12A) – Extra per person 4.20€ – Reservation fee 20€

In the heart of the Domaine de Cassagnole vineyards, near the river; the reception is in the domaine wine cellar.

Surroundings : 🐟 ⇇ 🌳🌳
Leisure activities : 🏊 🦯
Facilities : 🚿 – 52 private sanitary facilities (🚿 🚻 🚽 WC)

GPS Longitude : 4.21788
Latitude : 44.40158

CHABEUIL

26120 – Michelin map **332** D4 – pop. 6 568 – alt. 212
▶ Paris 569 – Crest 21 – Die 59 – Romans-sur-Isère 18

🏕 FranceLoc Le Grand Lierne

☎ 04 75 59 83 14. www.grandlierne.com 🐟

Address : Les Garalands (5km northeast along the D 68, follow the signs for Peyrus, turn left onto the D 125 and turn right onto the D 143 – from the A 7, Valence-Sud exit towards Grenoble)

Opening times : from mid April to mid Sept.

3.6 ha (216 pitches) flat, grassy, stony

Tariff : (2015 price) 39€ ✶✶ ⇔ 🖵 🗲 (10A) – Extra per person 7€ – Reservation fee 27€

Rental rates : (2015 price) (from mid April to mid Sept.) 🐟 – 207 🚐 – 3 🏠 – 13 tent lodges. Per night from 37 to 123€ – Per week from 147 to 1,316€ – Reservation fee 27€

🚐 local sani-station

Numerous rental options and pitches for tents and caravans in a wooded setting, with facilities suitable for families.

Surroundings : 🐟 🌳🌳
Leisure activities : 🍴 🗙 🏊 🎣 🚲 🏌
🏓 🛶 🎿
Facilities : 🚿 ⟶ 🛁 🍴 launderette 🏊 🦯 refrigerated food storage facilities

GPS Longitude : 5.065
Latitude : 44.91572

This guide is updated regularly, so buy your new copy every year!

CHALLES-LES-EAUX

73190 – Michelin map **333** I4 – pop. 5 073 – alt. 310 – ♨
▶ Paris 566 – Albertville 48 – Chambéry 6 – Grenoble 52

🏕 Municipal le Savoy

☎ 04 79 72 97 31. www.camping-challesleseaux.com

Address : avenue du Parc (take the r. Denarié, 100m from the N 6)

Opening times : from beginning April to mid Oct.

2.8 ha (88 pitches) flat, grassy, gravelled

Tariff : (2015 price) ✶ 4.15€ ⇔ 1.85€ 🖵 5.70€ – 🗲 (10A) 3.15€ – Reservation fee 10€

Rental rates : (2015 price) (from beginning April to mid Oct.) – 2 🚐 – 6 🏠 – 2 canvas bungalows. Per week from 250 to 554€ – Reservation fee 10€

🚐 Flot Bleu sani-station 2€ – 22 🖵 14.50€

Pretty pitches lined with hedges, near a small lake.

Surroundings : 🐟 ⇇ 🌳 ♨
Leisure activities : 🏊 🦯 🚲
Facilities : 🚿 ⟶ 🛁 🦯 🛁 🍴 launderette
Nearby : 🗙 🏊 (beach) 🐟

GPS Longitude : 5.98418
Latitude : 45.55152

CHAMONIX-MONT-BLANC

74400 – Michelin map **328** O5 – pop. 9 054 – alt. 1 040
▶ Paris 610 – Albertville 65 – Annecy 97 – Aosta 57

🏕 L'Île des Barrats

☎ 04 50 53 51 44. www.campingdesbarrats.com – 🐶

Address : 185 chemin de l'Île des Barrats (in the southwest of the town, opposite the main hospital)

Opening times : from beginning June to mid Sept.

0.8 ha (52 pitches) flat and relatively flat, grassy

Tariff : (2015 price) 30.80€ ✶✶ ⇔ 🖵 🗲 (10A) – Extra per person 7.30€

Rental rates : (2015 price) (from beginning June to end Sept.) 🐟 – 4 🏠. Per week from 1,025€

In a green setting opposite the Bossons glacier, but choose the pitches furthest from the road.

Surroundings : ⇇ Mont Blanc mountain range and glaciers 🌳 ♨
Leisure activities : 🏊
Facilities : 🚿 ⟶ 🛁 🦯 🍴 launderette

GPS Longitude : 6.86135
Latitude : 45.91463

🏕 La Mer de Glace

☎ 04 50 53 44 03. www.chamonix-camping.com – 🐶

Address : 200 chemin de la Bagna (at Les Bois, 80m from the Arveyron – direct access)

Opening times : from beginning May to beginning Oct.

2 ha (150 pitches) sandy, gravelled

Tariff : 31.90€ ✶✶ ⇔ 🖵 🗲 (10A) – Extra per person 9€

🚐 local sani-station – 40 🖵 31.90€

Surroundings : 🐟 ⇇ Mont Blanc mountain range 🌳 ♨
Leisure activities : 🏊 🦯
Facilities : 🚿 ⟶ 🛁 🦯 🍴 launderette

GPS Longitude : 6.89142
Latitude : 45.93846

CHAMPDOR

01110 – Michelin map **328** G4 – pop. 462 – alt. 833
▶ Paris 486 – Ambérieu-en-Bugey 38 – Bourg-en-Bresse 51 – Hauteville-Lompnes 6

🏕 Municipal le Vieux Moulin

☎ 06 50 54 28 98. www.champdor.jimdo.com

Address : route de Corcelles (800m northwest along the D 57a)

Opening times : permanent

1.6 ha (62 pitches) flat, grassy

Tariff : ✶ 3.30€ ⇔ 1.20€ 🖵 1.70€ – 🗲 (10A) 4.70€

Rental rates : permanent – (2 chalets) – 2 🏠. Per night from 90€ – Per week from 280 to 380€

In the Le Bugey hills close to two natural lakes – one for swimming, one for fishing.

Surroundings : 🐟 ⇇
Leisure activities : 🏊 🦯
Facilities : 🚿 (July-Aug.) 🍴 🍴 🛁
Nearby : 🗙 🏊 (pool) 🐟

GPS Longitude : 5.59138
Latitude : 46.023

CHANCIA

01590 – Michelin map **321** D8 – pop. 237 – alt. 320
▶ Paris 452 – Bourg-en-Bresse 48 – Lons-le-Saunier 46 – Nantua 30

⚠ Municipal les Cyclamens

⚲ 0474758214. www.camping-chancia.com – limited spaces for one-night stay

Address : La Presqu'île (located 1.5km southwest along the D 60e and take road to the left, where the Ain and the Bienne rivers meet)

Opening times : from beginning May to end Sept.

2 ha (155 pitches) flat, grassy

Tariff : (2015 price) ♣ 2.70€ ⇔ 3.50€ 🅴 3€ – 🔌 (10A) 3€
Rental rates : (2015 price) (from beginning May to end Sept.) – 2 'gypsy' caravans. Per night from 40 to 50€ – Per week from 200 to 300€
🚐 15 🅴 18€

On a tiny peninsula in the Lac de Coiselet; a rural site surrounded by beautiful cliffs.

Surroundings : 🌿 ⩿ 🌳	G	Longitude : 5.6311
Leisure activities : 🏠 🐎	P	Latitude : 46.34203
Facilities : 🚿 ⛽ 🗑 🚮 🍴 launderette	S	
Nearby : 🏊 🎣 🛶		

CHARAVINES

38850 – Michelin map **333** G5 – pop. 1 758 – alt. 500
▶ Paris 534 – Belley 47 – Chambéry 49 – Grenoble 40

⚠ Les Platanes

⚲ 0476066470. www.camping-lesplatanes.com

Address : 85 rue du Camping (take the northern exit along the D 50d, 150m from the lake)

Opening times : from mid April to mid Oct.

1 ha (67 pitches) flat, grassy

Tariff : 18€ ♣♣ ⇔ 🅴 🔌 (6A) – Extra per person 5€ – Reservation fee 7€
Rental rates : (from mid April to mid Oct.) ✂ – 5 🚐 – 2 🏠. Per night from 49 to 90€ – Per week from 290 to 525€ – Reservation fee 7€
🚐 local sani-station 2.50€ – 6 🅴 13€

Surroundings : 🌳	G	Longitude : 5.51545
Leisure activities : ✗ 🏠	P	Latitude : 45.43096
Facilities : 🚿 ⛽ 🍴 🗑	S	
Nearby : 🍽 🎯 🏊 (beach) 🎣 🛶 pedalos		

CHASSAGNES

07140 – Michelin map **331** H7
▶ Paris 644 – Lyon 209 – Privas 67 – Nîmes 85

🔺 Domaine des Chênes

⚲ 0475373435. www.domaine-des-chenes.fr – limited spaces for one-night stay

Address : at Chassagnes Haut (off the D 295, D 295A)

Opening times : from beginning April to end Sept.

2.5 ha (122 pitches) flat, grassy, stony

Tariff : 33€ ♣♣ ⇔ 🅴 🔌 (10A) – Extra per person 8€
Rental rates : (from beginning April to end Sept.) – 26 🚐 – 13 🏠 – 4 tent lodges. Per night from 37 to 183€ – Per week from 259 to 1,281€ – Reservation fee 25€
🚐 AireService sani-station – 🚐 🔌19€

Varied rental options, including some high-quality mobile homes, owner-occupiers, and pitches for tents and caravans.

Surroundings : 🌿 ⩿ 🗔 🌳		
Leisure activities : 🍴 ✗ 🏠 🏋 🏊 hammam, jacuzzi 🌊	G	Longitude : 4.13218
Facilities : 🚿 ⛽ 🗑 🚮 🍴 🗑	P	Latitude : 44.39899
Nearby : 🏊 🎣	S	

CHASSIERS

07110 – Michelin map **331** H6 – pop. 1 008 – alt. 340
▶ Paris 643 – Aubenas 16 – Largentière 4 – Privas 48

🔺 Sunêlia Domaine Les Ranchisses 👥

⚲ 0475883197. www.lesranchisses.fr

Address : route de Rocher (1.6km to the northwest, access via the D 5, follow the signs for Valgorge)

Opening times : from mid April to end Sept.

6 ha (226 pitches) terraced, relatively flat, flat, grassy

Tariff : 57€ ♣♣ ⇔ 🅴 🔌 (10A) – Extra per person 11.50€ – Reservation fee 15€
Rental rates : (from mid April to end Sept.) – 112 🚐 – 3 gîtes. Per night from 40 to 244€ – Per week from 280 to 1,708€ – Reservation fee 30€
🚐 local sani-station

The site is in two sections on either side of a road, connected via a tunnel. Choose those pitches near the river where it is quieter. A well-equipped spa area.

Surroundings : 🗔 🌳 ⛰		
Leisure activities : 🍴 ✗ 🏠 🎯 🏋 🏊 hammam, jacuzzi 🐎 🎾 🎣 🛶 🏊 ⛵ 🌊 multi-sports ground, spa centre, skate park	G	Longitude : 4.28536
Facilities : 🚿 ⛽ 🗑 🚮 🗑 🍴 launderette 🗑	P	Latitude : 44.56137
	S	

A chambre d'hôte is a guesthouse or B & B-style accommodation.

CHÂTEAUNEUF-DE-GALAURE

26330 – Michelin map **332** C2 – pop. 1 557 – alt. 253
▶ Paris 531 – Annonay 29 – Beaurepaire 19 – Romans-sur-Isère 27

🔺 Iris Parc Le Château de Galaure

⚲ 0475686522. www.chateaudegalaure.com

Address : route de St-Vallier (800m southwest along the D 51)

Opening times : from end April to end Sept.

12 ha (400 pitches) flat, grassy

Tariff : (2015 price) 43€ ♣♣ ⇔ 🅴 🔌 (15A) – Extra per person 8€
Rental rates : (2015 price) (from end April to end Sept.) – 192 🚐 – 110 tent lodges. Per night from 23 to 136€ – Per week from 161 to 952€
🚐 local sani-station 7€

In a pleasant green and shady location.

Surroundings : 🌳		
Leisure activities : 🍴 ✗ 🏠 🎯 🐎 🌊 skateboarding	G	Longitude : 4.95644
Facilities : 🚿 ⛽ 🗑 🚮 🍴 🗑 🗑	P	Latitude : 45.23029
Nearby : 🎯 🖼 🎣 fitness trail	S	

CHÂTEAUNEUF-SUR-ISÈRE

26300 – Michelin map **332** C3 – pop. 3 707 – alt. 118
▶ Paris 561 – Lyon 98 – Valence 13 – Privas 55

▲▲▲ Sunêlia Le Soleil Fruité ▲▲

𝒫 04758419 70. www.lesoleilfruite.com ✖

Address : Les Pêches (4km, take exit 14 Valence Nord towards Châteauneuf sur Isère, continue along the D 877; near the 'Les Folies du Lac' cabaret)

Opening times : from end April to mid Sept.

4 ha (138 pitches) flat, grassy

Tariff : (2015 price) 36.10€ ★★ ⇌ 🔲 🔌 (10A) – Extra per person 6€
Rental rates : (2015 price) (from end April to mid Sept.) ✖ –
34 🚐. Per night from 50 to 120€ – Per week from 720 to 899€
🚏 AireService sani-service 3.10€

Surroundings : 🐾 ▱ ♀
Leisure activities : 🍸 ✕ 🎠 ⛳ ⛸ 🎣 ⛵
🏊 ⛷
Facilities : ⊶🚿 ⛺ ♒ launderette 🛒 🚿

G P S Longitude : 4.89372
Latitude : 44.99707

CHÂTEL

74390 – Michelin map **328** O3 – pop. 1 213 – alt. 1 180 – Winter sports : 1 200/2 100 m
▶ Paris 578 – Annecy 113 – Évian-les-Bains 34 – Morzine 38

▲▲▲ L'Oustalet ▲▲

𝒫 04507321 97. www.oustalet.com – alt. 1 110

Address : 1428 route des Freinets (head 2km southwest following the signs for Le Col de Bassachaux; beside the Dranse river)

Opening times : from mid June to beginning Sept.

3 ha (100 pitches) flat and relatively flat, stony, grassy, gravelled

Tariff : 35.30€ ★★ ⇌ 🔲 🔌 (6A) – Extra per person 7.20€ –
Reservation fee 10€
Rental rates : (from mid June to beginning Sept.) ✖ – 16 🚐 –
1 apartment. Per week from 370 to 760 – Reservation fee 10€
🚏 Flot Bleu sani-station 6€ – 12 🔲 6€

The site is in two sections on either side of a small road, with a nice view of the Abondance river valley.

Surroundings : ❄ 🐾 ⋖♀
Leisure activities : 🎠 🕐daytime ⛸ 🐕
⛷ ✖ 🎮 🏒
Facilities : ⅙ ⊶ ⛺ ♒ launderette
Nearby : 🍸 ✕ 🚿 🚴 ⛏

G P S Longitude : 6.82981
Latitude : 46.25755

LE CHÂTELARD

73630 – Michelin map **333** J3 – pop. 645 – alt. 750
▶ Paris 562 – Aix-les-Bains 30 – Annecy 30 – Chambéry 35

⚠ Les Cyclamens

𝒫 04795480 19. www.camping-cyclamens.com

Address : Les Granges (north of the village, head north on the D922, following the signs for Le Champet (turning to the left))

Opening times : from mid April to end Oct.

0.7 ha (34 pitches) flat, grassy

Tariff : 17.50€ ★★ ⇌ 🔲 🔌 (10A) – Extra per person 4.40€
Rental rates : permanent – 1 studio – 1 cabin in the trees.
Per night from 78 to 98€ – Per week from 525 to 546€
🚏 local sani-station 4.50€ – 4 🔲 14.20€

The pitches are partly in shade, partly in sun.

Surroundings : 🐾 ♀♀
Leisure activities : 🎮 ⛸
Facilities : ⅙ ⊶🚿 🏒 ♒ 🎮

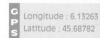

G P S Longitude : 6.13263
Latitude : 45.68782

CHÂTILLON-SUR-CHALARONNE

01400 – Michelin map **328** C4 – pop. 4 899 – alt. 177
▶ Paris 418 – Bourg-en-Bresse 28 – Lyon 55 – Mâcon 28

▲▲▲ Municipal du Vieux Moulin

𝒫 04745504 79. www.camping-vieuxmoulin.com – limited spaces for one-night stay

Address : rue Jean Jaurès (take southeastern exit along the D 7, follow the signs for Chalamont; beside the Chalaronne, 150m from a lake – direct access)

Opening times : from mid April to beginning Oct.

3 ha (140 pitches) flat, grassy

Tariff : (2015 price) 19.90€ ★★ ⇌ 🔲 🔌 (10A) – Extra per person 5€ –
Reservation fee 11€
Rental rates : (2015 price) (from mid April to beginning Oct.) –
5 🚐. Per night from 48 to 65€ – Per week from 333 to 455€ –
Reservation fee 11€
🚏 Flot Bleu sani-station – 16 🔲 14.90€
In a shaded green setting beside a river.

Surroundings : 🐾 ♀♀
Leisure activities : 🎮 ⛸ 🎣 multi-sports ground
Facilities : ⅙ ⊶🚿 ♒ 🎮
Nearby : 🛒 🍸 ✕ 🍴 🏊 ⛷

G P S Longitude : 4.96228
Latitude : 46.11654

CHAUZON

07120 – Michelin map **331** I7 – pop. 341 – alt. 128
▶ Paris 649 – Aubenas 20 – Largentière 14 – Privas 51

▲▲▲ La Digue

𝒫 04753963 57. www.camping-la-digue.fr – access difficult for caravans

Address : at Les Aires (located 1km east of the town, 100m from the Ardèche river (direct access))

7 ha/3 for camping (141 pitches) terraced, flat, grassy
Rentals : 37 🚐 – 8 🏠.

There are shaded pitches with some good-quality mobile home rentals.

Surroundings : 🐾 ♀♀
Leisure activities : 🍸 ✕ 🎣 🍴 🏊 🚿 ➰
Facilities : ⅙ ⊶ 🏒 ♒ 🎮 🔲 🏊

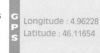

G P S Longitude : 4.37337
Latitude : 44.48437

LE CHEYLARD

07160 – Michelin map **331** I4 – pop. 3 289 – alt. 450
▶ Paris 598 – Aubenas 50 – Lamastre 21 – Privas 47

⚠ Municipal Le Cheylard

𝒫 04752909 53. www.camping-le-cheylard.com
Address : Le Vialon (off the D 120)
Opening times : from beginning April to end Sept.
1.5 ha (61 pitches) relatively flat, flat, grassy
Tariff : 13.50€ ★★ ⇌ 🔲 🔌 (16A) – Extra per person 6€

Rental rates : (from beginning April to end Sept.) – 4 🚐 – 2 🛏 – 4 canvas bungalows – 1 gîte. Per night from 65 to 70€ – Per week from 390 to 550€ 🚽 local sani-station

Surroundings : 🏞 ♨♨
Facilities : 点 o━╖ ⁿ¶ 🖼 ♨

GPS Longitude : 4.42011
Latitude : 44.9155

CHORANCHE

38680 – Michelin map **333** F7 – pop. 132 – alt. 280
▶ Paris 588 – La Chapelle-en-Vercors 24 – Grenoble 52 – Romans-sur-Isère 32

⚑ Le Gouffre de la Croix

✆ 04 76 36 07 13. www.camping-vercors-choranche.fr

Address : at Combe Bernard (to the southeast of the town, follow the signs for Chatelas; beside the Bourne river)

Opening times : from mid April to mid Sept.

2.5 ha (52 pitches) open site, terraced, flat, grassy

Tariff : (2015 price) 29.50€ ★★ ⇔ 🅴 ⚡ (6A) – Extra per person 5€ – Reservation fee 15€
Rental rates : (2015 price) (from mid April to mid Sept.) 🐾 – 2 🚐 – 1 tent lodge. Per night from 40 to 65€ – Per week from 200 to 520€ – Reservation fee 15€
In a natural wooded setting at the bottom of a valley.

Surroundings : 🏞 ⪡ ♨♨
Leisure activities : ♟ 🏊 🎣
Facilities : 点 o━╖ ♨ ⁿ¶ 🖼

GPS Longitude : 5.39447
Latitude : 45.06452

LA CLUSAZ

74220 – Michelin map **328** L5 – pop. 1 876 – alt. 1 040 – Winter sports : 1 100/2 600 m
▶ Paris 564 – Albertville 40 – Annecy 32 – Bonneville 26

⚑ FranceLoc Le Plan du Fernuy

✆ 04 50 02 44 75. www.franceloc.fr

Address : 1800 route des Confins (located 1.5km to the east)

Opening times : from mid Dec. to end April

1.3 ha (80 pitches) terraced, relatively flat, flat, grassy, gravelled

Tariff : 42.14€ ★★ ⇔ 🅴 ⚡ (13A) – Extra per person 6.42€ – Reservation fee 27€
Rental rates : (from mid Dec. to end April) 🐾 – 20 🚐 – 12 🏠 – 1 studio – 3 apartments. Per night from 58 to 112€ – Per week from 231 to 1,141€ – Reservation fee 27€
🚽 local sani-station 10€ – 40 🅴 24€
There are good-quality rental options in both summer and winter, beside an indoor swimming pool.

Surroundings : ❄ 🏞 ⪡ Aravis range ⌑ ♨
Leisure activities : ♟ 🏛 🏊 🖼
Facilities : 点 o━╖ ⁿ¶ ♨ ♨ ⁿ¶ launderette

GPS Longitude : 6.45174
Latitude : 45.90948

CORDELLE

42123 – Michelin map **327** D4 – pop. 896 – alt. 450
▶ Paris 409 – Feurs 35 – Roanne 14 – St-Just-en-Chevalet 27

⚑ De Mars

✆ 04 77 64 94 42. www.camping-de-mars.com

Address : Presqu'île de Mars (4.5km south along the D 56 and take road to the right)

Opening times : from beginning April to mid Oct.

1.2 ha (63 pitches) terraced, relatively flat, flat, grassy

Tariff : 25€ ★★ ⇔ 🅴 ⚡ (10A) – Extra per person 5€

Rental rates : (from beginning April to mid Oct.) 点 (1 mobile home) – 10 🚐 – 2 🏠 – 2 canvas bungalows. Per night from 45 to 110€ – Per week from 315 to 770€
In an attractive location overlooking the Loire river gorges.

Surroundings : 🏞 ⪡ ⌑ ♨
Leisure activities : ♟ ✗ 🏛 🏊 🚴 ⁿ 🎣
Facilities : 点 o━╖ 🅴♨ ♨ ⁿ¶ ⁿ¶ │ aunderette ♨
Nearby : 🎣

GPS Longitude : 4.06101
Latitude : 45.91668

CORMORANCHE-SUR-SAÔNE

01290 – Michelin map **328** B3 – pop. 1 051 – alt. 172
▶ Paris 399 – Bourg-en-Bresse 44 – Châtillon-sur-Chalaronne 23 – Mâcon 10

⚑ Le Lac

✆ 03 85 23 97 10. www.lac-cormoranche.com

Address : at Les Luizants (take the western exit along the D 51a and continue 1.2km turning to the right; at the leisure and activity park)

Opening times : from beginning May to end Sept.

48 ha/4.5 for camping (117 pitches) flat, grassy, sandy, wood

Tariff : (2015 price) ★ 5.60€ ⇔ 🅴 8.20€ – ⚡ (10A) 2.35€ – Reservation fee 7€
Rental rates : (2015 price) permanent 🐾 – 9 🚐 – 12 🏠 – 3 cabins in the trees – 4 tipis. Per night from 45 to 99€ – Per week from 165 to 529€ – Reservation fee 7€
🚽 local sani-station
Trees and shrubs surround the pitches, near a small but pretty lake.

Surroundings : ⌑ ♨
Leisure activities : ♟ ✗ 🏊 🚴 ⁿ 🏊 (beach) 🎣 ♪ entertainment room
Facilities : 点 o━╖ ♨ ♨ ⁿ¶ ⁿ¶ launderette ♨

GPS Longitude : 4.82573
Latitude : 46.25105

The pitches of many campsites are marked out with low hedges of attractive bushes and shrubs.

CREST

26400 – Michelin map **332** D5 – pop. 7 857 – alt. 196
▶ Paris 585 – Die 37 – Gap 129 – Grenoble 114

⚑ Les Clorinthes ♨♨

✆ 04 75 25 05 28. www.lesclorinthes.com

Address : quai Soubeyran (take the southern exit along the D 538 then take the road to the left after the bridge, near the Drôme river and the sports centre)

Opening times : from end April to mid Sept.

4 ha (160 pitches) flat and relatively flat, grassy

Tariff : (2015 price) 26.90€ ★★ ⇔ 🅴 ⚡ (6A) – Extra per person 7.40€ – Reservation fee 21€
Rental rates : (2015 price) (from end April to mid Sept.) – 10 🚐 – 4 🏠 – 2 canvas bungalows. Per night from 50 to 74€ – Per week from 322 to 693€ – Reservation fee 21€

Surroundings : ⪡ ♨
Leisure activities : ♟ ✗ 🏛 🕯 daytime 🏃 🏊 🚴 🎣
Facilities : 点 o━╖ ♨ ⁿ¶ launderette
Nearby : ✗ 🐎

GPS Longitude : 5.0277
Latitude : 44.724

RHÔNE-ALPES

CUBLIZE

69550 – Michelin map **327** F3 – pop. 1 242 – alt. 452
▶ Paris 422 – Amplepuis 7 – Chauffailles 29 – Roanne 30

🏕 Campéole le Lac des Sapins

📞 04 74 89 52 83. www.campinglacdessapins.com – limited spaces for one-night stay

Address : rue du Lac (800m to the south; beside the Reins stream and 300m from the lake (direct access)

Opening times : from beginning April to beginning Sept.

4 ha (182 pitches) flat, grassy

Tariff : 16€ ★★ ⇔ 🅴 🕪 (10A) – Extra per person 10€ – Reservation fee 25€

Rental rates : permanent – 24 ⛺ – 26 🏠 – 12 canvas bungalows – 6 tent lodges. Per night from 57 to 152€ – Per week from 399 to 1,064€ – Reservation fee 25€

⛽ 6 🅴 16€

Surroundings : 🌳 ⇐ 🛶
Leisure activities : 🏄 🚲 🎾 multi-sports ground
Facilities : ♿ ⊶ 🚿 🔥 launderette
At the leisure/activities centre : 🏖 🛥 🏖 🎣

Longitude : 4.37849
Latitude : 46.0132

In order for the guide to remain wholly objective, the selection of campsites is made on an entirely independent basis.

CULOZ

01350 – Michelin map **328** H5 – pop. 2 920 – alt. 248
▶ Paris 512 – Aix-les-Bains 24 – Annecy 55 – Bourg-en-Bresse 88

🏕 VivaCamp Le Colombier

📞 04 79 87 19 00. http://www.camping-alpes.net/

Address : ile de Verbaou (D992) (1.3km east, at junction of D 904 and D 992; beside a stream)

Opening times : from end April to end Sept.

1.5 ha (81 pitches) flat, grassy, gravelled

Tariff : 21€ ★★ ⇔ 🅴 🕪 (6A) – Extra per person 6€ – Reservation fee 15€

Rental rates : (from end April to end Sept.) – 6 ⛺ – 3 canvas bungalows. Per night from 38 to 80€ – Per week from 140 to 560€ – Reservation fee 25€

Situated near a leisure centre.

Surroundings : ⇐ 🛶 ♀
Leisure activities : 🍸 🏄 🚲
Facilities : ♿ ⊶ 🚿 🔥 launderette 🚮
Nearby : 🎾 🏓 🏖 🛥

Longitude : 5.79346
Latitude : 45.85158

DARBRES

07170 – Michelin map **331** J6 – pop. 252 – alt. 450
▶ Paris 618 – Aubenas 18 – Montélimar 34 – Privas 21

🏕 Les Lavandes

📞 04 75 94 20 65. www.les-lavandes-darbres.com

Address : in the village

Opening times : from mid April to mid Sept.

1.5 ha (70 pitches) terraced, flat, grassy, stony

Tariff : 29.90€ ★★ ⇔ 🅴 🕪 (6A) – Extra per person 4.50€ – Reservation fee 15€

Rental rates : (from mid April to mid Sept.) – 12 🏠. Per night from 54 to 60€ – Per week from 270 to 670€ – Reservation fee 15€

Near the centre of the village, with attractive vews from the bar's terrace, swimming pool and some elevated pitches.

Surroundings : 🌳 ♀♀
Leisure activities : 🍸 🍴 🏄 🏊
Facilities : ⊶ 🚿 🔥 launderette 🚮

Longitude : 4.50402
Latitude : 44.64701

DARDILLY

69570 – Michelin map **327** H5 – pop. 8 384 – alt. 338
▶ Paris 457 – Lyon 13 – Villeurbanne 21 – Vénissieux 26

🏕 Indigo International Lyon

📞 04 78 35 64 55. www.camping-indigo.com

Address : Porte de Lyon (10km northwest along the N 6, follow the signs for Mâcon – from the A 6, take the Limonest exit)

Opening times : permanent

6 ha (150 pitches) flat, grassy

Tariff : (2015 price) 27.60€ ★★ ⇔ 🅴 🕪 (10A) – Extra per person 5.20€ – Reservation fee 13€

Rental rates : (2015 price) permanent – 6 'gypsy' caravans – 61 ⛺ – 7 tent lodges. Per night from 41 to 115€ – Per week from 201 to 644€ – Reservation fee 13€

⛽ local sani-station 7€

Surroundings : ♀♀
Leisure activities : 🍸 🍴 🚣 🏄 🏊
Facilities : ♿ ⊶ 🍴 🚿 🔥 launderette

Longitude : 4.76125
Latitude : 45.81817

We value your opinion and welcome your feedback. Do email us at campingfrance@tp.michelin.com

DIE

26150 – Michelin map **332** F5 – pop. 4 357 – alt. 415
▶ Paris 623 – Gap 92 – Grenoble 110 – Montélimar 73

🏕 Le Glandasse

📞 04 75 22 02 50. www.camping-glandasse.com

Address : La Maldrerie district (1km southeast along the D 93, follow the signs for Gap then take the road to the right, beside the Drôme river). Note for access: maximum height 2.8m

Opening times : from mid April to end Sept.

3.5 ha (120 pitches) relatively flat, flat, grassy, stony

Tariff : 27€ ★★ ⇔ 🅴 🕪 (10A) – Extra per person 6€ – Reservation fee 10€

Rental rates : (from mid April to end Sept.) – 2 ⛺ – 15 🏠. Per night from 40 to 82€ – Per week from 280 to 574€ – Reservation fee 10€

Surroundings : 🌳 ⇐ 🛶 ♀♀
Leisure activities : 🍴 🏓 jacuzzi 🏄 🚲 🏖 🏊 🛥 🦆 multi-sports ground
Facilities : ♿ ⊶ 🚿 🔥 launderette 🚮

Longitude : 5.38403
Latitude : 44.73993

🏕 Le Riou Merle

📞 04 75 22 21 31. www.camping-lerioumerle-drome.com

Address : route de Romeyer (head north along the D 742)

Opening times : from beginning April to mid Oct.

2.5 ha (97 pitches) flat, grassy

Tariff : 27€ ★★ ⇔ 🅴 🕪 (10A) – Extra per person 6.80€

464

Rental rates : (from beginning April to mid Oct.) – 12 ⊞ – 3 ⌂. Per week from 252 to 650€

⊞ local sani-station

Surroundings : ⌒ ♀
Leisure activities : ♀ ✗ ⌂ ⌸
Facilities : ☞⌒✉ 🍴 launderette ⌇

Longitude : 5.37776
Latitude : 44.75441

In a wooded setting with mountains as a backdrop.

Surroundings : ⌒ ♀♀
Leisure activities : ♀ ✗ ⌂ 🏃 ⌸ 🚴
✗⌸ ♀♀
Facilities : ♿ ☞ 🍴 ⌇ 🍴 launderette
⌸ ⌇

Longitude : 6.1178
Latitude : 46.37137

DIEULEFIT

26220 – Michelin map **332** D6 – pop. 3 028 – alt. 366
▸ Paris 614 – Crest 30 – Montélimar 29 – Nyons 30

⚲ Huttopia Dieulefit

✆ 04 75 54 63 94. www.huttopia.com

Address : Espeluche district (3km north along the D 540 follow the signs for Bourdeaux then take the road to the left)

Opening times : from mid April to beginning Oct.

17 ha (140 pitches) undulating, flat, grassy

Tariff : (2015 price) 47.80€ ♣♣ ⇌ ▣ ⓖ (10A) – Extra per person 8€ – Reservation fee 13€

Rental rates : (2015 price) (from mid April to beginning Oct.) – 34 ⌂ – 40 tent lodges. Per night from 49 to 180€ – Per week from 258 to 1,260€ – Reservation fee 13€

⊞ local sani-station 7€

Surroundings : ⌒
Leisure activities : ✗ ⌂ ⌸ ⌸
Facilities : ☞ ⌇ launderette ⌇

Longitude : 5.05826
Latitude : 44.53987

⚲ Le Domaine des Grands Prés

✆ 04 75 49 94 36. www.lesgrandspres-dromeprovencale.com

Address : Les Grands Prés district (take the western exit along the D 540, follow the signs for Montélimar, near the Jabron river – direct access to the town along a pedestrian path)

1.8 ha (91 pitches) flat, grassy

Rentals – 9 'gypsy' caravans – 5 ⌂ – 6 yurts – 1 cabin in the trees – 2 tipis – 3 canvas bungalows – 4 tent lodges – 1 gîte – 2 cabin lodges on stilts.

⊞ local sani-station

Surroundings : ⌒ ♀♀
Leisure activities : ⌂ ⌸ ⌸ ⌇
Facilities : ♿ ☞ 🍴 ⌇ 🍴 launderette
Nearby : ⌇ ✗

Longitude : 5.06149
Latitude : 44.52141

DIVONNE-LES-BAINS

01220 – Michelin map **328** J2 – pop. 7 926 – alt. 486 – ⚓
▸ Paris 488 – Bourg-en-Bresse 129 – Genève 18 – Gex 9

⚲ Indigo Divonne - Le Fleutron

✆ 04 50 20 01 95. www.camping-indigo.com

Address : 2465 Vie de L'Etraz (3km to the north, after Villard)

Opening times : from end Feb. to mid Nov.

8 ha (253 pitches) terraced, flat and relatively flat, stony, grassy

Tariff : (2015 price) 29.90€ ♣♣ ⇌ ▣ ⓖ (10A) – Extra per person 6.10€ – Reservation fee 13€

Rental rates : (2015 price) (from end Feb. to mid Nov.) – 12 'gypsy' caravans – 38 ⊞ – 15 ⌂ – 28 tent lodges. Per night from 46 to 107€ – Per week from 226 to 749€ – Reservation fee 13€

⊞ local sani-station 7€

DOUSSARD

74210 – Michelin map **328** K6 – pop. 3 473 – alt. 456
▸ Paris 555 – Albertville 27 – Annecy 20 – La Clusaz 36

⚲ International du Lac Bleu ⚐⚐

✆ 04 50 44 30 18. www.camping-lac-bleu.com

Address : route de la Plage (follow the signs for Albertville)

3.3 ha (221 pitches) flat, grassy, stony

Rentals : 47 ⊞ – 2 ⊨ – 12 studios – 10 apartments.

⊞ local sani-station

Surroundings : ⌒ ∢ ⌒ ♀♀ ⌸
Leisure activities : ♀ ✗ ⊗ 🏃 jacuzzi ⌸ 🚴
⌸ multi-sports ground
Facilities : ♿ ☞ ⌇ 🍴 launderette ⌇
Nearby : ⌇ ✗ ⌂ ⌇ ⚓ ⌇ ⛵ paragliding, marina

Longitude : 6.21648
Latitude : 45.79103

⚲ Campéole la Nublière ⚐⚐

✆ 04 50 44 33 44. www.campeole.com

Address : 30 allée de la Nublière (located 1.8km to the north)

Opening times : from beginning May to end Sept.

9.2 ha (467 pitches) flat, grassy, stony

Tariff : 19€ ♣♣ ⇌ ▣ ⓖ (10A) – Extra per person 10€ – Reservation fee 25€

Rental rates : (from beginning May to end Sept.) – 56 ⊞ – 10 ⌂ – 40 canvas bungalows. Per night from 34 to 214€ – Per week from 238 to 1,498€ – Reservation fee 25€

In a pleasant setting beside the lake (beach), with a variety of rental options.

Surroundings : ♀♀ ⌸
Leisure activities : 🏃 ⌸ ⌒ ⌸ multi-sports ground, entertainment room
Facilities : ♿ ☞ 🍴 ⌇ 🍴 launderette
Nearby : ⌇ ♀ ✗ ⌂ ⌇ ✗ ⌇ ⚓ ⌇ ⛵ paragliding

Longitude : 6.21763
Latitude : 45.79014

⚲ La Ferme de Serraz

✆ 04 50 44 30 68. www.campinglaserraz.com

Address : rue de la Poste (in the town, take the eastern exit near the post office)

Opening times : from beginning May to mid Sept.

3.5 ha (197 pitches) relatively flat, flat, grassy

Tariff : (2015 price) 22€ ♣♣ ⇌ ▣ ⓖ (16A) – Extra per person 8€ – Reservation fee 25€

Rental rates : (2015 price) (from beginning May to mid Sept.) – 40 ⊞. Per night from 43 to 185€ – Per week from 305 to 1,295€ – Reservation fee 25€

⊞ local sani-station 5€

The whole site is well shaded, with numerous pitches run by tour operators.

Surroundings : ♀♀
Leisure activities : ♀ ✗ ⌂ ⌸ 🚴 ⌸
Facilities : ♿ ☞ 🍴 ⌇ ⌸ ⌇ 🍴 launderette

Longitude : 6.22588
Latitude : 45.77508

DUINGT

74410 – Michelin map **328** K6 – pop. 891 – alt. 450
▷ Paris 548 – Albertville 34 – Annecy 12 – Megève 48

⚠ Municipal les Champs Fleuris

📞 04 50 68 57 31. www.camping-duingt.com

Address : 631 voie Romaine – Les Perris (located 1km west)

Opening times : from mid April to end Sept.

1.3 ha (112 pitches) terraced, relatively flat, flat, grassy

Tariff : 27.50€ ✦✦ ⛺ 🔲 ⚡ (10A) – Extra per person 6€ – Reservation fee 5€

Rental rates : (from mid April to end Sept.) – 6 🚐 – 2 canvas bungalows – 1 tent lodge. Per night from 60 to 120€ – Per week from 570 to 900€ – Reservation fee 5€

🚰 Flot Bleu sani-station 4€ – 20 🔲 21€ – 🚗 21€
The pitches are laid out on terraces, sometimes with shade; a variety of rental accommodation.

Surroundings : 🌳 ⛰ 🌿🌿 Leisure activities : ⛵ Facilities : ♿ 🚿 🛒 🍴 launderette	Longitude : 6.18882 Latitude : 45.82658

ÉCLASSAN

07370 – Michelin map **331** K3 – pop. 910 – alt. 420
▷ Paris 534 – Annonay 21 – Beaurepaire 46 – Condrieu 42

⛰ La Via Natura L'Oasis

📞 04 75 34 56 23. www.oasisardeche.com – pitches accessed via steep slope, help moving caravans onto and off pitches available on request

Address : at Le Petit Chaléat (4.5km northwest, follow the signs for Fourany and take road to the left)

Opening times : from end April to beginning Sept.

4 ha (63 pitches) terraced, flat, grassy, stony

Tariff : 28€ ✦✦ ⛺ 🔲 ⚡ (6A) – Extra per person 5€ – Reservation fee 8€

Rental rates : (from end April to beginning Sept.) – 4 🚐 – 12 🏠 – 8 tent lodges. Per night from 78 to 105€ – Per week from 206 to 735€ – Reservation fee 8€

Pitches on natural-style terraces, some beside the Ay river.

Surroundings : 🌳 ⛺ 🌿 Leisure activities : 🍴 ✕ ⛺ ⛵ ♨ 🏊 ⛷ Facilities : ♿ 🚿 🏕 🗑 🍴 🏪 🛒	Longitude : 4.73944 Latitude : 45.17889

EXCENEVEX

74140 – Michelin map **328** L2 – pop. 988 – alt. 375
▷ Paris 564 – Annecy 71 – Bonneville 42 – Douvaine 9

⛰ Campéole La Pinède

📞 04 50 72 85 05. www.camping-lac-leman.info – limited spaces for one-night stay

Address : 10 avenue de la Plage (located 1km southeast along the D 25)

Opening times : from end April to end Sept.

12 ha (525 pitches) undulating, sandy

Tariff : 17€ ✦✦ ⛺ 🔲 ⚡ (10A) – Extra per person 10€ – Reservation fee 25€

Rental rates : (from end April to end Sept.) ♿ (2 mobile homes) – 84 🚐 – 20 🏠 – 57 canvas bungalows. Per night from 34 to 185€ – Per week from 238 to 1,295€ – Reservation fee 25€

🚰 local sani-station

In a pleasant wooded site close to a beach on Lac Léman, but choose those pitches furthest away from the road.

Surroundings : ⛺ 🌿🌿 Leisure activities : 🎣 🏖 🚣 jacuzzi ⛷ 🚴 ⛵ 🏊 multi-sports ground, entertainment room Facilities : ♿ 🚿 🛒 🍴 launderette 🧺 Nearby : 🍴 ✕ ⛵ 🎯 🚣 🐟 ⚓ pedalos	 Longitude : 6.35799 Latitude : 46.34543

FARAMANS

38260 – Michelin map **333** D5 – pop. 906 – alt. 375
▷ Paris 518 – Beaurepaire 12 – Bourgoin-Jallieu 35 – Grenoble 60

⚠ Municipal des Eydoches

📞 04 74 54 21 78. mairie.faramans@wanadoo.fr – limited spaces for one-night stay

Address : 515 avenue des Marais (take the eastern exit along the D 37, follow the signs for La Côte-St-André)

1 ha (60 pitches) flat, grassy

Rentals : 2 🏠.

🚰 local sani-station – 2 🔲

Surroundings : 🌿 Facilities : ♿ 🏕 🗑 🍴 🏪 Nearby : 🎯 🚣	Longitude : 5.17563 Latitude : 45.39348

FÉLINES

07340 – Michelin map **331** K2 – pop. 1 475 – alt. 380
▷ Paris 520 – Annonay 13 – Beaurepaire 31 – Condrieu 24

⛰ Bas-Larin

📞 04 75 34 87 93. www.camping-bas-larin.com

Address : 88 route de Larin-le-Bas (situated 2km southeast, along the N 82, follow the signs for Serrières and take road to the right)

Opening times : from beginning April to end Sept.

1.5 ha (67 pitches) terraced, relatively flat to hilly, grassy

Tariff : (2015 price) 21.80€ ✦✦ ⛺ 🔲 ⚡ (10A) – Extra per person 3.50€

Rental rates : (2015 price) (from beginning April to end Sept.) – 11 🚐 – 1 🏠 – 3 canvas bungalows. Per night from 35 to 85€ – Per week from 220 to 599€ – Reservation fee 12€

🚰 15 🔲 18€
The pitches on terraces are well shaded, but choose those furthest away from the road (a former national highway).

Surroundings : ⛺ 🌿🌿 Leisure activities : 🍴 ✕ ⛺ ⛵ ♨ 🏊 Facilities : ♿ 🚿 🏕 🗑 🍴 🏪 🛒	Longitude : 4.74665 Latitude : 45.3086

LA FERRIÈRE

38580 – Michelin map **333** J6 – pop. 226 – alt. 926
▷ Paris 613 – Lyon 146 – Grenoble 52 – Chambéry 47

⛰ Neige et Nature

📞 04 76 45 19 84. www.neige-nature.fr – alt. 900

Address : chemin de Montarmand (to the west of the village; beside the Bréda river)

Opening times : from mid May to mid Sept.

1.2 ha (45 pitches) terraced, relatively flat, flat, grassy

Tariff : 18.80€ ✦✦ ⛺ 🔲 ⚡ (10A) – Extra per person 5.90€

Rental rates : permanent – 2 ⊞ – 2 ⌂. Per week from 325 to 650€

⊞ local sani-station 18.80€ – 20 ▣ 18.80€

A green, well-kept setting.

Surroundings : ⚬ ⩽ ◻ ♀
Leisure activities : ⌂
Facilities : ᛃ �o⊣ ⊟ ♨ ⁱ ▣ ᛃ
Nearby : ⩲ (pool)

Longitude : 6.08331
Latitude : 45.3184

FEURS

42110 – Michelin map **327** E5 – pop. 7 741 – alt. 343
▶ Paris 433 – Lyon 69 – Montbrison 24 – Roanne 38

⚹⚹ Municipal du Palais

✆ 0477264341. mairie.camping@feurs.fr – ℝ

Address : route de Civens (take the northern exit along the N 82, follow the signs for Roanne and take a right turn)

Opening times : from beginning April to end Oct.

5 ha (385 pitches) flat, grassy, lake

Tariff : (2015 price) ⭑ 3.20€ – ⇔ 2.80€ ▣ 3.30€ – 🔌 (16A) 3.70€

⊞ AireService sani-station

In a peaceful area, close to the town centre.

Surroundings : ♀ ♀
Leisure activities : ⟋⟋
Facilities : ᛃ o⊣ ▦ ♨ ☂ ⁱ ᛃ
Nearby : ⤮ ⤲

Longitude : 4.22572
Latitude : 45.75429

FLEURIE

69820 – Michelin map **327** H2 – pop. 1 250 – alt. 320
▶ Paris 410 – Bourg-en-Bresse 46 – Chauffailles 44 – Lyon 58

⚹⚹ VivaCamp La Grappe Fleurie

✆ 0474698007. www.beaujolais-camping.com

Address : rue de la Grappe Fleurie (600m south of the town along the D 119e and take a right turn.)

Opening times : from mid April to mid Oct.

2.5 ha (85 pitches) flat, grassy

Tariff : 26€ ⭑⭑ ⇔ ▣ 🔌 (10A) – Extra per person 6€ – Reservation fee 10€

Rental rates : (from mid April to mid Oct.) – 2 'gypsy' caravans – 24 ⊞ – 3 ⌂ – 3 canvas bungalows. Per night from 45 to 100€ – Per week from 315 to 630€ – Reservation fee 25€

In the heart of a vineyard; some rental options have a local flavour (barrel-shaped).

Surroundings : ⚬ ⩽ ◻ ♀
Leisure activities : ⟋⟋ ⤮ ⤲ Finnish sauna
Facilities : ᛃ o⊣ ▣ ♨ ☂ ⁱ launderette
Nearby : ⤲ ⤮

Longitude : 4.7001
Latitude : 46.18854

LES GETS

74260 – Michelin map **328** N4 – pop. 1 254 – alt. 1 170 – Winter sports : 1 170/2 000 m
▶ Paris 579 – Annecy 77 – Bonneville 33 – Chamonix-Mont-Blanc 60

⚹ Le Frêne

✆ 0450758060. www.alpensport-hotel.com – alt. 1 315

Address : at Les Cornus (take the southwestern exit along the D 902 then continue 2.3km, following signs for Les Platons to the right)

0.3 ha (40 piches(very uneven,open site, terraced, flat, grassy

A small but quiet road crosses the campsite.

Surroundings : ⚬ ⩽ Aiguille du Midi, Mt Blanc mountain range ◻ ♀
Leisure activities : ⌂ ⟋⟋ ⤲
Facilities : ᛃ o⊣ ♨ ☂ ⁱ ▣

Longitude : 6.64296
Latitude : 46.15065

GEX

01170 – Michelin map **328** J3 – pop. 9 882 – alt. 626
▶ Paris 490 – Genève 19 – Lons-le-Saunier 93 – Pontarlier 110

⚹⚹ Municipal les Genêts

✆ 0450428457. www.pays-de-gex.org

Address : route de Divonne-les-Bains (located 1km east along the D 984 and take the road to the right)

Opening times : from beginning May to end Sept.

3.3 ha (140 pitches) flat and relatively flat, gravelled, grassy

Tariff : (2015 price) ⭑ 4.50€ ⇔ ▣ 6.50€ – 🔌 (10A) 3.50€

Rental rates : (2015 price) (from beginning May to end Sept.) – 4 ⊞. Per week from 298 to 538€

⊞ local sani-station 3€ – 96 ▣ 19€

in a pretty situation between Lake Geneva and the Jura mountains.

Surroundings : ⩽ ◻
Leisure activities : ✕ ⌂ ⟋⟋ ⊗
Facilities : ᛃ o⊣ ⊟ ▦ ☂ ⁱ launderette
Nearby : ⤮ ⤲

Longitude : 6.06841
Latitude : 46.33564

LE GRAND-BORNAND

74450 – Michelin map **328** L5 – pop. 2 195 – alt. 934 – Winter sports : 1 000/2 100 m
▶ Paris 564 – Albertville 47 – Annecy 31 – Bonneville 23

⚹⚹⚹ L'Escale

✆ 0450022069. www.campinglescale.com

Address : route de la Patinoire (east of the town, near the church and the Borne river)

Opening times : from mid Dec. to end Sept.

2.8 ha (149 pitches) terraced, relatively flat, flat, grassy, stony

Tariff : (2015 price) 26.20€ ⭑⭑ ⇔ ▣ 🔌 (10A) – Extra per person 6.80€ – Reservation fee 12€

Rental rates : (2015 price) permanent – 26 ⊞ – 30 ⌂ – 2 ⊫ – 8 studios – 20 apartments. Per night from 50 to 120€ – Per week from 340 to 890€ – Reservation fee 12€

⊞ local sani-station 28€

Numerous rental options beside a small, partially covered water park.

Surroundings : ❄ ⩽ ♀
Leisure activities : ⍾ ✕ ⌂ ⟋⟋ ⤮ ⊞ ⤲
Facilities : ᛃ o⊣ ▦ ♨ ☂ ⁱ launderette ᛃ
Nearby : ⚹ ⩲ sports trail

Longitude : 6.42817
Latitude : 45.94044

Do not confuse:
⚹ *to* ⚹⚹⚹⚹ : *MICHELIN classification with*
★ *to* ★★★★★ : *official classification*

⚠ Le Clos du Pin

☏ 04 50 02 27 61. www.le-clos-du-pin.com – alt. 1 015 – limited spaces for one-night stay

Address : 1.3km east along the follow the signs for Le Bouchet; beside the Borne river

1.3 ha (61 pitches) relatively flat, grassy

Rentals : 2 🚐 – 1 apartment.

🚾 local sani-station

There are numerous owner-occupier mobile homes. Choose the pitches the furthest away from the road.

Surroundings : ❄ 🦆 ≤ Chaîne des Aravis mountains ♀		Longitude : 6.44281
Leisure activities : 🏠	G P S	Latitude : 45.93971
Facilities : 🚿 ⚪ 🏛 🏕 🚰 launderette		

GRANE

26400 – Michelin map **332** C5 – pop. 1 730 – alt. 175
▶ Paris 583 – Crest 10 – Montélimar 34 – Privas 29

⛰ Flower Les 4 Saisons

☏ 04 75 62 64 17. www.camping-4saisons.com

Address : route de Roche sur Grane (take the southeastern exit, 900m along the D 113, follow the signs for la Roche-sur-Grâne)

Opening times : from beginning April to end Sept.

2 ha (80 pitches) terraced, relatively flat, flat, grassy, sandy

Tariff : (2015 price) 31.50€ ✚✚ 🚗 🔲 🔌 (6A) – Extra per person 6€
Rental rates : (2015 price) (from beginning April to end Sept.) – 6 🚐 – 10 🏠 – 4 tent lodges. Per night from 42 to 121€ – Per week from 210 to 847€

🚾 local sani-station – 🚐 11€

Surroundings : 🦆 ≤ 🏕 ♀		Longitude : 4.92671
Leisure activities : 🏋 🏕 🚰 🏊	G P S	Latitude : 44.72684
Facilities : 🚿 ⚪ 🆓 🏛 🏕 🚰 🚽 launderette 🛁		
Nearby : 🍴		

The information in the guide may have changed since going to press.

GRAVIÈRES

07140 – Michelin map **331** G7 – pop. 391 – alt. 220
▶ Paris 636 – Lyon 213 – Privas 71 – Nîmes 92

⚠ Le Mas du Serre

☏ 04 75 37 33 84. www.campinglemasduserre.com

Address : at Le Serre (1.3km southeast along the D 113 and take the road to the left, 300m from the Chassezac)

Opening times : from mid April to end Sept.

1.5 ha (75 pitches) terraced, relatively flat, flat, grassy

Tariff : 27€ ✚✚ 🚗 🔲 🔌 (6A) – Extra per person 7€
Rental rates : (from mid April to end Sept.) – 6 🚐 – 1 gîte.
Per night from 56 to 82€ – Per week from 390 to 670€

An attractive site set around an old mas (regional-style house).

Surroundings : 🦆 ≤ ♀♀		Longitude : 4.1016
Leisure activities : 🏕 🚰	G P S	Latitude : 44.41475
Facilities : 🚿 ⚪ 🆓 🆓 🏕 🚽 🔲		
Nearby : 🏊		

GRESSE-EN-VERCORS

38650 – Michelin map **333** G8 – pop. 394 – alt. 1 205 – Winter sports : 1 300/1 700 m
▶ Paris 610 – Clelles 22 – Grenoble 48 – Monestier-de-Clermont 14

⛰ Les 4 Saisons

☏ 04 76 34 30 27. www.camping-les4saisons.com

Address : 1.3km southwest, at La Ville, off the D 8D

Opening times : from beginning May to beginning Oct.

2.2 ha (90 pitches) terraced, flat, grassy, fine gravel, stony

Tariff : 25.40€ ✚✚ 🚗 🔲 🔌 (10A) – Extra per person 5.20€ – Reservation fee 6€
Rental rates : (from beginning May to beginning Oct.) 🏕 – 9 🚐 – 3 🏠. Per week from 395 to 725€ – Reservation fee 16€

🚾 local sani-station 5€

In a pleasant location at the foot of the Massif du Vercors plateau and mountains

Surroundings : ❄ 🦆 ≤ Massif du Vercors mountains		Longitude : 5.55559
Leisure activities : 🏋 🍴 🏠 🏕 🚰	G P S	Latitude : 44.8965
Facilities : 🚿 ⚪ 🏛 🚽 launderette		
Nearby : 🛶 🍴		

GRIGNAN

26230 – Michelin map **332** C7 – pop. 1 564 – alt. 198
▶ Paris 629 – Crest 46 – Montélimar 25 – Nyons 25

⛰ Les Truffières

☏ 04 75 46 93 62. www.lestruffieres.com 🏕

Address : 1100 chemin Belle-Vue-d'Air, Nachony district (situated 2km southwest along the D 541, follow the signs for Donzère and take the D 71, follow the signs for Chamaret)

Opening times : from end April to mid Sept.

1 ha (85 pitches) flat, grassy, stony, wood

Tariff : 26.20€ ✚✚ 🚗 🔲 🔌 (10A) – Extra per person 5€ – Reservation fee 15€
Rental rates : (from mid April to mid Sept.) 🏕 – 12 🚐.
Per night from 50 to 100€ – Per week from 230 to 760€

A wooded setting.

Surroundings : 🦆 🏕 ♀♀		Longitude : 4.89121
Leisure activities : 🍴 🏠 🏕 🚰	G P S	Latitude : 44.41163
Facilities : 🚿 ⚪ 🏕 🔲		

GROISY

74570 – Michelin map **328** K4 – pop. 2 976 – alt. 690
▶ Paris 534 – Dijon 228 – Grenoble 120 – Lons-le-Saunier 146

⚠ Le Moulin Dollay

☏ 04 50 68 00 31. www.moulindollay.fr

Address : 206 rue du Moulin Dollay (situated 2km southeast, junction of D 2 and N 203; beside a stream, at Le Plot)

Opening times : from beginning May to end Sept.

3 ha (30 pitches) flat, grassy, wood, stony

Tariff : 23€ ✚✚ 🚗 🔲 🔌 (6A) – Extra per person 5€
🚾 local sani-station 5€ – 10 🔲 17€ – 🚐 15€

Surroundings : 🏕 ♀♀		Longitude : 6.19076
Leisure activities : 🏠	G P S	Latitude : 46.00224
Facilities : 🚿 ⚪ 🆓 🆓 🏛 🏕 🚰 🚽 launderette		

HAUTECOURT

01250 – Michelin map **328** F4 – pop. 760 – alt. 370
▶ Paris 442 – Bourg-en-Bresse 20 – Nantua 24 – Oyonnax 33

⚠ L'Île de Chambod

✆ 0474372541. www.campingilechambod.com

Address : 3232 route du Port (4.5km southeast along the D 59, follow the signs for Poncin then take the turning to the left, 300m from the Ain (small lake)

2.4 ha (110 pitches) flat, grassy
Rentals : 7 🏚 – 4 canvas bungalows.

Surroundings : ⪡ ⌂ ♀
Leisure activities : ▼ ✕ ⚓ ♨ ⚓
Facilities : ৬ ⊶ ♨ ⁿ 🗑
Nearby : ⚓ sports trail

GPS Longitude : 5.42819
Latitude : 46.12761

ISSARLÈS

07470 – Michelin map **331** G4 – pop. 165 – alt. 946
▶ Paris 574 – Coucouron 16 – Langogne 36 – Le Monastier-sur-Gazeille 18

⚠ La Plaine de la Loire

✆ 0624492279. www.campinglaplainedelaloire.fr – alt. 900

Address : Le Moulin du Lac – Pont de Laborie (3km west along the D 16, follow the signs for Coucouron and take the road to the left before the bridge, beside the Loire river)

Opening times : from beginning May to end Sept.

1 ha (50 pitches) flat, grassy

Tariff : (2015 price) 14.50€ ✚✚ ⚎ 🅔 (10A) – Extra per person 3.50€
Perfect for those in search of peace, nature and fishing.

Surroundings : ⪢ ⪡ ♀♀
Leisure activities : ✕ ⚓ ⚓ ⚓ ⚓
Facilities : ⊶ ⌐ ⁿ

GPS Longitude : 4.05207
Latitude : 44.818

JAUJAC

07380 – Michelin map **331** H6 – pop. 1 212 – alt. 450
▶ Paris 612 – Privas 44 – Le Puy-en-Velay 81

⚠ Bonneval

✆ 0475932709. www.campingbonneval.com ✉ 07380 Fabras

Address : Les Plots at Fabras (situated 2km northeast along the D 19 and take the D 5, follow the signs for Pont-de-Labeaume, 100m from the Lignon and basalt columns)

Opening times : from beginning April to end Sept.

3 ha (60 pitches) terraced, relatively flat, flat, grassy

Tariff : (2015 price) 29.30€ ✚✚ ⚎ 🅔 (10A) – Extra per person 6.20€

Rental rates : (2015 price) (from beginning April to end Oct.) – 4 🏚 – 4 🏠 – 1 tent lodge. Per week from 210 to 695€ – Reservation fee 10€

Pitches in both sun and shade, various rental options and a good standard of sanitary facilities suitable for families.

Surroundings : ⪢ ⪡ Chaîne du Tanargue mountains ♀
Leisure activities : ▼ ⚓ ♨ ⚓
Facilities : ৬ ⊶ (season) ⌐ ▥ ♨ ⁿ 🗑
Nearby : ⚓

GPS Longitude : 4.25825
Latitude : 44.64168

JOANNAS

07110 – Michelin map **331** H6 – pop. 342 – alt. 430
▶ Paris 650 – Aubenas 23 – Largentière 8 – Privas 55

⚠ Sites et Paysages La Marette

✆ 0475883888. www.lamarette.com

Address : route de Valgorge (2.4km west along the D 24, after La Prade)

4 ha (97 pitches) terraced, undulating, grassy, wood
Rentals : 2 'gypsy' caravans – 24 🏚 – 19 🏠 .
The site is laid out in numerous small, individual terraces, in a natural setting with good shade.

Surroundings : ⪢ ⌂ ♀♀
Leisure activities : ▼ ✕ ⚓ ⚓ ♨ ⚓
Facilities : ৬ ⊶ ♨ ⁿ 🗑 ⚓

GPS Longitude : 4.22913
Latitude : 44.56662

⚠ Le Roubreau

✆ 0475883207. www.leroubreau.com

Address : route de Valgorge (1.4km west along the D 24 and take road to the left)

Opening times : from mid April to mid Sept.

3 ha (100 pitches) relatively flat, flat, grassy, stony

Tariff : 31.30€ ✚✚ ⚎ 🅔 (6A) – Extra per person 7.40€ – Reservation fee 9€

Rental rates : (from mid April to mid Sept.) – 29 🏚 – 2 🏠 – 2 canvas bungalows. Per night from 29 to 110€ – Per week from 200 to 770€ – Reservation fee 9€

🚐 Raclet sani-station 5€

Well-shaded pitches and rental options beside the Roubreau river, with good sanitary facilities.

Surroundings : ⪢ ⌂ ♀♀
Leisure activities : ▼ ✕ ⚓ ⚓ ♨ ⚓ ⚓
Facilities : ৬ ⊶ ♨ ⁿ 🗑 ⚓

GPS Longitude : 4.23865
Latitude : 44.55964

Some campsites benefit from proximity to a municipal leisure centre.

JOYEUSE

07260 – Michelin map **331** H7 – pop. 1 640 – alt. 180
▶ Paris 650 – Alès 54 – Mende 97 – Privas 55

⚠ La Nouzarède

✆ 0475399201. www.camping-nouzarede.fr

Address : north of the town along the rte du Stade, 150m from the Beaume – direct access)

Opening times : from beginning April to mid Sept.

2 ha (103 pitches) flat, grassy, stony

Tariff : 32.50€ ✚✚ ⚎ 🅔 (10A) – Extra per person 6.70€ – Reservation fee 14.50€

Rental rates : (from beginning April to mid Sept.) – 27 🏚 – 1 🏠 . Per night from 55 to 65€ – Per week from 280 to 860€ – Reservation fee 14.50€

Opposite a well-equipped horse and pony centre, good sanitary facilities.

Surroundings : ⌂ ♀♀
Leisure activities : ▼ ✕ ⚓ ⚓ ♨ ⚓
Facilities : ৬ ⊶ ⚿ ▥ ⚓ ⚓ ⁿ 🗑 ⚓
Nearby : ✂ ⚓ ⚓

GPS Longitude : 4.23526
Latitude : 44.48368

LAGORCE

07150 – Michelin map **331** I7 – pop. 700 – alt. 120
▶ Paris 648 – Aubenas 23 – Bourg-St-Andéol 34 – Privas 54

⚞ Les Castels Domaine de Sévenier (rental of chalets only)

Domaine de Sévenier

✆ 04 75 88 29 44. www.sevenier.net

Address : Sévenier district (1.6km south along the D 1, follow signs for Vallon-Pont-d'Arc)

Opening times : from mid March to mid Nov.

4 ha undulating

Rental rates : ⚒ (3 chalets) – 56 ⌂. Per night from 58 to 331€ – Per week from 350 to 2,030€ – Reservation fee 20€

An attractive chalet site, some equipped for very young children or large families, some on a hotel-style basis.

Surroundings : ⚲
Leisure activities : ▼ ✕ ⚓ ⚒ 丄
Facilities : ⚬ ⊪ ⊓ ⚐ ⚒

G P S Longitude : 4.41153
Latitude : 44.4338

LALLEY

38930 – Michelin map **333** H9 – pop. 205 – alt. 850
▶ Paris 626 – Grenoble 63 – La Mure 30 – Sisteron 80

⚞ Sites et Paysages Belle Roche

✆ 04 76 34 75 33. www.camping-belleroche.com – alt. 860

Address : chemin de Combe Morée (head south of the village following signs for Mens and take the road to the right)

2.4 ha (60 pitches) terrace, flat, grassy, stony

Rentals : 6 ⌂ – 1 cabin.

In a pleasant location opposite the village.

Surroundings : ⚲ ⩽ ⊡ ♀
Leisure activities : ▼ ✕ ⚓ ⚒ ⚒ multi-sports ground
Facilities : ⚒ ⚬ ⚐ launderette ⚒
Nearby : ✕

G P S Longitude : 5.67889
Latitude : 44.75472

LALOUVESC

07520 – Michelin map **331** J3 – pop. 496 – alt. 1 050
▶ Paris 553 – Annonay 24 – Lamastre 25 – Privas 80

⚠ Municipal le Pré du Moulin

✆ 04 75 67 84 86. www.lalouvesc.com

Address : chemin de l'Hermuzière (north of the village)

Opening times : from beginning May to end Sept.

2.5 ha (70 pitches) terraced, relatively flat, grassy

Tariff : (2015 price) 13.10€ ✯✯ ⚘ ▣ ⚡ (10A) – Extra per person 2.60€

Rental rates : (2015 price) (from mid May to end Sept.) – 5 ⌂ – 5 cabins in the trees. Per night from 40 to 50€ – Per week from 150 to 343€

⛽ Eurorelais sani-station 2€
Various rental options, some with rather old, simple facilities.

Surroundings : ⚲ ♀
Leisure activities : ⚓ ⚒ ✕
Facilities : ⚒ ⚬ ⚐ ⚐ ⚒

G P S Longitude : 4.53392
Latitude : 45.12388

LAMASTRE

07270 – Michelin map **331** J4 – pop. 2 501 – alt. 375
▶ Paris 577 – Privas 55 – Le Puy-en-Velay 72 – Valence 38

⚞ Le Retourtour

✆ 04 75 06 40 71. www.campingderetourtour.com

Address : 1 rue de Retourtour

Opening times : from beginning April to end Sept.

2.9 ha (130 pitches) flat and relatively flat, gravelled, grassy

Tariff : (2015 price) 23.96€ ✯✯ ⚘ ▣ ⚡ (13A) – Extra per person 4.98€ – Reservation fee 10€

Rental rates : (2015 price) (from beginning April to end Sept.) – 16 ⌂ – 3 canvas bungalows. Per night from 34 to 81€ – Per week from 238 to 595€ – Reservation fee 10€

Well-shaded pitches, near a small lake.

Surroundings : ⚲ ♀♀
Leisure activities : ▼ ✕ ⚓ ⚒ ⚒ ⚒
Facilities : ⚒ ⚬ ⚐ ⚐ ⚐ ⚒
Nearby : ⚊ (beach)

G P S Longitude : 4.56483
Latitude : 44.99164

Routes nationales are main roads and their identifying numbers begin with N or RN. Routes départementales are generally quieter roads and begin with D or DN.

LANSLEVILLARD

73480 – Michelin map **333** O6 – pop. 457 – alt. 1 500 – Winter sports : 1 400/2 800 m
▶ Paris 689 – Albertville 116 – Briançon 87 – Chambéry 129

⚠ Caravaneige de Val Cenis

✆ 04 79 05 90 52. www.camping-valcenis.com

Address : rue sous l'Eglise (southwestern exit, follow the signs for Lanslebourg; beside rapids)

Opening times : permanent

3 ha (100 pitches) flat, grassy, stony

Tariff : (2015 price) 15€ ✯✯ ⚘ ▣ ⚡ (10A) – Extra per person 7.10€ – Reservation fee 6€

⛽ Flot Bleu sani-station 4.15€
The site boasts excellent sanitary facilities.

Surroundings : ❄ ⩽ ♀
Leisure activities : ▼ ✕ ⚓ ⚒ ⚒
Facilities : ⚒ ⚬ ⚐ launderette ⚒
Nearby : ✕ ⚒

G P S Longitude : 6.90928
Latitude : 45.29057

LARNAS

07220 – Michelin map **331** J7 – pop. 97 – alt. 300
▶ Paris 631 – Aubenas 41 – Bourg-St-Andéol 12 – Montélimar 24

⚞ FranceLoc Le Domaine d'Imbours ⚌⚌

✆ 04 75 54 39 50. www.domaine-imbours.com

Address : 2.5km southwest along the D 262 – for caravans, from Bourg-St-Andéol, go via St-Remèze and Mas du Gras (D 4, D 362 and D 262)

Opening times : from beginning April to end Sept.

270 ha/10 for camping (694 pitches) relatively flat, flat, grassy, stony

Tariff : (2015 price) 36€ ✯✯ ⚘ ▣ ⚡ (6A) – Extra per person 7€ – Reservation fee 27€

Rental rates : (2015 price) (from beginning April to end Sept.) – 6 'gypsy' caravans – 412 🚐 – 64 🏠 – 96 🛏 – 32 tent lodges – 100 gîtes. Per night from 35 to 177€ – Per week from 140 to 2,072€ – Reservation fee 27€

Surroundings : 🌲 ♨
Leisure activities : 🍸 ✕ 🎦 📷 🏇 ⛷ 🚴 ✂ 🎯 🏊 🏓 multi-sports ground
Facilities : 🚿 ⚡ 🛒 🚮 ⚕ 🍴 🚰 🧺 🎣
Nearby : 🏇

GPS Longitude : 4.5764
Latitude : 44.4368

LATHUILE

74210 – Michelin map **328** K6 – pop. 960 – alt. 510
▶ Paris 554 – Albertville 30 – Annecy 18 – La Clusaz 38

⚞ L'Idéal

📞 04 50 44 32 97. www.campingideal.com

Address : 715 route de Chaparon (located 1.5km to the north)

Opening times : from mid April to mid Sept.

3.2 ha (300 pitches) gravelled

Tariff : (2015 price) 36€ ⚤ 🚗 ▣ ⚡ (10A) – Extra per person 8€ – Reservation fee 16€

Rental rates : (2015 price) (from mid April to mid Sept.) ♿ (1 mobile home) ✂ – 78 🚐 – 4 studios – 6 apartments. Per night from 90 to 150€ – Per week from 210 to 1,069€ – Reservation fee 16€

The site has plenty of space and a variety of rentals, beside an extensive water park.

Surroundings : 🌲 ♨
Leisure activities : 🍸 ✕ 🎦 jacuzzi 🏇 ✂ 🎯 🏊 (open air in season) 🏓 multi-sports ground
Facilities : 🚿 ⚡ 🍴 launderette 🎣

GPS Longitude : 6.20582
Latitude : 45.79537

⚞ Les Fontaines 👥

📞 04 50 44 31 22. www.campinglesfontaines.com

Address : 1295 route de Chaparon (situated 2km to the north at Chaparon)

Opening times : from mid May to mid Sept.

3 ha (170 pitches) terraced, sloping, flat, grassy

Tariff : (2015 price) 36.20€ ⚤ 🚗 ▣ ⚡ (6A) – Extra per person 8€ – Reservation fee 16€

Rental rates : (2015 price) (from mid April to mid Sept.) ✂ – 57 🚐 – 3 🏠 – 8 tipis. Per night from 105 to 431€ – Per week from 190 to 977€ – Reservation fee 16€

The site boasts some different and rather unusual rental accommodation.

Surroundings : 🌲 ♨
Leisure activities : 🍸 ✕ 🎦 📷 🏇 ⛷ 🏊 (open air in season) 🏓 multi-sports ground
Facilities : 🚿 ⚡ 🍴 launderette 🎣

GPS Longitude : 6.20444
Latitude : 45.80037

⚞ La Ravoire

📞 04 50 44 37 80. www.camping-la-ravoire.fr

Address : route de la Ravoire (2.5km to the north)

2 ha (124 pitches) flat, grassy

Rentals : 22 🚐 – 4 🏠.
Located in a pleasant, green setting near the lake.

Surroundings : 🌲 ♨
Leisure activities : 🍸 ✕ 🎦 🏇 🏊 🏓 multi-sports ground
Facilities : 🚿 ⚡ 🚮 🍴 launderette
Nearby : 🎣

⚞ Le Taillefer

📞 04 50 44 30 30. www.campingletaillefer.com

Address : 1530 route de Chaparon (situated 2km to the north, at Chaparon)

Opening times : from beginning May to end Sept.

1 ha (32 pitches) open site, terraced, sloping, flat, grassy

Tariff : 19€ ⚤ 🚗 ▣ ⚡ (6A) – Extra per person 6€

This grassy site has some shade and clean if somewhat old sanitary facilities.

Surroundings : 🌲 ♨
Leisure activities : 🍸 🎦 🏇 🚴
Facilities : 🚿 ⚡ 🍴 🖼

GPS Longitude : 6.20565
Latitude : 45.80231

LAURAC-EN-VIVARAIS

07110 – Michelin map **331** H6 – pop. 885 – alt. 182
▶ Paris 646 – Alès 60 – Mende 102 – Privas 50

⚞ Les Châtaigniers

📞 04 75 36 86 26. www.chataigniers-laurac.com

Address : at Prends-toi Garde (to the southeast of the town, recommended route via the D 104)

Opening times : from beginning April to end Sept.

1.2 ha (71 pitches) relatively flat, flat, grassy

Tariff : 21€ ⚤ 🚗 ▣ ⚡ (10A) – Extra per person 4€

Rental rates : (from beginning April to mid Sept.) ✂ – 14 🚐. Per night from 55 to 65€ – Per week from 240 to 670€

🚐 10 ▣ 21€

The upper part of the site has the most shade, the lower part has marked out pitches.

Surroundings : ♨
Leisure activities : 🎦 🏇 🏊
Facilities : 🚿 ⚡ 🍴 🖼

GPS Longitude : 4.29497
Latitude : 44.50429

LÉPIN-LE-LAC

73610 – Michelin map **333** H4 – pop. 407 – alt. 400
▶ Paris 555 – Belley 36 – Chambéry 24 – Les Échelles 17

⚞ Le Curtelet

📞 04 79 44 11 22. www.camping-le-curtelet.com

Address : Le Grand Pre (1.4km west of the village off the D921D)

Opening times : from mid May to mid Sept.

1.3 ha (91 pitches) relatively flat, flat, grassy

Tariff : 25.40€ ⚤ 🚗 ▣ ⚡ (10A) – Extra per person 5.60€ – Reservation fee 10€

Surroundings : 🌲 ♨ ⛰
Leisure activities : 🍸 🏇 (beach) 🎣
Facilities : 🚿 ⚡ (July–Sept.) 🚮 🍴 launderette
Nearby : ✂ 🎯

GPS Longitude : 5.77916
Latitude : 45.54002

LESCHERAINES

73340 – Michelin map **333** J3 – pop. 731 – alt. 649
▶ Paris 557 – Aix-les-Bains 26 – Annecy 26 – Chambéry 29

⚠ Municipal l'Île

🖉 0479638000. www.savoie-camping.com

Address : Les Îles du Chéran, at the leisure centre (2.5km southeast along the D 91, follow the signs for Annecy and take the turning to the right, 200m from the Chéran river)

Opening times : from end April to end Sept.

7.5 ha (215 pitches) open site, terraced, relatively flat, flat, grassy

Tariff : (2015 price) 19.50€ ✦✦ ⟷ 🔲 (10A) – Extra per person 4.60€ – Reservation fee 10€

Rental rates : (2015 price) (from end April to end Sept.) – 13 ⌂ – 5 ⌂ – 3 gîtes. Per night from 38 to 42€ – Per week from 264 to 610€

🖼 Eurorelais sani-station 1.50€

Situated beside a small lake and bordered by river and forest.

Surroundings : ⟨ < ⊙ ⚘	**G** Longitude : 6.11207
Leisure activities : 🛶	**P** Latitude : 45.70352
Facilities : ⚒ ⟷ ⟳ ☂ ⛺ ⛷ launderette	**S**
At the leisure/activities centre : ⛄ ✗ ⚓ 🚣 ⛷ ⛷ forest trail	

To make the best possible use of this guide, please read pages 2–15 carefully.

LUGRIN

74500 – Michelin map **328** N2 – pop. 2 260 – alt. 413
▶ Paris 584 – Annecy 91 – Évian-les-Bains 8 – St-Gingolph 12

⚠ Vieille Église

🖉 0450760195. www.campingvieilleeglise.fr

Address : 53 route des Préparraux (situated 2km west, at Vieille-Église)

Opening times : from beginning April to end Oct.

1.6 ha (97 pitches) terraced, relatively flat, flat, grassy

Tariff : (2015 price) 27.40€ ✦✦ ⟷ 🔲 (10A) – Extra per person 7.40€ – Reservation fee 7.40€

Rental rates : (2015 price) (from beginning April to end Oct.) ⚒ – 29 ⌂ – 1 studio – 1 apartment – 1 tent lodge. Per night from 50 to 110€ – Per week from 300 to 830€ – Reservation fee 5€

🖼 local sani-station 6€ – 🚽 16.90€

Some pitches have a view over Lac Léman.

Surroundings : < ⟨ ⊙ ⊙	**G** Longitude : 6.64655
Leisure activities : 🛶 ⚓ ⛷ ⛷	**P** Latitude : 46.40052
Facilities : ⚒ ⟷ ⟳ ⛺ launderette ⚓	**S**

LUS-LA-CROIX-HAUTE

26620 – Michelin map **332** H6 – pop. 507 – alt. 1 050
▶ Paris 638 – Alès 207 – Die 45 – Gap 49

⚠ Champ la Chèvre

🖉 0492585014. www.campingchamplachevre.com

Address : southeast of the village, on the D505, near swimming pool

Opening times : from mid April to end Sept.

3.6 ha (100 pitches) terraced, relatively flat, flat, grassy

Tariff : 29.10€ ✦✦ ⟷ 🔲 (6A) – Extra per person 7.50€ – Reservation fee 5€

Rental rates : (from beginning Feb. to end Oct.) – 6 ⌂ – 9 ⌂ – 6 canvas bungalows. Per night from 30 to 78€ – Per week from 185 to 740€ – Reservation fee 15€

🖼 local sani-station 3€ – 10 🔲 15€

Surroundings : ⟨ < ⊙	**G** Longitude : 5.70998
Leisure activities : 🛶 ⛷ (open air in season)	**P** Latitude : 44.6629
Facilities : ⚒ ⟷ ⟳ ⛺ ⛷ 🖼	**S**
Nearby : 🏇	

LES MARCHES

73800 – Michelin map **333** I5 – pop. 2 453 – alt. 328
▶ Paris 572 – Albertville 43 – Chambéry 12 – Grenoble 44

⚠ La Ferme du Lac

🖉 0479281348. www.campinglafermedulac.fr

Address : located 1km southwest along the N 90 (D1090), follow the signs for Pontcharra and take the D 12 to the right

Opening times : from mid April to mid Sept.

2.6 ha (100 pitches) flat, grassy

Tariff : ✦ 4.70€ ⟷ 🔲 5.60€ – (10A) 10€

Rental rates : (from mid April to mid Sept.) – 9 ⌂ – 1 ⌂. Per night from 55€ – Per week from 235 to 415€

🖼 local sani-station 4€ – 10 🔲 15€ – 🚽 11€

Choose the pitches furthest away from the road.

Surroundings : 🏕 ⊙ ⊙	**G** Longitude : 5.99327
Leisure activities : 🛶 ⚓ ⛷	**P** Latitude : 45.49595
Facilities : ⚒ ⟷ ⟳ ⛷ 🖼	**S**

MARS

07320 – Michelin map **331** H3 – pop. 279 – alt. 1 060
▶ Paris 579 – Annonay 49 – Le Puy-en-Velay 44 – Privas 71

⚠ La Prairie

🖉 0475302447. www.camping-laprairie.com

Address : at Laillier (to the northeast of the town along the D 15, follow the signs for St-Agrève and take road to the left)

Opening times : from mid May to mid Sept.

0.6 ha (30 pitches) flat, sandy, grassy

Tariff : (2015 price) ✦ 3.50€ ⟷ 1.60€ 🔲 4.70€ – (6A) 3.30€

Rental rates : (2015 price) (from mid May to mid Sept.) – 1 ⌂. Per week from 400 to 700€

🖼 local sani-station 4€

Well-kept pitches, positioned around the house.

Surroundings : ⟨ <	**G** Longitude : 4.32632
Leisure activities : ✗ ⚓ 🚴	**P** Latitude : 45.02393
Facilities : ⚒ ⟷ 🔲 ⛷ ⛷	**S**
Nearby : ⛳ 18 hole golf course	

MASSIGNIEU-DE-RIVES

01300 – Michelin map **328** H6 – pop. 591 – alt. 295
▶ Paris 516 – Aix-les-Bains 26 – Belley 10 – Morestel 37

⚠ VivaCamp le Lac du Lit du Roi

🖉 0479421203. www.camping-savoie.com

Address : at La Tuillère (2.5km north following signs for Belley and take road to the right)

Opening times : from end April to mid Sept.

4 ha (120 pitches) terraced, flat, grassy

Tariff : 28€ ✦✦ ⟷ 🔲 (6A) – Extra per person 7€ – Reservation fee 15€

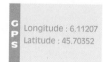

Rental rates : (from end April to mid Sept.) – 22 🚐 – 5 🏚 –
2 tipis – 3 canvas bungalows. Per night from 40 to 115€ – Per week
from 147 to 805€ – Reservation fee 25€

🚰 local sani-station

In a pleasant location beside a lake formed by the Rhône river.

Surroundings : 🦢 ≤ lake and hills 🔲 ♀ ⛰	**G** Longitude : 5.77001
Leisure activities : ⛾ ✗ 🛶 🚲 🐠 🏊 🎣 pedalos 🚤	**P** Latitude : 45.76861 **S**
Facilities : 🚿 ⛽ 🚽 💦 ⛳ 🔋	

MATAFELON-GRANGES

01580 – Michelin map **328** G3 – pop. 653 – alt. 453
▶ Paris 460 – Bourg-en-Bresse 37 – Lons-le-Saunier 56 – Mâcon 75

🏕 Les Gorges de l'Oignin

📞 0474768097. www.gorges-de-loignin.com

Address : rue du Lac (900m south of the village, neare the Oignin
river)

Opening times : from mid April to end Sept.

2.6 ha (128 pitches) terraced, flat, grassy, gravelled

Tariff : 25.80€ ⛾⛾ 🚗 📧 🔌 (10A) – Extra per person 7.10€ –
Reservation fee 16€

Rental rates : (from mid April to end Sept.) 🌊 – 2 🚐 – 10 🏚.
Per night from 110 to 126€ – Per week from 226 to 671€ –
Reservation fee 16€

Situated near a lake.

Surroundings : ≤	**G** Longitude : 5.55723
Leisure activities : ⛾ ✗ 🛶 🏊	**P**
Facilities : 🚿 ⛽ 🅲🏧 🚽 💦 ⛳ 🔋	**S** Latitude : 46.25534
Nearby : 🛶	

*The prices listed were supplied by the campsite owners
in 2015 (if prices were not available, those from the
previous year are given). The fees should be regarded
as basic charges and may fluctuate with inflation.*

LES MAZES

07150 – Michelin map **331** I7
▶ Paris 669 – Lyon 207 – Privas 58 – Nîmes 83

🏕 La Plage Fleurie ♨♂

📞 0475880115. www.laplagefleurie.com

Address : 3.5km west of the village (off the D579)

Opening times : from mid April to beginning Sept.

12 ha/6 for camping (300 pitches) terraced, flat and relatively flat,
grassy

Tariff : 51€ ⛾⛾ 🚗 📧 🔌 (10A) – Extra per person 8€ – Reservation
fee 20€

Rental rates : (from mid April to beginning Sept.) – 170 🚐 – 1
2 canvas bungalows. Per night from 45 to 235€ – Per week
from 315 to 1,645€ – Reservation fee 25€

🚰 Eurorelais sani-station

*Located beside the Ardèche river, with a sandy beach and an
area of grass and several luxurious mobile homes.*

Surroundings : 🦢 ≤ ♀♀	**G** Longitude : 4.3546
Leisure activities : ⛾ ✗ 🏠 ⛵ 🏃 🏄 🎿 🏊 🛶 (beach) ⛷ 🎣 paddling pool 🚤	**P** **S** Latitude : 44.40837
Facilities : 🚿 ⛽ 🚽 ⛳ 🔋 💦 🚿	

🏔 Beau Rivage

📞 0475880354. www.beaurivage-camping.com

Address : in the south of the village, off the D 579

Opening times : from beginning April to beginning Sept.

2 ha (100 pitches) terraced, flat, grassy

Tariff : (2015 price) 37€ ⛾⛾ 🚗 📧 🔌 (10A) – Extra per person 6.50€ –
Reservation fee 16€

Rental rates : (2015 price) (from beginning May to
beginning Sept.) 🌊 – 14 🚐. Per night from 70 to 90€ –
Per week from 299 to 835€ – Reservation fee 23€

*Located among the vineyards on the banks of the Ardèche
river, the perfect place for some peace and quiet.*

Surroundings : 🦢 🔲 ♀♀	**G** Longitude : 4.3649
Leisure activities : ✗ 🏠 🏃 🛶 🏊 🎣 🚤	**P**
Facilities : 🚿 ⛽ 🚽 ⛳ 🔋 🛒	**S** Latitude : 44.4103

🏔 Arc-en-Ciel ♨♂

📞 0475880465. www.arcenciel-camping.com

Address : in the west of the village, off the D 579

Opening times : from end April to mid Sept.

5 ha (218 pitches) flat and relatively flat, grassy, stony

Tariff : (2015 price) 39.50€ ⛾⛾ 🚗 📧 🔌 (6A) – Extra per person 7€ –
Reservation fee 20€

Rental rates : (2015 price) (from end April to mid Sept.) – 66 🚐 –
14 canvas bungalows – 10 tent lodges. Per night from 30 to 55€ –
Per week from 250 to 920€ – Reservation fee 20€

*Beside the Ardèche river with a sandy beach and grassy area.
A wide range of local rental options of differing standards of
comfort.*

Surroundings : 🦢 ♀♀	**G** Longitude : 4.3512
Leisure activities : ⛾ ✗ 🏠 🏃 🛶 🏊 ⛷ (beach) 🎣 🚤	**P** **S** Latitude : 44.41177
Facilities : 🚿 ⛽ 🚽 ⛳ 🔋 🛒 💦 🚿	

MÉAUDRE

38112 – Michelin map **333** G7 – pop. 1 321 – alt. 1 012 – Winter
sports : 1 000/1 600 m
▶ Paris 588 – Grenoble 38 – Pont-en-Royans 26 – Tullins 53

🏕 Les Buissonnets

📞 0476952104. www.camping-les-buissonnets.com – limited spaces
for one-night stay

Address : at Les Grangeons (500m northeast along the D 106 and
take turning to the right, 200m from the Méaudret river)

Opening times : from mid Dec. to end Oct.

2.8 ha (100 pitches) flat and relatively flat, grassy

Tariff : 20.30€ ⛾⛾ 🚗 📧 🔌 (10A) – Extra per person 5.50€

Rental rates : (from mid Dec. to end Oct.) 🅿 – 16 🚐. Per night
from 61 to 92€ – Per week from 304 to 610€

🚰 local sani-station 5€ – 20 📧 16.10€ – 🚐15€

Surroundings : ❄ 🦢 ≤ ♀	**G** Longitude : 5.53243
Leisure activities : 🏠 🏃	**P**
Facilities : 🚿 ⚡ 🍴 🚽 ⛳ 🔋	**S** Latitude : 45.12955
Nearby : 🎿 🏊	

⚠ Les Eymes

☎ 04 76 95 24 85. www.camping-les-eymes.com

Address : 3.8km north along the D 106c, follow the signs for Autrans and take turning to the left

Opening times : from beginning May to end Sept.

1.3 ha (40 pitches) relatively flat, terraced, grassy, wood, stony

Tariff : (2015 price) 23€ ✖✖ ⬛ 🅐 (10A) – Extra per person 7€ – Reservation fee 2€

Rental rates : permanent – 9 🚐 – 4 🏠. Per night from 53 to 106€ – Per week from 316 to 636€ – Reservation fee 10€

🚐 local sani-station 5€ – 4 ⬛ 19€

Surroundings : ⛵ ⬍	**G**	Longitude : 5.51574
Leisure activities : ✖ 🛝	**P**	Latitude : 45.14468
Facilities : ♿ 🚿 🆑 ⬛ 🚭 🍴 🔥 🛝 ⬛	**S**	

MEGÈVE

74120 – Michelin map **328** M5 – pop. 3 907 – alt. 1 113 – Winter sports : 1 113/2 350 m

▶ Paris 598 – Albertville 32 – Annecy 60 – Chamonix-Mont-Blanc 33

⚠ Bornand

☎ 04 50 93 00 86. www.camping-megeve.com – alt. 1 060

Address : 57 route du Grand Bois, Demi Quartier (3km northeast along the N 212, follow the signs for Sallanches and the Rte de la télécabine (cable car) to the right)

Opening times : from end June to end Aug.

1.5 ha (55 pitches) open site, terraced, sloping, flat, grassy

Tariff : (2015 price) ✖ 4.10€ ⬛ ⬛ 4.70€ – 🅐 (6A) 4.10€

Rental rates : (2015 price) permanent 🚿 – 4 🏠. Per week from 330 to 595€

🚐 local sani-station 2€

Wooden chalets very typical of the Savoyard style.

Surroundings : ⛵ ⬍ 🌳	**G**	Longitude : 6.64161
Leisure activities : 🏠	**P**	Latitude : 45.87909
Facilities : ♿ 🚿 🚭 🍴 launderette	**S**	

MENGLON

26410 – Michelin map **332** F6 – pop. 406 – alt. 550

▶ Paris 645 – Lyon 183 – Valence 80 – Grenoble 90

⚠⚠ Sites et Paysages L'Hirondelle 👥

☎ 04 75 21 82 08. www.campinghirondelle.com

Address : bois de Saint Ferréol (2.8km northwest along the D 214 and D 140, follow the signs for Die, near the D 539 – recommended route)

Opening times : from beginning April to end Sept.

7.5 ha (180 pitches) undulating, flat, grassy

Tariff : 41€ ✖✖ ⬛ 🅐 (6A) – Extra per person 11€ – Reservation fee 20€

Rental rates : (from beginning April to end Sept.) – 20 🚐 – 28 🏠 – 18 tent lodges. Per night from 44 to 186€ – Per week from 308 to 1,302€ – Reservation fee 20€

In a pleasant site and setting beside the Bez river.

Surroundings : ⛵ ⬍ 🌊	**G**	Longitude : 5.44746
Leisure activities : 🍴 ✖ 🏠 nighttime 🚴	**P**	Latitude : 44.68143
🛝 🛝 ⬛ (river)		
multi-sports ground		
Facilities : ♿ 🚿 🚭 🍴 launderette ⬛	**S**	

74290 – Michelin map **328** K5 – pop. 1 876 – alt. 482

▶ Paris 552 – Lyon 148 – Annecy 9 – Genève 51

⚠ Le Clos Don Jean

☎ 04 50 60 18 66. www.campingclosdonjean.com

Address : 435 route du Clos-Don-Jean

Opening times : from beginning June to end Aug.

1 ha (64 pitches) flat and relatively flat, grassy

Tariff : (2015 price) 21€ ✖✖ ⬛ 🅐 (6A) – Extra per person 4.70€

Rental rates : (2015 price) (from end May to mid Sept.) – 9 🚐. Per night from 60 to 80€ – Per week from 299 to 530€

The site has a view over the imposing Château de Menthon.

Surroundings : ⛵ ⬍ 🌳	**G**	Longitude : 6.19699
Leisure activities : 🏠	**P**	Latitude : 45.86298
Facilities : ♿ 🚿 🚭 🍴 ⬛	**S**	

We have selected the best campsites in France with our usual care, listing those with the best facilities in the most pleasant surroundings.

MEYRAS

07380 – Michelin map **331** H5 – pop. 842 – alt. 450

▶ Paris 609 – Aubenas 17 – Le Cheylard 54 – Langogne 49

⚠⚠⚠ Sites et Paysages Domaine de La Plage

☎ 04 75 36 40 59. www.lecampingdelaplage.com – limited spaces for one-night stay

Address : at Neyrac-les-Bains (3km southwest along the N 102, follow the signs for Le Puy-en-Velay)

Opening times : from end March to end Oct.

0.8 ha (45 pitches) terraced, stony, flat, grassy

Tariff : 40€ ✖✖ ⬛ 🅐 (10A) – Extra per person 8€

Rental rates : (from end March to end Oct.) – 25 🚐 – 12 🏠 – 3 apartments – 8 gîtes. Per night from 65 to 137€ – Per week from 250 to 960€

Below the road; choose those pitches beside the Ardèche river.

Surroundings : ⬍ 🏕 ♨	**G**	Longitude : 4.26067
Leisure activities : 🍴 ✖ 🏠 🛝 🚴 🛝 ⬛	**P**	Latitude : 44.67315
🚿 multi-sports ground, entertainment room		
Facilities : ♿ 🚿 ⬛ ⬛ 🚭 🍴 launderette ⬛	**S**	

⚠⚠ Le Ventadour

☎ 04 75 94 18 15. www.leventadour.com

Address : at the Pont de Rolandy (3.5km southeast, along the N 102, follow the signs for Aubenas; beside the Ardèche river)

Opening times : from mid April to beginning Oct.

3 ha (115 pitches) flat and relatively flat, grassy

Tariff : 26€ ✖✖ ⬛ 🅐 (10A) – Extra per person 6.50€ – Reservation fee 15€

Rental rates : (from mid April to beginning Oct.) – 19 🚐 – 1 🏠. Per night from 89 to 149€ – Per week from 199 to 790€ – Reservation fee 15€

🚐 12 ⬛ 17€ – 🔌 🅐 17€

Choose pitches beside the river, furthest away from the road.

Surroundings : 🏕 ♨	**G**	Longitude : 4.28291
Leisure activities : 🍴 ✖ 🛝 🚴 ⬛ (beach) 🚿	**P**	Latitude : 44.66757
Facilities : ♿ 🚿 ⬛ 🚭 🍴 launderette ⬛	**S**	

MEYRIEU-LES-ÉTANGS

38440 – Michelin map **333** E4 – pop. 839 – alt. 430

▶ Paris 515 – Beaurepaire 31 – Bourgoin-Jallieu 14 – Grenoble 78

⚠ Base de Loisirs du Moulin

✆ 0474593034. www.campingmeyrieu.com

Address : route de Saint-Anne (800m southeast along the D 56b, follow the signs for Châtonnoy and turn left towards Ste-Anne; near a small lake)

Opening times : from beginning April to end Sept.

1 ha (58 pitches) flat and relatively flat, terraced, grassy

Tariff : 21.30€ ♥♥ ⇔ 回 (10A) – Extra per person 5€

Rental rates : (from beginning April to end Sept.) ℗ – 3 ⌂ – 10 ⌂. Per night from 60 to 110€ – Per week from 252 to 735€ – Reservation fee 12€

⊡ local sani-station 10€

Pitches arranged on terraces looking out over the lake.

Surroundings : ⅏ ⌂ ♤♤	G	Longitude : 5.20175
Leisure activities : ⌂ ⚘ ⬡	P	Latitude : 45.5152
Facilities : ⚓ ⛏ ⌂ ⚐ ⚑ ▦	S	
Nearby : ♉ ✕ ⛵ ⚓ ⚓ ≋ pedalos		

MIRABEL-ET-BLACONS

26400 – Michelin map **332** D5 – pop. 904 – alt. 225

▶ Paris 595 – Crest 7 – Die 30 – Dieulefit 33

⚠ Gervanne

✆ 0475400020. www.gervanne-camping.com

Address : Bellevue district (situated where the Drôme and the Gervanne rivers meet, at Blacons)

Opening times : from beginning April to end Sept.

3.7 ha (150 pitches) flat and relatively flat, grassy

Tariff : 32.10€ ♥♥ ⇔ 回 (6A) – Extra per person 7.60€ – Reservation fee 15€

Rental rates : (from beginning April to end Sept.) ⚓ (1 chalet) ⬡ – 3 'gypsy' caravans – 3 ⌂ – 15 ⌂ – 1 cabin in the trees. Per night from 70 to 119€ – Per week from 315 to 885€ – Reservation fee 15€

⊡ local sani-station 4€

In a green setting beside the Gervanne and Drôme rivers.

Surroundings : ⅏ ♤♤ ⛰	G	Longitude : 5.08917
Leisure activities : ♉ ✕ ⌂ ⚓ ⚲ ⬡	P	Latitude : 44.71083
Facilities : ⚓ ⛏ ⌂ ⚐ ⚑ launderette ⚓ ⛵	S	
Nearby : fitness trail		

MONTCHAVIN

73210 – Michelin map **333** N4 – alt. 1 206

▶ Paris 672 – Lyon 206 – Chambéry 106 – Albertville 57

⚠ Caravaneige de Montchavin

✆ 0479078323. www.campingmontchavin.com – alt. 1.250

Address : at Montchavin

Opening times : permanent

1.33 ha (90 pitches) terraced, flat, grassy

Tariff : ♥ 8.30€ ⇔ 3.20€ 回 16.50€ – (10A) 10€

Rental rates : permanent ⬡ – 2 ⌂. Per night from 99 – Per week from 297 to 693€

⊡ local sani-station 10€

A superb location and view.

Surroundings : ❄ ⅏ ⥐ Tarentaise valley, Bourg-St-Maurice and Mont Blanc ♤♤	G	Longitude : 6.73933
Leisure activities : ⌂	P	Latitude : 45.56058
Facilities : ⚓ ▦ ⚑ launderette	S	
Nearby : ⚓ ♉ ✕ ⬡ ⌂ ⚓		

MONTREVEL-EN-BRESSE

01340 – Michelin map **328** D2 – pop. 2 363 – alt. 215

▶ Paris 395 – Bourg-en-Bresse 18 – Mâcon 25 – Pont-de-Vaux 22

⚠ La Plaine Tonique ♠♣

✆ 0474308052. www.laplainetonique.com

Address : 599 route d'Etrez, at the leisure center (500m east along the D 28)

Opening times : from mid April to beginning Sept.

27 ha/15 for camping (548 pitches)

Tariff : ♥ 7.30€ ⇔ 回 16.10€ (10A) – Reservation fee 10€

Rental rates : (from mid April to beginning Sept.) ⬡ – 21 ⌂ – 57 ⌂ – 54 ▭ – 8 tipis – 10 tent lodges – 1 gîte. Per night from 81 to 92€ – Per week from 458 to 861€ – Reservation fee 10€

⊡ Eurorelais sani-station 2€ – 10 回 13€

Beside a lake and an attractive swimming area.

Surroundings : ⌂ ♤ ♤♤	G	Longitude : 5.136
Leisure activities : ♉ ✕ ⌂ ⚗ ⚘ ⚓ ⥐	P	Latitude : 46.33902
⬡ ⚓ ⌂ ⚓ ⬡ ♫ sports trail	S	
Facilities : ⚓ ⛏ ⌂ ⚐ ⚑ ▦ ⚓ ⚓		

Michelin classification:

⚠⚠⚠⚠ *Extremely comfortable, equipped to a very high standard*

⚠⚠⚠ *Very comfortable, equipped to a high standard*

⚠⚠ *Comfortable and well equipped*

⚠ *Reasonably comfortable*

△ *Satisfactory*

MONTRIGAUD

26350 – Michelin map **332** D2 – pop. 496 – alt. 462

▶ Paris 560 – Lyon 97 – Valence 51 – Grenoble 75

⚠ La Grivelière

✆ 0475717071. www.lagriveliere.com

Address : route de Roybon

Opening times : from beginning April to end Sept.

2.6 ha (59 pitches) flat, grassy

Tariff : (2015 price) 25.50€ ♥♥ ⇔ 回 (6A) – Extra per person 5€ – Reservation fee 10€

Rental rates : (2015 price) (from beginning April to end Sept.) ⬡ – 4 ⌂ –1 ⌂ – 2 canvas bungalows. Per night from 43 to 107€ – Per week from 299 to 749€ – Reservation fee 10€

Surroundings : ⅏ ⌂ ♤	G	Longitude : 5.16711
Leisure activities : ♉ ✕ ⌂ ⚓	P	Latitude : 45.22176
Facilities : ⛏ ⚑ launderette ⚓	S	

MORNANT

69440 – Michelin map **327** H6 – pop. 5 438 – alt. 380
▶ Paris 478 – Givors 12 – Lyon 26 – Rive-de-Gier 13

⚘ Municipal de la Trillonière

☎ 04 78 44 16 47. www.ville-mornant.fr

Address : boulevard Général de Gaulle (southern exit, junction of D 30 and D 34, near a stream)

Opening times : from beginning May to end Sept.

1.5 ha (60 pitches) relatively flat, flat, grassy

Tariff : (2015 price) 16.80€ ★ ★ ⇔ 🔲 🔌 (10A) –
Extra per person 4.20€

🚐 Flot Bleu sani-station 3€ – 30 🔲 16.80€ – 🔋 🔌15.98€
At the foot of the medieval old town; bus stop for Lyon.

Facilities : ᵴ ⊶ 🏕 🍴 🔲
Nearby : ✂ 🎿
Longitude : 4.67073
Latitude : 45.61532

MORZINE

74110 – Michelin map **328** N3 – pop. 2 930 – alt. 960 – Winter sports : 1 000/2 100 m
▶ Paris 586 – Annecy 84 – Chamonix-Mont-Blanc 67 – Cluses 26

⚘ Les Marmottes

☎ 04 50 75 74 44. www.campinglesmarmottes.com – alt. 938

Address : at Essert-Romand (3.7km northwest along the D 902, follow the signs for Thonon-les-Bains and take D 329 to the left)

Opening times : from mid June to beginning Sept.

0.5 ha (26 pitches) flat, grassy, gravel

Tariff : 27.50€ ★ ★ ⇔ 🔲 🔌 (6A) – Extra per person 8€
Rental rates : (from mid June to beginning Sept.) 🚫 –
2 🛏 – 1 🛏 – 1 studio. Per week from 432 to 607€ – Reservation fee 15€

Choose the pitches furthest from the road, which is very busy during the day. There's a bus into Morzine.

Surroundings : ❄ ⋖ 🎋
Leisure activities : 🏛
Facilities : ᵴ ⊶ 🏕 🍴 launderette
Longitude : 6.67725
Latitude : 46.19487

MURS-ET-GELIGNIEUX

01300 – Michelin map **328** G7 – pop. 236 – alt. 232
▶ Paris 509 – Aix-les-Bains 37 – Belley 17 – Chambéry 42

⚘ Île de la Comtesse

☎ 04 79 87 23 33. www.ile-de-la-comtesse.com

Address : located 1km southwest on the D 992

Opening times : permanent

3 ha (100 pitches) stony, flat, grassy

Tariff : 25.80€ ★ ★ ⇔ 🔲 🔌 (6A) – Extra per person 7.50€ –
Reservation fee 14€
Rental rates : permanent – 20 🛏 – 12 🏡 – 6 canvas bungalows.
Per night from 70 to 120€ – Per week from 392 to 875€ –
Reservation fee 28€

🚐 Eurorelais sani-station 6€
Situated near the Rhône river (small lake).

Surroundings : ⋖
Leisure activities : ☕ ✗ 🏛 🎣 🚴 🎿
Facilities : ᵴ ⊶ 🍴 launderette 🔲 🌿
Nearby : 🚣
Longitude : 5.64876
Latitude : 45.63993

NEYDENS

74160 – Michelin map **328** J4 – pop. 1 486 – alt. 560
▶ Paris 525 – Annecy 36 – Bellegarde-sur-Valserine 33 – Bonneville 34

⚘⚘ Sites et Paysages La Colombière

☎ 04 50 35 13 14. www.camping-la-colombiere.com

Address : 166 chemin Neuf (east of the town)

2.5 ha (156 pitches) relatively flat, flat, grassy, gravelled
Rentals : 31 🛏 – 8 🏡.
🚐 local sani-station – 3 🔲
The pitches are well marked out; real wooden chalets to rent.

Surroundings : 🌳 ⋖ 🎋 🎋
Leisure activities : ☕ ✗ 🏛 ☀daytime 🎯
hammam 🎣 🚴 🎿 🌿 launderette
Facilities : ᵴ ⊶ 🏛 🍴
Longitude : 6.10578
Latitude : 46.11997

NOVALAISE-LAC

73470 – Michelin map **328** H4 – pop. 1 712 – alt. 427
▶ Paris 524 – Belley 24 – Chambéry 21 – Les Échelles 24

⚘ Le Grand Verney

☎ 04 79 36 02 54. www.camping-legrandverney.info – limited spaces for one-night stay

Address : Le Neyret (1.2km southwest along the C 6)

Opening times : from beginning April to mid Oct.

2.5 ha (116 pitches) terraced, relatively flat, flat, grassy

Tariff : (2015 price) 19.30€ ★ ★ ⇔ 🔲 🔌 (10A) –
Extra per person 4.70€
Rental rates : (2015 price) (from end March to end Oct.) ᵴ
(2 mobile homes) – 22 🛏. Per night from 65 to 85€ – Per week from 320 to 635€

A great deal of owner-occupier accommodation, but also some pitches for tents and caravans.

Surroundings : 🌳 ⋖ 🎋 🎋 🎋
Leisure activities : 🎿
Facilities : ᵴ ⊶ 🍴 🔲
Longitude : 5.78371
Latitude : 45.5683

This guide is not intended as a list of all the camping sites in France; its aim is to provide a selection of the best sites in each category.

NYONS

26110 – Michelin map **332** D7 – pop. 7 104 – alt. 271
▶ Paris 653 – Alès 109 – Gap 106 – Orange 43

⚘ L'Or Vert

☎ 04 75 26 24 85. www.camping-or-vert.com ᵴ

Address : at Aubres, quai de la Charité (3km northeast along the D 94, follow the signs for Serres; beside the Eygues)

Opening times : from beginning April to end Sept.

1 ha (79 pitches) small orchard

Tariff : (2015 price) 25.90€ ★ ★ ⇔ 🔲 🔌 (6A) – Extra per person 6.50€
Rental rates : (2015 price) (from beginning April to end Sept.) ᵴ –
7 🏡. Per night from 45 to 116€ – Per week from 260 to 810€ –
Reservation fee 10€

Surroundings : ⋖ 🎋 🎋 🎋
Leisure activities : ✗ 🏛 🎣 🎿 🎣
Facilities : ⊶ 🍴 🔲 refrigerators
Longitude : 5.16272
Latitude : 44.37273

⚏ Les Terrasses Provençales

☏ 04 75 27 92 36. www.lesterrassesprovencales.com

Address : Les Barroux – Novezan (7km northwest along the D 538, then take the D 232 to the right.)

Opening times : from beginning April to end Sept.

2.5 ha (70 pitches)

Tariff : (2015 price) 25.50€ ✶✶ ⇔ ▣ ⚡ (10A) – Extra per person 5.60€ – Reservation fee 8€

Rental rates : (2015 price) (from beginning Sept. to end Sept.) – 10 🚐 – 4 tent lodges. Per night from 40 to 65€ – Per week from 230 to 695€ – Reservation fee 12€

⚏ AireService sani-station 4€ – 6 ▣ 7€ – ⚓7€

Surroundings : ⚏ ≤ ♀
Leisure activities : ♟ ✗ ⛵ ♻ ⚓
Facilities : ♿ ⚏ ⚏ ⚏ launderette

Longitude : 5.08047
Latitude : 44.40949

LES OLLIÈRES-SUR-EYRIEUX

07360 – Michelin map **331** J5 – pop. 927 – alt. 200
▶ Paris 593 – Le Cheylard 28 – Lamastre 33 – Montélimar 53

⚏ FranceLoc Domaine des Plantas ♟♟

☏ 04 75 66 21 53. http://campingplantas.franceloc.fr/fr/accueil.htm

Address : 3km east of the town via narrow road, access near the bridge; beside the Eyrieux river

Opening times : from end April to mid Sept.

27 ha/7 for camping (172 pitches) terraced, stony, flat, grassy

Tariff : (2015 price) 36€ ✶✶ ⇔ ▣ ⚡ (10A) – Extra per person 7€ – Reservation fee 27€

Rental rates : (2015 price) (from end April to mid Sept.) – 2 'gypsy' caravans – 92 🚐 – 21 🏠 – 4 tent lodges. Per night from 40 to 117€ – Per week from 161 to 1,260€ – Reservation fee 27€

⚏ AireService sani-station

Various hostel-style rental options and facilities.

Surroundings : ⚏ ≤ ⚏ ♀♀
Leisure activities : ♟ ✗ ⛵ ♻ ⚓ ⚓ ⚏ ⚏
⚏ ♻
Facilities : ♿ ⚏ ⚏ ⚏ launderette ⚏ ⚏
Nearby : ⚏

Longitude : 4.63565
Latitude : 44.8087

⚏ VivaCamp le Mas de Champel ♟♟

☏ 04 75 66 23 23. www.masdechampel.com

Address : at the Domaine de Champel (north of the town along the D 120, follow the signs for la Voulte-sur-Rhône and take the road to the left, near L'Eyrieux)

Opening times : from beginning May to mid Sept.

4 ha (95 pitches) terraced, flat, grassy

Tariff : 29.80€ ✶✶ ⇔ ▣ ⚡ (6A) – Extra per person 7€ – Reservation fee 15€

Rental rates : (from beginning May to mid Sept.) – 35 🚐 – 1 tipi – 9 canvas bungalows. Per night from 50 to 140€ – Per week from 171 to 980€ – Reservation fee 25€

Various rental options of varying standards; a pleasant small beach beside the Eyrieux river.

Surroundings : ⚏ ≤ ♀♀
Leisure activities : ♟ ✗ ⚏ ⚏ nighttime ⚏
⚏ jacuzzi ⚏ ♻ ✗ ⚏ ⚏
Facilities : ♿ ⚏ ⚏ ⚏ launderette ⚏

Longitude : 4.6146
Latitude : 44.80603

⚏ Eyrieux-Camping ♟♟

☏ 04 75 66 30 08. www.eyrieuxcamping.com

Address : at La Feyrère (take the eastern exit along the D 120, follow the signs for La Voulte-sur-Rhône and take the road to the right; 100m from the Eyrieux river (direct access)

Opening times : from beginning April to mid Nov.

3 ha (94 pitches)

Tariff : 20€ ✶✶ ⇔ ▣ ⚡ (10A) – Extra per person 3.70€

Rental rates : (from beginning April to mid Nov.) ♿ (1 mobile home) – 25 🚐 – 29 🏠. Per night from 55 to 80€ – Per week from 200 to 300€

Various rental options, ranging from basic to more luxurious.

Surroundings : ⚏ ≤ ⚏ ♀♀
Leisure activities : ♟ ✗ ⚏ ♻ ⚓ ♻ ⚏ ⚓
♻ multi-sports ground
Facilities : ♿ ⚏ ⚏ ⚏ launderette ⚏
refrigerators

Longitude : 4.63072
Latitude : 44.80764

LA PACAUDIÈRE

42310 – Michelin map **327** C2 – pop. 1 078 – alt. 363
▶ Paris 370 – Lapalisse 24 – Marcigny 21 – Roanne 25

⚏ Municipal Beausoleil

☏ 04 77 64 11 50. lapacaudiere@wanadoo.fr

Address : at Beausoleil (700m east along the D 35, follow the signs for Vivans and take a right turn, near the sports field and the college)

Opening times : from beginning May to end Sept.

1 ha (35 pitches) relatively flat, grassy

Tariff : ✶ 3.80€ ⇔ 1.75€ ▣ 2€ – ⚡ (6A) 3.10€

Rental rates : (from beginning May to end Sept.) – 6 🏠 – 1 apartment. Per night from 56 to 73€ – Per week from 260 to 352€

⚏ local sani-station 12.75€ – 30 ▣ 12.75€

On the outskirts of the village, with a beautiful swimming pool and a pretty chalet village.

Surroundings : ⚏
Leisure activities : ⚏ ⚏ ✗ ⚏ ⚏
Facilities : ♿ ⚏ ⚏ ⚏ ⚏ ⚏ ⚏

Longitude : 3.87236
Latitude : 46.17562

A chambre d'hôte is a guesthouse or B & B-style accommodation.

PALADRU

38850 – Michelin map **333** G5 – pop. 1 044 – alt. 503
▶ Paris 523 – Annecy 84 – Chambéry 47 – Grenoble 43

⚏ Le Calatrin

☏ 04 76 32 37 48. www.camping-paladru.fr

Address : 799 rue de la Morgerie (near the exit from the village, towards Charavines)

2 ha (60 pitches) terraced, flat, grassy
Rentals : 2 canvas bungalows.

Surroundings : ⚏ ≤
Leisure activities : ⚏ ⚏
Facilities : ♿ ⚏ ⚏ ▣
Nearby : ♟ ✗ ⚏ (beach)

Longitude : 5.54673
Latitude : 45.47077

PETICHET

38119 – Michelin map **333** H7
▶ Paris 592 – Le Bourg-d'Oisans 41 – Grenoble 30 – La Mure 11

⚲ Ser-Sirant

✆ 04 76 83 91 97. www.campingsersirant.fr

Address : at Laffrey Petichet lake (take the eastern exit and take road to the left)

Opening times : from beginning May to end Sept.

2 ha (100 pitches) terraced, flat, grassy, stony, wood

Tariff : 26.90€ ✶✶ 🚗 🗐 🔌 (10A) – Extra per person 6€ – Reservation fee 10€

Rental rates : (from beginning May to end Sept.) – 7 🚐 – 6 🏠. Per night from 90 to 105€ – Per week from 280 to 715€ – Reservation fee 17€

🚐 local sani-station 5€ – 5 🗐 15€ – 🔋 12€

Surroundings : 🌄 ♨🗻 Leisure activities : 🍴 🏠 🛶 🎣 boats for hire Facilities : 🔦 ⛺ 🍴 launderette Nearby : 🎣	**GPS** Longitude : 5.77759 Latitude : 45.00038

LE POËT-CÉLARD

26460 – Michelin map **332** D6 – pop. 133 – alt. 590
▶ Paris 618 – Lyon 156 – Valence 53 – Avignon 114

⚲ Club Airotel Le Couspeau

✆ 04 75 53 30 14. www.couspeau.com – alt. 600

Address : Bellevue district (1.3km southeast along the D 328A)

Opening times : from mid April to mid Sept.

6 ha (133 pitches) terraced, relatively flat, flat, grassy

Tariff : (2015 price) 40€ ✶✶ 🚗 🗐 🔌 (6A) – Extra per person 8€ – Reservation fee 20€

Rental rates : (2015 price) (from mid April to mid Sept.) – 10 🚐 – 20 🏠. Per night from 60 to 180€ – Reservation fee 20€

🚐 local sani-station

In an elevated location with panoramic views.

Surroundings : 🌄 ← 🗕 ♨ Leisure activities : 🍴 🍽 🛶 🚲 🎯 🖼 (small swimming pool) 🏊 ⛷ multi-sports ground water park Facilities : ♿ 🔦 🏧 ⛺ 🍴 launderette 🌊 🔥	**GPS** Longitude : 5.11152 Latitude : 44.59641

LE POËT-LAVAL

26160 – Michelin map **332** D6 – pop. 922 – alt. 311
▶ Paris 619 – Crest 35 – Montélimar 25 – Nyons 35

⚲ Municipal Lorette

✆ 04 75 91 00 62. www.campinglorette.fr

Address : Lorette district (located 1km east along the D 540, follow the signs for Dieulefit)

Opening times : from beginning May to end Sept.

2 ha (60 pitches)

Tariff : 15.50€ ✶✶ 🚗 🗐 🔌 (6A) – Extra per person 3.50€

🚐 local sani-station

Situated beside the Jabron river.

Surroundings : ← ♨ Leisure activities : 🛶 🏊 🎣 Facilities : ♿ 🔥 🍴 🖼 Nearby : 🍽	**GPS** Longitude : 5.02277 Latitude : 44.52922

PONCIN

01450 – Michelin map **328** F4 – pop. 1 618 – alt. 255
▶ Paris 456 – Ambérieu-en-Bugey 20 – Bourg-en-Bresse 28 – Nantua 25

⚲ Vallée de l'Ain

✆ 04 74 35 72 11. www.campingvalleedelain.com – limited spaces for one-night stay

Address : route d'Allement (500m northwest along the D 91 and D 81, follow the signs for Meyriat, near the Ain river)

1.5 ha (89 pitches) flat, grassy
Rentals : 4 🚐 – 3 🏠.
🚐 local sani-station – 10 🗐

Surroundings : ♨ Leisure activities : 🍴 🍽 🏊 🚤 Facilities : 🔦 🍴 Nearby : 🍽 🚤 🎣	**GPS** Longitude : 5.40407 Latitude : 46.08996

There are several different types of sani-station ('borne' in French) – sanitation points providing fresh water and disposal points for grey water. See page 12 for further details.

PONCINS

42110 – Michelin map **327** D5 – pop. 869 – alt. 339
▶ Paris 446 – Lyon 77 – St-Étienne 50 – Clermont-Ferrand 109

⚲ Village Vacances Le Nid Douillet – (rental of chalets only)

✆ 04 77 27 80 36. www.le-nid-douillet.com

Address : at Les-Baraques-des-Rotis, route de Montbrison-es-Baraques-des-Rotis

2 ha flat, grassy
Rentals : 6 🏠.

Chalets set in a lush green landscape.

Surroundings : 🌄 Leisure activities : 🍽 🏠 🎣 Facilities : 🔦 🍴 Nearby : 🐎	**GPS** Longitude : 4.1615 Latitude : 45.7123

PONT-DE-VAUX

01190 – Michelin map **328** C2 – pop. 2 187 – alt. 177
▶ Paris 380 – Bourg-en-Bresse 40 – Lons-le-Saunier 69 – Mâcon 24

⚲ Champ d'Été

✆ 03 85 23 96 10. www.camping-champ-dete.com

Address : at Champ D'Eté (800m northwest along the D 933, towards Mâcon and take the road to the right, near a small lake)

Opening times : from mid March to mid Oct.

3.5 ha (150 pitches) flat, grassy

Tariff : ✶ 6€ 🚗 🗐 9€ – 🔌 (10A) 4€

Rental rates : (from mid March to beginning Nov.) – 2 🚐 – 30 🏠 – 2 tent lodges – 1 gîte. Per night from 60 to 75€ – Per week from 245 to 795€

🚐 Eurorelais sani-station 2€ – 5 🗐 13€

Leisure activities : 🏠 🛶 🖼 🏊 ⛷ Facilities : ♿ 🔦 🔥 🍴 🖼 Nearby : 🎣	**GPS** Longitude : 4.93301 Latitude : 46.42966

🏔 Aux Rives du Soleil ♣♣

📞 03 85 30 33 65. www.rivesdusoleil.com

Address : at the Port de Fleurville on the Saône-et-Loire ain (river)

Opening times : from mid April to mid Oct.

8 ha (160 pitches) flat, grassy

Tariff : 28 € ♣♣ ⬛ 🔲 🔋 (6A) – Extra per person 6.50 € – Reservation fee 15 €

Rental rates : (from end April to end Sept.) – 1 'gypsy' caravan – 11  – 8 canvas bungalows. Per night from 26 to 94 € – Per week from 182 to 658 € – Reservation fee 15 €

On a peninsula at the confluence of the Saône and Reyssouze rivers.

Surroundings : ♀ ⛺
Leisure activities : 🍴 ✕ 🎦 🎣 🤸 🏃 🚴
🏊 🛶 ⛷
Facilities : ᵫ ⚆⚊ ☂ 🚻 launderette 🧺

GPS Longitude : 4.89892
Latitude : 46.44701

🏔 Les Ripettes

📞 03 85 30 66 58. www.camping-les-ripettes.com

Address : at Les Tourtes (northeast of the town, off the D 2, D 58)

Opening times : from beginning April to end Sept.

2.5 ha (54 pitches) flat, grassy

Tariff : 22 € ♣♣ ⬛ 🔲 🔋 (10A) – Extra per person 4.50 €

Rental rates : (from mid April to end Sept.) 🦋 – 1 tent lodge. Per night from 40 to 60 €

🚐 3 🔲 22 €

A very well-kept camping area with lots of green space.

Surroundings : 🌳 ♀
Leisure activities : 🏊
Facilities : ᵫ ⚆⚊ ☒ ☂ 🚻 launderette

GPS Longitude : 4.98073
Latitude : 46.44449

For more information on visiting particular towns or regions, consult the relevant regional MICHELIN Green Guide. We also recommend you use the appropriate Michelin regional map to locate your selected campsite, to calculate distances and to work out the best route.

POUILLY-SOUS-CHARLIEU

42720 – Michelin map **327** D3 – pop. 2 582 – alt. 264
▶ Paris 393 – Charlieu 5 – Digoin 43 – Roanne 15

🏔 Municipal les Ilots

📞 04 77 60 80 67. www.pouillysouscharlieu.fr

Address : route de Marcigny (take the northern exit along the D 482, follow the signs for Digoin and take right turn; beside the Sornin river)

Opening times : from mid May to mid Sept.

1 ha (50 pitches) flat, grassy

Tariff : (2015 price) ♣ 3 € ⬛ 🔲 2.60 €

The site is on the edge of town and has a family atmosphere.

Surroundings : 🌳 ♀
Leisure activities : 🎦 🚴
Facilities : ᵫ 🚿 🚻 🚽
Nearby : 🍴 🎣

GPS Longitude : 4.11135
Latitude : 46.15101

POULE-LES-ÉCHARMEAUX

69870 – Michelin map **327** F3 – pop. 1 045 – alt. 570
▶ Paris 446 – Chauffailles 17 – La Clayette 25 – Roanne 47

🏔 Municipal les Écharmeaux

📞 06 79 30 46 62. www.pouleslesecharmeaux.eu

Address : to the west of the village

0.5 ha (24 pitches) terraced, flat, grassy

The pitches are arranged on individual terraces overlooking a lake.

Surroundings : 🏊 ← ⛺
Leisure activities : ✂
Facilities : ⚆⚊ 🔲
Nearby : 🎣

GPS Longitude : 4.4598
Latitude : 46.14871

In order for the guide to remain wholly objective, the selection of campsites is made on an entirely independent basis.

PRADONS

07120 – Michelin map **331** I7 – pop. 421 – alt. 124
▶ Paris 647 – Aubenas 20 – Largentière 16 – Privas 52

🏔 Les Coudoulets ♣♣

📞 04 75 93 94 95. www.coudoulets.com

Address : chemin de l'Ardèche (to the northwest of the village)

Opening times : from mid April to mid Sept.

3.5 ha/2.5 for camping (123 pitches)

Tariff : 37.10 € ♣♣ ⬛ 🔲 🔋 (16A) – Extra per person 7.50 € – Reservation fee 12 €

Rental rates : (from mid April to mid Sept.) – 35 – 4 gîtes. Per week from 300 to 890 € – Reservation fee 12 €

🚐 AireService sani-station

Well shaded near the river, with good sanitary facilities; entertainment for the family.

Surroundings : 🏊 ⛺ ♀♀
Leisure activities : 🍴 ✕ 🎦 daytime 🏃 jacuzzi
🚣 🛶 🏊 ⛷
Facilities : ᵫ ⚆⚊ – 4 private sanitary facilities (🚿 🛁 🚽 wc) 🚻 launderette

GPS Longitude : 4.3572
Latitude : 44.47729

🏔 Le Pont

📞 04 75 93 93 98. www.campingdupontardeche.com

Address : chemin du Cirque de Gens (300m west along the D 308, follow the signs for Chauzon)

Opening times : from mid March to mid Sept.

2 ha (80 pitches)

Tariff : 35.20 € ♣♣ ⬛ 🔲 🔋 (10A) – Extra per person 5.70 € – Reservation fee 11 €

Rental rates : (2015 price) (from mid March to mid Sept.) – 16  – 3 🏠 – 2 tent lodges. Per night from 45 to 65 € – Per week from 252 to 903 € – Reservation fee 11 €

🚐 Eurorelais sani-station

Choose the pitches near the steps down to the Ardèche river, further from the road.

Surroundings : ⛺ ♀♀
Leisure activities : 🍴 ✕ 🎦 🚣 🏊 ⛷
Facilities : ᵫ ⚆⚊ 🚻 🔲

GPS Longitude : 4.35337
Latitude : 44.47392

⚠ Laborie ♣♨

📞 06.43.24.90.76. www.campingdelaborie.com

Address : route de Ruoms (1.8km northeast along the D579, follow the signs for Aubenas)

Opening times : from beginning April to end Sept.

3 ha (100 pitches) flat, grassy

Tariff : 32€ ♣♣ ⬛ 📷 (10A) – Extra per person 6.50€ – Reservation fee 10€

Rental rates : (from beginning April to end Sept.) – 13 🚐. Per night from 45€ – Per week from 210 to 725€

Choose the pitches near the river, furthest away from the road.

Surroundings : 〰
Leisure activities : ♟ 🎣 ⛷ ♣ 🏊 🚣 ⛵
Facilities : ♿ ⚡ 🚿 🍴 📷

GPS	Longitude : 4.3783
	Latitude : 44.48161

PRALOGNAN-LA-VANOISE

73710 – Michelin map **333** N5 – pop. 754 – alt. 1 425 – Winter sports : 1 410/2 360 m
▶ Paris 634 – Albertville 53 – Chambéry 103 – Moûtiers 28

⚠ Alpes Lodges - Le Parc Isertan

📞 0479087524. www.alpes-lodges.com

Address : Isertan district (south of the village)

Opening times : from beginning Jan. to end Sept.

4.5 ha (152 pitches) open site, terraced, flat, grassy, stony

Tariff : 35€ ♣♣ ⬛ 📷 (10A) – Extra per person 7€ – Reservation fee 5€

Rental rates : (from beginning Jan. to end Oct.) – 2 'gypsy' caravans – 3 🚐 – 3 🏠 – 15 🛏 – 6 studios – 8 apartments – 9 tent lodges. Per night from 30 to 100€ – Per week from 190 to 1,150€ – Reservation fee 15€

🚰 local sani-station 4€ – 6 📷 15€ – 🚐 📷20€

In a pleasant location beside a mountain stream.

Surroundings : ❄ 🐾 ≼
Leisure activities : ♟ ✕ 🎣 📷
Facilities : ♿ ⚡ ▦ 🚿 🍴 🚸
Nearby : ♣ 🎿 🐎 🏊 ⛏climbing, skating rink

GPS	Longitude : 6.72883
	Latitude : 45.37189

---

*For more information on visiting particular towns or regions, consult the relevant regional **MICHELIN Green Guide**. We also recommend you use the appropriate Michelin regional map to locate your selected campsite, to calculate distances and to work out the best route.*

PRIVAS

07000 – Michelin map **331** J5 – pop. 8 461 – alt. 300
▶ Paris 596 – Alès 107 – Mende 140 – Montélimar 34

⚠ Ardèche Camping ♣♨

📞 0475640580. www.ardechecamping.fr

Address : boulevard de Paste (located 1.5km south along the D 2, follow the signs for Montélimar ; beside the Ouvèze river)

Opening times : from mid April to end Sept.

5 ha (170 pitches) terraced, relatively flat, flat, grassy

Tariff : 34€ ♣♣ ⬛ 📷 (10A) – Extra per person 8.50€ – Reservation fee 20€

Rental rates : (from mid April to end Sept.) – 2 'gypsy' caravans – 36 🚐 – 20 🏠 – 4 canvas bungalows – 4 tent lodges. Per night from 32 to 139€ – Per week from 224 to 973€ – Reservation fee 20€

Situated near the town centre with facilities suitable for families with young children.

Surroundings : 🐾 ≼ 🌿
Leisure activities : ♟ ✕ ⛷ ♣ ♣ 📷 🏊 🚣 ⛷ multi-sports ground
Facilities : ♿ ⚡ 🚮 🚿 🍴 📷 🚸
Nearby : 🛒

G P S	Longitude : 4.59698
	Latitude : 44.72597

RECOUBEAU-JANSAC

26310 – Michelin map **332** F6 – pop. 240 – alt. 500
▶ Paris 637 – La Chapelle-en-Vercors 55 – Crest 51 – Die 14

⚠ Le Couriou

📞 0475213323. www.lecouriou.fr

Address : at Combe Lambert (head 700m northwest along the D 93, follow the signs for Diè)

7 ha/4.5 for camping (138 pitches) terraced, relatively flat, flat, grassy, gravelled, stony, wood

Rentals : 22 🚐 – 15 🏠.

The site has a swimming area and a small but pretty chalet village.

Surroundings : ≼ 🏠 🌿
Leisure activities : ♟ ✕ 🎣 📷 🏊 jacuzzi ♣ 🏊 ⛷ multi-sports ground, spa centre
Facilities : ♿ ⚡ 🚿 🍴 launderette 🚸

G P S	Longitude : 5.41098
	Latitude : 44.65689

These symbols are used for a campsite that is exceptional in its category :

⚠⚠⚠ ... ⚠ *Particularly pleasant setting, quality and range of services available*

🐾🐾 *Tranquil, isolated site – quiet site, particularly at night*

≼≼ *Exceptional view – interesting or panoramic view*

RIBES

07260 – Michelin map **331** H7 – pop. 266 – alt. 380
▶ Paris 656 – Aubenas 30 – Largentière 19 – Privas 61

⚠ Les Cruses

📞 0475395469. www.campinglescruses.com

Address : at Le Champcros (located 1km southeast of the village, along the D 450)

Opening times : from mid April to mid Sept.

0.7 ha (47 pitches) terraced, stony, flat

Tariff : (2015 price) 30€ ♣♣ ⬛ 📷 (10A) – Extra per person 7€ – Reservation fee 7.14€

Rental rates : (from mid April to mid Sept.) – 2 'gypsy' caravans – 8 🚐 – 17 🏠 – 2 gîtes. Per night from 48 to 55€ – Per week from 336 to 865€ – Reservation fee 16.50€

🚰 Raclet sani-station, 10€ – 4 📷 13€ – 🚐 📷13€

Surroundings : 🐾 〰
Leisure activities : ✕ 🎣 jacuzzi ♣ 🏊
Facilities : ⚡ (July–Aug.) 🚿 🍴 🚸

G P S	Longitude : 4.20757
	Latitude : 44.4927

LA ROSIÈRE 1850

73700 – Michelin map **333** O4 – alt. 1 850 – Winter sports : 1 100/2 600 m

▶ Paris 657 – Albertville 76 – Bourg-St-Maurice 22 – Chambéry 125

⛰ La Forêt

✆ 04 79 06 86 21. www.camping-larosiere.com – alt. 1 730

Address : 2km south of the town along the N 90, follow the signs for Bourg-St-Maurice – direct access to the village

1.5 ha (67 pitches) open site, terraced, relatively flat, flat, grassy, stony

Rentals : 3 🚐 – 1 🏠 – 3 huts.

In an attractive location among pine trees, with a panoramic view.

Surroundings : ❄ ⛰ ≤ Mont Pourri, Aiguille Rouge, Arc 2000 ♤♤ Leisure activities : ♈ ✕ ⚓ ⚒ (small swimming pool) Facilities : ⚹ ⚮ ▥ ⚑ launderette Nearby : ✕	**GPS** Longitude : 6.85425 Latitude : 45.6234

We value your opinion and welcome your feedback. Do email us at campingfrance@tp.michelin.com

ROSIÈRES

07260 – Michelin map **331** H7 – pop. 1 121 – alt. 175

▶ Paris 649 – Aubenas 22 – Largentière 12 – Privas 54

⛰ Arleblanc

✆ 04 75 39 53 11. www.arleblanc.com

Address : Arleblanc district, southeast of Rosiières (take the northeastern exit, follow the signs for Aubenas and proceed 2.8km along the road to the right, beside the Intermarché commercial centre)

10 ha/6 for camping (167 pitches) flat, grassy

Rentals : 34 🚐 – 6 🏠 – 4 gîtes.

An extensive site set beside a 12th-century priory and beside the Beaume river. Ideal for swimming and fishing.

Surroundings : ⚘ ♤♤ Leisure activities : ♈ ✕ ⚓ ✕ ⚒ ⚒ ⚐ ⚑ Facilities : ⚹ ⚮ ▥ ⚑ ⚒ ⚑ launderette ⚒ ⚑ Nearby : 🐎	**GPS** Longitude : 4.27221 Latitude : 44.46552

⛰ La Plaine

✆ 04 75 39 51 35. www.campinglaplaine.com

Address : at Les Plaines (700m northeast along the D 104)

Opening times : from beginning April to mid Sept.

4.5 ha/3.5 for camping (128 pitches)

Tariff : 34€ ♈♈ ⚗ 🔲 ⚡ (10A) – Extra per person 6.50€ – Reservation fee 20€

Rental rates : (from beginning April to mid Sept.) – 50 🚐 – 2 🏠. Per night from 70 to 90€ – Per week from 210 to 790€ – Reservation fee 20€

A good amount of shade for the pitches and a small pool for anglers.

Surroundings : ⚏ ♤♤ Leisure activities : ♈ ⚑ ⚓ ✕ ⚒ ⚒ Facilities : ⚹ ⚮ ⚑ 🔲 Nearby : 🛒	**GPS** Longitude : 4.26677 Latitude : 44.48608

⛰ Les Platanes

✆ 04 75 39 52 31. www.campinglesplatanesardeche.com

Address : at La Charve (take the northeastern exit, follow the signs for Aubenas and proceed 3.7km along the road to the right, beside the Intermarché commercial centre)

2 ha (90 pitches) flat, grassy

Rentals : 27 🚐.

⚒ local sani-station

Pitches for tents and caravans beside the river, beneath hackberry trees; the mobile homes are across a small road.

Surroundings : ⚘ ≤ ♤♤ Leisure activities : ♈ ✕ ⚓ ⚓ ⚒ ⚐ ⚑ Facilities : ⚹ ⚮ ▥ ⚑ ⚑ 🔲 ⚒ ⚒	**GPS** Longitude : 4.27766 Latitude : 44.45702

⛰ Les Hortensias

✆ 04 75 39 91 38. www.leshortensias.com

Address : Ribeyre-Bouchet district (1.8km northwest along the D 104, follow the signs for Joyeuse, D 303, follow the signs for Vernon to the right, and take road to the left)

Opening times : from beginning April to end Oct.

1 ha (43 pitches) flat, grassy, sandy

Tariff : (2015 price) 27.50€ ♈♈ ⚗ 🔲 ⚡ (10A) – Extra per person 4.60€

Rental rates : (2015 price) (from beginning April to end Oct.) – 21 🚐 – 2 canvas bungalows – 1 gîte. Per night from 40 to 60€ – Per week from 240 to 740€

Surrounded by vineyards, a peaceful site, various rental options, but few pitches for tents and caravans

Surroundings : ⚘ ⚏ ♤♤ Leisure activities : ⚒ Facilities : ⚹ ⚮ ⚑ 🔲 Nearby : ⚒ (river) ⚑	**GPS** Longitude : 4.23976 Latitude : 44.48755

In order for the guide to remain wholly objective, the selection of campsites is made on an entirely independent basis.

RUFFIEUX

73310 – Michelin map **333** I2 – pop. 800 – alt. 282

▶ Paris 517 – Aix-les-Bains 20 – Ambérieu-en-Bugey 58 – Annecy 51

⛰ Saumont

✆ 04 79 54 26 26. www.campingsaumont.com

Address : at Saumont (1.2km west, access on the D 991, near the carr. du Saumont (junc. with D904/D55), towards Aix-les-Bains)

Opening times : from beginning April to end Sept.

1.6 ha (66 pitches) open site, flat, grassy, gravelled

Tariff : (2015 price) 17.50€ ♈♈ ⚗ 🔲 ⚡ (10A) – Extra per person 4.70€ – Reservation fee 10€

Rental rates : (2015 price) (from beginning April to mid Oct.) – 16 🚐. Per night from 87 to 110€ – Per week from 589 to 749€ – Reservation fee 10€

Some pitches are among trees and shrubs, by a small stream.

Surroundings : ⚏ ♤♤ Leisure activities : ♈ ⚓ ⚲ ✕ ⚒ ⚑ Facilities : ⚹ ⚮ ▥ ⚑ ⚒ ⚑ launderette	**GPS** Longitude : 5.83663 Latitude : 45.8486

RUOMS

07120 – Michelin map **331** I7 – pop. 2 249 – alt. 121
▷ Paris 651 – Alès 54 – Aubenas 24 – Pont-St-Esprit 49

▲▲▲ Sunêlia Aluna Vacances ▲▲

Sunêlia Aluna Vacances

✆ 04 75 93 93 15. www.alunavacances.fr

Address : route de Lagorce (2km east along the D 559)

Opening times : from mid April to beginning Nov.

10 ha (430 pitches) terraced, relatively flat, flat, grassy, stony

Tariff : 54 € ★★ ⬤ 🔲 (½) (10A) – Extra per person 13 € – Reservation fee 30 €

Rental rates : (from mid April to beginning Nov.) ♿ (2 mobile homes) – 237 🚐 – 2 tent lodges. Per night from 41 to 258 € – Per week from 287 to 1,806 € – Reservation fee 30 €

🚽 local sani-station

The Aluna music festival is held every year in mid June, with 4 to 7 concerts every evening; it attracts crowds of up to 35.000 over the 3 days.

Surroundings : 🦆 🗂 ⚲⚲
Leisure activities : ♟ ✗ 🏛 📺 🏃 ⛷ hammam, jacuzzi ⛷⛷ 🏹 🎣 🏊 🏊 multi-sports ground, spa centre
Facilities : 🚿 🛒 ⛺ ⛺ 🕯 launderette 🛒 🛠
Nearby : 🐎

G P S	Longitude : 4.3526 Latitude : 44.44962

▲▲▲ Yelloh! Village La Plaine ▲▲

✆ 04 75 39 65 83. www.yellohvillage-la-plaine.com

Address : La Grand Terre district (3.5km south of Ruoms, off the D111)

Opening times : from mid April to mid Sept.

4.5 ha (212 pitches) relatively flat, flat, grassy, sandy

Tariff : 47 € ★★ ⬤ 🔲 (½) (6A) – Extra per person 8 €
Rental rates : (from mid April to mid Sept.) 🚿 🅿 – 87 🚐. Per night from 42 to 202 €

🚽 local sani-station

Located near vineyards and the Ardèche river; well-shaded pitches and some high-quality rentals.

Surroundings : 🦆 ⚲ ⚲⚲⚲
Leisure activities : ♟ ✗ 🏛 📺 🏃 🏃 🏹 🏊 🏊 🎣 🏊 multi-sports ground
Facilities : 🚿 🛒 ▥ ⛺ ⛺ 🕯 launderette 🛠

G P S	Longitude : 4.33596 Latitude : 44.42666

▲▲▲ Domaine de Chaussy ▲▲
(rental of mobile homes, gîtes and hotel only)

✆ 04 75 93 99 66. www.domainedechaussy.com

Address : Le Petit Chaussy district (2.3km east along the D 559, follow the signs for Lagorce)

Opening times : from beginning April to mid Sept.

18 ha/5.5 for camping (250 pitches) undulating

Rental rates : (2015 price) – 190 🚐 – 40 🛏 – 17 gîtes. Per night from 42 to 160 € – Reservation fee 20 €

Numerous sporting activities for the family.

Surroundings : 🦆 ⚲⚲
Leisure activities : ♟ ✗ 🏛 📺 🏃 🏃 hammam, jacuzzi ⛷⛷ 🏊 🏊 ⛸ fitness trail, mountain biking trail
Facilities : 🚿 🛒 ⛺ 🕯 launderette 🛠 🛠

G P S	Longitude : 4.36913 Latitude : 44.4472

▲▲▲ RCN La Bastide en Ardèche ▲▲

✆ 04 75 39 64 72. www.rcn.fr

Address : route d'Alès, D111, by the bridge over the Ardeche river (4km southwest of Ruoms)

Opening times : from mid March to mid Sept.

7 ha (300 pitches) flat, grassy, stony

Tariff : 53.50 € ★★ ⬤ 🔲 (½) (6A) – Extra per person 6.75 € – Reservation fee 19.95 €
Rental rates : (from mid March to mid Sept.) – 45 🚐 – 30 canvas bungalows – 5 tent lodges. Per night from 39 to 169 € – Per week from 270 to 1,200 € – Reservation fee 19.95 €

In an attractive location beside the Ardèche river with a sandy beach, but choose the pitches further away from the road.

Surroundings : ⬔ ⚲⚲
Leisure activities : ♟ ✗ 🏛 🏃 🏃 🏹 🎣 🏊 (beach) ⛷
Facilities : 🚿 🛒 ⛺ ⛺ 🕯 launderette 🛠 🛠

G P S	Longitude : 4.32524 Latitude : 44.42326

▲▲▲ La Grand'Terre ▲▲

✆ 04 75 39 64 94. www.camping-lagrandterre.com

Address : La Grand Terre district (3.5km south of Ruoms, off the D 111)

Opening times : from mid April to mid Sept.

10 ha (296 pitches) flat, stony, sandy

Tariff : (2015 price) 40 € ★★ ⬤ 🔲 (½) (15A) – Extra per person 9.20 €
Rental rates : (2015 price) (from mid April to mid Sept.) 🚿 – 66 🚐. Per night from 51 to 119 € – Per week from 357 to 833 €

🚽 AireService sani-station – 15 🔲 12 €

Most of the pitches have a very wooded setting, with the added bonus of a beautiful sandy beach beside the Ardèche river.

Surroundings : 🦆 ⚲⚲⚲
Leisure activities : ♟ ✗ 🏛 📺 🏃 🏃 🏹 🚲 🎣 🏊 (beach) 🎣 multi-sports ground
Facilities : 🚿 🛒 ⛺ 🕯 launderette 🛠 🛠

G P S	Longitude : 4.33192 Latitude : 44.42522

▲▲▲ La Chapoulière ▲▲

✆ 04 75 39 64 98. www.lachapouliere.com

Address : at La Chapoulière (off the D111, 3.5km south of Ruoms)

Opening times : from mid March to end Oct.

2.5 ha (164 pitches) flat and relatively flat, grassy

Tariff : (2015 price) 38.60 € ★★ ⬤ 🔲 (½) (3A) – Extra per person 9.30 €
Rental rates : (2015 price) (from mid March to end Oct.) 🚿 – 21 🚐. Per night from 45 to 114 € – Per week from 312 to 794 €

A lovely grassy area beside the Ardèche river, with some pitches overlooking the water.

Surroundings : 🦆 ⚲⚲
Leisure activities : ♟ ✗ 🏛 📺 🏃 🏃 hammam ⛷⛷ 🏊 🎣 massages ⛷ multi-sports ground
Facilities : 🚿 🛒 ⛺ 🕯 🔲 🛠 🛠

G P S	Longitude : 4.32972 Latitude : 44.43139

The Michelin classification (▲▲▲ ... ▲) is totally independent of the official star classification system awarded by the local prefecture or other official organisation.

⛰ Sites et Paysages Le Petit Bois ♨

📞 04 75 39 60 72. www.campinglepetitbois.fr

Address : 87 rue du Petit Bois (800m north of Ruoms, 80m from the Ardèche river)

Opening times : from beginning April to end Sept.

2.5 ha (110 pitches) terraced, flat and relatively flat, grassy, stony, rocks

Tariff : 38€ ♣♣ 🚗 🔲 ⚡ (10A) – Extra per person 8€ – Reservation fee 20€

Rental rates : (from beginning April to end Sept.) 🛶 – 2 'gypsy' caravans – 27 🚐 – 11 🏠 – 3 tent lodges. Per night from 40 to 190€ – Per week from 280 to 1,330€ – Reservation fee 20€

🚐 11 🔲 16€ – 🔌 ⚡14€

Some rentals have a panoramic view over the Ardèche river and the gorge, and some are high-quality, with access to the river via a very steep path.

Surroundings : 🐟 🏕 🎯
Leisure activities : 🍴 🍽 🚤 🏓 ⛷ 🏊 hammam 🚣 🏊 (open air in season) 🎿
🛶 🚲 multi-sports ground
Facilities : ♿ 🚿 🏪 🍴 launderette

Longitude : 4.33789
Latitude : 44.45882

⛰ Les Paillotes en Ardèche

📞 04 75 39 62 05. www.campinglespaillotes.com – limited spaces for one-night stay

Address : chemin de l'Espédès (600m north along the D 579, follow the signs for Pradons and take road to the left)

Opening times : from end March to end Sept.

1 ha (45 pitches) flat, grassy

Tariff : 39€ ♣♣ 🚗 🔲 ⚡ (10A) – Extra per person 9€ – Reservation fee 10€

Rental rates : (from end March to end Sept.) – 30 🚐 – 5 canvas bungalows – 2 gîtes. Per night from 70 to 315€ – Per week from 180 to 970€ – Reservation fee 10€

Well marked-out pitches but little space for tents and caravans beside a large canoeing centre.

Surroundings : 🏕 🎯
Leisure activities : 🍴 🍽 🚤 🛶 🎿
Facilities : ♿ 🚿 🏪 🚮 🍴 🔲

Longitude : 4.34184
Latitude : 44.45938

⛰ Le Carpenty

📞 04 75 39 74 29. www.camping-ruoms-ardeche.com

Address : Fay et Carpenti, 3.6km south along the D 111

Opening times : from end March to end Sept.

0.7 ha (45 pitches) flat, grassy, stony

Tariff : 28€ ♣♣ 🚗 🔲 ⚡ (16A) – Extra per person 6€ – Reservation fee 3€

Rental rates : permanent – 30 🚐. Per night from 32 to 115€ – Reservation fee 5€

A lovely green site beside the Ardèche river, but choose pitches away from the road and the bridge.

Surroundings : 🏕 🎯
Leisure activities : 🍴 🍽 🚤 🛶 🎿
Facilities : ♿ 🚿 🍴 🔲 🚮

Longitude : 4.32842
Latitude : 44.42695

SABLIÈRES

07260 – Michelin map **331** G6 – pop. 144 – alt. 450
▶ Paris 629 – Aubenas 48 – Langogne 58 – Largentière 38

⛰ La Drobie

📞 04 75 36 95 22. www.ladrobie.com

Address : at Le Chambon (3km west along the D 220 and take turning to the right; beside the river, for caravans recommended route is via Lablachère along the D 4)

Opening times : from mid April to end Sept.

1.5 ha (80 pitches) terraced, relatively flat, stony, grassy

Tariff : (2015 price) 21€ ♣♣ 🚗 🔲 ⚡ (10A) – Extra per person 6.50€ – Reservation fee 5€

Rental rates : (2015 price) (from beginning April to end Oct.) – 3 🚐 – 10 🏠 – 1 gîte. Per night from 45 to 60€ – Per week from 315 to 605€ – Reservation fee 5€

Pitches beside the river, with good sanitary facilities. A good restaurant, open all year.

Surroundings : 🐟 ⚓
Leisure activities : 🍴 🍽 🚤 ✂ 🛶 🎣
Facilities : ♿ 🚿 🏪 🍴 🔲 🚮 🚮

Longitude : 4.04863
Latitude : 44.54368

SAHUNE

26510 – Michelin map **332** E7 – pop. 322 – alt. 330
▶ Paris 647 – Buis-les-Baronnies 27 – La Motte-Chalancon 22 – Nyons 16

⛰ Vallée Bleue

📞 04 75 27 44 42. www.lavalleebleue.com

Address : take the southwestern exit along the D 94, follow the signs for Nyons; beside the Eygues, in the southern end of the village

Opening times : from beginning April to end Sept.

3 ha (45 pitches) flat, stony, grassy

Tariff : ♣ 7€ 🚗 🔲 11€ – ⚡ (6A) 3.50€

Rental rates : (from beginning April to end Sept.) – 2 🏠. Per night from 50 to 60€ – Per week from 350 to 850€

Surroundings : ⚓ 🌳
Leisure activities : 🍽 🚤 🎣 🛶
Facilities : ♿ 🚿 🚮 🚮 🍴 🔲

Longitude : 5.26139
Latitude : 44.41148

ST-AGRÈVE

07320 – Michelin map **331** I3 – pop. 2 522 – alt. 1 050
▶ Paris 582 – Aubenas 68 – Lamastre 21 – Privas 64

⛰ Le Riou la Selle

📞 04 75 30 29 28. www.camping-riou.com

Address : Riou la Selle (south of the town, 2.8km southeast along the D 120, follow the signs for Cheylard, take the D 21, follow the signs for Nonières to the left and take the Chemin de la Roche to the right)

Opening times : from mid April to mid Oct.

1 ha (29 pitches) terraced, relatively flat, flat, grassy

Tariff : (2015 price) 22.50€ ♣♣ 🚗 🔲 ⚡ (11A) – Extra per person 6€

Rental rates : (2015 price) permanent – 2 🚐 – 2 🏠. Per night from 85 to 130€ – Per week from 300 to 590€

A peaceful, pleasant wooded site, with rental accommodation of a fairly basic standard.

Surroundings : 🐟 🏕 🎯
Leisure activities : 🍴 🍽 🚤 🛶
Facilities : ♿ 🚿 (July–Aug.) 🚮 🏪 🍴 🔲 🚮

Longitude : 4.40462
Latitude : 44.98892

ST-ALBAN-AURIOLLES

07120 – Michelin map **331** H7 – pop. 994 – alt. 108
▶ Paris 656 – Alès 49 – Aubenas 28 – Pont-St-Esprit 55

▲▲▲▲ Sunêlia Le Ranc Davaine ▲▲

Sunêlia Le Ranc Davaine

✆ 0475396055. www.camping-ranc-davaine.fr

Address : route de Chandolas (2.3km southwest along the D 208)

Opening times : from mid April to mid Sept.

13 ha (435 pitches) flat, grassy, stony

Tariff : 53€ ♦♦ ⇌ 🔲 🚽 (10A) – Extra per person 12.50€ – Reservation fee 30€

Rental rates : (from mid April to mid Sept.) ♿ (1 mobile home) 🚿 – 238 🏠 – 2 tent lodges. Per night from 44 to 228€ – Per week from 308 to 1,596€ – Reservation fee 30€

🚐 local sani-station

A good amount of shade is provided by oak trees; a partially covered water and play park, with direct access to the river.

Surroundings : 🐟 ⌷ ♉♉
Leisure activities : 🍷 ✗ 📷 🎢 🎣 ⛰ 🎿 hammam, jacuzzi 🚣 ⚔ 📺 🎱 🏊 🌊 disco 🌿 spa centre
Facilities : ♿ ⛽ 🏪 🛁 🚻 launderette 🛒🏪

GPS Longitude : 4.26868
Latitude : 44.40014

▲▲ Le Mas du Sartre

✆ 0475397174. masdusartre.fr

Address : at Auriolles, 5 chemin de la Vignasse (1.8km northwest along the D 208)

Opening times : from beginning May to mid Sept.

1.6 ha (49 pitches) terraced, flat and relatively flat, grassy, stony

Tariff : 29€ ♦♦ ⇌ 🔲 🚽 (10A) – Extra per person 6€ – Reservation fee 5€

Rental rates : (from beginning May to mid Sept.) – 10 🏠 – 4 🏠. Per week from 305 to 620€ – Reservation fee 5€

🚐 local sani-station – 6 🔲 10€ – 🔌 10€

Choose the pitches surrounded by shrubs and bushes, furthest away from the road.

Surroundings : ⌷ ♉♉
Leisure activities : 🍷 ✗ 📷 🚣 🎱 multi-sports ground
Facilities : ♿ ⛽ 🛁 🚻 🏪 🌿 refrigerators

GPS Longitude : 4.31477
Latitude : 44.43418

ST-ALBAN-DE-MONTBEL

73610 – Michelin map **333** H4 – pop. 605 – alt. 400
▶ Paris 551 – Belley 32 – Chambery 21 – Grenoble 74

▲▲ Le Sougey ▲▲

✆ 0479360144. www.camping-sougey.com – 🏮

Address : at Le Sougey (1.2km to the northeast, 300m from the lake)

Opening times : from end April to mid Sept.

4 ha (159 pitches) terrace, relatively flat, flat, grassy, fine gravel

Tariff : (2015 price) 28.80€ ♦♦ ⇌ 🔲 🚽 (10A) – Extra per person 4.40€

Rental rates : (2015 price) (from end April to mid Sept.) ♿ (1 chalet) – 7 🏠 – 8 🏠. Per night from 64 to 115€ – Per week from 305 to 765€

🚐 local sani-station

A small and pretty chalet village and pitches that are well marked out.

Surroundings : 🐟 ⌷ ♉♉
Leisure activities : 📷 🎢 🚣 🚴
Facilities : ♿ ⛽ 🏠🛁🎱 🛁 🚻 launderette 🌿
Nearby : 🎱 🍷 ✗ 🏊 🎣 pedalos

GPS Longitude : 5.79069
Latitude : 45.55562

Michelin classification:

▲▲▲▲ *Extremely comfortable, equipped to a very high standard*
▲▲▲ *Very comfortable, equipped to a high standard*
▲▲▲ *Comfortable and well equipped*
▲▲ *Reasonably comfortable*
▲ *Satisfactory*

ST-AVIT

26330 – Michelin map **332** C2 – pop. 326 – alt. 348
▶ Paris 536 – Annonay 33 – Lyon 81 – Romans-sur-Isère 22

▲▲ Domaine la Garenne

✆ 0475686226. www.domaine-la-garenne.com 🚿

Address : 156 chemin de Chablezin

Opening times : from mid April to end Sept.

14 ha/6 for camping (112 pitches) terraced, relatively flat to hilly, flat, grassy

Tariff : (2015 price) 26.50€ ♦♦ ⇌ 🔲 🚽 (6A) – Extra per person 7€

Rental rates : (2015 price) (from mid April to end Sept.) 🚿 – 35 🏠 – 7 🏠 – 6 canvas bungalows. Per night from 45 to 185€ – Per week from 250 to 1,200€ – Reservation fee 10€

Surroundings : 🐟 ⟨ ♉♉
Leisure activities : ✗ 📷 🚣 🎱
Facilities : ♿ ⛽ 🛁 🚻 🏪
Nearby : 🐟

GPS Longitude : 4.9549
Latitude : 45.20176

ST-CHRISTOPHE-EN-OISANS

38520 – Michelin map **333** K8 – pop. 123 – alt. 1 470
▶ Paris 635 – L'Alpe-d'Huez 31 – La Bérarde 12 – Le Bourg-d'Oisans 21

▲ Municipal la Bérarde

✆ 0476792045– access narrow, sometimes only possible using passing places – alt. 1 738

Address : at La Bérarde (10.5km southeast along the D 530; difficult access for caravans – steep slope)

2 ha (165 pitches open site, terraced, relatively flat, flat, grassy, stony, rocks

A very pleasant rural site beside the Vénéon river.

Surroundings : 🐟 ⟨ Parc National des Écrins ♀
Leisure activities : 📷 🐟
Facilities : ⛽ 🏪 🏠
Nearby : 🎱 🍷 ✗

GPS Longitude : 6.29205
Latitude : 44.93309

ST-CIRGUES-EN-MONTAGNE

07510 – Michelin map **331** G5 – pop. 248 – alt. 1 044
▶ Paris 586 – Aubenas 40 – Langogne 31 – Privas 68

⚠ Les Airelles

☎ 04 75 38 92 49. www.camping-les-airelles.fr

Address : route de Lapalisse (take the northern exit along the D 160, follow the signs for the Lac-d'Issarlès, right bank of the Vernason river)

0.7 ha (50 pitches) terraced, relatively flat, grassy, stony

Rentals : 10 🛖 – 9 🛏.

Surroundings : 🐟 ⛰
Leisure activities : 🍴 🏓 🛶 🎣
Facilities : ⚡ 🚿 launderette
Nearby : 🛷 ✕

GPS	Longitude : 4.0949
	Latitude : 44.75648

ST-CLAIR-DU-RHÔNE

38370 – Michelin map **333** B5 – pop. 3 886 – alt. 160
▶ Paris 501 – Annonay 35 – Givors 26 – Le Péage-de-Roussillon 10

🏔 Le Daxia

☎ 04 74 56 39 20. www.campingledaxia.com

Address : route du Péage – avenue du Plateau des Frères (2.7km south along the D 4 and take road to the left, recommended route via the N 7 and D 37)

Opening times : from beginning April to end Sept.

7.5 ha (120 pitches) flat, grassy

Tariff : (2015 price) 22.75€ ✶✶ ⛟ 🔌 (6A) – Extra per person 4.70€ – Reservation fee 15€

Rental rates : (2015 price) (from beginning April to end Sept.) – 5 🛖 – 2 studios. Per night from 60 to 75€ – Per week from 270 to 495€ – Reservation fee 20€

🚐 local sani-station 18.75€ – 6 🔲 18.75€

Pretty, marked out pitches; beside the Varèze river.

Surroundings : 🐟 🌳 ⛰
Leisure activities : 🍴 ✕ 🏓 🛶 🎣 🛷 🎿 🎣
Facilities : ⚡ 🚿 🛁 launderette

GPS	Longitude : 4.78129
	Latitude : 45.42128

ST-DONAT-SUR-L'HERBASSE

26260 – Michelin map **332** C3 – pop. 3 825 – alt. 202
▶ Paris 545 – Grenoble 92 – Hauterives 20 – Romans-sur-Isère 13

🏔 Domaine du Lac de Champos

☎ 04 75 45 17 81. www.lacdechampos.com

Address : Lac de Champos (situated 2km northeast along the D 67)

Opening times : from end April to beginning Sept.

43 ha/6 for camping (60 pitches)

Tariff : 20€ ✶✶ ⛟ 🔌 (10A) – Extra per person 4€

Rental rates : (from beginning April to beginning Nov.) – 21 🛖 – 4 tent lodges. Per week from 199 to 599€ – Reservation fee 15€

🚐 local sani-station – 5 🔲 17€ – 🚐 11€

In a pleasant setting beside the Lac de Champos.

Surroundings : ⛰ ⛲
Leisure activities : 🍴 ✕ 🏓 🛶 ✕ 🎿 🎣 pedal go-carts 🚲
Facilities : ⚡ 🚿 🛁 launderette

GPS	Longitude : 5.00543
	Latitude : 45.13615

🏔 Domaine des Ulèzes

☎ 04 75 47 83 20. www.camping-des-ulezes.fr

Address : route de Romans (take southeastern exit along the D 53 and take the road to the right; near the Herbasse)

Opening times : from beginning April to end Oct.

2.5 ha (85 pitches) flat, grassy

Tariff : (2015 price) 20€ ✶✶ ⛟ 🔌 (10A) – Extra per person 4.80€

Rental rates : (2015 price) (from beginning April to end Oct.) 🛖 – 8 🛖 – 3 canvas bungalows. Per night from 60 to 130€ – Per week from 295 to 680€

🚐 3 🔲 20€

Surroundings : 🐟 🌳 ⛲
Leisure activities : ✕ 🏓 🛶 🎣 🎿 🎣
Facilities : ⚡ 🚿 🛁 🚰 🛁 launderette
Nearby : 🍴 🎣

GPS	Longitude : 4.99285
	Latitude : 45.11914

ST-FERRÉOL-TRENTE-PAS

26110 – Michelin map **332** E7 – pop. 228 – alt. 417
▶ Paris 634 – Buis-les-Baronnies 30 – La Motte-Chalancon 34 – Nyons 14

🏔 Le Pilat

☎ 04 75 27 72 09. www.campinglepilat.com

Address : route de Bourdeau (located 1km north along the D 70; beside a stream)

Opening times : from beginning April to end Sept.

1 ha (90 pitches) flat, grassy, stony

Tariff : (2015 price) 28.50€ ✶✶ ⛟ 🔌 (6A) – Extra per person 7€

Rental rates : (2015 price) (from beginning April to end Sept.) 🛖 – 21 🛖 – 2 gîtes. Per night from 50 to 96€ – Per week from 250 to 850€

🚐 local sani-station – 3 🔲 28.50€

Surroundings : 🐟 ⛰ ⛲
Leisure activities : ✕ 🏓 🛶 🎿 🎣 🎿
Facilities : ⚡ 🚿 🛁 🚰 🛁 🎣

GPS	Longitude : 5.21195
	Latitude : 44.43406

ST-GALMIER

42330 – Michelin map **327** E6 – pop. 5 596 – alt. 400
▶ Paris 457 – Lyon 82 – Montbrison 25 – Montrond-les-Bains 11

🏔 Campéole Val de Coise 👥

☎ 04 77 54 14 82. www.camping-valdecoise.com – limited spaces for one-night stay

Address : route de la Thiery (situated 2km to the east along the D 6 and take the road to the left)

Opening times : from beginning April to end Sept.

3.5 ha (92 pitches) terraced, relatively flat, flat, grassy

Tariff : 12€ ✶✶ ⛟ 🔌 (10A) – Extra per person 10€ – Reservation fee 25€

Rental rates : (from beginning April to end Sept.) – 11 🛖 – 5 🛖 – 4 canvas bungalows. Per night from 32 to 99€ – Per week from 224 to 693€ – Reservation fee 25€

🚐 local sani-station 1€

Not far from the source of Badoit mineral water and the Coise river.

Surroundings : ⛲
Leisure activities : 🏓 🎲 🎣 🛶 🎿 🎣
Facilities : ⚡ 🚿 🛁 🛁 launderette
Nearby : 🎣

GPS	Longitude : 4.33552
	Latitude : 45.59308

ST-GENEST-MALIFAUX

42660 – Michelin map **327** F7 – pop. 2 916 – alt. 980
▶ Paris 528 – Annonay 33 – St-Étienne 16 – Yssingeaux 46

⚠ Municipal de la Croix de Garry

✆ 06 85 40 95 38. www.st-genest-malifaux.fr – alt. 928 – limited spaces for one-night stay

Address : at La Croix de Garry (take the southern exit along the D 501, follow the signs for Montfaucon-en-Velay; near a lake and 150m from the Semène river)

Opening times : from mid April to mid Oct.

2 ha (85 pitches) terraced, relatively flat, flat, grassy

Tariff : (2015 price) 20.50€ ★★ ⇌ 🗐 🄴 (6A) – Extra per person 5€
Rental rates : (2015 price) permanent ⅙ (1 chalet) 🏠 – 8 🏠 – 1 gîte. Per night from 100€ – Per week from 290 to 410€

A little way out of town; beside a small lake that is ideal for fishing.

Surroundings : ≤		
Leisure activities : 🏹	**G P S**	Longitude : 4.42258
Facilities : ⅙ ⚬⊸ ▥ ⑂ 🄴		Latitude : 45.33357
Nearby : ✂ 🎣		

To visit a town or region, use the MICHELIN Green Guides.

ST-GERVAIS-LES-BAINS

74170 – Michelin map **328** N5 – pop. 5 673 – alt. 820 – ♨ – Winter sports : 1 400/2 000 m
▶ Paris 597 – Annecy 84 – Bonneville 42 – Chamonix-Mont-Blanc 25

⚠ Les Dômes de Miage

✆ 04 50 93 45 96. http://www.natureandlodge.fr – alt. 890

Address : 197 route des Contamines (situated 2km south along the D 902, at a place called les Bernards)

Opening times : from mid May to mid Sept.

3 ha (150 pitches) flat, grassy

Tariff : 31.20€ ★★ ⇌ 🗐 🄴 (10A) – Extra per person 6.20€ – Reservation fee 10€
Rental rates : permanent 🏠 – 1 🏠. Per night from 220 to 260€ – Per week from 630 to 1,680€
🚏 local sani-station

In a lush green setting, on a field crossed by a small stream. One original Savoyard chalet, equipped to a high standard.

Surroundings : ≤ ♀		
Leisure activities : 🏹	**G P S**	Longitude : 6.72022
Facilities : ⅙ ⚬⊸ ▥ 🛁 ⑂ launderette ⚗		Latitude : 45.87355
Nearby : ⑂ ✗ 🚣		

ST-JEAN-DE-MAURIENNE

73300 – Michelin map **333** L6 – pop. 8 374 – alt. 556
▶ Paris 641 – Lyon 174 – Chambéry 75 – St-Martin-d'Hères 105

⚠ Municipal les Grands Cols

✆ 04 79 64 28 02. www.campingdesgrandscols.com

Address : 422 avenue du Mont Cenis

Opening times : from mid May to mid Sept.

2.5 ha (80 pitches) terraced, flat, grassy

Tariff : (2015 price) 21€ ★★ ⇌ 🗐 🄴 (16A) – Extra per person 6€ – Reservation fee 8€

Rental rates : (2015 price) (from mid May to mid Sept.) ⅙ (1 mobile home) – 7 🚐. Per night from 45 to 85€ – Per week from 280 to 560€ – Reservation fee 8€

In a green setting, with mobile homes on well-situated terraces.

Surroundings : 🌳 ≤ mountains 🖾 ♀♀		
Leisure activities : ✗ 🏛 multi-sports ground	**G P S**	Longitude : 6.3515
Facilities : ⅙ ⚬⊸ 🛁 ⑂ ⑂ launderette		Latitude : 45.2716
Nearby : 🚲		

ST-JEAN-DE-MUZOLS

07300 – Michelin map **331** K3 – pop. 2 444 – alt. 123
▶ Paris 541 – Annonay 34 – Beaurepaire 53 – Privas 62

⚠ Le Castelet

✆ 04 75 08 09 48. www.camping-lecastelet.com

Address : 113 route du Grand Pont (2.8km southwest along the D 238, follow the signs for Lamastre; beside the Doux river and near the Tournon St-Jean railway station)

Opening times : from mid April to mid Sept.

3 ha (66 pitches) terraced, flat, grassy, stony

Tariff : (2015 price) 27€ ★★ ⇌ 🗐 🄴 (6A) – Extra per person 6.50€ – Reservation fee 20€
Rental rates : (2015 price) (from mid April to mid Nov.) – 3 🚐 – 4 🏠. Per night from 75€ – Per week from 398 to 620€ – Reservation fee 20€

Pitches on terraces extending down to the river, below vineyards and the road.

Surroundings : 🌳 ≤ 🖾 ♀♀		
Leisure activities : ⑂ 🏛 🏹 ⚓ ⚓	**G P S**	Longitude : 4.78564
Facilities : ⅙ ⚬⊸ 🄴 🛁 ⑂ 🄴		Latitude : 45.0681

The pitches of many campsites are marked out with low hedges of attractive bushes and shrubs.

ST-JEAN-LE-CENTENIER

07580 – Michelin map **331** J6 – pop. 668 – alt. 350
▶ Paris 623 – Alès 83 – Aubenas 20 – Privas 24

⚠ Les Arches

✆ 04 75 36 75 19. www.camping-les-arches.com

Address : at Le Cluzel (1.2km west along the D 458a and take D 258, follow the signs for Mirabel then take the road to the right)

Opening times : from end April to mid Sept.

10 ha/5 for camping (177 pitches) terraced, relatively flat, flat, grassy

Tariff : (2015 price) 28€ ★★ ⇌ 🗐 🄴 (10A) – Extra per person 6€
Rental rates : (2015 price) permanent – 29 🏠 – 2 gîtes. Per week from 250 to 865€ – Reservation fee 10€
🚏 local sani-station – 65 🗐 28€ – 🚐 28€

Pitches and rental options in both sun and shade, situated with a view of or beside a small natural pool, near a waterfall.

Surroundings : 🌳 🖾 ♀		
Leisure activities : ⑂ ✗ 🏹 🚲 ⚓ ⚓	**G P S**	Longitude : 4.52576
Facilities : ⅙ ⚬⊸ 🛁 ⑂ 🄴 🚣		Latitude : 44.58759

ST-JORIOZ

74410 – Michelin map **328** J5 – pop. 5 716 – alt. 452
▶ Paris 545 – Albertville 37 – Annecy 9 – Megève 51

⚲ Europa ⚄

☏ 0450685101. www.camping-europa.com

Address : 1444 route d'Albertville (1.4km southeast)

Opening times : from mid April to mid Sept.

3 ha (190 pitches) flat, grassy, stony

Tariff : (2015 price) 40€ ⚄⚄ ⚗ 🔲 🔋 (10A) – Extra per person 8.50€ – Reservation fee 25€

Rental rates : (2015 price) (from mid April to mid Sept.) ⚅ – 55 🚐 – 4 🏠. Per week from 315 to 1,399€ – Reservation fee 25€

There's an attractive swimming area; rental of good-quality mobile homes.

Surroundings : ⚬⚬
Leisure activities : 🍽️✖️⚅🚣🛶🚴⛵⛸️ multi-sports ground
Facilities : ♿ ⚬⚬ 🚿 ⚅ 🧺 launderette ⚅
GPS Longitude : 6.18185
Latitude : 45.83

⚲ International du Lac d'Annecy

☏ 0450686793. www.camping-lac-annecy.com

Address : 1184 route d'Albertville (located 1km southeast)

Opening times : from mid April to mid Sept.

2.5 ha (163 pitches) flat, grassy

Tariff : 42€ ⚄⚄ ⚗ 🔲 🔋 (10A) – Extra per person 8€ – Reservation fee 23€

Rental rates : (from mid April to mid Sept.) ♿ (1 mobile home) ⚅ – 35 🚐 – 3 🏠 – 4 tent lodges. Per night from 38 to 146€ – Per week from 266 to 1,022€ – Reservation fee 23€

The site is in two sections on either side of the Voie Verte (green way).

Surroundings : ⚬⚬
Leisure activities : 🍽️✖️🚣🛶🚴⛵⛸️ multi-sports ground
Facilities : ♿ ⚬⚬ 🚿 🧺 launderette
GPS Longitude : 6.17845
Latitude : 45.83078

⚲ Le Solitaire du Lac

☏ 0450685930. www.campinglesolitaire.com – access difficult

Address : 615 route de Sales (located 1km to the north)

Opening times : from beginning April to mid Sept.

3.5 ha (185 pitches) flat, grassy

Tariff : (2015 price) 28.60€ ⚄⚄ ⚗ 🔲 🔋 (6A) – Extra per person 6.10€ – Reservation fee 8€

🚽 local sani-station

Set on a pleasant, green field stretching down to the lake.

Surroundings : ⚬⚬
Leisure activities : 🚣⛵🚴⛱️
Facilities : ♿ ⚬⚬ 🚿 launderette ⚅
GPS Longitude : 6.14875
Latitude : 45.84177

For more information on visiting particular towns or regions, consult the relevant regional MICHELIN Green Guide. We also recommend you use the appropriate Michelin regional map to locate your selected campsite, to calculate distances and to work out the best route.

ST-JULIEN-EN-ST-ALBAN

07000 – Michelin map **331** K5 – pop. 1 311 – alt. 131
▶ Paris 587 – Aubenas 41 – Crest 29 – Montélimar 35

⚲ L'Albanou

☏ 0475660097. www.camping-albanou.com

Address : chemin de Pampelonne (head 1.4km east along the N 304, follow the signs for Pouzin and take the Celliers road to the right; near the Ouvèze)

Opening times : from mid April to end Sept.

1.5 ha (87 pitches) flat, grassy

Tariff : (2015 price) 26.50€ ⚄⚄ ⚗ 🔲 🔋 (10A) – Extra per person 5.50€ – Reservation fee 3€

Rental rates : (2015 price) (from mid April to end Sept.) – 3 🚐. Per night from 46 to 94€ – Per week from 320 to 655€ – Reservation fee 5€

🚽 local sani-station 22.50€ – 6 🔲 22.50€

The attractive pitches are marked out.

Surroundings : ⚅⚬⚬
Leisure activities : jacuzzi 🚣⛸️
Facilities : ♿ ⚬⚬ 🧺 ⚅ ⚅
GPS Longitude : 4.71369
Latitude : 44.75651

ST-LAURENT-DU-PONT

38380 – Michelin map **333** H5 – pop. 4 496 – alt. 410
▶ Paris 560 – Chambéry 29 – Grenoble 34 – La Tour-du-Pin 42

⚲ Municipal les Berges du Guiers

☏ 0476552063. www.camping-chartreuse.com

Address : avenue de la Gare (take the northern exit along the D 520, follow the signs for Chambéry and take the turning to the left; beside the Guiers Mort – pedestrian walkway to village)

Opening times : from mid June to mid Sept.

1 ha (45 pitches) flat, grassy

Tariff : 17.50€ ⚄⚄ ⚗ 🔲 🔋 (5A) – Extra per person 5€ – Reservation fee 10€

A footpath leads to the village.

Surroundings : ⚬
Facilities : ♿ ⚬⚬ 🚿 🧺 ⚅
Nearby : 🚣⛸️✖️⛱️
GPS Longitude : 5.73615
Latitude : 45.39068

ST-LAURENT-EN-BEAUMONT

38350 – Michelin map **333** I8 – pop. 436 – alt. 900
▶ Paris 613 – Le Bourg-d'Oisans 43 – Corps 16 – Grenoble 51

⚲ Belvédère de l'Obiou

☏ 0476304080. www.camping-obiou.com

Address : at Les Égats (1.3km southwest along the N 85)

Opening times : from mid April to mid Oct.

1 ha (45 pitches) terraced, relatively flat, flat, grassy

Tariff : (2015 price) 28.20€ ⚄⚄ ⚗ 🔲 🔋 (10A) – Extra per person 6€ – Reservation fee 12€

Rental rates : (2015 price) (from beginning May to end Sept.) – 5 🚐 – 2 🛏️. Per week from 259 to 693€ – Reservation fee 16€

🚽 local sani-station 5€ – 4 🔲 14.30€

Surroundings : ⚬
Leisure activities : ✖️🏠🚣⛱️
Facilities : ♿ ⚬⚬ 🆑 🧺 🚿 ⚅ ⚅
Nearby : 🍽️
GPS Longitude : 5.83779
Latitude : 44.87597

ST-LAURENT-LES-BAINS

07590 – Michelin map **331** F6 – pop. 156 – alt. 840
▶ Paris 603 – Aubenas 64 – Langogne 30 – Largentière 52

⚠ Indigo le Moulin

🖉 04 66 46 02 03. www.campingleceytrou.free.fr

Address : situated 2.1km to the southeast along the D 4

Opening times : from beginning April to mid Nov.

2.5 ha (60 pitches) terraced, flat and relatively flat, grassy, stony

Tariff : 13.10€ ★★ ⇔ 🔳 (≬) (10A) – Extra per person 3.50€

Rentals : permanent – 12 🏠. Per week from 150 to 420€

In a charming location in the heart of the Vivarais Cévenol mountains.

Surroundings : ⅏ ≪ ♀
Leisure activities : 🎭 ✂ 🏛 🔥 🛶 🐟
Facilities : ⅍ ⊶ 🏕 ⌁ 🚰 🖳

Longitude : 3.97962
Latitude : 44.59922

To make the best possible use of this guide, please read pages 2–15 carefully.

ST-MARTIN-D'ARDÈCHE

07700 – Michelin map **331** I6 – pop. 886 – alt. 46
▶ Paris 641 – Bagnols-sur-Cèze 21 – Barjac 27 – Bourg-St-Andéol 13

⚠ Le Pontet ♣♣

🖉 04 75 04 63 07. www.campinglepontet.com

Address : at Le Pontet (located 1.5km east along the D 290, follow the signs for St-Just and take road to the left)

Opening times : from beginning April to end Sept.

1.8 ha (97 pitches) terraced, flat, grassy

Tariff : (2015 price) 25.80€ ★★ ⇔ 🔳 (≬) (6A) – Extra per person 5.80€ – Reservation fee 10€

Rental rates : (2015 price) (from beginning April to end Sept.) – 17 🔟. Per night from 40 to 80€ – Per week from 210 to 710€ – Reservation fee 26€

🚰 local sani-station 3€ – 4 🔳 8€ – 🔌 8€

The site is surrounded by vineyards, with plenty of shade; the swimming pool is on the other side of the small road.

Surroundings : ⅏ ♀♀
Leisure activities : 🍸 ✕ 🏛 🏃 🏄 🚴 ⛵
Facilities : ⅍ ⊶ 🆑 ⌁ 🚰 🖳 🛒

Longitude : 4.58453
Latitude : 44.30409

⚠ Les Gorges

🖉 04 75 04 61 09. www.camping-des-gorges.com

Address : chemin de Sauze (located 1.5km to the northwest)

Opening times : from beginning May to mid Sept.

3 ha (145 pitches) terraced, flat, grassy, stony

Tariff : (2015 price) 38€ ★★ ⇔ 🔳 (≬) (10A) – Extra per person 8.90€ – Reservation fee 30€

Rental rates : (2015 price) (from beginning May to mid Sept.) 🏕 – 24 🔟 – 1 gîte. Per night from 40 to 164€ – Per week from 280 to 1,150€ – Reservation fee 30€

🚰 local sani-station

A well-shaded site with access to the banks of the Ardèche river.

Surroundings : 🚣 ♀♀
Leisure activities : 🍸 ✕ 🏛 🏄 🛶 🐟
🏑 multi-sports ground
Facilities : ⅍ ⊶ 🏛 ⌁ 🚰 🖳 🛒

Longitude : 4.55547
Latitude : 44.31155

🏔 Indigo le Moulin

🖉 04 75 04 66 20. www.camping-indigo.com

Address : take southeastern exit along the D 290, follow the signs for St-Just and take a right turn (D 200); beside the Ardèche river

Opening times : from beginning May to end Sept.

6.5 ha (200 pitches) relatively flat, flat, grassy, sandy

Tariff : (2015 price) 34.20€ ★★ ⇔ 🔳 (≬) (10A) – Extra per person 7.10€ – Reservation fee 13€

Rental rates : (2015 price) (from beginning May to end Sept.) – 16 'gypsy' caravans – 8 🔟 – 55 tent lodges. Per night from 46 to 129€ – Per week from 226 to 903€ – Reservation fee 13€

🚰 local sani-station 7€

Surroundings : ♀
Leisure activities : ✕ 🏛 🏄 🛶 🐟
Facilities : ⅍ ⊶ ⌁ 🚰 🖳 🛒

Longitude : 4.57122
Latitude : 44.30035

ST-MARTIN-DE-CLELLES

38930 – Michelin map **333** G8 – pop. 157 – alt. 750
▶ Paris 616 – Lyon 149 – Grenoble 48 – St-Martin-d'Hères 49

⚠ La Chabannerie

🖉 04 76 34 00 38. www.camping-isere.net

Address : La Chabannerie, Passage de l'Aiguille (north of the village, off the D 252A)

Opening times : from beginning May to end Sept.

2.5 ha (49 pitches) terraced, flat and relatively flat, grassy, stony

Tariff : (2015 price) 23€ ★★ ⇔ 🔳 (≬) (6A) – Extra per person 4€

Surroundings : 🚣 ≪ 🔲 ♀♀
Leisure activities : 🏛 🛶
Facilities : ⊶ 🏛 🚰 🖳 🛒

Longitude : 5.61624
Latitude : 44.82574

For more information on visiting particular towns or regions, consult the relevant regional MICHELIN Green Guide. We also recommend you use the appropriate Michelin regional map to locate your selected campsite, to calculate distances and to work out the best route.

ST-MARTIN-EN-VERCORS

26420 – Michelin map **332** F3 – pop. 378 – alt. 780
▶ Paris 601 – La Chapelle-en-Vercors 9 – Grenoble 51 – Romans-sur-Isère 46

⚠ La Porte St-Martin

🖉 04 75 45 51 10. www.camping-laportestmartin.com

Address : take the northern exit along the D 103

Opening times : from beginning April to end Sept.

1.5 ha (66 pitches) terraced, sloping, flat, grassy, stony, gravelled

Tariff : (2015 price) 18.90€ ★★ ⇔ 🔳 (≬) (10A) – Extra per person 7€

Rental rates : (2015 price) permanent 🏕 – 3 🏠 – 1 gîte. Per week from 230 to 650€

🚰 local sani-station 9€

Surroundings : ≪ ♀
Leisure activities : 🏛 🚴 🛶 (small swimming pool)
Facilities : ⅍ ⊶ 🚰 🖳

Longitude : 5.44336
Latitude : 45.02456

ST-MAURICE-D'ARDÈCHE

07200 – Michelin map **331** I6 – pop. 312 – alt. 140
▶ Paris 639 – Aubenas 12 – Largentière 16 – Privas 44

⛰ Le Chamadou ♣♣

📞 0820366197. www.camping-le-chamadou.com ✉ 07120 Balazuc

Address : at Mas de Chaussy (500m from a lake)

Opening times : from beginning April to end Oct.

1 ha (86 pitches) flat and relatively flat, grassy

Tariff : 31.40€ ♣♣ ⬟ 🄴 🄷 (10A) – Extra per person 7.20€ –
Reservation fee 15€

Rental rates : (from beginning April to end Oct.) 🚫 – 24 🏠.
Per night from 32 to 172€ – Per week from 220 to 1,200€ –
Reservation fee 15€

In the heart of the Ardèche winegrowning area, with a pretty traditional stone farmhouse.

Surroundings : 🌳 🏞 ♀
Leisure activities : 🍴 🗶 🎱 🏇 🚴 ⛷ 🎿 ▵
multi-sports ground
Facilities : 🚿 ⛲🚼🗑 🔥 📷
Nearby : 🚣

G P S Longitude : 4.40384
Latitude : 44.50826

Some information or pricing may have changed since the guide went to press. We recommend you check the price list online in advance or at the entrance to the campsite and enquire about possible restrictions.

ST-NAZAIRE-EN-ROYANS

26190 – Michelin map **332** E3 – pop. 716 – alt. 172
▶ Paris 576 – Grenoble 69 – Pont-en-Royans 9 – Romans-sur-Isère 19

⛰ Municipal du Lac

📞 0475484118. www.saint-nazaire-en-royans.com

Address : 100B rue des Condamines (700m southeast, follow the signs for St-Jean-en-Royans)

Opening times : from beginning April to beginning Nov.

1.5 ha (75 pitches) flat and relatively flat, grassy

Tariff : (2015 price) 15€ ♣♣ ⬟ 🄴 🄷 (6A) – Extra per person 4.30€

🚻 local sani-station
Situated beside the Bourne river, where it widens into a small lake.

Surroundings : 🏞 ♀♀
Leisure activities : 🎱 🚣
Facilities : 🚿 🗑

G P S Longitude : 5.25368
Latitude : 45.05912

ST-PAUL-DE-VÉZELIN

42590 – Michelin map **327** D4 – pop. 303 – alt. 431
▶ Paris 415 – Boën 19 – Feurs 30 – Roanne 26

⛰ la Via Natura Arpheuilles

📞 0477634343. www.camping-arpheuilles.com – access difficult for caravans

Address : at Port Piset, 4km north of the village, near the Loire river (and lake)

Opening times : from mid April to end Sept.

3.5 ha (80 pitches) terraced, relatively flat, grassy

Tariff : 28.50€ ♣♣ ⬟ 🄴 🄷 (10A) – Extra per person 3.50€

Rental rates : (from mid April to end Sept.) – 8 🚐 – 7 🏠 – 3 tent lodges. Per night from 70 to 100€ – Per week from 200 to 695€

In an attractive setting in the steep valley of the Loire river, on a secluded and unspoilt site.

Surroundings : 🌳 ≤ 🏞 ⛰
Leisure activities : 🍴 🗶 🎱 🏋 🚣 🎿 🛶 🏊
Facilities : 🚿 ⛲🚼 🔥 🕯 launderette 🏕
Nearby : 🏊

G P S Longitude : 4.06314
Latitude : 45.91178

ST-PIERRE-D'ALBIGNY

73250 – Michelin map **333** J4 – pop. 3 269 – alt. 410
▶ Paris 587 – Aix-les-Bains 43 – Albertville 27 – Annecy 52

⛰ Lac de Carouge

📞 0479285816. www.campinglacdecarouge.fr

Address : 2.8km south along the D 911 and take a left turn, 300m from the N 6

Opening times : from beginning April to mid Sept.

1.9 ha (81 pitches) flat, grassy

Tariff : 23.50€ ♣♣ ⬟ 🄴 🄷 (10A) – Extra per person 3.50€ –
Reservation fee 10€

Rental rates : (2015 price) (from beginning April to end Sept.) –
11 🚐. Per night from 50€ – Per week from 300 to 700€ –
Reservation fee 20€

🚻 local sani-station 4€

A pleasant and shaded site near a water sports centre.

Surroundings : 🏞 ♀♀
Leisure activities : 🍴
Facilities : 🚿 ⛲🚼 🔥 🕯 launderette
Nearby : 🏖 🏊 (beach) 🚣 pedalos, cable wakeboarding

G P S Longitude : 6.17092
Latitude : 45.56057

The pitches of many campsites are marked out with low hedges of attractive bushes and shrubs.

ST-PIERRE-DE-CHARTREUSE

38380 – Michelin map **333** H5 – pop. 999 – alt. 885 – Winter sports : 900/1 800 m
▶ Paris 571 – Belley 62 – Chambéry 39 – Grenoble 28

⛰ Sites et Paysages De Martinière

📞 0476886036. www.campingdemartiniere.com

Address : route du Col de Porte (3km southwest along the D 512, follow the signs for Grenoble)

Opening times : from beginning May to mid Sept.

1.5 ha (100 pitches) open site, relatively flat, flat, grassy

Tariff : 27.90€ ♣♣ ⬟ 🄴 🄷 (10A) – Extra per person 6.40€ –
Reservation fee 8€

Rental rates : permanent 🚫 – 4 🚐 – 3 🏠 – 2 tent lodges.
Per night from 100 to 230€ – Per week from 250 to 750€ –
Reservation fee 8€

🚻 local sani-station – 3 🄴 21.90€ – 🔌11€

In a pleasant location in the heart of the Chartreuse National Park.

Surroundings : ≤ ♀
Leisure activities : 🎱 🏇 🎿
Facilities : ⛲🚼 📶 🔥 🕯 📷
Nearby : 🗶

G P S Longitude : 5.79717
Latitude : 45.32583

ST-PRIVAT

07200 – Michelin map **331** I6 – pop. 1 588 – alt. 304
▶ Paris 631 – Lyon 169 – Privas 26 – Valence 65

⚊ Le Plan d'Eau

🖉 04 75 35 44 98. www.campingleplandeau.fr

Address : route de Lussas (situated 2km southeast along the D 259)

Opening times : from beginning May to end Sept.

3 ha (100 pitches) flat, grassy, stony

Tariff : 30.80€ ✶✶ 🚗 🗐 ⚡ (8A) – Extra per person 7.20€ –
Reservation fee 20€

Rental rates : permanent – 25 🛖 – 2 tipis. Per night from
20 to 125€ – Per week from 140 to 890€ – Reservation fee 20€

Good shade cover; pitches near the Ardèche river.

Surroundings : 🐾 🗺 ♤♤		G
Leisure activities : ⓨ ✗ ♨ ⚓ ⚓ 🏊 🎣	Longitude : 4.43296	P
multi-sports ground	Latitude : 44.61872	S
Facilities : ♿ ⚬ᵣ ⛺ launderette		

ST-REMÈZE

07700 – Michelin map **331** J7 – pop. 863 – alt. 365
▶ Paris 645 – Barjac 30 – Bourg-St-Andéol 16 – Pont-St-Esprit 27

⚊ Domaine de Briange

🖉 04 75 04 14 43. www.campingdebriange.com

Address : route de Gras (situated 2km north along the D 362)

4 ha (80 pitches) relatively flat, flat, grassy, stony, sandy

Rentals : ♿ (1 chalet) – 1 'gypsy' caravan – 24 🛖 – 1 cabin in the
trees – 6 canvas bungalows – 6 gîtes.

*Many different rental options are available, some good quality
and many well spaced out.*

Surroundings : 🐾 ♧		G
Leisure activities : ✗ ⚓ ⚒ 🏊	Longitude : 4.5139	P
Facilities : ♿ ⚬ᵣ ⛺ 🔲	Latitude : 44.40615	S

⚠ La Résidence d'Été

🖉 04 75 04 26 87. www.campinglaresidence.com

Address : rue de la Bateuse

1.6 ha (60 pitches) terraced, relatively flat to hilly, grassy, stony, fruit trees
Rentals : 19 🚐.

*Situated very close to the centre of the village; a lovely natural
area beneath cherry trees.*

Surroundings : ≤ ♤♤		G
Leisure activities : ✗ ⚓ 🏊	Longitude : 4.50437	P
Facilities : ♿ ⚬ᵣ ⛺ 🔲 ⚒	Latitude : 44.39105	S

ST-SAUVEUR-DE-CRUZIÈRES

07460 – Michelin map **331** H8 – pop. 535 – alt. 150
▶ Paris 674 – Alès 28 – Barjac 9 – Privas 81

⚊ La Claysse

🖉 04 75 35 40 65. www.campingdelaclaysse.com – for caravans and
campervans, access via the top of the village.

Address : at La Digue (To the northwest of the town; beside the river)

Opening times : from beginning April to mid Sept.

5 ha/1 campable (60 pitches) terraced, flat, grassy

Tariff : 30.50€ ✶✶ 🚗 🗐 ⚡ (10A) – Extra per person 4.50€ –
Reservation fee 15€

Rental rates : (from beginning April to mid Sept.) ⚡ – 13 🚐.
Per night from 50 to 70€ – Per week from 220 to 700€ –
Reservation fee 15€

*Below the road, with some pitches beside the river. The
production and sale of olive oil on site.*

Surroundings : 🗺 ♤♤		G
Leisure activities : ✗ ♨ 🏄 ⚓ ⚓ 🚴 🏊	Longitude : 4.25085	P
🏊 🎣	Latitude : 44.29984	S
Facilities : ♿ ⚬ᵣ 🗑 ⛺ ⛺ ⛺ 🔲		
Nearby : climbing		

ST-SAUVEUR-DE-MONTAGUT

07190 – Michelin map **331** J5 – pop. 1 144 – alt. 218
▶ Paris 597 – Le Cheylard 24 – Lamastre 29 – Privas 24

⚊ L'Ardéchois

🖉 04 75 66 61 87. www.ardechois-camping.fr

Address : situated 8.5km west along the D 102, follow the signs for
Albon

Opening times : from beginning May to end Sept.

37 ha/5 for camping (107 pitches) terraced, flat, grassy

Tariff : 34.95€ ✶✶ 🚗 🗐 ⚡ (10A) – Extra per person 7.35€ –
Reservation fee 23€

Rental rates : (from beginning May to end Sept.) – 18 🚐 –
8 🛖. Per night from 75 to 130€ – Per week from 380 to 785€ –
Reservation fee 23€

Surroundings : 🐾 ≤ ♤♤		G
Leisure activities : ⓨ ✗ ♨ ⚓ ⚓ 🚴 🏊 🎣	Longitude : 4.52294	P
Facilities : ♿ ⚬ᵣ ⛺ ⛺ launderette ⚒	Latitude : 44.82893	S

ST-SYMPHORIEN-SUR-COISE

69590 – Michelin map **327** F6 – pop. 3 438 – alt. 558
▶ Paris 489 – Andrézieux-Bouthéon 26 – L'Arbresle 36 – Feurs 30

⚊ Hurongues

🖉 04 78 48 44 29. www.camping-hurongues.com

Address : 3.5km west along the D 2, follow the signs for Chazelles-
sur-Lyon, 400m from a small lake

3.6 ha (114 pitches) terraced, flat, grassy

In a pleasant wooded setting based around a leisure park.

Surroundings : 🐾 🗺 ♤♤		G
Leisure activities : ♨ ⚓	Longitude : 4.4282	P
Facilities : ⚬ᵣ ⚒ ⛺ 🔲	Latitude : 45.63481	S
Nearby : ✗ 🏊 🎣		

ST-THÉOFFREY

38119 – Michelin map **333** H8 – pop. 444 – alt. 936
▶ Paris 595 – Le Bourg-d'Oisans 44 – Grenoble 33 – La Mure 10

⚊ Au Pré du Lac

🖉 04 76 83 91 34. www.aupredulac.eu

Address : at Pétichet (hamlet), north of St-Théoffrey off the N85, by
the Grand Lac de Laffrey

Opening times : from beginning March to end Oct.

3 ha (96 pitches) flat, grassy

Tariff : ✶ 5€ 🚗 🗐 9€ – ⚡ (10A) 4€ – Reservation fee 8€

Rental rates : (from beginning March to end Oct.) – 4 🚐 – 3 🏠. Per night from 130 to 400€ – Per week from 240 to 770€ – Reservation fee 12.50€

🚽 local sani-station – 🔌 11€

Surroundings : ♀ ⚠
Leisure activities : 🍴 ✖ 🏛 🚣 🏊 🎣 🌊
Facilities : ♿ ⚡ 🏧 🚿 🍴 launderette 🧺
Nearby : 🍽 ⚓

GPS
Longitude : 5.77224
Latitude : 45.00454

ST-VALLIER

26240 – Michelin map **332** B2 – pop. 4 000 – alt. 135
▶ Paris 526 – Annonay 21 – St-Étienne 61 – Tournon-sur-Rhône 16

⚠ Municipal les Îsles de Silon

✆ 04 75 23 22 17. www.saintvallier.com – 🈺

Address : at Les Îles (situated to the north of the town, off the N 7, near the Rhône river)

Opening times : from mid March to mid Nov.

1.35 ha (92 pitches) flat, grassy, stony

Tariff : (2015 price) 🚶 2.80€ 🚗 🔲 4.10€ – ⚡ (10A) 2.50€
Rental rates : (2015 price) (from mid March to mid Nov.) – 4 🚐. Per night from 40 to 120€ – Per week from 260 to 420€

Surroundings : ≾ ⌷ ♀♀
Leisure activities : 🚣
Facilities : ⚡ 🏧 🍴 📷
Nearby : ✖ 🏊

GPS
Longitude : 4.81237
Latitude : 45.1879

STE-CATHERINE

69440 – Michelin map **327** G6 – pop. 911 – alt. 700
▶ Paris 488 – Andrézieux-Bouthéon 38 – L'Arbresle 37 – Feurs 43

⚠ Municipal du Châtelard

✆ 04 78 81 80 60. http://mairie-saintecatherine.fr – alt. 800 – limited spaces for one-night stay

Address : at Le Châtelard (situated 2km south of the village)

Opening times : from beginning March to end Nov.

4 ha (61 pitches) terraced, flat, grassy

Tariff : (2015 price) 🚶 2.30€ 🚗 🔲 2.60€ – ⚡ (6A) 2.90€
🚽 local sani-station 4.50€

Surroundings : ≾ ≺ Mont Pilat and Monts du Lyonnais
Leisure activities : 🏛
Facilities : 🚿 🍴 📷

GPS
Longitude : 4.57344
Latitude : 45.58817

SALAVAS

07150 – Michelin map **331** I7 – pop. 530 – alt. 96
▶ Paris 668 – Lyon 206 – Privas 58 – Nîmes 77

⚠ Le Péquelet

✆ 04 75 88 04 49. www.lepequelet.com

Address : at Le Cros (take the southern exit along the D 579, follow the signs for Barjac and continue along turning to the left for 2km)

Opening times : from beginning April to end Sept.

2 ha (60 pitches) flat, grassy

Tariff : 32.50€ 🚶🚶 🚗 🔲 ⚡ (10A) – Extra per person 8.50€ – Reservation fee 15€

Rental rates : (from beginning April to end Sept.) – 10 🚐 – 5 🏠 – 2 apartments – 2 canvas bungalows. Per night from 40 to 130€ – Per week from 280 to 910€ – Reservation fee 15€

🚽 local sani-station – 🔌 ⚡ 15€

Beside the Ardèche river and surrounded by vineyards.

Surroundings : 🚣 ⌷ ♨ ⚠
Leisure activities : 🏛 🚣 🏊 🎣 🌊
Facilities : ♿ ⚡ 🚿 🍴 📷

GPS
Longitude : 4.39806
Latitude : 44.39075

The Michelin classification (⚠⚠⚠ … ⚠) is totally independent of the official star classification system awarded by the local prefecture or other official organisation.

SALLANCHES

74700 – Michelin map **328** M5 – pop. 15 619 – alt. 550
▶ Paris 585 – Annecy 72 – Bonneville 29 – Chamonix-Mont-Blanc 28

⚠⚠⚠ Tohapi Les Îles

✆ 08 25 00 20 30. www.tohapi.fr

Address : 245 chemin de la Cavettaz (situated 2km to the southeast; beside a stream and 250m from a lake)

Opening times : from mid April to mid Sept.

4.6 ha (260 pitches) flat, grassy, stony

Tariff : (2015 price) 16€ 🚶🚶 🚗 🔲 ⚡ (10A) – Extra per person 4€
Rental rates : (2015 price) (from mid April to mid Sept.) – 74 🚐 – 12 🏠. Per night from 32 to 64€

A thickly wooded site, close to a large leisure complex.

Surroundings : ⌷ ♨
Leisure activities : 🍴 ✖ 🏛 ⊙ daytime 🏃 🚴
Facilities : ♿ ⚡ 🔲 🏧 🚿 🍴 📷 🍴 launderette 🧺
Nearby : 🏊 (beach) 🎣 ⚓ electric boats

GPS
Longitude : 6.65103
Latitude : 45.92404

LA SALLE-EN-BEAUMONT

38350 – Michelin map **333** I8 – pop. 297 – alt. 756
▶ Paris 614 – Le Bourg-d'Oisans 44 – Gap 51 – Grenoble 52

⚠⚠⚠ Le Champ Long

✆ 04 76 30 41 81. www.camping-champlong.com – help moving caravans onto and off pitches avilable on request

Address : at Le Champ-Long (2.7km southwest along the N 85, follow the signs for la Mure and take road to the left)

Opening times : from beginning April to mid Oct.

5 ha (97 pitches) open site, very uneven, terraced, flat, grassy

Tariff : 26€ 🚶🚶 🚗 🔲 ⚡ (10A) – Extra per person 6€ – Reservation fee 15€
Rental rates : (from beginning April to mid Oct.) – 4 🚐 – 14 🏠 – 3 ▭ – 3 studios. Per night from 52 to 105€ – Per week from 310 to 800€ – Reservation fee 15€
🚽 local sani-station 5€ – 4 🔲 18€ – 🔌 13.50€

Surroundings : 🚣 ≺ Lac du Sautet and valley ⌷ ♀♀
Leisure activities : 🍴 ✖ 🏛 ≋ 🚣 🌊 spa facilities
Facilities : ♿ ⚡ 🔲 🍴 launderette 🧺

GPS
Longitude : 5.84416
Latitude : 44.85725

SAMOËNS

74340 – Michelin map **328** N4 – pop. 2 311 – alt. 710
▶ Paris 598 – Lyon 214 – Annecy 82 – Genève 63

⚕ Club Airotel Le Giffre

℘ 04 50 34 41 92. www.camping-samoens.com

Address : at La Glière, by the Giffre river and the Lacs aux Dames

Opening times : permanent

7 ha (212 pitches) flat, grassy, stony

Tariff : 32.60€ ✶✶ 🚐 🔳 ⚡ (10A) – Extra per person 4.60€
Rental rates : permanent ⚙ –1 🚐 –6 🏠 –5 canvas bungalows.
Per night from 46 to 74€ – Per week from 195 to 665€
🚽 Flot Bleu sani-station 6€ – 14 🔳 22.65€ – 🛒 11€

In a pleasant location, near a lake and a leisure park.

Surroundings : ≤ ♀♀ Leisure activities : ☝🎣 Facilities : ⅙ ⊶ ⅢⅢ ♨ ⚴ ♈ launderette Nearby : ♈ ✕ 🛥 ⚼ ♨ 🏊 ≅ ⛷ sports trail, water golf practice	**GPS** Longitude : 6.71917 Latitude : 46.07695

This guide is updated regularly, so buy your new copy every year!

SAMPZON

07120 – Michelin map **351** I7 – pop. 224 – alt. 120
▶ Paris 660 – Lyon 198 – Privas 56 – Nîmes 85

⚕ Yelloh! Village Soleil Vivarais ♦♦

℘ 04 75 39 67 56. www.soleil-vivarais.com

Address : route du Rocher, off the D161, near bridge over the Ardèche river (follow the signs for Vallon Pont d'Arc)

Opening times : from mid April to mid Sept.

12 ha (350 pitches) flat, grassy, stony

Tariff : 55€ ✶✶ 🚐 🔳 ⚡ (10A) – Extra per person 8€
Rental rates : (from mid April to mid Sept.) – 254 🚐 – 5 🏠.
Per night from 39 to 385€ – Per week from 273 to 2.695€

Near a lovely beach on the Ardèche river; mobile homes ranging from good to luxurious.

Surroundings : ♨ ≤ ♀♀ Leisure activities : ♈ ✕ 🍴 ☝🎏 ♈ 🛥 🚲 ♈ 🏊 ≅ (beach) ⚓♨ Facilities : ⅙ ⊶ ⅢⅢ ♨ ♈ launderette ♨ ⚴	**GPS** Longitude : 4.35528 Latitude : 44.42916

⚕ Le Mas de la Source

℘ 04 75 39 67 98. www.campingmasdelasource.com

Address : La Tuillière, off the D161, near the Ardèche river

Opening times : from mid April to end Sept.

1.2 ha (30 pitches) terraced, flat, grassy

Tariff : (2015 price) ✶ 6.90€ 🚐 6.30€ 🔳 28€ – ⚡ (6A) 4.90€ – Reservation fee 8€
Rental rates : (2015 price) (from mid April to end Sept.) ⚙ –11 🚐 – 2 canvas bungalows. Per night from 35 to 104€ – Per week from 150 to 730€ – Reservation fee 10€

Situated on the Presqu'île de Sampzon – peninsula/large bend in the Ardèche river (access); pleasant and shady.

Surroundings : ♨ ▭ ♀♀ Leisure activities : 🛥 🏊 ≅ ♈ Facilities : ⅙ ⊶ ♨ ♈ 🏴	**GPS** Longitude : 4.3466 Latitude : 44.42242

⚕ Sun Camping

℘ 04 75 39 76 12. www.suncamping.com

Address : 10 chemin des Piboux (200m from the Ardèche river)

1.2 ha (70 pitches) terraced, flat, grassy

Rentals : 14 🚐.

On the Presqu'île de Sampzon (river peninsula) with good-quality mobile home rentals.

Surroundings : ♨ ♀♀ Leisure activities : ♈ 🛥 🏊 Facilities : ⅙ ⊶ ♨ ♈ launderette Nearby : ⚴ ✕ ⚼ ≅	**GPS** Longitude : 4.35352 Latitude : 44.42895

SATILLIEU

07290 – Michelin map **331** J3 – pop. 1 616 – alt. 485
▶ Paris 542 – Annonay 13 – Lamastre 36 – Privas 87

⚕ Municipal le Grangeon

℘ 04 75 67 84 86. www.lalouvesc.com

Address : chemin de l'Hermuzière (head 1.1km southwest along the D 578a; follow the signs for Lalouvesc and take turning to the left)

Opening times : from beginning May to end Sept.

1 ha (52 pitches) terraced, flat, grassy

Tariff : (2015 price) ✶ 2.60€ 🚐 1.80€ 🔳 2.80€ – ⚡ (10A) 3.30€
Rental rates : (2015 price) (from beginning May to end Sept.) – 5 🚐. Per night from 45 to 50€ – Per week from 188 to 343€
🚽 Eurorelais sani-station 2€

Both the pitches and the chalets have good shade; beside the Ay river and an attractive lake.

Surroundings : ♨ ▭ ♀♀ Leisure activities : 🛶 Facilities : ⅙ ⊶ ⚴ ♈ ♈ 🏴 Nearby : ≅ (fresh water)	**GPS** Longitude : 4.60389 Latitude : 45.14438

SCIEZ

74140 – Michelin map **328** L3 – pop. 5 269 – alt. 406
▶ Paris 561 – Abondance 37 – Annecy 69 – Annemasse 24

⚕ Le Chatelet

℘ 04 50 72 52 60. www.camping-chatelet.com – limited spaces for one-night stay

Address : 658 chemin des Hutins Vieux (3km northeast along the N 5, follow the signs for Thonon-les-Bains and turn left onto the rte du Port at Sciez-Plage, 300m from the beach)

Opening times : from beginning April to end Oct.

2.5 ha (121 pitches) flat, grassy, stony

Tariff : 23.50€ ✶✶ 🚐 🔳 ⚡ (10A) – Extra per person 5.80€ – Reservation fee 8€
Rental rates : (from beginning March to end Oct.) ⅙ (1 chalet) – 12 🏠 – 2 tent lodges. Per night from 29 to 139€ – Per week from 189 to 973€ – Reservation fee 12€
🚽 local sani-station 4€

There are some pitches for tents and caravans, but a good number of owner-occupier mobile homes.

Surroundings : ♨ Leisure activities : 🛥 🚲 Facilities : ⅙ ⊶ ⅢⅢ ♨ ♈ launderette Nearby : ✕ ≅ ♈ pedalos	**GPS** Longitude : 6.39705 Latitude : 46.34079

SÉEZ

73700 – Michelin map **333** N4 – pop. 2 332 – alt. 904
▶ Paris 638 – Albertville 57 – Bourg-St-Maurice 4 – Moûtiers 31

⚠ Le Reclus

🕾 0479410105. www.campinglereclus.com

Address : route de Tignes (take northwestern exit along the N 90, follow the signs for Bourg-St-Maurice; beside the Reclus river)

Opening times : permanent

1.5 ha (108 pitches) terraced, relatively flat, grassy, stony

Tariff : 22€ ♟ ♟ ⇔ ▣ (10A) – Extra per person 5.25€ – Reservation fee 5€

Rental rates : permanent – 1 'gypsy' caravan – 6 ⌂ – 2 ⌂ – 6 yurts – 1 apartment – 1 tipi. Per night from 50 to 80€ – Per week from 350 to 650€ – Reservation fee 10€

🚐 local sani-station 5€ – 6 ▣ 14€ – 🚲12€

Choose the pitches furthest away from the road in preference.

Surroundings : ❄ ♀♀
Leisure activities : 🏠 ♟
Facilities : 🛁 🚿 ▦ 🍴 launderette

Longitude : 6.7927
Latitude : 45.62583

SERRIÈRES-DE-BRIORD

01470 – Michelin map **328** F6 – pop. 1 143 – alt. 218
▶ Paris 481 – Belley 29 – Bourg-en-Bresse 57 – Crémieu 24

⚠ Le Point Vert

🕾 0474361345. www.camping-ain-bugey.com – limited spaces for one-night stay

Address : route du Point Vert (2.5km west, at the leisure and activity park)

Opening times : from beginning April to beginning Oct.

1.9 ha (137 pitches) flat, grassy

Tariff : (2015 price) 24€ ♟ ♟ ⇔ ▣ (6A) – Extra per person 5€

Rental rates : (2015 price) (from beginning April to beginning Oct.) – 5 ⌂. Per week from 400 to 550€

Situated beside a small lake near the Rhône river.

Surroundings : ⟨ ♀ ⚠
Leisure activities : 🏠 ⏰daytime 🏌 ♟ 🚲 🐟
Facilities : 🛁 🚿 ⛳ ⛺ 🚰 🍴 launderette 🏠
Nearby : 🍴 ✕ 🏊 ✂ 🏖(beach) ♣ pedalos

Longitude : 5.42731
Latitude : 45.81633

SÉVRIER

74320 – Michelin map **328** J5 – pop. 3 835 – alt. 456
▶ Paris 541 – Albertville 41 – Annecy 6 – Megève 55

⚠ Le Panoramic

🕾 0450524309. www.camping-le-panoramic.com

Address : 22 chemin des Bernets (located 3.5km to the south)

Opening times : from end April to end Sept.

3 ha (189 pitches) flat, relatively flat, grassy

Tariff : 29.50€ ♟ ♟ ⇔ ▣ (10A) – Extra per person 6€ – Reservation fee 10€

Rental rates : (from mid April to end Sept.) – 20 ⌂ – 14 ⌂ – 3 studios – 4 apartments. Per night from 50 to 90€ – Per week from 275 to 950€ – Reservation fee 10€

🚐 local sani-station 6€

Surroundings : ⟨ ♀♀
Leisure activities : 🍴 ✕ 🏠 ⏰daytime 🏌 🐟
Facilities : 🛁 🚿 🍴 launderette 🏠 🏠

Longitude : 6.1417
Latitude : 45.84308

⚠ Au Coeur du Lac

🕾 0450524645. www.campingaucoeurdulac.com 🚭

Address : 3233 route d'Albertville (located 1km to the south)

Opening times : from beginning April to end Sept.

1.7 ha (105 pitches) terraced, relatively flat, grassy, fine gravel

Tariff : (2015 price) 28.50€ ♟ ♟ ⇔ ▣ (6A) – Extra per person 5.50€

Rental rates : (2015 price) (from mid April to end Sept.) 🚭 – 10 ⌂. Per week from 290 to 730€ – Reservation fee 12€

🚐 local sani-station – 20 ▣ 18€

In an attractive location near the lake (direct access).

Surroundings : ⟨ ☐ ♀
Leisure activities : 🏠 ⏰daytime 🏌 🚲 🚭
Facilities : 🛁 🚿 ▦ 🏠 🍴 launderette
Nearby : ✂ 🐟

Longitude : 6.14399
Latitude : 45.85487

SEYSSEL

01420 – Michelin map **328** H5 – pop. 948 – alt. 258
▶ Paris 517 – Aix-les-Bains 33 – Annecy 41 – Genève 52

⚠ L' International

🕾 0450592847. www.camp-inter.fr

Address : chemin de la Barotte (2.4km southwest along the D 992, follow the signs for Culoz and take the road to the right)

Opening times : from beginning April to end Sept.

1.5 ha (45 pitches) terraced, flat, grassy

Tariff : 24€ ♟ ♟ ⇔ ▣ (10A) – Extra per person 4.50€ – Reservation fee 12€

Rental rates : (from beginning March to end Oct.) – 15 ⌂. Per night from 57 to 114€ – Per week from 240 to 714€ – Reservation fee 17€

🚐 5 ▣ 20€

A peaceful setting in an elevated location.

Surroundings : 🏊 ⟨ ☐ ♀
Leisure activities : ✕ 🏠 🏌 🚲 ♟
Facilities : 🚿 🍴 launderette 🏠

Longitude : 5.82349
Latitude : 45.94957

SEYSSEL

74910 – Michelin map **328** I5 – pop. 2 262 – alt. 252
▶ Paris 517 – Aix-les-Bains 32 – Annecy 40

⚠ Le Nant-Matraz

🕾 0450485640. www.camping-seyssel.com

Address : 15 route de Genève (take the northern exit along the D 992)

Opening times : from beginning April to end Sept.

1 ha (67 pitches) flat and relatively flat, grassy

Tariff : (2015 price) 16€ ♟ ♟ ⇔ ▣ (16A) – Extra per person 3.50€

Rental rates : (2015 price) (from beginning April to end Sept.) 🚭 – 1 ⌂ – 4 tipis – 10 canvas bungalows – 1 tent lodge. Per night from 50 to 80€ – Per week from 210 to 390€

🚐 local sani-station 5€ – 6 ▣ 16€

Choose the pitches overlooking the Rhône river.

Surroundings : ☐ ♀♀
Leisure activities : 🍴 ✕ 🏊 (small swimming pool)
Facilities : 🚿 🏠 🍴 launderette
Nearby : 🐟

Longitude : 5.83574
Latitude : 45.96339

TANINGES

74440 – Michelin map **328** M4 – pop. 3 414 – alt. 640
▶ Paris 570 – Annecy 68 – Bonneville 24 – Chamonix-Mont-Blanc 51

� Municipal des Thézières

𝒫 04 50 34 25 59. www.prazdelys-sommand.com

Address : les Vernays-sous-la-Ville (take the southern exit, follow the signs for Cluses; beside the Foron river and 150m from the Giffre)

Opening times : permanent

2 ha (113 pitches)

Tariff : (2015 price) 15€ ✱✱ ⇄ 🅴 🅙 (10A) – Extra per person 2.90€
🚻 local sani-station 4.90€ – 3 🅴 10.10€
Situated in a pretty green park with shade, near a fast-flowing stream.

Surroundings : 🌿 ⩽ 🌳🌳
Leisure activities : 🎣
Facilities : 🕭 ⚍ 🏢 🍴 launderette
Nearby : 🍽 🛴 🍴

GPS	Longitude : 6.58837 Latitude : 46.09866

This guide is updated regularly, so buy your new copy every year!

TERMIGNON

73500 – Michelin map **333** N6 – pop. 423 – alt. 1 290
▶ Paris 680 – Bessans 18 – Chambéry 120 – Lanslebourg-Mont-Cenis 6

⚠ Les Mélèzes

𝒫 04 79 20 51 41. www.camping-termignon-lavanoisecom

Address : route du Doron (in the village; beside some rapids)

Opening times : from beginning May to mid Oct.

0.7 ha (66 pitches) flat, grassy

Tariff : (2015 price) 18€ ✱✱ ⇄ 🅴 🅙 (10A) – Extra per person 3.10€
Rental rates : (from beginning May to mid Oct.) 🚫 – 4 🚗.
Per night from 65 to 80€ – Per week from 420 to 480€

The shaded pitches lie beside the Arc river.

Surroundings : 🌿 ⩽ 🌳🌳
Leisure activities : 🏠 🎣
Facilities : 🕭 ⚍ (midJune–mid Sept.) 🚿 🏢
🍴 🍽

GPS	Longitude : 6.81535 Latitude : 45.27815

LA TOUSSUIRE

73300 – Michelin map **333** K6 – alt. 1 690
▶ Paris 651 – Albertville 78 – Chambéry 91 – St-Jean-de-Maurienne 16

🏔 Caravaneige du Col

𝒫 04 79 83 00 80. www.camping-du-col.com – alt. 1 640

Address : 1 km east of La Toussuire, on rte de St-Jean-de-Maurienne

0.8 ha (40 pitches) flat, grassy

Rentals : 7 🚗 – 3 🏡 – 2 apartments.
🚻 local sani-station
There's a free shuttle service to the ski resort.

Surroundings : ❄ ⩽ Les Aiguilles d'Arves (peaks) 🌳
Leisure activities : 🍴🍽 🎠 🕗daytime ⛷
🛴 🎣
Facilities : 🕭 ⚍ 🏢 🚿 🍴 launderette

GPS	Longitude : 6.2739 Latitude : 45.25727

TREPT

38460 – Michelin map **333** E3 – pop. 1 741 – alt. 275
▶ Paris 495 – Belley 41 – Bourgoin-Jallieu 13 – Lyon 52

🏔 Sites et Paysages Les 3 Lacs du Soleil

𝒫 04 74 92 92 06. www.camping-les3lacsdusoleil.com

Address : at La Plaine Serrière (2.7km east along the D 517, follow the signs for Morestel and take the road to the right, near two lakes)

Opening times : from end April to mid Sept.

25 ha/3 for camping (160 pitches) flat, grassy

Tariff : (2015 price) 36.50€ ✱✱ ⇄ 🅴 🅙 (6A) – Extra per person 7€ – Reservation fee 10€

Rental rates : (2015 price) (from end April to mid Sept.) – 30 🚗 – 7 🏡 – 20 canvas bungalows – 4 tent lodges. Per night from 59 to 101€ – Per week from 414 to 924€ – Reservation fee 10€

🚻 AireService sani-station 12€ – 🔋🅙16€

Surroundings : 🌿 🌳 ⛰
Leisure activities : 🍴 ✗ 🏠 🕗daytime 🏃
🛴 🍴 🎣 🚣 🏊 (beach) ⛵ 🎣
Facilities : 🕭 ⚍ 🍴 launderette

GPS	Longitude : 5.33447 Latitude : 45.69039

TULETTE

26790 – Michelin map **332** C8 – pop. 1 915 – alt. 147
▶ Paris 648 – Avignon 53 – Bollène 15 – Nyons 20

⚠ Les Rives de l'Aygues

𝒫 04 75 98 37 50. www.lesrivesdelaygues.com

Address : route de Cairanne (head 3km south along the D 193 and take road to the left)

Opening times : from beginning May to end Sept.

3.6 ha (100 pitches) flat, grassy, stony

Tariff : (2015 price) 28.60€ ✱✱ ⇄ 🅴 🅙 (6A) – Extra per person 4.10€ – Reservation fee 10€

Rental rates : (2015 price) (from beginning May to end Sept.) 🚫 – 2 🚗 – 6 🏡. Per night from 42 to 96€ – Per week from 293 to 670€ – Reservation fee 10€

In a natural setting among vineyards.

Surroundings : 🌿 🏠 🌳🌳
Leisure activities : 🍴 ✗ 🏠 🛴 🎣
Facilities : 🕭 ⚍ 🚿 🍴 🏢 🎣

GPS	Longitude : 4.933 Latitude : 44.2648

UCEL

07200 – Michelin map **331** I6 – pop. 1 929 – alt. 270
▶ Paris 626 – Aubenas 6 – Montélimar 44 – Privas 31

🏔 Domaine de Gil ▲▲

𝒫 04 75 94 63 63. www.domaine-de-gil.com 🚫

Address : route de Vals (take northwestern exit along the D 578b)

Opening times : from mid April to mid Sept.

4.8 ha/2 for camping (80 pitches) flat, grassy, stony

Tariff : (2015 price) 40€ ✱✱ ⇄ 🅴 🅙 (10A) – Extra per person 7€ – Reservation fee 22€

Rental rates : (2015 price) (from mid April to mid Sept.) 🚫 – 52 🚗. Per night from 50 to 135€ – Per week from 250 to 945€ – Reservation fee 22€

🚻 local sani-station

Well-shaded pitches and mobile homes, in a very pleasant natural setting beside the Ardèche river.

Surroundings : 🐟 ⚘ 🎠 △
Leisure activities : ☂ ✕ 🏠 🎮nighttime 🎯 jacuzzi 🚣 ⛷ 🏓 🎣 🛶 🏊 multi-sports ground
Facilities : ♿ ⛽ 🚿 ♨ 🧺 launderette 🚐

G P S Longitude : 4.37959
Latitude : 44.64308

VAGNAS

07150 – Michelin map **331** I7 – pop. 521 – alt. 200
▶ Paris 670 – Aubenas 40 – Barjac 5 – St-Ambroix 20

🏔 La Rouvière-Les Pins

📞 0475386141. www.rouviere07.com

Address : at La Rouviere (take the southern exit following signs for Barjac then continue 1.5km along road to the right)

Opening times : from end March to mid Sept.

2 ha (100 pitches) terraced, relatively flat, flat, grassy

Tariff : (2015 price) 25€ ✚✚ 🚗 📺 ⚡ (6A) – Extra per person 6.50€ – Reservation fee 15€

Rental rates : (2015 price) (from end March to mid Sept.) 🚐 – 2 🏠 – 2 apartments – 3 canvas bungalows. Per week from 250 to 730€ – Reservation fee 15€

A spacious site in the heart of wine-growing country.

Surroundings : 🐟 ⚘
Leisure activities : ☂ 🏠 🚣 🎣
Facilities : ♿ ⛽ 🚿 🅿 ♨ 🧺 🚐

G P S Longitude : 4.34194
Latitude : 44.3419

We have selected the best campsites in France with our usual care, listing those with the best facilities in the most pleasant surroundings.

VALLON-PONT-D'ARC

07150 – Michelin map **331** I7 – pop. 2 337 – alt. 117
▶ Paris 658 – Alès 47 – Aubenas 32 – Avignon 81

🏔 Les Castels Nature Parc l'Ardéchois 👥

📞 0475880663. www.ardechois-camping.com

Address : route Touristique des Gorges de l'Ardèche (located 1.5km southeast along the D 290)

Opening times : from mid March to end Sept.

5 ha (240 pitches) flat, grassy

Tariff : 58€ ✚✚ 🚗 📺 ⚡ (10A) – Extra per person 11€ – Reservation fee 40€

Rental rates : (from mid March to end Sept.) – 25 🏠. Per week from 491 to 1,540€ – Reservation fee 40€

🚐 local sani-station 10€

In a green setting with some very well-equipped pitches and an attractive terraced layout, above the Ardèche river.

Surroundings : 🐟 ⚘ 🎠 ⚘ △
Leisure activities : ☂ ✕ 🏠 🎮 🎯 🚣 ⛷ 🏓 🎣 🛶 multi-sports ground
Facilities : ♿ ⛽ 🚿 📮 🚻 🅿 ♨ 🧺 launderette 🚐
Nearby : 🏇

G P S Longitude : 4.39673
Latitude : 44.39672

🏔 La Roubine 👥

📞 0475880456. www.camping-roubine.com

Address : route de Ruoms (located 1.5km west)

Opening times : from mid April to mid Sept.

7 ha/4 for camping (135 pitches) flat, grassy, sandy

Tariff : 54€ ✚✚ 🚗 📺 ⚡ (10A) – Extra per person 11€ – Reservation fee 30€

Rental rates : (from mid April to mid Sept.) ♿ (1 mobile home) 🚐 – 38 🏠. Per night from 65 to 245€ – Per week from 455 to 1,710 € – Reservation fee 30€

An attractive campsite beside the Ardèche river; some high-quality mobile homes and good sanitary facilities.

Surroundings : 🐟 🎠 ⚘ △
Leisure activities : ☂ ✕ 🏠 🎮 🎯 🛶 jacuzzi 🚣 ⛷ 🏓 🎣 multi-sports ground, spa centre
Facilities : ♿ ⛽ 🚿 🚻 ♨ 🧺 launderette 🚐 🚐

G P S Longitude : 4.37835
Latitude : 44.40636

🏔 Mondial-Camping 👥

📞 0475880044. www.mondial-camping.com

Address : route des Gorges de l'Ardèche (located 1.5km southeast)

Opening times : from beginning April to end Sept.

4 ha (240 pitches) flat, grassy

Tariff : 46€ ✚✚ 🚗 📺 ⚡ (10A) – Extra per person 9.50€ – Reservation fee 30€

Rental rates : (from beginning April to end Sept.) 🚐 – 24 🏠 – 7 canvas bungalows. Per night from 60 to 120€ – Per week from 340 to 1,200€ – Reservation fee 30€

🚐 local sani-station

A green site beside the Ardèche river, with some pitches well marked out.

Surroundings : ⚘ ⚘ △
Leisure activities : ☂ ✕ 🏠 🎮 🎯 🚣 ⛷ 🎣 🐾 multi-sports ground
Facilities : ♿ ⛽ 🚿 🅿 ♨ 🚻 launderette 🚐
Nearby : 🏇

G P S Longitude : 4.40139
Latitude : 44.39695

🏔 International

📞 0475880099. www.internationalcamping07.com

Address : La Plaine Salavas (located 1km southwest)

Opening times : from beginning May to end Sept.

2.7 ha (120 pitches) relatively flat, flat, grassy, sandy

Tariff : 40€ ✚✚ 🚗 📺 ⚡ (10A) – Extra per person 8€ – Reservation fee 10€

Rental rates : (from beginning April to end Sept.) – 14 🏠 – 2 🏠. Per night from 50 to 120€ – Per week from 250 to 820€ – Reservation fee 10€

🚐 local sani-station – 10 📺 20€

Choose those pitches beside the Ardèche river, furthest from the bridge.

Surroundings : ⚘ ⚘ △
Leisure activities : ☂ ✕ 🚣 🎣
Facilities : ♿ ⛽ 🅿 ♨ 🧺 🚐 🚐

G P S Longitude : 4.38203
Latitude : 44.39925

To make the best possible use of this guide, please read pages 2–15 carefully.

⛰ L'Esquiras

✆ 0475880416. www.camping-esquiras.com

Address : chemin du Fez (2.8km northwest along the D 579, follow the signs for Ruoms and take the road to the right after the Intermarché service station)

Opening times : from beginning April to end Sept.

2 ha (106 pitches) relatively flat, flat, grassy, stony

Tariff : (2015 price) 39€ ✶✶ 🚗 🗐 🗐 (10A) – Extra per person 8€ – Reservation fee 16€

Rental rates : (2015 price) (from beginning April to end Sept.) – 46 🚐 – 1 🏠. Per night from 46 to 167€ – Per week from 322 to 1,169€ – Reservation fee 16€

🚐 local sani-station 4€ – 6 🗐 12€

In a green setting, with space for relaxation and good-quality mobile homes.

Surroundings : 🛶 ≤ 🗐🗐
Leisure activities : ✗ 🗐 🛶🛶🛶
Facilities : 🖐 ⚬🗝 🖐🗐 🖐 🗐
Nearby : forest trail

Longitude : 4.37913
Latitude : 44.41536

⛰ La Rouvière ▲:

✆ 0475371007. www.campinglarouviere.com

Address : route des Gorges Chames (6.6km southeast along the D 290; at Chames)

Opening times : from mid March to mid Oct.

3 ha (153 pitches) terraced, relatively flat, sandy

Tariff : 32€ ✶✶ 🚗 🗐 🗐 (10A) – Extra per person 9€ – Reservation fee 12€

Rental rates : (from mid March to mid Oct.) – 39 🚐 – 3 🏠 – 13 canvas bungalows. Per night from 49 to 119€ – Per week from 290 to 940€ – Reservation fee 15€

Below the road, beside the Ardèche river, with well-organised canoeing activities.

Surroundings : 🗐🗐 ⛰
Leisure activities : ✗ 🏊 🛶🛶 🗐 🚣
multi-sports ground
Facilities : ⚬🗝🖐🗐🗐 🗐

Longitude : 4.42649
Latitude : 44.37796

⛰ Le Midi

✆ 0475880678. www.camping-midi.com

Address : route des Gorges de l'Ardèche (6.5km southeast along the D 290; at Chames)

1.6 ha (52 pitches) terraced, relatively flat, sandy, grassy

Rentals : 6 🚐.

Below the road, a spacious site near the Ardèche river, with well-organised canoeing activities. Groups are welcome.

Surroundings : 🛶 🗐 🗐🗐 ⛰
Leisure activities : 🛶🛶 🗐 🚣
Facilities : 🖐 ⚬🗝 🖐 🗐 🗐
Nearby : ✗

Longitude : 4.42093
Latitude : 44.37672

For more information on visiting particular towns or regions, consult the relevant regional MICHELIN Green Guide. We also recommend you use the appropriate Michelin regional map to locate your selected campsite, to calculate distances and to work out the best route.

VALLORCINE

74660 – Michelin map **328** O4 – pop. 419 – alt. 1 260 – Winter sports : 1 260/1 400 m
▶ Paris 628 – Annecy 115 – Chamonix-Mont-Blanc 19 – Thonon-les-Bains 96

⛰ Les Montets

✆ 0679021881. www.camping-montets.fr – alt. 1 300

Address : 671 route du Treuil, at Le Montet (2.8km southwest along the N 506, access via Chemin de la Gare, at Le Buet)

Opening times : from beginning June to mid Sept.

1.7 ha (75 pitches) open site, terraced, relatively flat, flat, grassy, stony

Tariff : (2015 price) ✶ 4.50€ 🚗 1.50€ 🗐 5.90€ – 🗐 (6A) 3.50€

In a pleasant setting near a stream and the small railway line connecting St-Gervais with Châtelart (Switzerland).

Surroundings : 🛶 ≤ 🗐
Leisure activities : ✗
Facilities : 🖐 ⚬🗝 🅿 🖐 🗐
Nearby : 🚲 🚣

Longitude : 6.92376
Latitude : 46.02344

Some campsites benefit from proximity to a municipal leisure centre.

LES VANS

07140 – Michelin map **331** G7 – pop. 2 805 – alt. 170
▶ Paris 663 – Alès 44 – Aubenas 37 – Pont-St-Esprit 66

⛰ Le Pradal

✆ 0475372516. www.camping-lepradal.com

Address : 1.5km west along the D 901

Opening times : from beginning April to end Sept.

1 ha (36 pitches) terraced, relatively flat, stony, grassy

Tariff : ✶ 6.50€ 🚗 🗐 20€ – 🗐 (6A) 3.90€

Rental rates : (from beginning April to end Sept.) – 5 🚐 – 1 🏠. Per night from 55 to 70€ – Per week from 220 to 700€

🚐 local sani-station 5€ – 3 🗐 20€

Numerous pitches on small, individual terraces enclosed by hedges.

Surroundings : 🗐🗐
Leisure activities : 🗐 🗐 🛶 multi-sports ground
Facilities : 🖐 ⚬🗝 🖐 🗐

Longitude : 4.11023
Latitude : 44.40809

VERCHAIX

74440 – Michelin map **328** N4 – pop. 661 – alt. 800
▶ Paris 580 – Annecy 74 – Chamonix-Mont-Blanc 59 – Genève 52

⛰ Municipal Lac et Montagne

✆ 0450901012. www.mairie-verchaix.fr – alt. 660

Address : 1.8km south along the D 907; beside the Giffre river

2 ha (104 pitches) open site, flat, grassy, stony

Choose the pitches furthest away from the busy road.

Surroundings : ≤ 🗐
Leisure activities : 🛶🛶 🗐 🚣
Facilities : 🖐 ⚬🗝 🗐 launderette
Nearby : 🗐 ✗ 🗐

Longitude : 6.67527
Latitude : 46.09001

VERNIOZ

38150 – Michelin map **333** C5 – pop. 1 182 – alt. 250
▶ Paris 500 – Annonay 38 – Givors 25 – Le Péage-de-Roussillon 12

⚏ Le Bontemps

☎ 04 74 57 83 52. www.camping-lebontemps.com

Address : 5 impasse du Bontemps (4.5km east along the D 37 and take the road to the right; beside the Varèze river, at St-Alban-de-Varèze)

Opening times : from mid April to end Sept.

6 ha (175 pitches), flat, grassy, lake

Tariff : 29€ ★★ 🚐 📵 ⚡ (10A) – Extra per person 7€
Rental rates : (from mid April to end Sept.) 🏕 – 10 🛖 – 1 🏠. Per night from 40 to 115€ – Per week from 180 to 805€

Surroundings : 🏊 ➰ ♨♨
Leisure activities : ♟ ✕ 🏠 🎣 🏊 🚴 ➰ ✂
🏛 🖼 (open air in season) 🎿 entertainment room
Facilities : 🚻 ⛟ 📧🛁 🚿 ♨ launderette 🚲

Longitude : 4.92836
Latitude : 45.42798

VILLARD-DE-LANS

38250 – Michelin map **333** G7 – pop. 4 031 – alt. 1 040
▶ Paris 584 – Die 67 – Grenoble 34 – Lyon 123

⚏ FranceLoc Domaine de L'Oursière

☎ 04 76 95 14 77. www.camping-oursiere.fr

Address : avenue du Général de Gaulle (take the northern exit along the D 531. follow the signs for Grenoble; pedestrian path to village)

Opening times : from beginning Dec. to end Sept.

4 ha (189 pitches) relatively flat, flat, grassy, gravelled, stony

Tariff : (2015 price) 22€ ★★ 🚐 📵 ⚡ (10A) – Extra per person 7€ – Reservation fee 11€
Rental rates : (from beginning Dec. to end Sept.) – 53 🛖 – 4 🏠. Per night from 58 to 82€ – Per week from 231 to 665€ – Reservation fee 27€

🚉 AireService sani-station 5.50€ – 34 📵 19€

Surroundings : ❄ ⟨
Leisure activities : 🏠 🏊 🏛 🖼 🎣 ⛷ 🎿
spa facilities
Facilities : 🚻 ⛟ 📧 🛁 ♨ 🚲 🚿
Nearby : bowling

Longitude : 5.55639
Latitude : 45.0775

VILLARS-LES-DOMBES

01330 – Michelin map **328** D4 – pop. 4 328 – alt. 281
▶ Paris 433 – Bourg-en-Bresse 29 – Lyon 37 – Villefranche-sur-Saône 29

⚏ Indigo Le Nid du Parc 👥

☎ 04 74 98 00 21. www.lenidduparc.com – limited spaces for one-night stay

Address : 164 avenue des Nations (southwestern exit, RD 1083 following signs for Lyon and take a left turn; near the swimming pool)

Opening times : from mid April to beginning Nov.

5 ha (191 pitches) fairly flat, grassy

Tariff : (2015 price) 26.90€ ★★ 🚐 📵
⚡ (6A) – Extra per person 5.50€

Rental rates : (2015 price) (from mid April to beginning Nov.)
🏕 – 4 'gypsy' caravans. Per night from 90 to 110€ – Reservation fee 10€

🚉 Flot Bleu sani-station 5€

In a pleasant setting in partial shade beside the Chalaronne river.

Surroundings : 🏊 ➰ ♨
Leisure activities : ✕ 🏠 🏊 🚴 ➰
Facilities : 🚻 ⛟ 🛁 ♨ launderette
Nearby : ✂ 🎣

Longitude : 5.03039
Latitude : 45.99749

VINSOBRES

26110 – Michelin map **332** D7 – pop. 1 109 – alt. 247
▶ Paris 662 – Bollène 29 – Grignan 24 – Nyons 9

⚏ Franceloc Le Sagittaire 👥

☎ 04 75 27 00 00. www.campings-franceloc.fr

Address : at le Pont de Mirabel (junction of D 94 and D 4, near the Eygues – direct access)

Opening times : from end March to mid Nov.

14 ha/8 for camping (274 pitches) flat, grassy, gravelled

Tariff : (2015 price) 45€ ★★ 🚐 📵 ⚡ (10A) – Extra per person 8€ – Reservation fee 27€
Rental rates : (2015 price) (from end March to mid Nov.) – 6 'gypsy' caravans – 159 🛖 – 61 🏠 – 4 tipis – 2 gîtes. Per night from 34 to 131€ – Per week from 168 to 1,603€ – Reservation fee 27€

There's an attractive swimming and play area.

Surroundings : ⟨ ➰ ♨♨
Leisure activities : ♟ ✕ 🏠 🎣 🏊 🚴
✂ 🏛 🖼 🎣 (beach) 🎿 multi-sports ground
Facilities : 🚻 ⛟ 📧 🛁 🚿 ♨ launderette
🍴 🚲

Longitude : 5.08002
Latitude : 44.22661

⚏ Municipal

☎ 04 75 27 61 65. camping-municipal@club-internet.fr

Address : district Champessier (located south of the town along the D 190; by the stadium)

Opening times : from end March to end Oct.

1.9 ha (70 pitches) flat, grassy, stony

Tariff : (2015 price) ★ 3.25€ 🚐 2.25€ 📵 2.25€ – ⚡ (8A) 3.15€
Rental rates : (2015 price) (from end March to end Oct.) – 1 🛖. Per week from 350 to 450€

Surroundings : ⟨ ♨♨
Leisure activities : 🏊
Facilities : 🚻 ⛟ 📧 ♨ 🖼 refrigerators

Longitude : 5.06594
Latitude : 44.32912

Michelin classification:

⚏⚏⚏⚏ *Extremely comfortable, equipped to a very high standard*

⚏⚏⚏ *Very comfortable, equipped to a high standard*

⚏⚏ *Comfortable and well equipped*

⚏ *Reasonably comfortable*

⚏ *Satisfactory*

VION

07610 – Michelin map **331** K3 – pop. 905 – alt. 128
▶ Paris 537 – Annonay 30 – Lamastre 34 – Tournon-sur-Rhône 7

⛰ L'Iserand

✆ 0475080173. www.iserandcampingardeche.com

Address : 1307 rue Royale (located 1km north along the N 86, follow the signs for Lyon)

Opening times : from mid April to mid Sept.

1.3 ha (60 pitches), terraced, stony, grassy

Tariff : 16€ ✦✦ ⛟ ▣ ⊞ (10A) – Extra per person 6€

Rental rates : (from mid April to mid Sept.) ⌇ – 8 ⌂. Per night from 40 to 90€ – Per week from 200 to 640€

🚐 local sani-station

Choose those pitches furthest away from the road in preference.

Surroundings : ⩽ 🛇🛇
Leisure activities : ✗ ⚓ ⋔ 🛝
Facilities : ♿ ⊶ ⌖ 🍴 📷 🐾

Longitude : 4.80027
Latitude : 45.12117

To make the best possible use of this guide, please read pages 2–15 carefully.

VIZILLE

38220 – Michelin map **333** H7 – pop. 7 592 – alt. 270
▶ Paris 582 – Le Bourg-d'Oisans 32 – Grenoble 20 – La Mure 22

⚠ Le Bois de Cornage

✆ 0683181787. www.campingvizille.com

Address : chemin du Camping (take the northern exit towards the N 85, follow the signs for Grenoble and turn right onto av. de Venaria)

Opening times : from beginning April to end Oct.

2.5 ha (128 pitches) terraced, relatively flat, grassy

Tariff : 22€ ✦✦ ⛟ ▣ ⊞ (16A) – Extra per person 5.30€ – Reservation fee 10€

Rental rates : permanent – 22 ⌂ – 2 tent lodges. Per night from 40 to 85€ – Per week from 190 to 485€ – Reservation fee 10€

🚐 local sani-station 3.50€

Part of the site is shaded by ancient trees.

Surroundings : 🛇 ⩽ 🛇🛇
Leisure activities : ✗ ⚓ 🛝
Facilities : ⊶ ▥ 🍴 📷 🐾

Longitude : 5.76948
Latitude : 45.08706

VOGÜÉ

07200 – Michelin map **331** I6 – pop. 917 – alt. 150
▶ Paris 638 – Aubenas 9 – Largentière 16 – Privas 40

⛰⛰ Domaine du Cros d'Auzon 👥

✆ 0475377586. www.domaine-cros-auzon.com

Address : 2.5km south along the D 579 and take road to the right

Opening times : from beginning April to mid Sept.

18 ha/6 for camping (170 pitches), flat, grassy, sandy, stony

Tariff : 49€ ✦✦ ⛟ ▣ ⊞ (6A) – Extra per person 7€ – Reservation fee 12€

Rental rates : (from beginning April to mid Sept.) ♿ (5 mobile homes) – 37 ⌂ – 4 ⌂ – 37 ⌂. Per night from 28 to 117€ – Per week from 357 to 1,036€ – Reservation fee 12€

🚐 local sani-station

The lower part of the site is near the river with shaded pitches, the upper part features the services: water park, restaurant, hotel.

Surroundings : 🛇 🖵 🛇🛇
Leisure activities : ⛾ ✗ 🎯 ▣ ⛹ ⚓ 🛝
🖥 🛝 🚣 ⛲ 🎣
Facilities : ♿ ⊶ ⌖ 🐾 ⛽ 🍴 launderette 🐾

Longitude : 4.40678
Latitude : 44.53178

⛰ Les Roches

✆ 0475377045. www.campinglesroches.fr

Address : district Bausson (located 1.5km south along the D 579; at Vogüé-Gare, 200m from the Auzon and the Ardèche rivers)

Opening times : from beginning May to mid Sept.

2.5 ha (100 pitches), undulating, flat, rocky, grassy

Tariff : (2015 price) 30.50€ ✦✦ ⛟ ▣ ⊞ (10A) – Extra per person 6.50€

Rental rates : (2015 price) (from beginning May to mid Sept.) ⌇ – 8 ⌂. Per week from 180 to 650€

🚐 local sani-station 4€

Shaded pitches on small terraces, in a wild setting among rocks.

Surroundings : 🛇 🛇🛇
Leisure activities : ⛾ 🎯 ⚓ 🛝
Facilities : ♿ ⊶ ⌖ 🐾 🍴 launderette, refrigerators
Nearby : 🚣

Longitude : 4.41406
Latitude : 44.542

⛰ Les Peupliers

✆ 0475377147. www.campingpeupliers.com

Address : at Gourgouran (head 2km south along the D 579 and take the road to the right; at Vogüé-Gare)

3 ha (100 pitches), flat, grassy, stony, sandy

Rentals : 10 ⌂ – 9 ⌂.

Some pitches are beside the Ardèche river; some of the rental accommodation is a little old.

Surroundings : 🛇 🛇🛇
Leisure activities : ⛾ ✗ ⚓ 🛝 🚣 🎣
Facilities : ⊶ 🐾 🍴 launderette

Longitude : 4.411
Latitude : 44.53765

⚠ Les Chênes Verts

✆ 0475377154. www.camping-chenesverts.com

Address : Champ Redon (1.7km southeast along the D 103)

Opening times : from mid June to mid Sept.

2.5 ha (37 pitches) terraced, flat, grassy, stony

Tariff : 26€ ✦✦ ⛟ ▣ ⊞ (16A) – Extra per person 6€

Rental rates : (from beginning April to end Sept.) – 26 ⌂. Per night from 58 to 120€ – Per week from 280 to 850€ – Reservation fee 25€

A well shaded site, laid out with terraces above the road, but few pitches for tents and caravans.

Surroundings : 🛇🛇
Leisure activities : ✗ ⚓ 🛝
Facilities : ♿ ⊶ 🍴 📷 🐾

Longitude : 4.42075
Latitude : 44.54425

Do not confuse:
⚠ *to* ⛰⛰ : *MICHELIN classification with*
★ *to* ★★★★★ : *official classification*

CANILLO

AD100 – Michelin map **343** H9 – pop. 4 826 – alt. 1 531
▶ Andorra-la-Vella 13 – Barcelona 207 – Foix 88 – Perpignan 152

▲ Santa-Creu

✆ (00-376) 85 14 62, www.elsmeners.com

Address : in the village (beside the Valira-del-Orient river, left bank)

Opening times : from mid-June to mid-Sept.

0.5 ha terraced, relatively flat, grassy

Tariff : ★ 4.20€ ⛟ 4.20€ ▣ 4.20€ 🔌 (4A)

In a green setting with plenty of shade, near the town centre.

Surroundings : ≤ ♀
Leisure activities : ♈
Facilities : ♿ ⚊ ⛏ ✉ ⚑ ▣

GPS Longitude : 1.59978
Latitude : 42.56579

▲ Jan-Ramon

✆ (00-376) 75 14 54, www.elsmeners.com

Address : carretera General (400m northeast following signs for Port d'Envalira; beside the Valira del Orient river, left bank))

Opening times : from mid-June to mid-Sept.

0.6 ha flat, grassy

Tariff : ★ 4.20€ ⛟ 4.20€ ▣ 4.20€ 🔌 (4A)

Rental rates : (from mid-June to mid-Sept.) – 5 ⌂. Per night from 51 to 179€ – Per week from 350 to 700€ – Reservation fee 99€

A pleasant and partially shaded site, but there is noise from the nearby road.

Surroundings : ≤ ♀
Leisure activities : ♈ ✗
Facilities : ⚊ ✉ ⚑ ▣ ⚙

GPS Longitude : 1.59975
Latitude : 42.56594

LA MASSANA

AD400 – Michelin map **343** H9 – pop. 9 744 – alt. 1 241
▶ Andorra-la-Vella 6 – Barcelona 204 – Foix 101 – Perpignan 164

⛰ Xixerella

✆ (00-376) 73 86 13, www.xixerellapark.com – alt. 1,450

Address : at Xixerella (3.5km northeast along the CG 4 then continue to Erts, taking turning to the left)

5 ha terraced, relatively flat, stony, grassy

Rentals : 13 ⌂ – 28 apartments.

A shady grass area for tents and caravans; a range of rental accommodation of good quality.

Surroundings : ≤ ♀♀
Leisure activities : ♈ ✗ ⛱ ≋ hammam, jacuzzi ⚓ ♨ ▣
Facilities : ♿ ⚊ ⫘ ⚑ launderette ⚙ ⚙

GPS Longitude : 1.48882
Latitude : 42.55327

ORDINO

AD300 – Michelin map **343** H9 – pop. 4 322 – alt. 1 304
▶ Andorra-la-Vella 8 – Barcelona 207 – Foix 105 – Perpignan 168

⛰ Borda d'Ansalonga

✆ (00-376) 85 03 74, www.campingansalonga.com

Address : carretera Général del Serrat (2.3km northwest along the follow the signs for Le Circuit de Tristaina; beside the Valira del Nord river)

3 ha flat, grassy

A shady grassy site, but choose the pitches near the stream and away from the road in preference.

Surroundings : ≤ ♀♀
Leisure activities : ♈ ✗ ⛱ ⚓ ♨
Facilities : ♿ ⚊ ⫘ ⚑ launderette ⚙

GPS Longitude : 1.52162
Latitude : 42.56855

Michelin Travel Partner

Société par actions simplifiées au capital de 11 288 880 EUR
27 cours de l'Ile Seguin – 92100 Boulogne Billancourt (France)
R.C.S. Nanterre 433 677 721

No part of this publication may be reproduced in any form
without the prior permission of the publisher.

© Michelin Travel Partner
ISBN 978-2-067208-84-1

Layout: Jean-Luc Carnet
Translation: JMS Books llp (www.jmswords.com)
Layout of English edition: Chris Bell, cbdesign
Printed: February 2016
Printed and bound in Italy
Printed on paper from sustainable forests